Shree Ramayana
Mahanveshanam

Shree Ramayana Mahanveshanam

Volume Two

M. Veerappa Moily

Rupa & Co

Copyright © M Veerappa Moily 2010

Chief Editor: Dr C.N. Ramachandran

Translated from Kannada: Dr C.N. Ramachandran, Padma Sharma, Dr Laxminarayana Bhat P, Dr C. Naganna, Dr Vijay Sheshadri

Published 2010 by
Rupa Publications India Pvt. Ltd.
7/16, Ansari Road, Daryaganj,
New Delhi 110 002

Sales Centres:
Allahabad Bengaluru Chandigarh Chennai
Hyderabad Jaipur Kathmandu
Kolkata Mumbai

All rights reserved.
No part of this publication may be reproduced, stored in a retrieval system, or transmitted, in any form or by any means, electronic, mechanical, photocopying, recording or otherwise, without the prior permission of the publishers.

Typeset by
Mindways Design
1410 Chiranjiv Tower
43 Nehru Place
New Delhi 110 019

Printed in India by
Rekha Printers Pvt. Ltd.
A-102/1 Okhla Industrial Area, Phase-II
New Delhi-110 020

Contents

||❀||

Book Four   1

Book Five   301

BOOK FOUR

Canto One Hundred and Thirty-six

'Arise, O Hanuma!
O Son of Wind, Arise!'

||⊚||

On the peak of the mountain stood Anjaneya,
Gazing with rapt attention at the vast ocean
That lay stretched wide and far beyond!
The towering waves beat high against the hill,
And they chased and clashed and fell into a ravine.
When would the volcano hidden in the ocean's womb
Explode – is beyond anybody's guess.

O, Look! The waves of the ocean of life
Gather force, swell up, and overflow similarly.
Now happiness and good fortune, and then sorrow;   10
Falsehood at one time, and truth at another;
This is natural and yet a contrived web.
Whatever is steadfast is also, truly, moveable;
It is a witness to all that moves and yet stands still;
It stands well above Dualism and Non-dualism.

At the peak of the Mount Mandara,
In his gigantic form stood Hanuma – the achiever.
He shook the long tresses of hair on his head,

Which looked like black clouds, planted his arms
On the mountain peak; and then, lowering his waist,
And bending his head in his yogic stance,
Fusing his inner energy with adamantine will,
Gazing the path that lay far ahead as if devouring it,
He stood firm, with his ears sharpened.

What a terrible sight he was!
As though the earth-bearing elephant stood trumpeting,
To crush the entire universe into pieces and dust;
As though the slabs of gem-stones split with a thud,
And the resultant lightning shot forth flames, as if
From the third eye on the forehead of Shiva,
Covering the entire universe with molten lava.

Looking at this magnificent sight
Of the son of Wind standing there, Jambava said:
'Like the lightning exploding from the pit of a volcano,
Like the fires of deluge springing the subterranean ocean,
Like the arrow leaping out from the bow of Shiva,
Arise, O Hanuma! Arise, O son of Wind!

'The peak of the Mount Anjana is close to you.
Like the acute pain of birth shoots up
To bring forth new life from the earth's womb
Through the heat of the blistering earth,
Arise, O Hanuma! Arise, O son of Wind!

'When the frozen drop gleams bright,
When the life within the womb attains immortality,
When the spring of life spreads as the seed of light,
Arise, O Hanuma! Arise, O son of Wind!

'Wherever you go wandering,
It becomes the garden of Heaven; and the world
Gets bathed in the spring of celebration.
The light of knowledge shall gush out by itself.
Arise, O Hanuma! Arise, O son of Wind!

'O you, brighter than millions of suns and moons;
You are the valiant one to accomplish
Shri Rama's cause. The world awaits you.
Arise, O Hanuma! Arise, O son of Wind!'

As if the earth itself went down,
As if the Mount Mahendra fell to the nether world,
As if Vasuki – the giant serpent supporting the globe,
Shook all of his hoods bending his head,
Hanuma looked majestic when he took his leap. 60

Flying high and flying low, moving with a loud roar,
Floating in the stream and straining through the valley,
Merrily through the plains and roaring through the hills,
Now visible, and then out of sight,
Crossing all bounds as if to swallow the world,
He, the son of Wind, moved on his way.

Like a river born of a tiny drop
On the mountain-peak and flowing downhill,
Becomes a stream, cascading into a water-fall,
And with greenery blesses the world, and flows, 70
Losing itself in the union with the ocean, and still,
Promises to provide succor to the world again –
So did Hanuma look.

Like the alter-image of the sun himself
Standing on the mountain-peak stretching his divine-body,
Beaming and gleaming like an alter-icon of
Pride, perseverance, courage, and determination,
Toning up his body in readiness for the heroic leap,
Stiffening his arms and balancing his body-weight,
Bending his knees and lowering the neck, 80
Radiating energy, power, and true valour,
Hanuma called out to the warriors who stood there
Gazing at him with astonishment, and said:

'O men of courage, listen!
I am the messenger of Rama; Rama's arrow am I;

I am the glow of Rama; Rama's life am I;
I move forward like the arrow shot from Rama's bow,
I shall cross the ocean be it hundred-*yojanas* distant;
I shall reach Lanka faster than the wind;
I shall crush Lanka to pieces.   90
I shall set it ablaze and spare nothing;
I shall seek the daughter of Janaka, and chanting
The name of Rama, I shall convey the message.

'If I do not find the "mother" at Lanka,
I shall reach *Patala* – the nether world;
If she is not there, I shall ransack the Seven Worlds
And spare neither the earth, nor the sky nor the ocean.
I shall push down all the ten directions into *Patala*
Pounding Dashamukha – the ten-faced one,
And pinioning him, I shall drag him and throw him   100
At the feet of Shri Rama; and as you all watch
I shall decapitate Ravana and throw away his head
Into the ocean.'

'Praising and bowing to Rama with devotion,
Hanuma said thus: 'You are the treasure of beauty,
And are pleasing to the eyes.
You have grown in the forest, and you dwell in my heart.
Like the flowing river restless to join the ocean,
I shall seek only you and shall be united with you.
As the flower of your love joyfully blossoms,   110
I shall become the bee and savour the nectar.
When you aren't there, I won't seek refuge in the world;
And the world shall be mine when you are there for me.
Why should I beg others for mercy? And, why do I need
Shelter offered by others!'

'Who else is there like you,
Devoted to the Master's cause, O Hanuma!
When Shri Rama shows mercy, nothing can be difficult.
Where there is the name of Shri Rama, there is victory;

Let victory be to Rama, let victory be to Hanuma;   120
Let victory be to the messengers, let victory be for all.
Hurrah, hurrah!' shouted the *vanaras*, in excitement.
The loud shouts of victory, like the high-pitched huge drums,
Echoed through the ocean, the sky, and the forest.

Anjaneya, hearing the victory-shouts,
Gleamed bright. Like a wild fire leaping up
To the snow-capped peaks, as the divine vibrations
Of the primal word '*Om*' reverberated,
Like the ocean roaring fiercely,
Hanuma took his amazing leap with agility!   130

Canto One Hundred and Thirty-seven

'Look! The Bird of Revolt Flies with Wings Spread out!'

||๖||

As Hanuma soared high chanting the name of Shri Rama,
The tusker of the northern direction, trumpeted;
The primeval Turtle and the sovereign serpent, carrying the world,
Trembled in fear; waves churned deep in the ocean-womb;
And Hanuma, looking like the God of Fire, floated high
As glorious as a million suns, leaving everyone wonder-struck.

Surpassing the radiance of Brahma – the Creator,
Bidding the winds to stand still by the power of Yoga,
Stretching his arms like the wings of Garuda – the carrier
Of Vishnu, as he moved swiftly warding off all impediments,　　　　10
Hills and forests here and there on the way,
Giant trees and flowers of many hues, and varied animals,
Flocks of birds – all flew following him, as if they felt
They could not stay back without their soul-mate Hanuma!
Fish, whales and other sea-creatures too, followed him
Like his shadow.

It looked as though a mountain itself
Was rushing ahead taking on the form of Hanuma;

As though, with its high tides, the ocean itself was flying;
As though the God of Wind himself, cleaving the clouds, 20
Was flying, with a fierce force to frighten the world.
Such was the grandeur of Hanuma.

'What a terrific form this is!
It must be Time himself ready to swallow the world,' –
Thus thought all, and shook with fear that the time
Of *Pralaya*, the end of the World was near; and
They cried out helplessly, from one end to the other.

While the wonder of Brahma's creation
Glitterred in the sky, Hanuma, the supreme *yogi*,
Resonating to the vibrations of the word *Om*, 30
Moved on and on, the supreme state of bliss radiant
In the form of Rama himself.

In the presence of Hanuma-yoga,
Cowardice is dead and small desires are extinguished;
Magnificent accomplishment is set to be achieved;
And the world appears small like an atom.
All the accumulated energy in the form of speed
Pervades the entire universe in yoga and
Reaches its point of culmination.

It is the will of the son of Wind: 40
It is like the steady crest of a glowing lamp;
It is the emotion of quietism and self-command;
It is beyond the dualities of self-mediation.

The great leap of the son of Wind
Shook the world and then calmed down the commotion.
As the ever-full vessel spread pleasure and enjoyment,
The Fountain of Consciousness swelled.
A new bud shot forth from the Tree of History;
The Bird of Rebellion flew spreading its wings.
A new song was sung and a wild dance followed; 50
The essence of good deeds overflowed the banks;

Window of the New Age was then opened.
Musical notes were struck in excitement;
And the Bird of the Epoch flew to the sky.

Hanuma, roaring aloud,
Moved towards Lanka with total confidence.
While the ocean too roared in great excitement,
And its huge waves swelled up and danced;
While the leaves of the Tree of Time fell down one by one,
While the greatness of Shri Rama was visible in full, 60
While the valour of a great soul came to work wonders,
As if all the latent energy in him was awakened;
All virtues and eminent qualities exploding,
And the spell of a rainbow was cast on the horizon,
Freeing himself from apathy and inertness, invigorated,
The son of Wind moved on.

While all the five vital forms of breath –
Prana, apana, samana, udana, and *vyana* –
Were in perfect equilibrium,
While the treasure of knowledge spilled over, 70
And the new path was open, as if he was, indeed,
The artistic bridge of communion, severing apathy
And inertness, and in a spirit invigorating,
Anjaneya moved on.

Like the five vital forms of breath,
Having discarded one body, but eager for another,
Reach a womb to live in, and, nine months being over,
As if all the aggregated past *karma* moves toward
The future *karma*, jump into the ocean of life, eagerly,
And, in the end, meeting the right Guru, ascend the steps 80
Of spiritual attainment, one by one, and finally,
Become one with Nothingness, just Light,
Free from apathy and inertness, in a spirit invigorating,
Anjaneya moved on.

Owing to his *ashtasiddhi* – the eight supernatural powers,
He shed the heaviness of his body, and became as light as a feather,
As light as cleaned cotton. Inhaling deep breath
Through the left nostril he held back his breath,
And shut the sky-principle within through *puraka* and *kumbhaka*,
   two kinds of controlled breathing.
His face turned red like the orbit of the rising sun;   90
Like the God of Fire his radiance was brilliant.
Gazing at the ocean and getting thrilled, and feeling
As if the bird of self-confidence stretched out its wings,
Free from apathy and inertness, in a spirit invigorating,
Rama's messenger moved on.

The sole hero of the world,
Efficient in every limb, his whole body pure,
Bringing back to his mind his vow, again and again,
Gazing at the tip of the nose in contemplation,
As the *ida-pingala* breath flowed in and out,   100
Transcending the *shatchakras* – the six centres of energy, one by one,
And, as if to awaken the power of *kundalini*
That lay coiled in the form of a serpent –
Free from apathy and inertness, in a spirit invigorating,
The dear friend of Saumitri moved on.

Like a being, at the level of physical body,
The earth-principle lying hidden, through the principle
Of air holding on to the fire-principle, focussing on
The sky-principle, ascending the chariot of energy,
Along with the five elements, like the monarch of the world,   110
Going through the cycle of births and re-births,
And, at last, resting united in the Universal Soul,
Free from apathy and inertness, in a spirit invigorating,
The beloved of the Supreme Soul moved on.

Like Bhaktamaheshwara, a devotee of Shiva,
Becomes one with His Soul, the *prana linga*,
With purity of mind, good manners, and equanimity,
Moving from *annamayakosha*, the first of the five sheaths

Of the living spirit, to *pranamayakosha*, and then
To the *manomayakosha*, and from *manomayakosha*   120
To *vijyanamayakosha*, and, finally, to *anandamayakosha*,
And, in the end, all the five sheaths dissolving,
He himself becomes the Supreme Soul,
Free from apathy and inertness, in a spirit invigorating,
The soul of Rama moved on.

'Shri Ramachandra – the Creator,
the Preserver, and the Destroyer – is the soul of all.
Victory to Shri Rama, and victory to Raghurama.
Mother Janaki is held captive; I shall free her;
I shall free her, who suffers the pangs of separation   130
From Shri Rama. I shall keep the light of life burning
With the oil of the message given by Shri Rama.
Could Ravana be a worthy equal? When I reach Lanka,
I shall crush Ravana and set Lanka on fire.
Who caused these giant waves here, in mid ocean?
Did the gentle breeze itself raise these waves?
I wonder!' Thus, full of varied thoughts and fancies,
Contemplating deep on Shri Ramachandra,
And also remembering the Sun-god again and again,
Like Garuda who carried the vessel of elixir,   140
The one with strong arms moved in the path of the Quest!

Jambava and the others gazed,
Without ever closing their eye-lids, as far as they could,
In great curiosity, excitement, and wonder
At the path Hanuma traversed, gliding and sliding.
Hanuma moved forward in the sphere of air,
Stretching his hands and beating his legs,
Looking like a wondrous bird with four arms,
And reflecting the journey of the Time-cycle.
'Is there anyone who has such strong arms as Hanuma?   150
Are there any other epoch-making men like Hanuma?
Are there any other exponents of Yoga like Hanuma?

Are there any other devotees nearer Rama's heart?
Are there any other heroes here who can crush Ravana?' –
Praising Hanuma thus in their own befitting manner,
And feeling elated, and increasingly buoyant,
Merrily they danced on the heap of sands!

Where does the ocean end?
It is a journey towards the unknown.
The ocean is the source of variety, and the Goddess   160
Of Nature strolls happily, there.

He is the son of Anjana:
The untiring hero, the crest-jewel of renunciation.
The spirit of the epoch breathed novelty, and curbed
All the evil deeds. The fresh air of revolution had spread;
It became the comet of doom for Ravana's life.
The dream of the impending colourful reign of Rama
Created there the delightful tapestry of rainbow.
The path ran there as was charted by divine will!

On seeing Anjaneya,   170
Gliding to carry out Rama's mission, the assembly
Of gods and demi-gods, the celestial troubadours,
And the nymphs, sang heavenly songs and performed
Bharatanatyam, and showered flowers on him.
They all praised the son of Wind as it pleased them;
They blessed that his mission be successful;
And they prayed for the victory of Hanuma.

Huge, heavenly drums were beaten; and the southern
Breeze blew, carrying fragrance. Up above, the sky
Was blue; below the ocean was deep blue; and Nilamegha,   180
The god with the complexion of dark-blue clouds,
Saw everything, and smiled gently.

Canto One Hundred and Thirty-eight

'The Ocean has no Path; We have to Explore One'

||६||

Flying above the ocean for long,
Hanuma descended into the womb of the ocean;
And looked as if wearing a garland of waves.
Subduing all forms of consciousness to remain motionless
In total tranquility, transcending the bounds of time and space,
A personification of supreme composure,
Squeezing the universe in deep meditation, Hanumanta swam across!

His mouth wide open as if to guzzle the ocean itself;
As if passing through the ocean of an epoch itself;
Like a young cobra moving in gentle sunshine;   10
Like Nataraja – Shiva performing *tandava* – the Wild Dance;
Like Vamana, incarnation of Vishnu about to measure all the
  three worlds;
Like Devendra swimming with his thousand arms;
Like Airavata, the celestial elephant, splitting water with its trunk;
Squeezing the universe in deep meditation, Hanumanta swam across!

Vibrations of melodious tunes are heard.
Look! The divine bugle is being sounded.

His arms are moving rhythmically.
Mountains shake as he moves his legs.
He feels as if he is casting away his body, the pot of sin. 20
As he sported in water, as the whole world sported with him,
It looked as if all the moving and non-moving objects
Took part in that happy sport of dancing.
Like the thunderous sound of Shiva's drum,
The ocean roared reverberating in all the directions.
Squeezing the universe in deep meditation, Hanumanta swam across!

All the wild aquatic animals in great hullabaloo
Came besieging to test the strength of Pavanaja – the son of Wind.
Embodying all the rakshasaic qualities
The ocean offered resistance, hurled insults, and caused annoyance. 30
Filled with Shri Rama's will in body and soul,
Shri Hanuma, destroying the wickedness of Lankesha – the king
   of Lanka
Squeezing the universe in deep meditation, Hanumanta swam across!

The sky looked splendid in dark blue hue;
The divine-parasol posed majestically encompassing vastness.
The lullaby of the swinging birds sustains the world;
The sweetness of their song is like the melody of strings of a *veena*;
The love of music floats in the enchanting waves of emotion.
Be you the *jalagara* – the one who washes away the dirt – of the
   world
And enter the sheath of my womb being transposed – 40
Thus invited Sagara – the king of the ocean.
Squeezing the universe in deep meditation, Hanumanta swam across!
Exceeding the speed of the raft, exceeding the speed of the mind
He is swimming across the ocean of life;
He is an exponent of Yoga; he is the devotee of Shri Rama;
As if immersing himself again and again in nectar and rising up –
Causing his body to be light once,
Becoming heavy like a mountain once again,
Bending his body, and shrinking his elements, being pushed by

The waves themselves, but himself appearing to be the cause of it,   50
Squeezing the universe in deep meditation, Hanumanta swam
   across!

That very vigorous swimming raised a storm
And the sea became rough with the rising waves.
He is pushing ahead breaking the garland of waves;
As if pulling out the earth and the sky and then throwing them
   away;
As if the ocean of milk rose up high in frenzied emotion;
It seemed like the autumn-clouds rising high above.
All the fish and the crocodiles, turtles and all the other aquatic
   creatures
Scattered away and disappeared fearing whose intrusion was it.
Squeezing the universe in deep meditation, Hanumanta swam across!   60

Whales, sharks and all the other wild creatures of the sea
Came rushing forward thinking that they got something to eat;
   and as the
Water swelled up by the forceful sweep of Hanuma's arms and
   gushed forth,
The creatures scattered away in fear on seeing ferocious Hanuma.
As if the new epoch itself made a loud proclamation
Squeezing the universe in deep meditation, Hanumanta swam across!

While Hanuma was swimming thus
Surasa – the mother of serpents was waiting with hunger:
'Some *rakshasa* of the water shall now enter my stomach' – thinking
   thus
As she came near with her mouth opened wide   70
Hanumanta swiftly changed course and while
He looked as if fear-stricken, tired, and quite exhausted
And while it seemed as though the rakshasaic-power would win
Like an arrow cast forcefully from a bow
And remembering Goddess Kali,
The great-pilgrim Hanuma jumped at the speed of lightning and
   was gone!

Closing her eye-lids, as Surasa waited with her
Mouth wide-open, she had nothing but disappointment;
When she opened her eyes and saw –
There was neither the prey nor anyone around;   80
Then she turned around and saw –
Hanuma was swimming in quietude feeling completely relaxed!

While Hanuma's passage continued thus –
In great happiness, the king of the ocean, thought –
This one is the messenger of Rama; he must be honoured;
Rama, the Kantupita – father of Cupid, must be helped;
Rama is an eminent king of the clan of Raghu,
The clan that elevated the land of Bharata, starting with King Sagara.
Here, Hanuma is exhausted by the exertion;
Let him rest for a while and then proceed – with these thoughts   90
The king of the ocean said thus to Mount Mainaka:

'Oh! You are prominent among the mountains.
You have prevented the *rakshasas* of *Patala* –
The nether world – from coming up.
Be a host to Hanuma who has come here on Rama's mission;
Give him shelter to rest.
Shri Rama's life has now become a sad story;
Janaki – the daughter of Janaka is suffering in grief;
Hanuma shall seek the gem of Truth and convey the message;
You shall make light the burden of his hard task;   100
O, the king of mountains! Rise up from the water and treat him kindly.
Hanuma is a great soul and an exemplary achiever.
He has vowed to explore Truth!'

That speech was appeasing.
Like the sun who appears bright
Piercing through the dark clouds –
Mount Mainaka came up in great excitement slashing the ocean!

Welcoming and treating Hanuma benevolently –
Mainaka spread fragrance, sprinkled perfumed water,

Offered fruits, radish and other roots to eat, and pleased him by 100
Offering flowers and betel leaf with areca-nut.
Like a charmer, Mainaka hid himself in the water once,
And surfacing yet again, played hide and seek with Hanuma.
The peak of the Mount Mainaka spread like the horns of a bull
And invited Hanuma, 'Come, and rest here happily
For a while and then proceed.' At the manifestation of such emotions
And such sweet-talk, all the hardships of the journey of Pavanaja
Disappeared instantly and he moved ahead!

Once upon a time
All the mountains had wings. 110
Without stopping at any place, they used to
Fly from here to there and there to here again!
When a mountain that was there today, disappeared tomorrow
The rains and the crops, the land and the waters suffered
  high fluctuations.
This caused great hardships to the people of the world.
When the people appealed for protection to Devendra – the king
  of Heaven,
He advised the mountains not to fly.
Turning a deaf ear to Devendra's summons, as the mountains kept
Flying, infuriated Devendra severed their wings.

Mainaka was frightened. 120
He appealed to Maruta – the God of Wind – for protection.
Maruta showed him the ocean in the south.
Mainaka remained immersed there and thus saved his wings.
This is the son of Maruta – the one who had protected him before;
With this feeling of gratefulness,
Mainaka offered hospitality to Maruti – the son of Maruta.

If extreme comforts are desired
It shall affect servitude; as I am a servant of my master,
Shall I immerse myself in comforts forgetting my master's
  mission –
Thinking thus, having enjoyed the hospitality, 130

Hanumanta moved ahead on the path of his journey.
Instantaneously, being afraid of *Vajra* – the weapon of Devendra,
Mainaka was set to hide himself in the ocean.
Devendra saw him and said: 'O, Mainaka, be not afraid!
Shri Rama's incarnation is for the good of the world.
Hanuma's journey is for a great cause, one could see that.
Pavanasuta – the son of Wind is greatly satisfied with your service.
Your kind words have made Pavanasuta highly satisfied.
Look! Here is the reward for the service you have done:
I am pleased, I shall not sever your wings – 140
With these words, he assured safety.

A surprise occurred.
Unknowingly Pavanaja, climbed up the back of a crocodile
Under the illusion that it might be the parched land;
At the very next moment he realised what it was;
Yet, Hanumanta sat there unperturbed.
And the crocodile, not being acquainted with the humans,
Remained indifferent considering
Neither friendship nor enmity.
Then, Hanuma himself jumped up 150
And moved ahead with great agility.

Not far from there
A gigantic whale was rushing with its wide-opened mouth
Eager to swallow him –
Remembering Rama, Hanumanta saw the approaching whale.
When it came near and was about to swallow him,
The sharp-witted Hanumanta, bound by his great task of seeking Sita,
Clutched the two jaws of the whale, opened them wide,
And pulled apart hard;
Then, both its cheeks were ripped off, the blood gushed out, 160
And it lost its life; Hanuma flung it away!

Like the Mount Meru,
The waves were rising up high and as the power
Of intellect was springing forth

Transcending all fatigue, Hanuma moved ahead surpassing all.
Like the future that grows out of the yard of the present
Like the tender shoots ripen into fruits from which seeds come
  splintering
Like the new vision that shines forth cracking the crust of the
  universe
Like the River of Time that flows between the past and the present
Like the womb of the barn of life pours out bounty through its
  wide mouth,   170
All divine emotions came into life.

Instantly, the dark clouds gathered
And a torrential rainfall followed.
A rainbow-like stage was set.
In the dark black clouds, and in the bright white clouds,
It seemed that the assembly of gods was holding in grandeur
Parasols of tawny colours.
Like the moon shone through
The clouds now and then, Hanuma –
Swimming, gliding, floating and beating his limbs –   180
Shone brilliantly emanating radiance.

Shri Rama has instructed *pranava* – the mystic syllable *Om*.
Saumitri – the son of Sumitra is an embodiment
Of *a-kara* – the first syllable;
Shatrughna – the enemy-destroyer is *vi-kara* –
A principal syllable – embodied;
Shri Rama is the sole form of Supreme Bliss;
Ayodhya's queen – Sita is Nature-incarnate.
Combining all in his mind in unison and being himself fully
  absorbed
In *Nadabrahma* – the all-pervading primal sound,   190
Hanuma, himself an embodiment of the Supreme Soul,
And a learned *yogi* – swam steadfastly.

The ever reverberating tunes
And musical notes make life itself musical;

It is full of accomplishments, and happiness.
As the intact energy ascends from the *anahata chakra* –
The mystical circle – the mental will-power is infinite
And the consciousness knows no boundaries.
The manifested form of the primordial power itself is this universe!
The mental faculty which resembles electricity is the cosmic
    power;   200
Encompassing all souls it has grown full!
Thinking thus, and knowing his path well, Hanuma moved ahead.

Are there any readily available paths
For realising Truth; Quest is inevitable.
Where is the pathway in the ocean; the path must be explored;
Without any well-drawn design, one must go on;
When the mind is filled with quietude and is free from worries
Where is the need for pre-meditated plans, and what value does it
    have?
Hanuma's Quest continues in perfect harmony!

Canto One Hundred and Thirty-nine

'As this body belongs to my Master, how could I offer it to you?'

||६||

Some unknown island it was, and Hanuma reached there.
Not being able to find any sign of where Lanka was situated
As he was searching for the path groping here and there
Finding an eminently pious sage there
In the solitude of that vast Empire of Silence
Feeling re-assured, falling at his feet in great humility and eagerness,
   Hanuma pleaded:

'O, great sage! Tell me
I know not which island is this. I am going in the direction of
Lanka where Ravana resides. O, venerable sage!
If you kindly tell me in which direction Lanka is situated   10
Much good shall be yours. The path is densely-beset.
I shall go there in great agility and swing the noose of time.
He is the thief of a *rakshasa*; abducting the venerable Mother –
Janaki on the sly, he brought her away; certainly the wicked one
   is he.
'I am called Hanuma; I am the messenger of Rama;
O, venerable sage! Be merciful!'

Then, the venerable sage said:
'I am Thrunabindu. Why do you seek this crazy task?
Of what use is a gem-mirror in the hands of a blind person?
Why does a deaf person need the grandeur of seven musical notes? 20
Should a crippled one need to be eager to climb up a
   mountain-peak?
Should the one who lives by begging desire the palanquin?
Why do you desire to enter the stomach of a python?
Why do you want to get burnt to ashes in the cave of wild fire?
Is it a child's play to go to Lanka?
You being *vanara*, leaving the game of climbing up trees,
It's a wonder that you have come with a desire for Lanka!
It has a fort with seven enclosures, and is heavily guarded.
To enter into that fort is not an easy task even for
The troop of spirits, and the fiend of Brahmins as well. 30
Do you have in you the courage to scale its heights?
Would you survive provoking the valorous warriors, tell me.'
He spoke thus trying to instill fear.

He is the master of firm mind.
Without getting agitated, Pavanasuta said:
'Is this body eternal; is this body not a mere log of wood?
This body shall be discarded one day or the other.
I shall enter Lanka slaying the valorous warriors.
I shall throw away all the *rakshasas* into the sea crushing them hard.
I shall seek Ravana and efface the writing on his forehead. 40
I shall crush him hard against the rocks, and push him down the
   valley.
I shall wipe out the name of Lanka itself.
What does it matter if I die performing my Master's mission?
Will I not attain the much desired Kailasa – the abode of Shiva,
   tell me.
O, wise sage! Tell me where Lanka is.
Just give me a clue, that's enough; I shall swim unto there.
I shall break the arrogance and conceit of the *rakshasas*.
I shall crush and grind them hard.'

Hearing the words of Anjaneya – the son of Anjana,
Sage Thrunabindu said: Are you the one known as Pavanasuta?   50
Are you the messenger of Rama? Be that so, and for good!
I am highly pleased by your firmness.
I have been doing penance secretly for a very long time;
I am sitting here stooping low as if rooted to the spot.
How could I show you the way?
If you lift me up and hold me straight,
I shall send you in the right direction gesturing by the hand.

Hearing those words,
Hanuma got up at once, and thinking thus –
'I shall lift him up by the hand;   60
Hoist him on my shoulder and ask him the path' –
As he tried to lift him up, Thrunabindu sat there heavy
With the weight of the universe. What a wonder!

'What a wondrous thing is this! He appears weak and very old.
But look at me, I am quite valorous;
Filled with the energy of youthfulness;
Also, I have got the power of Yoga;
Nevertheless, I am unable to lift him up;
I blabbered too much with the
Venerable Sage; I admit my folly.   70
In front of the sage's greatness, I am only worth a straw.
My conceit is tamed; I shall beg his pardon.
The saying – "virtuous men live at all times
Secretly somewhere" – has come true today and here!'
He thought thus for himself.

'O, venerable sage! Pardon me;
Pardon my impudence; I felt great in self-conceit;
Proclaimed my valour and felt big in my insolent might;
How could I forget your greatness, O, venerable sage!'
While Hanuma pleaded thus in great humility,   80
Thrunabindu said smilingly:

'Do not you worry, my son,
You are truly valorous indeed. Now lift me up on
Your shoulder and you can see the path,' said the sage.
Then, Hanumanta lifted up the great sage
Who was now as light as a flower.
Hanuma within himself appreciated the greatness of the sage!

As was seen at that very instance
Hanuma meditated on the name of Rama,
Recalled his own strength,   90
And grew tall up to the sky
Radiating valour in heroic stature.
'Look there! That's Lanka. Go in this direction;
This is the path' – saying so, the sage showed the way.

Folding his hands to the sage in veneration
Hanuma placed him down and went along on his way.
As he proceeded further, there was an island on the way.
Gandharvas, siddhas, and *kinnaras* – the celestial beings – live there.
A cruel *rakshasi* is the queen there.
She eats only humans; Surasa is her name.   100

What does Surasa look like, if you ask –
She is big like a mountain; her form is frightening;
What sharply pointed teeth! What fiery yellow eyes!
What a wide mouth that opens like the sky!
The news of someone's arrival had already reached her ears.
'Being hungry without eating human meat for long,
God himself in his mercy has sent me food;
Now I shall have a sumptuous meal' –
Thinking like this, Surasa beamed with great delight.

Coming near Anjaneya, she said: 110
'Good that you have come here; I shall not spare you; you're now
A good meal for me; all those who come to my place become my
   meal.
Better you come on your own.'

She called out to her soldiers –
'Place his head at the alter of sacrifice at once;
Put a garland of red flowers on him right away;
Let Shakini-Dakini – the blood-thirsty attendants on Kali be satiated.'
She ordered them thus.

Hearing those words, Pavanasuta, son of Wind, said:
'Rama's mission is to be accomplished – 120
A great task indeed. Put no obstacles, mother;
I am Rama's servant.
While I am in servitude thus,
Do I have the freedom to act on my own?
As this body belongs to my Master,
How could I offer it to you?
I am not afraid for my life;
I am not the one to offer lame excuses.
I shall find Mother-Sita and give her the signet-ring of Rama;
The message she would give I shall deliver it to Shri Rama; 130
Thereafter I shall return and be your meal willingly;
Believe my words; do not stop me now, stop me not' –
He spoke thus with gentleness,
Humility and all the dexterity at his command.

'You can not be believed.
You mortals are utterly selfish.
Would I allow you to run away deceiving me thus?
Don't you place before me the lame excuse of your Master's mission.
I have a vow to offer – to satiate Shakini-Dakini'
Surasa – the *rakshasi*, sternly said so. 140

She told her soldiers:
'You do not get charmed by his sweet-talk.
Put on him at once the garland of scarlet flowers.
Smear his body with the ashes of humans.
Beat the tom-toms, let the worship be done fast.
Let the festivity of human sacrifice be concluded together at once.
In this island with no traces of humans,

Providence itself has granted this good fortune.
He shall not be left free; it would amount to
Kicking the bounty with one's left foot.' 150
As Surasa along with her soldiers
Rushed forward to seize Hanuma –
'Though a *rakshasi*, she is a woman after all; why should I strike her?'
Thinking thus, by his yogic power
He sprang a surprise on them. Using his great power, he grew to
Gigantic proportions and showed them that wonderful physique;
Employing *anima* – the supernatural power
Of becoming as small as an atom,
He showed himself even smaller than an atom.
This kind of power to grow large and small frightened 160
And entertained Surasa. The petty desire of
Eating Hanuma goaded her no more.

Folding her hands in supplication, she said:
'How could I devour the one laden with
The weighty duty of Rama's mission?
I troubled you by my desire for human meat out of ignorance.
You are the Guru who has conquered desire and anger.
By the vision I had of you, I got discerning knowledge.
O, Master! I bow to your power and devotion.
You have come crossing the irrepressible ocean – 170
Who could prevent you from entering into Lanka?
You have now won *tamasa* – slothful darkness
By your *sattva* – purity and goodness.
I am wonderstruck by your eight supernatural faculties.
You have shown me mercy and spared my life, O master!
Let victory be to Shri Rama; let victory be to Shri Hanuma' –
Praising him thus and showing him the way to Lanka
She sent away Hanuma,
And she herself was afloat in the pond
Of Shri Ramachandra's devotion. 180
She rocked herself in the swing of happiness.

After that, Hanuma
Continued his swimming in the ocean and on seeing an island
He stopped and stood under the shade of a tree there.
As he was looking around thinking –
What next, and what else –
Simhika – a female with the ability to assume any form at will
Came there to seize Pavanasuta!

'This one is a rare animal.
After a long time it has come to be mine.   190
I have almost forgotten the taste of human meat.
I shall slash this beast, and separate the flesh
And preserve the meat by boiling; it shall last for four days;
It shall be a great festive cooking for the entire family' –
Thinking thus, she lifted up Hanuma and carried him away.

It dawned on Hanuma –
'What is this amazement, who is holding me?
Who has lifted me up? Have I become like a ship
That suffers in the tumultuous storm?' –
Thinking thus he slipped down and saw –   200
She looked like a ghost risen up from the depths of the ocean.
'O, Hanuma! Beware!
In the middle of the ocean there is an island;
And there lives a *rakshasi* who is fond of human flesh,'
Sugriva – the king of Kishkindha – had warned;
Hanuma recalled it. 'How true it is!'
Thinking how to handle her, Hanuma quickly
Enlarged his body by the power of Yoga
And kicking Simhika on the chest, he leaped forth.
It seemed as though *Patala,* the nether world itself had roared
   opening its mouth wide.   210
As she chased him here and there aiming to swallow him –
Hanuma is the grace of the Monkey-clan;
He is *vajradehi* – the one whose body is as hard as the diamond –

Enlarging and contracting his body, and scratching and tearing with his
Long nails like that of Narasimha – the man-lion, Vishnu –
Wrenching his fist and raining heavy blows on her vital parts like Narashimha tore at the body of Hiranyakashipu,
He slashed Simhika, the one who was a menace to the world.
There was a playful sprinkling of blood and the entrails lay scattered.

Canto One Hundred and Forty

'Amidst Hundred Afflictions, You Sprouted and Grew to be a Giant Tree'

||௬||

Cutting across all impediments, and barring all else,
Anjaneya saw Lanka and felt very happy.
What grandeur of the river joining the sea!
What grandeur of trees in the dense jungles!
What grandeur of the peak of the Mount Malaya!
What lovely rows of gardens!
What beauty in the flowers that spread fragrance there!
What bounty of fruits and nuts everywhere!
The city of Lanka as described by Thrunabindu and Surasa
Looked thus in all its grandeur.   10

As the waves of intense emotions
Coursed through Hanuma, he fell silent.
'Like thunder and lightning, you strike the *rakshasas*.
Amidst hundred afflictions, you sprouted and grew to be a giant tree.
As the world has sunken deep in inviolable chains,
As the oceans of blood are swelling up causing harm,
As the ever-burning lamp at the altar is extinguished
Spreading darkness all over;
As the sky has turned red in the scorching heat,

As the howling note is played at a high pitch, 20
As the crest of fire is hidden in the ribbed-cage of the heart of the world,
As Kalapurusha – the Time-persona has tied ankle-bells for his wild dance,
As the vampire of hunger has turned the bellies of the people
Into a dancing-floor and is performing its bizarre dance there,
As the memory of the fertile womb is fading in the mind,
As countless mothers' wombs are drying up,
As countless women are widowed and face a bleak future,
As the life's boat on earth has lost its course,
As the wombs and the backs are stuck with the spears all over, 30
O, God! How do you restrain the web of immense torture?
The light cast on earth is too meagre for it.
How many dark caves would you be lighting up?
When the branch of a tree blossoms sucking the sap of roots
How would you restrain the blows of a tempest?
In what way the spring of rain-water hidden in the
Depth of the womb of the earth be made to gush out and flow?
O, Viranjaneya – the valorous Anjaneya – you are the protector of the epoch.
O, the Great-one! Let the comforting deeds of benevolence happen aplenty.'
As the sound of this fervent wish resounded in all the directions 40
Hanuma stood there with heroic conviction!

Is there anyone who can equal Hanuma?
Could those who are a menace to the world survive today?
Could the misery of the world be stopped in the future?
In valour, purity of character, ethics,
In the ability to restrain passions, and in the simplicity of life
Are there any other brave-yet-gentle men who can equal Hanuma?
He gets engrossed in chanting the name of Rama.
He is Shiva; he is personification of intellectual happiness;
He is the one with pure intelligence. He is the Guru, 50
Nay, the great Guru of all heroic deeds.

Mount Anjana is his maternal home and
Vayu – the God of Wind himself is his father.
He is the manifestation of tolerance and endurance.
He has come crossing the irrepressible ocean!

Driven by the curiosity to see
What is there in Lanka, Hanuma swiftly
Climbed up the peak of the Mount Trikuta.
It is the land of tall coconut and areca-nut trees.
All the beasts and birds got frightened by the quick pace of
  Hanuma 60
And fearing that some misery awaited them
Ran away in different directions!
But soon realised that some venerable person has arrived there
And that there is nothing to be afraid of.
With this feeling, they all came back
To their homes yearning to see him.

Standing atop the peak
And watching with care the riches and grandeur of Lanka,
Hanuma forgot himself. It was the time of dusk.
The beauty of Goddess Lakshmi, surrounded by the ocean, was
  doubled. 70
As the rays of the Sun-god reflected in the water,
It looked as if the gold-smearing work was in progress
Inside the sea. Blowing gently, the God of Wind
Made his son Anjaneya's journey-fatigue disappear.
New enthusiasm swelled up.
The trees showered flowers with affection.
Filled with happiness, Maruti – the son of Maruta
Felt light like a flower.

Hanuma stands here.
There is no elation, dejection, pain, or pleasure. 80
Developing an attitude of mind to gauge
The past and the future; carrying and bringing along
Punya – the grace of virtuous deeds – of all the aeons with him;

Glowing bright and pulling out the inert element
And throwing it away,
Ploughing thunder and lightning, he sowed nectar.
He stands there shining bright like a lighthouse.

Hanuma stands here.
The valley of forgetfulness that swallows every epoch
Is lit up with the light of knowledge by this *yogi*. 90
Where is Heaven? It's in our own hearts.
Where is Hell? It's in our own hearts.
Hanuma practiced this in his life and showed it to the world.
He stands there shining bright like a lighthouse.

Hanuma stands here
Pulling out the very roots of Ravana-cult –
All the evils of Ravana – which diminish virtuous character,
And crush down life itself –
In order that the dream of *Ramarajya* –
The ideal kingdom comes true. 100
As the glitter of the lightning of the world's misery fades away
He stands there shining bright like a lighthouse.
Hanuma stands here
Giving up the path of earning wealth, gold and the other riches
In the eagerness to accomplish Shri Rama's mission;
Rushing steadfastly for the grace of god's love,
Moving ahead crossing the River of Life,
Crushing all impediments with the support of his strong arms,
He stands there shining bright like a lighthouse.

Hanuma stands here. 110
Looking back, one can see that
Surasa personifies extreme craving for food;
Nagajanani – the mother of serpents is the web of love;
Simhika, who swallows creatures grabbing them
By their shadows, is just another name for the alluring bait.
Hanuma has won all these through his sense of discrimination.
He stands there shining bright like a lighthouse.

Hanuma stands here
Becoming extremely light in weight
By invoking the supernatural faculty – *anima*;　　　　　　120
Becoming extremely heavy in weight invoking *garima;*
Shrinking his body into extreme tiny-ness invoking *laghima*;
Enlarging his body into extreme proportions invoking *mahima*;
demonstrating magnificently his will-power
By invoking *prapti – prakamya*,
He stands there shining bright like a lighthouse.

Hanuma saw:
The forest filled with fragrance, the pasture-ground for cattle,
The rocks and the hills here and there,
The mountain-peaks, the many valleys and the strong forts,　　130
The toddy-palm-trees in golden colours and
Their glittering reflections on the sands,
The calm deep-sea and its endearing silence,
The floating clouds in different forms and shapes,
The evening stars rising gracefully at sunset,
And a variety of trees – the pine tree; the *jambira*;
The *priyala*; *kodasu, kanagalu* – the medicinal shrubs.

As the dusk was setting in,
Birds were happily returning to their nests
And kissing their young-ones, were feeding them.　　　　　140
Mohana raga – the musical note that invokes affection –
Was rocking the swing of enthusiasm.
The leaves of plants and trees were washed clean in the rain.
The young bees were gulping down the
Last drop of nectar of flowers.

Chirping merrily
The water-birds were floating and swimming
In the pond full of lotus and lily flowers.
The birds were playing and singing in the pride
Of who could be more beautiful and charming than them.　　150

The garden opened by god himself was gleefully emanating
The fragrance of all-season flowers and fruits.

Lanka was a grand city
Decorated with golden door and pearly frame;
Every house had a garden filled with the grandeur
Of flamingos and herons and their sweet sounds;
The drone of ornaments of the delightful wives
Resounded here and there.
It looked as if some charm was cast.
There were many manors with rows   160
Of upper storey with golden pillars,
And eight-storeyed palaces with golden frames;
The amorous mansions of the *rakshasas* were thus looking grand
Decorated with diamonds, gems, pearls and golden arches.

Wherever one looked –
The grand palaces were kissing the sky;
The tall towers teased the rustics and the simpletons;
Flags were hoisted on all the mansions.
That was Lanka, the golden city, equal to the Heaven in grandeur.
The entire city seemed   170
Like a golden boat swaying in the middle of the ocean.

'Now I must enter the city' –
Thinking thus, Anjaneya leaped
And swiftly came to the northern door.
Fierce *rakshasas* were standing guard there.
They were armed with lances, spears, axes and iron-maces.
A large troupe of *rakshasas* was standing guard day and night.

He was immersed in worry:
'Could we, the *vanaras*, ever win this?
Could Shri Ramachandra attain victory?   180
Would Dashashira, the ten-headed one, ever pay obeisance
To *sama-dana-bheda* – negotiation-gift-dissention –
The three means of success?

Danda – punishment, the fourth means of success,
Alone seems to be the right choice
And not even *bheda* would be appropriate here.
Let alone the thought of victory;
With what tricks can I enter the city?
What could be the means of breaking the iron-walls?
The *rakshasas* are strong; 190
What could be the apt means to crush them?
Let all worries be put to rest.
As Shri Rama's name is there to provide solace,
And as Shri Rama safeguards us for ever,
Like an ignorant person,
Why should I doubt the power of Rama!

'I shall enter the city at night.
I must escape the gaze of watchful eagle-eyes.
Before sunrise I must accomplish my task.
I must steadfastly break the guard of the *rakshasas*. 200
When I am endowed with the mission of meeting Janaki –
The jewel of Rama,
I must have a good sense of discrimination
As I am the messenger of the king.
Disguising myself and attaining the form of a baby-monkey
I shall enter the city. I know of no other means to success' –
When Hanuma was rubbing hands in worry
And with a feeling of helplessness was
Groping around here and there in great bewilderment,
The moon appeared spreading moon-light. 210
Like a heron floating majestically in the pond,
The moon floated in the pond of the sky
And with great joy gifted his soothing light to the whole world!

Canto One Hundred and Forty-one

'Why Pollute the Great Rakshasa-culture?'

॥६॥

'There are extremely vigilant armed guards;
They stand guard day and night;
Indeed they are soldiers of Yama – God of Death.
I am unaware of the means of searching Mother Sita
And her whereabouts in this city.
I have come here alone leaving behind Dwivida,
Angada, Mainda, Sushena, Kumuda – all great warriors
Of the Monkey-clan; what shall I do now?' –
Thinking thus for a while, and in the very next instance,
Remembering the holy feet of Shri Rama,　　　　　　　　　　10
And the valour of Saumitri – the son of Sumitra –
His firmness, strength, confidence, boldness, valour were
All regained with renewed vigour.

The glow of the soul that would
Make possible the impossible, exploded suddenly with a bang.
'It is the peak of beautiful light and it welcomed with waving hands
That supreme confidence into the mind's peak.
I shall proceed quickly; I shall rush in speedily,
And breaking everything into pieces,
I shall see the mother,' – resolving thus,　　　　　　　　　　20
He moved ahead in great heroic spirit.

At that time, there itself,
The presiding deity of Lanka, a fierce *rakshasi* that she was,
Roaring aloud in intense anger rushed forward
Like the onslaught of a tempest.

'Who goes there? Who is it?
Stop, stop you creature of a monkey; what is this leaping about?
Are you ready for the attack? Wouldn't you mind losing your life?
I am Lankini; I shall not spare you; I shall not leave you thus,' –
Shouting this way and brandishing her sword,   30
She came there with a face full of anxiety!

Without feeling frightened, Anjanasuta – the son of Anjana,
Said thus in utter politeness and humility:
'Why do you cry aloud so, mother?
I am an amiable person; I haven't committed any mistake.
As I am only a little monkey, what are you anxious for?
Why do you stop me, and why do you frighten me?
Why are you scared, and why do you grieve?
Whether Lankesha – the king of Lanka has lost confidence
In his own strength?   40

'There is an emotional bond between
Kishkindha – the capital-city of the Monkey-clan and Lanka;
And there exists harmony and a treaty of peaceful co-existence;
When it is so, why are you plagued with suspicion?
I am not an offender; I mean no offence.
There is not any reason to stop me, in the first place!
After completing my task, without causing any harm,
Before sunrise, I shall return to my town
And shall not remain here.'

Hearing that, Lankini   50
Laughed aloud hilariously: 'Who do you think I am?
I am Lankalakshmi – the presiding deity of Lanka.
When I, Lankini, am here
Would I allow you to wander at will?

You shall be the moth that hops around the crest of fire
And finds its end in getting burnt alive.
By the orders of Ravana, I guard the city.

'The bridge of friendship between
Vali – the king of Kishkindha and Ravana was broken.
How could I trust that you are the messenger of Sugriva –   60
The present ruler of Kishkindha, tell me!
The news of Vali's death is indeed the bell that heralds war.
If you take a single step forward, I shall kill you, listen!

'Who called you here?
You creature of a monkey; having no one to control you,
And in fickleness of character,
Not considering the consequences,
Why did you come here leaping?
Why did you sneak in on tip-toe?
All your movements rouse suspicion.   70
There is something secretive; a great conspiracy, I am sure.
Would someone come with no purpose at all?
Your game is over; I shall not spare you;
I shall not leave you thus.
I shall cut you with a saw, and I shall strike you with a sword,' –
Shouting like this, splintering in anger,
Lankini frightened Hanuma.
Not abandoning the path of tolerance
And holding forth the abode of peace, Pavanasuta said:
'Why are you here? Why am I here?   80
Why do you shout so much?
I am the offspring of your womb;
I am the child of your mercy.
Heaven itself is here – so it is said.
This is the treasure-house for those
Who worship wonderful things – they say.
Ruminating on all these in mind, I came here.
I came to the abode that invites pilgrims stretching out its hand.

I came leaping over the ocean in valour.
I came here thinking that 90
This is the wealthy abode for the guests – invited or otherwise.
I came to Amaravati – the abode of Devendra
That attracts the whole world.
Is there any other land that equals this in greatness and grandeur?
The rich culture of Lanka is renowned world over.
How could you tarnish its glory thus in ignorance?
How could you taint it by your pettiness!

'Listen, O Mother! Listen!
I am the sun of Anjana; I am Anjaneya.
I am not afraid for my life or death in the least. 100
Whether all the soldiers of Sugriva are the enemies of Lanka?
If you are suspicious still, no doubt I shall return.
I came here to enjoy the beauty and charm of Lanka.
I came here on State affairs.
I am truly a simple and an innocent person;
Why do you think of destroying me?
You are like a mother to me;
Let me enjoy the grand views of Lanka
Happily under your hospitality.
I want to eat sumptuously; serve me a great meal. 110
You are Lankini, and that being so,
Why do you attack me like this?
I have heard the great fame of Lankini through my own ears.
Now it is my good fortune to see you with my own eyes.
Lankini's heart is filled with mercy,
And is home to the guest – all say so.
Is it fair that the mercy with which one welcomes
The guest lovingly with folded hands, should dry up?
How come the world-renowned Lanka is
Affected by the unpropitious stars? 120
Whether anybody uses *Brahmastra* –
The supreme weapon of infallible destruction –
On a sparrow-like *vanara*!'

Not being moved or touched in the least
And not showing any mercy, Lankini screamed:
'Goaded by capriciousness, you have entered the city.
Why pollute the great *rakshasa*-culture?
O, you *vanara*! Get out from here, out with you.
To enjoy the sight of Lanka is not a child's play,' –
Shrieking in anger thus, she rushed forward striking 130
And in readiness to catch hold of him.

Clenching the fist,
And collecting all her physical strength
As she readied herself to pound Anjaneya –
Hanumanta turned around quickly without getting caught
And struck a blow with great force on the *rakshasi*'s chest
With his diamond-fist, shouting – 'May you die – you *rakshasi*.'
Unable to bear the blow, as if the mountain had dropped down,
The *rakshasi* fell down to earth.
It seemed to foretell Lankesha that just like this, 140
Lankalakshmi – the presiding deity of Lanka,
Would also fall down very soon.
Recovering quickly, Lankini
Sat up and looked around.
'A woman shall be respected.
It is not proper at all to torment and batter a woman,' –
Such was the advice mother Anjana had given him –
Remembering that, he apologised to Lankini:
'Pardon me, O Mother! I wronged you.
I countered your attack in unbridled temper. 150
True, you are the mother; I struck you in anger.'

Lankini said with folded hands:
'You are truly valorous; you are heroic indeed.
I am a *yakshi* – the demi-goddess attending on Kubera;
Vishwakarma – the architect of the gods – has built Lanka;
Kubera himself has ordered and appointed me
To protect Lanka – this is my bounden-duty.

I stopped you in a spirit of protecting Lanka.
Now I am defeated, and therefore I shall not stop you.
March forward; may your great mission be accomplished! 160

'Whatever is said, what use does it have!
It is no fault of yours; you are truly a gentle person.
Great indeed is your forgiveness; I am appeased;
I pay obeisance to you.
You have called me mother,
And have shown your mercy and affection already
And thus you have become the offspring of my womb.
Before the spring of my good fortune dried up
You came in the form of water
That flows out from the depths of the sands. 170
O, Saumya – the calm one!
You came as a Guru; I bow to you.
You have come here as the foreword that proclaims
The end of Ravana who has brought Sita here!

'O, my son! March into the city.
Get yourself engaged in your mission of Great Quest!
Vaidehi – the daughter of Vidarbha, is waiting;
A virtuous woman is she.
Like *chataka* – the mythical bird that lives only on rain water –
She has been anticipating when the message of Shri Rama would
    come.' 180

Lankini is an ignorant sloth.
She surrendered to Hanuma in devotion.
Hanuma, the messenger of Rama,
With the ability to accomplish his mission,
Responding to the need of the hour,
Combined within himself the powers
Of *sattvika* – essence of purity;
Rajasa – intense passions; and *tamasa* – slothful ignorance,
And keeping them under his perfect control,
Struck hard all the evil-powers 190

That bring to naught any great achievement
Driven by the passions of love and hatred!
Now he was ready to explore his path.
And here, Lankini was free from the bad-company of Ravana.
She had the good fortune of seeing the messenger of Rama.
She moved towards the rainbow in the new horizon!

By the grace of Rama, for Hanuma,
Poison itself became ambrosia;
All the blazing heat became refreshingly cool;
Enemies became friends; 200
A giant rock was now only a speck;
The hundred *yojana*-wide ocean itself seemed to shrink
To the size of the foot of a cow;
The mission impossible now seemed achievable.
In this way, having gained victory over Lankini,
In order to crush the enemies under his feet,
Bending on his right leg,
He leaped over the fort and entered the city!

Canto One Hundred and Forty-two

'The Fire of Ruthless-indulgence is Burning in the Pit of the Stomach'

॥६॥

As Hanuma was walking along the main street
There were many buildings decorated with gems and charming ramparts;
Many types of designs and grandeur of sculpture were found.
There was *chaturangabala* – an army comprising
Of elephants, chariots, cavalry, and infantry.
There were stables for elephants and horses.
The natural fort surrounded by water on all sides looked grand.
The city was shining bright with greenery everywhere.
Kalasha – an ornamental dome – shone atop mansions
And they were glowing like light-houses. 10
The rows of entertainment-houses atop hills
Were gleaming like the crown of *Rajyalakshmi* –
The presiding deity of the State.
The rows of towers and the rows of lighted arches
Were glowing brighter through reflections.
The moon was looking magnificent among the stars;
Mitigating the heat of the world by his soothing light,
And causing high-tides in the roaring ocean,
He was supremely pleased.

There is the grandeur of gold. 20
It looked as if Lakshmi – the Goddess of Wealth,
Deserting the ocean of milk in bewilderment
And showering her grace on Lanka, settled there.
Hanumanta walked along viewing everything
And scrutinizing all with his sharp-sight.
'What is the use of having everything that one could wish for?
Lankesha has no character – what a pity!
He has invited death stretching his hands out.
He himself has lifted the veil of death.
What more!' – Hanumanta grieved thus. 30

In his eagerness to seek the mother,
Pavanasuta entered many mansions and thoroughly searched them.
It was the opportune season for the lovers to play the love-game;
It was the time of the night for them to come closer;
It was the happy-time for enjoying heavenly charm;
And as the melody of the orchestra was spread throughout
The couples, under the stupour of romance, were wandering
Happily in the empire of lustful indulgence.

What diverse views one could see there!
Some were arguing hard; some were screaming aloud; 40
Some were lost in infuriating anger and unbridled wrath;
Some were peevish, and some others were awake;
Some were tottering under the spell of heavy intoxication;
Some were dancing in frenzied excitement.
As the heat deep inside the mind was spreading out in dreams,
They were all immersed in the world of myriad dreams.

It was the kingdom of love and desire.
There were the charming, young damsels
And the mature women adept at *navarasa* – the nine tastes;
There were the beautiful women, who walked like swans, 50
And the charming women under the trees;
Young dames with slender waists;
Damsels with glowing long arms.

As the young damsels with shining faces
And enchanting breasts bared their beauty
In the cool breeze of the night,
Every shrunken limb was roused by the touch
Of Ananga – the God of Love.
In the garden of life, the flowers of smile bloomed
Spreading out the fragrance of love.   60
The swaying slender bodies got sprinkled
With that fragrance of love.
The fully drenched slender body
Was quivering in the excitement of kisses
And the spring of kisses was intoxicated with intense joy.
The feral stream gushed forth dancing in merriment.
The grandeur of the seven musical notes reached its peak.
As there were the fellowship parties
Of sipping the spirituous liquor at all lanes and by-lanes,
They were roaring aloud dancing in high intoxication.   70
Some were playing sprinkling coloured water on each other.
The fragrance of sandal-paste was all over the place.

In the many mansions called –
Padmaka, Svastika, Vardhamanaka –
Young charming damsels were singing excelling even the nymphs;
The jingling of their beautiful anklets resounded melodiously.
The light of exuberant beauty and wealth was glowing there.
The eulogy of Lankesha's glory was heard everywhere.
The soldiers were keeping vigil armed with
Mace, sword, bow, axe, and other such weapons.   80
Hanuma saw a white tusker in rut
At the far-off main-gate.

Hanuma was searching sometimes the
Main street, and some other times the various manors and palaces.
Many virtuous-women, feeling shy of the love-game,
Forgot the world in the embrace of their beloved men.
The skin-colour of the charming damsels engaged

In the act of love was glowing like gold,
And Hanuma on seeing all these,
Shut his eyes in utter disgust, 90
And recounted the name of Rama!

What a mean affluence is this!
The fire of ruthless-indulgence is burning in the pit of the stomach
And its rich echo is resounding everywhere.
Outwardly it all appeared laughter-filled merriment;
But deep down it was only writhing in agony.
It was as if molten lead was poured into one's eyes and ears.
Lanka was indeed home to the world's wealth;
Home of the lord of Lakshmi – the Goddess of Wealth;
It was as if the celestial city itself descended 100
To earth in the form of Lanka.
When such a Lanka was thus polluted,
What a disgrace!

The search was on.
Wherever Hanuma searched, Vaidehi was not there.
'Where could the holy mother,
She who loves the feet of Rama, be?
Where could the holy mother,
She who dwells in the mind of Shri Rama, be?
Where could she be, 110
The one who suffers from the pangs of separation?
Where could she be,
The one who abides by *dharma* and Truth?' –
Lamenting thus, Hanuma was vexed and fatigued.
Meditating on Shri Rama,
He fell asleep atop a mansion.

Canto One Hundred and Forty-three

'At the Will of its Master, moves *Pushpaka* – The self-propelling Aerial Plane'

||๑||

'What if I fell asleep, I shall certainly seek her –'
With this determination, charged with renewed vigour
And enthusiasm, Hanuma moved ahead.
He came near Lankesha's palace which was
Surrounded by glittering mansions!
The palace which was full of fierce *rakshasas*
Looked as if it was a forest inhabited by tigers,
Lions, and such other wild beasts.
Brave soldiers mounted on elephants, horses,
And grand chariots were standing guard at all places. 10

There were gymnasiums at all places.
The roar of the wrestlers, and the charm of their wrestling skills
By which they seized their opponents and pulled them to the ground,
And their challenging pose made the cowards cry out in fear,
And swelled up the spirit of valour in the brave.

There were chariots made of gold and silver
Decorated with tiger-skin.
In the mansion of that great charioteer,

Many rows of couches were looking grand
Decked with nine varieties of precious gems.   20
The jingling sound of anklets worn by the young damsels
Seemed like the echo of the roaring ocean.
The enticing fragrance was spread all over.
The sound of the gong, conch, drum
And kettle-drum were heard everywhere.

Hanuma entered the mansions
Where lived the prominent *rakshasas*.
He searched the gardens.
He steadfastly went round the swimming pools.
He searched the chambers upstairs;   30
He searched the inner enclosures.
He finished searching the palace of Prahasta –
The army-chief of Ravana;
The palace of Mahaparshwa was next;
He finished searching the palace of Kumbhakarna;
And the palace of Mahodara thereafter;
He finished searching the palaces of Vidyujihwa and Vidhyunmali;
The palace of Vajradamshtra was searched,
And so was the palace of Indrajit;
The palaces of Shuka, Sarana, Sumali,   40
And Jambumali were also searched.

Now, to the palace of Lankesha:
It is the epitome of beauty; who could describe that!
Adishesha himself – the sovereign of the Serpent race,
With his many tongues, admits defeat for failing
To describe the beauty of the palace.
It is home to exquisite sculpture decked with bountiful gold.
It measures one *yojana* in length and its width is half-a-*yojana*.
It is multi-storeyed and is heavily guarded.
The entire wealth of Kubera is settled there.   50
The riches of Devendra too settled there.
There is no comparison to Lanka's bounty
Of wealth in the whole world!

There is the superb glittering of diamonds and lopez.
Golden palanquin is there; so also the golden couch.
The creeper-houses there glitter in freshness everywhere.
Look at the art gallery! Look at the amusement-house!
As one watches them, emotions race through the veins pulsating.
The palace is home to *navaratna* – nine varieties of precious gems,
And *navanidhi* – the nine treasures of Kubera. 60
The palace of Kailasa – the abode of Shiva, with its rich
    white-glow;
The glitter of the abode of Devendra;
The gleam of the land of the moon;
The radiance of the land of the sun,
In unison have filled the palace of Ravana.
It is created by Maya – the architect of the *rakshasas*,
And is decked with precious gems.
There are many colourful and grand pavilions with
    rounded-windows;
The finesse and dexterity of sculpture and architecture
Are all seen manifested in the armouries and the upper chambers. 70

There are golden vessels filled with the juice of *soma*.
In merriment, it puts to shame the palace of Kubera himself.
Young charming damsels walk jingling their anklets.
The soft melody of *veena* soothes one's heart.
'How many women languished here imprisoned by wealth?
How many are still languishing in the
Lure of grandeur, charm and wealth of Lanka – I can't say!'
Maruti – the son of Maruta, lamented thus.

There, at one spot,
Pushpaka was gorgeously present and Hanuma gazed at it intently. 80
Bowing to the exquisite handicraft of Vishwakarma –
The architect of the gods –
And admiring – 'Bravo! Bravo! Well-done, well-done!!' –
Hanuma watched its beauty thoroughly.

He gazed at it once from the front,
And once again from the rear;

He watched it once from the sides,
Yet again circumferentially all around;
From the southern direction once,
And once again from the north; 90
Once from the top,
And once from below; and once again from all over.
Rich handicraft was present everywhere.
It stood there glowing but without touching the ground;
Hanuma, overcome with wonder,
Looked at it rubbing his own eyes.
How strange is this! It is not easy even for the gods
To get one such as this.
How shall I praise the fruit of Ravana's great penance!
At the will of its master, moves *Pushpaka* 100
The self-propelling plane –
And so it is said. What a Chariot of Life is this!
Only the very fortunate could have such a chariot.

As if the twang of a bow-string came
To rest on the mountain-peak,
As if the well-chiseled idol came out splitting the rock,
As if the beauty of the demi-gods was fused,
And as if it was the Flower-chariot of Manmatha – the God of
  Love –
Pushpaka stood there in such grandeur.

Look at the art gallery! 110
Many colourful paintings were there on the walls:
There was a row of mountains;
The moon and the other planets were there;
The trees on the mountains looked grand blossoming with flowers;
The dexterity of handicraft could be seen in every petal of a flower.
The painted mansion with upper-storey
Looked like the epitome of beauty.
There was a grand pond filled with lotuses.
Swans were flying spreading their wings wide.
There was the design of a bird glittering with the glow of gems. 120
It looked as if the sky and the horizons attained fullness.

There were parrots and peacocks everywhere
And spreading their feathers,
They played and remained wakeful.

There was a drawing.
It draws the onlookers' attention.
Gajalakshmi – Goddess Lakshmi was there.
She is *padmahaste* – holds a lotus in her hand;
She stands on *padma* – the lotus;
Two elephants stand on her sides lifting up their trunks   130
In readiness to offer water-lily to the goddess.
Pavanaja's eyes were drawn to that painting.
When Pavanaja saw the fragrant aerial-chariot there,
His mind jumped and leaped in excitement.
It looked as if the entire world was whirling at a great speed.
It looked as though the nether world cracked and the entire earth
   sunk below.
His eyes rolled fast in great wonder
And he stood rooted there in silence!

In the palace of Ravana
There were many women brought by force   140
By the invading *rakshasas*.
There were many queens of other kings among them,
So also many princesses.
Many varieties of aquatic animals were found there.
It looked like an overflowing ocean.

The stairways were gem-stacked.
There were windows made of gold with crystal-laid frames;
The walls were inlaid with corals; it looked as if
The wealth of the entire world was heaped up there!

What a beautiful! abode!   150
The Goddess of Beauty herself lay there as if her legs were broken!
Lankesha's palace is an embellishment par excellence.
Not having seen the holy mother Sita
Who lives recounting the name of Rama,
Anjaneya was immersed in the ocean of worry.

Canto One Hundred and Forty-four

'The Most Handsome and Lovable Man Shone Brilliantly!'

||६||

Night was getting darker and silence was spreading fast.
The mission of searching for the Mother was on.
The beautiful damsels in Ravana's palace
Having spent time in the love-game until past mid-night
And as the intoxication of *soma*-juice got subsided
And as the heat of lust having been diminished
Forgetting themselves, rolled down languidly wherever they were.
They – numbering more than a thousand – were all fast asleep.
Though not wished for, the World of Love,
And all kinds of love-acts and their aberrations too   10
Unfolded themselves before Maruti's eyes.

There were women whose faces looked beautiful like a lotus.
They were asleep with their lips half open.
The buzz of bees and swans in the darkness of the night was heard.
The lotus-pond was calm.
The charming damsels sleeping there
Looked as if they were the beautiful stars fallen on earth;
And it seemed as if they were the swans asleep on the river banks
After their immensely satisfying swim in the river.

Getting exhausted after the joyful sport of dancing 20
And the game of love, now they rolled down languidly
And they looked like the creepers pulled up and cast away
By a tusker in rut.
Their hair was dishevelled and the ornaments had slipped off.
The auspicious mark on the forehead was distorted
And the flowers worn on the head had fallen down;
The necklace of pearls, corals, and gems
That had slipped off, now remained spread
On the cleavage between the breasts;
The golden bells of their jewelry lay scattered. 30
The loose-end of the sari with its colourful paintings
That covered the breasts looked grand
Like a flag on their heaving bosoms.
Every jewelry worn by them –
The golden pendant on the forehead, the anklets,
The dangling ear-rings – was oscillating fast.
The air that had sucked in the fragrance of the *soma*-juice,
In their exhalation was now spreading that fragrance all around. 40

There are the beautiful women –
Some drawn by the valour of Ravana,
And some others drawn by passion –
Who left their husbands for the charming love of Lankesha,
And considered themselves fortunate to be so.

Among those women
Some are from the clan of the priestly-sages,
And some from the *rakshasas*;
Some are from the *gandharva*-clan.
It looked as though 50
It was a beauty pageant of many gorgeous
Damsels of all hues and clans.

All the beautiful damsels were happy
As they enjoyed a thoroughly satiating game of love
And beamed in their pride as the most beautiful women on earth.

As they were rolling in stupour, overcome by illusion,
They were embracing their own women-companions
Dreaming that it was their beloved Lankesha;
And how they kissed each other in ecstasy!
The rival-wives imagining that Lankesha himself had kissed them,　　60
Felt happy and overjoyed.
Some of them slept there using their arms as pillows;
Some rested their heads on the breasts of others;
Someone was in the arms of some other;
Someone slept on the thigh of some other.
They were so forgetful that they slept
In rows thus unmindful of each other.
Their entwined arms looked like a garland of flowers
Neatly woven and placed there.
Their shoulders were like the branches of trees;　　70
And ornaments, the flowers; their eye-brows
Looked like the bees sucking nectar.

The arm-bracelets worn by
Those beauties glittered like lightning.
The glow of their skin looked like that of an idol made of gold.
Their slim waists; long arms; pointed, ample breasts;
Long hair; broad faces; the charming supple cheeks –
All looked like the creepers entwining a tree.
It looked as if they were throwing
The nooses on their beloved men　　80
And making them fall at their feet;
And thus pretended to mock at them.
They moved about enticingly jolting the juice of their beauty.
Seeing these limitless beauty-mines everywhere
Anjaneya moved ahead and went very far.

There, at one spot, was
An ornamental arched structure,
Decked with gems and the sheen of golden tusks.

There was a large soft silken bed;
The white royal-parasol resembled the full-moon. 90
The hand-fan was swayed up and down.
The air was filled with the sweet-smelling fragrance of perfumes.
The swaying garland of flowers was spreading fragrance.
In the comfort of the bed-chamber,
On that soft couch, Lankesha was asleep.
He looked like the peak of the Mount Mandara.
Like the moon surrounded by a galaxy of stars,
Lankesha, the most handsome and lovable man, shone brilliantly!

The ear-rings glittered bright
On Lankesha's ears. The outstretched arms 100
Looked like Indra's flag.
Enjoying the love-game under the intoxicating
Soma-juice, he was breathing heavily
Like the hissing of a great serpent.
Then, Anjaneya leaped swiftly on to the
Stairway and saw the *rakshasa*.
His arms had grown like the trunk of an elephant.
On the side of his arms,
The scars made by the tusk of Airavata – Indra's tusker – could
 be seen.
The beautiful damsels smeared his body with sandal-paste 110
That looked as if his body was smeared with the blood of a rabbit.
His arms had turned red in the act of love goaded
By the charming damsels of all hues and clans –
Of the demi-gods, the *rakshasas*, the *gandharva*, and of the
Serpent-clan. His yellow-coloured silken attire
Had dropped down in a heap.

In the arched structure of his bed-chamber,
Lighted torches were burning in all the four directions.
Like a white cloud gleaming in the brightness of lightning,
Lankesha was looking grand with his wives asleep on both sides

Who lay there exhausted with dancing 120
And the all-consuming game of love.

There was a damsel –
Like a creeper of lotus afloat on a river
That feels secure entwining a boat –
She was asleep embracing a *veena* imagining it to be her beloved.
Another damsel held a drum close to her heart
Believing it to be her beloved.
There was a damsel who, in the imagined bliss
Of being alone with her beloved,
Held the flute in a passionate embrace. 130
Another damsel with the golden hue
Tightly embraced a drum with such passionate hug
That every part of her body intertwined with it.
Yet another woman held the cymbals
Close to her heart thinking it to be her man.
A pair of small drums was embraced by yet another woman
Under the illusion that one of them was her husband sleeping
 on one side,
And the other, a child on her breast, resting on the opposite side.
Seeing these women who were fast asleep in different styles and
 postures,
Pavanasuta moved ahead worrying 140
Where the "mother" was.

'Who could this most beautiful damsel be?
As if the wealth of youth itself slipping off its foothold fell
Into the harem of Lankesha bringing glamour, charm
And grandeur thereunto – who could this beauty be?
As if the beauty of the world itself manifested there
In Ravana's nuptial bed in the form of a woman
Resembling the pinnacle of glory – a *kalasha* –
Who could this woman be? Who was it?'
As Pavanasuta saw her, 150
He was struck with bewilderment

And as his head rolled in confusion,
Losing grip on his own posture,
He felt as if he was sinking down to *Patala*;
He felt as if he was tossed to the skies;
He sunk low to *Patala* as if he slipped from a mountain-peak
Down into the abyss of unconsciousness!

Canto One Hundred and Forty-five

'How Could I Sever the Path of Quest?'

||๑||

'Who is this most beautiful damsel sleeping on
The nuptial bed with Lankesha
So intimately and with such ease?
Could it be the "mother"? No! Never!
Then, who else is she?
Rama's wife is *pativrata* – the virtuous wife;
Could she ever sleep thus?
Could she ever sleep in the embrace of Ravana?
Nothing of the sort is seen here.
May the sins of such a qualm be put to rest. 10
That day Rama had informed me
The intimate subtle signs of Sita:
There are not any *padumarekha* –
Auspicious lotus-lines in the front of her feet;
There is not *matsyalanchana* – the fish-totem on the right thigh;
This woman is certainly not Janaki –
The wife of Padmanabha – Rama;
Look! On the back of her head
There are signs of widowhood!

I shall seek steadfastly; 20
I shall carry on the Great Quest;
If I can't see the "mother",
I shall uproot the city itself' – so he thought!

Spending just about two moments
In the upper chamber of the *rakshasa*'s mansion,
Hanuma moved ahead.
Look, look there! That's the kitchen.
Heaps of food-stuffs are there.
There are heaps of slaughtered deer, pig, peacock
And many other varieties of animals and birds. 30
Most of the food-stuffs have been eaten and only a little bit is
  left out.
There are food-items cooked in six tastes:
Sweet, sour, salty, pungent, astringent, and bitter.
A variety of juices were drunk and spilled over.
There were the fruit-juices mixed with sugar and honey.
The *soma*-juice seemed to invite the revelers to partake of it.
The distilled drink made of pomegranate and grapes –
The intoxicating liquor was frothing and foaming!

There was good taste, but cleanliness none.
Everything lay there scattered in disorder. 40
There were many empty vessels all over
And some vessels with a little bit of food too.
The pot that was fallen down, the pitcher that was broken –
Everything created an illusion
That there was great confusion and uproar at dinner time.

Not finding the queen of Rama
Despite the thorough search, beads of perspiration
Appeared on the forehead of Hanuma
And sitting down at one place, he began to reflect:
'What is all this? Have I committed any offence? 50
Have I come on the sly and watched the damsels?
Is that not a blemish on my vow of celibacy?

Am I not disturbed in the mind?
Has not the firmness of my mind been shaken?
Does it befit me to have seen the damsels
Shamelessly engaged in unbridled acts of lust!
Forgetting myself I wandered uncontrolled in Lanka.
I have become guilty and I have become sinful!'

Thinking thus, and finally
Consoling himself, Hanuma felt thus: 60
'I neither have any guilt; nor need I worry about virtue.
I have not transgressed the limits of decency,
Nor have I broken any rules.
I have not fallen for sensuality,
Nor has my self-restraint diminished.
I have not come here to see the damsels in such an unnatural state.
I have come here on my master's mission to seek the "mother".
This unnatural state of affairs fell into my sight involuntarily
And therefore I am not guilty in the least!'

Feeling composed thus, 70
Hanuma continued his search worrying all the while –
'Will I, or will I not see the "mother",'
He looked for the "mother" once in the creeper-house;
Once again in the art gallery; yet again in the garden,
One more time in the pond;
And thus he went on searching,
And felt completely exhausted!

'Whatever has happened to the "mother"?
In this over-indulgent, uncouth culture of the *rakshasas*
It is not possible for the good-natured, 80
Virtuous holy mother to take respite.
In the anger that she did not take a liking for him,
Whether Ravana had killed her and thrown her away?
Not having seen the "mother",
And not knowing anything about her whereabouts,
How could I return and present myself before Sugriva?

How could I show my face to Shri Ramachandra?
What shall I answer to the question of Saumitri?
The time-span given by Sugriva is already over.
Sugriva, the powerful king, won't leave me unpunished.   90
If returned empty-handed thus,
He won't spare any of the *vanara* warriors unpunished,
Including Angada – the son of Vali, for sure.
The order of Sugriva is harder than diamond;
Could anyone survive in the kingdom
Of Kishkindha disobeying his order!

'Whatever has to happen, will happen!
I shall search steadfastly. Why should I be fearsome?
Why should I be dispirited, disappointed and helpless?
Is there anything impossible for the spirit of enthusiasm?   100
I shall try again; I shall not mind the drawback.
I shall search again in the liquor-house, the art gallery,
The creeper-house, and the amusement-house;
I shall even use the hooked drag right into the womb of Lanka
And pull everything out and demonstrate my valour
To the *rakshasas*' – so he thought.

He searched in the basement cell and the square-porch;
He searched them again and again.
He searched all the mansions – big and small;
He searched them again and again.   120
He leaped from house to house;
And stopping at each door and opening it
He entered it silently and looking everywhere
He searched them again and again.
Descending here and ascending there;
Every street, every square and every platform
Every garden and every bank of a pond –
He searched them again and again.
What was the use of such a search?
There was no trace of the daughter of Mithila anywhere.   130

'Whatever has happened to the "mother"?
At the time when Ravana was bringing her here after the abduction,
Did she lose her life falling down from the chariot?
While crossing the ocean, did she die of broken heart?
As she did not take a liking for Lankesha,
Did his followers crush her in anger,
And with relish, ate her up roasted?
Did the other *rakshasies* eat her up fearing
That she would be a rival wife?
Wailing helplessly and recounting the name   140
Of Rama and Lakshmana,
Did she depart from the world in *prayopavesha* –
Fasting unto death as expiation?

'Where is the "mother"?
Where is she? How is she? Is she dead? Is she alive?
Whether Lankesha has secretly kept her
Like a caged parrot in solitary confinement?
Has he killed her? Has he eaten her up? What has he done?
Whether my crossing the ocean has gone futile?
Whether my loyal servitude to my master has gone waste?   150
Whether my valour and courage have gone waste?
O, my Great Quest has gone waste!

'Janaki is not there!
Suffice to say that she might be dead – then, instantly,
Shri Rama would certainly die of grief!
If Shri Rama dies, whether Saumitri would live?
Would Bharata-Shatrughna – the younger brothers
Of Rama, hold on to life then?
In the grief that they did not accomplish at all Shri Rama's mission,
Would Sugriva and Rumaa – his wife, survive at all?   160
When Sugriva dies, the entire *vanara*-clan
Would certainly die by smashing their heads against the rocks;
Would jump down from mountain-peaks and die;
Would even drink poison and thus discard the mortal frame;

Would even use swords and slash their bodies.
Kishkindha and the city of Saketa too would fall down
Being condemned to be even worse than the burial grounds.
I shall not return now.
What is the use of being alive?
I shall fall into the pit of fire and die being burnt alive;   170
I shall fast unto death, and breathe my last,' –
Pavanaja was lost in such worry and anxiety.

Thus he remained there
In the abyss of disappointment for a while.
But Pavanasuta cast all such dejection away
And relied on courage and valour.
'Vaidehi is not here. So what?
Ravana alone is guilty and he alone is the cause of "mother's" death.
I shall bind his hands and limbs and thus I shall slay him;
And I shall offer as festive-meal his torso and trunk   180
To the Goddess of Death,' –
He was lost in such anger and worry.
But soon shedding such thoughts
And relying on his sense of discrimination, said unto himself:
'Why should I get angry thus? I shall search again.
How could I sever the path of Quest?' –
Thinking thus, he resumed his search.

Canto One Hundred and Forty-six

'A Divine Imploration Took Hanuma to the Garden of Desire and Stood him there'

||◉||

O, Look! As the search continued, Pavanaja moved all around
And getting exhausted and feeling weak by the wanderings, he sat down.
Slowly the night faded away and sun appeared heralding a new dawn.
As Hanuma was moving ahead, cool breeze blew gently;
It appeared as if some happy news came floating with it.
Some unknown but pleasant-requital and some divine imploration
Took Hanuma to the Garden of Desire and stood him there.
That indeed was the Ashokavana!

A swarm of bees was
Moving fast kissing every flower. 10
As the buds bloomed, fountains of fragrance
Were springing up. The very essence
Of quietude was flowing out as light.
All the paths were lighted and all the directions were glowing.
The chirping of birds was soothing to the mind.
The *ashoka* tree with its thick mat of green foliage was

Drawing the mind of Pavanaja unto itself.
It seemed as if the regents of the eight cardinal points
And all the gods had settled there with great pleasure.

'O, Rama! What penance may be required 20
To win over the *rakshasas* to seek out Vaidehi!
Would I accomplish it? What greatness is there in me?
I bow to Shri Rama; I bow to Shri Lakshmana;
I bow a thousand times to the holy mother – Janaka's daughter;
I bow to Devendra; I bow to Rudra – Shiva;
I bow to Yama, *dharma* incarnate; I bow to my sire,' –
Thus he uttered unto himself.

As the light of the dawn was spreading
Surveying all the directions,
'What a quiet place is this! 30
How beautiful a place is this!
This place that Lankesha has created is basking in glory,
Grandeur, grace and excellence,' –
Thinking thus, Hanuma moved ahead under the shade of trees.

What grandeur of nature!
It was the thirteenth day of the lunar fortnight,
Of the twelfth lunar month; spring had just arrived.
There were rows of *champaka*-trees;
Mango-trees and jasmine-creepers;
Nagakesara and *uddalaka* trees were also there; 40
All varieties of trees were looking grand with full of flowers.
Like an arrow shot from the bow, Pavanasuta,
Leaping across the enclosures,
Entered the mango-grove interlaced
With flowery-creepers and wandered there.

Many a variety of colourful birds were
Chirping happily and their melodious notes could be heard all over.
Jack and citron trees were covered with fruits.
Hares and peacocks were running about sprightly

And the nightingales were cooing. 50
Birds were flying towards the flower-gardens.
Bees were abuzz sucking nectar from
Jasmine and the flowers of the fragrant screw-pine.
Swans were flying majestically and the flowers were oozing nectar.
The auspicious journey has been progressing well and is
  tempting too.
The green paddy fields stretched everywhere
And the ripe rice-stalks looked beautiful
As they swayed and stood bent heavy with grains.
The entire clan of birds was eagerly sucking
Juice from the straw-like ripe rice-stalks! 60

In his natural fickleness of mischief,
As Pavanasuta shook the branches of a tree,
The flowers, the leaves, and the unripe fruits
All fell down to the ground!
That tree looked like a gambler
Who stood there empty-handed having
Lost everything that he had.
Then the birds went off flying somewhere.
As Hanuma grasped another tree
Some small branches broke off and fell down to the ground. 70
As the big branches looked skywards helplessly
That tree looked like a damsel in disarray
With dishevelled hair, scratch-marks made of nails and teeth,
Parched lips and unkempt pale face.
'Why this mischief,' – thought Pavanasuta
And stopped his pranks.

There was a lake filled with
Crystal-clear water and aquatic birds were chirping happily.
The lotus-buds were blooming unfolding their beauty.
There was a hill and the stream gushing down from it 80
Looked like a damsel getting up swiftly
From the lap of her beloved and walking away in pretended anger;

The arched stone-structure, the slanting trees,
And the rocks and the hills on her path
Looked as if they were attempting to hold her back by
Comforting her saying – 'why play such pranks on him!'

  That stream flowed meandering
And its momentum was now checked –
It looked like a wife who, worshipping her beloved
On a pedestal made of gold and cheering him up lovingly,   90
Was happily on her way to her parental home – and thus
The stream flowed through in a sing-song fashion.

There was a *shimshupa* tree.
As the melody of jingling golden anklets was heard
Pavanasuta, becoming curious to know
Whether the Mother was there,
Climbed up a tree thick with flowers and buds
And looking all around with watchful eyes thought thus:

'I shall certainly seek Sita wherever she may be –
The one who is yearning to see Shri Rama.   100
In their anxiety-filled enthusiasm
To see the fierce vows and penance Vaidehi has undertaken,
All the aquatic birds, lotus creepers, *champaka* flowers, sandal trees –
All that are dear to Janaki have come
And settled here!'

Filled with the enthusiasm and hope
That Sita who is adept at journeying through the forests
And the one who suffers from the pangs of separation from
  Shri Rama
Is certainly somewhere near here,
Pavanasuta lost himself in deep meditation.   110
At that instant itself, there was a flash of self-realisation
On the peak of accomplishment.

Canto One Hundred and Forty-seven

'The Lamp of Broken Hope Seems to be Glowing Now'

||৬||

Ashokavana was set in glory resembling the spring-chariot.
All-season flowers and fruits were looking grand on the trees.
Like Gandhamadana – the mountain renowned
For its fragrance, scented air was emanating everywhere.
Ashokavana seemed grander than Heaven itself.
The palace of Ravana that Hanuma had seen at night was
Circular in shape and a high-rise grand mansion.
It was a snow-white mansion
And it looked like the palace in Kailasa, Shiva's abode
It had thousand pillars and the thresholds made of corals;   10
Its tower was so high that it looked as if it was piercing the sky;
The sparkle of its golden doors was so bright that
It pricked the onlooker's eyes even from far.

There, under the tree,
In the middle of the group of *rakshasies*
Hanuma saw a beautiful damsel who looked like a pious hermit!
Like the brightly glowing moon covered by a mask of thick smoke,
Like the lotus bloomed in mire,
The one with a moon-like face was wearing soiled dress

And tears were rolling down her cheeks –
Hanuma saw her with wide-opened eyes
In such a plight and wondering –
'Is she Janaki; is it true that she is the pious "mother"?'
He looked at her again and again.
She was wearing a white dress.
Like the lotus that had lost its gleam;
Like a frightened deer,
That beautiful damsel sat there with her eyes closed
In penance and with her mind focused on meditation.
As if the whole world was inert,
As if the entire ocean remained motionless,
As the internal glow sprang like a fountain
She sat there with her head bent down
And her gaze fixed on her feet.
Many days and nights passed thus,
And she was weak in body; her hair was dishevelled
And she was constantly burnt by the fire of separation;
She was steadfastly recounting the name
Of Raghupati – Rama, lord of the clan of Raghu.
Her desire to possess
The golden deer was dried up now;
With a feeling of deep disappointment,
And recounting the virtues of Shri Rama in her mind,
She was pleading in utter humility –
'Help me out of this imbroglio, my lord!'

There, as the peacocks danced
In rapture, Sita slowly opened her eyes.
Emotions that stir the waves of anxiety
Agitated growing hundredfold.
A peacock, desiring the affection of Janaki,
Moved about coming close to her.
Unable to resist, she took the peacock on her lap
And embracing it affectionately comforted it.

A *rakshasi* who was near Sita, saw all this.
'What kind of a woman is this one
Who defies the love of my lord, but loves a peacock?' –
So wondering, filled with jealousy and anger,
The *rakshasi* seized that peacock
And wringing its neck hard squeezed its life.
'Look! I have eaten it now. It's so tasty and truly so! 60
Look! It's dancing in my stomach now.
Give up your stubbornness; love my lord;
You shall be the queen,' – the *rakshasi* said so.

Having seen such a cruel act,
Janaki, pained deeply, shed tears.
She was overcome with many emotions:
The blame of being *ayonija* – the one not born of womb,
The episode of being deserted by one's own mother,
The spell cast by *maya* – in the form of the golden deer;
The deception of Ravana; 70
The death of Jatayu, the king of the Eagle clan;
The adversity under which she became
A doll in the hands of time;
And the pain of living like an orphan –
Trapped in such thoughts, the "mother" shrank in grief!

Looking at her own feet, she felt –
'For what did I cross the lines drawn by Saumitri?
These feet are ominous indeed.
Why I went crossing them over?
Did I cross the limits of Saketa's decency – the Code of Ayodhya? 80
Evil befell me as I desired that deer of fanciful hue.
I am ruined because I did not pay heed
To the presence of Raghupati, my consort.
O Rama! O Rama! I am utterly ruined,' –
Thus she said unto herself!

'She, the one with the face like a full-moon,
Was lost in pain and was shedding tears.

She recounted the name of Rama and Hanuma heard it.
No doubt she is *bhumija* – the daughter of earth;
She is the Light of Happiness of the entire world; 90
The lamp of broken hope seems to be glowing now.

'Yes, she is Janaki for sure.
There is no doubt in it anymore.
I have seen now Saketalakshmi – the queen of Ayodhya.
It is like seeing *pranavapanchakshari* –
The primordial sound *"om namah shivaya"* –
The mystic chant to appease Shiva;
I have seen Gayatri – the presiding deity
Of the sacred Vedic hymn so called;
I have seen the secret signs on her as told by my master; 100
As everything matches perfectly well, I now feel composed.
She is wearing ear-rings and has scanty ornaments on her.
I have seen all the ornaments the "mother" had thrown away tied
Into a heap at Rushyamuka –
The mountain where Sugriva had taken refuge.

'Yes, it is true; there is not any mistake.
Indeed she is *kanakangi* – the one with a golden hue;
Rama is fortunate indeed;
The Mother is fortunate; I am truly fortunate.
She is the crystal of fortune of this epoch; 110
She has been found after all!
Urmila – Saumitri's consort, the crystal of penance, is at Saketa;
Sita – the crest-jewel of mankind – is in Lanka.
She is truly the epitome of confluence
Of all virtues of this epoch' –
Praising her thus, Pavanasuta sang and danced
In the rhapsody of excitement.

'How shall I rescue the "mother"?
By what means could I take her to Kishkindha
Crossing the ocean? O Shri Rama! 120
Who could lord over you!

Protect me; protect me, my lord;
Lift me up with your grace and protect me,' –
Imploring thus, Pavanaja worried
Filled with the emotions of anxiety and conflict.
'How could one gauge the greatness
Of Kalapurusha – the Time-persona!
Not being unduly agitated,
The "mother" is sitting there in complete quietude.
Considering devotion to her husband the greatest virtue   130
And thus refusing all comforts and indulgences,
Shubangi – Janaki, the beautiful woman,
Came to the forest taking it to be the palace itself.
Shri Rama is the epitome of strength.
When would Rama take the "mother" home slaying all the *rakshasas*?
He has unparalleled strength;
He has slain Vali;
He has destroyed Khara and Dushana, Subahu and Trishira –
All were powerful *rakshasas*.
Rama, the one graced with infinite strength,   140
Shall certainly slay Ravana, and take the "mother"!

'Suffering loneliness, Janaki has become weak
Like *chakravaka* – the ruddy goose renowned for conjugal
   attachment;
Like a female elephant caught up in the centre of a pack of lions;
Like a *veena* discarded by the flutist un-played;
Like the moon covered by thick clouds;
Like Rohini – the most favourite consort of Moon
Surrounded by wild planets –
Thus Janaki is suffering greatly.
What a pity!' With such thoughts,   150
Pavanasuta got lost in the sea of compassion!

Having seen the "mother" at last
Pavanasuta was drenched in tears of happiness.
As the tearful drops fell on the *shimshupa* leaves

They glowed like pearl-balls.
'I am blessed by Shri Ramachandra.'
Feeling overtly happy in the emotion of fulfilment
And ascending high in such a sublime state of mind,
He became Gommata – the renowned Jain king turned ascetic,
   himself!

Canto One Hundred and Forty-eight

'Harnessing the Horse of Volition, She Drove the Chariot of Mind'

||௬||

When Maruti, the son of Marut danced with joy, the whole world danced too.
'Glory to the Mother of the Three Worlds;
Glory to the virtuous "mother";
Glory to the one who is strength incarnate;
Glory to the one whose ornament is fame itself;
Glory to the one loved by Rama;
Glory to the protector of the virtuous men;
O, Mother! I bow to you.
Could you ever be in the mansion of Ravana!
Why did I search for you there?   10
Why did I look for you there?
True, I carry the load of such sins now
That can't be washed off even after many re-births.
O, Mother! Absolve me, forgive me;
I implore you, O, Mother!'

There, at the palace,
Ravana remembered Janaki – 'Come what may,
I shall allure her to please me,' – so thinking
Ravana came to Ashokavana

Wearing grand ornaments
And dressed in grandeur, and glowing bright.
The maids fanned Ravana with *chowry*
That was drenched in moonlight.
Like the nymphs surrounding Devaraja – the king of Heaven,
The damsels with unruffled soothing faces surrounded Ravana.
As if it was the proclamation of his enormous fame,
They spread a figured carpet for him to walk on.

Befitting his high stature
Ravana walked majestically showing royal fortitude.
The white royal-umbrella held over him glowed like the moon.
The damsels were holding a golden pedestal
And they were carrying water in a golden jar;
The damsels were constantly fanning him with *chowry*.
The damsels walked gracefully jingling their anklets.
It all seemed so strange and curious to Pavanasuta.

In his eagerness to appease Janaki,
Ravana did not pay heed to himself; he was choked with desire.
He pulled at his hair, he twisted the garland;
Not having slept well, his eyes were like fire-balls.
Nevertheless, it looked as if beauty itself was manifested
In his persona, and he looked
Like Indra himself who descended to earth.
Having seen the beauty of Ravana thus,
Anjaneya was wonder-struck.

'Look at the charming beauty of the villain!
The twin mountain-cities have branched off forming his heads.
His flag has the fish-totem.
He looks like Mahadeva – Shiva.
He is radiating eminence,
And one does not feel inclined to rebuke him.'
Thinking thus, Hanumanta, hopping from branch to branch,
Moved closer to get a better glimpse of him.

On seeing Ravana,
Janaki looked like a plantain tree caught up in a whirlwind.
She was trembling and shedding tears with her head bent low.
She looked like a ship sinking by the weight of grief.
Harnessing the horse of volition,
She hastily drove the chariot of mind
Straight to the presence of Rama.

She sat there shriveled up – 60
Like a female serpent under the spell of magical chant;
Like Rohini caught by Ketu – the menacing *rakshasa*;
Like the fame crushed by false-accusations;
Like the faith withered under the pain of humiliation;
Like the intellect defeated by frivolous argument;
Like the unimplemented royal decree;
Like the platform for sacrificial offers defiled by sinners;
Like the bare garden deserted by the animals and birds;
Like the drying up spring; like the dying out flicker –
Janaki sat there lusterless. 70

Ravana spoke to her endearingly thus:
'Look here! Dashashira – the ten-headed one –
The one who built up this entire empire
Of the *rakshasas* – is standing before you.
Yearning for your love day and night, I have been waiting.
O, the gem of my heart! Be pleased with me.
I became wild with passion and submissive the moment
I saw you once at Mithila, and once again at Panchavati.
I will carry you everywhere in exaltation –
Be that the galaxies in the sky or the worlds above or below. 80
I will worship your lotus-feet and hold you in high esteem.
Would the fully blossomed flower last long!

'What shall I say, O beautiful damsel!
You alone are true and everything else is sapless.
Shri Lanka is home to all kinds of enjoyment and riches.
Maya is a big lie; I have come seeking your love.

How could I be fulfilled without you?
Without you, my mind goes blank,
And this world remains empty.
Purusha – the Masculine Principle is inert;   90
Prakriti – the Feminine Principle
Is indeed the spirit that breathes life.
You are the spirit that lights up my life.
You are beautiful in every limb
And make everyone happy.
Why do you waste your youth thus
In the prime of your life?
Come, and sit on my left thigh –
The coveted place of a loving wife.
Give up all worries;   100
Be the empress of the World-of-Beauty.

'Listen, O beautiful damsel, listen!
I will renounce this whole kingdom and be your slave.
Give up your reticence;
I shall protect and look after you with utmost care.
Would anyone punish one's supple body
By sleeping on the ground, with unkempt hair,
And not decking oneself with flowers?
What use is it to suffer from starvation?
There are exotic body creams;   110
There are exquisite ornaments; superb dresses;
Grand couches; excellent music and dance;
And grand water-sports –
All in abundance and at your command –
Come, be the garland of pearls round my neck!
Once this youth is lost, it is like water
That has flown down and united with the ocean;
Would it ever come back, O queen?
I am handsome and brimming with youthful charm
And now I am your slave in love.   120
Is it fair to relinquish the emperor, tell me, please.

'You are the epitome of my good fortune.
This empire, this treasury – are all yours.
My body and my life – are all yours.
O beautiful damsel! If I could get some cozy shelter
In your heart, I consider my life meaningful.
Who could equal, or even excel me in valour!
There is no equal to the grandeur
Of Shree Lanka, and none can excel it.
You have defeated me – 130
The one who is renowned as inviolable.
You are truly the unconquered goddess.
O, the epitome of my fortune!
Accept me, and marry me with love.

'I have been waiting for you.
What a beautiful smile you have!
And what beautiful eyes!
How beautiful are the pearly teeth!
And how lustrously white are they!
You are the queen of a peahen 140
Who makes my mind dance in ecstasy.
Come, be the queen of my harem,
O *sushroni* – the one with beautiful hips.
Strike the chord of my heart,
And let the melody flow into a stream.
All riches, grandeur, fame, and desires are awaiting you
In readiness to obey your command.

'Is Rama alive?
He is the chieftain of defeat. He has lost all wealth.
Giving up the hope of victory, 150
He has found himself in the forests.
He has bitten the dust. How could he ever see you now?
Shree Lanka is inaccessible;
And look here! It is impenetrable.
Who seeks moonlight in the thick black clouds?

Forget him; give him up; and give up your false dream.
Could Rama, the one who wears coarse clothes
Made of tree-fibres, ever knock at the doors of Lanka?' –
Speaking thus, Lankesha appeased and comforted her.

Hearing the words spoken by the *rakshasa*-king, 160
Shedding tears, and recounting the name of Shri Rama,
She placed a piece of straw in front of her
As if to suggest 'All your riches and comforts
Are worse than straw,' and said thus:

'Do not be ruined; be not ruined.
Do not be ruined becoming a sinner with no desire for salvation.
I am a devout wife; do not desire me; it is not proper;
As you protect the honour of your wife and become exemplary,
You be the emperor who follows *dharma* –
And be the protector of another's wife; 170
It befits you to live such a life.
When the ruler himself treads the path of evil –
The subjects follow suit – proverbially –
"*yatha raja tatha praja*" –
And undoubtedly the subjects too miss the righteous path.
The prosperity shall decline
And Lanka itself shall be burning.
I shall not become enamoured of wealth and comforts.
Is there any paucity of wealth and comforts at Saketa –
My husband's kingdom? 180
Is there anyone who has separated brightness from the sun?
Rama is the Lord of the Universe;
How could anyone separate me from him?
If you have any desire to live, cultivate Rama's friendship.
Knowing the subtle nuances of *dharma* exceedingly well,
Rama protects those who seek refuge in him.

'Don't you have any sense?
Rama's attack shall be fiercer than *Vajra* –
The most powerful weapon of Indra, the king of Heaven

Rama's attack shall be harsher than 190
That of Yama – the God of Death;
As Trivikrama-Vishnu's incarnation, he shall reach
Lanka just with three foot-steps and invade the fort.
Let the path of *dharma* be yours;
Stop all your evil deeds.
Do not crush under your feet *raja-dharma* –
The duties of a king; be warned!
Could life ever exist in this world –
If deviated from the path of *dharma*;
And also, if the sun, the moon and the earth deviate 200
From their own orbits?
Like the sun sucks away water from the oceans,
Shri Rama and Saumitri shall suck the sap of your life.
Like the tree that is struck by lightning gets burnt and falls down,
The giant tree of *rakshasas* shall be burnt
And shall fall down by the arrow of Shri Rama. Listen!

'When an elephant in rut
Rushes all over blindly causing havoc,
And losing its sense moves towards ruination
In the absence of *ankusha* – 210
A rod with iron hook to control the elephants,
Shri Rama's *ankusha* shall bring it to the right path.
Stop your fickleness.
Does this quirkiness of love befit an emperor?'

All the *rakshasies* there,
Desiring the love of Dashakantha, the ten-headed one,
And feeling elated in their eagerness
To cast Janaki under the spell of love of him, said thus:

'Enough of recounting the name of Rama.
He has strayed from his kingdom. 220
Forget him and desert him forever.
Enough of these coarse clothes made of tree-bark.
Get bedecked with ornaments;

Beautify eyes with lampblack;
And watch your face in the mirror.
First, get up and bathe; we are there to bathe you.
Wear a grand silk sari and a greenish blouse;
Comb your hair well and decorate it with flowers;
Wearing a golden waist-band
Walk into the royal assembly and sitting on the left lap   230
Of Lankesha, enjoy that coveted position in this world;
Be the Goddess of Lanka and set yourself afloat
In the lake of limitless riches and fortunes;
Lankesha has been waiting for you!'

As all the *rakshasies* there
Tried to appease her every moment,
Janaki being devoid of any passion and desire, said:
'Enough, enough! Do not throw those pointed darts of your words at me.
Listen, I shall never be a wife to the *rakshasa*.
Why has he such a delusion?   240
As Suvarchale follows the sun faithfully,
I have faith in Rama,
And I shall certainly be freed from this bondage.
Like Shachidevi follows her consort Devendra;
As Rohini follows Moon;
As Arundhati follows Vasishtha,
And Sukanya follows Sage Chyavana;
As Shrimati follows Kapila;
And Savitri follows Satyavan;
As Damayanti follows emperor Nala;   250
And Keshini follows Sagara – and thus
All of them have guided the world
By following their consorts faithfully.
Lankesha shall be consumed by the fire of desire.
Why shall he desire vainly!'

Unable to tolerate such words,
The wretched Vinata lifting up an axe said:

'Enough! Enough of this arrogance,
And the farce of love for Rama!
This in itself is the poison that hampers 260
The prospect of a natural, wonderful, beautiful,
And grand love-filled life.
Listen, this is not good for you.
Love Ravana, and be Goddess of the Three-Worlds.
Rama shall never ever come to you.
The ocean is insuperable and this fort is inviolable.
Would anyone allow the creeper of youth to wither away?
If you love Lankesha, gold shall flow
Like water kissing your feet.
Do not forget the grandeur of Lanka; 270
Do not wilt; and do not desert.'

Hearing those words
Hanuma who was sitting atop the *shimshupa tree*,
Getting wild with anger –
'Forthwith I shall jump down on the *rakshasi*
And crush her seizing her hard,'
Getting himself ready to jump down with such a feeling of anger,
'My mission shall not be spoilt;
I shall exercise restraint now,' –
Thinking thus, he sat there watching in silence! 280

Then, Vinata came there lifting her hand up
Ready to strike with her fist and said:
'You afflict everyone with your silence.
Is it great to die suffering in bondage thus?
The beauty of women is like the rainbow;
It is transient, and shall never come back again;
Do not forget that.
Wander with Ravana, and take him to the heavens.
If not, we shall kill you
And make a grand feast out of your meat,' – she shouted thus. 290
'Silence is golden, – it is said –

And I shall take recourse to silence,' –
Thinking so, the loving companion of Shri Rama,
Shut her eyes, and was lost in recounting the name of Rama.
Fierce with anger, Chandodari rushed in swiftly
Brandishing a trident –
'It's quite true that you have the eyes of a deer,
And vibrant breasts and tempting flesh;
We shall kill you and eat you;
We shall thus wipe out the lineage of Saketa,' –   300
She shouted thus and felt great.

Praghasa roared feeling – 'Am I any less?' –
'Why do you all stand there doing nothing?
Squeeze her by the throat and kill her, eat her up;
If not, as days roll by, her youth shall wilt
And she shall be reduced to bones;
And then, she shall not be fit for food.
How tasty her meat would be
If eaten along with cooked sesame-balls
And spirituous liquor!' – She shouted so.   310
In this way, as the *rakshasies* assembled there
Were afflicting Janaki using every means –
Sometimes placating, sometimes offering gifts,
Sometimes speaking softly, and sometimes vilely –
Another *rakshasi* said:
'Let us dance now and offer her as sacrifice
To Bhadrakali and finish her off.'
Not paying heed to any of these,
Janaki, the holy mother, with a feeling
Of – 'Do what you want' –   320
Resorted to recounting the name of Rama
And was fully engrossed in yogic-meditation.
Seeing the divine glow of Rama on her face,
Anjaneya was peaceful.

Canto One Hundred and Forty-nine

'Would Lotus bloom under the Light of a Glow-worm?'

||६||

Unable to bear her sorrow, Sita was grieving
Reclining against the *ashoka* tree.
Like a boat caught up in the whirlpool,
She was suffering intensely
Finding no way out of the imbroglio.
Like a black cobra, her long hair was swaying obliquely.
'This affliction is a great poison; I can bear it no more;
Now I am under someone else's custody;
How would I escape from this?
O Shri Rama! Protect me.　　　　　　　　　　　10
Fie to this life of mine, and to this living!
How would you come breaking all the barriers
Of these highly vigilant *rakshasa*-guards – I can't say!
You are the bank of my life's river; you are steadfast;
You are the beginning, middle and end of all;
As everything is in you, you alone are the core of Truth;
What other life do I have without you?
You are the light of my life,' – as she was shedding tears
Grieving thus, Ashokavana – the Garden of No-Sorrows
Turned into Shokavana – the Garden of Sorrows.　　　　　20

Attempting to console Janaki,
Among the women who had gathered there,
Ekajata said: 'Ravana is of the lineage of Pulastya.
He is the son of Vishravasu, and a great, valorous emperor.
Kubera is the son of Vishravasu by his first wife Ilabele.
His second wife – Kaikasi gave birth
To Dashashira, Kumbhakarna, and Shurpanakha.
Malini, a staunch ascetic is the mother of Vibhishana.

Trusting his own valour
And thus unmindful of Kubera, 30
Ravana has been ruling over Lanka.
There is not anyone who is equal to Ravana in this world.
This vast empire, wealth, and fame have all come
To stay with Ravana. He is dreadful to his enemies.
Do not neglect him and then start worrying about it.
You be his queen and lord over his wealth.'

Paying no heed to the words of Ekajata,
Janaki resorted to silence. On seeing this,
Praghasa roared in anger:
'He is valorous at war and very handsome too. 40
Forsaking countless beautiful women,
He has come here yearning for you.
Look! The golden door of your good fortune has opened up.
Do not be stupid to cast that away.'

Sita turned a deaf ear
To the words spoken by the *rakshasi*.
At that time, Vinata came and scolded thus:
'You are indeed short-sighted; truly you are an idiot;
He is the most exemplary valorous warrior,
And the king of kings who has defeated the *naga-gandharva* heroes. 50
How could you say "no" to him!
You are vile indeed!
Sun rises in the fear of Ravana's fury;
Wind blows in the fear of Ravana's fury;

Clouds pour rains fearing Ravana's fury
Rivers flow fearing Ravana's fury.
Listen to my advice, and be his loving wife.
There is no alternative left for you;
He will subdue you with his power.
It's certain that you shall ascend the lap of Lankesha.' 60

Having heard all these, Ravana said:
'In this world, when handsome men speak endearing words,
Beautiful women receive it with love;
But why do you push it away?
This is the moment when the fountain
Of love springs up, doesn't it?
As the coachman restrains the speed of an impudent horse,
I have somehow reined in my anger, O darling!
You are merciless and deserve to be slaughtered.
Give up sporting anger. 70
Be pleased with me and love me!

'The love of the golden deer made you blind.
When I appeared in the guise of an ascetic,
You became enamoured of me in your mind,
And on your own free-will
Came to me under the pretense of offering alms,
And kindled my desire.
My sense of discrimination
And power of restraint are lost completely.
You have come crossing the life-line of a wife. 80
You have come to me being pulled by desire.
Why delay the enjoyment of a sweet embrace now?
Is silence any tasty? Be merciful to me.
Look! I am the most exemplary person in the whole of creation!

'Does anyone let lose one's anger and rebuke thus?
Listen! O intelligent damsel! I am lost to you;
Why be stubborn with me?
With love I will put on you exquisite ornaments.

Beautiful women of Lanka will bring *kalasha-kannadi* –
Water-vessel and mirror, the auspicious symbols of royal welcome; 90
Lift up your face, and look at me with a gentle smile.
If you do not love me, I won't live;
Wipe out this fear of mine.
Comfort me in love, I implore you humbly.
I am a beggar for your love;
Why do you torture me thus?
Why do you destroy me?
You shall ascend the flowery conjugal bed soon, O damsel!

'If you do not love me when implored in gentleness,
I can subdue you with my power; but there is no charm in it. 100
Being a *kshatriya*-woman – the one belonging to the warrior clan,
You were united with Rama as a reward for his valour;
Now you become mine;
What does it matter if a dice used in gaming comes
Into the hands of someone or the other?
You are a puppet in the hands of Fate.
Why then worry about anything else?

'Be a traveller.
Wherever you are taken, it is just fine;
Whoever takes you, it is just fine; 110
The place you are in is the spring of your love;
There itself is the breath of your enjoyment.
Under my custody, your life shall be auspicious.
Would that petty Rama destroy the fort of my valour?
Having become impotent with diminished strength,
He is now bemoaning on the banks of the Tungabhadra.

'As you are with me now –
The one who was given to Rama as a reward for his valour –
Having become weak and desperate,
Your husband is waiting with a beggar's bowl 120
At the doors of Sugriva's palace begging for his mercy.
Is youth permanent? It flows like a stream.

Before it is over, you become one with me.
Like the moonlight in a forest, do not be useless.
O Bhujata – the Earth-born,
I am not the one to enjoy this beauty and grace of yours by force.
It's proper that on your own free-will
Be joined with the one strong in arms.
Is it not customary that all that is created grand in this world
Shall be offered to the Emperor? 130
You are a gem of a woman indeed.
You shall join me for sure!

'How much shall I beg of you?
Yearning for you with no respite
I am turned into a barren desert;
Pour down the rain of your love now on this desert land
Of mine and make me fulfilled.
As I come floating in the sky of emotions,
As the chariot of lotus is moving ahead,
O beautiful damsel, 140
Like the flash of lightning,
Do not emanate the fierce heat of anger!
O young damsel, grant me my heart's desire
And save me, please!
Make me one with you in love.
I desire the heavenly bliss of merciful glances
From the Goddess of Lanka's fortune.
Desiring nothing else save the moonlight of love –
I have become *chakora* –
The bird fabled to subsist upon moon-beams; 150
Why then delay anymore?'

Then, Sita said:
'It is true that I am born not of my mother's womb;
It is true that I am the one given as reward for valour;
It is also true that I shall burn the *rakshasas* to ashes;
Do not forget that.

Not to be dead being subjected to incessant suffering,
And to live rooting out exploitation –
I shall make it possible for women to live
Like the light of the epoch on the path to liberation. 160
A woman is endearing if she loves her man;
If not, she is Evil-incarnate. Beware!
Shri Rama – the saviour of the helpless –
Shall come to set free the women languishing in your prisons,
And he shall herald a new Epoch of Liberation.
Giving no scope for your own ruination,
Set free those helpless women
And be the harbinger of liberation yourself.'

As the women languishing under the
Captivity of Lankesha were all trying to comfort Janaki, 170
Gesturing through their faces, lips, and eyes, Janaki said:
'O mother Trijata, Listen! Tell him all of you –
Let alone today, even after countless re-births too,
I shall not love *nishachara* –
The one who roams about in the nights.
If the *rakshasas* feel elated in the illusion
That they are all valorous,
Would Rama spare them without throwing them into the abyss?
Listen, you all!
As Indra has Shachi as his consort, 180
Mandodari is there for Ravana;
Then, why should he desire the wife of Shri Rama?'

Having heard Janaki's words
Ravana became anger personified;
Spitting out flames, and with shoulders trembling in agitation,
He roared aloud:
'Would the stream that has flown forward come back ever?
Give up your pride and be the queen of Lanka.
As the fragrance of the garden has turned into hundred flowers,
As the joy of spring has blossomed in my mind, 190

As the nectar of beauty has showered rains spreading fragrance,
As the melody of the soul of music has roused pleasure
Reverberating in the heart,
And is coursing excitedly through every vein –
Come to me with love,
And set afloat the bright light of happiness on the ocean.
Would anyone bite the dust and get buried
In the womb of time wantonly?'

'You have not gained victory over yourself;
Then, how could you consider yourself victorious   200
Over the entire world!
You have brought me here like a thief. Fie to your valour!
Send me to Rama. He is the sole hero of the world.
Could you ever win over Rama?
You came to my *swayamvara* –
With the intention of marrying me,
But stumbled and fell down;
Have you forgotten that? Just recollect it.
You've abducted me in the guise of an ascetic;
Thus you've insulted the very clan of great ascetics.   210
Look what you've done!
You've summoned your own destruction.
The flame of my sorrow will burn you down,
And it shall burn to ashes this wealthy Lanka itself, listen.
Would you douse everyone in the well of sin?
Like your own wife, the wives of others too
Deserve to be protected; have you forgotten that?' –
Thus spoke Janaki with great agitation.

Enraged Dashakantha, the ten-headed one said:
'What an impertinent talk! I have lost patience.   220
As all means of pacification and the lure of gifts have failed,
You deserve punishment; do not compel me to resort to it.
You are the damsel who carefully counts your profit
And your good, aren't you?

How could Rama, who has lost his kingdom and riches,
And wanders in the forests, be my equal?' –
Ravana roared aloud thus in conceit.

'O Lankesha! Listen to me now.
Shri Rama is Maryadapurushottama –
The Supreme Being in morality and demeanour; 230
The protector of *dharma* – righteousness;
Destroyer of the wicked.
Will he not protect his faithful wife?
Your grandeur is worth only a straw.
Would lotus bloom under the light of a glow-worm?
I am the lotus bloomed in the magnificent splendor
Of Shri Rama – the one renowned as Bhanukulatilaka –
The crest jewel of the Sun-race.

'His glory and greatness are beyond description.
As Varaha – the Boar incarnation, 240
He had borne the earth.
Before his great power, what are you,
And what have you to boast about?
If you want to escape death from Rama's arrow,
If you have any desire to see good in life,
Worship Saketa-Rama with devotion.
He will forget and forgive all your wrong-doings.
In this land of Vishravasu enriched with *dharma* and culture,
Would anyone look at other's women lustfully thus?'

Paying no heed to the good words 250
As Ravana shouted aloud in anger,
Janaki getting infuriated said:
'You're the vilest of the vile!
As you were impotent in valour being unable
To cross over the limits of the lines
Saumitri had drawn with his arrow,
Why now this empty-pride, and why threaten thus?
Would anyone speak so vilely filled with the stench of lust?

If you attempt to embrace the wives of others,
Shri Rama shall cut off your arms without fail, listen.'   260
Janaki said so.

Ravana lost all patience.
'How dare you insult the most valorous among men!
You who were born somewhere, and grew up somewhere,
Wherever you may be, it is useless to lament thus.
Would that ordinary mortal Shri Rama chop off my arms?
Look here! Now I shall cut off your head and throw it away,' –
So saying, he rushed ahead.

Restraining Ravana,
Clever Trijata said: 'She has suffered the pangs of separation;   270
O, she has wilted and withered in grief.
When her anger subsides, she would certainly appease you.
You are the great lover who has won favours of damsels
Of the *gandharva-kinnara-naga* clan including the celestial nymphs;
Why do you act rashly now?
If you kill her, you get infamy;
But if you wait patiently, certainly she will be yours.
Do not crush the flower vainly.'

Looking at Surama,
Janaki said to Ravana in anger: 280
'He failed to lift up the bow of Shiva;
In the past, he was tied like a toy to the cradle
Of Angada – the son of Vali;
And why does he now boast himself to be supreme?
Abductors of other's wives are pierced with *dasi* –
A pointed wooden peg;
That is the law of Ayodhya, listen.'

Hearing the harsh words of Janaki,
Unable to control his anger,
As Lankesha rushed forward with a drawn out sword to kill her,   290
Surama came swiftly and somehow restrained him.

Not fearing the *rakshasa*
And calling out Surama again and again, Janaki said:
'Look at the cruelty of the *rakshasa*.
If tortured thus everyday,
Could anyone be able to live; tell me, please.
Days and months have rolled by
In the anticipation that Shri Rama shall come.
I have lost all hopes now
And I have no desire to live on this earth anymore. 300
O Surama, I shall enter the blazing fire.
Where would Shri Rama be now?
Where would Saumitri be?
Why am I alive? Why this life? Why this physical beauty?' –
Thus she lamented overcome with grief.

Canto One Hundred and Fifty

'The Wealth of an Empire Bows Down to Truth'

||७||

Later, Lankesha moved into the garden.
He summoned Surama and Trijata to his presence
Desiring to know the secret of Janaki's heart –
Whether or not Janaki would love him!
'O king! Give up the desire of Janaki; she shall not love you.
As her mind is always pervaded with the name of Shri Rama
And is home to his memory, would she, the dutiful wife, ever
   love you?
Would a cat grow horns? Would a crow turn white?
Would a serpent pour out ambrosia?
But if you so desire, even such things may happen.   10
But, Sita shall never ever love you!

'Even if a fly in elation swallows up a mountain,
Even if an ant sucks away the entire ocean,
And even if a lotus blooms on the rocks,
Sita shall never ever love you!

'Even if the sandal-wood
Emits heat instead of its natural cooling,

Even if the moonlight turns hot,
Even if the sun rises in the west,
Even if the trees grow legs and attain mobility,   20
Sita shall never ever love you!

'Do you now realise this, O king!
She considers all other men as poison.
The warning bell is ringing;
Listen, O king!
Sita shall never ever love you!'

Not able to tolerate
These unpalatable words, burning with anger,
He took the maids with him;
And throwing away the silken saris kept exclusively for Sita,   30
And throwing away in all directions *kalasha-kannadi*
That the women were carrying,
And spilling out helter-skelter all the perfumes,
And pulling away the women,
Threatening, scolding, and pushing them hard,
And getting himself wild with uncontrollable anger, he said:

'O insolent woman!
You are only a gnat;
Right away I will offer the Goddess of Death
A grand feast with the hot blood of your heart;   40
I won't spare you; I shall tenaciously accomplish
What I desire,' – so saying,
As he rushed near Janaki brandishing his sword to kill her,
Mandodari came there swiftly at that instant
And stood facing the sword of Ravana.
Shedding tears, and holding his hand in utter humility,
She pressed his hand against her eyes in supplication.
Then, the hand of Dashamukha got fully drenched in tears
And as Mandodari embraced him with both her hands
And crying silently lifted up her face to him,   50
And with that glance as she shot into

The inner recess of his heart,
The king got pacified. At that very instant
Mandodari led him to the harem.

As they were proceeding, Ravana said:
'The temple of my heart has turned into a battle-ground now.
Indeed you are the illustrious daughter of Maya; you desire my good.
Who else could I remember for clean habits and sense of propriety!
I could defeat Janaki only by tenacity;
That I shall do unfailingly,' – 60
As Ravana spoke thus, Mandodari fell at his feet
And begged him in utter humility:

'What is all this, my love!
Give up your desire and thirst for Janaki's love.
Shri Rama is the ocean of mercy; surrender to him;
When you submit Janaki to his care
And stand before him in humility,
He will forgive all your misdeeds; surrender to him.
O king of kings! Why this obstinacy to appease her in love?
Is it proper to suffer thus sacrificing our own peace and comforts? 70
Why give up our good habits?
Discarding the attire of vanity,
If we tread the path of Truth, victory shall be ours, for sure.
The wealth of an empire bows down to Truth.'

Looking again and again at Mandodari,
The adoring dutiful wife, a gem of a woman,
The crest-jewel of womanhood,
Hanuma said to himself:
'In good manners, she is an exemplary dutiful wife.
Filled with the courage of righteousness 80
She has protected Maithili –
The holy mother and Goddess of Saketa;
To such a virtuous woman, I salute repeatedly.'

Pained deeply at the harsh words of Dashashira,
Janaki told Trijata: 'The pointed arrows

Of Lankesha's vile words have hit me hard.
Set up a funeral-pyre and dousing it with the oil of your love
Light it up; and thus save me from this suffering; grant me salvation;
O Mother! I can't live thus any longer;
I shall take recourse to death; I shall surrender to death.'   90

Then, Trijata said humbly:
'O Daughter! Do not be frightened. I will safeguard you
Protecting your life and honour until Shri Rama comes.
What has been ordained in the dream shall come true
And it shall never be false.
Do not break the journey of universal conquest of Raghuvara –
The supreme one of the clan of Raghu,' –
Thus she comforted Janaki.

Then, Janaki looking at the
Sky and the earth with tearful eyes,   100
And giving up all hopes, and suffering great pain, said thus:

'The desire for the golden deer overcame me;
The inauspicious moment had come,
And I was separated from Rama.
As he alone is the wealth of my life, the wealth of my honour,
And the lord of all of mine, now this life is futile;
Why death does not come to me?
The heart of the world has turned into a stone;
The sap of life has dried up;
O Mother of mine, the Mother Earth!   110
Hide me in your womb.
I am being burnt in the fire of affliction.
It's enough if the assemblage of *rakshasies* chop off my body
And eat it up – it shall be my salvation.
I drove Rama away in the vile desire for the golden deer.
Abusing Lakshmana, I drove away him also.
My *karma* – the heap of past deeds is certainly stronger.
Who could save me from the consequences of my own actions!

I shall settle the burden of all my debts.
Do not blame Rama. He is not helpless, listen! 120

'He is the lion of a man.
Single-handedly he had slain an assemblage
Of fourteen thousand *rakshasas* at Janasthana, hadn't he?
Lanka is not inviolable. He shall conquer the ocean.
Fearing the arrow of Rama, the ocean itself shall open up
And pave the way; if not, it shall be dried.
As volcanoes lay hidden in the womb of Mother Earth,
The fire of anger in my stomach is ready to be exploded.
I shall kindle the light of the New Epoch
With the fat of the slain *rakshasas*, 130
And dance in ecstasy.
Listen! The land of golden Lanka
Shall become worse than the graveyard
Being filled with crows and vultures!
The servants of my lord shall certainly come here
To set ablaze Lanka, the land that has lost its reins.
The twanging sound of Kodanda – the great bow
Of Rama shall reverberate in all the four directions;
The sound of drums shall resound in all the four directions;
The hapless cry of the *rakshasas* shall echo in all the four
  directions; 140
The wailing of women shall resound in all the four directions,' –
Thus, Janaki foretold all the signs of evil –
The tragic events that were to follow.

Canto One Hundred and Fifty-one

'Listen, you all! The Bird of Good-omen is Singing'

||௬||

Maithili's decisive, razor-sharp words affected all.
Some were in worry; some others were in fear;
Many were angry and disappointed;
Deciding for themselves that –
'She is not the one to appease Ravana' – they all moved away.

Trijata thrashed and restrained in anger
The assemblage of *rakshasies*, who came to torture Janaki,
And told them threateningly thus: 'Stop this at once;
Do not play out the tragedy of cruelty and violence.
If you desire human flesh, eat your own well-fed bodies   10
Fattened with conceit. Life is transient.
I saw a dream; I was frightened and trembled in fear.
It foretold the beginning of total destruction, no doubt in it
  anymore.'
As she spoke these words, all the *rakshasies* got frightened
And trembling in fear asked, 'Tell us what it is. We are all ears.'
As they persistently tormented her, then Trijata told them thus:

'Listen with attention.
I saw a grand palanquin made of ivory and with beautiful carvings

Flying high in the sky.
I saw the grand spectacle of 20
A pair of white swans flying with great passion.

'Look there!
Shri Rama was wearing a garland of white flowers;
Wearing a white attire of finely woven silk, he was seen with Saumitri.
He was sitting atop a grand elephant with four tusks;
Along with Shri Rama, Sita was there under his complete protection.
It was the posture that assured blessings to the world.
I saw them moving ahead ascending the mountain
That stretched along the milky ocean.

'I saw a crowded assemblage of gods 30
As the grand chariot drawn by eight bulls with
Brahma, Vishnu, and Maheshwara seated in it
Was passing over Lanka.
At that very instant, there appeared *Pushpaka* –
The self-propelling plane in the sky;
Shri Rama ascended it as the other gods waited in attendance
And they too climbed up *Pushpaka* which moved
Towards the city of Saketa.

'I saw Lankesha –
His head pressed with oil, he was wearing blood-red attire, 40
And a garland of red flower.
I saw him falling into a valley and
Unable to get up, he was wriggling there.

'Our Master was driving his chariot
Drawn by a donkey to the southern direction;
He was laughing wildly and dancing madly;
And his body was smeared with red sandal paste –
I saw him thus.

'I writhed in sorrow.
He had fallen down on his head; he had discarded his dress; 50
He had fallen into the well of filth which stank like hell –
I saw him thus.

A dark woman of unclean body
Came there and putting a noose round Ravana's neck,
She took him away tightening the noose,
And dragging him along towards the southern direction –
I saw him thus.

'Kumbhakarna – his younger brother,
And Indrajit, and all the other sons of Ravana,
With their heads tonsured clean   60
And their bodies smeared with oil
Were wandering screaming aloud in a sorrowful voice –
I saw them thus.

'The dream was not over yet.
Ravana – the lord of Lanka was riding a boar;
Kumbhakarna was mounted on a camel,
And Indrajit on a crocodile;
They all moved thus facing the southern direction –
I saw this spectacle.

'With his attendants holding the royal white parasol over his head,   70
Wearing a garland of white flowers, and dressed in regal white,
Mounted on a white elephant,
And surrounded by a council of ministers,
Vibhishana – the devout brother of Ravana was radiating
Like the sun amidst grand festivities –
I saw the grandeur of all this glory.
A group of *rakshasas* was
Wearing garlands of red flowers and they were drinking oil;
They were all deserting Lanka,
And gathering in long lines,   80
Marched straight into the womb of the ocean –
I saw all this.

'Some envoy of Rama burnt Lanka to ashes
And the wives of the *rakshasas* were sipping oil
And jumping up and down wildly

Smearing their bodies with ashes and dancing fiercely –
I saw this dream of a nightmare.

'Go away, go away!
Go away in haste, Rama may not forgive you.
You will be in trouble; you will wilt away now.   90
Before the race of the *rakshasas* is wiped out
You all go away. Would anyone reproach the irreproachable?
My left eye is quivering; my left arm is quivering;
It augurs well to be so;
Rama shall come to protect Janaki –
The good omens foretell such a thing; look, you all!
The bird of good-omen is singing; listen, you all!'
As Trijata said thus,
All the *rakshasies*, trembling in fear, ran to the palace.

Sita muttered to herself: 100
'God is not on my side. Fire is far away.
Why does not the sky rain fire-balls?
O, the glowing moon! Pour down the crest of fire.
O, the reddish tender leaf! You give me the blazing flames.
Like a mountain that cracks as the thunderbolt strikes it,
Why my heart is not yet broken into thousand pieces?
Whether Truth and *dharma* have all gone in vain?
Whether the wealth of chaste wives has suffered a pitfall?
Whether all the vows, disciplined devotion,
Meditation, and ruminating silence,   110
Have gone waste without yielding any fruits?
O, Shri Rama! Tell me please.
This is a life of darkness; when would the light appear?
Neither poison, nor the noose,
Not even the weapons are in my hands;
My fortune has waned –
I do not even have the means to die.'

Lamenting thus,
And holding up her long hair, Maithili, the daughter of Mithila
   thought:

'Yes, yes, there is a noose here;   120
It is best to die; let me put an end to this body.'
Thinking thus, as she was readying to tie her hair
As a noose to the branch of that *shimshupa* tree
Recounting the names of Shri Rama, and Lakshmana,
Her fortune changed course!
Like the timely support granted to a good deed,
Good omens appeared to Janaki
Who was weak with suffering a joyless life.
Her hair turned loose;
Like a lotus that sways in water tickled by fish,   130
Her lotus-like left eye quivered.
The intimations of fructification of her desires were evident:
'Shri Rama and Saumitri will come for sure,
And steadfastly protect me.'
In the joy of such a thought, a smile appeared on her face
And like the full-moon, just liberated from the hold of Rahu,
    the monster.
She stood there attaining wholesome grandeur!

Canto One Hundred and Fifty-two

The Vow of Exploring Sita's Whereabouts Accomplished Successfully!

||๑||

On seeing Janaki lamenting, Hanuma,
Grieving over it, was lost in many worries.
The dream narrated by Trijata brought in happiness.
'I do not know through what tricks I could see the Mother.
If I see her, wouldn't she doubt me?
She would think that this is yet another deception by the *rakshasas*.
And, if not comforted, she would lose her life.
How could she, the one who is sorrow-stricken, be comforted?
Would the Great Quest done by the *vanaras*
Go in vain without fructification?' – feeling thus,   10
Hanuma remained engrossed
Waiting for the opportune time to see Sita.

At that time,
Some of the *rakshasies* gathered round Janaki
Fell asleep fast, and some others went away scattered;
Hanuma saw all this! As if he got such solitude
As to feel that he might be burnt by the heat of Janaki's sorrow,
And feeling happy that it was the opportune time as well,
In a sweet-voice he said:

'Let victory be to Shri Rama! 20
Let goodness prevail! Let there be beauty!
Let victory be to Mangaladhama –
The one who is home to all auspiciousness!
Let goodness prevail! Let there be beauty!' – proclaiming thus,
He sang the entire history of Rama in gist.

'I will sing the story of Shri Rama
And thus make the Mother happy.
By my actions, I will cause her to believe in me,
And I will present myself before her
And speak to her with devotion. 30
I will narrate to her the message sent by Shri Rama,' –
In this way, he sang with happiness:

'Dasharatha, the sagely-king,
And the one adored prominently in the clan of Ikshvaku,
Rules over Ayodhya.
He is endowed with all the characteristics required
Of crowned heads, and he is the light of the royal family
With well-groomed qualities, and a pious one too.
He has a complete army comprising
Of elephants, chariots, cavalry and infantry. 40
He has all kinds of wealth. He is the lord of the kingdom
That stretches up to the four oceans.
He is crowned in glory hitherto unparalleled.
Kausalya, Sumitra, and Kaikeyi are his wives.
To them are born Rama and Lakshmana, so also,
Bharata and Shatrughna.

'Rama is the eldest son.
He excels his own father in *dharma*, and in Truth.
He is merciful and protects all that is living in this world.
He has given up the kingdom for abiding by his father's words. 50
He has come to live in the forests with his exemplary dutiful wife.
As Saumitri accompanies him,

Rama glows in grandeur punishing the evil-doers
And protecting the good and the righteous.

'As things stood thus, Ravana –
Causing Janaki to be lured by the charm of the golden deer –
Abducted the Mother in the guise of an ascetic
And took her away to Lanka.
The whole kingdom is suffering in this grief.

'Then, Rama came to Rushyamuka   60
And gaining Sugriva's friendship there, he had slain Vali.
As *vanaras* are pressed into service to seek Janaki,
Hanuma, the devout servant of Rama, has come swiftly
Leaping across one hundred *yojana* distance over the ocean,
And has seen the Mother with great excitement.

'I am Anjaneya.
I am fortunate, and I am blessed.
Let victory be to Rama; let victory be to Janaki;
Let victory be to Saumitri, the valorous one.
The vow of my life is fulfilled; O the vow is fulfilled!   70
The vow of exploring Sita's whereabouts is accomplished successfully!
I have fulfilled my mission;
I am blessed, I am truly blessed!' –
Thus he sang in happiness.

As Hanuma jumped,
And leapt and hopped from branch to branch in great excitement,
Leaves and flowers fell down at that vibrant jubilation.
As all those falling leaves and flowers became offerings to Sita,
Happiness was spread all over.

There was song in praise of Rama.   80
As if the golden light overflowed from the womb of darkness,
The glow of daylight shot forth lifting up
And casting away the curtain of dark clouds, heralding a new dawn.
The wheel of *karma* turned and a refreshing new form became
  visible.

As if the auspicious moment of communion
Of soul with God approached fast,
Happiness was spread all over.

Anjaneya, the virtuous Guru,
Is untainted, having no vices of any kind;
He is engrossed proclaiming the communion   90
Of Shri Rama and Vaidehi, the daughter of Videha

Having heard the song in praise of Rama,
And the story of Rama, Janaki, the holy mother, was greatly excited.
Feeling elated with excitement, she looked in all the directions.
It seemed as though the name of Rama resounded in all the ten directions.
As that sound was heard once in a high pitch,
And once in a soft note, and yet another time
As the humming of the lute of Shiva,
The whole world responded to it.
'What is this charm? Whether Sharada –   100
The Goddess of Learning, played the lute in her hand?
Whether Narada – the sage, played the lute of Rama's-rumination?' –
Thinking thus, Janaki, lifting up her face,
Looked at the *shimshupa* tree.
'Yes, yes! Some devotee of Rama is sitting there
Engrossed meditating the name of Shri Rama.'

Thinking thus,
And on seeing the heroic Hanuma,
Who was sitting there in hiding, with a face full of smile,
Appearing like the flash of lightning,   110
And he – the devotee, looked like purified gold –
Janaki praised him heartily.

'What humility and what obedience!
With what intense devotion he sings the praise of Rama!
What a sweet voice and how articulate are his musical beats!'
With such wondrous feelings,

As she looked at him without winking her eyes,
Janaki instantly saw in him the omnipresent sublime form of
   her lord,
And she folded her hands in supplication!
'O Rama! O Saumitri!' –   120
She uttered these words rapturously.

Fully engrossed thus, she said:
'As I have been grieving and meditating on Rama day and night,
As my body and mind are filled with the name of Rama,
As my eyes are filled with the image of Rama,
As if awakened by the touch,
Rama's form is standing before me glowing in the
Light of divine appearance –
I saw such a grand manifestation.

'I saw the billow of music.   130
I saw the rhythm of the word of the source of birth and death.
Like the screen that lay between the eye and the vision is removed,
Like memory that comes to life from the abyss of forgetfulness,
Like the stream of Rama's name that keeps overflowing,
Like the forest that is freshly bloomed,
And like the mind that evolves,
Like the light of soul transformed itself into visible light,
The nectar of peace – the divine soul of Rama himself –
Is flowing all over manifesting itself into every conceivable form
Of a tree, a shrub, and all, and I saw its blooming here.'   140
Feeling thus, Janaki was afloat in the ocean
Of Shri Rama's Universal Appearance.

But, at the very next instant,
There was doubt in her mind: 'How could I believe this?
I do not know whether it is only a dream, or something real.
Could it be the magical spell cast by Lankesha?'
Thinking thus, she felt weak.

Canto One Hundred and Fifty-three

'O Mother! This is how Shri Ramachandra is! Isn't he?'

||๖||

Anjaneya, climbed down from the tree,
And with a very humble posture, went near Janaki;
Folding his hands over his head reverentially,
He spoke sweetly thus:

'Let victory be to Shri Rama.
O Mother! You, who meditate Shri Rama's name,
Tell me please, who you are.
I am the messenger of Rama and I have come seeking Janaki.
O Mother! Tell me please, whether you are Janaki.'

Having heard those words, 10
Janaki, expressing happiness, said: 'Yes, yes! I am Janaki.
I am wife to Rama and Dasharatha's daughter-in-law.
As Rama deserted the kingdom to abide by his father's words,
And as Rama desired to convince me not to come
To the forest, I told him that,
"Let me have an equal share in both your happiness and sorrows,"
And thus, like his shadow, I came following my husband.
Saumitri, causing Urmila, his wife, to live alone, came to the forest
Considering that Rama alone is the essence of his life.

Rama entered the dense forest 20
And at Dandakaranya, he punished the evil-doers
And protected the virtuous ones.
At that time, Ravana, the thief,
Abducted me deceitfully and brought me here.
He has fixed a term of two months within which
If I do not surrender my honour to the *rakshasa*,
Death sentence awaits me.' Thus, Janaki told Hanuma
The heart-wrenching tale of her woes.

Having heard Maithili's words,
Hanuma felt sad and spoke affectionately words of consolation: 30

'O Mother! Why are you sorrowful?
Why do you suffer the affliction, O Mother?
I am the messenger of Rama, and I have brought a message.
O Mother! Shri Rama and Saumitri are well.
Shri Rama is brooding over you without respite.
Serving the brother well, remaining together in grief,
And comforting with the words of courage,
Saumitri is taking care of Rama.'
Speaking thus, Hanuma moved near her.

Janaki was frightened. 40
Contorting her face, Janaki said: 'I am deceived.
You are not the messenger of Rama.
Surely, you are Ravana himself.
Have you come to deceive me in this guise?
Playing deceitful tricks, would you cause me troubles?
You are the cheater who deceived me in the guise of an ascetic.
You are vicious and hurtful to women.
Go away, go away from here, you lustful creature.
Fie to you!' Thus she told him in scorn.

Bowing his head low, Pavanasuta said: 50
'O Mother! O, Bhumija!
I am indeed the messenger of Rama.

This is the truth; believe me. There is not the slightest deceit in this.
Do not spoil the mission; I am bound by vow to Rama.'

Then, with great pain, Sita said:
'This is the magical city. How could I believe?
In the forest of cruelty, there is the cunningness to imprison someone.
Casting someone into the pond of evil, they clap their hands.
Here is witchcraft; deceitful tricks abound here.
How to believe you, Sir? 60
Here, they take on any form they wish.
The theatrical performance of Dashashira's deceit is here.
Even if Shri Rama comes here, it's doubtful that he may be believed.
O *vanara*! Forgive me.
Send forth Rama himself here.' Sita said so.

Anjaneya, in order to convince her,
Transformed himself into giant proportions like the Mount Meru,
And exhibited himself thus before the Mother.
He showed his exemplary valorous divine form
That encompassed the earth and the sky – 70
The form that radiated the glow of the sun,
The form that emanated the brilliance of a war-hero,
The form that was not even slightly different from that of Rama –
This was the kind of cosmic-form that Hanuma showed Janaki.
She looked at him in wonder;
She looked at him with anxiety.
She was convinced in her mind
That he was indeed the messenger of Rama.
'I feel delighted by your presence.
I feel happy as if I have seen Rama himself. 80
I wish you well. You are very calm
And look like Guha – a friend of Rama.
You are full of divine grace.
My mind is drawn to you in the love of Shri Rama.
Like the Guru who guides his disciple to cross over the ocean of life,

Like the divine hand that carries someone caught up in a stream
Safely to the river-bank, you have come to protect me.
I stand here feeling emotionally insane.
I am suffering the pain of frustrating disappointment.
O Hanuma! Tell me something more about Rama's-story.' 90
Thus she pleaded.

Hanumanta said:
'Be not afraid; do not be in a hurry; have patience, O Mother!
Indeed I am the messenger of Rama;
I am the servant of Rama.
Preparations for the battle are being made there
At Kishkindha in Karnata under the helpful guidance of Sugriva.
There is an army of millions of *vanaras* there.
Crushing Ravana's head, they will blow
The trumpet of liberation and grandly prove their valour. 100
Discard your anxiety, O Mother! Shed all your doubts.
I am the stage-manager for the liberation of Shri Rama's pious wife,
And, so also, for crushing Lankesha.
I am the charioteer of the giant chariot
Of Shri Rama's Great Quest.
Let the grace of your divine feet be on my head.
I am son to you. Do not drive me to *Patala*;
I've crossed the threshold of the world's fortune.

'O Mother! Believe me; trust me.
I have come crossing the ocean for crushing Lankesha. 110
I am the harbinger of death.
I am friend to Sugriva; I am the son of Wind.
I am the son of Kesari who resides in the Mount Malyavanta.
As I am born by the benediction of the God of Wind,
And thus I am called the son of Wind.
In the pranks of childhood, perceiving the sun to be a fruit,
I leapt into the sky hoping to eat the sun;
As a result of which I became Hanumanta –
The one with the protruded chin.

Shri Rama and Saumitri are at Mount Rushyamuka. 120
I am blessed by the sight of you, O Mother!
I am fulfilled by the sight of you.
O Mother! The pot of my fortune is filled to the brim.
Raghava will come; you shall be liberated.
We have vowed to take you back to Saketa!
Sugriva, my master,
Having been banished from his kingdom,
And suffering the pangs of separation from his wife,
Has been living in the Mount Rushyamuka
Becoming thin by enduring this affliction. 130
The common plight of their wives has bound Rama and Sugriva
In friendship. As a result,
Rama has fulfilled his vow of slaying Vali.
The ornaments that you had thrown away were collected
And we showed them all to Rama at the Mount Rushyamuka.

'Shri Rama, on seeing the ornaments,
Shed tears copiously, and as the fire of grief increased,
He fell to the ground; somehow, we comforted him.
As the earth shoots forth tremors, even the mountain begins to shake.
Shri Rama quivers in excessive grief. 140
Wherever he wanders – in every river, and in all the forests;
In every stream and all the mountains –
His mind and heart keep searching for you.

'In the kingdom of Kishkindha,
Preparations for the war are being done at great speed.
Day and night, the great *vanara*-heroes are searching for you
In every forest and every hill.
As the period set by Sugriva for this task is getting over,
We all live in the fear of being punished by our master.
Angada, the son of Vali; so also, Jambava 150
And the other *vanara*-heroes are awaiting my return.
O Mother! Bidding them to be stationed at the southern ocean,

I've come here;
Crossing over one hundred *yojana*-distance, I have come to you.
Believe me, O Mother! Trust me; and bless me.'
So said Hanumanta.

'Alright, alright. Now I have got faith in you.
If you describe how Rama looks in every limb,
Listening to that I will get great pleasure,' – said Sita.

'O Mother! I will carry your order on my head. 160
I am blessed that you have come to trust me
To be the messenger of Rama.
But, would I be able to describe the divine form of Shri Rama!

'He equals the sun in radiance;
His divinely graceful form rouses happiness;
His beauty is like the cooling of the moon;
He is the king of kings; he equals Vishnu in valour;
He is Manmatha – the God of Love in the charm of his physique;
He is adept at talking pleasantly;
He is unexcelled in wealth and brilliance; 170
O Mother! This is how Shri Ramachandra is! Isn't he?

'He is endowed with all great virtues;
He is husband to only one wife;
He is the lotus-eyed one;
In tolerance, he is Bhudevi – the Goddess of Earth;
In cleverness, he is Brihaspati – the Guru of the *devas*;
In fame, he is King Sagara;
He is the merciful one, who protects all the creatures;
He is the patron, who protects the culture of the people.
O Mother! This is how Shri Ramachandra is! Isn't he? 180

'He is the staunch performer of duties;
He is worshipful to the sages;
He is the benefactor of the virtuous,
And destroyer of the evil-doers;
He is the accomplished one in every good deed;

He is the treasure of humility and courtesy;
He is the exponent of State policy;
He is *karmayogi* – the acclaimed accomplisher of duties;
He is the exemplary scholar in *Yajurveda*, and the art of archery.
O Mother! This is how Shri Ramachandra is! Isn't he?   190

'He is robustly built;
He is endowed with all royal characteristics;
He has the colour of dark-blue clouds;
His chest is vast;
His arms are long and touch the knee-joints;
His neck is like the conch-shell;
His voice is resonant like the sound of a trumpet;
He is true to the Almighty; and is worshipped by all;
O Mother! This is how Shri Ramachandra is! Isn't he?

In his arms, there are three auspicious lines;   200
There are three corrugations across his abdomen and neck;
There are three whirls on his head that denote wealth;
On the underside of his big toe, there are four lines;
His calves and feet are strong.
O Mother! This is how Shri Ramachandra is! Isn't he?

'His jaws and teeth are strong and healthy;
He has a tall stature;
His eye-brows, nose, lips, hands and legs, claves, forearms, wrists,
His back and thighs – every limb is in perfect symmetry,
Perfectly-balanced, and in excellent harmony.   210
O Mother! This is how Shri Ramachandra is! Isn't he?

His lips and cheeks, eyes, ears, and nose,
His fingers and hair, his face, eyes, and palate,
His chest, nails, hands, feet and arms, ribs and back – all are
  beautiful.
He walks with heavy strides like a great bull.
O Mother! This is how Shri Ramachandra is! Isn't he?

He is such a virtuous person that only at the opportune time
He indulges in *dharma, artha,* and *kama* –

The three objects of man's desire;
Is it possible to describe such a one?   220
Not even Adishesha with his thousand tongues could do so!
O Mother! This is how Shri Rama is!
Saumitri, brother of Shri Rama, is charming;
He is equal to Rama in youth and beauty;
He is equal to Rama in valour and heroism;
He is equal to Rama in brilliance and grandeur;
He is equal to Rama is all virtues!

'What shall I say, O Mother!
I am fortunate; I saw the charming princes
On the banks of the Pampa Lake at the feet of God Virupaksha   230
In the land of Karnata; my eyes that sighted them are blessed;
For having been gifted with such eyes, I am doubly blessed;
They caused the lotus of my heart to bloom
And they remain etched there!

The faith grew stronger.
In the delightful excitement, eyes became moist
And swelled with tears of happiness;
At that instant, understanding the promptings of Sita's heart,
Pavanasuta, gave her Rama's signet-ring.
'O Mother! This is not any magical-charm;   240
There is not any deception, O Mother!
Shri Rama has given this divinely graceful ring.
Let victory be to Shri Rama;
Let victory be to the one who is the treasure-house of virtues.
Let victory prevail; let auspiciousness prevail;
Let there be benediction to all,' –
Thus Hanuma sang in delightful excitement.

On sighting the ring,
Sita looked at it again and again in great joy.
She was already in the company of Rama.   250
She looked like the full moon out of the eclipse.
She remembered the face of Shri Ramachandra.

Recalling the long-armed one, she felt happy in the mind.
Recalling the conch-shell like throat,
Recalling the lion-like shoulder,
Recalling the lotus-like eyes,
Recalling the pleasant smile,
Recalling all the charming beauty like that of the God of Love,
She pressed the ring to her eyes and bathed it with her tears,
And thus doing, she forgot herself!   260

'O, the most pious icon;
O, the exalted one in the clan of Raghu; O king of kings;
O, the virtuous Rama; O, the Universal Soul;
O, the one revered by the gods; O, the kin of the virtuous;
You have shown mercy by giving this ring, O my lord!'
Thus saying, she offered the lotus of her heart to that ring worshipfully,
And kissing it, she held it and closed it with her fist.

With a feeling of deep contentment
Janaki said: 'You are indeed valorous.
You are adroit in knowledge. I do not know how you came here!   270
As I was drowning in the ocean of pangs of separation, you have come.
You are the boat to protect me and take me to the banks, my child!

'How did you cross the ocean
That is one hundred *yojana*-wide,
And is full of cruel aquatic creatures?
With such ease you have come winning over fear and anxiety.
How is Shri Rama keeping? How is Saumitri keeping?
Are they angry at my behaviour, tell me.
How Shri Rama controlled his wrath against Ravana;
How Saumitri controlled his wrath against Ravana;   280
How did they do this, tell me!

'Tell me, O Hanuma, tell me –
What are their plans; what efforts they are making.

Has Shri Rama resorted to silence, you tell me.
Has he lost faith in human efforts?
Where are the four expedients to success against an enemy:
Sama, dana, bheda, and *danda* –
Negotiation, bribery, sowing dissension, and open attack –
Has he remained idle without employing any of these means, tell me.
Giving up his efforts, and growing weak in grief, 290
Has he sunk low without liberating me?
Has his valour disappeared?
Has his confidence got charred?
Has he lost the grandeur with which he had slain the *rakshasas*
At Dandaka-forest and demonstrated courage
Winning over worry, fear, and sadness?
With my mind steadfastly focused on Rama,
And with my breath devoted solely to Rama,
I have been waiting for him day and night.
Has Rama forgotten me? 300
I am aggrieved from deep affliction;
Tell me, O Hanuma, tell me!'

Folding his hands in supplication, Hanuma said:
'Shri Rama is not aware where you are.
If aware, would he sit quiet?
Without any delay, he would lead the *vanara*-army swiftly –
What limits the oceans could set for him?
What limits the forts could set for him?
O Mother! He does not reckon Lanka to be any great –
He shall pour hot water on the whole race of the *rakshasas*. 310
Would he spare them? He is steadfast in his resolution.
Like an enraged tusker that crushes everything on its way
And rushes forward,
In order to strike the enemies hard, Shri Rama –
The great tusker in rut, would come here charging, listen!

'I am the servant of Rama.
I swear by Mount Malaya;

I swear by Mount Vindhya;
I swear by Mount Meru;
I swear by Mount Chamundi; 320
I swear by Mounts – Sahyadri and Sheshadri;
I swear by Mount Hyma;
I swear by Mount Rushyamuka;
I swear by the sun and the moon; I swear by Maruta;
I swear by the food – edible tubers and roots;
I swear by Dandaka, the forest;
O Mother! You shall certainly see the lotus-face of Shri Rama.
In the vow and anxiety of looking for you,
Shri Rama eats only tubers, fruits, and roots sparsely
Just to keep his body and soul together, and has utterly waned. 330

'What shall I say, O Mother!
Looking at flowers and fruits, Rama laments – "O Sita!"
When he sees a deer, he laments – "O Sita!"
Waking up from sleep, he laments – "O Sita!"
While standing and sitting, he laments – "O Sita!"
He cries out saying – "here's the waterfall;"
Under delusion, he often says – "Sita, be careful!"
Like the moon covered by the autumn clouds,
In the pangs of separation from you,
Our lord has moved to the backstage. 340
In the eagerness of the very thought –
"When will I see Sita" –
He counts every fleeting moment
And sighs deeply looking at the sky.

'How shall I describe Rama's pangs of separation, O Mother!
The words uttered by him, cause me pain in the pit of my stomach:

"O Janaki, look at me!
In the pangs of my separation from you,
All have turned into my enemies.
All things that give comfort and happiness are now 350
Blazing hot and afflict me. With whom could I say this!

All the tender shoots of spring have turned into burning embers;
The summer breeze has turned into poisonous breath of a serpent;
The monsoon clouds rain fire,
And the winter nights cast dense darkness;
The autumn-moon spreads scorching moonlight;
And the peace of the cold season has disturbed my mind,
And I am drowned in deep anguish," – in this way, he laments.'
Having heard Hanuma's words,
Sita, feeling sad, said: 360
'Raghava is the pinnacle of mercy.
He is not at fault, none whatsoever.
He has suffered worrying about me, hasn't he?
Tell Rama how I have been suffering.
In the funeral pyre of worry, I am burnt day and night.
Life itself has become poisonous.
Won't Shri Rama come?
Ten months have gone by;
Won't Shri Rama come?
Ravana has set the period of two months within which to appease
 him. 370
Would I appease him? Never!
Even if I lose my life, it is alright.
Vibhishana has given good counsel to Ravana;
"You have invited death" – he has told Ravana so.
Anale – Vibhishana's daughter has told thus:
"A messenger of Rama shall certainly come
To herald the arrival of Shri Rama."
Look! This is the Supreme Truth;
My inner voice tells me so without respite.
Since you have come now, her words are proved right; 380
I am happy, and feel comforted.
The faith that you are the messenger of Rama,
And the faith that Rama will certainly come, are now confirmed.
I am blessed; indeed I am!'
So saying, Sita wiped her tears!

'O Mother! Let Shri Rama come in the direction of Lanka.
Today itself I will carry you on my shoulder
And crossing the ocean, I will carry you to Kishkindha
And proffer you to Rama.
Like Rohini eagerly joins Moon, her consort, 390
O Mother! Live happily being united with Ramachandra.
After that, Shri Rama will come invading.
He shall slay Ravana and thus rid this earth of dead-weight,
And bring happiness to all.

'What forts and ramparts could stop me!
What constraints the walls, the city-gate, and the army
Of *rakshasas* could pose!
What is so great about Kumbhakarna, let alone Ravana!
By the grace of Rama, I am endowed with enough strength
To lift Lanka off the ground and carry it! 400
That's the power of Rama; and I have nothing else to rely on.
Sit on my shoulder quickly; why delay any more?
I am the servant, who sifts the sorrow of Shri Rama and Lakshmana;
As I am here to serve you,
O Mother, be advised to oblige,' – he pleaded so.

Quivering with delight
She looked at him with wide-opened eyes:
'I understand that you are valorous.
In speed, you are the storm indeed, and I know that well.
In radiance, you are like fire; 410
In brilliance, you are the volcanic fire.
All strengths and diplomacy, all charms and spells
Have found their home in you –
The one who has crossed the ocean.
You've the capacity to hoist me on to your shoulder.
The same strength that is there in the arms and bodies of
Shri Rama and Saumitri is there in you too.
However, as I am the lawful wife of Shri Rama;
As I am a dutiful wife; as I am the daughter of Janaka;

As I am the loving child of Mother India; 420
As I am the daughter of the blessed earth;
Why should you carry me clandestinely?
Ravana brought me here; and I got disgrace;
How could I touch a stranger again, tell me?
You are son to me; would the world understand that?
Slander-mongering and baseness are the diseases that infect some;
Is the Saketa-tongue devoid of fickleness?
It will rest only after ransacking all rumours and ominous details, listen!

'Rama is highly valorous.
I desire salvation by his strength. 430
With the support of Saumitri, when Rama crushes Ravana
I will get the nectar of liberation.
Would Shri Rama stop until then?
As the region of Great Quest is spread wide,
As Saketa was deserted for the sake of punishing the evil-doers,
In the pretext of saving me, Rama will come here,
And slaying Ravana, Rama will ameliorate the world.
If I come with you, the Great Quest of Rama will be put off, listen.

'Let it not be so, my child.
Do not explode Rama's Quest at its summit. 440
Do not bury the luster of Rama's victory at some unknown spot.
Do not cast obstacles in the resolute path of ameliorating the world,' –
Janaki said so.

Canto One Hundred and Fifty-four

'This is the Message of Love; This is the Sweet Message'

‖☉‖

On hearing Janaki's words,
Hanuma's effulgence of happiness rose high.
'You have spoken words befitting a dutiful wife.
As my heart was wrenched by your afflictions,
I was eager to seek a solution to that.
As my devotion to Rama rose high,
I had the great desire to proffer you to him without delay;
Forgive me, O Mother!

'I shall return from Lanka, and go to see Rama.
"Have you seen Sita? What did she say?" – 10
Thus, when Shri Rama asks,
'What shall I say, O Mother!
What message shall I carry to Shri Rama, O Mother!' –
Thus he begged.

'This is the message, listen.
Is Shri Rama keeping well? Is Saumitri keeping well?
You tell Rama that this is what I asked.
Saumitri, who protected us in the forest forsaking sleep and food,

Treating me like a mother, and Rama like his father, –
And the one who is deeply hurt by my scornful words – 20
Tell him that I enquired about his well-being;
Whether Sugriva and the entire *vanara*-force are keeping well –
O Hanuma! You tell them that I enquired thus.
There is only two months period left now;
And within that time,
If Shri Rama does not appear here,
I swear by the divine feet of Shri Rama, O listen;
I swear by my father, O listen;
I swear by Truth, O listen; I shall not live – you tell him thus.
Before I lose my life, Rama is duty-bound 30
To be the volcanic fire to the forest of wickedness
By employing his valour befittingly – thus, you tell Rama.
When Shri Rama himself comes and crushes Ravana,
The dome of fame of the clan of Ikshvaku shall glow bright
And rising sky-high, it shall glitter grandly – you tell him so.

'O Anjaneya, listen!
This is the message of love; this is the sweet message;
This is the message that would appease Rama
By touching the chord of his heart.
When we were happily together at Chitrakoota – 40
A variety of fruits and flowers spread fragrance
Across the banks of the Mandakini;
Having wandered in the garden there,
As Rama was asleep resting his head on my lap,
A wicked crow, arrived swiftly from somewhere,
And started pecking at my breast.
I sat there motionless unmindful of the pain
So that the sleep of my beloved shouldn't be disturbed.
As the blood oozed out from the wound and was flowing down,
Rama's sleep was disturbed by the touch of that blood, 50
And getting up swiftly, he looked at the wound on my breast with fear.

Steadfastly he asked:
'Aha! What happened? Why the blood is oozing out?
Asking thus, and hissing like a serpent,
As he looked around, and learnt that
That was the act of the wicked crow,
He grew angrier, and twisting his eyes,
He blew the charm of *brahmastra* –
The most potent, divine weapon of annihilation –
On a streak of straw and as he threw it up, 60
It chased the crow emitting the fire of death.
Wherever the crow flew, the straw-weapon kept chasing the crow.
The crow couldn't escape the fate of being killed by that *brahmastra*.
'I shall seek refuge in Shri Rama himself and get a fresh lease of life,' –
Thinking thus, the crow approached Rama and surrendered itself.
Shri Rama looked mercifully at the crow that had surrendered;
And recalling *brahmastra*, he protected the crow.
When you tell Rama this episode, he will bloom in happiness.

He did not spare the crow.
Would he then spare Ravana? Won't he come running? 70
Why Rama, the pinnacle of mercy, has forgotten me?
It is impossible to describe the speed of Rama's arrow.
Naga, gandharva, asura, Maruta and the *naga* clan –
None could bear the speed of that fierce arrow.
Lakshmana does not like to remain inactive.
Has Rama prevented him?
The fruit of sin of abusing Saumitri scornfully on that day
Has pushed me to this affliction – tell him all that.'
Thus, while conveying the message,
Janaki unfolded her agony. 80

At that time, Anjaneya,
Comforting her, said:
'Why do you grieve over it, O Mother!
Rama will certainly come; Saumitri will come too.

They will annihilate the progeny of Dashashira;
Thus annihilated, they shall become manure for the epoch-tree.
Sugriva, the *vanaras*, and the heroic *bhalluka* – the Bear clan –
All will come to the land of Lanka and stand like rocks.
They will cross over the ocean at the speed of the mind.
If compared to others in the *vanara*-army,   90
O Mother! I am the one with the least valour and heroism;
All others are stronger than me,
And would rush in to Lanka in just a single leap.
Who could resist Shri Rama and Lakshmana
When they come invading like the rising sun and the moon?
Give up your sorrow; shed your worries;
Shri Rama's light will be lit here and it will glow brightly;
We all will see that, for sure.
Benediction will be yours; liberation will be yours.
You have the protection of Rama   100
Who is accompanied by countless valourous heroic clans.
O Mother! Shed all your worries.'
Hanuma said thus.

After that, Janaki,
Untied the magnificent *chudamani* –
The crest-jewel
Which she had tied with the loose end of her sari,

And giving it to Hanuma, she said:
'This is the pendent of my heart; give it to Shri Rama –
This is a magnificent jewel which will bring back recognition;   110
This is a jewel of consciousness which will remind everything;
This is a jewel of glowing ruby which will rescue from the ocean
 of sorrow.'

She was overcome with happiness.
'You have placed an altogether new ornamental dome on Duty;
You have become the officiating priest
Of Shri Rama's Great Quest;
In the task of punishing the evil-doers, you are in the forefront;

You have struck the kettle-drum of alerting the *vanaras*;
You have blown the trumpet of the awakening;
You have sounded the trumpet for the war of liberation; 120
You have guided the world on the path of righteous knowledge
By making them drink the celestial nectar and lighting up their path;
There is the prowess and radiance of a warrior in your words;
You have marched forward kicking off commotion
And alerting the land.

'How much could I praise you!
You are the full-river which flows spreading coolness
Pushing away the old water and running a stream of fresh water.
As the Chariot of New Age rolls, you have become its charioteer.
You have caused the Cloud of Mercy to pour down as soothing rain. 130
The fruit of your good deeds has become offering to the land.
O Hanuma! With the challenge of strength,
Brandishing the sword, you are on your way riding the Horse of Truth.
Striking the chord of the lute of liberation,
And becoming yourself its tune,
Spreading the nectar of happiness, and casting away inertia,
You have harvested a magnificent crop,' –
Thus Sita rained praise on Hanuma.

'In the courtyard of heart,
You have stepped in with the Feet of Peace, 140
And chanting *pranava* – the mystic syllable *Om* –
You have won the heart of this mother.
For you, the stars themselves are the tender mangoes;
And the sun and the moon are the fruits.
You have shone in grandeur as the one with unequalled strength.'
Thus, Janaki, praising Hanuma again and again,
Made him float in the wave of emotion that was most poignant!

Canto One Hundred and Fifty-five

'Ashokavana – the Garden devoid of Sorrow Turned into Shokavana – Garden of Sorrow'

||๖||

Hanumanta has been honoured by Janaki,
And has received the message; he has received a mnemonic sign;
He has received her blessings; he stands in great delight;
Then, he moved away from the presence of the "mother".
'I have seen the "mother"; my vow has been fulfilled.
Now the war-strategy could be devised steadfastly.
Would Ravana bend down to *sama* – the strategy of negotiation?
Would Ravana bow down to *dana* – the strategy of liberality?
Would Ravana fall to *bheda* – the strategy of sowing dissension?
They are the cruel *rakshasas*;   10
To curb their arrogance there are no other ways left
Except *danda* – the ultimate strategy of open attack.

'Well, I have seen the "mother".
The next task is to understand how strong the enemy-might is.
It must be compared with Rama's might;
All the differences must be thoroughly assessed.
'Shri Rama shall crush you to dust,' –

Such a foreboding should be given now itself.
Crushing the *rakshasas'* power of countenance,
We should stand victorious.   20

'How could the war be won?
The will-power of Ravana's *chaturangabala* –
Army of elephants, chariots, cavalry and infantry –
Shall be reduced to rubble; if not,
How could I be able to return to the presence of my Master?
How could I be able to return to the divine presence of Shri Rama?
Prior to designing all the war-strategy,
What is there deep down in the minds of Dashakantha's
Council of Ministers, should be thoroughly studied.
There shall not be any lapse in the strategy –   30
What is Ravana's might;
What weapons of warfare, spells and charms does he have;
What plans and strategies does he have;
What kind of war-skills and expertise does he have –
If all these are not understood,
The vow will become lax.

'In the ensuing war in Lankesha's kingdom,
What shall befall us –
Such a fear should be instilled now itself
I shall cause the entire clan of Ravana   40
To be weighed down by disbelief in their victory.

'Ashokavana looks pleasant to the eyes
And glitters like the celestial garden of Indra.
This is Ravana's favourite garden; I shall steadfastly destroy this.
Like the wild fire that devours the forest hungrily,
I shall now ransack and completely destroy this.
To overpower me, if enraged Lankesha
Sends forth a troupe of *rakshasas*
Along with elephants, horses, and chariots,
Armed with tridents, iron-bars, axes, and the like,   50

I shall wage a battle with them fearlessly.'
Thus he thought.

The heroic Anjaneya was already at his task.
In the row of trees, he broke the branches, and uprooted the trees.
He pulled down the arched-sheds of creepers and scattered them away.
He squeezed all the flower-buds and crushed them.
Leaping here and there, and climbing up the arched sheds,
He pulled down the entire festoon suspended across the gateways.
Roaring aloud heroically, he crushed the arched sheds,
And pulling hard at the swings, he broke them and threw them away. 60
Like a storm, he moved swiftly here and there
And crushed to dust the sports-hill constructed under simulation.
He despoiled the ponds and lakes that were
Looking grand with crystal-clear water, and ran ahead.
The garden for the damsels, losing its grandeur, wore a withered look.
The garden for the boys was completely ransacked.
The grandeur of the garden turned into dreadful graveyard.
The glitter of the art-gallery lost its sheen.
As if the fire of ultimate destruction exploded,
There were explosions spread all over. 70
As if some conspiracy got exploded,
Like the excessive sheen of lightning that is dazzling to the eyes,
As if simultaneously destroying everything by using the forces
Of thundering thunderbolts and clusters of lightning,
Anjaneya steadfastly rummaged through the garden.

Because of Anjaneya,
Ashokavana turned into Shokavana – Garden of Sorrow.
All the *ashoka*-creepers withered in sorrow.
The deer and birds crying aloud in fear
Ran helter-skelter in every direction. 80
Many bad-omens appeared in the city.

Consternation shrouded the *rakshasas*.
Shivering with the fear that *pralaya* –
The universal destruction might be on the anvil –
'What happened to the city of Lanka?
What pestilence that wasn't here ever before, has struck now?
This fort is inviolable. Who has entered here?
Where did the power to quell Lanka take birth?
What is this storm, and tempest?
Would it uproot Lanka and cast it away?' –   90
Thus they asked quivering.

All the women flocked together,
And coming to the streets they wandered in delusion.
They hastened to protect their babies
By clasping them close to their hearts.
'This is the progeny of Lanka; would it be wiped out?
Would our *kumkum* – the crimsoned saffron-powder
Applied on the forehead by married women –
The mark of wifehood be wiped out?
What can we do? We are women after all!'   100
Thus, they all lamented there in unison.

All the *rakshasies* who were surrounding
Janaki trembled in fear. They all saw Hanuma
Who was busy destroying everything.
They came near Janaki and asked thus:
'Who is this wicked one?
O Janaki! Tell us from where has he come.
Did he speak to you? Who is he to you?
He has caused this great upheaval by your order –
That is what we doubt in our minds.'   110

'I do not know; I do not know.
I do not know who has caused this great upheaval.
The trail of a serpent would be known only to one of its own kind.
How any other creature could understand that, tell me.
Being a *rakshasa* himself, he has blown this storm, I suppose.

Only the other *rakshasas* should understand that and curb him;
Listen, you all. Look at him! He assumes any form at will.
He becomes a dwarf once, and at another instance,
He grows to be a giant.
My mind fears him; I am scared,' she said.   120

All the *rakshasies*,
Scattering in all the directions, hid themselves.
Burdened with their duties, they entered the palace of Dashashira.
They were breathing heavily.
'We are alive; we are saved,' – so saying,
They fell at the feet of Lankesha.
'We prostrate ourselves before you, O king!
Someone – who he is, we do not know – he's fear personified –
Has entered Ashokavana, and not minding anyone,
Is marching ahead crushing everything to dust.   130
Is he the messenger of Devendra;
Or the messenger of Kubera;
Or the messenger of Rama, we do not know.
He seems to be omnipresent; going near Janaki,
And revealing some secret,
He has caused this fierce destruction.

'What shall we tell you, O king!
He has uprooted all the trees that were there
In Ashokavana, sparing none whatsoever.
No one knows the secret behind this.   140
Watch for yourself, O Master!' Thus, they all said.

Having heard those words,
Lankesha, blazing with rage, said:
'Should I watch that myself? It is not worth a straw to me.'
Thus saying, he pushed those maids with the powerful
Sweep of his hands, and sent for his servants.
'Who instilled fear? Seize him at once
And chop him to pieces, and throw the meat
To jackals, dogs, and crows;

Let them eat the meat to the brim right away.' 150
Thus he gave them strict orders.

Instantly, a big battalion of mighty *rakshasas*,
Brandishing swords, tridents, maces, and mallets,
Rushed to strike Hanuma, roaring aloud thus:
'Who is that great fool? Does he desire death?'

Would Hanuma be bothered!
He has no fear of death. All trees must shed their leaves
In humble submission to welcome spring.
Without selfless dedication, is it possible
To accomplish any great mission! 160

Steadfastly, Anjaneya,
Like an elephant in rut, grew his body to giant proportions,
And getting furious like a lion, he pressed his feet firmly to the ground,
And thumping the ground with heavy stride, rushed to strike, roaring thus:
'Let victory be to Shri Rama;
Let victory be to Lakshmana;
Let victory be to the dutiful wife;
Let victory be to Sugriva;
Let victory be to the valorous of the Monkey-clan.
I am the son of Wind. I am called Hanuma. 170
I am Kesari's son. I have come now
To annihilate the progeny of Ravana.
I will cause the entire encampment of *rakshasas* to shiver violently
And burning down Lanka, I will fulfil the mission.'
So saying, he marched against the *rakshasas*
And raining blows with his fist, hit them hard.

He looked around.
He saw the bolt of a size bigger than sugarcane
Fastened to the door of the main-gate,
And pulling it off with agility and 180

Brandishing it swiftly, he hit the *rakshasas* with it
And sent them to Yamapuri – the city of Yama, God of Death.
All this happened at the speed of twinkling of an eye.
'We will inform our master;
Let us not meddle with him.' Crying aloud thus –
'We do not know how to rescue Lanka.
Why did the god of universal destruction come today itself!'
Uttering thus, they retreated and ran away swiftly to save their lives.

Canto One Hundred and Fifty-six

'Assuming Form, Mount Mandara itself seems to have Come!'

||৬||

When Lankesha called Jambumali, the son of Prahasta,
To rein in Hanuma, there was enthusiasm.
Wearing yellow robes, and a ruddy garland,
And accepting *ranavilya* –
Betel-leaf as a token of formal invitation to go to war –
From the hands of Ravana,
And holding a sharp arrow,
And seated in a chariot that moved swiftly,
And making a loud war-cry,
He came to attack Hanuma! 10

All the valorous *rakshasas*
Armed with a variety of weapons
Like swords, mallets, large axes, and roaring aloud –
'We'll strike; we'll chop off; we'll cut and crush him with these weapons' –
Stood there encircling Anjaneya.

'O, *rakshasas*! Listen you all!
I am the messenger of Rama; Sugriva is my master;

I have come from Kishkindha;
Like me, many more valorous *vanaras* are there;
They'll come barging in tomorrow.   20
Abducting Sita, Ravana has sown enmity;
And has himself thus given invitation to massive annihilation.'
Thus, the valorous Anjaneya proclaimed loudly.

As Hanuma sat happily
On the transverse beam of the gigantic gateway
Casting a bantering look at Jambumali, the *danava* got infuriated:
'Who are you, O *vanara*?
Have you come here forsaking the desire to live?'
Thus abusing, he set a sharp crescent shaped arrow
To the bow and shot it with great force.   30
The sharp arrow hit the face of Anjaneya.

Yet another arrow with the shape of *ankusha* –
Elephant-driver's hook – had already hit his head.
With ten more arrows, Jambumali pierced the arms of Anjaneya;
Blood oozed out; then, the face of Hanuma turned red
And looked like a red lotus.

As the arrows got stuck on every limb,
It looked as though this great devotee was smeared with red sandal paste
And he was aglow with red all over.

'What shall I do to him?'   40
Thinking thus, Hanumanta lifted up a large rock,
And hurled it with great speed at Jambumali's face.
With the dexterity of his archery,
Jambumali cleaved that rock.

Aiming at Hanuma's chest,
With yet another five arrows Jambumali
Struck him, oh!

'He shall not be spared,'
Thinking thus, Hanuma pulled out a door

And swiveling it swiftly, struck him hard. 50
At that intense impact, the body of Jambumali
Got smashed, and he died instantly.
It was as though Lankesha's flag itself had fallen to the ground!

The battle-scene looked
As if it was the whirlpool that rose in the middle of the ocean.
In his extraordinary gigantic form,
Maruti flew boldly in the sky-way grandiosely
And roaring like thunder and lightning,
He knocked the others down.

As soon as that news reached Ravana, 60
His eyes turned into burning embers and emitted fire.
Summoning the sons of his seven ministers hastily
And enthusing them to be ready to set out on war,
Ravana said thus: 'You are radiant like the God of Fire;
You are indeed dexterous in all kinds of weaponry;
It is up to you to decide and devise strategies as to
How should you fight, and how should you put out
The fire that has engulfed Lanka.
A monkey has caused annihilation
And like a rock is standing against the main gate, it seems. 70
How amazing! And how ridiculous!
Go swiftly and put an end to it.

The young warriors set out together taking the *ranavilya*.
The flags fluttered as they ascended their grand chariots,
And they roared like thunder:
'We'll tackle this; we'll kill it and return.'
Shouting thus, and lifting up their bows
That glittered like the blades of lightning,
With ever-abiding readiness each one rushed ahead
Of the other towards Hanuma 80
Who was standing against the main gate.

The *rakshasas* shot arrows one after the other
In quick succession; It looked as though the sound

Of chariots was itself the sound of the thundering clouds;
And, the arrows themselves were the rains pouring down.
Just as he would leap skywards, Pavanasuta moved swiftly
Deftly avoiding getting hit by the stream of arrows
As if it was a mere sport for fun.
Roaring aloud and tightening his fist,
He hit some of them hard and thus gave them a taste 90
Of his powerful hands; he kicked a few others
With his legs again and again and pushed them out;
He cleaved some others with his nail
And squeezing some of them between his thighs,
He killed suffocating them thus.
When he roared aloud ferociously,
Some of them died as their hearts stopped beating frightened
By the fierceness of the roar.
Unable to bear the pain of the blows,
The herds of elephants roared; 100
Writhing in pain, the horses fell to the ground and died;
With broken limbs, the *rakshasas* rolled in pain;
As all the chariots were broken to pieces in the battle,
Their flag-poles lay there scattered and broken.

The remaining troupe
Ran helter-skelter in fear.
'There is a proverb – If alive, one can survive even by begging for food;
It is enough if our lives are spared now,' –
So saying, they all ran away.
As an old jackal howled raucously, it seemed 110
To herald the imminent end of Lankesha
And it was a bad omen indeed.
'Who are the other valorous men here? Come here quickly,'
So saying, Hanumanta grew himself tall
To the size of the main gate
And thus he stood there!

Ravana heard the news that
Hanuma had killed all the sons of his ministers.
He was overcome with worry. He summoned Virupaksha,
Yupaksha, Durdhara, Praghasa, and Bhasakarna, and said thus: 120
'Listen, you Generals! You are all veterans of war;
You all are proficient indeed in rushing in
And creating confusion in the enemy camp.
He is some unknown *vanara*.
If not fought with caution, calamity awaits us, no doubt.
Judging the situation cautiously, attack that giant monster
With all the *chaturangabala* –
A complete army of elephants, chariots, cavalry and infantry –
Punish him enough, but do not kill him;
Bring him here pinioning! 130

Kishkindha is home to many warriors;
There live Vali, Sugriva, Jambava, Nila,
And Dwivida – all are great friends to me.
That being so, I do not know why such a thing has happened.
In speed, radiance, valour and knowledge,
They are like the ocean; they are *kamarupi* –
Able to assume any form at will;
They appear in the guise of a monkey once;
Yet again, they appear in the guise of a giant monster;
They are unequalled in courage; 140
They are excessively fierce and violent.
Is Vali any ordinary? He laid his hands on me too once;
Do not be over-confident and lose yourself. Be warned!

Cast away fear.
Truly, you are such valorous heroes that
You can rein in the world of gods, the nether world and this world too.
Jayalakshmi – the Queen of Victory – is always capricious.
Do not feel conceited of your physical strength; control it constantly.
Attack shall be the last resort, remember;
If forgotten, you shall suffer affliction and die of grief.' 150
Thus said Ravana.

The Generals, having been appraised of the
War strategy and its appropriateness,
Sought Ravana's permission and set out
To the battle-front in their chariots that were kept ready for them.
Having seen valorous Anjaneya at the gate,
Beaming with radiance as if he were a fountain of enthusiasm,
They were all frightened, 'Where did this ghost come from?
How to harness and pinion it?
Assuming form, Mount Mandara itself 160
Seems to have come,' – so saying, they rushed forward
And attacked Hanuma with sharp arrows.

The *rakshasas*, in a fit of excitement thought –
'He shall fall to the ground any moment now,'
And as they were watching happily,
Hanuma roared aloud like a lion, which echoed in all the ten directions,
And, with the speed of lightning, attacked the *rakshasas*.
He broke to pieces all the sharp arrows and threw them away.
He grew himself into giant proportions and hit hard
At the chariots and broke them into pieces; 170
Hit hard the horses and killed them;
At that instance, the Generals – Virupaksha and Yupaksha –
Jumped out of the chariots and roaring in fury,
Cast mallets pointedly at Anjaneya's chest with a powerful sweep.
In retaliation, Hanumanta pulled out a *sal*-tree
And as he hit them with it, the *rakshasas* lay down dead.

Without losing courage, Praghasa and Bhasakarna
Rushed forward and as they stabbed Hanuma with spears,
He was wounded and the blood gushed out
As if the sun at dusk covered the horizon with crimson-rays. 180
Infuriated Anjaneya the brave steadfastly inflicted troubles
By hitting back in retaliation;
All the Generals then became the guests of Yama – the God of Death.
Hanuma then smashed down the infantry,

The elephants, horses and the chariots.
It looked as though the mountain
Of Ravana's conceit came tumbling down.
'Who else shall come to fight with me?' –
With such valour and rage he appeared like Kalabhairava –
The terrible form of Shiva – 190
Who engulfed the world at the time of *pralaya* – the Great Destruction.

Canto One Hundred and Fifty-seven

'On Which Wild Tiger's Milk has He Grown up thus!'

॥௦॥

Having heard that all the generals had died,
In silence, Lankesha became the sun at dusk.
Aksha, a dear son to his father, and a valorous warrior himself,
Having understood his father's intention,
Requested to be given *ranavilya*.

Shining brilliantly like Agni – the God of Fire –
Bowing to the feet of his father,
And then ascending the chariot that shone bright
Like the rising sun, Aksha moved in the direction of Hanuma.

Powerful knives and lances were all loaded in the chariot.   10
The flag was fluttering.
An army of warriors followed Aksha.
'Where is that enemy? When shall I see him?' –
He was in such haste to meet Hanuma.

He saw Hanuma.
Aksha felt that Hanuma's radiance was certainly more than his own;
Wondering at that, pooling together all his powers and strengths,

And beaming with conceit,
He pulled out a sharp arrow and shot Hanuma.
Paying no heed to that, Hanuma leaped to the sky
At the speed of Garuda – vehicle of Vishnu.
Asksha saw that and pondered:
'What a surprise! What a steady mind! What self-confidence!
There was not the slightest anxiety; no sweat in the face;
There were no fearful palpitations of heart;
There weren't any movements either;
With what graceful stance he stood steady like a sculpted idol of stone!
There were no lip-movements; there was no shivering in the hands;
His hairs did not stand on end in excitement; his feet did not move;
His eyes did not become red in anger; everything is calm.
To which land does he belong?
Of which womb is he the offspring?
Of which epoch's end does he desire standing here?
Of which wild tiger's milk did he drink, and grew up thus?
Of which elephant-womb did he come out cleaving?' –
Thus worried Aksha.

Proclaiming war
With the beating of drums as he stood in readiness, the sky reverberated.
The brilliance of the sun was hidden under the thick clouds.
The wind stood still; the mountain peaks trembled;
As the sky and the ocean converged at their own will,
Pulling out arrows from the sheath, Aksha attacked Hanuma
With sharp arrows in quick succession and felt elated.
The arrows filled the sky.
As Aksha shot the fierce arrows in quick succession
Superseding the speed of the mind,
Hanumanta leaped to the sky.
Wherever he went, Aksha's arrows followed him steadfastly;
Thus chasing him wildly,

Aksha offered Hanuma a treat of his swift and powerful arrows. 50
Hanuma was wounded; Hanuma suffered pain.

Hanumanta appreciated:
'Bravo! Well-done! You are indeed the son of
Dashakantha – the ten-headed one.
You gleam like the rising sun.
You are a skillful archer; you are truly a valorous hero;
You labour hard;
In valour and enthusiasm, you are at the
Pinnacle among the *nagas* and *yakshas*.
What swiftness! What courage and firmness! 60
What a superb stance that runs shivers in the hearts of enemies!' –
Thus Hanuma praised Aksha.

'When a spark is kindled
It is good to put it out before it engulfs the entire forest.
I shall kill this warrior employing the skills of warfare.' –
Hanuma attacked Aksha and hit hard his horses;
Broke the chariot into pieces and thus caused him panic.

Aksha jumped out of the chariot carrying his bow.
Like a sage who ascends to the sky
By the powers of his meditation, Aksha stood there up in the sky. 70
Like Garuda catching a serpent,
Anjaneya swiftly caught Aksha by the legs
And swiveling him fast, struck him hard against the ground;
Aksha's arms, thigh-joints, waist and neck
All got crushed badly; his necklaces,
Epaulets and badge of honour on the anklet
Lay scattered on the ground.

Ravana, the lord of Lanka,
Had till then sacrificed the sons of others in the war
And was afloat in the comforts of savage ocean. 80
But today, having sacrificed his own son,
Ravana was drowned by the weight of heart-wrenching grief.

Has the Goddess of Glory who held high the valour of Lanka so far,
Remains hidden now?
'How would I preserve this sovereignty?' –
Thus lamenting, and comforting himself,
And then grieving over –
'A tempest has struck; would I succumb and perish?' –

He sent for his son – Indrajit
And touching him with tender love, told him thus: 90
'You are indeed Adishesha – the sovereign serpent,
The protector of the wealth of honour of this nation.
You are adroit in the skills of weaponry;
You have exhibited your valour by defeating the gods
And the *rakshasas* earlier;
You are the jewel of a warrior who has secured *Brahmastra* –
The ultimate weapon of destruction – through hard meditation;
You are well-balanced in offering personal counsel.
The *vanara* has killed Jambumali and the other warriors;
The kingdom is lurking in danger. 100
Look! The entire *chaturangabala* – army – has fallen down.
Look! Your dear brother is slain.
I am drenched in the ocean of grief. What shall I do?
On the path of the gateway, the enemy is standing
Beaming with great conceit and bantering stance,
Challenging everyone to war;
Like the ferocious Shiva, the Destroyer,
He is standing there roaring aloud and eager to swallow all.

What shall I say, my son!
Not winning that one, I have sunk low into the abyss of
  disappointment. 110
I shall go to fight with that one *vanara* and that war is equal to death.
Even if the war is won, what is so great about it?
That is equal to defeat indeed.
He is the enemy who is equal to Agni – the God of Fire.
He will push me into the burning pit of fire, for sure;
Would I discard this body in an act of expiation?

I am caught up in the heat
Of the funeral pyre of worry. I have fallen into the Well of Futility.
O, I have lost my way in the Forest of Distress.
Tell me, what I could do now.   120
Look! To protect the honour of wealthy Lanka,
I shall offer my life itself.

If I die while fighting the enemy,
Glorious Heaven for the valorous heroes shall be mine.
Even if the battle is won, would I return?
I shall drown myself in the ocean.
Fighting with a single person and winning, is it any great victory?
You rule over the Lanka-empire well.
Ravana, the lord of Lanka was a shameless king;
He once ruled over Lanka – get all such tidings   130
Wiped out from Lanka's memory.'

So saying, Lankesha pulled out
A knife and was about to stab himself;
Meanwhile, Indrajit went near him in haste,
Took away the knife and throwing it out, said:

'O father, what are you doing?
Why this despair? Has the spring of Lanka's valour dried up?
Being the crest-jewel of Lanka,
Would you wipe out the *sindura* –
The auspicious mark applied on the forehead – yourself?   140
Grant me the *ranavilya*; and then watch my valour;
I shall not allow your fame –
The one who rules over the world – to be despoiled.'

He got ready for the battle.
Having received his father's permission,
Indrajit set out in the chariot feeling quite enraged.
As Hanuma heard the twang of Meghanada – Indrajit's bow-string
And the sound of his approaching chariot,
Maruti was excited at the prospect of the impending war

And floating in the pond of happiness at such an opportunity, 150
Felt quite elated.
To watch the grandeur of the war between the two valorous heroes
The *nagas, yakshas, siddhas*, and the great sages were all
   assembled there.

Indrajit rained arrows.
Hanumanta, exhibiting marvelous movements in the sky,
And moving swiftly like lightning,
Showed his war-skills deftly avoiding all the arrows.
'Would I bow down in fear and perish
If attacked with arrows in quick succession?' –
So saying, he caught the arrows with the sweep 160
Of his powerful hands, and breaking them to pieces
And throwing them all over,
He laughed aloud merrily!

All the potent divine weapons
Used against Hanuma turned like toys.
'You have won over Indra, haven't you? Do you know who I am?' –
In this way, it appeared as if Hanumanta mocked at him;
It was as if Indrajit's valour was provoked.

As his fuming rage crackled wildly, Indrajit shouted:
'Kill him; chop him off; stab him; pierce him to death; 170
Shoot him with arrows; he is a cunning *vanara*;
Break his teeth; tear out his entrails;
Knock him down with swords, tridents, lances,
Maces, millets, and spears;
Pinion him fast and throw him out into the ocean.'
As Indrajit cried aloud thus,
All kinds of weapons used by the *rakshasas*
Broke to pieces with a crackling sound
On approaching Hanuma, and were scattered away.

Indrajit thought for himself: 180
It is impossible to slay this *vanara*.

He is highly adroit; he is very clever; he is valorous too;
I shall truss him in contrivance; that would be better;
I shall now cause him to bend –
Thinking thus, as he employed *Brahmastra*,
'I shall not supersede this most divine weapon,' –
Showing such reverence,
Hanumanta allowed himself to be bound in submission
And sat down there as if he was defeated!

On seeing that, the *rakshasas* rapturously cried aloud 190
And danced in excitement –
'He is defeated; catch him' – shouting thus,
They pinioned Hanuma fast.
Indrajit, the one who had defeated Indra, is truly valorous –
Proclaiming loudly thus –
Bring the horses here; get the strongest of the carts;
Bring an elephant trunk; we ought to take him thus by force –
Laughing raucously and jeering at him thus,
The *rakshasas* took Hanumanta away
And threw him into the royal court of Ravana. 200

'I have got an opportunity
To see Lankesha; I will have a conversation with him.'
Thus thinking, Hanuma was engrossed in deep meditation
On Rama, and assumed silence.
Being amazed, the courtiers muttered thus:
'Who is this one? Whose son is he?
Where did this evil-doer come from?
He who has slain the *rakshasas* ought to be killed.
He ought to be burnt down;
He ought to be chopped off and thrown away; 210
Considering what he has done to Lanka,
He is Kalagnirudra – terrible form of Shiva as the Ultimate
  Destroyer –
Isn't he?'

In the middle of the court,
Lankesha was seated on the pearly throne;
He was glowing like the sun among the assembly of *rakshasas*;
Watching the wealth on display, the *vanara* was wonder-struck;
Looking at Ravana who was equal to Madana –
The God of Love, in his charming appearance,
As Hanuma folded both his hands in salutation,   220
It appeared as though he saluted Rama with great devotion.

Canto One Hundred and Fifty-eight

'O Look! The Shackle that Binds One to Life is Getting Unfastened'

॥६॥

Two eyes are not suffice
To watch the grandeur of Ravana.
He is wearing a golden crown studded with glittering
Precious gems. Pearly tassels are tied to it.
The glow of the golden ornaments is spread all around.

The pair of ear-rings is studded with nine precious gems.
The epaulets look like the five-hooded serpent in their charm.
The wonderful throne is studded with gems.
The carpet that is laid out is well embroidered.
Ravana is dressed in silk and wears finely woven raiment across
   his shoulder.   10
The fragrance of red-sandal and musk is spread all over.
Beautiful damsels who looked like the celestial nymphs are
   comforting
Ravana with hand-fans made of *chowry*.

Lankesha looked grand
Like the sun atop Mount Meru.
'He is radiant; he is the ocean of beauty;

All royal-characteristics are found in him;
As he sits in the royal throne with a charming smile,
He looks like the king of gods who rules over the world.
Valour is coupled with wealth of beauty in his person.   20
Is there anyone the likes of Ravana?' – thus appreciating,
As if Hanumanta was in the posture of dancing,
His feet moved rhythmically and his lips quivered in rapture.
'What madness has come over me?
Would anyone ever praise Ravana
Who has deviated from the path of righteousness?
Having deposed the sun and the moon and Agni – the God of Fire,
Ravana stands here as if being engulfed in the grandeur of darkness.'
Thinking thus, Hanuma sang in humble submission to Rama.

'Victory be to Shri Rama; Shri Rama, the ever auspicious!   30
Let victory be to Shri Rama;
Shri Rama, the most exalted of the clan of Raghu.
You are indeed moon to the lake of the clan of Raghu
O the consort of earth's-daughter! Let victory be to you.
Your radiance is greater than that of million suns and moons.
You are the most virtuous of all; and resolute on the vow of Truth.
Sweetness of your name is most charismatic.
The entire earth is filled with the brightness of your light.
You are a divine light; and I am only a tiny lamp;
You alone are the oil, the wick, and the glow of it indeed.'   40
Thus, at the centre of the royal court,
Hanuma sang in the reverberating tune of *Om*,
And as his excitement rose high,
Hanuma lost himself in dancing.

Ravana – the world-leader,
Looking at Hanuma anxiously, said to himself thus:
'Who could this one be? Who is he?
Is he Nandikeshwara – a chief attendant of Shiva in the form of
   an ape –
Who has come in disguise? Is he Brahma – the Creator himself,

Who has come in the form of a monkey? 50
Is he the instigator of the tricks designed by the enemies?'

Looking at the face of Prahasta,
Ravana asked: 'Who is this offender, and where did he come from?
Why did he destroy Ashokavana? Why did he slay
Our valorous warriors so frenziedly?'

Prahasta went near Anjaneya
And said: 'Be not afraid, O brave *vanara*!
Tell only the truth; it will do you good.
Who has sent you here – is it Yama; Varuna; or Vishnu?
Whose messenger are you? Whose servant are you? 60
You are brilliant indeed! If you tell lies,
It shall be the gallows for you; do not you forget!'

Looking at Ravana
Hanumanta said: 'Ask me directly who I am.
Why do you bid Prahasta to ask of me this?
Let thieving, lying, and wickedness all be solely
To the lineage of Ravana. Does anyone deceive
The very same hand that offered alms? Let that be so.
I will tell you presently who I am. I am not a servant
Of Devendra, Yama, Varuna, Kubera, or Vishnu. 70
I am just an ordinary *vanara*, and I am called Hanuma.
The renowned wrestler has effortlessly broken the bow of Hara –
The symbol that manifested cosmic mystery.
He has slain Khara, Dushana, Trishira, and Vali.
He is none other than Shri Rama; I am his messenger.
You have abducted Sita on the sly and brought her here.
Sugriva, my Master, has sent me here to find out all
And I have come from Kishkindha.
I have already seen the Mother
And got her message too. 80

'I am the royal messenger.
I am sent by Sugriva. I am duty-bound.

Why do you afflict me thus? Yes, to draw your attention,
I uprooted the trees and threw them up and thus
I have slain the wicked *rakshasas* who came to kill me
Without even asking me first who I am, and why I came.

'I can't be faulted.
As I have brought the message from Sugriva,
Why do you kill me? What kind of justice is that?
Is there such a royal policy that the messengers be troubled? 90
Where did you learn this kind of wicked craft, tell me.
Does anyone use *Brahmastra,* the ultimate weapon at a tiny sparrow
   just as me?
Brahmastra shall not be slighted;
As a mark of respect to it, I have come here; and not only that,
I wanted to see you as well.

'Listen to my words.
Shri Ramachandra is the most compassionate one.
He safeguards all those who seek his protection.
He has not the slightest mercy while punishing the wicked.
If Rama gets infuriated your house shall be on fire. 100
The chariots and the streets will be on fire.
Your army, wife and children,
Your brothers, relations, all your sons and grandsons,
All of your wealth and fortune, all your riches
Shall be wiped out, listen!

Do not test the patience.
I alone am suffice to destroy Lanka,
And all of your *rakshasas* including you.
But Shri Rama won't appreciate that; hence, I restrain myself. 110
Janaki is the dark night of Lanka's destruction,
And she is only in disguise; do not forget that!

'You are the emperor.
You are well renowned. Your clan is well respected.
Ruining all that prospects would anyone become a thorn to the clan?

Why should you suffer the ignominy of being an axe to the clan?
Cast away any such vile.

'Give up enmity with Rama.
Install devoutly the sacred feet of Rama in the lotus of your heart.
Hand over Janaki, daughter of King Janaka.   120
Give up the amorous fascination.
Sita is a virtuous wife; she shall not be yours.
What virtue is there in afflicting such a gem of a lady?
You are well-versed in the ways of how to conduct yourself
In *dharma*, *artha*, *kama*, and *moksha*, the four goals of life
You are the pinnacle of glory of the clan of Vishravasu.
By performing innumerable *tapasya*, you are blessed with many
  boons.
Would anyone bring to naught the glory of all that!

'If you ignore the good counsel,
You shall embrace death in the crest of war, listen.   130
Lanka shall be destroyed in the crest of war, listen.
The clan of Pulastya shall be wiped out completely, listen.
Have you forgotten that Rama has slain
Khara, Dushana, Trishira – all your aides – at Janasthana?
For the one who is truthful, there is neither the slightest fear, nor
  anxiety.
Truth alone triumphs – "*satyameva jayate.*"
Even *Brahmastra* shall be defeated when confronted with truth.
Why should there be *chaturangabala*, and why all kinds of
  weaponry
When there is no path of truth?
Everything shall be futile then.   140

Let the path of truth be yours.
You are the embodiment of a great soul. Don't you pollute that!
O king! You have the vision of the Universal Soul.
Spirituality is indeed the fusion of intellect and emotion.
That itself is the path to perfection. That alone is the soul of truth.
When Truth is perceived, all shackles shall be unfastened.

The soul-bird then will soar high in the sky
In a spirit of absolute freedom.

'Rama means Brahma.
Rama means Vishnu; Rama means Rudra; 150
He is the sole cause of creation, preservation, and destruction;
Be warned, O king! Be warned, O king of all the worlds!
A flame is burning bright on the horizon of life.
O look! The shackle that binds one to life is getting unfastened.
I have brought the torch. I will show you the path.
Tread the path of *dharma*.

'The amorous fascination for someone else's wife
That has disregarded the virtuous-path,
Leads to total destruction, no doubt.
Truth and perfection are all inherent in you. 160
You watch for yourself. Why do you get Lanka burnt?
I have come to forewarn you with good counsel;
I have come to take you on the path of truth;
I have come to lift you up from the well of sin;
I have come to bathe you in Shri Rama-Lake;
I have come to spread the moonlight of wisdom.
O the charming king of the three worlds, be warned and beware!'

Canto One Hundred and Fifty-nine

'Would the Glow of Face Look any Grand in an Unclean Mirror!'

||৬||

Would the glow of face look any grand in an unclean mirror!
Listening to the bold words of Anjaneya,
Foolish Lankesha, without getting discerningly any wiser,
Became enraged in vain: 'Having destroyed the grand garden,
And having killed my son Aksha,
What did you gain, tell me, O you fickle-minded *vanara*!
That being so, what deserving qualification you have to give advice!

What ethics have you?
Compassion, love, civility, humanity, and mercy
Of the noble Arya lineage – where have they all gone hiding, tell
 me! 10
Have you trampled them down into the northern arid land?
Or else, have they been imprisoned in the deep valleys of the forest?
Have they been caught up in the web of playful creepers woven
 by *karma*?
Have they reached the womb of dark clouds?
Have they gone into hiding in the flock of birds and herds of cattle;
In trees and creepers; in every speck of dust in the earth;
In the dark recesses of countless epochs;

Or, in the void of the ocean's playful waves?
Has the noiseless stillness in the edge of the sky,
Embracing mysterious silence, descended into the ocean?   20

You do not know; you certainly do not know!
You do not know the all-consuming fire of precipitated pain.
Having come from the enemy's camp into the territory of wealthy
   Lanka –
Like a spy and a seasoned thief,
You have wandered in every nook and corner unraveling the secrets;
You have wandered searching the harem every bit and probing
And prying all the secret spots
You have gone to Janaki and confided all the secrets;
Like a charmer, you have gone frightening everybody
And vandalised the beauty of Ashokavana;   30
You have killed my son Aksha brutally
And haven't spared the sons of my ministers either;
Like a rogue, you have gone round deriding all
By answering back adversely;
O wicked deceiver,
What deserving qualifications have you to give advice?

Don't let the vile one go.
Chop off his head and throw away the torso.
Who did he ask the permission to enter the city?
He would take the secrets of Lanka to Kishkindha.   40
He is cancerous to Lanka; chop him off and throw him away!

Why has the security become lax?
Who has committed this deception?
Who has trampled upon the strict vigil of Lankini?
How strange! How strange!
Look, how he could deceptively break into Lanka's fort!
How he could tame the guards on duty,
And gain passage to the verandah and reach the bed-chamber?
How he could go to the garden of merriment,
And how he could meet Sita and talk to her tricking the damsels
   there?   50

Conduct an inquiry; find out who is the culprit.
This one certainly deserves death.

Let there be strict vigilance.
What negligence is this? What kind of protection is this?
Ready the army at once.
Any future calamity should be prevented with great care.
I do not care who this Hanuma is, or even anybody else greater than him.
Put him on the scaffold and chop off his head.'
Thus Lankesha spoke harshly.

Having heard his brother speak thus, 60
Vibhishana, with humility, said what was apt ethically:
'Why to act rashly, your Majesty! Why to give in to anger?
Please listen to me with a calm mind.
It is not proper and prudent to kill a royal-messenger.
You are exemplary in royal conduct and policy, a scholar yourself,
And you are truly knowledgeable in the tenets of *dharma*;
Then, how could you behave thus!
Impose punishment with due consideration to
What is proper and what is not, your majesty.'

The brother's words were 70
Like adding fuel to the fire; Lankesha became angrier still.
'What did you say? When entry into Lanka was prohibited,
How did he come? Who gave him the permission?
Is he a blockheaded rustic? He is the minister of Surgriva!
He is a great royal diplomat no doubt,
And being well-versed in such diplomatic missions,
He has come here to desecrate Lanka.
As he supported the killing of my friend Vali,
How could he not be the enemy to Lanka,
And how could I forgive him? 80
The Kishkindha Treaty itself is violated. Look here!
I shall not spare him now.'
Thus Lankesha shouted aloud.

'O, brother, please listen! Have mercy.
Whether he is vile, or an enemy,
The royal messenger shall not be slain —
That is the prudent royal policy; do not forget that.
There are alternate punitive ways and forms:
Severing the limbs, whipping, cauterising, tonsuring
And such other practices to cause humiliation.   90
You are a world-renowned warrior. Who could your equal be!
You have forgiven innumerable persons
Who have done things unpleasant to you.
While you are thus acclaimed for sparing the lives,
It is not proper to kill this one.
Why should you get entangled in the prolixity
And suffer the accusation that Ravana was afraid
And violated the ethical code?

If the royal-messenger is slain,
And if the war does not take place, it is not befitting to take away   100
The growing war-excitement of the *rakshasas*.
When the new epoch is inviting you to open its door to the prospect
Of invading the land of the Aryans,
And thus rule over the land of Bharata,
Accept that challenge.
Don't fall into the abyss of futility.
Don't kill the royal-messenger.'

To mock at Ravana
As Hanuma seemed to have shown his tail,
Believing it to be true, Ravana himself made haste   110
To cause Hanuma's tail to be burnt and punish him thus
To be devoid of a limb!

Having heard his brother's words, Ravana said:
'Vibhishana! Your words are appropriate and I appreciate that.
You have said that there is the practice of dismemberment in vogue.
I shall give the same punishment to this *vanara*
Which that vile Lakshmana gave to sister Shurpanakha.

A *vanara* is called so because of his tail which is dear to him.
He is now mocking at me by wagging his tail.
Let us get it burnt. Let him be ridiculed as a tail-less monkey, and
   so on.   120
Let us see what happens!

Wrap up the tail with clothes
And soak it in oil. Setting fire to the tail,
Parade the *vanara* in all the streets
And city-squares, and push him down into the valley.
Do this so that no other *vanara* would ever dare
To set his foot into the city of Lanka.
Having seen the messenger of Rama in his true form thus,
Let our people be fearless.'
Saying thus, Ravana laughed aloud sarcastically!   130

This was proclaimed to the beating of drums.
The city was filled with the news of this procession.
They tore all the rags and wrapped round the tail.
As they went on wrapping it up with rags, the tail grew longer
   and longer.
The grandeur of the tail attracted all.
As all the clothes of Ravana's palace got over,
The servants appealed to the masters.
It was ordered that clothes should be given
From every household, and clothes came in large bundles.
Even so, how strange! All the clothes were exhausted.   140
'Except what is worn, give away all other clothes,' –
When the order came thus, everybody obeyed.
Everything was exhausted. What next? What else?
Now he will disrobe the women.
He would certainly take away even what is worn.
Thinking thus, Hanumanta stopped growing his tail any further.
The task of wrapping up the tail with clothes was now complete.

Canto One Hundred and Sixty

'The Foetus of Conceit Got Aborted on its Own'

||⊙||

Boys and girls, all the old men and women
Assembled quickly to watch the surprise:
'Who is that valorous hero who has enraged Ravana?
We must see him.' Thinking thus, people gathered
In large numbers at all places in Lanka.

Then Hanuma saw:
'There is not a match to the crafty deception of the *rakshasa*!
When I have come here on Shri Rama's mission
Let me see how Ravana in conceit could disfigure me
By employing evil tricks! 10
He has humiliated me. Would I spare this vile one?
I will show him the strength of Saketa-Kishkindha.
I will cut the ropes; smash the *rakshashas*.
He has laughed aloud sarcastically; would I spare him?
I will make his face go pale and cause his eyes to shed tears.
If I were to leave Lanka without curing Ravana of his offensive egotism,
And without deflating his vanity,

Let me not be the servant of Rama.'
Hanumanta vowed thus.

As ordered by Ravana, 20
The *rakshasas* put Hanuma in a cart;
Beating big drums and blowing conches
And loudly boasting of the many titles of Ravana, the lord of Lanka,
They took Hanuma in a procession in all the streets, lanes and by-lanes.
Then, they set fire to his tail wrapped up in oil-soaked clothes.
They clapped their hands as the flames blazed wild.
They danced in frenzy and the procession marched ahead.

Presently, the maids went near Janaki
And taunted her thus: 'O Mother Sita, look here!
The red-faced monkey is deservingly punished 30
For the havoc he has created.
They have set fire to his tail cursing –
Let the wicked monkey fall down dead.'

Bhumije – earth-born, became sorrowful.
The pain relapsed. She prayed fervently:
'O God of Fire! You are the protector of the world:
You are the revered Yajnapurusha!
If I have in me the power of *pativratya* – the strength of a dutiful wife;
And if I have served my husband with single-minded devotion,
By the grace of Lord Rama, become cool and soothing.' 40
Thus she implored devoutly.

The fire on the tail became soothingly cool
For Hanuma as if being sprinkled with rose-water.
His devotion to Shri Rama was thus well rewarded.
The meditation of the dutiful wife spread divinity.
Roaring like a lion, Hanuma swiftly leaped forward.
As he grew his body once, the knots that bound him were broken.
Swaying the tail, and leaping from one mansion to the other swiftly,

He set fire to them all.
The city went up in blazes instantly! 50

There was great lamentation.
There were loud screams and cries of pain everywhere.
There was commotion and horrible sounds of affliction.
There was terrible pushing around and pulling about in great haste.
Many *rakshasas* were burnt by the fire and fell down dead
And some were charred to death.
As Hanuma set fire to the warehouse of explosives,
With a terrible sound it got exploded in the heart of the city
And the cry of anguish reached the skies.
With his seven tongues, the God of Fire consumed rampantly 60
The mansions of the *rakshasas* and the ministers,
And everything else without any respite.

Maruta, God of Wind, blew fast aiding Maruti, his son.
And the tongues of flame were widely spread.
Who is there to check the blazing fire now!
Who will extinguish it now!
All the diamonds, gems, corals, and emerald,
All the gold, silver, pearls, and ruby, being engulfed by the fire,
Became molten and flowed down the streets.

All the citizens rushed out of their homes 70
And assembling in the streets, were crying hard.
The foetus of conceit got aborted on its own!
Loud lamentations reverberated everywhere
And the clouds of smoke shrouded everything.
The people of the city ran for their lives.
'Good heavens! Just like bringing evil itself into the city,
Why the king brought Janaki here!' – the women-folk cursed thus.

It was a mere play for Pavanaja, son of Wind.
The smouldering fire emitted thick smoke
And spread in all the four directions. 80
The crackling fire burnt down everything

And the snapping and crashing sounds were heard all over;
And the fire swelled and spread wild
Like the fire in the wide-opened third-eye on the forehead of Shiva
On the day he burnt to ashes Kama, the God of Love!

The magical sparks of fire
Turned into conflagration in Prahasta's mansion;
And the mansions of Vajradamshtra, Hruswakarna,
Kumbhakarna, and Makaraksha,
And Ghoramukha, Dhvajagriva, Hasti, and Karala,   90
Were all burnt down in the blazing fire.

The fire of ultimate destruction
Invaded the palace of Ravana:
Upper storeys of the mansion rolled down;
Windows flew away; ventilators slid down;
Doors came falling down with a thud;
All the beams and pillars were charred black in the fire
And came down tumbling.
It was a horrible sight; it looked as if a fire-ball
Rolled and brought down everything.   100
It made everyone shudder.

The great flood of fire flowed down.
As if the earth itself was set ablaze
A tiny spark of fire turned into a flame and the raging blaze
Burnt down everything completely.
As if frying Lanka in a frying-pan,
As if the red-hot embers came cascading down,
As if the rage of the world burst into splinters,
As if the vanity of Lanka melted into flames,
As if Shankara, unable to tolerate the evil-deeds of Ravana,   110
Heaved a sigh that turned into a fiery wave –
The fire cast by Hanuma engulfed the length and breadth
Of the earth and the sky!

As the conflagration touched the clouds,
It seemed as though the razing blaze would catch

And swallow up the moon.
Alas! As if the God of Fire himself has come
To swallow up Lanka in the guise of the heroic *vanara*, –
The crackling fire burst forth the vessel of the cosmos.

It is a lie that this one is a monkey. 120
It looked as if Devendra had come wielding his *Vajra* weapon;
As if Yama, Varuna, and Vayu
Together stood in the form of Hanuma;
As if Rudra, Agni, and the Sun themselves
Were personified in Pavanasuta;
As if the four-faced Brahma himself was in the person of Maruti;
As if Bhairava himself came; as if it was Kubera himself;
As if Vishnu, the Preserver himself appeared
Today in the form of Destroyer
In order to devour by fire the wicked *danava* clan; 130
As if the fiery grief in the belly of Janaki got itself manifested thus! –
It appeared so.
A country becomes known by just one able son of the soil;
So also, just one wicked man could easily be the bane of the land;
Only one person is sufficient to build a shelter for many;
And a single person could grow a big forest;
Only one Ravana brought glory to Lanka.
And the very same Ravana set it on fire!

It was as if lampblack was spilt all over the green forest.
Agitation and anxiety filled the earth and the sky.
Hanuma leaped to sky and danced – 140
It appeared like the game of love between thunder and lightning.

Lankesha's safe haven of indiscrete cruelty
Was completely burnt down in the crackling fire.
The cry of anguish and blood were like the dark shadows;
The ash-covered embers were smouldering deep inside;
The fire was stretching its fiery tongues of flame to the sky
Filled with hope and desire for a better tomorrow.

Just as the wild fire consumes the forest swiftly,
The golden Lanka became charred-Lanka!

Could anyone prevent such a thing! 150
Forgetting the entire world in the comforts of luxury and riches,
Enjoying the grandeur of being the emperor of the world,
Feeling proud that everything was his,
And there was none to equal him,
Crushing others in conceit,
And adopting exploitation as his sole means,
Robbing others of their riches, self-respect, and independence,
Sowing the poisonous seeds of violence and anxiety,
As Ravana lived in glory as if he was violence personified.
The tears of countless widows and a multitude of orphans 160
Flowed down in the form of a fiery-river
And engulfed Lanka.

The palace of the virtuous,
And the noble Vibhishana was the only one
That remained un-burnt, and unaffected by fire.
Everything else was destroyed.
All riches and wealth turned to ashes.

Wild fire broke into the forest
Of Ravana's wicked reign.
It rained burning embers into the unbridled vessel of supreme
   power. 170
The shelter of exploitation was burnt to ashes.
The blind vanity of self-importance was cremated.
Look! All cruelty shall thus get burnt.
Listen! All deception and cheating shall turn to ashes.
Watch out! This is the punishment for taking fancy
To somebody else's wife.
Be advised! This is how the uncontrolled selfish-ego
Shall meet its end. At the end of it all,
Everything shall sink into the abyss of darkness –
The roar of the God of Fire heralded thus. 180

Creation, Preservation, and Destruction are all
In the womb of fire which alone is the source
Of new life and that of all culture.
Fresh soil and life afresh begin as a tiny speck
And melting away in fire, once again they appear similarly
And grow up again; that is how creation manifests itself!

The charred bodies lay scattered everywhere.
Alas! Why the act of burning happened thus!
Ascending the peak of Mount Trikuta,
Hanuma was swirling his tail as if it was the orb of sun.   190
As the river of revolution flowed down,
All the citizens of Lanka witnessed the track of Hanuma's footprints
And they were all filled with consternation.
Lankesha stood there as if he were a silent statue.
It appeared as if his heart had stopped beating.

Canto One Hundred and Sixty-one

'Let the Torch of Truth be Your Guiding Light and Protect You'

||๑||

As Lanka became a tumultuous cage after it was burnt down,
A fresh worry afflicted Hanuma:
'Alas! What have I done!
Have I burnt Lanka without considering the safety of Janaki?
I have become a sinner, and a traitor. Fie to me!
Have I acted in haste without showing restraint!

'What have I done!
There is not a palace; there is not a grove that I have not burnt.
I have burnt down everything.
Is the Mother alive now?
If the grief of Sita's death reached Kishkindha,
Would Rama survive? Would Saumitri survive?
Surgriva, Angada, and Bharata, Shatrughna –
Everyone would die in succession.
How could I show my face! I shall drown myself in the ocean.'
Deciding thus, he reached the ocean.

At that very instance, charming Charana's – the celestial singer –
Divine voice proclaimed thus:

10

'Stop at once, O Hanuma, do not die.
You are an accomplished achiever indeed.   20
Bravo! What a great thing that the golden Lanka
Was burnt down in the fire set by you!
Would Agni burn the grandeur of conjugal fidelity!
Look at the power of her meditation! It has safeguarded you too!'

Hanumanta was at peace.
The gentle blow of the cool breeze brought peace of mind.
Setting aside the thought of death,
Hanuma immersed himself in the ocean.
He shed all the pollution of Lanka in the holy-bath;
As he was now filled with divine peace,   30
Hanuma sang the praise of Rama,
And he moved towards Ashokavana.

Having seen Lanka burnt to ashes,
The *rakshasas* stood there with a pale, sagging face;
Pavanasuta went past them as if he did not see them.
As though someone has erected a rampart of protection
The spot in Ashokavana where Sita was kept
Remained tender and bright.
Hanuma, with devotion, went near the Mother
Who, under the *shimshupa* tree, was engrossed in meditation   40
On Shri Rama's divine name.
Hanuma went round the Mother in devout reverence,
And folding his hands respectfully, said:

'Let victory be to Shri Rama!
I am fortunate that I am blessed to see you, O Mother!
You showed to the whole world the power of Shri Rama, O Mother!
I poured hot water into the roots of Lanka's vanity.
Filled with anxiety, I have come to see you.
Bless me, O Mother! Shri Rama is awaiting my return.
Saumitri is awaiting; Sugriva is waiting;   50
The whole world is waiting to hear the news of your well-being.
I will announce this news promptly.

I am your child, O Mother!
The beauty of the world rests in your safety.
With your emancipation, a lamp will glow bright;
And the epoch of Truth would bloom then.'
Hanuma said thus.

As Janaki's affection for Hanuma
Filled every nerve of her person and sprang up sprightly, she said:
'O Hanuma, come here! You are precious to Rama. 60
You have shed the darkness that shrouded my life.
As I was afflicted with grief for Shri Rama,
And was reduced to mere bones,
And as my mind was getting tempted towards death,
Without fearing for your own life,
You have come here breathing new life in me!

By shattering the fort of conceit,
Blowing the bugle of war, trampling down Ravana cult,
And hoisting the flag of *dharma* in Lanka,
You have become the harbinger of the New Epoch, 70
And are indeed a great diplomat.
I was afraid whether Ravana had beheaded you
And erected a triumphal arch out of it.
As I sat down exhausted, lamenting
Whether the light of devotion to Rama had got extinguished,
I prayed fervently that let the torch of Truth
Be your guiding light, and protect you
As you journey through the noble path of Great Quest.
Each passing moment seemed like an epoch;
But, now there is no cause for fear; you are protected by Rama. 80
Without realising the colossal vastness of Rama's strength,
The *rakshasa* obliterated the glow of Lanka-Lakshmi, the presiding deity,
Condemning her to suffer a wretched misfortune!

You have given the signal that the philosophy
Of Shri Rama's Great Quest –

Barbarity shall perish and benevolent humanity shall triumph.
I am filled with great admiration for you
That you are the messenger and devotee of Rama.
You are truly valorous. May you live forever.'
Thus Sita blessed him.   90

Seeing the Mother's happiness,
Hanumanta was filled with immense delight:
'Shri Rama will come along with Saumitri.
In the vast field of the sacred land of Karnata
Sugriva, Jambava, and the other valorous heroes
Of my clan are getting ready for the ensuing battle.
O Mother! I too shall come accompanying Shri Rama.'
So saying, Hanuma respectfully prostrated himself
At the feet of the Mother
And with unbound happiness,   100
Climbed Mount Arishta.

Canto One Hundred and Sixty-two

'Hanuma is the Tree of Wisdom Spread across the Sky'

||૬||

Mount Arishta was looking grand with the birch-trees
As if they were the apparels on it;
And the clouds at its peak seemed
Like the mountain's upper garments worn across the chest;
The rays of the sun stood as if they were saluting the mountain
With their hands folded in reverence;
The elements of red-mineral looked
As if the mountain opened its eyes wide.

The majestic sound of the mountain-river compares well
With the melody of the chanting of Vedic hymns.   10
The pine trees there look as if someone is standing with raised hands.
The jets of springs sing melodiously.
The roar of cascading water is filled everywhere.
The bamboo-bushes are whistling.
The poisonous snakes frighten with their hissing.
The fog-covered caves are engrossed in deep meditation.
As the clouds drift past the mountain peaks touching them gently,
It looks as though the mountain itself is stretching its limbs.

The bamboo-bushes and the timber-yielding *ashwakarna* trees
In the mountain appear grand like rows of *palmyra* trees. 20
The flowers spread their fragrance;
Edible tubers and roots are found aplenty in the mountain.
Hence, it is the favourite place of the ascetics and the mendicants.
The mountain is rich in minerals.
The crevices of rocks are the sources of cascades.
Lions and tigers roam about the mountain.
The grandeur of Mount Arishta is beyond description.
'When would I see the valorous clan
Of Shri Ramachandra's devout *vanaras*!' – filled with such anxiety,
As Anjaneya swiftly climbed up the mountain, 30
Big rocks came down rolling by his heavy strides.
Anjaneya climbed down the mountain from the other side
And reached the sea-shore.
He saw the vast ocean coloured jet-black.

His mind became calm.
Expanding his body he grew taller and taller.
'I have the grace of my lord; I have the blessings of the Mother;
I came here crossing over the vast ocean;
And now I will cross it again.' So thinking,
As if he is the symbol of the power of Yoga, 40
Hanuma leaped across the vast ocean.

What grandeur there!
The ocean-like expanse of the sky!
The moon himself is the white lily;
The sun himself is the water-fowl;
The conglomeration of Pushya, Shravana – the stars –
Were the clouds and the green moss;
The star Punarvasu was like a great fish;
The planet Mars itself was the mammoth crocodile;
Airavata, the royal elephant of Indra, was the island; 50
The star Swati was Garuda, the vehicle of Vishnu;
The storm was the waves; the moonlight was the waters;

The assembly of the *nagas*, the *yakshas*, and the *gandharvas*
  was the lotus.
Anjaneya floated happily in the ocean-sky
As if he was a massive vessel.

Is Hanuma any ordinary!
As if he was showing that he would similarly cross the ocean
  of life,
With great will-power Hanuma was crossing over the ocean.

O, what speed is this!
He is coming as if he sucks away the ocean; as if he pulls the
  clouds;   60
As if he pulls out the solar orb, and the rows of stars!
Like Shri Rama's arrow shot from the Kodanda,
Anjaneya is coming down from the sky cleaving the heap of clouds,
And descending into the ocean like the enchanting rays of the
  rainbow,
He comes wading through the waves.
The sound of great joy is heard in all the ten-directions!

The *vanaras* are standing at the seashore
With their gaze fixed to the horizon.
Angada, the son of Vali, and others have been anxiously waiting:
'What may have befallen Hanuma?   70
Has he seen the "mother" or not?
Have the *rakshasas* caught him?
Has Ravana crushed him?
Is Hanuma hiding himself in Lanka not knowing what to do?
When would he be coming?' – With such anxiety
The *vanaras* started counting time.

It seemed that the sky and the ocean would cleave
Under his feet at the speed with which Pavanaja was approaching.
At that instance, the roar of the pounding waters
Reached Mount Mandara and looked like a sparkling star.   80
As the *vanaras* looked with wonderment as to

Which new star was rising yonder the mountain.
Jambava recognised Hanuma, and with great elation
Told all the friends gathered there:

'O Angada! Come here.
O *vanaras*, look! Pavanaja is coming.
Look! He is coming at the speed of the wind.
By the swing of his arms and thighs, this loud noise is born; hear it.
He is an exemplary achiever; he is the man of the epoch!

It seems as if all the hills and mountains, 90
And all the mountain-peaks themselves come leaping fast.
Look! How grand Hanuma looks in the horizon.
Look at this great vision of the epoch with your eyes wide open!
In the eagerness to drench the thirst of the barren land,
Hanuma is coming pouring down the rain of happiness, look!
Look how the son of Kishkindha is approaching in glorious grandeur
Leaping swiftly and cleaving through the waves and winds!

Hanuma is revered by all.
Hanuma is personification of the soul.
He shall not be burnt by the fire; 100
He shall not be cut by the sword;
He knows well that body, beauty, glory, youth,
And wealth are but fleeting like lightning.
Hanuma is the Tree of Wisdom spread across the sky
With its roots firmly anchored in earth.
He knows no bounds and is a noble soul;
He symbolises *dashagunas*, ten supreme qualities:
Devotion, knowledge, *virakti* – absence of passions;
Wisdom, intellect, fortitude, propriety,
Disposition, vitality, and vigour. 110
He is Shri Guru – the supreme teacher;
The one endowed with the power to grant salvation.
O look; all of you look! Look without winking your eyelids!
Such a grand manifestation shall never be seen again. Look!'
Thus exclaiming, as Jambava rushed forward –

Not minding the edges of the mountain peaks –
As if he would fall into the ocean in the trance of that excitement,
Angada and the other *vanaras* held him back in tight embrace.

The trumpet of victory roared aloud.
As all the waves lifted Hanuma up and reached him to the shore, 120
Bharati – the motherland, felt fulfilled
As if she gave birth to the child of the epoch!
Saluting Jambava, Hanuma hugged Angada
And all the other valorous *vanaras*, and shed tears of happiness.
All of them shed tears.

'I saw the virtuous wife of Shri Rama – the Mother Janaki –
Imprisoned in Ashokavana.
Like a dove is guarded by the vultures,
The *rakshasies* keep a watch over her day and night.
Without eating food she is waiting for Shri Rama 130
And has become very weak.
I have returned after seeing and speaking to her.
I have come swiftly to tell everything to you all.
Are you all keeping well?
Let victory be to Shri Rama.'
Thus Hanuma said dancing in excitement.

The *vanaras* screeched and screamed with joy.
They roared aloud and embraced Hanuma again.
They hoisted Hanuma on their shoulders
And proclaimed aloud his victory: 140
'Who could equal Hanuma in valour and power!
Crossing the irresistible ocean, you reached Lanka
And have now returned after ascertaining
The whereabouts and safety of the Mother.
O brother! You have given life to us all.
You have spared Shri Rama the pangs of separation,
And prevented his rage.
You have thus prevented *pralaya* – the ultimate destruction.
You have protected the tree of pride of Bharata – the Motherland,

By watering it with the rain of your valour.   150
Who could equal you in all this!
You are the Kalpavriksha – the celestial tree that grants all desires;
You are Mukhyaprana – Hanumanta.
You have breathed new life into the spirit of the *vanaras*.
Who else could equal you in your devotion to the Master!'
In this way, all praised Hanuma.
Angada, Jambava, and the other valorous *vanaras*
Sat on a flat rock relaxing and getting thrilled
As they listened to the heroic deeds narrated by Hanuma.
They listened to the story shouting excitedly   160
'Bravo, bravo!' now and then.
They were drowned in the ocean of happiness
As if the flag of Bharata returned after a triumphant tour of the world.
They embraced Hanuma again and again
Praising him for his heroic deeds.
As this joyful news of Hanuma having seen the Mother
And spoken to her spread everywhere,
It was felt as if the severed jewel of life
Of the *vanaras* was restored once again.

Canto One Hundred and Sixty-three

'What a Heroic Deed, O Hanuma!'

||६||

As the *vanaras* were relishing the grandeur and excitement
Atop Mount Mahendra, Jambava asked:
'O Pavanasuta! Tell us elaborately;
We are all eager to hear how you crossed the ocean;
How you entered Lanka and searched and found Sita there;
What she said; and what you told her;
We all are curious to hear.'
Thus Jambava rained questions at Hanuma,
One after the other, with no respite.

'You are curious to hear, 10
And I am eager to tell. O brothers, listen.
After bidding farewell to you, I leaped across the ocean.
With great speed as I was soaring past Mount Mainaka,
Surasa, the mother of serpents, held me swiftly, saying
"Today you have come as my food;
I will satisfy my hunger of many days."
Then I beseeched her –
"O Mother! I am the messenger of Rama.
As Ravana abducted Janaki, the virtuous wife of Shri Rama,
And took her to Lanka, 20

I have come to seek the whereabouts of Janaki
As ordered by Rama. Do not stop me.
I have a great mission to accomplish.
You could eat me to your heart's content on my return.
I swear by the sacred feet of Rama; believe my words."
Yet she refused and in the imminent battle that followed
I thrashed Surasa, and surrendering herself, she said:
"I appreciate your valour; let victory be yours."
Thus she blessed.

'As I moved forward, not very far from that place, 30
Simhika, a *rakshasi*, pulled me down:
"You are food to me now; I have become weak with hunger."
As she afflicted me thus,
I killed her and moved ahead.

I reached Lanka.
As I slyly entered the fort, a *rakshasi* roared
Like thunder caused by dark clouds,
And came running swiftly to stop and crush me.
I saw her hair which were like tongues of blazing fire.
Without feeling frightened, with clenched fists 40
I pounded Bhairavi – the guarding deity of Lanka.
Alarmed by what happened, she said:
"Bravo, bravo! I appreciate you.
As you have defeated me, you will win over the *rakshasas*,
And there is no doubt about that."
So saying, she showed me the way to move ahead.

'As soon as I entered the city of Lanka,
I searched for Sita everywhere.
Then I went to Ashokavana, the wonderful garden with a variety
  of trees.
I was elated with happiness. 50
I saw Saketa-Lakshmi, the Goddess of Saketa,
Under the *shimshupa* tree lost in deep meditation on Shri Rama!

She is fasting.
Her entire face has become pale; her attire has become unclean;
She has become very weak afflicted
By the pangs of separation from Shri Rama.
Like a female deer surrounded by tigers,
A group of fierce *rakshasies* had encircled her and was threatening her.
Having sunk low into the well of disappointment,
She was contemplating to give up her life. 60

At that instant, Ravana, with great pride, came there
And said: "You have two months' time within which
If you do not appease me, I shall put you to the gallows.
Worrying and pining for you Rama will die from the pangs of separation.
If you do not appease me, the tree of your desire will be scorched."

As Ravana uttered these words, enraged Janaki said:
"You are the vilest of the vile; do not speak so meanly.
As you are a sinner, how could you be an equal to Shri Rama's majesty?
Do not provoke me and die. He is a great pilgrim travelling
On the path of Great Quest." 70

Not heeding the words of Sita,
In great fury as Ravana came forward twisting his eyes,
And lifting up his right hand shouting –
"I will kill her with the blows of my fist" –
Trijate, Dhanyamalini and the other women prevented Ravana and said:
"You are the emperor. Do not kill Sita.
You shall be scorched in the sin of slaying a woman, listen."
At those words,
Ravana returned to the palace.

At the time of sunrise 80
As all the *rakshasies* were fast asleep,

I sang the praise of Rama in a loud voice.
Janaki was elated with happiness.
She had a conversation with me: "Who are you?
How did you cultivate the bond of relationship with Rama?
You have come to my rescue
Like a giant tree of faith providing shelter."
Thus she said.

"I am the devotee of Rama.
And I am the minister of Sugriva.   90
With love, Shri Rama has given this ring as a token – so saying,
I gave the ring in her hand.
I will take you back safely, O Mother, come" – thus I beseeched her.
"O Hanumanta! I shall not come.
I shall wait until Shri Rama comes
And takes me back after killing the *danava*."
So saying, she gave this *chudamani* – a crest jewel, as a token.
"There is only two months' time-limit.
If Shri Rama does not come, I shall give up my life;
And this I swear in the name of Saketa, O listen."   100
Thus she said with great pain.

'The pitiable story of Janaki
Hurt and pained me intensely.
The mansion of patience crumbled and rage swelled within.
In the eagerness to show the power of Shri Rama
And the valour of Surgriva and Saumitri to Ravana,
I destroyed Ashokavana.

'As the servants of the *danava* came to attack me,
The latch of the great door itself became my weapon
And striking them hard with it, I killed them all.   110
Then, the army of the ministers' sons attacked me.
Akshakumara, the son of Lankesha, came to battle.
With ease, I crushed them all.
Finally, as Indrajit – the one who had gained victory over Indra –

Came and employed *Brahmastra*, without refusing,
I willingly submitted myself to be pinioned.

'As I was taken to the royal court of Lankesha,
I saw the wealth and grandeur of it.
"You do not know the power of Shri Rama.
Handover Janaki to Rama and surrender to him;   120
He will protect you; if not, he shall kill you."
Thus I advised him.

'As my advice did not go well with him,
In great fury, the *danuja* ordered –
"Kill him and throw away the body" –
Vibhishana said: "It is not proper to kill the messenger;
But dismemberment is allowed in the law-books.
There are alternate ways to punish."

'Dashakantha, the ten-headed one, agreed to this.
"Look at the fickle-minded monkey!   130
Wrap up the tail with rags and set fire to it." Thus he ordered.
They wrapped clothes round my tail deliberately grown long,
Soaked it in oil, and took me in a procession in all the streets and
    lanes.

'As they set fire to my tail,
I burnt down all the mansions and palaces of the Golden Lanka in
    a jiffy
As if it was enveloped by *pralayagni* – the fire of destruction.
But, I spared the palace of Vibhishana and the spot
Where Janaki lived and left them safe.
Once again, I met the Mother, and seeking her blessings,
I climbed up the Mount Arishta in order to cross over the ocean.   140

O *vanaras*, listen!
Physical power and power of meditation are in confluence in the
    danava.
He is an exceptional warrior who has won all the Three Worlds.
I had planned to bring back the Mother.

"Let Rama himself come; not otherwise," said the Mother.
I am capable of churning Lanka all by myself.
As you are all with me, what more is needed!
What if Indrajit comes? Do I fear him? Would I ever lose out to him?
Let us throw him into the bottom of the ocean itself.
Let us put to naught all the weapons he employs against us! 150

On the streets there at Lanka,
They proclaimed that I was the messenger of Rama.
I demonstrated at Lanka all the powers and ingenuity
Of Shri Rama, Lakshmana, Sugriva and the *vanaras*.
I caused fear in the hearts of the *rakshasas*.
I waged a symbolic war in order to make them
Aware of our strength. I gave them *ranavilya* – a formal invitation to war.
As the Mother had made up her mind and stood ready to end her life,
I prevented that and offered solace to her.
I gave the signet-ring of Shri Rama. 160
I have brought the *chudamani*, the crest jewel.
Now let us draw up a war strategy and attack Lanka;
Let us crush the *rakshasas* down.'
As Hanuma said thus,
Jambava praised Hanuma merrily:

'Bravo Hanuma, bravo!
You are an unparalleled accomplisher.
In just one broad day-light you leaped across the ocean.
Just as the moon was rising in the sky, you entered Lanka.
You explored Lanka during the night. 170
At dawn you entered the Ashokavana.
At sunrise you gave the signet-ring.
At that instant itself you received the *chudamani* with devotion.
You took up the task of destroying Ashokavana
And by afternoon you sent Aksha to Yamapuri – the abode of Yama.

Thereafter, surrendering yourself to *Brahmastra* employed by Indrajit,
You entered the royal court of Ravana.
By night you completely burnt down Lanka.
At dawn you saw the Mother yet again,
You climbed up the mountain 180
And during night-time leaped across the ocean.
By dawn you came back and joined us all.
What a heroic deed, O Hanuma!
Do I have the capacity to describe it!!

O Traveller in the path of Great Quest!
What a heroic deed! Am I capable of describing it?
Being Vital Breath personified, you protect all living beings.
You are the most intimate servant of Saketa-Rama.
It is enough to think of you devotionally – one shall be blessed with
Wisdom, physical strength, fame, courage, 190
Fearlessness, health, life, eloquence and all.
On your footsteps all the world blooms.
You have protected us like the mother who gave us birth.
When we were afflicted with difficulties one after the other
You came as our saviour and protected us.
Physical prowess, intellectual strength, and the vigour of life itself
Blooms tenderly like the luster of lotus at the very thought of you.
You are filled with the radiance of Supreme Bliss.'
Thus Jambava praised Hanuma.

Canto One Hundred and Sixty-four

'Play the Musical Instruments; play the Drum of Kannada'

||೬||

Listening to the details of the journey
Of Great Quest told by Anjaneya,
And ruminating over it again and again,
Angada said in a sober mood: 'Listen you all!
Hanumanta has come back after exploring Lanka; bravo!
He has killed the *rakshasas*; he has burnt them to ashes.
He has broken the security of Lankesha's fort.
So, why cause trouble for the valorous *vanara*?
Why should Shri Rama and Sugriva be troubled?
Are we helpless? Let us gain victory over Lanka. 10
Let us free Janaki from the clutches of Ravana;
Bring her back and unite her with Rama.'
Thus Angada said to all the valorous heroes.

Listening to those words, Jambava said:
'O Angada! It is true that you are the crown-prince.
If you order thus, who is there to disobey you?
Even then, would anyone forget
What the order of Shri Rama and Sugriva is?
Apart from the message, have they bid us the task

Of bringing Janaki back? 20
Would anyone do anything that Rama does not like?
Would anyone do any valorous deed not liked by Saumitri?
As restraining evil falls in the path of Rama's Quest,
Why should we interfere in that?
Have you not heard the words spoken by Hanuma?
"When Shri Rama crushes down Ravana in the battle
I shall come along with Rama" – Janaki has said so.
Let us remember that!

'Why do you exhibit valour in vain?
Let there be restraint and discipline. 30
Why to bear the accusation of being called fickle-monkeys?
This is the time to follow the regulations.
Do not forget that and be alert.
Haste is the cause of affliction.' Thus he advised
And everybody agreed to that.

'Well then, let us go now.
Let us walk the path leading to Kishkindha.
As they were coming, on the way they saw Madhuvana –
A forest belonging to Sugriva;
Its grand vineyard was full of flowers and fruits 40
And was indeed the abode of choicest spirituous liquor.
In its grandeur, Madhuvana put Nandana –
The celestial garden of Indra, to shame.
Dadhimukha is the maternal-uncle of Sugriva.
He is the overseer of Madhuvana and he protects it with great care.
The servants guard it like a fort.

On seeing the vineyard,
The *vanaras'* mouths began to water
And they implored compellingly –
'O crown-prince! Give us permission to drink the spirituous liquor.' 50
As Hanuma was with him, Angada happily agreed.

The drinking-bout was on.
The *vanaras*, intoxicated with happiness, were quite ecstatic.
Some were singing there and some others were dancing.
Some were jumping up and down there
And some others were running about.
Some were pushing there and some others were swearing.
Some were laughing there and some were lamenting.
Some others were prostrating themselves and rolling over and over.
The *vanaras*, intoxicated with happiness, were quite ecstatic. 60

They were jumping from tree to tree
And suddenly they were falling down from the trees to the ground.
While one was singing, another was trying to spoil it.
While one was laughing there, another was crying.
While one was laughing aloud, another was pushing him away.
In the assemblage of the *vanaras*,
There was not anyone who was not drinking the spirituous liquor,
And none who was not intoxicated and roamed about.
The *vanaras*, intoxicated with happiness, were quite ecstatic.

When the guards of the Madhuvana tried 70
To stop the *vanaras*, not heeding them,
They thrashed the guards and pushed them away.
The servants rushed fast and complained to Dadhimukha.
'Do not you worry; I will handle them. Let us stop the *vanaras*.
If they become unruly, let us thrash them hard.'
So saying, Dadhimukha came rushing.
'What mischief is this?' So shouting, he pulled out a *sal*-tree
And chasing *vanara*, he thrashed them all.
The *vanaras*, intoxicated with happiness, were quite ecstatic.

Would the *vanaras*, 80
Who were insolent like the elephant in rut,
Spare Dadhimukha? They started to fight with him.
They thrashed him with sticks and rained blows with their fists.
The arms, thighs, neck and the shoulders of Dadhimukha
Were all wounded and blood spilled out of them like a fountain.

The *vanaras* pushed and pulled Dadhimukha
And thrashed him black and blue.
'Enough of this companionship –
Not only for this life, but even for the ones that follow this.'
The *vanaras* made Dadhimukha suffer such a plight   90
And he lost the battle.
The *vanaras*, intoxicated with happiness, were quite ecstatic.

'Madhuvana is the abode of beauty and grandeur.
King Sugriva has fostered this garden with great love.
Succumbing to great joy, the *vanaras* have ruined it now
And fierce punishment awaits them.
I shall report this to the king and cause them
To be punished appropriately.
I shall cause their invigorating pride
To be tamed and teach them a lesson.'   100
So thinking, Dadhimukha, accompanied by his servants,
Marched towards the city of Kishkindha.

Sugriva, together with Shri Rama and Saumitri,
Was eagerly awaiting the arrival of Pavanasuta, Jambava, and Angada.
At that instant, Dadhimukha came in utter humility,
And saluting Sugriva, said:
'O Sugriva, listen! Pavanasuta
And the other valorous *vanaras*, goaded by the desire
To drink spirituous liquor, have rampaged Madhuvana
Which you have fostered with great love.   110
When I went to prevent them, they thrashed and chased me away.
They have beaten the servants and kicked them with their knees.
Look at the wounds. I have failed in my duty.
Hanuma, Angada, Jambava and all of them
Encouraged the mischief of the *vanaras*.
What shall I say! Madhuvana is utterly ruined
By these petty mischief-mongers.
Only you have to protect now.'
Thus he said overcome by terrible grief.

Without getting angry, Sugriva said: 120
'Let that be so. O dear uncle! Are you hurt? Forgive them.
Bravo, bravo! Accompanied by Angada,
Have Hanumanta, Jambava and all come to Madhuvana?
O uncle! You have brought happy news indeed.
Forgetting themselves in the ecstatic excitement
Of the deeply fulfilling emotion of having seen Janaki,
They have entered Madhuvana.
In the joy of momentous victory, they have drunk spirituous liquor.
Succumbing to great joy, they have played havoc.
I will forgive them. Summon them fast. 130
Welcome them with grand celebration.
Play the musical instruments; play the drum of Kannada.'
Thus he ordered.

Dadhimukha, the protector of Madhuvana,
Returned to Madhuvana with a long face.
On seeing Angada, he said:
'O *saumya* – the gentle one!
When you were crushing Madhuvana
I prevented you. Forgive me.
I attacked you without realising 140
The significance of the epoch's journey.
Your uncle, the king, is waiting.
Shri Rama and Saumitri are waiting eagerly –
"What the news might be."
Kishkindha is being readied to welcome you.' Thus he said.

'O *vanaras*! Stop now. You have had enough.
Stop drinking liquor. This is the order of my uncle, the king.
We must swiftly go to Kishkindha now.
If we delay any further, it would cause offence.
Happy news should be communicated quickly. 150
It is not proper to be lazy in discharging one's duty.'
When Angada said thus,
Everyone was quickly alerted and saluting Madhuvana,

Pavanasuta, Jambava and all the other valorous *vanaras*,
Appreciating Angada's timely presence of mind,
And proclaiming aloud
Victory to Rama, Sugriva, and Pavanasuta-Hanuma,
Marched quickly in the direction of Kishkindha.

Canto One Hundred and Sixty-five

'Urmila Stands like a Golden Idol'

||๖||

'O Shri Rama! Your mission has attained victory.
Look there! Having seen Goddess Maithili – daughter of Mithila-city –
All the *vanara*-leaders are coming this way exuberant with joy.
Their exhilarating words of happiness are reverberating there; listen!'
When Sugriva said thus,
The lotus-face of Shri Ramachandra bloomed
And Saumitri was elated with joy.

The *vanaras* led by Angada came near
Shri Rama and Lakshmana.
Sugriva embraced Angada, the crown-prince;   10
Shri Rama hugged Anjaneya –
The officiating-priest of the Great Quest.
Everyone bathed in the lake of happiness!

Thrilled with joy, Angada said:
'Let benediction be to you. Let victory be to Sitarama.
Hanumanta, who is Bhima in strength, saw the Mother.
The Sun of Great Quest was blessed
To see the auspicious presence of the flag of Saketa.'

Jambava, the great diplomat, said:
'By your divine grace, Jayalakshmi – the Goddess of Victory –   20

Was pleased with you. As your path is the path of victory,
Hanuma was blessed similarly.
The heroic deed of the *vanaras* became well-known all over the world.
Even Adishesha – the seven-hooded serpent –
Wouldn't know to tell its story.'
Then, Pavanaja, bowing his head in reverence, said:

'O *punyasholka* – the one who is always well-spoken of – listen!
O lord! Is there anything that equals the power of your name!
Meditating on your name, I leaped across the ocean.
I entered into Lanka and saw the "mother". 30
I saw the virtuous wife who is heavily guarded.
I saw the dutiful wife who meditates on you always.
I saw the one who holds on to life with the sole desire of seeing you
And has become weak due to her vow of fasting.
What shall I say, my lord! I saw the one who had made up her mind
To end her life being unable to tolerate the torture inflicted by Lankesha.
If your ring had not been seen,
Saketa-*kalasha* – the symbol of Saketa's honour –
Would have been destroyed;
Your *bhagyajyothi*, the light of your good fortune, 40
Would have been extinguished.

'O Purushottama – Supreme Being – listen!
I told Janaki, who is the epitome of *tapasya*,
The sign and history that you had told me.
I told her the secret sign.
I narrated the friendship with Sugriva that came
As a blessing in the path of Great Quest.
I told all your history earnestly.
When I gave her your ring and comforted her, she became happy.
She has given the charming *chudamani* for you.' 50
So saying, Hanuma gave it to Rama with great joy.

Shedding tears of joy,
Shri Rama kept the *chudmani* in the lotus of his heart and said:
'Like the cow secretes milk from its udder when the calf comes
    near it,
My heart melts when I see this charming fortune.
This rare gem is given by Indra as the rewarding-fruit of a *yajna*;
This gem is given by Janaka in the marriage-*pandal*.
This is the rarest of the rare gem born in the ocean.
This is the beautiful gem that decorated the hair of Janaki.
This charming *chudamani* has completely filled my eyes and heart   60
To the exclusion of all else in the world.
Is this life worth-living without Janaki?
O Hanumanta! Tell me some more news of Janaki.'

Then, with tearful eyes, Janaki asked Anjaneya –
"Tell me, why Shri Rama who had aimed at the crow
That was troubling me is now silent? What sin have I committed?
Why both the men who are brave like a lion are neglecting me
    thus?" –
To this, Anjaneya replied:
"O Mother! Shri Rama is terribly afflicted
From the pangs of your separation.   70
Saumitri is enduring pain in silence.
Forsaking food, shelter and rest,
Shri Rama has wandered in forests and hills searching for you,
And not able to find you anywhere,
He is now fully exhausted.
Now, when he learns that you are here, would he sit quiet?
Listen! He will come in full speed.
To kill Ravana and to protect you is his mission.
There is not the slightest doubt in this. Then, why should you cry?"
Thus I spoke comfortingly.   80
O lord! Janaki asked me again and again –
"Tell me, how is Shri Rama; how is Saumitri;
How is Bharata who is the epitome of *tapasya*;
How are Kausalya, Sumitra, and Kaikeyi, the icons of affection;

How is Shatrughna; how is Urmila, the epoch's epitome of *tapasya*;
How is the community of people at Ayodhya;
How are all the birds, animals, tigers, lions, and deer
At Dandaka-forest, tell me;
How the trees are; how are the creepers;
How the fruits and flowers are, tell me." – 90
Thus she enquired about the well-being
Of all the moving and motionless creatures.

Then, I told her:
"O Mother! Why to delay any more?
You will see all for yourself.
Climb on to my shoulder.
Like Garuda I will carry you to Kishkindha."
Thus I implored.

"Until Shri Rama, the visionary of liberation comes,
Until Lanka is won, until Lankesha is not slain, 100
And until the burden of the world is not eased,
How could I come? I will not come. I shall not be sullied.
Look! There is the world in the forefront for all to see
Which humiliates me that I am *ayonija* –
Not born of my mother's womb,
And that I am given as the reward for bravery.
I am only alive and I carry the burden of dishonour.
I stand in the row of countless such women.
Tell me, my child, who will take care of me?
Who will silence this mocking world? 110

Every stream of tears of the pitiable tale
Of women in every epoch, has joined the womb of earth,
And agitating greatly it is boiling hard.
For how many women, their own life has become miserable
And stabbed them like a pointed knife!
To mitigate all such evils and to give new light
To the world of women, why should there be any more delay?
O Pavanasuta! Ask him to come swiftly.

How much more shall I narrate the woes of women
That they are given away as rewards to – 120
Brave men, prospective grooms, and so on!
Let Rama come as Narasimha – the man-lion form of Vishnu –
Cleaving the womb of all vileness.
Ask him to come hoisting the flag of goodness
That women are strong indeed.
Enough of these vexing looks cast at women.
Ask him to come singing a requiem to all such evils.
Ask him to come to break away the array
Of cruelty that encircles women,
And to put an end to all affliction of exploitation. 130
If not, he shall not be called Shri Rama,
And I would declare him to be another Ravana; tell him that."
Thus she said roaring like Chandi – the most ferocious goddess.

Listening to the words of Hanuma with all seriousness,
Shri Ramachandra deliberated in his mind the future course of
    actions.
With great affection, he heartily praised Hanuma
And the entire clan of Sugriva, the king of *vanaras*.

River Tungabhadra is Bhagirathi – the sacred Ganga – of Kannada
Gushes through the Sahyadri Mountain
As if the heart of the mountain itself is opened wide. 140
Like Goddess Ganga herself has come down to earth,
Tunga flows through the state of Karnataka
Turning its soil into gold,
Opening up the highway of wealth as desired by all,
Without discriminating between people in the slightest,
And providing succour to all.
Assimilating every drop and offering handfuls
Springing high up to the sky once, and passing through the valley
    once,
Filling the *kalashas* of the sublime essence of beauty,
Emanating extraordinary delight, proclaiming equality, 150

Vowing to ameliorate the world,
And singing the praise of Bharati – the motherland –
River Tungbhadra flows majestically.

Sitting on her banks,
Saumitri, with his eyes closed,
Is engrossed in the thought of his virtuous wife Urmila,
Who was sitting on the banks of river Sarayu.
She has sacrificed all selfish desires.
The song of her grief of separation from her beloved
Is continually echoing   160
Like a divine song through the waters of the Sarayu.
To aid the Great Quest mission of Shri Rama and Saumitri
And with a self-willed vow to accomplish the welfare of the world,
She has submitted herself heart and soul at the altar of sacrifice.
That is truly boundless love that transcends the physical body!

Memory has gained strength there.
The sprout of childhood has emerged as a bud
And blossomed into a flower spreading its fragrance.
The touch that the body does not know has stirred the tongue.
The look that is unknown to the eyes,   170
And the song that is unknown to the ears
Have turned into a melodious song of the nightingale.
The coming of spring and the dream of union stood before her eyes.
Like purified gold, shedding all impurities
Urmila stands in the mind of Saumitri
Like a golden idol.

Canto One Hundred and Sixty-six

'Exercise Restraint; Let Not the Rule of Law be Despoiled'

||ॐ||

Rama liked very much the news conveyed by Hanuma.
'What an impossible task!
Yet you have accomplished it successfully.
There is none other in the world who is an accomplisher like you;
And none other to equal you in such meticulous planning
And execution of tasks.
O Hanumanta! Tell me how you broke into the inviolable fort;
How you spoke to Janaki; and how you killed the *rakshasas*.'
With great delight Pavanasuta replied thus:

'Why to speak in great detail now? 10
Meditating on your name, I leaped across the ocean.
Singing your history, I spoke to the Mother.
Believing in your power, I burnt down Lanka.
Remembering you again and again, I returned. O listen!'

'Bravo! I appreciate your heroic deeds.
Look, how have I sat forgetting you in the excitement of it all!
Tell me what I shall do for you; tell me what I shall give you.'
When Shri Rama asked thus, Hanumanta said:

198

'What shall I beg of you?
The good fortune that you have bestowed on me abounds here.   20
Grant me the undying devotion that would eternally rest in you.
Let my tongue keep uttering your holy name continually.
Devotion at your holy feet is all that I need
And I shall be delighted in the contemplation
Of your name deep in my soul.
I am blessed with the good fortune of seeing Bhuvanamata –
The Mother of the World. I feel deeply fulfilled
Having done what is proper.'

Being highly pleased, Shri Rama said:
'You are very dear to me.   30
Who else is there who has leaped across the ocean like you!
You are indeed Vainateya – Garuda, the son of Vinata;
You are truly Vayudeva, the Wind-god.
Trusting my power, you crushed Lanka.
Trusting my love, you spoke to Janaki.
What self-confidence and how heroic is this!

'How shall I praise you!
A servant who is ordered to do a certain task by the king,
If he returns spoiling the task, he is rated the lowest;
If he returns empty-handed, he is considered mediocre;   40
And when the task has great risks, if he returns victorious,
He is considered the best of all.
The task that you have accomplished shall last
As long as the sun and the moon last.
People shall praise you always.

'O Hanuma! This is the truth.
The clan of Raghu lives in the breath of Vaidehi.
Having set at high glory the duty of a servant;
Having saved *raja-dharma* – the king's duties;
You have set on fire Lankesha's exploitation. Bravo!   50
You have spread in all the four directions
The truth of the saying that

If anyone, beaming in arrogance, behaves unrestrained,
There is always someone to curb such a person.
You have hoisted the flag of *dharma*.'
Saying so, embracing Pavanaja, Shri Rama
Happily smelt the head of Hanuma with great affection.

As Sugriva looked at all this in wonderment,
Shri Rama said: 'Look here, O Sugriva!
If the success story of the impassable ocean of difficulties faced   60
By Hanuma, Nala, Jambava, Angada, and all the others
In the task of the Great Quest is recalled to mind,
Surely one would shudder at the very thought of it all.
Pavanasuta has leaped across such an ocean.
He has returned breaking the crown of glory of Dashashira.
Where are the equals to the heroes of Karunadu –
The land of the Kannadigas!
How to praise the grandeur of Karunadu!
It is the seat of volition of Bharata – the motherland.
I can't forget that the sacred land of Karunadu is the heart   70
Of Ramayana's Great Quest!

'O Sugriva, my good friend!
Janaki is suffering the torture of Ravana.
Just as a fleeting moment seems like an epoch to me,
Similarly Janaki is holding on to life waiting for me.
Tell me, what Ravana might do.
Disgusted by Hanuma's attack,
Would he kill Sita? How shall I bear the pangs of separation?
How shall we accomplish Janaki's liberation now?'
Thus spoke Shri Rama.   80

'You are indeed a great hero.
You are an intelligent scholar, and an exponent of royal-diplomacy.
Why this dejection? The whirl of sorrow will drown the boat
Of volition and swallow us up.
Lassitude of mind is harmful to self-realisation.
Let us build a bridge and cross over the ocean.

Let us lay siege on Lanka and crush the *rakshasas*.
Let us liberate Janaki and return happily.
These *vanaras* are efficient workers and are valorous too.
These *vanaras* are capable of attaining any form at will.
They shall accomplish great wonders.
I swear by Sun-god, my father that
I shall get this mission accomplished for you.'
Enthusing valour, thus spoke Sugriva heroically.

Listening to the re-assuring words of Sugriva,
And looking at Anjaneya happily, Shri Rama asked:
Tell me, how strong the fort of Lanka is and how it is protected;
How the gate-way is constructed and what is its design;
Tell me, how well-stocked the arsenal is;
How strong the *rakshasas*' army is
And what is the size of its *chaturangabala* –
The four-wings of a complete army comprising
Of elephants, chariots, cavalry, and infantry.'

'O Shri Rama, kindly listen!
What shall I say of the *rakshasas*' limitless devotion to their king!
The strength of the *daitya*-army, including the *chaturangabala*
Is enormous and beyond counting.
If one looks at the kinds of weapons,
Certainly it is frightening to the enemies.
Lanka is situated atop the mountain and is formidable.
It is surrounded by the ocean and the *rakshasas* beam
In the conceit that none could come there crossing the ocean.
All bastions and the fort are strong like the diamond.
There are four main gates in each of the four directions
And the main gates are secured with massive iron latches.
Large trenches are there all around
And water runs through them forcefully.
The crocodiles there frighten with their wide-opened mouths;
And moving about hungrily, they await their prey.
At the main gates, they have kept iron-*shataghnis* –

Weapons used as missiles.
Close to the main gates, there are great machines
That could rain arrows and stone-balls at the enemies.
The walls of the fort are covered with drawings
Studded with diamonds and gems.

Many wonders are there.
There are causeways connected to the trenches.
When the causeway is lifted up by the power of machines,
It provides security by preventing the crossing over by the enemies.
If so desired, the causeway could be readied and laid back in
   position 130
And only then the citizens could move in and out.
There are golden pillars in the trenches,
And there are platforms in them for the *rakshasas* to keep guard.
There are bastions to keep watch continually.
The army officers come in batches and are engrossed
In the task of providing security.
An army of spies is spread all over.
It is thus impossible for the enemies
To break into the fort and gain entry.

The city is located at the mountain peak. 140
It is secured by the water-fort; the mountain-fort; the forest-fort –
The three natural forts – and a man-made fort as the fourth one.
There is no marine route for that city and none other either.

If one looks at the eastern gate,
There is a troupe of more than ten thousand *rakshasas*
Armed with spears and swords. They keep guard day and night.
At the southern gate, there is the *chaturangabala* –
A full army of one lakh soldiers.
The troupe armed with swords and shields at the western gate
Has ten lakh soldiers. 150
The *rakshasas* are highly adept in the use all kinds of weapons.

My lord! By your grace, I have crushed
To pieces a few causeways there. Breaking the rampart,

I have filled up the trench here and there.
I have destroyed the *rakshasa*-troupe to some extent.

Even then, the *rakshasas*
Again and again turn their minds to lustful indulgences
And forsaking any fear of war, they remain indifferent;
Their morality is utterly ruined.
Their valour has melted down 160
And their war-preparedness is scanty.
They have forgotten all about the outside world,
And the awareness within has dried up.
At such a time like this, if we attack with ingenuity,
Jayalakshmi – the Goddess of Victory shall surely be on our side.'
Thus said Anjaneya.

'O Sugriva! Why delay anymore now!
Get ready the military expedition to Lanka swiftly.
Punarvasu is my birth-star; Uttara is my star for accomplishment;
And Hasta is my star for striking the enemy. 170
All are auspiciously disposed.
How would that vile Ravana escape being hurt by my arrow!
I shall slay him.'
When Shri Rama spoke thus, everybody agreed,
And as they were all looking at his face with the emotion
Of what might happen next,
Shri Ramachandra spoke again:

'Get ready you all.
Nila is quick to act,
And as the general of the troupe of one-lakh *vanaras*, 180
Let him lead the troupe. Your path is bountifully blessed with
Ample roots, tubers, water-holes and tanks.
In the dense forests, mountains and valleys,
Fierce *rakshasa*-troupes secretly lie in wait.
They will try to kill by poisoning the water.
Therefore beware, and march cautiously!
Leave behind the weak and sickly *vanaras*;

Take along only those who are fit and ever-ready
And may you be gallant and valorous.
Exercise restraint; let not the rule of law be despoiled.' 190

At that instant, Angada
Explained in detail the preparations for the war.
He got the war-proclamation announced aloud.
The declaration of war brought excitement to the *vanaras*.
At sunrise on the fifth-day of Margashirsha – the ninth lunar month,
The great military expedition marched off from Kishkindha!

Canto One Hundred and Sixty-seven

'When would She Show Her Smiling Face to Me'

||૬||

As their neatly arranged matted tuft of hair glowed in royal grandeur,
Carrying bows and arrows, as Rama and Lakshmana marched
Along with Sugriva and the *vanara*-chieftains in the excitement
Of the conquest-expedition,
They looked radiant like the moon.

Wherever one looked,
The troupe of valorous warriors was marching ahead roaring aloud.
A variety of trumpets were sounded loudly.
As the *vanara*-army was spread like the vast expanse of the ocean,
As the earth was vibrating with the heavy strides of the warriors, 10
As the ocean-waves rose high to the sky,
The cry of victory resounded continually:
Let victory be to Rama; let victory be to the brother of Rama;
Let there be victory to Sugriva, Angada, Jambava, and Hanuma.

'In this great military expedition,
Let Gaja, Gavaya, Gavaksha and the other powerful warriors
Stand in the frontline of the army.
Let Rishabha stand guard at the right side there.

Let Gandhamadana be on the left side.
Like Indra sits mounted on his elephant Airavata,
I will remain in the centre of the army seated on
Pavanaja's shoulders and march forward enthusing all.'
Shri Rama said thus in a loud voice.

The pre-eminently valorous *vanara*,
With folded hands devoutly bowed to Lord Virupaksha – Shiva;
On seeing river Tungabhadra flowing majestically
Like an excellent dancer,
They danced happily and climbed up the trees.
Eating mangoes, jackfruits, guavas, and honey sumptuously
They belched contentedly. Resting for a while,
They drank water in the river Tungabhadra –
The one who blesses the world with her bounty.
Hiding within herself the blazing misery of the world,
Offering her milky stream to all,
Spreading greenery – the breath of life – all around,
She flows nurturing the coconut and areca-nut orchards
And the paddy fields.

As they were coming in the Sahyadri-range,
Sushena – the renowned doctor of Ayurveda,
Showing some wonderful medicinal roots to the valorous warriors
And imparting in essence their special qualities, said:
'O *vanaras*, listen! Look at this medicinal root;
If you eat this, hunger and thirst won't afflict you for many days;
Look at it closely; it is highly nutritional, and you better know that.
Look at this yet another medicinal root –
If you extract its juice and spray it into the nostrils,
The one who is tired will regain the lost stamina.
Here is one more; look at it;
If the leaves of this root are crushed, made into pills
And put in the mouth –
Bleeding will stop; there is no doubt in it.
Here is yet another; if ground well and smeared,

The skin will not be burnt.
Watch this wonder! This is the divine elixir
Which has the power to save the one who is poisoned.'
Thus he moved ahead describing
All medicinal roots and herbs.

As they were afflicted by hunger,
There was food made of the finest row rice;
Chutney made of select variety of ripe round brinjal; 60
Mango-*chutney*; sweet-smelling tasty lemons;
Pickle made of tender bamboo-shoot; broth seasoned with chillies;
Gravy made of boiled split pulses.
With great love, the *vanara*-troupe was served with fresh curd
That gleamed like the autumn-moon.
In this manner, a sumptuous Karnataka-feast was spread before them.

The one-lakh strong army
Of the pre-eminently valorous *vanara* was under the command
Of Shatabali. He was entrusted with the responsibility
Of overseeing and protecting the entire army. 70
Sushena was there by his side to protect the army.
Jambava, flanked by the *bhalluka*-warriors,
Marched ahead along with Sugriva,
Protecting the centre of the large army.

Dadhimukha, Prajangha, Rambha,
And such other pre-eminently valorous *vanara*-leaders
Stood ready to lead swiftly the *vanaras*.
They crossed the Sahyadri mountains.
They went past the forest filled with flowers and fruits.
They crossed over the tanks and pools that looked grand 80
With a variety of flowers. The *vanara*-troupe appeared
As if the ocean itself overflowed its shores.
They all marched swiftly in great excitement.

Like the well-bred horses gallop
Whisked by the whip, the pre-eminently valorous *vanara*

Walked by the side of Shri Rama leaping.
Shri Rama and Lakshmana looked
Like the planets Jupiter and Venus.
The dust on the path was scattered high
By the heavy strides of the marching troupe 90
And clouded the rays of the sun making it look dull.
They all marched swiftly in great excitement.

The pre-eminently valorous *vanara*
Climbed the mountains; crossed the rivers; entered the valleys,
And went round the trenches.
Beaming with excitement, feeling elated in valour,
Exhibiting pride, and showing youthfulness
They all marched swiftly in great excitement.

The pre-eminently valorous *vanara* walked
Leaping with excitement and striding the path aggressively. 100
Gabbling aloud, challenging all, breaking the trees,
Throwing out rocks, chopping off bushes,
And pulling out creepers,
They all marched swiftly in great excitement.

They crossed the Velandhara Mountain
And walked towards the Suvela Mountain.
They spent a night in the Akshavana.
Later, halting at Hamsa-island, they continued their journey.
They all marched swiftly in great excitement.
They arrived at the Mahendra Mountain. 110

Shri Rama said:
'O Sugriva! Look at the vastness of the ocean!
How could we cross this?' Worrying thus,
They camped at the plateau of the Mount Mahendra.

Who the enemies were and where could they be hiding,
And in what way they could wage a war – fearing all these,
They stood guard in all the directions.

The roar of the ocean coupled with the uproar of the *vanaras*
Echoed in all the four directions.

The beauty of that plateau of the Mount Mahendra 120
Is beyond description. *Suragi* – tree with very fragrant flowers;
ketaki – the fragrant screw-pine; *madhavi*; *choota*; *patali*; *bakula*;
vasanti; *spurjaka*; *tilaka*; *arjuna*; *shimshupa*; *ankola*; *padmaka*; *sampage*;
nerile; *churnaka*; *nyagroda*; *anjula*; *hintalanipaka*; *raktakuravaka*;
dhavavarana,
And such other trees have grown thick there.
It had rained flowers there. The buzz of the bees resonated there.
The soothing breeze brought in delight.
The water-tanks and ponds were full and the water-birds
And the *krauncha* birds swam and floated fearlessly.
Saugandhika flowers, lotus, lily,
And other flowers bloomed majestically. 130

The glow of the sun disappeared.
As moon appeared, the Ocean-god danced ecstatically.
With his hands of waves, as the Ocean-god macerated sandal,
With his hands of rays, moon himself seemed
To be smearing the celestial damsels with that sandal paste
In an act of intense love.
Thus, in unison, the earth and the sky glowed in grandeur.

Many fierce water-creatures were there.
Crocodiles, whales, sharks, and serpents with the glowing gems
On their hoods were moving freely. 140
As the hurricane hit against the massive rocks,
The waves rose high and seemed to be dancing.
As if all the gems of the ocean were thrown up,
The gleaming stars appeared on the sky.
Which was the ocean, and which one was the sky –
It looked as if the difference between the two had melted away!

In Mount Mandara of such grandeur
The *vanaras* settled in silence

And watched everything with wonder-filled eyes.
Knowing the intricacies of war-diplomacy, 150
Nila – the general of the troupe, stood there
At the northern shore waiting with watchful eyes.
Moving swiftly all over,
Mainda and Dwivida, had taken upon themselves
The great responsibility of protecting the army.
As the moonlight filled the earth and the sky,
Suffering from the pangs of separation from Janaki,
Rama told Saumitri thus:

'O Saumitri! O the gentle-one!
My grief is rising high without seeing Janaki, my consort. 160
The light on the path of Quest of the world is dying out.
My heart is burning as if I have drunk poison.
I am enduring the pain as if the molten flames of fire
Have entered the crevices of my bones.
The flames are ablaze.
This body itself is becoming the fuel for the fiery pangs of separation.
Would I disappear getting drowned deep in the bottom of the ocean?
The news that Sita is alive has saved my life.

Being the daughter of Janaka,
The daughter-in-law of Dasharatha, and the wife of Rama, 170
Sita is helplessly caught up in the humility
Of spending her days in fear under the guard
Of the *rakshashis* in the imprisonment of Ravana!
O Fate! I know not when the moon covered
By dark clouds would come out of it and shine bright again.
When would she show her smiling face to me, I know not.
She has grown weak and tired in the vow of fasting.
She is engrossed in meditation. She thinks only of me.
The soothing cool breeze, coupled with fragrance,
The glow of the moonlight blending with the glow of the clouds 180
Are comforting the whole world.
But what does it to matter me?

Taking away all merriment,
It is only causing me immense pain.
I know not how this agony would end.
I do not see the hope of liberation.
How would my life's boat reach its shore,
And how this agony would end – I know not, O Saumitri!'
Lamenting thus, and thinking of Janaki again and again,
He lifted up the *chudamani* and pressing it to his eyes   190
He bathed it with his overflowing tears,
And assumed silence as if he were an idol.

Canto One Hundred and Sixty-eight

'I have Given the Freedom of Expression to All'

॥६॥

One day, as Vibhishana was engulfed in worry,
Surama, approaching slowly with measured steps, asked him:
'What is this distress?
To you who soothe the world with your soft, sweet talk
Why this kind of suffering from affliction?'
The pain has traversed down to the pit of my stomach.
When my elder brother was treading the path of truth and *dharma*
This Lanka stood as an inviolable nation in the whole of the universe.
Now, look around!
The best of the values have turned into graveyard-flowers   10
And everywhere the despicable Ravana cult is set in high glory.
When the citizens go wrong, the king is duty-bound to punish
   them.
When the king himself does wrong,
It is as if the fence itself is eating up the crops in the field!'
Vibhishana said so.

'Yes, there is indeed a blemish
In the personal ethics of Ravana. But what does it matter?
The nation is quite wealthy. There is everything aplenty

And the people are happy and peaceful.
Is there any dearth of fame? 20
Truly, the whole world praises Lanka.'
Thus said Surama in great enthusiasm.

'O Surama, stop this; enough of it!
I have great love for my elder brother.
But what of it? Unlawfully Ravana has brought here
The beautiful damsels of the defeated emperors,
And uses them as mere objects of lust in the harem.
This is a great moral degradation. O Surama!
When the king drifts from the path of righteousness,
That itself is cause enough for destroying the nation.' 30
Then, Surama said:

'How could I bear the destruction of Lanka!
O my lord, I can not do so. My whole body is burning in anguish.
Give some friendly advice, please.
I am confident that in the light of your
Good counsel Lanka shall glow bright.
Why do you suffer unnecessarily?
I am sure that everything will end well.'
Touched by the befriending words of Surama,
Vibhishana said thus smilingly: 40
'As you have spoken what is there in my mind,
I feel happy. I will give good counsel to my elder brother.
I will remain steadfast in that and keep trying again and again.'

One day, when Ravana was sitting on the throne in his court,
All the major leaders – Indrajit, Sharabha, Praghasa, Anala, Anila,
Vibhishana, Aviruddha, Prahasta, and such others –
Had assembled in that royal hall.
As the panegyrists stood eulogising Ravana's many titles,
The royal assembly resounded with such high praise.

In his sonorous, serious voice Ravana said:
'Shri Rama, the king of Saketa; 50

And Sugriva, the lord of Kishkindha,
Are advancing jointly to attack us.
They have encamped on the ocean-shore.
Do you hear the news of the enemies!

'Has Rama vowed to complete that war now at Lanka
Which he did not wage then on the pretext of Shurpanakha?
Forget the attacks committed by Hanuma. Do not lose courage.
The ocean has prevented the *vanara*-army from crossing it.
If they invade Lanka, we ought to slay them all.
Swiftly get all our forces ready! 60
A great war awaits us. The war is inevitable. What do you say?
I am eager to get your approval for the war.
The house is summoned for this very purpose.
Tell me frankly your opinions.'

'Is Shri Rama any ordinary person?
He has won the battle with Parashurama.
He has broken the bow of Shiva. You are defeated there.
All alone, he has slain one-lakh and odd soldiers
Including Khara and Dushana.
He is such a hero who has slain Vali – 70
The one who had pinioned you
And tied you to the cradle of Angada.
He has killed Maricha, Tataka, and Subahu.
He is the most venerable hero.
Is it syllogistic to win such a one?
Having killed all the *rakshashas* right from Ayodhya to Kanyakumari,
He is now advancing towards Lanka.
O my lord! Think it over for yourself.'
Malyavanta said thus in utter humbleness.

How could Rama be a hero! 80
He has chopped off Shurpanakha's nose clandestinely.
When he who killed Vali hiding himself behind a tree
Declares war on us, would anyone praise the enemy?
Thus Atikaya roared in anger.

Dashamukha, the ten-faced-one said:
'It is not praise at all. Let there be a debate now.
I have given the freedom of expression to all.
Tell me quite frankly what you all feel!'

At that instant, Anila got up and said:
'Would anyone forget the harm done 90
By the *vanara* single-handedly?'
Then, Prahasta said: 'Jayalakshmi – the Goddess of Victory
Has come appeasing you, always. The war should be waged.
This is not the time to buckle down.'
At that moment, Aniruddha said:
'This is not the proper time to wage war.
War is not advisable; undue haste is certainly not advisable.
Think it over calmly.'

Appreciating the words spoken by Aniruddha,
Malyavanta said boldly: 'Aniruddha has spoken the truth. 100
The act of keeping Sita imprisoned is the root cause of all evil.
Why do we need a war that spills out blood?'

Canto One Hundred and Sixty-nine

'Peace is Greater than War – Realise this, O King!'

||๑||

Listening with rapt attention to the friendly words of all,
And agreeing with Malyavanta's words,
Vibhishana got up and spoke thus in utmost humility:

'You are well-versed in the ways of the world
And know the intricacies of royal diplomacy.
Please listen to these words.
O brother! It is better to discard the house that leaks,
The servant who is jealous,
The wife who is vile, and the path that is unknown.
If you tread the path of truth, there is no fear of death.   10
Truth alone is the mother, the father,
The kindred and everything indeed!
It is better to walk the path of *dharma*
And hand over Janaki to Rama.
All that you had dreamt in the childhood will become a reality then.
It is better to safeguard the well-being of the citizens.
Don't wage a war; give it up.
Give up the causeless enmity with Rama.
Any rule that neglects *dharma*, truth, justice,

And morals is deplorable;
Don't you know this!
The well-being of the majority is indeed the base of all kingly duties.
Do not push the citizens to the abyss of dissatisfaction.
Shri Rama has come to take his wife with him.
If you release her yourself, would Rama wage a war still?
Janaki is the dutiful wife to Rama.
Is it proper to adduct and bring her here slyly?

Observing the ritual of *saptapadi* –
The sacred seven steps of marital vows,
And all the religious ceremonies,
They have become man and wife.
How did you become the victim of vile lust!
Would anyone separate the blessed couple in cruelty?
Do not trust the selfish and the conceited people.
Do not tread the path of destruction.
Think how the bow of Shiva,
Which you could not tame, was broken in the hands of Rama!
He has himself slain Khara and Dushana.
He is endowed with the divine weapons
That are given to him by the renowned Sage Vishvamitra.
Do not forget the words spoken by Maricha.

He is indeed Mahavishnu.
Assuming the form of Matsya – the Great Fish, he has slain Tamasura.
He has lifted up the Mount Mandara in his incarnation as Kurma –
The Tortoise. In the incarnation as Varaha – the Great Boar,
He has slain Hiranyaksha. As Narasimha – the Man-Lion,
He has slain Hiranyakashipu.
As Vamana – the Dwarf, he has pushed Bali to *Patala* – the Nether World.
As Parashurama – the one with the lethal axe,
He has wiped out the conceit of the Kshatriya-clan.

Now, in the form of Shri Rama,
He has stretched his holy feet in order to punish the evil-doers.
It is good to mend one's ways and behave well.
Do not push Lanka and the *rakshasa*-clan
To the abyss of unfathomable darkness.

'War in itself is the poison.
Standing in the grace of wisdom,
You rule over the world, O king!
Peace is greater than war; realise this, O king!
On the sandy bank, in the crevice of the rocks,   60
When the national-bird falls down facing the sky,
Its wide opened eyes are filled with broken rainbow;
With a pitiable wail when it flies
Spreading its wings towards the solar orbit,
O brother, protect it thus that it shall never fall down again.
Why do you remain silent as if you do not see anything?
Why should the wealth and power be lost in unbridled behaviour?

'O Vibhishana, listen!
You have embedded the core philosophy
Of *dharma* in your words.   70
Without the war-expeditions, the task of building up
An empire is only a mirage indeed.
Tell me, were you not there with me supporting me
In the victory-expeditions
And built up with ingenuity this Lanka-nation!
It is true that you are *sarvajna* – the one who knows everything.
Nevertheless, would you believe Rama
Who has come to grab our kingdom
On the pretext of *vanavasa* – the vow to live in the forest.
Give up such innocence.   80
Putting forward the lame excuse of offering
Fertile land to the sages, why did he kill Khara and Dushana?
Why did he allow Shurpanakha's nose to be chopped off?
Why did he kill Vali clandestinely?

For what reason did he kill Tataka and Subahu?
Why do you preach morals to me?
Why do you glorify his wretched valour now?
Sita's abduction is the means of refuting the
Morality of the war-expedition undertaken by Rama.
The political game of dice is being played now; 90
Sita will roll down as dice!

She is worth only a cowrie to me;
It is quite alright if she does not appease me;
I am not afflicted by that.
I am Ravaneshwara – epitome of the glowing national pride
That finds fulfilment in me.
I will live for hundreds of years.
This is the kingdom of the *danavas*.
It shall stand in high glory and not be wiped out.
Purposeful abduction is royal diplomacy indeed, listen! 100
Would I surrender! I will wipe out Saketa's evil desire,
And demonstrate my valour grandiosely!

Vibhishana said:
'You must search the root of who is guilty.
You have slain Vidyujihwa in a fit of jealousy;
And thus, who has taken away stealthily the *mangalya* –
The sacred symbol of marital status – of our sister?
Our sister Shurpanakha is unaware of the ways of the world.
You drove her to Janasthana, saying –
"Go, find your own consort" – 110
And thus you pushed her to a life of willful lust.
Like a courtesan in the prime of her youth,
You pushed Shurpanakha to the wantonness
Of loving whomever she took fancy for.
In the form of a parasitical plant that seed of sin is now
Sucking away the sap of Lanka and killing it.
Shurpanakha has committed evil deeds in the weakness of lust.
If looked from this perspective,
Rama hasn't done anything wrong.

O king! Would anyone forget the deeds of Anjaneya, 120
Who came here in the form of a messenger,
And though allowing himself to be bound by *Brahmastra*,
Nevertheless shook Lanka!
That by itself is a nightmare!
Countless *vanaras* with similar valour have jointly come now.
Tell me, how you would counter them.
Would you lose out in war this Lanka,
Which you got from Kubera as part of a treaty?
For want of taste, a patient
Of pulmonary consumption would rebuke milk. 130
A patient, who does not like dietary restrictions, would scorn medicine.
What if the good counsel I give is not to your taste?
It is bitter to the lips; but, sweet to the stomach.
Good advice is not sweet to the ears; but it is sweet to life indeed.
The fire of *pativratya* – the moral strength of a dutiful wife –
Would engulf Lanka.
Release Sita and surrender to Rama at once!'

'These stories that you have told
Are pleasant only to listen.
It is a befitting – though useless – advice meant 140
Only for the assemblage of children.
It is not fit for the royal court.
There are not any blockheads here.
This court is full of valorous heroes.'
Thus Prahasta said mockingly.

Vibhishana said again:
O Lankesha! Do not trust the council of wicked ministers.
Ascribing it to the "will of the king,"
They will conceal truth and by hiding the essence
Of the matter, they will write false accounts. 150
In order to provide for their kith and kin,
they will cheat the royal treasury.
They make the king believe that there is not anyone else

Who is more truthful than them in the whole world.
They deceive the king in this way,
And being driven by selfishness, they swindle the world.
They break the unity and sow the seeds of dissension.
They are accustomed to the tenet of "divide and rule."
Malyavanta, and such others, are venerable. Accept their words.
Do not rush to war in conceit.   160
Even if one could count all the sand-grains on the ocean-shore,
It is impossible to measure the strength of Lanka's army.
There is no limit to its valour. Even then, look here, and listen –
War is not advisable! Your own sins are fatal to Lanka.
If merely the empire gets bigger, what profit is there in it?
Safeguarding it is indeed greater than everything.
Wanton administration of a kingdom is not the tenet of stately rule.
Safeguarding peace alone is the foundation of a welfare state!

Just as the gift given
To an unworthy person produces adverse results,   170
Indiscreet action leads to one's downfall, listen!
You have now put your hand to the braid of *bhujata* – the
  earth-born.
Hanuma is *mukhyaprana* – the Vital Breath of life;
He will not spare your life.
If a black cobra is kissed, will not the poison shoot up?
Wear that inviolable amulet meant to safeguard *dharma*.
As you wear such a protective gear,
You can see for yourself its infinite power
To grant your wish and to safeguard you.
You will then be victorious and become perfect.   180
Thus, may you be the Adishesha
And bear this Lanka on your strong shoulders.

Do not rush to war insolently.
Whether the dice of politics is war – tell me that.
Be well focused in your mind solely on this point.
If one changes colour, character, and directions like a chameleon,

The downfall is certain. Caught up in the stream of insanity,
You will be washed away; you will be afloat dead.
Enmity and hatred have blinded you.
Look inwards; the lotus of your heart has faded away.   190
Whether the citizens appreciate the abduction of Sita?
The flame of patriotism shall be extinguished, listen.
In the ensuing battle, countless troupes
Of valorous heroes will bite the dust.
O king! Have belief in the light of Truth, and be blessed!

Smoke has engulfed all over.
Why do you deceive yourself thinking
That you would forget pain by indulging in enjoyment of all kinds?
Being mesmerised by the false words of ministers and sons,
Would anyone bid eternal farewell to cleverness, and skillfulness!   200

Closing your eyes that have appeased
Mandodari, my sister-in-law, would you fall to the
Abyss of evil infatuation like a hungry royal tiger!'

Indrajit said:
'When the enemy knocks at the door and calls out for war
Should we say "No;" we will be eunuchs then.
Rudraveena – Shiva's lute – is being played all over;
War-songs are resounding everywhere;
War-drums are sounded everywhere.
Tell me, would one survive   210
By rejecting the *ranavilya* – invitation to war!'

Vibhishana replied:
'Why should you become a victim of fate?
The city of Lanka will be destroyed in an instant.'
'What did you say, Sir? Do not speak harsh words.
You never came to the battle-front to protect the nation.
You have not sweated it out; and have never bled for the country.
You offer useless advice, and speak vainly!

You spend time happily indulging
In worship, prayers, meditation, yoga and observing countless feasts.   220

You are not inclined to repay the debt of the motherland.
If you defy Lanka, I will chop off your head.
My sword is eager to act. Get out of here.
Your followers shall not stay in the precincts of Lanka.'
Indrajit said thus sardonically!

'I am not a coward. I have only offered good counsel.
Your well-being, my well-being, Lanka's well-being, nay,
The well-being of the world itself is hidden in this counsel.
Restrain yourself.
Hand over Janaki and surrender to Rama thus.   230
Why should one listen to the words
Of people trying to stray one away from the path of righteousness?'
Unable to bear the insults anymore, Vibhishana said so.

'In this royal assembly, you are all alone.
Enough; speak no more.
The battle-field does not tolerate the words of a coward.
Enough of your advice.
The sap of heroism is boiling and my body is burning.
If you stand up in defiance, it shall explode you right away.'
So saying, Lankesha got up from the royal court   240
And swiftly went to the chamber
Of private consultation behind closed doors.

Canto One Hundred and Seventy

'Play the Lute of Vani for a while'

||◉||

Mandodari saw her dear consort walk in worried.
Understanding his state of mind,
Lovingly she seated him in the bed-chamber,
And offering him food and drinks,
And rendering satisfaction thus, she comforted him.
She is a perfect match to Ravana in beauty, age and thoughts.
Appreciating the valour of Lankesha wholeheartedly,
She herself has come here as his loving bride.
She has come here with much appreciation for the culture of Lanka.
There is no custom of worshipping many deities.　　　　　　　10
Parashiva is the Supreme Lord;
And Paravati is the supreme Mother-Goddess.
The freedom-tree, which proclaims men and women equal,
Is looking robustly elegant here!

Refuting the Ayodhya-culture –
Which, in the pretext of protecting their virtuous character,
Entangles women in the web of child-marriage and *sati*,
And thus crushes and discards them.
Mandodari has appreciation for the matchless culture of freedom.
Mandodari, such a blessed wife, caressing Ravana's forelocks,　　20
Said thus in endearing love:

'Listen to me, my beloved!
The treacherous hold of monolith culture is swallowing up
The pluralistic cultures of the *vanaras*,
The *rakshasas* and the Bhilla-tribesmen,
Who are dexterous in archery.
The game of dice of monolithic-culture is being held continually
Between Vali-Sugriva, and Ravana-Vibhishana.
The unique culture of the Lanka-island is getting drowned
In the ocean of the Saketa-empire. 30
It is true that Shri Rama is a noble person of virtuous character.
Nevertheless, he has been nurturing
The invasive tree of Ayodhya-culture.
That is the society which abuses women.
It is highly patriarchal. Women have no freedom there
And are treated like animals there.
The power of women is suppressed there
And is languishing in the valley of harems.

'Look! In Lanka
Dhanyamalini still retains her respect. 40
Shurpanakha, though widowed, without being pushed to the confines
Of the enclosures of the inner chambers,
Was made the empress of Janasthana;
Thus the stump of her life has blossomed once again!
This indeed is the noble culture of Lanka!
Here is harmony between husband and wife;
But the city of Saketa is the rock of oppressive dominance;
Enslaving thoughts there; but liberal thinking here.

'May you have this one virtue:
If you forsake the cruelty, 50
If you wear the crown of Rama's values,
If you break the fort of exploitation,
Look! You would certainly be the visionary of the new culture.
Break the chain of monolithic culture that tries
To bind Bharata within its confines,

And thus be the harbinger of the new epoch yourself!
Arise, and awake before the ghost
Of monolithic culture swallows up the world!

In Lanka there is no noise of *yajna* and *yaga*.
There is no fort of discrimination erected here –   60
Like – this is sin; this is virtue; this is Heaven; this is Hell;
This is superior; this is inferior, and so on –
Cut off the prolixity that tries to wipe out the fearless, liberal culture.
Come, O king, my beloved! Build up the Lanka-culture!
Cut off the creeper of the poisonous monolithic culture.
Break the ant-hill of the sin of secrecy.
Look, what happened there when it was time for Rama's coronation!
The Will of the Nation became the matter of inquisitive conjecture.
There was no trace of openness; it became an intensely secretive affair.
Betrayal showed its ugly head that resulted in great crime.   70
Bharata and Shatrughna, and all the citizens
Stood mute witness there, look!
In Saketa, the spring of citizens' will has dried up;
But in Lanka, being the source of life, it flows continuously.
Everything is transparent here;
Here is the true State; it is only a deceitful cage there.

It seems that Rama has built a bridge.
Rama, along with the *vanaras*, would come here.
He would put the chain of monolithic culture on everybody.
The pluralistic culture would be wiped out without a trace.   80
He would wreck the garden of liberal culture.
Rama is unaware of the sins that he commits.
Wipe out all that.' Mandodari said so.

'O my beloved!
I know everything: I am aware of the cultural conflict
That tries to convert the pluralistic culture into a monolithic culture;
Pushes to inertia the vibrantly pulsating emotions;
And the attempts to convert the multi-lingual society
Into a mono-linguistic one.

I am aware of the conspiracy to wipe out the creative energy   90
Of the whole generation by pushing them to war.
I vow to protect the Lanka culture valorously. I shall fight.
Would I tolerate the invasion by strangers?
Never! I shall not spare them!

'If Janaki is handed over,
The Lanka-culture itself would be wiped out.
War is necessary now to save it.
Rama and Ravana are only an excuse here.
The *vanara*-culture has surrendered itself to Ayodhya-culture;
Sugriva is responsible for this.   100

'Now I am declaring war on Ayodhya-culture; I will win.
Thereafter I will hand over Janaki to Rama.
If I die heroically, some other leader in the future will praise me –
"Ravana attained Heaven in the act of protecting the Lanka-culture" –
And thus spread my fame in the entire world!

'The self-confidence of Lanka has come down
Because of the scarcity of arms and ammunition;
It is caught up in the whirlpool of anxiety.
War alone is the royal way to restore it, listen!'

Mandodari said: 110
'You alone are the deity to protect;
You alone are the deity to destroy.
Seal the abyss of Aryavarta's fault.
Who else but you know the excellent grandeur
Of Lanka-culture which always brings to the fore
Newer and newer aspects keeping in tune with the spirit of the times.
It is only the lotus which knows the depth of the pond;
But would a tiny bee ever know it, tell me!
Chop off the poisonous branches, the poisonous trunk,
The poisonous roots and everything   120
Of the Saketa-culture which crushes all novelty.
There is none like you in the whole world

Who prides himself in balancing well *dharma, artha,* and *kama*
And enjoying the fruits thereof!
Would it be easy to win Lanka which is founded
On the culture of hard labour?'
Thus she began to appease him!

'Mandodari is a venerable, virtuous wife.
She is so pious that she deserves
To be remembered reverentially at day-break. 130
She has always appreciated the valour of Lankesha.
Condemning the vileness of falling for someone else's wife
And suffering the lassitude,
She stands as the icon of tolerance.
She is caught up in *dharmasankata* –
The hardship of choosing between the two equally valid,
But mutually conflicting issues.
She is engrossed in the task of leading her husband in the path
Of righteousness without causing any lapses in *dharma*!

'Why to suffer pain on account of Janaki's abduction? 140
Why do you spend the nights sleeplessly thus,
Having committed that great sin?
Due to the trouble of sleeplessness,
And suffering pain in the heart,
You have lost the balance of equanimity
Like a boat with the torn out sail.
This is highly vexatious.
How would you bear this, my lord?'

'Lanka is burnt, isn't it?
Humiliation has tormented my heart. 150
The Mansion of Love is burnt to ashes, Isn't it?
I will win the battle. Why do you fear?'
Lankesha said so.

The beautiful lady said:
'Lanka is burnt externally; *dharma* is burnt within.

What if Lanka is burnt? It could be built again.
If *dharma* is burnt, the whole world will be burnt to ashes, listen.
If the power of *dharma* resides in you,
What harm Rama, or anyone else can do?
But if *dharma* becomes lax, where would I be, 160
And where would you be?
On that day, how beautifully you sang the metrical *Sama*!
How well did you explain the path of *dharma* and destiny!
Then, why do you move on sacrificing *dharma* today?
My mind is in pain, and my heart is full of sorrow.
Other than you, who else is there to preserve Lanka!'

'What shall I say, my dear wife?
The guilty conscience is tormenting me every day.
Ravana is dead already; he is only a living corpse now.
When my deformed sister with her chopped off ears and nose 170
Stands before me, I sink low in the pond of sorrow.
I am burning hard with anguish and anger
In the whirlpool of *dharmasankata*.
Other than you, who else would offer me refuge?
As my sister is meted out with the punishment even worse than
   the slaves,
I abducted Janaki only in retaliation to that.'

Mandodari said:
'Why do you have the debasing idea of revenge?
It is an emotional aberration; it diminishes the national fame.
Do not forget that, O king! I beg of you humbly. 180
Fame outlives the mortal body – may you live like that.
Lift up Sita with the arms of *dharma*
And hand her over to Raghava with that affection
As if she were your daughter.
At that very instant, Kailasa, Shiva's abode shall descend to Lanka, look!
Everybody will sing your praise then.
This alone is *daivasampada* – the well-earned, blessed wealth.
Thus, may you live forever!'

'Do not be afraid, my wife.
By continuous Quest, today I will forge the radiance   190
Of the sun with the power of *tapasya*.
If not seen, I will create another sun.
In the radiance of the divine fire of valour,
I shall seek the glory of the sun.'
When Ravana spoke thus, the virtuous wife said:

'Let victory be to you.
I have happily bathed in the pond of your fame.
Like the *mandara* flower, my mind is gleaming bright.
O my beloved, indeed you are greater than diamond.
Mother Earth has the power to turn the ordinary thing   200
That is within her into diamond.
Similarly, you are endowed with the power and capacity
To create extraordinary things!

'Just as the lava, springing up from the womb of the ocean,
Creates a new island, you are endowed with the great power of creation.
As the abode of golden Lanka is Heaven in wealth, O my lord,
You must grow the fruits of eternal life with the water of pure emotions.
As humility imparts grandeur to valour, why do you step back?
Accept Rama!'

'O *priyabhashini* – the one who speaks endearingly – listen!   210
Discard the sorrowful words.
Play the lute of Vani, the Goddess of Learning – for a while.
Let the melody of music flow to quench the tired mind.
As my body is burning in fire now,
Cause the melody to flow in my veins.
You are well-versed in the ways of the world,
And quite a courageous one too.
Even if the sky falls down, even if the earth explodes,
Even if the mountains move about,
And let all the oceans join and turn the world upside down,   220

And let the whole world tremble,
I shall not give away Janaki!

'Would anyone forget the vow?
Appeasing my valour, you have forged a bond
Of love between *Patala* and this earth.
In order to place the ladder of valour to the sky, get up now,'
  said Ravana.
Then, 'O the Supreme Lord! Protect my husband,'
So saying, and suffering the affliction,
Mandodari, with her eyes closed, was engrossed in deep mediation.

Canto One Hundred and Seventy-one

'Truth and Fame are all Dharma-centric'

||☉||

'O the valorous heroes listen!
An ordinary *vanara* entered Lanka and committed amazing deeds.
He caused Lanka to suffer the grief.
Now, think well and tell me what the appropriate course of action is.
Tell me only the most effective path.
This secret meeting is summoned
Solely for this consultation and counsel.'
Ravana said so.
He, who sets out to accomplish the task,
By inviting suggestions from his well-meaning ministers and friends,   10
Accepts them after thorough consultations,
And moves ahead seeking divine blessings, is the best on earth.
He, who does not consult others, thinks for himself,
And sets out to accomplish the task reposing faith
In divine interventions, is considered mediocre.
He who does not discuss the pros and cons,
And sets out to accomplish the task beaming with conceit,
Unmindful of divine grace, is the wretched on earth.

'The decision taken jointly
By the ministers by consensus in accordance with the set procedures   20

And the rule of law, is rated the best in the world.
Even when there is dissension in deciding on the task,
The decision that is taken harmoniously, creating unity
Among all involved, is considered mediocre.
Harping on dissension and continuing argument on that count,
If trust and consensus do not emerge still,
Such a one is considered the most despicable.

'Rama would be coming now.
By all means, he would cross the ocean;
There is not the slightest doubt in it.   30
The highly valorous Saumitri is with him;
He would employ all his strength and diplomacy on a grand scale.
The war would be imminent and challenging too.
Are there any other ways?
An intense consultation that examines all options –
Both suitable and unsuitable – before arriving at a decision
Is indeed the base on which war is fought.
Before the enemy arrives,
How to device the appropriate war strategy
To combat and safeguard our position –   40
Tell me all these in great detail.
If we delay further,
It would cause us much greater harm,' said Ravana.

Folding his hands in supplication,
Aniruddha *rakshasa* said:
'O king! I make this submission respectfully:
There are the blockheads in this world
Who are not aware of the essence of royal diplomacy.
Without knowing in the least what is their strength,
And the strength of their enemy, they device the strategy   50
Of lowering the morale by frightening the enemy.
Are there any who succumb to it?
Weapons such as *parigha, pattisa, shula* –
Iron club; spear with sharp edge, and lance –

Are aplenty with us. When the enemy-army is ready to charge,
Why should we worry; why should we waver?
You have invaded *Patala*, the nether world
And conquered Bhogavati, the Ganga of *Patala*.
At the Kailasa-peak, you have won the *yakshas*
In severe wrestling and brought them here imprisoned.   60
Kubera himself has surrendered to you and gave you *Pushpaka*.
Maya, the *danava*-king, trembling in fear by your valour,
And as a gesture of friendship offered you
His daughter in marriage, and fostered your relationship,
Which is now popular as a heroic story.
You have crushed the *danava* known as Madhu.
You have defeated Kumbinasi's beloved.
You have reigned in the valorous heroes
Like Vasuki, Takshaka, and Shankajata.
You battled heroically with the Kalakeyas for a year   70
And held them captive. There is none to counter your valour.
You have gained victory over Devendra, and Varuna.
Would you ever care for Rama, or such others?
Wouldn't Indrajit alone wipe out all the *vanaras*!

'When the eleven Rudras, the twelve Adityas,
Along with the seven Marutas and the eight Vasus
Roared like tigers, and all the *chaturangabala*
Was beyond counting, and was spread
Like ocean all over, Meghanada had captured Indra
And brought him dragging along – this heroic story is well-known.   80
Meghanada alone is enough; why anybody else is required here?
He will kill the army of *vanaras* and throw their bodies away.'
Praising thus, Aniruddha sat down!

Prahasta, the commander,
Who looked like the fiercely destructive dark clouds, said:
'Among the *devas*, *danavas*, *pishachas*, and the serpents,
Who could counter you?
Hanuma deceived us; we stumbled then for want of adequate
    attention.

Give me orders; I shall efface the entire *vanara*-clan from
This earth that stretches unto the ocean in such a way 90
That wherever one searches none shall be sighted.
Trust my words.
I shall protect Lanka in such a way
That the offence committed by Hanuma shall not be repeated.'

Durmukha said:
'A *vanara* came here and provoked the valorous heroes.
Entering the harem, the *vanara* gloried in impudence.
We are shameless. Give me orders.
Even if the *vanara* have leaped to the sky, or descended to *Patala*,
I shall kill them all and demonstrate my valour.' 100

At that instant, Vajradamashtra,
Lifting up the iron club soaked in blood, said:
Hanuma is a coward; he sneaked in like a thief.
Should such evil ones, and the cunning tricksters, be spared?
I alone shall swirl up the *vanara*-army.
With my iron club, I will hit hard Rama, Lakshmana,
Sugriva, and all the others; and swiftly I will return safe.
Also, I will play a trick on them:
'O Raghunatha, look there!
I am the messenger of Bharata; 110
Now you must return to Ayodhya swiftly;
A great task has to be done; a mishap has occurred;'
if I say so,

At that very instant, Shri Rama,
Leaving the *vanara*-army behind,
Would rush in great haste towards Ayodhya.
Then, I will fall upon the
Vanara-army with my sharp-edged spear and many other weapons,
And send them to Yamapuri – the abode of death.
With such clever tricks, I will crush them, look' 120
Thus he spoke proudly of his valour.

With great fury, Nikumbha,
The son of Kumbhakarna, roared aloud:
'I shall slay Rama and Saumitri singlehandedly
And return victorious.'
On hearing that, Rabhasa, Suryashatru, Mahodara,
Agniketu, Suptaghna, Yajnaha, Mahaparshwa,
And Rashmisetu, and so also,
Indrajit, Atikaya, Dhumraksha, Durmukha, Vajradamshtra
And all the other *rakshasas* stood brandishing swords,   130
Lances, axes, iron clubs, spears, arrows,
And such other fierce weapons!

'Why to delay now?
Go and kill Rama, Saumitri, Sugriva,
And the entire *vanara*-clan and return swiftly hence.
Kill Hanuma, the fickle *vanara*
Who has burnt down Lanka, and return swiftly hence.'
As Ravana said so,
The *rakshasas*, carrying their weapons on the shoulders,
Made ready to leave. But Vibhishana stopped them,   140
And requesting them to be seated,
Humbly said thus with folded hands:

'O valorous heroes, listen!
Without properly employing the strategies
Of *sama*, *dana*, and *bheda*,
If we rush to act in haste, it is bad for the success
Of our mission. Indulging in the comforts of lust,
And thus guilty of not being on our guard,
And without divine blessings,
Why should we proclaim now the glory of our valour?   150
Is Shri Rama engrossed in lustful indulgence?
As he is desirous of victory, he has come fully prepared.
He has not come insolently enraged.
It is not possible to guess how valorous the enemies are.
Look at Hanuma!

He has crossed the ocean; and burnt down Lanka.
He has returned to his camp without even a hair being bent.
Has Rama committed any offence? The fault lies with us.
Why did he abduct Janaki from Janasthana
And brought her here? 160

'Look at Khara's fate.
With arrogant pride, as he went to fight on his own,
Shri Rama restrained him.
Could Rama be faulted for this?
You have touched somebody else's wife vilely;
You have disgraced yourself.
All your *punya* is lost and your life-span diminished.
Does anyone give invitation to war foolhardily?
Before the valorous *vanara*-army invades the golden Lanka
And destroys everything, 170
Give away Maithili.
I humbly implore you; stop the war.
Should we employ divine weapons
For killing someone without reasons?
The fury that destroys truth and *dharma* is
Like the scorching autumn sun.
Truth and fame are all *dharma*-centric.'
As Vibhishana said thus,
Ignoring the good counsel, and abruptly winding up
The private consultation, Ravana went away in silence. 180

Canto One Hundred and Seventy-two

'The King of Saketa is the Symbol of Perfection'

||६||

Not abandoning his mission
Of offering good counsel to his brother,
And trying again and again to bring him back
To the path of *dharma*,
On the following day at sunrise Vibhishana came
To the royal court that had assembled in all grandeur.

The cool breeze was blowing gently.
The sound of *Om* emanating from the conches,
And the resonant sound of various musical instruments
Filled the place. On the way to the courtyard,
The beautiful damsels were engaged in happy conversations.
In grandeur, the place looked like Bhogavati.
On seeing Dashashira seated on the throne –
'O emperor, let victory be yours' – greeting him thus
Vibhishana sat on the seat shown by the brother!

Many discussions were being held there;
The war-trumpet was sounded,
And as all stood ready on their toes highly excited,

Vibhishana got up and said humbly thus:
'Forgive me, O brother! 20
My mind is tormented. War is not proper.
Building the bridge of friendship among nations is the right
    dharma;
Why to afflict others? Why to wish others bad?
To treat even the enemy like a friend, is the right *dharma*!

'O Ravaneshwara, listen!
From the day that you have brought Janaki to this city,
Many kinds of bad omens are attacking us continually.
Burning embers appear in the heap of ashes;
A cobra freely moves about in the kitchen;
Cow-milk has dried up in the udder; 30
Elephants look at horses pitiably;
A crow is crowing in a harsh voice;
Vultures circle the sky;
Jackals howl looking at the sky;
Dogs cry barking hoarsely.
War is not proper, O king!'

'Exploitation has increased.
Anarchy has spread. There is a split in the army.
How would you motivate them to fight with valour, I do not know.
Where is justice and ethics? Where is the welfare of the people? 40
A void is filling up Lanka and is afflicting it.
The king of Saketa is the symbol of perfection.
War is not proper, O king!' He said thus.

'Enough, enough. Stop speaking.
I do not care for bad omens or whatever.
You have given enough advice; I know it all.
I am not afraid. I am ready for the war.
I never cared for the army of Devaraja;
Would I be now scared of ordinary mortals – Rama and Lakshmana!
I will crush them all and throw them into the ocean.' 50
Thus Ravana thundered aloud.

As it was time for the secret private consultation,
Terminating the meeting,
Ravana got into the chariot and moved away.
The valorous heroes gathered there followed Ravana
Brandishing their weapons – maces, iron clubs, lances, and such others.
The procession moved ahead thus.

Musical instruments were being played.
Pure crystals, white *chowries*, symbol of princely rank;
And the white royal-parasol that was as radiant as the full moon –   60
Were all looking grand.
The trumpeting of the royal elephant was heard loud.
The sound of victory-greetings was continually heard there.
As the people of the city stood on either side
With their heads respectfully bent down,
Ravana arrived at the chamber of private consultation.
Ascending the royal seat,

He called for the messengers and said:
'Summon the ministers and the chieftains at once.
To decide on the strength of Lanka,   70
Send for the counsellors immediately.
Proclaim to all the exciting news
That war has been declared.'

As the messengers went and informed the dignitaries,
They came to the meeting swiftly riding chariots,
And mounted on horses and elephants.
As they saluted the king with humility, Ravaneshwara,
Welcoming them with respect,
Offered them appropriate seats.
Vibhishana came swiftly riding the chariot,   80
And touched the feet of his elder brother as a mark of respect,
And with utmost humility
Occupied the seat gestured by the king!

Looking at the face
Of Kumbhakarna in that full house,
Rakshasendra – the lord of the *rakshasas*, said:
'Dasharatha's sons – Rama and Lakshmana –
Have planned to cross over the vast ocean!
Even before that, the *vanara* had created havoc here.
The heart of Lanka itself was shaken. Such an evil task shall not
  be forgotten. 90
You are a valorous hero. You shall emerge grandly victorious
In the tumultuous war.'

Kumbhakarna quickly said thus:
'Knowing the whereabouts of Janaki,
Rama and Saumitri have come.
An army of the *vanara* is with them.
Thinking on the means of crossing over the ocean,
They stand in waiting there.
Tell me, would it be easy for us to gain victory.
Did you consult us while abducting Sita? 100
You reap the fruit of your own wrong-doing now.
You forgot the princely duties.
You forgot what is right and what is wrong.
Overcome by lust, look what you have done.
Alas, you were insolent!
The enemy is powerful indeed.
Nevertheless, as you are my elder brother,
And as the time for destruction of the *rakshasa*-clan is nearing,
Pledging my own life,
I shall fight for the safety of the clan. 110

'The vicious hour has come.
What if Indra, Surya, Agni, Vayu, Kubera, Varuna,
Or any such others come invading!
I will fight courageously.

'When I am armed with the sharp-edged spear,
Devendra fears me. I will not spare Rama.

If he shoots one pointed arrow at me,
Before the second arrow hits me,
I shall slay him for sure.
I will suck out his blood. Would I count Saumitri? 120
I will eat him up. I will wipe out rest of the *vanaras*.
Stop worrying now.' As he said so,
Ravana's face went pale.

Mahaparshwa, the minister said:
'As soon as one enters the forest,
If one gets honey, but does not taste it,
Such a one is a fool indeed!
You are a renowned enemy-destroyer.
Who could stop you now? It is well beyond Shiva too.
The time to take recourse to the strategy of *sama*, and *dana* is over. 130
Now proceed with the strategy of *danda* or punishment
If you could accomplish the task successfully thus –
'The strategy of *danda* is appropriate for accomplishing the task' –
This would be well-known as your new axiom of success.
On that day at Mithila, Janaki was the reward for Rama's valour;
Today at Lanka, she is the reward for Ravana's valour.
Would Rama, the coward, get her now!
You are truly valorous.' Thus he praised Ravana.

Beaming with ecstasy, Ravana said:
'Bravo, Mahaparshwa! 140
I am pleased by your words.
I tell you a secret. On a war-expedition then,
I saw a celestial nymph called Punjikasthala.
Enamoured by her fire-crest like beauty,
I forced myself on her. Like a lotus torn from the creeper,
She reached *Brahmaloka* and stood there in silence!
As I slowly realised what had happened, and how,
Lord Brahma cursed me thus:
"If you make love to damsels by force,
May death befall you." 150

Like a tempest, the power of a dutiful wife is afflicting me.
Would I have spared Janaki otherwise?
Fearing death, I remain away from her.

'Rama is ignorant.
He does not know the depth and range of my powers.
He has provoked the hungry lion in the den.
A sharp arrow that hisses like a venomous serpent would
Strike him like lightning; Rama is not aware of this.
Like the lighted torches cause fear in the mammoth elephant,
I shall blow out the trembling Rama.
As the stars stand dull losing their brilliance at sunrise,   160
Rama will stand pale in front of my radiance.
Let Sahasraksha – Devendra, the thousand-eyed one – come,
Or Varuna rush in,
I shall not bend down in the battlefield.'
Ravana roared thus.

Canto One Hundred and Seventy-three

'Venomous Foetus is Afloat in the Womb of Earth'

||๑||

Having heard everybody speak, the highly eminent Vibhishana,
Discarding the placatory exaggeration of high-sounding praises,
And looking straight in the face of Ravana,
With courage, spoke of the truth of reality thus:

'O emperor, listen!
Sita is a female-serpent which you have tied round your neck.
Remember, her tender body is the body of a serpent.
Listen, Sita is the affliction, which itself is the serpent-venom.
Her long, slender fingers are the hoods of that serpent.
Look, her smile is the fierce fangs.   10
Why do you die in vain; give her up!

'Before Shri Rama and Saumitri invade Lanka,
Give away Janaki. Before all the lightning-arrows come
Striking with great speed and cut off the heads of the *rakshasas*,
Send Maithili to Shri Rama.
There in the battlefield, in front of Rama,
There is neither Kumbhakarna, nor even Indrajit, or Mahaparshwa,
Nor Mahodara, Kumbha, Nikumbha, Atikaya,
And none else stands; everyone would die!

When Surya, Maruta
And such others are not the lords of Rama,
Where would you hide?
Even if you hide in *Patala*, it is not safe.
Do not cut off the roots of freedom-culture.
Walking haphazardly, do not crush the flowers.
Mount Trikuta is burning as the poison of love of war is rising.
Having performed one hundred *yagas*,
You are an accomplished harbinger;
Beware; you shall be the sacrificial lamb for the final *yaga*.
Rama stands beyond the visible ocean;
He is indeed the formless Brahma;
Now he has appeared in human form!

'Shri Ramachandra has shed his innocence
Of childhood in slaying Tataki.
He has spent the time of his exciting youth
In the sorrow of *vanavasa* – dwelling in the forest.
Now, firmly resolved to take Sita back with him,
He stands in the vacuity where the earth meets the sky.
You trust only strength, power, and cruelty.
You have cast away humanity and justice into the valley.
You have drowned the character – our national wealth – in the ocean.
The citizens are lamenting questioning the propriety of this war.
You have forgotten the *mantra* of unity!'

In great conceit, Prahasta said:
'Do you think that we are all a cowardly flock of sheep?
We will not bend down whether they are *yakshas*,
pannagas, *gandharvas*, or whosoever they may be!
In Lanka, there are not people who have seen even the shadow of fear.
Would we ever care for Rama,
Or anyone else like him?'

Hearing the words of the vicious people,
And feeling sad, Vibhishana said:

'O Prahasta, it does not befit you to speak lightly thus!
Do not ever push Lankesha, Mahodara, Kumbhakarna
And all others to the edge of destruction.
In front of Shri Rama – whether it is Ravana, Kumbhakarna,
Indrajit, Trishira, Akampana, or Nikumbha and others –
All would be defeated.
When a thousand-hooded venomous serpent coils
Encircling Ravana tightening its grip,
He will succumb to its poison; 60
You will not be able to save him then.
Would it be fair to push him to the abyss of *Patala* thus, O listen!
As ministers, you must advice the king that does him good!
Without judging properly the strengths of both the parties,
Without understanding the possible losses and gains,
And without comparing what is similar and what is not,
Do not give harmful counsel!

'O king! You are the elder brother of Kubera.
Why have you cultivated enmity with Rama?
The time to mend your ways slips past. 70
Beware, O king, beware!
Would anyone desert ethics thus for the sake of fleeting desire?
Do not be caught in the alluring web of *karma*.'

Vibhishana, the crest-jewel of the Paulatsya clan,
Is indeed devoutly loyal to the king.
His soul is yearning and grieving.
The fire of rebellion is growing stronger in his mind;
But there is none to support, and none to share.
What accomplishment can there be in mere wishing?
If there is no power of sacrifice, everything will be barren. 80
He is greatly intelligent; he is Brihaspati –
The celestial teacher in wisdom;
Nevertheless, there is none to support Vibhishana!

Indrajit heard the words of Vibhishana.
He thundered in anger:

'Uncle dear, stop at once!
Why this cowardliness?
Would anyone from the Paulatsya clan speak thus?
Would anyone speak thus giving up one's self-esteem?
We have dragged Indra himself down to this earth and imprisoned
   him;   90
We have pounded Iravata and as it roared in pain, pushed it away;
We have tamed completely the pride of the celestial beings;
We have reigned in all the renowned valorous heroes and ruled over.
Rama and Saumitari are just ordinary princes;
We do not care for them; we do not reckon them at all!'

'O Meghanada, listen!
You are truly a valorous hero;
Even so, you do not know the heroic deeds
Of Shri Rama and Lakshmana.
Open the eyes of discernment at once.   100
Do not be like an enemy to your own father.
Prevent the total destruction at once.'
Thus Vibhishana offered him good counsel.

Then, looking at Ravana, Vibhishana said:
'How will you face the sharp arrows of Raghava?
How will you win over Rama, the Kalagni Rudra –
Shiva regarded as the fire of ultimate destruction of this world?
Rama is the primordial Brahma; how will you face him?
Rama is the primordial Vishnu; how will you fight him?
Rama is the primordial Rudra; how will you win over him?   110
Give up your stubbornness;
Prevent the destruction of the Paulatsya clan.
Being a devotee of Shiva,
And well-versed in all branches of learning,
Would you behave like a senseless man, tell me, please!
First, through your messengers, gather intelligence
About the enemy's strength;
After that, decide for yourself
Would it be proper to wage a war or not!

In order to win over Shri Rama,   120
Do you have within you the required will-power,
The forces to combat, and the resoluteness of mind, tell me.
Your mind is now polluted.
Your will-power and physical strength are now diminished.
Your sense of discretion of what is proper and what is not, is now lost.
The strength of Lanka itself has now shrivelled.
The strength of *dharma* and truth has now bitten the dust.
Look, your obduracy is now the root-cause of total destruction!

'If you feel ashamed to hand over Janaki,
Leave it to me; I will go there myself.   130
When we hand Janaki over to Shri Rama,
He would forgive all our wrong-doings.
When that *vanara* entered Lanka all alone and caused havoc,
Where was the heroic army?
What happened to the valorous warriors?
Do not be fooled by the vainglorious words of the flatterers
And be ruined!' Thus Vibhishana said.

'It is possible to live together with one's enemy;
It is possible to live trusting an enraged serpent;
But it is impossible to live with a sibling and secret enemy   140
Like you who speaks in favour of the enemy-camp.
Would a *dayadi* – the rival heir – tolerate the glory of the other sibling?
He would dance with joy when the other one is in trouble;
Without opening up his heart in kinship,
He would wish the highest treason;
And he would inflict anxiety most cruelly.

'We have no fear of fire and weapons;
There is no fear of being caught by a net; no fear of lions either;
But look! Here is a rogue born to the clan of *dayadi* –
The one who has joined the humans and got accustomed to their ways;   150

This *dayadi*, though born of the elephant clan, betrays us;
We are afraid of him,' –
On seeing the hunters in the Padmavana-forest
Feeling sad, thus the wild elephants seemed to have said once!
Same thing has happened to me now;
I am caught in the cruelty of *dayadi*-jealousy;
I have no desire to live.

'You have not understood me.
I stand strong crushing the enemy-head;
You can not tolerate that, listen! 160
Your behaviour and attitude is like the water droplet
That does not stick to the lotus-leaf on which it falls.
Like the bee that flies away after sucking the nectar of a flower,
You have become selfish.
Like the elephant that splashes dust on itself after bathing well,
You are causing destruction to your own clan.
Fie to you, the destroyer of the clan!
Had anybody else spoken thus, would I have spared them?
Sucking away their life, I would have pushed them far.
But my affection for you as a brother prevents me.' 170
Thus roared Ravana in great fury.

In a very sober mood, Vibhishana said:
'I agree that you have the power.
Nevertheless, it is not proper for the king
To act as he pleases and revel in glory unrestrained!
There is not that kind of a dictum in the rule of sovereign governance.
It is but inevitable for the king to understand the pulse of the people
And respond accordingly.'
Unable to bear these words of Vibhishana,
Brandishing his sword, Indrajit roared thus: 180
'Stop, you traitor! Enough, and scream no more.
As you have spoken thus in the royal court,
Severe torturous punishment awaits you now.'

In extreme anguish, Vibhishana said:
'Lanka is dear to me; you too are dear to me O brother, hear me!
It is my duty to protect both of you.
I beseech you again and again; do not wage a war.
Do not ruin the fame and the kingdom.
I am not afraid of you; none can restrain me.
Even if they desire to kill me 190
By humiliating me as a coward and a traitor,
I have forgiven the children,
And have restrained myself with patience.

'I shall not stay back in Lanka.
I am duty-bound to protect you;
I will take leave of you now.
I am not a traitor; nor am I weak.
I am not the one to cut off the tree of patriotism.
I am not the one to crush the flower of brotherly love.
It is my sacred duty to save you, hear me. 200
It is my sacred duty to preserve the clan, look here.
It is my sacred duty to save Lanka, hear me.
It is my sacred duty to prevent the war, look here.
You are spreading violence and it will swallow you up!
If you destroy the light of life in others,
Finally, your own light will burn bright for a while
And then be extinguished.
What can be achieved through violence?
We can not survive.
Only the reign of love is the *mantra* – 210
The sacred incantation that can save us!

'Is there any saving grace for us?
If we employ the natural powers in the path of essential goodness
Science shall bloom and become the light of the world.
But if such powers are employed in the path of wickedness,
It shall push us down to *Patala*.
The vital air in the atmosphere has turned poisonous

And is blowing thus.
Venomous foetus is afloat in the womb of earth.
Every tiny speck of Bharata is an atom in Lanka. 220
The blood coursing in our veins is the pure water of this land.
Do not disturb the peace of this land,
And do not provoke unnecessarily.
Shri Ramachandra is supreme bliss indeed!

'You have the freedom.
O emperor, listen! You are my elder brother.
You have the power to say anything that pleases you.
Would anyone desert the path of *dharma*, and thus remain
    shameless?
Desiring your welfare, I have spoken harshly.
Caught in the current of fate, we have lost our senses. 230
Why should you be killed by Rama's arrow!
By giving Sita away, forge friendship instead!'
Thus Vibhishana said repeatedly.

Hissing with fury, the enraged Indrajit said:
'What did you say? Why have you forgotten the heroic tradition
By which one becomes the lord of all the riches won through the
    battles?
It is not proper to hand over Sita, the jewel among women.
She is not a mere woman; she is an empress.
If we win her, it is like winning the Aryavarta –
The entire land of the Aryans. 240
As a reward for this valour, the entire land
Of Bharata shall fall under Lanka's sovereign rule;
Are you such a blockhead not to be aware of this!'
Unable to bear such harsh words that cut like diamond,
And not being afraid in the least, Vibhishana said thus:
'Though you are son to me in kinship,
You have become a secret enemy now.
You have become afflicted with the heady lure of power.
It is my misfortune to see with my own eyes the destruction of
    Lanka

By Saumitri's arrows. How could anyone live being tied up 250
With a venomous serpent round one's neck?
Rama and Lakshmana are endowed with such powerful arrows
That are strong like diamonds, capable of flying across oceans,
And those that can even reach the solar orbit.
I do not understand how you will win over them.'

'You are an evil-monger,'
Saying thus, as the enraged Ravana came rushing
With his sword drawn out, the warriors stopped him!
'The harsh words that you have spoken are
Burning me. Get out of here at once! 260
How dare you insult me, the one renowned
As the hero in all the three worlds!
What evil has befallen you?
Today, the kinship of our brotherhood by blood is severed.'
Roaring thus, Ravana swiftly went out of the royal court!

Canto One Hundred and Seventy-four

'Be the Protector of Dharma and the Torch-bearer of Truth'

||௬||

It was an auspicious day in the hermitage of Sage Vishravasu.
Peace was reigning supreme all over.
Like a carpet, greenery was spread everywhere.
Fragrant flowers like oleander,
Jasmine, *champaka* were in full bloom.
Deer and antelopes were happily chewing the cud
With their eyes closed.
As the initiated-youth were performing *yajna*,
The God of Fire was burning bright there!

Kaikasi was deeply engrossed worrying about something. 10
Seeing her sad face, Ravana and the others asked their mother:
'What sadness afflicts you, O mother?
When we are there – your brave and valorous children –
Why should you shed tears!
Seeing your grief, our blood is boiling.
Give up your worrisome agitation. Wipe your tears.
Tell us right away the cause of your worry!'

On hearing the words of her children, and sighing hard,
Kaikasi said thus in great anguish:

'Have you seen Kubera revelling in the luxury of great riches?   20
Sumali is my father. He should be the ruler indeed.
He is the emperor, and the lord of fortune and wealth.
But what is the use of it all?
Kubera is revelling in the grandeur of Lanka!
As the anguish is burning within me, who could I say this to?
I wash my hands in copious tears,
And am drowned in the ocean of grief.'

Bouncing up in fury,
Ravana comforted the mother thus:
'I have realised the true state of affairs now. I will not sit quiet.   30
I will cause the earth tremble and shrink.
By becoming the pre-eminent emperor,
I will cause the retinue of Kubera serve me humbly.
I will hoist the flag of glory high.'

'I am fortunate.
Tapasya – profound contemplation – is the source of all knowledge.
My son, now you proceed to achieve that.
If you could gain control and knowledge of warfare
And weaponry and become adept in them,
And secure god's blessings too,   40
You will win the entire world.
The path of sacrifice has enjoyment
Of all comforts as its true reward;
Do not forget that.'
Said the mother in great joy.

'You have opened the door of knowledge for me.
Darkness has been dispelled; the dark clouds have dispersed;
And the thick fog has melted away.
I will seek a quiet place to perform *tapasya*
And gain knowledge by diligent pursuit.   50
We will come back thus equipped,
And you will see that we will dethrone Dhanada – Kubera –
And steadfastly establish empire of the *danavas*, for sure.'
Ravana said thus resolutely.

Ravana, and Kumbhakarna,
And so also Vibhishana, went together swiftly
And stood there performing *tapasya*.
Having gained power and strength, the brothers,
Haughty with their triumph, returned happily.

Sumali, the father of Kaikasi, said: 60
'I am caught in the blaze of Kubera's wickedness.
I am compelled to live incognito thus. I can not win.
'I shall annihilate the *rakshasa* clan itself,'
He has vowed thus. Having been defeated very badly,
I live in *Nagaloka* – the land of the serpents, in hiding.
I heard the news of your arrival and felt happy.
You are pre-eminently valorous indeed.
Lift up the *rakshasa* clan and make it stand firm.
Why should you be living in the hermitage?
Ascend the the royal throne in grandeur, 70
And ruling over Lanka, bring the progeny of Kubera down.
Set out on a war-expedition forthwith.'

Ravana, the one who loved Lanka, said:
'Yes, I agree with you. I shall not rest contented.
O grandfather, why should you be living incognito?
I would see you living in grandeur in Lanka.
I will eradicate the suffering endured by the people of our clan.
O Prahasta, go now and tell Kubera thus:
'Return the kingdom of the *danavas*;
This is the order of Ravana.' 80

Protesting against that speech,
Vibhishana candidly said:
'O brother, what is it that you are doing? Is Kubera a stranger?
He is our elder brother; we are all born to the same father;
Do not act in haste.'
As Vibhishana was giving good counsel thus,
Ravana taunted him saying,
'When he is ruling over our kingdom

Having abducted it unlawfully,
Should we bear with our *dayadi*, tell me! 90
Death is better than living without self-respect.'
Saying thus, Ravana, quite excited with the prospect
Of a war-expedition, arrived at Lanka.

Feeling depressed, Vibhishana said to Vishravasu:
'Caught in the lure of kingdom, Ravana is ruined.
I will stay at the hermitage itself and serve you.
O father, when Ravana treads wrong path,
How could I live happily and prosper at Lanka!
I will stay in the thatched-hut and spend my days in meditation.
Why to get soaked in the well of injustice and sink low? 100
Would anyone get caught thus in the whirl of darkness knowingly!
Would I subject myself to the riches and comforts
And the unbridled life of the golden Lanka!
As Kubera rules justly following the tenets of *dharma*,
Should I nurture Ravana who treads the path of violence
And strike a note of discord!

'O father, hear me again.
Why should the most powerful Ravana need Lanka?
He has the power to build another empire.
Why to take Lanka by force and why to transgress *dharma*? 110
How would I live with a brother such as this one?
There is the council of wicked ministers who advice wrongly.
How would I bear such a thing?
My life has become a puzzle now.'

Stroking affectionately the son
Who had respectfully bowed down to touch his father's feet,
Vishravasu said:
'Why do you have this depression?
Why do you have such maddening thoughts?
Why do you wish to live in the hermitage? It is not proper for you. 120
You are the protector of *dharma*.
This kind of a saying is not proper for you.

Would anyone get engrossed in meditation forgetting one's
  stately *dharma*?
When Kubera has run away deserting Lanka,
There still have remained a few people who think and act righteously.
If ill-treatment increases, such good people will desert Lanka
And they will surely perish.

'Therefore, I tell you –
Be the protector of *dharma*, and the torch-bearer of truth
And holding the umbrella of *dharma* high, 130
Do such acts by which the good people could live fearlessly.

'Spread the grandeur of truth and *dharma* in Lanka.
Make the stream of love and affection flow unobstructed in Lanka.
Dispel the darkness of evil. Lanka is like a prized gem.
Good people are there in Lanka, O hear me.
If you fail in this, you forge ahead in a new path.
You have love for your brother. I appreciate your heroism.
Who else but you could bring him back on the path of righteousness?'

Like the gentle breeze,
The words spoken by his father soothed him and dispelled his
  ignorance. 140
'I will dwell in Lanka. I will steadfastly sail ahead in the
Boat of volition determined to fulfill all your wishes.
Even if the Quest of *dharma* becomes futile,
I will seek the path that suits me and move ahead.'
Thus saying, he respectfully bowed and touched his father's feet.

Lifting up Vibhishana and stroking him affectionately,
Vishravasu said shedding tears of joy:
'You are dear to me indeed. Let benediction be to you.
Dharma protects them who protect *dharma*.
Let there be victory; may it be auspicious; 150
And let there be benediction for all.
Blessing his son thus, Vishravasu bid him farewell,
And was deeply engrossed in meditation.

Recollecting all such past incidents again and again,
Vibhishana, feeling very sad, told unto himself,
'O is it my plight to be thus ordained!
I have not been able to bring back my brother
Who has deviated from the path of *dharma*.
I have not been able to nurture the good people.'
Vibhishana was caught in *dharmasankata* – 160
The dilemma of deciding between two equal,
But mutually contradictory courses of action,
And the noble man was thus afflicted!

Canto One Hundred and Seventy-five

'Lay Down Life to Protect the Nation'

||௬||

As his mind was disturbed on hearing
The harsh words spoken by his brother
In the chamber of secret consultation,
Vibhishana was worried:
'What next? What else?
What wrong meanings my words might have generated?'
Continuing with such worrisome thoughts –
'In order to save my elder brother, in order to change his mind,
And in order to protect Lanka, as another attempt yet again,
I will go to mother Kaikasi forthwith' – he went out swiftly.   10
On seeing the pale face of her noble son, the queen-mother asked:
'What is the matter, my son, tell me; do not be afraid.'

'What shall I say, O mother!
My plight is quite distressing.
I do not know what Lanka's plight is.
I am afraid that I may lose the favour of serving you.
As the bad ethics of my elder brother is ruining Lanka,
Where shall I go? I thought that by succumbing to Rama's arrow,
I will cast away this mortal body here in Lanka itself;
But my brother does not allow that as he has ordered me –   20

'Do not remain in Lanka; do not stay in my presence' –
When asked, "Why do you need the wife of Rama
Who is a staunch follower of *dharma*?"
My brother abuses me angrily.
I will go to Shri Ramachandra forthwith and beseech him –

"Grant Lankesha-Ravana the gift of life as a favour" –
To this end, O mother, I set forth now,'
Saying thus, as Vibhishana respectfully touched his mother's feet,
Embracing him tight, Kaikasi said:
'Wait, my son, and be patient.
You are the eminent son of the family. 30
I will dissipate the misery that you are suffering
By soliciting your brother earnestly,
And also the danger that lurks Lanka.
Do not lament; do not be afflicted.
Won't he honour my words?
I will unite the two of you in the kinship of brotherhood.'
Sobbing and shedding tears, Kaikasi said so.

There, Ravana was engrossed
In secret consultation with his favourite ministers.
As Kaikasi rushed in greatly agitated, 40
Ravana got up from his seat and saluting her with respect,
And offering her a befitting seat, asked in a jeering tone:
'What brings you here, at this odd hour, O mother?
Has your loving son Vibhishana sent you here, tell me, mother.'

'Whoever the sender is, what does it matter?
You are my loving son. Why won't I come on my own?
Though monarch of the three worlds, you are a blessed son to
the mother.
Kumbhakarna is an extraordinarily strong son;
In this world, who else can equal Vibhishana in *dharma*?
I am an unfortunate mother now. 50
How could you think of severing the umbilical cord
And throwing it away?

Would anyone deport from Lanka such a righteous man!
Would anyone forget the suffering I endure by that?
Would you expel your younger brother from Lanka,
The one who beseeches you
To give away the wife of another man
And thus safeguards your own welfare?

'What shall I say?
Abduction of Sita is a terrible sin in itself. 60
Expelling the younger brother is yet another offence.
Give up your obduracy. Give up the lure for another's wife.
You are fortunate that Mandodari has come like Lakshmi –
The Goddess of Wealth, being pleased with you; that being so,
Should you take a liking to somebody else's wife?
Sita's abduction is a disgrace to the clan itself.
Supposing that Shri Rama has committed treason,
Why should you torment Janaki in retaliation?
Being the grandson of Pulatsya, the son of Vishravasu,
And a great ascetic yourself, why do you commit a sin? 70
Do not push me to the well of such an accusation –
"Which mother has given birth to such a wretched sinner?" –
Your brother's good counsel is quite appropriate; accept it.
Tread on the path of *dharma*;
Give Janaki away and thus may you live long,' so she said.

Having heard his mother in silence,
Lankesha asked: 'What is all this, O mother?
It is true that you are the mother who has given birth to me;
But are you such a rustic woman who does not know
The intricacies of royal demeanour? 80
Why have you come to the royal court, O mother?
Have you come with a desire that Lanka be safe?
Whether it is the motherly affection that has brought you here?
When the empire of Shri Lanka stands shaken by the invasion of Saketa,
Why your maternal feelings do not stir up, tell me, O mother!

He has chopped off
The nose of your daughter – Shurpanakha; do not forget that.
Having lost Janasthana, the kingdom has shrunk.
The doubt that Lanka may be nearing its destruction is tormenting
    me.
I am an obstinate wrestler; I am your son;   90
And I have a high self-esteem.
Could I ever bear to live under the servitude of Rama?
I am your loving son; I am the lord of the world.
Would I ever die surrendering myself
Like a nameless, faceless coward?
Living under servitude is not proper even in the wildest of dreams.
As I have the all-pervading protection of your blessings,
I will crush Rama;
Do not lose courage, O mother.
Why should you diminish the courage of the monarch yourself?   100
One should lay down one's life to protect the nation.
It is not proper to offer the task of our destruction to Rama.
Am I a coward like Vibhishana?
This is an evil ploy played by Kubera and the others.'
Thus Ravana said harshly.

Lankesha, comforting his mother with such words,
Embraced her and offering to perform *padapuja* –
Homage paid to the feet –
Led her out of the royal assembly
And took her to the queen's quarters.   110
Realising that the good counsel of the mother was thrown
To the winds, Vibhishana said unto himself:

'It is true that Ravana is well-versed in the Vedas.
He is caught in the web of self-conceit.
Without caring for the welfare of the nation,
He has led Lanka towards its own downfall.
I will go and meet Rama now.
People may accuse me as –

"The one who has forsaken his brother;
A traitor to one's brother and nation" – 120
Nevertheless, I am left with no other alternative.
Having relinquished the path of revolution,
And treading on the path of exploring peace,
Tomorrow I will go to Rama carrying a message of peace.
Rama is the protector of him that seeks his refuge,
And he is the infinitely kind visionary.
Is there anyone else to protect us, save Rama?' Thinking thus, Vibhishana remained
Anticipating the sun of Lanka's liberation to rise!

The night went past then.
At day break, as Anala, Sharabha, Anila, Praghasa, 130
And all the others assembled in Vibhishana's palace,
With a sad face, Vibhishana said thus:
'As my mind has gone blank,
I am unable to find the path.
Like a lamp that flickers in the wind, my mind is wavering.
I am suffering from endless agony.
Not paying heed to royal-ethics,
Ravana has adopted the path of annihilation.
It is difficult to live with him. Yet, when I think of forsaking him,
Affection of brotherhood and love of Lanka pull me back.' 140
Then, Praghasa spoke thus:

'As *dharma* has eroded, *adharma* –
Unrighteousness is raising its ugly head.
As the evil counsel of Indrajit, Atikaya, Prahasta,
And others is getting prominence,
And as Lankesha is ruining himself without realising the true path,
O Vibhishana, establish Dharmarajya – a just State in Lanka!'

Then, Anala said:
'Is establishing a State such an easy task, O Praghasa? In order to cause revolution,
Do we have a strong army and weaponry with us? 150

Is it easy to appease and draw the army chieftaincies to our side?
They are all steadfastly loyal to Ravana.
We are under the shade of a serpent's hood!
We will surely be condemned to death.
It is enough if they get the slightest indication of our revolution,
All our heads would be swinging on the gallows in the streets of Lanka!'

At that instant, Vibhishana said:
'No, never! The revolution will not happen!
Is it possible for us to forsake them all?
The citizens would call us traitors.' 160
Then, Anala said:

'Cast away all your doubts.
Now Lanka stands on the threshold of liberation.
We must jump from darkness to light and move ahead.
We must rush forward unfastening the handcuffs.
We must put down all kinds of suffering and pain.
We must establish a life of harmony.
We must joyfully swim in the milky ocean
Of love, peace, happiness, friendship, and harmony.
We must wipe out the inert-slumber of the epochs. 170
We must walk playfully on the path of death.
We must beat the drum to put down ignorance.
We must water the sapling of desire that has withered!

'He is an unethical person.
By causing the people to revolt,
We must get hold of the rein of administering the State.
With no consideration to the kinship of brotherhood,
He has insulted you by expelling you from the royal court.
All the citizens would favour *dharma*.
Let us sing the invocatory song of revolution now itself. 180
Let us give wide publicity.
By earnestly converting the chieftaincies to our side,
Let us dethrone Ravana,

And send Indrajit, Kumbhakarna, Prahasta,
And the others to prison.
By welcoming Rama, and by handing over Janaki,
Let us make friendship with Rama.
Let us cut off the web of disgrace and cast it away.'

Vibhishana asked in grief:
'Would anyone drown in the ocean of baseless decision? 190
Would it be fair to cause Lanka to be swept away in the canal of blood?
Would anyone wage a war of insurgency against one's own brother?'
At that instant, Anila said:
'Let us live in hiding in the middle of forests
And mountain-caves, and consolidate power
By garnering a strong army and weapons,
And then attack Ravana.
Let us work hard, at all levels, for the liberation
In unison with the *vanara*-army that is accompanying
Shri Rama and Sugriva.' 200

Vibhishana resolutely said thus:
'No, let there be no war.
Would anyone fight with one's own brother?
I will cross the ocean, and taking refuge in Shri Rama,
I will build a bridge of friendship between Sri Lanka and Ayodhya
And thus bring them together.
Why should we accumulate sin?
Why should we entertain the bad thought of calamity?
Beseeching the gift of peace, let us unite the hearts.
As the friendship between Rama and Ravana lights up the world, 210
The poverty of the epoch would vanish
And peace would be restored.'
A rainbow showed itself clearly
On the edge of the sky of welfare!

Canto One Hundred and Seventy-six

'Even for a Moment, Stay Not in a Place Where There is No Peace'

||६||

At the foot of the Mount Mahendra,
Shri Rama stood gazing at the sky and at the ocean alternately.
Like the conglomeration of celestial planets that orbit the sun,
The *vanara* chieftains sat around Rama.
The army was stationed close by.
Shri Ramachandra sat with his eyes fixed
On the horizon where the sky embraced the ocean
As if there is neither a beginning, nor an end
For the rejuvenating power of the spectacular sight and creation
That emerges from the blending of the earth and the clouds. 10
At the eastern sky, the morning light seemed to be smiling.
The song of a white heron seemed like *mantra*.
The cascading water was coursing through hard rock making deep
   cuts.
All the mountain-flowers were spreading fragrance.
The inert hill stood blooming full.
At the summit, the light was glowing bright.
It seemed as if Mother Nature herself was in a playful mood
And smiled benevolently.

Sugriva, Saumitri, Nala, Angada,
And all the others were sitting silently.   20
Breaking the silence, Sugriva said:
'During the time of war, as conflicting news keeps flooding in,
Confusion prevails generally;
And if it defies analysis as to what is true and what is not,
And if enemy's designs are not grasped well,
The entire mansion of war-strategy collapses.
Therefore, without losing any time,
Let us grasp the core of truth and see things as they are!'

Appreciating this, Saumitri said:
'There are many kinds of emulations in a war.   30
If there is a fog, the environment becomes hostile.
If the enemy-army is stationed close by –
That is also not a viable option.
In a war of archery, at the appropriate time
If we do not shoot sharp arrows in quick succession,
The cavalry, caught in the ensuing chaos,
Would not be able to march forward,
And thus losing proper direction and morale, we would fall down.
When well-experienced troupe
Of valorous warriors search for the enemy   40
In all the directions using their knowledge prudently,
And fight steadfastly, it will surely lead us
Towards the purpose of the Great Quest.'

Looking at the face of the *vanaras*, Sugriva cautioned:
'Use your ingenuity, and march ahead cautiously.
Understand the volition of the chieftain.
Rush forward bearing cold winds, and scorching heat.
Exhibit your valour grandly
Without being caught in the whirl of defeat.'

At that very instant it seemed that   50
A hazy figure on the edge of the ocean
Was approaching leaping fast,

And it looked like a wave of emotion swelling up
In the lake of a poet's heart,
And as the *vanaras* were looking in wonderment,
And as the valorous Nala was cautioning them –
'Be ready; be prepared'–
And as it became quite obvious that a group
Of *danavas* was coming in a boat waving a peace-flag
That signaled 'No danger,'   60
And as Sugriva asked Hanuma – 'who they were,'
Hanuma said thus:

'I now realise.
He is a devotee of Shri Rama, and the brother of Lankesha.
He is a messenger of peace indeed.
He is a virtuous noble man.
He has come seeking the friendship
Of Saketapati – the lord of Saketa.
He is gentle in friendship,
And a follower of high ethical principles.   70
He is an icon of truth, and very fierce at war.
He is Vibhishana.'
Then, Sharabha said:

'If he is the younger brother of Lankesha,
No doubt he is trickster of a *rakshasa*;
Do not forget that, and do not trust him.
They wait for the opportune time, and then commit treason.'
As uneasiness spread through the *vanara*-army
With whispers heard loud,
Jambava said in a comforting voice: 80

'O *vanaras*, hear me!
Be not afraid; be not frightened.
Hanuma, who set the great Lanka on fire;
The one who meditated on Rama's name to safeguard Janaki,
Has assured us so!
Is not Prahlada the son of Hiranyakashipu?

Isn't Bali, a *danava*? Nevertheless,
Weren't they all the illustrious devotees of god, tell me.
Do not send them back.'
'These words are gems, and are worthy of acceptance;   90
Apply discretion and step forward,' said Angada.

Sushena said:
'He has come to the enemy-camp at war time.
He is a traitor to his own people.
How could he be a virtuous man?
How could there be any refuge to the traitors in Shri Rama's camp?
He has seen the strength of Hanuma with his own eyes.
In the downfall of Ravana, with an eye on the throne of Lanka,
Has come here scheming for such favours by taking refuge in Rama?
Whatever it may be,   100
We should be alert and stand on guard.'

Hanumanta, who was hitherto silent, said:
'Vibhishana is a man of pristine purity,
And is radiant, and unblemished.
He is the one who saved my life with great ingenuity
When Ravana was about to kill me in Lanka;
He is the virtuous person who has protected Janaki.'

At that instant, Sugriva –
'Let us think well; and wait patiently;
Let us approach Rama, and come to a decision' – saying so,   110
He went to Rama and spoke thus:
'O lord! Vibhishana is waiting at the seashore.
We all beseech your order now.
The charming golden deer had pushed you to affliction;
They are *kamarupis* – able to assume any form at will;
How could we believe them, tell us.'

Shri Rama said with a smile:
'Would anyone forget the words spoken by Hanuma, tell me.
Vibhishana is a man of great eminence;

He is very dear to me; he is an honest ascetic.   120
Because of him alone, *tapasya* has reached its fruition in Lanka.
He is the crown prince of Lanka.
Why should we doubt him?
In the absence of Ravana,
He would be the king to rule over Lanka.
Welcome him lovingly, and treat him with respect.
This is my sacred duty, hear me.
If Lankesha himself comes,
And repents, I will forgive him heartily.
I will not counter a rogue with similar roguishness; hear me.   130
Play the ensemble of auspicious musical instruments.
Blow all the trumpets loud
And let them resound in all the four directions.
Bring him here happily in a procession.
Get ready to worship the Goddess of Lanka's empire;
This is a befitting honour to Saketa!'

Sugriva, still doubtful, said:
'O king! It is not Vibhishana alone who has come.
He is accompanied by armed soldiers.
They are *kamarupis*; I do not know why they have come.   140
Could they have come to deceive us in their web of fraud?
Let us arrest them; let us ask them why they have come;
If not, we would be in danger.'
'You are an exponent of high principles.
I have vowed that I shall never desert those
Who come surrendering themselves.'
Thus Shri Rama said.

Hearing the words of the eminent lord,
Pavanaja said in happiness:
'You are the protector of him who seeks refuge in you;   150
You are the protector of *dharma*.
The political point of view is based not on trust;
The point of view of Satya-*dharma* is based on trust.
I am blessed, my lord; Vibhishana is unblemished.'

Saumitri said solemnly:
'It is alright even if Dashashira – the ten-headed one himself
Has sent them all.
Even if all the *rakshasas* of the world come united,
There are such powerful warriors in our camp
Who can crush them in a moment.   160
Then, why should there be any anxiety?
It is our duty to protect those who come to seek refuge in us.
It is sinful to fail in such a duty.
Have you forgotten the valour of Shri Rama
Who has cut *sapta tala* – the seven Palm-trees with a single arrow?'

Hearing such words, and smiling benevolently,
Shri Rama said, 'Well, why are you still in doubt?
Bring them in.'
As Sugriva went out to bring Vibhishana in,
Vibhishana himself approached near saying,   170
'Do not be afraid; I have not come for war.
I am Vibhishana, brother of Ravana;
I am Rama's devotee; I am the messenger of peace.
May I see the one renowned as the crest jewel of the clan of Raghu?'

Coming near Shri Ramachandra,
Vibhishana saw the radiance of Rama without blinking an eyelid.
'O the protector of them who seek refuge in you,
O the one vowed to duty,
O the one with the divinely auspicious form,
None other than you could protect us in the whole world.   180
Trahi mam – protect me – O lord of the Raghu-clan, protect me,'
Saying thus, Vibhishana respectfully bowed to the feet of Rama.

Shri Rama, lifted him up,
And embracing lovingly, and stroking him affectionately, said:
'I am aware that you are caught in a moral dilemma.
It is good that you have left the abode of impoliteness.
You are welcome here.
Even for a moment, it is not good to stay
In a place where there is no peace!'

Choked with emotion, Vibhishana said thus: 190
'O my lord, O the merciful!
I am blessed at the sight of your lotus-feet.
My fear has gone away; every lure is now severed.
As the illusion of conceit, the illusion of greed and fraud,
The illusion of evil-power filled in the mind,
And the owl of amour and hatred,
Are all ruling the heart of my elder brother,
O the one armed with *kodanda*! Be kind as to reside there.
Dispel the darkness of evil by your light.
Wipe out all the dance of wickedness with your love. 200
Crush to dust the mountains of selfishness and egoism.
Be the sun of Lanka's heart,
And be the sun of Lanka's good fortune.
You are the embodiment of bliss!
I offered good counsel to my elder brother.
I implored him to give away Janaki.
I asked him to save the *rakshasa*-clan.
I even pestered him to stop this war.
Not paying any heed to what I said, and speaking jeeringly,
He drove me out of the kingdom. 210
I have come here to beg of you how to save
And ameliorate the *rakshasa*-clan.

'O the accomplisher of Supreme Knowledge!
As the world moves riding on the shoulder of ignorance,
You have filled the earth and the sky
With your all-pervading presence, my lord.
The sky is pleased here; smile is spread there;
Clouds are aglow with multiple hues;
The milky stream flows through and joins the stream of wealth;
Truth manifested itself, and showed us the path of virtue. 220

'Lanka, the golden land, has grown beyond
The borders of truth and *dharma*.
Beleaguered with faults and wickedness, Lanka shudders.

As you have come here now,
Your ray of mercy comes flowing into a giant stream, my lord.
Is mere living for long any beauty for the world sans peace?
When the sky was covered with dry grey clouds,
And when the whole earth stood waiting eagerly for water,
You showered copious rains and protected the parched earth.
Thus you came to be known as Dharmameghana – 230
The virtuous cloud-bearer.
Light itself has come bearing your form.
Like the waters showered from the sky reach for the ocean,
Every stream of life takes refuge in you and dwells there.
There is knowledge in *satvaguna* – the quality of purity;
And there is amnesia in *tamoguna* – the darkness of ignorance.
The chirping of a bird evokes crimson colour;
Similarly, one's vitality blooms on seeing you.

'My elder brother Dashashira is valorous,
But he doesn't have the slightest discernment. 240
He is the personification of hatred and revenge.
He does not tolerate the strong ones;
He has killed the husband of his own sister – Chandranakhi –
The one with the red nails, and drove her away to Janasthana.
When she lustfully desired Rama, and got her nose chopped off,
Using it as a pretext, Ravana abducted Janaki,
And has blundered terribly.
Reproaching the words of mother Kaikasi, wife Mandodari,
And my own good counsel,
His sanity is lost in trusting his own valour. 250
By lighting the light of knowledge in the heart of Ravana,
Prevent this fierce war and all that evil!'

Shri Rama, understanding the mind of Vibhishana,
Said thus in kindness: 'O my son!
How did you live in the kingdom of Lankesha?
The vessel of poison was mixed with nectar.
Would anyone spill burning embers on *champaka*-flowers?

Lanka thirsts after lust and unbridled indulgence in luxury.
Discipline is the boat; right thinking itself is the oar.
Without any of these, how could you live, tell me. 260
He who is afraid of war,
And he who is afraid to protect the virtuous *dharma*,
Both of them are cowards indeed!
Understanding oneself is the virtuous *dharma*,
And it is salvation indeed.
There is need for devoutness and willingness to listen;
There is need for meditation and prayer;
There is need for worshipping the sacred feet;
Worship and veneration are the true source
Of surrendering one's self humbly. 270
When the excesses of egoism are wiped out,
The all-pervading godliness rises high.
When it is said that I reside in god,
Isn't it equal to saying that god is within me?
Dharma that is within me,
And that which stretches up to the abode of god is one and the same.
All *karma* is god; and everything that exists is god.
O *vanaras*, look! Here is Ravana's brother.
He is second to none in protecting *dharma*.
That being so, not accepting his brother's wickedness, 280
He has come with the sole aim of protecting *dharma*.
After Ravana's death in the battle, He is the ruler of Lanka;
   coronate him.'

'No, my lord, I do not accept it.
I do not have the desire or craftiness to capture any empire.
Lead us in the path of peace; protect the *danavas*;
May you initiate the process of averting war!

'Why should there be pain, suffering and torture?
Why to burn down the wings of humanity?
Killing is at the root of every war; violence is its mammoth form.
Cast away into the ocean the frenzied surge of violent thoughts! 290

Let peace be the *bijamantra* – prime principle – of the land of
  Bharata;
And let peace be the *mahamantra* – greatest principle – of the world;
Stop this violence!

'O the merciful! Break the horn of war and protect the world.
When you are the king of Sri Lanka and Bharata,
When the power to ameliorate all rests in you,
When the light of universal love is aglow in your mind,
Why to proclaim war that will swallow up the world, O king?
By proclaiming the path of peace,
Make tranquility, prosperity, quietism, self-command, 300
And *yajnas* reign and come to fruition in the world.
As the world is caught in the web of abnormality,
Cut it off and let the era of welfare come to glory!
I do not have the great desire to rule over the kingdom
By killing my elder brother; forgive me,' implored Vibhishana.

Watching his anguish, Shri Rama said solemnly:
'When Ravana dies, is it fair to allow anarchy to spread in Lanka?
You must ascend the throne, and that is your *dharma*.
Ravana is wicked. He would certainly die in the battle;
There is no escaping it. 310
We have not come here with any desire for invading
Any kingdom and to seize its wealth.
To put an end to the wickedness of Ravana
And to liberate Janaki –
That is our sole duty!

'Hear me!
Soon after this is fulfilled,
Not even a single *vanara*,
And not even for a minute, would stay back in Lanka.
Shri Rama is duty-bound to bring peace to this world; 320
And Shri Rama does not have any desire to acquire kingdoms –
The world will come to know the truth of this only after

You ascend the throne! All vain accusations will then cease!
Let the righteous Lanka war be waged under your leadership.

'I shall proclaim now.
Listen you all. Vibhishana is the sovereign lord of Lanka.
Saumitri, make haste. Conduct the coronation.
This coronation is righteously consecrated to Vibhishana.
To establish *dharma-samrajya* –
Empire founded on the tenets of *dharma* –   330
Is the innate desire of the epoch!'

The *vanaras* heard this divine conversation.
Breaking their serene silence,
And wondering at the supreme sacrifice,
The *vanaras*, quite bewildered, said:
'O Shri Ramachandra! You are the lord
Who helps us cross the ocean of life.
You have united Heaven and earth.
You have united the minds of the people.
Being born on earth, you have risen to divinity.   340
By accepting Vibhishana,
By building a bridge of friendship,
And by becoming the touchstone
Of forgiveness, tolerance, and generosity,
You have illuminated the path of Great Quest by your divinity!'
Shri Rama went near Vibhishana and embraced him.
As the tree of *dharma* spread its soothing shade,
He remained thus engrossed!

Canto One Hundred and Seventy-seven

'Gentleness is Melting Away; Humanity is Fading Away'

||๏||

Having bathed in Shri Rama's ocean
Of love and becoming pure,
Vibhishana said with joy:
'O Shri Ramachandra! Do not kill Ravana.
Stop the war; save Ravana.
I do not know who else but you can protect us.'

Shri Rama replied:
'O Vibhishana! I have got three brothers.
In the town of Shrungavera, there is Guha, the fourth brother.
Sugriva is the fifth brother. As you have joined now, 10
We have become six brothers in all,
And our celebration knows no bounds.
I appreciate your demeanour and gentleness,
But it is impossible to save Ravana.
Would he be pleased with good words?
Would the arrogant one bend before *sama, dana* –?
He could be tamed only by power and not by any other means!'

'O eminent-one of the Raghu clan, Listen!
Dashakantha – the one with ten necks, is very strong.

All the *devas* and *danavas*, 20
Being unable to win him, are afraid of him.
Kumbhakarna is radiant. Prahasta is terribly fierce.
Indrajit is an exponent of war; when he wears iguana-skin,
And the finger-protector, it is impossible to win him.
There are men in Lanka who are as strong as Bhima.
Mahodara, Akandana, and Mahaparshwa
Are all equal to *dikpalas* – regents of the eight quarters of the world.
When war is waged, both *vanara* and *danava* clans would die;
Save them, lord!
O the lotus-eyed one! Keep them in your lotus-heart and save them! 30
Pull out Ravana principle, and plant well the tree of *dharma*
In the holy city of Lanka.
When one Ravana dies,
Millions of Lankesha-*danavas* will be born again and again;
Do not forget that.
Erect the pillar of peace yourself.'
When Vibhishana said so, Saumitri replied thus:

'O Vibhishana, listen!
Shri Rama is the guiding spirit of the *vanaras*;
His spirit flows in every vein of the *vanaras*; 40
Shri Rama has filled life in them and made them strong.
That being so, without realising the valour of the *vanaras*,
Ravana is sitting on the peak of conceit.
He is fast asleep in high conceit thinking
Whether the *vanaras* would ever cross the ocean and come here.
When we invade Lanka, it would dawn on him how strong we are!
Forgive me, brother. I appreciate your patriotism;
I appreciate your love for your brother;
Nevertheless, Ravana can not win, nor can he live on.
But you are honest; I salute you heartily!' 50

'Saumitri has spoken the truth.
We shall build a bridge; we shall reach Lanka.
Then, Lankesha's conceit will melt away.
At that instant, let us move the peace-mission;

Let us hold out Sri Lanka's grandeur in the whole world then;
Let us proclaim peace to the world through war.'
When Shri Rama said thus,
Moved deeply by Rama's gentleness,
Vibhishana told Rama thus:

'We must win Ravana through our experience   60
Of the ways of the world. Why to wage a war?
Why to cause bloodshed?
Why should there be violence that fosters hatred among the clans?
Stop the war and be the universal leader.
The earth is hissing hard and is ablaze.
All the towers of comforts are crumbling down in Lanka.
The statue of happiness is melting away like ice.
Gentleness and humanity are fading away.'
Stopping him, Shri Rama said:

'You have deserted Lanka.   70
Why are you still bound by affection for your brother?
Give up fondness.
Would the wicked Ravana listen to sane voice?
Let us make all efforts; indeed you wish good for others;
But would your vow be fulfilled?'
When Rama spoke thus,
Vibhishana was lost in grief.

'I am your devotee; you may soak me in milk or water –
You may cause me good or bring me to harm as it pleases you –
The nectar of your words has freed me from fondness.   80
Here is a heart that loves you;
Dwell in my heart spreading the luster of your happiness,
And protect me showering your blessings
Of sunshine and soothing drizzle!'

Offering all the flowers of devotion
To your feet, I worship you.
Spreading the golden light, open the door;

Make the moon shine bright, and let the stars twinkle;
O my lord! Open the door of your heart and bless me.'
Thus he implored.

Ignorance was dispelled; 90
The light of true knowledge shone bright;
The dark clouds of fear were dispelled already!

When this kind of thinking was in progress,
Shardula, the spy, saw the *vanara*-army at the seashore.
He went back to Lanka and respectfully explained everything
To Ravana thus:
'O the lord of the *rakshasas*, listen!
The great *vanara*-army is camping at the seashore.
Rama and Saumitri are exceedingly radiant.
The *vanara*-army is spread in a whopping ten-*yojana* area. 100
If war is proclaimed without proper scrutiny and thought,
The city itself will sink;
Without a shadow of doubt, defeat is a certainty.
Sama, *dana*, and *bheda* are the better options to be considered.'
Ravana questioned, 'Why are you afraid thus?
Tell me what happened in the enemy camp.'
Shardula explained in great detail thus:

'Approaching Sugriva, I asked –
"O Sugriva! You are very heroic.
You are the son of Ruksharajassu, the renowned *vanara*. 110
If Ravana has abducted Janaki and brought her to Lanka,
What is it to you? If you help Rama, what is your gain?
Return to Kishkindha at once with your army.
Never ever come to golden Lanka.
It is impossible to cross the ocean and reach Lanka.
When it is impossible for even the *deva*, *gandharva*, *yaksha*, 120
Kinnara, *kimpurusha*, and such others to gain entry into Lanka,
Why should you make vain attempts?
Would the *vanaras* be able to cross the ocean?"

Hearing those words,
The *vanara*-army came at me angrily; 130
Pulling me hard and raining blows,
They pounded me and knocked me down.
Unable to bear the pain, I implored Rama, saying –
'I am the royal-messenger.
Is it fair to torture and kill me by hitting hard?
I have come to convey the message of Ravana; protect me' –
Then, Shri Rama came there swiftly! He said –
"It is not proper to torture the messenger of Ravana.
Why do you forget the royal ethics and behave violently thus?
Stop it now. 140
Wickedness does not befit us" –
These words saved my life!'

'O Sugriva, what good message
Should I carry to Ravana, tell me" –
When I asked thus, Sugriva said:

'Messenger, tell him thus –
O Ravana, listen! You are not our friend;
We have no love for you; you do not deserve any mercy.
Whoever is Shri Rama's enemy is my enemy too; hear me.
We have come to uproot your entire clan. 150
We have brought a massive army with us.
Breaking the ant-hill of sin, we shall burn Lanka.
Be it *Chandraloka*, the world of moon;
Or the *Suryaloka*, the world of sun; or *Patala*, the nether world,
Wherever you may stay in hiding,
We shall find you out and kill you.
Who is there to save you in these seven worlds?
By killing the king of the Eagle-clan, you abducted Sita like a thief;
And you consider it a heroic act!
Your valour should be subdued well. 160
Where was your valour when you attempted
To lift up the bow of Shiva?

Where was your valour while you fought Vali?
As the clan of Raghu and the *vanara*-clan are united now,
Your game is over in the land of Karnataka!"

'Later on, Angada, doubting my credentials, said:
"This one is not a royal-messenger; he is indeed a spy;
Standing at a distance he was sizing up our army."
Immediately, they came on me and started to beat me again.
Calling me a trickster, they pinioned me and began to torture me.   170

'When I implored Rama saying –
"Don't you see my suffering, O Rama?
Who else but you is responsible for this act of the *vanara*-clan" –
Shri Rama stopped them and said –
"What does it matter even if he has assessed the strength of our army?
What does it matter whether he is a messenger, or a spy?
When he says that he is a messenger, do not beat him up" –
These words of Rama saved my life;
Thus I came to be afraid.
Think well before you proceed to wage a war.'   180
Thus Shardula explained at great length all that happened there.

Canto One Hundred and Seventy-eight

'Volition and Unity are the True Source of Victory'

||६||

As the preparations for constructing a bridge
Across the ocean were in progress,
Shri Rama desired to obtain
The goodwill of Samudraraja – Varuna, the lord of the Oceans.
In order to offer prayers to him,
Shri Rama reclined on *darbhatalpa* – a bed made of *kusha*-grass –
And was lost in deep reflection:

'Conflict is gaining momentum.
The stream of life is shrinking in the blazing flames of revenge.
All the musical strings are broken and lay scattered. 10
Losing rhythm and strength, the glow of life is withering away.
The stream is getting dried up at its very source.
Buds must bloom and fragrance must emanate.
Extinguishing the flames of revenge,
Life must shine forth from the city of Saketa to the land of Tataki,
And from the base of Panchavati towards the kingdom of Kishkindha.
Today, it is the turn of Lanka.
What awaits me in the future?
Having blown the conch of war, I have now become miserable.

What a pity that I moved ahead getting drenched in violence!   20
I failed to understand the true meaning of the bird
That flew high happily in the sky singing melodiously
And wishing well all the while.
I considered the strength of all life insignificant.
I failed to show the slightest mercy and goodwill.
I do not know how many sins I may commit in the future.
I do not know how to find salvation in a world filled with violence!'

He told Hanuma:
'O Hanumanta, look what my life has come to be!
It's only a drop in the ocean where foamy waves rise and fall.   30
Like a thin cloud that floats in the endless expanse
Of the sky for a while and then vanishes out of sight,
Like the leaves that fall down from the trees in the forest get rotten
And become manure in the valley,
Whether my life is well-lived?'

Then Hanuma said:
'When I was wandering in Lanka searching for Janaki,
A nightingale sang in its nest there.
On that night, the young ones of the nightingale became the food for
A black cobra and were silenced forever.   40
As the morning melody spread gradually, day-light broke as usual.
Destiny proclaimed the volition to which it vowed allegiance.
I do not know what it really means!'

Shri Rama reflected:
'Bees of disappointment are flying in the sky with a resounding buzz.
The greenery in the garden of life is smouldering struck by lightning.
The stench of burning is spread all around.
The waves of desire are crushed being struck against the shores.
There is no sign of light.
As darkness spreads, all kinds of impediments   50
And obstacles spring up
And the garden of desire is fenced with thorny milk-hedges.
The spread of tender sunshine is severely curtailed.

The heat of hatred is felt everywhere;
The goal of life is severed.
With removing the veil of darkness,
Without the face of dawn shining forth,
Without opening the door of the heart,
Without the sapling of life sprouting,
Without the blooming of flowers, 60
Without the sin melting away,
Body and mind are scorched in the heat;
I know not how to prevent this!'

Comforting him, Saumitri said:
'You attained victory at Janasthana
By destroying the countless army
Of Khara and Dushana. By killing Vali,
You made friendship with Sugriva
And paved the way for Lanka's Quest.
You sent Hanuma and got the seeds of fear sowed 70
In the hearts of the *rakshasas*.
Now, you have set the army for a decisive battle.
Lankesha's strength has now diminished.
Now when the countdown for the defeat of Ravana
And the victory of Shri Rama has begun, march ahead boldly.
Cast away all doubts and misgivings from your mind!'

Sugriva said:
'In war, the General is the most vital accomplisher.
Considering the greatness and welfare of the nation,
And devising a suitable war-strategy, 80
He will lead to flawless perfection.
Searching the most vulnerable spot for attaining victory,
Like an eagle that pounces on its prey with precision,
Arrows should be shot with great speed, and dexterity.
Like the war machines that move ahead swiftly causing great noise,
The enemy-heart should tremble in fear with the roar of war-cries.
Volition and unity are the true source of victory.
If not, we shall be like the dry leaves that fly off aimlessly!'

'Yes, it is true indeed.
We shall cross the ocean; we must reach Lanka. 90
We must set the battlefield at once and stand in readiness.
We must gain victory by weakening the enemy's stamina.
If we stay back here wasting away time,
Victory will only be a mirage and defeat is certain.
When the enemy army stands in the battlefield ready to fight,
If we tactfully recede for a while,
And then rush forward to strike swiftly,
There will be chaos and commotion in the enemy camp then!'

'Let us keep aside such tactics now.
Let us first think how we could cross this vast, fierce ocean. 100
If we go in boats, it is a great distance of hundred *yojanas*.
Ravana's maritime force is standing guard there.
The *rakshasa*-army with its millions of soldiers will certainly surround
And kill us; the battle will then be difficult to win.'
Thus Lakshmana alerted the mind
Of Rama by cautioning about the impending
Trials and tribulations!
Three days passed since Rama reclined for meditation
On the bed of *kusha*-grass to appease Sagara, the king of the oceans.
Though, like an ascetic, Shri Rama sat meditating 110
On Samudraraja in purity,
Restraining *karanatraya* – body, speech, and mind –
With utmost concentration, patience, and peace,
As the king of the sea did not appear before him,
Shri Rama was perplexed.

There was a storm; the waves rose high
And touched the feet of Shri Rama.
Giant crocodiles rolled on their backs and lay scattered.
The heady clouds rained heavily; it thundered aloud;
And lightning flashed brightly, 120
Catching everybody in the vortex of anxiety.

Shri Rama saw that Sagara became greatly annoyed;
And Rama was overcome with anger at that insolent act.

I shall cause Sagara to dry up completely
And thus root out his conceit.
Let me reach Lanka on foot through this pathway –
With such thoughts, Rama sent forth *Brahmastra* –
The ultimate weapon of destruction;
The entire world jolted tumultuously!

The king of the sea appeared instantly.   130
'Forgive me, I am late.
I will cooperate with you in your mission.
I will bear the bridge; I will protect all.
Let Ravana-principle end and Rama-principle stand to glory.
Let the task of constructing the bridge progress
Without any impediments.'
It appeared that the king of the ocean said so.

Shri Rama retrieved the *Brahmastra*.
The ocean became calm; the sky became calm;
And all the seven worlds attained quietude!   140
As though the assemblage of *devas* appeared on the sky
To watch with their own eyes,
The grandeur of *setubandha* – the act of constructing the bridge –
Serenity spread all around.

Canto One Hundred and Seventy-nine

'Bridge of Emotional Unity and Culture'

॥६॥

'The task of *setubandha* should begin auspiciously.
How the bridge shall be constructed;
Who shall be the sculptors and architects?
Who will construct it and what shall be its plan?'
When Rama was engaged in such consultations,
Sugriva said:

'The land of Karnataka is the hometown of sculpture;
And it is the laboratory for a variety of architecture.
There are great exponents of the art here.
At the time when the whole world knew nothing about bridges,　　10
The sculptors of Karnataka constructed bridges.
There is no dearth of expertise, and there is no comparison either.
Nala is indeed a great scholar.
It appears as if Vishwakarma – the architect of the gods –
Has himself come here in the form of Nala.
He is an eminent sculptor indeed.
Nala is such an expert who could construct
Such a bridge that can take Rama across the ocean –
Rama, the one who helps people to cross the ocean of life.'

'Let me see who is Nala,' said Rama. 20
At that instant, Nala, getting up from the midst of *vanaras*,
And folding his hands respectfully, said:
'O Shri Rama!
Let me have the grace of your mercy.
I will construct the bridge that unites Lanka and Bharata;
I will use all the available scientific knowledge for that.
I will open a new epoch in the art of building bridges.
There are eminent *vanaras* here; they will help and support me.'

'O Shri Rama, Raghurama!
O the protector of him who takes refuge in you! 30
O the one who is gracious to the devotees!
I will construct the bridge;
Let there be your blessings and protection to me;
I will pour out all my expertise to this cause, my lord!

I will churn the ocean, my lord.
I will cause the flashes of lightning shine bright.
I will work hard day and night and continuously reform
The path of Great Quest. I will hoist the flag high.
We must seize the lightning; we must drink the ocean;
With clenched fist and fixed gaze, 40
We must march ahead walking on the ocean-bed.

On the strength of your name,
I will make the coral rocks float.
On the strength of your arrow, the ocean will open up.
On my left, and on my right, in front of me, and at my back,
Up and down and wherever I turn or see
The strength of your name shall protect me.'
Thus getting Rama's blessings
Nala, the sculptor was engrossed in the task.

The *vanara*-army surged into the forest. 50
They broke a variety of trees and put them in the ocean –
Ashwakarna, red-*matti*, bamboo, *kodasu*, *matti*, Palm-trees,

Tialak, tinisha, bilwa, saptavarna, mango, *ashoka, punnaga* –
And such other trees they cut,
Pulled out some others, and put them in the ocean
As if they were all the flag-pole of Indra!

The ocean was tumultuous.
They started construction of the giant bridge
That was ten-*yojana* wide and hundred-*yojana* long;
Some were holding the measuring scale; 60
'Be quick to finish the work,' saying so, some waved sticks;
Some others were busy straightening, and levelling the mound;
Allowing none to be lazy, all were pressed into work there.

Wherever one looked, one could see the *vanara*-troupes
Bringing trees swiftly; some *vanaras* brought rocks and hillocks
Pulling them away from their base and cast them into the ocean fast.
What a commotion!
Everybody was filled with a feeling of fulfillment!

Nala, the great sculptor, is highly knowledgeable about rocks.
He collected the coral rocks 70
That have the quality of remaining afloat in water
And put them together in the ocean.
The string of floating rocks looked
As if it was a necklace of Mother Earth.
It looked as if the heap of coral rocks was beckoning Shri Rama.

Lord Varuna, on seeing the bridge being constructed, felt elated.
The wave of musical notes – *Sa, Re, Ga, Ma* – spread all around.
The music of the ocean resounded and spread all around.
The sweetness of Shri Rama's name spread all around
And the bridge stood firm on the strength of Rama's name. 80

As Nala inscribed Rama's name on the coral rocks
And thus offering his prayers placed them in the ocean,
They stood steady floating.
Bathing in that ecstasy,

Vanaras went on placing the rocks in the ocean
Picking them up one by one.

At that instant, a squirrel soaking itself in the ocean,
Came out of the water and rolling over the sand,
And once again it went into the ocean
To place that sand in between the rocks already laid there. 90
The service of that little squirrel
To Rama's cause became proverbial devotion.
Shri Rama went near the squirrel in great happiness
And stroking it affectionately showered his grace copiously on it!

At that time, a baby *vanara*, lifting up a rock
Scribbled Rama's name on it and threw the rock into the ocean;
The rock floated well.
Shri Rama too picked up a rock
And as he threw it into the ocean, it sank with a thud.
'All the rocks are floating on the strength of my name; 100
Then, why did the rock that I threw sink to the bottom?'
As Rama thought over it, Hanuma then said:

'O Shri Rama, your name is great indeed,
And is very soothing;
It can unite all the three worlds.
As you hold the rocks by the grace of your hand,
All of them remain afloat;
But if you yourself let go of them out of your hand,
Would they remain without sinking?
That is why the rock that you threw out of your hand 110
Reached the ocean-bed.

'Your name alone is enough;
Your presence is not needed;
We will win Lanka today.
We do not count how strong the enemy-army is;
We will kill them all.
Why to lament and why to worry over it, my lord?'
Thus Hanumanta praised Shri Rama.

The construction of the bridge
In the path of Great Quest was steadily progressing.   120
On the first day, fourteen-*yojana*-long bridge was completed;
Twenty-*yojana* length was over on the second day;
On the third day, it was twenty-one *yojana* length,
And twenty-two *yojana* on the fourth day;
The remaining twenty-three *yojana* length was completed on the
  fifth day.
With that, the bridge got connected to the Mount Suvela in Lanka
And everyone felt a sense of fulfillment.
The bridge in its grandeur looked
Like the radiant path of Swati – star Arcturus.
Vanaras jumped and danced with joy shouting –   130
'Nala has done it' –
The construction was indeed a wonder;
Its grandeur was beyond imagination.
The glow of rainbow spread across the sky.

It looked as if the bridge stood kissing the horizon.
It seemed like the parted hair of Mother Earth.
The bridge was beautiful; it was strong; it was enchanting;
Shri Rama, highly pleased, went ahead;
The *vanara*-army followed joyously.
The path of Great Quest reached its success.   140
Looking all around, Saumitri said:

'O *vanaras*, arise!
Your radiance is hidden; move ahead towards the goal.
Unveil the clouds, and come forward flashing the light of your valour.
Darkness has shrouded in the heady wine of power.
The spark of revenge is ready to engulf Lanka.
Striking the chord of millions of hearts,
Come here playing the musical notes that awaken us to a new dawn.
O the valorous heroes of revolution! Come forward
To give light to the New Epoch;   150
Come to serve the land without losing courage;

Fearlessly leap forward, and surge ahead;
Be confident of yourself; and have faith;
Have faith in god; have faith in the Supreme Soul;
Have faith in life; have faith in service.
Look! In times of trouble,
Sacrifice and faith shall always protect us.

'The abyss of differences, and conflicting interests
Between the continents, and the islands
Shall be sealed now – such is the spirit of this venture; 60
The island-culture will now have communion with other cultures;
In unison, the motif of give-and-take shall be fostered;
The bridge of a collective culture's emotional unity has been
   constructed here!'

Canto One Hundred and Eighty

'They Carried the Vessel Filled with the Nectar of Love'

॥६॥

In the life caught between birth and death,
The bridge of sacrifice is constructed;
There is forbearance of earth and sky;
Shri Rama has undertaken his amazing journey through all this.
Rama is of the clan of Sagara;
He has the complete blessings of Sage Agatsya;
Rama moves ahead in great radiance.
Rama, the most propitious lord,
Addressed the *vanaras* thus:
'O Sugriva, listen! 10
O Jambava, listen! All *vanaras* listen!
There is no match to your valour and heroism.
Look at the heap of sand; countless grains of sand,
When put together, form the massive sand dunes.
Look at the ocean; countless drops have joined together
To form the vast ocean.
When each drop is closely examined,
One attains the grand realisation
That the universe lay concealed in an atom.

Why to foster egoism?
If we consider that every 'I' jointly forms 'we,'
It will certainly yield beneficial results;
Trust is born thus; purity spreads;
Only when the *panchabhutas* – the Five Principles –
Fire, Air, Water, Earth, and Sky – are joined together,
We grow from the tiny embryonic state to the full-fledged form.
When this wonder is seen in perspective, egoism will disappear;
With no room for selfishness, the desire to serve others blooms.
You all are incomparable.
I am Rama, the selfless accomplisher.
Now it is my duty to liberate my wife.
I will prevent all the wickedness that may appear in the future.
Ocean is the holy place where all rivers converge.
Ocean's water transforms itself into clouds and pours down as rain;
That being so, ocean's water is the source of all water.
Whatever we have received from the world,
Shall be returned to the world again and again –
That is what I have vowed;
I will teach all of you the same.'

Hearing those words, Jambava said:
'We are blessed, my lord.
Let victory be to Shri Rama; let victory be to Janaki;
Let victory be to Shri Lakshmana; let victory be to Hanuma;
Let victory be to Sugriva; let victory be to Nala, the sculptor.
Your grace is great; the bridge is constructed.
Ravana's fall is now nearing soon!'

Vanaras became very ecstatic
About their accomplishment in life and climbed on to the bridge;
Their roar of their joyous hailing resounded in all the four directions.

Malyavanta said:
'In Lanka, such unreal, distorted news has spread
That due to the invasion of Ayodhya-culture,
The island-culture will perish.

I do not know the means of how all minds
Would be united in harmony.
Clouds of fear have shrouded
And the smoke of enmity has spread.'

'You have spoken the truth.
I am vowed to stop all cultural conflicts.
We shall nurture culture; we will not break hearts;   60
We will indeed unite heats.
We will do the task of uniting the island-culture
With the culture of the sub-continent.

'Strengthening the process of give-and-take in the world,
We have constructed the bridge.
We will break all fences; we will wipe out all differences;
We will seal every kind of abyss;
Henceforth the lonely islands will never remain isolated;
We will unite all in the same spirit;
The world can not prevent this; selfishness will not engulf this;   70
This is my innermost desire;
O Malyavanta, listen!
This alone is the path of Quest;
We must rush ahead!
For the task of bringing in unity,
Let this is the mode of communication.
Our volition is to unite all;
What is so great about breaking or destroying?
This is the kind of history of the land of Bharata:
In the conglomeration of diversity,   80
Unity alone is the life-blood.
There is no haste and compulsion by the great forces.
The strength of the eminent ascetics, great poets,
And the exponents of various arts is pressed into service here.
The construction of the bridge in itself is a process
Of uniting the Little Culture with the Great Culture.
Satyam-Shivam-Sundaram –

Truth is auspicious and pleasing – is the life-sustaining *mantra*.
Every culture's root is similarly potent.
Every culture is the treasure-house of divinity. 90
Henceforth, there shall not be conflicts; harmony is the sole aim.
The task is of uniting all diverse factions into one unified whole.
When the feeling of unity dwells in every heart,
Like the bird of life, it will protect all.
This is not a war-expedition;
This is a friendly expedition.
Considering non-violence to be our sole aim,
You all march ahead subduing violence and uniting hearts.'
Thus spoke Saumitri.

As everyone got ready, 100
Saumitri walked ahead;
Shri Rama was in the middle flanked
By Vibhishana on his right, and Sugriva on his left;
Malyavanta, Nila, Tara, and Angada were on his side.
There were not any weapons;
There were not any spears, lances, and axes;
There was not the evil design to annex any kingdom;
Uniting the hearts, they carried the vessel
Filled with the nectar of love.
The great exponents of dance, sculpture, 110
And painting too walked swiftly.
It was indeed a fair of the collective culture;
There was a group of doctors walking on the great bridge
That aimed to weave the island-culture with the culture of the
    main-land;
There was a large army too.

Shri Rama and Saumitri,
Together with *vanaras*, have opened a new chapter
In the path of Quest; they have constructed the bridge.
The whole of Lanka-island is a prison without light;
They have lighted the lamp of liberation there to dispel the darkness; 120

As the path was covered with smoke and looked hazy,
Carrying the light of friendly message, they were moving ahead.

Lanka stood there as an idol of lonely island.
They moved ahead cutting the thorny milk-hedges
And cleaving through the sickly darkness
That formed obstacles for humanity;
The voice of destruction has faded;
The voice of nurturing has risen high;
New emotions, new life,
And a new momentum were seen everywhere;   130
The boat of laughter was sailing in the ocean of cries.
They were moving ahead in the eagerness of quenching the heat
By fostering the blooming of the
Flower of emotions in the forest of human-hearts.

Walking on the bridge, Jambava said:
'Whether we are in the clouds, or in the lap of the ocean,
Living a great life is our aim; such a good life is proper for us –
Not spoiling our resoluteness to live like that,
Today we have started to move ahead crossing the ocean,
And likewise crushing all the other obstacles –   140
Whether they be water, fire, or storm –
And searching for the path of liberation
Endowed with a new vision for fostering cultural links in the new land!
As our minds are rejuvenated with the new spirit for a new life,
And as time ticks away at the speed of light,
We pray to you, O Lord Hari, kindly make us float
In the ecstasy of harvesting such a delightful revolution!

'In the pursuit of such a pure life,
Let us swiftly cross over the vast expanse of the green fields;
Let us cross the mountains and let us cross the borders   150
And step into the new land;
Let us march ahead uniting all our strength towards
That new destination.
O Lord Hari, kindly make us float in joy!

As the auspicious sound of the conch is heard;
As the sound of the vital syllable *Om* is inviting to rejoice
In the well-accomplished task of constructing the bridge;
As the hitherto dormant science is now swinging its outstretched hoods;
And as the blooming vital conscience is rising high
Climbing on the ladder that connects the earth with the clouds above,   160
O Lord Hari, kindly make us float in joy!

'Arising from this earth, and soaring high in noble emotions,
Elevating the spirit from the physical sphere
To the sphere of supreme bliss,
Enlivening love of the world from the concrete to the abstract,
Fusing life-sustaining emotions with religious sentiments,
Driving the golden chariot of visionary dreams
You are born here with a vow to ameliorate the soul of every man.
You have quenched the thirst of this land of Bharata
By your supreme sacrifice.   170
O Lord, the desire for this mundane world
And its rewards are now satiated.
Come to us holding out your beautiful hands
That will always support us;
Come to us as the soothing wind, and water.
O Lord Hari, kindly make us float in joy!

'As each stair is ascended,
The creative spirit soars high before ebbing away to attain stability.
As the blissful realisation sprouts in the expanse of the clouds
Causing the juicy crops to stand smiling in full bloom,   180
There occurs manifestation of the supreme perception
That when perfection is drawn out of perfection,
What remains is perfection.
The auspicious sound of conch and gong is heard.
The knowledge of taming the lightning,
The knowledge of seizing the sun,
The knowledge of ransacking the bounty of the ocean,

The knowledge of shaping the good deeds
For causing the new revolution –
O Lord, all such knowledge has dawned on us now. 190
O Lord Hari, kindly make us float in joy!

'Like standing engrossed in a dream
In the intense silence of the forest;
Like the windy storm screeching through the glitter of green shoots;
Like the vast ocean creating multiple perceptions
In the awakened conscience,
O Lord, you have led us through gleaming light and glory.
With the mystic symbol born of ancient truth
You have awakened the inert mind
And elevated it to the summit of happiness. 200
O Lord Hari, kindly make us float in joy!

'Before we were consumed by the fire of disappointment,
We have completed the task of constructing the bridge.
We will reach Lanka in just one long leap.
Kicking on the hearts of *danavas*,
We will break their arms and shoulders.
Before the new blood coursing fast in our veins turns cold,
We will construct a new kingdom in the land of liberation.
O Lord Hari, kindly make us float in joy!

'This is not the sweet chirping of birds; 210
It is the powerful roar of the invading wind.
This is not the soothing breeze.
The whisper of good minds, the resounding laughter
Of the forest-wealth is heard.
The land's thoroughfare has opened here today.
The path of Quest has now been made easy.
Leaping out from the depths of the ocean in the form of vapour,
The beautiful rainbow is formed among the clouds.
As you are omnipresent, which other world need we seek?
O Lord Hari, kindly make us float in joy!' 220

BOOK FIVE

Canto One Hundred and Eighty-one

'Don't Blame the Darkness; We must Light the Lamp'

||❀||

Atop Suvela hills, Rama gazes at Lanka
That stands resplendent, mocking all the treasures
Of the world. The Goddess of Wealth lies there crippled.
Through his power of penance, Ravana glories there
In luxury and comforts; and he beams vainglorious,
Unmatched and unrivalled.

The leaping and jumping *vanaras* are full of
Unbridled spirit and enthusiasm, as though
They are not going to war but are in a peace-march.
Still, Mother Earth shudders with the loud blare   10
Of the war bugles being blown; and fearing
That the *rakshasas* will cause rivers of blood to flow,
She reaches the ocean for shelter.

Listening to the roar of the ocean,
Shri Rama stretched his arms, embraced
His brother Lakshmana, and said: 'Dust storms
Are whirling, uprooting the trees. Look!
A dark cloud looms large, with threatening

Thunder; and dark rings are being formed round
The sun. Alarming omens are seen all over, 20
Signalling the doomsday. With the battle raging,
Spears and swords clashing, the whole world
May be swept off!

'Brother, how can I bear this cry of pain?
How can I accept, dear brother, this devastating
Bloodshed? Brother dear, where has the music
Of the stars fled? Where has the music of birds
In flight disappeared? Has the bridge of friendship
Built with great joy collapsed?' So said Shri Rama,
Full of anguish. 30

Intending to comfort Shri Rama, Saumitri,
The son of Sumitra, spoke solemnly:
'Don't blame the darkness; we must light a lamp.
When the world is clouded by ignorance,
I don't see anyone but you who can light
The lamp of peace. Like a huge tree
Hidden as if in a seed, peace lies in void.
We have to dig it up and churn; and then,
Knowledge that transcends the senses
Will rise up like fresh butter. 40

'Look! Time has come
For slavery to end in Laṅka, slavery akin to hell!
A free and democratic nation is
Greater than Heaven. March ahead, O King!
Who else but you can free virtuous people?
Who else is the greatest archer of the Raghu
Dynasty but you? March ahead, O King!

'New leaves and fresh flowers
Will bloom noiselessly on the path you tread.
Ours are truthfulness and the upright path. 50
During the short period you live on this earth,
Give, with a large heart, light to the whole world.

'Territorial desires aren't yours, not at all.
Wealth, gold, and women do not interest you.
Sugriva and other kings like him, with your help,
Have amassed riches of varied kinds.
Your path is to redeem the world;
Service to humanity is your religion;
It is for you to safeguard them from debasement.
Then, you will see the main portals of truth,   60
Righteousness, and peace opening up for you!

'You declared to Kaikeyi then, "O mother!
I do not want this throne; I have given it up.
Ahead of me lies the path of achievement."
That's what you said; why do you hesitate now?
When the entire world is crumbling, devoid
Of righteousness, you should go ahead,
Unmindful of your personal pains.
Before the world crumbles completely,
Lift it up, with the holy *kalasha*, on its top.   70

'What did you say, then, to your brothers
Bharata and Shatrughna? "This kingdom
Along with its power and wealth, I reject.
Mine is the path of renunciation."
Why do you fear now? The path of renunciation
Stretches right in front of you.

'When the ideals of *Ramarajya* are strong,
Do not forget the task ahead. A few black spots
Amidst soothing moonbeams, O Lord,
Don't hinder the radiance of the beams.   80
Get ready for a just war.

'You have viewed sorrow and happiness,
And birth and death alike. Look! The wheel
Of this world turns round, continuously.
Why this emotional turmoil? Stamp on it,
And arise.'

Overcome with anguish,
Replied Shri Rama: 'What shall I say dear brother?
The words of Vaidehi have struck me deep
"Raghava, why should you kill animals? 90
You are a man of good deeds, and honest.
You have never lied in the past; you will not do so
In future. Now, under the pretext of protecting
The hermits, you have entered the forest and
Have killed the *rakshasas*. In the guise of fulfilling
The pledge to your father, you have sold yourself
To violence. Why should you meddle with weapons
In exile? In the land of peace and penance,
Should there be an exhibition of valour?
Why continue the sinful path, my husband 100
Once the exile is over and you reach the city,
Display your weapons; but here, renounce them.
Follow the ideals of sages, and scale the sublime
Heights of virtue" – these are her words, my brother.

'What shall I say, brother?
Caught in the web of violence, I am suffering.
It's like sitting peacefully under the mango tree,
And suddenly hearing thunder and lightning.
Having lost all the pleasant emotions of sunrise,
I have become blood-thirsty, facing a violent war. 110
This mass hysteria will push me into further
Violence, destroying all my longings for peace.
Songs I wished to sing remain unsung,
The notes from the violin remain muted.
Searching for Wholeness, I am blinded by darkness;
With memories of Janaki, I am reduced to emptiness;
A tempest has gathered around me and hurled me
Into a world devoid of love and amity.

'Had I listened to the words of Janaki,
Would there have been this chain of violence? 120

Janaki's abduction and the coming massacre?
In this cold, cruel, and endless journey,
Where will courtesy, fear, and compassion be?'
Thus bemoaned Rama, full of anguish.

Responded Lakshmana:
'Enough, brother, enough of it.
Your mind is disturbed and I can understand it.
Can I dare advise you – my elder brother?
Just as friendship is righteous, so is war.
Weeding out evil and the wicked is a duty. 130
Why don't you remember our Guru Vasishtha,
And his advice, and the ethics of war taught
By Vishwamitra? Remember Parashurama,
Whose sole goal was destruction of evil?

'In order to protect the world,
Lord Shiva incarnated as Bhairava.
Who saved the Vedas, in the form of a giant Fish?
Who preserved the ambrosia, becoming a Tortoise?
Who lifted up the earth incarnating as the Boar?
Who slew the *rakshasa* Hiranyakashipu, 140
Incarnating as "Man-lion," coming out of a pillar?
Who grew to reach the clouds and stamped down
King Bali? Who redeemed the universe as Bhargava,
Destroying all wicked kings?

'Radiant Lord of the world, it was you;
You are unrivalled. You, the sun of the universe,
How can you fear the clouds? My brother,
Just as compassion is part of righteousness,
Destruction of the wicked is also a part of it.

'There is only one Shri Rama born in an epoch. 150
The world is wearied and full of suffering;
Set forth to nurture the tree of *dharma* and
Rejuvenate it with the spirit of life.

Do not delay; to fecund the Scriptures and rituals,
Arise, O Rama, and begin your noble work,'
The son of Sumitra pleaded.

'Desires of my heart are dead,' Shri Rama replied,
'My mind is disturbed, and I am at a loss
To discover contentment and equanimity.
My search for fulfilment has been shattered;   160
I pine under the accusation that the members
Of the Ikshvaku clan are busy, forcefully
Expanding their kingdom. Caught I am like a fish
In the deceptive net of Fate. Brother, look there!
The bloody waves on the western horizon
Foretell some impending catastrophe.
Stars appear like cadavers afloat on those waves;
And the sun goes down, in utter despair.
I don't know how we will be freed from
The tempting cords of the *rakshasa* called war.'   170

'Brother, listen!' continued Shri Rama:
'We have to end these violent emotions,
And achieve the state of joy through *sattvika* or noble qualities.
Let's rise higher than *annamaya kosha*,
The gross material body, and reach the state of *ananda*,
The perfect state of joy, the final stage of our search.
That's the blissful state of *sachidananda*,
The pure and everlasting state of joy.'

Lakshmana retorted:
'Who else but you, being free from worldly desires,   180
Can discern the nature of truth and *dharma*?
Frogs are prey to snakes, birds to hunters,
Snakes to kites, and cattle to tigers –
All living beings are food to one another,
And this is inevitable, oh elder brother!
Can anyone leave the wicked free who constantly
Molest the good people?

'Disregarding all advice,
Ravana has reached the height of foolishness
And savagery. How can Ravana ignore 190
Shri Rama who broke the bow of Lord Shiva,
Disfigured Shurpanakha, set Lanka on fire,
And built a bridge across the huge sea?
Blind to Rama's valour, plunged in delusion,
He has challenged Rama, unprovoked,
For a war, without any concern for his subjects.
Warfare devours all the bystanders
As well as those who participate in it.
Alas! Peace and non-violence are only a mirage!'

Rama replied: 200
'Should the rivalry between Rama and Ravana
Be a cause to offer all living beings to the Goddess of War?
We have to totally erase the history that tells us:
"Just as famine and affray, earthquake and pestilence
Are natural, so is war." Let the dark shadow of death
Caused by the impetuous war, thirsting for blood,
Be rooted out. Should warfare be part of any culture?
Should one dance in ecstasy singing heroic songs?
Should volumes of poetry be written that describe war?
No! Not at all, brother! 210

'Let war and fighting come to an end.
A revolution that stems war must take place.
Why should there be books that teach warfare?
Why should there be "Hero-stones" that glorify war;
And *masti*-stones that commemorate
Self-immolation on the part of poor widows?

'Spirited youths, driven by emotions, succumb
To the temptations of war. Savagery and violence
Perform a wild, brutal dance on the battlefield.
Enough of this strife and conflict and hassles; 220
I don't enjoy swimming in the pool of blood.

'O Saumitri! Don't pour *ghee* and aggravate the fire of enmity.
Pitch-dark nights are filled with terror and horror;
Stars have fallen to the thunderous lightning.
Let the foam of ambrosia rise up with hymns of peace.
Is it fair to condemn married women to widowhood?
Why should a graveyard be crowded with tombstones?
Is it fair to offer blood as gift to Mother Earth,
Who suckled us with her breast-milk? Tell me!
Is it fair to burn the children's jasmine-garden? 230
Is the human sacrifice I indulge in pardonable?

'There is a white gleam of the stairs of skeletons;
There is mindless celebration of Lanka's violence;
And the hoarse wailing of jackals is heard, look!
Where is that heroic land,
Where there is a garden with new saplings?
Where can we find laughter, mirth, and happiness?
I cannot look back; nor can I take a step forward.
Dig a deep trench in the Suvela Mountains
And inter me there. The peace I don't find in my own land, 240
I may find that in Lanka's soil, O Brother!'

Dejected, as Rama continued
With his emotional outburst, Saumitri replied:
'Do not sing this song of renunciation, my brother;
You are the harbinger of the welfare of the world;
You are the upholder of the flowering of humanity.
Come, ushering enthusiasm and dynamism;
Bring fresh flowers into the human heart.
O the Turtle-incarnation! Do come and lift up
The human spirit trapped in the quagmire of brutishness. 250
As the chain of hope for the welfare of humanity
Is drowned in the slush, get ready to lift it up!

'Get ready to light the lamp of confidence;
To promote the culture of common weal,
Get up and bring cheer to the suffering world.

'Get ready to cleanse Bharata, clouded
By religious dogmas and conceit!
Come, brother, to dispel the darkness of ignorance,
And enhance the spirit of rightful action.
Let valour course through every vein here; 260
Let people stand strong against death and pain;
And bring the rain of ambrosia that quenches
The thirst for worldly life!'

Shri Rama replied:
'I am a pilgrim who passes through all the epochs.
I view life and death as the twin banks of Life,
And I continue my journey.
I am the river-water that flows continuously,
Meandering through both good and evil,
Now angry and now calm, now rich and now poor. 270
Who can understand the mystery and mind of Time?
I do not want this war; I do not,' thus, in despair,
Shri Rama collapsed on the ground.

Canto One Hundred and Eighty-two

'To a Prudent Achiever, Body is the Abode of God!'

||६||

Looking at his brother lovingly, but with courage,
Lakshmana said: 'If you abstain from war fearing infamy,
Another ignominy will befall you for sure.
"There is a black-spot on the Moon, and cruelty in a Lion" –
Thus the world will blame you.
Different people, different views.
Do not forget the principles of Truth, Goodness,
And Beauty, and the *Yoga Vasishtha*,
Taught by the revered sages.
Remember, those tenets were addressed to the brave-hearted.' 10

Shri Rama replied: 'Suffering afflictions,
I am drowned in sorrow. How can I remember,
Dear brother, the words of my revered teachers?'
At that moment, Lakshmana recollected
The conversation that had taken place between
Shri Rama and Sage Vasishtha sometime ago,
And recounted it to Rama.

'"Push away Fate;
Keep away the sycophants; and be a complete man.

Action and Knowledge are like the wings of a bird. 20
When one acts, submitting oneself to God's Will,
It shall naturally lead one to the door of Knowledge.
Move ahead with discipline, testing everything;
And prosper, goaded by reason and enthusiasm.
These four qualities will certainly free the soul
Imprisoned in the body; this is Truth.
If you think that you are not within this world,
But the entire world is within you, you will conquer
The cycle of Life for sure." When the sage said thus,
You had queried: "I am only a minuscule particle; 30
How could the universe dwell in me? I am confused.
I am bewildered at such a dual paradox." To this,
The teacher had replied:

' "The three states of being –
Sleep, Dream, and Consciousness – are experienced by all.
If you are asleep, can you see the world? When awake,
Consciousness enables you to see the universe.
Don't say that even when you are asleep, the world
Still exists, because it is contrary to your experience.

' "You are like Brihaspati, the preceptor of gods; 40
Oh! You possess extraordinary ingenuity and ideals.
Destiny is nothing but the consequences of past actions.
The long chain of Creation runs through the past
And in the future; but it cannot be understood only
In the present. You know what awaits the man,
Who says, 'the well dug by my grandfather is old;
This water is stale, and this is not Ganga-water.'
What else, but his downfall! The art of quest
Lies within oneself, in one's being righteous.
Self-happiness comes only from self-examination. 50
You see, it is the only panacea!
You explore that path.

' "O Son! Do not give up.
Uproot the tree of sin; and, on the path of achievement,

'"Do not succumb to despair in mid-course; do not look back.
Just as the teeth mash all eatables,
Readying them for digestion,
If you move ahead crushing all impediments,
Who can equal you?

'"How could a king rule without fighting a war? 60
The world is filled with brutality, and it trembles.
When high ambition and low desire stand before us
Tempting, if we opt for the higher one, with pure intent,
It shall certainly be accomplished. If we blame *karma*,
Will the fruits of *karma* be done away with? Tell me.
Whatever foolishness had been there in the past,
Shall now be wiped out by sound values of the present.
Through supreme human effort, Sage Kaushika
Scaled new heights and reached the summit, earning
The title – *Brahmarshi*, the Sage Supreme. 70
Believers of Fate sink low into a world of despair,
And become weaklings. Do not depend on others' strength.
Unaware of your own valour, do not drown yourself
In the whirlpool of weakness.

'"Treading on the path of valour,
Achieve supreme success, and be the harbinger
Of change! God is not far from you, but close,
Very close to you. Just as the pot gets its form
From the soil, Godliness does not exist without you.
Divinity lies within you, and you are divinity. 80
'Tattvamasi' – 'You are That' – the Vedas proclaim.
Ignorant of this truth, fools drown in fear and doubt,
Peace remains a mirage, and they disappear in slush.

'"For the noblest of men,
Work is worship, and that itself is *karmayoga*;
Indolence is not much different from evil.
It's like fetching water in a porous basket.
One must keep one's mind focussed on the Supreme;

If pompous worship is considered great by some,
Well, that is merely being childish.   90

'"Look! Virtuous people shower
The world with peace, and glorify happiness.
They live not caring for riches or poverty;
They have no past regrets or future worries;
Believing in the present, they move on with faith.
Not greedy of wealth, they are content with themselves;
Clearing the muddles of the world, they gain happiness.
Even if the scorching sun loses his heat,
Or the cool moon swelters, or the fiery flames blaze,
Would the saints feel ruffled?   100
Would crossing an ocean make one a great leader?
The one who conquers one's senses is a leader indeed.

'"When equanimity and tranquility
Dwell together with good sense, that is called restraint.
Would ghostly *rakshasas*, enemy tigers or huge
Pythons trouble an ascetic, the man of restraint?
Just as all the water on earth reaches the ocean,
All knowledge merges with the doctrine, beyond
All logic. Listen, O Raghava!
The wealth of noble thoughts,   110
Is the real wealth to be acquired.

'"If something good is spoken even by a child,
One must accept it; even if Brahma tells one
Something unacceptable, one should reject it totally.

'"Look! Illusion is the root
Of all diseases. One must reject all notions of witchcraft.
Truthfulness could never ever be at a loss.
Even if one bites and throws out pieces of jaggery,
Tell me, would it ever lose its sweetness?
When the illusory feeling of ego is wiped out,   120
You will dwell in the abode of eternal truth.
Raising your arms high proclaim steadfastly:

'Let everyone get to know the path of living,
Responding fully to one's inner voice.'"
As the great sage said thus, evincing interest
To know more of that philosophy, Shri Rama said:

'"O, revered one!
I yearn to know more of birth and death,
Even when a man is endowed with high intelligence
And physical strength, if he is obsessed with ambition, 130
It will throw him into the streets, like a piece of straw.
What could one say about such instances?"

'The great sage replied:
"The root of birth and death is sin and virtue.
Sin sends one to hell, and good deeds to Heaven;
When sins and good deeds are balanced, one is born
On this earth. This is an ever-turning wheel.
'Enough of this birth, enough of this death,
Enough of fecundating in the mother's womb' –
When such a desire for deliverance gets rooted 140
Firmly in the mind, one should take to the path of knowledge,
And gaining self-awareness and burning all desires,
One attains *moksha*. Listen! Salvation means,
Becoming one with God! Neither birth nor death."

'Then he went on:
"Brahma is nothing but a state of mind, the root of all creation.
Whether it be happiness, or pain,
Mind is the one that experiences both.
Mind is responsible for bondage and liberation alike.
Win over the mind, you win the Universe. 150
No one has the strength to turn such a man into a sod
And throw him on the streets!
All the seven worlds are hidden in the mind.
Without mind, what work and actions could there be!
Realise that man himself is the mind, and live accordingly.

'"Discern what mind means!
It is the precious gem which looks dull
When it is part of the soil;
If polished, it shines bright.
Taking shelter in the body, the mind becomes exuberant. 160
The human body with its nine outlets is the means
Of experiencing happiness and sorrow;
It is also the means to attain salvation.
To a prudent achiever, the body itself is the abode of God.
A learned one will witness all the hardships suffered by the body
And yet remain calm.

'"The tremulous response
Travels far, ascends high, and descending low,
It merges with the void of unity that doesn't have
Any beginning, middle, or end. 170
Mind is the origin for the rising of the spirit;
It manifests itself as conceived in the womb.
You are the Perfect One, and indeed
The personification of Perfection.
Realise that your pilgrimage is from perfection to perfection,
And thus become the one revered by the whole world!

'"What is meditation?
It is that wondrous state where it blooms
As a flower in the solitude of mind;
That is, getting bathed in the glow of light. 180
Meditation is the rudder that enables a wavering ship
In the mid-ocean to steady its course.
What is a soul but the light that lights up the world
And it is the Supreme Soul indeed.
Meditation is that divine path which fixes the mind
In the emotion of *tattvamasi* – that you are the Absolute!
Meditation is the supreme potion that strengthens the mind.
When faced with trials and tribulations,
Running away from them isn't the
Proper alternative, O Raghava! 190

'"Don't you know the ways of the world?
There are countless worldviews:
Sometimes it appears to be high-spirited,
And horrible, at another time;
Gentle and pleasing at one time,
And terrifying at another instant.
You become spiritual not limited by the mortal body,
And none can afflict you then.
Cast away all doubts, and proceed swiftly.
The lute of the heart will strike a fresh note. 200
Earth, Water, Air, Fire, Ether,
Mind, Intellect, and Ego together constitute
All forms of life in this world, you see!

'"The three basic qualities of nature are –
Sattva, rajas, and *tamas* –
Virtue, passion, and ignorance – *rajas* tramples down *sattva*,
And ignorance triumphs trampling on passion.
Vitiating the mind, ignorance pushes one
To the well of sensual pleasures
And making one dwell in hell, it afflicts thus. 210

'"Be you the mine of good traits.
Let there be a firm mind, piety and the company
Of saints and ascetics.
Serving the father and mother is the noblest work.
Purity of mind and body is essential.
Let there be limits on what one should accept
And let there be humility.
Helping others, being charitable,
A smiling face, gentleness,
The feeling that I am not great, 220
Balanced mind and compassion are essential.
Pettiness of looking for others' fault isn't good.
Self-restraint and contentment are certainly needed.
Silence, fearlessness, seriousness, a firm mind, discernment,

And generosity are essential.
One must give up all improper deeds.
One must view honour and disgrace with equanimity.
Robbing others should be shunned, and one should
Appreciate the good quality in others.

' "Observing abstinence and chastity, 230
Exhibiting fearlessness and forgiving mistakes,
Performing meditation and oblations with fire,
Extending warm hospitality to guests,
Remaining unenvious, serving the highly eminent ones,
Meditating at heart on bondage and salvation,
Enduring the paradoxes and getting rid of avariciousness,
Treating all as equal to oneself,
Empathising with the suffering of others and helping them –
To live life thus is the means to attain salvation.

' "O, the crest-jewel of the Raghu dynasty! 240
Why are you hesitating to go to war?
Burning down emasculation be a valiant soldier in the battlefield.
Running away from war in the pretext
Of viewing war as violence is the trait of a coward.
Is it so simple to decide what is violence
And what is not one's duty?
Forgetting the dignity of a soldier and the ethics of war,
In the fickleness of mind.
How can one be ignorant of one's duties, tell me!
Why are you wailing like a weakling? 250
Look, war is the abode of supreme peace!

' "What else can I say?
Cross the mire of affection. Do not waste time.
Is it fair to lead a life caught up
In the net of confusion, remaining unresponsive, and
Losing all memory and reasoning?
Just like a tempest stealthily steers a ship to an unknown destination,
An unsteady mind takes away everything
And pushes one to dwell in hell.

To strive for attaining the Supreme Soul 260
That is Formless, Traitless,
Could there be any other ways than
Discharging one's duties with the feeling
Of complete surrender to the Will of God!
This body is the chariot; intellect is the charioteer,
Senses are the horses, mind is the reigns,
Sound and other sensual aspects are the tracks of the chariot.
Discerning this, if one proceeds,
What else could one get but victory?
Discerning this, if one proceeds,
What else could there be but Salvation? 270
Be you the epoch-making man to provide impetus
To the world and thus coalesce with
The Supreme Soul of Eternal Bliss.

'"Can there be enemies for you?
You are your own friend and foe.
Your success lies in your own hands.
If you proceed concentrating on your duty,
The brilliance of a rainbow will be yours.
The soil will turn to gold and poison into ambrosia! 280

'"In the land of Bharata,
Nationalistic feelings must bloom to the full.
All creed and religions must live and thrive.
The roads of common good must open up.
Brotherhood must flourish amongst all clans
And uniting with the mainstream nationalism,
All must live in harmony.
Racial discriminations must perish.
Ignorance, superstition and pomposity must be destroyed."'
Recalling the words of Sage Vasishtha thus, 290
Saumitri tried to instill the desire in Shri Rama
To wage war.

Canto One Hundred and Eighty-three

'Pacifying the Grief-stricken, Embrace Them Lovingly!'

||६||

Saumitri, who resembles Adishesha –
The sovereign of the Serpent race
Who safeguards the treasures of the world –
Said to Shri Rama:
'If you do not jump into war,
It would seem like an invitation to anarchy!
Do not be afraid of any blame.
When barbarism has taken over the Lankan culture,
Is it right to grieve bitterly abstaining from your duty?
Is it fair to turn a deaf ear when the epoch's bugle is sounded?   10
Like the sword that has come out of its sheath,
In the charming shape of half-moon the bridge is looking grand.
O Raghava, look!
The bridge appears like an edict of the strength of *vanaras*;
It appears like the parted hair of the goddess of your fame
And it stands radiant as a symbol of the universal consciousness.
Clip the attractive wings of Ravana's empire
And throw them away.'

Shri Rama replied:
'The Lankan army stands in the zeal of nationalism.
It has moved swiftly like a stream.
Do you think the city Ayodhya is near to us?
I do not know how it is possible to
Invade the Lankan fort with pride as we are
Dependent entirely on the strength of *vanara*-army!'

The very next moment Shri Rama's mind got distracted.
Gazing at the expansiveness of the sky,
Filled with intense emotions,
He turned into a poet and spoke thus:
'Look! The skylark is flying higher and higher, and
Piercing the blueness of the sky, it soars up like a deer.
Rising and singing, singing and rising
It is losing itself in the prime state of bliss!

'What shall I say, O Brother?
The vessel of my life is shattered and scattered here.
I have become like the heifer tethered to a post.
Not able to rise higher, I have drowned in the gorge of existence.
Rising up from the depths of my mind,
The grandeur of the Sarayu waters
Disturbed me as a dream; my heart is broken.

'My dreams of bringing humanity to fruition is
Shattered completely.
I do not know whether I am an idol of love or violence;
But have become the idol of paradoxes.
Dear brother, enough of this wily massacre of human lives.
The thirst for war-commotion should disappear.
Janaki has wisely said – non-violence is the supreme *dharma*.
Dear brother, how can I forget those words that
Explore the path of meaningful existence in this world!'

Saumitri replied:
'What is this, O brother?

You are the irresistible, irrepressible elephant in rut,
And as a man of equanimity,
How can you drown in such a paradox?
If Adishesha feels the pain of the weight borne by him,
Can he put down this universe, tell me?
By burning himself, the sun lights up the world.
To carry out the vital responsibility bestowed on you by the world is
Your bounden duty indeed! That being so,
Why this hesitation? 60

'*Karmayoga* is yours – you are duty-bound;
And the fruition of it will be the offering to God.
Working hard, but still feeling energetic as if never worked at all,
Sweating, but not wearied –
This is the way to exhibit dexterity in *karma*.
This war is inevitable to install justice.
The future of the epoch lies hidden in this war.
The mind of men is like the slippery staff;
If you forget yourself even for a second,
You will slide down swiftly. 70

'War is a daily festival.
Life is a battlefield where war is waged
Continually between good and evil.
As the war-music satiates the three worlds,
Traversing that path, can one fall short of contentment?
One should not worry about victory or defeat!
Silence sans argument, and mere surrender
Make life in the world like stagnant water.
If one thinks merely of one's own well-being,
Duty is easily forgotten. 80
Cowardliness is nothing but stupidity.

Life in lawless Lanka should be cleansed now.
Valour should rise, why do you hesitate?
Surge ahead to wage war.'

Rama reiterated his stance
Of abstaining from war:
'The piled up sins are now ready to bear fruition.
The wailing of men is heard everywhere,
The roots of peace are in shambles.
How can one redeem the humans through bloodshed?'   90

Saumitri replied:
'Shri Rama, what can I explain to you
About the features of *dharma*?
Evil should be punished without respite.
Where has the fragrance of the teachings
Of Sage Vishwamitra gone?

Shri Rama replied:
'War is violence-ridden.
We need a new strategy of winning without war.
Let us throw all the armaments to the sea.   100
Now we need conscious thinking that instills valour.
Science and knowledge have scaled new heights;
Nevertheless, good will, not having flourished, suffers badly.
Who can equal me when I am surrounded
By people who are well-meaning thinkers and honest friends!
There exists a world outside, and there is an inner world as well.
The heart is burning like a *yajnakunda*, the pit of sacrificial fire;
To protect that fire from getting extinguished
Is the true worship of Fire.
He who knows the taste of freedom would be liberated;   110
What benefit does war have?'

Lakshmana said:
'No, my Lord, no! It's impossible.
To punish the wicked and save the good, please do arrive;
Not forgetting to establish *dharma*,
Arrive to respond and voice the need of the epochs.
The sun is scorching and the earth lays waiting,
Rivers and ponds have dried up

And trees and shrubs have withered,
The mind of the universe has shrunken 120
And the clouds have dispersed.
The wealthy Lanka is waiting to
Receive the ambrosia of your love.

'Why are you in doubt still?
Defeat is the stepping stone to the thoroughfare of a new life;
It is possible to halt the journey for a while and then proceed.
Come forward to light a million lamps in every nook and corner.
I am speaking in your own tongue!
I am a blockhead.
Pardon me, O King! 130

'Because of you, even the blind have seen the world now,
The dumb have become great orators,
Valour has flowered and ignorance has disappeared,
A variety of desires have emerged joyfully.
The lotus of a new dawn is blossoming merrily.
Spreading the net of peace through war,
Give solace to the hearts of all and console humanity.'

Lakshmana continued:
'At the very first response, strength is
Emanating in all the ten directions of the world. 140
Assume the complete form.
The wheel of the new religion,
The religion of the epoch, stands ready.
Take charge of it and let it start rolling;
It is the unseen, it lies dormant,
And it is the essence of new energy,
It is resplendent with the glow of the New Epoch
That is fast approaching.'

Shri Rama got up.
Both walked silently and climbed the hill. 150
Saumitri spread tender foliage like a mattress.

As Shri Rama reclined there resting his head
On the soft animal-hide
And slept in the divine posture as Anantashayana,
Saumitri sat near his feet.
Just then, the moon rose in the east
On a Poushya day, the asterism being a full moon.
Just as a lion tears apart the forehead of an elephant in rut,
The moon emerged cleaving darkness.

Has Shri Rama reclined contemplating 160
A well-suited strategy to slay Ravana who dwells in darkness?
As if having discerned well Rama's intimate thoughts,
Saumitri said: 'Like a father you have showered
Love on your brothers, and giving a place to them
In your heart, you have nurtured them.
By killing Vali, you protected Sugriva.
The job of killing Ravana is inevitable.

'O Shri Rama! Arise!
Dashashira, the ten-headed one, has set the universe on fire.
The women in his captivity are burnt day and night 170
In the the fire of separation from their loved ones.
Ravana deserves to be punished.
Give up worrying. No affliction can bother you,
O Lord!

'Enough of this joking, O the one vowed to volition!
Arise, Shri Hari! Why delay anymore?
The mind of the epoch is filled with the strength of the epoch.
Bring it out.
Due to the pounding of the roaring waves
The ship of universal Life is swirling; 180
Save it fast and be the leader of the world.
The song of the birds is heard; tender sunrays are spreading.
Awaken the world from its slumber.
With the power of knowledge
Enliven the lives of people.

Swiftly generate in every mind the strength to wage war
And sound the drum to signal liberation of the world!'

The words of Saumitri were
Readily agreeable and breaking his profound silence,
Shri Rama said in contentment: 190
'Listen, O Saumitri, your words are soothing.
Setting aside lethargy, I will wage war.
I will sing the benedictory verse
For liberating the universe this instant.
I will fight in Lanka till my last breath
To ensure equality for all.'

As Shri Rama's words conveyed his
Firm decision to wage war, the hills and the valleys
Of the entire earth were lit up in sublime grandeur;
With thundering and lightning, and with powerful winds 200
It rained heavily; darkness enveloped,
And the fierce Goddess of Night became most fearsome!

On hearing the words of Shri Rama,
Plunging into the sea of joy
Saumitri praised Rama profusely:
'You are steadfastly truthful;
You are the embodiment of Soul;
You are soft-spoken and your speech is pleasant;
You are the embodiment of good conduct;
You have control over your emotions and you are brilliant; 210
You are the comforter to all living beings on this earth.
I shall never ever forsake you.
Reside, O Lord, in the temple of my mind!

'You are the spirit that brings inertness back to life;
You are the source of devotion.
The entire universe is waiting to see you.
A necklace of well-chosen pearls of virtue is
Adorning your neck.
Reside, O Lord, in the temple of my mind!

'You are both *saguna* and *nirguna* – the one 220
With and without attributes;
You are the driving spirit behind this universe;
Like the proverbial *chataka*-bird,
The hearts of all devotees are yearning for you.
Reside, O Lord, in the temple of my mind!

'You are Hari in the form of a human;
You are mercy incarnate;
The vitality of all living forms flows into you;
You are the shrine of love.
You are the one who fills the strength of thunder in a cinder; 230
Reside, O Lord, in the temple of my mind!

'You are free from all agitations
And emotions that afflict mortals;
You are the immaculately Pure One
Who tears away the web of illusion;
You are the one who has crushed treachery,
Arrogance, and deceitfulness
For the common good of all.
Reside, O Lord, in the temple of my mind!

'You declared: 240
"Longing for another man's wife and wealth
Are akin to deadly poison."
Beautiful, amazingly wonderful, is your mind.
Pacifying the grief-stricken,
You embrace them lovingly.
Reside, O Lord, in the temple of my mind!'

Canto One Hundred and Eighty-four

'Why do You Pour Hot Water on the Tree of Friendship?'

||๑||

Surfeited with impudence, Ravana resides in Lanka
Ostracising those who advised him well.
Compassionate life has collapsed in Lanka.
Ravana's son, Indrajit, has nurtured the tree of wickedness
And has vowed to root out the power of enemy's valour.

Prahasta arrived at the court of Ravana
And with folded hands, said:
'There is fresh news, O Lord!
Having constructed the bridge,
Shri Rama and Lakshmana, along with *vanaras*, 10
Are now camping in the Suvela Mountain!
The time of destruction has come.
The valour of the invading *vanara*-army
Matches the valour of the *vanara* that set Lanka ablaze.
Approaching Lanka, they are thundering:
"We will slay the clan of Lankesha."
I do not know how you would stop them.
These are hard times indeed.

As the wealthy Lanka is now wilting in danger,
I do not know the means to save the kingdom.'   20

At that instant, summoning
The spies Shuka and Sarana, Lankesha said:
'Assess the strength of Rama's camp immediately.
Find out the strength of their unity
And the kind of war preparations.
Learn all that happened after Vali's demise;
Find out whether they have arrived under compulsion
Or with love;
And how massive is their wealth, gold, gems, and women;
Go secretly and find all this out   30
And return swiftly.'

Leaving the court
He reached the palace. Sweet-talker Mandodari
Who discerned the situation very well
Spoke to Ravana lovingly:
'Enough of this enmity.
We can surely win over Rama with love.
As he is Dinakara, the sun, why do you foster enmity?
He is Shiva, the Destroyer; he is Kamadhenu,
The celestial cow that grants every wish.   40
He is manifested in a multitude of lives,
And he is the one and the only Supreme Lord.
He is the protector of all and is ever-ready to grace the devotees.
There is no fear of being punished; he does not punish.
By surrendering Janaki,
It is better to move on in friendship;
And that is good for everyone.'

Not heeding the advice,
Lankesha replied in anger:
'The crimes committed by Rama and Lakshmana   50
Are countless, and you know it all.
In the eagerness of gaining victory, he has disturbed peace.

Their net of cheating is expansive.
I am not a fool who is ignorant of the attacks
Of the Aryans. When I wage war, the world
Shouts oppression. But when Rama fights, it is called
War of justice! What is this law of the world?
Under the guise of fulfilling the father's vow
Kaikeyi has planned the extension of their kingdom.
The uncrowned king of Ayodhya is Rama for sure. 60
Kaikeyi, Bharata, and Shatrughna are all pawns
In the game of dice; do not be under any illusion.
As I am bestowed with the title – 'Controller of Time,'
Shattering the evil designs of the Aryan brothers,
The radiance of the soul of Lanka has
Emerged exhibiting profound valour in all its grandeur.

'Pouring the oil of *danavas*' blood,
I will safeguard the flame of Lanka's fame
From getting extinguished.
I will not allow the Dravidian valour to fade. 70
As I have allowed multiculturalism to flourish,
Will I allow the onslaught of monoculture to thrive?'
Beaming with pride, Ravana said thus.

Disappointed, wife Mandodari once again spoke to her
Husband in a pacifying tone:
'Why do you sprinkle hot water on the tree of friendship?
I had a bad dream and I am frightened.
I dreamt that a large serpent was holding me
In its tight grip for a long time, and I sweated.
I am afraid all the time in my mind 80
That something dreadful might happen
And this has been disturbing me since then, O love!
A volcano is smouldering in my mind.
O my Lord! Knowing full well the power of Shri Rama,
Why have you fallen into the gorge of arrogance?
Look! Lanka will be a victim of your pride.

How many *mangalaya*s, marital threads will reach the ocean,
I do not know; how many intestines of young ones will be ripped
And gutted, I do not know.
Your cruelty has no beginning and end.' 90

Not caring for her words,
Lankesha said: 'To me, Lanka is the
Playground of my childhood, it is the garden of my youth.
It is the wealthy home for the entire clan of *asuras*.
I will now unravel the evil designs of those
Who set out to destroy it.
I will not fail to sound the drum of victory.
The war between Rama and Ravana is only a pretext.
To disperse the dark clouds of oppression
That have engulfed the Indian continent is my aim, 100
And I am vowed to do that.
I will destroy for sure the ploy hatched
In the pretext of war for justice.
Look! The root of Brahma's creation
Is rotting there. Darkness has enveloped everywhere.
As fresh buds haven't sprouted, superstition is on the rise.
The old loam has become home for the termites.
I will respond to the sufferings of the people.
I will light the lamp of exploring Truth.
Watch! I will bring all the worlds' knowledge 110
And science here!

'I will clear the fog of faults and loopholes,
Melt the worries; trust my volition!
I will root out the ill fame that, "Lankesha has
Drowned himself in sensuous pleasures."

'Look! Lanka will be home for the virtuous.
Is the obsession of boasting one's fame rightful?
Lankan culture is the tree of fragrant flowers.
Stripping the body bare, filling the mind with darkness,
And losing oneself in troublesome trivial worldly pursuits – 120

Will I allow such things to flourish? I will not be afraid.
I will fight unto death.'

Mandodari said:
'It is true; it is true that nobody can match your love
In this entire universe.
Nevertheless, abducting Janaki,
You have lost peace and honour;
You have become lonely like the meteor
That has fallen from the sky;
Is your proclivity an anthill of pollution? 130
If you turn it into an abode of the Creator by harnessing it well,
It will play the melodious music.
Expel all sins from your heart, O Lord!
You have won my heart with love;
But why this obstinacy now?
Play the music of a life that is forever pure.
Conduct an ensemble of sweet melodies
In the yard of the garden.
Give away Janaki; make me float in
Your world of immortality, O Lord!' 140

Ravana said:
'By breaking the mighty bow of Shiva,
Shri Rama married Maithili;
After winning over me, let him carry Sita to Saketa.
Suffering the pangs of separation from Sita,
Shri Rama has become weak.
The wearied Rama will not get his Sita.
Do not worry about what happens in the future.
Can he win over me! I will destroy all the secrets
Of Fate. Look, who could crush me!' 150

Mandodari spoke to her husband in a pleasing
And entreating way:
'Discern my suffering; do not be adamant, O Love!
Many doubts and worries frighten me.

The cruel voice of an imminent upheaval is heard here.
Before the sinful sprout grows into a plant and yields fruit,
It is better to extirpate it. Inordinate affection
Is quite intense indeed.
The butterfly loses its life desiring the crest of light.
Tempted by the palate, the fish gets caught in the hook and dies. 160
Abstain from passionate love.'

Ravana got disturbed and his
Self-confidence sank low. Not wanting
To reveal the turbulence of his mind to anyone,
He kept shuffling between
The royal court and the harem, lost in thought:
'What shall I do? What shall I do?
I will not give away Janaki; I will defeat the enemy.
I cannot cut down the tree of self-esteem.
Even if the earth becomes topsy-turvy, the ocean disappears, 170
And the sun rolls down, I will not give away Janaki.
I will turn all the royal power of Ayodhya futile.'
Soliloquising thus, he moved about lamenting and blabbering.

Mind clouded with delusions
Mandodari started seeing many violent scenes:
Sniffing out, the carnivorous evil spirits running around;
Thousands of bodies burning in the funeral pyres;
Lined up skeletons mocking here and there;
The crowns that slipped from the severed heads
Shining brightly, blinding the eyes; 180
Eagles, jackals and dogs dragging the cadaver
And pulling out the gut, have created a horrible scene.
Mandodari shuddered in fright!

Seated at the centre of the royal court,
Dashakantha, the ten-headed one, said: 'Listen, my kith and kin!
Building a bridge, the sons of Dasharatha – Rama and Saumitri
Have invaded Lanka now
Along with their *vanara* army. If you have

Any strategic plans to counter their attack, speak out now.'
Hearing the words of Ravana, 190
Nikumbha replied with humility:
'As only the trivial humans and *vanaras* have come,
Why should we fear them?
We have complete confidence in your strength,
Why wait, surge ahead.'

Opposing the words of Nikumbha,
Prahasta got up hurriedly and said:
'O King! Those are not the words of discretion.
Do not heed to the words of sycophants and be in a hurry.
These are foolish people who are ignorant of the laws of war. 200
Is violence a feature of valour?
Instituting justice through bloodbath is cruelty.
When Hanuma set fire to Lanka,
Where were these valiant commanders-in-chief?
Valiant soldiers, who are equal to Hanuma in valour,
Have all lined up in countless numbers.
Look at Kalanemi, the commander-in-chief!
Frightened on seeing the *vanara*-army, he has returned in haste.
Shun your illusions, O Lord! Give away Janaki.
Not agreeing to the soothing words of Vibhishana, 210
You banished him then. The freeing of Janaki
Would be the auspicious beginning of good for your own soul,
For Lanka, and for the good of the world.

'After surrendering Sita,
If Rama still wants war, the whole
World will discern that Rama is greedy of annexing kingdoms.
Think of this for a second – with the surrendering of Janaki
The revenge for the humiliation meted out
To sister Chandranakhi would be complete;
The entire world will discern the truth 220
That Ravana does not yearn for another man's wife.'

On hearing the advice of Prashasta
Ravana got wild. Anger welled up in him,
And he said: 'Stop, stop this nonsense.
Who taught you this foolish discourse?
Are you born to the clan of bad instruction
That teaches one to love the enemy?
You were not born of the iron-hot sperms
Of the *danavas*, but a worm born out of mixed blood.'
'To a man caught in the web of Time, 230
Good counsel doesn't taste good.'
So saying, Prashasta left the court!
The assembly dispersed.

To forget the burden of sorrow,
Seizing *rudraveena*, the lute,
Ravaneshwara lost himself in the world of music
And forgot everything!

Canto One Hundred and Eighty-five

'Put an End to the World that Doesn't Live Making Obeisance'

||६||

Just as shade spreads on the lawn,
Flowers from the trees that are in full bloom are falling down.
The yellow green earth resembles a silk carpet.
Fragrant cool breeze is blowing gently.
Flowery creepers have entwined the trees passionately.
The buzzing bees have turned all the shrubs and trees into flutists.
The rhythm of life and emotions of love are so united
As if nothing else exists!

But this pleasant and wonderful atmosphere
Is mocking at Rama, increasing his pangs of separation;
Tender buds were looking like the fiery tongues of lost love.
Shri Rama lamented:
'In the pangs of separation from Sita,
To me the world appears vacuous;
Now I do not know how I could fight the battle with zeal.'

Saumitri replied:
'You are the pinnacle of the world, the end of endless ocean,
And the everlasting One.

As if the stream of liberation is flowing in the land of internment,
When confidence is springing up creating 20
A radiant tapestry in the mind,
Unmoved, why are you worrying, O Lord?
Arise with zeal, this instant!
In the land where you do not exist
The sun does not rise;
The moon does not rise, stars do not sparkle;
Lightning does not gleam, and thunder does not roar.
You alone are the beacon of light to everything!'

Lakshmana continued:
'The world is suffering 30
From sorrow beyond all limits.
The world is waiting for your mercy; bless it!
Put an end to the world that does not live making obeisance,
And impede the mind that does not retract fearing impropriety.'
Hearing these words, Rama got up instantly,
And looking happily at the camp, whispered to himself:
'Enough of wasting time;
The task must be accomplished.'
Deciding thus, he summoned the chief
Of the *vanaras* and said: 40

'Though I have promised Vibhishana
That destroying Ravana-cult through the path of non-violence
I will safeguard Lankesha, that opportunity is missed.
If there is no truce, get ready for the war.
If Lankesha gives away Sita, there will be no war and
The bridge built for war will turn into a bridge of friendship.
The war must be avoided!

'The advice of the brother,
The good words of the loving wife
Might force Ravana to introspect. 50
I believe that he might agree for truce. Listen,
There is a saying –

"If you kill after warning sufficiently, it is not a sin.
The strategy of administering justice by punishment
Should be the last option." That is the law of the monarchs.'
Sending an intelligent emissary,
Let's put forth our proposal for reconciliation
And try for a truce. Friends! Advice –
Who could be sent as the emissary?'

Responded Jambavanta with folded hands: 60
'Listen, Shri Rama!
You are a brave man marching towards victory.
If Anjaneya is sent for peace talks,
Recalling the fashion in which he set Lanka ablaze,
Ravana might get angry;
Ravana cannot tolerate Sugriva either.
As he has deserted Lanka,
Ravana's brother Vibhishana is not a right choice.
I have grown old and do not know the nuances of politics.
I entreat you to send Angada, the son of Vali. 70
He has mastered logic, and like mercury, is quick to act.
Respecting him, Ravana might agree for peace talks.
If the truce fails, it is infamy for Ravana
And the world will bestow fame on you for sure.'
'Bravo! Bravo! We give our consent,'
Shouted all in unison rejoicing.

Jambavanta went on:
'The one who maintains self-esteem,
The one who guards the fame of his master,
The one who speaks good words of advice 80
Without getting fooled by the enemy's tricks,
The one who does not get allured by women and material riches,
The one who is fully conversant with the pros and cons
Of the mission undertaken,
The one who does not blame others,
The one who speaks pleasantly,

And the one who treads cautiously meditating on Rama
In the depths of his heart, is the one fit to be an emissary.
And that is none other than Angada indeed.'

Shri Rama beamed in happiness, 90
And calling Angada near him, whispered thus:
'O Angada! There are three types of emissaries in the world:
The first type is the one who
By settling an accord between two kings,
Builds a bridge of friendship, and thus unites them;
The second kind garners support for his king from others!
The third kind is the one who creates pandemonium
In the enemy-kingdom, takes away the wealth
And attracts the officers of the king towards him!
I grant you the power of carrying out the peace talks; 100
Get into the city of Lanka at once!

'A peaceful agreement is viewed as truce;
The method of strife is to take control over the situation;
A temporary inaction is called a stance;
If one sets out to attack, it is called a military march.
Seeking refuge in another king is a protective step!

'The ethics of Economics make the one
Who is weak, settle for a truce on one's own initiative.
If one is a powerful king, one will take control of the situation;
If a king feels that he is equally powerful, 110
He will take the right stance.
If one really desires to take control,
It is good to march ahead with full force.
When caught up in a helpless situation, it is good to seek refuge.
When in need of cooperation from another king,
It is better to follow the precept of give and take,
And it is the secret path of success, dear son!

'Beneficial results will be achieved
Through good deeds and cultured behaviour.

If sensual pleasures rise high, and riches are aplenty, 120
Like undigested food that causes sickness,
Foolishness creeps in and the mind gets inebriated.
Getting boons through hard penance, and then perishing
By taking recourse to the wrong path –
This is the routine history of the *rakshasas*.
Portend Ravana that he shall fall –
Patiently convince him of this blatant truth.
Even if one is very intelligent, one stumbles at times,
Transgresses the boundary of lust without cognizance,
And falls into the abyss driven by sins and destiny. 130

'Listen, O son of Vali!
As you possess intelligence and strength of character,
Discerning the purpose of the mission,
Carry out the peace talks.
You are very intelligent and will do the task
Assigned and I have that confidence in you.
Lankesha's hands that gently rocked your cradle
When you were a babe,
On seeing you, will certainly embrace you that instant
And the assigned task will be successfully accomplished for sure.' 140

'Will Lankesha agree for the truce?
He stands there desiring war.
His enmity for Rama has grown like a giant tree.
I do not know what I will do!
Discerning the secrets of battle,
I will sow the seeds of fear in the minds of *rakshasas*
And infuse my efforts with those that
Hanumanta has already inflicted
And return!' Thinking thus in his mind,
He prostrated himself before Rama and said: 150

'O Shri Rama!
By sending me for the peace talks,
You have infused exuberance.

With your blessings, the love for Rama will grow.
All have grown and flourished under the grace of your blessings.
What you desire shall be achieved;
We are there only as a pretext
To carry out the tasks assigned by you.'

On hearing this,
Shri Rama proudly embraced Angada, 160
Caressed him and planted a kiss on his forehead.
Then Sugriva, lifting up Angada who had already bowed to him,
Smelt his forehead and blessed him:
'Be successful, dear son,
Emerge victorious in the task assigned by Rama.'

Canto One Hundred and Eighty-six

'When You Tread the Path of Truth, the World will be with You!'

||௬||

Like thunder that strikes the herd of sheep,
Like a surging whirlwind that engulfs, roaring aloud,
Valiant Angada entered Lanka.
People looked at him with fear
And recalled the destruction of Lanka by Hanuma.

Seeing Angada,
Women ran in different directions, hid their sarees and
All the oil barrels, and by pouring water into the oven,
They put off the fire. Opening their
Deer-like eyes, they watched him hiding. 10

'Who is this, who is this –
The one who walks fearlessly, holding his head high?
Who is this valiant youth who walks with pride?'
Such whispers were heard in Lanka city.
Scared, they shut the doors of their shops.
Not fearing, the children came forward and
Offered bunches of plantain to Angada,
And followed him with excitement.

Prahasta, who was patrolling the city streets,
Spotted Angada strolling on the road.
'By provoking, we were ruined previously.
It's better to win over him through soothing words' –
Contemplating thus,
He approached Angada and said:

'O valiant traveller!
Tell me who you are and why you have come.
I don't see anger in you; you are all smiles.
Seeing your smiling face,
I feel drawn to you with affection.
Through your looks alone you exhibit enough valour and pride.
A feeling of respect for you is growing within me!
You haven't come as a thief; you are out in the open.
Are you moving towards the palace of Lankesha?'

With great excitement, Angada replied:
'I am the son of Vali; Angada is my name.
I am the messenger of Rama;
I am the crown-prince of Kishkindha.
I have not come to wage war or to set fire to Lanka;
I have come carrying a message of peace.
I must succeed in settling a truce, and avoid war.
Shri Rama does not desire any senseless violence.
I like you immensely; I like your affection.
Your benevolence is great;
Your sophisticated demeanour is great indeed.
Your sweet words have touched my heart;
Tell me who you are.
I am awe-struck by the splendour of Lanka.'

Prahasta felt great admiration for Angada.
He approached him and smelt his forehead affectionately,
And spoke endearingly thus:
'Hatred for Rama has grown into a giant tree
In the mind of Ravana.

Can you sow the seeds of comfort in a hot desert?
Once, when I pleaded for a peace proposal,
Not tolerating the good counsel, he walked out in great fury!
Your function as a messenger will be
Like pouring clarified butter to Ravana's fire of fury.
Your truce will not succeed;
Be quick to save your life as Ravana has
Passed a strict order to – "kill the *vanaras* at sight".
Enticed by the sight of your sweet face,   60
We have failed in our duty by not killing you already.
Leave at once, my child.'

Angada said:
'You are a well-informed person.
I am pleased by your affection; but I am not scared.
Being the son of Vali,
I have come now to make yet another attempt
For Ravana's own good.
When as a babe I was sleeping comfortably in the cradle,
Ravana, rocking the cradle, had sung a lullaby for me then.   70
He will receive me affectionately and
Not kill me. If you dispatch me
Not allowing me to call on Ravana, will he not be angry?
Lead me quickly to the palace court.'

Discerning the intentions of
Angada, Prashata agreed and did all the preparations.
With all royal splendour and grandeur, he led
The valiant Angada to the palace in a procession.
What blowing of trumpets! What *kalasha*, and sparkling mirror!
What beauty of the maids carrying the pails!   80
Citizens viewed the procession with wonder!

Hearing the news of Angada's arrival,
Dashashira, the ten-headed one,
With great excitement came to receive him
And shedding tears of love, hugged Angada affectionately.

Offering him an exalted seat,
Ravana spoke to him tenderly:

'You are the crown-prince indeed.
Lanka is blessed by your arrival!
Not tolerating the friendship among the confederation 90
Of Lanka, Janasthana, and Kishkindha,
Rama and Lakshmana killed your father so that
The *vanaras* and the *rakshasas* shall never be friends again;
Having accomplished that, they have camped here now.
If not today, I will destroy the hegemony
Of the Aryan culture soon. Now, tell me, Angada,
What brings you here?

Angada said:
'Listen, O Ravaneshwara – Lord of Lanka!
The burden of your love is on me. 100
Lord Shiva and Brahma have all given you boons.
You are a monarch, and an idol of success.
I have arrived here as the messenger of Rama.
Desiring your good, I have come for peace talks.
As you are the son of Pulastya, whether the abduction
Of someone else's wife brings you any glory, tell me;
Give away the mother.'

'What is this dear son?'
Interjected Lankesha hurriedly.
'Being the son of my dear friend Vali, 110
How can you be a valet to Rama, the wrong-doer!
He has sent you here as an emissary only to be killed.
You are like my son, I cannot kill you.
Beware! Rama is a charlatan;
Do not be a prey to the trap waylaid by him.
He is dreaming of becoming the sole monarch.
Desert his companionship.'

Angada said:
'One neck to ten heads; one head to ten necks –

The form of *brahmarakshasa* – 120
I remember such strange stories
My mother had told me in my childhood.
Before I saw you, I had strange
Feelings and thoughts about you.
But I am happy today:
You are not what I thought you would be.

'Set those words aside.
Cast away the illusion that Rama is a trivial human being.
He is a one-man army and a fiercely valorous man
Who has killed great warriors belonging to your camp. 130
This chance for truce has come to you unasked.
I am your well-wisher
And I haven't come here as your enemy.
Give away Sita; prevent the massive annihilation.'

Lankesha said:
'O Angada! You are ignorant of Rama's tricks.
He is a charlatan, you see.
He has slain your father deceitfully.
Sugriva has no love lost for you.
Plotting truce as a pretext, he has sent you to be killed by me. 140
Rama and your uncle Sugriva are your secret enemies.
Let that be so. Listen to my words now.
I'll make you the king of Kishkindha
And perform your coronation at once.
With the blowing of trumpets, and the beating of drums
Beautiful damsels will welcome you in a grand procession,
And perform the pearly *arati*.
The time is ripe now to teach a lesson to the rogues
Who are power-mongers.
Dasharathi, son of Dasharatha, is dreaming 150
Of crossing the sea in a raft instead of a ship!
How can he stand against my army?'

Angada replied:
'I am young and I am like your son.

I don't possess the strength to advice you, O King!
What annexing of territories,
What a life of pleasures you have led!
Under the pretext of the humiliation meted out to Chandranakhi
You abducted the mother and tortured her in many ways.
You have banished the one who advised for your own good. 160
Tataka, Subahu, Maricha, Khara, Dushana
Have all given up their lives in the task of fulfilling your desires.
I have come as a messenger to caution you.
Thinking that there is a treasure beneath,
You went on digging deeper and deeper,
But found only a vessel of worthless cowrie.
You have fallen into the pit of suffering!

'What is so great about riches?
That wealth is only a visor.
It has fattened you up and blinded you as well. 170
O King! Holding on to the path of peace,
Abstain from violence;
Tread on the path of seeking justice.'

'Shri Rama has said:
"The doors of downfall are – atheism, falsehood, anger,
Lack of devotion, indolence in work,
Deserting the company of good people,
Sensuous temptations, taking unilateral decisions,
Consulting the inexperienced;
These are all weaknesses in a king." 180
Aren't you aware of these, tell me.
You have become a nest of poison for all the wrong doings.
A giant serpent resides in you.
Be quick to act on truce, and escape from danger.
You have made yourself trivial; acquiring virtues
Be a normal person.
Yours is a wicked plan.
The allies are not with you anymore.

If you tread the path of truth, the world will be with you.
If you behave indiscreetly, you will be left alone. 190
Which state has the chance to expand its commerce
And wealth other than Shri Lanka, tell me?
When there is an opportunity to build an extraordinary empire,
Show political prudence for the welfare of the state.'

Listening patiently to the words
Of Angada, Ravana said:
'Peace without justice is useless like the flower in the graveyard.
Raghupati is a python that devours every kingdom.
I wonder how you have become his emissary for peace!
Are you giving me bitter pills coated with sugar? 200
Why don't you see the wickedness of the Aryan culture?

'Is Sugriva a good man?
He has taken your mother under his control.
In the ensuing war, he will send you with a weak army
And get you killed for sure.
I am not ignorant of the strategies of Economics!
Desirous of conquest, when an army arrives to attack,
Whichever ruler it confronts first on its way, will be the enemy;
In this case, it was Chandranakhi.
Later on, it was the turn of Khara, Dushana, Trishira and others. 210
Again, when Sugriva extended the hand of friendship,
Rama killed Vali hiding behind a tree.
Vibhishana came crying for help.
Being well-versed in the precepts of Economics,
With a pre-planned course, he stands there filled
With the desire of extending his kingdom.
As he has said, attack on Lanka
Is the final phase of that course.

'I have decided to wage a war.
Do not ensnare me in the net of truce and obligation. 220
Keep quiet. Surrendering, I will not live.
I will fight till I am exhausted.

My victories have been etched on
The rocks in the mountains and hills everywhere.
I who have reigned as the supreme monarch of the world
For ages, can I tolerate them who have killed
And humiliated my people and have come
To invade Lanka! I will give away Janaki
If Rama surrenders like a coward and implores!
Only then there shall be no war.' 230

Discerning that the time was right
For exercising the strategic principles of truce,
Angada replied:
'You see, all anger, flaws, anxieties, as well as bad tongue
That could cause war should be shunned!
Why are you cutting the tree of fame with a saw?

'Soul is the river;
Virtue is the milestone;
Truth is the water that flows;
Good behaviour is the bank; 240
And compassion is the wave.
Taking a holy dip in such waters,
If you get rid of your sins,
Good days are ahead for everyone!

'To the edifice of kingdom,
Righteousness is the foundation;
If you do wrong, the edifice will collapse.
If you lead a life of dedication, possessing
All the eight good qualities –
Giving alms, meditation, truthfulness, 250
Fearlessness, perusal of scriptures,
Forgiveness, not being greedy, and being honest –
The very source of salvation will be yours.
In the absence of culture, ego surfaces in full glory.
If you give up ego, humility will flourish.
Be full of humility; your fame will not diminish.

Come with me; I'll take you to the Suvela Mountain.
To a valiant person, humility is the most befitting ornament!

'Do not ignore the *vanaras* and humans
As merely trivial. By weaving together reeds of straw 260
Into a rope, even an elephant in rut can be tethered with it!
The tree of courage grown on the banks of the river of life
Will be washed away by the waves of lust, you see.
Though a king of all the three worlds,
If he becomes a slave of desires,
He ends up being the slave of the world!

'A new light has emerged
In Lanka, envisioning a new dawn.
They have crushed dictatorship to dust.
They are contemplating to build a new nation 270
By destroying the ramparts that curtail freedom!
The battle between the *devas* and the *rakshasas*
Is indeed the battle between darkness and light.

'O King! As you are a slave to the vices,
I do not know the way to stop Lanka's downfall.
Like the bee that is drawn by the aroma
Dies being entrapped in it,
Why do you invite the Goddess of Death?
Why do you become an axe to the clan of Sage Pulastya?
Do not crush Lanka's lotus of fortune!' 280

Losing his restraint
Lankesha said: 'O Prince Angada, listen!
As I am Lankesha, the one whose name alone
Causes tremors in all the three worlds,
Your oratorical skills will not succeed in binding us –
Rama and Ravaneshwara – the sworn enemies, in a truce.

'What is there in Rama?
Is Ayodhya with him? Is earth's daughter by his side?
By sheer indiscretion, he has lost one after the other.

As all kind of wealth is with me now, 290
Desert that empty-handed Rama; sit on my lap;
I'll protect you like a son.
Do not say no! I warn you!

'May you be accursed!
Why do you live at the mercy of Rama –
The one who killed your father deceitfully?
Killing Sugriva, I will coronate you as king, for sure.
Vali's soul would have sunk low in disgust
Viewing your surrender to Rama;
Console your father's soul; it will be good for you. 300
Do not fall into the trap waylaid by the Aryan tricksters.
You are an innocent boy! If you are with me,
You will conquer the world. Is Rama any match to you?
Abstain from the life of a valet and deserting
The slavish obligation,
Be an indisputable sovereign.'
Saying so, Ravana approached
Angada and caressed him affectionately.

That instant, Angada
Discerned the meanness and vileness of Ravana; 310
He became aware of the secrets of divide and rule policy;
And of being pushed into the whirlpool of enticement.
Not losing confidence, Angada said with great restraint:
'I am reminded of a wise-saying:
"One can bring back a gem caught
Between the teeth of a crocodile;
One can cross the seas riding on a wave;
One can tie a ferocious serpent on one's braid of hair;
But it is impossible to mend a foolish man."
Don't be like that, O King! 320
Accept these as words of good counsel from Angada,
The son of your dear friend Vali.
Sita is like thunder; she will burn you to ashes.

You have become the abode for the sinful deeds of the *rakshasas*.
Having received many boons, you have misused their powers.
Give up enmity; give away Sita, the daughter of earth.

'Being my father's dear friend,
I beg you with all humility:
Before Lanka gets destroyed for your sins,
Before your kindred get killed, 330
Before your kingdom and all its treasures come to naught,
Before you dig your own grave,
Go to Rama. He will forgive all
Your wrong doings,
And protect you.

'Yes, I am the son of Vali.
My father died having taken recourse to wrong doings;
But my father realised his mistakes lying on his death-bed;
And he breathed his last repenting.
But you are fortunate to get this opportunity 340
To make amends while still living!
Accept my words of advice.
You are the shrewdest among the shrewd,
And most intelligent of them all.
If your great worldly achievements do not ennoble you,
Your heart would be home to envy and desire
And they will destroy you.
Considering me a kid, do not neglect my good counsel
And die. Do not shut the windows of a better dawn.'

Anger welled up in Lankesha. 350
But not wanting to lose the son of Vali,
He spoke controlling his anger:
'Though having been born in the clan of great warriors,
You have joined the enemy camp;
It is like a lion-cub joining the herd of sheep.
Desert their company, be the king of Kishkindha
And sound the drum of Kannada, dear son.

There is no end to a man's wants;
They are like the waves of the sea
That keep chasing one after the other, 360
And how to satiate them!
Rama is caught in the vortex of desires.
We should mow him down and hoist the
Flag of Karnataka's valour. Do not fear. Be not afraid.
You are young, and you do not know Rama's past.
He is cruel at heart, but has a sweet tongue.
For outward appearance, he looks pure like milk,
But possesses fiery poison within.
Forging a bond between Mithila and Kosala through marriage,
Annexing the kingdoms of the north and north-east, 370
He has pushed your *vanaras* into the forest-city
Of Kishkindha. That is his gift to you.
Hoodwinking you, he has drawn you all
Under the shade of his compassion. Do not forget that.
Join hands with me. Together we will celebrate the victory
Of *vanaras* and *rakshasas*.
Let us put an end to the ploy of expansion
Of Aryan empire through annexation of other kingdoms.'

As Ravana thus tried to open
A new chapter in the life of Angada, 380
It seemed as if the mountain peaks were clouded
By countless shadows. Angada spoke:

'Listen, O Ravaneshwara!
Shri Rama, the valiant one of the Raghu clan,
Is housed in my heart.
By attempting to poison and distract my mind
Advocating divide and rule policy, you are trying
To pull me to your camp. I will not join you.
All the witchcraft and magic will fail, you see.
It is not a fair desire to drown me in the well 390
Of ignorance where you are drowned already.

Reposing faith in me, Shri Rama has sent me for peace talks;
I will not think of deceiving him even in my dreams.
You do not know the graceful personality of Shri Rama;
He is the embodiment of goodness;
He does not desire harm even to his enemies.

'Look at Vibhishana!
He has done the greatest sacrifice!
The instant you banished him
He approached Rama not with the lure of becoming a king. 400
He is living peacefully under Shri Rama's protection.
When Shri Rama said: "I will crown you the king of Lanka,"
With folded hands Vibhishana replied, "No!"
He has found fulfillment in leading a life of renunciation.

'You said repeatedly that Rama killed my father;
You are trying to make vain attempts to win me over.
You are the traitor who drove away your brother.
Deserting the benefits of good company, you have ruined yourself.
Lead a life that kindles light in your soul;
Live a life perceiving the grandeur of Shri Rama!' 410

Protesting the words of Angada,
Lankeshwara said thus:
'He has no genuine love for Lanka.
Then why did he get Lanka burnt treacherously by Hanuma?
I know his game plans very well.
If he had no intentions of war, why the bridge then?
Don't I know his plans of annexing Lanka?
You have spoken harsh words.
I have tolerated you because you are the son of my dear friend,
And also killing the messenger is against the ethics of warfare. 420

'I am advising you again.
Do not be a slave of Rama and lose your self-esteem.
I am there to support you;
Be the most eminent of the *vanara* clan;

Be the crest-jewel on the crown of Bhuvaneshwari –
The patron Goddess of Kannada.
Who are the valiant men there to fight me?
In the pangs of separation from his wife,
Rama has lost all his bravery and valour;
Saumitri too has sunk in the sorrow of his elder brother;   430
Are you and Sugriva any match to me?
Vibhishana is a coward; Jambavanta is old;
And Hanuma has lost his face and ethics.
Where do you find valour
And war strategies for this trivial cause?'

Angada replied:
'You do not know Hanuma.
When he set fire to Lanka in front of your eyes
Where was your valour hiding, speak!
Had you lost your valour, or did you collapse awe-struck?   440
Did valour in Lanka get evaporated then, tell me!
The valour you did not exhibit then, would you show it now?
Not able to subdue a trivial monkey, you have lost.
What happened to your arms, ammunition,
And magical powers and strengths?
If it were any other emperor, unable to bear this humiliation,
Renouncing all, would have taken recourse to meditation!
Making your friendship, my father suffered.
Why should I suffer now knowing you well?
I will not leave Rama, the one who fulfills his father's wishes,   450
And the one who is the protector of virtuous people.
He has given new life to the women who were deserted;
He has ameliorated the unfortunate ones.
Uncle Sugriva is valiant and upright,
He has treated Tara, my mother, like his own mother.

'Who is not aware of your weaknesses?
Sahasrarjuna thrashed you with his mace,
Subdued you and when he was taking

You to the city as a prisoner,
Pulastya begged him to free you, and he did so.   460
Everyone knows this.
When I was a baby, my father brought you captive
And tied you to my cradle.
You were humiliated then being kicked on the head.
The entire world knows about your valour!'

Hearing this, Ravana thundered:
'Enough, enough of this, you wicked one!
Misusing my leniency shown to you as the son of my friend,
How dare you mock at me!
You do not know the ways of the world, immature boy!   470
Enough of this stupidity!
Speak not! The world shudders at my strength.
I am an ardent devotee of Shiva, and I am valiant.
Just as a raft vacillates when an elephant in rut climbs on it,
The entire globe wavers when I walk!
Not knowing my powers, why do you chatter?
Discern my fame, glory and valour first,
And speak only then, you young brat!

'Mighty Kumbhakarna is brother to me;
Indrajit, the one who defeated Indra, is my son.   480
Building a bridge by placing floating-stones together
Is a great work for you, uh!
Birds cross the ocean easily;
There is nothing great about Hanuma crossing it.
Stop this praise of Rama's valour and do not brag.
When one has valour, why should one act
Cowardly and feign a truce?
I will fight; I will kill them all and flaunt my valour!'

'When I have come as a messenger,
It is not good to be angry,' thought Angada and said: 490
'Vali in Kishkindha, and Ravana in Lanka, both share many
Similarities with Rama; I intended to save both

And yearned to promote goodwill among them all.
Without waging a war, I wanted to bring Ayodhya,
Kishkindha and Lanka together culturally and politically,
And make each one a sovereign kingdom so that
Each one would flourish and accomplish great things.
I had a great desire to see such things happen.
I do not have any ploy to put down Ravana 500
And glorify Rama. Why do you spoil my
Big dream of promoting parallel cultures
And see them flourish together?
Why are you obsessed with the thought that
All the living creatures created by Brahma
Should be under your control,
I do not know! How egoistic you are!
Would any one beam in valour
By abducting another man's wife?
What greatness lies in being adept at theft?' 510

Biting his lips in anger, and
Brandishing his huge sword,
Ravana rushed to kill Angada instinctively.
A well-known proverb is proved right once again here:
'When facts were laid bare, the irate listener got up
And kicked the speaker on the chest.'
'What shall I do now? The messenger should not be killed.'
Pressing his hands in helplessness, Ravana said:
'You stupid boy, stop this praise of Rama; enough of it.
Deserting his rightful throne, 520
He roamed in the valleys and forests as a coward.
Setting eyes on my kingdom, he killed my kith and kin.
He destroyed the prospects of multiculturalism.
He is a commoner; what harm could he bring to me?
You rely on the support of such trivial humans,
The likes of whom are devoured by the *rakshasas* in my camp.
What's Rama to me? Go, go away, you fool.
I have seen enough of your childish pranks!'

Angada got furious and said:
'It is not proper to hear the insults hurled at Hari and the Teacher. 530
There is a saying, "either one should punish the abuser,
Or quit the place at once." Let that be so. I shall not slay you.
And Shri Rama has not ordered your killing either.
But I will cut that accursed tongue of yours.' Saying so,
Angada mashed his teeth in rage and raising his
Arms high, stamped the floor with all his might.
The earth shuddered at that.
Seated courtiers rolled down from their chairs;
Fear-stricken, they all ran away.
Feeling as if somebody had pushed him, Dashakantha, 540
The ten-headed one, fell from his throne
And as he rolled on the floor,
His royal crown too dropped down.

'O wicked Ravana! The arrow
Of Rama is thirsty for your blood.
I myself could finish you off.
But Shri Rama would not be pleased by that.'

Not tolerating Angada,
Ravana shouted: 'Fool, shut up! Stop your bragging.
You have become garrulous by joining company
With those roamers in the forest. 550
Your father never bragged.
Considering that you are an emissary,
And also the son of my dear friend,
I have let you scot free without killing you.
Go, go away this instant.
Tell Rama what I desire.
I will surrender Janaki after winning the war;
If not, fighting valiantly I will die
In the battlefield and reach Heaven.
To uphold the honour of the *rakshasas* 560
I will fight till my last breath.

'Slavery is not the Lankan culture and
I don't agree for a truce.
Daring the enemy's arms and ammunition
With fierce valour and pride,
And not caring for the blood that would flow like a stream,
I will surge ahead.
Breaking away from the past, I shall march into the future;
I don't care what lies in store for me.'
Speaking thus, Ravana made his intention 570
Clear to Angada.

Angada looked at Ravana and contemplated:
'He is the greatest fool among the fools;
And the most wicked of them all.
He will not mend his ways
Even if advised by Lord Brahma himself.
He will die in the battlefield; death is awaiting him.'
Issuing forth an invitation to a fierce war, and exhibiting courage,
Angada returned alone to Rama's camp
At the Suvela Mountain. 580

Canto One Hundred and Eighty-seven

'Do not Praise the Enemy, Do not Look Down Upon Me!'

||६||

Climbing up the terrace of the white-mansion,
Ravana viewed the Suvela Mountain intently.
Summoning Shuka and Sarana, Lankesha queried:
'Among the *vanara* army, tell me frankly
Who are the valiant soldiers who can invade Lanka?'

Replied Sarana:
'Listen, O Ravana! Look over there!
There stands Nila, the commander-in-chief,
Towering like a mountain peak.
Next to him stands Angada, the crown-prince.   10
Look over there, O King!
There stands the strong-armed Nala, an expert
In building bridges.

'Look at Rajatavarna!
He is fair complexioned; he is an expert
In the formation of a military array.
There stands Kumuda, the one who has built a kingdom
On Sankocha Mountain!

He is a dangerous *vanara*; he stands roaring 20
In the eagerness to crush your entire army.
Look at Rambha there! He always wanders
In the Vindhya, Krishna, Sahya, and Sudharshana Mountains.
He is eager to raze down Lanka to dust.
Sharabha, the king of the Salveya Mountain,
Stands trembling in anger with his ears stretched straight.

'Panasa, the king of Pariyatra
Stands there radiant like the sun.
The one who stands like an irresistible mountain is Vinita;
And the one who shines with the golden hue is Gavaya. 30
Yakshavanta and Haradhumra too are there.
Look at Jambavanta, chief of the Bear-clan,
Who fought on Indra's side
When the war between the *devas*
And the *rakshasas* took place.
Next to him are the soldiers
Who can effortlessly scale the mountain peaks
And throw massive rocks on the enemies;
They proceed not caring and fearing anyone.

'Look over there, O King! 40
There is Dambha on one side and Sannada on the other;
They are so valorous, that each one can cross
A mountain in a single stride;
When they stand up, they cover nine miles
With their mammoth form.
Krathana and Pramathi appear like elephants in rut;
They can move at the speed of a tempest.
Look at Shatabali! He stands in the excitement
Of winning over the entire Lankan army singlehandedly.
In Rama's camp, there are such great valorous soldiers 50
Who can crush a mountain to dust, and cast it away in an instant!'

As Sarana finished,
Coming forward, Shuka said to Ravana:

'Look at Mainda and Dwivida!
They can assume any form at will;
They are terrifying in the battlefield; who can match them?
When angry, the son of Wind can drain the ocean.
He is equal in strength to a meteor.
There is none who has measured the strength of Sugriva;
He is equal to Vali in valour and has mastered 60
The craft of warfare immaculately.

'Saumitri is beyond all description.
He is a great warrior equal to Adishesha –
Sovereign of the Serpents;
He is learned in the Vedas and mastered the *Brahmastra* –
The ultimate weapon of destruction;
He can split open a mountain and does not spare
Anyone who instigates him.
Lakhs and lakhs of *vanaras* have assembled;
They are moving ahead like a stream! 70

'Look, O King Ravana!
Rama is engaged in a private conversation with Vibhishana.
Next to him stands Lakshmana holding two bows in one hand.
The one who stands pointing his hand
To the east is Sugriva.
Even though he is old, Jambavanta is the most efficient one.
Look at Jambumali who stands with all humility.
Look at Anjaneya, one who set fire to Lanka!'

Listening to the description of
Rama's army, Ravana lost patience 80
And said thus reproachfully:
'Enough of this tale of glory!
Is it fair to praise the valour of the enemy, you trivial sods?
I am the king responsible for your prosperity and destruction;
Why do you make me lose confidence and why this vile talk?
Standing on the soil of Lanka,
Like traitors, how dare you praise the enemy!

I will kill and throw you out!
Do not stand in front of me.
Let Shardula come here immediately.   90
I want the reports from him this instant.
Shardula appeared before him and stood with folded hands!

Spoke Shardula entreatingly:
'O King! Please do believe what Shuka and Sarana have said.
Look, as if Death itself has taken the form of a *vanara*,
Dhurmukha stands there!
Gaja, Gavaksha, Gandha and Madana,
All appear as sons of Yama, the Lord of Death.
Setting up the military array in the form of an eagle,
They stand ready to strike.   100
Give away Janaki and stop this terrible war.'

'Listen, Shardula!
Even if the *devas*, the *danavas* and the *gandharvas* come together
And fight against me, I will not give away Janaki.
Summon Vishwakarma, the architect of the gods,
And strengthen the fort.
Make the walls slippery so that the enemies
Slip off when they attempt to climb up.
Throw boulders and iron balls on the soldiers
Who come through the secret entrance.   110
Let the fierce vampire-like *rakshasa*-archers
Stand guard at various points in the seven-walled fortress.
Let the old people stand at one corner
Ready to spray powdered calcium, mustard,
Soap-nut and red chillies on the enemy,
And make them run helter-skelter.
Alert the young boys, and give them slings
To throw stones on the enemy!

'Tell me Shardula, is it difficult
To wage a war with monkeys that climb trees?   120
Would clouds ever stand against the sun,

And a frog against a snake?
Would the *vanara* army stand against
A complete army comprising
Elephants, chariots, cavalry, and infantry?
Would the one who knows all be challenged by a halfwit?
Would anyone instruct a mother of ten, how to give birth?
Why fear when I, the lord of the three worlds, stand here?
One valiant soldier is enough for all those monkeys!   130
I will teach a lesson to those who boast of slaying
Khara, Dushana, Maricha and Trishira.'

Ravana said in anger:
'Look there! Why are they not stopping those crossing the bridge?
Is there a breach in the defense strategy?
Have they plotted against me?
I will hang them!'

Replied Shardula in mock humility:
'The sin committed by you will devour you.
Why are you blaming others?   140
Are there any friends for you?
When I described the strength of Rama's army,
When all the chieftains explained the greatness of Rama's army,
Not caring for our words, showering abuses,
You made us shut our mouth.
Shri Rama is strong like a lion;
All the brave soldiers at Janasthana have bitten the dust.
Lakshmana is an excellent archer;
Can Devendra, the chief of Heaven,   150
Stand in the path of his arrows?
Listen, the fair-complexioned Jyotirmukha, is the son of Sun-god;
Hemakuta is the son of Varuna, the Rain-God;
Nala, the son of Agni, God of Fire, is the commander-in-chief;
Can anyone match the strength
Of Angada and Hanuma in this world?
Within seconds, they will crush Lanka to dust.

Rama is Narahari, Lord Vishnu in human form;
Do not regard him as mere a human being!

'This mortal body is made of the five elements, 160
And is home to the seven essential ingredients.
Body is transient but fame is permanent.
Yearning for momentary pleasure, you have ruined yourself.
O King! Even death fears to venture into
The *vanara* army and sunrays too are scared to enter it!

'One can even enter the fire of destruction and come out safe;
One can survive even after drowning in the sea of poison;
One can even pass through the door of death unharmed;
But it is not possible to destroy and win over the *vanara* army!
They have come crossing the seven seas. 170
Constructing a bridge across the ocean,
They have arrived conquering the expansive sea.
They are about to invade the fort,
And they will crush it and surge ahead.
Give away Janaki, O King!
Otherwise, get ready to die.
The good counsel of the brother was displeasing to you;
You put blame on that great patriot.
Not accepting factual information,
You paid attention to the words of sycophants. 180
Forsaking your sense of discrimination, you march towards death.
Who can protect you now, O King!'

Ravana was caught in the vortex of anxiety for a moment,
But regaining confidence, he said:
'Are the city-guards negligent?
Why do you blame me for their dereliction of duty?
Do not praise the enemy; do not look down upon me.
I will burn the *vanaras* with arrows of fire.
Just as the sun sucks the light of the stars,
I will suck all the strength of Rama. 190
I will exhibit all the crafts of warfare this instant.

Like the letters written on water,
I will destroy the toy bridge built by the monkeys
That spreads flat without the support of pillars and
Wipe it out altogether!

'Let them first cross over and reach here;
I will break the bridge immediately thereafter.
Not able to go back, the *vanara* army will be incarcerated
And certainly they will all die.
Who is going to provide them food? 200
Being hungry, they will all die for sure.
The death of Rama is nearing fast.'

As Ravana was guffawing and ranting thus,
Shardula interjected:
'All your calculations are wrong.
They have stocked fruits, rations, and medicines
That would last for three months.
Valiant Rama and Lakshmana
Are aware of all the crafts of war; they are not fools.
Look at the bridge built by Rama! It is solid 210
And it withstands the weight of the army without getting saggy.
Be aware of the true state of affairs;
Do not shut your eyes and ears to reality.
Do not be under any illusion and your raving is in vain.
The biting nails of the *vanaras* can split open the universe,
And the entire Meru Mountain will collapse!
When the war between the *devas* and the *rakshasas* took place,
They say that Sushena, the doctor of gods,
Saved all the *devas* by administering *sanjivini*,
The medicinal herb that brings back one's lost life.' 220'

Wounded, Lankesha said:
'What is this nonsense?
What madness is this that all are praising Rama!
I do not doubt your loyalty.
It appears that by continually hearing the stories that praise Rama

You all dwell in a world of illusion!
But I am not the one to succumb to these stories.
If crows, owls, bears and monkeys
Come together, can you call it an army!

'Would an elephant in rut be scared of an army of ants? 230
Would a tiger tremble in fear and collapse in front of a cow?
If I don't defeat Rama, I will cast away my titles.'
Ravana thundered.

Shardula replied:
'Think, O King!
Bringing the coral rocks, the *vanaras*
Have built a ninety mile-long bridge.
They are shouting war-cries in great excitement;
Each one of them will fight like Kalabhairava,
The Lord of Destruction, 240
And raze the enemy's pride and strength.'
But the words of Shardula did not touch Ravana's heart a bit.
'It is not good to be here anymore.
We cannot remove the mask of foolishness.
Time has to run its course.'
Contemplating thus, and bowing to the king,
Shuka, Sarana, and the other detectives left the place in silence.

Canto One Hundred and Eighty-eight

'One should Love Life, and so also Death!'

||6||

Deeply agitated and sullen,
Ravana climbed up the terrace of the mansion in the evening
And watched the Suvela Mountain intently.
He contemplated:
'Though a monarch, have I become lonely?
Everyone is praising the enemy head over heels.
Their words of caution – Do not wage war; give away Janaki –
Are reverberating in all the ten directions of the world;
What kind of destiny is this?'

Feeling shocked at something, his heart shuddered; 10
His confidence sank low and fear gripped him.
With his body shivering, he felt like crying hard.
The mind was clouded by fears – such strange fears
That he had experienced never before.
As thunder and lightning roared aloud,
He got down from the terrace with a hope of getting some peace.
Fearing whether he would hear words of appreciation or ridicule,
He got into the harem.
Holding his hands, Mandodari received him lovingly,

Made him sit and caressing his hair, she 20
Spoke endearingly:

'Fear is writ large on your face,
Walk the path of Truth; you will get peace.
If you win over your mind, you will surely win the world.
Extirpate the poisonous weed that is weakening you day by day.
Embrace the path of Truth and give away Janaki.
You who could not cross the line of control drawn by Lakshmana,
How can you evade Rama's sharp arrows, I do not know.
Valour will melt like ice in the blaze of truth. 30
Look at Hanuma! All alone,
Setting foot on Lanka, he killed Akshaya,
Destroyed the garden, and set Lanka on fire.
As he returned triumphantly beaming with pride,
You remained a mute spectator.

'Look! Hanuma
Crossed the expansive sea like a cow crosses a pit!
How can you rest contented under the delusion
That what he did was only trivial!
I don't think there is anything to match the strength 40
Of Shri Rama in all the seven worlds!

'He is the Lord of the Universe.
Think of the episode of Maricha;
Recall the episode of how Shri Rama broke
The mighty bow of Lord Shiva;
Did you not you collapse attempting to lift the bow?
Recollect how he killed Vali with a single arrow;
He has built a bridge across the sea;
What a wonder! Finished it like it was a child's play!
What shall I say about Shri Rama sending Angada for peace talks? 50
You spoiled the truce turning your heart into stone.
Look, what has happened now:
Shri Rama stands fearless at the Suvela Mountain!

When the enemies set foot
On your land, without restraining them
Why are you sitting thus doing nothing?
Are all your crafts exhausted? The Suvela Mountain
Provides a vantage point to examine
The activities in Lanka!
You have neglected your duty of protecting the city.   60
Being lost in the pursuit of pleasures,
You forgot your duty as a king.
Having lost the Lankan provinces one after the other
The danger now lurks at the capital city itself!

'Give up the over-confidence you have reposed on
The strength of your men.
Abstain; abstain from ego;
Give up enmity against the one who is valorous by birth;
Abstain from the lust for Janaki;
Abstain from the obsession to wage war;   70
Abstain from the pride that you'll win over Rama;
Abstain; abstain from being carried away by delusions.

'Do not waste time anymore;
Apply your mind to the comforting truce.
As your capacity to think well is lost completely,
Take refuge in Rama, the pre-eminently virtuous one,
And attain fame.

'Falsity is the root of destruction.
Truth is the supreme *yajna*;
Vedas and scriptures proclaim Truth;   80
Truth is nothing but self-restraint;
Truth is righteous conduct;
The world and its ethics flourish because of Truth;
If Truth collapses, everything else collapses.'

Ravana said:
'One should love life, and so also death.

Night is a cave of darkness, a place enveloped by darkness;
Stretching my sight afar, I take a step forward.
I have no illusions that somebody will lead me on;
Nor will I beg anyone helplessly 90
To hold my hand and lead me kindly.
What if I die now? All will say
"Lankesha, the one who highly valued his honour and firmness,
Died a valiant death and reached Heaven."
That is enough for me. As you have an equal share in
My happiness and suffering, forget your appeasing words.'

Mandodari replied:
'It's alright, my Lord!
Lord Shiva will protect you. It's time for the
Royal banquet; get up to savour it, my Lord.' 100
But while dining, as Lankesha was lost in grief,
The food did not taste good.
Beads of sweat lined up on his forehead! Mandodari,
As if warding off all his adversities, speaking endearingly,
Swiftly wiped Ravana's forehead with a soft fabric!

Ravana spoke comfortingly:
'Don't you worry, O the queen of Lanka!
It doesn't matter if I sweat on the forehead; wipe out your tears.
You are indeed a valiant wife; why do you fear war?
Is Prashasta, the valiant warrior, any ordinary? 110
Crushing the *vanaras*, he will return victorious.'
Delving into silence for a moment
Ravana continued:
'In the middle of the night, I had a dream.
Just as Vedavati jumped into fire,
Sita's body too turned to ashes; and as the breeze blew gently,
I saw a heap of ashes flying towards me.
At that instant there appeared an idol made of marble.
I saw the soul of Rama's wife in it.
Waking up from the dream, I perspired profusely 120

And dismissing it as whimsical, I laughed at myself!
Whatever it was, I wanted to see for myself
Whether Sita was alive or dead;
Worrying thus, I entered the garden
Early this morning to clear my doubts.
On seeing Sita being safe there as usual,
I felt reassured.

'O dear wife, listen!
You understand my feelings very well.
I fell in love with Sita at Panchavati for the first time.   130
But in Lanka, I have taken care of her as a daughter.
This is my volition to protect her until I return her to her husband.
First, I will defeat him in the battle,
And then I will give away Sita.
How can I tell this decision to others?'

As Ravana poured out his heart,
Mandodari said: 'This is the dream
That should alert your conscience.
Trijata has had a different dream.
Anala told me about that which I will tell you now.   140
She saw Vaidehi entering the hermitage
In the form of a recluse in dreadful silence, with eyes wide open.
At that instant, she turned into a holy flame.
Unaware of the outer world, Maithili spoke as if in a trance
And the all-pervading presence of Maithili was felt then.
She is the creative energy and the driving force of the world.
When the hand of that virtuous wife touched Anala
And woke her up,
Rama's wife said: "May you be fearless, O daughter!
By the kind deed of your father Vibhishana, Lord Rama is alive.   150
The danger is over now!"'

Said Ravana:
'She rambles something, and cooks up stories;
Believing them herself, she makes others believe them too.

Do not trust the words of Anala.
Tell her this instant, "Ravana does not desire Sita;
His lust has dried up and the desire for war has shot up."
Believe my words. O dear love!

'Wishing good luck for Sita, I will win the war.
My aim is not to kill Rama in the battle. 160
By destroying his chariot in the battle,
I will bring Rama and Saumitri here as captives.
And then take them to my royal court with all honour.
As all can see, I will bring Janaki
And make her sit on my lap. Inviting Rama,
I will hand over Sita just as a father sends away
His daughter after the marriage.

'How will the enemies believe when I speak
Of the transformations that
My heart has undegone? Will my words 170
Touch their hearts? It is enough if you understand me.
I will fight the war wholeheartedly; I will win over the brothers.
Even if I die in the battle, I am not worried.
I will reach Heaven with a calm mind.
With a volition to win, when one strives hard to fulfil it,
If one fails, why should one collapse and sit sullen?
Even if a fierce danger befalls, I will face it.
I have shed the love of myself and I am
In the blissful state devoid of all passions.
Now I am not weighed down by likes and dislikes. 180
My mind is now ripe to welcome with equanimity,
Whether it is ambrosia or poison,
Without discriminating between the two.
As mentioned in the scriptures, this indeed is the trait of the man
Purified by knowledge and freed
From the cycle of births and deaths.'

Canto One Hundred and Eighty-nine

'To Protect the Virtuous, this War is Inevitable!'

||๖||

As Angada returned to the Suvela Mountain all alone
At night, everyone was curious to know
What happened in Lanka. 'According to the scriptures,
It's not proper to discuss political affairs
During the night,' thinking thus, Shri Rama
Summoned Angada next morning and enquired all the details:
'Are you well, son? Is Ravana angry?
Does he want war or truce? Tell me everything, my son.'
Bowing to Shri Rama's feet with all humility,
Angada replied: 10

'Listen, O King of Kosala!
Dashashira, the ten-headed one is mean, and lacks character.
Whatever one advices him, he is not ready for truce.
Through this truce I discerned that a fool
Cannot be convinced even if advised a hundred times.
Even if the Lord of Death tells him
To stop the war and surrender Sita, Ravana will not listen.
There is no other option but war, my Lord.'

Discerning that war was inevitable,
Rama asked for the complete details 20
About the enemy-fort. Summoning Sugriva and the other
Commanders-in-chief, Rama discussed the secrets of
'How to invade the four main gates of the Golden Lanka,'
And he queried further:

'Tell me how to seize the Lanka city;
Tell me how to take it under our control.
The fashion in which Hanuma and Angada singlehandedly
Waded through the army secretly is quite different from
Countering and thrashing the enemy
Through formation of a military array. 30
If we invade mindlessly, many deaths will occur for sure.
No doubt, the *vanaras* are excited. Even then, they have
Neither witnessed great wars, nor have they won any.
This is not like the guerilla warfare of the hills
Where the enemy is thrashed sometimes by ambushing them,
And sometimes by fighting them in the open.
While waging war in the open battlefield,
We should gain victory
By destroying the arms and ammunitions,
And by quelling down the magical evil spell of the enemy. 40

'To give alms wholeheartedly when beseeched,
To protect when someone seeks refuge,
To crush to death when confronted –
These bring fame to a king.
He is the most valorous warrior, and he has sought war;
How we can defeat this impetuous warrior of immense strength?'

Listening intently to Rama,
Jambavanta said: 'Are *vanaras* any ordinary!
They will wade through the battlefield with ease
As if it was a field to be readied for ploughing; 50
They will raise a sumptuous crop of success with humility,
And glowing like precious pearls, they will harvest victory.

Lord Shiva's beauty, the rising sun
In the east, illuminating the universe,
The ocean of life, the radiance of the limitless sky,
The touch of your feet, the air filled with the breath of Hanuma,
The blow of the cool breeze across river Sarayu
And the light of Rama's soul – if all these do not touch Lanka,
Would there be salvation for it? War is just a pretext!'
Jambavanta said endearingly. 60

Angada said:
'O Lord Shri Rama!
I will unravel the defence secrets of the Lankan army
Which I have learnt well and returned.
Prahasta guards the eastern entrance;
Commanders Mahaparshwa and Mahodara
Guard the main gateway of the south, my Lord.
As Indrajit guards the main door of the west,
Soldiers of great strength, carrying shield,
Sword, bow, spears and hammer, 70
Stand next to him supporting him constantly.
Lankesha himself guards the northern entrance.
A large army of *rakshasas* under Virupaksha's command
Stands guard at the centre of the city holding
Spears, swords, and bows. All stand in readiness
To take part in the ensuing war.

'A thousand soldiers mounted on elephants,
An equal number riding the chariots,
Twenty thousand horsemen, an infantry
Numbering more than a crore, 80
A separate army comprising ten lakh *rakshasas* – this kind of troupes
Are stationed at every vantage point.
Such is the variegated nature of the army.
People say that defeating Kubera, the King of Wealth,
Ravana brought sixty lakhs soldiers.
Who can match Ravana in his grace and grandeur?

The task of destroying the *rakshasas* isn't trivial at all;
We must be extremely cautious now.'

Shri Rama replied:
'Because of one adamant person, 90
Countless *rakshasa* battalion will die
Resulting in blood-bath – quite a heart-rending scene!
How can I fight?' Hearing this,
Saumitri said:
'Do not show sympathy to Ravana; it's not fair.
Many well-meaning persons have advised him.
The advice of Angada for truce was the last of it indeed.
War is the only *mantra*; war is the only strategy now!
Let us think of ways to thrash the enemy;
I will tell you that; listen to me. 100
Let Hanuma, the best among the *vanaras*,
Confront Prashata;
And let Angada take on Mahodara and Mahaparshwa;
I will counter Indrajit;
Let Jambavanta and Vibhishana stay at the centre of the army.
Lankesha will meet his end at the northern gateway, for sure.'

Look! There is happiness in Rama's camp.
All thoughts about war have come to a halt.
As the sun went down, the moon appeared shining bright.
As Nala approached him, Rama said: 110
'War is like a cruel planet, you see.
What else is there but the killing of humans?
The motif of establishing peace seems to be an illusion.'
Nala replied that instant:
'Why do you worry, O Lord? War is inevitable
To punish the wicked and to protect the virtuous.
It is Ravana who is instigating this war.'

'The *vanaras* are
Filled with the excitement of war.

Dreams of exhibiting their valour are dancing wild; 120
Their hearts are ready for the forthcoming war.
Without turning our backs, we will fight fiercely in the war;
What if the head is severed, the trunk itself will surge ahead
Chasing the *rakshasas* and kill them.'
Thus they remained committed to their volition.

'The *vanara* army
Appeared like a wildfire to the woods of *rakshasas*;
It looked like a wildfire of destruction
To the ocean of Lankan army!
There is no limit to the adventures and valour of Angada; 130
If he touches with his nails, the entire universe will crack!
The world will turn topsy-turvy if he stamps his feet!
The Meru Mountain will turn upside down
If he kicks it with his knees!
Golden Lanka will be ransacked and destroyed
Like a plantain-orchard invaded by an elephant in rut.

'In the army of the *vanaras*
Shatabali is very persistent and is known for his immense strength.
Sharabha is waiting for Rama's command.
Gavaya is waiting to repay his debts of gratitude.
Gaja, Gavaksha, Ganda, Madana, Sumukha, and 140
Durmukha are on their toes, waiting impatiently
To suck the life of the *rakshasas*.
Dadhimukha is eagerly counting the
Hours to jump into the fort.
Is it possible to speak about the excitement
Of Sugriva and Lakshmana?'

Hearing the reports of the detectives,
Shri Rama ordered thus:
'Getting the support of Mainda and Dwivida,
Let valiant Nila confront Prashasta in the 150
Eastern part of Trikuta Mountain.
Taking the help of Gavaksha and Rushabha,

Let Angada take on Mahaparshwa in the south.
Accompanied by Vinata,
Let Anjaneya confront Indrajit.
Accompanied by Darimukha,
Let Nala fight Akampana!
Let Gaja and Gawaya jointly
Resist the attack of Agniketu in the south-east.

'Joining Kesari, let Taradeva be stationed in the south-west. 160
Let the army of Shatabali fight Suryashatru in the north-east.
In the north-west, let Suptaghna fight Brahmaksha, and
Let Sushena take on Makaraksha.
Studying the situation well,
Let Saumitri and Jambavanta support
The main army and provide help to all constantly.
As supreme commander,
I will guard the entire army in such a way that
Our soldiers do not fall into the
Death trap laid by the *rakshasas*. 170
I'll command the war in such a way that the fame
Of the *vanara* army would appear hundred-fold more!'

As the *vanara* army stood ready thus,
Their roar of excitement was greater than that of the sea and
Incited even the cowards to fight.
Rama, the harbinger of the new dawn of Bharata,
Has set out to shatter the mean ones.
As the drums and trumpets roared aloud,
The hearts of the enemy experienced a chilled shudder.

Discussing together, all the commanders 180
Of Rama's army said in unison:
'We will unravel all the tactics
Of the Lord of the *rakshasas* now.'

Canto One Hundred and Ninety

'The Root of Humanity Can Never be Severed!'

||6||

Maternal grandfather Malyavanta advised Ravana:
'The one who follows the path of morality will reign
Exhibiting his riches, winning over his enemies
And rule his kingdom ensconced in fame and name.
His kingdom will witness peace and harmony.
Scrutinising carefully who is the enemy,
It is better to agree for a truce and achieve success thereby!
Rama has the support of many people.
Ravana is only a wax doll; he has nurtured
Cheating and violence – opine the people! 10
The giant serpent of immorality is devouring you.
Ascetics are angry for your wrong doings.
Ascetics are always pure in mind and soul;
They chant Vedas and perform meditation and *yajnas*;
They always bless people to get rid of evil forever;
The smoke from their holy fires spread far and wide
Sucking the strength of the *rakshasas*.
Goodness gets established and peace spreads.

'Listen, listen my son!
Various kinds of portents are frightening us.   20
There is no end to having bad dreams.
Warm blood is flowing in golden Lanka.
Flags and banners have lost their hue.
Black-faced ominous women afflict in dreams;
They mock and guffaw revealing their crooked teeth.
Dogs are eating the sacrificial food;
Donkeys are born from the wombs of cows;
Mice are born in the wombs of mongoose;
Birds are flying screeching hoarsely;
Antelopes are screaming looking at the sun;   30
A baldheaded disfigured person, dark in complexion,
Goes visiting every house.

'Creation subsists on Truth;
All existence thrives on Truth;
Sun exists because of Truth; air exists because of Truth;
And all the five elements exist because of Truth.
You give up your lust for Sita and give her away.
If antelopes, elephants, butterflies, bees and fish
Die caught in the attraction of just one of the senses,
How can a human being save himself   40
From the attraction of all the five senses?
Do not cause the massacre of the people of Lanka
As an offering to the evil war.
A new chapter is being opened in the history of Bharata.
Do not succumb to the words of sycophants and slanderers.
Poison kills one; a weapon kills quite a few;
But an evil counsel devours the entire nation
Along with the king!

'Shri Rama is not an ordinary human.
Do not fight with Hari – the supreme Lord; surrender Janaki!   50
Fear the infamy the world will bestow on you
And proceed accordingly; it is good for you.

Relying too much on worldly life,
Do not forget the purpose of human life.
The lust for another man's wife is like adding fuel to the fire
And it destroys the perpetrator mercilessly!'

Ravana was enraged:
'Rama is asphyxiating the culture of Lanka.
This truth will be known today or tomorrow.
I am not ignorant of the evil designs
Of Rama who tries to establish his creed over Lanka.

'I will quell down the culture of
Ayodhya and uphold the culture of the folks, and
I will uplift the downtrodden.
I will make the spirit of rebellion course through the veins
Of the downtrodden and the marginalised.'

'"*Dharma* triumphs forever" –
It's a magnificent doctrine.
Dharma is the ultimate philosophy; *dharma* sustains the universe;
The riches, fame and splendour of a king
Who is ignorant of *dharma* are akin
To the light of a lamp held against the blowing wind.
Awake, awake dear son, and protect *dharma*.'
Malyavanta advised thus.

Ravana lost his patience, and said:
'Do not spoil the fortunes of my life
With the poisonous precept of Destiny.
Belittling human effort
By putting forth the doctrine of fatalism,
Why are you tarnishing humanity?
Man is a creation of god, and embodies his strength, you see.
By exhibiting ignorance, why do you wreck my confidence?'

Malyavanta replied:
'Love for humanity springs from high ethics;
Love generates wealth; from wealth all other necessities are met.

All these jointly constitute *dharma*;
And *dharma* brings victory;
Dharma makes the gods happy, and this happiness
Brings harmony between Heaven and earth.

'Snatching away wealth, honour and strength   90
From others, how long can you enjoy it all?
Whoever climbs up, inevitably comes down too.
The wheel of ups and downs rotates perpetually.
Rama yearns for peace in the entire world.
What do you yearn for?'
Malyavanta retorted.

Not allowing his self-esteem to be hurt thus,
Ravana thundered: 'The dark secrets
Of the mind are imprisoned
In the labyrinth of the unconscious,   100
And are not easily discernible.
At the conscious level, by evoking my sense of discrimination
Between the good and the evil
I shall never surrender what I have sought to pursue.
I will not sacrifice the soul of Lanka's self-esteem.
Do I not know the happenings of the world –
The strife, the pains, and the other afflictions
That always entangle the world?
I have had a taste of all these myself.
Such being the facts, am I not aware   110
Of the cunning political designs
Of kings of the Raghu dynasty to expand their empire
By annexing the kingdoms of the gullible?

'Are we the fools
To be ignorant of Rama's tactics of sowing the seeds of conflict
Among kings by exploiting their hatred and enmity for each other
To further his own selfish motive!
Listen! Rama is filled to the brim with the conceit
That he alone is wise, and he alone is the valiant warrior.

Coming together, all of us kings 120
Will stand united as a giant rock and resist
The invasion by the clan of Raghu;
We will unmask their plot.'

Worried, Malyavanta said:
'Do you have any friends
Who are going to stand with you?
Friendship with Vali's camp is severed already.
All are your enemies now, and you are all alone.
As all have condemned the abduction of another man's wife,
What options are open to you to win over Rama? 130

'Your birth in the
Rakshasa clan, dawned a new fortune for the clan.
You provided an opportunity for the *rakshasas*
To live in self-esteem
At a time when they had none.
Would you destroy the fame that you yourself have built?
The moment you surrender Janaki,
Everything will be set right: Kishkindha
Will join us in friendship; your brother will return to you;
And you will become a powerful monarch of the universe, for sure. 140

'By responding to the needs of your people
You brought in revolutionary changes; very good.
But now you have faltered completely.
Discerning the situation, be well advised, and correct yourself
And lead the citizens on the right path. If that happens,
You will be the true leader of the people.

'Not knowing your well wishers
You have been trapped by transient allurements.
When danger befalls, the man who decides how to guide
The people at the crucial hour, becomes the real leader. 150
What is there in publicity? Thinking of the past,
And comparing it with the present situation,

The man who plans well the future
In the light of his own experience, becomes the real leader.
Eliciting the opinions of the citizens,
And weighing its pros and cons, if you proceed respecting them,
There will be success for you. Otherwise,
The dilemma will become worse
And Lanka will be destroyed for sure.

'The *sal* tree, once chopped by Vali's arrow 160
Sprouted again. But Rama's arrow was not of that kind.
When he shot through the tree, it died out completely.
He is the true liberator; therefore,
The seed will be destroyed, you see!
A lifeless seed, if sown, will not sprout again.
If rice is sown, will it sprout?
If the husk of paddy is sown, will it sprout, tell me.
If fried paddy is sown, will it sprout, tell me.
When the soul receives Rama's grace
What springs forth isn't a re-birth but a sure salvation from it. 170
Tell me what Rama's blessings cannot do!

'Do not waste time.
Get up fast and think of the truce.
Shri Rama has vowed to preserve
All the diverse cultures of Bharata in their pristine forms,
And harmoniously fuse them with each other.
His goal is to bring unity in diversity.
Rama has the divine power to achieve this harmony.

'You have transgressed the *dharma*
Of Treta *yuga*, the second of the four ages of the world. 180
This transgression has become Rama's strength.
If you give away Janaki,
The Goddess of Victory will come running to you;
Rama will be marginalised.
May you be the man of the epoch!

Can one split the Meru Mountain with a chisel made of lead?
When it rains fire, can one hold an umbrella for protection?
When awareness, *dharma*, forgiveness
And self-restraint are struck by vileness,
How can you defend yourself and your honour?   190
How can Shri Lanka defend itself?

'Hunger and desire are the twin shafts of Creation;
They goad men into constructing forts and also demolishing them;
Luring with various worldly enticements, they push men towards
Destruction and thus put an end to everything.

'In the deluge of Time
Many cultures, many civilisations,
And many laws of morality have been washed away, my son!
Whatever be the momentum of the epoch
And the state of affairs of the world,   200
The root of humanity can never be severed.

'Let the stream of ambrosia,
Flow from one era to another.
Let the tenets of humanity be vastly established on earth.
All awareness is sliding fast; what will you do now?
If you desire another man's wife,
Lakshmi, the Goddess of Wealth, will desert you.'
Saying so, he watched Ravana's face intently.
He realised that his advice did not touch Ravana.
'When Destiny has boiled our broth with poison,   210
Who is there to protect us?'
Feeling the pain of such a contemplation,
Malyavanta assumed silence.

Bursting with anger, knitting his brows
And rolling his eyes, Lankesha addressed
Malyavanta and his favourite ministers:
'It is not fair for the grandfather to be
On my enemy's side, and hurt me thus.

Rama has come to the forest as an exile;
How can he be my equal? 220
I am truly the crest-jewel of the *rakshasa* clan
And fearsome to my enemies;
Before the start of the real war in the battlefield,
Rama has waged a psychological war
And has disturbed the minds of our men, for sure.
Falling prey to the astuteness of Rama,
Our men have lost their strength and collapsed.

'Therefore, we should plan
A new war strategy and steadfastly infuse confidence in the minds
Of our people. Who has the 230
Strength to confront Lanka? Do not fear!
Very shortly, the monkey-army will fall to the
Spear of Lanka and all of you just watch:
I will cut the heads of Lakshmana and Sugriva
In the battle and throw them to the sea.
I will split Rama into two halves in a duel;
If not, I shall not be Ravana; I shall not surrender.'

Canto One Hundred and Ninety-one

'An Earth-cracking Roar Reached the Skies'

||ॐ||

Meanwhile in Lanka, Vaidehi called
Her dear friend Sarame, and said:
'Tell me how is Shri Rama; how is my brother-in-law?
Are Sugriva, Hanuma and Angada fine?
How can I be rescued, tell me.
If the deadline given by me to Hanuma is crossed,
I will seek death by fasting.
Doing penance and meditation,
I will become one with Lord Shri Rama.'

Sarame replied: 10
'Listen, O Mother! Good time is approaching;
Goddess Durga is pleased with you and blesses you now.
The dark cloud of suffering is disappearing on its own.
Fragrant cool breeze is blowing across.
There it rains flowers and it augurs well for you.
Shri Rama has built a bridge across the sea.
Leading the *vanara* army, Shri Rama
Has reached Lanka and is camping at
The Suvela Mountain. He is moving swiftly
On the path of destroying the conceit of Lankesha! 20

Something wonderful has occurred!
As Angada arrived with a peace proposal,
Seeing him the citizens of Lanka were scared.
Ravana has ignored the peace proposal and
War-commotions are heard in Lanka. Listen!
The assembled valiant soldiers are beating the drums
And are blowing the war-trumpets excitedly,
And they are getting ready for war!

'Look over there, O Mother!
Elephants in rut are thundering like dark clouds.   30
All the charioteers are setting the horses ready;
Horsemen are ready with spears.
It is a fierce scene that indicates how keen they are for the battle.
Soldiers on foot are adorned with armour;
Roaring like the ocean-waves, they are advancing;
Wearing military uniforms, they are brandishing
Their shining swords, lances, and pikes in full force.
Awestruck, and with lurking fear,
The citizens stand watching them!

'The sound of the bells tied to the elephant's neck,   40
The creaking of the chariot wheels, the neighing
Of the horses, make one feel excited.
Whatever be the grandeur
Of Ravana's army, what is the use?
The Goddess of Victory is on the side of Rama.
A great fear is sown in the mind of Ravana.
As this fear is transformed into anger in Ravana,
Citing reasons of treason, he is punishing
Many *rakshasas* wantonly.

'Shri Rama is like Devendra, the chief of Heaven.   50
Killing Ravana valorously, he will protect the world;
There is no doubt in it.
He will surely come to you swiftly; there is no doubt in it.
Resting your head on the chest of Shripati,

You will shed tears of joy and that
Auspicious hour is fast approaching.
Uniting with you, Rama will feel blessed.
Fervently pray to Sun-god – the one who dispels darkness –
For the speedy arrival of Shri Rama!'
Sarama spoke such soothing words of advice. 60

As clouds pour rains
On earth and bring along coolness and freshness,
The good words of Sarama brought happiness to Janaki:
'Ravana is wicked. He inflicts pain
On his enemies by torturing them.
He cannot touch Rama. But listen! I am worried that
He may catch hold of *vanaras* and torture them.'

Sarama replied:
'True, Ravana is cruel. His mind has turned wild,
And foolishness is coupled with it! 70
His dear wife advised him; Prahasta too advised him;
Grandfather Malyavanta also counselled him in many ways.
In unison all have pleaded with him thus:
"Do not wage war; if you surrender Sita, it will be good for you."
But ignoring the advice of kith and kin,
Dashashira has put faith in war!
Angada's efforts for truce are utterly ruined.
By trying to entice Angada to be on his side with a proposal –
"I will crown you as the king of Kishkindha" –
Ravana has failed in his strategy of divide and rule. 80
The vessel of Ravana's life has
Cracked now and it is going to burst open shortly!'

Approaching near, Trijata said with excitement:
'A fierce war between Saketa and Lanka is in the offing.
Listen! The war instruments have been sounded.
The sound of the trumpet of victory has mingled with
The rattling sound of your shackles.
Listen to the roaring war-cries;

Listen to the twang of the strings of Kodanda, the mighty bow of
  Rama!
Listen, Lord Shiva himself is sounding his drum!'   90

Janaki replied:
'My fear is allayed; my Lord has arrived;
He will release me from this imprisonment,
And I dreamt of the same. I saw a burning fire
In the centre of the battlefield. I saw the burning
Tongues of flame taking hills and valleys in their sweep,
Spreading swiftly to the skies, and razing the entire world to ashes.

'I saw Rama disappear and I began to wail:
"Where did he go, the one who broke the bow of Lord Shiva?
Where did he go, the one who broke the pride of Bhargava?   100
Where did he go, the one who received
The consecrated instruction from Sage Kaushika?
Why should I live now? I will consume poison."
At that point, I awoke from the dream and my mind was
Filled with anxiety of what evil may befall.'

'Forget about that fear and anxiety.
Shri Rama is arriving; Raghunandana, son of the Raghu clan,
Your beloved is arriving;
The one who is thousand-folds more charming
Than Smara, the God of Love, is arriving;   110
With matted hair and twisted plaits,
Wearing apparel made from the bark of a tree,
Holding Kodanda, the mighty bow,
Swinging an arrow in his hand,
With a quiver slung on his back,
Rama, the enemy of *asuras*, is arriving,' said Trijata.

Immersed in deep thoughts,
Thinking of the inevitable war,
Thinking of the inevitable violence and bloodshed,
Janaki cried and hot tears rolled   120
Profusely down her cheeks. An earth-cracking
Roar reached the skies at that instant!

Canto One Hundred and Ninety-two

'Let the War-preparations Take Place Meticulously!'

||৬||

Climbing the bastion, Ravana looked
At the Suvela Mountain. The *vanara* army
Was marching ahead swiftly;
He then spoke to Prahasta who had accompanied him:
'Tell me in detail how we have readied our army.'
Prahasta replied: 'Why should we fear, O King?
Even if there are'countless dry leaves,
Would the storm mind it?'

Ravana replied:
'I appreciate the way you have formed the military array.   10
Let Vajra and Rahu guard in the east;
In the south, let Mahaparshwa join Mahodhara and resist;
And let Shonitaksha guard the western entrance;
Let Akampana in the north, and Saptaghna
And Makaraksha fight in the north-east.
In the south-east, let Agniketu and Durmukha,
And let Suryashatru wage war in the south-west;
Let both Brahmaksha and Dhumraksha guard
And protect the north-west;

The remaining commanders Chandikadhwaja, Darpadashraya   20
Stand in the middle of the *gulma*, a body of assorted troops.
I, the supreme commander of all the forces,
The architect of the victory of the *rakshasa* clan,
And the one vowed to lead the war,
Will stand in command!
Look, the Goddess of Victory
Will be on our side and the war will thus end on its own!

'An extraordinary strength of the epoch
Is now manifested in the minds of the entire Lankan people;
Whether Rama's army has the valour to quell that?   30
I will see whether Rama possesses the strength to put out
The divine light of such self-confidence.
Now I should destroy the advancing arrogance
Of annexing kingdoms.
As I am determined to save
The small as well as big kingdoms, a powerful
Leadership is inevitable. Get the
Entire war machinery ready quickly!

'Let the singers and merry-makers be present;
Let jesters, tassel wavers, barbers, servants holding   40
Chowries and spittoons be at various places;
And all the courtesans and women remain inside their quarters.
Let a platoon guard them!

'Let all the singers, orators, musicians, scholars
Panegyrists, minstrels, bards, Brahmins,
Courtesans, jesters all be present.
Let the war-preparations take place meticulously.
Let all the charioteers also be present.'

'There are ways of waging war:
If one fights the enemy in the battlefied, it is known as "open war"; 50
Not giving any clues, if one attacks, it is called "plot";
If one quells the enemy through deceit, it is called "silent war".
If the enemy is powerful than the king, go for the "open war";

If the enemy is weak, then the "plot",
And in all other cases, it is the "silent war".

At that instant, arriving at the royal court,
Prahasta said humbly:
'O Lord! What have you done!
Why have you brought Janaki to Lanka?
Will a mountain ever melt away in flowing water?   60
Rama and Saumitri are extraordinary warriors.
To take revenge for the humiliating episode of Shurpanakha,
And also to punish Rama, there were other ways.
But getting angry, you chose the wrong path.
Weighing the pros and cons and correcting your mistakes
If you move consciously with conviction, it is good for you.
But you chose the wicked path and it has grave consequences.
Not knowing the strength of Rama, you have erred.
Would any king conduct the affairs of the State thus!
Subrahmanya, the commander-in-chief of the Heaven's army,   70
Is extraordinarily powerful; once, while waging war,
He shot a pointed arrow forcefully;
It struck the Krauncha Mountain and created a huge hole.
And this helped the serpent clan to sneak in there!

'Your lust for women has
Been your undoing and this
Weakness of yours is akin to that hole.
The enemies will easily get at you through that hole
And destroy you without fail.
Has anyone survived eating poisoned meat? Be that so.   80
Do not fear now; anyhow war has been proclaimed already.
What else can you do now? Return Janaki;
We are there to take on Rama and his followers in the battlefield.
Leave it to us.' Hearing those words,
Indrajit got up and thundered:

'Whether the ruler is good or bad
He cannot come under the scrutiny of the citizens.

It's the bounden duty of the citizens to support the king.
Citing introspection as a pretext,
Could the king be ever reproached?' 90

As all the commanders had assembled,
Ravana ordered them to get ready for the war;
The sound of the war trumpets reached the skies.
The sound of trumpets blown by the valorous soldiers
Reverberated in all the city, forts, hills and forests.
The valorous soldiers freed themselves with great difficulty
From the loving embraces of their wives.
'If I lose the battle, not bearing the humiliation, I will die.
If I win killing the enemy, I will return;
Listen, O my love, I will hug you tightly then!' 100
Making such promises, the soldiers
Collected their arms, headgear, and donning
The armour, they marched to the battle.

Elephants, horses, chariots, and soldiers
Were equal in number in Ravana's army.
As the entire Army was comprised
Of assorted troupes called *gulma, chamu,*
Anikini and other forms, could anyone
Describe the grandeur of Ravana's army?

If comprised of one chariot, one elephant, 110
Three horses, and five soldiers on land,
It is designated as *patti*; three such *patti* put together
Is counted as *sene*; the joining of three such *sene*
Is called *senamukha*; a battalion of three *senamukha* make a *gulma*;
Three *gulma* constitute *pratana, chamu,* and *anikini*;
Ten such *anikini* make one *akshohini*.
As Ravana's army is made up of a variety of such *akshohini*,
Is it possible to describe the grandeur of war preparations?

Shuka, Sarana,
Vibhatsa, Vajraksha, Nakramakara, 120

Vibhrama, Nikumbha, Sandhyaksha, Sunda,
Malyavanta, Jambumali, have all congregated!
Shibhivira, Durdharsha, Shukrabhi, Vajrodara,
Vighatodara, Subhishana, Dhumraksha, Vidyujihwa,
Mahadhutha, Prachanda, Dundhu, Dambara, Thunda
Halahala and Sarpabahu are all present there!
Vidyakaushika, Shanka, Mahadyuti, Prashankha,
Pushpachuda, Hemagaura, and Shilimukha
All moved swiftly harnessing the highly agile horses,
Shouting 'Victory! Victory!' 130

Canto One Hundred and Ninety-three

'All the War Trumpets Sounded Loudly!'

||⊚||

The valiant feudatory chiefs like Kadamba, Vitapa, Bhima,
Bhimanada, Shardula, Vikridita, Chalanga,
Chalapa, Chola, Vidyudambaka,
And Chala harnessed the chariots drawn by elephants.
Lankesha's dearest son Indrajit, resplendent as the sun,
Was a great warrior and he was ready holding a trident.
They readied a magnificently glowing chariot called Jyotiprabha
For the use of valarous Indrajit.
Chariots drawn by lions, hogs
And such other animals were also kept ready.   10

It is the war of the millennium!
The war trumpets were sounded aloud in all the corners.
Lankesha summoned Maya that instant
And ordered: 'Prepare the fort for defence!
Ah! The height of the bastion reached the sky!
It appeared as if the multiple scaffolds would reach the sun,
And in between the bulwark was shining,
At the centre the angled doors were looking grand.
The upper storeys were beautiful like a pitcher.
Surrounding the fort, there were large trenches   20

Resembling the depths of the nether world!
It was a seven-walled grand fort.
Spears, swords, shields, arm-shields,
Flagstaffs, huge drums, knives, daggers, bows, moon-shaped axes,
Sharp-edged spears, axes, iron clubs, giant maces
And such other weapons were stored there.
Mustard powder, red-hot iron balls,
Cauldrons of heated wax, huge vessels containing snake venom,
And lots of arms were all well stacked there!

The assemblage of lions, *sharabha*, hogs, 30
Wolves, tigers instill fear!
There were huge syringes that sprayed poisonous liquid.
Heaps and heaps of sling-stones were kept ready.
Sharpened knives, and pointed spears were stacked.
Heaps of logs, stone-balls, strong nets and ropes,
Assorted cudgels for beating and thrashing were all heaped in the fort.
Huge earthen vessels filled with red ants and hornets,
Huge mud pots filled with hot slush and boiling oil,
Sacks filled with itching-powder,
Various kinds of traps and nooses, horseshoes, 40
Wooden bars for fastening doors, cartloads of arrows,
Bulls carrying the quivers of arrows,
Soldiers in hiding all over the fort
Ready to shoot with sharp-edged spears,
Alert warriors adorning armour
And wearing protective headgears were all there.
War bugles, flat drums, and huge drums,
And all kinds of war trumpets sounded loudly!

Look there!
A wall of fire akin to death! 50
And poisoned water that can cut the hand if touched!
Giant warriors like Taraka, Tarakaksha
Jambanamuchi and Nikumbha and such other
Danava chieftains jointly began the battle.

Canto One Hundred and Ninety-four

'I Offer my Heart and Soul to the Success of Saumitri'

||६||

Like the swan in the lake of love,
The fusion of hearts lost in intense love for each other
Played the musical notes which reverberated in all the directions;
Like a stream of honey flowing from the sky to the earth
The love of Urmila had filled the heart of Saumitri.
Awaking from her meditation on the banks of the Sarayu river,
Urmila said:

'Look over there, O friend!
Look at that bee – lovelorn like me,
It is sullen, and is waiting for the arrival of its lover – the sun –   10
Just as I am waiting for the arrival of Saumitri!
The sun is provoking the earth and
The wearied earth is gazing with frightful eyes!

'O my Love, how hard is your penance, look!
The flames of your penance are burning;
Feeling thirsty, animals are suffering and the lakes
Have all dried up! Let the tears in the thirsty eyes
Not dry up. The parched earth is waiting.

Dust is rising high because of the gusty wind.
The bubble of heat of Destruction is bursting, and prodding all.   20
Not worrying about me, submit yourself wholeheartedly
To serve Rama; may you accomplish the epoch's desire!

'What is this, dear friend?
Why are you shedding tears and why are you sweating?
If you pour out your emotions,
The pangs of separation will increase.
Making me think of my lover, you made me feel light.
Recalling those sweet memories,
I forgot the bitterness of my love-sickness.
My yearning to be with my beloved is on the rise.   30

'All the fruits of my meditation
I offer to my dear love Lakshmana.
O the chance of uniting with him appears a distant dream!
My excellent voice is drying up;
Give me my true voice.
I will spend the time thinking of my beloved.
Let your sweet voice continue; do not stop.
These salty tears offer enormous value to your voice.
Make your voice flow mellifluously.
Listening to your voice,   40
Past memories come back to life and my
Cheeks turn crimson like the morning sun.
Thousands of dreams have surfaced.
The entire earth and sky appear vacuous.

'Have you seen the *chataka*,
The bird that thrives only on raindrops?
Have you discerned my pangs of separation
Which others have failed to notice?
The lute of Nature is playing gently.
The sigh of a lady languishing in love is heard in the clouds.   50
Clouds give back earth's own water in the form of rain,
Fill the world with happiness,

And are remembered kindly for this favour!
Ah! Someone toils to redeem the world,
And someone else takes the credit! How strange!
It is Nature itself that has taught man to be thus self-centred!

'Let that be so.
Ignorance is getting dispelled;
And new thoughts are emerging.
All the dark clouds are telling new stories   60
In a soft, pleasant voice,
And fill the world with enthusiasm.
O Clouds! Pour the rain of happiness.
I will add to it my tears in profusion.
Whether it is rainwater or tear-drops –
Both waters belong to the earth.
Will you manifest before me now?
The sun scorches the earth in summer;
During monsoon, may you pour in rain and bring happiness.
Your drops will turn into pearls during Swati-star.   70
On seeing you, the peacocks dance.
Your arrival has such magical charm.
Let all the dormant spirit come to life!

'Let the juice of life flow;
Do not obstruct it. Rainbows and glowworms
Are all yearning for you; come pouring in copious rain.
O tufts of grass, *henna* plants, tendrils
And fresh shoots, do not rot but grow;
O the double-Jasmine, take shelter entwining the *kadamba* tree.
Let not anyone languish like me;   80
It is not fair to lead a solitary life,
Nor is there any charm in it!

'O you are the gentle wind,
That has come to me after touching Saumitri!
I bow to you a thousand times for bringing to me that soothing touch.
I hear the sound of clouds that resemble my beloved's voice.

O flowers, blossom like the smile of my beloved.
O wonderful clouds! Come showering in rains!

'One day, when my beloved was
Rocking the swing excitedly and as he swung it harder,
The swing soared higher and higher,
And as I was overcome with fear,
He then said with a smile,
"It appears as if you are mounted on a horse without the reigns."
O wonderful clouds! Come showering in rains!

'The flower of heart's desire
Is blossoming silently;
The desire to unite with the son of Saketa
Is growing rapidly. My red lips
Are trembling eagerly to offer my love to him.
One night, when it was raining incessantly,
When a gentle breeze was blowing
With the fragrance of screw-pine,
When the beetle was abuzz like the sound of the anklets,
A lightning glowed bright! At that very instance,
My beloved stood gazing at me with such intense love.
How can I forget that look, and that love!
O wonderful clouds! Come showering in rains!

'O Moon! Keep smiling always.
O *champaka* flowers! Blossom and keep swaying in the wind.
Let the pain of my tears not touch you.
Together with Rama, Saumitri will come back any time now
Treading the path of Great Quest.
O wonderful clouds! Come showering in rains!'

Urmila looked as if
She was the personification of immortality on earth!
She has encompassed the sky, the earth
And the nether world through the power of her deep penance!
She is that great explorer herself

Who brings to fruition the tenets of Saumitri. 120
'I offer my heart and soul to the success of Saumitri,
And will wait till you return accomplishing
The pilgrimage of the epoch.
O wonderful clouds! Come showering in rains!'

'What shall I tell you, my beloved?
Come dispelling the darkness of the epoch;
Come ushering in the light of supreme bliss;
Come spreading the peace of the night;
Come evoking pleasant dreams,
And come playing the strings of the lute; 130
Come joining with the sound of my heart,
And come spreading love all around.
I will gaze at the dark blue sky with the dream of your arrival.
I will hoist the flag of sparkling lights.
Ah! The pangs of separation from my beloved are afflicting me!

'What is this, O my beloved?
There is no sound of the chariot-wheels on the path of your arrival!
There is no cry of victory; there isn't any crowd.
I wait here every day, every night, every moment, every year
For your arrival and I hope that you will surely come. 140
Like the forests spread the fragrance of springtime all over,
You will come swiftly riding on the clouds
And I am waiting fervently with such hopes.

'Filling the sunrise and sunset
With excitement, flaunting the chirping
Of the birds with joy, with a smiling face,
I stand waiting, hoping that you will arrive.
With intense love, I stand yearning for you.'

Canto One Hundred and Ninety-five

'In the Path of Light, the Souls are United'

||◉||

'Your smile is captivating.
It appears as if you are standing in front of me.
You are the pervasive light of all lives.
Ah! I hear the sweet music
And the pleasant sound of musical instruments.

'As the daylight shines through wilted leaves,
Pigeons mutter as if to mock at me
That I am a deserted wife!
And mocking accusation has pierced my heart.
What if I sit in the shade of the hermitage? 10
Sleeping on the bare earth,
Your memory is prodding me constantly.
O son of Sumitra! You are my life,
And with conviction I am staying here.
You tread on the path of Truth every day;
You are a visionary indeed.
You have been a wanderer in unfamiliar terrains for ages now,
And I am confined to be here.
Give me a little space to lead my life.

I got up at daybreak 20
Hoping you would arrive.
I heard the sound of approaching feet,
And heard a voice say "I am a thirsty traveller".
As a bird was chirping hiding among the leaves,
I peeped out to see whether you were there.
Not finding you there, I delved into meditation.

'Later I realised
That you are housed in my soul!
In the path of light, the souls are united.
O the light of the world, O the captivating light, 30
O the light issuing forth the melody of the heart,
O the great light that dances in my whole being,
I came to the banks of the Sarayu to set afloat the light.
As you were not there, I was feeling lonely.
I walked slowly carrying the lamp of your memory,
And at once I set afloat that lamp of memory itself.
Accept the lamp that lights the heart, my Lord!

'This heart has been waiting for so long;
Let the flower of the epoch blossom;
Let it spread the fragrance in the path of Quest. 40
I don't know at what instant I stepped on the threshold of life.
It was an invisible power that made life bloom
Like a lotus in a pond in the thick of the forest.
Getting up at dawn as I looked around,
You were not there. My heart missed a beat!
The soul within and the Supreme Soul
Are playing hide and seek with me!

'I introspected – who am I?
I realised that I am a traveller in the path of Great Quest.
I won't cry, nor will I burn myself in the pangs of separation! 50
Overcoming love-sickness, and tearing off the veil of *maya*,
I will play the strings of my heart.
I will play the auspicious song of my heart.

The breath of life will spontaneously flow quite rhythmically;
It will rise and fall, like the waves of the sea;
It will dance rhythmically to the beat,
And it will revolve round the universe.

'Play on the strings of love.
The melody will spread to the sky like a creeper.
Gentle breeze is blowing.
Pigeons are flying far into the ocean.
Clouds pour in rains kissing the earth tenderly.
Memory springs up great excitement.
The love of my beloved is flowing nearby
In the form of the waters of the Sarayu!

'The divine glow of your eyes
Is reflected in mine and is shining bright springing up
Happiness in the depths of my heart
And has encompassed the entire earth and sky.'

Urmila stood in a trance
Gazing at the mountain peak of her dreams.
Her sight merged with
Saumitri's who was at the Suvela Mountain!
Unmoved by the world at large,
In profound silence she introspected
And experienced the wonder of her own inner self!

She contemplated:
'You are indeed the epoch's explorer.
Come rocking in the swing of vacuity.
There is a blind alley that is hanging on the periphery,
And the feathers of tempest are fluttering constantly.
As the thundering clouds poured in rain heavily.
Perhaps I can chance upon a rainbow!

'I have become the prisoner
Of human frailty. I don't know
When I will see the lustrous light! I am still searching for it;

Worry has taken over me and it's frightening.
It appears that my life is a closed chapter now.
Strife is raking the nerves hysterically,
And a horrendous deafening sound is spreading fast   90
Threatening to split the universe into two halves.
Nightmarish ghosts are dancing afar;
And the coffins are all lined up.
The sword of Lankesha is piercing the universe!
Mind is roaming aimlessly and shouting in fear.
The dark crystals of sorrow
Are approaching near crawling like cruel insects.

'Primordial idols are dancing wildly
Threatening with their horrendous forms.
Your silence is piercing my heart fiercely;   100
Don't you have any mercy on me?
The bird of Time is flying yonder stretching its beak
Writing and re-writing the epoch's destiny,
Opening the doors of fortune and fluttering its feathers,
Trudging on the conceit and grandeur of empires,
Plotting to encompass the universe and split it.

'As I open my eyes
Hoping to see the new seasons, I stand cheated and wearied.
Do not stir out from my heart even for a second.
Dear love, I will enthrone you in the gem-studded altar   110
And worship you. Do not move
Until I open the doors of my heart.'
Expecting the auspicious moment,
Urmila stands waiting past midnight!

In the Suvela Mountain
Saumitri remembers his dear wife and recalls
The words spoken by Urmila when he left Saketa:

'O the noble son of the clan, listen!
A forest is full of thorns and flowers,

And also countless trees that provide shade. 120
There is a rich variety of tasty roots and fruits.
Fragrant cool breeze blows there constantly.
It is indeed a palace kept wide open by the Creator himself!
It appears as if sympathy flows like a stream there!

'The canopy of vines and flowers
Shower affection by providing us with shade.
Birds and animals entertain by singing songs endearingly.
The sound of the cluster of clouds resembles the drum.
Peacocks dance to their hearts' content.
But look at the palace! It is filled with pain and anxiety. 130
The woods are filled with serenity, and are the
Abode of accomplishment.
O my beloved! I have the confidence to win over even death;
Do not worry about me. As you are vowed to tread
The path of Quest, be resolute in your task,
And move ahead peacefully.
Nature is looking at me like my beloved.
The heat of her heart has spread like hot sun in the woods.
Lotus have blossomed in the ponds,
And as the dew drops have settled on them, 140
It appears as if they are about to offer pearls to Sun-god.
The river is flowing as if
My beloved is coming to unite with me.
A conflict is going on in the estuary.
Rolling in the sand on the sea-shore, I have laid down there.
When I looked up I saw Urmila with her face pressed against
The window of the hermitage.
In the pangs of separation from me
Her face has turned pale and looks withered.
She has become weak in body and she's lost her courage. 150
Her dishevelled hair appears matted and is scattered by the wind.
Urmila stands there resembling the brightness of a lightning!'

Urmila is sitting on the banks
Of the Sarayu heaving a deep sigh.

'What an outstanding beauty is carved in the sky!
It appears as if the entire galaxy of stars is laid open!
Tell me dear maid, have my days of happiness arrived?
Will I be able to see happy days soon, tell me, O dear friend!
Will I see my beloved Saumitri, tell me, O dear friend!
Will he arrive; or will he not? 160
He has become the babe of destiny and keeps wandering.
I have drunk the ambrosia of hope that he will come.
My whole body is trembling with the desire of seeing him.
You are the eternal witness to the entire Ikshvaku clan!
Tell me, dear Sarayu, the news of my beloved.
Are you angry with me? Have you taken a vow of silence?
How can you push me thus into sorrow?
Keep flowing forever, and let the stream of love flow in my heart.'
Thus beseeching humbly she sat down there!

Gold-complexioned damsel Urmila 170
Is on the path of sublime love.
Holding herself high, she has scaled
The summit of intelligence through devout meditation.
The stillness of the night has enveloped
And clouded the mind making it difficult
To discern the earth from the sky.
It appeared as if the wind itself has lost its breath;
The air was motionless and remained dense!

Canto One Hundred and Ninety-six

'All Preparations were Made to Ignite the Cinder of the Epoch'

||६||

Getting down from the Suvela Mountain swiftly,
Shri Rama examined the preparations for the war
And spoke to Saumitri thus:
'Listen, Saumitri! Let some of our
Commanders stand forming an array.
Would the *bhallukas*, the *vanaras*
And so also the *danavas* be
Wiped off this earth, I wonder!

'The earth is trembling.
As the mountains shake, trees keep falling down.　　　　10
Giant clouds resembling the *rakshasas* soar high
And pour in blood, thundering.
No doubt, the crimson horizon at dusk is bathed in blood!
Fire of destruction is bursting in the solar orbit.
Gazing at the sun, herds of animals and flocks of birds
Are hoarsely wailing in fear.
The dark halo of the sun has encircled the moon.
The stars have lost their glitter and are not twinkling.
Eagles, owls, jackals are all

Crying hoarsely even during the daylight.　　　　　　　　20
The entire province will be sprawled
By flesh and blood like slush and
I don't know who can stop this!
Let that be so. We must lay siege on Lanka quickly
And take control of all the forts and bastions.'

As commanded by Rama,
The great army of *vanaras* comprising
Of Anjaneya, Sugriva, Nala, Nila
And other *vanaras*, and *bhallukas*, headed towards Lanka
In great excitement.　　　　　　　　　　　　　　　　30

Rows of flags fluttered there
In that grand city of Lanka. The forts and bastions
All had high walls. The city-gate seemed inviolable.
Under Rama's command
The *vanara* army surrounded all vantage points.
Accompanied by Saumitri,
And readying his mighty bow Kodanda,
Shri Rama stood at the northern entrance.

Nila, Dwivida and Mainda
Along with Pavanasuta, the son of Wind,　　　　　　　40
Laid siege on the eastern entrance,
While Sugriva, Pramathi, and Praghasa
Attacked from the western entrance.
Sugriva's army encircled from the north-west,
At every entrance there was an army of thousand *vanaras*.
All preparations were made to ignite the cinder of the epoch.
Like swarms of locusts,
The army of *vanaras* was beyond reckoning!
As the *vanaras* surged ahead roaring like the ocean waves,
Unable to bear it, the golden city of Lanka shuddered.　　50

Shri Rama commanded:
'Attack! Invade! Why should there be any delay?

Finish the task of crushing the enemy as swiftly as possible.
As the peace talks have all failed,
This war is inevitable.
Let us fight with good intention.
Let us cut off the heads of the enemies
And purify Lanka, bathing it with the blood of the traitors!
Destroying the citadels of bad traits,
And establishing the throne of Justice,   60
Let's proclaim victory to *dharma*.'

'Let victory be to Shri Rama' –
Was heard everywhere and the earth
Shuddered at that loud roaring.
All worshipped their arms silently in their minds.
As instructed by Nila,
All the *vanaras* screamed aloud
Stamping the earth with their feet
And bowing to Shri Rama and Sugriva,
They marched ahead.   70

All personal guards at service,
Sushena, and Prabha, the team of expert doctors,
Stood on one side; magnificent medicines
Of all varieties – pastes, creams, potions,
Powders, unctions, tablets,
And all types of mixtures – were kept ready there.
Saumitri and Pavanasuta watched over it.
A team of attendants also accompanied them.

As doctor Prabha brought sweet water
From the small streams, deep wells, lakes, and ponds,   80
They cleaned it and stored it well.
With the faith that Shri Rama would
Protect them, everyone was singing the song of victory.

'Let victory be to the killer of Tataka,
And victory to the slayer of Maricha!

By killing Khara, Dushana, and Trishira,
You protected the sages and ascetics.
Let victory be yours.

'O, the one who tamed the conceit of Parashurama –
Let victory be yours! 90
O, the one who made the virtuous people happy,
O, the one who protected the learned men
By allaying all their fears,
O, the Supreme-bliss-incarnate,
Let victory be to you, the beloved of Janaki!
Let victory be to the slayer of the magical-deer;
Let victory be to the saviour of Shabari;
Let victory be to the slayer of Kabandha;
Let victory be to the slayer of Vali!

'You are soul-mate to the entire clan of Sugriva. 100
You built the bridge to cast away the suffering of Janaki.
Let victory be yours.
You have given refuge to Vibhishana.
Let victory be yours!'

Praising Shri Rama thus,
Roaring like lions, they climbed the rampart
And filled the gorge with soil. Breaking open
The main entrance and destroying the cupola, they shouted:
'Victory to Rama, victory to Lakshmana
Victory to Janaki, victory to Sugriva,' 110
And surged ahead thundering and roaring.

Damaging the outer fortifications
Of Lanka, Virabahu, Subahu, Nala and other commanders
Surged ahead forming a military array.
Collecting a thousand soldiers, as Kumada stood ready
In the north-east, chieftains Praghasa, and Panasa
Advanced briskly. Shatabali in the south-east
And Sushena in the south-west, stood in readiness.
Ah! Well-equipped, all were ready!

The war trumpet sounded. 120
Blowing the conches aloud, the *rakshasa*-army
Moved briskly. The roar of the elephants,
The neighing of the horses, the screaming of the charioteers,
And the commotions of combat, resounded everywhere.
Climbing up, the *vanaras* invaded the fort
And razed down the forts and its embankments.
Smashing the dome of the fort with their weapons,
And not caring the wounds caused
By the spears of the fort-guards,
They climbed up the ramparts. 130

Many *vanaras*
Had their legs broken and ears torn;
Bathing in the pool of blood, they surged ahead
And breaking the main gateway of the fort, they went in.

Look there!
Shouting Victory to Lankesha
The strong-shouldered *rakshasas* were astride
Their horses. Carrying flags
That resembled the blazing torches, they climbed
Into chariots that glowed like the sun. 140
Adorning armours and roaring like lions
At which the earth shuddered,
They arrived to resist the attack of *vanaras*.

Hailing victory to Rama
The *vanaras* entered into a face-to-face
Combat with the *rakshasas*.
Indrajit took on Angada.
Andhaka encountered Trayambaka
And Sampati countered Prajangha.
Pavanasuta, son of Wind fought Jambumali 150
While Gaja resisted Tapadaitya.
Nila fought Nikumbha and Sugriva confronted Praghasa.
Saumitri countered Virupaksha.

Angered Mainda and Dwivida took on
Vajramushti and Ashaniprabha.
Nila confronted Durdharapratapa.
Sushena stood ready to slay Vidyunmali.
Ah! The fist-to-fist wrestling began with excitement,
The battle turned fiercely horrendous!

Goaded with a desire to win 160
As everyone was fighting fiercely, blood flowed out
In a stream from the bodies of the *vanaras* and *rakshasas*;
Bodies were strewn like piles of wood.
As Angada chopped the enemies
And threw their bodies away,
Enraged Indrajit went on killing the *vanaras*
Yielding his *vajra* weapon.
When Prajangha injured Sampati
Shooting three arrows at him,
Angered Sampati killed Prajangha 170
Striking him with *ashwakarna* tree!

Getting into his chariot as
Jambumali hurled Shakti weapon at
Anjaneya's chest, dodging it deftly, Hanuma smashed
Jambumali's chariot with his bare arms at that very instant!

Roaring continuously when Ghorapratapa
Attacked Nala, with his long nails
Nala plucked the eyes of the *rakshasa*.
As Laguhasta seriously injured Gaja with a sharp weapon,
Gaja smashed and killed Laghuhasta with his fist-blows! 180
As Praghasa rushed to confront Sugriva,
Striking him with *saptavarna* tree, Sugriva
Killed Praghasa that instant!
Virupaksha attacked Lakshmana showering him with arrows,
Lakshmana killed him with a single arrow!

On the other side of the battlefield,
Agniketu, Rashmiketu, Suptaghna, Yajnakopa faced Rama;

With arrows resembling fire, Rama killed the *rakshasas*
By chopping off their heads with an arrow each!

When Nila, who resembled the Nilagiri Mountains, 190
Was struck by Nikumbha with pointed weapons,
He evaded them tactfully and hit back
Showering hundreds of arrows.
The chariot got mashed up; Nikumbha and
His charioteer fell on the ground with their heads severed!

As Ashaniprabha
Advanced like a thunderstorm,
Dwivida hit him hard and his body was festered with wounds.
Uprooting a *sal* tree as Dwivida struck him with it,
The horses and the chariot got crushed 200
And the *rakshasa* died.

Arrived Vidyunmali
Roaring like a lion and shot
Pointed golden arrows at Sushena.
But Sushena smashed his chariot and stood bracing.
Jumping down the chariot, with a mace
The *rakshasa* attacked. Resisting him, Sushena
Rained blows with his strong and big fist
That resembled a boulder!
With his bones smashed, the *rakshasa* 210
Reached the kingdom of death.

The battle turned horrendous!
Strewn all over were broken swords, lances,
Chariot wheels, and the bodies of *rakshasas*.

The battle turned appalling!
Jackals and wolves were haunting the place;
Severed heads were rolling in heaps;
Skulls were scattered like cinders;
Blood was flowing like a stream.

The battle turned terrifying! 220
All around the severed arms of *rakshasas* had fallen;
All around heaps of thighs were strewn;
All around mounds of heads were thrown;
All around the entrails and brains lay scattered.

The battle turned ghastly!
The bodies that were slaughtered like sheep were stacked
As if readied for a sacrificial offering.
The severed head of the enemy
Dangling on the flagstaff on the howdah of an elephant
Appeared like a flag of valour! 230

The battle turned dreadful!
As the severed heads of the enemies looked like hailstones,
The gleam of the weapons flashed like lightning,
And blood flowed like rain,
The battlefield exhibited solemn grandeur of the rainy season!

At the back, in the front
To the left and to the right, troupes
Of valiant bodies fought bravely!
Who could take count of the lost lives?
They fought unmindful of their own lives 240
And paid with their heads.
Wailing and wriggling in pain,
They awaited the horrible death.
Who could describe the sufferings of a battle?
Vultures were pecking at the cadavers.
Poor soldiers were writhing in pain.
Having lost their hands, legs, eyes and noses,
The wounded warriors appeared like hillocks of flesh.
The place reverberated with the sound of clashing swords,
The swish of the arrows and the wrenching of the catapult. 250
Dead bodies were strewn in every nook and corner.
Smoke spread far and wide from the simmering fire.
The celestial regents of all the eight quarters rubbed their eyes

And the tusks of the mammoth elephants stationed there, turned dark.
Black thick smoke reached the clouds!

The main gateway was broken open.
It was as if a wolf had got into a flock of sheep;
It was as if an elephant in rut entered into a sugarcane field.
Violence and killing were on a rampage.
Fireballs exploded continually. 260
Pointed arrows were shot; elephants were killed.
The gorge of poisoned water was closed down.
How the *vanaras* invaded and how they ambushed
The fort leaping swiftly like leopards!

Fist-to-fist fights,
The fierce clashing of swords, axes and
Tridents went on constantly.
Climbing over the dead bodies of the *rakshasas*
vanaras killed the enemies and surged ahead!

As dusk approached, 270
Anxiety clouded Ravana's mind.
Rakshasas rushed forward shouting war-cries;
Donning the golden armour, they moved fast like lightning!
As the *rakshasas* surged ahead in anger killing the enemies,
The *vanaras* blocked them and fought back with the same vigour.

Jumping on the *rakshasas*,
The *vanaras* pulled down the crowns of the *rakshasas*;
They pulled and tore the shining flags;
Pulling down the mahouts, they pricked the elephants hard
And smashing the chariots, 280
The *vanaras* broke them all.

The loud sound and roar of war instruments,
The beating of drums, the blowing of conch,
The blowing of stringed and wind instruments,
Loud wailing, hoarse shouts and commotion deafened the ears.
The battleground appeared
Like the graveyard of ultimate destruction!

How splendid was the battlefield!
Desiring a war of ethics and justice,
Rama and Lakshmana declared – 290
'Let this battle come to a halt at nightfall';
And as they proceeded towards the camp at the Suvela Mountain,
Not heeding, the *rakshasas* trespassed the rule!
The *vanaras* wailed and the *rakshasas* screamed endlessly.
There wasn't any room even to set foot on that death-land!
It turned out to be a horrendous night for all
'Dark night is convenient to us,' averred the *rakshasas*
And showering arrows they attacked hard.
The commotion rose high
Like the wild waves of the seven seas. 300

As Sugriva attacked
Hurling a powerful weapon, the *rakshasas* got scared.
Severely wounded, they backtracked.
A fierce, hoarse cry resounded
In the gorges of the Trikuta Mountain.

On the other side,
A fierce battle ensued between Indrajit and Angada.
The war became intense and as his chariot got smashed,
Indrajit moved towards the palace.
Rama dispatched Nila, Sharabha, Jambavanta, Sanuprastha, 310
And Rushabhaskandha to search for Indrajit.
As they spread to all corners and searched,
They found Indrajit. He stopped
The *vanaras* from advancing
By shooting arrows, and like the sun among the clouds,
Disappeared in darkness evading everyone!

With sharp arrows
As Indrajit hurt Shri Rama and Lakshmana,
Their bodies were full of wounds and blood flowed like a stream.
The brothers appeared like red *muthuga* flowers in full blossom! 320
The *rakshasa* said:

'I am Indrajit. Could Indra stop my advancements!
I will shower arrows and send you to the kingdom of death.
Remaining invisible, I would wage war.
Can you stop me?
What harm the two of you can do to me!'

The army of *vanaras* was frightened.
Vanaras were afflicted by the blows of Indrajit.
Guffawing, Indrajit got into a magical chariot
And moving skyward as he showered arrows like rain, 330
The strength of the *vanaras* vanished completely!

The *vanaras* tasted the bitterness of defeat.
Axes, bludgeons, swords, spears, lances,
All clashed heavily. Arrows were shot from all directions.
Harsh cries like 'catch, thrash, and kill' hit the ears.
Dumbstruck, not knowing who was smashing them,
And not knowing what was happening, the *vanaras* shuddered.
Mustering all courage, the *vanaras* threw
Hillocks, hummocks, and huge trees in the direction of the voice.
Instantly, Indrajit, the charlatan disappeared. 340
Frustrated, the *vanaras* got wearied.

The expertise of Indrajit
Looked as if it rained fire from the sky,
As if water gushed out incessantly from the earth,
As if earth got engulfed in fire from all the directions,
And as pitch darkness enveloped and grew thicker,
The *vanaras* got caught in the magical web of Indrajit.

'Stop, O Indrajit!
Stop this war of cheating.
Does it befit a warrior like you?' 350
Thundered Lakshmana. Anger welled up in him
And he fought with the *rakshasa* fiercely.
Indrajit was hurt. As his chariot, horses
And soldiers got destroyed quickly,

The *rakshasa* got worried and feeling desperate,
He hurled a highly potent weapon called *Ghatini*
And it came and struck Lakshmana's chest with great speed.
Screaming 'Ah, Urmila!' with excruciating pain,
Lakshmana fell down and fainted!

With the pride of victory, 360
Indrajit shouted: 'I shot arrows, and Saumitri is dead.'
Worry enveloped Rama's camp.
As voices shouting 'Saumitri is hurt,' hit his ears,
In glee Indrajit said:
'Lakshmana is killed; he can't be hurt anymore.'
Bracing with pride and exhilarated with such an illusion,
He headed towards the palace swiftly.
'I have sent Lakshmana to the city of death, O Father!'
Said Indrajit. Getting up instantly, Lankesha
Came forward and saying, 370
'I am blessed; I am blessed indeed,'
He embraced Indrajit.
Caressing the head of Indrajit endearingly,
Lankesha was lost in himself!

Canto One Hundred and Ninety-seven

'The Essence of Happiness Lies Hidden in the Womb of Sorrow!'

||६||

Mind filled with the thoughts of Saumitri
As Urmila sat engrossed in deep meditation,
The cry of anguish – 'Ah, Urmila' –
Struck her heart like a thunderbolt.
Wailing aloud, she swooned and fell down.
Filled with anxiety as her maid attended to her,
She opened her eyes slowly! Resting Urmila's head
On her lap, caressing her hair gently,
The maid asked, 'What happened?
Why this anxiety? Tell me.' 10
Urmila replied in all humility:

'My head started reeling and
Darkness enveloped. I had a horrible dream:
My beloved was caught in a stream;
Raising his arms, he cried "Ah, Urmila!"
As I rushed to help him, there was silence;
No sound nor any sign of him.
There was a play of sun-light and shadow;
And the stream disappeared!

'I stood there watching.
Hills, woods, and trees were on fire.
As the smoke hovered like a mist,
Buds lay scattered all over. It became dark then
And as if destroying the world
A bright lightning struck blinding the eyes.

'The mind was ruffled.
The trees entwined by tendrils got uprooted
And fell down and the bunch of creepers got crushed too.
The cry of bees reached the skies
And the universe was splintered into pieces then!
The spell of my dream too was broken at that instant.'

Stroking her body gently
And comforting Urmila thus, maid Sulakshana said:
'Abstain from worries, stop this fickleness.
Aren't you the bold one? Drown the sorrows.
Drinking milk humans have lived;
Sucking blood *rakshasas* have lived;
Drinking ambrosia *devatas* have lived;
Your beloved lives well drinking poison.
Though the fire of sorrows afflicts you badly,
It will provide light for others.
The essence of happiness lies hidden in the womb of sorrow.
Enduring the heat of summer, Mother Earth
Flourishes when the rainy season starts.

'In the Ikshvaku clan
Shri Rama became a sage and your beloved Saumitri
Embraced a life of sacrifice willingly;
Though he took on the reins of the kingdom,
Bharata remained bereft of all passions;
And Shatrughna stood supporting the brother;
He is indeed the blessed one.' Urmila replied:

'Bad dream has afflicted me.
Look! The white dust has enveloped the sky.

A violent storm has spread in all the directions.
My Lord was fettered with iron shackles.
His face was pale with grief.
I don't know when I will see him.
Would the sun of my heart dispel the darkness?
To whom shall I express my anguish?
Would my penance be in vain?   60
The banks of the Sarayu river look like an illusory dream.
The entire universe seems to have a solitary form!

'I don't know what kind of life is this.
Swans are in deep slumber on the banks.
As the stream flows ahead steadily
The influx is washing the womb.
The moon in the sky is spreading his soothing beams
And wears a garland of stars.'

As the lute of her heart resounded
With the premonition that some evil has befallen her beloved, 70
Urmila, struck by grief,
Remained engrossed in deep meditation.

In the trance of her devout meditation,
Urmila envisioned splendid scenes:
All the great *vanaras* stood in sorrow
Surrounding the fainted Saumitri.
Some of them were standing near Rama.
Consoling the entire army,
Hanuma, Angada, Nila, Gaja, Gavaya,
And Jambavanta stood nearby.   80
Fearing that the *rakshasas* might attack suddenly,
Some of them were restlessly moving here and there
Keeping vigil on all directions.

Saumitri has collapsed;
He is soaked in blood and his face has turned pale.
Lamenting in sorrow, Rama said:

'Oh God! What is the use of my being alive now?
Look! My brother has lost his life;
How could I return to the city now'?
If Kaikeyi, Sumitra and Kausalya question me   90
Where is Lakshmana, what answer shall I give them?
"O Shri Rama! Thinking that you would protect him,
I had sent Lakshmana with you;
Leaving him behind, why have you come back?" –
Wailing like an osprey,
If Sumitra repeatedly asks thus,
Who would console her?
How could Shatrughna and Bharata be pacified?
I shall give up my life.

'O Saumitri! Where have you disappeared?   100
As I am grief-stricken, without comforting me
Why have you disappeared thus?
Whenever I cried in sorrow,
You had consoled and guarded me.
Why are you silent now? Being valiant
And capable of crushing the *rakshasas*,
How could you get wounded?
Why have you reclined on a bed of arrows?
Your body has been tormented.
You look like the west-bound sun.   110
You who had followed me without respite even for a moment,
You who would follow me even to the kingdom of death,
Should such a brother like you meet with this kind of death?
This indeed is the result of my unethical stance that has devoured you!

'What shall I do now?
You had never spoken harshly or unpleasantly.
You were an excellent archer and you had the power
To shoot five hundred arrows at a time.
You possessed the strength
To defeat the mighty Karthaviryarjuna.   120

You had the firmness to counter the weapons
Of Devendra, the chief of Heaven.
Has my volition to crown Vibhishana
As the king of Lanka failed!
Have I become a man of broken promise!

'O Sugriva! Set off
Towards Kishkindha. Knowing that I am not there,
Lankesha would invade your city. Set off at once.
Along with Nala, Nila and other *vanaras* cross over the bridge.
Many valorous soldiers like Gaja, Gavaya, Sampati   130
Sharabha, Kesari, Mainda and such other valiant men,
Not caring for their lives, stand here supporting me.

'O Sugriva! You are virtuous and god-fearing.
You have done your duty.
I am sunk in the well of failure.

'What shall I say, O brother!
Deserting your dear wife, forsaking the kingdom
And disowning the riches,
You followed me like a shadow.
You protected me like a mother   140
And led me like a teacher.
Why should I wage a battle
When the valiant one such as you are dead?
What will I achieve by killing Ravana?
Yearning for Sita I came here; but by sacrificing you,
Alas! I have fallen into the nether world!'

As Rama was lamenting thus,
Tears rolled down from the eyes of the *vanaras*.
Vibhishana sunk into deep sorrow.
Approaching Sushena, Sugriva said: 150
'Hear me. Waging war is my responsibility now.
Let Rama and Lakshmana set out
To Ayodhya this instant.

I will crush Ravana and all his kith and kin.
I will free mother Sita
And give her away to Shri Rama
And thus pay my gratitude to him.'

Sushena replied:
'O Sugriva! Why do you speak thus?
Brihaspati's *mritsanjivani mantra*, the life-infusing hymn,   160
Sanjivakarani and *vishalyakari*, the life-restoring medicinal herbs
Which grow in Chandradrona Hills are all there to help us.
Sunk in deep sorrow, have you forgotten all these?
Saumitri is not dead; he is deeply unconscious.
He should be treated with *mantra* and medicinal herbs forthwith.
There is no room for laziness.
Summon Anjaneya and dispatch him to the Hills.
Hundreds of medicinal herbs are there
And Anjaneya knows them all.
O Sugriva! Make haste to get them here quickly.'   170
Speaking thus, Sushena infused courage in everybody.

At the command of Shri Rama
Hanuma reached the Chandradrona Hills with lightning speed
And collecting all the medicinal herbs within seconds
He returned swiftly
To Rama and Lakshmana!

Sushena and others,
Along with Prabha the physician, cleansed the medicinal herbs
Swiftly. Then they prepared potions
And readied all the required medicines.   180
In the presence of Rama and other prominent leaders
Saumitri was given the best treatment.
They were all overcome with the worry wondering
Whether Saumitri's life would be restored or not;
But as the *mritasanjivini* powder was put in his nostrils,
Saumitri who was lying as if dead,
Started breathing and opened his eyes.

Rama felt relieved as if his own life was restored;
Hanuma felt relieved as if his own life was restored;
Sugriva felt relieved as if his own life was restored;   190
All felt relieved as if everyone's life was restored!

Because of the *vishalyakarani* herb,
The bits and shreds of weapons that had struck deep in the body
Of Saumitri came out effortlessly;
The broken bone got joined and the pain vanished due to
The administering of the herb *sandhanakarani*;
The wounds healed because of *suvarnakarani* herb
And the normal complexion of the skin returned.

Shining with full radiance
Saumitri got up that instant.   200
He was filled with the excitement to wage war
And he stood in readiness! At that instant,
Feeling extremely happy,
Shri Rama embraced his brother tight
And shed tears of joy.

'Blessed am I.
My valiant brother has come back to life.
He who is dear to all has come back to life.
He who is the crest-jewel of Ayodhya has come back to life.
He who is a man of character,   210
He who is the apple of his mothers' eyes
He who has none to match him,
Has come back to life!' Proclaiming thus,
Shri Rama hugged his brother
Over and over again and blessed him.
Anjaneya, Sugriva, Angada
And other valiant *vanaras* hugged
Lakshmana lovingly. The sea of sorrow receded
And the sea of happiness swelled.
The pale faces of the *vanaras* bloomed in happiness   220

And filled them with enthusiasm and valour once again.
The war-commotion knew no bounds and spread all over!

Sitting engrossed in deep meditation
On the banks of the Sarayu river,
Urmila envisioned all these
As if it all happened right in front of her eyes.
Breaking the meditation Urmila exclaimed:
'O my beloved! You are the embodiment of spirit
And you have come back to life!'
Then she went into deep silence. 230

The potency of the magical herbs
Brought by Anjaneya drew the attention of *vanaras* immensely.
Sugriva, Angada, Hanuma, Jambavanta, Vibhishana
Gaja, Gavaya, Sampati, Sharabha, Kesari
Vaidya Prabha and all her team of doctors were wonderstruck
And shook their heads in appreciation.
They beseeched Sushena
To describe the strength and power
Of all the six hundred magical herbs that were there.
Showing each herb to the assembled crowed, 240
Sushena explained in detail:

'This is *brumhaniya* herb
Which enhances the strength of body and mind immensely
And bestows longevity. This is *sandhaniya* herb
Which fixes broken bones.
Dipaniyaki herb increases appetite
While *balya* herb has the strength to heal the wounds.
Varnya has the strength to enhance the glow of the skin.
Kantya is good for cough and asthma.
For heart problems there is *hridya* herb 250
And *triptighna* quenches thirst.
Harshoghna is good for piles and fistula.
Kushtaghna herb is used for skin diseases,

And *kandughna* cures body itches.
Krimighna is the best medicinal herb for all kinds of infections!

'There are still many more
Herbs like *stanyajanana* which increases breast-milk
While *stanyashodha* purifies breast-milk.
Shukrakshodha enhances virility.
Shukrajanna increases sperm count. 260
Snehopaga repairs and steadies joints and cartilages.
Svedopana controls sweat and *vamanopaga* is anti-venom.
Virechanopaga cleans the bowels
While *astapanopaga* stops diarrhoea.
Anuvasanopaga is used for ulcers.
Shirovirechanopaga is administered for migraine
And headaches. Similarly, there is *trishnanigrahana*
For quenching thirst, and *hikkanigrahana*
Is administered to stop hiccups.

'If herbs like *vidanga, vacha,* 270
Nimbagala, manjishta are burnt,
The smoke that emanates from them spreads out
And brings good health for everyone!
Again, herbs like *jambira, nirgundi, dashamula* and such others
Are mixed and made into a potion
And the patient is bathed in it, he will feel elated.
If one's head reels, here is the herbal powder
That will provide relief.'

Vaidya Prabha explained to Hanuma and others
The various methods of treatment that she knew: 280
'*Mutrasangrahaniya* is the kind of treatment used
For curing infection of urinary bladder.
Similarly, *kasahara* is for treating cough,
Shwasahara is for asthma, and *shothahara* is used
For treating the inflammation caused by a mace.
If the eyes are injured by an arrow,
Sadyovrana treatment is quite effective.

To bring down fever, there is *jwarahara*.
While *dahaprashamana* is used for relief from dehydration,
Shithaprashamana cures ailments caused by cold.   290
Angamardaprashamana is used for treating body-aches.
Shulaprashamana treats the wounds caused by an arrow.

'How shall I explain the greatness of it all!
Shonitasthapane is used for blood purification
While *vedanasthpane* is used for subsiding pain.
To regain consciousness, *samjnasthapane* is used
While *prajasthapana* is for easing out
Labour pains and easy delivery of babies.

'Look at Jambavanta!
He is well advanced in age. To such people   300
We have *shaktivardhanasthapana* for revitalising their infirmity!

The treatment of wounds is a different section altogether.
If the wound is deep, one has to suture it
With silk thread or the gut of a sheep.
Later, it should be covered by a well-ground
Paste of *lodra* and bandaged.
If a blood vessel doesn't function well,
The ashes of mango leaf in an alkaline base
Shall be applied and covered with a bandage.

'Burn-wounds would be treated by   310
Spreading a tender plantain leaf and tying it
With a cloth around the wounds.
This man – Duja by name – who is with us here
Knows the medicinal qualities of various herbs
And is adept at treating the injured with a variety of bandages.'

In the battlefield
As the soldiers were wriggling with pain,
Shri Rama looked at them mercifully
And all the injured were treated well.
As the soldiers crawled with broken bones, using   320

Madhuchistha grass, the physicians treated them
Providing proper support to the broken bones.
Giving them meat-soup, milk, rice, and honey,
The wounded soldiers were nursed well.
Rama, Saumitri, Sugriva, Angada, Hanuma, and Jambavanta
Went round the battlefield treating the wounded soldiers
With utmost care and love and made them happy!

Canto One Hundred and Ninety-eight

'Would the Cowardly Cross that Kind of a River of War?'

||௬||

The roaring of *vanaras*
Deafened the ears of Ravana in Lanka.
He queried the courtiers assembled there:

'What is this noise and ecstatic commotion
As if the ocean waves have overshot their bounds?
Have Rama and Lakshmana freed themselves from the confines
Of the serpent-weapon? This is surprising, absolutely surprising!
Has the strength of our espionage declined?
Has the armour of Lanka's protection become weak?'

Climbing the rampart10
And viewing everything, the valiant *rakshasas*
Said to Ravana: 'Yes, yes, O Lord!
Rama and Lakshmana have freed themselves
From the straps of the serpent-weapon and moving ahead
Like an elephant in rut, they now stand ready for war!'
Anger welled up in Ravana and summoning Dhumraksha
He gave a stern command:
'Come, Dhumraksha. Do not show me your face
Until you have killed Rama, Lakshmana and the *vanaras*.'

Bowing to Ravana, Dhumraksha said:
'I shall obey your command, O Lord!'
Dhumraksha, the most dreadful *rakshasa* that he was,
Set out excitedly taking an army of valiant soldiers with him.
Holding spears, hammers, huge staffs, giant pestles, bludgeons,
Large lances, swords, daggers,
Roaring and brandishing their weapons,
The valiant soldiers surged ahead.

In the army of *rakshasas*, there were
Elephants carrying cords and long ropes;
Sharp daggers were tied to their tusks;
The bells tied round their necks made jingling sounds.
There were well-painted chariots drawn by donkeys.
There were chariots harnessed with fast-moving horses.
Readying themselves,
The valiant soldiers moved on.

The soldiers harnessed the chariot
Of Dhumraksha with fiercest donkeys having faces
Like lions and wolves. The disgusting *rakshasas* moved
Like wildfire and whirlwind, and
Like giant tigers, the valiant soldiers went along.

Vanaras, led by Hanuma, roaring like lions,
Countered the *rakshasas*.
Hitting the *vanaras* with their hammers, maces and spears
As the *rakshasas* proceeded briskly,
The *vanaras* retaliated by throwing large rocks
And smashed the chariots of the *rakshasas* to pieces.
As the *vanaras* thrashed the horses and elephants,
Hit hard at the horsemen and bruised
The faces of *rakshasas* by scratching with their nails
Causing them to bleed profusely,
Shouting in anger the *rakshasas* hit back with their strong fists
And smashing the *vanaras*, they advanced briskly.
But as the *vanaras* beat them up severely,
Unable to bear the blows, the *rakshasas* took to their heels.

Gazing fiercely, Dhumraksha stopped
The valiant *rakshasas* from fleeing.
He attacked the *vanaras* with all his strength.
Smashing the *vanaras* and making them spit blood,
He wielded the hammer and hit the *vanaras* hard.
Smashing with bludgeons and piercing the *vanaras*   60
With pointed lances, pulling out their entrails,
He soaked the *vanaras* in blood.
The battlefield turned awful and appeared
As if someone was playing the lute of destruction.
The sound of bows shooting arrows was spread everywhere.
The cries of agony, the pitiful pleas for help,
And the heavy sobbing of the wounded *vanaras*
And *rakshasas* echoed everywhere.

As Dhumraksha, holding the bow, advanced fiercely
Like a wild bison; as he rushed ahead like an elephant in rut;   70
As he stood like a tempest that shattered the entire earth;
Like the Lord of Death, as he stood firm to crush the enemies;
And as he pounced on Shatabali and injured him causing his fall;
It looked as if a huge tree fell down rolling!

Then, at the
Southern entrance, like a big wildfire,
As he attacked the army of Angada,
A large number of *vanaras* were burnt to death!
It seemed as if the monsoon clouds scaled the western mountains
And thundering aloud rained fireballs.   80
As the wheel of Time turned against them thus,
The wearied army of *vanaras* backtracked.

Raising the sharp axe
As Angada struck hard on the heads of the *rakshasas*,
Their skulls broke and heads rolled down.
Groaning and hissing like a snake
Dhumraksha rushed in and attacked!

Look! At the western entrance,
The *rakshasas*, pushing open the huge door,
Fastened the hanging bridge to the trench. 90
A large troupe of *rakshasas* came out running.
Akampana confronted Nala; Darimukha too rushed in;
And Nala countered Akampana
And pushed him back fiercely!

The battle was in full swing.
It rained blood causing the dust in the battlefield to settle down;
The earth turned slushy. Darimuka stood yawning
Opening his mouth wide and it appeared
As if the door of the nether world was open!
Like an elephant in rut fiercely swings its long trunk, 100
Dhumraksha swung his huge hands with great force.

What a gruesome scene!
Like a lion fighting with another lion,
Like a tiger fighting with another tiger,
Like a snake raising its hood hissing and striking another snake,
Like a bull bellowing and attacking another bull,
They wrestled with one another.

Fearing for their lives as the *vanaras* took to their heels,
The *rakshasas* laughed at them mockingly.
Unable to bear this, with bloodshot eyes 110
Valiant Hanuma hurled large boulders at the *rakshasas*.
Then, the wheel of Dhumraksha's chariot was shattered;
The shaft of the chariot was broken; the flag was torn;
And pierced by sharp arrows, the horses died.
With a mace in hand, Dhumraksha slipped out from the chariot.

Maruti – son of Maruta, the Wind-god,
Mashed the enemy with tree-trunks.
Lifting a huge boulder, as Hanuma hurled it,
Dhumraksha deftly dodged
And roaring, Dhumraksha swung his thorny 120

Mace at Anjaneya's head with all force.
Not caring about the blow, Pavanasuta, son of Wind,
Dropped a huge boulder on the head of Akampana.
Unable to bear the blow, shuddering, he
Ran towards Lanka. Blood flowed profusely
And there was the silence of the graveyard!

Honouring the command of Lord Lankesha,
Bracing with pride, fearless Dhumraksha surged like a storm.
Like the lightning that strikes during monsoon,
He proceeded uprooting the trees. 130
Roaring aloud as he rushed to slay Shatabali,
The *vanaras* threw trees at him and smashed his chariot.
As they hurled stones, the elephants died
With their skulls split open.
Dhumraksha jumped out of the chariot;
Shatabali rushed in and repeatedly hit on
The head of Dhumraksha.
The *rakshasa's* head was smashed
And he drew his last breath!

Hearing the news of Dhumraksha's death 140
Lankesha got highly disturbed.
Summoning Vajradamshtra, Ravana said:
'Valiant of the valiant, go swiftly. Slay Rama,
Saumitri and the *vanaras*.' Commanding him thus,
Ravana dispatched him swiftly.

Saying 'I am Blessed'
Vajradamshtra assembled an array
Of elephants, horses and donkeys.
He decorated the chariot with flags
Of variegated colours, and donning a bracelet of the upper arm, 150
Putting on the armour and the headgear,
He entered the battlefield.
An army of valiant *rakshasas* followed him
Holding maces, giant pestles, and sharp lances.

As Angada began to thrash the enemy,
The battle turned fierce!

As the monsoon rains thundered with
Lightning in the Sahya Mountains,
Rotating his handheld wheel violently, the *danava*
Chopped the heads of the enemies   160
And he appeared like a farmer harvesting the crops in the fields!
Vanaras retreated in fear!

Stamping the earth heavily
As Angada, weilding a heavy axe, roared loudly
And aimed blows at the head of Vajradamshtra,
The *rakshasa* prodded and dodged the blow
With his handheld wheel. Frustrated,
Angada hit the forehead of the elephant;
It collapsed trembling at the blow.

As the strength of the *rakshasas* weakened,   170
Wild with anger, Vajradamshtra shot with arrows;
The frightened *vanaras* ran to Angada for protection.
Pacifying everyone, Angada glared at Vajradamshtra's face.
Both fought fiercely like a lion fighting an elephant.
Angada's whole body was covered with blood.
As Angada hurled trees at the *rakshasa*,
He chopped them into pieces midway.

Viewing the craft of the *rakshasa*,
Angada picked up a heavy boulder
And hurled it at the chariot of his adversary;   180
The wheels and the shaft were broken
And the chariot collapsed to the ground.
Both fought fiercely like Mars and Mercury.
They appeared like the *muthuga* tree in full blossom.
Jumping off the chariot, as the *rakshasa* pounced
On Angada attacking him with his mace fiercely,
Angada picked up another boulder

And hurled it at the *rakshasa*.
Spitting blood, wailing and screaming
The *rakshasa* fell to the ground. 190

As their leader died,
The valiant *rakshasa* army, overcome with anger,
Encircled Angada. In the commotion that followed,
Several soldiers from both the camps were soaked in blood
And collapsed to the ground.
As the *rakshasas* advanced with bludgeons,
The *vanaras* attacked them with trees and boulders.
The fierce sound of the clashing of metals spread everywhere.
With the armours on their bodies gleaming,
The soldiers looked like a painting 200
Of the star-studded sky in autumn night.
Succumbing to the ferocity and the pace of the *vanaras*
The *rakshasas* scattered like clouds caught in the storm.

Hearing the news of
Vajradamshtra's death in the battle,
Lankesha summoned Prahasta and gave a stern command:
'Take Akampana with you and go the battlefield.'

Look! As the massively built Akampana,
Wearing diamond-studded ear-rings, proceeded swiftly
Leading an army of *rakshasas*, he encountered bad omens: 210
His left eye twitched, voice became faint,
And his face turned pale.
Darkness enveloped during daylight and a storm blew fast.
Frightened animals and birds screamed hoarsely.
The horses harnessed to the chariot became dull in spirit.

Not caring about the bad omen,
Akampana jumped into the battle with the fury of a giant tiger.
As the dust rose and covered the sky,
It seemed as if a white silken cloth had been spread out.

Both the *vanaras* and the *rakshasas* 220
Got completely confused as to who they should fight.

As the place was covered with dust,
Unable to see the enemy, *vanaras* killed the *vanaras*
And *rakshasas* slaughtered the *rakshasas* thinking
That they were indeed attacking the enemy!
Blood flowed profusely.

In the camp of the *rakshasas*,
Countless deaths occurred. The battle turned hideow.
Angered Akampana encouraged the *rakshasas*
Constantly and took them along with him. 230
Countering Nala, Mainda and Kumuda,
He surged ahead engaging the enemy as if in a sport.
His charioteer drove the chariot swiftly
According to the instructions of the valiant warrior.

Then, like the heavy rains
On the peak of the Mahendra Mountain,
Akampana showered arrows and killed many valiant *vanaras*.
He then surged ahead aiming to crush Hanuma.
Not caring for the shower of arrows, Pavanasuta
Determined to slay the *rakshasa*. 240
Stamping the earth with his heavy strides,
Radiant like the sun, roaring like a lion,
Swinging a huge tree, Hanuma moved briskly
Like Devendra, the chief of Heaven,
Rushed to kill Namuchi with his *Vajra*-weapon,

The *rakshasa*, looking intently,
Cut off the tree with crescent shaped arrows and leaped forward.
Filled with terrible anger,
Hanuma uprooted a huge *ashwakarna* tree,
And roaring aloud, he smashed the *rakshasa* army 250
And killed the elephants and charioteers.
Chopping the soldiers on foot coming his way,
Hanuma severed the head of Akampana and cleaved his body.
He glowed with a rare radiance!
Hanuma appeared like Lord Vishnu –

The slayer of *rakshasa* Kaitabha!
He then surged ahead with determination to slay all the *rakshasas*.

Dropping down their weapons and shivering in fright
The *rakshasas* ran with their backs to the battlefield.
As Hanuma chased them mockingly 260
It appeared that the *rakshasas* were
In a race and ran fast competing
With each other fearing that they might be caught by Hanuma.
As the *rakshasas* ran for their life, Hanuma thundered:
'Today I will spare you,' and returned roaring like a lion!
As the sun went down that instant,
The battle ended for the day.

The next day
Summoning Prahasta, Ravana said thus:
'Look at the marvellous strength of the *vanara* clan! 270
The magic of Meghanada did not bear fruition.
Vajradamshtra, Dhumraksha and Akampana are dead.
What shall I do now? You are my only hope now!
Tell me whether we have erred in our war strategies.'
Prahasta replied:

'The army of *vanaras* has viewed
The *rakshasas* like a trivial entity, O King!
Driving away the brother, you did a wrong thing.
Succumbing to sycophancy, you broke the peace talks.
I was one among those who advised you 280
To surrender Janaki. As everything has gone out
Of our control now, war is the only way left for us.
Why do you worry, O King? Do not blame anyone.
Just as the seven musical notes have high and low pitch,
Rise and fall in battle is natural for every valiant warrior.
I am vowed to wage war
And I know that this mortal body is ephemeral;
I will offer myself wholeheartedly to the service of my lord.'

As Prahasta proceeded to the battle,
Narantaka, Mahanada, Samunnata, and Kumbhaha 290
Marched along on his either side.

The oblations of fire got consummated
And with the offerings made to the sacred fire,
The fragrant smoke rose high and spread everywhere.
The *rakshasas* decked themselves with the flowers offered to them
Sanctified by chanting the victory-hymn.
'Today we will certainly offer the flesh of the *vanaras* to the birds,'
They shouted. Bowing to the king of *rakshasas*
And receiving from him the formal royal decree to wage war,
Along with Prahasta they marched happily beating the war-drums. 300

Something untoward happened!
Bad omens appeared: vultures circled in the sky
Over Prahasta's chariot in the contrary direction.
Birds screamed spitting out fire.
The clouds thundered and it rained fire.
Meteors fell down. It looked as if all the planets were in conflict
And all the warriors remained crestfallen.
The reins slipped out from the hands of the charioteers.
The horses faltered even on flat grounds.
The roaring of the *rakshasas* and *vanaras* reverberated all over. 310
And they stood opposite to Rama's army.

Shri Rama asked:
'Tell me, O Vibhishana!
Who is this warrior with such a great physique?
Who is this *rakshasa* jumping into war now?
Who is this valiant warrior?'
Vibhishana replied:
'He is Prahasta, the commander-in-chief
Of the *rakshasas*. He is a highly renowned valiant warrior
Well-versed in the dexterous art of weaponry.' 320

As Prahasta surged ahead roaring fiercely,
The angry *vanaras* resisted and attacked him.

Rakshasas waged war wielding a variety of maces, bludgeons,
Darts, lances, bows, giant pestles, and axes
While the *vanaras* attacked the *rakshasas*
Hurling boulders and trees at them.

The *rakshasas* killed the *vanaras*
Piercing their rib-cage with pointed spears,
Chopping them with sharp wheels, thrashing them with bludgeons,
And striking with giant axes, they dispatched   330
The *vanaras* to the city of death.
Pulling the heads with bow-strings, they chopped off the heads
Of the *vanaras* with swords.
Squeezing the neck hard,
They killed the *vanaras* cruelly by smothering them.

The *vanaras* were enraged.
They retaliated by thrashing the *rakshasas* with trees.
Pounding with the fists, they smashed the faces of *rakshasas*;
Their teeth fell down, and the eyeballs
Popped out from their sockets.   340
Dwivida swung a branch and with it killed Narantaka.
Durmukha destroyed Samunnata that same instant.
Aiming blows at Mahanada's chest
Jambavanta made him disappear from the scene.
The attack of Tara killed Kumbhaha.
The war-commotion took various forms
And like the whirlpool in the sea,
The battle turned dreadful.
Like the bright red *muthuga* flower
That bloomed in summer, the redness   350
Of the battlefield struck the eye fiercely.

Blood flowed profusely
From the dead bodies that lay in heaps
And the weapons lay scattered all over.
It seemed that the river of blood was flowing
To join the ocean of death.

Ripped livers and spleens were the slush;
Entrails were the green moss;
The torn limbs that floated in the pool
Of blood appeared like fish; 360
The marrow of dead bodies appeared
Like froth in the stream of blood;
The severed bodily organs and parts were all
Like the grass in the river;
Vultures were the swans and herons;
The wailing of the wounded was the roar of the river.
Would the cowardly cross that kind of a river of war!

Prahasta appeared as the one
Surfaced from the depth of such a river!
On seeing the savagery in Prahasta to slay the *vanaras*, 370
The valorous Nila confronted him.
Prahasta, moving like a tempest that scatters the clouds,
Wounded the body of Nila with his sharp arrows.

Seizing a huge tree,
Nila smashed the horses of the *rakshasa*
And pulling the bow of Prahasta,
Nila broke and threw it away.
Seizing a giant pestle, Prahasta jumped out from the chariot.
Both warriors fought like lion and shardula.
The Goddess of Victory appeared to be on Nila's side once, 380
And on Prahasta's side at another instant.
Each valiant warrior chose his equal from the other side.
A fierce battle ensued from dawn to dusk.

The steam of blood in the battlefield
Turned into clouds and rising high in the sky
Appeared like the saffron cloth worn and discarded
By a saint vowed to win over death through penance.
The hue of the sky ushered in excitement.

Not caring the attack of Nila,
Prahasta moved forward and smashed him with a giant pestle 390

And blood spurted out from Nila's forehead. Not fearing,
Nila cleverly moved and smashed the chariot.
Kicking the charioteer, Nila turned the chariot upside down.
Fastening the *rakshasa*-minister and appearing
Like Narahari, the Lion-incarnation,
Nila slit open the armour
And wrung the neck of the *rakshasa*.
Then, with his strong nails,
Nila pulled out the entrails and sprawled it on the battlefield.
With his anger swelling up, as he swung and threw away the body,   400
The head of the *rakshasa* shattered into a hundred pieces.

All the strength having been weaned,
Crestfallen and all senses having failed,
The *rakshasa* hit the ground like a felled tree.
Warm fresh blood spurted out from the body of the *rakshasa*.
Viewing the death of Prahasta,
The army of *rakshasas* collapsed with dwindled spirit.
Like water gushes out, roaring from a broken dam,
The *rakshasas*, frightened like jackals, ran helter-skelter.

Canto One Hundred and Ninety-nine

'Discern that this is the War of the Epoch That Cleanses the Dirt of the Universe'

||૬||

The news of Prahasta's death shattered Ravana.
Bad dreams in the night caused him enormous pain.
Getting up at dawn, he offered prayers to Lord Shiva,
And presiding on the royal court, said thus:
'I do not know how the valiant Prahasta –
The one who quelled the strength of Devendra,
The chief of Heaven,
And the one who was the most fearsome to his enemies –
Could be slain!
It is impossible; it is incredible. 10
Alas! Alas! What could be done now!
Just as the wildfire burns down the forest,
I will now burn to ashes Rama, Lakshmana and the *vanaras*
In the battlefield with a sea of arrows!
I will not keep quiet until I satiate
All the spirits that are there on earth and in the sky
With the blood of the *vanaras*!
As the forest-dwellers keep killing my sons and ministers

Would I spare them! I will chop them into pieces
And make an offering to the Goddess of War.' 20

On the command of Ravana as the
Army set out, the war drums sounded
As if the time of ultimate destruction approached fast.
Adorning bracelets and armlets with bells,
And bowing to Lord Shiva
As Ravana stood brandishing his sword,
Damsels performed *arati* for his victory and put *sese* on him.
Lankesha climbed into the grand chariot swiftly.

Roaring aloud, as the valiant *rakshasas*,
Surrounding Ravana, proceeded in great excitement, 30
Ravana appeared like Lord Shiva himself
Who had set out with his *ganas*.
His mountain-like physique and fair complexion were charming;
His eyes blazed like fire-balls.

Coming out of the fort
Ravana watched with his own eyes the oceanic *vanara* army
Standing in readiness armed with *shaila* trees.
'Who is this radiant, valiant, well-built man?'
Shri Rama asked Vibhishana.
Vibhishana replied: 40

'He is my elder brother, Ravaneshwara.
Just as Lord Shiva stands radiant amidst
His attendants – the *pramatha ganas*,
Adorning the golden crown, glowing with radiance,
Extraordinarily well-built Ravana stands firm
Like the Vindhya Mountain.'

Shri Rama replied:
'Oh! What a surprise! What a magnificent form!
His radiance is extraordinary. Tell me whether there is
Anyone who is as radiant and as powerful 50
Among the *devatas* and the *rakshasas*!

The door of my fortune is opened. If at all one needs to fight,
One should fight such a valiant man as this.
My life is blessed and also the epoch's desire is fulfilled today.'

Later, Ravana commanded:
'Guard the main doors without fail;
Protect the fort-towers, the rampart and the royal quarters
Without fail; do not fear; be not afraid.'
Saying so, like a giant whale,
Ravana stormed into the oceanic *vanara* army. 60

Staring at Ravana,
Sugriva unearthed a hillock and flung it on Ravana.
Arranging the golden tipped arrows,
Dashakantha, the ten-headed one
Shot at the hillock and it split into five pieces.
Then he shot another arrow which traversed towards Sugriva
With such speed as if it was Indra's *vajra*-weapon
Which Lord Shanmukha – the six-faced son of Shiva –
Had used once
To slit the Krauncha Mountain. The arrow moved swiftly 70
Towards Sugriva and hit him hard. Unable to bear the blow,
As Sugriva fell to the ground with a thud,
The *rakshasas* shouted with joy.
Carrying mountains with them
Leaders like Rushabha, Jyotirmukha, Gavaya, and Gavaksha
Chased Ravana to attack him; by shooting sharp arrows at them
Ravana deterred them from advancing and surged ahead.

Licking bones and stems like snakes,
Sowing the seeds of death,
Crushing the strength of the enemy, impairing the power 80
Of Yama, the God of Death, ripping the labyrinthine Time itself,
Ravana showed his splendid valour to the enemies.

Ravana's blows got harder and
Unable to withstand the ferocity of the blows,

The valiant *vanaras* got severely hurt
And fell down then and there.
Shuddering with fear, they ran helter-skelter shouting desperately:
'O Shri Rama! We are at your mercy; protect us.'
On seeing this, as Shri Rama got ready for the battle,
Saumitri said: 'I will slay Ravana   90
And extirpate the entire *rakshasa* clan;
Grant me permission.' Shri Rama said:
'O Saumitri! Be careful.
If the mighty Ravana gets angry, all the three worlds tremble.'
Embracing him endearingly, and granting permission,
Shri Rama sent Saumitri.

In the meantime, the son of Wind,
Stopping Ravana in the battlefield said:
'You are a dead man now!'
Has anyone survived in this world fighting the *vanaras*?   100
Abducting Janaki you have invited death;
You will not live anymore. I will drive out your soul
That has sheltered in your body for so long.
This is the volition of the epoch.'
Thus Hanuma mocked at him.

'Stop, stop at once, you monkey!
I will test your strength first, and then I will slay you.
The monkey pranks that you played in Lanka
Won't be any good in the battlefield; I will make you bite the dust.'
As Ravana thundered thus, not fearing, Anjaneya said mockingly: 110
'It is alright. I have seen your strength. You have become the king
Of a country of cowards. To a village in ruins,
Any survivor would be the headman; you are one such.
When I challenged you in your court then,
You were sitting like a stray dog, why do you brag today?

'You are such a shameless one
Who did not even stir to save the blazing Lanka.
You are the thief who abducted mother Sita.

Enough of your ploys; your game is over.
It isn't late; surrender Janaki at least now!' 120

Hearing the incisive, humiliating words of Hanuma,
Getting wild with anger, Ravana struck Anjaneya on the chest.
Pavanasuta was ruffled at the blow, tottered and almost fell.

Recovering that instant and enraged,
Hanuma hit Ravana with all his might.
Like the hills and mountains that shudder during an earthquake,
Wounded Ravana fell tottering; he shrunk in shock.
The *vanaras* shouted in excitement.
Recovering, Ravana said:
'Bravo! Your valour is great indeed. 130
Your prowess is praiseworthy; you are a valiant foe.'
Hanuma retorted: 'Shame on your valour!
This blow of mine will shove you
To the city of death this instant.'

Not able to bear the harsh words,
Ravana hit Hanuma ferociously.
As Hanuma stood tottering and trembling,
Ravana turned his chariot swiftly
Towards Nila and attacked him.
Is Nila any ordinary! 140
He is an expert in military array formation,
And an ingenious commander par excellence in the art of warfare.

But now, by the ferocious attack of Ravana
Nila suffered badly. He retaliated by hurling mountains
And hillocks at Ravana. At that instant, recovering fully
And desiring to fight, Hanuma came searching for Ravana.
As he approached Nila, he saw Ravana there, and said:
'I will take on you. Why do you fight Nila?
Fight with me and that will be the end of you!'
Not heeding the words, Ravana shot seven 150
Arrows at the mountains and hillocks Nila hurled at him

And shattered them into pieces. Uprooting the trees,
As Nila continued to hurl them all at Lankesha,
Showering pointed arrows,
Lankesha retaliated by smashing everything to pieces.

Exhibiting his craftsmanship
Nila moved briskly and climbed onto Ravana's flagstaff.
Roaring aloud, he got on top of Ravana's crown.
Viewing this, Rama, Saumitri and Hanuma
Exclaimed in appreciation: 160
'What craftsmanship! What speed!
He is moving on Ravana's body
Obfuscating and ruffling him all the while!'

Not able to grasp or seize Nila,
Ravana thundered: 'Enough of these pranks, you monkey!
Stand in front of me, fight fairly and I will slay you.
I will burn you to ashes with the arrows of fire;
Let me see who is going to protect you.' Saying so,
As he shot the great arrow, it struck Nila hard on the chest
And he fell from the top of the flag-staff   170
To the ground and became unconscious.

Leaving out Nila there
On seeing Lakshmana,
Ravana set out twanging the bow-string and killing the *vanaras*;
As if to diminish the radiance of the entire colour spectrum,
Twanging the bow-string again and again,
Ravana said thus:

'Oh! Lakshmana!
I am fortunate indeed that I sighted you today!
Naming Chandranakhi as Shurpanakhi   180
You disfigured the young girl by chopping off her nose and ears.
Will I spare you? Stop! Stop, you villain!
There is a saying – "When the hour of destruction approaches
One begins to think and act eccentrically!"

The proverb suits you very well.
Showering arrows, I will dispatch you to the city of death.'

Saumitri replied:
'I know your bravery very well.
Don't be boastful. You bit the dust in the battle with Sahasrarjuna;
Have you forgotten that? 190
When trying to lift the bow of Lord Shiva, it fell on you
And you lost your honour then.
Have you forgotten that too, tell me!
You are the Lord of the *rakshasas* who abducted the mother.
Where was your bravery hidden then?'

Listening to the mocking words of
Lakshmana, anger welled up in Ravana
And he shot seven arrows at Lakshmana.
Saumitri broke the arrows and threw them away instantly.
When Lankesha tried to entrap Lakshmana with a host 200
Of fierce arrows, destroying them all
And without feeling exhausted or agitated,
Saumitri stood his ground smiling!

Angered Ravana
Shot the blazing *Brahmadatta* arrow aiming at Saumitri's forehead.
Lakshmana tottered and the bow slid from his hand.
Recovering the next moment, when he hit the *rakshasa*
With three pointed arrows,
The *rakshasa's* bow broke into pieces and he swooned.
Recovering with difficulty, as Ravana swung the most 210
Powerful and radiant *shakti* weapon, it came forcefully
And struck the chest of Lakshmana
And he fell and lay unconscious on the ground.

With high excitement
Ravana thought: 'I will lift Lakshmana up
Onto my chariot, reach Lanka,
And throw him at the feet of Chandranakhi.'

Thinking thus, he came running,
And trying to lift him up, seized Lakshmana by the arm.
Can Lankesha lift up Lakshmana who is indeed Adishesha? 220
It is true that Ravana has lifted up Kailasa mountain;
Perhaps he would lift up even Meru,
Mandara or such other mountains.
But unable to stir Lakshmana even slightly,
He suffered the loss of his pride!

Viewing the *rakshasa's* struggle,
Anjaneya said: 'Leave, leave him out, you villain!
Who are you to touch Lakshmana?' Saying so,
He hit Ravana with his fist powerfully.
The *rakshasa* shuddered; blood oozed from his eyes and ears; 230
His head reeled. Climbing the chariot, he reclined there.
The *vanaras* yelled in excitement
While the *rakshasas* waited sullenly.

Carrying Lakshmana
On his shoulders very devoutly,
Valiant Anjaneya brought him to Rama and refreshed him
By fanning and offering cool scented water, fruits and flowers.

In the meantime, gaining consciousness
Ravana shouted: 'I won't spare Lakshmana,'
And advanced like a storm. The *vanara* army suffered. 240
When Shri Rama himself got ready to attack Ravana,
Pavanasuta, son of Wind, pleaded: 'Climb on to my shoulder
As you do with *Garuda*, the vehicle of Lord Vishnu.
Shri Rama denied with all humility and climbed his chariot.
Seizing his bow Kodanda, and twanging its string,
He approached Dashashira, the ten-headed one, and said:

'Stop! Stop, you *rakshasa*!
You watered and nurtured enmity.
What if you seek refuge in Devendra, Yama, and Sun?
What if you surrender to Brahma and Shiva? 250

What if you go into hiding in all the corners of the world?
What if you stayed away in Patala, the nether world?
I will not spare you; you shall not be alive.
Mother Earth has collapsed not able to bear you.
The door of death is wide open for you.'

Gazing intently,
Shri Rama shot arrows continuously.
One arrow shattered the chariot-wheel;
Another arrow killed the horses;
The third arrow hit and cut the flag pole of the chariot; 260
The fourth arrow killed the charioteer;
The arrows of Ravana proved futile.
The fifth arrow broke the white royal parasol
And Lankesha collapsed to the diamond-like sixth arrow.
Aiming another arrow, Shri Rama broke Ravana's bow into pieces
And with yet another arrow caused Ravana's crown
To fall to the ground.

Viewing the magical powers of Rama's arrows
All the valiant soldiers were awe-struck.
Like a snake that has lost its venomous teeth, 270
Ravana appeared pale and sullen.

Shri Rama said:
'You are exhausted killing the *vanaras*.
You are without a chariot and you have weapons none.
Return to the palace, rest and come back tomorrow.
If *dharma* awakens in you, come with an offer of truce;
If stubbornness and hoodwinking gratify you,
Come with the volition to wage war;
Come riding a new chariot and come seizing a new bow.
I desire a war of Justice. As you are helpless now, 280
I will not slay you.
I will prove my valour and take back Janaki.
I haven't come here as a beggar.

This is not a war of self-interest; discern that
This is a war of the epoch that cleanses the dirt of the universe!'

Lankesha was afflicted.
His chariot was broken and so also was his fervent desire.
As the *rakshasas* watched their king without the crown,
He walked to the palace in silence.

Canto Two Hundred

'In the Vessel of Poison, Look for Ambrosia!'

||६||

Having been subdued by the intensity of Shri Rama's arrow,
Ravana returned to the palace suffering great pain.
The humiliation of being defeated
Pierced his mind like a wasp.
Like a wild elephant defeated by a lion,
Like a serpent overpowered by an eagle,
Enduring the pain of defeat,
He contemplated the magnificent powers
Of the arrows of Raghavendra, the crest-jewel of Raghu clan.
Ascending the royal throne and addressing the valiant warriors,　10
Ravana said:

'Listen, my companions.
Undertaking fierce penance,
I have received many boons. But the glory of my fame
In priding on who could equal me has now bitten the dust!
I have lost to a trivial human called Rama.
What is the way out for me now?
Succumbing to my arrow then,
The dying monarch of Ikshvaku clan cursed me thus:

"O despicable creature! A man will be born in my clan;
He will slay your sons and ministers in the battle!"
When I violated the modesty of Vedavati
She said, "reincarnating I will slay you in my next birth".
It appears that all curses are coming true.
Who is there to protect the accursed Lanka?
Is it worth living fearing like sheep?
We now need the services of Kumbhakarna,
The extraordinarily powerful and valorous warrior;
Send for him at once!
Standing firm like a flagstaff in the battlefield,
He will protect everyone; there is no doubt in it.'

At that instant, a group of soldiers
Entered the palace of Kumbhakarna and looked for him.
The palace was beautiful and filled with fragrance.
He is engrossed in penance for six months in a year.
'How will we awaken him;
He is a scholar and an honourable man.'
Thinking thus, not able to violate Ravana's orders,
They brought in countless trumpets,
War-bugles, drums, cymbals and bells.
Blowing and beating them all, they generated a loud sound.
Not stirring a bit, Kumbhakarna sat unperturbed!

'What shall we do now?' They wondered.
Thinking wisely, they played on the seven-stringed
Veena evoking the seven musical notes melodiously.
As the *rakshasa* heard the melodious composition,
He woke up and looked around.
Everyone was surprised!
They praised him:
'He did not wake up for the loud noise;
But how did he wake up to the melody of the seven strings;
He is a supreme being for sure!

'He is the idol of supreme goodness
And valiant among the valiant.

His face and eyes are radiant like fire.'
With anxiety he asked, 'I was engrossed in penance
To ward off the oncoming impediments.
Is Ravana well? Has any danger befallen?'

Folding his hands, Yupaksha said:
'Building a bridge with the help of the *vanaras*,
Rama and Lakshmana have invaded Lanka.
The fort and the trenches have all been destroyed. 60
Listen! Lanka has collapsed due to the intense battle.
The *vanaras* resembling Hanuma who killed Akshakumara
Have come in large numbers. Ravana himself
Has been subdued and has retreated!

'An ascetic named Agastya
Has come to the south traversing from the north.
Having learnt all the crafts of warfare of the *danava* clan,
And with a determination to surpass the *rakshasas*,
He has created, through intense research,
An assemblage of great weapons. 70
He has revealed the secrets of *Brahmastra*, the ultimate weapon to Rama.
He has taught them the methods of
How to use the medicinal herbs
To heal the wounds suffered in the battle.
He is now engaged in teaching the art of novel warfare
To Saumitri and *vanaras* to empower them.'

Determined to break the
War crafts of Rama and Saumitri,
Kumbhakarna had requested Ravana
Earnestly then: 'Give me six months' time!'
At that instant, Indrajit had said mockingly: 80
'Uncle, listen! What could you discover in six months?
It is a sheer waste of time. Why engage in useless research
That does not come to our help in times of danger?
Desert that desire for research through penance.
To destroy the trivial humans, the magical powers I possess suffice.

Who has got the strength to cross the seas?
Is building a bridge across the sea a child's play, tell me.
Can the trivial humans withstand the spell of magic?
It is good to undertake penance during the time of peace
And it's not fair to engage in research during the time of war. 90
If there's a danger from radiation in the research centre
How can one survive it? Why this misadventure now?
The confidence of the citizens of Lanka will collapse.
You are not the only commander-in-chief
And all will be destroyed with you. As this is the right time
To discern the secret activities of the enemy.
Our war strategies will not bear fruition if we do anything else!'

Hearing these childish words,
Kumbhakarna retorted: 'Look at the relevance of science
In the life of human beings! 100
Then, how could you speak so derisively?
The fiercest weapons that can burn the whole universe
To ashes are all on the rise!
When Maricha cried, "O Rama! O Sita!"
Rama shot an arrow in that direction
Merely listening to the sound
Of Maricha and killed him. Can you forget that episode?
Wherever the ships may be,
The strategies of exploding them merely
By studying their movements have been successfully developed. 110

'Along with the craft of employing missiles guided by sound,
There also exist such other similar tools
Like the missiles guided by light, and motion,
How can your witchcraft be successful? Today,
Rama possesses the strength to quell all your magical spells.
When Lanka was set ablaze,
Where were your magical powers hidden?
Abstain from this foolishness, and think wisely!
Do not dip Lanka in the ocean of misery.'
Kumbhakarna had then pleaded with Ravana, 120

'Give me permission.
Six months are more than enough. I will carry out
An appropriate scientific research in the most secret of places.
I will teach all our commanders the art of destroying
The entire army of Rama.
Listen! It is precisely for this purpose
I will do penance and gain the requisite knowledge and expertise.'

The permission was of course granted.
But what is the use of it? Before the research
Got completed, the battle ensued and Kumbhakarna's   130
Penance ended without bearing fruition.
'I was about to achieve victory in my goals,
But precisely at that instant,
My penance was interrupted and cold waters
Were thrown on my research.
Not exhibiting the shrewd diplomacy of postponing the battle,
Lankesha has erred miserably. Alas! He is doomed!'

Rolling his eyes fiercely
Kumbhakarna said, 'Yupaksha, I will come,
Do not worry, and be not afraid. I will slaughter the   140
Army of *vanaras* and slay Rama and Lakshmana
And later I will visit my elder brother.'
Bracing with pride, and snarling ferociously,
He got up and came out!

Mahodara said:
'Visit the king first! That is the order of the king.
You can't go to the battle straightaway.'
Treading valiantly and appearing like Yama, the God of Death,
Kumbhakarna walked towards the palace of Ravana.

Anticipating the arrival of the younger brother,   150
Lankesha got the streets colourfully decorated
And raised slogans of praise. Beautiful ladies showered flowers
From the top of the buildings. As a mark of respectful welcome,
Auspicious instruments were played aloud.

Arati was performed; the sacred vase and mirror were held
   respectfully.
As the citizens stood folding their hands,
It appeared as if the cupola of golden Lanka's confidence itself
Moved on the streets in the form of radiant Kumbhakarna.
As he entered the royal court, descending from the throne,
Lankesha embraced his brother tightly
And made him sit on a chair akin to the throne.   160
The council of ministers briefed all details of the war.

'Why did you send for me?
My penance was interrupted and my research was spoilt.
I was engrossed in penance for your own good.
It appears that we do not have the blessings of Lord Shiva.
What can we do? Who can discern the ways of destiny!
Abstain from worry. I cannot rest until I rid you off the pain
That has been afflicting you,' said Kumbhakarna.

Dashavadana, the ten-faced one, said:
'Listen, O the one endowed with great strength!   170
A trivial wanderer of a human called Rama has built
A bridge with the help of *vanaras* and has severely wounded
The very soul of Lanka. Who else but you can protect us now?
Because of this, disturbing your penance, I got you here.
All great *rakshasa* warriors have died in the war.
Several young women have now become widows here;
Several mothers have lost their children now.
Only the aged, the invalid, and babes are left out.
Our strength has diminished
And strength of the enemy has increased.   180
I lost the war yesterday and collapsed.
I do not know how to live with dignity now.

'You are a highly valiant warrior!
In the war between *rakshasas* and *devatas*,
You are the incredible warrior who defeated the *devatas*!
Vibhishana has joined the enemy-camp.
You must safeguard us!

Ignoring your advice
I have come to this plight. I am not inclined to surrender to
The enemy and give away Janaki. 190
Only after defeating Rama in the battle, I will give away Janaki.
You are the one to save the honour of Lanka.
Like the autumn clouds get scattered by a tempest,
You must cause the *vanara*-army run helter-skelter.'

'Not weighing the pros and cons thoughtfully,
Not discerning the prevailing ethos of the society,
You have wasted all the powers gained through
Penance and meditation by abducting Janaki.
Not knowing the obligations of your various duties,
You are guilty of dereliction of your bounden duties. 200
Not understanding the meaningful symmetry
Of *dharma, artha,* and *kama,* you are ruined.
You could not employ *sama, dana,* or *bheda* at the opportune time.
A king who listens to the good counsel of his ministers
Who guide him on the right path, lives in peace and prosperity!
Ministers who are immature and are ignorant of the true meanings
Of scriptures, and those who
Wag their tongues eloquent foolhardily
Are indeed the enemies of the king.
They only appear to be wishing the good of the king; 210
But failing in the assigned task, they cause great harm.
Some of them turn traitors and join the enemy-camp.

'The enemies would enter the fort
Like birds entering through the hole in the Krauncha Mountain.
A king who fails to discern who is a friend
And who is a foe will falter.
Having neglected the good words of the brother,
You are on the path of your own downfall.
There is no other way left for you now.
If god's grace is lost, which other power can protect? 220
Good deeds lead to *dharma*; *dharma* leads to fame;

Fame leads to wealth, and wealth itself is victory.
Are you ignorant of all these!

'Listen, O elder Brother, to your own inner voice now!
What answer would you get!
You are gifted with riches and good fortune;
The palace is filled with beautiful women;
You have a virtuous wife in Mandodari.
Such being the situation, why did you bring
Mother Janaki who will raze the *rakshasa* clan to the ground? 230
She is the Mother of the Universe and Rama is its Supreme Lord;
He is not the one rejected by his father
Or the one exiled from his kingdom!'

Kumbhakarna continued:
'Look at Shri Rama!
He is not the one who utters a lie
Or the one who breaks his promise;
He is not greedy or vile; he is not cruel or deceitful;
He is not a blot for the clan. To fulfil the wishes of his
Father, deserting all the luxuries of life, he has come to the forest. 240
He has won over his senses and quelled his fickleness.
He is an embodiment of *dharma*, and the noblest of men.
Do not accuse him of bad qualities!
In the trees of enmity, there exist seeds of love.
Explore the subtle mystery of creation,
Preservation, and destruction.
In a world of contradictions, look for harmony.
In a vessel of poison, you must look for ambrosia!'

'Ah! time has run out.
There is no going back now. 250
We should avenge for the humiliation meted out
By the Raghu clan. Victory and defeat
Are quite common in any war.
What is there in being righteous
Or not being upright? Does absolute righteousness

Exist in the world? Is victory or defeat permanent, tell me!
Expanding his kingdom is *dharma* for Rama;
And for us, protecting Lanka is the *dharma* of our clan.
Giving away Sita is a treacherous act against Lanka.
Who gave the right to Rama to propagate *dharma*? 260
Let bygones be bygones. Why talk about it now?
How could a past event or water that has flown down return!
Failed truce is like a broken glass.
Recalling the events of the past, it is not fair to collapse now.
The flaw is in me and there is repentance too.
I am caught in trouble and who else but you can help me?'
In the stern words of Lankesha,
Love for the brother became discernible
And the lotus of his heart bloomed.

Pacifying the elder brother
With soft-spoken words Kumbhakarna said: 270
'Calm down dear brother; desert your depressing worries.
As you are a dear brother to me, I spoke these soothing words.
Do not feel hurt. War is inevitable!
I know what to do. I will rush into the battlefield
And thrashing the *vanaras* as well as Rama and Saumitri,
I will throw them into the sea.

'I will crush the strength of the enemy.
How can I be defeated? Let Indra, Yama,
Maruta, Agni, and Varuna come; raising the spear
If I roar loudly, Devendra will shudder. 280
What shall I say? Why do I need any weapons?
My strong arms are enough! I will squeeze Rama;
I will devour Agni and pull down the sun;
Throwing the moon away, I will cross the horizon;
I will slay Indra and drain the sea by drinking;
Pounding the mountains, I will pierce the earth!

'I will bring the head of Rama
And wipe the sorrowful tears of the

Rakshasas and the kindred. Being soaked
In the blood of Sugriva, the sun will roll down from the sky 290
And you will see this with your own eyes!
The festival of Rama's death will take place without fail!'

Listening to the boastful words
Of Kumbhakarna, Mahodara said in pain:
'O Kumbhakarna, no doubt you are valiant, but listen!
Fruit of the bad deeds is burning Lanka now.
You begged your elder brother in the royal court then
To return Bhumija, the earth-born, but listening
To the words of sycophants, and not you, Lankesha erred.
How could we save him now? 300
For the love of your elder brother, you have set out for the battle.
There, Rama is burning like the fire of ultimate destruction.
Lanka is shuddering at the blows of the *vanaras*.
Saumitri is equal to Adishesha;
With his thousand hoods, he emits poisonous breath.
Our strength is declining; enemy's strength is on the rise.
Chitragupta, the clerk of the God of Death,
Leaving out the dead in the *danava*-army,
is counting only those who are alive!
What a misfortune has befallen us! I don't know 310
How you will gain victory against the army of Shri Rama.'

Kumbhakarna replied:
'Mahodara has spoken the truth; yet war is inevitable.
I will deploy all my strength to this crucial test.
This body is dedicated to the service of Lanka.
But my inner voice says you better give away Janaki;
Send away the destructive goddess staying in Lanka.
Then the Goddess of Lanka will adorn me
With the garland of victory.
When I am in the battlefield, Janaki shall not be in Lanka. 320
Then victory is mine for sure!
May you live long peacefully enjoying all the riches.
Now hoist the flag of fame and ethics as advised by us all.'

Steeped in worry
Lankesha said: 'How could I give away Janaki now?
Seizing the spear, return after slaying the enemy;
Thrashing like Yama, return victorious;
Then I will release Janaki.
If I give her away now, the world will view me as a coward.'
Speaking no further, with great excitement, 330
Wielding a gold hilted spear –
The spear which had killed many
Deva, danava, yaksha, gandharva, kinnaras –
And decorated with red flowers,
Kumbhakarna moved like a wild elephant born
In the Malaya Mountain, and stood ready to attack!

'Abiding by the orders of the king
I will carry out the task; I have no other volition;
I will not desert Lanka. In bringing good to Lanka
Even if I have to go to hell, I will not spare the enemy. 340
I will fight in such a way that all the three worlds would shudder.
I will bathe my blood-thirsty spear with blood from
The chest of the one who killed Khara.
With my prowess, I'll grow up to the sky
And knock down the heads of my enemies!
Waging a bloody battle with the army of *vanaras*,
And slaying them like a flock of sheep,
I will make an offering to the Goddess of War.
May the great Shri Lanka live long!
I will proceed to the battle single-handed. 350
Let the army stay back in Lanka!'

Hearing the valourous words
Of Kumbhakarna, the *rakshasas* clapped in excitement.
Victory slogans resounded everywhere;
Mansions trembled in the sound of that commotion!

Ravana said:
'Do not go to the battlefield all alone.

Brother! Proceed taking the soldiers with you.
Vanaras are clever; they move with agility;
They are a fiercely determined lot 360
And will slay the *rakshasas* with their sharp teeth and nails.
Finish them off. Be a fierce threat to the *vanaras*.
Feed the enemy with the poison of defeat fast.
Make the stream of victory flow
And may you be the beloved of Lanka's Goddess of Victory.
May you be the rising sun of the Pulastya clan.'
Blessing thus, Ravana offered him
The formal royal decree to wage war.

Canto Two Hundred and One

'Rudra who Arrives during *Pralaya*, has Arrived well in Advance!'

||६||

As excitement was on the rise, endearingly Ravana
Dressed Kumbhakarna with rings, amulets,
Ear-rings, studs, garlands, bracelets of the upper arm,
And waistband. Readying his brother
With armour and shield, he flaunted him thus.
Like the fire that blazes bright when oil is poured to it,
Kumbhakarna appeared glowing bright.
Hugging the elder brother affectionately,
Circumambulating him thrice,
And bowing, he rushed to the battlefield swiftly. 10
Kumbhakarna was a massive *daitya*!
As he sat on the chariot drawn by eight elephants
That resembled the celestial elephants stationed in every quadrant,
The wheels screeched and the shoulders of the elephants drooped;
Rows of mansions trembled. As he roared aloud,
It echoed in all the directions.

Valiant *rakshasas* climbed horses, elephants, camels and donkeys;
The charioteers climbed onto their wonderful chariots!

Raising their spears, swords, bludgeons, maces,
Giant pestles and axes, they surged ahead. 20
As they sounded a variety of wind-instruments and stringed
  instruments,
The entire earth shook violently.
Shouting with excitement, Kumbhakarna enthused them all:
'Valiant soldiers, listen! I will squeeze the monkeys alive.
Prodding them with spears, I will soak them in blood.'

Bad omens appeared that instant!
As the meteors exploded, the earth shook violently.
Jackals howled spitting fire,
And vultures flew in a line right in front of Kumbhakarna.
His left eye twitched and the left shoulder shook. 30
Not caring, the *rakshasa* emerged from the fort
And stood facing the army of Rama!

Shri Rama saw him and asked Vibhishana:
'Who is this giant who shines like lightning in the dark clouds?
Who is this valiant soldier with such a great physique
Donning a shining bracelet on the arm?'
Vibhishana replied:
'He is Kumbhakarna –
The younger brother of Ravana and my elder brother.
Who can match his strength and valour? 40
None among the *rakshasas*!
He is equal to Yama, the God of Death.
He is the valiant hero who has subdued the warriors of every race:
The *gandharvas, rakshasas, yakshas* and the serpents!'

Looking at Kumbhakarna,
The *vanara* army was wonderstruck and shook
With fear. Some ran while some fell to the ground.
Like clouds scattered by a storm,
The *vanaras* ran helter-skelter and rolled down haphazardly.

At that instant, Shri Rama 50
Summoned commander Nila and said:

'Pacify the frightened *vanaras*;
Ready the army with discipline. Do not
Enter the fort blindly; there are trenches. Make the soldiers
Stand near the bridge to cross those trenches.'
The next instant, Nila readied the army as directed.

On seeing the frightened *vanaras*,
The *rakshasas* braced with immense pride
And stood roaring in excitement. As Kumbhakarna
Roared aloud, the astounded *vanaras* 60
Fell to the ground like uprooted trees!

Watching this, Angada said:
'Where are you running? What is this cowardice?
Look! Kumbhakarna is only a scarecrow.
He is like a decorated garden for all outward appearance
But is full of weeds inside;
I will take care of him, follow me!' Saying so,
He filled them with confidence.

The valiant *vanaras* proceeded
Seizing trees and boulders. 70
As anger welled up, like elephants in rut,
They attacked Kumbhakarna. Climbing on his body,
They hurt Kumbhakarna
Scratching with their nails and bit him hard.
Not caring, the *rakshasa* seized the *vanaras*
And squeezing their bodies hard, did them to death and threw them away.
Like wildfire, he crushed them and
The *vanaras* fell down like *Palasha* trees
With bloody bruised bodies!
Scared and shuddering, 80
Some *vanaras* leaped into the sea.
Putting their lives at risk of being seized alive by the *rakshasa*,
Some *vanaras* crossed over the bridge.
Shuddering with fear, some *vanaras* hid themselves

In valleys, caves, and behind giant boulders.
Not able to run, and not able to stand, some collapsed
And withholding their breath, they lay as if dead!

The arrows stung the *vanaras* hard;
Their faces were thrashed with maces;
They were pierced with lances; 90
Old wounds turned sore and their skin peeled off.
The injured *vanaras* ran to physician Prabha's camp for treatment.

Varied treatments were carried out
In the medical camp. Smearing herbal pastes,
They bandaged the wounds; they gave potions to drink;
They sutured the deeply cut wounds;
They set the broken bones.
The camp resounded with the agonising cries of the wounded.
As some of the *vanaras* had their ears and noses chopped off,
Suturing them with a sewing implement, the doctors applied
   medicine 100
And bandaged the wounds. Vaidya Prabha's team
Treated all the injured relentlessly.

Stopping the *vanaras* who took to their heels,
Angada said: 'Do not run. Get ready to fight.
What has happened to your valour? Is this life permanent?
Do you have a life-span of thousand years to live?
Evading the battle if you run, women will mock and chide you;
Death is far better than that!
If one dies killing the enemies in battle,
One gets fame as well as reaches Heaven heroically. 110
Should a multitude of *vanaras* be frightened of a lone *rakshasa*?
Have the *rakshasas* who have entered the battlefield returned alive?
Now, watch what happens to Kumbhakarna!
Shri Rama will arrive and slay
The *rakshasa* like a locust put to fire!
Listen, *vanaras*! You have fought and had a series of victories
When the time of victory has arrived,

Why do you behave like this?
Karnataka is your land; Kannada is your language;
Can you tolerate humiliations meted out to Karnataka? 120
Your act of cowardice will definitely drain all the water
Of Tungabhadra river!
There will be a blemish on your valour, for sure!'
Hearing the brave words of Angada,
The *vanaras* returned forthwith.

The war turned nightmarish!
Hissing, as Kumbhakarna swung his mace,
Hundreds and thousands of *vanaras*
Got their hands and legs broken by a single blow
And collapsed! Seizing a boulder, 130
As Dwivida, the illustrious *vanara*,
Rushed towards the *rakshasa*,
He appeared like the heavy cloud
Rushing towards the mountain peak.
At the impact of that boulder,
The *rakshasa's* elephants and chariot got smashed.
As Dwivida threw another boulder, the battlefield
Was splashed with the blood of the *rakshasas*!

Raising his spear,
As Kumbhakarna advanced, the valiant Anjaneya 140
Hit him hard with a boulder and bloody fat flowed out
From the body of the *rakshasa*. In retaliation,
As the *rakshasa* pierced the chest of Hanuma,
Blood splurted out like a fountain!
The *rakshasas* danced with joy and the *vanaras* scattered.

Using all his strength,
Nila pulled a hillock and flung it fiercely at Kumbhakarna.
The *rakshasa* smashed the hillock with his fist as if it was a ball.
Emitting fire, the hillock was shattered into pieces!
Gandha, Madana, Rushabha, Nila, and Gavaksha, 150
Confronted the *rakshasa*, one by one.

Would the *rakshasa* mind them!
Ah! Their blows were like the rotund jasmine buds
Showered on his body!

Advancing, as Kumbhakarna
Seized Rushabha and squeezed hard,
Vomiting blood, he fell down.
Kumbhakarna then hit Sharabha fiercely,
And mashed Nila with his knee.
He then pounded Gavaksha with his fist, 160
And tossed Gandhamadana like a ball!
Kumbhakarna appeared like Indra wielding his *vajra*-weapon;
He appeared like Yama holding his snare!

As the cry of pain and desperation
Spread in the *vanara* camp,
Lifting a boulder and surging ahead, Angada hurled
It at the head of Kumbhakarna and hurt him.
Anger welled up in the *rakshasa* and he moved fiercely
Towards Angada to pierce him with the spear.
Stepping aside, Angada dodged his aim 170
And as the *rakshasa* faltered, leaping fast,
Angada hit the chest of the *rakshasa*.
Ruffled, the *rakshasa* lost control,
And recovering the next moment,
As he smashed Angada with his fist, he fell unconscious!
The *rakshasa* was about to kill him with his spear;
Sugriva confronted him and said, 'I will take you on.
Leave that kid.' Saying so, as Sugriva hit him
With a boulder, it got smashed to pieces!
The *rakshasas* shouted in excitement. 180

The killing spree
Of the *rakshasa* continued unabated.
He cut innumerable bodies,
Pierced and plucked eyes, chopped many shoulders,
And severed several heads; it appeared as though

The sluicegate of the blood-tank was lifted up!
Appearing like the fierce Shiva, the *rakshasa*
Frightened the *vanaras*; it was like an elephant in rut
Entering a sugar-cane field!
Ah! Rudra, who arrives during *Pralaya*, the ultimate destruction,   190
Has arrived well in advance!
It appeared as if Narahari,
The Man-Lion incarnation of Lord Vishnu,
Emerged from the pillar!
The entire battlefield shuddered and shivered struck by fear!

As the *rakshasa* surged arrogantly
To kill Sugriva, leaping quickly, Pavanasuta, the son of Wind,
Pulled the spear of the *rakshasa* and breaking it with his knee
Threw it away. The *vanaras* who were running away with fear,
Returned to the battlefield shouting 'bravo, bravo!'   200

Not able to bear the attack,
The *rakshasa* swung a boulder at Sugriva which hurt him badly;
Sugriva fell unconscious. Immediately, the *rakshasa*
Tucked Sugriva under his arm and moved
Towards the city of Lanka. The *rakshasas* gleefully sprinkled
Sandal-water on him. Gaining consciousness,
And realising where he was, Sugriva started scratching
The face and ears of the *rakshasa* with his sharp nails;
He then bit and smashed the nose and wounded his body immensely.
Ah! Blood spurted from all parts of the *rakshasa's* body!   210
Unable to bear the pain,
Kumbhakarna dumped Sugriva on the ground.
As the *rakshasas* crowded around Sugriva,
Jumping over them, he reached Shri Rama's army!

Frustrated at not getting Sugriva,
Kumbhakarna returned to the battlefield
And started devouring the *vanaras* rapidly.
Saumitri interrupted him showering pointed arrows
And slit open the *rakshasa's* armour. Kumbhakarna said,

'I appreciate your valour; I don't want to fight you; 220
Show me where Rama is.'

Saumitri said:
'All right, all right! You have invited death.
Your wishes will be fulfilled.
Look! There is Shri Rama, the inviolable treasure of valour.'
As Kumbhakarna attacked him,
Rama struck a sharp arrow on the chest of the *rakshasa*.
Not able to bear the pain, roaring loudly,
He collapsed on the ground!

Anger welled up in him. 230
Getting up quickly, not viewing whether they were *rakshasas*
Or *vanaras*, he started hitting and kicking everyone around
And killed them all. Not able to dodge the fierce arrows
Of Rama, his entire body was covered with wounds;
Swaying a huge boulder, the *rakshasa* hurled it at Rama.
Shri Rama shattered the boulder into pieces
By shooting it with seven-curved arrows.

Moving about the battlefield
Like the the Meru or the Mandara Mountain,
The *rakshasa* thrashed and smashed the *vanaras*. 240
Colouring the flowing stream of tears with blood,
He appeared like the Lord of Death vowed to destroy all;
He appeared like the lord of ultimate destruction and death.

Later, seizing a huge mace and raising it high,
The *rakshasa* swung it fiercely with all his might.
One thousand heads of *vanaras* rolled at a single stroke!
Wriggling in pain, the *vanara* army retreated.
Angada who got hit by the huge mace suffered injuries,
And he vomited blood. Enraged at this,
The *vanara* army attacked with renewed vigour. 250

At that point in time,
Dwivida's rib bone was fractured;

Sharabha was gasping for breath; Nila was unconscious
By the kick he suffered;
The pain of the injured arm was taking the life out of Rushabha;
Gavaksha was pounded and soaked in a pool of blood;
And Panasa mashed and squeezed Tara.
Kumbhakarna appeared like the wildfire burning down
A dried-up forest during hot summer.

Shrugging and snarling and pulling a hillock, 260
Anjaneya smashed it against the head of Kumbhakarna.
The gems on the *rakshasa's* crown fell on the ground
Like hailstorms of varied hues. The chariot got shattered;
The charioteer died, and the elephants roared in pain.
A fountain of blood jetted out from Kumbhakarna's head.
Recovering soon, the *rakshasa* got up and swung the giant mace
At Hanuma's chest. Screaming and tottering, Hanuma hit the ground.
The *rakshasas* shouted aloud 'hurray, hurray' excitedly.

Deciding that enough was enough,
Hissing like Adishesha, Saumitri 270
Showered pointed arrows on Kumbhakarna.
The *rakshasa's* mace slipped out of his hand
And the arrows struck him deep.
The *rakshasa* appeared like a porcupine!
Roaring like a wounded tiger, he climbed onto an elephant
And brandishing the spear, he rushed
Towards Rama and Lakshmana.
As they both made the *rakshasa* wander
Here and there, escaping from his sight all the while,
He looked like the Trikuta Mountain 280
Performing a wild dance like Lord Shiva!

As Kumbhakarna spat
Fire from his mouth, his long tongue
Appeared like a syringe issuing forth blazing fire
And the army of *vanaras* was scorched.

At that instant, Nala created clouds from water-mills.
Thinking that they were wrong in trusting Rama's valour,
As the monkey-army took to its heels, Jambavanta prayed:
'O Lord Shri Hari!
Kumbhakarna is a staunch devotee of Rudra. 290
None can stop him in all the three worlds.
To protect the army of *vanaras*, finish him off
With a powerful divine weapon!'

Listening to the hoarse roar
Of Kumbhakarna, Shri Rama thundered:
'Come to me, O *rakshasa*!
I am the proper match for you in the battle.'
Beaming with pride, Kumbhakarna thundered:
'Don't show your valour. Have you counted me
Like Viradha, Kabandha, Khara, Dushana, Maricha, or Vali? 300
I am Kumbhakarna, and I do not fear anyone!
Enough of this task of killing the innocent *vanaras*!
Look! This is the giant mace, a great weapon indeed
And these are my great arms! Exhibit your valour now!'

As Kumbhakarna roared thus,
Shri Rama aimed pointed arrows akin to *Vajra*, the great weapon
Of Indra, the chief of Heaven, the *rakshasa* guffawed mockingly.
It was like the heavy rains in the mountains.
Swinging the huge mace, he shot several arrows.
Shri Rama got wild with anger. 310
With the powerful *Vayuvya* weapon
Shri Rama cut the arm of Kumbhakarna holding the huge mace.
Roaring violently, the *rakshasa* trembled
And fell with a large thud amidst the *vanara* army!
Next moment, he got up and uprooting a *sal*-tree with a single hand,
He swung it forcefully at Rama. Like a tiger hit by a bullet,
The *rakshasa* rushed towards Rama.

Determined not to spare him,
Shri Rama aimed the potent *Indrastra* at the *rakshasa*.

The left arm of Kumbhakarna got severed! 320
Not able to bear the pain, shouting and wailing,
As the *rakshasa* moved about like the Lord of Death,
Rama then cut each of the legs of the *rakshasa* using *Chandrastra*.
With a huge thud, the *rakshasa* fell to the ground rolling.

That great sound reverberated in all the directions,
Oceans and caves. Like Rahu devouring the moon,
The *rakshasa* came roaring angrily rolling
Like a razing fire to devour Rama!

At that instant, Shri Rama
Aimed a divine weapon at the *rakshasa*; 330
It shot forth like the scorching sun, and like thunder
And lightning in a storm.
Blazing like a smokeless fire, and lighting up
The ten corners of the world, the magnificent weapon
Severed Kumbhakarna's head
That resembled the peak of a huge mountain!
Like Indra severed the head of Vritrasura and cast it away,
The severed head of Kumbhakarna
With its gem-studded ear-rings shot up high in the sky
And it shone like the rising Punarvasu star! 340

Later, the severed head of Kumbhakarna fell
On the streets of Lanka, while his body
Fell into the ocean! Like the sun freed
From Rahu dispelled darkness, by killing the *rakshasa*,
Rama gave immense happiness to the *vanara* army.
Everyone praised Rama.
The face of *vanaras* bloomed like the lotus.
Shri Rama, the Supreme Lord of the Universe,
Was engrossed in divine bliss.
As the war-bugle sounded, 350
It brought the battle to a halt.

Canto Two Hundred and Two

'What Fortitude in a Puny Body!'

||६||

In the Ashokavana,
Worried Janaki queried Trijata humbly:
'What is this wailing and crying?
What is that thick smoke?
Why have the funeral drums been sounded?
Why this sorrow on the face?
Where has Anala gone?'

Trijata replied in deep agony:
'What shall I say, mother?
The war turned nightmarish and countless people have   10
Died on both the sides. The piled up dead bodies
Appear like hillocks. And there is a mass-cremation
Of the bodies. I do not know whether the smoke
From my own father's dead body is a part of it.
I do not know when I will see my husband.
It appears that the good fortune
Of offering my services to you is coming to an end.'

Vaidehi replied in all humility:
'I am the cause for all the sufferings of the world.
My father lifted me up from the earth and gave me to Rama.   20

We came to live in the forest in exile, and my father-in-law died.
From Ayodhya to Lanka, I rocked on the swing of suffering.
I don't know which episode I should remember!
I don't know how many sorrowful episodes to recall!
Many beautiful girls have turned widows in Lanka.
What shall I say to this?
If this plight of mine is the result of *karma* committed by me,
How can I blame anyone else for it?
O mother Trijata, listen!
Abstain from all anxiety. The day I become a widow   30
You will also be one. Even if hit by Brahmastra,
Your husband will not die.'
With these words, Janaki pacified Trijata.

Trijata replied:
'It is alright, Mother! I am at peace now.
You are my mother; you are my teacher.
To be at your service is my only penance.'

In the meantime, Anala,
Yearning for peace, came out from Lankesha's mansion of sorrow,
And approaching Sita, bowed to her.   40
Lifting her up endearingly and embracing,
Janaki said: 'How could I tell you not to cry?
How shall I comfort you?'

Anala replied in all humility:
'No, Mother, no! Your grief is greater;
Your tears have dried up;
If you shed tears, each teardrop of yours,
Transforming into a flood, will drown Lanka.
To avenge the death of uncle Kumbhakarna,
My brother Indrajit has undertaken *Nikumbhila-Yaga*   50
And has vowed to take away hundreds of lives.
Who can stop him once he completes the ritual successfully!
Sister-in-law Tarakshi, Mandodari and Chandranakhi
Are all assisting my brother in completing the *yaga*!'

Anala continued:
'What shall we do now?
As Lankesha's strength has diminished
And he has mellowed down now, let us try for a truce.
I will try for a truce in such a way as
Not to cause him any disgrace.' 60
Hearing these words, Sita exclaimed:
'What fortitude in a puny body!
I appreciate you for that.
Courageous women like you should
Grow in number in Lanka. What help can I give you?
All I can do is pray for your peace talks
To be successful. That is all.'

'Why this disappointment?
Lankesha will arrive here to see and talk to you.
Are the *vanaras* fools? Would they keep quiet 70
By not causing impediments
To the *yaga*? Advise Ravana as you would advise a child.
Put some sense into him. Speak to him
In such a way that his heart should melt.
Make him see that all his valour
And fame are subservient to sympathy.
I know my uncle is beaming with pride!
But his heart will give way to love and affection, for sure.'
As she went on thus, caressing her forehead affectionately,
Janaki said: 'Alright, my child! I will do as you say. 80
When Lankesha arrives here, I will advise him so.
Have no doubts about it.'
With these words, Janaki consoled Anala.

Canto Two Hundred and Three

'Peak of the Himalayan Mountain Collapsed and Rolled Down!'

||૬||

Bowing with folded hands, the soldiers
Brought the tidings of Kumbhakarna's death to Lankesha:
'Listen, listen O King!
Kumbhakarna, akin to Yama, the God of Death,
Smashed and killed the *vanaras* and proceeded
With great enthusiasm blowing away the enemy camp,
And flaunted his valour well.
But, at the end, he succumbed to the
Arrow of Rama and attained eternal peace!

'Half of his body has reached the sea; 10
His neck, shoulders and thighs are all severed and lay scattered.
The remaining parts of the body have
Fallen obstructing the main entrance of Lanka.
The national hero who tried to protect Lanka,
Being faithful to you, has laid down his life.
That is all we say of that great martyr, O Lord!'

Ravana swooned to the ground
In sorrow. Recouping, he spoke laden with grief and pain:

'You are indeed an eminently valorous warrior, dear brother!
O Brother! Partaking in my afflictions and waging war
You have deserted me now. Ah brother! It's living-in-death for you
And death-in-living for me.
The very source of my strength has been severed.
Reposing trust in your strength,
Not caring for anyone, trampling the pride of
Devas, *rakshasas* and humans, I flaunted
Like Rudra, the destroyer.
Who is going to be there for me now?

'A warrior who did not care even for the
Wound caused by *vajra*-weapon, how were you killed
By the arrow of a trivial human?
Now the *vanaras* will invade
The inviolable fort of Lanka, for sure.
The wealthy Lanka is as good as gone from our hands.
Why do I need Lanka now when you are gone?
Why do I need Janaki, why this empty pride?
If I do not kill Rama who killed you,
Why should I be alive?
Death is far better than that.

'Recalling the past enmity
When *devas* and humans will mock at me clapping their hands,
Will I tolerate it? Not heeding the words of brother Vibhishana,
Lending ears to the words of sycophants and turncoats,
I have drunk the poison.
Words of good advice were cacophony to my ears then.'
As Ravana was wailing thus, Atikaya came to him and said:

'You viewed uncle Vibhishana
As your enemy. See how Saumitri has
Sacrificed everything for the love of his elder brother.
Like him, Bharata too is in Nandigrama.
You should have treated your brothers
The way Shri Rama has treated his.
Why have you tread on the wrong path?

There is still time.
Stop this battle at once and give away Janaki.
Come out of the illusion that your status will suffer a setback.
Call uncle back; all reasons for the war will die out.
There is harsh truth in my words
And not the slightest hypocrisy.'

Ravana replied: 60
'Listen, Atikaya, my son!
Your words are full of propriety and justice.
What if Vibhishana has deserted me severing all ties of kinship?
He still is the crown prince of Lanka!
If he were to be here now, I would have discussed
The matter of handing over Janaki with him
And I would have treaded the path of righteousness!
Look! The entire world is blaming me now.
Even if I return Janaki, the blame of abduction will stay!
Will Kumbhakarna return? Will Vibhishana return? 70
Will Khara and Dushana come back to life?
When the time to wage war has approached,
Fearing for life, if I backtrack, I will lose my grace!
It is only proper that I should wage war with Rama now.
Let him defeat me and win Sita!
It is not for me to tread the path of Rama, my son!
Do not disturb my mind now.'

Atikaya replied:
'What shall I say father? I will follow your footsteps.
There goes a saying, 80
"A father gets assimilated into the soul of the son."
How can I survive without you?
Bless me to enter into the battle this instant.'
Ravana said, 'As you have set an example,
Let the duty of a son be held high on this earth in your name.'
Hugging Atikaya endearingly,
Ravana sent him to the battle with his blessings.

Ravana was filled with worries soon after,
And as he was lamenting, his son Trishira approached him
And said humbly: 'Do not lament over the death 90
Of uncle Kumbhakarna and lose heart.
You possess the great weapon *Shakti* gifted by Lord Brahma.
Great bows, arrows, armours and chariots are all still with you.
You are the most exalted warrior in the world.
You have the fame of killing
The *rakshasas, devas* and humans even
Without wielding any weapons.
Is it any great task to kill Rama wielding all your great arms!
You do not go to the battlefield, but allow me to go instead!
Like an eagle pouncing on and destroying the serpents, 100
I will destroy the enemies in the battle.
Rama will collapse and die in the battlefield for sure.'

Listening to the encouraging words,
Ravana was filled with newfound excitement.
All the sons of Ravana – Devantaka, Narantaka,
Atikaya and Trishira – are inviolable and possess the strength
To quell the enemy. Glowing like the sun,
They stood surrounding Ravana waiting eagerly for his permission
To enter the battlefield at once.
Ravana shone like Devendra, the chief of Heaven. 110
Hugging each one tightly, saying encouraging words,
And blessing them all,
He sent them to battle and felt quite relieved.

Ravana sent his brothers –
Mahodara and Mahaparshwa – for protecting his sons.
Bowing to Ravana, all the valiant
Warriors set out to the battlefield!

Mahodara climbed onto Sudarshana,
The elephant resembling the dark blue clouds;
Narantaka got onto a white horse resembling Ucchaishrava, 120
The magnificent steed of Indra,

And shone like Lord Shanmuka, the six-faced son of Shiva;
Atikaya and Trishira got into a chariot
Resembling the Meru Mountain and shone like the sun;
Wielding his mace ferociously,
Devantaka appeared like Lord Vishnu;
And Maharnava appeared like Kubera,
The Lord of Wealth himself!
As the war bugle sounded, the entire earth and sky splintered.

On the other side, the *vanaras*   130
Carrying boulders as weapons and roaring aloud, came running
Towards the *rakshasas*, overcome with the excitement to fight.
As the *rakshasas* attacked showering arrows,
The *vanaras* resisted hurling boulders in retaliation.

As the strife proceeded,
Vanaras threw cudgels and smashed the *rakshasas*.
Advancing further, they hit them with their fists and smashed
Their chariots, horses, elephants and the armours.
As the eyeballs of the *rakshasa* leaders
Popped out of their sockets, they screamed in fear.   140

In return, the *rakshasas* shattered
The *vanaras* with spears, giant maces,
Swords, lances, and bludgeons.
The battlefield turned into a pool of blood.
Launching a ferocious attack, the *rakshasas* kicked and
Pushed the *vanaras* back, dragged them along violently
And chopped them ruthlessly.

The *vanaras* retaliated
Slaying the *rakshasas* mercilessly. Blood dripped from
The bodies like the sap from a tree trunk.   150
The battle turned gruesome.
Boulders rolled everywhere;
The bodies of *rakshasas* were strewn everywhere;
Uprooted trees lay scattered everywhere.
Wherever one looked, the *vanaras* attacked the *rakshasas*.

At that moment, Narantaka
Moving at the speed of wind, thrashed the army of Sugriva
Slaying seven hundred *vanaras* every second.
Vanaras rolled down like the hillocks.
Just as the wildfire devours a forest, flaunting his valour, 160
Narantaka devoured the *vanaras*.
That nightmarish scene caught everyone by surprise.

Viewing the downfall of the *vanaras*,
Sugriva moved to Angada and said:
'This shall not be tolerated anymore. Finish him off quickly
And protect the *vanaras*.' At that instant,
Like the sun appears rupturing the thick clouds,
Angada confronted Narantaka and said:
'Stop, stop, O brave one! Let me see your lance
And let me have a taste of it.' Hearing this, the *rakshasa*, 170
Rotating the lance, struck Angada on his chest.
The lance shattered into pieces.
At the same instant, Angada, pounding with his fist,
Killed the horses. The *rakshasa's* limbs got
Shattered and the eyeballs came out of their sockets.
As the *rakshasa* hit Angada's head angrily,
Wearied, the son of Vali rolled down.
Recovering the next moment and gathering strength,
He hit the *rakshasa's* chest with great force.
Not able to bear the pain, the *rakshasa* died that instant 180
And fell on the ground. The *vanaras* danced gleefully;
The cloud of darkness was dispelled.

The tiding of Narantaka's death spread quickly.
Arriving there swiftly, the enraged Mahodara
Confronted Angada showering arrows on him.
Not fearing, Angada thrashed with the bludgeon!
The elephant's tusk was broken. As Devantaka attacked him,
Angada hit him forcefully with the bludgeon.
Unbale to bear the blow, both Mahodara and Devantaka,
Fell to the ground vomiting blood. 190

Arriving there, Trishira, the three-headed one,
Aimed and shot three arrows at Angada's face.
Viewing this, Hanuma and Nila
Arrived on the spot. Nila swung a
Tree at Trishira at that instant. Roaring aloud,
The valiant Anjaneya rushed in with intense anger
And smashed the head of the *rakshasa* with his strong fist;
Trishira's teeth fell down and head got smashed, eyes popped out
And tongue rolled out. Wailing loudly,
The *rakshasa* fell to the ground. 200
Recovering fast, as he was getting up,
Pavanasuta, the son of Wind, jumped on Trishira
And seizing his three heads, severed them all
And flung them away. The severed heads rolled down
Like the splintered meteor from the solar orbit.
Frightened, the *rakshasas* took to their heels
And the *vanaras* shouted in excitement.

Spitting out fire in anger,
Mahaparshwa chased the *vanaras* hitting them with his mace
And killed them. Later, he smashed the chest of Rushabha 210
And made him spit blood. Somehow,
Rushabha regained balance and moving swiftly
Towards the *rakshasa*, thrashed him forcefully.
Not able to resist the blow,
Mahaparshwa rolled down like a felled tree.

Scared, the *rakshasas*
Ran for their lives. The eminently powerful Atikaya
Saw all this. He got on to a chariot that glowed more radiantly
Than the sun and chased the *vanaras*.
The *vanaras* shivered in fright. It appeared as if 220
Regaining life, Kumbhakarna himself
Had returned to the battlefield.
The *vanaras* ran in large groups
Shouting, 'O Saumitri! Save us.'

Seeing Atikaya, wonderstruck, Shri Rama
Called Vibhishana and queried:
'Who is this lion-eyed one who spits fire?
Who is this one holding the spear, bludgeon and lance?
Who is this one glowing like lightning
And comes readying the bright arrows? 230
Who is this one looking like the visage of Death?'

Vibhishana replied:
'He is Atikaya, the son of Dashagriva, the ten-headed one,
A great and a brave warrior
Adept at sword fight, archery and
All kinds of warfare. He is an expert in capturing
The enemy swiftly. He is the son of Dhanyamalini.
Slay him quickly.' The next moment
Kumuda, Nila, Sharabha, Dwivida, Mainda, and other
Valiant *vanaras* all joined together. Seizing boulders, 240
They advanced. Gazing at them, casting a
A sympathetic look at the *vanaras*, and not confronting them,
Atikaya moved towards Rama and said:

'Listen, Raghava!
Sitting in the chariot I am holding the bow and the arrows.
Why should I kill the ordinary soldiers on foot?
Show me the most powerful among you,
I will fight with him.'

Hearing these words, and bursting with anger,
Saumitri made everyone shiver at the twanging of his bow 250
And confronted Atikaya.
Drawing a sharp arrow, the *rakshasa* said:
'O Saumitri! You are only a kid. How can you match me?
What do you know about warfare?
Move aside and show me the one who can match my strength.
Walk away throwing the bow; go away, you boy.
Not heeding, if you fight me in arrogance,
I will send you to the city of death.

My pointed arrows are equal to the trident of Lord Shiva.
Just as a ferocious lion sucks the blood of an elephant in rut,   260
This weapon will suck your blood.'

Listening to the arrogant words
Of Atikaya, Saumitri got wild and thundered:
'Stop this babbling, you mean one.
Give up this vain talk and arrogance.
Exhibit your strength, if you have any.
Forget about me being a boy.
Do not forget that Vamana,
The Dwarf-incarnation of Lord Vishnu,
Measured all the three worlds with only three steps!   270
Like the gentle wind causes the ripe palm fruits to fall down,
I will make your head roll down!'

Bursting with anger, Atikaya advanced
Like a snake emitting fierce venom
And shot an arrow aiming at Lakshmana's head.
Saumitri effortlessly stopped it mid-way and cut that arrow swiftly
With his crescent-shaped weapon.
Snarling like a tiger at that, seizing five arrows together
As the valiant *rakshasa* shot them with full force,
Saumitri, breaking the arrows into pieces,   280
Shot an arrow back aiming at the neck of the *rakshasa*.
The arrow struck the forehead of the *rakshasa* in full force.
When Shiva shot arrows at Tarakaksha and his companions,
The tower of the three cities shook violently;
Shuddering similarly, Atikaya collapsed and fell to the ground.
Getting up the next moment, he blurted out:
'Enough! I am pleased. You are indeed the best in archery.
Can one envy the merit of a person, even if he is an enemy!'
Praising thus, arranging three, five and seven arrows at each time   290
He showered arrows at Saumitri.
The arrows moved swiftly like the snare of death!

Saumitri stopped all the arrows
Half-way and cut them down.

But one arrow struck the chest
Of Saumitri fiercely. Saumitri pulled out and threw away
The arrow instantly and warm blood spurted
Like ichors from the temple of an elephant in rut,
Not losing heart, Saumitri shot gold-feathered
Weapons at the *rakshasa*. Both Saumitri and Atikaya 300
Fought fiercely, shooting various weapons at each other.

At one point Saumitri fell unconscious.
Regaining consciousness soon, he shot four arrows killing
Atikaya's charioteer, the horses and broke the flagstaff.
Not losing heart, the *rakshasa* fought fiercely
Appearing like the Lord of Death once,
And like the Lord of Destruction at another instant.
Thus he infused new excitement to the war.

Everywhere heads lay severed;
Broken limbs and headless bodies were strewn around. 310
Blood flowed in a stream and dead bodies were afloat.
Atikaya stood firm filling the entire battlefield
With his imposing presence
Like the fierce Rudra during the time of ultimate destruction.

What can one say?
Atikaya is the most powerful of the *rakshasas*;
Even the *devas* are frightened of him;
An expert on war ethics,
He is the crest-jewel of the young *rakshasas*.
Roaring aloud, he moved away from Saumitri. 320

Look! He made Nala fall with
Six arrows and with three arrows
Jambavanta fell down unconscious.
Viewing this, Lakshmana thundered:
'The troubles caused by the *rakshasa* can't be tolerated anymore,'
And aimed the mighty *Brahmastra*;
The weapon surged ahead like fire of destruction;

Thick smoke clouded the sky and the entire universe felt the heat.
Atikaya swung various weapons in succession.
All the weapons turned out to be useless! 330
Brahmastra came in great speed and
Severed the neck of the *rakshasa*; his head flew into the sky.
As if the peak of the Himalayan mountain
Collapsed and rolled down,
The *rakshasa's* torso fell down from the chariot.

The entire earth shuddered.
The death of Atikaya marked an end of a heroic epoch
In the annals of Lankesha's life.
The *rakshasas* ran in fright.
Beaming with pride, the *vanaras*, 340
Shouting joyously, danced in excitement!

Canto Two Hundred and Four

'I Must Put Out the Fire I have Lit'

||๑||

Hearing that Saumitri slayed Atikaya,
Getting agitated, Lankesha told the warriors:
'How strange and unbelievable!
Dhumraksha was an expert archer;
Akamapana was outstanding among the warriors;
Prahasta, Mahakaya, and Kumbhakarna were insuperable.

'The fact that Shri Rama slayed
Such valiant warriors so easily, is indeed my misfortune!
Listen soldiers! Protect Lanka carefully;
Do not allow anyone to enter Ashokavana without permission;   10
Be careful! Be on high alert! Keeping a strict vigil,
Protect the fort constantly. Keep me informed
Of all the secret news of the enemy frequently.'

Boiling with anger,
Accompanied by the chief of the city,
Ravana viewed the city and informed him about the strategies
Of allaying fears from the minds of the citizens.
As the war bugle sounded, he returned to the palace.

Chandranakhi arrived there in tears
To see her elder brother. Falling at Ravana's feet, she said: 20
'O elder brother! I am the sinner, forgive me.
I am boiling with pain for the trivial mistake I did
In bringing that virtuous wife here. Indeed, I am responsible
For all the misfortunes of Lanka.

'What shall I say, elder brother?
All the valiant warriors have died because of me.
I have drowned the valiant ones like Kumbhakarna,
Atikaya and others in the sea of death.
Saumitri abused me as 'Shurpanakhi' then,
And it has proved right today. I beg a favour from you: 30
Enough of this sacrificing of countless lives;
Enough of this battle; protect your life now.
I must put out the fire I have lit.
Protect Shri Lanka; this is the favour I beg of you.
If surrendering Janaki, daughter of King Janaka,
To Rama is any disgrace to your valour,
Let me do that task;
I will protect your honour without fail.'

Ravana replied:
'Listen, Chandranakhi! The fire lit by you 40
Has crossed all limits and it is burning the whole world.
If one desires to put it off now,
The harm it would cause is beyond imagination!
The time is now past and my amorous yearning
For Sita has dried up; I will win over Rama in the battle;
Imprisoning him, I will bring him here and offer him as a gift
  to Sita.
Later, in the same way Videha, the king of Mithila,
Had given her away to Rama then,
I will hand her over to Rama today – that is my wish.
I cannot perform a cowardly deed and cannot abandon war!' 50

Chandranakhi replied:
'Just because people may call you a coward,
Should you tread the wrong path? Desert this empty pride.
Listen to the inner voice and tread the path of righteousness.
Your radiance that has appeased Lord Brahma
Through penance is losing its sparkle.
Dear elder brother, be careful, be careful!'

'I will impede Raghupati's evil design
Of annexing kingdoms. I will stifle the Aryan sovereignty.
The words of Maricha that "Sita will never be yours",   60
Has turned out to be true. Listen to my words carefully now.
You climb the Trikuta Mountain
And watch the grand scene: You will see there
The world's unparalleled warrior Rama being
Imprisoned in the battle and returned
To his own wife Maithili as gift;
You will see this grand scene, the likes of which the world
Has never seen before! The time is now ripe for that
And I will be the blessed one,' said Ravana.

Listening to those words,   70
Chandranakhi was filled with excitement
And praised Ravana endearingly:
'You are the most talented one;
Who else but you can script such a great happening!
You are your own match.
Let me be blessed to see the fruition of such a dream of yours.
I pray to Lord Shiva for that and surrender myself to you.'

'I have garnered all my resources
And strength for this final battle. I will fight until
The title Dashamuka, the ten-headed one,   80
Becomes Shatamukha, the hundred-headed one,
And finally gets transformed befittingly into
Anantamukha, the one with infinite heads.
O Chandranakhi, you proclaim

To the world this new history of Ravana.
Listen! There goes the war bugle," said Ravana.

What is the use of saying all this?
The valiant army is dying in the battlefield.
I don't know the means of winning over Rama.
Thinking thus, overcome with extreme grief, 90
His eyes filled with tears. At that instant,
Meghanada came there and pacifying his father said thus:

'O Father! Give up this worry and sorrow.
I am there to recompense your loss.
The serpent weapon turned out to be a waste then.
I'll exhibit my valour and dexterity once again.
Why this concern?
I am there for you! My arrows will hurt
And sever the bodies of the enemies
Aand they will fall in the battle; 100
I will not spare Rama and Saumitri;
I won't return showing my back to the battlefield;
I will fight unto death!
I will protect the fame and name of Lanka.
I will live like the pillar of your throne;
If not, I will lay down my life.
I vow to do this with god's grace
And trusting my own valour!'

As he prostrated himself
To the feet of his father, Ravana said: 110
'Be victorious, my son,
Defeat the enemy and return victorious.'
Blessing him thus,
Ravana gave him the formal royal decree to go to war.
He bedecked Meghanada with medals, wristband, amulets,
And armours. Beautiful girls raising *kalasha*
Performed *arati* and showered him with flowers.
The panegyrists praised him with the titles of his accomplishments!

He got into a great chariot harnessed
With horses that moved at the speed of wind.　　　　　　120
As the valiant Meghanada set out,
A huge army of valiant warriors,
Seizing weapons, followed him riding the horses and elephants
And beating the war-drums. The city which
Wore a haunted look suddenly turned vibrant!

As he neared the battlefield,
Getting down from the chariot,
Indrajit performed oblations of fire.
Consecrating the fire, chanting verses,
He worshipped the holy fire offering sandal paste and flowers.　　130
Later he offered puffed paddy and clarified butter
To the holy fire prayerfully!
As the malicious ritual got completed,
Strangling the neck of a black sheep,
He made an offering to the fire and circumambulated
The consecrated fire devoutly.
As the ritual had a malevolent purpose,
On its completion, the entire universe shook!

The next moment, riding the chariot,
He moved towards the battlefield and waged a fierce war.　　140
He chopped and killed many *vanaras*.
With a single arrow, as he slayed countless *vanaras*
And surged ahead, the *rakshasas* felt elated.
Shivering with fright and whimpering,
The *vanaras* took to their heels.

Recouping in a minute, the *vanaras*
Resisted flinging stones and striking with large tree-trunks,
They smashed the horses. As the magical arrows shot by Indrajit
Showered on them, the heat of the deadly venom
Of black cobra spread in all the four directions.　　　　　　150
Climbing the hill, the *vanaras* showered boulders
And the valiant Indrajit quelled them all.

A fierce battle ensued.
He shot eighteen arrows at Gandhamadana
And nine arrows at Nala standing afar.
With seven arrows, he hurt Mainda and
Five arrows pierced the body of Gaja.
He aimed ten arrows at Jambavanta
And struck Nila with thirty arrows.
He shot a fierce arrow obtained by godly boon 160
At Sugriva, Rushabha, Angada and Dwivida;
It hit them all like the fire
Of ultimate destruction and made them unconscious!

Afflicted with the fierceness of the battle,
The *vanaras* felt wearied. With their bruised bodies,
They wandered aimlessly wailing aloud.
Their ears turned deaf by the sound of swift arrows
And they felt choked by the smoke
And they ran seeking fresh air to inhale.

As the magic spell spread, 170
A strange behaviour surfaced in the monkeys:
Some bent like snakes and wriggled,
Some leaped like frogs and swam like fish,
Some climbed up like smoke and rolled down like stones.
Hit by arrows, some reached the kingdom of death.

As Indrajit shot the *Amogha*-weapon,
Emitting fire, the arrow split into two;
Two became four; four became eight;
Eight multiplied into multiples of eight
And transformed into countless arrows. 180
As the *vanaras* rolled down succumbing to the arrows,
The battlefield turned into a sea of silence!

As if to cleanse his blood-drenched body,
The sun descended into the ocean in the west.
Taking recourse to witchcraft, Indrajit decided to destroy

The war strategies of the enemy.
'Before the night is over, I will wipe out the *vanaras*,'
Thundering thus, he rained arrows; all the three worlds trembled;
All the water of the sea rose up skywards;
Mountains shook violently and leaped to the sky! 190

All the corners of the universe trembled.
As thick clouds ushered in darkness,
Lightning splashed across and thunder struck.
It rained hailstorms pounding the earth
And Indrajit felt immensely pleased with
The powers of his witchcraft!

Delusion prevailed in the battlefield.
Struck with arrows shot at the speed of lightning,
Shattered bodies of the *vanaras* were sprawled
All over in the battlefield. Everywhere arrows swished 200
Like lightning and struck one after the other injuring everyone.
As Rama and Saumitri were caught in this intense rain of arrows,
Not caring for them, Shri Rama said:

'O Saumitri! Have you noticed Meghanada's witchcraft?
Through black magic, he is afflicting the *vanaras* and killing them.
Showering arrows, he has blocked all the daylight.
Through my arrows I'll light up the battlefield
And unraveling the witchcraft of Indrajit thus,
I will teach a lesson to the vile *rakshasa*.'
Saying so, as Rama shot a divine arrow, 210
Bright light flashed as if the sun had risen.
As the valorous warriors like Hanuma and others jumped skywards
To strike the *rakshasa*, undeterred by the attack,
The *rakshasa* showered arrows akin to lightning.

Spitting red-hot beams,
The arrows of Indrajit surged thundering aloud.
It appeared as if boulders of thunder rolled
From one corner to the other.

The striking arrows shone like daggers.
A nightmarish sound reverberated as if Lord Shiva 220
Struck his drum during the hour
Of the ultimate destruction of the world.
Hailstorms struck with such force as if to crack the skulls!

Canto Two Hundred and Five

'Humanity Flew Away like a Bird!'

||௬||

The *vanara* army shook with fright.
Holding a torch, Vibhishana walked around
The battlefield in the night looking for the wounded
And sent some of them to *vaidya* Prabha's medical camp.
Severed hands and legs were strewn everywhere;
Chopped thighs, feet, fingers were all sprawled across.
Sharabha, Angada, Nila, Dharimukha, Gavaksha,
Mainda, Ahuka, Jyotirmukha, Nala, Panasa, Dwivida
And others lay down in the battlefield wounded and wearied.
With anxiety, as Vibhishana was looking for the aged Jambavanta,   10
He spotted him lying down struck by a pointed arrow.
As Vibhishana pacified him, Jambavanta queried:
'I could recognise your voice. But where is dear Hanuma?'
Vibhishana asked in surprise: 'Instead of asking about
Rama, Lakshmana, Sugriva or Angada,
Why do you enquire about Hanuma so particularly?'
Jambavanta replied:

'Who do you think Hanuma is?
He is the warrior supreme, the very breath and life of the world!
If he is alive, we will be alive too; the earth cannot exist without him.   20

Look! If Hanuma dies, we are all dead!
In valour, he is Vaishvanara, the God of Fire;
He is the very breath of Rama; that is why I enquired about him.'
As Jambavanta spoke thus, Pavanasuta, son of Wind,
Came crawling slowly to Jambavanta, touched his feet
And said: 'I am right here, bless me.
Your blessing protects everybody.'

Jambavanta replied:
'You are the breath of the universe, the life-sustaining air!
Who else can save us but you? 30
Because of that charlatan Indrajit, we are in this plight today.
Saumitri has got the strength to slay him.
You now walk fast; meet Shri Rama, Saumitri, and Sugriva
And humbly remind them of what they need to do!'

Pavanasuta did what was asked of him.
Sugriva said: 'Let us invade Lanka in the night.
Ravana is drowned in deep sorrow thinking about the death
Of his sons, kindred and valiant warriors.
Let us attack Lanka this night!'
At his command, holding torches, 40
The highly agile and strong *vanaras*
Entered Lankan city breaking its fortress!
They carried out the tasks as commanded by Sugriva.
Seeing the *vanaras*, the sentries ran helter-skelter screaming.

Lanka was set ablaze once again.
Mansions, buildings, dance halls,
Theatres and all were up in flames.
The entire Lanka was blazing with fiery tongues of flame!

Gold vessels and gold ornaments
Embroidered paintings, handicrafts and artefacts, 50
Decorative ornaments of horses and elephants were all set on fire.
The entire Lanka was blazing with fiery tongues of flame!

The armours of soldiers, decorative ornaments of chariots
Swords, bows, arrows, lances, hooks
Umbrellas, royal fans, flagstaff were all up in flames.
The entire Lanka was blazing with fiery tongues of flame!

The royal stable and the royal kitchen,
Treasure-house stacked with incenses and musk of the musk deer,
The gem and pearl-studded mansions were all up in flames.
The entire Lanka was blazing with fiery tongues of flame! 60

Tongues of flame spread across swiftly!
Wailing aloud, women-folk ran in fright
To save their babies from the fiery flames.
The mahouts freed the elephants from their fetters;
The horsemen freed the horses
And the cowherds unleashed their cows.
Frightened, the animals ran in all directions!
Seeing the elephants, the horses ran wildly;
Seeing the horses, the donkeys ran;
Seeing the donkeys, the cattle ran in fright, goring the citizens! 70
Lanka appeared like an ocean on fire.
It seemed as if a volcano had erupted and the whole earth was on fire.

The wailing and screaming of women
Spread and reverberated as far as ten *yojanas*.
As the *rakshasa* army guarding Lanka confronted the *vanaras*,
The entire city turned into a battlefield.
As Saumitri twanged his bow-string,
He appeared like Rudra himself – the fierce Destroyer,
The one so propitiated in the Vedas – stood there seizing his trident.
As the arrows shot forth swishing, 80
The *rakshasas*, shuddering in fright, fell to the ground.
The screaming of the *rakshasas*, the glee of the *vanaras*,
And the twanging of the bows
Resounded in all the directions!

Sugriva said:
'If Indrajit followed unethical means of warfare and

Hurt the *vanaras*, are we cowards to sit back without retaliating?
Let the war proceed! Wipe out the *rakshasas*!'
Hearing this, the *vanaras* roared aloud in unison.

Waking up, Ravana dispatched such valiants   90
Like Yupaksha, Shonitaksha, Prajangha,
And Kampana to the battle.
Seizing weapons, roaring loudly, they attacked
Pushing hard and chopping off the *vanaras*.
The light of blazing Lanka
Helped them to fight in the night.

The *rakshasas* brandished the
Swords and giant maces in anger
And severed the heads of the *vanaras*.
In retaliation, the *vanaras* hit them with their fists.   100
Pulling away the weapons from the hands of the *rakshasas*,
They smashed them with the same weapons
And flung them into the burning fire.

The fight got intensified.
The one, who killed someone, got killed by someone else;
The one, who bit someone, got bitten by someone else;
The one, who pushed someone, got pushed by someone else;
The one, who abused someone, got abused by someone else.
Both the *vanaras* and the *rakshasas* fought each other
In fierce competition and the battle turned nightmarish.   110
The clothes and armours of soldiers got slit and fell off
And their hair was dishevelled.
It appeared that humanity had flown away like a bird!

As the excitement of war exceeded all limits,
Angada fought Kampana and Kampana
Smashed Angada with his mace. Tottering but recovering at once,
Angada, seizing a boulder, smashed it on Kampana
And he died instantly!

Viewing this, Shonitaksha swiftly shot
A razor-sharp arrow which cut like a sword.   120

He shot a crescent shaped arrow
And a long, pointed arrow
And many other powerful and unique arrows.
Enraged Angada smashed all of them into pieces
And he smashed the *rakshasa's* chariot too.
Hopping from here to there,
The *rakshasa* fought with his sword and shield.
As Angada pulled the weapons away,
Shonitaksha seized a giant mace and pounced on Angada.
As Yupaksha barged in from one side 130
And Prajangha rushed in from the other,
Angada, fighting with them both, appeared radiant
Like the luminous moon amidst the Vishaka star.

At that instant, the valiant *vanara* leaders,
Mainda and Dwivida, rushed to the rescue of Angada
And mowed down the *rakshasas*.
They threw large trees in the garden at Shonitaksha.
Prajangha, seizing a large sword resembling a trumpet,
Jumped on Angada.
Angada smashed him with his fist. 140
Again, as Yupaksha advanced,
Angada hit him fiercely; unable to bear the blow,
Tears rolled down the cheeks of the *rakshasa*.

As Shonitaksha attacked steadfastly
And smashed Dwivida with his mace,
Dwivida snatched away the *rakshasa's* mace
And smashed him with his fist.
The *rakshasa* dropped down dead that instant!

As the *rakshasas* scattered away
In fear, advancing, Kumbha swiftly 150
Shot the gold-feathered arrows.
Struck by the arrow, Dwivida fell unconscious.
Viewing his fall, Mainda seized a huge boulder
And hurled it at the *rakshasa* forcefully.

The *rakshasa* shattered the boulder
Into a hundred pieces with his arrow
And hurt Mainda with a pointed arrow.
Regaining consciousness, Angada threw several boulders
At the *rakshasas* and blood oozed out from their bodies.

As the *rakshasa* Kumbha 160
Struck Angada with seven pointed arrows,
The son of Vali fell unconscious and rolled on the ground.
When this news reached Shri Rama,
He sent Nala to protect Angada.

At that instant, Sugriva arrived
And pulling the *rakshasa's* bow fearlessly,
Broke and threw it away. Applauding the *rakshasa's* skills
Of archery, Sugriva said: 'Bravo, bravo!
Your skills of archery are truly magnificent!
You are indeed a perfect match to the eminent kings 170
Like Prahalada, Bali, Varuna, Devendra, and Kubera.
If you stand seizing your bow, who can gain victory over you!
You are equal to Indrajit and Ravana.
You have subdued the *vanaras*.
If I kill you, the world will blame me.
But unfortunately, you belong to the camp of the wicked people
And you are caught in the stronghold of immorality;
What shall I do?'
Hearing this, Kumbha's conscience pricked
And he said: 180

'I appreciate your words, O venerable one!
I have learnt prudence and am aware of what is good and what is not!
But during the times of war, what can one do?
I have the will to set things right.
Is this the right time to question Lankesha's ethical stance?
I am bound by my allegiance to my nation.
I have put my life at stake to protect my nation.
War is my only *mantra*!'

Moving close to Sugriva,
Kumbha embraced him! Why should one envy merit? 190
Later they fought like two tuskers in rut.
All of a sudden, Sugriva lifted Kumbha swiftly
And squeezing him hard, threw him into the sea.
As if Mandara Mountain had fallen into it, the sea overflowed!
The *rakshasa* got up that instant and rushed to attack Sugriva.
With his powerful fist Sugriva struck him on the chest.
Sugriva's beatings are fierce indeed.
The *rakshasa* fell to the ground dead!

Viewing the death of his elder brother,
Nikumbha stared angrily at Sugriva 200
As if to burn him down to ashes.
Seizing a bludgeon with a golden hilt studded with diamonds,
That resembled the sceptre of Yama, the Lord of Death,
He lifted that bludgeon and rotated it fiercely. It appeared
As if Alakapuri, the kingdom of Kubera was rotating fast;
As if Amaravati, the kingdom of Devendra was rotating fast;
As if Ashwini and other stars were revolving rapidly;
As if Venus, Mercury, and the Sun were rotating fiercely!
All were frightened.

Valiant Anjaneya, 210
Treading fearlessly, advanced towards the *rakshasa*
And the *rakshasa* smashed the bludgeon on the chest of Hanuma.
The weapon exploded and flew like a meteor spitting fire!
The earth shook as if an earthquake had occurred!

Before the *rakshasa* seized another weapon,
Advancing swiftly, Pavanasuta, son of Wind,
Planted a fierce blow on the chest of Nikumbha.
Not stopping at that, lifting him high, smashed him onto the ground.
Stamping on the chest and not allowing him to get up,
Hanuma danced on Nikumbha's chest. 220
The ribs and the other bones broke with a rattling sound
Under the heavy stride of Anjaneya's feet.

Wailing aloud, the *rakshasa* died!
A nightmarish sound spread and echoed in all the directions.
The *vanaras* shouted hailing victory to Hanuma.
The visage of the *rakshasas* turned sullen.

Canto Two Hundred and Six

'I Have the Good Fortune of Avenging Today'

||⊚||

Hearing of the death of Kumbha and Nikumbha,
Ravana was overcome with grief and anger.
Summoning Makaraksha, son of Khara,
Ravana said:

'O my son! Go to the battlefield.
You have to win this war and come back victorious.
Two trivial humans called Rama and Lakshmana have
Killed your father brutally. Remember that!'

Listening to those words,
Beaming with pride, son of Khara said decidedly: 10
'I will slay the enemies.' Bowing to Ravana,
He set out to the battlefield. Gigantic *rakshasas*
Resembling wild elephants followed the son of Khara
Blowing conches and war-drums. They surged ahead
Challenging their enemies and shouting violently.
The earth shuddered at their heavy strides.
The *vanaras* awaited in excitement to fight them.

Killing the *vanaras* fiercely,
Makaraksha moved ahead searching for Rama.
'I will not spare the one who has killed my father at Janasthana.' 20
Roaring aloud, he proclaimed:
'I have the good fortune to avenge my father's death today.
I will offer libations to my dead father with the blood of his slayer!'

Refusing the call of the other
Vanaras to fight, riding on his chariot here and there,
He spotted Rama in the battlefield.
Beckoning Rama with his hand, Makaraksha said:

'Oh! You are the one called Shri Rama, aren't you?
Stand there still! If you have the courage, fight with me!
The way you killed my father deceitfully at Janasthana 30
Won't succeed here now.
I have made all preparations to take away your life
And I am waiting for you here with sharp arrows.
The raging fire of Janasthana will burn you to ashes.
Just as a hungry tiger lies in wait for its prey,
I am awaiting you. Stop, stop, you evil one!
Showering arrows, I will send you to the grave.
Let everyone watch our fight.
Tell me the kind of warfare you prefer –
Archery, mace, or wrestling?' 40

Listening to the boastful words
Of the arrogant *rakshasa*, Shri Rama said:
'O Makaraksha! Stop this bragging!
Can empty talk yield victory in the battlefield, tell me.
To win a war one must have a strong arm
And know the art of warfare.
I have singlehandedly slain Khara, Trishira,
And the other countless warriors. Will I spare you?
You all lack truth and morality.
All your learning is futile like building an edifice with sand. 50
Yours is a misadventure indeed. Seize an arrow and fight;

Stop jabbering; all your questions will be answered thus.'
As Makraksha showered arrows, stopping them half-way,
Shri Rama broke them into pieces.

The fight intensified.
Everyone watched the fight
Between Shri Rama and Makaraksha with wonder.
Harsh sound filled all the directions.
Countless arrows pierced the *rakshasa's* body
And wounds appeared on Shri Rama's body as well. 60

Destroying the arrows of the *rakshasa* swiftly,
Shri Rama shot eight arrows killing the charioteer and the horses.
Jumping from the chariot, seizing a lance,
The *rakshasa* rushed to kill Shri Rama.
Shri Rama shot an arrow and the lance flew skywards.
Shooting more arrows, he destroyed the lance into pieces and
Like meteors they fell from the sky!
Mashing his teeth Makaraksha thundered:
'Enough of these weapons;
I will smash you with my fist and suck your breath.' 70
Saying so, as he surged ahead,
Shri Rama shot him with a fiery arrow;
Like lightning, it struck the *rakshasa* and pierced his chest.
Roaring fiercely, the *rakshasa* hit the ground
Never to get up again!

Hearing the news of Makaraksha's death,
Disturbed, angered, and sullen with worries, Ravana decided:
'Now there is no other go. I must send Meghanada to the battle.'
Summoning him, Ravana said:
'Who can equal you? Who else but you can exhibit 80
Your valour now and kill Rama and Saumitri?' Saying so,
Ravana sent him to the battle with a formal royal decree.

Indrajit was performing *yajna*
Invoking the evil spirits with magical chants

For his success in the war.
Satisfied with performing the ritual successfully,
He appeared contented and well-pleased.
Then he climbed onto a chariot drawn by four horses;
The chariot was filled with numerous sharp arrows and weapons.
Radiant like the sun, surfeited with arrogance 90
That he was inviolable
By his possessing the *Brahmastra*, he contemplated:
'They are the fraudulent ascetics;
Killing them in the battle,
I will bring victory to my father.
I will wipe out the *vanaras* from this world.'

The charlatan Indrajit,
Being visible to the enemies once,
And remaining invisible again,
Swiftly spread evil spell in the entire battlefield. 100
He covered the battlefield with his fierce arrows.
Not able to see where the arrows came from,
Shri Rama and Saumitri shot arrows skywards.
All the directions were covered with dark smoke.

The screech of the chariot wheels
And the sound of hooves of the horses couldn't be heard.
The battlefield was covered with darkness;
Arrows showered continuously.
Watching the direction from where the weapons were coming,
Rama and Saumitri shot arrows in that direction 110
And quelled the strength of Ravana's son and his arrows.
None could see Indrajit or grasp his movements;
None could see the bow of Indrajit, or his arrows;
None could comprehend or see Indrajit's actions;
But Indrajit's arrows wounded the *vanaras*
Piercing their bodies from all the directions!
Unable to bear the heat of the arrows,
Some of the *vanaras* were wriggling in pain;

Badly wounded, some were wailing aloud;
Soaked in blood, some were writhing with pain; 120
Feeling thirsty, with parched lips, some were shivering;
Like the deer caught in a wildfire,
Some *vanaras*, sighing deep, were crying out for help!

Watching all this, Saumitri said:
'What a bad situation we are facing today!
It isn't fair to spare the *rakshasa* anymore;
I will shoot the *Brahmastra*.'
Consoling him, Shri Rama said:
'In order to slay one, is it fair to burn the entire world?
Will you repeat the sin committed by Bhargava earlier?' 130

Watching the *vanaras* run helter-skelter,
Stopping them, Pavanasuta, son of Wind, said:
'Why are you all scared thus? Aren't you all brave?
How can you run with your backs to the battlefield?
I will proceed first, follow me!'
Hearing this, seizing rocks and boulders,
The *vanaras* proceeded.
Appearing like Yama, the Lord of Death,
Valiant Anjaneya killed many *rakshasas*.

As the spell of his black magic diminished, 140
Indrajit became visible; the *vanaras* threw boulders,
And using slings, catapulted stones,
And thus attacked Indrajit fiercely. As his strength lessened
And his confidence took a beating, Indrajit thought:
'Let me get back to Nikumbhila
To revitalise myself with the powers of black magic.'
Contemplating how to do that in the midst of the battle,
He spread a rumour:
'Janaki is dead in the Ashoka garden.'
Hearing this and believing it to be true, 150
Hanuma suspended the battle for a while
Awaiting Shri Rama's order!

Discerning that his plan had worked,
Indrajit proceeded to Nikumbhila.
Chanting magical verses and offering
Sacrifices to the consecrated fire,
He prayed for the success of the *rakshasas*.
Viewing that the battle had stopped,
Shri Rama summoned Jambavanta and asked
The reason for it. At that moment, 160
Hanuma arrived stricken with grief and spoke thus:

'What shall I say, O Lord!
Slaying the *rakshasas* as I was waging war,
The hearsay of Mother Janaki's death in the
Ashoka garden spread widely.
Why to wage war when Saketa's crest jewel itself is lost?
Feeling sad, stopping the war abruptly, we have returned.
Whatever is your bidding, we will follow it.'
As he spoke, tears rolled down his cheeks.

Hearing the news that 'Janaki is dead', 170
Shri Rama swooned.
The *vanaras* brought scented water
In lotus leaf and sprinkled it on Rama's face.
Opening his eyes, Shri Rama sat up.

'Listen, dear brother!
This is the trick of the *rakshasas*;
Mother is alive, for sure.
Believe my words; give up sorrow.
Come what may, Ravana must be slain.
You have always upheld *dharma* faithfully. 180
Has *dharma* come to your rescue?
Where is *dharma* in the world, dear brother?
Animals live sharing happiness and sorrow;
Lions and *shardula* live killing their prey violently;
Do they think about sin and virtue, tell me.
You are the protector and upholder of *dharma*;

But why you are caught in troubles, tell me!
Doing all evil deeds, is Ravana suffering badly for it, tell me!
Today, as *dharma* is transformed into evil-doing
And is spreading steadily, 190
An upright person's suffering is constantly on the rise.
The belief that *dharma* yields good results is an utter lie!

'Discerning that being truthful is *dharma*,
You set out to fulfil your father's words;
But what has come of it? It is befallen us
To dwell in the forest in exile.
Were you able to make father follow *dharma*?
Can giving up the throne be viewed as *dharma*?
You have indeed severed the very roots of *dharma*!

'The root of success lies is wealth. 200
Just as a river is born in the mountain peak and flows down,
All good deeds happen because of adequate funding.
Without finance, if man sets out to achieve things,
Everything will come to naught
Like the trickling stream in summer.
A penniless man in the world commits only sinful things!
A rich man is the most respected, and honoured person;
He is seen by the world as a scholar, a man of virtues,
A daring man and an intelligent person.

'Overcome with pain, and deeply agitated, 210
I have spoken thus. You know and discern everything!
Get up, be bold, nothing bad has happened to the mother.
This must be the doing of Indrajit's evil spell.
You are a man of convictions;
You are unblemished; you are unaffected by grief.
Arise, and set out what you are vowed to do.
Give me orders; I will slay the son of Ravana.
I will destroy Lanka and reduce it to dust.'
Hissing like Adishesha, Saumitri thundered.

Canto Two Hundred and Seven

'The Enemy of the Gods has Arrived; The Formidable Warrior has Arrived'

||◉||

As the death news of Janaki drowned
Shri Rama in sorrow, Saumitri got agitated
And anger welled up in him.
Vibhishana, having discerned all the deceitful deeds
Of Indrari, the enemy of Indra,
Accompanied by other ministers,
Came to meet Shri Rama:

'Listen, O Shri Rama!
The death news of Sita is not true;
It is only a rumour created by Ravani, the son of Ravana.   10
Janakaje, the daughter of King Janaka, has not died;
She is engrossed in meditation in the Ashoka Garden.
She knows all the news about the ongoing war;
She is yearning to meet you.
The spies have brought the true tidings;
Do not lose courage and suffer.

'If you drown yourself in sorrow,
The morale of the entire army will sink low.

This sorrow that is the result of an illusion will
Enhance the enemy's strength two-folds.   20
Give up all your worries;
Do not lose heart; engage yourself in action.'

Vibhishana continued:
'Casting a spell on the *vanaras*,
Indrajit has returned to the temple at Nikumbhila
To perform the malevolent *yajna;*
If the *yajna* is completed successfully,
None can stop him and he will be invincible.

Send Lakshmana with an army
To Nikumbhila this instant!   30
Shooting pointed arrows let him see to it
That the malevolent *yajna* is not completed.
Then Ravani, the son of Ravana, can be killed easily.
Saumitri's fiercest arrows will swiftly cloud Indrajit
And suck his blood. If there is the slightest delay in
Killing the enemy, we will be in great danger.
If Ravani gets the blessings of Goddess Durga –
She lives in the precincts of Lanka –
All of us would be dead for sure!'

Shri Rama replied: 40
'Your words are soothing. I am aware
Of Indrajit's black magic; he is a cheat.
Listen, brother Lakshmana! Readying the army,
Go along with Sugriva and Pavanasuta, the sun of Wind,
And slay Indrajit this instant.'

Bowing to the feet of Rama,
Saumitri said: 'With your blessings,
I will shoot such sharp arrows that would cast away
The body of Indrajit into Lanka city.'
Saying so, seizing the bow and arrows,   50
He proceeded with the army
In the company of Hanuma, Jambavanta, Nila and Sugriva.

The archery of Saumitri
Made Indrajit shudder in fear.
Determined to win the war
By hook or by crook, slipping out from the battlefield,
He was performing, as advised by Shukra,
The eminent *guru* of the *rakshasa* clan,
The malevolent *yajna* by making oblations
Into the fire with the evil intention of annihilating the enemy. 60

They had set up the *yajna*-altar,
In the cave under a banyan tree located in the deep valley
Of the Trikuta Mountain.
The altar was protected with seven circuitous forts.
At each enclosure of the seven-walled fort,
Like a serpent guarding a treasure,
Giant *rakshasas* stood holding lances and other sharp weapons;
Besides these, there were two squads of vampires;
Two rows of elephants and chariots;
And two rows of broad-shouldered *rakshasas* 70
Stood so close to each other,
Not allowing even air to pass through!

They had drawn magical diagrams to invoke strength;
With a volition to annihilate the enemy,
Ravani, the son of Ravana, was engrossed in meditation
In the centre of the diamond-studded high altar
Erected in the shape of thousand-petalled lotus surrounded
With an enclosure of blazing fire.
Controlling his breath according to the precepts of Yoga,
Perceiving the potent mysterious laws that sustain the universe 80
And making its colossal energy an offering
To the Primordial Deity,
Indrajit was trying to accomplish all his volitions.
The fire of his intense desire blazed in the altar of his mind –
His unswerving intention was the pole to which was bound
All his five senses perceived collectively as the sacrificial lamb –

And thus set, he was ready to perform the oblations of fire
To acquire such powers that would turn
Him invincible even for the gods!

Ravani had brought all things required 90
To perform the *yajna*.
The consecrated fire was set in the southern direction
And the malevolent *yajna* began with it.
The officiating priest administered the volition
To annihilate the enemy and Ravani bowed in submission.
His entire body was smeared with blood;
He wore the apparel soaked in blood;
He wore a garland of red oleanders, a garland of human skulls,
And wore the human entrails as the sacred thread.
The officiating priests were also attired similarly. 100
Among the officiating priests, there were also the fiends
Of Brahmins who had led wicked lives.

Besides the firewood soaked in blood,
Meat of sheep, oxen, and horses were mixed and kept ready
For making oblations to fire.
Chanting the magical *mantra* from the *Atharvanaveda*,
Invoking the spirits, they made sacrificial offerings;
Thus, they offered propitiatory prayers to Goddess Maheshwari.

Thinking that it would be impossible
To slay Meghanada if allowed 110
To complete the malevolent *yajna*,
Saumitri was filled with anxiety;
Placing the army under the charge of Nala,
And accompanied by Hanuma and Jambavanta,
Saumitri went searching for the altar
Where the *yajna* was in progress.

Moving swiftly like wind,
He slew the *rakshasas* guarding all the
Seven-walled circuitous fort and entered the hall

Where the oblations of fire were in progress.   120
Meghanada – the one who roared like clouds –
Was surprised and enraged.
Stopping the *yajna* that instant, getting up
And seizing the bow, Indrajit confronted Saumitri.
As they got the signal, the *vanaras* led by Nala,
Marched in to the *yajna*-hall roaring!

The battle got fierce
And the entire Lanka shook. Climbing onto a chariot
As Indrajit surged ahead,
He appeared bright like the mid-day sun.   130
Awestruck, everyone watched Indrajit.
The *rakshasas* praised Indrajit:
'The enemy of the gods has arrived;
The formidable warrior has arrived;
The tormentor of gods has arrived;
The infinitely valorous one has arrived;
The invincible one has arrived;
The valiant hero who can win Yama –
The Lord of Death, has arrived.'

As arrows were showered on both sides,   140
It appeared like the flash of lightning on a pitch-dark night;
It appeared as if the venom of the serpent king flowed into a stream;
It appeared as if the earth shuddered like a shaft-less wheel;
It appeared as if Death itself stood
In readiness to destroy everything.

Resembling the fire of destruction,
Swinging a tree and smashing the *rakshasas*,
Valiant Anjaneya surged ahead.
Seizing lances, swords, axes, maces, wheels, and spears,
As the *rakshasas* jumped on Hanuma,   150
Not caring, Pavanasuta smashed the *rakshasas*
With his powerful fist that resembled the *Vajra*-weapon of Indra,
And dispatched them to the abode of Death.

As he confronted Indrajit,
Hanuma thundered: 'O son of wicked Ravana!
If you are a valorous warrior,
Abstain from magical warfare
And fight with your own prowess.
Fight a duel with me and exhibit your strength.
If you can endure the pace of my fight, 160
I will accept that you are indeed
The crest jewel of the *rakshasa* clan.'
As Pavanasuta, the son of Wind,
Thus went on mocking at Ravani, the son of Ravana,
Saumitri intervened and showered arrows.

'Listen, O Saumitri!
Forget that a ruler is good or bad;
Following the king is the bounden duty of a citizen.
As Ravana is my father, to show him obedience is my *dharma*,'
Indrajit said thus in such a tone 170
As if to prove that his stance was the noblest one.

Because of his blind devotion to his father,
Indrajit had employed all his strength
In the malevolent magical warfare.
Hence, his natural strength was on the decline day by day.
As he was lost in mid-night orgies, alcoholic drinks,
Making animal sacrifices, offering prayers to evil spirits,
Performing malevolent *yajnas*, and witchcraft,
Magical warfare became dear to him.
All his natural strength, prowess, 180
And radiance were thus burnt out.

Shouting that he would slay Saumitri,
Indrajit surged ahead thundering,
'Hit them and thrash them, seize them,
Kill them, cut their heads, and tear apart their shoulders
And push them out.' As the fighting continued,
The heads of *vanaras* rolled, and in retaliation,

The bodies of slain *rakshasas* fell down.
In the gorges of the valley blood flowed profusely.
By the sound of hooves of the horses 190
And by the speeding wheels of the chariots,
The battlefield turned into deep furrows.

As thousands of chariots,
Horses and elephants got smashed due to Saumitri's valour,
Indrajit became sullen and furious and lost himself in thought
Worrying what he should do next.

Canto Two Hundred and Eight

'The One who has Conquered his Passions Conquered Indrajit'

||६||

The radiance of heroism of Rama's brother looked splendid.
He shone like the rising sun.
All kinds of war-instruments like horns, trumpets,
Drums and kettledrums sounded loudly.

Angered Saumitri said to Indrajit:
'Running away from the battle,
You have taken shelter under witchcraft.
Have you forgotten the ethics of war, tell me.
Hungry for war, I have come here as a guest.
Honour the dictum that "Guest is God." 10
Would you employ witchcraft to slay the innocent ones?
Abstain from worshipping the evil this instant.
Set aside the arrogance of your black magic.
Look! The hour of your death has come.'

Wild with anger, Indrajit shouted:
'Who told you the path to reach my altar?
Will I fear you? I follow my *dharma*.
I have discerned the many faces of *dharma*;

An individual is bound by duty towards
Self, family, community, and the nation. 20
You have forgotten my colossal strength.
You have just come back to life from death!
Why this exhibition of pride now?
Stop there! Do not move.
I shall conclude the *yajna* by sacrificing you at the altar
Of this consecrated fire and thus bring the rites to fruition.'

It was a magnificent battle:
The sound of the clashing weapons was like the musical notes;
Sounds competed with sounds;
Weapons competed with weapons; 30
And blows competed with blows.
Not caring for death, everyone fought fiercely
Hoping that victory would be theirs.
As Goddess of War danced wildly in the battlefield,
Everyone swayed under the heady spell of war.

Saumitri said in a sober tone:
'Do not utter words of hatred;
Do not spit venom anymore;
As life is a battle,
Death is like discarding the old clothes 40
And wearing the new ones.
It's only fair that you suffer for the
Crimes perpetrated by your father.
The strength of Mother Sita as a virtuous wife
And the power of Urmila's penance are enough
To assure our victory in the war. Stop this blabbering
And protect yourself.'

Wild with anger, Indrajit thundered arrogantly:
'Caught in my magical web, you will die
And your requiem will be sung today. 50
Showering pointed arrows,
I will pack you to the city of death,

Like the parched paddy roasted deeply on a frying pan.
Have you forgotten your pitiful plight when you fell unconscious?
Death is approaching you. When Rama comes here,
He will see your chopped body, torn armour, smashed head,
And knocked out teeth; he'll see your body being dragged violently
By jackals and dogs.
Get ready to die.'

Saumitri thundered: 60
'Can the task be achieved through empty talk?
Stop boasting about yourself.
Making the opponent unconscious through magic and witchcraft
Doesn't befit a valorous warrior like you.
Bravely I stand before you.
Shoot the arrow and exhibit your valour.
Don't be arrogant and stop your derisive talk. Watch out!
I will dispatch you from this world
To the abode of your forefathers!'

As the fight ensued, 70
The valiant warriors adept at using all kinds of weapons,
Pulling the strings of the bows till their ears,
Shot arrows forcefully;
Like the heavy clouds pouring down incessant rain,
They showered arrows at each other.
Their fierce fight appeared like the clashing of two planets;
Like the fight of Devendra
With *rakshasa* Vritra, his perpetual enemy;
And like the fighting between two ferocious lions.
Wielding various kinds of weapons, they fought fiercely. 80

To Rama and Lakshmana,
The war had to be waged against all adversities;
Would it be a child's play to fight the enemy
In his own home land?
Arms, ammunitions and the valiant army are all
At the beck and call of Ravana stationed

At arm's length in Lanka city!
There are chariots in large numbers
And troupes of cavalry ready to march.
The fire of hatred is blazing to raze the enemy. 90
How to fight a battle pitted against such adversities!

But Angada went on
Smashing the *rakshasas* with his fist, kicking
Them, thrashing them, locking the *rakshasas*
Sometimes in his arms and proceeded
Killing the enemy swiftly.
Viewing the fierce fight,
It was difficult to say who slaughtered whom;
Nobody could say for sure as to who died,
Who pushed and fell and who got hurt. 100
Who is there to keep count of the dead ones?
Who is there to enquire and pacify?
Tired and wearied of writing the accounts of the dead,
The ink in the ink-pot of the Chitragupta –
The clerk of Yama – got emptied.
Even the gateway of Heaven was pulled out
And thrown away!
Dwivida rolled down there;
Mainda got wearied somewhere else;
As Mahodara was injured, the army retreated. 110
Angada fought fiercely there.
Confronting Pavanasuta, son of Wind,
Shakrajit, the one who defeated Indra, was humiliated.
Deciding to wage a war using witchcraft,
He retreated in haste and waited for the night to fall.

The passion to wage war was roused.
Surging ahead angrily Angada thundered:
'I shall wipe out the savagery
Of the *rakshasas* and drain out their blood
And lighten the burden of Mother Earth.' 120

Viewing Saumitri confronting Indrajit,
Angada became confident that
Saumitri would kill Indrajit for sure.
The face of Indrajit was sullen with worries.
As Saumitri's arrows caused him great pain,
He became weak in all his limbs.
But concealing all that and putting up a brave face,
Indrajit spoke harshly:
'Do you remember that I had fastened
You with the snake-snare? 130
If you have forgotten, better recall it now.
Do not move; stop there!' Saying so,
Indrajit shot seven arrows at Lakshmana.

Lakshmana said:
'While waging war, why are you shooting weak arrows?
As they touch my body, I feel highly soothed.'

Each one's arrows hurt
The body of the other and fell on to the ground.
Clashing against each other in the sky,
The arrows fell. As the dry blades of grass 140
Lay strewn all around the altar of *yajna*,
The battleground was filled with the arrows
Of Indrajit and Saumitri.

No one was emerging victorious;
None succumbed to defeat either.
Fighting tirelessly, each one anxious to kill the other,
They shot arrows continuously.

The two brave men
Were visible now and then
Like the sun and the moon covered by the passing clouds; 150
They shot arrows shifting the bows
From the left hand to the right.
Thus they flaunted their skills of archery
Like Arjuna, the proverbially great archer of all times!

An arrow resembling the *Vajra*-weapon of Indra,
Killed the charioteer of Indrajit.
'What if the charioteer is dead,
I myself will be the charioteer,'
Thundered Indrajit and driving the chariot himself
As he shot arrows, watching his skills of archery,   160
The *vanaras* were awe-struck. Viewing this,
Deciding to kill the horses harnessed to the chariot,
Saumitri aimed an arrow.
At that instant, four eminently valiant *vanaras*
Jumped on the four horses and pounded them with their fists;
Vomiting blood, the horses and fell to the ground.
Next moment, they smashed the chariot too.

'What if the chariot is broken?
My legs are my chariot!' saying so, Indrajit
Disappeared at once and spoke thus to   170
The *rakshasas*: 'Listen, you are all inscrutable warriors.
Are the *vanaras* any match to you who have won the world?
Victory is ours, and the *vanaras* will certainly lose the war.
Fight with determination and endurance.
I will go to the city now and return with another chariot;
Keep fighting till then. The news that
I am not here should not reach the enemies;
Behave that way!' Commanding thus,
Indrajit, invoked the magical spell
And reached the Lankan city.   180
Without any delay, he swiftly returned
To the battlefield in a chariot drawn by well-bred steeds
And moved around exhibiting his valour.
The *vanaras* and Saumitri viewed in wonder.

As Saumitri showered arrows
Continuously and broke the bow of Indrajit
Before the agitated *rakshasa* could ready
Another weapon quickly,
Saumitri's arrows tore apart Indrajit's armour and he swooned.

Recovering, as Indrajit showered arrows, 190
Saumitri stopped and cut them half way.
Aiming a curved arrow, as he severed the head of the charioteer,
Not getting disturbed, the horses continued to pull the chariot
In a circular manner and everyone watched in surprise.
Saumitri shot arrows again, and vexing the horses,
Killed them at once!
The arrows of Indrajit hit the
Armour of Saumitri and fell down broken.
Discerning that it is an impenetrable armour,
Indrajit aimed three arrows at Saumitri's forehead; 200
It struck hard and blood spurted out!
Anger welled up in Saumitri
And with five arrows, he pierced the cheek of Indrajit.
Both got soaked in blood and appeared
Like the fully bloomed silk-cotton tree.

At that juncture, Saumitri aimed
varunastra and Indrajit responded with *agneyastra*;
In return, Saumitri shot *saurastra*;
Discerning at once that it was impossible to win,
Indrajit shot a *ghorastra* in desperation. 210
Saumitri destroyed the *ghorastra* with *maheswarastra*.
The battle turned horrendous!

Then Saumitri seized
Aindrastra to kill Meghanada;
He chanted the verses propitiating Indra,
The patron-god of that arrow;
He bowed devoutly to Rama in his mind;
He bowed reverentially to Sage Kaushika, their *guru*;
He prayed: 'Shri Rama is the upholder of *dharma*
And he is truthful; 220
Is there any limit to his valour?
If Rama is truly eminent, O Arrow!
I bid you to sever the head of Indrajit!'

Chanting thus, as he shot the arrow,
It surged ahead like thunder and lightning,
Spreading fire and causing the entire earth to shudder,
And it struck the neck of Indrajit severing it
From the torso at great speed!
Blood spilled out and the torso tottered!
The *vanaras*, like the rising ocean-waves, roared excitedly; 230
'The devil of our affliction has gone off,' relaxing thus,
They danced in joy.
'The Sun of Lanka has set; who else can save us now?'
Their hearts filled with vacuity,
The *rakshasas* ran away shuddering in fear;
Some jumped into the sea, some scaled the mountains,
And some hid themselves in the caves.
The battlefield wore a deserted look!
The one, who has conquered his passions, conquered Indrajit.

Devotion, knowledge, absence of desires, 240
Control over the senses, and sacrifice are great virtues.
Saumitri is the symbol of all these virtues, whereas
Indrajit is the symbol of lustful indulgence and black magic.
It is indeed the victory of virtue over vice!
Everything was offered to the holy feet of Shri Rama!

Canto Two Hundred and Nine

'My Valour is Crippled; the Life of my Clan is Nipped in the Bud!'

||☉||

After killing Indrajit, with his body soaked in blood,
Saumitri came to Shri Rama accompanied
By Hanuma and Jambavanta and said endearingly:
'Your blessings saved me;
O Shri Rama! I have killed the *rakshasa*.'

Embracing his brother tightly, Shri Rama,
Overcome with emotion, spoke thus:
'Well done Saumitri!
I am highly pleased; you have accomplished a magnificent task!
Now, Ravana is like a dead man, though alive;   10
By killing Indrajit, you have crippled Ravana's valour.
In this great task, Hanuma, Angada, Jambavanta
And other valiant warriors have fought supporting you.
Well done, well done! The battle with Meghanda started
On the tenth lunar day at the fourth quadrant of the night;
The battle was horrifying on the eleventh and the twelfth day;
On the thirteenth day at the fourth quadrant of the night
It ended in victory!
This marks a turning point in the war of the epoch!'

As Saumitri was wounded, 20
Shri Rama summoned the physicians – Prabha and Sushena –
And said: 'Your are all expert physicians;
Saumitri is afflicted with the wounds caused
By the poisonous arrows. Treat the wounds
By removing the pointed splinters
Of the arrows struck in the body
Before the poison causes any harm!
Do treat all the wounded *vanaras* as early as possible;
If delayed, it is like inviting death!'
Shri Rama went on: 30
'O Hanuma! Come here; let me see your body.'
Everyone praised him saying that no pointed arrow has struck
The body of Anjaneya. Bowing to Shri Rama,
Hanumanta said: 'This is all because of your blessings.'
Shri Rama embraced Pavanaja, son of Wind,
Sugriva and other valiant *vanaras* endearingly.

Prabha humbly requested:
'O Valiant Saumitri! Do come to the medical camp;
We will treat you.' Accompanied by Jambavanta and other *vanaras*,
Saumitri walked towards the camp. 40

In the medical camp,
Countless wounded soldiers –
The *vanaras* and the *rakshasas* as well –
Were receiving varied treatments and nursing care
Without any discrimination!
Extracting the juice from an excellent medicinal herb,
Sushena applied it on the forehead
Of Lakshmana and put a bandage.
Removing the splinters of the arrows
From different parts of the body, 50
Sushena gave him a scented herbal root for smelling.
Inhaling the medicinal aroma of the root given by Sushena,
Saumitri stood .hale and hearty regaining his normal strength!
All the other wounded were also treated in the same fashion.

In Lanka, the tidings of Indrajit,
Ascending his heavenly Elysium shrouded Ravana's heart
With fierce darkness. The grief of losing the dear son
Pierced his heart and not able to endure the pain, he lamented:
'My valour is crippled; the life of my clan is nipped in the bud.'
My enemies would rejoice and laugh at me now. 60
'Has the one who defeated Indra died in the hands
Of a trivial human being?
Has my weakness for the woman cost me my dear son?
Why do I need this Lanka and riches any longer?
Why do I need any praise and fame?
Why should I live? Why this life? Why this war?
Shame on my valour; I am disgraced to be a womanizer!

'Ah, the eminent commander-in-chief!
Has Yama become dearer to you than me?
Without you, the entire world is a vacuum to me. 70
Everything looks bare and barren.
The citizens of Lanka were very dear to you;
Deserting them where have you gone, O dear son!
Deserting your mother Mandodari, deserting your dear wife,
Where have you disappeared, O brave one!
The son performs the death rites of his father;
Alas! Reversing this natural order,
I am condemned to do it for you!
Rama, Lakshmana, Sugriva, and Hanuma
Were the lances that pierced your heart; 80
Without rooting them out,
Where have you gone, O son!'

Just as the female elephant roars in grief
When its consort, the tusker, is slain,
The wailing of the ladies in the harem of the palace
Touched Ravana's heart and he felt deeply sad.

As Ravana heard this wailing,
All his sorrow got transformed into anger;

Just as the ocean becomes turbulent
At the time of ultimate destruction, 90
Fierce anger coursed through his veins and he frowned:
'Janaki is responsible for the death of my sons;
I will kill her.' His eyes turned red in anger
And emitted fire; mad with anger,
He mashed his teeth fiercely.
Seeing him thus, the *rakshasas* scattered in fear
And hid themselves.
As if to devour the world and challenge Death itself,
Drawing out the sword from the sheath, he thundered
Like the rattle of the chariot-wheels running on a rocky path: 100
'Listen, all you ministers! Dragging her into the street,
Mocking and hustling, I shall slay that evil of a woman
Who has reposed faith in that wicked warrior – Rama;
And offer her as a feast to the evil spirits.'

'Sita shall not be slain,' the citizens pleaded.
But not heeding, pushing his confidants aside,
Enraged Ravana rushed into Ashokavana looking for Sita.

Janaki watched him from afar
And lamented: 'He is arriving wielding his sword angrily.
He will not spare me; who will save me now? 110
Alas! Though Shri Rama is in Lanka now,
Am I condemned to die like an orphan?'

Discerning the hapless plight
Of Janaki and sympathising with her,
Suparshva, the minister, stopped Ravana boldly and said:
'O great King! You are born in a noble clan;
Overcome with rage, you have come to kill Sita;
You are well-versed in the Vedas;
You have performed many *yajnas*;
You very well know that killing a woman is a heinous sin; 120
Turn your fuming anger on Rama.
Tomorrow is the new moon day.

Declare war; slay Rama; keep Sita with you
As the reward for your valour
And be happy ever after; why do you fear?'
He spoke thus appeasing Ravana.

The soothing words of Suparshva
Placated Ravana. His anger then turned to Rama.
As he came to the palace, Mandodari's wailing reached the sky.
Wiping the tears of dear Mandodari, he said: 130
'Forgive me, O dear one!
By giving birth to Indrajit, you placed the pearly cupola
On the golden temple of the Lankan empire.
Ah! You are indeed the blessed one.
I am the cause of your terrible anguish.

'Power, wealth, kingdom, and all material pleasures,
Can be won again; but would it be possible
To get an eminent son like Indrajit once again?
Turn your heart into stone.
Do not burn the roots of my courage 140
With the fire of your wailing.
Valiant Indrajit was deceived;
Lakshmana has slain him while he was meditating.
Tomorrow is a new moon day;
I shall avenge his death.'

At that point, there arrived
A female messenger and said:
'Queen Dhanyamalini has fainted;
I am afraid whether she will be alive.'
Making Mandodari sleep on the bed, 150
He ordered the maids to take care
Of her and arrived at the palace
Of Dhanyamalini. Caressing her hair
As she sat with a mind fixed elsewhere, she spoke
In a hushed voice:

'Listen to my entreaty, my Lord!
Succumbing to passions, I offered my body to Lankesha;
But, O Lord, I gave him only my body, and not my mind.
All my dreams were shattered, O Lord.
I am separated from you because of my bad deeds. 160
You are everything to me, O Lord.
Sita is the mother of the world.
The *rakshasa* has brought her;
Would the virtuous wife ever fall for him?
She has not lost her chastity. The dust of the holy feet
Of Mother Sita have given me salvation.
I offer hundred salutations to her.' Saying thus,
She closed her eyes. Like the quiet pond sans ripples,
Her face shone with tranquility.

'She became a victim of my lust,' thinking thus, 170
Ravana was deeply anguished. His sympathy increased.
As if seeking forgiveness for his sins,
He was drowned in silence.

At that instant, a female messenger arrived
And said: 'O Lord, Listen!
Having lost her husband Indrajit,
Tarakshi, his queen, has decided to undergo *sati* –
The practice of jumping into the funeral pyre
Of the dead husband.'
Hearing this, like a gusty wind that brings in heavy rains; 180
He got up and rushed to her palace.
The loud wailing and screaming deafened his ears.

'I am doomed!
O the handsome one, where have you gone?
O the breath of my life, where have you disappeared?
Ah! Dear, my beloved, I am orphaned.
You were the most desirable treasure of virtues;
I had hidden your love deep in my heart;

And my heart is broken now.'
Saying so, she wriggled and rolled like a female serpent.   190

Lifting up the dear daughter-in-law,
With a heavy heart and a choked voice,
Ravana consoled her:
'O daughter, control your sorrow;
The entire Lanka is drowned in the ocean of sorrowful tears;
I am caught in the wildfire and will be burnt to ashes soon;
You are the saving grace of Lanka; protect the clan;
O daughter, be patient, and live long;
You are the valiant mother of Vajrari;
It is your duty to protect him.   200
You must nurture your progeny
To bloom and prosper.' Pacifying her thus,
Ravana embraced Vajrari dearly,
Kissed him tenderly, and felt immensely happy!

Continuing, he spoke thus:
'This baby is the commentary on life;
Watching his childish pranks, forget your grief.
Viewing Lanka as Heaven on earth, live your life well.
Abstain from the selfish thought of following Indrajit to Heaven.
Get up and cuddle your babe.   210
Do not make him an orphan, O daughter.'
Consoling her thus, Ravana returned to his palace.

Hugging Vajrari endearingly
And kissing him tenderly, Tarakshi went into raptures
Like a tendril exhilarated by a soft touch.
Steadying the tumultuous thoughts in her heart,
Gazing at her son, she delved into silence!

Canto Two Hundred and Ten

'This War is only to Quench the Thirst for Self-esteem'

||௬||

Summoning the courtiers to the royal assembly,
Seated on the throne, not able to bear the pain,
With a deep sigh, Ravana told his ministers:
'Release all the prisoners and distribute all the wealth
In the royal treasury to the poor and the humble.'

Later, arriving at the palace
And getting ready for the battle, he came
To Mandodari and asked:
'I am going to the battlefield;
Won't you wish me good luck?' 10

Mandodari replied:
'How will you win over the *vanara* army?
How will you win over Rama and Saumitri?
How will you win over Hanuma and Jambavanta?
How will you win over Sugriva and Angada?
Building the bridge across the ocean,
They have set foot on Lanka,
Destroyed the fort and slain the valiant warriors;

They have stored food that can last for more than three months;
They have arrangements for treating all the wounded; 20
Facilities have flown into the *vanaras*
From distant islands like the river of Time.
They are fighting with a single-minded focus to free Janaki.
The *vanaras* are supporting Rama, viewing him
As the man of the epoch who leads the
Great Quest for universal peace.
Just as the fire blazes bright consuming
The sacrificial offerings made to it,
The desire for indulgence cannot be quelled
By yearning for more, my Lord!' 30

Listening to the counsel of Mandodari
Ravana said: 'I feel that I have lost the war already.
Time and again, you tried hard to warn me
By shattering my vanity at every stage;
Not heeding, I have ruined myself.
The very precept of "Aryan versus Dravidian"
Is of conflicting interests;
I do not know how to tame the seed
Of hostility contained in it.
Listen! The war between Rama and Ravana is just a pretext; 40
Hence, any introspection will not bear fruition now.
Look at Kumbhakarna, who loved peace greatly.
Being caught in the vortex of war, wearied, he died.
Having sacrificed Khara, Dushana,
Indrajit, Atikaya and others, how can I be happy?
My mind is vacuous sans sense of discretion,
And a great void stares me in the face;
Death is all that I seek now;
The Ganges keeps flowing fast.

'I am aware of myself. 50
I am neither vile nor am I highly virtuous;
Fortitude and valour are my religion

And at the core of my thinking;
I cannot have a truce with Rama;
I have no desire for Sita now.
I am waging a war to protect multiculturalism.
Till today, everyone has fought and died
In the battle to pay their debts to me.
I shall now fight to protect my nation and sacrifice my life
At the altar of my nation.   60
Listen, O my beloved! Rama isn't any virtuous or courteous.
Right from the episode of Tataka-garden to Panchavati,
In the pretext of establishing *dharma*,
Rama has done nothing great, only gimmicks.
He slew Tataka and Subahu; he humiliated Chandranakhi;
He killed Vali deceitfully; why should a monkey
Come to Lanka and burn it?
Why should I surrender to the one,
Who himself has deviated from the path of *dharma*?

'Wars have taken place since   70
Times immemorial only to quench the hunger of self-esteem;
But alas! In this game, countless states,
Nations and even cultures
Are all wiped out without leaving a trace.

'If you look at me,
I have many good qualities and only a couple of bad ones.
Look at Rama! He has more vices than me.
I'm condemned to be punished; but Rama is idolised!
Why this discrimination? Why this bias?
I shall wipe out racism; I shall wipe out the concepts of sin and
    virtue;   80
I vouchsafe living life most naturally;
People have forgotten the philosophy of true religion;
In a world given to all kinds of weaknesses,
I will infuse the light of this new awareness this instant.
Valiant men are there to fight the war.

Listen, war shall not cease;
Trusting my valour, I will slay Rama,' he said.

Discerning that advice will not bear fruition,
Mandodari prayed: 'O Lord Shiva!
You have blessed my husband
And gifted him boons and weapons. Grant him wisdom
To tread the path of *dharma,* O Lord.'
Saying so, she bathed him in tears;
Her deep sighs were the incense and her soul was the lamp;
Her sobs were the *mantra* and her wailings were the prayers;
And her *mangalya,* the symbol of holy matrimony,
Became the sacrificial offering to the Lord.

Making Lankesha sit on
The golden bed-stead, she offered him
Cow's milk in a golden bowl.
Then she put on him suitable protective gears
And armour for the battle.
Smearing his forehead with the holy ash of Lord Shiva,
She performed *arati* and put flowers and consecrated rice grains to ward off evil.
She hugged him lovingly and touched his feet with reverence.
Then, she prayed, 'Listen, O my Lord!
Let your path be smooth
And may you be successful.'
Dashakantha, the ten-headed one, hugged and kissed her.
Seizing the Chandrahasa weapon, accompanied by Mandodari,
He arrived at the royal court.
All his kith and kin, the citizens, the chieftains of army,
And all the courtiers had congregated there.
Ravana spoke:

'O, my dear citizens!
As you all have reposed faith in me,
I led the Lankan Empire on the path of progress.
The flag of the *rakshasas* fluttered high in the sky.
Because of me you are all suffering now.

Having lost your children and kindred in the battle, 120
You have all drowned in the ocean of grief.
I have lost many a valiant men
Including my own son, Indrajit;
What more can I say now?
I will go to the battlefield forthwith and fight.
I will win the war as Lankeshwara, the Lord of Lanka;
If not, I will sacrifice my life. The auspicious hour has come;
The war expedition will proceed with *chaturangabala*.
Surrounding the *vanara* army from all sides,
Showering arrows, slay the enemies steadfastly. 130
I will not spare Raghava, the son of Raghu clan;
I will slay him as the world would look on as witness.'
Nodding silently, they sent the army to the battle.

Ravana reached the battlefield.
Readying the *chaturangabala*, he invaded.
A terrifying battle ensued at sunrise.
As *vanaras* pulled out bludgeons, sharp-edged spears,
Giant axes and swords from the hands
Of the *rakshasas* and slaughtered them,
Blood flowed in a stream there! 140

Next moment, the *vanaras*
Shattered the flagstaff along with the chariots
And crushed all the weapons to pieces;
With their canines, they bit the *rakshasas*
And scratched the bodies of the *rakshasas*
With their sharp nails;
Tearing the ears and hair of the *rakshasas*,
And smashing their faces,
The *vanaras* annihilated the *rakshasas*.

At another end, Rama and Ravana 150
Showered arrows at each other.
As Shri Rama shot *roudrastra* at Ravana,
He retaliated with *asurastra*.

As Rama shot *agneyastra*, Ravana, in turn, shot *krurastra*.
Rama proceeded with *gandharvastra*
While Ravana retaliated with *saurastra*.
Both fought fiercely.

Both were determined to win.
As Ravana flaunted his valour shooting serpent-arrow,
Shri Rama subdued it with *garuda*-arrow; 160
When Ravana shot *yamya* filling the world with fear,
Shri Rama neutralised it with *rudra*-arrow,
Roaring, as Ravana shot *parvata*-arrow,
Shri Rama quelled it with *vajra*-arrow.
As Ravana shot *tama*-arrow,
Shri Rama shot *surya*-arrow and the entire world was lit up.
Finally, when Lankesha shot *sammohana*-arrow,
The *vanaras* swooned and fell down.
At once, Shri Rama broke the magic spell
And waking up the *vanaras* thus, 170
Filled them with enthusiasm.

The *vanaras* shouted in excitement:
'Shri Rama is our protector;
Let Victory be to Rama.'
Readying his bow – Kodanada,
Rama barged into the army of the *rakshasas*
And showered arrows
That emitted fire and destroyed them.

To the swift attack of Rama
The valiant *rakshasas* rolled like the 180
Trees in the woods caught in a gale;
The heaps of severed heads reached the sky.
As the soldiers were looking for Rama to see how he fought,
A big surprise awaited them.
Just like the soul, shrouded in mystery, remains concealed
In every limb of the body,

Shri Rama, not becoming overtly visible,
Waded through the army
Of the *rakshasas* and slew them!

As one said, 'Rama is here,' 190
Another one said: 'Aye, Rama is there!'
As Shri Rama became ubiquitous,
Each *rakshasa* perceived the other to be Rama;
Shouting aloud, the *rakshasas* started
Fighting among themselves
And killed each other. As one asked:
'Are there thousand Ramas
In the battlefield?' another shouted,
'No, no. There's only one Rama.'
The bow Kodanda held by Rama revolved 200
Like a wheel of fire and everyone saw it.

Rama was not visible,
But they saw that wheel killing the *rakshasas*.
Look! Rama's body itself is the navel
Of the powerful wheel;
And his strength is the flame of the wheel;
Arrows themselves are the sharp scything teeth
And the bow itself is the circumference of the wheel;
The loud roar of victory,
The power of Shri Ramachandra's intellect, 210
His prowess and the glow of his body
Together imparted radiance to the wheel.
The grandeur of that wheel transformed itself
Into the Wheel of Time, the ultimate destroyer of all!

Sweeping the battlefield like
A tempest, the great wheel crushed
Thousands of chariots; thousands of horses;
Thousands of elephants and thousands of horsemen.
The *rakshasas* felt utterly miserable!

As Raghava broke Ravana's bow, 220
He seized another one; Raghava broke that arrow too.
In this way, Raghava swept through the battle
Cutting Ravana's arrows continuously;
As thousands and thousands of arrows were broken,
The battlefield was filled with the broken arrows.

That war ended for the day.
The *chaturangabala* was scattered helter-skelter,
The battlefield appeared like the playground of Lord Shiva.
As the *rakshasas* headed towards the city,
Watching the archery-skills of Rama, 230
Sugriva, Hanuma, Jambavanta, Vibhishana
Mainda, Dwivida, they were all awe-struck!

The morale of Ravana's army
Had sunken low. As Lanka was losing itself
In the wilderness of war, Vibhishana was the only one gifted
To pacify and restrain Ravana.
But Vibhishana was not in Lanka
At this crucial hour. When patriotic emotions are roused,
The path of victory could be found.
Disappointment had spread widely in Ravana's camp 240
And the vigour had sunken low.
The valiant *rakshasas* had all succumbed to Rama's arrows.
The soldiers who had seen and experienced all this,
Will they have any excitement to wage war?

In Lanka, the grief-stricken women
Were collapsing under the burden of widowhood;
Mothers who had lost their sons were suffering terribly.
Embracing each other, they are shedding tears.

They wailed and lamented:
'Shurpanakha is the root cause of all this misfortune; 250
Why was she born here?
Why did she desire to be charming like Cupid?

She nurtured this hatred and deserves to be condemned.
Bringing Sita to Lanka, she has brought death to all.
Can anyone live instigating Shri Rama,
The one who has never known defeat?
Shri Rama has destroyed Ravana's *chaturangabala*.
There is no end to our catastrophe;
Bad omen surfaced before each fight;
Not caring, Ravana continued to wage war 260
And defeat was inevitable.
Sita has arrived here to destroy the *rakshasas*.
The bad ethics of Ravana are destroying all of us.
Who will protect us now? Who will save us now?
Our life has become like the plight
Of the hapless female elephants
Caught in the midst of a raging forest fire.'
Deeply distressed and heart-broken,
They were lamenting thus!

Canto Two Hundred and Eleven

'To Destroy the World, Now I will Fight like Rudra'

||৬||

As the fifth day of the dark fortnight
Of the lunar month dawned,
Determined to get boons to decimate the enemies,
Ravana visited the shrine of the mighty Goddess Durga –
The eight-shouldered goddess,
Holding fierce weapons in her hands,
Adorning the garland of human skulls
With blood dripping from her protruded tongue –
He praised the Goddess thus:

'O Mother Bhuvaneshwari! 10
Your long hair is like the fierce black cobra;
You are the three-eyed one;
You are the Mother of the three worlds;
You are the Nature; you are the *maya*;
Your *lila* is magnificent;
You are the Creator, Protector,
And Destroyer of the Universe;
You are the presiding deity of the *rakshasa* clan;

You are the Time-incarnate Durga;
You govern the affairs of the world at your bidding!' 20

Focussing unswerving attention on Goddess Durga,
He performed the oblations to fire.
As he stood waiting for the auspicious hour of blessing,
It appeared as if the three worlds stood still
Under the glare of a planet.
Dashashira, the ten-headed one, returned contented that
The mother granted her grace and blessed him.

From every household as Ravana heard
The heart-rending cry of grief-stricken women
Who had lost their near and dear ones, he felt deeply hurt. 30
Anger welled up in him and his eyes turned red.
Gnashing his teeth, he entered the royal court like Rudra,
As if to burn the world to ashes and thundered:

'Listen, valiant men!
With the arrow that is red-hot like the sun,
I will etch the death warrant of Rama and Lakshmana.
My arrows will shower like the clouds that spread across
The earth, sky, rivers and oceans, and sever the *vanaras*.
Fierce tempests will sweep through the battlefield
And the ocean waves, rising high, will wash away the *vanaras*. 40

'I will chop off the bodies of the *vanaras*
And throw them as food for dogs, jackals, and vultures;
I will cover the entire earth with their bodies.
I will wipe the tears of every woman in my city
Who has lost her husband, sons, brothers and the kindred.

'Listen, brave men!
I am grateful for the love you have shown me.
Many lives have been lost in the battle
Save the one, and that is my own life.
Today, like Rudra, I will fight single-handedly 50
For destroying the world.

'I will lay down my life; if not,
I will suck away the lives of all the enemies.
You all remain as spectators, do not wield any weapons.
Let the great fierce battle between Rama and Ravana
Take place and let the three worlds stand watching it.
Is Lanka short of valiant soldiers?
Everyone is a fighter; everyone is excited to fight.
Look! Our ultimate goal is of great value,
You cannot discern it now, nor can I say it! 60
It will be unravelled tomorrow! It isn't my selfishness
To drink the ambrosia of the celestial cow all by myself!

'Listen! The hour is fast approaching –
To scale the tower of victory and
To ascend the summit of fame,
With head held high, and beaming with pride,
To proclaim that wonderful news to the whole world.
Wait patiently for that auspicious hour!

'Do not cry for me;
Do not grieve for me; my life is 70
Well-protected in this strong body.
I have got the divine chariot and horse;
I have got the divine bow and sword,
Great physique and great prowess.
As everything of mine is divine,
Is there anyone in the world who is similarly blessed?
I can counter Lord Shiva in the battlefield.
Even if I venture into the battle all alone,
I will appear as the Infinite.
Come, let us offer prayers to the quiver and arrows! 80
Climbing on the northern fort,
You feast your eyes watching the war!'

In the arsenal,
Anointing them with blood,
All the weapons were worshipped

In the form of Goddess Durga.
They sounded the bells, clashed the cymbals
And blew the trumpets and war bugles.
The *rakshasa* army offered prayers to the goddess:
'O Mother Supreme! You are the all powerful one; 90
Get up to protect us, O Mother;
Get up to drink the blood of the enemies;
Get up to save Lanka; get up to destroy the enemy;
Raise Ravana, the eminent sovereign
Of the *rakshasa* clan, to glory.
You are the one who grants courage and confidence;
You are the radiance of our lives and the valour of our arms;
You are the very source of our lives;
The chariots and horses are yours indeed;
The zeal to fight the enemy is your gift; 100
You are worshipped as Durgi, Chamundi, Ranakali
Savitri, Gayatri, Shivani, Narayani,
Gauri, Shakambani, Varahi, Vaishnavi,
Katyayini, Raudramukhi, Vikatangi and Jatodari;
Get up to bestow upon us the strength to win the war.
Lankadhipa, the Lord of Lanka, has ascended
His divine chariot that is the wonder of the three worlds
And the entire world is shuddering in fear;
O Mother! Get up this instant and bless him!'

Swords, arrows, amulets and armours shone 110
And the great chariot appeared
As if a divine spirit descended on earth.
The neighing of horses resounded all around
And the entire atmosphere was filled with excitement.

As awe spread across, he climbed onto the chariot
That resembled the peak of the Golden Mountain;
The white horse appeared like the dazzling peak
Of the Silver Mountain;
The flag fluttered with a garland made of human skulls;

Many chariots, stacked with weapons, followed him; 120
Ravana wore a garland of *mandara* flowers
And the vermilion on his forehead resembled
The third eye of Lord Shiva;
As the chariot moved ahead at the auspicious hour,
The entire Lanka shook. As the waters of the river Sarayu
Of Ayodhya swelled up and struck the banks,
The *vanaras* gazed at the grand chariot with awe.

Viewing the *Chandika*-flag,
Darimukha, cautioned the *vanara* army:
'Look! Ravana is arriving all alone to the battle,' 130
And got ready to confront him.
Can he match Ravana?
First of all, Ravana was angry
And he was eager to slaughter the enemy.
Opening his eyes wide, he stared fiercely:
Darimukha's mace got cleaved; his arms got chopped off;
His eyes were plucked out; his cheeks were bruised;
Moving his hands and legs violently,
The valiant warrior Darimukha succumbed
To the blows of Ravana and reached Heaven! 140
The enraged *vanaras* fought fiercely.
Like Rudra, slaughtering them all,
Ravana surged ahead and the frightened *vanaras* ran
For their lives without fighting back.

Valiant Anjaneya and Angada
Watched the ghastly death of the *vanaras*.
Jambavanta tried to stop the fleeing *vanaras*.
Grieving over the death of Darimukha,
Rama called Sugriva and said:

'Listen, O the king of *vanaras*!
Let none of you fight with Lankesha now; 150
If Nala, Nila, Jambavanta, Hanuma, Mainda and others
Attack Ravana, they will certainly lose their lives.

Do not push the *vanara* army to be slaughtered like sheep;
The loss of Darimukha is more than enough. Keep quiet.
Call back Hanuma; tell Angada, Jambavanta,
And Nala not to fight. The king of the *rakshasas*
Is looking for me steadfastly.
Today's war is set apart for me.
Just as the river looks desperately to join the ocean,
Losing patience, Ravana is looking for me. 160
Beware! Ravana will devour you all in no time! Beware!'

As Ravana proceeded
Looking for Rama and Saumitri,
The sunlight faded and all the directions turned dismal;
The earth shook; vultures and other birds cried hoarsely;
It rained blood and the horses faltered;
A vulture alighted on the flagstaff of Ravana's chariot;
Jackals hooted; Ravana's left eye twitched;
His right shoulder shuddered;
His voice became weak and his face turned pale; 170
Vultures screeched and crows quarrelled.
Not heeding the bad omens,
Lankesha surged ahead swiftly.

Canto Two Hundred and Twelve

'Feast Your Eyes on the War of the Epoch'

||६||

Stationed at the centre of the battlefield, Ravana said:
'Charioteer, swiftly drive the chariot ahead now.
I will slay Rama and Saumitri and thus eliminate the afflictions
Of the women grieving over the loss of their dear ones.
I will root out the tree called Rama
Filled with fruits and flowers called Vaidehi
With its glowing robust branches called
Sugriva, Jambavanta, Gandhamadana, Kumuda,
Hanumanta, Nala, Dwivida, Mainda, Sushena, and Angada!'

The rattle of the chariot spread everywhere   10
And gushing like a river, it resounded in the hills and the forests;
The earth shuddered; the animals and the birds got frightened;
And the *vanaras* were scattered.

Rama appeared
Along with his brother Lakshmana:
Seizing the bow, Rama stood
As if he would size up the entire sky with his bow;
Rama, the lotus-eyed, the one with long hands

That reached the knees,
And the one who destroys the enemies,   20
Stood there like Mount Meru.

Shri Rama queried:
'Who is this, the one who is advancing
Towards me staring fiercely?
Is he Ravana's chieftain, or son, or kin?
Who is this ferociously dreadful one who is advancing in grandiosity?'
Vibhishana replied quickly:
'Have you forgotten, my Lord? He is Lankesha himself.
He is arriving emanating more radiance than ever before
And I am afraid to describe him,   30
The one who is Rudra in the battle.'

As Shri Rama swiftly
Twanged the strings of his bow,
A great sound emanated as if to split the entire universe.
Listening to the terrible sound, the *rakshasas* fell down.
As Ravana stood facing Rama,
It appeared as if Rahu, the monster stood clouding
The sun and the moon on a new-moon day.

With an excitement to fight,
Lakshmana confronted Ravana   40
And shot an arrow that resembled a fireball.
Valiant Ravana broke it into pieces half-way in the sky.
For every arrow shot by Lakshmana,
Ravana effectively retaliated.
Ah! Ravana's archery-skills outsmarted Lakshmana!

Viewing Rama with blood-shot eyes,
Ravana showered arrows.
But the agile Rama, fixing pointed spears,
Shot back in quick succession. Like venom,
The weapons killed the *rakshasas*.   50
Both fought moving round and round in circles

And moving back and forth and in reverse motions;
They fought for long. In radiance,
Once Shri Rama appeared like Yama;
And once Lankesha appeared like Rudra.
Just as the dark clouds cover the sun,
Heaps of arrows covered the sky.
As if the sun had set,
The battlefield was covered with darkness
And fear gripped both sides. 60
Both were of equal strength and both fought fiercely.
Just as the waves swell up when a gale strikes,
Their skills of archery outwitted each other
And the arrows surged fiercely.

As Ravana shot many arrows
At Rama's forehead, not losing heart,
Wielding Raudra-weapon and chanting propitiatory verses,
Rama attempted to tear apart the armour of Dashashira.
Ah! The armour was impenetrable and the arrow fell down in vain.
Angered, as Rama shot another fierce arrow at Ravana's forehead, 70
It moved hissing like a five-hooded serpent.
Ah! Ravana cut it into pieces half way.

As the *danava* aimed *Asurastra*,
It shot forth like the tigers, lions, jackals,
Wolves, vultures, and eagles
With their mouths opened wide, and exploded.
In retaliation, as Shri Rama shot *Agneyastra*,
It moved with great speed creating
Sun, moon, stars, and meteors on its course.
Ravana stopped it mid-way and shot *Asurastra* again; 80
As Rama cut it into pieces,
The *vanaras* shouted in excitement.

Angered Lankesha shot *Raudrastra*;
Lances, maces, giant pestles, and pointed weapons
Sprang up from it like a tempest. Shri Rama retaliated

With the divine *Gandharvastra* and quelled it.
As Ravana shot *Saurastra,* the wheels of fire shot forth
Like the blazing sun. Shri Rama quelled it
Showering pointed arrows.

Not losing heart, Ravana 90
Aimed ten arrows to the vital parts of Rama;
Not fearing, Shri Rama pierced Ravana's entire body
With his sharp arrows. At that point,
As Rama took respite from war,
Saumitri surged forward and confronting Ravana,
He said thus revealing all the secrets:

'Aha, Dashashira, the ten-headed one!
You have desecrated many *yajnas* and oblations to fire.
Being a coward, you have abducted women
And you have raped them; 100
Violating their chastity, you have afflicted them;
Drowned in sorrows, they have all cursed you;
You will suffer for afflicting them;
Your end is imminent now!'

Saumitri shot seven swift arrows
And they tore away the flag fluttering on the chariot.
With another arrow, he shot the charioteer down.
With five pointed arrows, he broke into two
Ravana's bow that resembled the trunk of a tusker.
He shot five more sharp arrows and 110
The horses fell down dead.
Immediately, jumping off his chariot,
As Ravana hurled *Shakti*-weapon,
Saumitri broke it into three pieces
And they fell down emitting fire.

Seeing the weapon failing to strike its goal,
Ravana drew another great weapon and hurled it swiftly.
Saumitri retaliated with alacrity and the weapon

Of Danavendra, the king of the *danavas*,
Broke into pieces in no time. 120

Trying hard,
As Ravana once again shot *Shakti*-weapon,
It struck Saumitri's heart like a thunderbolt.
The anxiety of the *vanaras* rose high.
Saumitri swooned.

Rama came running.
Saumitri lay down soaked in blood.
Pavanaja, son of Wind, tried to pull out the *Shakti*-weapon;
But it had struck so deep into the chest
That it pierced the earth too! 130
What an appalling sight!
Shri Rama – the idol of brotherly affection –
Languished in sorrow;
Tears rolled down his cheeks copiously.
Seizing the *Shakti*-weapon with both his hands,
Shri Rama pulled it out and flung it away.
With his anger soaring high, Rama said:

'Listen, you eminent *vanaras*!
Accompanying Saumitri, you all have fought with fortitude.
Time is now ripe to punish the wicked *rakshasa*. 140
The insipid darkness will disappear and a new dawn will rise;
I am the proverbial *chataka,*
And I wait for that opportune time.
Ravana's life-span is racing
Towards the inevitable end.

'What shall I say of my lamentations!
I lost my kingdom; it befell on me to dwell in the forests;
I wandered in the Dandaka-forest;
Vaidehi was abducted;
I bore the atrocities of the *rakshasas*; 150
Vali was slain; and the bridge across the sea was built.

Saumitri is dear to me more than my own life.
Arriving here now, will I spare the life
Of wicked Lankesha?
No, never; he will live no more;
You will see Rama's valour in the war.
All celestial beings – *devatas, gandharvas,*
charanas, Kinnaras, kimpurushas – and the sages
Will witness the excitement and grandeur
Of the War of the Epoch; 160
This has neither happened in the past,
Nor will it ever happen in the future.
Let all the three worlds
Feast their eyes on the War of the Epoch!'

Engaging Ravana in a fierce fight,
Shri Rama showered pointed arrows continuously.
In return, as Dashashira, the ten-headed one,
Shot arrows swiftly, the arrows clashed in the sky
And produced a deafening sound.
The *rakshasas* got frightened 170
And Lankesha was frightened too!
Fighting continuously and getting wearied,
Ravana thought – 'I cannot fight any longer' –
And thus departing from the battlefield,
He reached the palace.

Canto Two Hundred and Thirteen

'Defrauding in a Hundred Ways is Your Forte'

||૬||

Watching Saumitri fall, Shri Rama said wailing:
'When Saumitri is dead, why should I live?
My massive valour is shattered;
As I am grief-stricken, my arrows have become unsteady.
Why this great war? Why do I need Janaki now?
Why do I need the kingly crown? Why should I live?'

Sushena replied:
'Why do you worry, O Lord?
Saumitri is not dead.
He has just fainted and is still breathing.   10
As the great medicinal herb brought
By Pavanasuta, son of Wind,
Is readily available for treatment,
Why do you worry?
When I am here, and so also *vaidya* Prabha,
Why this wailing?'
Thus assuring, Sushena summoned Prabha.
Grinding the medicinal herb,
As he squeezed its essence into Saumitri's nostrils,

Saumitri opened his eyes and sat up
As if awaking from sleep!
The *vanaras* danced in excitement,
And whole-heartedly praised Hanuma,
Vaidya Prabha, and Sushena.

Overcome with joy
Rama spoke endearingly with tears in his eyes:
'Come, dear brother; I want to embrace you.
Blessed am I, for you have emerged
Severing the snare of death.'

Bowing to the feet of Rama, Saumitri said:
'You are truly the valiant one.
Do not forget your volition.
Moved deeply by your affection for the brother,
Do not forget your duty.
Can a tusker confront a roaring lion?
Get on with the war and slay Ravana before sunset.
This is what I wish for;
This is what the world desires and
This is the desire of every man of virtue.
It is not fair to neglect the wish of the people
Who are suffering under oppression.
Otherwise, Janaki will jump into the fire!'
Alerting him thus, Saumitri reminded Shri Rama
Of the epoch's volition and his commitment to it.

Shri Rama said:
'Get up; get up, O the valiant one!
Am I afraid of death? Will I shy away
From any impediments?
How can one get a vision of Truth
Without quelling one's ego?
You are an extension of my mind
And you are my soul-mate and all the events
Keep unravelling as they ought to.

Ravana has arrived mustering all his strength
And will aim to destroy the *vanaras* mercilessly.'

As the fierce battle ensued,
Confronting the army of Ravana,
The *vanaras* thrashed the horses, smashed the elephants,
Shattered the chariots, and broke the swords.
Slaying the *rakshasas*, they surged forward   60
And blood flowed into a stream.
Each side witnessed victory and defeat consecutively.
The *rakshasas* invaded like hounds
And the *vanaras* took to their heels.
Watching this, Anjaneya said:

'Listen, O *vanaras*!
Do not fear, do not run.
Death might descend today or tomorrow;
Can anyone survive by running away?
I will give up my life for accomplishing the Master's mission.   70
I will unburden all my worries this instant and make myself agile.
If I do not stop the impediments
That thwart my Master's mission,
Why should I be alive?
Life will be fulfilled only when it is dedicated
To the service of Shri Rama!'

As Shri Rama stood tall like a tower,
The *vanaras* jumped in excitement.
On the other side, the *rakshasas* too jumped in excitement
Watching the towering figure of Ravana.   80
The battle turned horrendous.
Valour and fortitude coursed through the veins
Of the onlookers; the sky cracked, the hills shuddered,
The rivers gushed out, and their reverberations shook the forests.
The forceful army of Ravana surged forward
Pushing back Rama's army steadfastly!

The greatest battle of the epoch turned into
The nightmarish dance of Shiva
At the time of ultimate destruction.
Thunder and lightning struck; 90
The Meru Mountain shuddered;
Cold and misty mountain peaks swayed continuously;
The elephants stationed at the eight directions of the universe
Roared loudly and fell down exhausted.
The valiant warriors like Rahurosha, Saptaghna
Brahmaksha, Shonitaksha, Mahodara and Agniketu
Stood at the front line of the military array!
Ravana donned the apparel that glowed like fire;
Ravana forgot the grief
Of losing his sons in the battle; 100
Ravana pushed aside the cloud
Of his deep disappointment;
Ravana flaunted his colossal physique
That exuded his supreme strength!

The sea of army stood ready for the combat.
Kettledrums and war bugles sounded aloud;
War slogans were shouted at high pitch.
A wide variety of weapons shone and flashed across.

Dashamukha, the ten-headed one, spoke:
'Now, Lanka is like the pain-stricken wild hog; 110
If Lanka's national pride is provoked, it will pounce
Roaring like a lion and quell the enemy.
The power of penance and the accomplishments
Of meditation secured over the decades,
The power of magical charms,
And the inventions of science are all
In my possession and control;
Can the *vanaras* withstand it all?
In my *chaturangabala*, there are countless
Soldiers, charioteers, horses and elephants. 120

The amazing strength
Of Ravana's volition will stimulate them all!

'If our determination is not lost,
Great warriors like Gandhamadana, Anjaneya, Nala,
Jambavanta, and Angada will be burnt to ashes like grass.
What if Indrajit, Atikaya, Kumbhakarna, Dhumraksha,
Mahaparshwa and Prahasta are dead and gone?
Each one of you is equal to me in valour.
Let every drop turn into an ocean in the *danava* army.
Surge ahead and rock in the swing of victory!' 130

Hearing Ravana's words,
The valiant *danava* army gave a loud victory cry and clapped;
Horses neighed and elephants roared;
The chariot-wheels screeched,
And the war of the epoch began.
A smile flashed across Ravana's face.

As the battle turned gruesome,
Gandhamadana fell; Gaja and Gavaya became weary;
Jambavanta was gasping for breath;
Angada retreated hesitatingly; 140
Nala wailed and Pavanaja, son of Wind,
Moved away from the battlefront.
Who else but Rama could confront
The great army of Ravana!

Ravana flaunted
As if he was the all powerful supreme lord of the universe;
As if he was the embodiment of Will
To achieve everything he desired for;
As if he was Shiva, the Lord of ultimate destruction;
As if all Knowledge resided in him; 150
As if he was the embodiment of the supreme yogic prowess.

Viewing Ravana's colossal strength,
His power of penance, unswerving volition and steadfastness,

The son of Maruta — Hanuma, felt wearied and contemplated:
'Alas! It is better to die than live shouldering the burden
Of shame and defeat. Why should one live when
There is nothing worthwhile to live for?'
Musing thus, Hanuma rushed to Shri Rama
And prostrating himself at his feet said:

'What is this, my Lord? 160
In the epoch-making process, can anyone
Punish the *vanaras* vainly?
When a tusker is trampling everyone fiercely,
Can you be merely viewing the end
Of the epoch for the fun of it?
I do not know whom I shall come across
On the threshold of a new epoch.
Arise, and save the life of the *vanaras*.'
Hearing the caution sounded by Hanuma,
And being in perfect agreement with his views, 170
Rama steadfastly got ready for the battle and
Set a sharp arrow to his bow!

Lankesha revealed his prowess
Shooting a *Vayuvyastra*; a gale shot up
And the earth trembled.
In retaliation, Rama shot a *Varunastra*;
Heavy rain lashed out and darkness enveloped.
Rivers, ponds, tanks overflowed and inundated the fields
And the heavy rains destroyed all the standing crops.
Relief work went on simultaneously. 180

Ravana surged into the sea of army
Wielding his weapon *Chandrahasa*.
What exhibition of valour and
What grandeur of destruction!
Fire-balls enveloped the battlefield;
The killing of *vanaras* went on with ferocity;
With its spirits dwindling at the onslaught,

Wriggling in pain, the *vanara* army rolled like a wave.
The battle got exciting!

As the Lord of Lanka shot 190
Gandharvastra, in retaliation, Shri Rama too
Shot a similar weapon and countered it well.
As Ravana shot *daivastra*, Rama matched it
With a similar weapon and destroyed it.
As Ravana hurled a *rakshasastra* in anger,
Fierce serpents emerged out of it;
Emitting poison and spitting fire,
They came rushing towards Rama.
Rama retaliated by shooting *Garudastra*;
Eagles came out from it and 200
They flew decimating all the serpents.

With anger swelling high,
As Ravana showered arrows,
As if the ocean was set ablaze,
A meteor struck the sky.
As there appeared the rotund solar orb,
With bow in hand, frowning and with blood-shot eyes,
Rama stood like the Mainaka Mountain and said:
'Lankesha, get ready to pay for your sins and bad deeds;
All evil shall end today; henceforth, 210
It shall not exist in the world!'

Ravana retorted:
'You nurture all wrong doings;
You call me the ten-headed one.
Your heart is filled with envy akin to hell.
It is you people, who possess hundred heads that think of evil;
Turning into a snake you raise the hood and hiss once;
Next moment, you roam about roaring like a tiger;
Then, turning into a frog you hop and croak;
And becoming a deer, you run off in fear. 220
Defrauding in a hundred ways is your forte.

It is you who killed the women and humiliated them;
It is you who sheltered traitors to the brother.
It is you who killed the valiant warrior hiding behind a tree!

'Invoking the ethics of valour,
I brought that gem of a woman; but I haven't
Attempted to violate her honour;
Like a serpent guarding the precious gem,
I have protected her; I am not an abductor of women.
You are the fool who went after the golden deer. 230
You plotted to get the innocent Angada killed
Under the pretext of peace talks, but it failed.
Like the frog in the well,
You are an ignorant fool who is not
Able to decipher the constant transformations
That occur in the world.
Devendra, the chief of Heaven,
Who enjoyed another man's wife,
How can he be your idol of reverence?
Go and fight with him; 240
Why have you come here instead?
Tell me, which *dharma* you uphold!

'You are indeed the chief of all deep-plotting;
You are the head of all fraudulent people
Who trample the poor, the destitute and the meek.
You have cultivated a coterie of sycophants
Who praise and worship you. You are all
Traitors who have labelled us '*rakshasas*',
We are indeed the well-bred, eminent warriors
Who have built our kingdom relying on 250
Our own strength – an empire built
With a desire for the welfare of all.
You curb freedom by quelling the spirit of rebellion;
What kind of royal ethic is this?
When the world discerns your wickedness

You'll be dethroned from your high altar!
How can your *dharma* which is full of contradictions,
Idiosyncrasies, and deceits, be called
A universal religion, tell me!

'If the *kshatriya* emperors   260
Do not beget children,
Getting children through the Brahmins
Is considered ethical;
Is this is not promiscuity, tell me!
Since the time of your great-grandfathers,
It is common among your clan
To abduct good women and enjoy them;
You are all the heinous progeny
Of such an evil practice.
Such being the case, when I shrewdly brought here   270
The wife of the one who has lost the kingdom,
And protected her safely in Lanka,
How can I be called unethical?
Young Kaikeyi was brought and married
To the old lustful king
And her youthfulness was thus destroyed;
This is history now!
How many lovelorn, how many destitute might have
Shed tears helplessly and how much
Of their tears might have   280
Joined the Sarayu waters!
You are fighting this war for the sake of a woman;
What virtue could there be in such a war?
In your journey, there isn't an iota
Of sacrifice or the good of others.'
Ravana said so mocking with pride.

Shri Rama replied:
'You cannot comprehend the good deeds of mine;
On the order of my Guru, I killed Tataki

Who tried to disrupt the *yajna* performed 290
To establish peace and harmony in the society.
To subdue oppression, and to safeguard the one
Who sought my shelter, I killed Vali;
Why do you blame me for that?
Chandranakhi suffered because of her lust;
You are least inclined to know the truth.
If cheating, suppression, and arrogance
Of oppression are your *dharma*,
Let that be yours gladly!'

Thundered Ravana: 300
'Listen, you beggar!
Do not boast of your empty valour to me.
I am not like those valiant men whom you claim to have won.
Winning over many kings, I have established
My vast empire and rule over it as Lankesha, the Lord of Lanka;
I have earned this throne solely on my own strength.
I am not one of your kind who lord over a piece of land
Handed down by the forefathers. Speak no more!
Ascetics and bards have praised you immensely;
But all that fame of yours is like a water bubble. 310
Waiting like a hunter, hiding behind a tree,
You killed the valiant Vali;
And you killed the other valiant warriors deceitfully.
I well slay you this instant and avenge the death
Of my kith and kin. Do not run away;
You are caught in the stronghold of Ravana;
Your death is certain!'

Provoked by the harsh words of Ravana,
Shri Rama replied: 'The garb of the true ascetics
Suffered humiliation because of your faking. 320
I have come with the responsibility of quelling down
The wicked; fight you must, and die you shall.
But before that, listen to my counsel.

There are three types of people in the world:
Some only speak but do not know
How to execute what they say;
Some speak and also know
How to execute what they say;
Some never speak but reveal their capacity through their work!
Pagade tree has just flowers but bears no fruits – ripe or unripe. 330
While the mango tree has both flowers as well as fruits,
The jack tree has no flowers at all but only fruits.
People who speak not, but perform, are the best in the world;
Those who speak, and also perform, are rated just average;
Those who speak, but never perform, are considered the worst.
Tell me, which is your path;
Abduction of women is an act of cowardice;
It is the abominable path the world has not known till today.
Though the entire world is mocking at you, blissfully unaware,
You roam about flaunting; yours is the wicked path.' 340

Beaming with pride, Ravana shouted:
'Who are you to advise me?
The fear of death that was not there when you set out
To fight, has it surfaced now?
Whether the compassion and ethics of the Aryan *dharma*
Flowed into the sea now? The evil tasks you carried out
And the deceitful actions you did are indeed countless.
Why this pretence? Stop this farce at once.'

Getting enraged, Shri Rama said:
'Stop! Enough of this empty boast, Lankesha! 350
Remember, when you attempted to lift the
Bow of Lord Shiva in Mithila city,
Spraining your ankles, you collapsed there
And the bow slipped off.
What happened then? The guards tried very hard to lift you up.
Later, hanging your head in shame,
And without looking back,

You returned to Lanka! I singlehandedly slew
All your wicked associates –
Tataka, Subahu, Maricha, Khara, and Dhushana. 360
Not fighting me, you abducted Janaki like a thief.
What kind of a mischief is this? What a mockery!
The valour of Ayodhya is greater than the ocean.
With a mind shrouded in darkness, and laying your body bare,
How will you fight? Like a blind man, you wander aimlessly.
I know very well your strengths and weaknesses.
You boast in vain!'

Canto Two Hundred and Fourteen

'Shri Rama Stood Ubiquitous'

॥६॥

Watching the infuriated face of Shri Rama,
Everyone got frightened.
The earth, the hills, the trees shuddered;
The sea overflowed; the clouds thundered
Signaling the impending catastrophe;
The birds cried hoarsely.
Fear gripped Ravana too.
The *danavas* and the *vanaras* assembled in the battlefield
Watched the fierce battle and shouted victory slogans.
As Lankesha wielded a pointed lance,   10
It appeared to be the destroyer of the enemy
And fear gripped the hearts of the onlookers.
The lance shone like lightning.
Emitting fire and smoke,
The sharp lance shone bright.
The rest of the soldiers fought
Wielding swords, axes, maces, spears and catapults.
The clashing sound of the weapons filled the battlefield.
Blood spurted out profusely and flowed in many directions.

In the battlefield,   20
As the jackals hooted and the vultures screeched,

It appeared that Lanka would be razed
In the grip of hatred and lust.
As Shri Rama surged ahead,
The enemy camp appeared
Like blades of dry grass that would be burnt to ashes;
Who is there to rescue them?
It appeared as though the radiance of the sun
Stood there manifested in the form of Rama;
The arrows from his great bow – Kodanda,   30
Glowed like the beams of sunlight.

As Rama fought fiercely,
It appeared that Time stood still;
It appeared that he quelled all the evil of the world.
Holding his large bow pressed firmly to the ground,
Bending it towards his right thigh, twanging the strings
Of the bow with his left hand, as he shot the arrows,
It sounded like the twanging of the *rudraveena*;
The courage and confidence of devouring the entire world
And draining it completely, manifested there.   40

Seizing a great lance and holding it high
The gigantic Ravana stood upright.
He stood thundering fiercely like Lord Shiva.
The valiant *Danava*-army stood surrounding him.
Hearing the demoniac roar of the *rakshasa*,
The world trembled; the *ganas* shuddered,
Looking at Shri Rama, Ravana spoke hoarsely:

'Look at the lance I am holding;
Ferociously I will hurl it at you now;
It will suck the life out of you   50
And your dear brother's as well.
I will avenge the death of the valiant *danavas* you have slain.
I will annihilate everything of yours and
None shall recall even your name.'

It was a lance with eight bells;
It surged into the sky like a bunch
Of lightning emitting fire and smoke.
As Shri Rama showered arrows,
The lance burnt them all like the blazing fire burns locusts.
With its bells sounding aloud, emitting bright light, exploding 60
Like a meteor as the lance approached with a brisk pace,
Shri Rama was infuriated and aimed pointed arrows at it.
Losing its luster, the lance broke
Into pieces and fell to the ground.
The *vanaras* shouted in excitement.

Later, Shri Rama aimed
More arrows at Ravana; the arrows struck him on the face,
Shoulders, temple, arms, and his entire body
Was covered with arrows.
Blood oozed out profusely; Ravana appeared 70
Like a freshly bloomed flower
Of sorrow amidst the battlefield.
The *rakshasas* felt dejected. Ravana stood perplexed:
He saw Rama everywhere – in front of him, at his back,
And by his sides; as he looked up, he saw Rama there;
As he looked down, he saw Rama there;
On earth and in the waters too he saw
Rama's all-pervading presence;
Shri Rama stood ubiquitous!

Ravana was bewildered 80
Not knowing in which direction to shoot his arrows.
As the spell of Lord Hari dispelled,
Regaining his self-control, Ravana fiercely shot fresh arrows.

Shri Rama was fully covered
With the arrows shot by Ravana.
Just as the mountain stands unshakeable
And resists the powerful beams of the sun,
Raghava stood firm and countering the arrows of the *rakshasa*
He broke them all into pieces.

As some arrows aimed at Lakshmana 90
Struck Rama, he got soaked in blood
And looked like a freshly bloomed coral tree.
As heaps of arrows were showered at a time,
Ravana could not see where Rama was
And neither could Rama!

Shri Rama thundered:
'You are the vilest *danava*;
You have brought Janaki to Lanka slyly.
What kind of a valiant warrior are you?
You are lustful of another man's wife; 100
You are a great coward indeed;
You are a brute without shame and character.
You are an evildoer and you are immoral.
You have invited death in arrogance.
Now reap the fruits of all your evildoing.
Had you touched Janaki in my presence,
I would have put you to the same plight meted out to Khara!
Today, I will push you to the abode of Yama. Beware!'

Ravana was shocked at the swiftness
Of Shri Rama's arrows and felt terribly frightened. 110
He wasn't able to invoke the propitiatory hymns
For wielding the weapons.
His hands felt too weak to twang the bow.
As the lamentations of countless soldiers echoed within,
He wasn't able to come to terms with himself.
He felt that he was drowning in the sea of life
And was sinking into a bottomless abyss;
Trying to wriggle out of the chaos,
He waded unsteadily through the heaps of *vanara*-corpses.

As the swiftness of Rama's arrows went on unabated, 120
Ravana sat down helplessly.
As his entire body was bruised and his strength weakened,
He reclined in the chariot, wearied.

The clever charioteer saw his master and
Thundering like clouds, he drove the chariot
In a different direction and went out of sight swiftly.
Recovering within seconds, Ravana looked around.
Turning blood-shot eyes at the charioteer, he said:

'Why did you bring me here?
Am I weak, and am I devoid of valour?   130
Do you think that the power of my charm
And the strength of my great weapons has declined?
Driving back the chariot, are you humiliating me?
You have tainted my reputation of being a great warrior.
When I was readying myself to fight,
By taking me away from the battlefield
You have helped the enemies.
You have not done any good to me.
Why do you stand still? Battlefield is my only goal;
Drive the horses in the direction of the battlefield at once!'   140

With a yearning to do good to his Master always,
Ravana's charioteer spoke with humility:
'I am not scared of war nor is this a deed done in haste.
I am a devout servant of my king.
When the sea swells in high tide,
The water in the river flows backwards.
As the battlefield was swelled up by Rama's strength,
I brought you back only to safeguard you, my Lord!

'Fighting continuously,
Your face looked pale and your excitement had waned.   150
You appeared like the cows that roam aimlessly in sun and rain.
Bad omens afflicted you!

'The charioteer has a great responsibility.
He must discern every wish of his master.
He must keep watch over his Master's weaknesses and worries.
He must be in a position to judge what is happening around him.

He should know when the situation is conducive and when it is not.
If one doesn't know when one should drive
The chariot near the enemy
And when to drive it away at an opportune hour, 160
How can one be called a charioteer at all?
I felt that you and the horses needed some rest.
I did not do this in haste.
I'll obey your command. Thinking carefully,
You move ahead;
Do not surge in arrogance. I will not hesitate
To fulfil the obligations to my master!'

Listening to the words of the charioteer,
Ravana's anger simmered down.
Gifting a gold chain to the charioteer 170
And getting excited to fight again, Ravana said:
'You are very loyal to your master;
I am pleased with you, O charioteer.
You are indeed an expert in warfare and military formations.
Drive the chariot to the battlefield swiftly.
Look! I will not return without slaying the enemy.'
The chariot of the Danavendra, lord of the *danavas*,
Moved into the battlefield and stood facing Rama!

Canto Two Hundred and Fifteen

'Land Explosion, Landslide, and Wild Dance of the Sea'

||௬||

Wearied with fighting in the battlefield,
As Shri Rama thought of the ways to win over Ravana,
He recalled the great *Adhityahridaya* hymn
Taught by Sage Agastya. The chanting
Of the hymn would bring to fruition the task one undertakes;
Wash away all the sins; wipe out all worries;
Bestow longevity, and lead one to victory
And everlasting success.
Chanting that divine *mantra*, Rama invoked the Sun-god:

'O Lord! My prayers to you, who lights up the world;   10
You bring in good luck; you are worshipped by all;
You dispel the darkness;
Devas, and Danavas worship you;
Brahma, the Creator; Vishnu, the Protector;
Shiva, the Destroyer; Skanda, son of Shiva;
Indra, the chief of Heaven; Yama, Lord of Death;
Prajapati, the progenitor, Chandra, the moon;
Varuna, the Ocean-god;
Pitradevatas, the forefathers; Vayu, the Wind-god;

Vahni, the Fire-God
Are all manifestations of your radiance.'

As Rama chanted thus, his worries melted away.
He looked up at the sun and took three sips of water devoutly.
He felt as if Sage Agastya himself appeared before him
And performed the initiation
Of the holy *mantra* – *Adityahridaya*.

He then regained the strength to confront Ravana
And his volition grew stronger.
Viewing the fast approaching chariot of the *danava*,
Rama showered arrows.
The chariot wheels rotated so fast
That the entire earth shuddered.
As Rama twanged his bow, sharp arrows
Shot forth like lightning
Breaking the hearts of the onlookers.
Everybody watched holding his breath in awe.
At that point, Lankesha shot *tamasastra*.
The great sound reverberated in the city, at the fort,
And in the hearts of the Lankan people;
It shot like a meteor striking the *vanaras*.
Some caught fire; some were burnt to ashes;
Some became blind; some deaf
And some were scattered away.
Nila, Maruti, Nala, Sugriva, Jambavanta, Angada,
And Lakshmana attacked Lankesha wielding their weapons.
Signalling them with his eyes not to fight,
Shri Rama countered the *rakshasa's* arrows with the *Aditya*-arrow
And he shot the highly potent fiery arrows swiftly.

Elephants and horses ran directionless
And the Danavas screamed.
On the one side, there were the warriors strengthened
By the power of penance;
And on the other, there were the divine accomplishers – the Great Explorers;

The Goddess of Victory was bewildered and swayed in indecision
On which side she should be.
While the *danavas* shouted 'Victory to Ravana',
The valiant *vanaras* retorted by shouting 'Victory to Rama'.
Trikuta and Suvela Mountains resounded
With the shouts of the warriors.

It appeared as if 60
The entire world had assembled there
To watch the battle between Rama and Ravana.
Everyone gave a loud victory shout.

Viewing the huge *vanara* army,
Ravana shot *asura*-weapon. It produced a jet black
Smoke and spread like the tumultuous ocean waves.
Invoking the *mantra*, Shri Rama employed *agneyastra*.
With its outstretched tongue resembling the comets,
The weapon swallowed the *Asurastra* shot by Ravana.

Angered Ravana 70
Shot *Raudrastra*; hundreds of maces, lances, and giant pestles
Emerged from it and hit the arrows of Rama.
Shri Rama swiftly destroyed them all with his *gandharva*-arrows!
Viewing Asurendra – the chief of *asuras* – gazing angrily,
Vibhishana said: 'Before Ravana shoots another great arrow,
O Saumitri, despoil him.'

Shooting a powerful arrow,
Saumitri killed Ravana's charioteer instantly.
The Chandika-flag on Ravana's chariot was broken
And the horses too fell down! Ravana jumped from the 80
Chariot angrily and hurled the powerful *Astaghanta*-weapon
At Lakshmana's chest. He fell down vomiting blood.

Shri Rama dashed to the spot.
Pulling out the sharp arrow, he wailed:
'You gave up your life at last!'
Lamenting thus, he said: 'O Sugriva! Carry Lakshmana

To *vaidya* Prabha's camp at once.
Is it possible to slay Ravana before sunset?
Call Nila, Angada and all others at once.
I will not spare Ravana. Climbing the peaks 90
Of hills and mountains,
You all watch the grandeur of the Great War.'
Saying so, he wiped his tears.

Angered Shri Rama took out
An arrow resembling the radiance
Of the sun and twanged the bow.
The arrow struck like a thunderbolt
And darkness enveloped all around.
Shrieking hoarsely as the mountain birds
Hovered over Ravana's chariot, 100
It signalled bad omen to Ravana;
But it augured well to Rama!

Raghupati, Lord of the Raghu clan,
Aimed a pointed arrow at the flag
Of Dashagriva, the ten-headed one;
It tore the flag into pieces and hit the ground.
Going mad, Dashashira, the ten-headed one,
Shot arrows avidly;
But Rama destroyed them all!

As Ravana stood guffawing, 110
Shri Rama contemplated:
'What is this strange event?
The arrow by which I had slain Khara and Dushana,
The arrow by which I pierced the seven *tala*-trees
And killed Vali,
The arrow by which I threatened the ocean –
How could such arrows now go in vain
Without slaying Ravana?'
He wondered.

The next moment, a fierce duel ensued 120
Between the two great warriors.
The seven seas got turbulent and the sun appeared dull.
The wind stood still and the entire universe trembled.
The *vanaras* and the Danavas exclaimed:
'Sky alone is a match to the sky;
Sea alone is a match to the sea;
The fight between Rama and Ravana
Is a match only unto itself!'
The battle brought in excitement.
As the sun went down, 130
The battle ended for the day.

It was well past midnight.
Lankadhisha, the king of Lanka, had a nightmarish dream
Just before sunrise:
There was no sign of wind, but a thunder struck.
The loud sound of a gale afar was heard.
Atop the Trikuta Mountain, Ravana stood gazing
At the ocean waves. The waves swelled up
Roaring fiercely and then subsided.
It appeared that the earth's protective sheath was 140
Torn apart and the ocean exploded within,
And the entire water body engulfed the universe!
As Adishesha shook his head,
Everything was shattered to pieces – shrubs, trees,
Men, women, and children – young and old alike –
Belonging to every caste, creed and religion –
Were thrown afar!

The Goddess of War is hungry
And she is devouring everyone.
Are tempests, earthquake, *Pralaya* 150
And such other catastrophes occurring simultaneously
To destroy the world?
Shaking his hoods, is Adishesha emitting a stream of poison?

The Goddess of Destruction is smashing, hitting and razing
All the things she comes across; turning the boats upside down
She causes them to sink; she is making everything drown
In the sea of darkness and advancing fiercely.
Whether the glean of love, and the light of peace too
Are drowned in the abyss of the sea!

Variegated forms and scenes flashed before him: 160
Serpents rocking him with their outstretched hoods;
Strange infuriated faces attacking with swords;
Colorful springs jetting out all of a sudden, and so on!

Later, the serpents coiled round Ravana tightly;
Suddenly there was darkness; the heavy sound
Of the waterfall in the dense forest was heard
Like the requiem sung by the million voices
And it resounded in all the directions!

The light from the sky,
Flashing intermittently appears to be driving away the darkness; 170
But, at the next moment,
The engulfing shadow swallows everything.

The battle to gain control
Over the Five Elements is fought continuously.
Nature in all its fury stands devouring everything.
At the last scene, all life-forms are steadily moving
Towards the burial ground and everything meets
With its inevitable end.

The Trikuta Mountain is turned
Into a heap of ashes and has collapsed. 180
Drowned in the ocean of fear and violence,
The hearts of the *rakshasas* are full of deep silence.
A horrendous fear is drilling the hearts of humans
Turning them hollow, draining all their emotions.
Caught in the tempest, the ships are wrecked.

As the *danavas* are sinking,
The *vanaras*, climbing the trees, are rescuing them, offering
Their hands to the *danavas*.
Will this kind of benevolent attitude fill the world?
Can there be an end to racial hatred? 190

Islands and continents have
Submerged in the sea without leaving a trace.
If one's pride clashes with the pride of another,
What happens next?
Nothing but endless pain and suffering!

Does the Lord of Destruction have any mercy?
Everything perishes; but Nature always triumphs.
The entire Lanka is washed away in the fury
That exploded from within.
Everything is covered under water. 200
There will be no more twanging of bows;
No more swishing and clashing of metals;
No more shooting of magical weapons;
No more showers of arrows; and,
No more blowing of trumpets and war bugles.
Aha! The smoke of the graveyard has engulfed
The earth and the sky!

Wailing and crying is heard everywhere.
The waves carry the dead bodies
And smash them against the shores. 210
There is landslide, explosion, and wild dance of the sea.
Everything that is old is washed away
As if a new culture will dawn shortly.
The Nikumbhila-shrine is getting submerged and only
Its cupola is visible now!

As Lanka started
Collapsing, and getting submerged under the sea,
Falling on the ground, Lankesha cried vehemently.

He slid fast on the epoch's downward slide.
He shouted: 'Alas! I am sinking; hold my hand and lift me up.'   220
Sliding from the bed, as he fell on the floor,
The dream got shattered.
Approaching Ravana, beloved Mandodari asked:
'What happened, my Lord?'
Later, she comforted him, fanning and offering him scented water.

Canto Two Hundred and Sixteen

'Win, Win; O the Supreme Being! Let Victory be to You!'

||६||

The army of Ravana comprised millions and millions
Of soldiers; indeed it was beyond anybody's reckoning.
'Which country has this kind of a well-trained army?'
Flaunted Ravana with all his pride.

The king's elephant carried a golden *howdah*.
There were hundreds of chariots loaded with arms and ammunition.
The valiant soldiers wielded an assortment of weapons.
There were personal body-guards to shield the king.
The war-trumpet was sounding aloud.
Bedecked with ornaments, queen Mandodari   10
Bowed to the king's feet and performed *arati* to ward off evil.
Flowers and consecrated rice grains dipped in turmeric were showered
On the king as a blessing.
Seizing the trunk of the elephant,
Ravana got into the *howdah* and was majestically seated there!

Priding on their valour, the *danava* army
Got excited and went berserk in its wild frenzy to wage war fiercely.
Striking their arms excitedly in a challenging fashion,

Roaring loudly and stamping their feet heavily,
The valiant *vanara* warriors too surged forward. 20

Shri Rama saw Ravana
Swinging his sword wildly and felling the heads of his enemies.
With fierce arrows, he was killing the *vanaras* who came invading,
Leaping and jumping. Fuming with anger,
Ravana went wild on a killing spree and appeared dreadful.
Thinking of Sage Agastya and the other great sages,
As Shri Rama twanged his giant bow – Kodanda – the earth shuddered.
The valiant *vanaras* shouted in excitement.
At that instant, Rama and Ravana stood facing each other!
Each one outsmarted the other in twanging their bows; 30
Frowning harder and roaring louder than the other, they fought fiercely
As if they were representing the *danavas* and the humans collectively.
Everyone watched the fierce battle with awe.
The sound of war instruments of the *danavas*
Coupled with the loud roaring of the valiant *vanara* army
Struck like the lightning of ultimate destruction.

As each one outsmarted the archery skills
Of the other, countless arrows whizzed and fell.
As both were ambidextrous,
They steadily wielded arrows with equal ease and ferocity 40
And the entire sky was covered with the rainbow of arrows.
The war of magnificent magical weapons ensued:
As Ravana shot *Agneyastra*, it whizzed emitting smoke and fire;
It blazed as if to devour everything on its way.
Rama, king of the Sagara clan, chanting the Varuna *mantra*,
Shot the *varunastra* in retaliation; as if made of corky wood,
The entire world was afloat in the deluge caused by the weapon.
Swiftly as Lankesha shot *vayuvyastra*, the water drained out completely.
As Shri Rama aimed *parvatastra,* a wild tempest erupted
And stood blocking like a solid mountain. 50

Roaring aloud,
As Ravana shot the magic wheel given by the charmer Maricha,
Shri Rama shot *vaishanvastra*
And dispelled the magic!

Next, as Shri Rama revealed his Omnipresent Form,
The earth, the sky, the planets, and the stars revolved at great speed
And exploded. All the five elements appeared to have converged
In one place; they seemed to be moving away scattering in all
   directions,
And again, appeared to be blending into each other harmoniously.

Dashakantha, the ten-headed one, 60
Viewed in rapture the colossal form of Vishnu
Adorned with thousand heads that measured up to the sky.
Ravana was awestruck for a moment and viewed contentedly
The grandeur of that gigantic form – the embodiment of great
   prowess –
And felt as if he was stung by thousands of scorpions all at a time.

Memories of his past deeds came flooding to him
All at once: Vedavati, Rambha, Dhanyamalini,
And the other women all flashed across his mind.
The innate strength of womanhood took a fierce shape
And getting wild with frenzy, it began to gnaw away at his body 70
With its pointed canines and sharp nails.
Hundreds of vultures pecked at his body.
As Lankesha tried to lift up his hand to drive them off,
His hands stood motionless!
His voice went sore and his legs shuddered.
He felt as if he was repeatedly bitten by hundreds
Of poisonous snakes and the venom spread fast in his body.
As Rama retrieved *vaishnavastra*,
Lankesha regained his consciousness
And the battle resumed at once! 80

As the fight between Rama and Ravana
Intensified, arrows lay heaped like hillocks.

It appeared that neither of them was losing or winning!
Once, Lankesha's strength was on the rise;
And Shri Rama's valour was high another time.
It was a war that seesawed –
Sometime the balance tilted towards the *danavas*,
And sometimes toward the *vanaras*.
The Goddess of War moved across the battlefield
Dancing wild with frenzy.   90

Due to the horrendous nature of the war
The earth shuddered, the horizon swerved,
The planets and the stars got disturbed.
It appeared as if the entire universe was sweltering in the heat
Of the magical weapons; the wind was still;
The sunbeams lost their luster,
And the water resources dried up!

Angered Lankesha hurled
Shaktyayudha and Shri Rama fell unconscious!
The *vanaras* wailed and cried.   100
As Saumitri rushed forward angrily, stopping him,
Pavanasuta, son of Wind, said:
'Let us treat Rama first; later we will fight.'
Vaidya Prabha and Sushena came running to the spot
And administered proper treatment using medicinal herbs.
Pavanasuta stood fanning Rama.
Regaining consciousness, Rama pulled out the arrow and said:
'I am feeling better; you may stop attending to me now.'
Saying so, he got up and twanged his mighty bow – Kodanda;
The *danava* army had a glimpse of the Lord of Death!   110

Seizing a lance swiftly,
Ravana aimed at Rama and prayed fervently in his mind:
'O Divine Mother! Listen to the secrets of my heart.
Swollen with pride, I did not pray to you.
The spring of my entire prowess is dried up now.
Forgive me, O Mother. Show me the way
To capture Rama unharmed and alive

And thus protect Lanka.'
Praying thus, he hurled the lance at Rama.
Frightened *vanaras* ran helter-skelter.   120
The golden radiance of the lance flashed across the sky
And the vision of the onlookers got blurred.

Jambavanta said:
'Wasting no time, shoot a magnificent weapon at once.
The mighty lance has sucked the blood of the regents of Heaven.
It is a deadly lance; you alone should protect us.
I do not know any such valiant one
Who has countered this lance ever before.
This mighty weapon has defeated Kubera, the God of Wealth,
And it has subdued Indra, the chief of Heaven.   130
This is the ultimate weapon of Lankesha
And his future depends on it.
Shoot a magnificent weapon at once.
This is the auspicious hour; if missed,
Such an opportune hour will never come again.
Act with discretion before it is too late.
Look! A good omen is appearing
At the far end of the western hills.
This indeed is the most opportune moment to strike.'

Yonder the far off mountain   140
A huge cloud appeared in the shape of a serpent's hood;
Its posture appeared to be a divine blessing.
Viewing it, Anjanasuta – son of Anjana – said:

'This is the blessing of the universe for you;
It is a symbol of divine script etched only for you.
Not knowing the Truth, Ravana is immersed in illusion.
Employ the *Brahmastra*, the weapon of ultimate destruction –
The infallible Rama-arrow – and usher in the new epoch.
Ah, look! Death in the form of lance is rushing towards you!'

Shri Rama replied: 150
'Wait, wait; Hanuma! I will chant *Adityahridaya* taught

By the eminent Sage Agastya; the power of penance
Will pulsate and exert naturally.
O Hanuma! Get ready to view the grandeur of the scene ahead!'

Saying so, he took out the
Mighty *Brahmastra* from the quiver and shot it.
The mountains shuddered, the sea became turbulent,
And the volcanoes emitted lava.
The *Brahmastra* embodied the prowess of all the three gods:
The radiance of Brahma, the Creator; 160
The will-power of Vishnu, the Preserver;
And the power of penance of Shiva, the Destroyer.
It appeared that Lankesha's end had come!
Brahmastra was created by Brahma; it possessed an amazing halo;
In its feathers, Maruta, the Wind-god was installed;
In its blade, the presiding deity was installed;
Its body was the sky, and its weight was enormous.
Its size was synonymous with the Meru
And the Mandara Mountains.
Such is the great weapon *Brahmastra*! 170

It blazed like the sun;
It emitted fire; it possesses the strength to destroy the *chaturangabala* –
All the four divisions of an entire army – in a single stroke!
It can shatter to pieces the gateway of the fort and
All the weapons in an instant;
It has the power to shake the entire world;
It is the messenger of Yama, the Lord of Death
That can provide sumptuous food
For crows, jackals, and vultures in the battlefield daily.
Such a fearsome weapon is *Brahmastra*! 180
'Win, win; O the Supreme Being! Let victory be to you.' –
Shouted the *vanaras* in excitement!
The army of the *danavas* and the *vanaras* wriggled
And the entire world – animate and inanimate – ruffled.
The battlefield shone like the crimson glow of the setting sun.

Not fearing, Ravana thundered:
'I will seize and break him; I will pin him down;
I will squeeze and crush the beloved of Janaki.'
As he boasted thus and surged ahead frenzied,
The giant arrow approached and struck Lankesha fiercely. 190
As if the darkness of his heart was spilled out
By the luster of the weapon
And engulfed all the three worlds,
The darkness of the moon-less sky spread thickly.
The great weapon pierced Ravana's stomach
And jutted out from his back.
Shri Rama watched that scene.

The *Brahmastra* tore the heart
Of Ravana, and drenched in blood, it pierced through the earth.
The bow of the *danava* slipped from his hand 200
And his life escaped from his body.
Lankesha slid from the chariot and fell on the ground dead.

Good triumphed over Evil.
It was a historical victory at the dawn of the new epoch.
All the darkness was dispelled and Shri Rama glowed like the sun.
The *vanaras* shouted in excitement signalling the victory of Rama.
As the wind blew pleasantly carrying with it the divine fragrance,
Flowers were showered on Shri Rama.

The shuddering of the earth disappeared;
Peace filled in all the directions; 210
The entire sky became clear
And the sunbeams shone brightly.
Sugriva, Vibhishana, Sushena, Jambavanta,
Angada, Nala, Nila, valiant Anjaneya, and *vaidya* Prabha
Bowed to the feet of Rama.
Shri Rama embraced Saumitri endearingly
And later, Lakshmana fell at the lotus-feet
Of Rama with a feeling of deep contentment.

Canto Two Hundred and Seventeen

'Evolution is Life; Diminution is akin to Death'

||౬||

This world is the human-zoo and is home to cruelty;
Strife is a daily routine here;
The wild dance of horrendous destruction has been taking place
Since times immemorial;
Life on earth is wasted away in the frenzy of hatred and enmity
And pleasant gardens are turning into burial grounds.
Insatiable desires are lined up like tombstones
And the flowers of emotions wither away in the sweltering heat.
The loser is subverted in the poison of defeat
And the winner is consumed   10
With the demoniac arrogance of success.
This monstrous vileness never dies even if slain a thousand times
And innocent lives are burnt down like a house of wax!
Evolution is life; diminution is akin to death.
Shri Rama has vowed to make life blossom forth.
Shri Rama has extirpated all forms of false desires.
Shri Rama has scaled the peak of creativity.
Shri Rama has crossed the ocean of life!

When would Shri Rama
Come to live in the heart of every person?　　　　　　　20
How can *Ramarajya* – the ideal State – be established
If truth, righteousness, sacrifice, and peace won't be widespread,
And racial enmity and violence don't end?
When lawfulness and ethics become one's second nature
Ramarajya comes into being on its own.
It is the temptations of the sensory organs
That afflict people continuously
And lead them astray; subduing them
Is a great achievement indeed
And that should be the supreme goal of life!　　　　　　　30

Which is the true source of victory?
Would physical prowess, enormous wealth,
Or the power of penance suffice?
Would *chaturangabala* – a complete army – yield victory?
Kumbhakarna is an example of what physical strength could achieve;
Lankesha is an exemplar of what material wealth could do;
Indrajit is a testimony of what the powers of penance could accomplish!

As Lankesha fell to the ground dead,
Truth triumphed and
The devotees praised Shri Rama:　　　　　　　40

'You alone are the source of all happiness.
Bestow on us the strength to control our senses –
Desires, arrogance, anger, greed, envy and material pleasures –
And fill our lives with success.
O Shri Rama! Reside in the temple of our body;
And bless us, O Lord!

'O Lord Shri Ramachandra!
You viewed praise and blame, happiness and sorrow as equal;
You desire the good of all;
Your victory has instilled a new awakening in the land　　　　　　　50

Of Bharata; all darkness has been dispelled;
Come and bless us, O Lord Shri Ramachandra!

'It is a new dawn for all of us and
The world has witnessed the vision of this new dawn.
As you are the monarch of the world,
Bless us with the strength of body and soul
To turn the wheel of the new epoch.
Liberate us from maya, O Lord!

'O Lord! You are the Supreme Light.
Grant us the goodwill to treat the wives   60
Of other men like our own mothers;
To treat others' wealth like poison;
And make us feel the pain and sufferings of others as our own.
Protect us with love, O Lord Govinda!

'O, the Supreme Being!
You are dear to all and your demeanour is praised by all.
Being truthful in body, mind, and soul
You tread the path of Truth.
You are the traveller on the path of the Great Quest.
You being the Light of the World,   70
Deliver us from all sins, O Lord!

'O, Lord Shri Rama!
You have opened a new door on the path of Great Quest.
Infusing great strength in both young and old alike,
You have guided Bharata to tread
On the path of sacrifice and service.
You are worshipped by all communities and
Thus you bind us all in a spirit of oneness.
Listen to our prayers, O son of Kausalya!

'You are the fountain of life, O Lord!   80
You are the immortal Soul.
You are like the wind that cannot be caught in a net;
You are like the lotus leaf that does not get wet in water;

You wander all over with zeal, yet are not attached to anything;
And you emerge victorious always!
When our lives and senses take the wrong path,
Help us restrain ourselves and bestow on us new values of life.
Help us scale the peak of perfect life.
O Lord! We beseech you; listen to our prayers!

'O, the dweller of Saketa! 90
You are the destroyer of three kinds of afflictions;
You are the protector of those who seek refuge in you;
You deliver us from all evil;
Grant us devotion to you; grant us strength;
Take away our sorrows; you are merciful to the meek;
We pray to you devoutly; dwell in our hearts, O Lord!

'The Wheel of Dharma runs its course at your bidding.
Fill our hearts with the emotion of equality for all;
Wipe out the evil desires, fear and envy from our minds;
Teach us the merits of humility and detachment; 100
Inculcate in our hearts the lofty ideal –
"Helping others is a virtue; causing afflictions to others is sinful."
Grant us the devoutness to cross the ocean of Life.
O, The azure-bodied God! We bow to your lotus-feet!

'O Lord! You are the great embellishment of the world.
You took on many incarnations; Janaki is Shakti-incarnate;
Being united with her,
You are the sustaining force of all life forms.
You are the magnificent one; you are the most charming one.
Protect us, O Lord Raghava, Shri Hari! 110

O Lord! You are the protector of the downtrodden.
We bow to your name and your divine form.
All virtues reside in you; you ameliorate us from all anguish;
Bless us to be in the company of noble souls;
O Lord Keshava! You are the ocean of mercy; be pleased with us!

'Benediction to the one who slew Dashamukha;
Benediction to Lord Vishnu who slew Mura;
Benediction to Saumitri's elder brother;
Benediction to Madhusudana;
Benediction to the son of Dasharatha; 120
Benediction to the son of Kausalya;
Benediction to the one who is revered by the eminent sages;
Benediction to the slayer of the *asuras*;
Benediction to Madhava;
Benediction to Lord Vishnu!'

Calling Saumitri, Shri Rama said:
'Tell the *vanara* army that in the excitement of slaying Ravana,
The wealth of golden Lanka shall not be plundered;
That is my order.
It is not fair to destroy a culture akin to Rama; 130
There is no scope for further attack,
And there is no room for exploitation;
Anyone who disobeys the order, shall be punished with death.
The citizens of Lanka shall not be tormented.
What if Ravana is not alive?
The kingdom of Lanka shall live forever;
O Saumitri! Proclaim to all –
Universal peace is our goal;
Do not be overjoyed by victory; and do not lose heart at defeat;
Do not hurt the minds of others 140
In the joy of celebrating your victory;
And do not drown Lanka in the fire of anxiety.
Look, O Saumitri! This indeed is the spirit of Treta *yuga* –
The epoch of Rama!

Canto Two Hundred and Eighteen

'You have Destroyed the Bridge of Friendship that You have Built'

||๑||

As the *Brahmastra* was sucking Ravana's life,
Grief-stricken Mandodari came running and offered him solace.
Ravana regained consciousness, and wriggling in pain
He turned to his left, and to his right.
Looking calmly at the face of beloved Mandodari, he said:

'Decorate the city with festoons of young leaves.
Let the auspicious musical instruments be played aloud.
Let the women-musicians sing the victory song of Ravana.
Look here! I have won over Rama;
I have seized the matchless valiant warrior   10
Of the world in the stronghold of my fist;
This is my tribute to Janaki; take this and give it to her.
Making Janaki sit on my lap, I will offer her to Rama in holy matrimony.
The volition of the epoch has come to fruition.

'Fill *Pushpaka* – the flying chariot –
With ornaments and gold coins;
Let Rama be crowned the sovereign of Janasthana

And let that be the gift to the bride-groom.
Let the strife end with the union of Lanka and Ayodhya
And let peace prevail all over.' 20

Mandodari said:
'You have spoken from the bottom of your heart.
The entire world was looking at you with
Suspicion and you bore the yoke of blame.
Alas! Not discerning your well-meaning emotions,
The world deceived you and the epoch of Great Quest
Remained completely blind.'

Speaking thus, Mandodari – the virtuous wife,
Pulled out the *Brahmastra* and threw it away shuddering.
Ravana closed his eyes, his head turned sideways, 30
And blood jutted out like a spring.
'Ah! I am doomed; I'm doomed' – lamenting thus
She drowned in the sea of sorrow.

'O King! You, who defeated all the three worlds, were
Capable of assuming any form at will. How could you die?
Though many cautioned you that
Shri Rama was not an ordinary mortal,
You failed to realise that.
He is the Supreme *Yogi*; the eternal God.
He has no beginning and no end. 40
He is Lord Vishnu, the Protector.
He is the consort of Lakshmi, the Goddess of Wealth.
He is the Lord of the Universe and the Incredible Achiever.
By fostering enmity with such a One, you lost your life.

'What shall I say, my Lord?
You were the victor of the three worlds,
But were a slave to the senses.
You lost to Rama, who has won the senses.
I cautioned you many times not to foster enmity with Rama;
But you did not heed my counsel. 50

Making me endure sorrow and suffering,
You departed from this world!

'Janaki has surpassed such virtuous women
Like Arundhati and Rohini in her exemplary character.
You brought her here on the sly.
The sigh of the virtuous wife hit you hard;
Janaki is just an excuse for your destruction.
Let the desires and riches be damned!

'You shone like the moon;
You were a perfect match to Manmatha, the God of Love; 60
And you were radiant like the sun.
But what is your plight today?
Where has your handsome nature
That attracted my eyes disappeared?
Where has your sweet voice that drew my ears hidden?
What has happened to your lustrous eyes?
What has happened to your beautiful, smiling face?
Struck by the arrow of Rama, you are soaked in blood;
Your face has turned sullen covered with the dust of the chariot.
Alas! The accursed widowhood is my plight now! 70

'Till now I was fearless; but no more so;
The pillar of my courage itself has collapsed.
Your body shone like the sapphire;
Your body stood upright like the mountain peak;
Your body was adorned with the many ornaments;
Your body shone with great brilliance;
What happened to your great body in the battlefield?

'Like a porcupine,
Your entire body is struck with arrows;
Your body is all torn apart; how can I see that, my Lord! 80
You appear like the hill split by Indra's Vajrayudha.
Is it true that the kind-hearted Rama has killed you?
You defied even death; how could you succumb to it now?

You shook the three worlds by your valour;
You quelled the eight regents of the directions;
You punished the arrogant ones;
You countered your enemies befittingly;
You nurtured your kith and kin lovingly;
You were highly valiant; you were an incredible achiever.
How could such a one like you bite the dust! 90
My lord, where have you disappeared on the path of no return!

'Look at my sorrow!
Grief-stricken, how can I live without you?
Couldn't you take me along with you?
"The tears of a chaste woman would usher in great sufferings";
There is truth in such a saying.
For bringing Sita stealthily, you were labelled "chief of the thieves."

'Not heeding the words
Of Vibhishana who could foresee even the future
You became a victim of death.' 100
Lamenting thus, she swooned.

Not able to bear the grief,
Vibhishana lamented:
'O valiant elder brother!
Your valour is renowned all over the world;
You who sat on the magnificent throne
Have fallen in the battleground today.
Ah! Your strong shoulders adorned with amulets
Are stretched sideways lifelessly;
Where has that valour disappeared? 110
Where has the idol of righteousness gone?
Ah! Where has the crest jewel of fame vanished!

Has the sun fallen down?
Has the moon sunk down? Has Agni, the Fire-God, turned cold?
Has the shelter of valorous enthusiasm collapsed?
The robust tree that stood majestically,

With flowers of stubbornness, sprouts of bravery,
Fruits of intense penance, and roots of valour, is now uprooted
By the gale called Shri Rama!
Has the elephant in rut been killed by the lion! 120
Has the wind called Rama put out the
Blazing fire called Ravana?
Has the wild bison been killed by the tiger!

'O Lord! I became helpless.
Believing that the path of Truth is visible afar,
I sat crying like a babe in the dark
Goaded with the yearning to take you on the virtuous path
By mitigating your vileness;
How unfortunate that such a desire remained only a mirage!

'Why do I need the throne? 130
Why do I need the Lankan kingdom? I am only a seeker of Truth.
Just like Bharata, I too will stay at Nandigrama
And spend the rest of my life doing penance.
I don't want anything else.
I can't stay in Lanka even for a moment.
Permit me to leave at once.' Wailing thus, he collapsed!

Pacifying the grief-stricken Vibhishana,
Shri Rama said: 'You have rooted out the vileness, no doubt;
But you were not able to save Ravana and fulfil your wish.
Forgive me; I can't sever the link of kinship with Shri Lanka. 140
Ravana was a great patriot; highly valorous and brave;
And a great warrior who defeated Devaraja, the chief of Heaven.
Embracing heroic death, he has attained the heavenly abode.
Abstain from sorrow. You are the eminent elder
To the surviving warriors.
Get up and console all your kindred and the citizens of Lanka!'

'Listen, O Raghava!
Ravana was such a valiant one
Who steadfastly defied the combined attack

Of *devas, yakshas,* and *kinnaras* and emerged victorious; 150
Today, he is killed by you.
What could I say to that!
Who could match such a righteous king who
Looked after his citizens lovingly;
Gave away his wealth in charity;
Carried out the royal duties faithfully;
Read the Vedas, and comprehended its intrinsic philosophy
And lived accordingly,' said Vibhishana ruefully.

Mandodari said:
'Listen, Vibhishana! You were dear to Ravana 160
And a well-wisher of Lanka. Do not desert Lanka!
Who else is the crown prince of Lanka but you?
Ravana had thought of crowning you as the King of Lanka.
Everyone knows how hard you tried to protect the life of Ravana.
Without killing him in the battle,
Ravana had plans to bring Rama a prisoner;
Making Sita sit on his lap,
Ravana desired to give her away to Rama.
You never wished anything bad to your elder brother.
Though you departed from Lanka, 170
Ravana did not want anyone else to be the crown prince of Lanka.
He waited for you to come back to be crowned the king.
After that, he wished to join Vishravasu
And spend the rest of his life doing penance.

'He brought Sita to Lanka
To avenge the humiliation meted out
To Chandranakhi at Janasthana,
And the slaying of the *danavas*.
He was enamoured of her only momentarily;
Without despoiling, he safeguarded the chastity of Sita. 180
Not discerning his high ideals, the world blamed him.
Who could rule like him?
Who else knew so well the art of warfare?

Would such a one like him be born again?
His death is the greatest catastrophe of the epoch!

'The world counts me one among the
Five virtuous women in the world;
Vibhishana is truly a righteous person;
That being so – Ravana who is our own soul –
How can he be so vile!   190

'O Shri Rama! Heeding to the
Words of some ascetics and the calumny of some small chieftains
Why did you kill my beloved and snap my holy matrimony –
I do not know; is there anyone who can answer?
Perhaps this is the path of the Wheel of Time;
Who is there to stop it?
There was a lack of understanding between the two of you;
That lacuna resulted in such a catastrophe!
In the guise of punishing the wicked,
I do not know how many more such massacre lay in wait;   200
The bridge of friendship that you have built is destroyed by you.'
Wailing thus, Mandodari poured out the deep anguish
She suffered in her heart.

Shri Rama replied:
'O my sister Mandodari! You are a virtuous wife indeed;
If it is my fault, forgive me but blame me not.
This is not the time to worry about
What is right, and what is not.
Let us talk about Vibhishana's coronation sometime later.
Let us get Vajrari here and perform the final rites of Ravana.'   210
Hearing this, the officiating priests readied the funeral pyre
With fragrant roots and sandal-woods; spreading the hide
Of the black antelope, they placed
The body of Ravana on the pyre.
Setting up the three sacred fires and
Readying wooden vessel and pestle
They sacrificed a sheep to the holy fire as was their wont.

And dipping its flesh in clarified butter,
They put it into Ravana's mouth;
Shedding tears, all his kindred poured puffed paddy 220
Onto the funeral pyre.

Vajrari, son of Meghanada,
Wearing a wet dress lit the funeral pyre.
Later, he offered obsequies to the dead.
Everyone bowed and returned to the camp.

Truth and righteousness are the foundations
Of good government;
Could a strong army, physical prowess,
Material wealth or authority safeguard any kingdom!

Not discerning this basic principle, 230
Lankesha's kingdom collapsed!
Not discerning the timeless principle that
Righteousness alone triumphs,
Many kingdoms have been vanquished
And are confined to the annals of history.
If one exploits the people neglecting the principles
Of good governance, and beams with pride
That none can match him,
One is sure to bite the dust;
Has anyone seen such a person ever thriving? 240
Righteousness alone saved Rama and gained him victory;
Oppression and exploitation led Ravana to his inevitable end;
And Shri Rama is only a pretext in this entire episode.
Ideologies and laws of the State should guide the king to the right path;
If the king goes astray, the lake of peace will turn turbulent for sure.
The entire world fears the savagery of man's beastliness.
Bravery, self-restraint, wishing others well, truthfulness,
Character without blemishes, forgiveness,
And purity of mind would lead one in the path of progress.
This volition of Shri Rama gained him victory steadfastly! 250

Canto Two Hundred and Nineteen

'When the Entire World is Suffering, Can I Alone be Happy'

||௬||

As the funeral rites got over,
Sun.moning Lakshmana, Shri Rama said:
'Listen Saumitri, as I cannot enter the city,
Discuss Vibhishana's coronation
With Mandodari, and get it done quickly.
Time is running out; I am worried about what may happen
To Janaki and Bharata.
Mandodari is like our mother; bring her to the Suvela Mountain;
I will bow reverently and wash her feet with my tears!

'Vibhishana is a virtuous man   10
And is worthy to be the king of Lanka.
He is balanced in mind, emotion and thoughts.
Handing over the reins of the kingdom to Vibhishana,
Ravana went on many war expeditions; don't you know that!
No one can match Vibhishana's skills of administration.'

To carry out the orders of Shri Rama,
Accompanied by Hanuma, Angada, and Jambavanta,
Lakshmana reached the camp of Vibhishana and said:

'O revered one! Get up; let us go to Mandodari;
You should be crowned the king of Lanka at once.   20
The deadline set by Bharata and Janaki is approaching fast
And I am worried what might become of them;
Every moment is counted and we cannot afford to lose time.'

'What shall I say, dear brother?
It is my misfortune that I couldn't save Ravana
By purging him of his vileness.
I won't come to the city of Lanka.
I have no desire for either the Lankan kingdom, or the throne.
There is no scope for second thoughts.
That is why I arranged Vajrari to carry out the final rites of Ravana.   30
Accompanying Shri Rama, I will reach Nandigrama
And spend the rest of my life doing penance.
The desire to be the king is no longer there in me.
Let Vajrari be crowned the king;
Let Mandodari be the queen-mother;
And Lanka will be ruled well,' said Vibhishana.

Listening to the words of Vibhishana
Everyone was awe-struck; feeling dejected,
They delved into silence.
After a while, Sugriva spoke: 40

'Why do you speak thus?
Shri Rama desires that you alone should be the king of Lanka;
How can you say defy it?
When the voice of the epoch desires you to be the king,
How can you turn your face away and not respond to it?
Drowning in the sorrow of elder brother's demise,
Can one forget one's responsibility, tell me.
Your ascending the throne will not be seen as selfishness;
When the Lankan citizens desire you as their king,
If you turn your back to them, the folks will not forgive you.'   50

He was drowned in worry.
As the emotions of renunciation rose high,

And material wealth and wishful indulgence
Appeared as intense darkness,
The liberal-minded Vibhishana spoke:
'What will I achieve fighting for the throne?
Life is transient; is the throne any permanent then?
The day I deserted Lanka, my responsibility
And bonds with it are severed.
I will not enter Lanka again.   60
Ravana's fame is permanently etched;
He is immortal. Let me not live bearing the brunt of blame that
For the love of the kingdom, Vibhishana got his brother slain;
Let me not be a thorn to the clan;
Let me not be a dead-wood on earth;
And let me not fall into hell in such disgrace!
I must cleanse myself of all such blames;
This torment is unbearable!'

Saumitri said:
'He who is born shall die; that is inevitable.   70
If one runs after wishful indulgence,
One is sure to be afflicted with sorrow.
Youth is followed by old age and everyone knows this.
Forget all such worries. Even when leading a normal life,
One can certainly live like a recluse. Do not fear!'

Baring his heart, Vibhishana said:
'Is there any other fire that is equal to ardent desire?
Is there anything else that is equal to destructive hatred?
My life has turned out to be mean
For getting my elder brother slain.   80
One must win over oneself;
Such a one is truly valorous in the world.
I am guilty of hurting my elder brother.
My mind has become blunt, can it be honed now?
I will burn my sins in the fire of fasting;
Gaining discerning knowledge,
I will try to live a worthy life.'

Saumitri said:
'When you deserted Lanka, reserving the status
Of the crown prince for you,   90
Ravana waited for your return.
When you have become the pinnacle
Of Shri Rama's Great Quest, how can you
Disown your responsibility?
You have tasted things sweet and sour in life;
You have experienced happiness and sorrow.
When you are strong in mind
And are endowed with enviable qualities,
Why do you turn away from the call of duty?'

Vibhishana spoke resolutely: 100
'Enough of this life, yearning for wishful indulgence;
Ruling a kingdom makes one beam with pride,
And pride leads to war.
Is there an end to war and violence?
Deserting all the riches of the world, my elder brother
Ravana walked the path of salvation!

'When the entire world is suffering
In violence and senseless massacre, can I alone be happy?
What grandeur could there be in a throne
That is installed on the granary of dead bodies?   110
I don't know how I can gain knowledge to wash away my sins!

'Diverged roads are beckoning me
Let me snap the ties of bondage.
All-pervading darkness has engulfed me;
There isn't a ray of light or hope.
My soul is engulfed in darkness and my heart has lost all love.
Just like a bird that has lost its way flies through the clouds,
Yearning to purge, my soul is wandering
Everywhere with faltering steps.
Through severe penance I shall burn down this body   120
That has rebelled against the elder brother

And attain salvation.
Why do you force things on me now?

'I will subdue all desires and selfishness;
Do not make me veer off.
I have the desire to dwell near Shri Rama –
The Supreme Being, who sublimating his spirit
From the mundane, has attained perpetual happiness and peace.
Saumitri, you are a *yogi;* discern my intentions
And forgive me.'   130

Listening to the words of Vibhishana
Saumitri was shocked. Discerning the magnanimity
Of Vibhishana, he contemplated in all humility:
'Supreme bliss resides in Vibhishana;
Not fostering the lure of the kingdom in his heart,
He has shed all worldly desires
In his unblemished volition for virtue.
He has shown to the world the grandeur
Of such a strong will.
Through meditation and penance,   140
He upholds virtue of self-restraint.
Renouncing the kingdom with nobility,
He has turned into a *yogi.*'
As he stood contemplating thus,
Vibhishana spoke again:

'Tell me, how I can enjoy the kingdom that isn't mine.
Shri Rama has prophetic knowledge even of the future.
He discerns my mind and would forgive me.
If I enter Lanka, peace will be elusive and torment me for sure.
In Nandigrama I will be in the good company of holy men.   150
Subduing the temptations of the senses,
Quelling the ego, and following
The path of Yoga, I will live in the grace of Shri Rama.'

Saumitri listened to the words
Of Vibhishana – embodiment of supreme sacrifice – dumbfounded.

'I can't convince him anymore,'
Pondered Saumitri and delved into silence.
At that instant, there appeared a bright light in the horizon
And it shone magnificently.

With the lustrous light of the soul 160
A torch burns there – a torch that is imperishable;
A torch that doesn't have any infamy and pollution;
A torch that doesn't have any superstition and anxiety;
A torch without blemish; a torch of guiding light;
A torch that enthuses fresh hopes, instills new courage,
And infuses fresh volition, and meekness;
A torch that signifies the five facets of devotion:
Tranquility, serving the master resolutely, friendliness,
Affection and amiability.
The torch of sacrifice burns in the form of Vibhishana! 170

Saumitri, Sugriva, and Pavanasuta, son of Wind,
Reached the palace of Mandodari swiftly and bowed to her feet.
Not seeing Vibhishana amidst them, she queried:

'Where is Vibhishana?
The hour of coronation is fast approaching.
Janaki is getting ready to give up her life by jumping into the fire.
Ravana's dreams are all shattered.
We should prevent the impending catastrophe!'
Hearing this, Saumitri said:

'Listen, O mother, listen! 180
Vibhishana has said that he doesn't desire the throne of Lanka.
He has decided to go to Nandigrama and do penance;
He feels that it is a befitting atonement for Ravana's death.
Let Vajrari become the king and you be the queen-mother.
Agree to this immediately; do not break the wish of Vibhishana;
This is the auspicious time to act with prudence; if delayed,
Janaki will die, and Bharata too.
Then, will Shri Rama live and will I be alive?
The entire Ikshvaku clan will die, O mother!'

Mandodari replied: 190
'I must fulfil the desire of my beloved.
I will come along with you and make
Vibhishana agree to my words.'
Everyone proceeded carrying the auspicious *kalasha* and mirror.
On seeing the sister-in-law, Vibhishana got up
And bowed to her feet. Lifting him up and wiping his tears,
Mandodari comforted Vibhishana
Just as a mother comforts a stubborn child:

'Stop behaving like a child and be a man.
Ameliorate the *danava* clan. 200
Why do you push Shri Lanka to anarchy?
Do not make the Goddess of Lankan Empire an orphan.
Vajrari is very young and I am drowned in sorrow.
I don't have the energy to hold the scepter and discharge the duties.
If you don't take up the reins of the kingdom now, Lanka will collapse.
Do not push all of us to disappointment. Agree to what I say!'

'O mother! To me, you are highly respectful.
I have extirpated all desires for the kingdom from my heart;
Being a recluse in spirit, how can I fulfil your wish now!
Accompanying Shri Rama, I will go north. 210
I will spend my life responding to the call of the epoch
To forge the culture of friendship and harmony between
Lanka and Ayodhya. What more shall I say, O mother!
You know everything; do not compel me;
Do not be an impediment to the call of the epoch.'
Said Vibhishana resolutely.

Canto Two Hundred and Twenty

'She's Emerged Victorious from the Ordeal by Fire; Accept Her.'

||☉||

All preparations were ready for the coronation ceremony.
The valiant *danavas* and *vanaras* brought holy water
From the four seas and poured it into the golden *kalasha*!
Vajrari was prominent among the assembled crowd;
There was the council of ministers;
The citizens stood watching with excitement.
Mandodari was serenely silent.
At that moment, the royal priest lifted up the golden *kalasha*
And chanting the Vedic hymns poured the holy water
On the head of Vibhishana. 10
The crowd cheered gleefully.
All anxiety vanished into thin air.

Overcome with anxiety as to
What might be the plight of Sita,
Anjaneya and Mandodari moved towards Ashokavana.
They saw Sita circumambulating the holy fire.
As Trijata, Surama and all others helplessly viewed Janaki,
To their utter dismay, Janaki jumped into the fire.

Viewing Sita's act, Mandodari rushed in
Exclaiming, 'what a ghastly act,' and without looking back 20
She entered the womb of fire and lifting up Sita
Safely brought her out of the flame.
Everybody praised Mandodari for her brave act.

Pacifying Sita, making her sit on the lap,
And touching her chin affectionately,
Mandodari said endearingly:
'What is this, O daughter?
You jumped into the fire, and pulled me too into it.
Are you not satisfied with the fiery ordeal
Of life we have tolerated 30
And endured as women till now?
The man of the epoch should arrive and
Put an end to women's ordeal!'

'O Mother! Why this ghastly act!
I am the servant of Rama; I have brought
Shri Rama's message to you:
"Shri Rama has succeeded in his avowed mission;
With your good fortune, we have gained victory in the war.
Saumitri, Sugriva, Hanuma, Jambavanta,
And the other valiant *vanaras* 40
Have fought day and night for my victory.
As I am not supposed to enter a city during the period of exile,
I will wait for you at the foothill of Suvela Mountain."
O Mother, this is the message from Shri Rama,' said Hanuma.

Janaki said:
'I have heard the tidings of Shri Rama's victory.
The deadline was over and I couldn't stay alive;
As Rama's volition was fulfilled in the slaying of the *danavas*,
I am only an excuse for the task of Great Quest.
Being engrossed in his kingly duties, Rama has forgotten me. 50
Why should I live? Why this life?
I decided to sacrifice women's sufferings in the sacred fire.

I will wash away the blemish of abduction.
Do not push any woman to the kind of sufferings that I've endured.
This is my only plea and the only goal of my life.
The virtue of mother Mandodari has saved me
And restored me to life!'

'Lankesha had the noble intention to
Give you away as a daughter making you sit on his lap.
Not discerning this, the world blamed him squarely! 60
He was enamoured of you only initially; soon, he realised his folly
And abstaining from food and sleep, he suffered greatly
In the fire of repentance hoping to make amends!
Your blood-shot eyes too burnt his desires.
Later, Shri Rama refined him through his arrow.
He is like your own father Janaka to you.
Forgive him. Let the anger and desire
Of Dashashira be washed away
In your tears.' Overcome with anxiety,
Mandodari said so. 70

'The touch of your lap has comforted me
And I feel that I am in Heaven; I am blessed indeed.
The feeling that Shri Lanka is my maternal home has grown stronger.
The hatred that got sprouted in Panchavati grew up into a big tree;
And I cursed you then; forgive me, O mother!
I wasn't able to discern the truth.
All the past episodes are flashing across my mind one by one.
It was stupid of me not to discern the fatherly love
That was latent in Lankesha's heart.

'I am the sinner who has severed my mother's holy matrimony. 80
I do not know what ghastly punishment awaits me.
I was not able to understand the gracefulness of his heart
Who put me under the care of the loveable damsels
Like Trijata and Anala.
I've become an exemplar to the popular belief that
Women have very limited understanding and are short-sighted!

Your chastity saved me from fire.
Now, as parents, both of you have given me a new life.
O mother, my salutations to you and to Lankesha,' said Janaki.

'O daughter, let us go to the palace. 90
I will bedeck you with ornaments and take you to Shri Rama
In *Pushpaka,* the flying chariot.'
Janaki replied: 'No, mother; Shri Rama is an ascetic.
Hence I will see him wearing the humble apparel made of tree barks;
That is how he lives and I follow suit.'
Later everyone set out for the Suvela Mountain.

As soon he saw Janaki,
Shri Rama's joy knew no bounds.
Mandodari said: 'O Shri Rama, appear before Maithili –
The daughter of Mithila city; she is wearied a great deal; 100
Fire wouldn't burn her; I have brought her here from the blazing fire.
Look! Her character is without blemishes; she is pure and chaste.
She has emerged victorious from the ordeal by fire; accept her.'

Rama shed tears of joy.
Janaki, the virtuous wife, who had emerged victorious
From the ordeal by fire leaned against Rama's chest
And at once Rama embraced her endearingly.
What could be said of that sweet moment of union!
The eyes and the faces said it all!
Silence drew them together beyond the realm of words. 110
The earth was thrilled and there was serene silence everywhere.
As dusk approached, the horizon turned crimson.
As two hearts became one in the warmth of love,
The wind blew gently.

As the night descended,
Mother Earth felt great joy!
The palm fronds swayed like the fan.
Faces bloomed with happiness; minds felt elated;
All the senses awakened;

The roar of the springs sounded like the musical notes 120
Cheering the union of Rama and Sita;
Like festoons, the clouds hung in the sky;
There was laughter and jubilation in the air.
The union of Rama and Sita brought immense joy to all!

As the call of duty beckoned him,
Shri Rama summoned the team of doctors Prabha and Sushena
To the Suvela Mountain and in the presence of Hanuma,
Sugriva and Angada spoke thus: 'Let us walk through
The battlefield and treat the injured and console them.
Vanaras and *danavas* are all like one family now. 130
Bring the severely wounded to the camp.
Hand over the dead bodies to their families;
If no one claims the bodies, perform mass cremation.
Provide shelter and food
To all the orphans in Lanka and Kishkindha
Without any discrimination; everyone is equal.
I am vowed to live a life of universal brotherhood!'

Accompanied by Janaki and
The valiant *vanaras*, Shri Rama came to the battlefield.
The task of nursing and treating the injured gathered momentum. 140
Viewing the dead bodies, Rama spoke
In great pain choked with emotion:
'Look at the lifeless bodies of the great warriors!
They laid down their lives fighting for their country
Forgetting their own families and comforts;
Patriotism coursed through their veins
In every drop of their blood.'

Along with *vaidya* Prabha,
Janaki nursed and treated the wounded with her own hands
In the battlefield. 150
Someone's hair was dishevelled;
Someone else's neck was broken and tilted sideways;
Somebody's mouth was gaping;

Someone else's eyes were wide open;
And many lay there soaked in blood.
The horrendous sight of the dead made the onlookers twitch in pain!

Climbing over the mounds of cadavers,
Crossing the river of blood tottering, panting for breath and crestfallen
Shri Rama, Saumitri, and Sita walked in the battlefield
Unmindful of the splinters of arrows and other weapons   160
That pierced their feet as they moved.
Nursing and treating the wounded soldiers with great compassion,
And pacifying them,
They returned to Suvela Mountains.

Cautioning Shri Rama who was lost in compassion,
Saumitri said: 'Listen, O dear brother!
Bidding adieu to the *vanaras*,
Let us proceed to Nandigrama swiftly.
Bharata is waiting there for us; if the deadline is crossed,
He will jump into the fire and sacrifice his life.   170
Let us send the valiant Anjaneya at once to pacify Bharata.
Let us not be unduly blamed that we are here to expand our empire.
Let us depart from Lanka quickly.'
Rama heard Saumitri silently and nodded his head approvingly.

The queen-mother arrived at Suvela Mountain with Vajrari!
Vajrari bowed to the feet of Shri Rama, Janaki,
Saumitri, Sugriva and Jambavanta!
Embracing him, Shri Rama blessed:
'Following the path righteousness
And spreading the fame and grandeur of Shri Lanka,   180
May you live long, my son.'
Janaki blessed Vajrari and all others blessed him too.
Tears of joy filled everyone's eyes.

'Give us permission to depart;
To me, you are venerable like mother Kausalya.

I cannot repay the help you have done to me.
Vajrari is the king now; you are the queen mother.
Let the glory of Lanka shine bright in every epoch.'
Saying thus, Shri Rama bowed to the feet of Mandodari.
All others followed suit. 190

'All right, all right, Rama!
I do understand you and your actions;
You are the Lord of the Universe in human form;
Let your blessings be on us.
Let the blessings of Janaki, the Shakti-Goddess, be on us too.
I'll gift you *Pushpaka*, the flying chariot; do not refuse it.
I have the responsibility of ensuring Janaki's safe return to Ayodhya.'
Saying so, she bowed reverentially.

As the *Pushpaka* got readied,
With a heavy heart, Rama spoke to all who had assembled there: 200
'O Sugriva! I will not forget the help that you have done to me;
O Pavanaja! I will never forget the help that you have done to me;
O Angada, Jambavanta, *vaidya* Prabha and Sushena!
You have all worked hard and worn yourselves out day and night for me;
How can I forget it!
I won this inviolable Lanka because of you all.
I built the bridge across the sea with your help.
Lanka is liberated because of you.
I am an ascetic. What can I give you now?
Ravana's treasure is not ours. 210
Return to your camps and rest well.
Do come to Ayodhya for the coronation ceremony.
I will host a banquet in your honour and reward you well.'
Hearing this, tears of joy filled everyone's eyes.
As the chariot moved in the direction of Nandigrama,
All watched the chariot with eyes wide open until it disappeared from sight.

Canto Two Hundred and Twenty-one

'Stop, O Venerable One! Shri Rama is Arriving'

॥६॥

Pushpaka, the flying chariot, moved under the command of Shri Rama.
Viewing the environs, Shri Rama said to Janaki:
'Look over there dear;
Look once again at Shri Lanka situated in the Trikuta Mountain
Like the peak of Mount Kailasa.
Lanka is a magnificent city built by the great sculptor Vishwakarma;
But now, caught in the ravages of the war,
Lanka is sprawled with the slush of flesh and blood.
The *vanaras* and the Danavas were massacred,
But it was inevitable! 10

'This is the place where Ravana was killed in the fierce battle;
This is the place where Kumbhakarna was slain;
Look at the place where Prahasta was killed by Nila;
Hanuma killed Dhumraksha in this very place;
Look there! That is the heroic land where Sushena quelled
　Vidyunmali.

'Look over there, O dear!
That is the place where Saumitri killed Indrajit;

Look at the monumental spot where Virupaksha,
Mahaparshwa, Mahodara, Akampana,
And such other great warriors and patriots laid down their lives. 20

'Look here! This is the grand bridge
The *vanaras* have built with great acumen
Under the leadership of Nala
To cross over the holy waters of the mighty ocean.
That is the Mainaka Mountain which provided a resting place
For Hanuma while he was flying across the ocean.
Look! We are approaching Kishkindha, the city of Sugriva –
One of the most wondrous places of the world with its
Magnificent mountain ranges and verdure forests of exquisite flowers.

Janaki said: 30
'My Lord! Let the chariot stop;
Let us take the *vanara*-ladies with us and go!'
At Sugriva's behest, Ruma, Tara and the other damsels climbed
The chariot in great excitement; Janaki was overjoyed
And the chariot moved ahead.

As they were passing through the
Places at which they had stayed during their exile in the forests,
Shri Rama and Sita recollected the past episodes.
Shri Rama spoke:

'Look! What you see there is 40
The magnificent Rushyamuka Mountain rich with minerals of gold;
It was here that I first saw Hanuma;
This is the place where forging friendship with Sugriva,
I had vowed to kill Vali.
Lotuses have blossomed in the Pampa Lake;
Sitting on its banks, I had wept profusely
In the pangs of separation from you.

'I met the pious old lady named Shabari in this holy place.
This is the place where I had killed the long-armed Kabandha.
In the same place there exists a huge tree; 50

It is the spot where Jatayu, the giant eagle, fought with Ravana
To rescue you and gave up his life.

'Look over there!
That is the warfield where I killed Khara, Trishira, and Dushana.
Look there! It is the hut of leaves we had lived in.
Goddess Nature is in full bloom like a charming, youthful damsel;
She is drenched in rain and is looking
Enticingly colourful for your sake.
Clouds in the western direction look
Like hills hanging from the sky.   60
Look at the grandeur of the setting sun
Playing hide and seek amidst the clouds!

'Look! This is the Godavari river.
On its banks, the hermitage of Sage Agastya looks resplendent.
View the hermitage of ascetic Sutikshana.
Look, here is the sacred land of the eminent sage Shrabhanga.
That is the place where I killed the gargantuan Viradha!

'View the place where Atri and Anusuya did their penance.
I cannot forget the beauty of the Chitrakuta Mountain!
This is the very same place where Bharata,   70
Accompanied by the mothers, had arrived
To take me back to Ayodhya!

'Look at the beautiful hermitage
Where Bhagirathi river flows meandering in three directions.
View the green woods and the birds flying in flocks
To nameless distant lands; they are free from all desires and bonds;
They sing the song of all cultures and fly yearning for peace.

'This is the town called Shringavira where the
Great devotee Guha resides.
Look at the banks of the Sarayu river and the sacred hermitage 80
Of the eminent Sage Bharadwaja
Where oblations to fire are performed always.
Trees, shrubs and flowers all stand in pristine beauty here!'

On the fifth day of spring,
Shri Rama came to the hermitage of sage Bharadwaja.
Everyone bowed to the feet of the eminent sage.
As Rama exchanged pleasantries, the sage spoke:
'All your mothers are safe and healthy;
The citizens of Saketa are overwhelmed with joy.
Listen, O Raghava! Offering prayers to your footwear everyday   90
Bharata, like an ascetic, has been carrying out his kingly duties.
He stands waiting with a yearning
For your arrival day in and day out!

'You wore the garment made out of the bark of a tree;
The boon of Kaikeyi had hurt and pained me then.
I felt very sad worrying whether Rama was destined to wander
In the forests eating roots and tubers;
By killing the *rakshasas*, you ameliorated the world from evil
And moved on the path of Great Quest;
As you have now returned fulfilling your volition,   100
All my pains have disappeared.
Today, Kaikeyi's boon has become the boon of the epoch;
What a pleasant surprise!
The way the *vanaras* searched for Sita,
The way the son of Wind set fire to Lanka,
The way you built the bridge across the ocean,
The way you fought and won the great battle,
And the thrilling story of how you slew Ravana –
All these great tasks of yours are magnificent history!

'You are eminently virtuous.   110
Your history is a great epic indeed.
Sage Valmiki will write that epic
And become an immortal poet laureate;
The world will worship him!'
Hearing this, everyone was happy
And bowed to the eminent sage!

Hearing the news of Shri Rama's arrival,
Guha came running to Bharadwaja's hermitage.

Prostrating himself at the feet of Rama and the eminent sage,
Guha lamented: 120

'O Lord Shri Rama!
You have won over many hardships;
I couldn't come with you.
Compared to the immeasurable services Saumitri has done to you,
What I have done is so trivial;
I am a great sinner!'

Rama consoled him thus:
'Guha, why do you worry?
You followed my commands like *yogi* Bharata and settled here.
You helped me cross the river Ganges then 130
And thus wrote the preface to the great history of ameliorating
   the world;
You are indeed the stage-director of Rama's Great Quest.
Your help has been great indeed; do not feel sad.'

The trees of the hermitage, heavy with fruits and flowers,
Spread fragrance all around. The beehives were abuzz
And the aroma of fresh honey dribbling from them filled the air.
The rivers were overflowing and formed many magnificent waterfalls.
Shri Rama and all others ate sweet-smelling fruits sumptuously
And danced happily!

As commanded by Rama,
The valiant Anjaneya, seeking details of the road leading 140
To Nandigrama from Guha, and worrying
What might happen to Bharata
As the deadline was fast approaching,
Rushed to give the good tidings to Bharata.
Overcome with immense joy and excitement,
Watching Mother Nature on his way, Anjaneya contemplated:

'Nature's bounty suffers no loss here;
The infinite energy latent in the soil
Breathes life into trees and plants.

Millions of living organisms thrive on these trees and plants 150
And the Wheel of Life turns around; in its downward motion,
Millions bite the dust and become one with the soil again
Only to be re-born in various new forms.
This endless life-cycle is the great Wheel of Nature!

'Mother Earth has immense strength to bear and protect.
This progressive, marvellous energy is the driving force
Of all creations in Nature; it proclaims over and over again
The existence of God. By the blessings of Shri Rama,
Everything is virtuous!'

As he travelled further, 160
He came across the sacred Parashurama Lake.
Later, he crossed the Gomati and Valukini rivers.
Arriving at Kosala, and greeting the citizens on the way,
He reached Nandigrama. Fragrant flowers welcomed him.
Wherever one turned one's eyes,
One could see there beautiful gardens with a variety of flowers.
Men and women, young and old, were all relaxing merrily.

Bharata is an embodiment of sacrifice.
He was wearing a garment made of tree-barks and his hair was
  matted.
He had become weak suffering the pangs 170
Of separation from his dear brother.
Living frugally on roots and tubers, winning over his senses,
Worshipping the footwear of Shri Rama every day,
Bharata has carried out the kingly duties
In the name of Shri Rama
As if Shri Rama himself was present there.
Living like an ascetic with purity of mind and soul
He appeared like *brahmarshi,* the sage supreme.

The enlightened citizens carried out
Their duties efficiently and with responsibility as advised 180
By the council of ministers, commanders-in-chief, and the priests.

Thus, the citizens tread on the path of righteousness.
Ah! The framework of political administration in the new epoch
Has already in vogue in the form of Bharata!

'Ah! The deadline is over;
I cannot stay alive anymore: I will enter the fire.'
Deciding thus, Bharata raised a huge fire
In the front yard of the hermitage.
As he was circumambulating the holy fire with folded hands,
Pavanasuta, son of Wind, 190
Arrived at the spot like a tempest and said:
'Stop, stop, O venerable one! Shri Rama is arriving!
I am the servant of Rama. Do not enter the fire;
This is the command of Rama!'

As Bharata came near him,
Bowing to his feet, Hanuma stood with folded hands.
Bharata's joy knew no bounds and he asked:
'What did you say? Has Shri Rama arrived?
Tell me the truth!'

Hanuma spoke: 200
'Everyone calls me Hanuma;
I am the messenger of Rama.
I bring you good tidings.
Slaying Ravana, accepting mother Sita, accompanied
By Saumitri, Vibhishana and the *vanaras*, he is coming;
He will be here in no time!'

Listening to the good news and
Forgetting himself, he reclined for a minute.
Regaining composure, he embraced the valiant Anjaneya tightly.
Tears of joy rolled down his cheeks 210
And soaked Anjaneya's shoulders.
Bharata spoke:

'O Hanuma! You have brought the happiest news;
How can I reward you, O Hanuma!

I have been worrying whether Shri Rama would arrive or not;
I feared what might have befallen him –
Was he drowned in the ocean;
Where on earth was he hiding, and so on –
As there was no news of Rama's whereabouts,
And as the deadline was fast approaching,   220
I was determined to enter the fire.
As if my own life has come back, you have arrived here.
O my soulmate, tell me everything about Rama.'

Hanuma said: 'How can I describe that virtuous history!
Shri Rama entered the dense forest of Dandaka inhabited
By the wild animals like lions and tigers;
The forest is inaccessible to the humans.
As *rakshasa* Viradha attacked him, he killed Viradha.
Later, he reached the hermitage of the eminent Sage Sharabhanga.
Giving Rama the volition to protect the virtuous people,   230
The sage moved to Heaven.

'While Rama was living in Panchavati,
Surfeited with lust, Ravana's sister Chandranakhi tormented
Shri Rama and Lakshmana. As her desire was not fulfilled,
She became angry and rushed to attack Janaki
And was punished rightly by Lakshmana.

'That led *rakshasas* like Khara, Dushana, Trishira
And others to attack Shri Rama;
But he killed all of them single-handedly.
As Chandrankhi complained to Ravana,   240
With the help of Maricha, Ravana made him roam in the form
Of a magical deer; Sita desired the magical deer
And Shri Rama went after it.
Fearing that some danger might have befallen Rama,
Sita sent Lakshmana, who was guarding her, to find Rama.
At that moment, Ravana arrived there
And abducting Sita, took her to Lanka city.

As Jatayu, the giant eagle, arrived to protect
Sita from Ravana and fought with him,
Ravana killed Jatayu. On reaching Lanka, he placed Sita   250
In the Ashokavana and began to pester her to be his wife.

'Not finding Sita in the hermitage,
And getting the news from Jatayu,
Rama and Lakshmana set out into the wild forests in search of Sita.
Killing the *rakshasa* Kabandha
As they reached Rushyamuka Mountain,
I was very fortunate and blessed to meet them there.
Befriending Sugriva, Rama killed Vali.
With the support of the *vanara* army, Sugriva searched for Sita.

'As Rama's servant,   260
I crossed the sea and set Lanka on fire.
Discerning Janaki's whereabouts, I delivered her
The message of Rama. Receiving *chudamani* –
A jewel worn on the head –
As a token of recognition, I returned.

'What shall I say, O Lord!
For liberating Janaki, a bridge was built across the sea to reach Lanka.
Later, a fierce battle ensued in which Rama killed Ravana.
The Goddess of Victory blessed us and Rama reunited with Janaki!

'What shall I say, O the venerable one!   270
Vibhishana was to be crowned the king of Shri Lanka.
Giving up the throne, he desires to be with Shri Rama.
He will come to Nandigrama now;
And like you, he would lead the life of an ascetic.
Vajrari is now the king of Shri Lanka
And Mandodari is the queen-mother!

'To look at, Ravana's army was huge
When compared to ours. But as the morale of the
Lankan army was on the decline,
It turned out to be a boon for us.   280

As we had the protective blessings of Shri Rama,
And the valiant *vanaras* on our side,
And determination and faith were our forte,
Ravana's progeny suffered a humiliating defeat and collapsed.
The epoch's door of Fortune opened up.

'Rama will arrive at Nandigrama any time now.
He will narrate all the magnificent incidents to you in greater detail.
He will embrace you tightly and praise you immensely.'

The deadline was about to get over.
Anxiety gripped Hanuma and he narrated Shri Rama's feat a
  little longer. 290
As he felt that he heard the sound of hooves approaching near,
Thinking that *Pushpaka* chariot was approaching Nandigrama,
He gazed in that direction stretching his neck out.
He saw only a cloud of dust, and nothing more.
Deeply agitated, Bharata said:

'Enough, enough, O Hanuma!
What is the use? Time has elapsed beyond reckoning.
You are honest and your words aren't lies.
But the truth is that I am bound by my vow.
The world shouldn't blame me that with a secret desire to live, 300
Bharata spent time listening to the story of Rama,
And failed to fulfil his promise!

'It is the hour of Pushya star;
I shall not be stopped now; I will jump into the fire.
Salutation to the God of Fire; salutation of love to you;
And salutation to the virtuous citizens of Saketa.
Before my death, I heard the good tidings
Of Shri Rama, Janaki and Saumitri.
Now I can die in peace.
My vow is fulfilled. Why should I live anymore?' 310

Saying thus, with folded hands, bowing to
The holy fire as he circumambulated one last time,

The citizens looked at him dumbfounded.
Agitating in pain, Hanuma said:
'Alas! I couldn't save Bharata, crest jewel of the Ikshvaku clan;
This is the most awful failure of my life;
What's the use me being alive anymore?
I will follow Bharata into the fire
And give up this body.'
Vowing thus, he stood determined to follow suit! 320

Canto Two Hundred and Twenty-two

'You set in Motion the Great Wheel of Ramayana'

||६||

The fire blazed as if to devour
The most precious jewels of the universe;
Bharata circumambulated the holy fire thrice
And Hanuma followed him.
As they decided to jump into the holy fire,
All the directions resounded with the wailing.
With tearful eyes, Mothers Kausalya, Kaikeyi and Sumitra
Prayed to the Sun-god to protect Bharata and Hanuma.
As the citizens pined and wailed,
The sound of their wailing reached Kailasa,   10
The abode of Lord Shiva!

At that moment, like lightning flashing bright
In the dark of the night, there appeared a radiant light.
Everyone watched it awe-struck.
Shatrughna jumped in joy shouting –
'Victory to Shri Rama; victory to the Virtuous One' –
And embracing Bharata tightly, said:
'Shri Rama has arrived; O Bharata, stop and wait!
Pavanasuta has spoken the truth and hasn't lied.

Look there! It is *Pushpaka*, the flying chariot; 20
Look at the magnificent chariot crafted by Vishwakarma –
The architect of Heaven.
Look how it is shining like the sun at dawn!
Ah! Look over there! Shri Rama, Saumitri, our sister-in-law,
Sugriva and Vibhishana are all there.'
Hearing Shatrughna, Bharata danced with joy
And everyone acclaimed victory to Rama in unison!

The auspicious hour of union
Of the wonderful brothers has come.
Glowing with radiance like the full-moon, 30
Shri Rama got down from the chariot.
Choked with emotion and pleased with seeing Rama,
Like a stone, Bharata stood still for a moment.
Recovering, he fell at the feet of Rama, and said:

'O Raghupati! You have arrived at last!
You ameliorate the world; being merciful to me, you have arrived;
Come, come dear brother, bless me; I have regained my life now!'
Lifting Bharata, Raghupati embraced him endearingly,
Cuddled him lovingly, and forgot himself for a while.
Recovering soon and resting the head of Bharata on his chest, 40
Rama stood comforting him and rid him of all his weariness
   and sufferings
Of the past fourteen years!

Later, Bharata went to Janaki
And bowed to her feet with tears of joy.
Next, he went to Saumitri and hugged him lovingly.
He bowed to the feet of the mothers.
Overcome with gratitude, Bharata lovingly hugged Sugriva,
Jambavanta, Mainda, Dwivida, Angada, Nila, Vrishabha, Nala,
   Sushena,
Gandhamadana, Sharabha, Gavaksha, and Vibhishana.

Then, Bharata spoke with supreme happiness: 50
'Look Sugriva! We are four brothers;

And you are the fifth one now;
Your help is great indeed; you looked after
Shri Rama, Lakshmana and Janaki;
You brought them to Saketa safely.
I do not have the words to praise and thank you enough.
You have built the bridge of friendship
Across Lanka, Kishkindha, and Ayodhya.'
Looking at Vibhishana, he said:
'You have helped us, and it is my good fortune
That Mother Janaki has returned safely;
Ah! That was indeed the most difficult task,
But accomplished with ease.'

The agony of the past fourteen years has ended.
The vine of sorrow had now yielded flowers of happiness.
The fragrance of flowers had spread everywhere.
Everyone donned the mantle of excitement.
Approaching Kausalya, Kaikeyi and Sumitra,
Everyone bowed to them with tears of love.

Overcome with happiness,
Shri Rama said: 'The journey of fourteen years
Has come to an end today.
We roamed the forests, crossed the seas, and won the battle.
Where can one find a liberal person like you, O Bharata!
On seeing you, sorrow welled up in me;
Brotherly love is an intense emotional bond.
You all have suffered the pangs of separation from us.
Let us bid farewell to the pangs of separation, and sing songs of joy;
Let us dance in happiness; let us forget all the pain.'

Approaching Kausalya, Shri Rama bowed to her feet.
Looking at her grief-stricken, sunken face,
He spoke thus with great compassion:
'I transgressed your command and went to the forest.
I am responsible for the death of my father; forgive me.
Experiencing all kinds of sufferings, we have returned now.'

Hearing Shri Rama, overcome with joy,
Kausalya stood in serene silence.

As Rama approached Kaikeyi,
She said: 'Come, my dear son.'
Touching her feet reverently, 90
And with a smile on his face, Shri Rama said:
'You faced the blame of the people and
That turned out to be a boon for me.
Maid Manthara is fortunate; goading you to seek the boon,
She bore the brunt of abuse; the kind act
Of you both was a great help for me.
I learnt many things during my sojourn in the forests.
I travelled far on the path of Great Quest.
It helped me to liberate Lanka from the grips of Dashakantha.
With my volitions fulfilled, I have returned home safe. 100
You helped me to accomplish all these; you aren't guilty at all.
Your blessings helped me to spread my message
In the form of Ramayana; it is indeed your gift to the world
And it will become an immortal one, for sure.
You are the motivating force of this fame and glory.
You suffered in the mire of blame for all these fourteen years
And endured great sorrow;
But it has given me a sweet fruit at the end of it all.
O mother how incredibly affectionate you are!

'Because of you, the fame and glory 110
Of the Raghu clan has spread to all the corners of the world
The king's love for the son has been proclaimed all over the world.
The sacrifice and love of Bharata, Saumitri
And their brotherly love, have all become well-known in the world.
The virtue of Janaki as a dutiful wife is shining bright in the universe.
The valour of the son of the Wind has spread far and wide.
The world got to know the power of Rama's arrow.
You set in motion The Great Wheel of Ramayana!'

As Rama praised Kaikeyi thus, she said:
'You are the noble man who viewed both sorrow and happiness alike. 120

Has the fault of sinful Kaikeyi appeared to be a virtue to you!
You bore the yoke of the epoch's existence;
You bore the pain of the world, and saved it from destruction.'

Later, Rama bowed to the feet
Of the clan Guru, the eminent Sage Vasishtha.
The throng of citizens that stood there with their hands folded
Appeared like lotus buds; Shri Rama saluted them all.
At that instant, placing the footwear in front of Rama, Bharata said:

'O Lord, listen!
It is indeed the citizens, and not I, 130
Who safeguarded the kingdom of Ayodhya
That you had trusted into my care.
The citizens are the preservers of righteousness;
Following the doctrine of
"Equality for All in Prosperity, Life, and Justice"
And upholding the philosophy of the "Common Good of All,"
They have built an ideal State.
There is no greediness, envy, or fear of theft;
There is no robbery or murder for gain.
Such is the greatness of the new State they have built. 140
They proclaimed this ideal State as *Ramarajya* – the kingdom of Rama –
The likes of which neither existed in the past, nor is it likely in the future!
Ah! Building such an ideal State during all these fourteen years
They have etched a magnificent history!

'There are no law courts;
No lawsuits; all houses keep their doors always open;
There isn't theft in the least; no contemptible acts;
No harsh punishments; no death sentence;
No torment of policing either; cheating
And kidnapping don't exist at all; 150
No arrogance or pride of power;
No scope for exploitation in the name of religion;

None is affected with the discriminatory feeling of being high or low;
No inferiority or superiority feelings either;
No racism, no partisan attitude;
No room to suffer humiliation and no need
To live in fear of afflictions;
None fears the challenges of living life
With dignity and self-respect!

'Listen, O Lord of Kosala! 160
The tree of *Ramarajya* has spread its fragrance;
The tree of *Ramarajya* has yielded sweet fruit,
The tree of *Ramarajya* has spread its grandeur throughout the world
And up to the sky.

'The bounty of the kingdom has grown ten-fold by your grace.
I will hand over to you the kingdom, the treasury,
The complete army, and all;
Please accept and bless me.
The land is blessed by your arrival;
The blame that was hurled at me has disappeared!' 170

Viewing Bharata's unflinching devotion,
Astounded Vibhishana, with tears rolling down his eyes, said:
'O Bharata! You seemed to be an embodiment
Of Bharata, the mother-land!
Blessed are you! You have built a shrine –
Not with bricks and mortars –
But within your own heart – your body is the temple of Rama;
You have built mansions of harmony in every mind.
You are the architect for building such shrines in the citizens' minds
You have dusted out the dirt and smoke of envy and fostered love. 180
You have etched a tapestry of diversity governed by the voice of
   the majority
And you have sanctified such a world-view of inclusiveness!'

Bharata said:
'The lure of the five senses and the afflictions

Of "the group of six enemies" –
Lust, anger, greed, infatuation, conceit, and envy –
Are natural for everyone; but restraining all these follies
And sublimating them is the secret of one's success;
Just as the moon spreads pleasant moonlight
Absorbing the scorching heat of the sun,   190
If we extract the immortal Juice of Life from the world itself
And dedicate it to the world again for sustenance,
Ravana-ism – violence – will die a natural death
And Rama-ism – peace – will be on the rise.
This is the great, grand message of *Ramarajya*.'
Hearing this, everyone nodded their heads in appreciation.

The notion of what you call *Ramarajya* should be
A universal one; it must go beyond the barriers of time and place,
And should exist for ever. It should not be construed
That *Ramarajya* is limited just to the kingdom of Ayodhya   200
And be attributed only to Rama, but should go beyond both.
This doctrine is applicable to the entire universe.
Ayodhya-Shri Rama is only a symbol!

'Why do you all glorify me?
This sort of eulogy isn't fare.
I am a king, and I have done my duty.
Do not build mansions of victory.
Why should there be victory celebrations?
Spend the money on welfare activities;
Serve the poor and the needy and keep them happy.   210
Let everyone realise that wiping the tears
Of the grief-stricken, in itself is an act of worshipping me;
That itself is an act of chanting hymns in my praise!

'As life is a continuous churning
And a coming together of nature and man,
One should carefully monitor the outcome of such a joint venture;
Whether life-sustaining technology emanates or
Only life-threatening acrimony is spewed out, needs to be watched.

Be on your guard always, and proceed in the right direction.
  Beware!'
As Shri Rama advised and alerted them thus, 220
Everyone was witness to such a noble vision of the epoch!

Canto Two Hundred and Twenty-three

'Urmila and Lakshmana are the Paragons of Love and Sacrifice'

||६||

In the thatched hut on the banks of the Sarayu river
Urmila sits upright in excitement.
The arrival of Saumitri fills the forests and hills with excitement,
As the pangs of separation of all these fourteen years has come to
   an end,
In the sea of Urmila's heart, waves of happiness swelled
And dancing with joy hit the banks.
As the early morning's dream turned into a reality,
Donning white apparel, Urmila sits with a smile on her face.

'O Mother! This is the hour when the pangs of separation
Have disappeared; I will bedeck you;   10
Come here,' said the maid.

Urmila said:
'As the wick of magnificent amour has become dull,
Do you try to make it shine bright once again?
As my youthful fourteen years have slithered fast,
Would your decking up bring back those years of my youthfulness?
Money, precious gems, and riches could be got back;

But can the charm of lost youth be brought back, tell me, O friend!
My beloved won't approve of mere beautification.
When the hour of union of our hearts has come, 20
What value the pompous external ornamentation has, tell me,
   dear friend?'

The maid spoke:
'Listen princess! When the mind is happy,
Beauty and youthfulness are instinctively felt in the body.
All your pain will disappear then.
You have been lovelorn for long enough.
If you are waiting eagerly for uniting with your beloved,
Why this indifference?
When he sees you in a soiled dress,
He will be overcome with grief. 30
But if you appear before him bedecked with ornaments,
You will catch his eyes and it will make him happy, for sure!

'Forget the song of lost love; sing the song of union.
Like the lotus that blooms with the appearance of the sun,
O the lotus-faced princess! Be like the freshly bloomed lotus.
Your tear-drops have turned into pearls,
Ah! Pick up the pearls like a royal swan.'

Urmila replied:
'The sorrow of separation is over;
The time of happy reunion has come. 40
I'll bathe my beloved with tears of love.
Now, I am no longer the young princess that I was years ago.
Give me fresh clothes. I will offer my body and soul to my beloved.
As I am overwhelmed with joy,
Why do I need any ornaments at all?'

At that instant, her beloved arrived there.
As Saumitri stepped in, the maid moved aside.
'Like my own life is restored to me, you have come, O my beloved!
You are the treasure of my life and you have come.

You are the treasure of sacrifice and you have come.
You are the treasure of love and you have come. 50
You have come; yes, you have come; O my beloved, you have come!
You are the apple of my eyes and you have come.
You are the epitome of happiness and you have come.
You are the epitome of virtue and you have come.
You are the love of my life and you have come.
You are the source of my strength and you have come.
You've grown in beauty and you are laden with love.
You are indeed the symbol of Great Quest.
You are the infinite source of salvation.'
Saying so, she coyly melted into the arms of her husband! 60

Years of separation ended in a timid reunion.
In the ocean of their hearts, both sailed happily in the
Boat of oblivion; discovering the dream-world in the union of
 their hearts,
They were engrossed in unfathomable bliss.
Awakening from the stupor slowly,
Saumitri spoke to his beloved tenderly:

'In you, I see the lovelorn idol of Love.
In you, I see the guiding light that lighted my path with the
 torch of love
When I traversed the Dandaka forest in intense darkness.
In you, I see the *yogini* who offered her all 70
To the holy feet of Shri Rama and Janaki.

In you, I see the great ascetic who has grown weak in body
Through intense penance.
I see my own soul in you and I see myself in you!
In you, I see the moon without the halo.
In you, I see the flower glistening in dew.
In you, I see the grandeur of natural beauty sans any ornaments.
Youth surges like the overflowing monsoon stream full of dirt and
 slush.

But now we have matured in love
And everything appears pristine like the calm autumn lake!' 80

Urmila said:
'Tell me, whether my memory tormented you in the forest.
Tell me, whether it became an impediment in serving Rama.
Tell me the story of Rama and Janaki in detail.
Tell me all about your great expeditions.
I stayed on the banks of the Sarayu doing penance
And my dear friend looked after me day and night.
You must have suffered enough in the forests.
How you confront the wild animals and the savage *rakshasas*;
How you endured hunger and thirst; 90
How you bore the intense pain of separation from the city of Ayodhya,
The citizens, the mothers, and the kindred; tell me, my Lord!'

Saumitri said:
'Forgive me, my love.
I deprived you of the comforts and luxuries of the palace.
I put you through suffering and loneliness.
I punished you by making you lovelorn for long.
I forced you to live like an ascetic while still young.
In the spring of your life, you endured the chill of winter.
Should anyone be punished for no fault of theirs?' 100

Urmila said:
'Do not speak like that.
Through meditation, I am enriched in my soul.
I've discerned the ways of the world.
Life and greatness are all transient and they pass off.
Life fades away at every passing day.
Love is the only truth. Love defies time.
Is mere enjoyment of all pleasures the sole aim of life?
The last of the four objects of a man's desire – salvation – is our only goal.'

As night fell, 110
Moonlight spread across.
Fragrant breeze blew across gently.
Urmila and Lakshmana, the paragons of love and sacrifice,
Were engrossed in the bliss of reunion
As if they did not exist in the world but the world existed in them.
As they melted into each other's arms in deep contentment.
Urmila's face shone bright, lit by the moonlight.

Canto Two Hundred and Twenty-four

'You should Sing the Magnificient Song of Unity'

||◉||

Summoning the attendants, Bharata said:
'Mend the stretch of road from Nandigrama
To the palace of Ayodhya;
Sprinkle water on the road and
Let the road be strewn with flowers;
Decorate the road with festoons and hoist flags all along.
Let all decorations be over before sunrise.'

All preparations were done well.
All the eight ministers of the council
Were bedecked with gold ornaments; 10
In all grandeur, they got into their chariots.
Commanders were holding weapons in their hands;
Mounted on horses, they were holding the flagstaff.
All the queen-mothers climbed into palanquins.
The screeching of the chariot wheels, the blowing of the conch
And the excitement of the grand preparations filled the place.
Grooming their matted hair, and donning a silk robe
Shri Rama and Saumitri stood ready.
Donning a splendid dress Janaki walked along

Accompanied by the wives of the *vanaras*.
Wearing a wonderful dress and magnificent ear-rings,
The valiant Anjaneya, glowing like Devendra,
Stood next to Shri Rama.

Shri Rama climbed into the chariot,
And none other, but Bharata himself was the charioteer.
Shatrughna was holding the Royal Umbrella;
Vibhishana was waving the moon-shaped fan.

The procession moved on.
All were singing and dancing joyfully.
Sugriva was mounted on an elephant;
The rest of the valiant *vanaras* were astride horses.
The sound of trumpets and the victory shouts
Of the citizens filled the place.
Rama was surrounded by the council of ministers.
Grandly decorated cows marched right
In front of the procession.
Beautiful damsels were carrying sweets.

'What a strange thing I see!
The road is lined up with camping tents.
Whether the people who came out of the city
To see me off when I left Saketa –
Have they all been living on the banks of the river
For all these fourteen years and not returned to the city?
Have they lived donning garments made of tree barks?
Have they carried out meditation and penance?
Have they stayed back thinking –
"Let Shri Rama return; until then
What work do we have in the city"?
Is that what they have on their minds?
When deaths have taken place in their homes,
They have not returned.
Where are the tears in their eyes to shed?
Enduring thirst and hunger,

Have they lived turning into skeletons?
Who can match these citizens in such sacrifice
And penance in this epoch?'
Saying so, getting down from the chariot,
Shri Rama hugged each and everyone, wiped their tears,
And bowed to the elderly.
Sumantra then spoke: 60

'The children born since the day you left the city,
Haven't been christened; obsequies
To the dead haven't been performed;
Auspicious ceremonies haven't been observed;
And gold and apparel shops haven't been visited.'
Hearing this, dismayed at such show of love and affection,
Rama shed tears copiously.
Pacifying the virtuous citizens, he proceeded.

The tree of Ikshvaku clan was attacked
By parasitical plants. The banks of the lake 70
Where Raghupati used to swim and play were broken.
And the water was contaminated.
The cow-shed that king Dilipa
Looked after so well was covered with cobwebs
And was filled with eerie silence.
The gardens where king Aja roamed
Were all deserted and dilapidated.
With the news of Rama's arrival,
What a marvellous transformation now!
Ah! Saketa now stood resplendent with its former glory. 80

It is a journey of happiness and exuberance –
A journey that unlocks the shackles of sufferings and slavery;
A journey that proclaims libertation;
A journey that signals that none is a weakling;
A journey that proclaims the ultimate Truth;
A journey that lights up the torch of magnanimity;
A journey that wipes out greed and amour;
Ah! It is Shri Ramayana Mahanveshanam –

The Journey of Great Quest.
The noose of tempting amour was severed.   90
The gateway of the new dawn was wide open.
Requiem for all the evils was sung
And the onerous anxiety disappeared.
The time to lead a new life with new vigour was nearing.
It was indeed the time to sing a new song for the new dawn
And all the stone-hearts melted away.

As the procession moved further,
A cool breeze of dynamism and enthusiasm blew afresh
And the strength to imbibe the precept
Of values increased a hundred-fold.   100
As the ladies showered the place with fresh flowers,
Women carrying the holy water-pots said in unison:

'Blessed are we,
As the upholder of Truth and Righteousness
Shri Rama has returned;
Good days have come again;
The lost riches and splendour
Have returned and the eclipse is over.
The city of Saketa was all lit up and looked resplendent.
Though Shri Rama is the monarch,   110
He appears simple like a common man;
Though married, Shri Rama appears like an ascetic;
He dwells in everyone and he is endowed with everything.
Today, all our dreams have come true.
All hearts are overflowing with pleasure and excitement.'

Shri Rama left Ayodhya on the fifth day
Of the bright fortnight of the first lunar month
And has returned now after fourteen years.
The adventures of Hanuma have become a household talk.
Watching Sugriva and the other valiant *vanaras* with awe,   120
Everyone is praising them.

The procession entered the city.
The streets were decorated with colourful *rangoli*
And the fragrance of musk filled the place.
They sprinkled rosewater and fragrant incense of bdellium
Filled the place and brought joy to everyone.
They erected variegated festoons all over
Ladies performed *arati* and sprinkled Rama with flowers
And rice grains dipped in turmeric.
To ward off all evil,   130
The women waved pearls and gems in front of Shri Rama
And cast them away.

The entire palace bustled with activities.
Elephants with golden howdahs, chariots, horses,
Soldiers on foot – all moved in a line with grandeur.
Ladies were all dressed greatly for the occasion;
Adorning colourful dresses, glittering ornaments,
And wearing flowers on their heads,
They walked with a slight stoop in the procession
As the weight of their ornaments coupled with the weight   140
Of their heavy breasts!
Some ladies, fearing the suspicious looks of their husbands,
Disappeared into the palace coyly.

Raghupati entered the city in the procession
And then came to the palace.
He brought happiness to both the citizens and the kindred.

On the command of Shri Rama,
Bharata respectfully led Sugriva
To the mansion surrounded with *ashoka* trees
And seated him on a magnificent bedstead.   150
As Saumitri made all arrangements for the comfortable stay
Of the *vanaras*, everyone was happy.

On the orders of Sugriva,
Vegadarshi, Rushabha, Panasa and others
Set out to bring holy water from all the four corners.

Shri Rama said:
'When I was to be anointed the crown prince then,
And when I relinquished it in your favour,
You abdicated the throne saying, rather sternly,
That it wasn't of any use to you; 160
But the time for it has come now.
In the coronation ceremony that is going to take place now,
Customarily, you would be anointed the crown prince,
And that is inevitably so.
You are the eldest of the brothers after me;
Do not say 'no' now.'

Saumitri replied:
'O brother, you know me well!
Have you forgotten how we have lived
In the past fourteen years? 170
When the entire world is praising
That Rama and Lakshmana are inseparable soulmates,
Calling me crown prince,
Why should you separate me from you now?
When all the footprints in the path of Great Quest
Have blended into one,
Why are you segregating me now, tell me!
Don't say ever that this is the reward for my services!
It would be the last straw that I would ever wish to hold on to;
Do not entice me with this as the well-deserved reward 180
And sever the path of Great Quest.
Bharata must be anointed the crown prince.
That was what our father wished for; fulfil the father's wish!'

As she listened to the abdicating words of her son,
Sumitra started shuddering.
Her mouth went dry. As her son's stoicism struck
Her heart painfully, she said:

'You are the upholder of Truth!
You glow in the radiance of Truth.

Having lived with Shri Rama, you have scaled 190
The highest peak of culture!
You are glowing like the crest jewel of Adishesha
And you are radiant like the sun.
The glow of infinite creation resides in you.'
Saying so, she hugged her son endearingly,
And choked with emotion, she forgot herself.

Hugging Lakshmana tightly,
Bharata said with pain: 'Listen, O elder brother!
What is so great in the status of the crown prince?
Does the power of authority bring any happiness? 200
Do riches bring any peace?
When you abdicate that status, if I accept it,
I would only be a doll in a lifeless garden.
Could a calf ever carry the burden easily borne by a great ox?
Could any other bird mimic the majestic walk of a swan?
What should I do now?
Does the shaft that churns soot,
Ever show the grandeur of lightning?
O Noble Soul! If only I had come after you that day,
My bond with the kingdom would not have existed. 210
Oh, I was hoodwinked!
Since you abdicated the throne,
I got entangled in the kingly duty of administering the State.
I have become like a caged bird in the bargain,
Whereas you have grown
Like a free bird that flies high uniting earth and sky!'

'Blessed is Bharata, the motherland,
That has witnessed your sacrifice;
Blessed is Bharata, the motherland,
That has witnessed Urmila's sacrifice. 220
Let the path of Lakshmana turn
Into Lakshmanayana and protect everyone.'
'Victory to Lakshmana; victory to Urmila;
Victory to Shri Rama; victory to Janaki,'

Proclaimed the people in excitement,
And eagerly awaited the auspicious hour
At the break of dawn!

As Urmila and Lakshmana retired
To their private chamber,
They were overcome with a sense of fulfilment.   230
Viewing her beloved intently –
He who was aglow with the unparalleled virtues of the world;
He who was radiant with sublime spirituality;
He who was resplendent with everlasting piety –
She said:

'Ah! The great dream has turned into a reality today.
You have quelled the insatiable power-mongering among nations;
You have become an upholder of Truth and Righteousness.
In the land of plenty, tears of the poor and the miserable,
And the blood of martyrs, are flowing like a stream;   240
They all are waiting to be consoled;
Lift them up from misery and guide them well.

When the bountiful earth stands
Inert yielding nothing great
You infuse her with strength
And make her exuberantly vibrant again.
Be the harbinger of harmony and well-being;
Build the golden bridge that is unaffected
By the ravages of time.
Let all new forms emerge from the old.   250
Put down the impediments and quell the temptations
And you surge ahead steadfastly.
Discover the secret treasures hidden in the soul of man,
And reveal it to the world through your Great Quest.
Let the dried up tree, grow roots and branch out well!
Let all good things on earth flourish profusely and grow skyward!

'Let your mind traverse all barriers of time and space.
Imbibing strength from the old, show them the new path.

The poor are afflicted and ruthlessly exploited
By the greedy bloodhounds.   260
O beloved! Surge ahead and protect them
And cleanse the world of all oppressions and inequality!
Drive away violence in all forms
And bequeath the sweet fruits of religion and culture.
Through sacrifice, you have accomplished perfection.
By renouncing wealth and power,
You have gained contentment
And you have discerned yourself!

'You are blessed!
Give away to the world the knowledge   270
That you have gained through penance and hardships.
Cultivate universal love and brotherhood
In the minds of the people.
Teach the world the joy of selfless service and sacrifice.
Let the vision of unity be imparted by you
To unite all hearts in love!
Let all the qualities and emotions of universal friendship,
Peace and harmony be bestowed to the world by you.
Be you the magnificent poet who envisions such a New Dawn.
Be you the great explorer of Science and Aesthetics.   280
O Lord! Lead the world towards the horizon of eternal evolution!

'Having obtained such profound perceptiveness
Being in the company of Shri Ramachandra,
You are endowed with the task of reforming the minds
Of the people caught up in the vortex
Of power, greed, and selfishness.
Everyone should re-discover Rama in their souls.
This self-revelation alone can liberate us from all evils.
When that realisation dawns on us,
The difference between the knower and the knowable   290
The seeker and the sought shall no longer exist!
Let us all strive for such discernment!

Ah! You have gained great spiritual strength.
When caught in the whirlpool of pleasures,
Deviating from the path of virtuous evolution
Man falls into the abyss of debasement.
Today's world is enmeshed in revenge and anger;
It is caught up in the vortex of hatred and discrimination;
There is disparagement and strife
Among religions, sects, and cults; 300
Senseless violence is causing bloodbath;
And man is pushed into the abyss
Of frustrating disappointment.
O Lord! You should sound the bell of awakening.
You should sing the magnificent song of unity.'

Canto Two Hundred and Twenty-five

'The Great Song of Shri Mahanveshanam Reverberated Everywhere'

॥௬॥

As hymns and prayer songs were recited at the auspicious daybreak,
As birds sang the glory of Rama,
As the musicians sang and played on their instruments excitedly,
Shri Rama woke up, and attending to the morning rituals,
He stood ready for the coronation ceremony!

The throng of citizens gathered in the palace with excitement.
Holy waters of the Ganga, Godavari, Kaveri,
And the Narmada was brought.
Sacred waters of the oceans from
All the four directions was fetched.   10
The bouquets made of lotuses and lilies were readied.
The holy fire was set up and
The auspicious instruments were sounded.
Scented waters and precious gems were kept ready.
Eight damsels, tuskers, horses, chariots, swords, bows,
White royal umbrella, *chowries*,
And a bull with a golden chain,
Were all ready for the ceremony.
The throng jumped and danced in excitement!

Look! To the right of Rama's throne, 20
Royal chairs are placed for the
Crown Prince Bharata and Princess Mandavi.
Holding the holy *kalasha* and mirror,
Damsels sang benedictory songs.
Shri Rama, Janaki, Bharata, and Mandavi
Entered the royal hall majestically.
As they occupied their respective thrones,
Victory slogans were proclaimed aloud
And the Brahmin-priests chanted Vedic *mantras*.

Eminent sages – 30
Vishwamitra, Bharadwaja, Durvasa, Jabali
Jaimini, Matanga, Mrukandu, Agastya
Vasishtha and Vamadeva – were all present there.

Sugriva, Jambavanta
Angada, Sushena, Nala, Nila,
Gandhamadna were all assembled.
Lakshmana and Shatrughna were standing there.
Sita is Goddess Lakshmi indeed;
She remained seated on Rama's lap on the left.
Beautiful ladies performed the *arati* to Rama. 40
At that point, Sage Agastya stood up and blessed Rama heartily:

'Shri Rama has won over the inviolable Ravana.
Who can match Rama in all the three worlds?
He is compassionate; he will protect all the fourteen worlds.
He is the lord of the lords, and the consort
Of Lakshmi, the Goddess of Wealth.
May he live long and protect the citizens!'

As the oblations to fire and other rituals
Of coronation took place, the people watched it all
In great excitement. 50
Chanting the holy verses, sage Vasishtha
And the other sages poured holy water from

The *kalasha* ritualistically on Rama's head.
In the presence of all the ministers,
The sages put the diamond-studded royal crown
That came as a legacy from emperor Manu in succession,
On Rama's head and the coronation ceremony culminated with it.

On that auspicious occasion
Shri Rama gifted millions of milch-cows
To the poor, the destitute and the deserving; 60
Further, he also gifted thirty crores of gold coins
And a variety of glittering ornaments.
None who beseeched gifts was ever refused
And as no one heard a 'no' from Shri Rama,
Everyone felt extremely happy.

Later, he honoured Sugriva
With a gem-studded gold chain that shone bright
Like the sun. He gifted to Angada magnificent epaulettes
That shone like moon-beams.
He called Mainda, Dwivida, Nala, and Nila 70
And gifted them grand dresses and ornaments
And expressed his happiness.
Vibhishana and Jambavanta received gifts
That befitted them and they felt extremely happy!

At that moment,
Taking out a pearly chain from her neck,
Janaki looked at her husband and the assembled *vanaras*.
Discerning her mind, Shri Rama said:
'Gift the chain of pearls to someone
Who is courteous, fearless, efficient, valiant, radiant, 80
And intelligent, and with whom you are extremely pleased.'

The blue-eyed Sita, calling Hanuma,
Gifted him the chain of pearls endearingly;
As the valiant Anjaneya donned the chain on his neck,
He looked like the majestic Himalayan mountain
Resplendent with silver clouds!

Those who do not love and respect other religions
And spread communal disharmony will be punished and sent to jail.
Those who harm the lives and property of the people, 190
And those who torment others goaded solely
By self-righteous attitude, shall be punished severely.

'If the citizens wish to take on themselves
The responsibility of protecting the barrages,
Ponds, and highways,
I will provide them financial aid.
It is essential to curb all vices
Like immoral trafficking, gambling and alcoholism.
I'll sternly subdue all the evil forces
That harm the welfare of the people! 200

'I will provide quality education to people
Of all castes, creed, and religion without any discrimination;
And there won't be any partiality in dispensing justice.
Priority will be given to safeguarding health
And supplying pure drinking water.
I will provide jobs to all those who wish to work.
It isn't right to have separate laws for every person;
I will propagate a uniform civil code for all.
You as conscientious citizens should curb exploitation,
Extirpate all ignorance and quell all the evil forces with determination. 210
Patriotism will protect us to live freely as a nation.
Let every one of you live zealously nurturing the spark of life.
Let the notion of fatalism that prompts one
To accept one's lot helplessly
And to shirk responsibility being driven
By a sense of hopelessness be eradicated completely.
Do not be ignorant like a frog in the well!
Do not glorify the notion that God would
Descend on earth in one or the other incarnations
And liberate you from all bondage and grant you salvation! 220

'When your mind is elevated into a shrine of virtues,
Why do we need temples of brick and mortar at all?

As the councils of citizens are ruling in every province and village,
As a king, I shall reflect only the collective will of the people
And I shall remain only a symbolic head of State,
And like a lighthouse, watch over the affairs
Of the State dispassionately.
When a single drop of elixir turns into an ocean,
I shall feel fulfilled. 160
I shall be the guardian of your awakened conscience.

'There is only one God for the entire universe.
He is solely responsible for creation, preservation,
And destruction. He is free from birth and death.
He is ubiquitous and He is eternally new.
There's no other religion; no other path for *Ramarajya*;
Eminence alone is its religion.

'Protecting the nation, and achieving progress
In all spheres, are the twin goals of Economics –
This awareness is essential to a king 170
And he must also discern what the nation wants most.
When a king is thus guided,
Where is the scope for dictatorship!
Would treating the citizens as slaves be called ethical?
Whether governing a State in a self-willed fashion
By imposing military rule be considered a sign of sovereignty?
Should anyone flaunt himself as a king?
Everyone praises Bharata as the Land of Righteousness.
Decentralisation of governance is the best policy.
It's not fair to curb the thoughts of the citizens. 180
Let's uphold the principles of
Cooperation, peace, harmony, and equality!

'There will be no room for corruption
And I won't tolerate even the slightest
Inefficiency, dishonesty, and laziness.
If a farmer does not toil, I will impose penalty on him
And I'll confiscate his land and give it to the one who toils.

Food was served without any discrimination.
Savouring the delicious meal, everyone ate sumptuously.

In the evening,
All citizens assembled, curious to know
What Shri Rama would speak
And what his message might be.
Everybody was waiting eagerly.
Shri Rama spoke in a solemn, resonant voice:

'Look! The power of the throne
Is like a razor-sharp sword; if vested in good hands, 130
Everyone is benefited.
And in the hands of a fool, it is a great catastrophe.
The ruler should always be guided by magnanimity and prudence.
Just as a mother looks after all her children equally well,
A king should treat people of all races without any prejudices
Whether they are high or low, rich or poor!
Just as mother earth nurtures all humans without any discrimination,
A king should shine possessing such a quality of munificence.

'You have called this *Ramarajya*, the ideal State.
I will protect its greatness befittingly. 140
If you remain alert, lethargy will disappear;
Everyone will discover the new path.

'Let us console the afflicted.
Let us ease out the hardships of hunger and thirst.
Let us eradicate oppression, suppression,
And exploitation of all sorts.
Let us protect the lives of all.
Let the vision of universal brotherhood guide us all.
Do not think that I am the sole king and will rule over you.
It is the power of the community of citizens that empowers the ruler. 150
Did Bharata rule the kingdom? How did the kingdom run?
Why then, this sovereignty now,
And why this scepter of authority?

The valiant Anjaneya praised Rama devoutly:
'O Raghurama! You hold Kodanda bow in your hand;
Protect us. You are brave and valorous;
Let victory be to you always. 90
You are the one who killed Trishira, Khara and Dushana!
You are the one who mitigated the burden of evil on earth!
O Lord! You are upright, noble and an ocean of compassion.
You are the protector of the meek and the destitute
And you are the inexhaustible source of all grandeur and charm.
You make the gods happy.
You allay the tormenting dilemmas of the human minds.
You are kind-hearted like a soft flower,
Yet you are tougher than a diamond.
O Lord! Free our minds from all temptations 100
O Lord! Cure us of all suspicions in our minds.
O Lord! Dispel all darkness.
O Lord! Quell the lust and anger in us.
O Lord! Destroying our conceit and arrogance,
You reside in us, O Lord!
O Lord! Protect your disciples; allay their fears.
Help us to cross the sea of mundane existence, O Lord!'

As the coronation ceremony was well-accomplished,
The banquet was readied.
There were golden cauldrons filled with rice; 110
Huge pails were filled with milk, curd,
Clarified butter, *payasam*, and a variety of sweets.
Spicy eatables, sweet made of jaggery,
Fruits, *papadams*, pickles, buttermilk were all kept
Ready to be served. Enticed by the aroma
Of mouth-watering dishes,
Everyone sat down for lunch.

Tents were pitched everywhere.
In the precincts, extensions, lanes and by-lanes, halls,
In the front-yard of the palace, and in all the places 120

Why should there be a temple for me?
The time for change has come.
Cultivate liberal attitude and come out
Of the confines of parochialism.
Listen! Here's the message of *Ramarajya:*
Let it be your goal to treat others as your own.
Treat the sinful ignoramus with compassion.
Let your heart throb with a feeling of fellowship for all.   230
Allow knowledge, education, and the wealth of power
To flow freely in the public domain of mutual trust
For the greater good of all.
Open the door of *Ramarajya* to each and everyone
And sing the anthem of *Ramarajya* everywhere.
Write a requiem for all kinds of exploitation.
Let not calamities deter you.
Let sacrifice and equanimity be your guiding light.
Truth alone is supreme
And the one who knows it,   240
Attains self-realisation and godliness!
Respect the eminent sages
Who always meditate on such noble tenets!'
This message of Rama was cherished by all the citizens.

Love all and treat everyone equally –
Shri Rama has shown this to the world by his own example.
Did he not get friendly with the untouchable Guha?
Did he not develop friendship with the king of eagles?
Did he not bow to the love of the aged tribal-woman Shabari?
Did he not treat the mountain and forest-tribes as his own?   250
Did he not empower Vanaja and the other women
By imparting education?
Would the likes of eminent Shri Rama, Saumitri,
And Sita be born again and again?
If the king is righteous, his citizens will tread the path of virtue.
But if the king is sinful, his citizens too will tread the path of sin.
Remember the proverb – 'As the king, so his subjects'.

In *Ramarajya*,
All the citizens have abstained from vengeance and envy.
Subduing the temptations of the senses,   260
They live adoring each other.
Believing that each one is a seed of the universe –
A light bestowed to the world –
Each one shines being a speck of
That great blazing Universal Light!

The cycle of life is boundless and eternal;
It revolves like the spokes of a wheel.
The ways in which the human mind thinks
And the ways in which beauty may be perceived are
As infinite as the tempestuous ocean;   270
The one who seeks something tangible in it is a scientist.
The poet describes the emotions
Of truth, beauty, and benevolence.
He spreads the message to end exploitation and oppression.
He harmoniously unites the hearts of people
Belonging to different classes, castes and creed.

It is not easy to describe *Ramarajya*.
Wherever one looks, one can see the bright gardens
Filled with fruits and flowers all through the year,
In all the seasons. Animals and birds have forgotten   280
Their natural enmity. The bees are abuzz
Sucking the honey from the flowers.
Gentle breeze is soothing everyone.
Swans and cranes are all dancing in joy.
All differences between castes, creed,
And races have disappeared
And the emotion of universal fellowship
Has bloomed everywhere.

There is no drought or pestilence,
No excessive rains; no tempests and floods;   290
No inundation, earthquakes or fire disaster

And *Ramarajya* is not blighted by freezing cold
Or sweltering heat!

Though Ravana is dead,
The vestiges of such vileness still permeate the world
And devour the whole world just like cancer.
Therefore, it is inevitable
That war between Rama and Ravana –
The battle between Good and Evil –
Takes place in every epoch. 300
The search for truth and righteousness is therefore eternal.
The chaff should be blown off
And all the good grain shall be carefully preserved and saved.

If the vital energy that is latent in the hearts
Of people belonging to all castes and creed is tapped,
It will be like unearthing a gold mine!
The epoch's strength hitherto suppressed shall explode
And Shri Rama, Sita, Saumitri, Urmila, Anjaneya,
And Vibhishana will manifest in every human heart,
Paving way for the common good of all, 310
And that's what I desire most!

Man appears to be the same since
The time of his creation; man has undoubtedly
Become more intelligent;
But has become beastlier than the beasts themselves!
Becoming a slave to unlimited wants,
Man is enmeshed in suffering devoid of peace and happiness.

Though man successfully rules over the external world,
Not discerning and ruling over the inner world of his soul,
He finds himself caught up in strife and endless pain. 320
When the path of Great Quest becomes expansive
With the sole aim of ameliorating the world,
Results undreamt of will emerge.
That is what I yearn for – the fruition of volition!
Bharata, the mother land, is home to Vedanta philosophy.

But today, divisive sectarian tendencies raise their ugly heads
And haunt like a specter pushing us to slavery;
The very edifice of the nation is collapsing.
If we extirpate parochial sectarianism,
And embrace our rich heritage, 330
We shall stand upright holding our head high,
With our feet anchored firmly on the solid ground of tradition.
That is what I yearn for.

The desire to wage war is born in
All the human minds; the dark cloud of terrorism
Engulfs us all. The time has come
To build a strong fort of peace against the invasions
Of fear and violence into the human psyche.
That is what I yearn for.

What can one achieve through violence? 340
We need compassion today.
What is the use of a doctrine?
One needs a diagnostic way of thinking today.
If one takes the path of war,
Everyone will be a loser, for sure.
Friendship among the nations should flourish.
If values perish, the entire world will turn
Into a desert and that should be avoided at all costs.
I am not alone in this mission.
I will join those who tread on the path of peace 350
And take recourse to the path of Great Quest
In whatever ways I can – big or small –
And I endeavour to do my best!

I will recite the *mantra* of Unity now.
This indeed is the theme song
Of the epic – *Shri Ramayana Mahanveshanam* –
The Journey of Great Quest!

O Shri Ramachandra!
You are the protector of those who take refuge in you.
Quelling dictatorship, you have established
The rule of righteousness.
Punishing the arrogant, wicked people in the world,
You have opened the door of happiness
For the well-meaning people!
The unbridled Libido hunts the brutish man
With an arrow of lust.
Subduing Libido, you have protected those
Who have fallen out of grace.
Revealing the unfathomable abyss of mundane life,
You have ameliorated all those who have sunk
In the ocean of pleasures!
O Lord! continue to protect us forever like this.

O Lord! You are equitable to all.
The earth on which you trod has turned into gold.
Your very breath is melodic and your very being is radiant.
You have triumphed over *maya*
And you dwell in the hearts of the sages.
You are the protector of those who surrender at your feet.
You are the slayer of *rakshasas*.
You arrived on earth as a blazing light
And you shed light everywhere.
You are the inspiration for the poets and artists.
You feed people with the honey of knowledge.
You are the all-encompassing idol
And you are the manifestation of the Absolute.
O, the compassionate One! Protect us.

You are Supreme Bliss incarnate.
Like the moonlight, shed on us the wealth of beauty.
Let the Ganga, Godavari, Krishna,
And Kaveri flow with full force;
Like the sweet milk enriched with honey,

Let truth flow out pleasantly.
Let the flag of truth flutter high radiant with bright light.
Let your sweet name fill our hearts.
Subduing the kingdom of the senses,
As the whole world is aglow with the awakened vital energy,
O Lord, walk into our lives!

O Janakanandini, daughter of King Janaka!
You resemble Jahnavi – the Ganga – in purity.
You are the ocean of happiness. 400
You are revered in all the three worlds.
You are the Goddess of Wealth.
You nurtured all the flora and fauna of the forest;
And you taught them all how to live.
You are the Guru even to Rama,
And taught him the tenets of philosophy.
You bring benediction to the world.
You are Bhuvaneshwari, the Goddess of the World.
O Mother! Be merciful and bless us!

O Saumitri! You are the paragon of sacrifice. 410
You are Adishesha, the primeval serpent.
With your thousand tongues, you sang the great song
And made the world dance with joy.
Your musical notes have innumerable melodies and rhythms.
At the beating of your hood,
Arrogance of food, wealth, power, beauty, and clan
Have all got quelled. Treading on the path of Great Quest,
You destroyed the whole mountain of pollution.
You quelled – quite forcefully – anger, conceit, and lust.
Exploring Science, Philosophy and the Fine Arts with discernment, 420
You have accomplished success in all the three fields.
We bow to you, O Lord!

O, the breath of Life!
You are the auspicious Hanuma!
Who else but you can protect the poor and the destitute?

You are the valiant, who crossed the turbulent ocean!
Hold our hands and help us to cross the ocean of Life.
You are free from any blemishes
And you are the epitome of all virtues.
People, who know you well, are permeated   430
With the grace of Rama.
You are the source of all knowledge;
You blessed me with the strength and devotion
To write this epic of Rama.
Reside in our hearts forever!

The gargantuan spectre
Of turmoil is devouring the garden of peace.
Mind, intelligence, and emotions
Have turned into a gale of enmity
And have become a psychological disorder.   440
Ethnic clashes are rampant in Central Asia.
The stronghold of cultural hegemony and colonialism
Has enslaved people and teases the world
With its oppressive hands.

The desire for wealth and fame
Add fuel to the fire of warfare.
War is the root-cause of mass destruction.
War is the weed sown in vile minds
And, like wildfire, it spreads to the entire world.
War turns the fertile land into a desert.   450
War destroys the emotions of brotherhood!

O, the Goddess of Muse!
Teach us that war isn't inevitable.
Free us from the fetters of hegemonic culture.
Destroy the forts of slavery.
Wipe out the frenzy of war.
Let peace prevail and blossom well without war.
Let all arms and ammunition be thrown to the sea.

O Goddess! Rooting out anger and subduing beastliness,
Purify our minds and weed out the sufferings of the world. 460

Let good deeds flourish
As the epoch's gift to the world.
Let the lava of revenge and communal hatred be wiped out
And inspire us to build a tower of peace.
Bharata, the motherland, is held in high esteem
Being home to righteousness and exquisite arts and crafts.
Let Bharata be gloried now as the lighthouse
Of the universal religion
With the polyphony of multiculturalism,
And let it be aglow with new meanings 470
And motifs for the New Epoch!

O, the Goddess of Muse! Forgive me.
Description of war is not dear to me.
I have described it with absolute detachment.
The true path traversed by Buddha, Ashoka, Mahavira,
Jesus, Paigambar, and Basava is shining in front of me.
When the fear of war has gripped the universe,
Is there a way for salvation?
The widening gap between religions and castes,
Fanatical nationalism, the stubborn desire 480
To establish one's own superiority,
Have all brought the world to the verge of extinction.

Everyone should prosper; exploitation must end;
Universal brotherhood is the key for survival.
Leaders like Abraham Lincoln, Martin Luther, Gandhi,
And Nelson Mandela who fought
For universal peace and brotherhood
Shall be our presiding deities;
They are the beacons to dispel the darkness.
Rama, the protagonist of this epic, has lit the same lamp; 490
He has ushered in the common good of all!

O, Lord Shri Ramachandra!
I had the desire to write an epic on you.
But what strength and what skills do I possess?
You blessed me with the poetic zeal and you wrote the epic.
I, Veerappa Moily, along with my wife Malati,
Became your scribe and sang your history
And offering it to the world, feel amply blessed.
Taking me to the world of stars,
Making me stand amidst the sun, moon and the stars,   500
You bestowed on me a magnificent eye.
O Lord! You caused even the tiniest particle to
Shine most brilliantly in front of my eyes,
And things became quite evident to my mind.
O Lord! You drenched me in the ambrosia of compassion
Of Sita, Saumitri, Bharata and Anjaneya!
O Lord! You made every word of Kannada
Turn into a precious pearl in writing your history.
O Lord! You turned all the embers into stars.
O Lord! All the Kannada words used in writing your epic   510
Are amply blessed and revered.

Meditating on you day and night,
Malati inspired me to write your epic
And ascended all the five stairs along with me
And dedicated herself wholeheartedly
To the writing of this epic.
Bowing to Shri Rama and Janaki, Lakshmana, Maruti,
And the patron Goddess of Kannada,
I offer this work to the world.
May the discerning lovers of poetry appreciate it well   520
And with infinite pleasure,
May they be pleased and sing it forever!

May Shri Rama, Janaki, Saumitri, and Maruti
Reside in the hearts of the readers
Of this epic and bless them amply!

May the desire of nation-building get strengthened.
May the evil of racial discrimination
And the wicked notion of high and low disappear altogether.
May good sense prevail.
May the urge to serve the poor,   530
And the downtrodden take centre-stage.
May the desire for quest persist;
And may peace, harmony and happiness flourish in this world.
May the patron Goddess of Kannada –
The daughter of Mother India –
Accept our services for a long time to come,
And bless us!

Benediction to Shri Rama, the noblest of the Raghu clan;
Benediction to Mother Janaki and Lakshmana;
Benediction to Hanuma, the son of Wind;   540
Benediction to the Perfect One, the Supreme Being.

Thus ends the Epic
Shri Ramayana Mahanveshanam
– The Great Quest of Ramayana –
With Five Books and Two hundred and Twenty-five Cantos
Written by Veerappa Moily

Members of the Translation Committee

||௦||

1. Dr B.A. Viveka Rai, Chairman

B. A. Viveka Rai (B.Sc., M.A. and Ph.D. in Kannada, Mysore University) is a renowned Tulu-Kannada scholar. Having served in Mangalore University for three decades—as Chairman and Professor of Kannada for twenty years—he later served as the Vice-Chancellor of Kannada University, Hampi, and Karnataka State Open University, Mysore. Currently, he is the Visiting Professor Chair of Indology in Wurzburg University, Germany.

A writer in Tulu, Kannada and English, Rai has to his credit 25 scholarly and critical works, the most notable of which are his path-breaking analysis of Tulu epics (Ph.D. thesis, published); collection, documentation and translation of the *Siri*-epic (Tulu) along with Prof. Lauri Honko and others; and his collections of essays on Kannada literature, culture and theatre. He has been a member of many prestigious project teams, including the Project on 'Studies on the Western Ghats of Karnataka' and 'Heritage Village'. He has been awarded the DAAD Fellowship (Tubingen Univ., Transcription & Translation of Tulu oral epics); Tulu Sahitya Akademi Lifetime Achievement award; Karnataka Sahitya Akademi Award, and Rajyotsava Award (instituted by the Government of Karnataka).

2. Dr C.N. Ramachandran, Chief Editor and Translator

C.N. Ramachandran (B.A. and M.A. in English from Mysore University, LL. B. from Shivaji University, and Ph.D. from Miami University, Oxford,

Ohio (1982), has taught English language and literature in India, Saudi Arabia, and the United States. He retired from Mangalore University as Professor Emeritus in 1996.

Primarily a critic-translator, Ramachandran has published both in English and Kannada, and has attended International Conferences in San Francisco, Tokyo, Turku, Frankfurt, and New Delhi. His works in English include a study of British Drama (*Shifting Perspectives*) and monographs on Shivarama Karanth and Triveni (major Kannada novelists). His works in Kannada include post-colonial criticism (*Vasahatottara Chintane*), comparative criticism (*Taulanika Sahitya*), study of oral epics (*Hosa Madiya Mele Chaduranga*) and a monograph on Edward Said. Among his translations, the most ambitious are the translations into English of the famous Kannada oral epic *Male Madeshwara* and *The Edge of Time* (a novel in Kannada by Dr Veerappa Moily).

He has won many awards including Birla Fellowship, *Rajyotsava Award* (instituted by the Government of Karnataka), and Karnataka Sahitya Akademi Award for lifetime achievement.

3. Padma Sharma, Translator

Ms Padma Sharma (M.A. in English, Mysore University) is a major translator from Kannada into English. She has translated till now *Return To Earth* (a great Kannada novel by Shivarama Karanth); *The House of Kanuru* (by Kuvempu, translated with Ramachandra Sharma); *Strings And Cymbals* (translation of selections from Kannada oral epics, along with C. N. Ramachandran); and many stories of Vaidehi and others. She is the recipient of awards from Sahitya Akademi and Katha.

4. Dr Laxminarayana Bhat, P., Translator

Laxminarayana Bhat (M.A. and Ph.D., Mangalore University) is aProfessor-cumRegistrar(Evaluation) at School of Social Work,Mangalore. He has translated along with
 Dr C.N.Ramachandran the famous Kannada Oral Epic *Male Madeshwara* into English and the award-winning *Relationship* by Mahapatra into Kannada.

He has also edited and translated into English *Selected Poems of S.R. Ekkundi*. His poems in Kannada, English and Tulu have been published in various journals.

5. Dr C. Naganna, Translator

C. Naganna (M.A. and Ph.D. in English, Mysore University), is a Professor of English in Mysore University. He is a well-known poet, critic, translator with as many as twenty books to his credit. His translation of Chinua Achebe's *Things Fall Apart* has been very well received in Kannada. His chief preoccupations include African, Caribbean and Latin American Literatures besides Indian Writing in English. He has participated in many national and international seminars, and is very much a part of repertory and amateur theatres in Mysore.

6. Dr Vijay Sheshadri, Translator

Vijay Sheshadri (M.A. and Ph.D. in English, Mysore University) is, at present, an Associate Professor, Mysore University Centre at Mandya. He has presented papers at various International Conferences and National Seminars and is the recipient of the Mysore University Golden Jubilee Publication Award 2001-2004. His awards include 'Indian literature golden jubilee literary translation prize-2008' by Sahitya Akademi, New Delhi. He has published widely in literary journals and has translated two books into English: *Myasabedas (2007)* and *Visage in the Dark and Other Stories (2007)*.

Shree Ramayana
Mahanveshanam

Shree Ramayana Mahanveshanam

Volume One

M. Veerappa Moily

Rupa & Co

Copyright © M Veerappa Moily 2010

Chief Editor: Dr C.N. Ramachandran

Translated from Kannada: Dr C.N. Ramachandran, Padma Sharma,
Dr Laxminarayana Bhat P, Dr C. Naganna,
Dr Vijay Sheshadri

Published 2010 by
Rupa Publications India Pvt. Ltd.
7/16, Ansari Road, Daryaganj,
New Delhi 110 002

Sales Centres:
Allahabad Bengaluru Chandigarh Chennai
Hyderabad Jaipur Kathmandu
Kolkata Mumbai

All rights reserved.
No part of this publication may be reproduced, stored in a retrieval system, or transmitted, in any form or by any means, electronic, mechanical, photocopying, recording or otherwise, without the prior permission of the publishers.

Typeset by
Mindways Design
1410 Chiranjiv Tower
43 Nehru Place
New Delhi 110 019

Printed in India by
Rekha Printers Pvt. Ltd.
A-102/1 Okhla Industrial Area, Phase-II
New Delhi-110 020

To Her,

Who sowed the seeds of this epic poem, Mahanveshanam,
Who lighted in my mind the lightning-lamps of varied
Emotions and figures of speech endowed with rasa
And dhvani, *and thus enabled me to go deep*
Into the milky ocean of Imagination;
Who became one with me, sharing equally the radiance
Of the son of Sumitra; who, disregarding the pains
Of poverty, walked beside me in the path of my life;
Who, striking the chords of metaphysics in the world
Of Kannada, stood firm in my heart, throughout –
To her, Mala, my wife and partner in Dharma,
This sindoor *of Mahanveshanam is dedicated.*

Contents

||☉||

Foreword .... *ix*
Preface .... *xiii*
Introduction .... *xix*
A Note on Translation .... *xxxiii*
A Guide to Pronunciation .... *xxxv*

Book One 1
Book Two 297
Book Three 579

Foreword

||☉||

My happy relationship with Hon'ble Veerappa Moily is decades old; it goes back to the days when he began his profession as a young advocate at Moodabidri, near Mangalore. He is not only a politician with a vision but also a gifted writer. He has written four novels till today (two of which have been translated into English and several other Indian languages), besides plays and collections of poetry. I am happy to say that he has involved me, in one capacity or another, in almost all of his literary endeavours. Hence, when he suggested that I take up the responsibility of getting his ambitious epic, *Shri Ramayana Mahanveshanam*, translated into English, I was both happy and uneasy.

I was uneasy because what he suggested was a very challenging task. The epic, divided into five books, runs to about 43,000 lines; also, the author uses a kind of language that is both highly Sanskritised and terse in expression. It is the result of the author's decade-long research and meditation. But, again, it was for these very reasons that I finally accepted his suggestion so that a great Kannada work would be, through translation, made available to non-Kannada readers.

Two years ago, Shri Moily and I met and decided to form a committee of five translators; we persuaded Dr C.N. Ramachandran, a common friend and the translator of Shri Moily's celebrated novel *Tembare* into English (*The Edge of Time*), to accept the responsibility as Chief Editor. Then, the three of us together constituted the following committee of translators for the Project: Ms Padma Sharma, Dr C. Naganna, Dr C.N. Ramachandran, Dr. Laxminarayana Bhat, and Dr Vijay Sheshadri.

The first formal meeting of the committee took place in my office at Mysore on 17 February 2008; matters related to translation and other details were discussed at length. The chief editor reviewed two sample passages of translation from each and offered helpful suggestions. A time-frame of one year was fixed for the completion of the project.

The Committee accepted the principle of striking a balance between total fidelity to the original text and intelligibility of the translated work to non-Kannada readers; it was this principle that helped us to come to a reasonable compromise while translating culture-specific terms and concepts, synonyms and compound words in the original, and such other issues. In our opinion, glossary was to be kept to the minimum; and if a term or concept had an equivalent in English (however remote), it had to be used.

I am happy to say that thanks to the cooperation and interest on the part of all translators, the project was completed within the framework of time fixed by us in the first meeting. I have gone through the translated text completely, and I am convinced that all the members of the committee have done a commendable job. I specially commend the dedication, hardwork and scholarship of Dr Ramachandran, who harmoniously blended both the jobs of a translator and chief editor, and who is primarily responsible for the present form of the translated epic. I congratulate him and all the other members of the committee on their sincere effort and rich critical sensibility.

Since a detailed introduction to the text by the chief editor follows, I shall be very brief in my comments on the text. There have been, in the course of the last two millennia and in different languages, innumerable versions and counter versions (or 'tellings' as Ramanujan says) of the 'original' *Valmiki Ramayana*. Countless Puranas, epics in prose and verse, plays and novels based on 'the story of Rama' have been written and re-written. Even if I confine myself to Kannada poetry, I find that 'the story of Rama' has fascinated Kannada poets since long, beginning with the Jaina version of the *Ramayana* by Nagachandra *(Ramachandracharita Purana*, early 12th century). Shri Moily's *Shri Ramayana Mahanveshanam* belongs to this great tradition.

Although Shri Moily never deviates from the broad contours of Valmiki's work, in texture he has taken plenty of liberty. He has introduced scores of new characters and incidents, and has brought into discussion many issues which appear to be totally modern. As he interprets it, the *Ramayana*-narrative is very relevant today as it depicts an ideal society (*Ramarajya*), nonviolent and secular, governed by egalitarianism; a society in which every person, irrespective of his/her sex, class, caste, and religion, has equal rights and responsibilities; a new society, in fact, which was envisaged by the 'fathers of Indian Constitution'.

I am happy that owing to the conscientious work of the translators and Shri Moily's help, whenever needed, I have been able to successfully complete the project I undertook two years ago. I thank all the people concerned, especially the poet Shri Veerappa Moily and the translators. I hope the non-Kannada readers will receive this work with as much enthusiasm as the Kannada readers have done since its publication five years ago.

B.A. Viveka Rai
Chairman, Translation Project

Preface

||☉||

Today, man's mind has grown beyond imagination, and so has the *Ramayana*. What had been, once, the work of an individual's mind has today become the work of collective mind of mankind. A metaphysical history is hidden in the womb of man's evolution; and, today, we cannot fully understand what the nature and form of that history were in the beginning. Had it been possible to fully understand that history, Rama and Ravana would have become part of 'real' history, and the *Ramayana* would have been a documented chronicle instead of poetry. What is available for us today is not 'history' but a symbolic representation of man's psyche.

The world of poetry is neither a part of the real world nor its imitation; it is a distinct world by itself—autonomous, self-sufficient, and total. Before we enter that world, we have to leave behind, at least for a brief while, the laws and conventions of the real world and obey the laws of the new world. However, such a view does not imply that the new world of poetry is opposed to the real world. In fact, the poet has to be the sensory organs of his land and society; he has to be their eyes, ears, and heart; he has to be the voice of his age. He cannot afford to sit in an ivory tower, sending out messages.

As the great poet Kuvempu (Dr K.V. Puttappa, modern epic poet in Kannada) says, the works of great poets are the symbolic structures that embody eternal truths and life-giving values. Though they appear to be an individual's vision and creation, they are, in truth, the manifestations of collective consciousness, an ocean of creative energy. Hence they come to be revered as great epics and classics; they constitute the image of the epochal energy; they give a corporeal form to the formless imagination of the epoch's collective consciousness.

The Sanskrit term '*dharma*' includes all these meanings: law, custom, duty, rights, justice, character, and right action. Violation of any one of these results in *adharma* or loss of *dharma*. Hence, it is high time we realised that equating religion with *dharma* is the result of ignorance. Religious doctrines are only the frozen concepts that arise in the course of the cultural evolution of a people; they do not constitute *dharma* or the total culture of the particular people. Religion, divorced from culture, ends up as a barren island inhabited by barbarians. There, in that barren island, are bred avarice, selfishness, and animal instincts. No single religion inherits the culture of a particular community and region; if it comes to be viewed as such, it leads to blind religiosity or religious fanaticism.

Valmiki and Homer: these two are the rich symbols of two ancient and renowned cultures. *The Iliad* and the *Odyssey* are the records of the great achievements of the Greeks, the founders of Western culture; and Homer's epics are the eternal sources of inspiration for Western poets. *Ramayana* is the sacred source from which all Indian literature has originated.

According to historians, Valmiki's period stretches from 6000 BC to 300 BC; Homer is supposed to have lived around 900 BC. The encomium '*manasaa karmanaa vaachaa bhutapurvam na kilbisham*' bestowed on Valmiki establishes the kind of man Valmiki was – free from all kinds of sins (or faults) in mind, action, and speech'. Though Rama always thought of himself as a human being, Valmiki has portrayed him as an incarnation of God. '*Dharmohi paramo loke dharma satyam pratishthitam* (*dharma* is the greatest ideal in life; Truth resides in dharma)—this was the motto of Rama throughout his life.

Despite being the ruler of a huge kingdom, Ravana couldn't rule over his inner world. As opposed to him, in the beginning, Rama couldn't become the king of even a small province like Ayodhya; but he was able to rule over his inner self. Unravelling the different phases of *dharma*, voluntarily retreating into the forest in order to obey the words of his father, subduing the demons in order to protect the sages, killing Vali and Ravana – all these constitute the triumph of *dharma*. This is what the *Ramayana* is about; it is a chronicle of the triumph of *dharma*. *The Iliad* is the chronicle of 'Anger';

and the qualities admired in the Heroic Age, like valour and friendship, are the qualities of an individual. In an individual-centred age, scores of ideals come into being and disappear after some time without leaving any trace behind. But the *Ramayana* is characterised not by individualistic qualities but the ones of a community, of a whole culture. This is what I have attempted to unravel in my work.

The quest for the principles governing a *Ramarajya* that I have undertaken in this work may be a mere dream of mine. But, what was only a spark in the beginning grew to the stature of the glory of the sun's radiance, and my work was a witness to the way a dream could grow to envelop both the sky above and the earth below. Now I have placed my dream before you. Look at it through the eyes of my heart; and may your response to it be an honest one. Step cautiously on my dream unfolded before you. If, one day, my dream becomes the dream of our country and the goal of our national consciousness, I will feel truly blessed.

Glorification of the war-field is not the one I cherish. Although accounts of wars warranted by the narrative were unavoidable, it is my firm belief that there is no greater enemy to humanity in the modern world than wars. In order to satisfy one's ego or to avenge a heinous crime committed by one, if a war is declared to exterminate a whole community or race, there can be no justification for it. What is direly needed today is for all the world-leaders to come together and discuss various means of getting rid of wars and conflicts, for the sake of establishing peace in the whole world.

'War originates in the mind of Man; hence fort-walls to protect peace have to be built in the mind of Man' – this is the declaration of the world-body, the United Nations Organization. In the land of Gautama Buddha and Mahatma Gandhi, the work of building such protective fort-walls is yet to begin. This task acquires all the more urgency today as the war-clouds of terrorism hover over the whole land. We find in the edicts of emperor Ashoka, for the first time in the world, a victorious king giving up war and shaping that principle as his political doctrine. There is no other account of the quest for the psychological roots of war than that of Ashoka. Another universal truth that he discovered in his quest was that one should not hate another's faith, that one cannot conquer hatred through hatred, and that one can win over another only through love.

Many wars for one reason or another have been waged since the beginning of man's history: aggressive war, war to pre-empt war, patriotic wars, religious wars, cold war to save one's business interests, wars in self-defence – all these are only different forms of rationalising wars. But the fact remains that all these originate from prejudiced minds and fear. The only alternative for wars is the quest for that kind of freedom which liberates one's mind from fear. It is this quest that was undertaken by great people like Buddha, Mahavira, Gandhi, Martin Luther King, and many others who achieved victory through the path of non-violence. The cruel weeds of wars are nurtured in our minds by our irrational beliefs regarding purity or greatness of blood, race, and land. In the present times, when our social and secular values are being crushed by the onslaught of such doctrines, it is all the more necessary to explore such paths of peace that lead us beyond anxiety, fear, and self-interest. When Martin Luther King visited India in 1958, a journalist present in the press conference, posed this question to him: 'Where is Gandhi today? He is not to be seen anywhere!' This was King's reply: 'Gandhi is necessary for us. If humanity has to move on the path of evolution, Gandhi is necessary. If we forget Gandhi, we are inviting danger for mankind.'

Shri Rama, Buddha, Gandhi, and such others do not belong to any one race, religion or region; they are eternal symbols of those principles that guide us in the evolutionary path. Great works of literature and art are the storehouses of such symbols and principles; they unfold before us the myriad possibilities of life amidst authority and domination. Hence, such chronicles of evolutionary quest never become outdated; they are always contemporary and relevant.

◆

Many scholars and friends have helped me in many different ways during the course of research and composition of this work. In particular, my wife Malati has given me confidence, encouragement and advice; my elder brother, Shri Narayana Devadiga, was responsible for my interest in the great story of Shri Rama since my childhood; Dr K. Anantharamu, my Guru, has constantly helped me, critically going through my drafts and revising them in terms of metre and rhythm. Again, I will be failing in my duty if I do not acknowledge the help extended to me at every stage by the following scholars: Dr N.K. Kulakarni, Dr V. Prabandhanacharya, Dr B.A. Viveka Rai, Dr K.T. Pandurangi, Prof M.H. Krishnaiah, Dr G.S. Shivarudrappa, Dr T.V. Venkatachala Shastry, K.R. Kamalesh, and many others. I am indebted to all of them.

May Bhuvaneshwari, the daughter of Bharata and Mother of Karnataka, be pleased to accept this humble gift of mine, and bless us all.

♦

When Shri Kapish Mehra, Managing Director of the prestigious publishing house, Rupa & Co., New Delhi, expressed his desire to publish the English version of *Shri Ramayana Mahanveshanam*, I was both elated and hesitant. I was hesitant for the simple reason that translating a work running to 43,000 lines spread over five volumes involved massive and consistent work over a period of at least ten years.

However, I realised very soon that my hesitation was unfounded when towering scholars like Dr B.A. Viveka Rai and Dr C.N. Ramachandran came forward to undertake this challenging task.

A committee was constituted under the chairmanship of Dr Rai, former Vice-Chancellor of Karnataka Open University, Mysore, and Dr C.N. Ramachandran, Professor Emeritus and a great critic, agreed to be the chief editor and also one of the translators. The other members of the committee also were all well-known scholars and translators of proven ability. They took up the challenging task so sincerely and did their work so competently that I was really taken by surprise when, after a period of just two years, they completed the project and submitted to me the copy of the entire translated work. When I glanced through the pages of the translated work, all my earlier apprehensions melted away and I was immensely pleased. It was practically my dream (of which I have spoken earlier) come true. I am always beholden to all the members of this translation project for their exemplary work.

M/s Rupa & Co., with their dynamic MD Shri Kapish Mehra, mentor Shri R.K. Mehra, and a dedicated team comprising Ms Kadambari Mishra,

Shri Vijay Sharma and many others have done a great job in their production of this massive work. I acknowledge my gratitude to all of them. On this occasion, I again remember my Guru, Prof K. Anantaramu, for his constant guidance and advice.

I earnestly hope the readers of this English version will respond to the work with the same enthusiasm that the Kannada readers extended to the original work.

M. Veerappa Moily

Introduction

||☉||

1

A popular Indian myth says that the entire earth is borne by a five-headed primeval serpent called Adishesha. Playing upon this motif, a great 16th century Kannada poet, Kumaravyasa, explains, in the beginning of his epic *Bharata Katha Manjari,* why he chose to write in Kannada the *Mahabharata-*story and not that of Rama. He says, '*tinikidanu phaniraaya raamaayanangala bhaaradali*'; that is, by his time 'there had been so many Ramayanas that the Adishesha, carrying the earth on his head, began to totter owing to the weight of the Ramayanas.'[1] Coming to the modern age, one of the most insightful essays by A.K. Ramanujan, 'Three Hundred Ramayanas', begins with these two questions: 'How many Ramayanas? Three hundred? Three thousand?'[2] These two instances bear a testimony to the amazing and inexplicable hold the story of Rama has had on the Indian psyche for over two millennia. When we realise that the story of Rama has been told, retold, and re-fashioned in every language of India (and of South Asian

---

1. Kumaravyasa, *Karnata Bharata Kathamanjari;* ed. Kuvempu & Masti Venkatesha Iyengar (Bangalore: Dept. of Kannada & Culture, 1985). Compared to Vyasa Bharata, Kumaravyasa has told the story of only the first ten Books, up to 'Gadaparva'. Composed in 'Shatpadis' (a stanza form of six lines, with initial rhyme scheme), this is the most popular epic based on *Mahabharata* in Kannada.
2. A.K. Ramanujan. 'Three hundred Ramayanas: Five Examples and Three Thoughts on Translation,' in Vinay Dharwadker, ed. *The Collected Essays of A.K. Ramanujan* (New Delhi: O.U.P., 1999).

countries), in poetry, drama, fiction, dance, puppetry, painting, sculpture and musical compositions, the following statement of Ramanujan in the same essay does not appear exaggerated: the Ramayana constitutes as it were 'a second language of a whole cultural area'[3].

Over the millennia, three major traditions of the Rama-story are noticeable in India and abroad: the classical tradition that includes *Valmiki Ramayana, Adhyatma Ramayana, Adbhuta Ramayana, Ananda Ramayana, Bhushundi Ramayana, Shesha Ramayana,* and such; the tradition of retelling the Rama-story in Indian languages other than Sanskrit: Vimala Suri's *Pa-uma Chariya* in Prakrit, Swayambhu's *Pa-uma Chariu* in Apabransha, Nagachandra's *Ramachandra Charita Purana* in Kannada, Kampan's *Iramavataram* in Tamil, Tulasidasa's *Ramacharitamanas* in Avadhi, and such; and, the oral folk-tradition that includes *Bhil Ramayana, Kukana Ramayāna, Gonda Ramayana, Tamburi Ramayana,* and such.

Among these three categories, as Hiltebeitel, Paula Richman, and others argue, the works in the second category can be called 'subversive' or 'oppositional' texts.[4] However, we have to consider the works in the third category (Oral-folk tradition) 'different versions' and not subversions since the communities which gave birth to these works cannot be presumed to have had a prior knowledge of the works of Valmiki, Vimala Suri, and such others to go about consciously opposing their worldview.

On the basis of their doctrinaire orientation, we can group the works on the story of Rama in a different way also: the Vedic-Brahminic tradition (*Valmiki Ramayana* in Sanskrit, *Torave Ramayana* in Kannada by Kumara Valmiki, etc.), the Jaina Tradition *(Pa-uma Chariya* by Vimala Suri in Prakrit, *Ramachandra Charita Purana* by Nagachandra in Kannada, etc.), and the tribal Ramayanas (*Ram Seetmani Varta* of the Bhil tribe, *Ramayana* of the Gonda tribe, etc.). Even within the Jaina tradition, scholars have noted two different streams: one following the Digambara tradition of Jainism,

---

3. A.K. Ramanujan, p. 157.
4. Alf Hiltebeitel, *Rethinking India's Oral and Classical Epics* (Chicago and London: University of Chicago press, 1999), p. 9. 45–47, etc. The phrases used by him are 'reenplotted ruptures', and 'counter-cultural, non-Brahminical, and anti-imperial'. Paula Richman, Ed. *Many Ramayanas: The Diversity of a Narrative Tradition in South Asia* (Berkeley, L.A.: Univ. of California. Press, 1991), p. 14.

which includes the works of Vimala Suri and Ravishena, and the other the Shwetambara tradition of Jainism, which includes the works of Gunabhadra and Pushpadanta.[5]

Of these innumerable Ramayanas, which is 'the first work' or 'original' of which the others are variations? The consensus of scholars today is that it is not a relevant question at all. For, even before Valmiki, 'the First Poet' (*aadikavi*), parts of the Rama-story were to be found in the Buddhist *Tripitakas*: Dasharatha Jataka, Vessantara Jataka, and Jayyavirya Jataka, which, themselves, were the written accounts of popular tales in the oral tradition.[6] Even coming to *Valmiki Ramayana,* Romila Thapar argues that originally, the *Ramayana* by Valmiki did not contain the 'Bala Kanda' and 'Uttara Kanda', which were later additions.[7] Hence, convincingly, Paula Richman posits:

> 'while Valmiki's importance is undeniable, we learn more about the diversity of the *Ramayana*-tradition when we abandon the notion of Valmiki as the Urtext from which all the other Ramayanas descended. We need instead to consider the 'many Ramayanas,' of which Valmiki's telling is one. ...'[8]

Ramanujan makes this point very succinctly: 'In this sense, no text is original, yet no telling is a mere retelling – and the story has no closure, although it may be enclosed in a text.'[9]

2

Since it is almost impossible to consider in this introduction, even briefly, all the Ramayanas in the three categories mentioned above, I would like to

---

5. Mirji Annaraya (Kannada), *Ravisena Ramayana* (Shedbal: Shanti Seva Sadan, 1968), p. i (Introduction).
6. Mirji Annaraya, Introduction, p. 5.
7. Romila Thapar, *The Exile and the Kingdom: Some Thoughts on the Ramayana,* Mythic Society Lecture, 1978.
8. Paula Richman, p. 9.
9. A.K. Ramanujan, p. 158.

limit the discussion only to the history of Kannada Ramayanas, of which Moily's *Shri Ramayana Mahanveshanam* is the most recent. The history of Kannada Ramayanas begins with Nagachandra, whose *Ramachandra Charita Puranam* is the oldest, written in the beginning of the 12th century. It follows the Jaina tradition, and is indebted in both characterisation and incidents to Vimala Suri's *Pa-uma Chariya* in Prakrit and Ravishena's Sanskrit work *Padma Puranam*.[10] The major characteristics of the Jaina Ramayanas as in Nagachandra, are, briefly, the following:

a) Lakshmana, and not Rama, is the 'hero' of the work; it is he who, finally, defeats and kills Ravana. Neither Rama nor Lakshmana is monogamous; both have many wives. (Interestingly, in almost all the oral-folk versions of the *Ramayana* also, it is Lakshmana and not Rama who is the hero of the work.)

b) Ravana is not all evil like Satan; he is noble and virtuous, fatal attraction for Sita being his only weakness. Nevertheless, when he cannot dent Sita's fidelity to her husband despite varied attempts, he sincerely repents and resolves to atone for his deeds. Even when he dies on the battlefield, he remains noble. In other words, Ravana's depiction by the Jaina poets resembles the Greek tragic heroes who, despite their otherwise noble qualities, fall and suffer due to some tragic flaw in them.

c) The *vanaras* such as Vali, Sugriva and Hanuman, and the *rakshasas* like Ravana and Vibhishana are not monkeys and demons; they belong to a race called Vidyadhara who have many superhuman powers including flying in the *sky* (Khechara).

d) Many familiar incidents and characters in Valmiki like the 'Putrakameshthi' ritual, the character of Vishwamitra, Maricha turning himself into a golden deer, and such are missing.[11]

The next Ramayana in Kannada following the Jaina tradition was *Kumudendu Ramayana*, written in the latter part of the 13th century, by Kumudendu. However, only certain parts of it are extant, and they

---

10. R.S. Mugali (Kannada), *Kannada Sahitya Charitre* (1953; rpt. Mysore: Geetha Bookhouse, 2002), p. 123.

11. (Kannada) *Ramachandra Charita Puranam*, ed. R.S. Mugali (Bangalore: Kannada Sahitya Parishat, 1976), Preface, p. ix–x.

follow Vimala Suri. Other works in this tradition are: *Ramavijayacharita* by Devappa Kavi in the 16th century; *Ramakathavatara* by Devachandra in the 18th century; and *Jinaramayana* by Chandrasagara Varni in the 19th century.[12]

The major work based on the Rama-story in the Vedic or Brahminic tradition in Kannada is Narahari's (better known as KumaraValmiki) *Torave Ramayana* in the second half of the 15th century. His work is a free translation of *Valmiki Ramayana* in a concise form. Though he is faithful to the original to a great extent, he has made a few changes also, probably influenced by Jaina Ramayanas.[13] For instance, he has tried to show some virtues in Ravana; before leaving for the decisive war, Ravana distributes all his wealth to the poor, and, at the time of death, he repents for all his misdeeds. Also, in his version, Manthara is an incarnation of Maya; and, just before his coronation, Rama tells the sage Vasishtha that he had a dream in which he saw himself going to the forest. The major tone of the poem is one of *bhakti*, as he lived in an age of Bhakti.

Curiously, even the modern period in Kannada begins with an extraordinary retelling of *Ramayana*. Nandalike Lakshminarayana (pen name, Muddana) wrote his ambitious work *Shri Ramashwamedha* in prose in 1896. This is a brilliant self-conscious work in the sense that this work has a frame consisting of a court poet called Muddana and his wife Manorama; and this frame interrupts the narration of the story now and then, posing questions, commenting on certain incidents, and, occasionally providing humour. Such a narrative in which narration and commentary on it alternate was a very new technique (at least in Kannada) that the writer introduced. Through the Muddana-Manorama dialogue in the frame, the writer raises such questions (similar to the ones raised by modern Readers' Response theorists) as 'who is the reader and what are his expectations in the changed (that is, colonial) circumstances? Should a modern poet write in verse or prose? And how does one view certain incidents in the story like Rama's desertion of Sita?' The inset story is

---

12. Mirji Annaraya, Introduction, p. 76.
13. R.S. Mugali, *Charitre*, pp. 237–241.

based on *Shesha Ramayana,* which, mainly, focusses on the story of Rama after the death of Ravana and Rama's coronation.[14]

There are two more epics written in the 20th century, retelling the story of *Ramayana:* Kuvempu (Dr K.V. Puttappa, Jnanapith awardee) wrote *Shri Ramayana Darshanam* (1949) and Srinivasa (Dr Masti Venkatesha Iyengar, Jnanpith awardee) wrote *Shri Rama Pattabhisheka* (1972). Kuvempu's epic, running to about 21,750 lines, arguably the most representative work of the post-independence ethos, re-interprets Valmiki's Ramayana from the perspective of modern history, Vivekananda's Advaita philosophy, and Aurobindo's concept of the 'Super Soul'.[15] We can analyse the nature of re-interpretation of the classical epic by Kuvempu under these heads: incidents and characters, worldview, and response to colonialism.

a) Incidents and Characters: The very act of 'selection' and 'exclusion' of incidents and characters in a work is a pointer to the operating sensibility of a writer.[16] When we read Valmiki's classical epic today, we find many embarrassing incidents in it: the burning of Lanka, Shurpanakha episode, desertion of Sita, and such. Paula Richman calls these incidents 'nodal points', which, every poet after Valmiki has attempted to either exclude or re-interpret in his work.[17] Kuvempu leaves out both the incidents of setting fire to Lanka and desertion of Sita. The episode of Shurpanakha-disfigurement is too important as a turning point of the story to be left out; hence Kuvempu pictures it as an accident:

'He (Lakshmana) swung his arm at her. It held
An arrow. By inadvertence, it chopped off her nose.'

---

14. (Kannada) Tekkunja Gopalakrishna Bhatta, ed. *Muddanana Shriramashwamedham* (Mangalore: Sharada Press, 1972). For a detailed discussion of this point, see my article (in Kannada) "Swabhimukha Sahitya," in *Bayalu-Rupa* (Bangalore: Swapna Bookhouse, 2006, Vol. I, pp. 128–142).

15. English translation: S.M. Punekar, *Shri Ramayana Darshanam* (New Delhi: Sahitya Akademi, 2007).

16. I have borrowed these two terms from Foucault's discussion of 'Discourse'.

17. Paula Richman, p. 10.

Sita's 'Fire-ordeal' to establish her fidelity to Rama is a typical reflection of a patriarchal society. Kuvempu includes that incident, but makes Rama also go through the same ordeal.

Coming to characterisation, the striking feature of Kuvempu's epic is the importance he gives to those characters marginalised in the classical epics. Manthara, the maid of Kaikayi, is usually depicted as a mean and wicked woman. But Kuvempu pictures her with great understanding: since she is mocked at and rejected owing to her physical deformity by everyone except Kaikayi, Manthara develops an abnormal attachment to her, and hence she attempts to block Rama's coronation. Similarly, Urmila in Kuvempu's work appears a greater woman than Sita since, all alone, she has to suffer for fourteen years for no fault of hers. The poet calls her a 'silent sufferer' and 'an image of perfect womanhood'. The most meaningful touch of modern sensibility is found in the characterisation of Ravana. Kuvempu's Ravana is not a symbol of evil; he is a great scholar and ruler, whose only weakness is lust for Sita which, as he confesses once, is hereditary. Both Rama and Ravana, according to Kuvempu, are complementary to each other, Ravana representing the '*asat*' in Rama. Sita's influence changes him completely, and he wages war with Rama only to get her re-united with Rama.

b) Worldview: Kuvempu rejects the Vedic view of Rama-Ravana opposition as absolute opposition of good and evil. Mounting a strong critique of the Brahminic worldview inherent in the entire '*avatara*' concept, he declares that Rama does not become 'Shri Rama' just by killing a wicked king:

'Did the demons he slayed
Make for Rama's greatness? Nay, forget that. Great
For the hate? Nay, nay! ...
Let people
With low savour for battle admire Rama for slaying
Ravana. A poet cannot afford that delusion.' (p. 122)

In short, Kuvempu's modern epic is shaped by the ideals of Gandhi: *sarvodaya* (progress of all), *samanvaya* (co-existence), and *poornadrishti* (holistic vision).

c) Response to Colonialism: It is interesting to see how Kuvempu, living in the colonial world (while writing the epic, in the thirties and forties of the twentieth century), subtly subverts the colonial concept of 'Progress' and 'Modernity'. Ravana's Lanka, with all of its splendour and material comforts, stands for progress and development as defined by the industrialised West. The description of Lanka and of Ravana's subsequent conference brings to our mind Milton's description of Pandemonium and Satan's conference in his *Paradise Lost*–and it is meant to do so. Lanka is intended by the poet to image a modern Western city like London or New York:

'The main demon metropolis filled with high-rising structures,
Snuggled on the vast slopes of the central peak.
...
Homes lit up with bunched chandeliers glowed, in circular rows,
Streets lit up with cupped and bunched lamp clusters.' (p. 355–356)

This description, read together with the later descriptions of Kumbhakarna's war (compared to the mechanised, mass-destructive wars of the West) and modern weapons of destruction, establishes the point that the poet here is juxtaposing two definitions of 'modernity' and 'progress'. Ramarajya or the ideal society, the poet indirectly answers the hegemonic colonial power, need not necessarily be either rich or powerful.

3

M. Veerappa Moily: *Shree Ramayana Mahanveshanam*[18]

After Kuvempu, the next significant interpretation to come in the 21st century is Moily's *Mahanveshanam*. Moily's work is stupendous from any point of view. To start with, there has gone into the work an astounding amount of reading and research. Secondly, even the size and sustained effort

---

18. M. Veerappa Moily (Kannada), *Shri Ramayana Mahanveshanam*. Five volumes of this work were published one each year, beginning with 2001 (Vol. 1) and ending with 2005 (Vol. 5). Then, all the volumes put together as one text were published in 2006.

of the work are striking. The entire epic is divided into five volumes, running into about 43,000 lines.

The title of this ambitious epic is '*anveshanam*', literally meaning 'quest' and 'examination'. That is, the main objective of the author of this work is to explore the '*Ramatattva*' or the true principles of the Rama-story, from a secular and modern perspective. Though he closely follows the path of Valmiki, he introduces many new characters and incidents, and he re-interprets many familiar incidents from the point of view of modern sensibility, drawing freely from Jaina and folk traditions.

a) Nodal Points: The most important of these are the episodes of Ahalya, Shurpanakha, and Sita's ordeal of fire.

In Valmiki, Ahalya, the wife of sage Gautama, is tricked by Indra; and later, she is cursed by her husband to become a rock. She remains in that condition till Rama steps on the rock and she comes back to life. This punishment meted out to Ahalya strikes us today as very harsh and undeserved. In *Mahanveshanam*, Ahalya is shown as having had a fascination for Indra from her childhood itself; and hence, when Indra approaches her disguised as Gautama, she immediately recognises him for what he is but cannot control her passion. She, in that sense, becomes a willing partner. Later, overcome with repentance, she gives up her home and husband to go to a lonely place and spend the rest of her life in penance. When Rama meets her, he finds her a real *tapasvin* (ascetic) purged of all weaknesses, and he witnesses the reunion of Gautama and Ahalya.

Similarly, the disfigurement of Shurpanakha in the classical Ramayanas strikes us today as barbarous and undeserved. For, if Rama and Lakshmana did not want to marry her, they could have just refused her request; there was no need to punish her cruelly, chopping off her nose and ears.

Moily handles this difficult incident very adroitly. In his work, Shurpanakha is a philistine who does not believe in sin and virtue. For her, what matters is the pleasure of the moment, issues of morality being beyond her. Moily depicts her disfigurement as an 'accident' as Kuvempu does. When Shurpanakha begins to harass Sita so as to make Rama marry her, Lakshmana unsheathes his sword and, in the ensuing melee, accidentally wounds Shurpanakha's nose and ears.

Sita's ordeal of fire is the most difficult as well as embarrassing incident in Valmiki for us, today. For obviously, Valmiki's Rama is the product of patriarchy; and his world is so male-centred that women there are really (to use a phrase of Simone de Beauvoir) the 'second sex'. In fact, he even proclaims proudly that he has fought the war not for her sake but for the honour of his lineage, and that now that he has proved his worth, she may go wherever she desires.

Moily retains this incident but interprets it differently. After the Lanka-war, Rama is so preoccupied with restoring normal life in Lanka that he does not find time to meet Sita. She, unable to wait for Rama beyond a particular period, loses interest in life and voluntarily attempts to give up her life through fire. But, at the right moment, Mandodari happens to come there and she rushes to pull back Sita from fire and save her. On this occasion, the words of Mandodari (who, as Ravana's wife, has gone through all kinds of experience) are very meaningful:

> *'...What are you doing, my daughter?*
> *You have entered fire and you have dragged me also into it.*
> *Isn't the ordeal of fire that all of us, women, go through*
> *Throughout our lives –isn't it enough?*
> *It's only a great man, who comes to this world*
> *Once in a millennium, who can put an end to our ordeals.'*
>
> (5: 614: lines 27-33)

In fact, the poet's concern for the condition of women in a male-centred society and his respect for the 'woman's point of view' reverberate throughout the epic.

b)   New Characterisation:

Lakshmana: Patriarchy automatically privileges the eldest son and treats others as his shadows. According to the *Smritis*, the first son is *dharmaja* (born of *dharma*) and the others are only *kaamaja* (born of lust). Hence, in Valmiki, Rama is the hero of the epic and Lakshmana is only his shadow. But modern Ramayanas, like Maithilisharana Gupta's *Saketh* (and folk-narratives) treat Lakshmana as the 'hero' of *Ramayana*. Moily's epic follows this tradition.

Some of the most poetic and touching scenes in the epic are those that depict the deep love between Lakshmana and Urmila and their suffering in separation. When Lakshmana goes to the forest with Rama and Sita, Urmila also abandons her palace, builds for herself a cottage on the banks of the river Sarayu and spends her time in prayers and penance. When, after fourteen years, Lakshmana returns to her, she just collapses into his arms, overcome by emotions; and he tells her:

'I have seen today the moon free from ash-coloured circle;
I have seen today the dew-drop on the flower, free from dust;
I have seen today a woman radiant though unadorned;
...
Everything today is pure, like the autumn-sky.' (5: 641: 75–80)

Ravana in Moily's work (in the tradition of Jaina Ramayanas) is neither a villain nor a great tragic hero. He is enamoured of Sita for some time, and he does kidnap her. But later, due to the advice of his wife Mandodari and brothers, he changes his heart. He decides to hand Sita over respectfully once the war is over. But, unfortunately, he does not survive the war.

c) Contemporary Relevance:

From this point of view, Moily's epic is a work of this age: it upholds the values of secular, multi-cultured and egalitarian modern India.

It is very interesting to see the way Moily introduces burning contemporary issues so unobtrusively into a two-thousand-year old story. Just to take a few glaring examples:

i. Labourers and Manual workers: During Rama's wanderings in the Dandakaranya forest, once he comes across a sage called Sharabhanga (a new character), who publicly enters fire and ends his life. Taken aback, when he inquires of the onlookers, he is told that Sharabhanga was a friend and guide of mine-workers and that, finding them totally exploited by both Indra, the king of gods and Ravana, the king of demons, Sharabhanga organised them and made them demand better wages. In turn, the poor miners were set upon by the owners and were massacred. Owning up responsibility for such manslaughter, Sharabhanga sacrifices his life. This incident makes Rama realise the duties of a king toward all of his subjects and he vows he will in future strive for the upliftment of the poor and manual workers. Also, we come across here labour leaders like Mandakarni, who, bribed with wine and women by the owners, forget their duties and abandon workers to the mercy of the owners.

ii. Alcoholism: Once in the forest, Rama and Sita hear the cries of a poor woman being beaten up by her husband. When they rush to the woman's help, they find the husband dead-drunk. Sita gets so angry and upset with this incident that she urges Rama to put an end to such incidents, banning the consumption of liquor throughout his kingdom.

iii. Education: When Rama enters Sugriva's land, the poet gets an opportunity to depict the various administrative reforms carried out by Sugriva as opposed to the tyrant Vali.

Sugriva's motto as the king of Kishkindha is: '*I will build a new society free from all kinds of exploitation.*' He follows this ideal with determination and introduces new reforms in all fields – economic, cultural, and educational. His inviolable orders to his officers are:

'These are my orders: close down all liquor shops,
Houses of prostitution and gambling dens;
Make it the responsibility of the law-enforcers
To root out corruption in all spheres.' (3: 96: 123–126).

To encourage cottage industries, to heavily tax luxury goods entering his kingdom from Lanka so that native industries will thrive and some such are the all-inclusive objectives of Sugriva's rule. But, the one objective he holds the most important is education – to provide an opportunity for all for free education. Of course, even in Kishkindha, as in other societies, there are cynics who wonder if rustics and manual workers ('monkeys living on trees') deserve formal education; but Sugriva silences them all and declares:

'... This new policy of education
Is in all respects progressive to Kishkindha kingdom.
All men and women have a right to get education.
When we have a cluster of Agastya's disciples amidst us,
Why should we lead the life of animals, uneducated?

*While good education is available in nearby Lanka,
For all irrespective of sex, should Kishkindha continue to live
Fallen into the dens of ignorance and superstition?'* (3:96:16)

The ambition of Sugriva is to modernise his kingdom to such an extent that it can compete with other modern countries like Lanka and Ayodhya.

What is interesting here is the way the poet collapses the past and the present, and while narrating the story of Rama, actually narrates the story of modern India. Indirectly, he equates Lanka with the Western countries (particularly America), that have achieved unbelievable progress in science and technology; and Ayodhya with a country of immeasurable artistic achievements. Sugriva's ambition is to build a new society in Kishkindha which fuses together the achievements and values of both Lanka and Ayodhya.

Isn't the attempt, on the part of the poet, to introduce issues like co-education, total prohibition, casteless society, etc., into an ancient story too anachronistic? This is a difficult question to answer. However, such re-interpretations, especially of the two ancient classics, have become so common that, if we can accept Vimala Suri, it appears, we can always accept any other re-interpretation. Also, in a highly civilised and rich society like that of Ayodhya and Lanka, how can we be very sure that the above problems didn't exist then? It seems, literature, like any other art, is, simultaneously, both contemporary and timeless.

The Vision:

Above all, Moily's epic is concerned with a lofty vision for India in future. According to him, this is what the present-day India has to learn from the *Ramayana* – to build a nation of many voices, many cultures and many peoples.

On one occasion, Rama declares: 'Mono-cultural doctrine dumps us into a well of darkness.' When Ravana tricks Rama and forcefully abducts Sita with him, Jatayu confronts him and tells him why exactly he is an evil king:

*'...Having forcefully occupied Janasthana,
Destroying forest culture with cruel measures,*

> *Razing to the ground tribal culture and way of life,*
> *You are bent upon establishing only your demon culture.'*
>
> (2: 75: 48-51)

At the time of coronation, Rama unfolds before his subjects his vision of Ramarajya:

> *'Irrespective of the differences of caste, class and creed,*
> *I shall provide quality education to one and all;*
> *There will not be favour or prejudice in the rule of law;*
> *Public health, drinking water, and defence are my priortities;*
> *I shall provide employment for all capable of work;*
> *...*
> *God is one for the whole world,*
> *Responsible for its creation, maintenance and destruction;*
> *Neither birth nor death has He; there is no place without Him;*
> *He is a part of everyone, everything; He is ever new;*
> *'Ramarajya' has no other creed and no other goal*
> *But progress and upward evolution.'* (5: 225: 163-202)

In short, Veerappa Moily's *Shree Ramayana Mahanveshanam* is a great work which, though rooted in the present and the Indian context, transcends time and place in its concerns and vision.

Let me conclude this fairly long introduction with a few lines from the most successful modernist poet in Kannada, Gopalakrishna Adiga. In his seminal poem 'Bhoota' (literally, ghost/ past), Adiga explores the past of India and the way we can relate it to the present. The relevant lines are:

> *'At the time of digging, the soil is in foetus form.*
> *Deeper and deeper thrust of the pickaxe*
> *might show us the shining golden ore.*
> *Excavating it, smelting it and purifying it,*
> *at least now we should learn the art of*
> *Shaping it into the images of our personal Gods.'*[19]

---

19. Tr. Sumatheendra Nadig, *Selected Poems: Gopalakrishna Adiga* (New Delhi: Sahitya Akademi, 2005), p. 30.

That is precisely what we find Muddana, Kuvempu and Moily doing: moulding the rich but remote heritage (in the fields of poetry, art, and ideology) to suit our present-day needs and ideals.

A Note on Translation

A translator, according to A.K. Ramanujan, has to obey three sets of conflicting allegiances: to the reader, to the culture of the original text, and to the text's historical context or tradition. Since they are conflicting allegiances, often the translation, like Marvell's 'love seems to be begotten by despair upon impossibility'.[20] Hence, it is with trepidation that we undertook this challenging task of translating into English a voluminous Kannada text.

Before embarking on this task, we, the translators, decided, rightly or wrongly, that our first allegiance was to the non-Kannada reader; and all our subsequent decisions related to translation were corollaries of this basic principle, some of which can be stated as follows:

i. The Kannada text is highly Sanskritised, and gender in Sanskrit depends on grammatical forms, not on meaning. While 'Raama' would be masculine (connoting the hero of this epic), 'Ramaa' would be feminine (connoting Lakshmi, the Goddess of wealth). In other words, length of a vowel in Sanskrit is highly functional. Still, open to misreading and misunderstanding, we decided not to use diacritical marks in the text so that a reader may not be distracted with such marks.

However, for the sake of scholars and those interested in the way Kannada/Sanskrit words are pronounced, we have given a 'Guide to Pronunciation' at the end of the text, in which we have shown the pronunciation of such words using both RPA script and diacritical marks.

We still faced a problem with the transliteration of proper names, as different translators in course of time have spelt proper nouns differently (e.g. Sita/Sitha/Seeta/Seetha/; Shri Rama/Shree Rama/Shrirama/Srirama, etc.). We decided to use the most common forms in transliteration.

---

20. A.K. Ramanujan, "On Translating a Tamil Poem," in Dharwadker, p. 219.

ii. We have kept the transliteration of culture-specific terms to the minimum, and we decided not to give a glossary since, we hope, the context explains such terms (used in italics in the text).

iii. Regarding synonyms, we have translated them literally so as to bring out their contextual connotations: 'Saumitri' as 'son of Sumitra'; 'Raghava' as 'of the Raghu clan'; 'Bhumije' as 'Earth-born,' etc.

iv. Since we did not want to give our translation a false aura of bygone ages, we decided not to use either archaic or obsolete terms (like 'thee' and 'thou'); we have used simple day-to-day language, with the hope that the narrative has its own force to carry the reader along with it.

v. Wherever possible, we have accepted modern interpretations of the *Ramayana;* hence, we have desisted from using such terms as 'Eagle' (to denote Jatayu and Sampati), 'monkey/ape' (to denote Sugriva, Vali, Hanuman, and such), and 'demon' (to denote Ravana and his followers), to the best possible extent. We have understood them as denoting different clans, and therefore used the Sanskrit terms like *Gridhra, Vaanara* and *Rakshasa*.

I shall be failing in my duty if I don't place on record my appreciation of and thanks to the editors at Rupa & Co., for their competence and dedication in preparing the final form of this text. I also thank Shri Kapish Mehra for producing this book with personal care and interest.

If this translation reaches a few more readers than the original text and enables them to understand that a classic, capable of innumerable interpretations, is both 'rooted in specific time-place' and also 'of all times and places,' our objectives will have been fulfiled.

C.N. Ramachandran
Chief Editor

A Guide to Pronunciation

‖௭‖

Proper Nouns Places/Mountains/ Rivers	Pronunciation
1. Ayodhya	əjɔːðjɑː / Ayōdhyā
2. Mithila	mɪθɪlɑː / mithilā
3. Lanka	ləŋkɑː / lañkā
4. Kishkindha	kɪʃkɪndʰɑː / kiṣkindhā
5. Rushyamuka	rəʃjɑːmuːkə / Ṛśyamūka
6. Panchavati	pəntʃʌvətɪ / Pancavati
Proper Nouns: Sages	
7. Vishwamitra	vɪʃwɑːmɪθrə / viśvāmitra
8. Vasishta	vəsɪʃtə / vasiṣtha
9. Sharabhanga	ʃərəbʰəŋgə / Śarabhaṅga
10. Matanga	mɑːθəŋgə / Mātaṅga
Proper Nouns: Tribesmen	
11. Shabari	ʃəbərɪ / śabarī
12. Guha	gʊhə / guha
Proper Nouns: Rakshasa clan	
13. Ravana	rɑːvənə / Rāvaṇa
14. Mandodari [wife]	məndɔːðərɪ / Maṇḍodari

15. Vibhishana	vɪbʰiːʃənə / Vibhīṣaṇa
16. Kumbhakarna	kʊmbʰəkərṇə / Kumbhakarṇa
17. Indrajit	ɪnðrədʒɪθ / Indrajīt
18. Khara	kʰərə / Khara
19. Dushana	ðuːʃəṇə / Dūṣaṇa
20. Maricha	mɑːriːtʃə / Mārīca
21. Shurpanakhi	ʃuːrpənəkɪ / Śūrpanakhi
Proper Nouns: Ikshwaku/Raghu clan	
22. Shri Rama	ʃriː rɑːmɑː / Śrī Rāma
23. Sita [wife]	siːθɑː / Sītā
24. Lakshmana	ləkʃmənə / Lakṣmaṇa
25. Urmila [wife]	uːrmɪḷɑː / Ūrmilā
26. Bharata	bʰərəθə / Bharata / Bhārata (country)
27. Shatrughna	ʃəθrʊgnə / Śatrughna
28. Mandavi [wife]	mɑːndəvɪ / Māṇḍavi
29. Dasharatha	ðəʃərəʈʰɑː / Daśaratha
30. Kausalya [wife]	kaʊsəljɑ / Kauśalyā
31. Sumitra [wife]	sʊmɪθrɑː / Sumitrā
32. Kaikeyi [wife]	kaɪkeɪɪ / Kaikeyī
Proper Nouns: Vanara clan	
33. Vali	vɑːlɪ / Vāli
34. Tara [wife]	θɑːrɑː / Tārā
35. Sugriva	sʊgriːvə / Sugrīva
36. Rume [wife]	Rʊme / Rume
37. Anjaneya	ɑːndʒənejə / Āñjanēya
38. Nala	nɑːḷə / Nala
39. Nila	niːlə / Nīla
40. Sushena	sʊʃeɪṇə / Suṣēṇa

Others	
41. Jambava [of the Bear clan]	dʒɑ:mbəvə / Jāmbava
42. Jatayu [of the Vulture clan]	dʒəta:jʊ / Jaṭāyu
43. Sampati [of the Vulture clan]	Səmpɑ:θɪ / Sampāti

Courtesy: Ms. Flora Noronha, School of Social Work, Roshni Nilaya, Mangalore.

BOOK ONE

Canto One

'Life of Renunciation is Bliss'

||๖||

The story of Shri Rama, flowing like a pure stream
In the land of Bharata, sets the *veena*-heart-strings
Of all people resounding. It connotes
History, and the conflicting dualities
Of virtue and vice, selflessness and selfishness,
In the pages of the First Poem.

The mind is joyous, gratified is the heart,
The divine poetic power flashes; from the womb
Of the sky, imagination leaps down to the earth,
Now roaring, now jumping and flowing on,
In turbulence and expanse surpassing the sea,
Springing to the sky, to the lofty Himachal
And the Gangotri, resounding and frolicking
And flowing, in the divine presence
Of the Ganga of enlightenment.
Truth, amity, compassion, mercy, forgiveness,
Peace, courtesy, love and sacrifice, great reverence
For the Guru, restraint, dignity, valour,
Self-examination – all these are unfolded here.
It is the forge in which the vision and contemplation

Of the Creative Spirit are moulded.
For poets through the ages, the concept of grandeur,
Inspiration, strength, the source of a new awakening,
The stages of righteousness of an inner vision,
The all-knowing image of eternal truths,
The divine blend of charm and melody – it has revealed.

Like the energy latent in the silent, inert stone,
Brilliantly sculpted out, this poetic artefact,
Stands pure and shining in the grand peak
Of the Divine Spirit within me.   30
While the First Poet, Valmiki, a cuckoo of vitality,
Prancing among branches, sweetness and melody
Personified, chanting the name of Rama, lost in itself
In a true act of devotion, overflowing and mellifluous,
Sings the nectar of song, virtuous, meaningful,
My mind has become one with him, in total concentration.

When the presence of bees and the breeze carrying
The fragrance of flowers, raise in my heart-sky
The spiritual radiance of Rama's brother,
Sailing in a barge of love over the expanse of the sea,   40
I shall compose a befitting epic of Lakshmana,
Singing his paeans.

I salute respectfully the pipe Shri Rama granted me;
And as Adishesha listens swaying his hood,
Undisturbed, and boundless peace, fraternity
Beyond bounds, the consciousness of community
Welfare and the values of truth, love and compassion
Spread over the universe, the rays from this epic-ocean
Rise high and reach the summit of the horizon.
There are those who have plucked strings,   50
Have bathed in it, swum in it, internalising
The beauty of knowledge, the culture of Ayodhya.
The five divine principles – austerity, meditation, religious rituals,
Sacrifice and self-surrender – a have been

Etched firmly in the five pillars of Indian life.
The essence of Rama accrued and that of Ravana
Abandoned, the ambrosia of brother Lakshmana's life
Has been offered here.

Rama's brother Lakshmana is a symbol of ideals:
Of service to Ramachandra, of unfailing probity, 60
Conscientious duty, profound gravity, unshaken courage,
And readiness to share the joys and sorrows of others.
He, the brother of Rama, is a gem among men,
Enriched with love, beyond the reach of senses,
Righteous in action and courteous in behaviour.
Very loving, very wise, valiant and radiant.
One who finds happiness in renunciation, he is
A jewel in the crown, possessing dazzling values.
Bold and courageous, beyond the reach of senses,
An ascetic, simple and handsome, patient, 70
Guileless, purposeful in life, truthful, intelligent,
Moral and affectionate — all such virtues and more
Have come together in him.

Brother Saumitri is like the primordial serpent,
Adishesha, carrying the entire earth on his head.
An embodiment of values needed for a glorious life;
He is one who, even in adversity, remains unchanged;
A special yardstick for an ideal life, the ocean of culture;
An unwavering light. In rain or heat or hurricane,
He is not the one to surrender, even if the deity 80
Of destruction arrives roaring, forcing its way.
He is the idol of divine beauty in all the ages,
An ocean in gravity, the Sahyadri in adventure,
The peak of all sacrifices, detachment and
Generosity—

This is the story of one who renounced everything;
One who exemplified the principle, 'Let me bear
The burden of all the sinners in this Kali age',

While others believed that 'it was better for one to die
Than cause the death of all'. Such a story is unique.
Ramayana is the epic of the universe, an inspiration
To noble poets, showing them the path of nobility,
The establishment of righteousness by Ramachandra.
Such a story, like a river, a stream, a forked brook,
Has flowed everywhere on this earth.

Has the world learnt any lesson?
The ideal of *'Ramarajya'* has remained a dream.
Has there been peace? Has man found happiness?
The game of life goes on, unceasing, on this earth:
Schemes for victory and defeat, union of birth and death,
The sorcery of separation, the continuum of dualities.
The earth trembled here, flames blazed there,
Devastation roared and devoured life somewhere,
The fire of communal hatred, the lava of odious vengeance
Brought down three domes. The culture of the epochs,
Treta, Dwapara and Kali *yuga*, the endless chants of
The great cultural conquest – what did all these yield?

When the nation's womb burst, a wild fire blazed,
Fountains of blood splashed around, and anarchy
Exploded, tearing the sky apart. To establish peace again,
Would not Adishesha himself rise in the eastern
Horizon of a new epoch and hold up the spirit of Bharata?
His bow of bravery has the string of sacrifice; his arrow
Has stamped upon sensuality; and in the crucible of truth,
He will mould truth and peace to save the world.

He will teach the world,
'Tyaagenaikena amritatvamaahuhu'
(Only through renunciation does one achieve divine bliss).
He will make the world learn the essence of Vedantic vision,
And thus liberate all from sensual pleasures.
Fulfilment of life lies in renunciation,
And selflessness is *yajna,* the sacred ritual, in which

Energy is the master, earnestness is the wife,
Heat of anger is the horse, the heart is the pillar
Of sacrifice, a life fully lived the ritual-place,
And the final offering is total renunciation.
The blessed mother, Sumitra, with the sinless body,
Completed such a *yajna* and took her bath at the end.
Lakshmana came into being in such a holy womb.

The soul of the Vedas, the law-giver, 130
The serpent-king Adishesha leaped into this earth,
From the ocean of milk, from joy to sorrow,
For the welfare of the earth, to hold the royal umbrella,
Suppliant to Rama, incarnating himself as Lakshmana.
Many a civilisations has bloomed and faded
Burnt out in a sacrificial fire, and wheels of epochs
Have rolled on and disappeared. The great witnesses
Have been Vyasa, Valmiki, and such men of renown.
They are there to hold up, yet again, principles of virtue,
And the culture of the Vedas as well. 140

In a magnetic field, suffering becomes meditation;
All the pain becomes an act of austerity to please god.
Bharata's power of action joined the renunciation
Of Lakshmana. Shatrughna's righteous conquests,
The great Sage Vishwamitra's dedicated teaching,
Sugriva's friendship, Vibhishana's righteousness,
Hanuma's service, the truthfulness of noble Sita,
Religious sacrifice, meditation, charity, observance
Of austere rites, and egalitarianism – all these
That can lead to man's progress resound in every atom. 150

At a lovely point of a river-source, Valmiki-mount,
Originated this Ganga of poetry, full of delight.
Moving smoothly, not pausing anywhere, this river
Has flowed in the vales of poetic elegance and imagination.
On this sacred earth, it overflows its banks, swelling
With floods, and it races on its course, full of joy,

Through rocks and crags, like the river of gods.
This indeed is the noble epic of divine *Ramayana*.
It is the truth, cognizable with joy, for all times.
'Nate vaaganruta, kaavye kaachidatra bhavishyati' 160
(Not a word of falsehood is to be found in this poem.)
The virtue of the poet's truthful words, the Ganga
Of *Ramayana*, flows on earth forever, cleansing
The minds of all men, and watches over the eight
Directions of this land, like Sahya and Himavat
Mountains, and the oceans. Like a strong fortress,
It protects itself. This is a poem of truth and morality
For all times, of the principle of virtuous living,
The true epic that blends all religions and sects.

A devotee of people, called Veerappa Moily, 170
Has recounted this epic of new thoughts, by name
Mahanveshanam, the great and noble quest,
For the people of the new epoch and new sensibility.
Falling at the feet of Saumitri, longing to create
'Lakshmanayana', I bow to Ganapati and Sharada
Of Shringeri. I touch the feet of Janaki and Shri Rama;
I touch the feet of Valmiki, the First Poet and Vyasa,
The lotus feet of Shankara, Ramanuja, Madhva and
Basaveshvara. I bow to the Absolute, to Truth.
I bow to all connoisseurs of poetry, who will wear 180
This divine garland of poetry, with joy and satisfaction.
I bow down to all the powers which remove all obstacles
And grant me the strength to complete this task.

Nagachandra, Narahari, Lakshmisha, Muddanna,
Parti Subba, Masti, Kuvempu, Gundappa, Bhasa,
Bhavabhuti, Kalidasa, Tulasidasa, Krittivasa,
Maithili Sharana, Kohili, Meera, Kamban,
Tyagaraja, Vishwanatha, Veerarama Varma –
These, the true poetic-sons of the great First Poet,
Have brightened the world of *Ramayana* as great poets. 190

In order to step in the path of these noble minds,
O, Bhramarambike, the Goddess of Kateel!
Bless me, your loving child of Moodabidare,
Born to Tammayya and Poovamma;
Grant me the light of imagination, hold my hand
And guide me. Anantharamu is my mentor,
And Malati is my good wife, close companion,
Who instructed me to move in the right way, in life
As well as in this epic, *Mahanveshanam*.

In the waters of the Tamasa river, 200
As saint Valmiki was getting ready to bathe,
A pair of Krauncha birds flew around freely,
Cooing in pleasure and companionship.
Suddenly, the male fell down to earth shot by
A hunter's arrow and the female cried in agony.
The great saint, enraged, cursed the hunter:
Maa nishaada pratishthaatvam agamahshaashvatheehi samaaha /
Yat krauncha mithunaadekam avadheehkaamamohitam //
(O, tribesman-hunter! For the reason that you have killed
One of the pair of Krauncha birds making love, 210
May you suffer from infamy and homelessness, for ever.)
But the next instant,
He was contrite for the way he had cursed.
When the female bird's pain filled the world,
And pained everyone, setting the heart in turmoil,
The ocean of compassion took the form of poetry;
The dark clouds enveloping the sky melted away,
Staging a prelude to the rise of the sun of poetry.
All the people chanted Rama's name in praise,
The world's morality, valour and character were purified. 220

There is none to equal or surpass Saumitri, the achiever,
The nobility of righteous poetry has permanence,
Like a hill, a river, and the vast expanse of an ocean.
The varied sounds of drums echo and resound

In all the four directions joyously. In the depths
Of the ocean, there was churning; and there emerged
The voice of culture, divine and immortal.
While selfishness and bigotry hurt the world,
Heroism being assaulted relentlessly,
The essence of history was lost; and greed   230
And ignorance dealt a death-blow to the beauty
And grace of great poetry.

Today, when caste, religion and class have built
Clay mansions; when righteousness has become
A house of lac; when within the constricting frames
Of religion, the vast earth burns fiercely; when religions,
Sects and sub-sects move like the waves of the sea;
Poetry alone, in these times, moving along the lines of truth,
Can save life like divine elixir. Like the essence of nectar,
Saumitri's renunciation is the spirit that can revive ideals;   240
He is the poet of this epoch, the brave leader.
In deep poetic meditation, I have acquired the treasure
Of divine revelation. While the essence of experience
Of earthly life spills over, hearts sprout and bloom.

To portray the conflict in the physical
And cultural fields of Lanka and Ayodhya,
To tear open the illusory web of Heaven and hell,
To beat the tabor of the eternal doctrine that truth wins,
This poem was born. While power, law and conduct
Of nations sit cowering before the seat of truth,   250
My poetic journey moves on without sacrificing truth
Under the pretext of a nation.

When I was disheartened and about to slump,
Unable to cross the twin-flow of Ganga and Yamuna,
The stories of Shri Rama and Lakshmana,
The name of Rama became a bridge for my task;
And I walk on with my head bowed in devotion.
I am not a poet; Saumitri strengthens my pen.

When I am sunk in ignorance, at a loss for words,
That valiant man becomes my companion, 260
Holds my hand with compassion and leads me on.

While the fountain of music springs in the heart,
The *ketaki* flower blows the wind laden with pollen,
The blue autumnal sky gleams like a burnished sword,
Then, the spark of imagination lights up on its own,
And, intellect and emotion being blended, reveal
Transcendental experience; and I bow to Saumitri.
I supplicate at the feet of Saumitri.

Saumitri bore all the troubles and suffering
In the sea of life; like Adishesha, he held up 270
A precious umbrella, and became immortal.
He became the tallest peak in the royal Himalayas,
And stopped the rush of the great river of emotions.
Renouncing everything, he brought upon himself
Separation from Urmila for fourteen years;
Forsaking sleep in the forest, all the time,
He dedicated himself to the search for truth.

The newly-wedded Urmila, a noble woman,
Young bride, sacrificed all the comforts and pleasures
Of a kingdom, and spent life as an ascetic, all alone, 280
In the city of Saketa, being the most loyal wife.
Gentle and beautiful, shy and of a good lineage,
She felt fulfilled desiring the welfare of the world.
She discarded jealousy and hatred; and considered
Her husband's happiness, her own. She acquired
Permanent bliss and prosperity; she became, indeed,
A symbol of noble love and the Kshatriya spirit.
'What fear, worry or anxiety do I have,
When my heart has the power of thoughts about you?
While my soul stands steady as in an austere ritual, 290
Your ascetic, peaceful energy will protect me everyday' –
With such thoughts, she spent fourteen long years.

I shall scoop from my hands the nectar-shower
Of Shri Lakshmana's story, and, after drinking it,
I shall easily cross the seven seas of life.
Climbing higher and higher, seeking eternal peace,
I shall build a bridge, crossing the expansive ocean
Of poetry of *dharma* and *karma*.
While the dance of blood and fire rages,
And live coals burn the body, and the flames,   300
Thirsting for blood, stretch their tongues, hungrily;
While religiosity burns people's power and the light
Of secularism is dimmed in smoke; while humanity
Crashes down on earth like a giant tree,
To resist and stop all such catastrophic misdeeds,
I shall sing with all my heart
The epic of Shri Lakshmana's Great Quest.

My ambition is to see the flower of the twin principles
Of equality and egalitarianism bloom and spread
Its fragrance. The horizon of the poet's experience   310
Is vast and wide; I shall climb higher and higher,
And present in modern Kannada, divine nectar
To the human multitude.
The world is their home, humanity is their family.
Adapting the essence of *Ramayana* in all languages
Transcending the consciousness of earthly life,
And reaching supra human consciousness,
Illuminating the awakened conscious energy,
While I listen to the sweet notes of the larks that utter
Poetic truths, while the divine voice of awakened energy,   320
Splicing the womb of epochs, floats across in waves,
I have narrated in this epic, the sacred story
Of Lakshmana, a song of victory, so vast and high
That it equals the sky and the sea.

Primeval Energy, free from attributes and form,
Is an endless ocean, with neither beginning nor end.

The same element of energy, with the principle of joy
Blended, has infused the earthly body with divinity.
All the five elements are united here, happily.
Energy begets the Sky; the Sky the Wind, 330
The Wind Fire and the Fire Water,
Water the earth, the earth plants,
Plants food, and food Man –
This is the order of creation of the physical world.
All static forms become the embodiment of energy.
Energy itself is solidified and assumes a new shape.
A lotus-like scientific image is formed.
This is the achievement of mankind, as corroborated
By the physical sciences.

This staff of Rama will not bend under any pressure, 340
Illusion or any trap of temptations. Lord Ramachandra,
Is incomparable, in the conflicts of joy and sorrow,
In the arena of happiness and anguish. There is Saumitri,
His right shoulder, the light of the sun in the dense,
Dark forest of despair, a refuge, a succour, as tall as
Himachala and Sahyadri. He is the Ganga of self-confidence,
The stick supporting the life of Shri Rama; the bridge
For Shri Rama's march.

Saumitri is the conscience all along the amazing path
Of the epochs. In the moving wheels of method 350
And system, in the task of churning new thoughts,
His story is both ancient and contemporaneous.
He is the yardstick for generosity and virtue;
He is the seer of the principles of Shri Rama;
He is the leader of the quest; he is the noble pillar
To save civilisation from the edge of destruction.
He is like the sun for the fortunes of the earth;
He is an ascetic, who has renounced everything.
My aim is to worship him through the pure waters
Of poetry. Search for Sita is the everyday search 360

For the rescue of helpless women; it is an archetype
Of destroying the spirit of Ravana and upholding
The essence of Rama, the image of truth.
I shall extricate from the womb of time,
An epic of the Great Quest. Let the nations, gloating
In brute strength, feed on the nuclear mire.

Uprooting the differences between caste and creed,
Colour and money, eliminating the destructive feelings
Of high and low, friendship and enmity, of duality itself,
Flies the triumphant flag of Shri Rama, the noblest man.   370
His royal staff of authority stands tall and stiff, high
In the sky; and all people salute it and sing paeans.

The brute-like nations wallowing in the atomic mire,
Their horns are caught and held
By Bharata, like shivah the lord of the Bull, in a story of peace.
Because of this country, peace in the world, the loftiness
Of spirituality, and the awareness of peace
Will come alive again. A radiance full of energy
Will envelop the sky of this world. The deep secret
Of Ishwari, a search for truth, this poem undertakes.   380
I have seen the vision, the awakened human
Consciousness, exemplified by Shri Rama
And Lakshmana. O, Saumitri! God of Peace!
Guide me so that the culture of this epoch,
Ideology, social consciousness, righteousness,
And decency – all come together, along with
An awareness of the pains of the weak and downtrodden.
You are the poet, Girivajra, the master-writer.
I shall only be the ink and hold the pen just in name.
The bird in my heart sings a sweet song   390
Without any pause. The month of Spring is nearing
Fullness. My mind is perturbed as to how words
Can be put together, which tune to match, and
Which rhythm to choose. Look! There, I have seen

The world lit up by your song. I shall enjoin my feeble
Voice to your great melody.

I shall light the spark of mass-upsurge to lead
To a blazing flame. In all living creatures,
I shall awaken deep poetic sentiments.
Let the lives of people acquire the three-fold *rasa*   400
Of the Erotic. Championed by this epic of Lakshmana,
Let there be a whole new creation, in which values
That brighten up life – self-control, scrutiny,
Learning, valour, courtesy – are born again.

Saumitri has blessed me, causing the flow of poetry,
Which contains the nine life-giving gems, hidden
All these years in my heart, the story of the Great Quest.
When the bud of aesthetic emotion blossomed
In my inert heart, waiting for an outlet, years together,
Saumitri, you freed it from the prison of the 'six foes',   410
Sprinkled nectar on it, taught me the way of poetic
Movement, and brought to life the Goddess Saraswati.
While the peacock-mind spreads its feathers,
To show me the new creation; and the music
Of 'OM' reverberates in my heart, in the horizon
Of my mind stands the glorious sculptured image,
An embodiment of fulfillment.

Canto Two

'I am Tortured in the Fire of Anguish'

||๖||

In the kingdom of Kosala, the blessed city of Saketa,
Built by Manu and ruled over by King Raghu –
The crown of the Ikshwaku lineage, appears to be
A great vision of brave Kshatriyas of a radiant,
Royal lineage, of men of action and valour,
Performers of holy rituals, and seekers of might.

The city of Saketa, the abode of truth,
Is known as Ayodhya. Impregnable against
Any enemy, it is a symbol of heroism and courage.
There are stories in the pristine Ikshwaku lineage 10
Of emperors who gave up sons to save the kingdom's wealth.
There is the renowned story of Harishchandra,
Who sold himself to protect the integrity of his vow.
There is the blessed story of the saint-king Dilipa,
Who performed many a ritual and rejected
The status of Indra. There is the demeanour of Raghu,
Who performed Vishwajitu Yajna and gave away
Everything in charity.

Like the ends of a sari of a woman embodying fame,
Flags fly on tall mansions and palaces flaunting excellence, 20

Kissing the clouds. Gods reside in gold-domed temples
Of Saketa, and refuse to leave it. On the ceilings and walls
There, pleasing, artistic pictures are carved gracefully.
Creepers grow on the ledges of upper storeys
Filled with masses of various fruits and flowers.
Maidens in the city sprinkle flowers on the heads of kings;
They draw pictures of flowers, leaves and creepers
Around the windows. Believing the flowers and creepers
To be real, bees surround them and caught in great attraction,
They delight amongst them. 30

The brightness of lightning goes through the window,
And it is light everywhere. Doves and pigeons enjoy themselves
On the ledges at their own will in conjugal attachment.
Peacocks dance happily with feathers spread out,
As if giving intricate lessons in hair-styles.
The palace glitters in grandeur, like a shining example
Of skilled sculpture.

Jealous of the clouds that can assume any shape,
Many structures have reached the sky,
Many temple-dome shaped structures 40
Stand up amidst the fort-like marvels.
Birds are lost in wonder on the domes;
The song of the gently blowing wind is melodious;
The water of Sarayu river is mixed with perfume,
Used by women after bathing and glitters with many hues.
Enchanting waves sparkle with the radiance of a rainbow;
As if telling a soothing story to good people,
Sarayu flows with a murmuring sound. On both the banks
Of the river, the line of temples appeals to all senses
Of the onlookers and glitters. The path of kings is fragrant 50
With sweet water sprinkled on it, and Ayodhya
Is the pride of Lakshmi, the people's goddess; it protects
Her pride, being the home of prosperity, of gold and grains.

Saketa is the yardstick to measure
Truth and righteousness and the moral path.

Six-*yojana*-long and three *yojanas* wide,
It was a new experimental ground for architecture,
With nine entrances, nine pure Sudarshana *chakras*
Hidden in the womb of the city.
It is a city where nectar fountains spring forth, 60
In the middle of which there lies the golden palace.
The palace as well as the city is full of light always.
It is invincible and impenetrable,
Even for an unrestrained crowd of enemies.
Ayodhya is decorated like the checkered cloth
Used in dice-games. There are the main roads
Bedecked with lines of trees on either side.
The whole path is colourful with fallen flowers;
It is like a silk sari spread to walk on.
Nectar-sweet fruits are there in the orchard, 70
And all seasons gather there with great pleasure.
While the movement of horses raises dust,
Scented water is sprinkled all over the city roads.
Rows of houses close together, crowded alleys,
The music of *veena* and small drums resound here.
Rich paths, oceans of charm and love,
Are like swings for a worshipper of beauty.
Fort and bastion, the moat, elephants, horses and army,
All these protect the city of Saketa.

Dasharatha's palace is resplendent 80
With seven storeys, and it shines like a high mountain
Shaped with the skill of building multi-storeyed mansions.
These are the places for sport where the expertise
Of skilled architects is embodied. A happy mix of
Music from drums, *veena* and pipes pleases all there.
Misers, betrayers, cruel people and atheists,
And those denied education are unknown in Ayodhya.
There are people proficient in the Vedas and Vedanga,
Those virtuous priests maintaining *Aahataagni*,
And Pramathas who are blessed with six noble qualities, 90

Such as tranquility and self-restraint.
There are great warriors, experts in war,
And a multitude of quick and shrewd Siddhas.

Dasharatha is the son of Indumati and Aja;
And he has cultivated peace, tranquility and renunciation.
He is one with foresight as well as is virtuous, compassionate
And brave; and he looks on everyone with equal respect.
A tiger among men, a man of truth, he is adept at all skills.

All admire and trust him,
Praising him with love and respect, they are proud of him.   100
'Who is equal on earth to this king?' they ask proudly.
Tributary kings walk with heads bent, and all enemies
Tremble with fear. Noble kings are his great friends;
And he rules with a wealth of compassion.

Gaining victory over thousands of enemies,
He is a brave warrior equal to Indra, the king
Of gods. The king knows the essence of the Vedas
Being with a group of quick-witted scholars.
He is ascetic, radiant, and only he can match himself.

Once he was about to shoot an arrow at a deer,   110
When it stood up jumping like distress personified.
Seeing it, Dasharatha's heart melted with compassion;
He put the arrow back in the quiver.
Seeing the brightness of his wives' eyes
In the eyes of the deer, he gave up hunting deer.

The people in Saketa came to the palace once,
Troubled greatly by tigers, and other wild animals.
They begged him for help; and Dasharatha left the city
To hunt those animals. Reaching the banks of the Tamasa,
He shot an arrow following only the sounds he heard.   120
The arrow, travelling at lightning-speed, wounded Shravana,
The son of a sage. The good son, who had come to fill a pot
With water, screamed in pain and fell to the ground,

Like a small plant, beautified by sprouts and buds,
Breaking and collapsing on the earth.
Behind the shrubs, it seemed as if an elephant
Had come to drink water. It was the result of an illusion.
The gurgling sound had led to the killing.

'Alas! Was the glorious life of the sage's son
Sacrificed to my ignorance? Did I pluck off the bud, 130
Which was about to bloom?' Lamenting thus,
Aja's son Dasharatha, with his heart in his mouth,
Dropped down like a giant tree, knelt and picked up
The young boy, embraced and caressed him,
While the fire of sorrow raged and burnt the heart,
Paternal love wringing the body and haunting him.
Not knowing the depths of love of Shravana's parents,
The great hero carried him on his shoulders.
Stepping on the ground with a heavy heart,
The noble man walked towards the blind couple. 140

Unable to bear the misery of thirst,
They sat exhausted, water being a mirage.
The environment burning with the heat of sighs,
Sprouting plants wilting in the heat of the sun,
Blind eyes suffering in despair. King Dasharatha
Went near the couple and stood in fear and hesitation,
While cold wind pierced him like a knife,
And his body was cold.

The sage and his wife, bewildered in anxiety,
Smelt blood and were scared. Sensing someone's 150
Arrival, the wife came forward. 'What is it?
What has happened?' she screamed,
Groped and stroked the lotus face of her son.
As if the innards had been squeezed,
As if the womb that carried him had split
As if the heart and eyes had cracked into pieces.
The river of tears broke its banks and flowed madly.

All the desires of her heart, chopped off by a hatchet,
Met with dust in a rush. Clutching her son to her breast,
The mother rolled down to the earth, 160
Like a creeper that had lost its support.
The sage groped and unable to see, tripped,
And fell on Dasharatha, attempting to feel his son's face.
King Dasharatha felt as if a thousand scorpions
Bit him all at once. He begged them with folded hands:
'O sage, I have committed a crime unknowingly.
I am the son of Aja. I have killed your lovely son.
Please forgive me, revered teacher, great sage,
I am tormented in the fire of anguish.'
The sage drowned, caught in the terrifying, fast eddy 170
Of the sea of sorrow. He moaned in pain:
'Has the fortune of hearing the voice of my son,
Whom I cannot see, ended today?
Has the treasure of our life been lost today?
Has life bid the last farewell today?
Without offering us water at the end of our lives,
Did you long for water for us now?
Where have you disappeared, my child?'

The innards of the sage were cut, lamenting
The death of his son; his throat full and breath choked. 180
Years of austerity had turned into anguish for the couple;
Like a ball of fire, it had tormented their minds.
The earth, burnt and blackened in the heat of the sun,
Had split in anger. Staring at the sky, open-mouthed,
The blind father burst out:

'Don't you know the burning anguish of losing a son?
The feelings of an aged mind burning with agony?
When riches, fame and grandeur go to your head,
How can you care for the life and living of the poor?
Are you aware of all their desires being pulverised, 190
Caught in the spokes of wheels? Does it become

Ruling kings to hunt humans and taste fresh blood?
Did you tear my son apart to decorate your door?'

Sorrowing thus, he cursed the scion of the sun
Dynasty, in anger and despair: 'May your life be such
That you will have no children near you when you die.
May your cattle become barren; may the pyre of worry
Burn your happiness of having sons; may your life,
Full of tears, regrets, sighs and suffering,
End with the loss of your sons.' 200

Dasharatha was drained of all compassion and remorse.
Empty of breath, in the cracked, arid expanse of the sage's heart,
As if molten lead was poured into his ear,
Struck by thunder out of nowhere,
Dasharatha went back to Saketa, stupefied and
Depressed, carrying an empty heart.

Canto Three

'I Commend You; the Yajna is Fruitful'

||๖||

The god Brahma himself, it is said, called Dasharatha
To exterminate Shambara, a *rakshasa*. When the *rakshasa*
Was defeated and he began to run towards his city,
Dasharatha pursued him. On the way, in the thick,
Enveloping darkness, the axle-nail in the chariot-wheel
Of the king broke; and Kaikeyi, the beloved of Dasharatha,
Drove the chariot with great skill. Dasharatha, victor
Of all the three worlds, remained undefeated, and
Was renowned as one of the greatest charioteers.

Pleased, he granted Kaikeyi two boons: 10
'Gods are witness to my words, I shall keep my promise;
I shall not hesitate to fulfill it, Please ask me,' he said.
With great joy, admiring her husband, she said:
'I shall ask for them later when I need them'.

Vasishtha, the priest of the clan, a jewel among sages
Conquering the five senses, is the one who pacified,
With his chant of peace, the hatred, envy and egotism
Of the son of Gadhi. He is the one, the embodiment of patience,
Who gifted the status of Brahmarshi to Sage Vishwamitra.
When Vishwamitra got angry, and all the sons of Vasishtha 20

Were killed, he suffered quietly, with his heart on fire.
No one could survive against the law of nature,
He thought and swallowed the poison of pain,
Unperturbed, unruffled. He was, luckily, available as
The royal priest for the Ikshwaku lineage; and
He continued as a sage, protecting the values of tradition,
In a state of detachment.

Dasharatha had eight ministers: Drishti, Jayanta,
Vijaya, Siddharta, Artha Sadhaka, Mantrapala,
Ashoka and Sumantra. Suyagna, Jabali,   30
Kashyapa and Markandeya were the priests.
The ministers, councillors were gentle and courteous;
Refined in government, winning over anger and pain;
Achievers who could work for the welfare of the people.
They were scared of disrepute, radiant, scholarly,
Well-versed in precepts, firm of mind, forgiving,

Aware that service for the country was service to god.
Never telling a lie for selfish ends,
They were shrewd, coming to know in time all the news from
Other lands as well as from their own, intelligent,   40
And skilled. Whoever turned treacherous, be he son
Or relative, they would punish him, strictly following
Existing laws. Strengthening the entire army, adding to
The royal treasury, they were like trustees.
Skilled in politics, brave, valiant heroes,
Always assisting to protect good citizens,
They would not hurt the innocent, and they would view
Even the surrendering enemy with mercy.

Pure in mind, speech and action, without blemish,
Embodiments of compassion, carrying on   50
Without giving any room for internal strife,
United in political work, without disagreement,
Statesmanship and sensitive action and talent –
These qualities characterised all of them,

Where everything is tested – in Ayodhya.
Revered Kausalya, faithful Sumitra,
And beauteous Kaikeyi light up Dasharatha's palace:
The eldest, Kausalya, silent, full of love,
And a woman rich in good qualities;
Sumitra, of a good character, embodying sacrifice;   60
And dear queen Kaikeyi, beloved of Dasharatha.

While the ship of Dasharatha's life moved on,
Like a stream of honey, happily, one day,
In the grand palace garden, he saw a mother sparrow,
Feeding its fledglings. It was then that the anguish
Of being childless touched him deep inside, with pain
As well as the desire for offspring. This longing grew
Into a huge tree, unbearable; and Dasharatha
Spoke of his heart's desire to Vamadeva,
Vasishtha and other sages: 70

'Revered teachers, a crack has appeared
In the golden vase of my heart. The nectar of my life
Is dripping away, empty is the body.
My life is troubled and tired in darkness;
How can the wick of the lamp of progeny
Be brought to life again? Should the lineage of Ikshwaku
Get erased with me? What is left for me now?
I have become blind. Without direction, my heart is dead,
Like a mango tree seized by parasitic plants.
I am despondent. The opulence of this kingdom   80
Is like the decoration carried out on a corpse.
My life is like a mirror handed to a blind man.'
Dasharatha spoke thus in all piteousness.

Vamadeva called, at once, Sumantra
And Vasishtha for a meeting, and all the sages
Decided to perform Ashwamedha. Sage Jabali
In acute distress, said: 'Let there be Ashwamedha but no violence.
Beings of love are not born out of violence of any kind.

Call Rishyashringa, and worship the gods of fire
With gentleness. Honour everyone, rich or poor; 90
Let them be content and let them bless you.
Your vow will reach god and love will manifest
Itself in the pious act, performed in the presence
Of Rishyashringa. Words of blessing will be for you,
Yours will be the good fortune of having sons.'

Dasharatha was soothed with the pearl-like
Words of Jabali. Quickly, he invited with great honour,
The great Sage Rishyashringa, the embodiment of asceticism,
The very holy bank of the river Sarayu was chosen;
The construction of the ritual hall went on in ceremony. 100
The town was full of parks, springing fountains,
Platforms for drinks, markets of flowers.
They proudly decorated the town and alley.
A continuous line of crores of earthen bricks
Arrived in a grand procession, from all four directions.
Shouts of victory echoed, an elixir to the ear,
Flaunting the victory of Ayodhya's culture.
They were not bricks for a building that cut open the nation;
It was a journey for building a great mansion of unity.

Janaka, the kings of Kashi, Sindhu, and Kekaya, 110
Romapada, and the kings of Saurashtra arrived there.
To provide comforts for the royal guests, a stable
And a kitchen were specially built. They all came
From the east and the west of Bharatavarsha;
From the south and north, south-east and south-west,
From the north-east and north-west, from all directions possible.

Heads held high, brown and well-built,
Eyes radiating light, broad-chested,
Great strength of body, strong shouldered,
Wearing *dhotis*, cloth over their shoulders,
They sit in the south – *vanaras*, *rakshasas*, 120
Aryans and Dramilas, all together.

Women wearing *suragi*, jasmine, *jaji, champaka*,
Clothes ever so colourful, silk in shimmering gold,
Plaited hair adorned, ornaments in the neck, were there.
The beauty of silken thread, the brightness of a rainbow
Pashmina from Kashmir, Chanderi from the north,
Colours of Vairani saris, like the sea expanding,
They spread the message of unity.
The throng of many cattle was so beautiful,
With the gold foil tied to their horns. 130
Milk in gold vessels caught the eyes and shone.
Dasharatha stood there as the ceremonial head.

No one in pain, none in hardship,
The wealthy and the weak were not discriminated.
To establish equality in life and equal sharing,
A stage was set on the banks of the river Sarayu.
Victorious shouts of praise rent the sky.
Each and every branch stretching towards the sky,
Each and every root descending to the nether world,
The sacred fig tree of Bharatavarsha arose there, 140
A symbol of great unity.

As different countries and regions gathered there,
As a symbol of universal brotherhood,
As the keynote of unity was embodied in Ayodhya,
The great tree of culture stood high, in contentment.
Everyone was honoured; there was no displeasure;
Hospitality, contentment, and affection reigned there.
It was the divine chant for hospitality for everyone.
'Just as the cultured ones in all castes deserve honour,
Honour the Brahmanas, the Kshatriyas, the Vaishyas, 150
The Shudras, and all the great men of all the countries' –
Following this motto, everyone there was treated with respect.

Singing the praise of Somaraja, destroyer of sins,
Six Parashara posts of sacrifice were built; one from
Shleshatmaka tree and two of *devadaru* tree

Were joined together. The grandeur of the ritual platform
Was indescribable; all the sages praised it with joy.
They carried on the ritual with the sacrificial fire,
Following each and every prescribed rule.
Oblations were offered to gods in devotion; and   160
To those well-versed in the Vedas and others
Of the whole community were given in charity,
Herds of cows, lakhs in number, and ten crores
Of gold coins.

Dasharatha, an ornament of the Sun-lineage,
Felt fulfilled, while a priest filled with greed,
Went near the king to test him, and begged him:
'Give me the gem-studded bracelet you are wearing.'
He pleaded even as the final rituals went on, and soon after,
The king gave away the sparkling ornament to the priest.   170
Sages praised him saying what he did was good;
And all the citizens praised him in admiration.
Abundant food, special and tasty,
Everyone ate his fill and wished the king well.

An emaciated beggar in rags,
His back bent like a bow, nourishing a great desire
To eat a good meal, with his stomach harassing him
Like a heated pan, his lips cracked and bleeding,
A black body, a frame of ribs showing,
A child with him, a face withered in hunger,   180
Exhausted and crying, the tears of father and son
Now dried up and barren, crept inside eager for a meal.

The guard at the entrance stopped them in anger,
Pushed the father and son and made them fall on the floor.
'You, without a bath, wearing stinking, torn clothes,
Go away from here, this meal is not for you.
It is only for those who are clean as rituals demand.
Move, move away now. Our master is coming here.
Everything will go wrong with you in this sacred land' –

Thus he roared, scolded and mocked them. 190
Where could they bathe? The river had dried;
Where was the good fortune of new clothes for them?
When they lifted their heads, they could see,
Waving to them, the left-overs of delicacies eaten.
The mammoth of poverty was laughing uproariously.
While the whole universe harassed them in the form of hunger,
Rolling about with hands pressed on the floor,
They got near the remains of the grand meal and ate,
The father feeding the delicacies to his son.
Why a bath or cleanliness for the stomach? 200
Why decorate a heated frying pan?
Why clothes to wear, why worry about being clean?
It is supreme joy if hunger is quelled.

Anxiously, Dasharatha hastened there.
'What is all this? Why did you ask for the left-over,
Without coming to the dining hall?
This should not happen. I cannot bear this sin of lapse.
Alas! Alas! I have not seen a sight like this ever.
All are equal here, there is no discrimination;
Where there are exploiters, there will be the exploited.
Eating together, deliberating together, thinking together, 210
When brotherhood was such, the righteous earth cracked,
Slumped in the depth, the fruit of the ritual is lost.
A mishap through discrimination, Alas! Alas!
How did the poisonous seed sprout?
There are weeds everywhere, why this difference?
Who built the impenetrable fort of poverty?
Without hesitating, bring down and burn this
Dome of difference so it does not raise its head again.

'Nothing is lowly, nothing is superior; mankind is one –
Thus this sacred land proclaims. Priests, the low-born, 220
The king and the common man, all are equal here.
The mean custom of discriminating among people

Is unacceptable; pull it out even as it sprouts.
That exploitation is a cruel spear, and that it is
Death for those that are guilty of it,
Proclaim everywhere; it is the king's order.
This law exists to pull down and destroy
The ramparts that have risen between hearts.'
The king made the announcement and walked away.

He picked up the old man and consoled him: 230
'Please forgive me; I have committed a great injustice.
Great soul, did you eat the fruit of my sin?
Did you swallow poison and punish your body and mind?
After drinking the brew of hatred and envy of all,
Did you bless the world? To get rid of the sins of the world,
To make the *yajna* bear fruit, keep your feet
On my head. The dust of your feet is holy.'

Taking the child in his arms, stroking it with love,
Holding the old man's hand with compassion,
And leading him on, he gave him a bath, clothed him, 240
And served him grand meals prepared for the *yajna*.
Then, offering him diamonds, opals, coins and cattle,
He felt he had received fulfillment in the *yajna*, and
He was content and very happy. So was the whole world,
And the joy reached the sky.

There was quiet in the ritual hall;
The priest and Dasharatha were in deep meditation.
A moment later, from the platform of worship,
Agni, the God of Fire, emerged radiant.
Enveloping the earth and sky, he shone, 250
Red eyed and clothed in red, with ideal features.
Wearing fine ornaments, his radiance matching
That of the sun, the Lord of the earth said:
'I am pleased, O king. I shall give you a sweet dish;
This is the divine gift. Your devotion has borne fruit.
Give this to your wives, sons will be born,

Truthful and bright lights of the lineage.
'Prajapatyam naram vidhdhi mamihabhagyatam nripa'.
Saying so, he gave the king the shining golden pot.

While Putrakameshti ritual went on there, 260
Over here, among the people a great fair of prosperity
Was held. It was the Great Quest for the power of nature.
Songs and great poetry praising the plenitude
The women of Saketa sang in joy.
The song *Holi holi holiyo holi holi*
Resounded, expressing their desire for plenitude
For Ayodhya, plentitude for Kosala, and abundance
In their fields and farms. It was their Putrakameshti,
A festival celebrating the fruitful efforts of farmers.

Another observance in praise of fertility 270
Was 'the worship of the serpent,' called 'Nagamandala'.
The petal of Areca flower called *hingara* and
Likewise coconuts are symbols of fruition.
Actors representing the serpent and the half-woman-half-man
Ishwara danced in abandon round the intricate
Designs, drawn in many powdered colours.
There was an orchestra accompanying it,
With various instruments; and all of them endeavoured
To satisfy Nagaraja, the serpent-king, in order
That the glory of progeny may be theirs. 280

As they celebrated fertility,
There was also a festival called *'Keddaso'*,
To celebrate the coming of age of the earth-Mother.
Later, when seeds are sown, there will be a big harvest.
'Do not cut what is green, nor break what is dry;
The earth will become barren, take care' –
Songs with such messages resounded.
The kingdom of Ayodhya had become a great
Hall of religious observance, celebrating
Fertility of both man and earth. 290

Canto Four

'Four Flowers Bloomed in a Bunch'

||௬||

Southern wind blew clothing the king softly;
The thick web of anxiety was shed and a new tune played;
The severed life-line had rejoined in beauty; and
There was music with a new tune and a new beat.
Joyful and blessed with good fortune,
Radiant like the Fire-god, Dasharatha bowed
Before Rishyashringa, got his blessings and left
In haste for the palace.

The barren cow is fertile now, the stumps will sprout;
The flower of fortune for Raghu's lineage will bloom;　　　10
The barren will conceive and the soil of the desert
Will cool, and the fragrance of the earth will spread.
Thinking so, the king distributed the *payasa*:
Half of it, first, to the senior queen Kausalya;
Half of what remained to the faithful Sumitra,
The calm and intelligent gem of the lineage;
And what remained to the beloved Kaikeyi.
Having thus distributed the gift of Agni,
Dasharatha felt buoyant with joy.

Nine months were over, the body and mind were joyous.　　20
On the ninth day, during the bright lunar fortnight,

In the month of Chaitra, under Punarvasu star,
While the planets, the Sun, Mars, Jupiter, Saturn,
And Shukra shone at their highest peak,
In Karkataka *lagna*, while the Moon and the Jupiter
Rose, Shri Ramachandra was born to Kausalya.
In Ashlesha, Lakshmana and Shatrughna were born to Sumitra,
And, under the star Pushya, at an auspicious moment,
Bharata was born to Kaikeyi.

While all the three worlds were joyous, 30
The cuckoos sang, and the light of countless stars
Seemed to have come down to the earth, glittering.
Generous in mind and in a charitable mood,
Dasharatha donated diamonds and opals
Which sparkled on earth and in the sky.

Those imprisoned were freed right away,
Happiness, comfort and desires conjoined.
Harassment from thieves, from deceitful imposters,
From gamblers, lustful men, imposters,
And from traitors will never be found in the city 40
Of Saketa.

Four flowers blooming in one bunch,
Grew up as symbols of love and care:
Ramachandra, endowed with all good features,
The saviour of the Raghu lineage, refuge for the world.
A symbol of life for all, like shadows
Of one another, the brothers grew up.
Incomparable commitment to the welfare of all,
Learned in the Vedas, knowledgeable about everything,
Treasures of goodness, well-versed in rituals, 50
Of good character, and detached from temptations.
Lakshmana was handsome and prosperous,
Free from the envy and conflict of royal families.
With proper values in life, conquering weaknesses,
The brothers became invincible.

Sumitra, the second wife of Dasharatha,
Appeared thin like a wild oleander branch.
Observing rituals strictly, praying and fasting,
Living free from envy with Kausalya,
She found endless self-satisfaction, contentment and peace. 60
Ayodhya became a prison for her, and she was
A prey to a feeling of helplessness; but, she transcended
All these trivialities, and rose high, the virtuous woman.
Having understood the essence of Vedantic wisdom.
Not getting caught in temptation, a sense of duty
Was always awake in her. In the rain of present and future,
She was like an earthen doll, melting into nothingness.
Brave in consciousness, conscious of others' pain,
Turning away from censure of others, generous, controlled,
Wishing well for others, looking at joy and sorrow 70
With equanimity – that was Sumitra.

Canto Five

'Ayodhya Became a Charming Garden'

||6||

In strength of character, good looks and virtue,
Saumitri became the life and soul of Rama.
He became a great symbol for a complete vision
Of Rama's power. Without Rama sleep, food and sport
Were rejected by Saumitri. His sense of self-sacrifice
Was as endless as the Sahyadri mountain range.
Like the waves of the sea, swelling unceasingly,
He would take the name of Rama. Like a fish out of water,
Struggling and rolling on the sand, but which would heave
A sigh of relief only after getting into water, 10
Lakshmana shared an inseparable bond with Shri Rama –
The bond of birth and rebirth and epochs.
While Rama slept,
Lakshmana would keep awake to protect him.
The soul as witness, steadfastness not getting infirm,
Shri Rama would be happy within. Pushing aside food
Offered to him, he would cajole Kausalya and
Thrusting Lakshmana forward, he would feed him and
Dance with joy. As Rama's hair was combed,
Saumitri would go in. Lakshmana would be 20
Sent by Rama for a bath before him. He would be full of joy.
The bond between Rama and Lakshmana was unbreakable.

One day while Dasharatha was resting,
Rama, Lakshmana and Bharata came in running.
The king opened his arms to fondle them,
And called them all to him, with great joy.
Rama got on to his right lap and Bharata sat
On the other side. Lakshmana felt sad.
His heart wept and eyes were moist.
'Where can I sit? Where is place for me?'   30
He yearned, there was neither right or left.
His mind was upset and swayed like a monkey,
In the branches of the tree, seeking love,
Flew around, became still again and stood grieving.

Rama got down, embraced Lakshmana,
Wiped away his tears, gave the warmth of his heart
To his brother and filled with love
The emptiness that was seen. The salt image of Rama
Melted in the brotherly love of Lakshmana,   40
Becoming one with the ocean of their love.
Imbibing the sweet honey of the love between them,
King Dasharatha felt proud and Ayodhya
Became a charming garden, rich with love.

Canto Six

'Do Not Fear, I am Indra's Commander'

||☉||

Dasharatha's life-ship sailed as if on a river of honey
In the sea of sweetness, in uninterrupted light,
With a loving view of life, awareness of art
Filled with enticing beauty of royalty,
Pleasure and austerity, harmony of fruition,
Attachment and devotion, a pleasing creation,
Comfort, beauty and dignity, rapture, and grace,
Truthful Harishchandra, Raghu, Dilipa, Sagara,
Bhagiratha – a tradition of strength and refinement.
Dasharatha, the royal swan of the Ikshwaku lineage   10
Shone in the royal court.

'O Sumantra! I am enveloped in worry.
I cannot sleep nor can I relish any food.
Old age has assaulted me. I feel detached.
"Your son shall enjoy the pleasure of being a king,"
Thus I announced in madness at Kaikeyi's wedding.
How can I break the tradition of Raghu-lineage?

'Fear of war does not bother the kingdom;
I have offered enough charity and achieved people's welfare.
I am satiated with all pleasures the earth has to offer.   20

But the anxiety about Rama's coronation brothers me,'
Said the king.

Sumantra tried to console him:
'Shri Ramachandra, full of courtesy and politeness,
Is considered their own son by all the three mothers.
He has shown brotherly love, and his brothers won't disagree;
They will be pleased. Moreover, people love Rama.
Stop worrying, king; there are no obstacles.'

Vasishtha was there, radiant in glory;
Vishwamitra, the great sage, arrived then,   30
Well-versed in chants and prayers. Dasharatha,
Giving the venerable man offerings, washing his feet, said:
'I am happy at the arrival of a holy man
Like nectar churned from the ocean of worldly existence.
Like drizzling rain falling on dry and cracked earth,
Like a lost treasure tugging one's hand again,
Like delight overflowing at the time of a great festival.
I feel fulfilled by your celestial appearance.
What is your pleasure, great mentor?
What is your command? Why do you hesitate?   40
I shall carry it out dutifully, Please tell me.'
He pleaded with courtesy.
Kaushika was doubtful. Thoughts of Mankind
Flooded his mind; and he said: 'The Aryan kings
Have become pleasure-loving and lazy.
With many wives and sons and daughters,
Selfish desires are dancing in their minds.
The sea has not been crossed; Kishkindha
Has not been reached; and none has gone beyond Aryanvarta.
They have no navy or jungle troops or even a well-equipped army.   50
There is no strain of heroism in them,
No light of sacrifice, justice or rational thinking.
There is neither creativity nor energy; and
Moral values are extinct. Lowly greed has gained respect.

Vasishtha is the symbol of purity of virtue,
Founder of a lineage, tempering worldly business
With tradition. The culture of virtue is imprisoned;
All indulge in words, not action. Reigning in victory
Outside Aryanvarta, Aryan kings have become frogs
In the well.   60

'For Shri Rama, in managing the state,
Hunger, thirst and the experience of pain
Will be of help. The throne that has not stepped
On the hardship-nails, will collapse. Experience is the peak of truth.
Only through sacrifice can one see the real world.
The great Sage Kaushika has arrived
To make Shri Rama aware of it.'

Full of expectations, Sage Vishwamitra
Has come to Ayodhya. Self-confidence flashes
In his heart, in his eyes, in his physical strength.   70
Muscles stand stiff, ready for any situation.
Sculpted by Vishwamitra's will, all doubts
And dilemmas are shaken off.

Dasharatha spoke again. 'Great teacher!
I wait for your command, give me directions.
If the services of a layman like me are not offered to you,
They are futile.'
'Maricha and Subahu have become impediments.
Tataka and Sunda, are the *rakshasas* who can take any form
At will. Extremists they are and drop blood and meat   80
On the fire of sacrifice and ruin our rituals and *yajnas*.
All observances and vows taken are wasted.
Ravana has spread out his net of soldiers and colonised
Many places, and our freedom is lost.
No new religious observances can go on;
Debates and arguments about knowledge and science
Have become impossible. New experimental weapons
Cannot be tested. They seize divine weapons from us;

And establish their empire by force. My mind reeling,
I have come here, helpless and depressed,'   90
Vishwamitra narrated his woes.

The sage continued: 'You have Shri Rama;
An ocean of truth and valour, strong and radiant,
Embodiment of strength, terror for the *rakhashas*.
Rama destroys enemies, brings peace to the world.
There is none to compare with him at times of war.
I know none other brave one who can protect us.
I want Rama for ten days, O, supreme among men.
If you fulfill my desires, you will be benefited.
You are a truthful man who will keep his promise.   100
Rama will be with me for the welfare of the world!'

Struck by the spear of Kaushika's words like lightning,
Dasharatha collapsed on the ground in sorrow,
In anticipation of separation! The heart trembled,
The whole body broke out in a sweat. The dam of love
For Rama had burst. Unable to stand the weight of sorrow,
Falling and getting up, fainting again, silent,
His heart was split by Vishwamitra's thunderbolt.
Like a banana stem, the womb of filial love
Had burst. The tender creeper of love rooted   110
Under the ground was nipped, charred and tormented.
Getting up, humbly, Dasharatha
Begged: 'He is just a boy. Can he be sent to a forest?
It is not for him to fight with *rakashasas*. Venerable sage,
Trust me, I shall come. I have the well-equipped army
Of Ayodhya; I have soldiers brave and courageous,
Unequalled in the whole country.
My valour is reputed through all the three worlds.
I shall come with you, fight against anybody, and
Protect your *yajnas* and other rituals. Do not fear;   120
I am the commander of Indra himself.

'Rama is my life; Rama is my gold;
And I cannot live in this world without Rama.

In the absence of Rama, this Ayodhya,
This kingdom, this treasury, all are dead for me.
For this weakness of mine, born of my love for the son,
I beg your pardon, O great sage.

'Ravana, of Pulastya lineage and the son of Vishravasu,
Is a very powerful man. If he, or the ones assigned by him
Like Maricha, Tataka and Subahu, come there   130
To disturb your rituals, I shall annihilate all of them.
You are like a god to me; O sage, have mercy on me.
Ravana is a powerful king and a great conqueror;
Rama is only a boy, and I cannot send him against Ravana.
Though I am not a coward, I am telling you the truth;
I beg you, kindhearted sage, to save Rama's life.
I will pledge my life and protect your rituals.'

Hearing these words of Dasharatha,
Vishwamitra exploded with uncontrollable anger.
Like the fire burning bright after *ghee* is poured into it,   140
He was terrifying in his anger. Holding his *kamandala*,
He got up and roared: 'Have you forgotten your promise?
Have you got caught in excessive love for your son?
No, such shameless behaviour does not befit kings
Of the Raghu-clan. Are your sense and wisdom eclipsed?
Of what use is living for a hundred years, if the life
Is tainted by broken promises!' roared Kaushika.
Kaushika's anger seemed to spread all over the earth
Like a forest fire. His nostrils flared and lips trembled.
His anger grew like fire, consuming forest after forest.   150
As if the great tree of the Raghu-clan was struck by thunder
And fell on the ground. Watching the sage's anger,
Fearing that Aryanvarta would be sacrificed
To the spear of Vishwamitra's determination,
Dasharatha rushed to Vasishtha, the great teacher, a jewel in the crest,
And fell at his feet, filled with anxiety.

Then the great sage becalmed his turmoil.
With love and regard, he spoke to Dasharatha:

'Send with him Shri Rama, the one with the all-conquering bow,
The noblest man. Renounce fear; Vishwamitra   160
Is the embodiment of righteousness, a treasure
Of knowledge, always experimenting with new ideas,
Assiduous in meditation and austere. He shall give
Rama great weapons. He is an achiever, very strong,
Radiant, and well-versed in the use of weapons.
Faced with the bright fire of his meditation,
What can *rakshashas* do but fall?
They will burn like moths and get destroyed,
In the pit of fire built by Kaushika.
He can see the past, future and the present.   170
Rama is a treasure of the earth, a life-saver;
Put aside selfishness, and do not limit Rama
And Lakshmana to the region of Aryanvarta alone.

'It does not become you,
To save the sea-water, holding it in your palm.
Burn away attachment; personal ego should not stand
Against the interests of the world! Desire is dirt.
A mere touch of its breath will put out the light
Of good work and harmony. Why should you
Embrace attachment calling it your own?
At sunrise, Shri Rama will set out early on his journey,   180
In a chariot; do not stop him. His journey of righteousness
Will cross dense forests of obstruction. While the golden-stringed
Kinnari gives out sweet musical notes, early in the morning,
Why do you cut the strings harshly?'

The nectar of Vasishtha's speech comforted him;
He visualised the divine nature of Shri Rama's story.
Bowing to the mystic sage, Dasharatha begged for forgiveness.
He touched with love the foreheads of Shri Rama
And Lakshmana, and bade them farewell.
With her eyes full of tears, Kausalya broke down;   190
She fell on the ground like a plantain tree with its head cut off!

A sense of duty that they had left for a great cause,
Was awakened in her, and austere Sumitra
Looked like dry wood suppressing fire within.

Canto Seven

'We were Born as Tongues of Fire'

||⑥||

The magnificent chariot rolled on along the royal path
With great speed. As soon as it went past the main gate,
Kaushika ordered the charioteer to stop it for a while.
Shri Rama and Lakshmana got off the chariot,
And the charioteer was told to go back to the palace.
'Come, my son Shri Rama, come my child Lakshmana.
Our journey has to be continued on foot from now on.
Blood may spurt from being pierced by sharp stones;
But, all that must be borne for the noble acts that lie ahead.'
So spoke the sage, with joy.   10

Their journey on foot continued.
Vishwamitra in front, Shri Rama following him
With Lakshmana carrying a bow, quiver on the shoulder.
They looked like the king of serpents with three hoods.
The boys were wearing animal skin and finger guards –
Far from Ayodhya, they walked as the sun reached the west.
They thought they had travelled enough,
And rested on the southern bank of the Sarayu.
'Rama, did I hurt your soft feet making you walk?
Are you tired, O son of Sumitra? On feet,   20

That walk on carpets, are there blisters?
As the sun blazed on your heads, did you suffer,
Unable to bear it?'

'We were born as tongues of fire, O Guru!
Does live coal feel the heat of the sun?
We shall destroy the *rakshasas*. We shall unburden
The earth of its weight of sin. Mother Sumitra
Has initiated us not to be scared of cold or rain
Or heat, and to serve the sage with body and soul.'
As Lakshmana spoke thus, the sage was happy. 30
'Did Sumitra say so? Is this true Lakshmana?
She is a great ascetic, a visionary,' said the sage.
'Yes, great teacher. This is what she said –
She of good character, free from sin, energetic,
Ready to accept new things,' said Lakshmana.

Sage Vishwamitra
Fell silent, and looked within himself.
Overcome with emotion, he said to the boys:
'I have made you walk through impassable forests,
On rocks, over pits. You have had experience 40
Of the pain and death among common people,
Their sorrows and acts of devotion. Too much comfort
Can be a curse, taking men into a world
Of forgetfulness. Kings, emperors and courtiers
Will all be drowned in pleasure and luxury,
And live without knowing the pain in the world.

'They see the world from the outside, unaware of the pain within.
Enamoured of various pleasures, they move on,
Oblivious of the continuous conflicts between
Justice and injustice, honour and shame. 50
The plight of the millions who wish to live
And their cries of pain, they do not see or hear.
Hence I have brought you both here, walking all the way,
So that you can hear the voice of pain.

If you have ears and heart, you will find stories
Everywhere, all over the world.
Stoop and put your ears to the ground at night,
And listen. You shall hear the low moans of pain.
All people in penury are great storytellers indeed.

'How can you hear, in your palace, 60
Their piteous songs? In the colourful reflections
In shiny mirrors, in the artificial life
Full of games of love, on marble walls,
And carpeted floors, everything lies hidden.
How will you learn the essence of experience
On earth, in the city of Saketa?'
The sage's heart was full, his voice was broken.
Deep emotion turned his eyes watery.
Rama spoke with contentment:
'We feel fulfilled, O sage! We are cleansed 70
By your vision of the ideal path, we shall be on the right path
In the scrutiny of justice and truth, in the search
For righteousness.'

'Children, finish your prayers and rituals here;
And I shall instruct you about skills to achieve great power.
Do not delay, follow them and prosper.
The power of scriptures will impart you a divine experience;
You will be free from lethargy, fear and fever;
Rakshasas will not overcome you even in sleep!
In the strength of mind and body, in the power of weapons, 80
In philosophical thoughts and in the will to act,
In arguments and counter arguments, in talk and discussion,
In fortune and prowess – in all these,
There will be none to equal you on this earth,
And you will conquer all,' said the sage,
Imparting them the sacred *mantras* with great joy.
Radiance flowed through the veins of the brothers.
They shone like the thousand-ray-sun in autumn.

That night, on the bank of Sarayu, under a banyan tree,
On a bed of leaves and grass, without a care,   90
They slept, the lights of the lineage of Sagara.

'Kausalya supraja Rama purva sandhya pravartate'
('O worthy son of Kausalya! Rama, the dawn is breaking') –
They heard the voice of the sage early in the morning
And got up and walked to the bank of river Sarayu.
They bathed, bowed to the sun and giving him offerings,
They chanted the sacred Gayatri verses.
The expanse, depth and grandeur of Ganga,
They saw, in wonder and amazement, in that lovely river.
They listened to the river flowing gently like the strings   100
Of *veena* being plucked, and became conscious of nature
Awakening the light of knowledge, enchanting.

Vishwamitra said, 'Son, in the shadow
Of parents and relatives, within the lines
Drawn by Guru Vasishtha, Reason crystallises
Like an iceberg of tradition. The mind-garden
Will grow robust and abundant.
But, like the abundant trees and plants of the forest
Not bearing fruit, the masses are sunk in pleasure.
When sovereignty loses its strength, vice prevails,   110
And divine power is destroyed, caught in the illusion
Of pleasure and celebration. All sages and saints
Think only of filling their bellies, and desirous of fame,
They end up barren like stumps of wood.
Differences have cropped up, internal feuds
Have, among the Aryan kings, raised anxiety;
And powers of evil on the prowl, having subdued the world,
Have pushed righteousness to the nether world.

Then, Shri Rama asked him:
'Who are they, great teacher? Is it Tataki,   120
Maricha or Subahu or any such other *rakshasas*?'
'None of them. They are mere branches. It is Ravana,

Who is very strong. The roots are where he is.
He is here, in the golden land of the island of Lanka.
Ayodhya, Videha, Siddhashrama, Kamashrama –
Nothing is far off for the one with ten heads.
He has the sharp sight of *rakshasas*; his influence
Is spread in every direction of Bharatavarsha.
He has bored into the ancient venerable culture
Like a ferocious insect and made it hollow.   130
He is matchless in the skill of spreading wrongs;
And the terrible army camp of his is pitched right in the heart
Of Aryanvarta. He cannot discriminate between
Right and wrong, just and unjust.

'Full of greed for wealth, power and selfishness
Governance is centred in the hands of one man.
Animal rule reigns all over;
Morality and materialism rub against each other;
Saketa has forgotten truth and principle.
Responsible consciousness is no more and concern   140
For humanity is dead, supplanted by 'master-slave'
Insolence. In the guise of Ravana's culture,
Dicatatorship reigns supreme.
'There is no place for communication, discussion,
Or analysis; there is no meeting of ministers, or assembly
Of wise and learned men. No freedom of the individual,
And no expression of culture; and there is none
To listen to the cries of the downtrodden.
Before the powerful, unrestrained king, Ravana,
All have become deaf and blind; and strife, riots,   150
And confusion have disturbed peace among the people.'
'We are ignorant, O Guru, of either Aryan governance
Or the nature of the *rakshasas*' crafty conduct.'
'People tolerate Ravana's cruel oppression,
As it is backed by wealth and heartless power.
In the intoxication of power, in the river of greed,
Morality, order and principles are swept away.'
'Why don't the people protest, O sage?'

'Do they have the strength to stop cruelty and wickedness?
Brahmins, Aryans, leaders among men, 160
All are silent. Equality in justice and conduct
Has disappeared. Who will look after the land,
Vast and distant, where, Shabara, Vanara, Kola,
Kiratha, Yaksha, Bhilla, Nishada and such other
Non-Aryans live? Blinded by 'Aryan vision',
The vision of Bharata as a nation has been forgotten.
Janaka, Seeradhwaja, and Dasharatha are indeed
Brave warriors; but their coming together to fight
The *rakshasas* and to establish justice
Is only a mirage.' 170

'You speak the truth, O Guru!
Aryans seem to be in a hurry to reach death's door.
The *rakshasas* must be pursued and attacked;
But Aryans appear to lack self-confidence.'
'Son, if the enemy is not destroyed,
If what they have occupied is not taken back,
And if time is wasted, cultural downfall
And calamity are certain.'
Gazing at the innocent faces of Rama and Lakshmana,
Looking into their eyes, Vishwamitra, the great sage, 180
Felt a sense of fulfillment, and smiled, charged with emotion:
'You are indeed the best among the Kshatriya clans,
Raghurama! You are the dome of Ayodhya's empire!
Understand others' pain, fight against aggression,
And be ready to sacrifice your life to vanquish
The *rakshasa* clan. This is the Aryan vow
That you have undertaken!'
'O Guru! Here I pledge
To fight against the lawless, even at the stake of my life.'

Canto Eight

'You are Amazing'

||☉||

While the sages of the hermitage a kept the boat sailing
The brothers travelled on with Kaushika;
And their thoughts flowed like the river:
'Without fear or suspicion, the sages carry on
Their penance. No violence in their minds; I have seen
Peace embodied in them. Then, why are you depressed,
Great sage? Why is there a shadow of grief?
Why is there a lack of enthusiasm and liveliness?' –
Thus, Saumitri asked Kaushika politely.

'I desired a peaceful forest for prayers;   10
For intense meditation, discarding a life of pleasure,
I reached Dandakaranya. I nursed my ambition
Of making the whole world Aryan, establishing
Peace, and then to rest. I attempted to negate
Violence, conflicts and war. The actions of a sage
Were mine; and I did away with kingly qualities.
Would they let me do so? I dreamt at night
They were pulling the Mount Meru, as heavy as the earth;
Like a temple car of idols.

'While the festival went on with joy and excitement,
The car grew huge, covering the earth and the sky;
I saw people getting caught under the wheels and dying.
Unable to watch the slaughter, I shut my eyes in despair.'

'My eyes opened again. With great speed,
The chariot rolled on inside my pupils.
Coming down from the eyes, it rushed into my heart,
That chariot of heartlessness. I screamed in pain;
As I stayed yelling in the cave of darkness,
It echoed and hurt my own ears excruciatingly.
At that moment, like clouds dispersing, the dream broke.
Unable to forget the chariot and unable
To forget the bloodied corpses, I am depressed.
Son, whatever may happen, I shall not look back.
Protecting *dharma* is an unavoidable duty,
And I must carry it out!'

Rama's searching eyes watched
The shadow of pain and despair on the Guru's face.
The sage spoke again: 'I am not thirsty for blood;
I do not desire either war and acts of violence
Or wealth and pleasures, not even fruits of meditation.
I longed for fulfillment of pure dreams of well-being,
For the joyous evolution of a peaceful environment;
And the progress of knowledge and new ideas.
There should be opposition to war, opposition
To conflict and series of suffering!'

'We understand this, O sage! Who can deny it?'
'That is true, my son.
If it is an all-time truth, no one can oppose it,
Or say it is unacceptable. Today the way of war
Is different. The forms of physical or mental strength
Will not yield fruit. Now is needed the skill
Of using weapons, confabulations and trickery.
For victory or defeat, to depend on physical strength

Is a thing of the past. But, are the Aryan kings concerned?
Are swords, spears and arrows enough for victory?
Look at Vali. What does he have apart from his nails
And teeth and an army of monkeys? Faced with weapons
Of divine power, how can he fight for self-protection?
Defeat is certain.
'Look at the *rakshasas*; 60
With severe austerity, they have acquired great weapons
From celestial beings; these deathless beings have built
Chariots for them. In the magical, impenetrable armour
They are safe and prepared to conquer any enemy.
They are well prepared, spreading the smoke
Of cold war. They are slaves of sensuality
And luxurious living. The determination and strength
For austerity and meditation are lost to Aryan kings!
I have celestial weapons with me, young men;
But I am not sure if they will not go wasted 70
If I grant them to you; I am worried.'

Full of admiration for the sage, Ramachandra said:
'O great sage! Your noble personality is wonderful.
You are an ocean of profundity; your words
Have thrilled us. They are the nectar of experience,
The very essence of austere meditation.
We are grateful for what you have said,
And we have understood your mind. Do not doubt us!'

Saumitri asked again: 'Shall I, O great man,
Tell you about my suspicions? Cleanse me of my anxieties 80
And illusions. You as fast as the wind, why are you silent
Like someone powerless? What has happened to you
Who shines like a spear of fire? Have you cast away
The clothes of revenge and become free from enmity?
Where is the awesome, deep roar of the ferocious being?
Like dry wood burning itself in touch with fire,

Why these tears, why this silence?
Do you tolerate the injustice in this world?'

'I appreciate your question, Saumitri;
Listen and I shall tell you why I do not want war. 90
Nature's sense of justice and injustice are strange.
Thinkers, intellectuals, men of action – the very
Existence of these men of different natures is unique.
While discussions, arguments and counter-arguments
Go on, real action is pushed to the background.
If the will to act does not grow strong, it will collapse,
And the sharpness of thinking will get blunted.
This is the ethos of today, and I cannot fight it.
I shall bow down, and accept the human nature
Of action and the way of the world.' 100

Canto Nine

'What a Great Universal Brotherhood in the Forest!'

||૬||

'Whose hermitage is this, in this divine spot,
An embodiment of virtue?' asked Shri Rama.
'The God of Love sings while swinging here;
This is the glorious place where he sings and dances.
In a playful manner the learned people call him "Manmatha",
"The one who churns our minds." When Shiva,
In a strict regimen of prayers and meditation,
Was engrossed, forgetting himself in contemplation,
The beautiful heavenly region, floated in joy
And sprouted on earth; the bonds of desire in man   10
Got strong and the feast of spring took place here;
Rati played ten enticing musical scales on her *veena*;
Joy beyond sensuality, music beyond time and place,
Flourished; the other-worldly fragrance spread
Everywhere in the Brindavana of pleasure; the spring
Of playful glances showered joy and happiness;
And Shiva's meditation was disturbed.
In great rage, when he opened his fiery eye,
Manmatha, the God of Love, was reduced to ashes, here.

This is Anga region, where Shiva meditated; 20
This is the dancing grand of angry Shiva;
This is Kamashrama.'

Shri Rama and Lakshmana
Listened to the sage's account, with wonder.
The night was spent there. The next day,
After completing morning ablutions and rituals,
They sailed on. In the roar of the lashing waves,
The brothers heard what seemed to be the loud sound
Of a thousand conches blown together; and, astonished,
They asked Kaushika: 'What is this uproar? 30
When waves dash against waves, does such a sound
Of turbulence emerge?' The sage replied:
'The holy river created from Brahma's heart
Flows on here; Offer your obeisance to it.'
The princes obeyed him devotedly.

As they got off the boat and walked into the forest,
They lost their hearts to the grandeur of the forest:
'Oh! There is no place to step here, bees buzzing;
Various creatures of the forest roam around freely;
Parrots, peacocks, cranes, bats, owls and birds 40
Are making varied noises. Tigers, lions, cheetas,
Elephants, deer, and bison move around, fearless.

The harmony of nature, the great song of coexistence,
Goes on in concord of tone and rhythm.
'The resonance in nature
Of universal brotherhood rings in everyone's ears
The oneness of man; oneness is everlasting.
Division is false, and that is the truth.
'*Vasudhaiva kutumbakam*', 'the whole world
Is one family' – that eternal truth is in the womb of nature; 50
Teak and sandalwood, animals and birds are all one.
Why does man not possess this benign light!
How lovely this belonging to one another is!

That is the essence of life on earth, that great voice
Is resounding in all four directions. No one
Can bring it down. The way it reverberates
Is different. *Beete, thinduka, bilwa, kaggali* and *matti*,
All these trees sway in love, kissing one another playfully.
The bamboo grove, feeling that the world belongs to it,
Spreads its hands in pride and flourishes. 60
In the conflict and hardship of a lonely life,
The bamboo will burn and turn into ashes.
It proclaims that coexistence is the secret of life
Amidst the vast ocean of life.
If there exists a lonely island, high tides will advance,
The island sinks and becomes part of the ocean.
Without equality and harmony, a life
Of fulfillment will be hard to gain, unnatural;
The life of harmony is the only life to be led;
This is the divine message being spread.' 70

While Shri Rama and Saumitri
Were engrossed as they admired the awesome glory
Of the forest, the sage stroked them with affection:
'We shall cross the hillock and reach Siddhashrama;
That is the place of my work. There you will see
Tataka, Subahu, Maricha and all other terrorising
Rakshasas; you will see varied forms of their anger
And hate; arrogant leaders unaware of defeat,
Bloated with pride, and possessing magical powers,
And evil trickery; those that roar like the wild bisons 80
Making menacing noises; those that throw to the winds
The ethics of war, and split open the stomach and
Pull out the innards. Without using divine weapons,
You cannot defeat them, following the rules of war.
You need the light of the lamp of knowledge. How can I
Give you the divine weapons of the light of wisdom?'
Said the sage, swayed with worry and doubt,
To test the faith of Raghuram and Lakshmana.

'Why the dilemma? O, sage, please grant us
The knowledge. Be free from doubts,' said Saumitri.　　　90
'Black clouds of conflict are spread across the mind-sky.
Will the weapons I give be effective? Would they save
The human race? Otherwise, if my divine weapons
Are rendered useless, all my austere achievements
And dedication will be wasted and lost in nature.'

Reassuring the sage, Lakshmana said:
'If the mountain of dedication splits and the volcano
And lava spurt out, we shall close the hole in the rock.
If the flood does not stop, we shall thrust our chests
And hold it back. To face the dance of destruction,　　　100
We shall stake our lives and move ahead with dedication.'
Still the sage tested them: 'I don't want doubtful words
And conflicting thoughts. Will you stand up, renouncing
Everything, to fulfill my aspirations? Can you promise
That you will not fall prey to the greed and desire
For an empire? Otherwise, heavenly weapons
Become futile on the base of sensual pleasure!'
'The sword of our self-restraint has a sharp edge.
Sacrifice is Yoga for us. We shall face falsehood
And injustice, successfully. Bless us great teacher!'　　　110

'In your palace and in the courtyards of every home,
With no ground for suspicion, you should establish
Love and trust; you should infuse the joy of love
In every atom of the world; without discrimination,
Among the poor and the rich, wisdom should be cultivated;
Truth must be born of wisdom, truth should lead to
Ultimate Truth, knowledge should be another name
For courtesy, and total knowledge should be inseparable
From total power, and the world should live free
From all fears.　　　120

'When meditation is Brahman
And Brahman is supreme delight, all elements are born.

Living in the womb of happiness, they merge in the end,
In the endless sky. This is truth visualised;
This is the law of nature. The rivers and streams
Flow continuously and achieve fulfillment.
What does it matter if a mountain confronts them?
Will the river get scared and flow backwards?
This is the law of nature, constant, everlasting.

'At the edge of life, stands truth. Beware! 130
The inclination to change the evolution of values
Is without end. Compassion and cruelty,
Nectar and poison, love and hate, good and evil,
The mystery of dualities confounds the world,
Like fabric created by two twisted threads,
Like a plait designed with beautiful strands.

'Mice have holes, singing birds have nests;
But man doesn't have an inch of space to lie down and sleep.
To live carefree in sunlight is what man desires.
He is half-animal, his mind is fickle and indifferent, 140
How can he hope to achieve equanimity?
Consciousness should evolve through action and reaction.
Truth, righteousness and morality constitute
The backbone of a meaningful life; and a feeling
Of equality and coexistence make the music of life.
From the Himalayas to Kanyakumari,
Sages are deep in meditation with the wish
Sarvejana sukhino bhavantu
('May all the people be blessed with happiness').
But their longing for peace is a mirage and they are caught 150
In the whirl of anxiety and the web of attack
By the *rakshasas*.

'Barbaric acts are being committed;
Sages have been killed and their bones and flesh have been eaten;
The *rakshasas* are arrogant, unmindful of everything;
Free thinking has dried up, and life in this country,

Based on justice and culture is choked.
Have no doubts, be stone-hearted, move forward,
Determined to save the culture of righteousness.'
'Why should one pause and ponder? Why wait for order?   160
This is auspicious and this is a virtuous deed.
What more is needed, Oh, great teacher, when you
Have opened the eyes of the blind and showed a new path?'

Canto Ten

'We Will Hold High the Flag of Life-giving Values'

'I have fully realised,' the wise sage continued,
'The meaning of life and universal values.
It is easy to protect, with the strength of your army,
The capital and the king's throne. But attacking enemy forces
And fighting a war is not that easy; is the work
Assigned by your teacher very difficult?

'Begging to save their lives,
Bereft of their self-respect, the sages will not come to you
Of their own accord. The king should know himself
The difficulties and pain suffered by sages living in forests,　　10
And common people. In the ideal state, the king
Should give them self-confidence, wooing them.
Was there ever a golden age? I do not know about that, son,
Nor will I try to explore. If it was there, why this misery
And suffering for people? Would such a state befall them?

'If one breaks his head believing it to be the sign of times,
Will heavenly bliss come to one, seeking?
The Heaven people want is before them; they themselves
Have to achieve it with care; you be the navigators.
If one waits for tomorrow, it will be stale.　　20
Let new tradition be mixed with what is valued and old.

'There is a collapse; the moth of the epoch
Is being sacrificed at the fire. Stop it!
Receiving and offering, experiment and science,
Let the principle of making man divine, grow;
Let the farce of caste and creed be entombed.
In the search for the light of science, in the Great Journey,
Let the world see light. Promise me that you will
Establish an ideal governance. Promise me
That you will renounce the kingdom and
Destroy the *rakshasas* wandering around forests.
Before Ravana attacks Ayodhya, pledge me
That you will go into the battlefield and protect truth.'

'We shall carry the flag of values.
Do you disbelieve us? We shall continuously assess,
And examine our quest, forsaking everything else.'

'Understand the tone of my voice clearly,
Its deep echo, son! Having made a promise,
Do not grieve later. It is not easy, my boys!
When you try to leave the family, parents will stop you,
So will the wife and children. Do you have the strong will
To break the shackles of kinship? I have not known till now
Any instance of a king who has come out of the bonds
Of love for kingdom and kingship.'

Shri Ramachandra's mind
Was full of joy after listening to the sage's words.
It travelled in many directions, climbed
The tallest peak and settled there with a divine feeling.
'O, sage!' he said, 'We did not leave Saketa
Seeking joy! We discarded the chariot at the entrance
Of the city itself, and walked along a path of thorns
And stones, getting hurt, with the belief that the rough path
Had to be traversed to realise truth! Have we not, with joy,
Stepped on the state of fear and accepted it?
The search for truth is our commitment in life.'

'My dilemma is over. A tower of trust
Has come up! I have seen the virtuous radiance
Of the purity of thought born in your mind,'
Said the sage, contented.

'Great teacher, we shall shun selfishness,   60
And live fighting for strict justice; we shall bring down
The huge tree of injustice. Forsaking royal luxuries,
We take an oath, here, with determination.'

Saumitri said: 'Brother, I am with you
In the promise and fulfillment, in the search for truth;
In the thorny, stony path, I shall be your companion.'

Kaushika saw for himself
The radiance of the Kshatriya and its fierceness.
What remained was the final test of weaponry.
As if striking a hammer on hot iron, he struck   70
The feelings of Rama and Lakshmana, to test them.

'I shall say bitter words now, the last warning.
Not enough trust is found in royal families,
In the lineage of Ikshwaku! In a rock fallen down,
Stricken with fear, like a valley opening up,
There is none who has discarded familial pulls
And bonds of love. The more I talk about doubts
And anxieties, Rama, arising in the path of truth,
Much more remains to be talked about and understood.'

'That is natural, O revered one!' responded Shri Rama: 80
'The warning is accepted, it is appropriate.
We shall transcend this attachment towards
Wife and children, the traditional ramparts,
The great undertaking is rewarding, the diamond armour
Of self-confidence that you have helped us wear
Is impenetrable.'

Shri Rama hurled the sharp spear of sacrifice;
The screen of temptation was drawn, the cataract removed,

Now they were victors over sense organs. The stream
Of fulfillment flows in the heart, in search of a new epoch 90
Of the path of unending action.

In the body of the visionary Kaushika,
There was a flash of lightning; radiance overflowed;
A multitude of sun's rays sparked and shone,
Like a holy image cast in the radiance of the sun.
Like a water lily blooming in the pond in Janakpuri,
Like sapphires poured out by the blooming lotus petals,
Like flames whirling blue and moving up,
A great vision was seen of a divine figure.
Who was she? She was Sita, the pious woman, 100
Adorned with royal culture; the radiant ring of womanhood;
The jewel in the crest of mankind; the great woman
Hovered in the mirror of the sage's mind.

'My children!' said Vishwamitra, pleased with them:
'This alone is the proof for the future; no need
For any other evidence. Freed from doubts and dilemmas,
The sky of my mind is clear and pure. Divine weapons
I have acquired with the power of Gayatri hymn.
There was, earlier, some doubt that it might go waste.
If they fall into the hands of weak and evil men, 110
Humankind will collapse. The tree would dry up
And fall to the ground. I thought so in fear, and hence,
I tested the sap and power of your commitment.
I hurt your minds. Do not think badly of your teacher.
For the boat to reach the destination of the divine
Journey, I shall give you with love, Rama and Lakshmana,
The total knowledge of the divine weapons.'

Canto Eleven

'Your Acts Will Benefit the Whole World'

||๑||

They walked across the forest;
The sage tied his clothes tight;
He smoothed his beard and moustache;
Tied and twisted his hair. The brothers saw
The divine vision of the teacher. 'Take out your bows.
Set the arrows in them; who will be equal to you in the world?
Let the weapons of fortune sustain you,'
Preached the sage. They drank it in, understanding
With their senses, mind and intellect. The unknown
World of knowledge and science was seen in its entirety,   10
With the thunder of drawing the bowstring
Echoing in the earth and the sky.

Lakshmana said: 'Do not worry, O, teacher!
We shall make the Aryan empire impenetrable.
To the culture moaning in a wretched state,
We shall instill fear among the *rakshasa* clan.
We shall spread like a forest fire to destroy the *rakshasas*.
The flood waters of destruction
Cannot put out our roaring fire.'

'I am gladdened Saumitri! 20
Put out the fire in your speech. Planted in my mind
Is the great flagpole of stability. In the sky,
The universal flag of Aryanhood is flying.'

The journey went on, undisturbed,
To the environs of Siddhashrama.
Saumitri looked around, amazed at the forest.
'Which is this forest?' he asked in eagerness to know,
'The home of birds, animals, lions, elephants and shepherds?'

Vishwamitra said:
'This forest is the fertile hilly home of the Karusha. 30
The aggressive, terrorising sorcerers have occupied it,
Making it a haven for their despicable acts.
Tataki has plundered all. Sunda is her husband.
He died becoming a prey of his own game of deceit.
Maricha is their son. Big head, a bloated body,
Round arms, terrifying figure, ugliness incarnate,
Maricha is an expert in trickery and magic.
The law of the land has become a clay-toy
In the daily game of destruction. Magic, deceit
Murder, extortion and lawlessness constitute 40
The mechanism of governance. No work of welfare,
No mercy or comparison; cruel anarchy everywhere.'

As the sage was talking,
Tataki arrived there roaring:
Massive in form, terrifying looks, unbecoming face,
Scary canine teeth, ugliness which could not be faced.
From up in the sky, she rained
Stones and thorn, blood and flesh on the ritualistic fire.

Kaushika said in great anger
To Rama, 'Cut off her head. 50
Move forward, do not be scared, cut up Tataki;
Fearing killing a woman, do not forget your duty.

It is no crime to kill a woman who has given up righteousness.
This is the rule of the righteousness of the Kshatriya!'

Then and there, Rama twanged the bowstring.
The directions trembled. 'It is not good to kill a woman.
My mind is unwilling. I shall cut off the ears and nose
And hands and feet, and render her immobile.
She is secure as she is a woman.'
So speaking, while merciful Shri Ramachandra moved 60
Forward, Tataki, spreading smoke all around quickly,
Like smoke erupting from a forest fire, disappeared.

The brothers were startled and amazed by the guile of
The *rakshasi*. Slightly angry, Rama shot
Arrows in great speed and her hands were cut; and
Tataki roared in pain; the earth trembled
As she roared over and over, the earth and sky became one
As the rain of flesh and blood poured.
'Forget compassion! The sinful *rakshasi* deserves to die.
Finish her off before the sun sets. If night falls, 70
It will be difficult to kill her,' commanded Kaushika,
Prodding Rama.

Rama in the radiance of the Kshatriya, along with Saumitri,
Stiffened, grunted in anger, got his arrow ready,
Prayed, aimed and let it go.
It moved with the speed of the wind and pierced Tataki.
She roared and collapsed like a mountain or a tower
Breaking open suddenly, smashing against the earth.
She rolled and jumped, the wife of Sunda; and the shrines
In the hermitage were razed to the ground. 80
As she screamed and rolled over,
Her head bent to the right. A chapter was closed
In the lives of the *rakshasas*.

The sage ran to the brothers in joy,
Touched their heads in affection and said with love:

'Rama and Saumitri, you have done a deed
For the welfare of the world. Your mission is fulfilled.
The sages are pleased. You are adored by them.
In ritualistic observances, in the good work
Of universal welfare, one great step has been taken.'   90

Canto Twelve

'The Sage Bestowed Celestial Weapons'

||๑||

With the master-sage, Rama and Lakshmana
Spent the night in Siddhashrama, free from anxieties,
In a garden like the Spring-chariot of Kubera,
The God of Wealth. They roamed without a care
On the lovely stage of a dreamland. Going up the rocks
And springing, wriggling and swaying in the middle of the forest,
Like a new bride, the divine river Ganga flowed,
Gurgling and flowing with waves of sweet music.
Like a morning melody, the swing of music
In the chirping of many birds, swept into   10
The minds of the brothers.

Like melodies on pipes, it pleased their ears.
Bowing to the holy river, full of joy,
They completed morning prayers and other rituals,
Bowed to Kaushika who was like Kamadhenu,
The heavenly cow among sages,
In all purity of heart.

Vishwamitra, the eminent sage,
Full of self-confidence, initiated the brothers,
In secrecy, to the various divine weapons and chants,   20

That would make them invincible on the battleground.
Danda Chakra, Dharma Chakra, Kala Chakra, Vishnu Chakra
Vajrastra, Shoolavarastra, Brahma Shirostra
Aishikastra, Brahmastra, Kapali, Kankala
Musali, Kankana, Dharmapasha, Kalapasha
Varunapasha, Shushkashani, Ardrashani, Shikhara
Painaka, Narayana, Prathana, Hayashirassu and
Krouncha were granted.
Modaki, Shikhari, Gadaprayoga Shakti
Nandana Khadga, Rudra Shakti, Vishnu Shakti 30
Manavastra of celestial beings, *Praswapana,*
Santapana, Vilapana, Mousala and *Mohanadi*
Tanasa, Sowmana and *Samvartha* weapons
Satya, Mayadhara, Tejahprabhu, Shisira
Twashtra, Daruna, Sheeteshu – such fifty
Divine weapons were given. Rama and Lakshmana
Felt fulfilled and fell at the feet of their great Guru
And eulogised him to no end.

Kaushika embraced the boys in affection;
They rested happily in the arms of the great sage. 40
In the generosity of heart, in universal sweetness
He stroked their curly hair gently.
With love, he stroked their backs and faces,
He blessed them and fondled them with a pure mind.

In the embrace of the range of the Himalayas,
In the foothills, in the valley, like thick, black clouds,
Vegetation shone in profusion. In the free environment,
Animals of all kinds moved around.
Rama and Lakshmana beheld such a scene and said:
'This pleases the eyes and the mind as well. 50
In the melodious Mohana *raga*, birds of many kinds
Are all singing. The large expanse of water,
The music it makes is thrilling; and it pleases
All the five senses.

'We crossed the treasure of wonders, the wealth of the forest.
Whose hermitage was that? Whose land of rituals?
Winning over love and hatred, glorying in truth and virtue,
The vision of the universe is embodied there!

'Forgive me, mentor!
My mind is curious like a monkey. I have not seen 60
Such riches in a forest. Some memory of my previous birth
Pulls me back, and my legs stand unmoving as if chained.
What enchanting fascination! What jostling in the mind,
Which is calling out to discover the wonder?'

'This is the Siddhashrama, son! The land
Of my attainment, the land of Vishnu's meditation.
The chosen land for meditation of all the three worlds,
The glorious, holy land that attracted the God of gods.
Look there, the hermitage of Vamana, the land of victory,
Resting after Bali was stepped upon and crushed. 70
The land of fertility, where trees flower,
This is the radiant life-giving land for your victory.'
Thus, as the sage explained the land's greatness with joy,
Rama and Lakshmana stepped in, shining
Like the stars Punarvasu and Pushya, never covered by clouds,
Like the spotless moon knowing no black shadow,
Lighting the lamp of knowledge and science
Of the sages, of the temple of their minds,
Making the hermitage sacrosanct.
They entered it. 80

Vishwamitra was there,
Silent and thoughtful, in total concentration,
Immersed in the waters of the milky ocean of meditation,
Still aware of the outside world. Unified in mind
In observance of rituals, his expression was one of peace.

A new light had spread. It was as if
The circle of light itself had brightened the environment.
Contentment spread among the sages as Rama
And Saumitri were the guardians of the hall of rituals.

Canto Thirteen

'Fruitful Has Been the Sacred Rite We Undertook'

||๑||

While the sacred rite went on in peace and glory,
They guarded the hermitage with care, day and night.
Neither food nor sleep nor rest they needed;
While the world slept, they stayed awake,
And for six whole days, they kept the *rakshasas* away.
Thus passed days and nights like one moment,
And the auspicious moment of culmination arrived.
'Beware, Shri Rama! Be alert, Saumitri!,'
Said all the sages in great excitement.
The brothers, full of enthusiasm and high spirit, 10
Watched for the *rakshasas* in all the directions.

Cooked rice, *ghee*, and *kusha* grass were offered
To the Fire-god in the appropriate manner, and so were
Flowers and fig-twigs; and the rite was conducted
As the precepts ordained; it was so grand that
Such a ceremony was never seen before nor to be seen in future.
The Fire-god burnt bright and his tongues leaped to the sky.
It was then that the black clouds of anxiety gathered.
With the clash of thunders and lightning flashing,

With commotion and noise ear-splitting, 20
The terrible hordes of the *rakshasas*, led by Maricha
And Subahu, descended on the holy scene.
With their dark-skinned bodies and fierce faces,
Flattened noses and moustaches reaching the ears,
With their bodies swaying with intoxication,
Their dishevelled hair making them more fearsome,
Their blood-red eyes emitting cruelty,
Like dark clouds suddenly appearing in the sky
And pounding the earth with rain, relentlessly,
The *rakshasas* swooped on the scene. 30

Suddenly startled, all the sages got up,
In anxiety and fear. They pleaded to Shri Rama:
'What is this noise and disturbance, this commotion?
Son! It appears, the terrible situation of war is on us.'
No sooner did the sages cry in anguish than the *rakshasas*
Rushed forward, spilling blood everywhere.
Sharp swords they had in their hands, and raw meat in their mouths,
They threw all over pieces of flesh torn from living bodies;
And they were on a rampage, showering live coal everywhere.

When Maricha and the other *rakshasas* 40
Flew straight, like an arrow, towards the ritual-platform,
Shri Rama thundered: 'Watch me, Lakshmana!
I shall scatter the *rakshasas* like clouds in the wind,
Beyond the four corners, beyond the seven seas,
With the use of this *vayavyaastra*, "the weapon of the wind".
I shall explode the womb of their pride and throw them out.
Now, watch me,' said Rama, and, fixing an arrow as strong
As ten thousand horses, drew the bowstring to his ears.
But, immediately, unwilling to take the life of another,
He thought: 'Patience and restraint become a Kshatriya; 50
How can I take the life of another till his span of life is not over?'
Thinking thus, he fixed the arrow to his bow,
Chanted the prayers to the Wind-god, and shot it.

Maricha's chest being split open by the arrow,
And blood gushing out, Maricha screamed, roared,
And collapsed in the forest, writhing in searing pain.
'Look, Saumitri! This is the retribution of one
Who used to obstruct the rituals and disturb peace.'
'It is not enough, my brother,' said Lakshmana,
'Do not leave him half-dead. Like a wounded snake   60
Seeking vengeance, he will be after greater wickedness.
Take away his life.' But Rama replied calmly:
'Killing is not the only way to root out evil, my brother.
Let us show a little of humanity in all of our deeds.
Only love and compassion are the magical powers
To save this earth. Why should we hurry? There is the Wheel
Of Time to erase the history of evil. Let us not go to an extreme;
Come, let us be patient,' thus Shri Rama consoled his brother.

With increased alertness, while Rama and Lakshmana
Awaited any possible counter-attack of the enemy,   70
Subahu rushed in, and, taking out his sword from its sheath,
Swiped at Rama, with all his strength. Immediately,
Rama readied *agneyastra*, 'the weapon of fire,'
And shot it aiming at the chest of the *rakshasa*.
It pierced him hard and Subahu collapsed on the ground.
Blood sprouting out in a flood, twisting and turning
Like an animal, crawling in pain and roaring,
Subahu was burnt out. The last link of the chain of wrong-doers
Was broken, and Siddhashrama was freed
From the steel-grips of evil-doers.   80

The main platform of the sacred rites
Remained pure, unpolluted by the *rakshasas'* deeds;
And the final sacrifice was completed in peace.
The entire world was blessed, and the whole assembly
Of the sages was overjoyed.

The great Sage Vishwamitra, was very happy.
He lifted up the two brothers who fell at his feet;

Embraced them with affection, and praised their deeds.
He declared: 'The observances of the sages to explore truth
Have been fulfilled; and you are blessed, O Rama and Lakshmana! 90
You have carried out, satisfactorily, your Guru's orders,
However, difficult they were. We applaud your achievements.
It is befitting now to call this place "Siddhashrama",
"The hermitage of achievement". This land has been sanctified.'
Listening to the words of the great sage,
Rama and Lakshmana felt ecstatic and were contented.
The sage, glowing like the God of Fire, embraced
The brothers, again, and caressed them fondly.

Canto Fourteen

'The Aryan Aura is Dimmed'

||6||

Then they came, they came running
Gagan and his sons, the common soldiers of the Nishada tribe.
They had chased away the *rakshasas* beyond the borders.
They bowed and stood respectfully, and said:
'Master of the Aryan lineage, forgive us;
Sage, we are late in coming back. Simple villagers are now
Soldiers, and they are plunged deep into the war
For righteousness, and they have shown their valour.
When they become soldiers, the freedom and
The fortresses of enemies shall not last.   10

'Forgive our lapses, and bless our sons.
We have imprisoned Sakalashwa's son, Devapriya
And his wicked companions; Do not slight us,
Saying we are impertinent, great teacher!
These are murderers, who have committed atrocities;
Sinners who do not deserve to be forgiven.

'They have teased the young girls in the village,
Stalked them and spoilt them. They are lascivious.
Just because Sakalashwa is the commander; can illegal,
Lawless behaviour become justice? In cruel ways,   20

Should they dishonour innocent maidens?
If the fence devours the field, if the law makers
Break the law, where can we ask for justice, O, teacher?
Like a deer wandering thirsty in the sun
Seeking water, following a mirage, throat gone dry,
Wriggling in desperation, we are suffering.
Can you not give us justice? Isn't silence an approval
Of the unrighteous?'

The teacher listened and spoke:
'It is one's duty to protect the honour of women,   30
And what you have done is praiseworthy. It is good
That you have caught and imprisoned Sakalashwa's son,
And his wicked companions. Do not be afraid.
Do not hesitate. Though you are not of Aryan blood,
You have become protectors and guardians
Of Aryan culture; You are people's emperors;
You have become the heirs of the rich Aryan culture.
Of caste and creed, of connections and wealth,
There is no place in the matters of justice.
Justice will be meted out to all those who are moral,   40
Virtuous, righteous and rich in character.'
Gagan and his fellow hunters presented
The group of Aryan young men to Rama and Saumitri;
And they paraded them. Fair, tall and handsome,
Was Devapriya; but in his character, in morality and
Craftiness, he resembled the *rakshasas*.
On his face, distress, waywardness and ugly trickery
Were clearly visible. When he saw Rama, the glory
Of the Ikshawaku clan, he screamed, jumped and
Hopping, flying around and bouncing, he shouted   50
With great zest: 'These mean Nishadas have caught me
And brought me here; they have dishonoured me
With their arrogance. Such wicked acts of these lowly people
Do not befit Aryanvarta; put an end to it, O Aryan scion!
I am blessed by your sight, and I am freed from all pain

And from the net of these Nishadas. Vishwamitra
Is an enemy of the Aryans and the old man is a friend
Of these savages. He, a hypocrite, instigates
Dangerous maladventures. Save us from him, O son
Of Dasharatha! The Aryan aura is dimmed; 60
Give us justice.'

Canto Fifteen

'No Comparison Between us; I have an Army'

||๖||

Shri Rama told the people calmly:
'I shall save the Aryan honour; I shall protect
Law and Order. In the life of the Aryans, compassion
Is the everlasting value. For the divine, it is self-restraint;
Charity for the humans; and compassion for the *rakshasas*.
Among the Aryans, noble values must be sustained.
The Aryan culture should nourish the triple values
Of '*Satyam, Shivam, Sundaram*' (Truth, Goodness and Beauty),
In Bharata, like the deep resonance of the sublime sea.

'When a man is born, 10
The mother suffers pain; at death, he is in pain;
The hardship of living between these two is the rule.
Forgetting one's sorrow, if one fights and lives
To alleviate others' pain, then will flourish Aryan culture.
Do you not know this, Devapriya?

'What else can I give except justice?
O Aryan son! Does any other way befit me?
You are living in darkness, molesting helpless women.

If you do not possess goodness, what does it matter
That you are a child or grandchild of an Aryan commander? 20
The roots of the essence of Aryan culture have been pulled
Out and cut up; losing its value, it is mere firewood now.
Can life be lived without the essence of life?
The word "Aryan" does not connote caste, creed,
Or shape; it has no geographical boundaries –
son of Aryan!

'Without protecting the gem of Aryan values,
You have desecrated the basic values, committing atrocities,
Violence on Nishada men and women.
Like *rakshasas*, you committed crimes of various kinds; 30
You deserve to be killed; I have given you the punishment of death.
For the protection of righteousness and Aryanvarta
In a thick forest, distant and uninhabited,
Let the killing go on Saumitri. Take care, let not
The Siddhashrama become defiled with the splatter
Of this evil blood!'

The community was jubilant, acquiring
Joyful freedom, praising Shri Ramachandra's
Sense of fairness, ability and dedication to justice.
But Aryan Vishwabandhu was distressed, 40
Worried and upset. The face turned dark;
The voice choked and overcome by sadness,
It struggled to come out from the depths of the heart.
He spoke:

'Rama, think, protector of the good Aryan people!
This haste is unseemly. Is it right to punish
The Aryan in such a manner?
The complaint of the Nishada is childish.
The punishment of destroying the Aryan lineage is harsh!
Does one tie up live coals in what one is wearing? 50
Let there be no conflict. Would Sakalashwa leave Siddhashrama?
If they attack, who will stop them?

Would anyone desire the destruction of the Aryans,
It will do no good. Stop the violation of justice!'

Rama was calm of mind,
Strong of will. Without replying, he called Gagan
With affection. 'Brave people, I admire
Your bravery and strength! Stopping injustice that
Cannot be tolerated is the Aryan way of life!
Come, another duty awaits you.   60
You fulfil it right now.
Is Maricha dead? What has happened to him?
We need proof as we are uncertain about it.
Let our journey of winning over people
Move on. If lessening the weight of earth
Is inevitable, if righteousness is followed,
Maricha should die: carry on the search
All over the earth.' Bowing with pleasure,
The Nishadas went hurriedly to search.

Suddenly, soldiers on horses rushed in   70
From all directions of Siddhashrama. Rama
Gazed astonished and worried at their manner
The commander was sitting on a white horse,
Breaking down courtesy, civility and virtue,
It was startling to see an army with weapons.
Would an Aryan commander transgress rules!
Near the group of sages and Vishwamitra,
They stopped the horses, got down and with ear-splitting noise,
Rushed as if kicking them on their chests.
Everyone was scared, there was silence all around.   80
In fury, looking red-eyed in all four directions
The soldiers stood haughty and conceited.
Sage Vishwamitra asked in bewilderment,
In anxiety, 'Sakalashwa, why are you here?'

Sakalashwa spoke; 'I am the Aryan commander.
Getting to know of the arrival of Rama and Lakshmana,

I have come here to see them. I bow to the kings we love,
To the crowning glory of the Aryan lineage. This is the culture
Of the Aryans. But I am surprised; kidnapping the princes,
Imprisoning them with the power of your magic wand   90
In the area within the limits of our authority,
With stealth – is that worthy of you? You are a great sage,
Aware of the laws and principles of the world;
Should you attain your selfish aims, planning in secret?
Should you challenge the power and authority of empire?
Does this action befit you? I am worried.
The evil Nishadas have imprisoned my son,
Devapriaya, and his companions, in madness;
They have harassed them and taken them away.
Better, free them now. To which world does such a law belong?   100
Can royalty be imprisoned?' The words of Sakalashwa
Were impertinent, harsh, and severe.

'Are you not an Aryan commander?'
Asked Shri Rama, 'Are you unaware of duties and rules?
Entering Siddhashrama with armed horsemen –
Is that acceptable? Is this the culture of the Aryans?
Where did you learn the principles of politics?'

'Forget it; you can believe
That I do not know culture, the patterns of limitations.
The Aryans know how to use their power well.   110
We also protect our tradition, and stand up to protect
Its forts and bastions. You are a mere boy; should you ask
Childish questions without prior knowledge?
Whatever I do is law! My word is law!
Do you not know this?'

Rama said in derision:
'You have spoken the truth. If you are the symbol
Of Aryan culture, who can match you?'
'I do not want an argument with you;

Neither do I need any analysis of civility or its lack. 120
Tell me, where is Devapriya?' asked Sakalashwa.

'I have awarded him the punishment of death.
For the destroyers of culture, doers of bad deeds,
Breakers of law, in the realm of Ikshwaku,
There is only one end – total ruin.'
Rama's voice rose high, authoritatively.

'Who gave him the punishment of death?
Mad pranks to get an opportunity to attack the Aryan rule?
Only I have the right to punish, who else can do so?
Who will give such punishment to anyone? 130
The right to punish does not belong to Ayodhya.
It is overstepping its limits; it is an onslaught!
I shall chop off the heads, cut the arms, and thus
I shall subdue rebellion and end this revolt.
I shall make sure it shall not raise its head in Aryanvarta.'
Sakalashwa's face was burning with rage.

'Do you not know the limits
Of power of the Aryan commander who upholds law?
Why did Sage Vishwamitra arrive in Ayodhya?
Unable to bear violence and cruelty, he appealed to me. 140
If the *Brahmarshis* begged for protection like this,
Was there need for such weak governance?
This is in return for the sin you have committed.'

As Shri Rama spoke, Sakalashwa,
Boiling in rage, gnashing his teeth,
Roaring, pulling out the sword from the sheath,
Flashing it and waving it about,
Jumping up as if to destroy, flaunting,
Glaring in anger, said:

'What authority do you have Rama? 150
You have crossed the limits. To judge what is just and unjust,
I am here, Sakalashwa, the commander of the Aryans,

Don't you forget that I am the general. In the place
Where my orders prevail, who gave you the power to punish?
This is not the arena for flirting with maids
In the women's quarters in Ayodhya; this is not
Fun you get out of a game of 'hide-and-seek'
With little boys in the courtyard; it is not a 'Chenne' game
You play with little girls and red seeds; neither is it a game
Of dice, and certainly not entertainment for princes! 160
Where is Ayodhya and where is Siddhashrama?
There is no comparison between us. I have an army.
Do not try to swim in a river in flood; do not wipe out
The Raghu-clan. If the army does not arrive here to aid you,
You will squirm like helpless fish and die on a sand bank
Or in the heart of a forest.'

Watching the arrogance of Sakalashwa,
Shri Rama burst out in anger: 'Where were you
Sleeping, Sakalashwa, while I arrived here crossing
The Sarayu and the Ganga a few days ago? 170
I have come to the forest at Dasharatha's command;
With Saumitri, without any fear for life. Malada,
Karusha, Kamashrama and Siddhashrama
Had become safe havens for *rakshasas*.
While those evil people were harassing sages here,
Where was your army? Weakening the power
Of Aryanvarta, king Ravana was domineering.
Tataki, Maricha and Subabhu, in all viciousness,
Ruled here in continuous anarchy!
Plundering honour, lives as well as power and status. 180
Faced with *rakshasa* ways and arrogance,
The power of the state crawled, losing honour.

'While innocent people became targets of violence,
Reeling underneath, and their blood flowed,
Where were you then, Sakalashwa, the commander?
This turned into a land of evil progeny of Tataka,

Anxiety and bewilderment among people ran deep
And gave them endless misery. Killing countless elephants
For ivory, cutting down countless sandalwood forests,
Killing wild animals and drinking their warm blood,   190
Eating and dancing unrestrained – while all this took place,
Where was your acumen of Aryan law hiding?
Had you sold the power of authority?
Did you sacrifice all the honour of Aryanvarta
For the gold coins of Lanka?'
Even while Rama was speaking,
Sakalashwa's army, raising wonder and fear,
Surrounded the hermitage, scattering the inhabitants
Here and there.
Smiling in self-confidence,   200
Rama spoke again: 'What does it matter
Where Ayodhya's army is? It doesn't matter to me
Whether it be far or near. I am neither anxious nor worried.
Doing things justly as righteousness and morals dictate –
That is my protective armour. I shall build an army
Wherever I am, among the people, in the middle of the forest!
Are you not aware, Sakalashwa, that to destroy the *rakshasas*,
Leaving the army behind, I have come to the forest.
Filling the hearts of people living in villages
With strength of mind, I shall build an army;   210
This is Rama's goal. This is unchanging truth.'

Sakalashwa was incensed, fiercely angry
At hearing Rama announced his purpose.
Like a terrible hurricane raising dust,
Like a forest-fire spreading and burning the forest,
Like a volcano exploding and fireballs
Bursting out, spreading for miles around,
Like the earth and the sky spitting out red flames,
Like a tiger burnt by fire, roaring in anger, Sakalashwa shrieked:
'Do I not know Aryan culture? I shall not let go   220

The killers of my son,' Sakalashwa roared, and
Scratching the earth with his nails, he attacked.

Not tolerating it, Shri Rama spoke again:
'You have made friends with the *rakshasas*
And destroyed peace; instead of ending their atrocities,
You have made them grow. Being an Aryan commander,
You have done evil deeds. In return for what you have done,
No other punishment for you but death. You should not live
As a burden for the earth. You are caught
In a web of treason; and the temptation of women 230
And gold offered by Ravana has pushed the Aryan army
To the nether world of more collapse.'

'I shall test your arrogance, Rama,
Your insolence of power, and show you
What Aryan culture is, and what justice is.'
So saying, Sakalashwa declared war.
Positioning his army in circular formations in eight directions,
He pulverised the hermitage and razed it to the ground.
People scattered everywhere in the forest,
Trembling in fear. 240

Unable to tolerate it any longer,
Aware of all principles, Rama fixed an arrow,
Pulled the bowstring and shot it. Sakalashwa's chest
Was split; the arrow, going out of his back, flew far off.
Its force felled the body down to the ground
At the speed of lightning.
The wicked, on death bed, see the distant horizon,
They sight the hell hidden behind the veil of sins,
And thus realise the fruits of desire, fear and anger.

Canto Sixteen

'The Number of Evil-doers is Endless'

||๑||

When Sakalashwa died, being punished by Rama,
Vishwabandhu, hurt and sad, hurled these questions:
'Did your tolerance reach its limits, Shri Rama?
Should you have killed the able commander of Aryan rule?
Should you sing the prelude to feuding among the Aryans?
Which righteousness is it that you have protected?
Which is the moral law that you have upheld?'

'O Guru! I do not claim I have protected any moral law.
As he was the wrong-doer, I gave him the death penalty,
Acting on the laws of the Kshatriyas. What wrong is there?   10
Can I forgive him because he is the commander
Under Dasharatha? I cannot kill justice. Let the glorification
Of criminals be stopped. Caste and colour are only pretexts.
Surgery, as you are aware, is the only remedy for cancer.
Devapriya and Sakalashwa are enemies of Reason,
Enemies of Humanity. Why should they be protected?'

Vishwabandhu asked at once, 'Tell me,
What was their offence? Did it deserve death?'
'It is better to react before any danger arrives;
It is necessary to be watchful every moment.   20

If we just let things happen, destruction is certain.
If they are not nipped in the bud, the offenders
Grow as huge trees and give poisonous fruits.
They will swallow people like a python,
And the number of evil-doers will be countless.
The progeny of heroes who will protect values
Like the sons of Dasharatha, are they born everyday?
While human beings suffer, asking them to wait a while,
Is to treat them like animals to be experimented upon.
Sakalashwa's progeny must disappear, and   30
Destroying the wicked is my duty.'

Listening to Rama's words,
Vishwamitra was thrilled: 'Rama, the giver of good,
And the one who grants grace, may your flag of *dharma*
Be always victorious. The punishment you have given
Is a judgment that the whole world will praise.
When Vishwamitra praised Shri Rama thus,
Vishwabandhu could say nothing. He kept quiet.

Shri Rama and Lakshmana
Listened to the pain and pleasures of the people,   40
Immersing themselves in the news of their welfare.
As the environment in the hermitage was
Peaceful and joyous, Gagan's companions arrived,
Bowed and said: 'We have searched for Maricha
In very village, in every street, but in vain.
Some said they saw him tottering with wounds,
Bloodied all over, moaning and rolling about,
Looking depressed, going alone towards
The south. He is certainly not anywhere around
Siddhashrama. As all the companions of Ravana,   50
Who spread fear, have abandoned Aryanvarta,
It is purified. Razing the *rakshasa* camps to the ground,
The people themselves hunted them. People woke up,

Became soldiers, and rooted out every evil-doer.
Immorality and lawlessness have ended O, king!
Since you came along with Lakshmana,
All the hearts have become soft, and the bodies lighter.'

Listening to these words of felicity,
The great teacher felt happy. Feeling contented,
There came tears of joy into his eyes: 60
'Like brave brothers, you fought for the people.
People were given the rule of justice and righteousness.
The inspiration you showed will move the swing,
And blessed sons like you will be born here.
Making their own the three concepts of truth, joy,
And beauty, they will imbibe the essence of Rama
And dance being drowned in it.'

Shri Rama and Saumitri
Listened with joy to what the mentor said.
With devotion and gratitude, they felt fulfilled 70
In the loving waves of the sage's trust flowing
Like a river. They floated on it and moved on.
Becoming a wandering ascetic looking for truth,
The great sage originated a true intellectual revolution.
From the nest woven with cords of love and attachment,
He released the brothers and made them stand up
On the broad cultural stage of Bharata.
From the heat of jealousy among Dasharatha's wives,
From the quarrels among flatterers and relatives,
From the pulls of inviting beds and comforts, 80
He freed them; and prevented them from becoming dwarfs.
In the furnace of austerity, he purified them,
And helped them shine with inner radiance.
Assuming the form of a tortoise, the God Vishnu
Gave the universe stability. Similarly, Kaushika saved
The people of Ayodhya by lifting them up
From the well of ignorance.

He gave Rama and Lakshmana stability and strength,
Unshakable steadiness like the Mount Meru,
The power of action as well as magical charms. 90
He made them realise the fruits of punishing the body,
The sweetness of duty, the fulfillment of serving people.
He taught them to act without seeking credit,
To be in the path of meditation.

In meditation, in silence, in renunciation of pleasure,
The Guru sat, with a peaceful expression on his face,
Constantly searching within his mind the ways of
Being freed from weak moments of temptation.
As he kept pondering, Shri Rama asked him:
'Is your plan fulfilled, O, Guru? 100
Will you permit us to go back?
We shall carry out whatever commands you give!'

Breaking his silence, the great sage said;
'What are you now thinking of, children?
Did the cord of love pull you towards Ayodhya?
Great moments of achievements await you.
Destroying the *rakshasas* is just a beginning.
The harvest of the change of epoch is yet to come,
I wish to teach you the mystery of the Great Quest,
And all the principles that need to be followed. 110
Mithila, where the great King Janaka reigns,
Will be to where you will travel tomorrow.'

Rama and Lakshmana bowed to him.
There was firmness, hardness and gravity;
There was briskness and a sense of achievement.
Like Adishesha swaying to the music,
Of the great wizard, they stood in joy.
In the mind of the sage, a desire was born;
The bark-clothes and loin-cloth pulled him to the hermitage.
Like Menaka, leaving the baby in the forest, 120
Experiencing deep pain of separation, Kaushika said:

'How will you go if I do not come with you?
Love for Siddhashrama has caught me.
I cannot cut it, I cannot walk forward;
The dilemma, the pyre of worry, is burning me.'
'Stop worrying, O Gurudeva,' said Rama,
'We are to your left and right. Saumitri is there
For me and I am there for you. We will sweep away
All your worries. What is your worry
While there is peace all around?' 130

'Vishwabandhu is the head of the hermitage.
He is a teacher greatly respected by his disciples.
I need to leave the hermitage in his care if I come with you.
He is still caged in his concerns for caste and creed,
And tradition. The dark clouds of preference to Aryans
Have enveloped him from within. Unable to digest
The punishment given to Sakalashwa and his companions,
He is sad and in two minds. I am worried about the hermitage.
Is this sacred hermitage a playground for caste and creed?
In the land of revolution, will earthquakes and counter 140
Revolution be born? This may become a lonely island.
It is such a thought that is paining my heart.'

'I have seen it, Gurudeva. Vishwabandhu
Is a slave of tradition, customs and orthodoxy.
But, Time will teach him, Time will correct him,
Let us resolve: *Kalaya tasmai namaha*'
(Let us bow to the all-conquring Time).
What else bothers you? Please tell us,'
Rama implored Kaushika.

Kaushika said gravely: 150
The helpless women in the *rakshasa* camps
Are insulted and looked down upon.
They have been raped and are pregnant.
Having gone through awful times, they are miserable
And they are pained. The lives of their children,

Are in jeopardy. Will those unfortunate women be given
The soothing acceptance of being a housewife?
Will the partisan society be generous towards them?

'Condemned to a life of exploitation and ill-treatment,
These women, sinless, find their lives an awful burden.   160
They huddle up in a corner, washing their hands with tears.
Will there be any kind soul to turn their wail of suffering,
And to respond to their misery, sympathetically?'

Consoling the Guru, Rama said:
'Do not worry, great sage; they are not destitutes.
Gagan's protection will be given to them.
He is a gem of a man with generosity and gentleness;
He will give them love and affection in a gentle manner.
He has suffered pain and hence he is fit
To soothe the burns of molestation.   170
He has courage, and he will rehabilitate them,
And he will bring back dignity to them.'

These nectar-like words of Rama
Alleviated the poison of pain in the Guru.
'You have spoken the truth, Rama. As a guardian,
Gagan will protect these helpless women.
He is the one who shows righteousness to the world.
Now I am free from any worries. Let us go to Mithila;
The path is straight,' the sage said.

Canto Seventeen

'Like Shiva, Remove the Poison from our Lives'

||๖||

The brothers and the sage woke up early in the morning,
Finished morning rituals, and got ready for the journey.
Shri Rama and Lakshmana fell at the feet of the elders.
With the sage in the middle, and the brothers on either side,
They began their journey, the ascetics and the holy men
Walked ahead in excitement. Leaders and people
Came to bid farewell and the community roared like the sea;
With slogans of victory reaching the sky,
Tears of joy flowed like a river.
Consoling everyone, offering friendship to all, 10
Stopping at the main entrance of Siddhashrama,
Kaushika, Rama and Lakshmana turned back and looked,
As if they were breaking free of the chain of love
That had continued through for many births.
They sighed, bade farewell and entered the forest.

At that moment, came rushing
Vanaje, a representative of the exploited women.
She fell at Rama's feet, and rolling over and over,
Kissing his feet, she washed them with her tears!

She was choked with the emotion of devotion.
'Who are you? Why these tears?' – asked Rama,
Full of compassion.

The woman, having suffered as a prisoner of the *rakshasas*,
Was free; but her freedom gave her no hope. Despair reigned
Supreme in her shattered life. Plunged in the well of darkness,
She found her life a burden; and she waited, helplessly,
Thirsty for love and yearning for companionship,
Wondering which window would bring light,
She, like a lonely deer, suffered in utter solitude.

Vanaje spoke in a choked voice:
'The cruel *rakshasas* ate away my husband, O king!
I was helpless and they took away my honour,
And, now, I bear the fetus of a nameless *rakshasa*.
People call me a fallen woman; they scold me and mock me.
Who else but you can redeem the women who have fallen
Into a well of shame and suffer, ingloriously?
There are many unfortunate ones like me.
True, we found our freedom because of you;
But, is that enough? Is your duty over?
How can you forsake us Rama? Who will protect us?
We have fallen into the fire from the frying pan!

'We have lost ourselves; the fountain of life is drying up;
The innards are at our mouth; life is full of poison.
You be the one to alleviate the poison from our lives!
Give us rebirth and renewal of life, O king!'

Shri Rama consoled them with compassion:
'Do not grieve, O woman; you are not refugees.
We are the unfortunate ones. In the form of Gagan
I will look after all of you. Be confident;
You will be lost if you lose faith. Do not despair.
Do not torture yourself with such fears as
"When will Rama come, and whether he will come or not."

I shall come to you whenever you remember me.
May your minds be strengthened. I give you my assurance
That I shall protect you. Be with ease.

'Get up, mother! Become the dynamite to explode around
Community awareness. Think of your suffering
As a bad dream; it will not recur. For all women,
You be the model. Take on the form of Durga,
The destroyer of the wicked and evil. 60
The edge of selfishness blunts it; break it immediately.
Throw the fiery spear of sorrow into the ocean.
Let the frozen water melt and overflow again!
Shake off the censure of fate and arise!
Let there be light in your life again; and let it light others.
Guilty consciousness will prick you like an arrow;
But, forget all that. Forget all old memories.'

Thus did compassionate Shri Rama console her.
He showed her the love and affection of a father.
The touch of his nectarine words filled every atom 70
Of Vanaje's body. Joy rose and overflowed;
Mind and body were soothed. Vanaje stood up;
There was contentment in her eyes,
Which expressed her feeling of gratitude.
Her lotus-like eyes were wide open and tears flowed.
While a smile shone, the cry for helplessness turned
Into a divine song!

On behalf of the exploited, Vanaje spoke:
'We are blessed. You have cured our suffering.
Your compassion has healed the sores in our mind. 80
We, women, must walk with care; otherwise,
Burning fireballs will come rolling onto our path.
We shall rise above exploitation, and become
The harbingers of revolution.' So saying,
Bowing to Shri Rama, Lakshmana and the sage,
Bowing to Gagan, the woman departed.

Canto Eighteen

'Life is a Sailing Boat Caught in a Whirlwind'

||६||

Observing the way Rama consoled
Helpless Vanaje, Sage Vishwamitra was joyous.
'Walk on, Shri Rama; walk on, Saumitri!
I am not worried about those ill-treated women
Any longer. I admired the way you consoled them.
Siddhashrama will become the home of truth,
Joy and beauty. I have given up worrying about it.
Let Time itself correct the mind of the preceptor.
Joy, conflict and confusion await you ahead.'

They reached the river Shona before sunset;   10
They camped happily on the banks of that river.
The sage woke up after midnight. The boys were asleep;
Animals and birds were sleeping; and the stars shone
On a clear sky. Light was faint and the cool wind
Cheered up the sage's body and mind.
Kaushika savoured memories of the past,
And the chain of events unwound itself.

Everything was fresh in his memory.
We are of the earth, and we wear the garland
Of life and death, a whole bundle of past lives.   20

Countless dead bodies rolled on the battlefield!
Life is a sailing boat caught in a whirlwind.
Memories prick us like the stings of honey bees.
Comfort and joy that are no more, joyous sights that are lost,
Show up in the shadow of dreams and trouble us.
The shade of sunset red comes treading on the morning.
Black mountain ranges loom large on the sky;
Silence envelops the valley and forest; and,
While quietness reigns, like drops of water falling,
Only breathing and the heart-beat are heard.   30

Past memories scowl at life in the present;
Hidden consciousness of guilt burns fiercely;
Misfortune pushes one into the depths of misery;
Troubled mind finds life like walking on a tight-rope.

Again the moonrise, again the sunrise;
The sound of horns and trumpets fills the sky.
The sea of earthly life should be crossed in a boat;
And it should be anchored once the journey is over.
No birth, no death, there is salvation then.
As such thoughts hovered in the sage's mind,   40
The night was over.

They bathed in Shona and cleansed themselves;
And, completing the daily rituals, moved on.
As soon as they entered Gautama's hermitage,
Bitter memories troubled Kaushika's heart.
The urgency of narrating what had happened seized him.
He sat telling a story from the past, and the boys listened
With all attention.

'Gautama rose to the position of the preceptor,
A dream had become a reality for him. In his hermitage,   50
Of scholars, sages, erudite men and experts,
Preparations were on to hold a *dharma* conference.
Great scholars such as Seeradhwaja and Janaka

Were entrusted with the responsibility of organisation.
For the position of preceptor, they chose Gautama.
The presiding deity, Indra, was also to come.
When doubts arose about his participation,
The good news of his coming arrived.
Gautama felt relieved and comforted.
Expectation, joy and excitement beyond limits 60
The sages experienced at the arrival of the king of gods,
Like the first rain in summer, falling on the ground.
Coconuts, areca and all other offerings,
Befitting Indra's status were kept ready. To Seeradhwaja
And Janaka, the gathering was an arena for status,
A symbol for grandeur.

Indra's path was decorated
With leaves and festoons. In the hermitage was spread
The sweet scent of the beautiful flower garden.
Near Gautama's cottage a unique and spacious 70
Cottage was kept in readiness for Indra.
A flower-decked pandal was built; food and drinks
According to Indra's taste, all objects of luxury
Were all kept ready; and the hermitage of Gautama
Sparkled like a bedecked young bride.'

As they listened to the sage,
Shri Rama and Lakshmana were astonished,
Hurt and upset. The comfort and luxury offered
To the king of gods, the celestial beauties,
His indulgence with them in sensual pleasure, 80
They heard all. Should a pleasure-seeking person
Like him be invited for the great meeting of sages?
Saumitri wondered, and interrupted the sage roughly:
'What did the performance of such rituals achieve?
Did you sages degenerate into such a state of mixing
Worthy and unworthy acts? What release did you expect?
Did you really hope to see the vision of truth hidden in gold?

Evolution is life, devolution is death.
When the mystery beyond reach waved and called you,
Did you respond and travel in that direction?
When the human journey moves away from truth
Towards decline, the rituals for freedom are in vain.

'Please stop, great teacher, we cannot hear any more.
It is harsh on the ears. Should the hermitage not follow
Rules and show integrity? Have all righteous precepts
Become shields for such illegal, immoral,
Vicious and sensual fulfillment? Why invite Indra
To an assembly of sages?'

'What can I tell you Saumitri?' said the sage.
All Aryan culture has become totally blind,
Morality has curdled and become blurred.
Sacrifice and rituals appear to have become
Means for gaining luxury. Is that not ignorance?
Good behaviour, strength of mind and the desire
To serve have vanished. When honesty declines,
And everyone moves in a world of illusion,
Should we not ascribe it to the theory of *karma*?
To whom can I go for succour, Shri Rama?

'The meek do not question, being subservient to tyranny!
They have bowed and accepted servitude in their minds.
They will not rebel against injustice and disorder!
Helpless, weak, experiencing grim difficulties,
Hoping for happiness and justice in the next birth,
They dream on,' recounted Kaushika, sadly.

'Why should immoral people be honoured?
Do wealth, power and status represent values?
Are their lives not disgraced? When it is so,
Why should the morality of Aryan culture,
Possessing both wisdom and science be distanced?'
The sage was dumbstruck at these words of Saumitri.

His eyes were filled with tears, tears of joy
As well as of sorrow.

Vishwamitra spoke:
'I am not the one to support Gautama's ambition.
A reputed sage, a wise man, a philosopher,
He is not blind to reality; nevertheless, the spark
Of revolution does not get ignited in his mind.
Whatever be the reason, Gautama has been punished,
So have the sages and ascetics.' Even while he spoke thus,
Kaushika shook in great pain as if his innards 130
Had been plucked out!

'Why are you in such a strange mood, O Guru?
Were you hurt so much? Forgive me for what I said,'
Said Saumitri, apologetically. But Kaushika remonstrated:
'No, Saumitri! Your words are as precious as rubies.
I remembered the sad story of what happened to Ahalya,
Gautama and Indra, when this holy assembly met.
It came to my mind, and was painful.' Immediately,
Rama and Lakshmana desired to listen to the entire
Story, and the sage began. 140

Canto Nineteen

'In the fire-pot of Lust Bloomed a Red Flower'

||☉||

Gautama and Ahalya stood with all the sages
Waiting, at the main entrance of the hermitage.
As soon as Indra arrived, they welcomed him.
The king of Heaven saw the immensely beautiful Ahalya.
Enamoured of her, he went on speaking of their welfare.
His mind was somewhere, his speech somewhere else:
'O respectable lady, Ahalya! Isn't hermitage-life difficult?
Aren't meditation and asceticism too demanding?
Does the environment suit you? You are the most beautiful
Woman in all the three worlds. Tell me, is this place   10
Suitable for you?'

'Forgive me, O king of gods! Why do I need luxury?
I am not a slave to sensual desires! I am the wife
Of a preceptor, I have acquired respect, and asceticism
Is enough for me. What else do I need?' Saying so,
Ahalya picked up her son Shata, walked to her cottage,
And went in! The conference was conducted successfully.
Gautama ascended to the status of the preceptor, and all
The sages praised him profusely. Vedas and Vedanta,

Varied codes and myths, and matters relating to them 20
Were discussed in the conference.

Husband and wife should work together for salvation.
That is the secret of life. Ignoring a wife is not proper conduct.
In longing for achievement, should one hate life?
While Gautama practised severe meditation, thirsting
For knowledge, he had to suppress all worldly desires.
Ahalya's ways were different, her desires were not dead;
That she also renounced desire for sensual pleasures
Was only apparently true; but her heart was open
For a hundred appetites. The waves of mind-sea would rise 30
In a high tide, and the strings of seven notes were plucked
In secret. In a language of silence, Cupid provoked her
Relentlessly. The yearnings of youth, hundred-fold,
Harassed her; and loneliness froze her life-stream.

When the eyes of Ahalya and Mahendra met
At the time of welcome, their hearts had slipped.
Indra's butterfly mind had flown seeking nectar
Into a forest, and had begun wandering in the bowers of love.
Ignoring the bond of being a guest, passion
Had turned impertinent; the lust within had screamed; 40
And in the fire-pot of lust, a red flower had bloomed.
Sensuality had spread like a fire, triumphantly.

Naked was Reason; the cobra slithered
In haste, in impatience, to satisfy its lust.
Looking at the head of a mongoose at the mouth
Of an ant hill, and deeming it to be a cobra, in the dance
Of blind passion of feasting on heavenly beauty,
Seeking a mirage of happiness, it had ended an easy prey.
Like a butterfly embracing a burning wick,
Deeming it to be sweet light and falling down burnt 50
Into a cinder, one becomes a prey to the fire of beauty,
Destroying one's self in the end.

As the bird of lust ruffled its feathers
In the form of Ahalya, nerves and pulses shaking,
Blood getting hotter, beauty unknown, passion unfelt,
Among the green foliage, at the edge of black clouds,
It yearned to climb the rainbow and slide down.

Deathless youth rising, beauty of the body brimming,
The bouquet of wild flowers filling with honey,
Bees flying around humming and the ocean of nectar   60
Dashing against the garden of multi-coloured flowers,
Its waves hit hard the heart of the king of gods.

While the king of seasons flowered and sparkled,
As if the desire for union transcending that of sight,
Came down from Heaven in the form of moonlight,
The cool wind stroked the body, tickled and teased.
The net of desire was spread and beauty was a curse.
Though Indra's conscience pricked him that falling
In love with another man's wife was not right,
Buffeted by the force of the lustful stream,   70
The dam of morality cracked and crumbled.
It was swept off by Ahalya's enticing youth.
Like twigs burning and spreading in the fire of *yajna*,
Sensual fire leaped high, and burnt fiercely;
And in the valley of lust, Indra, alas! lost his way.

It was midnight;
Silence enveloped the whole hermitage.
In the peace of deep sleep, the whole world was sunk.
But Ahalya was awake, her mind in turmoil.
Thoughts of Indra melting the mind, making it sad,   80
Unfulfilled desire swayed its hood.

Absorbed in rigorous penance for fulfillment,
Gautama had ignored the desire of a young woman.
His inner eyes were open, but the outer eyes were closed.
Not wanting to bother him with her sensuality,

Ahalya spent her days in self-restraint.
A child was born, Shata was his name;
He grew up happily being the gem of her eyes.
She was uneasy at the sight of Indra, the king of gods.
In despair, repulsive passion, delusion and oblivion, 90
The way Indra looked at her while entering the hermitage,
She couldn't erase that scene from her mind.
What if Indra approached her! Such unexpressed
Desire and anxiety troubled her.

'Kamaturanam no bhayam no lajja'
(Those overpowered by lust know neither fear nor shame).
Thus Indra planned many unwholesome tricks,
And ways of getting near beautiful Ahalya.
It was past midnight, and Indra was uneasy.
What should he do and when? He decided, 100
In an instant, to crow like a cock for Gautama to hear.
Why would he not become a cock or a crow
While Cupid's arrow had struck his heart?
Gautama woke up thinking the sun had risen,
Getting caught in the net Indra had spread.
He took the path to the river for morning ablutions.
After the rains, the receiving earth longs for seeds.
In the guise of Gautama, Indra slipped in.
As Ahalya tossed around, mumbling in sleeplessness,
The king of gods appeared right before her. 110

Excited that her husband had come,
The beautiful woman, like the sea rising, longing
For the sight of the moon, mad with ebullience,
Rising and falling, sinking and coming up,
While the lustful uproar filling the mind and body,
Like finding a mirage in the middle of a desert,
She closed her eyes and, madly, embraced him.
As she feasted on the delicious offering, a newness,
A new abundance, and ecstatic response she experienced.

While the honeyed kiss lingered on her lips,   120
While the assault was hot, the embrace tight,
Sinking and surfacing in a sea of joy, oblivious of oneself,
Her mind flew around like a free bird in the vast sky.
Her clothing was loosened, body slackened,
She was not at all sure if it was a dream or real.
While the body yielded, the mind retreated in caution:
Whom am I united with? Who is with me?
This is a new game never seen before.
Would the sage break the ascetic rule and indulge thus?

A man of self-control who could please even the Sun-god;   130
This is the moment just made for severe austerities;
His is the mind that will not flare up, Cupid cannot hurt it;
And he will not swim in the sea lit up by passions.

A hero who has blunted the point of Cupid's arrow,
Would he come to me like this? – wondered the woman,
Opening her eyes. Light was dim but recognition was instant.
In the guise of her husband, another man had approached her.
Startled, she withdrew in shock;
Benumbed, losing strength, trembling in fear,
She asked fuming in anger: 'Tell me, who you are?   140
You have deceived all and entered this cottage in stealth.
You have defiled me and made me a sinner.'

Canto Twenty

'In the silent forest, Sang the Cuckoo'

||☉||

Indra politely told Ahalya:
'I am Indra, the king of gods. I have come to surrender.
I am the slave of your Rati-like beauty.
With your dreams are my mind and body suffused;
I desired you in my mind, longed for union.
I have come to quench your desire, do not push me away;
I have broken through your fort of detachment and got in.
I shall make you float in unending joy and save you;
I shall dip my gentle love in all nine emotions.

'In the varied hues to paint a colourful world,   10
We shall bathe, and forget forever the rest of the world.
When the wood is damp, the fire is hidden in smoke;
Lust, likewise, hidden in the body, emitting smoke,
Kills with smoke, and bursts into flame all of a sudden,
And swallows the entire body. Do not move away,
My beloved, do not disappear from the field
Of my loving heart.

'O, my Beauty!
You are a gold pendant on a string of diamonds;
You are the smiling plant in a barren field;   20

You are a bee tasting sweetness full of desire;
You are the silver-edged lightning in a sky
Covered with black clouds.

'You are the passion of the rainbow in the sky-temple;
The divine cow of love yielding a stream of milk;
The cloud-maiden dancing in the blue sky;
The dream chariot taking one on a journey of flowers.'
Such honeyed words spoken by the king of gods
Resounded in Ahalya's mind!

'Do not do this, O conjurer, do not tune 30
The strings of the *veena* of my heart, do not pluck them.
Do not cross limits. Don't you tease and tempt
The cobra of my desires lying hidden in the anthill.'
While the fortress of passion for Indra imprisoned her,
The woman begged and pleaded for freedom.

Indra could not leave; Ahalya too was half-hearted.
He has to satisfy her and go, she has to be satisfied.
Both their bodies roasted in the heat of desire.
The fire in her heart was turning the sprouts of wisdom
To ash; the sensual desires, entombed till then, 40
Were dancing madly caught in inner commotion.
While attempting to come out of herself, the dam of restraint
Broke, and the tidal waves swept through the soil.
The celestial king was aware of Ahalya's state;
He could certainly divine the capricious mind of a woman.

'Let go of anger, beloved. If you break
The *veena*-strings of love, you will not hear the music again;
If this blessed moment is lost, it will not come again.'
Saying so, Indra disappeared.
Then, hiding in the bed of green foliage, he gazed 50
At the oscillation of Ahalya's emotions.

Ahalya was born the daughter of Sage Mudgala;
An embodiment of beauty, intellect and erudition.

In childhood, all the grandeur of Indra, the celestial king,
She had heard, and he was implanted in her mind.
Once, looking at his charming daughter, Sage Mudgala
Had exclaimed: 'Who else but Indra can match her beauty?
She should enter his palace, sit in the palanquin,
And live a life of splendour.'

The seed sown then, stayed in the subconscious, 60
Sprouted, bore leaves and had become a huge tree.
When she could not see him, the fever of lust rose in her;
His words of love echoed in her mind like a message
From the clouds. Like a lamp exposed to the wind,
Her body and mind were restless and trembling.
In pangs of separation, her mind turned dark,
And became hot iron. While fresh memories
Haunted her, she crossed the marital threshold.
'Foolish woman, what have you done?'
Mind taunted her. But her heart had been taken in; 70
The womb of faithfulness cracked; and, in the hurricane
Of lust, she became a dry leaf!

While the forest fire ranges, can cool wind put it out?
For thirst like a volcano's, will a drop of water suffice?
For the rainfall at the time of deluge, will an umbrella do?
Will arguments and philosophy solve earthly problems?
Will the Upanishads overcome the fever of lust?
The woman was imprisoned in a web of passion;
In the courtyard of Ahalya's heart, the celestial king
Drew patterns of passion yet again! 80
He appeared again,
Before the gem of a woman to know how she felt.
'What are you thinking of? What are you craving for?'
Questioned Indra and she gave herself to him, unquestionigly.
The burning heat cooled down, the night became moonlit,
The river of life flowed and the field became receptive,
In the silent forest, sang the cuckoo.

While thoughts of trust and fidelity strangled her,
And the fear of afterlife was all tangled and knotted,
Ahalya surrendered herself yet again to Indra. 90
Leaning against his broad chest and shoulders,
Amazed at the sensual ways of the celestial king,
She drank deeply of passion in bed.
When the search for joy and fulfillment became intense,
Sailing in the ship of ecstasy, she went into oblivion,
On the peak of contentment!

Over there, Gautama
Walked to the river bank and looked at the sky.
It was dark everywhere with no sight of the sun.
Silence reigned all around, and life was still passive. 100
Within the mind, doubts arose, anxiety increased,
And it disturbed the mind. Over and over again,
Ahalya's passionate sporting came to his mind,
And the sage was confused. All lustful feelings
Suppressed until then, awoke; and the intense desire
To please his beloved and caress her grew strong.
The discipline of asceticism was toppled;
The creeper of former love stretched its hands and called him;
The fountain of love sprang up, again, and overflowed.
Telling himself that he couldn't control himself anymore, 110
He returned, following the path to the hermitage.
Weakened was his asceticism, so was his will.
The lascivious contours of his wife's body got stamped
On his mind, pressed and prepared him to seek love,
And brought him home.

In a voice filled with love and passion,
He took her name and called her fondly, opened the gates
Of the cottage, and went in. It was too late.
The strings of the *veena* had been cut. It was all dark.
In the dim light, he dimly saw the woman in Indra's arms; 120
The celestial king's arms had encircled her slender body.

Thunder and lightning struck Gautama.
Joy and sorrow, smiles and tears, doubts,
Anxiety, wonder, disturbance and anger –
All emotions confused and shattered the sage!

Ahalya woke up, startled.
There was a scream of fear deep within her heart;
She pushed aside Indra from her chest;
The bed of love and glamour broke and turned into an abyss.
It was like a volcano exploding. 130
Like a banana tree uprooted, the woman
Rolled over on the ground, exhausted!

The morning cock was crowing then,
As if to awaken Ahalya's conscience!
Her face breaking into a sweat, she shook herself and stood.
The intoxication of lust had burst like a water bubble;
Like a kite, floating in the sky, suddenly crashing
Onto the ground with the string snapped.

In great sorrow, breathing hard, Ahalya bemoaned:
'What a disaster! Vanquished, I slipped for a moment 140
Of pleasure! Drinking in heavenly bliss greedily,
Caught in an illusion, did I forget my vow itself?
In the sparkle of golden leaves, in the songs of birds,
Did I delude myself that there was endless spring?
Did I become a fly, jumping up to consume poison?
Desiring nectar, did I embrace a poisonous snake?
Did I sacrifice my good name for momentary pleasure?
My life has become loathsome.' Thus crying,
The woman wilted in the fire of remorse.
The great Indra stood quietly, head bowed. 150

In great anger, Gautama screamed:
'You were the king of gods, Indra, and yet you cheated.
You have blackened the holy clan of women.
You, who should protect the world, have misbehaved.

Did you stab my wife with a golden knife?
This country, Bharatavarsha, considers a guest god;
Have you insulted the Aryan culture and defamed it?
Have you done something which will not
Let wives and daughters of sages live in honour?
Did you think their honour and lives were mere toys? 160
Creeping in like a night creature, looting their honour,
Did you make the hermitage look like a graveyard?'

The news had spread and there was anxiety in everyone!
Sage Gautama, the embodiment of humility,
Assumed silence for the time being. Later, when everybody
Had gathered, he told them: 'Listen to the terrible deed
That someone called the king of gods has committed.
Dancing and prancing during the preceptor's meditation,
He has been responsible for the faithlessness of a woman!
While I stood meditating for the welfare of the world, 170
Instead of guarding an innocent, deer-like wife,
He has seduced her like a lustful, evil tiger.
Speak up sages, saintly, scholarly *Brahmarshis*!
I ask everyone, what punishment does Indra deserve?'

A betrayer, a heretical sinner;
Shall I curse him so that he loses his masculinity?
That he should suffer in agony and rot?
I shall move a resolution that he is without character,
In this great gathering of good people.
He has overstepped righteousness, punish him. 180
He does not deserve to be the celestial king;
He should lose his status, somehow or the other.'

Silence enveloped the sagacious gathering.
Gautama watched the sages and celibates.
In the gathering, some bowed their heads,
Some slipped away. They were deaf to the supplications
Of Gautama for justice. Without siding with justice,
Unmoved and detached, were the great scholars;

They were the slaves of tradition, without a sense of duty.
Some sat quietly as if in ridicule; some closed windows,
And started meditating; and some threw sharp arrows
Of mockery; they were the ones who could just imitate!

'Ahalya is a fallen woman. The fault is only hers.
Should anyone invite Indra to the preceptor's abode,
While he, with an unclean mind, is ready to rush
Ahead with open arms? What happened to Ahalya?
She is one who has cut the binding of loyalty.
In her excessive lust, she has stained the holy place.
There is no redemption. The hermitage is not acceptable
Anymore. The sage's wife should be a model of virtue;
But now she has fallen into the web of passion.
She is the fallen woman, and she has crossed the bounds
Of morality. This is forbidden in Aryan culture,
And in the conduct of the hermitage as well.'

They were the shadows
Of Aryan and Vedic culture; with reactionary ideas,
They had built the foundation of tradition; though they
Spoke progressive words, they could throw a magical net
Of Aryan culture: 'Indra is the crown of celestial beings,
A god worshipped during rituals, a receiver of all sacrifices.
Who are we to displace his power?'

Listening with emotion to the story,
Shri Rama and Saumitri lost patience.
'How strange! Without upholding justice,
And becoming powerless, inactive, static rocks –
Are these sages and scholars?' questioned Rama in dismay.

'Does one become an ascetic only by wearing saffron robes?
Does one become a poet piling up words?
There is no alternative to a steady character, my son!
All outward performance is a false game,' replied Kaushika.

Saumitri's question was more pointed:
'At that time, you were there in the hermitage.
A witness; why were you silent?
Why did the fire of your protest go out?
Why did you live on, ignoring the violence done to a woman?
While the invitation to fight came your way,
When everyone in the learned gathering looked away,
Why did your conscience desert you?'
'Why do you remind me, Lakshmana!'
Kaushika was in agony: 'The wheel of time continues   230
To stab me endlessly. Look! I am a Kshatriya.
Longing for the status of a *Brahmarshi*,
I dedicated myself for a long time to penance.
As a result of meditation, I acquired the status;
It brought me joy and a sense of fulfilment.
Did I get caught in the allure of status and forget duty?
What did it matter that I was in Gautama's hermitage
On that day? I lay in a corner like a lump of meat.
The violence took place right before my eyes,
The ineffective chastisement of scholars.   240

Enamoured of my status, scared
And shrinking, I could not protest! I could not
Raise my voice against the system, as I was
Scared of losing what I had gained over decades.
While the celestial king was the master of the clan
With absolute powers, who would be brave
Enough to put him in the place of an offender?
He has the power to grant the status of *Brahmarshi*
To thousands! What if my status was reviewed
And it was taken away by priests? I was scared.   250
I was the only Kshatriya in the hermitage,
Who was a *Brahmarshi*. Saumitri, my wits were dull.

'The leech that stuck to my conscience that day
Is sucking the essence of my soul, even today.

I cannot bear the pain, and I don't know when I shall be freed.
The woman's cry for help burns my heart even now.
Protect me, Rama, before it burns me up completely.
I know none else but you. Give me salvation, Rama!'

Feeling sad at the great teacher's helplessness,
Shri Rama and Saumitri were deeply touched. 260
Breaking the silence, Saumitri asked;
'Tell us what happened next, O venerable Guru!'

'Nothing was said about punishment for Indra.
Thinkers, wise men, and sages left Gautama's hermitage,
Going away one behind the other, into the deep forest.
Later on discussion and argument went on there.
'Amitalabha said: "Ahalya must be punished,
And Indra must be forgiven. Otherwise, enmity
Will grow between the celestial beings and Aryan power.
It is never any good to discard tradition. 270
This is the hermitage of the highest level
In the kingdom of Mithila, and it is the centre of scholarship.
The scales of justice should lean towards Authority.
Ahalya's fickleness spells peril to the Aryan clan itself.
If the wife of the preceptor is sinful and stays
In the hermitage, the hermitage becomes corrupt.
Study and instruction, meditation and scholarship,
All end up futile. If we take on Indra, we shall be
Reduced to ashes like a parrot flying near the sun.
The fruits of a thousand rituals will be washed away 280
In the flood of Indra's anger."

'Jnanapriya did not like these words:
"Ahalya was helpless. There was atrocity committed
By an evil-doer. Why should the hermitage become corrupt?
Why is she a sinner? What is this morality, this virtue?
Having committed a crime, does one blame others?"

"The preceptor's wife tripped and fell.
When the idol of an ideal gets broken and falls,
What is the point in blaming others? Will any rule
Survive a convention the world has accepted?" 290
Reacted Amitalabha.'

Canto Twenty-one

'Ahalya Stood Still like a Stone'

||6||

While Ahalya searched her mind in inner struggle,
There were deep feelings of disgust and contempt.
Her self-respect, culture and purity were shattered;
The desire to live had withered. The sad state
Of having to go into the pyre of worry was hers.
Gautama was not angry or pained
For her helplessness, he showed sympathy and understanding.

In weariness Ahalya said to Gautama:
'The span of my life is over, sir!
Leave me in loneliness. In anguish, I shall   10
Perform strict penance. This is the best healer for me.
I shall become inert like a stone, curbing passion and greed.
I shall find new energy in religious observance.
You are thirsty for knowledge; if you stay away from scholars,
You will be like fish fallen on sand;
You will be restless, life will be meaningless,
Like the skin of sugar-cane after the juice is taken out.
Train disciples in another hermitage, and become
The preceptor there; achieve what you are capable of.

'Can anything be achieved in disgrace and anger? 20
When Shata grows up, they will mock him,
Calling him the son of a fallen woman. I cannot bear that,
I shall not become a stumbling rock in the path of his life.
His education must go on. He should become
Shatananda, a *Brahmarshi* with great radiance,
Respected by all, he should become the royal priest of Mithila.
Please grant me the initiation of freedom!
In order that another Indra shall not dishonour women,
I shall stand speechless, like a pillar of honour'.

Gautama looked at Ahalya, 30
With divine sight of a seeker and a scrutiniser.
With awakened radiance, with a philosophical view,
He saw her rising from ruin and admired her.
Her will to live had not died in the fire of anguish.
Self respect, steadiness and refinement
Had not been destroyed in violence against her.

Gautama spoke in a grave voice:
'I accept the grandeur of the future you see.
I shall give up the desire to be the preceptor
Of the hermitage, when you become the sculptor 40
Of our beautiful future; I shall renounce fame, honour,
Status and respect, all for you. Patiently,
I shall cross hills and banks and great rocks.
While the rivers of new life meet, the sweet music
That sings a prelude to it will join the main stream,
At the edge of the earth, the sound of victory
Shall spread the message of the woods.
I approve of your austerity, my beloved!
The rock at the bottom of the river gurgles,
Listening to the pain in your heart. Let the rain of solace 50
Pour on you. For that moment, I shall wait for years
On end, in the fire of austerity! Tell me, my wife,
To win in this trial by fire, what price should I pay?'

With a steady voice Ahalya said:
'When the aim is high, one should pay with life!
The path of our journey is difficult.
If the path of search is difficult, should one be scared!
Shata should not become a creeper without support.
He should become Shatananda and grow tall like a huge tree.
He is precious to us. He should climb the peak of honour.　　　　60
You are his father, you are his mother as well!'
Sage Gautama's heart melted with love.
He said: 'You are helpless. How will you live
A lonely life in the middle of a thick forest?
While the wound has not healed, suffering unending,
Pain enveloping body and mind, who will
Offer consolation to you? How can I leave you
In the middle of this forest? Am I so ungrateful?
For the selfish aims of the male society, like a sacrificial animal,
Will you offer yourself as the wick of the world's lamp　　　　70
And burn? Will you spend a life on fire?
Without you, how can I live a barren life?
How can I move on, how can I bear the pangs
Of separation? Tell me, beloved Ahalya!'
'Do not worry, I have seen life's injustice
As well as suffering; I have heard the terrifying sounds
Of the bells round the neck of Yama's buffalo.
While the fields of corn with the sweat of scores of centuries
Wave their heads; while, in the search of poets, scientists,
And revolutionary philosophers move in impassable paths,　　　　80
Dreams are burnt in the fire of wild eyes; should I be scared?
Should one be frightened of the painful cries of helpless humanity!

'Behind thick black clouds of sharp sounds,
While hunting dogs in the human world break their chains
And run, while the seven horses of the morning sun
Gallop in a spurt of power, while the cruel lions, lusting gold,
Roar and spring, if Indra's elephant rushes, trumpeting

In heat, I shall plant the hook and stop it;
I shall drag aside Amitalabha and Vedavedya, 90
And, with vigour, I shall move forward; I shall hold and pull
The elephant's tusk and fell it down; I have Aryan power.
I am not weak, and I shall enter the cave of danger
And fight the great fight of life.'

Gautama realised Ahalya's determination
And walked on ahead. Unable to leave his home and Ahalya,
Carrying Shata on his shoulder, dragging heavy steps,
Shrunk in sorrow, watching his wife Ahalya holding up
The green flag of the auspicious dawn of new life,
He moved on. 100

Till the shadow disappeared,
Ahalya watched steeling her mind. Then she walked in,
Closed every door of the hut, went up the roof, and sighing,
Saw her life evaporating. In a moment, she was like a tree
Falling on the ground with its trunk being cut!
Like water falling in the middle of sand and not sinking,
A stream of tears poured down from her eyes.

In the womb of the darkness of the forest,
She hears the sound of heavy drops falling as drizzle.
While over the wet cheeks hot tears roll down, 110
Years pass without her eyelids closed.
Like epochs gone by the hot salty land,
Her desires for happiness and comfort ended.
Free from desire and hatred, like a symbol of millions
Of pleading, weak women, harassed and despised,
Ahalya stood there as a stone.

The holy inauguration
Was over in the environment of Gautama's new hermitage.
The instruction to make him preceptor was given
By Seeradhwaja, King Janaka. In the preceptor's seat 120
Sat Gautama in the hall of rituals, and Jnanapriya was

His deputy. The position was not given to Amitalabha.
While Seeradhwaja and others gave instructions,
The rituals went on systematically. Gautama changed
The order of chants. During the rituals, the final sacrifice
Was not offered to the celestial beings; they were all ignored.
Taking the holy water in his palms, standing facing the sun,
Gautama pronounced in a grave and rough voice:

'I am the preceptor Gautama.
The Sun-god as my witness, with this water, 130
A curse I shall place on Indra, the king of Heaven:
His character is flawed, hence he is not worthy
Of being worshipped by the Vedas. He has shattered
The dreams of women and has disturbed the world's peace.
He is heartless. Hence, he will no longer be worshipped;
He will be forbidden from all the future rituals and
Conferences; he will no longer be invited in the rituals
To get his share of offerings.'

Water was poured on earth;
The sages watched this wonder of the epoch in silence. 140
The great king, Seeradhwaja accepted Gautama's
Pronouncements, and proclaimed them as the law of the land,
Thus was the king of Heaven punished.

Canto Twenty-two

'Mother, Open the Door'

||⑥||

Ahalya's story of grief saddened their hearts.
The pain of a woman killed raised its serpent hood.
Some voice in pain called out and the wind
Sounded like a sigh of agony. The very next moment,
The voice changed and the cry of pain appeared
To be a slow song. Watching in curiosity,
Shri Rama kept thinking, the treasure of
Mother Nature seemed to have collapsed. There was
Silence, peace, quietness spread all over. It was
A wonderland itself. Ahalya waited   10
Inert, stone-like, hoping for release,
With the desire to regain her respect in society.

'This is the hermitage that Gautama abandoned!
It became a graveyard because of Indra's sensuality,'
Said the sage. 'Corrupt, capitalist, destroyer
Of Aryan culture,' mocked Saumitri,
In great anger. 'Mentor, will you permit us?
We are eager to see mother Ahalya.'
Asked Shri Rama with courtesy. 'Ahalya is
Waiting for release! You do not need permission.   20

Those who cannot carry their own burden
Need permission. Go forward, Raghava,
Who will question your decision?' said the sage.

His words were soothing.
Self-confidence emerged in Rama. The pure
Wind of release blew joyfully and danced.
Shri Rama and Saumitri walked towards the hermitage,
Trees and plants growing like a fortress.
Right in the middle of the forest was the preceptor's hut,
Appearing unique in shape and structure.
Raghava knocked on the door gently.
The door did not open, there was no answer.
Worried, like an infant calling its mother with love,
'Mother', he called and knocked on the door again.
Shri Rama can pluck the strings of the heart-*veena* in everyone;
Does he not know this truth in life? He called again,
'Mother, open the door.'

As the boys stood before the door,
The sage watching like the chataka bird for rain,
The door opened. What was seen inside!
In such brilliant radiance, enough to attract the whole world.
Like a flame of fire within smoke,
Like the blinding sun amidst water,
Like the moon covered in mist and clouds,
The luckless woman Ahalya lay there like a rock.
They saw her like a great witness for purification of the soul!

Ahalya gazed
At the great men who had come in stepping gently;
In peace, she opened her heavy eyelids.
The wheel of time appeared dim;
Decades had passed as if they were epochs
Since human faces were seen. She had forgotten the world.
Someone sinned and someone else was punished.
Blind justice of the world, people appeared dead.

The woman engrossed in meditation was anxious
Recognising *Brahmarshi* Kaushika.

'Was not Kaushika the one who protected
The honour of men? An embodiment of humanity?
Where were his self-respect, sense of discrimination,
Compassion and humanity hiding?' She wondered inwardly. 70

Longing to speak, she stammered.
While her voice had dried up in the depth of her mind,
Awakening it, she said, 'Sage Vishwamitra, I bow to you.
Am I not a fallen woman? When will the trial by fire end?
I cannot express the feelings in my mind.
My tongue has been bound by elephantine fetters.
I am in the pit of sin the world has dug and pushed me in.
Who will cut the knots of customs and release me?
Who are these radiant and energetic boys?
I bow to the radiance, I bow to their form. 80
I bow to the kind people who have come to see me.'

'The sons of Dasharatha, the jewel of Ikshwaku clan;
Rama and Lakshmana they are called; they are the liberators,'
Said the great sage.

They saw the ascetic,
Mind and body burnt, a spotless divine consciousness,
A great woman chiselled like a great work of art.
Pain had mellowed in the fire of ascetic achievement.
Fair complexion, a shapely nose, silver hair like snow,
Sharp eyes with the message of pain – that was Ahalya. 90
Bowing their heads, they showed their respect
To the good woman, and they said, 'Supplications to you,
Bless us, mother! We are your children.
You have given us serenity in your abode.
We have received in the shade of a great tree,
Ease, peace and solace. We have experienced in you
The divine presence of Kausalya and Sumitra.'

Within Ahalya's mind
A wave of excitement arose and roared aloud.
Bowing low to a fallen woman? She was amazed   100
At the courage of the boys and saw with great joy
The edge of liberation: 'While King Seeradhwaja
And sages moved away in weakness,
Pledging their souls to the strictures of blind faith,
Disregarding opposition, the boys have come here.
Brave hearts, sage-like revolutionaries of Aryavarta!
They are not ordinary people walking on trodden paths,'
Thinking thus, she got up in excitement.

In a rush of devotion, Ahalya fell
At the feet of Shri Rama, Saumitri and the sage: 110
'You are beyond measure on earth, you have
Shown me the great path. You are the navigators
Of the Great Quest. You are men of the epoch,
The pole stars of the Treta epoch!
Fortunate am I that you touched my feet,
Fortunate am I that I touched your feet.
How can I offer my gratitude across many births?
I have spent years like epochs and waited
For a celestial vision, the opening of the door
Of liberation. Lying inert like a stone, I am not   120
The only one on earth to do that. The whole of Aryavarta
Is inert. You are great heroes. If you go forward without fear,
Energy will flow in every vein in the world!
You have granted self-respect to exploited people.
You have granted a new, blossoming gift of life.
Your search is complete. My asceticism has borne fruit.

'I am fearless now. I shall see my husband and son,
Free from the consciousness of guilt, O Shri Rama!
With your nectar-like touch I am free from worry;
I feel extremely happy, the frozen pain   130
Has melted and flown away like water.

Inertness of mind and body has departed;
I am one with the divine radiance.
The cataract has fallen from my eyes and they shine.

While a smile that could melt stones
Flashed over his lips, Shri Rama said:
'We are representatives of the society that ruined you.
Why should we say that? We are princes of Ayodhya.
We beg you, please forgive the wrong, mother;
The law of punishing the innocent and protecting   140
The wrong-doers is ours alone!
Looking at this, heads should be hung in shame.
Law cannot tolerate dishonouring women.
Should the innocent be punished through ostracism?
For the Ikshwaku clan, this is a stain. This is chaos,
And not governance. Sages who should teach
Mortality and comparison to regimes closed their eyes
And sat in silence. Why?'

Listening to Rama's words, Ahalya lost herself.
As waves of emotion rose in her heart, there was   150
No sound, shape, depth or height for them.
No words to give it form. She shed tears of joy;
Floating and drowning in the acme of divine joy.
'Your mission is fulfilled Rama, you have become brave
Growing tall beyond expectation. You are the man
Of the epoch, climbing the peak of a fruitful life,'
Thus Sage Vishwamitra praised Rama.

'Forgive me, children. I forget in my worries,
To give you seats and offer hospitality.
I shall bring a bouquet of flowers and fruits.   160
If I give you fruits, will you eat them?' so saying,
She went out. Kaushika, filled with friendliness, said:
'While Shri Rama smiles gently in love,
That is hospitality enough for us, mother!
Nothing more is needed. Fruits you have

Brought in the cup of your heart and offered.
We are satisfied, Shri Rama and Lakshmana
Have tasted the nectar of your hospitality.'

'Is this much of hospitality enough?
Bless me. My Gautama, the ascetic, how is he? 170
Is my son Shata well? How tall has he grown?
Is he handsome? Gentle? Does he resemble Rama
And Lakshmana?' Such breathless questions
She asked, with excess of love and care.

'Do not be scared or startled. Rejoice.
Your loving son has become Shatananda now;
He is a scholar and the world looks at him in amazement.
A *Brahmarshi* in wisdom, the pole star in radiance,
He has grown taller than his father. A royal priest
To the sage-king Janaka, he shines and has won all hearts. 180
Gautama thinks of you and waits;
His sorrow burns him like the heat of asceticism.
Cursing Indra, taking away his status,
Denying him the major part of offering in rituals,
He has totally weakened him. He has only taught
The way to control violence and follow morality.
He has become a great sage, respected the world over,'
Kaushika said.
'O great Guru! We want the story
Of mother Ahalya's achievement, the painful 190
Story of women; Tell me about it.
Forget your sorrow and tell the story,'
Said Saumitri with great concern.

Canto Twenty-three

'They Met Like the Ruddy Swans'

||⊙||

'How can I tell the tale?
The pain suffered by a luckless woman?
I cried for some days in the corner of the hut.
Restless, I rolled over on the mat;
Burnt out dreams danced hideously;
Ghosts and spirits rose and danced pompously.
Desires, animosities, friendships and harmony
Were choked and collapsed in the fortress of tradition
Like corpses, went across the screen of memory.
The sun-rays of joy had drowned in the black sea.　　　　　10

'The power to think was lost and turned into confusion.
The shadow of a tree assumed form and screamed in dissonance;
It wandered in forbidden places without peace;
Losing direction, thrashing and clashing;
Black tears spreading like insects of cruel mockery,
Donning many forms, moving to seek shelter
Not finding refuge, they came back to me,
Trudging the same trodden path, exploding,
They walked on in the distorted form of humour!

'The golden idol of my life had cracked 20
With a terrifying noise, ears, nose, arms and legs
Lay, severed, scattered, in horrifying forms.
Determination swung to and fro, in the valley of ups and downs.
Becoming a shadow of dissonance, a ghostly spectre mocked.
Weeping with mad laughter, to vanquish
The specters, as I rushed forward with courage,
Each and every form vanished.
While despair turned into a ghost, all was nothingness.
I lay exhausted, but hunger and thirst aroused me.
Crawling outside, I would search and return; 30
Plucking fruits from trees, I would store them.
I had a few cows of mine, like Kamadhenu, the heavenly cow;
They were my great protectors; my everything.
So I tended them with love and devotion.
Was I for them or were they for me?
In such engrossment, years rolled away.

'Rolls unwind on the screen of my memory;
Day and night I would spend in meditation.
Once in a while, I would be indisposed. In fever,
The body would shake and the head would burst with ache. 40
I would search for a doctor and ask for medicine.
Once, wandering along, I reached a village;
I knocked on the door, the woman of the house came out,
And screamed as if she had seen a ghost.
People left their houses and ran berserk,
Without even touching my shadow. When I followed,
They ran ever faster and reached the fortress of tradition.

'The chained locks
Were tightened and made secure, unaware
That they were imprisoning themselves! Raining stones, 50
Soaking me in the flowing red blood!
In the deadly fear that anything might happen any moment,

I spent nights and days awake; in dreams and sleep,
Fear haunted me at all times.

'In my action and thought, a black shadow had spread,
Hiding like a snake in a hole in the inner space of my heart.
It would rise again and again, hiss and scare me;
Raising its head and hiss as if it was going to spew out venom.
I saw terrible pictures which aroused anxiety
Like pointed arrows, questions deep within my mind,   60
Would fly around, not finding answers.
They would come back and pierce me inflicting
Permanent wounds. In the shade of the hermitage trees,
Like a wax image, I spent decades burning and suffering.'

The saga of lone diligence
Was listened to by Shri Rama with equanimity.
The sage stood unmoving like a statue!
Saumitri could not bear it, he was angered.
'Raining stones on mother Ahalya?
Is there no limit to viciousness? Traitors, betrayers,'   70
He roared, forgetting himself.

'How can I complain? They were not the ones,
Who called me a fallen woman; They were innocent.
The sages and scholars were the ones who chastised me
And drove me away. In pain, returning to the hut,
I fell over in despair. The world was empty.
Without moving out, I sought for support
And stayed within the hermitage. Unaware of the meaning
Of life and death, I became like a log of wood.
I have lived here in death, I have died here living.   80
On a lonely island, I ruminated on morality and righteousness.
'Was I alive or dead? Did I eat or starve?
There was none in the world who wanted to know.
This is a cruel world, son; Being flattered,
They get on to grand chariots and show off.
Leaders who have climbed high serving people,

Are trodden upon, thrown around, kicked about
With envy, to find sadistic pleasure.
Look, Lakshmana! The clothes I am wearing
Tell the story of my suffering: spinning the cotton
And flax I grew myself, I wove them with my own hands. 90
Look here, my child!'
Saumitri reacted yet again, sharply:
'You are a good woman, mother, full of divine qualities.
"Kshamaya dharitri" (as forgiving as the earth).
You are her virtuous daughter. Offering Gautama
And Shatananda to the world, you have filled the treasury
Of knowledge. You have sacrificed a lot. Forgive all those
Who ill-treated you mother.'

'I have no hatred, son!
Who will forgive whom? This is a tragedy 100
Played out by fate; can the actors be held responsible?
If the puppeteer's circle of poison does not stop,
Constant attack will continue to take place – assault
On women, and exploitation of the weak Aryans
As well as the non-Aryans.'

The sage said, soothingly:
'The sorrowful chapter of your life is over.
Listen to the happy prelude of the auspicious morning.'

Ahalya was released;
The auspicious time of re-union drew near. 110
Sage Gautama is in expectation; a ripened fruit,
He waits for a new life. Standing in the sun's heat,
He has now grown like a tall tree giving shade to people.
Energising lives of others, he has become immaculate.
The time for trial by fire of faithfulness being over,
He has come rushing, looking for Ahalya,
To behold the unchained hands of his wife.

He is there, eager, to accept her,
And lead her away to the courtyard of a new life.
'Under the pressure of devotion to precepts, 120
Forgetting the heart of mankind, unaware of
The depth of Ahalya's love, I neglected my duty.
Like a blinkered horse, I became deadwood, Rama.
Sacrificing the desires of the heart to the wheel of fate,
Deaf to the tunes of emotion, I became a buffalo
Submerged in mire, Ramachandra.' Thus bemoaned
Gautama, grieved in his heart and mind.

He saw Ahalya, craving for re-union, who,
Having punished her mind and body in asceticism,
Yearning for relief, for the curse to end, 130
Was longing for the time when anguish would turn
Into music.

Ahalya's soul sought Gautama
In every hut, constant and unceasing, in the stupor
Of plants and trees, in the blowing cool breeze.
As conjugal love became a mirage,
Love grew like a huge tree as decades went by,
Youth turning into a dry lump of mud in times of drought,
Gazing at the sky hoping for cool rains,
Her womb dark and suffering in separation. 140
It was like a deer, weary and weak, tortured in the sun,
Jumping into fire and losing its life.

Did she step on the boundaries of suspicion without love?
Was she prey to the commotion created by a battle?
Did she become a burning desert breathing hot breath?
Like fuel touched by fire, there was smoke in the mind;
Eventually, desire turned smokeless and became the flame of love.
Suffering long to wash away the sin, like gold purified by fire,
She bathed in pure love, and blossomed,
Cleansing the world of its dirt and grime. 150

Spotless purity is the game of supreme nature.
Like rising early in the morning and bathing in its light,
While the series of sights shone in the island of wisdom,
She looked in them for her soul in the manmade
Pot of fire, in the depth of the solemn sea;
In the lonely cavern of the heart,
In the mine of beauty in creation;
In the blue sky, in gurgling, flowing water,
At the tip of the burning tongues,
In the edge of a truthful sentence. 160

The eddy of heart-breaking sensitive voice was there.
It was not a call from the throat, not an enchanting flute,
That was the howling of the soul, a soft whisper
Of a whirlpool. Like the cry of an infant,
A sound that wrenched the heart, from far away,
It called Gautama.

Hearing it, when Gautama
Came running, he saw the gem of a wife.
Cleansed after a long time of asceticism!

The divine wife, a good woman of great talents, Like the shining
Flame, after the smoke-screen is swept off, 170
Like the moon out of mist, like the sun clear of clouds –
Gautama saw his beloved, radiant and dazzling.
He felt his search had been, finally, fruitful.
Looking at Sage Gautama,
Shri Rama and Saumitri, were extremely happy.

Sage Viswamitra declared his mission fulfilled.
Tears of love sprang in the eyes of Ahalya and Gautama.
While the sea of joy was in full tide, speech was banished.
In the royal path, while tender feelings and sacrifice
Were like steps, joy had been overflowing. 180
In the compatibility of souls cast in love,

Determined to live together, Ahalya and Gautama
Met like two inseparable ruddy swans.

'O, Rama, ocean of compassion, saviour of the fallen,'
Praised Ahalya and sang his glory, lost in devotion.
She came again and fell at the holy feet
Of Rama, Lakshmana, Sage Kaushika,
And Gautama. 'O Sachchidananda, protect us,'
Begged the husband and wife, chanting Rama's name.
Shri Rama's journey of victory moved on again, 190
With the great vision of the quest for Mithila.

Canto Twenty-four

'The Bridge of Love that Unites the World'

||๖||

On the way the sage instructed them thus;
'Know that the body is the chariot, intellect its charioteer,
The mind is the reins, the senses horses,
Objects of sensual pleasures are the road to travel,
The soul is the master of the chariot, the syllable "Om" bow,
And self-realisation is the ultimate goal.
This is the secret of salvation and righteousness.
"*Uttishthata, Jagrata, Papyavaran nibodhata*"
(Arise, awake, and stop not till the goal is reached).
Crush the obstacles of laziness and indifference. 10
Eliminate greed and move in the path of action
Free from desire, move ahead having ideals.

'Wicked people will not harass
Those that are full of forgiveness and are secular in outlook.
Fire goes out on a barren land, where no grass grows.
Each act has a cause, it is comforting to know and follow that path.
To achieve the four *purusharthas* – *dharma, artha, kama,*
And *moksha* (righteousness, wealth, love, and bliss),
Is the miracle that occurs in a man's life.

Sin and virtue take form in the creator's workshop. 20
The search for joy and peace in the truth of creation
Is the aim of science and philosophy. Harmony
Is the source of universal righteousness. To move on
In this joyous world, breathing excitement, is a journey
Of adventure. My search will be completed in Janaka's city;
When my vow is fulfilled, I shall walk back to my hermitage.

'Listen to Mithila's history, very sweet on the ears.
Janaka is the ruler there, a very virtuous man,
An abode for love and affection, a saint – king, a seer.
Once, a *yajna* had begun and the intitial rites, 30
Like purifying the field, were going on with speed.
While Janaka was in the front with the plough,
It stopped all of a sudden, the tip was caught in earth.
Amazed, Janaka sank on to the ground, unable to push!

'All the priests and sages gathered, and wondered
How the field was chosen, and why the work was hindered;
And they were worried that it was a bad omen.
With crow-bars and hoes, labourers rushed forward.
The attempt was in vain. Public announcements were made.
A group of skilled stone-cutters was called, experts 40
In planning were called. The attempt bore no fruit.
An army of elephants and horses, of brave soldiers –
All pulled but the plough did not budge.
Lines of worry formed on Janaka's forehead;
In expectation and anxiety the eyelids blinked;
The sound of the gongs reached the depths of ears.
Everyone was astonished as a box was visible
From the line of the plough. In it they saw
A divine, auspicious female infant, the one born of earth.

In a bed of soft silk, golden in colour, 50
As if Brahma himself had sculpted and gifted her
To the earth. Seeradhwaja saw the child glowing thus.
Picking up the unknown baby as if it were his own,

Fondling it with love and compassion, holding it close
To his chest, he kissed it! Nectar of love overflowed
In the fountain of his heart. "My dear daughter,"
He said and took her to the palace.
As he placed the child in his wife Sunayana's arms,
She rejoiced, feeling the *yajna* had borne fruit.

Sita, she was called, 60
She grew like a tender creeper and became a young woman;
A gem of a girl, beautiful and virtuous, was Janaka's daughter.
The fame of her beauty spread in all eight directions,
Among the *devas, danavas, gandharvas, kinnaras* and *nagaras*.
For Seeradhwaja, it was as if a drying, dying tree
Without offspring had suddenly flowered and borne fruit!

"Who is this Sita?" The mystery of her birth
Spread like wild fire, and such issues as her caste,
Sub-caste, family, lineage, high-born, low-born, and such
Troubled people's minds. Was she an orphan? 70
Did her parents discard her and walk away unmoved?
Found in earth! How strange! People talked.
To find out the source of her birth, Seeradhwaja
Carried on a search. But, on finding no clue, he decided
She was not born of any woman. He cared for her a lot;
And the time for her marriage approached!

Ministers and courtiers went seeking a husband for her;
Wandered around in Aryavarta and came back weary,
Not finding anyone suitable! Seeradhwaja's heart was full
Of apprehension! The picture of the infant in the field, 80
Crying, saddened his mind. In anxiety and sorrow,
He decided on the wonderful plan of Shiva's bow.
"Whoever lifts the bow and strings it will be offered Sita;
That will be the test, with Sita at stake," he announced.'

Rama listened to the story, and whispered thus:
'How strange, O sage! Do princes lack intelligence?

Is the beautiful daughter of Janaka, not born of a woman,
An orphan? Not finding a suitable bridegroom!
Who is responsible for her not knowing her parentage?
What wrong did she do? Why this prejudice against women? 90
Vanaje experienced the anguish of molestation;
Ahalya faced world's ostracism, becoming a prey
To Indra's web of deceit; has the turn of Sita arrived today!'

Rama's thoughts continued:
Who is this Sita? Is she the daughter of an unknown
Common peasant? Some have overflowing prosperity,
Some die of hunger. For equal distribution of wealth,
Did she arrive as an infant? Would a mother abandon
The flesh of her flesh? Who were her parents?
Did they turn away from their duty? Could she not become 100
The bride of the son of the Raghu-clan of Ayodhya?

Is she not a princess with culture and education?
Is she not worthy of becoming Rama's wife?
Is it fitting to talk about Sita as payment for valour?
Without being aware of her heart's emotions and desires,
Should she be pushed to the sacrificial post?
Should there be violence on her tender mind and body?
Can her life's desires be neglected!
The symbolic mysteries that the mentor had given him
Flashed like lightning and Rama was disturbed. 110

Sage Vishwamitra spoke:
'Into a violent forest, to protect righteousness
I have brought you Rama. Janaka's vow
Invited me. My inner voice has accepted
The challenges of the world. Sita is second to none
In character and beauty. Her heart is saddened
With the considerations of rigid class-caste hierarchy.
Between the two rulers, Janaka and Dasharatha,
Enmity and rivalry have developed; it has assumed
A giant form and will swallow all. 120

They should get together and with combined power,
Forget enmity and destroy the *rakshasas*.
You, Shri Rama, should become the bridge of love
To bring together these two and the whole world.'

Listening to these words, Shri Rama and Saumitri
Gazed intently at the great sage.
'My child. Think, there is time. Do not rush;
I shall not force you. Think before you give me your word.'
A tiger among sages, Kaushika spoke,
And turned to meditation.   130

'The mentor is not one to withdraw from duty.
I have not seen the bow of Shiva. The daring
Move would be futile childishness. I do not know
The bride Sita; I am the groom she does not know.
How can there be feelings? Don't the princes have desires
And dislikes? I have told you, O teacher, of my doubts.
We should get to know the hidden powers of
The bow of Shiva,' Rama said with a sense of determination.

The sage spoke with excitement:
'Sita is not born of woman, she is the loving daughter   140
Of Seeradhwaja. She is the perfect bride for you.
You will have all the fortune in the world; have no doubts.
She has agreed to the rules and regulations
That her father has laid down. An explosive power
Is contained in Shiva's bow. It is enough to touch it
With intelligence. I shall teach you the necessary skill
And technique. I desire to render it inactive eventually.
If the *rakahasas* possess it, the whole world
Will be destroyed. We have to prevent it.
For this epoch, it is the final step in our quest.   150
The expectation is a pledge. Shatananda
As well as King Janaka will arrive here. Then,
You should convey to them your decision.'

The dilemma in Rama's heart disappeared.
In a moment, the sky was clear. The sun rose
In a new epoch. The joy of an unearthly radiance
Grew and spread across the face of Shri Rama.
'I feel fulfilled. Kausalya and Dasharatha gave me life;
And, you have shown me the right path and vision,'
Said Shri Rama. 160

'Vishwamitra's arrival at Janaka's city was not new;
The wonder was the coming of Rama and Lakshmana!
Many decades had passed since rulers of Ayodhya
Visited Mithila. They had proclaimed excommunication
Between the Aryans of the west and the clan of Janaka.
Communication was cut, enmity had grown.
The tidings of the wedding had not been sent,
Yet Rama and Lakshmana had arrived. There was surprise,
Combined with fear: how can there be friendship
Without knowing their intentions? 170
Was that a secret trick to increase enmity?
Janaka was caught in a pool of anxiety, bewildered.

He had felt sorrow for Ahalya's misery;
He had been infuriated by Indra's foul behaviour.
The consciousness of guilt was burning Seeradhwaja.
Giving deliverance to Ahalya, Rama had
Cooled her with the water of Sarayu. So Janaka
Wanted to see Rama, the eagerness
Had sprouted clearly in his mind.

Seeradhwaja went to the place 180
Where Vishwamitra was staying and spoke,
Feeling blessed at his sight: 'I am fulfilled, O teacher!
You have redeemed Ahalya by bringing in the brothers.
You broke the fort of discord between Ayodhya and Mithila.
Shatananda praised you for the good that you did.
You have hoisted the flag of unity in Aryavarta.

To Ahalya, who was lying like a stone,
You gave a new life.'

Memories of childhood
Came back to Shatananda unrolling like a scroll.   190
Then Gautama had embraced Shata and wept,
Cursing Indra relentlessly. The father had wilted in pain.
In study and search he pushed back
The pain, each moment was like an aeon.
Now, there was a lot of comfort in his mind.

Seeradhwaja saw
Matchless radiance, glowing in the faces of
The brothers, sturdy, strong, with strict practice.
The noble personages had learnt to use weapons.
Dark-bodied, attractive with wide eyes,   200
Broad foreheads, shapely noses and lips,
Smiling all the while, cheeks flaunting determination,
They were the complete embodiment of masculine power.
Seeradhwaja was thrilled with the feeling of fulfilment!

'Great teacher, you must come to the palace
In the morning. These princes, celibates, must show
Enough kindness, to let us see them,' Seeradhwaja said.
'We shall come, king, we shall;
These young men have come with great hopes.
Shri Rama will see the bow of Shiva and try his prowess.'   210
The sage spoke thus; Shatanada and Seeradhwaja
Were overjoyed.

While Sunayana and Seeradhwaja
Were looking for Aryan sons for Sita's wedding,
In everyone suspicion and discordant notes arose;
Discussions went on the story of Sita's birth.
Some people, handsome but without virtue,
And some libertines were not entertained; and they,
Exploding in anger, plotted an attack, all together.

Such cries as 'Get Sita married,' echoed everywhere. 220
Seeradhwaja and others, who were not to be scared
Of being imprisoned by force, did not sacrifice
Janaki's future under the pretext of saving the kingdom
But stood up to the challenge, bravely!

The philosopher-king Janaka believed in non-violence.
Hence, when the challenge to war was given,
The state, being neutral, possessed a very small force.
While the soldiers of enemy kings surrounded like floods,
There was no way out except tenacity and strength.
They fought determined, and drove away the wicked kings. 230

The worry about Sita's wedding bothered him.
Sita was restless watching the anguish of her father.
Caught in the eddy of lineage he struggled;
Eventually, he spoke thus;
'There is no fear in me, I do not care
About superior or inferior caste. Are the kings
Born in Aryan lineage upright men? They are fallen rakes.
Falling into the well of sin, they suffer relentlessly.
What will stop me? I shall give her away
Even if they are not Aryan. Mithila kingdom 240
Has abolished caste-creed differences.
This is not a state of slavery. It is the home of freedom for all.
To mould one into a real and true man is the aim
Of *dharma*. Never has it meant harm to others.
Why be afraid, then? Why anxiety?

'They may clap and mock;
They may pierce you with sharp arrows of infamy;
We will bear pain and difficulties for the sake of Sita.

The fort of non-violence had cracked; there was human sacrifice.
Blood flowed freely; enough of violence. War 250
Is not needed anymore. Mother earth has suffered enough.
Should land, water and women be sacrificed

For status and wealth? Enough of it; Mithila
Does not want the commotion of war.
This is not the battleground for Aryan status.
That is why I have put at stake Shiva's bow for a test;
The victorious man shall receive Sita from me!
My daughter has agreed to this so that this war
Could be stopped, once and for all.'

Canto Twenty-five

'Rama and Sita become an Incomparable Pair'

||௬||

'Think, my daughter; later, in your journey of life,
Do not have let there be no regrets. I have proclaimed that you
   are the reward
For the winner in the test of strength and character.
That will bring in straits; be prepared to face them.
Do not be sad if the choice of your beloved is not done in haste.
If he can win over the bow of Shiva, he will win you over too.
Age, character, looks, lineage,
All these are worth nothing; be careful. If there is
None to triumph over Shiva's bow, will you stay single,
Walking warily on the tightrope of life and be strong?'   10
Janaka asked Sita.

Forgetting food and sleep,
Unmoved by emotion, climbing the peak of seriousness
Sita thought about the future day and night
While the contesting brave men arrived, it felt like
Going to the gallows. 'O, great Shiva! Will your bow
Bend? What if the power of the *rakshasas* bends it!
Should I marry the undeserving, an infamous scamp?

Do not show me the undeserving. Show compassion, O Shiva!
You are an ocean of compassion. Do not give strength
To the shoulders of the *rakshasas*. Let your bow not move.'
Sita appealed thus, in her heart.

She had heard Rama's story,
The holy tale of his victory. The fragrance of his name
Was like the rain-bearing wind, blowing gently.
He removed obstacles from Kaushika's rituals;
He upheld the self-respect of the Nishada and other
Non-Aryan tribes; he gave rebirth to Vanaje and such
Other women; he freed Ahalya from her state of frozen life;
When Sakalashwa turned arrogant, the death penalty was ordered.

Shri Rama is a great figure of radiance;
He is the heroic being, who will put down injustice;
Protector of the downtrodden, the symbol of truth,
Happiness and beauty; seeking a universal way of life,
Carrying on a quest, he pulled down all the walls
That constrict mankind. Hearing all this, Sita was thrilled!

Is Rama ready to wed Sita?
Will the one, not born of a woman, find direction?
Such discussions were everywhere. She had
Not dreamt of sleeping on a soft bed in a palace;
There was a higher purpose in the source of her birth!
Why should she, not born of a woman, take birth
And suffer like common men and women?
Her father being Seeradhwaja, a sage-king,
Would the ship of her life loses direction,
Break up and dash against the shores?
Having seen Shri Rama,
Seeradhwaja said when he came into the palace,
'Rama and Sita will become a unique couple in the world.'
The woman born of earth was content to hear those words.
The next minute, there was turmoil: while lifting the bow
Of Shiva, would he win? Doubts sprang in her mind.
Will the cool radiance in the mind disappear among dark clouds?

Will the tower of hope tumble down like a meteor?
Such was the distress and fevered expectation Sita was in!
The auspicious moment of choosing a bridegroom arrived.
For the exhibition of daring to string Shiva's bow,
The enclosure was all set. Janaka was confident
That Rama would string the bow.

Sita saw Rama and Saumitri 60
Sitting to the left and right of Kaushika in the gathering.
Broad shouldered, Shri Rama was handsome and dignified.
Feeling shy naturally, she was joyous.
In shyness, her lotus-face shone red,
Lips trembled, eager to say something,
She stayed quiet on her own!

'Let the test begin. Let the bow of Shiva
Be brought to the assembly,' said Seeradhwaja, firmly.
The cart with the bow was pulled in by hapless captives;
Pulling and pulling, exhausted, they brought it over! 70
Hearing the proclamation of the test of strength,
A few withdrew, bending their heads. The efforts of the *danavas*
Did not bear fruit. Not knowing what to do,
Defeated and exhausted, they sat quietly!
Breaking the silence, the sage said:
'To the brave one who will lift and string the bow,
Janaki will be given. That is the promise.
Since Kodandarama, the renowned bowman is here,
Could he be given the first opportunity?'
As he said that, Seeradhwaja looked at Vaidehi's face 80
With eagerness. A gentle smile was the sign;
Father and daughter's eyes met, there was consent.
Minutes rolled by in the dilemma of hope and despair;
Thorns pricked the depth of Seeradhwaja's heart;
For a moment he lost courage watching his daughter's anxiety!

While eagerness overflowed, Shri Rama waited
For permission from his mentor. 'Get up child! I shall bless you.

Do not delay. May the great Shiva bless you,' said the Guru.
Walking with firm steps, he moved forward.
His eyes turned towards the daughter of Mithila in joy.   90
Confidence of winning the test radiated in him.

'If the mind wavers, arms become weak.
The only thing I should think of, now, is lifting Shiva's bow.
The unstable mind should be completely focussed;
All strength should get united in the arms.
This bow is a machine, many powers and strategies
Must be hidden here; the special fuel may be concealed;
The machine parts, springs and such should be examined;
The mind should use intelligence and grasp minute things.'
Thinking thus, Shri Rama looked at the bow.   100

The superb structure of the bow
He admired and bowed to it in devotion.
In his mind, he praised the way it was moulded.
'Such expertise has not been seen in Aryanvarta;
This is a wondrous mechanical bow, controlled by precepts.
The bow must be strung. That is definite.'
Thinking thus, he admired the achievement of the craftsman!
Shri Ramachandra, gathering all his powers to his arms,
Gripping the bow with his hands and wanting to string it,   110
Tried hard to pull the instrument toward him.
But it did not move, and stayed secure in its place.
The first attempt appeared fruitless.
But Rama stood firm, without despairing.

Kaushika's words echoed,
Resounding like a bronze bell ringing:
'Control your mind! With your strength,
Use your intelligence. If both combine, success is certain.'
Shri Rama recovered and pressed with his thumb
The mechanical part of the bow. Bodily power had quickly   120
Divided into two parts in an equal manner.

Later the bottom part of the machine, with care,
He pressed down with his thumb, a unique balance
Triumphed. Powers of the body, the mind, science
Technique and skill gathered together,
And victory appeared to be close. All muscles in the body
Became taut, blood rushed to the face making it red.
Saumitri felt anxious.

Feet on one side, hands on the other.
Power pulling him in opposite directions, 130
Rama was subjected to unimaginable pain.
Feeling as if his body had been sliced at the navel,
The frightening picture of breaking apart
Flashed across his mind. Shri Rama struggled!
How could he prevent the tragedy of the epoch?
Saumitri's mind screamed in pain.

The anxiety in Janaki's mind was burning her heart.
Rama was fighting with a mountain of steel.
'Why doesn't the mechanical bow fall down pulverised?
Then I would stand before Rama, and Heaven of living 140
Together will be mine. May this steel fortress
Be broken by the strength of Shri Rama, the best among men,'
She consoled herself. 'Rama, Shri Rama! Are you fighting
A difficult battle for me? Are you bearing intolerable pain?
Let all the powers in the world come to your aid;
Let them strengthen your arms,' she begged.

Shri Rama pressed at once the centre
Of the mechanical bow. A divine strength flowed in the body
As the court watched in amazement, unblinking
A limb of the bow was rising. 150
The sage had said it was the shoulder of the bow
Equivalent to the God of Death for enemies
Like a steel elephant raising its trunk in a grand manner
And sweeping it, the great effort of stringing the bow
Was in action, as if the noble bow reacted.

Going into action, there was a sudden explosion
Of the hidden power that was within the bow,
As if a pot that was closed had exploded.
The great bow broke into pieces, never to be strung again,
Breaking down the *rakshasas* out of action.   160
All the people were delighted by that wonderful feat.

The wealth of the whole world in the form of the earth-born
Was given to the farmer, Janaka; in his search for wealth,
He had found Mahalakshmi, the Goddess of Wealth herself.
Today, she had accepted Rama.
The bow of Shiva was the symbol of mind-control;
Would Mahalakshmi accept anything else but the radiance of virtue?
Would she accept the *rakshasas* who came to loot, the ignorant,
The capricious of mind, the lustful, and such others?
From all of them, the treasure of gem-like Sita was protected   170
Until then by the bow of Shiva, a divine serpent.
The pride of the Raghu-clan was now its master.
Sita was not born of woman, undeserving –
With such excuses, like proverbial sour grapes,
All other princes were envious and frustrated;
With heads bent, they left the courtyard in silence.
Sita looked at the lotus-face of Rama, for long.
The steel mountain had crumbled at Rama's might;
Unparalleled, unique, and incomparable power it was.

In great joy, Seeradhwaja and Shatananda stood still   180
Like ministers, courtiers and all sages.
The people wanting to see the unique sight,
Had longed for it for many years. Not seeing it,
They were in the moss of disappointment. But that day
Truth was victorious and every one enjoyed
Complete bliss. The only bridegroom for Sita
Was Shri Rama, they said, and danced with joy.
Seeradhwaja, in a flush of affection,
Forgot himself, rushed to Rama and hugged him.

Janaka saw the depth of Rama's valour;   190
His greatness. The pledge was fulfilled.
'Let the ministers travel fast in chariots,
Go to Ayodhya and tell Dasharatha
The good news; we need permission for the wedding.
Let the invitation be given,' he said.
'Salutations to King Dasharatha.
I have decided to get my daughter Vaidehi married.
She has been won through valour. "If the bow of
Shiva was lifted and strung, she would be given to him" –
This was my proclamation. Everyone lost; but   200
Shri Rama has broken it and won Sita.
Permission is needed for the grand wedding of the epoch;
With friends and relatives, sages and priests,
Please come to Mithila.' Carrying a letter
With such content, ministers entered Ayodhya.

Canto Twenty-six

'Wouldn't the mind be sorrowful?'

||६||

Shri Rama and Saumitri left with Kaushika, the sage.
The ten days that passed after their leaving Ayodhya
Were like ten epochs for Dasharatha. Janaka's ministers
Arrived at the court and told the tale of victory.
Dasharatha was immensely happy. Respect grew
For Vishwamitra. The king had seen him
Narrow-minded and limited, without realising
What was within. Caught in the love of sons,
He was not aware of the strength of Rama and Saumitri.
Getting to know of their wondrous deeds   10
He was thrilled. Breaking the great fortress
Of enmity and misunderstanding between the two empires,
Singing a prelude for universal welfare, a new epoch
And eternal peace, the architect of the grand wedding,
Kaushika's many forms were remembered with gratitude.
The wedding party left joyously with relatives and town's people
Dasharatha was not aware of the road being traversed
They reached Janaka's city with a mind pure as jasmine.
With affection, King Janaka welcomed them.   20
Seeing Shri Rama and Saumiti there
Dasharatha's joy knew no bounds.

'Dasharatha, excellent in the Raghu-clan, a hearty welcome.
With the touch of your feet, Mithila is sanctified.
We are kinsmen now, let us live in friendliness.
No more anger in the face, no more distrust.
Shri Rama has won Sita as he did the bow of Shiva.
Under the auspices of the coming Uttara Phalguni star,
The wedding of Shri Rama has been fixed
By Shatananda and other priests. I request   30
You to agree to it,' said Janaka with courtesy.
Words failed Dasharatha.
Silence with a gentle smile was the answer,
The excitement of the town's people overflowed;
Each and every road was decorated.
Fresh green leaves, festoons, flags and banners,
The fragrance of perfume, designs on the floor,
Flower garlands, streamers, dance and music,
The thundering of instruments, divine songs radiated,
There was a shower of petals, the women dressed for the occasion,   40
Moving around joyously.

In the space where the rituals would take place,
They made a beautiful platform for *homa*;
Kept golden sacred vessels and decorated them
With sprouts, and arranged conches, even number of pots
Filled with water, spreading dry grass with chants,
The priests gave a habitation to the Fire-god.
They kept incense pots with holes here and there.
Coloured rice, puffed rice and other auspicious materials
Were kept ready, and so were large plates   50
Filled with fruits and flowers.

Gathered there were
Priests, sages, ministers and statesmen,
Subordinate kings, commanders, Brahmins as well as
Relatives, kinsmen, the retinue, and town's people.
The poor and the rich, the lowly and the upper class alike;

Everyone gathered, *'Sumuhurte Savadhana'*
(In the auspicious moment, with all care)
Chants resounding, the wedding took place,
Following all rituals in order! 60

Adorned and bejewelled, Sita
Was brought before Shri Rama.
'This is Sita, respectable as a goddess. A faithful wife,
She will follow you forever like a shadow;
An understanding wife, speaks well,
She is your wife. Let the marriage be performed.
May you fare well. May there be joy for you,'
Said Seeradhwaja, placing Sita's hands
In Shri Rama's hands, and pouring holy water on them.
The auspicious moment of the wedding was celebrated with joy. 70
'Victory to Sita and Rama,' was the proclamation,
Made by those had gathered in the *pandal*.
Many musicians played auspicious instruments;
Flowers were showered on the bride and the bridegroom!
The celebration of the wedding continued,
As Janaka, bringing Saumitri in joy,
Gave him the hand of his elder daughter Urmila.
Bharata was married to Mandavi, the daughter
Of Janaka's brother; and Shrutakeerti became
The wife of Shatrughna. 80
Once the rituals were over,
The princes along with their wives went around the fire.
The sound of *nagaswara, mridanga* and drums reached the sky.
The grandeur of dance and music was unbounded.
There was a grand meal to satisfy all;
Everyone blessed the newly-weds.
The very next day, Vishwamitra
Spoke to Shri Rama and Saumitri:
'My quest is over. I have fulfilled my ambitions.
Now, I shall go to the Himalayas, meditate deeply, 90
And I shall reach the empire of salvation.

You have become the pioneers in Treta age,
I have given you the initiation. I cannot stay back
Even for a moment. The vision of my life in this epoch
Has come alive.'

Hearing what the sage said, Shri Rama and Saumitri
Seemed thunderstruck. It was as if a streak of lightning
Had flashed across the chest, 'Do not go, O Guru!
Do not make us orphans. Our paths of victorious journeys
In future will be in darkness! You should show the light.   100
Illusion will envelop us, Do not go, O Guru!
In mid water, in the middle of a terrifying sea,
Do not put out the light in the divine tower of the future.'
In humility, they fell at his feet and pleaded.

In anticipation of the divine vision,
Vishwamitra spoke with a peaceful expression.
'The past is over. The future is not in our hands.
Without being overcome by the troubles of the past and future
Being happy is the right path for the soul.
I have had enough of the path of conflict.   110
The path of love which unifies human beings
Is what I want; welding everyone in love,
A peaceful revolution, a universal life is what I want.
"The principles of a preceptor must be one with that of a ruler"
That is the *Ramarajya* everyone desires!
If built with caution,
The Bharata of dreams will become a beautiful garden,
It will become the cradle of universal human civilisation
In the East, there is the striped shirt to wear,
Something else in the West. The time is near   120
For the meeting of the East and West. Egotism,
Hauteur, obstinacy and bad decisions should be set aside.
The West must be joined in the way the bride and groom
Get together, and both should live with love and amity.
The movement of a man, with his feet in his hands, is pure;

The sight of a man, with his hands in his eyes, is clear;
The heart of a man, with his eyes in his mind, is pure.
The one who turns all those emotions to detachment
Will become a free seer. There is no doubt
That you will travel towards a new epoch like that.' 130

'You are the one who fashioned our character and culture;
We are small streams and you are the great river of life.
You are the ocean to which great rivers flow and join.
In a Great Journey, you became the great light.
You are like the sun, the source of energy for life;
Do not go. How can we live without you,'
Said Saumitri without pausing anywhere.

Kaushika addressed them with finality:
'While the discontent of being a Kshatriya
Enveloped me like smoke, I clasped Brahminism, 140
And achieved the status of *Brahmarshi*. Able to speak
But unable to act, caught in such helplessness,
The Brahmins had become weak in my hermitage.
In protecting their rituals you acted for universal welfare.
By protecting them, when I was troubled by earthly matters,
The heightening of your radiance brought me
Self-realisation; the turmoil in the mind had stopped.
'On the body boiling in hate and envy,
You sprinkled love. Throwing away the cup of poison,
You filled it with divine nectar. I was ignorant 150
But very arrogant, and believed that I would tell you
The secrets of the world. You were wise and all-knowing.
You have become perfect, I believe firmly.
In the fetters of attachment freedom evaporates.
When the journey of my life has come to a stop,
When the duties and action in this epoch have been completed,
I am leaving to reach my goal, do not stop me now;
I cannot stay, neither can I accompany you!

'Like the tip of a flame and the flash of lightning,
Like a bright diamond and a coral creeper, 160

Like millions of moons and suns shining,
In stages of knowledge and wisdom, let the light
Of your fame shine. The peace that resides within nature,
Let it stay in your heart wholly,
Forever and ever.

'Unless a peaceful world is established,
There is no hope for mankind. This is the truth.
As long as you two are together, there is hope for the world.
Upholding truth and justice, protecting morals
Of the epoch, you are the representatives of the great God of Time. 170
Why are you stopping me? My being here is meaningless,'
Said the sage, in a determined voice.

Shri Rama and Saumitri
Were moved deeply listening to the divine words of the sage!
No words came forth; bidding farewell to the sage
Was inevitable. As everyone looked on
With great devotion at the lotus feet,
Washing them with tears,
Shri Rama and Lakshmana offered mind and body
Worshipping the sage's feet   180
Stretching out their arms in a flood of emotion
As if concealing in the lotus of the heart
An ocean of love breaking limits, in total absorption
The rising waves drowning the rock of the vow
Of asceticism, roaring wildly
The tiger of a sage controlling himself, groping
Looking at the lampstand of pledge, woke up,
Stroked the hair on the foreheads of Rama and Saumitri.
Like a mother in pain at the separation
Of children, unable to bear the parting,   190
Kaushika walked on savouring fulfillment,
To the peak of the Himalayas.

Canto Twenty-seven

'Retract the Red Tongue of Violence'

||๖||

A farewell for Dasharatha was arranged in éclat.
With Sita Devi there were Urmila, Mandavi and
Shrutakeerti. With Shri Ramachandra there were
His dear brothers Saumitri, Bharata and Shatrughna.
There was pain for the parents when daughters got ready to leave
Janaka Seeradhwaja, Sunayana and everyone else,
From everyone's eyes tears flowed.

While the wedding procession
Moved fast, many strange things happened on the way.
Birds screamed all around in fear;   10
That disharmony planted fear in the king's retinue.
Animals running helter skelter appeared as if encircling
The people; a whirlwind blew, shaking the earth
Great trees were uprooted and fell to the ground;
Dust rose, the four directions were enveloped in darkness.
There was turmoil as if there had been an attack nearby.
In a horrible, deafening, rough noise,
Horses and chariots trampled on the people,
Creating an echo like rushing with the speed of war.
Bringing out the bow and arrow, Saumitri got ready   20
For the danger to come!

Unable to bear the anxiety
That was terrifying, Dasharatha asked Sage Vasishtha:
'Why these bad omens? What pain awaits us?
Please protect us.' 'Do not worry, O king.
There maybe bad omens; still, the animals are going
Round in the right direction. That is auspicious
For your family and everyone. It indicates
That all will be well,' said Vasishtha consoling him.

Furious and terrifying 30
He appeared then, shining in radiance, matted hair,
The fierceness of Rudra on the face, the axe shining
On his shoulder, the radiant Vaishnava bow in hand,
Everyone wondered wide-eyed, who was it?
Parashurama, the destroyer of the Kshatriya clan,
The sage himself had appeared before them!

Like Shiva, the destroyer of the three demon-cities,
Bhargavarama had a fierce bow. Like million suns,
He lights up the sky and the earth. Dasharatha
Was pricked by anxiety and perils, not knowing 40
What was afoot, a thousand doubts troubled him.
Sage Vasishtha said, 'Do not be scared, O king;
Kartaviryajurna, a Kshatriya king, was arrogant
And killed Parashurama's father. Furious, Bhargava,
Desiring to wipe out the whole Kshatriya clan,
Moving like a whirlwind in all four directions
Of Bharatavarsha, has killed all the arrogant.
There is no more killing; the chapter of violence is over.
With sweet words, let us welcome him. Let us show hospitality;
Let us do all we can to please him.' 50
He gave courage to Dasharatha.

'O, noble Bhrigu, Why are you so angry!
In the anger at the killing of your father,
You destroyed the Kshatriyas twenty-one times.
Are you not at peace now? You are a sage.

Give us protection now! Leave all weapons.
Do not forget your vow of giving up all weapons;
Hatred and weapons do not befit you.
You put down the Kshatriyas and gave the earth
To Kashyapa, relinquishing love for the world.   60
Intending to meditate, you are on your way
To the Mount Mahendra. Please stay calm.
Do not invite Rama for a duel. If Rama dies,
We cannot live on. This is the truth,'
Begged Dasharatha in all humility.

Bhargavarama spoke in anger;
'Are you pretending now as if you know nothing, Rama?
Why did you break Shiva's bow?
Shaiva and Vaishnava were the great bows
Acquired in the land of the divine. They are beyond   70
Holding, matching and negotiation. Vishwakarma made them
With great effort. In the battle with Tripurasura,
He had given the bow of Shiva to Trayambaka.
You have broken it now, and thus you have insulted
Shiva, the God of all gods. Here is the Vaishnava bow.
Vishnu gave this to Ruchika of the Bhrigu clan.
That great sage gave it to my father, Jamadagni,
For safekeeping. String this bow and get ready for a duel.'
Listening to those words, Dasharatha felt helpless;
Realising the seriousness of the situation, he was anxious.   80

At that time Saumitri,
Unable to tolerate Bhargava's roar, insolence,
And his father's anxiety, and the fear in the wedding party,
Holding his bow and determined to break the arrogance,
Rushed forward. 'I am Ramachandra's brother,
Saumitri. Enough of your senseless daring;
Why swim against the current? You have challenged us
To pick up the Vaishnava bow. My father has agreed,
Rama will do it. Then I am there to break your arrogance.'

He roared but Rama held him by the shoulder. 90
'No, Lakshmana. Say nothing. Let go of your anger,'
He pacified Lakshmana.

Bhargava was angered at Lakshmana's behaviour.
'Do you not know that hearing Bhargava's roar,
The wombs of Kshatriya-mothers were split?
Do you not know my pledge to destroy the Kshatriya clan?
Do you not know that there is none in the Kshatriya clan,
On this earth, who is not scared of me?'
With lightening speed Rama stopped Parashurama,
Held his shoulders and with voice filled with love 100
Said, with courtesy:

'Why are you angry, O Guru, I am there to serve you;
Who does not know your greatness?
The evil Kshatriya, Kartavirya, who was against people,
Has been destroyed by you. Lawless, arrogant Kshatriyas
Have been dessimated and you have opened up a new path
For righteous war; you are a revolutionary hero.
We lower our heads before you.
Bloodshed was needed then. Now, what is needed is
Non-violence for a total victory of righteousness. 110
It is enough. Retract the red tongue of violence.

'Having killed Kartavirya,
Going round the earth twenty-one times,
Killing the Kshatriyas, giving away the whole world
To Kashyapa, you have given up all obligations.
Going to the ocean and with the help of *Agneyastra,*
The mystic weapon of fire, creating a new world
From the bottom of the ocean, you have achieved all this.
Why do you need the new bondage of this earthy life?
Why do you imprison yourself in the fort of earthly 120
Passions like hatred and jealousy?'

Pacified, Bhargavarama, responded:
'Shri Rama, you are the embodiment of politeness.

Look at Saumitri, what impertinence,
What brashness, how childish!
Does one attack elders with such passion?
To lighten earth's burden of sin, I carried
Out destruction of the Kshatriyas. The evil was destroyed.
The burden on the earth was lessened. My work,
Carefully protecting the morality of the epoch, 130
Would anybody look down upon it?'

So saying, Bhargava lowered the terrifying axe.
'I agree, O Guru. Lakshmana should have shown
Respect and affection towards you. If you do not speak with love
How will the young ones of the new epoch grow fond of you?
They want respect, they ask for blessings.
Observing the sensitive feelings of a new epoch,
One should act. Otherwise the *rakshasas*
Will obstruct with boulders and halt the journey
Along the righteous path. We have freed Siddhashrama,
Released Ahalya from her bondage, 140
To women like Vanaje who had been raped,
We have given back respect in society.
We solved the moral conflict within Seeradhwaja.
Did you congratulate us on what we did?'

Shri Ramachandra's sensitivity,
His discernment were like a flash of lightning
In the mind of Parashurama and he regretted his brashness.
'You spoke the truth Rama, my ability to see the unseen
Is worn out. Revolution is a process of continuous action;
I could not recognise it. Without accepting what is new, 150
I sat, vain in the grandeur of the past, a fossil.
One should change with the times. It is inevitable.'

Rama felt pain within.
'Forgive me, O Guru, I may have spoken harshly.
Tell us right now if our actions were wrong.
Was it wrong to be born in the Kshatriya clan?

Wrong to have broken the bow of Shiva?
If it was not done, the bow would have been in the hands
Of the *rakshasas*! Where did I go wrong?
Please tell me without hesitation. We have surrendered 160
To the power of your asceticism!' he said fervently.

Parashurama's mettle was weakened.
'Unaware of propriety, my mind in a turmoil,
As you said, my mind is inert and solidified;
I admired Shiva's bow, and you broke it.
My self-esteem was provoked. While in arrogance,
I realised what I really was and my pride vanished.
You did the right thing, Rama. Breaking the bow,
There was the welfare of the world in your mind.
I was obsessed with the past; I must get across the past 170
And become aware of responding to this new epoch.
Otherwise, I shall become useless like the ancient
Bow of Shiva. To put down injustice and to adapt
To the new epoch, you are the right one;
You can bring about revolution and usher in a new epoch.

'My dull mind is anxious to test.
You broke Shiva's bow. If you can string this Vaishnava bow,
My mind will be at peace,' said Bhargavarama.
Shri Rama pressed the bow on the ground;
Holding down what was on the ground and pulling 180
The top part towards himself, he begged:
'I shall do it, O Guru; give me permission.'
That bow appeared to be another variation of Shiva's bow.

But, before Shri Rama could finish his task,
Bhargava said quickly: 'Enough, Shri Rama!
I have no more doubts about your prowess.
Realisation of my life's search is complete now.
I shall give this Vaishnava bow to you,'
He said in a peaceful frame of mind.

'The desire in this epoch is fulfilled; 190
My anxiety about who would punish the wicked
Is over. While you are there to punish the wicked,
The righteous shall lead lives without fear.
I shall offer the fruits of my righteousness to you,
And walk towards the manifestation of truth!'

Rama's incarnation was the manifestation
Of divine state for Bhargava's eyes:
'O Rama with the famous bow! You will protect Aryanvarta,
And, I am reassured it will attain prosperity as *Ramarajya*,
The Ideal State.' With this wondrous thought, he left. 200
The sky was at peace, the ocean was at peace,
The divine form grown beyond the sky
Merged into the edge of the horizon!
The wedding procession moved on with sighs of relief,
Towards Ayodhya.

Canto Twenty-eight

'From the Atom to the Expanse of the Nebula'

||๑||

Shri Rama, always well-spoken and righteous,
Ahead of Brihaspati in knowledge and flow of speech,
Understanding the essence of righteousness, the values of life,
Is invincible, like mother earth in patience,
Indra in valour, in military array equal to Shanmukha.
In music, poetry, drama and fine arts,
He is highly skilled in all.
In the company of good people, he tastes honey
He showers love on all living creatures
In appearance, in character, in behaviour, he is pure. 10
He is a kind man responding to the pain of citizens
He is the moon that makes the joy of people overflow
He receives the love of all, generously and without envy,
Speaks well, though austere in speech, thinks of good things;
He is intelligent, looks ahead and is a scholar;
Well-versed in the Vedas, firm in mind, a brave warrior,
Skilled in the use of arms, he is one who expresses his emotions
In a fresh manner. An artist who stirs up emotions, a natural poet.
Janaki spreads like a creeper of nectar around the sculpture

Of Shri Rama, showering the coolness of sandalwood. 20
Relatives, town's people and everyone else
Admire and sing the praises of Rama and Sita.
That is not a union of bodies but of minds.
He is the beloved of the woman and she the beloved of the man;
They float on the waves of pure joy,
A life of milk and honey.
No trace of suspicion, no mist of the unclear;
A unique manifestation of light in their life
Music resounds from a divine source.
The fragrance of spring flows like a river. 30
Which poet can describe the beauty of Janaka's daughter?
The whiteness of her shining teeth, the sweetness of her glance,
The pearls she wears, the sandalwood paste smeared on
The folds of silk add to the whiteness.
Breeze from the mountains, of sandalwood and mangoes
Of *champak* and jasmine, soaked in nectar
Churning the sea of beauty from three worlds
Smeared over by the whiteness of the moonstone,
She is like a doll crafted with delicacy.
In the stream of nectar from flowers, bees buzz 40
Floating smoothly on the boats of lotus leaves.
Water-fowl and the krauncha birds bathe in honey;
Once clothed in white, once in red
Delicate as the lotus once, like a golden creeper,
Vaidehi is radiant with joy.
Urmila stands in greatness in the palace.
Her eyes overcoming the loveliness of the lotus,
The beauty of the union of souls, of the mind;
Loving admiration, friendship, compassion
As well as patience mixed like an ocean. 50
The amorous playfulness of Saumitri and Urmila
Starting form grassroots to the height of the Himalayas,
From the atom to the expanse of the Nebula,
It has spread and grown.

The mind longs and cries out for the touch of beauty
Thirsty for sentiment, it desires the spirit.
It waits for the door of the mind to open.
The spirit of the skylark moves within
Urmila's spirit in quietness and meditation
Dances, enthralled by the sight of Lakshmana.   60
Eyes await the sight of Lakshmana;
Ears long for the words he speaks;
Within and without, Urmila is filled with Lakshmana,
Like the Pole-star of unwavering light!
The movement of trees stops, the buzzing of bees ceases,
So do the voices of birds and the ambling of animals.
When total quietness filled space all around,
Drowned in still, profound sleep, was Lakshmana,
Like the mythical primeval serpent raising his hood
From the nether world to the skies!   70

In the life of Saumitri and Urmila,
There is love, joy and tenderness.
The wave of love caste them on the shore with force.
The wind of passion whistles past.
When a young cobra crawls in the gentle sun, it is a lovely sight.
'We shall go to the stream of beauty and bathe
In the enjoyment, we shall forget the earth;
When the joy turns into rain and pours on the way,
We shall all drench in it as wayfarers, beloved!'
Said Lakshmana; gripped by poetic spirit,   80
He speaks to his beloved.
The handsome Saumitri floats
In the amorous lake. The principle of beauty
Being the main goal, welding the world
Encircled by the fort of romantic dalliance,
Lakshmana is lost in the state of divine bliss.
He is held in grand imagination
In the great search for self-realisation:
'The light within is the light of lights,

The source of all brightness, the very essence of worship, 90
A bunch of radiance, the light of the great luminosity.
The sun sparkles there, the moon shines there,
The starts twinkles there, the lightning flashes there,
The fire is radiant there, that is the great truth.
That is the truth, there is nectar, that is what is heard.
Plants and creepers are there, so are flowers and fruits;
Flowing streams are there, incomparable in
Time or place, the divine radiance is there.
That is where creation meets, a treasure of complete joy.
Embracing the world, holding up the umbrella of righteousness, 100
Adishesha radiant with his thousand hoods!
He was there, so was Urmila,
Love breaking all boundaries, everything was just there!'

Waking up her husband in deep meditation,
Urmila said: 'What is this divine feeling!
Are you drowned in the honeyed vision of love's treasure?
Lost in the touch of love's chant? In the sweetness
Of your nearness, I woke up. Wakefulness, dream,
And deep sleep – in all the three states,
What course is followed? Explain to me, O virtuous man!' 110
'Crossing the three states,
Becoming one with god is the true meaning
Of life, say the sages. In the stream of love
Everything is beautiful, good woman!
Your beautiful form and radiance have thrilled me;
You are the idol that my heart will be devoted to in constancy.
I am a devotee of love, give me the love I beg for.
In the fragrance of flowers on the banks of river Chandrika
A queen bee, a human form enticing the three worlds.
Standing in beauty, ruling the golden land 120
Of my heart. Bathed in beauty, full of joyous
Sentiment, in the freedom of diversion is wisdom.
In the wave of playfulness and beauty,
Floating and sinking, sinking and floating I shall

Acquire the experience of true sentiment.
To the lotus of your heart, I shall offer
The food of love. Accept it with joy, noble woman!'
In love, Saumitri became a poet!
Like a poetess, Urmila said:
'Praising a weak woman, you raise her desire   130
Using an arrow of flowers, you make me lose myself.
I carry on my head your order of love,
Be it a bouquet of flowers or a crown of thorns,
I shall wear it. I shall offer everything at your feet.
We are maidens, we are like creepers,
Desiring support. We desire a beloved who knows
The joys and sorrows of the mind within;
One who will make the weight of life, flower-light.
When love is god, we shall discover victory in defeat.'
'I shall walk with care, protect dreams.   140
You are not weak. You are solemn and very strong
If you harbour anger, the whole world will burn.
At the movement of your eyebrows, my mind melts;
In the cool rain-brining wind of your loving glance
I shall find the joy of Heaven,' he said.
The words spoken in love brought happiness to both.
Meanwhile, one day Urmila
Got ready with love a gem-studded, golden pedestal
Offering a pedestal in the heart itself.
Quickly she made him sit there and gave him   150
A unique picture. The wonder, the style and colours,
The expression of feelings, struck him dumb.
Whatever was in the picture was indeed a marvel.
The palace court was decorated,
The diamond throne shone in the middle,
The white umbrella sparkled at the top.
A silken bunch hung from above in majesty,
A cluster of pearls and rubies shone swinging;
It was decorative like pearls on the parting of hair.

There was radiance as if diamonds and opals were strewn around.   160
The flag of the sun, the ancestor, flew above.
In the sky was spread the colour of happiness;
The earth was gladdened by showers of flowers.
Boys danced with joy to the music of instruments,
Drums resounded with the sound of victory.
The guards at the gate were a joy to behold;
In royal seats, lotuses bloomed
The foot-stool covered in tiger-skin was readied,
Shri Rama and Sita sat on the throne.
Vasishtha and other sages, priests and holy men   170
Accompanied by Dasharatha, conducted the coronation
Ceremony with great joy and thrill. Sita seemed to be bowed
Down with the weight of having to protect the world.
Grandeur shining in the picture,
Purity of imagination, the variety of colours
Made Saumitri smile in wonderment.
The grandeur portrayed in the picture
Made him long to see Shri Ramachandra's ascension to the throne.
He was lost in the divine imagination!
Urmila knew what was in Lakshmana's mind;   180
Divine devotion and loyalty were the pledge
They had taken. The path of Lakshmana's Great Quest
Was known to Urmila; that was why she became
The secret stream, the source of Lakshmana's prowess.

Canto Twenty-nine

'Joy and Sorrow Are the Heart of a Spinning Wheel'

||௬||

While with wives, sons and daughters-in-law,
Dasharatha ruled his kingdom happily,
According to the adage, *'Kalaya tasmai namaha'*
(All have to bow to Time),
Time brought in changes.
Omens appeared indicating future troubles.
In the sky, a falling-star was seen,
That was a symbol of calamity and pain;
The web of clouds spread, the earth shook and darkness fell.
Animals and birds screamed out of tune.
Good deeds and bad, outcome of all deeds   10
Dasharatha remembered and lamented,
'I have become the heart of a spinning wheel,
Of joy and sorrow.'

His mind was inclined towards detachment;
He began to wonder about the use of money, gold,
And vehicles; they would not accompany one in death,
Only the good deeds and the bad would.
Desiring salvation, he called his ministers, Vasishtha, and other sages
To confer with.

When the court was full, 20
He expressed the anxiety and worry in his heart:
'I have ruled the land for a long time righteously;
My mind is disturbed, the heart is agitated.
Age has come upon me. I need to leave all.
Like a true creeper, Shri Rama is to me
I shall give him the responsibility of ruling.
Birth and death are illusions; I shall break free.
I shall join the sages who have moved away from the mundane.
I shall search for the inner principles of life
To undertake this pledge and to crown Rama, 30
Please allow me to do so,' he asked and everyone
Admired his plan and without objecting,
They approved of it. 'This is excellent. Is he not
A great proponent of democracy?'
They praised him with all their heart.
Without delay, the king
Called Rama and told him. 'Son, carry the weight;
My father Aja made me a king
And left to conquer the kingdom of asceticism. You
Are radiant, you are the moon. Fulfill 40
My mind's desire to acquire the wealth of meditation;
None in Ikshawaku clan has disobeyed the father.'
Rama was disturbed when he heard it.
Shri Rama spoke with equanimity
'What is the hurry, father? Did you have to call
An emergency meeting to decide the future
Of the kingdom? Why all the secrecy?
Bharata and Shatrughna are not here;
They have gone to Kaykaya kingdom. Shouldn't Janaka
And Kaikeya be invited to this celebration? 50
Do not belittle the troubles to come.
Call mothers, friends and relatives to think it over!
Is not the council of our kingdom expensive!
It is not right to neglect the people's opinions.

They will scorn us saying we are despotic and selfish.
Should one imprison the stream of a clan within a pot?
Holding a handful of water from the ocean,
Can one flaunt and delude himself saying it is the ocean?
Follow the path of righteousness. If the state has to get strong
It is inevitable. Righteous conscience, ritual, practice,   60
Tradition, advice of a teacher – all these
Must suit the decision. I know your wish:
"My very dear Rama must ascend the throne."
That is your decision. Do not get caught in the web
Of attachment; do not neglect the greater morality
Of the State, father!'

Even after hearing Shri Ramachandra's noble words,
Dasharatha appeared as if he had not heard him, and said:
'Do not worry, son! All the people have granted permission.
The council of people is a representative body,   70
I have given it freedom and paramount power.
It will suggest an alternative, if any, and benevolent plans
Within the confines of righteousness.
The seal of agreement from the people, democracy,
The citizens of Ayodhya are everything to me.
The great values of political righteousness
Are held aloft. Why are you worried son?
All citizens want you and your duties are here.
I fear I am at the end of my life;
The demon of fear bothers me. Give me release!   80
This Chaitra season is holy, the right time for coronation.'
In the awareness of duties of kingship
In the respectful attitude of obedience to a father's orders
In the manner of one who carries the weight of a debt
In the manner of who has renounced power and desire,
Rama was quiet and that became acceptance.
Sumantra and other ministers were happy
Thinking of Shri Rama's face, as beautiful as a lotus.
Shouts of 'Victory for Rama' were already resounding.

While preparation went on for coronation, 90
Dasharatha called Shri Rama in privacy.
'Be careful tonight; a great abyss of thorns, stones,
Poisonous creatures and impediments surrounds
Any great happening. Let all the gods and well-wishers
Protect you. Surrounding the throne of power,
There appears a conflict from within.
If there is a conflict between right and wrong
The victory of truth over falsehood is certain;
There will be illumination of values.
The real characters of all, the inner 100
Essence will be sought.
Between temptation and restraint, greatness and discernment
There will be commotion of war.
A search will go on for what can control incitement
Leaving Punarvasu behind, the moon
Will come to the star Pushya tomorrow. You will ascend
The throne of the Raghu-clan, the throne in the hearts of people.
Fasting at night, sleeping on a bed of straw;
Sita should also follow the rituals with you.
Like the ministers, informers are also 110
Examining. The wealth of people's love is with you.
Ayodhyalakshmi will be sanctified by you, son!

'You must win over organs of sense. Desire and anger
Should be driven out; Do not get caught in
The whirlpool of women, gambling, hunting animals and drinking,
You should find your own joy in the happiness of people.
When you control your mind, you can control the world;
When you rule over your mind, you can rule over the world.
If realised, this is for life as well as ruling,
A divine principle. 120
'Bad dreams and bad omens are seen
Planets are cruel to me, Kuja and Rahu trouble me.
Astrologers have told me of the effects of the bad omens
I do not know what troubles may befall!

Who will protect if death will swallow?
I shall watch you being crowned king.
Then I shall die, son! May all good things happen to you!'
Shri Rama took in the nectar of his father's advice.
He left in silence after bowing to him.

As the festivities were about to start, 130
The king said that the whole city should have a festive look.
Workers came, dug the earth and levelled it,
Cleaned up the yard and walls.
Sculptors arrived, carved idols and
Placed them at the main entrance;
Painters came and filled them with colour.
The frame of the pandal was made beautiful
Festoons and tassels made it radiant.
Inviting kings from eight directions,
Tabors, drums and percussive instruments were beaten. 140
Many a king arrived in haste and joy.
Elephants, horses and palanquins arrived,
Instruments of all kinds played.
A play on tunes was spread by the orchestra;
The granary and hall of weapons expanded.
Material for worship, gems and golden herbs,
Garlands of flowers, honey, puffed rice,
Sandalwood, betel leaves and nuts were all gathered.
A hundred and eight rows of sacred gold vessels,
Oxen, elephants, a well-equipped army, 150
Banners and flags, umbrellas and fans
Were ready and waited joyfully for the auspicious event.
The hall for fire rituals was prepared.
The fragrance of perfumes reached the highway.
Festoons in each house, festoons in trees;
Temples, squares, shops and palaces, all festooned.
For all castes and the impoverished,
Grand meals were prepared along with
A treasury of coins to be gifted as charity.

At sunrise there were incantations for welfare. 160
Great musicians, merchants, dancers,
Groups for *yakshagana*, puppets, horses dancing,
Groups of costumed people walking and making others laugh,
Everyone had gathered for the king's coronation.
Everything had come alive for the event!
Outside the palace where it was to take place,
Soldiers, with swords tied around the waist,
In the splendour of their uniform, were performing
Exercises of many kinds with great respect.
Carrying the news of crowning, 170
Shri Rama walked to mother Kausalya,
To her chambers. Wearing a silk sari
She was praying for her son's welfare. The news
Brought her joy. In the company of Lakshmana
Arrived Sumitra, the embodiment of sacrifice. Sita was
called for to share the joy.
'I may be the king, but you are the alternate
Treasure of life. You will reign with me,
An embodiment of tolerance.
You are the ruler of the earth, my treasure,' 180
Saying so, Shri Rama embraced Lakshmana.
Everyone's eyes filled with tears of joy.
With sages and ascetics
Vasishtha walked towards Shri Rama's dwelling
For sacred chants. Along the highway
Shouts of joy resounded. The waves of the
Sea of joy echoed. Children were excited.
So were the elderly. Everyone was excited
Waiting for the ceremony. Worshipping the feet of Vasishtha,
Rama received the sacred chants. His abode 190
Was in great happiness like Saraswati's dance hall.
Fair women gave the auspicious bath to Rama.
Shri Rama, the crown of the Raghu-clan, wore golden robes.
Bracelet and waistband were put on him, whose soul was full of delight

Sandalwood and musk were applied on him
Chanting Gayatri *mantra*, Shri Rama
Prayed to Vishnu and bowed deeply.
Sacred chants were recited by Brahmins,
Chanting of Veda spread in all directions.
The courtiers praised him for long.   200
Everyone admired the wealth beyond limits.
Saumitri's love spread wide everywhere.
While everyone bathed in the fountain of Rama's love
The earth was blessed by Rama, the highest of his clan.
Ikshwaku clan achieved fulfilment!

Canto Thirty

'Slander Causes a River of Tears'

||⊙||

In the night, a star fell from the sky.
Kaikeyi's maid Manthara went up.
She looked with concern at the grandeur of the highway,
The dancing of the flags, the excitement of the people.
The streets sparkled with sandalwood water,
Beauty shone hundred-fold with painting.
People sang verses about the coronation,
Instruments of felicity and chanting of Veda
All sounded jarring to Manthara.
Open-mouthed, she gazed in wonder at the sky;   10
Losing patience, she was taken aback and was furious.
It was like jumping from the height of Kailasa,
To the depth of the netherworld.
Grossing the corridor, the short woman
Entered Kaikeyi's quarters like an ill-omen entering a house.
The beautiful Kaikeyi, wearing soft silk,
Like a coral creeper in an ocean of milk,
Lay on a white bed, relaxing.
Feet and hands were like lotuses
An attractive face, eyelids closed   20
Appearing as if she was in contemplation.

The elements of energy in equanimity.
The mind was pure and all evil thoughts
Lying low scared to come near her.
Like a comet, like ugliness personified,
Manthara came in.

Like a flower fallen form the blackness of sky,
Like the wife of a man painting darkness,
Like a pen of fate thrown from the womb of darkness,
Like writing dipped in and written with the ink of blood, 30
Manthara spoke in great agitation:

'Listen, Kaikeyi, you foolish, luckless woman; get up
From worthless sleep. Your prosperity has tumbled down;
Your dreams are shattered and desires are laid bare.'
She said that, tripped and fell on the floor,
Wriggling in despair.
Seeing Manthara screaming so,
Kaikeyi was bewildered, not knowing what caused it:
'It is Shri Rama's coronation and everyone
Is happy. Why are you exhausted? 40
When whole town is joyous and a sense of fulfilment
Is everywhere, why are you so disturbed?'
'Your riches are like a summer stream.
After sucking the nectar, does the bee bother
About the flower? While Shri Rama is being crowned
How can you be without worry?' asked the hunchback woman.
With excitement Kaikeyi stood up and said:
'I am not without worry. Bharata is not here.
That is the only worry. To see the joy today, 50
Two eyes are not enough; you need two more –
My dream has become a reality. Shri Rama
And Bharata all like *chakravaka* birds.
Where is the difference? What better news is there?
Here, this is a gift for you; you are not a hunchback.

You are victorious,' said Kaikeyi and gave
Manthara a gold necklace.

Manthara's anger rose from the sole of her feet to her forehead!
She pulled off the necklace and threw it away in anger and hatred.
'While terrifying troubles surround you, 60
While a string of difficulties are like bees boring into you
Are you sitting feeling ecstatic about your good fortune?
Your husband pretending to be righteous is a cheat,
Saying sweet words, he is a cruel being within.
The tongue is jaggery but the heart is scissors-like,
Sweet words were for you, profit was Kausalya's.
While Bharata has been sent off to your parents,
Should they crown Rama here in secrecy?
Do you call this great love and good fortune?
A great enemy is in the form of your husband 70
Will you keep a snake in your care and sing it a lullaby?
Where is the invitation for Keikaya? What is the hurry?
Is this the right thing to do? Tell me.

'Bharata is in great trouble;
His lineage will be lost, will end.
He will become humble and weak and send to exile.
If you ignore it, the black serpent will kill, take care!
Kausalya will be the king's mother and you,
A maid to Kausalya!'

With a serious face, Kaikeyi thundered: 80
'Dwarf, why are you spewing out your anger
On Rama? Walk away, serpent. Into nectar
Are you mixing venom? Do not splash on me hate-mire.

'Shri Rama is righteous.
To teachers and elders and relations as well
He shows humility. He is grateful, truthful,
Clean in mind, speech and body.
The eldest son of the king, worthy of the throne,

The throne of the king is naturally his.
Why feel envy then? He is good to me; 90
I am very fond of him! As far as love is concerned,
I love him no less than Bharata.'
The dwarfish woman was furious as a tigress.
'Stop your senseless talk, Kaikeyi! In the city of Saketa,
You have become death for Bharata.
In Rama's rule, you will be a menial like me.
In truth, in righteousness, Bharata alone should
Ascend the throne of Saketa. Dasharatha himself
Has promised it to your father, Kaikeya.
He was a slave to your beauty. 100
In a hurry to marry you, he forgot the rules of his clan,
Promising that your son, Bharata would reign
As the king.

'Has King Dasharatha forgotten his promise?
Why was Bharata's kingship stolen?
Much before the birth of Rama
Was the promise given.
Why break it? Why the silence?
Why should the interpretation of what is right be distorted like this?
When the whole kingdom has been given away as bride-price. 110
Why break a promise? Why secrecy? Why forgetfulness?
Shri Rama is a virtuous man. People will accept him
Putting forward the weakness of love for him,
Waiting for the time and situation when Bharata is not here
Should one taunt fate by breaking a promise?

"I shall marry secretly; hidden, you blow the pipe"—
Dasharatha's way of functioning is akin to this proverb.
The king has lost his mind, nearing the end!
If Rama becomes the king of Ayodhya,
You shall become dirt under Kausalya's feet, do not forget. 120
Drive Bharata to the forest and me as well.
Sheltered by him, I shall serve him all the while.
You stay on here washing Kausalya's feet,
Drink the holy water every day and chant praises.

'This city of Saketa is a desert of promise-breakers.
I cannot stay here a moment, I shall see Bharata,
And I shall bathe in the fountain of his love.
Among the Ikshwaku kings, justice and righteousness
Are an illusion like a mirage.
You are the mistress, I am the slave. I am not self-serving.   130
What rights have I over Bharata?
The dream I dreamt is worth nothing;
Tolerate the king's betrayal of Bharata! I am
Not that generous. I cannot bear the insult,
Let that be for you; with the speed of thunder,
Death will attack you, remember then what I said.
Total distruction awaits you in readiness!'
The tip of Manthara's poison dart
Had struck Kaikeyi deep. Every atom in her body
Was pierced. She was bewildered as if struck by an evil spirit.   140
She was helpless and collapsed like a tree for a moment;
But woke up the next moment and became a whirlwind!
'God! What are you making me hear?
In the abode of a peaceful mind, lava is boiling.
Even if an ocean is poured over, this flame will not go out.
Why should I be humble? Why become a slave?
My fortune is under my control, I shall achieve victory.
The exit is a flame, pushing ahead in madness.'
Kaikeyi became unwell with such feelings.

She was enveloped with envy regarding the other wives   150
Of her husband. The poisonous flame had spread,
Swallowing the town. Kaikeyi's mind was prepared.
The poisonous seed sprouted: the decision that Bharata
Should be crowned was embedded in her mind.
It is strange in this world
How the slanderous serpent kills people:
'Aho Khalabhujangasya, vichitroyam vadhakramaha!
Anyasya dashati shrotram, Anyaha pranairviyajyate'
(Look at this serpent; its ways of killing are strange.

It bites the ears of someone, but someone else dies. 160
Slander is an enemy of co-existence;
Slander has caused rivers of tears to flow;
It has devoured and fed on families and empires, alas!
In the sea of slander, the ship of the Raghu-clan is sinking;
The Octopus-arms of hatred and temptation
Have embraced Kaikeyi; she has forgotten to distinguish
Between what is appropriate and what is not.
It seems as if a deaf rock is much better!
'Why did this happen, why suspicion
About gentle Bharata? Is he not free from desire? 170
Was he not born of my womb of no envy?
In the fire which has neglected him, why is this body
Not turned to ashes? Let the underworld swallow me!
This is betraying trust! How can I bear the humiliation?
Was not Bharata the very life of Rama?
No one is for another. Fate has been treacherous.
The good name of sun's clan is blackened, alas!'
Thus, Kaikeyi's mind was greatly disturbed.

The hunchbacked woman fanned the fire of hate:
'In the past, in the battlefield of the *devas* and the *asuras*, 180
You had gone with the king towards Vaijayanta city.
Dasharatha's fight with Timidhwaja and Shambarasura
Became fierce, he was badly hurt, he fainted.
You became his charioteer and rescued him.
The king was pleased and granted you two boons.
"I shall ask for them when the time comes," you said.
Now the right time has arrived. Ask for the two boons.
Rama should be sent to a forest for fourteen years,
And Bharata should rule the kingdom. This should be
Your demand. This is the principle of morality. 190
Do not be scared of what people may say!
Bharata will gain in these fourteen years people's love.
His kingdom will be strongly rooted;
People will admire him forgetting Rama.

Fear comes chasing us; get up, beautiful woman,
You are vain about your beauty; along with your beauty,
Everything you possess is being swept away!

'Walk to your room. Venting your anger,
Fall on the floor. Wearing dirty clothes, weep aloud.
Do not be scared. Rama will now rule the forest! 200
Can you not understand the severity of power?
His radiance will diminish and he will be dull;
How can he then stay the king of Ayodhya?'
The hunchback advised her mistress thus,
Manthara, the maid-servant from Kaikeyi's maternal home,
To forget her own ugliness, let her affection
Flow towards Bharata.

She planted the venomous seed of envy in Kaikeyi's mind
For the other wives of her husband. The hunchback tended
The seedling pouring the water of love of her son, 210
And gained the benefit of sending Rama away to the forest.
Thus, the boat of milk and honey Sita and Rama
Were to sail, was caught in the whirlpool
Of Manthara's hatred, and reeled fast, helplessly.

Saketa was drowned in astonishment and fear,
Like a broom of fire and red, live coals,
As if the torch held by the God of Death burnt bright,
A fearful comet moved fast.
Looking at the omen in the sky, a divine writing,
Dasharatha trembled. 'Is the Raghu-clan in peril?' 220
The citizens of Ayodhya were sorrowful!

Manthara herself churned with Kaikeyi as the churning rod.
The ocean being *Treta* yuga and Bharata's love
Turning into the churning rope like Adishesha.
Nevertheless sweet words about Sita, Rama and Lakshmana
Were sweet to hear for one and all.

Drunk on the wine of Manthara's evil advice,
Kaikeyi lost her way like a wild horse!

In anger she assumed the form of fury,
With loose, ruffled hair falling down to the heels; 230
The pearl necklace broken, all the pearls
Falling on the floor like teardrops.
Like a female elephant, crushing the garland of flowers,
She threw pictures and images in all directions;
Hissing like a snake, she emitted the fire of envy.
Good, lovable things appeared distasteful,
Looking only at faults, she dipped them in attachment.
Her light silken saris were spread all over the floor.
The king's mother Kausalya, in arrogance and pride,
Smiling before her and mocking her 240
Was what she saw in her imagination.
Like a sharp edge, it planted itself in her chest.
The soft, swaying body, trembled in rage.
Gnashing her teeth, rubbing her hands,
Stamping her feet, bursting out in anger,
She leant back exhausted. Like a serpent hurt,
She kept hissing every moment.
Anger and darkness enveloping the face of the queen
Like a wounded deer, struck by a poisonous arrow,
Losing the radiance, saddened, the face became dull. 250
The veil of Manthara's joy had slipped and spread.
She fell at Kaikeyi's feet and shed pearls.
'You are my mistress, you are my protecting angel.
Do not be scared. Do not pause until you reach the goal.
Thereafter, Bharata will taste Heaven. He will be the ruler
Of the whole earth, no one to compare with!'

Manthara was not the one to accept defeat.
Her love for Bharata had made her obsessive.
A hungry tiger thirsts for warm blood;
Manthara's thirst was for Bharata's love. 260

Canto Thirty-one

'Having saved my life then, why do you kill me today?'

॥ ६ ॥

On the eve of coronation,
Many kinds of dreams troubled Dasharatha.
The lamps lit up to brighten the palace
As well as those lit up to brighten the kingdom,
All appeared to walk on the edge of death and go out.
Wind, tainted by evil, enveloped the city
Watching the disaster faced by the scion of his clan.
The Sun-god burnt bright, became a circle of fire
Spreading the signs of war in all four directions,
Threw a weapon of fire and retired. 10

Dreams are amazing. They warn one;
They are the signs of the future, milestones of psychology,
Embodiments of desire and frustration,
Bridges and links between wakefulness and sleep.
Progress, property, purity, revolution,
All these cyclical processes embody experiences.
The *agnachakra* seen between the eyebrows
Is the awareness of the states of sleep and wakefulness;
The mind is the machine beyond time;

It is the secret of sleep and wakefulness in life. 20
Brave as the high Himalayas is Shri Rama,
Dignified as the boundless ocean, a sea of knowledge.
Nevertheless, there was a war going on within
'If I sit on the throne, the king will go
To the forest to spend his old age,
I shall have no father. I shall be an orphan, truly
Ayodhya will be like an orphan. Why do I need the kingdom?'
While he was experiencing pain, Vaidehi
Saw his face clouded and spoke to him:
'Until now, you brothers, 30
Under the shade of your father's umbrella of love,
Enjoyed happiness, without worries, without any lack.
This will change when you become king.
We have to bow before the system
Like a fish thrown up on the bank from a royal lake.
The mind is in turmoil. How can one grow fond of
The power of the ruler and luxuries?'

'Holding the reins of power in a kingdom is not a luxury.
One should experience it without needing it.
I am the eldest son. It is my responsibility. 40
Let me use it for the welfare of all people.
Why do you worry, Sita. Even if I become king
The power shall not separate us and our brotherly love.
Is there anyone who can say that he has
Cut up and separated water by a sword?
In the sea of play of feelings
We are all sailing. Like waves of water,
We shall live happily together without separation.
Lakshmana is all powerful; an advisor who will
Help to push back enemies. Bharata is all-knowing; 50
He will help in administration. Shatrughna, a mine of affection;
There are no limits to his power. Everything is
His responsibility. I am a king just in name;
This is the transparent administration of trustees!'

Over there, Urmila with her beloved husband
Lakshmana, reflected in this manner.
'At this auspicious moment, there is pain
In Saketa that Bharata is not here. Finding no other
Auspicious moment, the king is in a hurry.
Are you not with Shri Rama, 60
Bharata and Shatrughna, gems of your clan?
If the coronation takes places in the presence of Bharata,
We shall all be very fortunate! Let Shri Rama
Get rid of our worldly distress and grant us
Transparent administration of the kingdom.'
In deep consultation
With the great Sage Vasishtha, Dasharatha spoke:
'Bharata's absence in the palace, brings me sadness.
But then, this is an auspicious moment for the coronation.
The mind is saddened by bad omens. 70
Will the curse of the sage come true? Is death nearby?
The absence of Bharata and Shatrughna is pushing me
To that end. Let this happy event take place at any cost.
This body, obviously, is transient.' The sage replied:
'Do not lose heart, O king! With the blessings of god,
Everything will go on undisturbed. Saketa
Will become an embodiment of fulfilment.'
The sage spoke comforting words.
The light of the sun disappeared from the sky.
Eager to find out what sort of game would be played, 80
The Night queen, wearing the moon on her forehead,
Descended slowly like an elephant into Saketa!
To inform Kaikeyi about the good news of the coronation,
Dasharatha entered her quarters with joy.
Struck by Cupid's arrow, the awareness
Of what was fitting and what was not, his mind was filled
With lustful desires!
In her 'Chamber of Anger,' he saw
The beautiful woman lying down like a volcano,

After spewing out fire. Her hair all dishevelled, 90
The face appeared dejected. She looked like a star
Wanting to shoot up in darkness, but falling from the skies.
She was restless like a hungry lioness.
The anger which had squeezed out her life, was mollified.
She was the black cobra. Who had offended her?
The king was shocked and startled with fear.
Not knowing what to do but trying to console her,
He went near her and stroked her hair.
Then he spoke to her in gentleness:
'Beloved, tell me why you are angry. 100
Why are you distressed when I am your slave?
Saketa is like Heaven itself, everyone is happy.
To increase the sweetness of life, there must be
Sourness with it. That is what I believe.
The time for love-fights is past; we are now beyond them.
We are liberated from passion and are respected by our sons.
Bharata is not in the city. Are you wanting him here?
His welfare is in the coronation of Rama.
If you are sick, tell me, I shall call the physician.
I shall place before you whatever you want. 110
I shall get heavenly nectar. What is impossible for Dasharatha?

'The umbrella of my power
Is spread as far as sun's rays reach. Do you want to give gifts?
The treasury of gems in Ayodhya is full.
Queen of my heart, what can equal your love?
When I was injured in the war between *devas* and *danavas*
You had saved my life and were given boons.
On that day, you were the Goddess of Victory and brought success.
You saved my life that day, why are you killing me now?
Speak to me beloved, I shall do what you want!' 120

'Stop your false talk of love, O king!
Put away your crafty schemes and then come here.
What promises did you give? What have you done now?

Were your boons mere colourful words!'
Kaikeyi said, showing hurt.
'Do not shoot words like arrows, Kaikeyi!
How can I open up my heart to show you?
What did you ask for? Have I said no?
Why have you brought me pain for no reason?
Do not make false accusations, ask for what you want;   130
Why the distrust? Listen to my pledge,
Divine beings as witness, the sun and the moon as witness
I shall speak only the truth. Truth is the source of the world.
If you ask for the kingdom, I shall give it to you.
I shall offer you my life, I shall give you all I have.'
Caught in the fondness for Kaikeyi,
Caught in the net of his own promise,
Not knowing what to do next, he spoke.
'Why mere talk now? Grant me the boons.
On this auspicious moment itself, Bharata   140
Must be crowned king. For fourteen years
Shri Rama should go to live in a deep forest,'
Kaikeyi said in a firm voice.
Listening to the terrifying words, Dasharatha collapsed.
He was thunder-struck, the body was in smithereens.
Hitting him where it hurt most, Kaikeyi said,
'Why the silence? Why are you sitting still like a statue?
Is this the way of keeping your word? If you cannot,
Just say you have broken your promise. The only
Way open for me is to kill myself.'   150
'Why should you die?' said Dasharatha, 'Live and enjoy
The power over the kingdom. You have been granted
Your boons anyway! I shall myself die like an orphan,
Betrayer of a son!

'Did you misuse the boons that were given?
Why should men be proud enough to offer boons?
Whom should one believe? What I thought was
A necklace of divine gems turned out to be

A poisonous snake, alas!' When you are hungry
For the kingdom, why are you angry with Rama? 160
Is not the scion of the Raghu-clan a son of yours as well?
Light of the Ikshwaku clan, a superior being,
Oh Rama, Oh Rama,' moaned the king in pain!

As Kaikeyi was like death, the palace became a graveyard;
The moonlight that shone around appeared like a shroud;
Light twinkled like sparks from a funeral pyre;
He trembled thinking of what the next day would bring.
As he collapsed suddenly, his head was between his knees;
It was as if he dared not show his face.
The king was caught in the misery between life and death. 170
As if he were half alive and half dead,
He twisted around in immeasurable pain.
'Sensing a herd of cattle in the field,
Did you turn into a tigress, lying in wait,
With your mouth open? These poisonous teeth
Have been planted in me. It is like mixing drain water
With the milk of the divine Kamadhenu and drinking it.
Alas, what a fate!
'You wicked one, if Shri Rama goes to the forest
I shall not live. You will become a widow. 180
Have evil times struck my palace, Oh fate!
If I die, do not touch my dead body;
Let Bharata not touch it either, swear it.
The promise I gave you has swallowed me up.
Pulling out my eyes, did you push me into darkness?'
Thus he moaned like a deer caught in a net.
Clothed as an ascetic, for fourteen long years,
How could Rama live in a forest? He thought,
And, with worry and dismay, he suffered!
Was it a dream, delusion, an evil spirit taking over, 190
Or a disease of the mind? Not knowing what had hit him,
Like a helpless deer caught by a ferocious tiger,
Like a serpent caught in a magician's circle,

The king suffered greatly.
'It is not right to break a promise, O king.
This will bring bad luck to the Raghu-clan.
Do not forget its honour. Did not King Shibi
Cut up his own body to keep his word,
Giving away those pieces happily? In the same way,
Emperor Alarka gave away his eyes and found salvation.   200
The promise that he would not cross the boundary
Was kept by the ocean king. Follow the path
Your ancestors followed,' said Kaikeyi again.
Realising her stubbornness as well as his own promise,
Screaming 'Shri Rama', like a huge tree cut down,
He fell, got up again; seeing Kaikeyi
Was like seeing the vision of an evil spirit.
'You became a rope round the neck, a black serpent
Spewing out poison, it was my foolishness
That I cared for you so much and was deceived.   210
Let your elegant body turn dry at once,
Let it burn in the fire with crackling sounds,
Let it be in pieces and mix with the earth.
Your inhuman actions are intolerable,'
Said Dasharatha and like Shiva granting a boon
To Bhasmasura, like an ageing ox,
Carrying the yoke and being whipped,
He became sorrowful!

'O sinner, I took your hand with fire as witness.
I let it go now. You are no more my wife.   220
With the material got ready for the coronation,
Let Shri Ramachandra complete my funeral rites.
I am caught in the shackles of honour. My energy
Is sapped. My head is swinging in a noose,'
Said the king and fainted again.
Without any hesitation,
Kaikeyi shot another arrow with these words:
'If you love righteousness, send Rama to the forest.'

Canto Thirty-two

'We Pledge to Fulfil our Father's Words'

||☉||

Dasharatha lay unconscious all night long.
Minister Sumantra went to Kaikeyi's palace.
'Night is over. Day has dawned.
O king, get up. The time of coronation is approaching.
Vasishtha and other sages are chanting
Sacred verses, preparations are afoot.
Water from all seas and springs in the world,
From the confluence of Ganga, Yamuna and Saraswati
From, Vapeekoopa lake, water from rivers flowing
Eastwards like Kaveri, Godavari   10
Those flowing South like Gandasi, Shona and
Bhadra have been brought with excitement.
Water from springs as well, leaping up like a rainbow
Have been filled in golden pots and brought over.

'Everything is ready, O king!
An auspicious throne made from Oudambara wood,
Gems, corn, fragrances, curds and milk.
Puffed rice, straw and flowers of many kinds,
Eight beautiful maidens, domineering elephants
Four horses, swords, bows, palanquin,   20

White umbrellas resembling the moon, two white fans,
A white ox tied up in golden chains,
A lion with four fangs, throne and tiger skins.

'The stage is bright, instruments playing,
The star Pushya is sparkling; get up, O king!
Bathe and adorn yourself. Like the sun
Who shines rising from Sumeru mountain
Show yourself, come out from these quarters
We are all waiting for your permission.'

'Sumantra, do not stab me with hurtful words.' 30
When Dasharatha said that, hearing the pitiful
Words, startled Sumantra just stepped
Back. Then Kaikeyi spoke deceitfully:
'Sumantra, in the anxiety of crowning Rama,
The king has lost sleep and is exhausted.
Do not worry. Bring Rama right now;
Let good things happen to Ayodhya.' Believing
It to be true, Sumantra went away, very happy!

Sumantra brought the brothers;
With Saumitri, Shri Rama in a joyful mood 40
Entered the palace, walking like a brave man!
Looking at their handsome faces, Dasharatha
Was energised. 'Come Rama, come Lakshmana,
Come, embodiment of virtue, my darling son,'
So he cried out, in a piteous voice.
Kaikeyi appeared to be the embodiment of misfortune,
Like clouds darkening the sky on a bad day indicating peril.
Murmuring like a man dreaming.
'Rama, Rama,' he said. Unable to get up from the bed,
He faltered, rolled over and crawled. 50
Rama felt miserable.
'Get up father, open your eyes and give orders.'
Dasharatha gazed at him piteously, without
Speaking, his lips trembled and tears flowed in silence.

The king's life was a boat caught in a whirlpool.
He stroked Rama and Lakshmana and embraced them.
Drenching Rama with his tears, he said,
'I was deceived, I was struck a blow;
Poisonous arrows are embedded in my heart.'
He looked at Kaikeyi with contempt. 60
Not knowing the reason for such behaviour,
Shri Rama asked mother Kaikeyi in all politeness;
'What is the matter, mother? why is father like this?
If you tell me the reason, I shall remove the anxiety.
His heart is like a gentle flower. I shall take away all the misery.'
Kaikeyi answered, 'Listen Rama. The reason is this:
I asked for the boons your father had granted earlier.
Bharata should be the king of Ayodhya;
You should go to the forest for fourteen years.
He is sad now because he cannot keep his promise.' 70
She said all that ridiculing Dasharatha.
The king thundered in anger:
'What are you doing, you miserable destroyer of the clan?
Looking at the lotus-like face of Rama, the noble man,
Doesn't compassion arise in you being a mother?
Has a woman's heart burnt into cinders merged with darkness?
Why do you push the loving child into the wild fire
Of life in a forest!

'For the momentary mirage-like joy of kingly power,
Will you kick away the permanent divine bliss? 80
Will you become stone-hearted and bore
Into the deep bondage between Rama and Bharata?
In a kingdom without Rama, will Bharata
Find happiness? He is now prey
To the burning anger of the people, will you pour *ghee* into it?
Repentance awaits you.'

Dasharatha's river of sorrow broke its banks and flowed.
Kaikeyi was furious. She appeared like a hurricane.

Shri Rama was composed. There was no pain in him;
The radiance on his face had increased. 90
The thunder of Kaikeyi's words had no effect.
He was not the one to lose his way or get distressed.
There was no frustration, no trace of discontent.
Like first showers on the heated earth,
Like cooling the hearts of one and all,
Shri Rama, prepared for a dialogue, spoke:

'Where is the sorrow father? Where is the difference
Between me and Bharata? When he has the duty
Of ruling Ayodhya, let me maintain righteousness
In the forest. Why should you suffer and punish the body? 100
We shall become the priceless gems in a necklace
Of those who renounce everything. Why do you worry father?
The great vision of my life is this. Grant me permission at once.
Why do you blame the venerable mother Kaikeyi?'
Saumitri became angry,
Like the primeval serpent with his hood spread out
And hissing, he said: 'Are you hurting us with a pointed needle?
Do you not know how devoted we are to our father!
A thousand Parashuramas will be born,'
He thundered like a cloud of devastation. 110
Without feeling scared, Kaikeyi replied:
'See, I stand like Renuka, do your duty.'
'Are you showing off your power as a mother?
How did you ever reach the city of Saketa?

'If Bharata desires the kingdom,
I shall behead him; I shall destroy your mean brother,
Yudhajita. This is a secret conspiracy to swallow Ayodhya.
I shall make you eat its fruits. Do not bring virtuous
Bharata into your cunning scheme. In the mire of Kaikeyi,
He has bloomed like a lotus. If he was here today, 120
He would be anguished; he would mock at you as a serpent
Breaking and eating its own offspring. Day would turn into night,
He would wander around, covering his face like a fool!

'Do you have the authority to rule the kingdom?
What right does father have to give it to you?
Ayodhya is in the hearts of crores of citizens.
It is not autocracy. It is not something to be handed out
To those who beg. The eldest has the right;
Why snatch it? I shall fight to save what is right.'
With the terrifying arrows of Lakshmana's words, 130
Kaikeyi was shattered. While the poison in her heart
Was struggling to come out from her lips,
Shri Rama spoke gently:
'Patience, Saumitri. Do not be swept away
In the flood of anger,' and tried to soothe him.

'How can I bear it? How can I forgive
This injustice? To fight against injustice
Is the duty of the clan. Do not stop me.
Rejoice among courtiers; ascend the throne;
It will be accepted by the righteous gathering. 140
I shall deal with the enemies. Let the war
Of righteousness go on. Like Vishnu with Mahashesha,
You are with me. Why do I need
The help of heavenly beings? If you are there,
It is enough for me!

'Let me look after your welfare.
I shall rush forward without worry and destroy any enemy,
So that they cannot rise again! Even if the whole world
Turns against me, I shall fight like your slave.
Who can snatch away the right to fight? I shall revolt, 150
Never bending my head before immorality.
She is a serpent. I shall pull out the poisonous teeth.
No peace for me unless I put down this immorality.
Do not pull out the divine fire in my heart,
And make me impotent, do not be heartless!

'This king is not our father; he is the slave
Of the daughter of a slave. He has destroyed

The divine tradition of the Ikshwaku family.
Unholy, a stump of wood, undeserving, a betrayer
Of the clan, he has lost the right to give orders.   160
When being swept away in the river of immorality,
Why stay quiet? Do not try to suppress
My feelings, Shri Rama. To lighten the burden
Of the earth, I have taken the pledge and stand here;
Give me permission. I shall destroy the enemies.
I shall become Bhargava, behead the enemies.
What is the point of living? I shall not rest
A moment until I crown the one who reigns in my heart;
Who can question my decision?

'I do not approve of going to the forest.   170
Why should the noble Kshatriya surrender to fate?
My valour will stop fate running
Wild like an elephant showing off its power.
I shall pull out the creeper of greed, the coronation will go on.
I shall drive out the faithless trying to send Rama away
Right into the forest. When there is agitation
I shall protect the kingdom, give me permission.
Are the bows and arrows, swords merely for decoration?
Give up the dishonourable emotion and concentrate
On being a Kshatriya!   180

'Your equanimity, the detached emotions
Of Vasishtha and other sages, Bharata's absence,
Kaikeyi's envy and Manthara's evil magic,
The dance of destruction has got together,
Dragging you towards life in a forest!'

Having shouted these words,
Lakshmana picked up his bow and twanged the string.
At that tremendous sound, Saketa trembled
As if struck by thunder. The jewels that Saumitri wore,
Sparkled; split the sky, rainbow colours appeared   190
In the sky, dazzling eyes of the beholders,

Like the flash of a sword, like a streak of lightening,
The necklace and pendant shone around the neck.
Like all-destroying fire, Lakshmana's fury blazed.

Shri Ramachandra, an embodiment of peace and compassion,
Like the wind dissolving dark clouds into rain,
Dissolved the clouds of anger enveloping Saumitri,
And swept them away like gentle breeze from the hills.
In a delicate and gentle manner, he began
The act of soothing: 200

'Control your anger, hold back the rage.
Get ready for the Great Quest! Do not speak
Hurtful words. When you are faced with difficulties,
Is it acceptable for a hero to become unsteady?
Lowering the family in blind brotherly love,
Why should you put your mind in a state of turmoil?
"*Matru devo bhava, Pitru devo bhava*"
('Mother is like god; father is like god')
When such things are said, why do you insult parents?
Should one scold the father, caught in a moral dilemma? 210
Whatever promise is made, should be kept.
To uphold righteousness, he will die and live
Otherwise he will be like the dead while living.
If a mistake is made, will the righteous son of Aja live?

'No water in rivers, no crops in fields;
When everything is a desert, does one blame
The rivers and fields? The turning wheel of time
Moves all. When the movement is such,
Why should you chastise mother and father?
Brother! What crime has Bharata committed? 220
The Great Journey and welfare of the world
Call us. Is it right to slam the door with the foot
And get back inside?

'While we are the sons of King Dasharatha
Why should we rule the kingdom straying from the right path?

No more doubt. What elders say is not untruth.
To pay back what we owe our father is our duty.
Our pledge is obeying our father's words.
Are you not moved by the quiet pain of father!
The kingdom and its treasury mean nothing to me. 230
Why the desire for the kingdom, anger and obduracy?

'Let us act with restraint. The world is our empire.
Let the tree of your mind grow in my friendship.
The kingdom will be safe in Bharata's rule;
Why should we be sorrowful? Forests are dear to me;
Life in a forest offers us the joy of art.
Is there another world apart from the search
Of the power of seeking wisdom? The great chance
Of pulling the chariot of the world calls us;
Should we ignore it, Saumitri? Only righteousness; 240
There is no other wealth and prosperity.
How can one live in a palace where there is no righteousness?
It is comparable to a terrifying graveyard.

'In the flame of hatred, the lotus-heart will wilt.
Protest against immorality, take a pledge.
Why nurture vengeance? Love is the principle of victory.
When you have the divine spark in you to light up man,
If that is not enough, absorb all the knowledge on earth,
Open the windows of the mind as well as
The eyes of wisdom. Then you are truly great among men! 250
You will become the initiation of the epoch and walk
In the path of universal victory. While you play in
The sea of wisdom, the world will praise you.
'If you stumble during independent thinking,
The crocodiles of conflict in a pond disturbed by doubt and fear
Will devour you. Only the value of harmony
Will take you up to the summit. Weakness will push you
To the depths of a valley!
'The whole world is breaking in violence;

The world should become home and must be reached. 260
Evil, distortion, greed and egotism will surely
Lead to defeat, that is the truth, Lakshmana!
Wake up from your dream, take off your shackles and be free.
That is a road without obstacles, do not worry
If the heat of the sun is on. Scared of your own shadow,
Why should you keep attacking it and feel exhausted?

'Your radiance is reflected everywhere in the world.
Wise men will break the shackles of the world and come out.
Let the world's sorrow be driven away and the light of love spread.
The stars have gone out, dark clouds gather, 270
The hurricane roars, darkness dances.
The ocean overflows, lightening flashes,
Do not be scared of all these. Until you light up the world,
Keep moving on, carry on with the Great Quest.'

Canto Thirty-three

'Why a Life in a Forest for Rama if Bharata Rules'

||६||

Shri Ramachandra advised Lakshmana in this manner;
He spread his arms wide like the branches of *tamala* tree,
And embraced Lakshmana, as if taking the whole world
Into his heart. Rama, a tree of mercy, and Lakshmana, his shadow.
Tears welled up. The black cloud of Lakshmana's anger
Had melted and he surrendered to Rama.

Like the night of the new moon
Darkness had enveloped Dasharatha's heart.
Losing everything, he suffered in frustration
For haste and hesitation, infatuation for a woman,   10
Gentle, virtuous Dasharatha was prey to all.
Manthara's hatred had set the city on fire.
It was like a wildfire for the Raghu-clan.
Kaikeyi's mind had gone sour with what Manthara had put into it.
The essence of Dasharatha's family was in smithereens.
While kings were invited for the coronation,
They would all laugh at the news of a life in the forest.
'Go ahead Shri Rama, in the path of stars
You have become my soul, go on virtuous one.

Go where there is freedom of thought 20
Nothing will come in your way. I am always with you!
I have taken the pledge of creating a new epoch
I shall offer myself at your feet as a sacrificial stone
I shall not break the strict rules of your deep desire
O king, the building of a new Ayodhya
Will take place. The world
Will not know of it. I know the way
The wheel of time turns. I shall honour the valour of a man.
Whatever is acceptable to you will be to me as well;
Everything is tolerable for those who know you!' 30
Listening to Lakshmana's words of restraint,
Shri Rama spoke with great love:
'Let me go to the forest Lakshmana;
Parents are here. So are Bharata and Shatrughna,
Here in Ayodhya. If you stay with them,
It will be good for everyone. There is wealth here
Equal to the three worlds. Protect everything!
Protect righteousness, father is shattered.
To console and protect him is your duty.
In the forest, there will be the company of sages. 40
Lakshmana, I am not worried at all. Do not be anxious!'

'Why should I bid you farewell?
Can I tolerate being parted from you?
This life and body are yours. If you do not take them
Kill them and go; You will not have sinned.
This life is under your control. Do not create distance;
It will be a life of an exile, a graveyard,
I shall live like a ghost, it is not right.
Do not be cruel and forsake me, I beg you Raghuvira!

'You are my mother and father, my relatives 50
My brother and my everything, do not stop me.
In art, in sport, in forays into the jungle,
In discussions at meetings, in making decisions,

In making judgement, I have been with you.
Why the distance? I shall be your shadow
In the forest, I shall honour your command.
After having tasted nectar in your proximity,
Why do you make me drink the poison of separation!

'You are fully within me – inside and out;
The pangs of separation are like being in hell; 60
I shall turn into ashes with sorrow!
Let it be Heaven, let divinity come.
Let there be immense wealth, O king!
Whatever is not for you, whatever is not you
Is not acceptable to me, not comforting.
Aham sarvam karishyami jagarataha swapnatashchate
(In wakefulness, in sleep and in every state,
I will do everything in your service!)'
After being nursed by Rama and Lakshmana,
Dasharatha regained consciousness and said, 70
'I have lost the status of a father!
Saumitri, save me. Imprison me right now
You conduct Shri Rama's coronation.
Follow political morality as well as concern for people;
This is the path of kings of the Raghu-clan. Do not abandon it.
Do people realise who Rama is and what his character is?
He has grown larger than the kingdom;
He is the emperor of the world. Protect righteousness,
Hold up the moral of universal man. You are indeed Adishesha.'

Silence was the answer to the father's words. 80
Looking at the lotus-face covered with dew,
Shri Rama melted and spoke with compassion:
'Let go of sorrow Lakshmana, come with me
To the forest. You will become my other half;
You become my companion and a friend as well.
Let the bond of love between us stay forever!'

As Shri Rama and Lakshmana walked away,
'Will you turn your face and leave me, Shri Rama?
I am facing death, do you not feel pity?'
Said Dasharatha and the brothers sighed.   90
It did not denote pity. It was an indication
Of release from paternal love.

From the wombs of their mothers
Rama and his brother came down to earth.
With great excitement, Saketa kingdom had fastened
The shackles of good fortune and pushed them
Into the prison of a palace.
Kaikayi opened the doors of the prison.
The brothers were happy and excited.
They left Kaikeyi's palace then and there
To Kausalya's palace they went like a pair of swans.   100
Minister Sumantra was outside. 'I wish you well',
He blessed them and spoke in a choked voice.
'Do you not know Sumantra, all is well;
Kaikeyi asked for power over the kingdom.
For me, she asked for fourteen years in the forest.
Saumitri is coming with me.'

Hearing that, Sumantra stood amazed.
He was bewildered as if a snake had fallen on him.
Unable to breathe, he started panting
'Oh, why did Kaikeyi become so evil?   110
Killing her husband, she killed the clan.
Moving on like a mountain, undisturbed as the sea
Is the king. How can he bear the sharp thrust!

'Like a fall of hailstones on a field ready for harvest'
Like a ship breaking into smithereens just before reaching the shore,
Did destruction come to him in this manner?
Does Bharata desire the kingdom and the treasury?
He will give up everything in great pain.
Did this lapse happen without knowledge of his inner feelings?

How can one stop this? When this is the path of righteousness, 120
How can I stop it?' He thought in great pain.

Kausalya had bathed, worn silken clothes,
And was worshipping god, with Vaidehi by her side;
Her veil sparkled with diamond embroidery;
Her clothes glittered and her unearthly beauty
Was beyond all limits!

On her face was spread
A pure feeling like a peaceful sky.
In her speech, there was the intelligence of Saraswati,
The Goddess of Learning; her lotus-face was radiant. 130
The riches of a budding jasmine had been caught in her lips.
Forelocks moved about beautifully on the face
Eyelids protected the eyes, tender as flowers,
Cheeks were full and radiant.
Like wealth, the Goddess of Beauty appeared
To have caught felicity too in her being.

For Kausalya,
The inside of her palace was a world of divine joy.
With Sita assisting her in her worship,
She was peaceful and pure within and without. 140
While a nectar stream of divine emotions flowed
Shri Rama was on one bank and Sita on the other,
Like Kartika ahead and Margashira behind,
Shri Rama arrived there with Lakshmana!
Mother Kausalya blessed them with great joy
'Sita, bring the holy rice here and sandalwood paste.
I shall put *tilaka* on their foreheads. Let them
Receive the offerings from the *puja*; prosper and live long.'
Sita looked at Rama and smiled.
She bent her head. On her face, a little shyness 150
Was mixed with joy and the blush was beautiful.

He is the embodiment of righteousness and heroism
Shri Rama spoke with the deep voice of thunder
'I feel fulfilled mother. You are wise; what can I tell you?
Selfishness has ended and the great truth radiates.
Blissful life in a forest proffered by righteousness is mine.
Bharata is king here. For fourteen years,
I shall travel to the riches of life in a deep forest.'

Kausalya did not trust enough;
Thinking it was banter, she smiled and said, 160
'Say nothing, Shri Rama. Do not speak of inauspicious things.
Will Bharata ever snatch your throne,
Sending you to live in a deep forest?
You tell me, Lakshmana, is your brother telling the truth?
Is he trying to test the strength of my mind, tell me.'

Unable to bear his sorrow, Lakshmana broke down.
Kausalya was disturbed and doubtful
When silence was the answer, she was shocked.
Thinking of the cruelty of fate, she collapsed.
Eyes heavy with tears, the world seemed empty, 170
The decorated chariot in her mind was in pieces
Wringing her hands, her womb twisted.
Her voice was choked and there was no sound.
From deep within her womb the turmoil of motherhood
Sprang out!

Unable to watch Kausalya's sorrow,
Sita went near her. Consoling, she wiped her tears.
'Take heart mother, Are you not strong?
This is a journey to conquer the whole world.
What does one gain from keeping selfish power?' 180
She spoke in a heart-warming manner.

Kausalya's grief crossed boundaries.
'Is this true, son? O, fate. Have they driven
You to the forest? For all who live in the kingdom of Ayodhya,

You were a loved treasure! What wrong did you commit?
Were you a victim of your father's anger!
I shall go to your father and beg forgiveness, Do not go
Lakshmana, you come with me,' she said.

Consoling her, Saumitri spoke;
'Shri Rama is one who will drive away faults,   190
He is the sustenance for all good qualities.
He is good, righteous and benevolent
Blessed with integrity, the brightest in the world,
Full of restraint. Can a fault touch the great power!
To fulfill Kaikeyi's desire and his father's promise,
He has abdicated all and leaving for the forest
Pushing everyone into the deep waters of anguish.'

Controlling herself, Kausalya spoke:
'I now understand Kaikeyi's new political morals.
I admire her supreme love for her son.   200
In the whirlpool of anxiety, I am not at all pained
That Rama will not ascend the throne.
I do not see any difference between Rama and Bharata.
While Bharata rules that kingdom, why should Rama live in a forest?
Let him stay in Ayodhya. I beg for Rama;
I do not want power nor do I want luxury;
If Shri Rama is with me, it is Heaven enough!'

'That will never happen. This humility should stop.'
These words echoed in radiance then and there.
While everyone looked in amazement where   210
The voice came from, Sumitra arrived there with Urmila.
Shri Rama and Lakshmana touched her feet in reverence
'Taste fame and live for a long time.'
The brave Kshatriya woman blessed them so.
She blessed them with the dignity of a lioness.
Then she spoke:

'Let love for Bharata be there. Begging for
Autonomous power is not proper; such things are not done.

Let high thinking be awake; Let the steam
Of Kshatriya valour flow in everybody;   220
Why should one beg to preserve power?
Heroic death is better than that.
Such abasement will not be forgiven by the Kshatriya clan
Prey to weakness, without any shame
Should power by given away!
To bear injustice in silence is the source of immorality.
Where is your valour in hiding, Lakshmana!'

Lakshmana heard what his mother said.
'What can I do mother? I have no permission.
Is there anything impossible for me in this world?   230
If Rama allows, I shall demolish all his enemies;
I shall put up streamers and guard righteousness.'
He said that wondering whether Rama would assent
And give a sign, he gazed at his radiant face.

The son of the Raghu-clan stood in magnificence and said:
'Wait brother, listen to what I say.
Bharata should rule and the forest is for me;
Is it wrong? Where will moral strength be?
A blemish on the glory of Kshatriyas and on emblems
Of morality; would anyone accept a father's   240
Forced imprisonment and take over power?
Should one rule over Kaikeyi, Bharata and Shatrughna?
Why should one break the promise of a father,
As precious as life, and the desire of mother Kaikeyi?

'Do not be upset. Listen to me, mother;
Felicitation and honour have been received now
Why should it be sold for establishing grandeur?
This is a difficult situation. How can it be overcome, mother!
Your son Shri Rama is not weak, he is strong enough   250
To protect righteousness. Do not be scared.
You are the one who can sacrifice. When awareness of duty
Is honoured, grandeur and wealth are ignored.

Mother Kaikeyi desires, conscious of worldliness,
Her son's upliftment as the bride-price, and that is
Appropriate. For me, kingdom is not a luxury;
It is the trellis of a dream, I shall fulfill father's promise,
I shall go to the forest. Principles, sacrifice and righteousness –
Why should I turn my face away from all of them?
I shall protect all. In the search in life, they will all help.   260
Let me have the support of your blessings.
Please bless me, mother!'

Canto Thirty-four

'A Forest is a Palace Opened by God Himself'

||૬||

In the words of radiant Shri Ramachandra
Was hidden the great message of life on earth.
The dark clouds of anger and hurt had dispersed;
The ornament of the Raghu-clan shone like the sun.

Kausalya blessed in calmness: 'May good things happen!
Lakshmana and Rama, for what you sacrifice itself
Is wealth. Go into the forest. Righteousness everyday
Is what you should achieve. Let peace remain in Saketa;
Let noble Dasharatha's promise be fulfilled.
A mother's heart, with the pangs of separation,   10
Burns. We shall bear it somehow!'

Sumitra spoke with courage:
'Do not be afraid sister. They will all come back from the forest,
Let that hope be in our life like a thread,
Like the great Himalaya, let your mind be firm. Rama!
Let Lakshmana's support be with you always. May you be
As fearless as lions. If Lakshmana is the body,
You, Rama, are the breath in it! When breath and body are fused,
You are indeed impenetrable, this is the truth.

'Lakshmana, become Shesha to protect 20
The treasure of Rama's name. Be it in pain or in joy,
Rama is your support. You were born for a life in the forest.
Do not be scared. It is righteous to serve an elder brother
With great love. There should be no wrong actions.
Charity, practice of religious rites and honourable
Death on the battlefield – these constitute
The age-old morality for the Ikshwaku clan.

'Rama is Dasharatha, the forest is Ayodhya,
Janaki is the mother equal to me. Think so and live.
Let there be victory in your search and well-being.' 30

By then minister Sumantra
Came rushing in with anxiety and haste!
'Unrest is growing in the kingdom;
The fire of rebellion is setting off sparks;
People are not accepting Bharata's rule;
Your stay in the forest is not to be tolerated.
That the throne of Ayodhya is not merely the personal
Matter of Dasharatha's family is the cry everywhere.
There is fear in all directions, will administration be easy?
Dasharatha's mind is weakened and hence 40
There is no strength to quell springs of rebellion.
Bharata is not here.

'Even if he were here, people's fury might burn him.
"Burn Kaikeyi alive," is what they say.
Saketa has turned into the mouth of a volcano;
People's minds have cracked in an intense quake;
The kingdom will be swept off in the stream of anger
Notwithstanding Sahyadri and Himadri.
Heads will roll, kingdoms will be destroyed.
Internal conflicts have swallowed up 50
Civilisations of the world. Ayodhya will surely fall.
Can you not stop this destruction, Shri Rama?'

'Sincerity, righteousness –
Which is to be followed now, Sumantra?
Did love for me give place to rebellion?
What did Bharata not do? What did I do?
What have we really done? Anything great?
My mind is in pain listening to Bharata being scolded.
It is like poisonous arrows piercing my mind.
Blaming him is like blaming me too.   60

'O great minister, Sumantra!
You are an ocean of wisdom, protector of the Ikshwaku clan.
If I do not go into the forest, the epoch of *dharma* will end.
If I leave the kingdom in search of the Great Journey,
It will be the inauguration of a new epoch, a new age,
Do you not know its secret?'

'What shall I say Rama,
God shall protect us. I am helpless. Let good things
Come your way. I shall bear the weight of governance
To face the difficulties in future with courage;   70
We shall pray. You are installed in the minds of people!
A divine light shines in your heart,
You have showered power that is out of this world.

'How can the turbulence of this epoch be calmed?
"Sumantra, you take them to the forest in the chariot"
That is what the king has ordered me. "If I am alive
Until Bharata comes, I shall give him the kingdom
To join Rama in the forest." He said so with confidence
Breaking the hearts of people, Raghurama;
How can I take you to live in the forest!'   80

While Sumantra stood with his head bent,
They brought clothes made from fibre; Sita stretched her hands;
'Stop Vaidehi, these clothes are rough.
Your delicate body will be hurt if you wear them.
You are like a swan grown up in Manasa Sarovara;

None has punished you with a life in the forest.
How can you come to a forest with thorns and stones.
If you are not here, Ayodhya will lose her charm.

'It would be difficult for you to bear the sun, rain and cold;
Fourteen years of life in the forest is difficult. 90
There is great anxiety in an uninhabited place, in a forest
There will be no food at proper times,
Wild animals like tigers, bears and such others are there.
Sleepless nights will have to be spent there.
When you weep in sorrow, there will be none to share your sorrows,
It will just be a cry in wilderness.'

Sita answered Shri Rama:
'Why do you tire yourself by speaking,
I came with you out of love,
Was I enamoured of your father's palace?
I am the daughter of a brave sage-king. 100
If I need to live in the forest,
Do not be anxious. Be strong and peaceful. It is good for you.
I shall walk with you in the forest, unafraid
Like a shadow. The soul is asking for a new horizon.
Life in the forest beckons me
I am one with you. Why break the oneness?

'A companion in joy, why not in adversity?
Your happiness is my happiness, your pain is mine too.
Let half of the respect acquired by you be mine.
Death in this forest of Ayodhya is better for me 110
If you leave me. It will also break your pledge, O king!
Kaikeyi's desire, the promise given by father
Will all be fulfilled by my coming with you.
Sister Urmila is friendly towards your parents;
She is a sage of the epoch; self controlled,
She will complete the good work half done by me.
The terror of the forest does not frighten me;
It will bring the fruit of the great search!

'Stones and thorns? There are flowers in between;
There are shrubs and trees here,
Which will provide fruit and shade; 120
In roots oozes honey. I shall find something tastier
Than palace meals. What if I fast? I shall bear it all.
The women of Bharata are used to austere living.
I shall practice all rules in the middle of the forest.

'The forest is a palace kept open by god.
There is cool breeze and capacious sky;
Many rivers here and there, music here and there;
Like fluid kindness, waterfalls cascade down;
Creepers spread there, there is a shower of coolness.
Animals and birds living together in harmony. 130
There is pleasing music there.'

'Lakshmana, carrying the bow day and night,
Protects cautiously like Adishesha. The cuckoo
Sings in a melodious voice; the clouds pass by,
Making sounds like drums; peacocks gather,
Spread their feathers and dance.
Wild animals have given up violence there,
And have taken the pledge similar to the one of sages:
"Let us live together and live in peace."

'I shall bring flowers and fruits; 140
There will be no domestic arguments or revolution
And illusion there. When you are near me, I have everything.
You are the strings of my *veena*, the wheel of the chariot.
The good fortune of being near you knows no limits.
When you are near, the forest is Vrindavana;
When you are there, even the wilderness becomes tolerable;
I do not even fear entering fire and being burnt.'

Meanwhile, good wife Urmila,
Overcome with sadness, becoming emotional,
Fell on the floor. Giving her quick attention, 150

Sita stroked and consoled her, calling out to her.
Overcome with feelings, Lakshmana closed his eyes,
While Kausalya and Saumitri seemed like statues.
The mine of virtue, Shri Rama felt the moment
Stretched to an epoch. Tears of love sprang in everyone's eyes.

Rama spoke in a peaceful manner:
'Urmila will become the sage of this epoch;
Matchless and a symbol of sacrifice and meditation.
Her being alone is greater than Sita's austerity.
Her asceticism is greater than Ahalya's. 160
Her life is great, she is the embodiment of ascetic victory.
Fickleness, fear, depression and frustration are not there for her
She is a good wife and the bright peak of radiant Saketa.'
In this manner, Shri Rama praised Urmila;
Kausalya embraced her, burdened with sorrow.

Sumitra blessed them again:
'You may leave, children. We shall face everything
If we are alive till you come back, we shall be together again;
Let the Great Search be fruitful. Let the path of truth be gained;
Let your fame spread in all four directions
For your righteous victory. 170
Let the earth be fulfilled learning the secret of your life.
Like you, let all men achieve greatness
May you be worshipped all over the world!'

Forgetting the weight in her heart,
Mother Kausalya wished him well;
'Raghava, may the righteousness you follow, protect you.
Your vision of universal brotherhood, equality and
Compassion for life will be good for the world.
This is the strong will of fate. Be victorious over cruel death!
You have rich qualities of control over the mind and body. 180
Farewell sons, I wish you well
I wish Lakshmana well, I wish Sita well,
The forest will truly turn into Heaven because of you.'

The royal chariot was ready
At the palace gate; Sumantra stood there.
There was mentor Vasishtha as well: Shri Rama,
Saumitri and Sita fell at his feet with great devotion.
With great emotion, in a broken voice,
The sage said these words:

'The honour of the world is enhanced, son! 190
This is a touching moment that Treta *yuga* has seen
I am honoured, I am purified.
My right eye is twitching ceaselessly.
But the vow is yours, it is not right to stop you!
The claims of duty are welded in the heart.
The wheel of the epoch-maker will not get stuck in mire.
Protecting the sages, do god's work.
Let the weight on earth be lessened by you, son!'

Canto Thirty-five

'You are the Polestar of Goodness'

||૬||

Shri Rama, the benevolent, sat in the chariot
Like the rising sun along with Sita and Lakshmana.
Saddened by the journey to the forest, the cooking fires went out;
The fragrant sandalwood lost its sweet scent;
Birds stopped taking food and were exhausted in the sky.

Babies cried as their cradles were not rocked,
The strings that brought out waves of music were snapped,
The bells of temples stilled their tongues,
The hot breath of frustration spread in the city.

The war was all over, there had been death and pain;   10
Saketa was like a battlefield. All citizens,
With tears in their eyes, wetted the highway everywhere.
The glory of the city seemed to have disappeared with Rama.
Like a cow running, looking for its calf
Kausalya and Sumitra ran behind the chariot,
Watching it until they disappeared in the dust.
'Oh Rama, Sita, Lakshmana,' they cried out.

Minister Sumantra's mind was caught in a whirl,
Housewives seemed dipped in intolerable pain.

Praising the daughter of earth, they scolded Kaikeyi. 20
Where Rama is, there we are, they said,
Packing up their belongings, they ran behind
The chariot. The anxiety in everyone was limitless.
The city was in turmoil. Stopping here and there,
Consoling people, slowly, Shri Rama moved on in the chariot.

The citizens kept praising Rama;
'There is no touch of selfishness among kings of the Raghu-clan;
There is no sacrifice greater than giving up a throne.
Is there any other like Shri Rama, devoted to the father so!
Truth is the breath, righteousness is the path 30
In righteousness, truth, sacrifice, love,
Valour, power, radiance and virtue,
Who can equal Rama, who is greater than him?
He considers life in the forest a gracious gift.'

Praising him in this manner,
Unable to turn back, surrounding the chariot,
Rolling on the ground, singing praises of Rama
Running at the same speed as the chariot
'There is no way we shall send you away. You must return.
Drive the chariot over our bodies. If you are not there 40
Of what use is life? Do not reject our request,
This is the wish of the people, do not tread on our emotions.'

They lay down on the path;
Horses stopped, forelegs lifted high.
The great love of the people melted.
Shri Rama stopped the chariot and said
Calmly, like the resonance of a conch,
Like the waves of the sea, resounding:
'Get up, citizens, get up and let go of attachment.
Why are you carrying on a strike like this? 50
What do I have that is dearer to me than you?
Is not the relationship between us eternal?
Why are you anxious, you are the life for my body

When our joys and sorrows are entwined
How could the emotional bond be broken?

'When righteousness is my life, I shall not turn back
From my duty. If you admire me, worship
These ideals and values. In the grief
Of separation, do not become blind. I understand
The pain within you! Do not make me turn away
Once in an epoch comes such an act of righteousness,
I am not going to the forest because of anger in the palace.
There is no fear, no weakness; There is no lack
Of friendliness among you. Why fight for transient happiness?

'Bharata, who will ascend the throne, is no ordinary man;
He is worthy. If not, I would myself have protested.
I would protect your well-being. All of you
Should accept Bharata. See me in him
You will forget your anxiety; The love I have for him
Will be doubled by it.

'Please, clear the way. I am not one to cheat.
I am leaving, eliminating evil people, protecting righteousness,
I shall smite obstruction and fear and bring security.
We are from Bhageeratha's lineage. Power is not a treasure for us.
Like Bhageeratha bringing down Ganga to earth,
I shall establish a new treasure equal to that.
Our only aim is to achieve our goals;
Do not hinder us. You are impartial. Give us
Encouragement. I shall leave behind signs of ideals.'

Like naughty children,
Throwing toys all around and the mother picking them up,
The nectar of Shri Rama's words made the people get up,
Who were lying in front of the chariot. They looked up and saw.
The chariot moved away with the speed of wind:
The turning wheels could not be seen.
There was a bend and at that moment,
The chariot disappeared.

The parks of Saketa,
Rivers and streams, lakes and fields were left behind.
The chariot arrived at the border and stopped.   90
He looked back and saw Saketa.
Deep within was the love of the motherland
Then his eyes were filled with tears!

He spoke to the queen-mother with great respect,
'The pillar of your fame is eternal O, mother!
We shall leave you now and do our duty;
We shall then come back and meet you, mother!
Like birds coming back to the nest.
You are so beautiful. We can never leave you;
Our hearts are filled with your   100
Love, compassion, courtesy, goodness, kindness.
We shall use them all in our journey of righteousness!

'Your pure air has filled our lungs,
Your water is blended with our mind!
Fire in exhalation, in detachment, the sky
The earth in steadiness, this body is made of five elements.
In every form and part, you exist.
In every atom you are me and I am you.
We have fallen and arisen in your yard
Playing and jumping around, we have grown up.   110
Which path is difficult for us to traverse?

'You are the one giving birth to great values, mother!
You are the benevolent polestar, of good character
A dancing peacock. In the great book of your life
Every page is printed with constant virtue. We are children
Playing around you!

'In your home,
In Ayodhya, the regulations of social life
Have been sculptured in a grand manner.
Like Mahashesha in the ocean of milk.   120

We are there, mother, to protect you always;
We shall be victorious. In variety, we shall
Achieve unity. In your goodness, there is peace.
Comfort and prosperity are there in excess.
Enemies will burn in dazzling light.
You are the swing, you are the house of flowers,
You are the treasure of diamonds in the ocean of life
Beautiful as art, giver of happiness, an abode,
And a spring of imagination. Wherever I bloom,
I am a flower offered to you. 130

'Holy Ayodhya is comparable to Heaven.
An unconquerable city, that is Ayodhya!
Save for us mother, that name, until I come back.
Motherland is the mother. There are no other parents,
No other brothers and relations do I have!

'With righteousness, the wilderness is a palace;
Without virtue, even a palace is worse than a graveyard.
There are many ways of doing good.
The call of the forest has opened new doors for me;
Closing the doors of power, listening to the call of the Age, 140
I shall move on.'

The praise of the motherland rising high,
The chariot moving on in the stillness of the forest,
Cool breeze bringing in the sweetness of music,
Knowledge holds the hand of devotion firmly,
Righteousness holds the hand of action!

A flower fell on Rama's head
As if the Wind-god himself had offered it.
In the music of birds, there was compassion.
They reached the river Tamasa, and Saumitri was awake 150
Protecting everyone. His sleep was left behind
With Urmila in Ayodhya!

Looking at the crowd coming behind him,
Rama was enveloped by anxiety at night.

'Crowns of Aryan lineage, I shall keep my promise,
Where there is desire, there does fear harass.
Bharata is a righteous man. Trust in him and move on,'
He consoled them and slept peacefully.

'Unconcerned about their families,
They have come with me; they sleep under trees, 160
Determined to take me back home. They are ready
Even to lose their lives. While they sleep,
Let us cross Tamasa,' said Shri Rama.
In the darkness, they travelled on towards the south.
Shri Rama, Sita, Lakshmana and Sumantra,
Were tired and rested under the *ingudi* tree;
From the womb of darkness, golden light emerged,
The scenes around made their appearance quickly.
The black blanket was drawn aside and the sun appeared
A new dawn of poetic creation emerged. 170

Is there a pause for the wheel of action?
A new dawn from creation, a new experience;
When there is devastation, there is a new world,
As lives move on, they bear stamps of waves in their hearts;
Assuming many forms, they imbibe beauty.

When nature herself is a great artist in colour,
Grand forms are created in many colours.
The blue bend of the sky, the smoothness of the moon,
The ebb and tide of the sea, the swaying of plants and creepers,
Moving clouds assuming myriad shapes. 180
Like memories hidden in the subconscious,
Sweet-voiced ripples emerging from the throats of birds
In the wheel of seasons in many an epoch
Holding an eternal tune, in the game of singing,
Millions of bird-bodies have been shed like dry leaves.
The voice of great music discovered in the search
Is echoed in every living creature in the forest.

While the deep blue of the sky remains mute,
Mountain ranges and thick forests wear rough clothing,
They are in a great search like meditating sages. 190
Boring through mountains, all rivers flow
Towards the sea; at the tip of the tongue of devastation
Kingdoms rise and fall, agonise and disappear
In the womb of time, man in his desire for wealth
Moves on becoming oil to nourish the wick of time.
Who cares for the sun when wealth becomes greater?
Man is dwarfish and cannot climb high.
Taking a divine pledge to attain victory
Sita, Rama and Lakshmana walked on
Like a million shining stars. Greater than the sun 200
In the rule of exist, enveloping the sky
With clusters of stars, with confidence
Like the lighted pillar in the west!

In the light of the rising sun,
They saw the divine river, mother Tamasa, appearing
To stop with expanding waves, flowing as if braided,
Shining as if showing the navel in a whirlpool,
Flowing slow here and fast there, once with a gentle noise,
And roaring at another time. The swan, the *sarasa*,
And *chakravaka* birds with sweet music, crocodiles, fish, 210
And other water animals move about. Wild elephants,
Bears, monkeys and deer move about without fear
On the banks of the river. Sita gazed at everything
In amazement, describing it all to Rama in joy.

Canto Thirty-six

'The Infinite Grandeur of Chitrakoota'

||௬||

Over there, the devotee of Rama, the honour of the hunter clan,
Guha, was the ruler of Shringiverapura.
He was a bosom friend to Shri Rama! He heard the news
And came with joy to meet him. 'With your coming
This land is sanctified; What are your orders, Tell me,'
He said preparing delicious food.
Then Shri Rama told him in friendship:
'Fulfilling father's orders is our duty.
So we are living in the forest like ascetics;
We are wearing rough clothes and cannot eat sweets;   10
Roots and fruits are enough for us. Give food and drinks
To the horses and I shall be happy. We need
The milk of the banyan tree.' Guha brought it.
Rama and Lakshmana smeared it on their hair,
Twisted it into a knot and shone with divine braids!

'Tomorrow at dawn,
Minister Sumantra must return to Ayodhya.
We have to cross the holy Ganga river.
A boat should be prepared for us.'
Guha agreed happily to what was said.   20

Learning about Shri Rama's life in the forest,
Guha's flower-soft heart had melted.
Shri Rama spoke words of advice:
'Good friend Guha, I admire your devotion
You have crossed the sea of worldly existence;
Let the path of devotion be yours. Be one with salvation;
Keep inertness at a distance; be vigilant always.
Between life and god, illusion stands strong
The mind must stay in action without reward;
Illusion must be won over.'   30
At sunrise, Rama said
Farewell to Sumantra lovingly. The pain of separation
Bothered Sumantra but duty pulled him away.
Unable to leave Shri Rama and Sita, horses
Neighed in sorrow as if they had lost their lives!
Wearing rough garments, as soon as they stepped
Into water, Ganga rushed towards Rama's feet with great excitement!
With Lakshmana and Sita,
Shri Rama started getting into the boat.
Guha came in a hurry. 'Stop, stop, O king.   40
This is a poor man's boat, do not step on it.
How can I praise the dust of your feet?
Everyone says that stone itself turned into a girl.
A boat made of wood is soft, where can I seek shelter?
What shall I do if the boat turns into a woman?
I have a wife at home. How can I live with two wives?
Without the boat, the sole means of my livelihood?',
That was what Guha said.
What could be done then?
Wondered Sita, Rama, Lakshmana, greatly perplexed   50
Guha brought a plate and placed
Shri Rama's feet in it. With tears of joy,
He bathed the feet. 'I am not afraid any more.
You may get on the boat. I have washed away
The dust on your feet,' he said joyously.

All the people watched with excitemen,
Dancing, feeling that life had been worthwhile.
The boat journeyed on over Ganga.
Radiant like sages,
Shri Rama and Lakshmana completed rituals 60
And bowed. In a proper manner, Sita begged of Ganga:
'Victory to you, Ganga. O mother, with waves of joy
Full of holy water, with banks of purity,
Full of divine melody, you were born in Heaven
Daughter of Bhageeratha, because of your movement,
The land of Bharata is blessed with wealth.
I beg for the everlasting fortune of seeing and touching you.
As soon as life in the forest is over, I shall offer you full worship.'

Crossing Ganga, saying farewell to Guha,
They went on to the forest. Cool, gentle, fragrant 70
Wind blew and Vaidehi's forelocks
Kissed her eyelids, the mind was pleased
In a beautiful environment, footpaths were seen
Appearing radiant like parting of hair on the head of a goddess.
Shri Rama saw beehives here and there
Among branches of trees. 'A tiny little insect
Doing such great work!' Rama was thrilled
At the grand vision of truth!

Shri Rama said: 'Let the life in a forest be for us.
Saumitri, you be there for Sumitra and mother Kausalya; 80
Go back to the town, Urmila is thinking of you.'
Thus did he try to send him back.
Lakshmana would not agree. He bowed and said:
'Saketa is like a night without the moon.
I cannot return, brother. Why are you anxious?
I cannot live even for a moment without you.
I shall die like a fish thrown out of water!
As you say Lakshmana, let us move on.
What does it matter if there are people or not in the forest,

Perform your duty of protection.
This is a strange place for us. We must always be on our guard.
You walk in front, Sita behind you
I shall protect you both from behind.
We should protect one another, not be careless.'
They spent that night under a banyan tree;
The next day they travelled towards Prayaga,
To the hermitage of Sage Bharadwaja.
Like the flag of the Fire-god, the holy smoke
Rose and filled the sky from the *homa*.
It was the place of the confluence of Ganga and Yamuna,
The radiance of quietness shone.
Entering the hermitage, they saw
The effulgent, meditating strict ascetic
Endowed with divine knowledge. They fell at his feet
Begging for blessings and benediction.
The saint blessed them with great joy.
'We wish to be near the people of Ayodhya.
Please tell us of a secluded holy hermitage, O Guru.'
That was Shri Rama's request.
'Listen, my child. There is a mountain
Beyond river Yamuna, five leagues away.
It is a holy place where a sage lives.
It is a place where *langoor* and bears move about.
It is Chitrakoota, beautiful as sandalwood.
Mountain peaks give incentive to good work
Untouched by sins, many are ascetics
Immersed in meditation, it is the motherland of morality.
It is a land where deer and peacocks go around;
In the mountain ranges, there are waterfalls;
There are many caves and dazzling springs.
It is suitable for your stay in that forest.'
Listening to the description, feeling happy within,
They walked towards the beauteous treasure of Chitrakoota.
They arrived at the banks of Yamuna.

Watching the speed of its flow, they were worried.
Constructing a raft with cane and firewood, they spread
Straw, the fragrant root of *lavancha* and tree branches;
Then, they crossed over safely.

Where did the grandeur of Chitrakoota begin or end?
Shri Rama moved on, describing it excitedly: 130
'Vaidehi, look there, the blooming *palasha* tree;
There are flowers everywhere shining like fire.
The cashew tree sways, fruit trees of many kinds.
Look at the beehive, pots full of honey.
Heaps of flowers have fallen and formed a bed.
This forest is a holy land for meditation.
Lakshmana, build a hut here.
Do not cut living trees. It hurts the environment.
Search for logs of dry wood and bring them over.'
Rama said so and that was what Lakhsmana did.   140
He built a beautiful hut there.
Chitrakoota shone resplendent.
Animals and birds of many kinds, colourful flowers,
Payoshni flowed there with water in abundance.
In one spot, it flowed in the shape of a half-moon,
Curving and gliding, emanating beauty.
Wild flowers dropping at the bank, floated on
In the river.

Varied flowers like *bakula, mandara, padari, karnikara,*
suragi, kuruvaka, kovidara, karaveera, champaka,   150
shireesha, sevantige and *mallige* appeared grand.
Unable to stand the sun's rays, *jaji* wilted;
Samapige danced intoxicated at the touch of the bee;
Increased its fragrance, adding to attraction,
Adirmutte's beauty grew hundred-fold when worn in the hair.
Trees of many kinds – *bilwa, nelhi,* mango,
Coconut, arecanut as well as banana, jackfruit, and
Promegranate – being hit by the trunks of elephants,

Branches were broken here and there. Lion's roar echoed
Here and there. Terror reigned there along with beauty.   160

In the drizzle, the wind was cool,
Blowing the forelocks of huntresses
the swan and heron playing in the pond,
Golden lotus flowers attracting the mind,
The blossoming forest and its beauty
Stretching towards the sky to embrace the moon.
Wonder, joy, truth and happiness
The great and the supreme, divine emotions
It was an instigation for the opening of eyes.

At the time of sunrise,   170
Morning sun filling spaces all around, the tops
Of mountain ranges shone like a ruby, and like coral
In the fresh leaves of trees.

At the time of sunset,
The setting sun appeared to be turning fast
Like a whetstone, the emanating red rays
Like the mouth of a roaring lion,
Like the dust of a brick held at a whetstone.

The beauty of the moonrise
Split the darkness around, appearing to ruffle up red rays.   180
Like a lion showing its red mouth while yawning,
The moon comes up from the peak of Udayachala,
Unmoving quietness was everywhere.

Moonlight could be filled up in pots and carried
Or could be scooped up by hands and drunk
Through the canal of the heart, it could
Be taken to the filed of life as well. Using oars,
The river of earthly life could be crossed. Jumping into the deep,
One could swim across and win. Such was its beauty.

Thus, in Chitrakoota,   190
Shri Rama, Sita and Lakshmana, spent days

In peace and joy. All the peaks, that appeared like pots,
Wished to bathe him. In combination with the sun-rays,
Drops of water spread here and there,
Looked like clusters of diamonds everywhere.
It seemed as if nature herself had seen the beauty
Of Shri Rama, Sita and Lakshmana, and protected them.

Canto Thirty-seven

'A Hundred Thousand Lights Went Off in the Palace'

||๖||

Bidding farewell to Guha, Sumantra
Left Sringaverapura, and travelled towards the city
Of Saketa; but Sumantra seemed to be completaly lost.
The chariot was empty, so was his mind.
He moved on, a prey caught in the shackles of fate.
Horses with speed of wind moved hesitantly
Pulling the chariot without Rama, unwillingly
In a static state devoid of all energy,
They shed tears and were getting tired.

The cold wind disturbed Sumantra's mind; 10
It was like the sky suddenly falling upon him.
Like ghosts opening their mouths and swallowing,
Sumantra was beset by fear. Mother nature
Was shaken and sat in a corner, dumb-founded.
Saketa had collapsed under the weight of great sorrow,
Burnt in the fire of sadness and suffering in separation.
A sea of joy had descended to a dark cave.
All protectors of the city had shrunk sapless
They sat with their heads hidden between their knees

'After everything was looted, why bother about protection?' 20
Appearing to be thinking in this manner, they lived
Like living corpses!

Sumantra's mind
Went back to the forest, remembering Rama and Sita.
Their faces were drawn in the heat of the sun.
The difficult path had exhausted the fair woman
Alas! She stopped, she sat, she sighed.
Shri Rama consoled her: 'Sita, look! The forest there
Is spread as far as the eyes can see; also are seen a lotus pond,
And a bunch of fruits. If we go there, the sun 30
Will not be so fierce,' he said. Holding a large leaf
Against her face, Shri Rama led her towards the lake.
When heat surrounded them, they got into the lake
To wash their faces and drink the clear water.
Under the lovely shade of a mango tree there,
They overcame the tiredness of the journey.

The beautiful and pure daughter of the earth,
Who, like nature, summoned new thoughts of
Unworldly generosity and feelings for those who suffer.
The daughter of nature was divine, always 40
As fragrant as the jasmine.

Pushing each other into the lake,
Deciding to have fun in water, quickly
The daughter of earth would jump about saying,
'The king has lost.'
Wearing rough, clean, white clothes
Radiant with a shining *tilaka* on the forehead
Rama himself would pick up flowers,
Adorn Janaki and admire her beauty.
'Look there, Sita, bears, baboons, tigers and lions 50
Over there, elephants, lions, tigers and leopards,'
'The wealth of this forest, exceeds that of

Saketa as well as the grandeur of Heaven,'
She would say in joy.

Imagining all this,
Sumantra, like the fire within the tree,
Burning the tree itself, agonised, would
Blame what was done in a previous life.
He would blame himself that his duties in Ayodhya endangered him.

Like a thief, stealing all, 60
Sumantra entered the town stealthily.
The sorrowful citizens surrounded him and asked:
'Where is Rama, Janaki and Lakshmana?
Alas! Rama. We are ruined. All our happiness
Has been snatched by fate! Dasharatha's dear treasure is stolen!
Stop Sumantra, have you come away
Leaving behind the ocean of compassion making our lives barren!
Did you give away everyone's joy?
Do not come into the city. If Shri Rama is not there,
A demon hides there, the house is broken. 70
Take the chariot back, bring back again
The fortune of the earth.' As they said it,
Horses shed tears in silence.

Sumantra got off the chariot,
Crossed the seven sectors of the palace and
Entered the eighth, he saw Dasharatha lying
Collapsed on the floor! The boat would sink,
It might not cross the ocean of worldly existence.
He was sad. Like a great elephant caught in the mire
Struggling to come out but unable to do so 80
Like female elephants trumpeting to bring him out
Sumantra saw such scenes before him, helpless!
'Have you left behind the breath of my life?
Minister, I shall come with you and see his lotus-face.
How can the faithful wife walk in the forest?
Are not her tender feet covered in blood, tell me.

Lakshmana is still a boy. How can he face the burning sun?
There are wild animals in the forest, how will they live?
What message did Shri Rama and Lakshmana send me?
Tell me, please do,' demanded the king.   90

'Let go of sorrow, king. You shall see
Victorious Sita, Rama and Lakshmana returning.
We should await the happiness to come.'
Sumantra consoled the king and spoke of
The message Shri Rama had sent.

'I am eager father, to give up all rules,
Come near you and serve you.
The heart longs for the joy of the touch of your hands.
Alas, the restraining hook of duty
Is stopping me. I shall come, be at peace!   100
I shall acquire spiritual power and peace in the forest.'

The message for Kausalya:
'Mother, think of what is righteous, let worship be carried on;
Let the king's welfare be your ritualistic rule.
When he is god, do not let go of his feet.
You are the eldest, be patient and controlled.
Treat the other mothers with concern.
If Kaikeyi is the king's mother, follow her;
If Bharata is king, give him high respect.

Sumantra thought within   110
Kaikeyi has done the right thing. The king has killed Shambara;
Shambara's sons live in the forest;
The wild fire of revenge would burn Saketa.
The daughter of Kaikeya had plotted well;
Rama will go there and destroy them.

The king heard what Sumantra said
'Where is peace for me? Where can I find it?
I am battered, caught in the hands of rebellious Kaikeyi.
The embodiment of courtesy and obedience, mass of sympathy.

Should one think nothing of being a king and go away? 120
My ambitions are broken, the chariot is empty.
Oh, son! Shri Rama, destroyer of evil, Abhirama,
Established on the throne in everyone's heart;
Did you go away to the forest instead of caring for me!

Courteous daughter of Videha, who is
Holy Saraswati, Shakti Maheshwari, great Gayatri.
Vishwambharikumari, Varahi, Vaishnavi, Durgi, Chamundi,
Paramasati, Savitri, Sandhya Taruni, the embodiment
Of Adishakti, daughter of milk and curds,
The goddess who brings all that is good to Ayodhya, 130
What did she say, Sumantra?'

'What can I say, O king!
No words would come out. The daughter of the earth stammered.
She remembered Saketa over and over again and lowered her gaze.
She gazed at the sky and bowed to the sun.
Tears filled her eyes.
While Rama stood at the back, she appeared
Like salvation standing near a sage.'

'Giving me a life in the forest, should Shri Rama leave?
It is too much, my hands are broken, 140
My eyes don't want to see, disjoined
All joy is a mirage, life will not go.
Is this flood of sorrow not enough,' said the king
Beating his forehead, he cried.
'Not willing to leave Rama,
The horses were stubborn. I consoled them and brought them back.
I have brought sorrow itself in the chariot, O king!
While I was with Guha in Sringaverapura
The hope that Rama would change his mind;
Was lost. I returned alone!' 150

Dasharatha was drowning in the sea of sorrow;
'Rama, Lakshmana, Sita', he wailed aloud.

The pain of separation was striking like a wave;
Lamentation resounding like the roar of the sea.
The words of short Manthara had swallowed all like a crocodile.
The boat of life had struck the rock, Kaikeyi, and was in pieces.
Kausalya was begging Sumantra to take her
To the forest.

'Do not feel sad, mother,
Shri Rama and Sita are happy in the forest;   160
Janaki is with her beloved, fearless.
Though there may be a hurricane or the burning sun,
She enjoys herself like a bird in the sky.
For the jangling of her anklets,
All animals and birds dance.'
Sumantra consoled Kausalya with such words.

In silence, Urmila slept.
Like a lotus separated from water, rubbed roughly
With hands and thrown away. In the flush of youth,
She was clothed like an ascetic. The hope of Lakshmana's   170
Return dried up when Sumantra came.
'Pardon me beloved for my untoward thoughts
Remembering you, I shall gain the power of forbearance.
While Sita and Rama sleep, while you are awake
Think of me, that will be like a fountain of love for me.' –
She remembered all she had said.

Sumitra remembered what she had said
When Rama and Lakshmana left for the forest:
'Dasharatha is your natural father, Rama is the true father;
I am the mother who gave you a body, Sita is the mother   180
To you, anywhere and always. Let the narrow concept
Of ego die in that which is without death. Saumitri, do not lose
This treasure on earth.'

The agony of the people overflows;
Mothers who had children cried for their being born

After Shri Rama was driven to the forest.
Slack were all the elements
Of Dasharatha's senses in great sorrow.
'Were the boys sacrificed to the madness of my lust?
Did I drive away the three gems of my life to the forest?   190
The one who is capable of freeing one from life's cycle;
The other who can make the whole world tremble;
And Sita, who can save all the sinners in this world;
Did I drive them mercilessly into the forest!

'Beauty, youth, grandeur, good fortune and longevity
Are like lightning, rainbow and a bubble in water.
Prey to the momentary joy of Kaikeyi's companionship
Have I pushed the pinnacles of fame of the Raghu-clan
Into the precipice? Tell me Sumantra, did Rama say
He would come back, did Sita say so, and Lakshmana?   200
My life is without essence. It is like a dry leaf.
Set it on fire, let everything turn into ashes.
Tell me, how can I live without my sons?
What other meaning is there to my life?
Immorality is running. It is chasing
Death and has caught it. I need justice,
Beauty, goodness and enlightenment all supreme
To console my burnt-out heart, my forefather
Have come with Indra. See them. This is Dilip Chakri.
This is my father, Raghuveera, the king of Aja.   210
They have come to lift me up and
Take me to the path of righteousness.

'Sita, Rama and Lakshmana are young and delicate;
Can they stand life in a forest! After eating a fine meal,
Should Maithili eat just rice in a forest?
How can they sleep with only arms as pillows!
Will not my heart break into a thousand pieces!

'In the fifteenth year,
Will Rama come back, will he accept the kingdom?

When nectar is served who will eat left-over food?
Will the lion eat meat discarded by another animal?
Will the offerings used in one *yajna*, 220
The *ghee*, the flour, straw, *kaggali* wood, and the pole
Be used in another ritual, Sumantra?
The kingdom ruled over by Bharata,
Will Rama accept it, tell me!'

Unable to bear the pain, Kausalya spoke:
'When the husband is the primary god to a wife,
The son is the second support and relatives, the third.
There is no fourth path for a wife. O king,
In lustful haste, did you drive Ramachandra to the forest.
The kingdom of Ayodhya could be caught 230
In the whirlpool of anarchy!'

'Are you not kind-hearted? I beg you with folded hands.
Forgive me. I am unfortunate. If not you,
Who else will console me,' said Dasharatha
In a most pitiful manner.
Like rain water flowing along the roof
Kausalya cried, tears streaming over her face.
She held Dasharatha's hand and placing it on her head
She said, 'I beg you with my head bowed, I gave you pain
Stricken by anguish about my son, I blamed you hastily. 240
The turmoil of sorrow has swooped down and ruined judgement.
The five days without Rama have hurt
Me as much as five years would.'

Losing consciousness over and over again
He would be dipped in a sea of sorrow and come up again;
Like Rahu grabbing the sun and swallowing him.
The separation from Shri Rama and Lakshmana was doing the same.
At midnight on the sixth day, he remembered the evil deed
As he cried saying he would give up his life:

'Without thinking of right and wrong, 250
I began something and am paying for it now.

Taken in by the grandeur of the *palasha*, I cut down the mango grove
I was foolish. Thinking I was the master of shooting by sound,
I was vain and was cursed for it.
It is swallowing me like a black cobra.
Like the river in its rush breaching the banks,
Sorrow is boring into all senses.
Why does the eye not see nor the ear hear!
The senses of touch, feeling, and smell are all dead.
A poisoned arrow has entered my body and the venom is
   spreading.   260
There is no cure. I am defeated and wasted.

'Where are you, Shri Rama, my beloved child?
You are the light of my eye. Lakshmana, where are you?
Where are you daughter of Janaka, why do you not see me?
Shri Rama with strong arms, can you not embrace me?
Like a lamp without oil, my energy is going down;
I am the river about to join the sea
I cannot see nor can you.
O Rama, O Sita, O Lakshmana! Today
My life will end!'   270

The agony of death had enveloped him;
It was like thunder striking from the womb of dark clouds.
Each and every nerve in Dasharatha's body stiffened.
Shaking in anxiety, tears rolled down,
There was brightness and eventually the bright light went out!
Thus, in great pain, the king breathed his last.
The light of the Ikshwaku clan
Had gone out. Separation from sons had taken life away.
Shabdavedhi, the art of shooting, focussing on sound,
Had turned into a prelude for a curse, it had borne fruit.   280
A hundred thousand lights went off in the palace;
Everything was drowned in darkness!

Canto Thirty-eight

'Did the Huge Tree of the Raghu Clan Fall Prey to Slander?'

||☉||

The mind was empty, so was the world;
The terrible sorrow-filled cry spread through the palace.
The queens were like creepers burnt in a forest fire.
Calling out for the king, they fell to the ground,
Like a female elephant trumpeting at the death of the elephant king,
And rolling on the ground, the queens rolled on the floor,
Hiding his face in his hand, Sumantra wept.

There was a bond between birth and death;
Joy at birth and sorrow at death.
The great Sage Vasishtha knew all that   10
Nevertheless, he collapsed in grief.
The loftiness of Hemadri peak was on the king's face.
He was asleep and would see his sons
In his dreams, that was the emotion on the face.
It was soul gone beyond dream, wakefulness and sleep
Set free from bondage, a chapter of Ikshwaku clan
Was completed and the preface for a new chapter was ready.

Kausalya kept the king's head on her lap:
'Did the huge tree of the Raghu-clan fall prey to slander?

I shall fall into fire. My life is empty.' 20
She wept in great sorrow
'The world is an illusion. Everything is ordained by fate.
Time will devour everything.
No one is there for anyone else. Can fate be changed?
When the sun has set, who will take away the darkness?
Console yourself, Kausalya,' said Vasishtha
In order to soothe her.

Lustreless like stars fallen from the sky,
All the women in the palace were grieving;
The sound of lamentation grew and spread. 30

The sorrow of separation from Rama
Was not over or faded; they worked like machines,
The panegyrists and singers all greeted the morning
And praised the king. They sang of times past
And moved on gently; here and there, birds
Joined the music; everyone waited to see the king.
Women walked slowly in doubt and suspicion;
Hearing the news of death, they trembled!

Like wild fire, the news of the death spread;
The sound of crying was all over Ayodhya;
Saketa was drowned in the sea of sorrow; 40
A multitude gathered before the palace!

Markandeya, Moudgalya, Vamadeva, Kashyapa,
Gautama, Jabali and all other sages gathered.
All citizens of importance held a meeting
Along with Vasishtha: 'Shri Rama and Lakshmana
Have gone to the forest; Bharata and Shatrughna
Are at their grandparents'; there must be a king,
And coronation must be held at once.
Otherwise, everything will be upside down.
No clouds will gather and no rain will fall. 50
There will be no sowing and morality will be lost.

Sons will not obey their parents,
Nor will wives listen to what their husbands say.

A wrong path will be taken and work will go on;
All people will spend their days in fear;
Worship in temples will go on haltingly;
Rituals will stop with the fear of the *rakshasas*;
Listening to holy stories and meetings of goodwill will stop.
Dancers and actors will become dull and withdrawn;
There will be no art, no joy or lively meetings. 60
Commerce and business will weaken without progress;
The people will fall into depression and sleep.
The guardians of all eight directions will feel exhausted!
Without a king, the land will become a wilderness.
Call Bharata to be crowned as king; until then,
The king's body should be kept in oil drums and protected.

'Siddhartha, Vijaya, Jayanta, Ashoka, Nandana,
Let us go fast in a horse chariot to Rajagriha.
Bharata should not be told the news of the king's death;
He should only be told that he needs to come without delay. 70
Kaikeyi's beloved son should be brought in safety.
Hiding the disastrous news, gold jewellery should be
Offered to Kaikeya.'

The five messengers travelled
At the speed of wind in chariots, westwards.
Crossing hills and hillocks, crossing river Mahini
To the north of Pralambagiri, near Hastinapura
Crossing the river Ganga, moving west
Travelling through the middle of Kurujangana
Reaching Panchala, on the way seeing
The clear waters of the radiant Divyasharadanda river 80
Bowing to the holy tree, shelter of diving beings
Crossing Kalinganagara, Tejobhi *bhavana*,
Seeing Tamasa river served by the Raghu-clan
They reached Bahleeka land.

Looking at the learned Dwija
Drinking water from cupped hands,
Remembering the Aryan saying
That it was not the right thing to do,
They reached Sudamaparvata, bowed at the feet of Vishnu.
The emissaries from Ayodhya crossed Vipasha Shalmali river,
They arrived at Girivajra Rajagriha,   90
The capital of Kaikeya kingdom, the abode of wealth.

Bharata was not at ease,
Many a bad dreams troubled him at night.
Wearing soiled clothes, hair dishevelled
Dasharatha climbing a hill, falling into some
Pit of filth and swimming around in it,
Laughing wildly and drinking oil with cupped hands
Bending his head, eating sesame seeds,
Wearing black clothes, sitting on an iron throne,
Red sandalwood smeared all over.   100
Wearing a garland of red *kepula* flower
Dark women smiling widely
Looking at all that.

Like the tusks of the imperial elephant getting pulverised,
Like climbing a chariot harnessed by an ass
As they travelled south, it was as if a horrid
Rakshasi, wearing a red sari, laughing wildly
Was pulling the wheel away from the chariot.
As if the sea had dried and the moon fallen on the ground
Like a brightly burning fire suddenly going out,   110
Like burnt out mountains spewing smoke!

Dreaming such terrifying dreams,
Bharata woke up in fear and was worried.
His throat went dry and joy was lost.
What might have happened to his father, and to Rama?
How were Saumitri and the mothers?
Waking up in the morning, Bharata
Wandered up and down in the palace.

By that time,
The emissaries from Ayodhya entered the palace. 120
Bowing to Kaikeya from a distance, when they saw him,
They offered the gift of jewels respectfully.
'We are messengers from King Dasharatha;
We bow to Bharata and Shatrughna;
We carry an order from the king,
That Bharata and Shatrughna should immediately
Return to the kingdom. It is his order.
We beg you to send them without delay.'
So said the messengers expressing a feeling of joy.

King Kaikeya gave gifts to Bharata and Shatrughna. 130
Blessing them with love and embracing them,
With all excitement, he sent them off.
Bharata travelled back at the speed of wind.
As the bad dreams kept troubling him,
They arrived near Saketa.

'O charioteer, control the speed of the chariot;
My mind is trembling in fear. Like a bow strung,
The body is trembling, sorrow overflows;
Inexpressible pain has weakened me;
A silence like that at midnight is all over this place. 140
The sight of darkness in the evening has become
A net of illusion. There is no sign of wind.
The leaves on trees are still, and appear to stand
With their heads bent. Ponds and lakes appear lifeless.
Gathering of citizens, music and entertainment
Are all stilled, alas! The reason is unknown.

'The gurgling of river Sarayu is not heard.
Why is the chanting of the Vedas not heard?
There is the silence of a graveyard everywhere.
All the eulogists appear like living corpses; 150
Joy has faded. Birds do not sing; with wings folded,
They are lying in their nests in silence.

'There is not a soul walking on the road;
There is gloom everywhere and anxiety as well.
Smoke and fragrance of incense and sandalwood aren't there;
My heart is breaking. I am unaware of what is happening.'
While Bharata felt troubled and anxious,
The chariot entered the city through the main entrance,
Vijayanta. As the chariot stood before the palace,
Minister Siddartha held his hand out for the son   160
To welcome him. Bharata asked him: 'Why this anxiety?
What has happened to Raghu lineage? Why do you look tired
Like someone getting out of a tiger's cage?'
He raised questions and Siddhartha spoke:
'It is a truth for all times, the path is difficult
To a place where all mysteries are hidden,
A place difficult even for the sages to reach,
Dasharatha has gone to that place.'

It was a riddle and Bharata could not understand.
He entered the palace and worried at not seeing his father,   170
He ran to his mother's palace. Kaikeyi, sitting
On a golden throne embraced him and stroked his head.
'How long was the journey? Are you tired, my child?
Is my father Kaikeya well? How are Yadhajith
And all the people of the kingdom?' She asked with love.

'Seven nights were spent on the journey; I rushed in haste.
Everyone is well in grandfather's kingdom;
Why is everything here enveloped in deep sorrow?
Why are the servants and maids sad?
Why is the golden bed empty?   180
Where is father? He is not in the palace!
I must touch his feet and show respect;
Is he in mother Kausalya's palace?
Where is Rama and where is Saumitri?'
Asked Bharata greatly distressed.

'He is a king with radiance, he had performed *yajna*;
He has gained a natural end, my son!
With Sita and Lakshmana, wearing fibre cloth,
Rama has gone to the forest to live there.
Listen to the final message from your father: 190
"Valiant Rama will return with Sita and Saumitri;
Those who set eyes on him then are blessed".
Saying so, he breathed his last.'

Canto Thirty-nine

'I am the Bee at the Lotus Feet of Rama'

||৬||

Listening to those words, drowned in sorrow,
Bharata said: 'Shri Rama is pure in action. What is the stain?
What Brahmin's property did he steal?
He is righteous. Did he desire another's wife?
Did he destroy a foetus? Did he kill the helpless?'
When Bharata asked, Kaikeyi answered him;
She spoke proudly of what she had done:
'Rama has done nothing wrong. He will not do so either.
While his coronation was about to take place,
I reminded the king of the two boons he had promised me.   10
For one, your coronation as the king; the second,
Rama leaving for the forest. Without straying from truth,
Rama left for the forest; Janaka's daughter and Lakshmana
Went with him. When the curse he had been given bore fruit,
Shattered without the presence of his sons,
He breathed his last and achieved salvation!

'Bharata, accept your right, the kingdom.
This is a natural status gained as bride-price.
You have not snatched anyone's treasure;
I thought of this plan to get you the kingdom;   20

This is Manthara's cleverness. One should praise her.
Get on the throne. Lakshmi is fickle-minded;
The Dwija will not help you, attend to obsequies;
Do not weep, do not get tired, do not let go of courage.'
Bharata was thunderstruck when he heard all that;
Unable to bear the pain, he said in anger:

'What did you do, mother? I am so luckless.
Father cannot come back. An elder brother like a father,
What kind of justice is it to send him to a forest?
Did you sprinkle salt on a wound? 30
Did you come into the palace like a dark night?
Not knowing the secret of your character,
Father embraced flames of fire and was taken by death.
Proving hurtful to the clan, you have swallowed
The embodiment of love and now become a widow.
Did mother Kausalya plan something evil for you?
Exploding the fort of righteousness with jealousy,
Did you make the great man wear fibre cloth?

'Were you foolish, mother?
Who can carry the weight that the Mount Meru can? 40
Can a small calf pull the load that a bullock can?
Caught in your wickedness and greed,
I cannot carry the burden of ruling a kingdom.
Rama is the eldest son. He should be given
The throne and power. That is the conduct of the Raghu lineage.
What you have committed is a terrible crime.
While Rama is the king, I shall be a slave;
The punishment of exile should be given to you.
You are a gland of poison; get away from here, you traitress!'
So, in great fury, 50
Bharata scolded Kaikeyi and roared.
His voice echoed throughout the palace,
Eyes were red as live coal.
Clothes were loosened; jewels scattered.

Like an elephant in heat controlled by a hook,
Like a cobra hissing with the hood spread,
Bharata appeared and Kaikeyi was fearful!

Not stopping her efforts,
Kaikeyi went near him and stroked him:
'Do not say anything, child. You are not so foolish
That you cannot understand the depth of a mother's love.
Do not refuse the throne and treasury of Ayodhya.
Let the whole world censure me. I can withstand the pain.
I desire love, faith and trust.
I shall go through hell seven times over;
You reign over seven kingdoms and live.'

'What is this obduracy mother?
Your words pierce me as a sword would;
It is harassing me like a monster.
Blind love for the son burns and consumes.
Death sentence is too lenient for you;
You should suffer in a hundred hells!

'Should one forego righteousness,
Caught in greed for kingdom? The boons granted
By the king have become curses to the lineage.
If I want kingdoms, I shall fight and acquire them.
With the strength of my arms, I shall build
A hundred Ayodhyas. A wrong path is not to be followed
To become a king. I shall be accused of being a conspirator.
The bond of a mother – but you are not my mother;
If I die, you shall not mourn for me;
I shall not mourn you if you die!

'Sacrificing Shri Rama's joy,
Did you try to partake of the heavenly drink?
My pledge is selfless service.
Nature herself is trembling at your behaviour.

Will the moon and all the stars fall off?
I feel too detached to sit on the throne.
All seats of selfishness will be destroyed;
You will see the birth of a new epoch; 90
Kings will fall and only men will be left.
The island of selfishness will sink; greed
And arrogance will be destroyed; differences of
Caste and creed will be erased in the world!
Talking of one lineage, one land, and oneness in all,
The world will assume a divine form.

'Mother, listen. I shall take two vows.
On the king, on the sun, on father Shri Rama,
The kingdom of Ayodhya is meant for Shri Rama.
Even if father descends to earth, I shall not rule; 100
I shall neither relax nor sleep, until Rama
Is enthroned! I shall burn in the fire of separation
From brother. This is in reply for your boons, mother.
Listen! Let the kingdom of Ayodhya move on in step
With the epoch. This is a crown worn by Raghu,
Bhageeratha and Sagara; if the son of Kaikeyi
Even touches it, he will himself turn into ashes.
The aim of the kingdom is joy and peace for citizens.
The officials of the kingdom are servants of the people.'
Said Bharata stating his decision. 110

Bharata, a jewel of righteousness,
Desired progress whereas Kaikeyi devised success.
One was the north pole, the other, the south,
Very distant, very far, a link never to be had.
The mother felt sure Bharata would like what she did.
Kaikeyi dreamed of being the king's mother;
Bharata broke the dream with the saw of sacrifice.
The tree of blind love had fallen; in Kaikeyi's
Heart, a tree of wisdom had sprouted.

Listening to what Bharata said, 120
The dirt in her mind was cleansed and became fresh.
The mind was born again in the flames of anguish.
What was done for her son's welfare had become
An evil deed. Her mind was given to rethinking.
It was good. She was sanctified and shone.
There was the beginning of change.
Good people are born from bad wombs as well;
Why are bad people born of good people?

Hearing of Bharata's arrival,
Kausalya and Sumitra, eager to see him, 130
Came there, minds filled with sorrow.
Kausalya collapsed with renewed grief.
Getting up herself she spoke to Bharata:
'You have got the kingdom. There are no dangers;
Rule with firmness, we wish you well.
You do not know why Rama went to the forest.
I beg you to grant me my son quickly.
Without Rama, breath certainly will forsake my body.'

Listening to these harsh words,
Bharata did not know what to do. His mind swayed, 140
The earth and sky became one. With eyes streaming
With tears, almost fainting, he rolled on
To Kausalya's feet and spoke:

'Am I not your son? Is there anything lacking in love?
That I am Kaikeyi's son is just an accident of life.
I am a bee at the lotus-feet of Rama.
I am brother in name, I am your slave.
I wear the armour of his compassion at all times;
I shall move on in the path of devotion, in search of Truth.
I have done nothing wrong. Do not blame me mother! 150

'I do not approve of Shri Rama's going to the forest.
If I am at fault let all the knowledge I have gained

From my mentors be nullified. Then, let the sins
Of the world envelop me and drive me mad.
If I am the wrong-doer, punish me, mother;
Give me permission to wear the dust of your feet
On my head. I shall be destroyed, I swear on the sun,
The god of our lineage; I swear on Dasharatha,
The ocean of Ikshwaku clan.'
Hurt in sorrow, swearing in a rough manner,   160
Bharata wept in grief.

Kausalya's mind melted with love. She said
In affection: 'Do not swear on anything, son.
It is enough. I feel anguished. Grief will increase.
Do I not know the minds of my children.
You are from Raghu lineage, you are truthful,
Your soul is pure, you love your brothers;
I was empty without Rama and you filled the vacant space.
For me, there is no difference between you and Rama,
You are both gold images cast in the same mould,'
She spoke and embraced Bharata.   170
She cried aloud and the heart was squeezed dry.

With the weight of sorrow, Bharata fell down in a faint.
Kausalya and the mothers trembled in fear,
As if they had trodden on a snake, sprinkled water on him;
Stroked his body and comforted him.

'Until I make Shri Rama sit on the throne
Of Ayodhya, I shall live to bear the accusation
Of the world. Until the black cloud of sin melts away,
I shall live to expiate my sins,'
Bharata proclaimed.   180

The night was spent in grief.
At the break of dawn, Sage Vasishtha arrived
'May good things befall you Bharata. Do not be sorrowful.
Will the river that has reached the sea, turn back again?

In future, the welfare of the world will come about.
All action has the sense of managing.
The world will acquire immense joy gathered by sacrifice.
Remember Rama, the jewel of Raghu lineage,
Remember Saumitri and sister-in-law Janaki.
Saumitri's sacrifice is unswaying and difficult,   190
Shri Rama's ideals have opened a golden path.
The image of a universal vision will unfold.
Let the funeral rites be done. It is not right to delay.
The citizens are immersed in anxiety.'
The sage consoled them with such words.
Weakened by sorrow,
Sumitra and Kausalya were consoled by the sage.
'Do not grieve, mothers. Do not ask how
The weight of widowhood can be borne.
Now you have love without involvement,   200
Prosperity inspired by a pure mind,
The feeling of lust is burnt and the mind will
Choose devotion. You are full of fire now.
The memory of your husband will give you all
A new life and expansion.' Thus, he consoled them.
Approaching Bharata,
Kausalya said, 'Look at yourself
With introspection, Do not run away!
I have won over emotion and passion, I am passionless.
Your sacrifice is big. You have given up the kingdom,   210
As if it was straw. Lakshmana, Bharata, Shatrughna,
Urmila, Sumitra, you are the pinnacles of humanity.
It cannot be said who is greater in good action.
'Adishesha, your good qualities cannot be counted.
Become brave and get up. Move on without losing courage.
The grief of father's death and the grief of brother's separation,
Endure them as if they were the arrows of an enemy.
Face difficulties and retain your individuality;
Do not forget your duty in your great grief.

The Goddess of Death admires a man of action. 220
May the citizens of Ayodhya imbibe your strength;
Let there be millions with souls like Bharata's.

Canto Forty

'If there are Brothers, They must be Like Bharata'

||६||

Dasharatha's body, in a boat-shaped container of oil
Was taken out, cleansed and decorated well.
Sunrise arrived waking everyone.
Sages and priests hastened everyone,
Those who performed *yajna*, brought everything out
From the palace to where the sacred fire was.
Helpers moved on, shedding tears.

Placing the body in a decorated palanquin,
While the shoulders of Bharata and Shatrughna were steady,
The procession moved on enveloped in silence,   10
Waves of sorrow surging in Bharata's heart.
Mother Nature had a grief-stricken countenance,
A light drizzle fell from the sky,
As silver and gold coins were tossed at the palanquin.
The citizens crying, overcome with sorrow,
The funeral procession moved on towards the banks of Sarayu.
The sound made by the rushing river was one of sorrow.
The funeral pyre was prepared from *devadaru* and firewood.
The fragrance of sandalwood, perfume and incense spread;

Priests chanted verses about the father's funeral;　　　　20
The body was taken down from the palanquin
And laid on the pyre. Everyone was sad.
They went round the body with respect.
Filled with devotion,
Everyone offered the final obeisance to the son of Aja.
Bharata lit the fire and it burnt fiercely.
People who had gathered read *Samagana*.
The cloud of smoke appeared to envelop the sun.
The flames were reflected in the river;
They went round the pyre from the right,　　　　30
Bharata, Shatrughna, and priests and ministers.
Sumitra, Kausalya and Kaikeyi were immersed in sorrow,
Grief overflowing, Bharata put his hands together respectfully;
A stream of tears flowed form his eyes.
'Where did you go father, who will look after me
Without elder brothers, I am really an orphan.
I do not want the kingdom my mother acquired for me.
To whom can I speak of the pain within me?
I carry the censure of stealing Rama's treasure;
How shall I spend my days in the fire of worry?　　　　40
You are free, I am bound;
I cannot stay here. I shall leave right now,
I shall bring my brother back and crown him.'
So cried Bharata piteously.
The queens were in anguish like *krauncha* birds;
The grief of citizens had crossed all boundaries!

The body disappeared in the fire.
They bathed in Sarayu river then,
Going back to the palace, they spent
Ten nights performing rituals. On the eleventh day,　　　　50
The special rituals for the dead were performed.
Charity, money and things of value,
While goats, gifts of cows, houses and land
Were given to the receivers. In mass feeding,

The people of Saketa were satisfied. Then they
Prayed for peace for the departed soul.
Bharata and Shatrughna
Conferred about what was to be done next.
The dwarf, fully adorned with jewels was seen at the east gate;
She had smeared perfume all over her body. 60
She wore a silk sari worthy of queens,
Variously shaped bands were around her waist,
She was flaunting herself as if she had done a great deed.
The guard became furious.
Wild with anger, they scolded the hunchback:
'She alone is the cause for the calamity.
She is like an axe to the lineage. Punish the sinner.'
Saying so, they stopped Manthara.
As soon as he saw Manthara,
Shatrughna was enveloped in anger. 70
Dragging her by force from among other women,
He flashed his sword shouting he would kill her.
Manthara screamed loud enough to shatter the palace.
'Pay for what you have done. You must be punished
For your crime.' At his roar, the whole palace trembled.
'Stop, stop,' said Bharata,
Rushing there and standing like a rock to protect Manthara.
'It is not right to kill a woman, brother!
Forgive her. She is the daughter of a maid.
Rama will not like this. What does she know? 80
She is just a cause.' Shatrughna's anger subsided.
He walked away.
On the fourteenth day,
Mentors, priests and ministers spoke to Bharata.
This is the kingdom of Ayodhya. It is now without a king
You must look after the Saketa kingdom;
The citizens wait. We request your permission.
You have done nothing wrong. Ascend the throne,
Everything needed for the coronation is ready.

In a serious voice
Bharata spoke: He understood the feelings of the people gathered.
'Do you not know the tradition of the Ikshwaku lineage?
When the eldest son is alive, how can a younger son become king?
It is not as if you do not know. Is it right to cross limits?
I shall bring Rama and seat him on the throne.
Let the army go in search of Rama,
Let us crown him there. Bring everything over,
I shall bring Rama back here.
I shall make him ascend the throne,
There is no blemish in him from beginning to end.
Shri Ramachandra is a divine form;
If he does not agree, I shall stay back in the forest.
Let preparation be afoot,
Make the road to Dandakaranya better,
Rama will come back in a grand palanquin,
Have protective armies in dangerous places.
Proclaim this as my order in the city.'
Everyone liked Bharata's stand and blessed him,
Tears of joy were in their eyes.
Everyone was set to leave.
Preparation was carried out with speed and zest.
Those that knew the land were the leaders;
Behind them were efficient guards
Experts in making machines and sculptors.
Labourers, carpenters, road-building experts,
Masons, basket-weavers, blacksmiths
As well as those experts at digging wells were all there.

Cutting down huge trees, pulling away bushes,
They built a road in the deep forest.
Pits and raised ground, burrowed holes
Were flattened, building bridges to cross streams,
Making reservoirs here and there, they moved on
Digging canals, building tanks,
Pouring lime water on either side of the road.

Camps were built and flags flew high.
They built frames and constructed places to stay.
On the fourteenth day the people of Ayodhya
Went on with enthusiasm.
An elephant leading, the great path
For the great search was formed thus.   130
Everyone moved on happily determined to bring Rama.
The army chief, mentors, priests,
Yudhajit, Sumantra, mothers, Bharata, Shatrughna,
Yajnavalkya and other sages as well –
Everyone moved on chanting Rama's name.
'Dasharatha sent Rama for the sake of truth;
He went to the world of truth himself. He is the truth.
This is a pilgrimage for truth to bring back Satyarama.
Truth here, truth hereafter.   140
Let us achieve truth, joy and happiness;
The ornament of Ikshwaku lineage, Bharata, is our mentor.
His sacrifice is something for us to follow;
If there are brothers, they should be like Bharata.'
Praising him thus, everyone moved on.
Bharata proclaimed in a loud voice.
'I shall bring Shri Rama back from the forest.
This is the goal of my life, this is the Great Quest.
Let us all bow to Shri Rama, that great man,   150
That god from Saketa! He is the master
Of all the three worlds and I am his slave.
Let not temptation catch me in its magic net.'
Listening to Bharata speaking in such a manner,
Admiring his brotherly love, they moved on.

Canto Forty-one

'In a Hut there, lives Shri Rama'

||๑||

Bharata got ready to see Shri Rama
Along with ministers, priests and the army.
Mothers Kausalya, Sumitra and Kaikeyi,
Potters, weavers, goldsmiths, blanket-makers,
Washermen, tailors, boatmen, people who could make arms,
Artisans and priests, scholars, all gathered together,
In great excitement, eager to see Rama
With increasing joy they travelled on.

They reached the banks of the Ganga.
Thinking of how to bring Rama back 10
Bharata spent the night conferring with others.
Over there, the king of hunters had deep
Consultations at midnight. 'The army of Bharata
Is spread out like an ocean. On chariots,
Flags with the emblems of Bharata,
The *kovidara* plant, are flying. Has he come to kill Rama?
If he wants war, we shall stop him from crossing the Ganga,'
Said Guha.
Along with his wife,
Guha took fish and meat, fruits with honey as 20

Offering and acted with love!
Guha's wife Saumya was a heavenly beauty.
Both showed respect to everyone
'Friend, you tell me. Will Rama return?
He should be brought back to Ayodhya's palace.
That is why I have come. You be with me.
The nooks and corners of Dandakaranya
Are well-known to you. Show me Rama.'
Guha was happy when he said that. 30

When the serpent of suspicion
Swayed its hood in his mind, Guha said to Bharata:
'I am gratified. Consider this land of hunters
A garden in your own palace.
The forest is difficult to walk through. My people will show you
The way with care. I shall come with you.
I was suspicious when I saw the big army.
Was there a plot here to harm Rama?
I was eager to find out. Forgive me for my harsh words.'
Bharata was anguished when he heard it. 40
'Do not doubt, Guha,
Shri Rama and Sita are like father and mother to me.
I want to take them back from the forest. That is the truth.
This is mine, that is someone else's; this is sweet, that is bitter;
This is fair, that is not. This should be taken out, discarded.
When a wild dance like this with such differences
Goes on, I have given it up and learnt to see the whole
In each part; I have built-up the truth of non-duality!

'While the dream of Rama's coronation
Turned to dust, father's desire to live died. 50
He would not eat, sleep was abandoned;
The palace of Saketa was immersed in silence;
Food does not taste good any more,'
Said Bharata weeping copiously.
Guha felt glad and satisfied.

'You are a fortunate man and incomparable.
You have reached the peak of self-sacrifice, O king!
Would anyone let go of a kingdom offered?
May your fame be steady and long-lasting,'
Guha praised him. 60

'Where was my brother, where was my sister-in-law?
How did they lie down on hard earth?
Where was Lakshmana, he is fortunate!
What did they eat, how did they spend the night?
Tell me everything, Guha. That will be sweet for me to hear,'
With those words, Bharata fell to the ground
Like an elephant, and lost consciousness.
Seeing that, mothers surrounded him at once.
Shatrughna held his brother in tight embrace;
Overflowing with sadness, Kausalya hugged him 70
And consoled him. 'We trust you. You are the support
For our lives. After the king died, you are our protector,'
Thus she comforted him in every way possible.
Watching the intensity of brotherly love,
Guha said in relief: 'Shri Rama was with me last night.
He would not eat the food offered since a Kshatriya
Should not accept it from others.
Shri Rama ate the fruits that Saumitri brought;
Sita and Lakshmana followed Rama and did the same.
Then with great piety, they said the evening prayers. 80
Saumitri brought straw and prepared a bed
Under the *ingudi* tree that you can see.
Without a worry or discomfort, Sita and Rama slept.

'Saumitri with the quiver tied to his back,
Held the great bow in his hand and all night without blinking,
Guarded them. To be of support, I stayed here with him.
The very next day, I helped them cross the Ganga.
"Living for fourteen years in a forest is difficult;
The burning sun in the thick forest is unbearable.

You stay here, mother; let Rama fulfill his promise," 90
Suggested Saumya to mother Sita, who soothed her,
And said quietly that living in a forest brought her joy.'
Bharata listened
With concern to all that had happened.
Calling the mother, he walked quickly to the *ingudi* tree.
'Mothers, look. This is where Rama slept.
I can see the signs of his sleeping and rolling over.
Alas! The dear son of Dasharatha, the eldest in the lineage,
Having the good fortune to sleep in a palace bed,
Is it his fate to sleep on the ground in the forest? 100
The loving daughter-in-law of the king, mother Sita,
Has slept on hard ground, on a straw bed,
The crumpled straw says it all, her disturbed sleep;
The thread from her upper garment is seen here.
I am ruined, utterly ruined, now.
Who is there to protect the kingdom?
The city has no one to govern it.
When that is like poisonous food, I cannot wait;
I shall somehow make him agree. I will implore him,
Perform Rama's coronation at the earliest,' 110
Bharata spoke, choked with emotion.

The night was spent on the banks of the Ganga.
Waking Shatrughna at the break of dawn,
Bharata said, 'With Guha's help, we shall cross the river.'
Guha showed five hundred boats immediately.
In the boat bearing the *swastika* sign
Bharata, Shatrughna and the queen mothers sat.
The boats sailed in the Ganga like an army of flag-bearing
Elephants. Like a mountain with wings sailing along,
The boats crossed the river. 120
A league away after crossing the Ganga,
He halted his troops. Along with Vasishtha and other mentors,
He walked barefoot to the nearby Bharadwaja hermitage.
As soon as he saw Vasishtha, Bharadwaja got up,

And showed great respect and hospitality.
Bharata fell prostrate before the sage.
They enquired about each other with affection.
'Why have you arrived forgetting Saketa?
A brave father, instigated by a woman
Drove Ramachandra, who has not even dreamt of a sin,　　　130
Into the forest for fourteen years.
Tell me the reason for your coming.
Why the army? Why this excitement?
Has your governance been obstructed
By Shri Rama! Why can you not leave them
In the forest, at peace?' asked the sage.
Listening to the harsh words of Bharadwaja,
Bharata was overcome with grief:
'I am undone, O sage, can wise people speak like this?
My mother's craftiness has pushed me into this anguish;　　　140
Why do I need the throne of Ayodhya, why?
I want to fall at the feet of the great man;
I have come to take him back to Saketa, bless me,' he begged.
Vasishtha and other sages spoke with concern;
They reassured Bharata that there was no flaw in him.
Bharadwaja was pleased:
'I spoke so to test the steadiness of your mind;
Do not be depressed. You have protected the glory of your lineage;
You are able to sacrifice, you are a gem among men.
When you are so righteous, I have no doubts.　　　150
Shri Rama and Sita are in Chitrakoota.
Spend the night here and continue your journey tomorrow,'
Said the sage with affection.
'Why should peace in the hermitage be disturbed?
If the army comes over, the sanctity of a hermitage,
Plants and trees of land and water will be spoilt.
That is why I left it far away, and have come here alone.'

The sage called the army, and treated it
With all hospitality. From across the hills,

Fragrant, gentle wind blew caressing the bodies; 160
A rain of sweet-scented flowers poured on them;
The celestial sound of drums was everywhere.
The army stayed there, in the garden.

The night was spent happily.
'Show me the path, O Guru. Where is Chitrakoota?'
Bharata inquired and the sage told him.
'Many miles away; among the forests, a river flows
Towards the north; flowers and fruits abound on its banks.
There is a hut there and Rama stays there.'

Seeking Bharadwaja's permission, 170
Bharata praised him and went on his journey.

Canto Forty-two

'Saumitri Has Taken Them to a New Epoch'

||६||

One day, while getting water from a stream,
Sita saw a young woman, Sumedha, of the hunter's tribe,
Who asked fondly about her welfare:
She called Sita '*devi*' who asked her to address her
As 'sister'. So grew their affection for each other.
One day, Maithili
Stroked Sumedha affectionately and talked to her.
She asked her to stay. 'I cannot, sister;
If I am late, my master will beat me,'
Said Sumedha and started to leave, looking depressed.   10
Why should he beat you? Is he your husband?'
Asked Sita. 'He is not my husband; but he owns my father.
He has bought me with a little money,
The mind and body are sold.'
Hearing it, Sita was pained at her piteous life.

'I want a pot like the one you have,'
Sita said. 'I shall bring the potter tomorrow.
He will bring you a pot,' said Sumedha.
The very next day she brought a handsome potter.

He had a pot in his hand.
When Sita asked him what his name was,
He said, 'I do not know what my name is.
I have no parents. The *rakshasas* killed them.
I am the child of this forest and have grown up alone;
I am nameless.' Janaka's daughter remembered
Her own birth and felt as if a thousand scorpions
Had bitten her all at once. She broke into a sweat.
'You bring your father, Sumedha, to my king
Shri Rama. Let this potter also come,' said Sita affectionately.
The very next day,
Along with the potter and her father Junguru,
She came to the hut. Shri Rama and Lakshmana
Welcomed them and made preparations
To eat together. Junguru was anxious and worried.
'No, sir. We are untouchables. How can we eat
With the Aryans?
'Are we your companions?
We were born as slaves and we live as slaves.
We shall conclude the business of life as slaves.
We shall be born again as sons of slaves.
The wheel of life turns round and round,
And we shall always be slaves. It is the law of life,
Which cannot be broken. It is our fate to suffer in silence.
Do not tempt us with freedom. Forgive us.
Freedom will trouble us more than bondage.'

His voice becoming faint in fear,
Junguru looked this way and that, perspiring:
'If we plough and sow in our own land, still we cannot
Collect the crops. "We own this," they say,
And steal our food, pushing us to the jaws of hunger.
My lord! We gain nothing by our labour.

'Viciousness is the natural law of ownership;
We have become slaves in our own motherland.
Does eating together with you bring freedom to us?

Are you not the princes of Ayodhya?
Did you come to the south to extend your kingdom?
Now, if there is conflict with the *rakshasas*,
Do not make us animals of sacrifice.
The peace of a graveyard is enough for us.
The price you pay for peace and people's rule 60
Is huge. We cannot pay it, O king!'

Junguru spoke with humility.
Saumitri spoke without getting angry:
'Do not be scared. We do not desire kingdoms;
We have given up our own kingdom; we shall get you
The kingdom. In Tatakavana, we gave the Nishadas liberty;
We gave them self-confidence and self-rule.
We drove away the *rakshasas*. When the Aryan
Commander of Ayodhya turned wicked,
We punished him with death penalty. 70
Malada and Karusha kingdoms
Were liberated and we developed democracy there.
Do not be worried. Your motherland will be yours.
Anarchy will end. A host of plants of freedom will sprout.
We are not invaders, and we are not thirsty
For the expansion of our kingdom.
Our pledge is to give you a life of liberty,'
Said Saumitri and thus reassured them.
He ate with them. 'You will not be called a potter.
Let your name be Mukura,' said Saumitri, 80
Giving him a name, and making the spark of self-confidence
In him shine brightly.
Meanwhile a demon called Boodara
Roared and attacked the huts of Junguru and Mukura.
He flashed his sword everywhere and Saumitri,
In anger, shot a sharp arrow and killed him.
Within Junguru and Mukura grew self-confidence,
And admiration for the brothers.
The drum of liberty sounded in the hearts

Of the Kola Bhilla. Teaching the principles of revolution, 90
Saumitri tore away the layer of passivity in slavery.
The ideal of Sage Kaushika's life was spoken of.
With the belief that the welfare of the common man
Was the principle to follow, he gave them the pledge of liberty.

Saumitri taught Mukura and others the knowledge of war.
The radiance of the Kshatriyas grew. Mukura was
The guardian of the hall of weapons built by Saumitri;
Junguru was the one to build a web of spies.

In the company of Janaki,
Sumedha became an adept at handicrafts. 100
Chitrakoota was a workshop for handwork:
Baskets, mats, furniture and many varieties
Of things were made by the people in that place.
Maithili was extremely joyous.
When the sages were given such articles,
They appeared a little hesitant. 'Are you still
Infected by the thoughts of untouchability?'
Asked Janaki. Ashamed of their mean emotions,
The sages received the new things that were made.
The essence of precepts and rules 110
Were taught to Sumedha and other girls
Of Kola Bhilla tribe by Janaki. Mukura was the leader;
He organised a colloquy about *kshatra dharma*.
Filled by a new light, their minds flowered.
Laziness disappeared and attention to work was instilled.
Waves of music filled them with zest;
Janaki gave them spiritual refinement;
Saumitri realised the value of Kaushika's words.
Will the salaried staff of the army accept
The process of change? Saumitri helped the free flow 120
Of awareness among people, taking the Kola Bhillas
To a new epoch.
There is a principle behind a glorious life:

Deer for the sound of the hunter, an elephant in heat
For the touch of a female, a moth for flame,
Flowers for the bee, fish for taste,
Thus they get caught and lose their lives.
If each sense of sound, touch, form, taste and scent
Can cause so much harm, man with five senses,
Can never be too careful about his sensual pleasures;   130
His self-control has to be extremely strong always.

Ignorance and sinful deeds breed fear;
Infatuation, worry, arrogance and egotism
Push us into terrible worldly bondage.
Unfailing truthfulness, avoidance of unnecessary speech,
Purity of body and mind, peace toward others,
Ability to face difficulty, righteousness, and humility –
Such qualities will surely liberate man; and then,
Life will become beautiful as an eternal garden.
Poverty checks the tongue and   140
Makes the head low. Mouths and hands are tied;
Slavery envelops the poor; and the blanket of darkness
Covers the body. Eyes are blinded, ears turn deaf.
Misspent money, extravagance and gambling
Are unwelcome. Search for truth, experience of beauty,
Skilled workmanship, benevolence – these are good traits.
Non-violence, control over senses, compassion
For all creatures, mercy, peace, meditation,
Reflection and truth – practice of these eight virtues
Is real worship. Devotion is the best means of worship.   150
Renunciation of everything and self-surrender
Protect the devotee like an armour. The principle
Of the Almighty is within one's heart. Discovering it
Is self-realisation, the final goal of life.
The values of life must shine again;
The fountain of sweet thoughts must spring up.
The dirt within must be washed away;
Bad thoughts and bad motives must be put out.

The essence of such principles was taught in many ways
By Sita to the girls of Kola Bhilla clan. 160
Watching Bharata arrive
With his whole army, the *rakshasas* were worried.
In Kalikacharya hermitage, fine celibate young men –
Jaya, Ananda, Trilochana, Kushala and Shashanka –
Had acquired from Saumitri the skill of fighting with arms.
'This is the conspiracy of the sages. Saumitri has made
Everyone a traitor,' cried the *rakshasas* in great fury,
And attacked Kalikacharya.
'What is this treachery?
We shall tear up the sages. We shall destroy 170
Their rituals. We shall raze the hermitage to dust.'
When they said that, Kalikacharya did not protest.
He thought that philosophical thought was better,
Rebellion was the source of evil and so he kept quiet.
Dragging along the young men,
The *rakshasas* roared at them: 'You are liars.
Why should Bharata come to Chitrakoota?
Is such a big army needed to placate Shri Rama?
He has come to destroy the *rakshasas*; that is the truth.
In his conspiracy and deceitful games, you are partners, 180
You young sages.' They pounded, hit and hurt them;
They took out their enmity towards Rama and Lakshmana,
On the young men. Kalikacharya
Did not come to their aid. There was great violence;
The skin on the face and the body was peeled off.
Kalikacharya said in anxiety:
'Treachery is not needed. There will be no peace,
Contemplation cannot go on. This is not a laboratory
To test Kshatriya valour; let us go away from here.
Let us seek a peaceful place.' 190
But the young men would not agree:
'Saumitri is our mentor, and we have pledged to him.
Rushing forward with Kshatriya valour,

We shall destroy the *rakshasas*. All that we need
Are power and strategy. Saumitri is a thinker,
A harbinger of change, a sensitive person
Full of the awareness of reality.

'Birth and death are boats that sink and rise
In the winds of Time. On the sandy shores are seen
Some footprints of immortal men. They must be explored, 200
And their principles must be understood.

'Saumitri is the winner.
Putting down the evil doings of the *rakshasas*,
He has trained the minds of people. Filling strength
In the minds of the weak, he has mobilised people.
He will build a lovely garden of good work.
Our stand and yours are different. We shall not come
With you, swallowing injustice,' said the young men.
Hearing this, Kalikacharya walked away from them.

Canto Forty-three

'Kingdom has been Given as an Offering'

||६||

Fearless and steady was Sita, the mother of the world,
In the environment of the hut, watering plants,
Her face appearing misty due to drops of sweat.
Shri Rama saw her and cast a loving glance at her.
Like an ascetic excited at the sight of the soul's light,
He felt joyous in his mind looking at Sita's radiance.

When the hut in the forest became their palace,
Her husband being the king and the brother-in-law minister,
She herself the queen and the tribals being citizens,
The daughter of Mithila forgot Saketa and Mithila.   10
The peaks of Chitrakoota having built a fort,
The flowing stream making sounds like a watchman,
And spreading awareness in the world of mysticism,
Sita was enjoying herself.

Shri Rama was an inspiration with his affection.
In the service of Lakshmana, there was a new horizon.
Were fruits needed, were bulbs and roots needed,
Saumitri would get everything ready.
There was no limit to joy, no dearth of humour.
Animals and birds were now friends with Sita: 20

'Peacocks, you dance; Swans, swim freely;
Deer, jump around; Parrots and cuckoos, sing';
So would Sita talk to them and both would be happy.
The lion and deer had forgotten their enmity;
Together, with love, they were drinking water.

Sensing Rama's mind,
Sita would act. Clearing his path of thorns and weeds,
She was the gardener showering flowers!
'Here in the forest, all plants grow freely and lusciously;
They are not cut down here as in towns.   30
Here, rivers flow without hindrance; there they build dams.
They destroy the environment. They pollute air and water.'
Sita would complain.
'No, beloved. Building dams is necessary
For the welfare of people. If we move on within limits,
Good will be done. You pluck flowers for garlands'
Are the plants hurt? Everything should be within limits.
If wealth is dedicated to the world, then it is worthwhile.
Sowing seeds of greed, if man becomes selfish,
Then harm is sure to follow!   40
There is gold beneath the earth.
How is it useful? A mine should be dug,
Gold should be brought up and cleansed,
And be given a form; only then, does it become precious.
When it becomes a jewel, there is fulfilment!
All rivers born at mountain-tops are beneficial;
They flow on and join the sea finally.
Trees and plants are with the weight of fruits and flowers
Pulled down; that is the law of nature.
That is the secret of benevolence. Good of others   50
Is at the source of the world. Clouds in the sky
Shower pure water over hot earth; Mother earth
Receives it with joy and gives her children
Food and drink,' said Shri Rama. His words
Were pleasing to the ears.

Saumitri nodded his head with joy, and then said:
'We must cross Chirakoota and go to Dandakavana.
The wicked *rakshashas* behave cruelly there.
They are arrogant and uncontrollable, doing wicked things.
We have to establish peace there; and should see that 60
The practices of asceticism and meditation are conducted
Smoothly. Only then, we can travel on.'
He explained the blueprint of their future action.
Shri Ramachandra was
Comforted by the environment in Chitrakoota.
'Animals of many kinds, a variety of birds,
Many kinds of trees that bear fruit.
In Sita's company and Saumitri with me
I can spend fourteen years like so many days
Why do I need Saketa? Why the coronation? 70
Is there a Heaven better than this?
Everyday, the fountain of joy is springing,'
Thus he described to Sita and Lakshmana,
The wealth of Chitrakoota's beauty.
Then they saw at a distance
The red dust covering the sky. An uproar
Was heard. Wild animals scattered in fear
As if hunters were chasing them!
'My loving parrot is screeching in fear;
My mind is trembling. What could this commotion be?' 80
Asked the daughter of the earth, trembling.
Saumitri got up at once, climbed
The big tree and looked in all directions:
'There is an army. It looks like the army
Of Ayodhya. I can see the Kovidara emblem on
The chariot. Bharata is coming. We do not know why
Horsemen are coming galloping fast.
There are people on elephants, on chariots;
It appears like preparation of war to me.

'After ascending the throne, 90
Is Bharata coming to fight with us and kill us?
When the thirst for the kingdom was not quenched,
Did thirst for blood breed boundless infatuation
And wickedness? Is it not enough to drive us into a forest?
I shall kill Bharata. I shall take revenge
Like an elephant in heat pulling out trees,
And throwing them away here and there.
I shall throw out Bharata and lessen the weight on earth,'
Lakshmana spoke in great fury.

Shri Rama said in all seriousness: 100
'Why should Bharata be killed? You are wise.
We have given up the kingdom; even hate should be given up.
I shall touch the weapon and speak the truth.
I do not desire the kingdom. No children or
Grandchildren who follow will want it.

'Has Bharata come to fight!
He has come with love; he has come to return the kingdom.
Why do you not think with good feelings?
Suspicion is like cancer. Cut off its roots.
Do not speak harshly. You cannot doubt 110
The love of Bharata. Perhaps father is coming
Himself. Who knows? Do not be hasty.
Father is the embodiment of kindness.
He might have come to take us back.
Look at the horses, look at elephant Shatrunjaya.
However, the white umbrella is not seen;
I am filled with anxiety. Come down, brother.
Giving up the kingdom, Bharata himself is coming.
He has set aside Kaikeyi's desire and has arrived.'
Lakshmana got down from the tree: 120
'If he is coming with love, why the army?
Why the court eulogists and why the retinue?

Why the pompous walk, why the noise.
It is difficult to go up to Heaven. It is easy to descend to hell.
My mind is still immersed in suspicion, brother!'
Bharata stopped the Ikshwaku army
Within the limits of Chitrakoota and came
Walking with Shatrughna. 'We shall search
In one direction, Guha in another direction.
Without seeing the one with eyes like lotus petals, 130
I am not the one to return. Without laying
My head on the feet with all royal features
I shall not live!

'As long as there is a drop of blood in the veins,
As long as there is breath in me, I shall look for Rama!
When shall I see the one I worship in my heart!
Lakshmana is fortunate, Janaki is to be respected;
They have gained the fortune of being with Rama,'
Bharata said as he moved forward.

Going round the trees, crossing hedges, 140
He looked beyond a garden of flowers and saw
Signs of smoke. Right then, the hut came into sight.
Guha joined the brothers right there.
They were happy seeing that it was Rama's hut.
Bharata spoke with excitement:
'There is a pile of cut firewood before the hut;
There are many flowers, there are water pots;
Fibre cloth has been hung up here and there;
Straw-seats among plants, bows, quivers like sunrays;
Two swords with gold handles, 150
Shields covered with diamond dots,
A platform for fire in the south-east.
Let mothers come with Sage Vasishtha;
We have arrived at the spot mentioned by Bharadwaja.
I shall now set eyes on Shri Rama's feet,
I shall now see Rama who pleases the eyes,

I shall now see Rama, the Lord of the earth.
I shall see Sita, the mother;
I shall see my brother Saumitri!'
Over there, Saumitri 160
Was soothed by Shri Rama with affection.
'See, Bharata and Shatrughna arriving
Look at the turn, stars coming down
With my features, my own form
I feel as if I am looking at myself!
When it is so where is trickery, deformity or wickedness
At the splendid heights of emotion and feeling, tell me
Let go of suspicion regarding Bharata!'

'Let my birth which drove Shri Rama
To the forest, be condemned. My life is censured. 170
My life is barren. The greatest among us
Was driven by me into the forest. The body of
A righteous man was punished. Royal raiment
Was lost and deer skin was given!'
Bharata was lamenting thus,
Running with arms outstretched,
Strength being lost in excess of sorrow,
He saw Rama and called out 'Anna' in a feeble voice
Touching Rama's feet and embracing him,
He collapsed on the ground, agitated 180
Shri Rama picked him up, stroked and soothed him
Like hundreds of rivers flowing from a mountain of love
He let the waves of affection flow.
Shri Rama was absorbed
In the mixed feelings of compassion and love:
'Bharata with matted hair, wearing fibrous clothes.
Is this Bharata, it is difficult to recognise him.
His face has lost colour. The body is thin.'
He pulled Bharata near and asked about his welfare.
'How long it has been since I saw my beloved brother. 190
Have you come from far away? Are you tired?

Is father well? Are the people well?
How are our mothers? How are the people in the palace?
Leaving aside administration and service to father
Why did you come to the forest?
'How can I tell brother,
A sorrowful story! I was not at home.
Mother asked for two boons.
That became the cause for a chain of sorrows.
"Throne for Bharata, life in a forest for Rama" 200
She said, and to keep father's promise, you came here.
With you came sister-in-law and Saumitri.
After you left, father was in terrible sorrow,
He floated and drowned in it!
The curse had worked and life flew away then.

"Alas, Rama, Sita, Lakshmana", he cried
Thinking of you, he gave up his life!
We are orphans now, what can I say Rama!
They called me without telling me the news.
When I came back happily I was struck by thunder. 210
Kingdom is now something to be given away.
Why do I need Saketa kingdom, my brother
When you are there, an elder brother like a father,
Should the younger one be crowned?
Should the morals of the Ikshwaku clan be wiped away?

'Caught in mother's love, I became the sacrificial animal;
I have come here after completing father's obsequies.
I beg you with folded hands. Answer my prayer:
Come back, brother and ascend the throne;
Remove the harsh censure that I carry; 220
I shall serve you and hold you up.
I do not have the strength to bear the burden
Of the kingdom; and all citizens desire your return.'
Begged Bharata in all humility.
Hearing the news of their father's death,

Rama and Lakshmana were deeply grieved.
'Why the city? Why the throne? Why live at all
After father is no more? I was not fortunate enough
To carry out the obsequies. Even when life here is over,
Why return to the city? The treasure has dried up. 230
You were fortunate that you completed the rituals.

'When I left for the forest,
Father came stumbling, crying not to take away his life;
He came begging with open hands, came running.
How can I forget his great love?
How can I forget his honey-sweet words?
"Sumantra, do not stop. Move ahead"
Was what I said firmly; I abandoned father cruelly.
For the truth that was told, was his life sacrificed?
Saumitri could have stayed near father; 240
But I dragged him along, separated him and
Increased father's pain. Who is to give us succour now?
Who will advise us?' said Shri Rama,
Grieving so much that all hearts melted.
Along with Vasishtha,
Kausalya, Kaikeyi and Sumitra arrived.
Looking at the mothers, his grief increased.
Every one consoled Rama. Vasishtha consoled him
With soothing words.
Going near Shri Rama, 250
Kaikeyi stroked and with tears flowing, said:
'My son, having committed a sin, my soul
Has committed treachery. When I do not know myself,
What will my maid Manthara know?
"A bad son may be born, but not a bad mother"
So the saying goes; but I have disproved it;
And have become a bad mother, I am unfortunate.
The world will have something new to say
For my behaviour. Even though he is my son,
I did not really know Bharata; I knew the outside. 260

Now I understand his mind. You will cleanse the sinner.
For the crime I have committed, please forgive me.
Let not my selfishness live eternally in the world;
Let not my story be known to people at large!

'Sandalwood turned into fire because of me.
Shri Rama, I beg you; return to the city,
Free from the net of infatuation, I have been reborn;
Test me. I am not the Kaikeyi of old. Saketa
Is burning in grief; the waters of Ganga and Yamuna,
Of Sarayu and Tamasa are not enough to put it out. 270
May the sweet-stream of Rama's name flow in Ayodhya!

'Let the fire I started be extinguished, Rama.
At the sad end of my life, I won't have anybody
To call my own; these will only be darkness all around me.
After having harassed others and strutted vainly,
Now I beg you humbly, please save me;
Grant me the alms of forgiveness!'
Rama spoke in a tender voice:
'You have done nothing wrong mother,
You are the reason for my entering the stage of duty. 280
Under the pretext of a boon, you set me off
On a Great Journey, on a grand quest.
The pride of action was mine. My mind attained maturity.
When father has given up his life for truth,
If I come back, everything will be spoilt, mother!
Should one throw away the diamond of father's words
In the deep forest and return to Saketa?'
Shri Rama repeated his decision.
Mentor Vasishtha arrived there;
'Perform the water-ritual for your father, Rama,' he said. 290
Everyone went towards the river in great sorrow;
With tear-filled eyes they got into water.
'Father, this is offered to you,' said Shri Rama.

Libation was offered. 'Lakshmana,
Bring me a ball of *ingudi* seeds,' Rama said.
Mixing *bore* fruit with *ingudi* seeds, placing it
On the straw that was spread, he said with pain:
'This is our food. If you like it as well,
Eat and be satisfied,' he said offering it.
Then it was as if the sorrow touched the sky. 300

Canto Forty-four

'Whatever Fortune Brings, Should be Faced as Such'

||6||

'A king who ruled across four seas
Has to be offered *ingudi* seeds as fate willed.
Will my heart not be broken into pieces?'
Mother Kausalya wept aloud. The women of the palace
Came there and consoled her.
Shri Ramachandra touched
The feet of the mothers and bowed to them.
Even as he cried, Lakshmana prostrated before them.
While Janaki in deep sorrow came, the mothers
Felt as if their innards had been pulled out;   10
'Born as Janaka's daughter, Dasharatha's daughter-in-law,
And having married Rama, should you be suffering
In a lonely forest! Your lotus-face had faded in the sun.
Did we have to see this?' They lamented.
To mentor Vasishtha, Rama
Showed respect and there was a gathering held.
Bharata, Shatrughna, Saumitri and mothers,
All ministers and people gathered in silence.
'What will Bharata ask for? What will Rama say?

What will the news be at this moment?'
Everyone awaited eagerly.
With his hands folded,
In a humble manner, Bharata begged again:
'Mother did something that is against truth.
Father reached Heaven, I fell into the pit of sin.
To cleanse the stain on me and my mother,
You must take over the kingdom.
Mother is burning in the flames of anguish.
We are here to beg for your blessings.
Preserve the honour of the lineage, redeem everyone;
Do not ignore people's heartbeat. All have placed you
In their hearts, giving you the throne,' he sighed,
And fell on the feet of Shri Rama.
'Bharata, listen.
It is not right for anyone to blame mother Kaikeyi;
You can consider it as blaming me.
What is wrong with Kaikeyi asking for boons?
When my father's promise ordered life in the forest for me,
You have been given the kingship of Ayodhya.
Whatever action and duties have been given to us,
Should be conducted without damaging morality.

'The wealth of the world may be lost.
So also power. Life finds fruition in death.
When the fruit is ripe, it separates itself and falls
On the ground. Death stays at the back, and sucks life.
When it is so, I cannot reject righteousness.

'After joining the sea, does the river flow back?
We are all logs floating in a stream;
We meet once and go away elsewhere.
Birth is an accident, meeting is an accident.
Do not lose heart because you are facing sorrow.
Where is the decline of morality, where is the lapse?
Carried away by your love, if I break father's promise,

That would be the decline of morality!'
While Shri Rama thus consoled Bharata,
Sage Jabali spoke words of advice to persuade Rama:

'Use your judgement, Rama. No one can live for another.
Man is born alone, he is alone as well when he dies.
What are parents, siblings, relatives and homes?
They are just stopovers along the journey. 60
They show up and fly away, do not trust them.
Whatever fortune brings, should be faced as such.
Why should you discard the position offered?
You have not looted someone else's treasure!
The man called father is only a means.
A woman called mother grows in the womb
A union of sperm and blood, an instrument for birth!
Has anyone cast in mould the feeling of love?
Dasharatha is one with the five elements. Similarly,
Others would be so when the time comes. 70
Why should one worry, feel anxious or sad?

'This is a position justly given, ascend the throne!
Does one turn away from joy and embrace sorrow?
In the name of truth, does one wander around in a forest?
Speaking of truth all the time, does one have a meagre meal?
Your hardship makes me pity you.
What are obsequies? Does a dead man eat?
Clever people will come, eat well and go.
To earn money in the form of charity or offering,
It is just a means! 80
"Worship gods, give charity constantly;
Perform *yajna* and meditation, become an ascetic,
And, eventually, attain salvation." These are written
In useless, ancient legends; do not be deceived by them.
When the kingdom of grandeur is in your hands,
On this earth, closing your eyes and thinking of the other
World is the path of foolishness. Ascend the throne.'

Rama heard the words of Jabali;
But, within his heart dwelt truth and morality.
Whatever others said, he followed his conscience. 90
'O, sage! Fidelity to truth, compassion for all beings –
These are the precepts upheld since ancient times.
Truth is the basis of the world. It is righteousness,
Charity and *yajna, agnihotra*, meditation,
And austerity that are the foundation of truth.
The one, straying from the path of truth will fall into hell.
Can one ignore the father's order and ascend the throne?
Wealth goes towards a truthful man;
Should one discard truth at difficult times?
Would the virtuous desire the path of sinners? 100
Carrying the load of sins, would they seek terrible hell?
I shall follow all the rules of food in the forest;
Meditation and silence will be practised in the forest;
Duties and obligation will be carried out in the forest;
I have within myself all joy and treasures,'
He said in a manner without guile.

Sage Vasishtha spoke then:
'Jabali is not an atheist. Do not be upset.
He has spoken about the circumstances in life.
He is wise. Do not harden your heart. He has spoken 110
About how things happen in the world.
People have come from Ayodhya to the forest
In large numbers, like a sea. Should one ignore
The needs and feelings of people,' he said.
Sumantra also folded his hands and begged Shri Rama;
But Rama did not waver at all.

Jabali spoke again:
'This is the philosophy of materialism;
Do not belittle it as advocating sensual pleasures.
Will the body which turns into ashes get revived? 120
It is not right to spurn comfort; physical ailments,
Need, medicine and values. Why should they be separated

From comfort? Comfort is hidden in the heart of sorrow.
Materialism explains the truth of the world;
It is the great message of changing the world.
The mind is everything. The essence is bringing
Action into practice everyday.
The meaning of food is understood in breath;
Of breath in the mind, the meaning of mind
Is in that which is beyond cognition, 130
And that state is one of pure delight.
Keeping various schools of thought limited,
The world has become the land of conflict.
Now is needed a symbol that will bring all together,
Under one principle. Carrying the burden of the sins
Of the world, the free man walks. Experience has value.
The path of evolution is discovered with the strength
Of the Great Quest.
The soul has its existence only in the body;
That energy called soul disappears at death. 140
The body is the soul. In the Vedic contradictions,
Truth is lost. There is no rebirth.

'Dictatorship has lost the touch of gentleness;
Oppression and exploitation are its qualities.
Hence it is that it mounts an assult on meaningful living.
The huge tree of humanity has been attacked by termites!
In the name of morality, people are kept in ignorance.
You should not stop any attempt to uproot all that,
And to sow seeds of revolution in an unequal society.'
To the new principle of Sage Jabali, 150
Sage Yajnavalkya gave this answer:
'Vedas, Upanishads, myths, and moral codes –
Is there any basis to blame them as being untrue?
Why should wrong-doing be interpreted as morality?
Bitter is sweet, alcohol is nectar, night is day,
Adversity is well-being, ignorance is science –
Does one become wise by such perverse logic?

Have you any knowledge of the other world,
To declare that it doesn't exist? Have you, scholars,
Solved the mystery of the world? Is offering temptations 160
And breaking bridges of truth good advice?
What was done in the previous birth is related
To a man's life in this birth. Some are sad,
Some are sick, some are poor, and some are rich;
Why is there such discrimination?'
Sage Jabali's words
Were digested by Saumitri and then he spoke:
'What is the foundation of faith, religion and principles?
Is it animal sacrifice, vows and worship, rites,
Yajna and *yaga* performed in a grand manner? 170
When the essence of humanity has disappeared,
What is there to do with a pile of principles?
When father Dasharatha committed a mistake,
Unknowingly, should he be sentenced ever so cruelly
To death?

'Suffering in remorse,
Did he not seek forgiveness? Was he forgiven?
Is there a greater penance than remorse?
Will morality take it into account?
When the king is punished, what of the others? 180
Remorse is the punishment for wrong-doing.
Tell me, when will such compassionate epoch be born?
There must be space for change in morality.
Otherwise it will be static. For a new morality to rise,
That is the reason; another man of the epoch
Will be born on earth.

'*Nahi Jnanena Sadrusham*'
(Nothing equals enlightenment)
When you believe so, to a Dalita, Shudra,
And everyone else, it should be available. 190
To deny it is not morality. '*Atmavat Sarvabhootani*'

(Love everyone as you love yourself)
To proclaim this Aryan principle yet again,
In the world, should another great man take birth?
'Sarve jana sukhino bhavantu'
(May all people achieve happiness)
Can the essence of these words be narrowed?
Why do you build a monotoned fort?

'What are *yajna* and *yaga*?
They are for charity and money; what does it mean   200
When the Kshatriya performs the Ashwamedha *yajna*,
The ritual of horse sacrifice? It is provoking war;
It is bloodshed. While the horse runs ahead
In preparation for war, stepping on crowns,
Looting treasuries, placing marks on the foreheads
Of women with blood, is it a sacred ritual?
What if the status of Indra in Heaven is gained!
When one enjoys oneself, what about the crores of people
Who are poor? Are positions taken away only by the rich?
Is this enough return for the Vedic actions?   210

'O Shri Rama! You become the man of the epoch.
Build a mansion of love; along with fear,
Wipe away slavery among men and exploitation too.
A hornet while building a nest of mud brings in a worm
From a plant, keeps pecking it over and over again,
Until the worm screaming "hornet, hornet,"
I itself turns into a hornet. Our father Dasharatha
Got caught in the fear of Kaikeyi; being her slave,
Became fear himself and gave up his life.
In the coming days,   220
Caste will itself become a strong fort,
Divide people, sow enmity and spoil everyone.
Who is there to protect the exploited and the downtrodden?
Breaking the fort of caste,

Teach brotherhood and non-violence, Rama!
When devotion is
The best path to see you, calling your name,
Thinking about you and reaching your height,
Preaching morality and devotion, a great devotee
Will be born.' 230

Janaki's heart was full.
Expressing her feelings she spoke:
'Saumitri has talked of the condition of the exploited
And Dalits. He has spoken the truth. But consider women.
If we are not creators of morality, religious freedom
Will be completely denied to us.

'A man can perform obsequies,
A woman does not have that right. We are also slaves.
If the soul is the same, why this difference
Between man and woman? The pain that women suffer 240
Must be alleviated by you. Do you not know
The torment inflicted upon Ahalya?
End sex-discrimination, and become the harbinger
Of giving the pledge of equality to all.'

'Listen Saumitri, listen dear Janaki!
The yoke of duty towards the Raghu lineage
Is upon me. How will the fetters of tradition be cut?
When there is no place for individual liberty,
I cannot answer the thoughts within the mind.
The interests of ready models swallow me, 250
The nails of the system break me. I am wearing
The armour of morality, and righteousness of the epoch
And tradition must be protected. I cannot
Agree with your arguments,' said Rama.
The feelings of Saumitri and Janaki receded
Into the background.

As a last resort,
Bharata gave orders to Sumantra:
'Spread straw on the ground. I shall lie down fasting,
Until Shri Rama consents.' When Sumantra, not being sure
What he had to do, stood in silence, Bharata himself
Collected straw, spread it and lay down:
'Life in a forest and the duties of a Kshatriya
Do not go together; fibre clothing and governance
Do not go together. Brothers, why do you work
In opposing directions?' Bharata spoke,
And appeared like someone lying before a debtor's door.
Shri Rama came near him immediately:
'It is not fit that a Kshatriya should fast unto death.
It is outside of morality and hurts me as well.
Let father's words not become false. Free me from debt,
O Bharata, Have you forgotten what was told to us in Gaya?
"Whoever frees one from a hell called "*puth,*"
Is known as "*putra*", the son." Free father from hell.
Let people acclaim you throughout the world, that
"Dasharatha was a truthful man; so was his son Bharata."

'I cannot come now.
I shall spend fourteen years in the forest;
This is the truth and this is eternal.
No one can force me anymore,' said Shri Rama
With determination.

Canto Forty-five

'Jaya Jaya Shri Rama Jayatu Mangaladhama'

||๖||

The people who were quiet till now spoke:
'Enough of Bharata's insistence. We know now
Rama's temperament, virtues and values. What
Power do we have to bring him back to Saketa?'

Shri Rama said:
'Bharata, did you see the moral view of trusted people?
Are they not great? Are they not the good sons
Of the sacred land? Do they not know the divine tradition
Of land and water? Give up fasting and get up;
Drink this holy water and touch me.'   10
Bharata followed what he said.
'My brother citizens!
I did not ask father for the kingdom's treasury;
I did not ask mother for kingship;
Now I wish to be in the forest for fourteen years,
And serve the greatest among men.
I beg for Shri Rama's permission to do so,'
Proclaimed Bharata.
Shri Rama's mind softened:
'What mother Kaikeyi asked for, should be fulfilled.   20

Father's orders must not be ignored. Trust me;
I shall return to Saketa when my term here is completed.
I shall ascend the throne with all of you.
Until then, not making Kosala rudderless, you shall
Take care of it. Father's words must not be disobeyed.
Moonlight may be separated from the moon;
Himavanta may give up snow; the ocean
May cross its limits. But I cannot move on
Ignoring father's rule and morality,'
Shri Rama proclaimed and all were happy. 30
'You have the power to protect the earth;
Ayodhya is not barren! Starting from Sagara,
To King Dasharatha, she is the blessed one
Who has given the earth limitless clusters of power,'
Rama praised the land in this manner.
Shri Rama's decision
Seemed firm and Bharata accepted it.
He had accepted another decision in his mind:
The wooden footwear he had brought so carefully
From Ayodhya, were kept before Shri Rama 40
And he pleaded: 'Step into these, and then
I shall keep them on the throne and govern.
I shall give the responsibility of governance to them.
Dressed like an ascetic, with matted hair and fibre cloth,
Eating roots and bulbs, staying outside Saketa,
I shall await your return.

'Brother, after fourteen years
Of life in the forest are over, the very next day
You should return to Saketa. If you do not,
I swear by our family god, the sun, I shall jump into fire 50
And end my life.' A terrible pledge was made by Bharata.
For Bharata,
That was the last stage in seeking Rama.
Looking at the extremity of brotherly love,
Shri Rama was amazed, bowed his head,

And put his feet into the wooden sandals.
Bharata seemed satisfied then. With great affection,
Going near Bharata and Shatrughna,
Shri Rama embraced them in great joy.
While Bharata prepared for the journey, 60
Shri Rama advised him thus:
'When a duty has to be done, brother, do it.
You must have such ministers with you who know
Your mind; consultations are the basis of victory.
You must win over sleep and be careful;
Work that gives maximum results with minimum
Effort must be undertaken. One wise man is better
Than a thousand fools. This must be in your mind.

'Corrupt, dishonest people,
Lustful people who take advantage of innocent women, 70
Should be under control. Greedy priests, doctors, ministers,
And servants who complain about their masters
Should be kept at a distance. People devoted to the king
And those who are honest should be honoured.
If you nourish the desire for fame of those skilled in war,
Then their ability to fight will increase!
In giving salaries, housing,
And free grocery to workmen, there should be no delay.
If there is a delay, troubles will crop up, and they
Will fall into evil ways, resulting in calamities. 80
There should be affection towards relatives
And scholars. A king's messenger should be intelligent;
An atheist will not do. In the enemy camp,
Spies should be appointed in secrecy; and the work
Of the ministers should be examined carefully.

'Army chiefs must be beyond question in behaviour;
Their movements should be observed often.
Exiled enemies and criminals should not be
Ignored. They will never be friends again.

When time passes, they may come to you humbly;
Do not simply consider them weak.
"Na vishwasedavishwaste vishwaste na ativishwaset."
(Don't trust those unworthy of trust; regarding even
The trustworthy, don't trust them completely.)

'Transparent governance is the duty of a ruler;
In earning money, there should be no immorality;
You should know the value of time and work with care;
Atheism, lying, anger, lack of concentration,
Delay in work, lack of good company, laziness,
Sensual desire, deciding without consultation,
Postponing work that has been decided upon,
Fighting with many enemies at the same time –
All these must be abandoned.
Treading the path of our ancestors is the best way.

'Let Kosala become very sacred;
Let the water of tanks and rivers give it good harvest;
Let agriculture be enriched with the help of Science.
Animals and birds, men and women, let them be
Free from troubles. Let mines and treasury be rich;
Let money and crops be abundant inside the fort;
Let mechanics, weapon makers and archers
Live well. Let not the innocent be punished.
Let there be no partisan views like
"These are my people; those are not.'"
Shri Rama gave such advice and Bharata
Gained self-confidence. All were in peace.
Bidding farewell to Bharata,
Shri Rama's eyes were filled with tears.
Venerable Bharata decorated the wooden footwear,
Put them on his head, went around Rama, saying,
'Victory to Rama, the great bowman and the king of Saketa.'
While the chant of victory went on,
He kept the wooden footwear on the royal elephant,

And walked on. Mothers shed tears in silence.
Feeling choked, unable to talk,
Shri Rama bowed to them and, with Sita
And Saumitri, he entered the hut right away.
Bharata travelled on
To the north of Chitrakoota, by the holy river
Mandakini; he went round the mountain and 130
Continued his journey to the east. Arriving
At the hermitage of the Sage Bharadwaja,
He got off the chariot, touched his feet,
And recounted to him all that had happened.
The sage was happy,
And praised Bharata: 'You are fortunate;
Like water collected in a pit, let good qualities
Always be with you. Having a righteous son
Like you, Dasharatha was indeed fortunate.
Having a devoted brother like you, 140
Shri Rama is fortunate. Live for a hundred years.
May all that is auspicious happen to you,' he said,
Blessing him. Everyone was thrilled; and,
The journey went on.
Bharata reached Ayodhya.
Like a ruined city, its glory had faded;
There was no sound of joy, silence everywhere, and
Cave-like darkness like the dark half of the lunar month.
Was there a hurricane that had destroyed everything?
Had the hot sun of summer burnt everything? 150
Had the sea risen and swallowed everything?
Had all living creatures fallen into eternal sleep?
Were they shattered, caught in an enemy attack?
No chirping of birds, no song and dance,
No fragrance of flowers, no incense and sandalwood.
With Shri Rama's exile to the forest,
Ayodhya was without lustre. But, with the arrival
Of Rama's wooden footwear, a little energy entered it!

Leaving Ayodhya,
Coming to nearby Nandigrama and staying there 160
Was his decision. He told the mothers
And Sage Vasishtha: 'In brotherly love,
and righteousness, who can equal you?'
Everyone praised and blessed him.
The journey continued
To Nandigrama. Vasishtha, revered sages,
The army and citizens as well went along.
'This kingdom of Ayodhya is a pledge of Shri Rama.
The weight of governance will be borne
By the wooden footwear; I am just an instrument,' 170
He said. Keeping them on the throne, he performed
The ceremony of coronation with all excitement.
Everyone proclaimed victory for Shri Rama and Bharata.

The royal umbrella and fan were at service
To the wooden footwear. Trusting that Rama's presence
Was felt in them, daily matters of governance
Were discussed before them. Bowing in devotion,
Serving and worshipping them, following rules
In the attire of an ascetic, Bharata was humble enough
To proclaim that Shri Rama's coronation 180
Was the final goal of his Great Quest.

'Victory to Shri Rama, victory to the abode of sanctity;
Victory to him who protects his devotees; victory to the Great Quest;
Victory to you O god, whose form is divine and auspicious;
We wish you all pious victory; may all of you be blessed'

Singing such paeans every day, Bharata ruled over his kingdom;
And *Ramarajya* was established in Kosala.

BOOK TWO

Canto Forty-six

'O Dome of Truth in Saketa!
O Lamp of Divine Light!'

||६||

Bharata looked after the kingdom from Nandigram,
And, yet, he was now totally detached;
Chanting the name of Rama,
He himself had become an embodiment of Rama.
Shatrughna was no less a hermit, and
Urmila, in the absence of Saumitri,
Had become a *yogin,* yearning for him.
Now, their loving glances met only when they
Gazed on the full moon from where they are.
The people of Ayodhya all chanted   10
The name of Rama, day in and day out.
'When will Rama come?' they pined,
'When will he arrive, our Saumitri?
When will Janaki be here?' – thus,
Yearning for them, they passed their days.
Mothers Kausalya, Sumitra and Kaikeyi
Suffered greatly at Shri Rama's absence.
'When will we see the one who
Carries out the pledge given to his father?

When will we see him, the man of all virtues?
When do we embrace that idol of affection?
When do we see him, the life-breath of Dasharatha?
When can we behold him, the idol of his subjects?
When can we sing of him, the soul of our souls?'
Thus they sighed and thus they pine,
And lived listless, counting each day and month.

Here, in Chitrakoota,
Every particle chants the name of Shri Rama.
The trees say, 'Shri Rama, Shri Rama,'
The birds sing, 'Shri Rama, Shri Rama.'
Flowers of all types bloom for Shri Rama,
And Mother Nature manifests herself
In myriad forms, and, being reborn each day,
Rejoices to see Rama, Lakshmana, and Sita.

The Summer season arrived in full force.
The feathers of the birds, singed, turned black;
The forehead of the elephant got cracked,
Shiva moved away from Gauri to be with Ganga,
And unbearable summer-heat enveloped the forest.
The earth burnt in the sun and the sky no less.
Whichever way you turned, you came across only heat.
Janaki hid her delicate face under tree-shades;
But the brothers were indifferent to the summer sun!

When the rainy season arrived,
The dark clouds covered the whole sky and earth.
Clouds of many hues – bee-black clouds,
Blue clouds, clouds of peacock colour,
And of dusky *honge* trees – covered the sky.

It is impossible to describe autumnal beauty.
When the gentle breeze wafted carrying the pollen
Of *kadamba* and *ketaki* flowers; when the autumnal
Blue sky shone like a sword, burnished afresh;

When the white clouds enveloped the sky
Gleefully; when the bees sang on *shali* trees;
Gods witnessed the sight from the sky above.

When Winter arrived, all the leaves fell.
Behold the sacred fig tree – a symbol of life,
With its roots upwards but its branches downward:
'Oordhwamulamadhah Shakhamashwattham Prahuravyayam.'
When their time is ripe, leaves of all beings fall; 60
And Spring brings them back and renews life.

What is there in the palace?
Royalty is within one's heart and the wilderness
Cannot wither inner richness.
The self-same palace turns into a desert
In the absence of aesthetic pleasure in life.
A man of taste converts the forest into paradise.
In the company of his dearest wife, a brother
Full of understanding, and an eye for beauty
The leafy hut became the abode of art 70
To Shri Rama.

Everything that is inert has changed
Into throbbing vitality; the treasure
Of the wild forest has attained a new aspect;
Entering the domain of memory, shedding
All grossness, life is a vast field of celebration.

The rocks appear to be meditating monks
To the daughter of Janaka. The butter-coloured cloud
Embraces the peak; unwilling to loosen its hold,
It stands still. Sita salutes the mountain 80
That is adorned with the cloud as it seemed
To be the veritable *shikhari*, the father figure
Who is god Seshadri in a sublime posture.

From the mountain peak,
The water cascades with uncontrolled speed,

After being released from the constricting
Locks of Rudra. Likewise, the bliss that is
Beyond description is enveloping the world.
Love fills the mind of men up to the brim.
When the forest fire blazes atop the mountain 90
During night time, the terrible dance of flame,
Unquenchable, Sita, who is innocence personified,
Gazes at it, continuously.

At the expiry of night,
The day dawns with an unparalleled splendour.
The reddish young sun rises in the east,
Ascending the chariot drawn by seven horses.
The maiden of directions offers him *arati,*
While the earth adorns him with a garland of blossoms.
He spreads golden hue everywhere. 100
The gentle breeze awakens the world,
As if a giant fan cooled it from end to end.
Even as the cuckoo's song woos the listeners,
All the birds respond to the call; and the trees
Nod their heads in assent that their decision
To give shelter to the winged friends was right.
The woodpecker continues to peck the giant tree;
The cackle of peacock and the murmur of bees;
The carefree sauntering of the wild animals;
The blooming of buds manifest in plenitude; 110
What fragrance, what elegance!
What vivid beauty of colours!!

Beauty blooms at the foot of the hill,
Colourful sky and the rhythm of music
Please the heart; the whole world wakes up
At the melody, and bathes in the golden rays
Absorbing the tender tenor of nature.
This is the way the sun disseminates pleasure
To the world from his inexhaustible treasure.

Shri Rama, Sita and Saumitri spend time 120
In this manner with no anxiety, in Chitrakoota,
Amidst its heavenly environs. One day,
The brothers saw monks sitting in groups
Discussing in low tones something of dire
Import. They were a picture of worry.
The brothers saw them as a flock of harassed deer.
'Why this harassed look, why this fear'
The brothers looked at them in dismay,
Ashwayati leading the group.

'Tell us what the matter is. 130
What is the trouble, what is the worry?
The sages are sitting in groups,
Coming out of their respective cottages;
They are heading elsewhere in silence.
Have we committed any mistake?
Have we done anything wrong,'
Shri Rama asked them in earnestness.

'You can never go wrong, O Shri Rama,
As you are blessed with all noble qualities.
We are very well protected under your governance. 140
The peaceful atmosphere of the hermitage
Is disturbed today and the reason for that is this:
The brothers of Ravana, Khara and Dushana,
Are in Dandakarayna; their cruelty knows no bounds.
These cannibals are accompanied by their
Terrible associates. Sinful souls they are,
And ruthless. Assuming ghastly forms,
They torture the sages relentlessly;
They pour meat and wine to the vessels for oblation,
Breaking all that is used in sacrificial rituals. 150
They are already unnerved by your prowess;
They cannot stand the dominance of the righteous.
They are afraid that Ravana's empire

Would be in ruins as Rama has arrived
Along with Sita and Lakshmana,
To expand his domain in the south.
This fear has prompted them to attack us
Labelling us as traitors.

The fear of the black cobra has driven them
To desperation and they are rushing in haste 160
Polluting our hermitage and its surroundings.
There is nothing but violence where there was peace.
Who can carry out the sacred rituals
In an atmosphere of conflict? Penance,
Meditation and chanting are our objectives,
Religious sacrifice being our honoured routine.
That is the reason why the sages are forsaking
Chitrakoota in search of peaceful refuges.
You are a strong man and assiduous one too;
You are determined to punish the law-breakers; 170
Suppress this violence and establish peace.
May you emerge victorious, O Shri Rama,'
Thus Sage Shatavruddha entreated.

Shri Rama was pained at this,
And he consoled the sage: 'Do not have fear
And anxiety, I am going immediately
To where the demons are. I will overcome them,
Destroying their pride. Listen to my words.'

Rama had intended to leave Chitrakoota
As it was narrated by Lakshmana to Sita: 180
'The memory of Bharata, Shatrughna and
Mothers come to the fore here in this hermitage!
Chitrakoota is the place where all the affection
Of people of Ayodhya flows in a flood.
The elephants, the horses and all the four wings
Of the army tread on this land. The voices of dear ones
Ring in the ear. There is a constant concourse

Of the citizens, here; they beg and entreat us
To return to the city; they shake our very pledge
Tempting us with the glory of the golden throne. 190
We shall leave this place and go where they cannot
Reach us, where we can earn our salvation.
We shall go where there is a place for our redemption.
We will find out the demons and bring to the lives of the sages
Peace and serenity,' thus Rama spoke touched to the core.

Listening to these utterances
Of Rama, Sita sat in silence and in great anxiety.
Rama looked at his wife's face and began again:
'Why are you silent, my wife? What doubts have gripped
Your mind? Can't you unburden your heart to me?' 200

'My lord, I do not have any doubts;
But I am only thinking of what is right and what is wrong.
I have told the sages that I myself will root out
All the demons. But, they are not your foes,
And they have done no wrong to you,
You have always followed the righteous path.
I am not stubborn, neither am I headstrong;
It brings pain if we tread the path of vice.
It is always good to follow what is virtuous.
This is the reason for my depression,' said Sita. 210

Lord Shri Rama liked those words
Of Sita. He went near her and said lovingly:
'You tell me, being the bright crest lamp of Saketa,
And also, you are the one who cleanses the mind.
When you guide me, only then I can fulfill my life.
Don't forget that I am a mere human being;
If gold is not refined, it will remain just mud.'
Hearing these words of Shri Rama, Sita said:

'As you are not the king of Saketa now,
Why does an ascetic need the association of the city? 220

You are clad in barks, and your hair knotted;
But you are wielding bow and arrow. As you pull
The bow-string once, the entire forest shakes
And all the birds and beasts of the forest run for shelter.
Having come here to suppress violence,
Why do you fill the atmosphere with fear?
Birds are vexed by the sound of your drum!

'If you sow the seeds of passion,
You will only cause the growth of a poison tree.
Chitrakoota is agog with the rumour   230
That you have come to expand the kingdom
Of Ayodhya, and hence you are a trespasser.
Truth and morality should not mix with violence.
If war ensues, it becomes a great catastrophe.
Everywhere there is fear and everywhere
There is anxiety; whichever direction you turn
You will witness new modes of aggression and onslaught.

'The weapons are new, and the methods are new;
The skills of war ever fresh. There is a need for new truth
And new knowledge; together with new rhythms,   240
And a new *mantra* of peace. Tell me,
What is the use of war?'

Listening to the words of Sita,
Shri Rama approached her and said gently:
'I have grasped all that you said of righteous path;
That is full of wisdom. But Vaidehi, the ascetics
Are in a dire state and protecting the helpless ones
Is the virtuous way. When the ascetics seek our help,
We must respond. You are my most intimate consort
And Saumitri is our unfailing companion.   250
Let there be no room for anxiety.
We have to protect the rituals and practices.
We cannot forget Sage Vishwamitra's advice
On the duties of a king, received at Tatakavana;

Neither can we afford to go against his directions.
'Apyaham Jeevitam Jahyam tvam va Sita Salakshmana
Na hi pratignam Samshritya brahmanebhyo Viseshatah'
(I am ready to give up my life; I will give up even you,
Sita, and Lakshmana; but, I will not violate
My pledge given to the sages to protect them.) 260
And that is the guiding principle of my life.'

Sita understood that Rama's aim was not
To expand his kingdom but to establish peace.
That every being should focus on god as it was
The only way to transform earth into Heaven,
That that was the only path for salvation,
And that that was the pledge Rama had taken
And remained silent!

This is the moment to punish the demons,
And this is the moment to protect the righteous. 270
So saying Sita, Rama and Lakshmana
Bowed to Chitrakoota and to Mother Nature;
They bowed to the huts of the hermits,
And moved along the path of Panchavati
In pursuit of truth and *dharma*!

Canto Forty-seven

'The Power of a Chaste Wife is the Greatest'

||૬||

As they were climbing the mountain
Amidst a thick forest and passing beside huge trees,
They saw pendent roots from the banyan trees,
Which appeared like huge pythons, and heard the sound
Of the bamboo trees swaying in the wind. The gigantic trees
Inspired awe in them. The roaring beasts and enveloping
Darkness daunted their spirit, impeding their progress
And causing fatigue.

As they plodded their way in the jungle,
They saw at last the hermitage of Atri and Anasuya,   10
That appeared to them like a symbol of culture
And *dharma*, and they were thrilled to the core.
There lived in the huts the hermits and their spouses,
Creating artifacts of culture and giving the onlookers
A sense of peace and illumination to the mind.
The chanting of the *mantras* echoed all around,
The ever-flowing stream of good culture that had come down
Since ages, including other tributaries on the way.

Atri and Anasuya have hidden in the womb of time,
Friendship, affection, pain, pleasure, desire, longing, 20
Selfishness, cunning, and all that. Now they have realised
The mystery of life beyond existence and have caused
The lotus of divine and blissful truth bloom.

When Atri and Anasuya
Saw Sita, Rama and Lakshmana, and embraced them
In joy, the trio fell very humbly at their feet.
The rest of the ascetics came running, joyful and excited,
To the hermitage of Sage Atri; and they stood speechless
Looking at the resplendent beauty of Sita, Shri Rama,
And Saumitri! Rama's face had the sheen of the blue sky 30
With lotus-like eyes, and his arms touching the knees.
He shone as the God of Love, and they all praised him
In great wonder: 'This handsomeness is celestial;
This is out of the world!

'Oh, Rama! you are a veritable
Wishing Tree; you have come especially
To bless us and to free us from three types of agony.
You will erase all sources of worry
And will quell six types of enemies;
You are blessed with a delicate body, 40
You are handsomeness personified;
You are kind and will free us from all anxiety.
You are immeasurable and you are like
Mount Mandara which churns the nectar
Of the ocean of life. You are wearing on your
Chest the priceless jewels called devotees,
Whom you got during the churning of the ocean,
By the gods on one side and the demons on the other.
You are the one who won Sita, the most beautiful maid,
With heroism; you are the Lord of the Three Worlds. 50
You have the form of three states: the dream state,
The awakened state and the deep-sleep state.

You are the light of the universe;
You are the Enlightened One
Attaining the highest state,
You grant liberation to all.
You are the one who bestows infinite pleasure.'
So prayed Sage Atri, plucking the chords of devotion,
And praising him to his heart's content.

Then the ascetics described   60
The manner in which the demons troubled them:
'The followers of Ravana are killing the ascetics
Everyday causing untold sufferings to them
Even when they are observing their ritual practices.
Look at our bodies which have been subjected
To such violence – we are beaten and bruised.
The sages are dying, this torture is unendurable.
Protect us, Shri Rama; we take refuge in you.
You have come as a great deliverer and we are saved.'

Shri Rama told them: 70
'You are the wise ones, you deserve our worship;
And you may order me to do things.
I prostrate at your feet and carry your command
On my head; you rest assured about my action.
I have pushed the wise ones to the bottom of sorrow
By forgetting my royal responsibilities;
I have tarried in executing the obligations.
You may pardon my error.
It is imperative that the kingdom of Saketa
Must be protected by all means.   80
Even as the tears are rolling down
I will wash your feet with them.
You have said that the demons' atrocities
Are intolerable.
Rest assured that I will root out them completely;
You may kindly carry out your virtuous oblations

Without any fear,' so saying Rama gave
Reassurance to the ascetics.

Rama, Sita and Saumitri are immersed
In the stream of devotion with Atri and Anasuya. 90
When the sage left for the river, Shri Rama and
Saumitri sauntered in the environment of the forest
Enquiring about the well-being of the inmates
Of the hermitage.

They say it is Sage Atri's wife Anasuya,
Who caused the swelling of the Ganga when
The river was lean and withered; and thus
She could drive away the ill-effects of drought.
They also say that she contracted ten nights into one.
Her body is emaciated owing to strict observance 100
Of rituals but her face is resplendent
With divine glow!

When Janaki found herself with Anasuya
The latter explained in detail in her nectarine
Voice all the essential ways of a devoted wife:

'Listen to me, Vaidehi! The husband offers
All happiness along with the fruit of life,
And hence to serve him is to obtain a condition
Of blissfulness. As he provides wealth and riches
In addition to his mind and body, 110
He is a relative par excellence.
Being his spouse, you can only derive
Half of the merit he earns.
Though it sounds strange, it is true
That the husband shares half of his wife's sins
And therefore, they ought be alert
As their destinies are linked.
They have equal share in fame and in slander,
They share everything equally.

Don't anticipate trouble in advance; 120
Never forsake the path of righteousness;
Make your husband a strong refuge;
Never leave his side.
Always observe rituals.

'Further, listen to me, Sita!
When the spring of love wells up in your heart,
Give it to your husband in abundant measures.
Understanding him with equanimity will lead
To greater heights and welding of the couple's
Souls in love and harmony will pave the path 130
Towards perfection.
Man and woman complement each other;
They are the symbol of consciousness
And creative power indeed.
If one forgets their equality, it is a tragedy.
The eyes are filled with rays of light
Heralding fruition of life.

'If the wheels of a chariot are asymmetrical,
It will surely wobble and finally fall.
Sacred is the discipline guarding the wedded life. 140
Life without jealousy is pleasant;
Ill-will and envy are equally harmful.
The deity of strength is in the form of a mother.
Man is inert and the woman is dynamic.
The power of a chaste wife is beyond comparison.
She is sacred and a priceless jewel to womanhood.
Dear daughter, you are indeed fortunate to have
Shri Rama who kept up the words of his father.
If you safeguard the principles of a house,
You will be protected always.' 150

'O noble one, how shall I describe
My husband Shri Rama, who is compassionate
And a conqueror of senses; he is a possessor of all

Good qualities; totally dedicated to me, his wife;
He is attached to his father and he worships his
Mother equally; he is an embodiment of *dharma*
And truth; so blessed I am being his wife.
Like Rohini ever inseparable from the moon
I am with Shri Rama experiencing the joy of
Chastity and devotion,' so said Sita to Anasuya,   160
And the latter was overwhelmed to hear these
Words of wisdom.

When it was evening time,
The sun ambled towards the western hill.
The scattered birds collectively flew
Chirping their way back home,
Desiring to sleep in their cosy nests' sans care.
After their bath, the sages, clad in fresh clothes,
Carry the pots of water. They arrange for the *homa*   170
With Sage Atri.

The wind caused the fragrant smoke
To engulf all around. Not knowing which
Way to turn, the animals of the hermitage
Approached sacred platforms; slept thereabout
With no anxiety or fear.
The moon illuminated the world with his light.
Then came Shri Rama and Saumitri!
'Come dear child Raghurama, come Lakshmana,
The hermitage has become sacred as you are our guests,'
So said the noblest sage with unbounded affection.   180

Sage Atri, who appeared to have been
An embodiment of peace and tranquility,
Blessed the brothers chanting all-time enveloping
Mantras. The ascetic representing continuation of
Tradition was in a state of transcendental meditation.

'A beautiful idol will not emerge
Unless a sculptor chisels a block of stone,' with these

Words, Sage Atri told the secret of human well-being.
He also told them about the hidden paths amidst
The impenetrable wilderness and other spots of 190
Withdrawal including the bloodthirstiness of
The demons and the barbaric people.

After bowing to the ascetic couple,
When Vaidehi sat in their vicinity,
Atri and Anasuya were happy that they learnt
About the circumstances of Janaki's birth and
Upbringing and her wedding.
The night in the hermitage was spent in plenitude
Of hospitality.

They arose from their beds 200
Next day very early. After finishing their
Morning ablutions, Shri Rama, Sita and Lakshmana
Approached Atri and Anasuya in great devotion
And said, 'You are like the ancient banyan tree
That has sent its innumerable aerial roots into the
womb of earth,
Spreading its countless branches across the sky.
You are the proverbial elephant carrying the globe.
We are fortunate to come near you.
You have enabled us to climb the peak of fulfillment. 210
We will move now towards Dandakaranya.
O noble one, grant us permission to
Take leave of you,' thus they prayed in humility.

In a mood of divine affection,
Then Anasuya took out the jewels fashioned
By the celestial goldsmith and adorned Sita
To enhance her natural elegance. She tucked
Fragrant blossoms to her tresses with a smiling face.
Sita's joy knew no bounds as she was
Decked in grandeur by Anasuya. 220

'Devoted wife of Dasharathi,
Return kindly to the palace at Ayodhya after
The fulfilment of your vow. Lead a life of happiness.
You have renounced your relations,
The pride that you are a princess,
You have renounced all your riches,
Accepting the proximity of your husband
As everything; you are aware that no one
Could be closer than the husband and you have
Followed him as a part of your penance   230
To the forest; thus you have earned
Immense merit by your action.'
So saying, the wife of Atri blessed Sita
With unbounded affection.

'On the path of the forest
There are cannibals, ogres and demons;
There are bloodthirsty beasts; be alert
While you move around. If you follow the way
Where the sages gather to collect fruits,
You will surely reach Dandakaranya.   240
And my blessings are with you,' said Atri
Bestowing his benediction.

'Listen Shri Rama,
The woman is exploited in the society
Whether she lives in the palace as queen
Or as a mere servant.
Everywhere, the womankind is in deep sorrow.
Look at your own mother, Kausalya.
Is she not undergoing agony?
Have the sages treated their wives with dignity?   250
Raghava! You alone must try to annul
This discrimination between man and woman.'
When Anasuya asked him in so many words
Rama promised her: 'I give my word mother,
Your wish will be carried out.'

In search of an elevating idealism, the vision of Atri
and Anasuya had goaded Sita and Rama
Towards a new horizon. This was in tune with
Their pursuit of achieving fulfillment
Of universal peace beyond the limiting 260
Target of individual salvation.
The sprinkling of perfect love had purified
All that was dross and gross between
The trusted couple; they overcame the impact
Of separation, the tinge of hate, the touch
Of sorrow and unacceptable desire and all
That drives a wedge between the trusted souls.
Now, everything was bright and beautiful
With resplendent rays of purity and accord.

Sita and Rama turned back 270
To get a last glimpse of Atri and Anasuya,
Whose countenances were grand and sublime.
As if they were made of great light,
The duo with immeasurable merit,
The duo with divine light,
Approached the advancing Rama and Sita
Becoming liquified light and assuming
The form of nectarine rain,
Entered Rama and Sita at once.
The effulgence redoubled itself in this merger. 280

Thus, Shri Rama, Sita and Saumitri
Left the hermitage of Atri and on their way
To a distant destination, they made frequent
Stops to pay salutations to the hermits,
Getting the view of all that was the essence
Born out of penance and meditation.
The birds fly freely and the beasts roam
Without hinder. The flowers bloom of their own
Accord. The lotus ponds ooze coolness.

The plantain and mango trees show their 290
Readiness to serve the hermits in the manner
Of *ashwatha* and *bilva* trees.
There is chanting of the Vedas from ritual *mandaps*,
Deer-skin, sacrificial grass and other requirements
For sacrifice along with pots of water and pots
Of *ghee* are seen. The songs of devotion
Are wafted in the air.

Witnessing the walk of that
Wonderful light, the wives of sages, the virgins,
And all those who could see that divine sight 300
Were awe-struck calling it the procession
Of the celestial moon and the star!

They bend at regular
Intervals receiving the hospitality of the ascetics.
'Blessed are we, blessed is this forest,
Blessed is our hut, O righteous one!
You are a refuge to the helpless;
You are the famed one.
Being a great warrior, you are beyond
Comparison. After quelling the lawless, 310
You have installed yourself in the hearts of the subjects.
Raghunatha, thus you are worshipped by the world.
You are the protector of the city and the forest.
Conquering the senses we have attained
Equanimity; we have subdued anger and
Attachment and hence we are least inclined
To punish the outlaws.
We cannot curse them, neither can we be harsh
And therefore we need your help and protection,'
So the ascetics solicited. 320

Sita, Rama and Saumitri are moving in
Search of a new pattern of salvation, amidst
Bud-filled bowers and the womb of gentle fragrance

Where there are nectarine dreams,
And beauty that endures
In the forests at the foot of the Shatashringa mountain,
Or the thousand-peak-mountain,
Where there are deer and wild stags,
And crystal streams that elevate the spirit.
Bearing the burden of the world, Sita, Rama and   330
Saumitri went to the abode of learning
In order to protect mankind.

Canto Forty-eight

'We have no Desire to Usurp any Kingdom'

||௬||

As they were walking amidst the impenetrable
Forest of Dandaka, they chanced upon
A spot where there was a huge mountain of
Human skeletons as if it was a mound of sin
Accumulated over centuries. 'What is this
Mountain of bones which is mocking us?' Rama
Asked the ascetic and the latter told him about
The demon, Viradha:

'He has killed the ascetics and
Has eaten their flesh and drunk their blood.   10
He has piled up their bones in this fashion.
We have been harassed like hell.' Thus they
Narrated their woes.

Just then there was commotion
All around as the wild beasts ran helter-shelter;
The shrubs shook violently and there was
Thundering sound which echoed in the forest;
Viradha manifested himself.
His eyes were like fireballs,
And he looked like the demon causing cataclysm.   20

His aspect was dark and terrible:
Deep-set eyes and bulging paunch,
The opened jaws gave out a deafening roar;
He bore a spear in his hand.
Rushing towards Rama like Rudra, the destroyer,
He roared:

'I am Viradha and my parents are
Jaya and Shatahrada, and I possess
All the weapons with the required *mantras* and
Techniques and hence I am invincible.   30
Now let me know who you are!
Why this pretence of unkempt locks of hair?
Why this simple vesture of mendicants?
Having a bow in your hand, why roam secretly?
Wearing a mask of *dharma*, why should you suffer?
Are you imposters, planning to kidnap women?
By the way, who is this maiden,
Who is like a creeper being pulled down
By the weight of her breasts?
Why is she alone amidst two of you?   40
Let me have her who is like a philosopher's stone.
You are taking away, forcefully, the maiden of my land;
I will drink the blood from your chest;
I am glad to have you for my meal.
I eat up those who wander in my kingdom
Without any fear and without any resistance.
She belongs to me and you have no right
Over her. This is the law of the jungle,'
So said Viradha.

Shri Rama responded   50
In a dignified tone: 'We are the sons
Of king Dasharatha of the Ikshwaku clan.
He is Lakshmana, my dearest brother;
She is Janaki, my wife, who is not born of any woman.

We have to live in the forest for fourteen years
To follow the dictum of our dear father.
We have come to Dandakaranya, renouncing
Our throne in order to fulfill that expectation.
They call me Rama.

'I am not attached to the throne;   60
Neither have I any inclination to usurp others' land.
We have come in pursuit of Truth, and to
Protect the same, we are bent upon rooting out
The very source of violence.
Therefore do not resort to violence;
Do not follow the path of immorality;
Do not advance to touch the lady, I warn you!'

But Viradha surged forward
And held Sita firmly and began to run,
Roaring like fire in unquenchable anger.   70
Sita was completely overtaken by fear.
When she blinked her eyes like a stricken
Deer, Shri Rama taunted her with these words:

'We told you not to come to the forest,
But you wouldn't listen; now you are held
Captive by this unspeakable demon.'

'Look Saumitri,
The demon may harm Sita if we tarry;
Do not delay; wouldn't you have quickened
Yourself if Urmila were in Sita's position?   80
Now take up your arms and act at once
And make the demon free Janaki,' so said
Rama in a raised tone.

'Listen, brother,
The reality is different. Mother Sita is beyond
Her corporeal form; she is not a woman born;
She is an embodiment of the Divine Mother,

And therefore she is, in fact, carrying
The demon like a mother and the sight that he is
Abducting her is only an illusion,' so said 90
Saumitri at the barbaric behaviour of
The demon and roared at his excesses:
'I'll quell Viradha's breath mercilessly;
I'll drink his blood as he holds Sita
Like a hawk. Just as Indra pulverised
The mountains with his *vajra* weapon,
I will break his chest; throw out his entrails,
And therefore you are not helpless,
Neither am I forgetful,' so said Saumitri
And began aiming at the demon quickly. 100

When Viradha roared,
In the womb of the forest it appeared as if
A thunderbolt had struck its environs.
But Shri Rama aimed at him drawing
All the seven arrows to his famed bow, Kodanda,
And they all penetrated the demon's body, deep.
Viradha fell to the ground with a huge thud
As if a mammoth tree was uprooted from the earth.
Sita gently slid to the ground like a delicate flower
After the demon's hands let go their grip. 110

Shri Rama rushed to the spot
And raised Sita gently, sprinkling water on her,
Even as she regained her breath slowly.
Shri Rama's neck was garlanded by her delicate
Arms and he, in turn, held her fast,
Dispelling anxiety and the ascetics heaved a sigh
Of relief at the conquest of the terrible demon.

Viradha uttered wailing,
In pain: 'Listen Shri Rama, I am a *gandharva*,
A heavenly being, in reality; this is the result of a curse. 120
In the absence of constitutional rules and the

Instruments for a livelihood; with least
Inclination to follow the path of knowledge
I followed the alternative arrangement of
Violence shown by the demons who revel
In conflict and confrontation. They were
Nurtured by little camps aiming at subverting
The machinery of governance.'

Shri Rama took pity
Hearing Viradha's antecedents. 'Tell me, Viradha, 130
Whether you have Ravana's help and guidance.'
When he asked thus, Viradha replied with
Great difficulty being on the verge of death, 'Never,
My lord. At every step, the followers of Ravana
Are adopting the lawless methods.
In the absence of proper
Governance, even a law-abiding citizen would
Turn into a ruffian; and the weak people
Would be their victims.'
As he was summoning strength to utter these words 140
Viradha's breath ceased and he was no more.

'Gear up Saumitri,
We must show a proper destination to Viradha's
Dead body.' Listening to Rama's inclination,
Lakshmana dug out a big pit in the ground
And pushed the demon's corpse into it;
Filled the gorge with mud and stone,
And it looked as if a thief of idols was put
Behind bars!

Canto Forty-nine

'I Will Slough off My Skin Like a Snake'

||6||

'Saumitri, march forward and we cannot tarry
Here in the forest as the path is exacting.
We can see our new path with the help of
The great Sage Sharabhanga,' said Shri Rama
And they saw the hermitage of Sharabhanga
After they traversed some distance.

Sita, Rama and Lakshmana
Derived fulfilment on seeing Sage Sharabhanga.
The sage, on his part, was overjoyed
And hence treated them with great affection: 10
'My dear Shri Rama, my life's ambition is complete
Now. You are the royal swan that swims
In the consciousness of Shiva. I have been waiting
For your arrival. The news of your coming
Was so elevating and now that I have seen you,
My eyes are filled with delight.
I was ready for the journey to the world of Brahma;
And now my state is greater than that after seeing you.
Your grace is beyond comparison
And I surrender my last offerings at your feet.   20
Kindly accept the roots and shoots.

'I was living like breath
Lodged within the cage of the body in the manner
Of a bird that is unable to go out of
The enclosure. But now I have overcome
The cycle of birth and death and therefore
I will go to the world of Brahma, making myself free
From this eternal cycle.
Until then, kindly stay before me with Sita and
Saumitri. Lodge within my heart so that 30
Your vision gets permanently etched there.
The one with the hue of a blue sky and lotus-like
Eyes; having all the noble qualities and capable
Of giving everything that one asks for.
The noblest of all beings, who has blessed names.
Stay, stay within my vision,' so saying
The ascetic meditated upon the divine form.

Sita, Rama and Saumitri
Were overjoyed. The great sage had attained
Ripe old age and the body reflected the passage 40
Of time and his heart was mellowed with wisdom.
Devotion had brought the fruits of penance.
His mind was crystal clear and consciousness
Had bloomed likewise.
Whenever he opened his mouth, the speech
Is full of sagely utterances accompanying
Eternal song of liberation.
'Listen Shri Rama, listen Saumitri,
I have travelled all over this country,
Continuously, and I have seen the plight and 50
Suffering of the poor and their ignorance.
I have pitied them. My soul burns for
Their deliverance. Many of us, hermits, have
Yearned for the well-being of the world
Through our penance and sacrificial
Oblations. But in the absence of real concern,

The service of the people will go to waste.
Everywhere there is foolishness and
What is needed is the will to bring succour
To those who suffer in poverty and indulgence!
The fount of compassion must spring from the heart;
We can't preach spirituality to a hungry man.
The soul of virtuous living is to live as we speak.
'Listen again;
Whatever a person earns, by way of riches
And wealth, does not strictly belong to him.
I have sown the seeds of compassion and kindness
In many a heart; many will sprout and
Grow into sturdy trees. All wealth must flow
In order to lift the lowly and the downtrodden.'
So saying, the great Sage Sharabhanga withdrew
Into silence for a while even as his eyes
Were brimmed with tears. His tongue
Became dry and the words stuck in his throat,
And he began to shake.
He overcame his silence
And spoke: 'Shri Ramachandra and Saumitri,
You should grow like a great banyan tree and
Provide shelter to all those who need help.
That alone delivers you from the grip of life.
It is a sin to harass others, whereas
Love brings merit. Fear is more dreadful than death,
Fear leads one to hell.
Through fearlessness you can obtain cosmic vision.
May you have a glimpse of the cosmic form!
'We need to sow the seeds of
Universal brotherhood; as everything is filled
With divinity, cut all that is illusory.
You are the lamp of assurance to the needy.
Overcome all those who harass the poor;
Let the suppressed subdue all obstacles

And spring from their miserable conditions;
Let the garden called New Bharatavarsha
Manifest itself right now with million blooms;
You become the bubbling source of love.
When the muscles of iron and nerves of steel
Are ready, Renaissance is close at hand,
Ramarajya is an undoubted reality!
Life is a penance, life is a ceremony!

'In the womb of violence itself   100
Will loom the horizon of peace; march ahead
Without pause; let hunger not retard you,
Let not thirst tax you; you be one with everyone,'
Said the ascetic with divine intent.
'We don't need any wealth and comfort.
While we enjoy your grace, the huts of leaves
would do; we will overcome all troubles,'
Replied Shri Rama.
'I am no longer burdened by body-consciousness,
I will leave this coil right here and go. Shri Rama,
March ahead and you will see the hermitage of the Sage
Sutheekshna. It is an abode of beauty and very close   110
To the banks of Mandakini. You may have to
Cross the river with a rafter as the auspicious time
Is at hand. The great sage will reveal the path
Of truth ahead. Let me continue to have your grace,
Lord, I will slough off this body like

A snake. I will attain the state of eternal bliss."
Uttering these words the ascetic entered
The ritual fire like the sacrificial matters offered
To the blazing fire. Side glance of the sage dazzled with intensity;
Renunciation is the wick and devotion is the *ghee*;   120
When awareness is the flame there is effulgence
Of experience revealing the divine path of
Liberation; and the sage's body was lost

In that all elevating light!
Within no time it flew to the celestial sky
Like an arrow shot by a god.
Many ascetics and villagers
Saw that wonderful sight of Sage Sharabhanga
Plunging into fire and turning into light
Before turning into void. With an unbounded affection,   130
A sage called Jnanashreshta addressed
Rama who was lost in thought:

'The scenes of
Self-immolation may take place here everyday;
Sage Sharabhanga had postponed his end
Until this day; he had freed his mind already,
And today he freed his body as well!
Humanity burns everyday and every night.'

Saumitri could not contain himself;
He approached the ascetic in great devotion and asked him: 140
'Please do tell us the reason for his self-immolation.'
The sage said, 'Now that you have asked me,
It is imperative that I explain to you.
'Mining is going on
In the forest. The labourers are exploited
By the gods as well as by the demons;
The wages are meagre; they suffer from hunger
Along with their children.

'They used to narrate
Their saga of sorrow to Sharabhanga every   150
Now and then! The sage went to their huts
And saw their plight at close quarters; he
Suffered greatly at their agony and did not
Sleep properly, always thinking of alleviating
Their pain. The labourers thought their lot
Would be improved by Sage Sharabhanga.
Sharabhanga waited

For the arrival of the king of gods to the hermitage.
As he is endowed with all the wealth in
The world, the sage thought, he would help the poor.
'His wish was fulfilled, in a way, after Devendra
Came to the hermitage; the sage sat with him
Alone and discussed the matter in detail, explaining
To the celestial being the plight of the workers.
"The labourers are invaluable wealth;
Should they he exploited in this manner?
Ever a great protector, you have to save them.
The cat plays, but the mouse is in agony;
Determined are the selfish to exploit the poor.
They are the enemies of humanity, the cruel ones;
We trust you, don't forsake them, don't ignore them.
Help the poor and the downtrodden", so saying
He prayed in all sincerity.

'Devendra, the king of Heaven, was deaf
To the pain of the poor, and mocked Sharabhanga:
"Whatever wealth I have earned is for the gods
And not for human beings." His words were
Curt and he left for his world in alacrity.

'Sharabhanga's citadel
Of hope had crumbled at once. Devendra had
Pushed him into the pit of desperation. His mind
Became empty and he looked into the void
And said with pain in his voice: "The rich
People and those in power — whether they are gods
Or demons — they evolve a stratagem together to
Suck the blood of the helpless. The workers
Suffer inconsolably and they have joined
The ranks of the animal world as they are
Unable to figure among human beings.
Ravana kills the intellectuals and
Devendra buys them up! On the ocean of the poor,
He sails and finds it entertaining!"

'And then Sharabhanga
Waited for your arrival contemplating, "Shri Rama
Will come and listen to the woes of the oppressed;
Shri Rama, who is the hero par excellence
Being born in the redoubtable Ikshwaku clan."
He held his breath within the frame of his body
For such a day.
What more can I relate – the rest you have seen   200
With your own eyes. He should have lived
To see your deeds, but it was inevitable that
He had to journey towards Brahma's world.'

The saga of Sage
Sharabhanga had engulfed the mind.
The sage entering the fire haunted him
Like a picture constantly in his consciousness.
The rest of the ascetics were happy beyond
Words that they could see Rama in person.
They related to him all the pain and   210
Suffering they were undergoing at the hands of
The demons; they showed him the wounds
And scars imprinted on their bodies.
'You must remove all these pains and
Stop all atrocities. The town protectors are
Taking one sixth of the subjects' earnings;
And if they fail to provide security to people
Treasury is nothing but a sinful hoard.
The ascetics offer to the king one-fourth
Of what they earn in the righteous way.   220
But there are no protectors and anarchy
Is indulging in its murderous dance.
Why, Saketa is lost in pursuit of sensual pleasure!
We are orphans and there is dissipation
Of discipline everywhere,' the sage told Rama
In great anguish.

The words of the ascetic
Pierced Rama like fierce arrows. 'I see now
The errors of the palace of Saketa as in a mirror.
I am pained; I have seen death and pain close at hand. 230
I have understood everything; I will carry out your
Words as law and I have come in pursuit of *dharma*.
I will quell and conquer the troops of demons
Who are pestering and persecuting the good people,
And uphold the discipline of righteous living.
Your wish will be fulfilled and there will
Be peace and tranquility all around,' so said
Rama with sturdy determination.

Rama couldn't sleep that night
As the pictures swirled in his mind in a 240
Panoramic fashion. Sita too was changing sides
Intermittently, and Lakshmana was seething with
Anger; he was immersed in pain. He visualised
The atrocities in front of him. His soul shuddered
To encounter the cruel aspect of exploitation.
Violence mocked at him. Siddashrama,
Thatakavana, Gauthamashrama, Janakapuri,
Saketa and Chitrakoota got mixed up with
Dandakaranya in a relentless whirl.

Looking at Rama who was 250
Overtaken by worry, Sita said in a gentle tone:
'Why this despondency, o noble one?
You have determined to put an end to the demons
And with Saumitri, you will accomplish the task.'
'Sita, that is the source of my worry.
When the common men took up arms
To counter the aggression of the demons,
The sages did not tolerate it, deeming
It as unacceptable. This has put the common people
In a fix. My dear lady, I am at a loss to understand 260
How to protect all my subjects,' replied Rama.

Sage Jnanashreshta was haunted
By the thought that the immolation of Sharabhanga
Would enhance the activities of the demons.
If Rama stayed in the hermitage, it was
Likely that this would anger the demons further,
And they would attack with an increased aggression.
Therefore, the ascetic prayed for Shri Rama's
Departure from the hermitage.

Canto Fifty

'Do Not Give Up the Pursuit of Truth'

||6||

The next day, in the morning,
When Shri Rama got ready, after his ablutions,
To leave the hermitage, a young hermit called
Dharmabhritya came to him and said in
Earnestness, "The hermitage of Sutheekshna is very
Far from here; my hut is nearer in comparison;
If you could accompany me till then, I will show
You the right destination.' 'As we have many
Weapons with us, we may not be your ideal guests,'
Said Rama. But Dharmabhritya persisted,   10
'Weapons are not unwanted and, moreover,
Your fame has spread far and wide and, hence,
Many have come to have a glimpse of you,
And many seeking your help; some in sheer
Devotion and others to test your prowess.'

Smiling gently Saumitri said,
'Tell me, what is your perception of Rama?'
His question was straight and unequivocal.
'I am not a hero, neither am I a tried warrior;
I do not possess strength to pursue divine knowledge   20

I am only a devotee of the heroes;
Now it is up to you to put me in any slot Saumitri.'
Saumitri said in appreciation, 'I like the way
You put things in perspective; but the life of
Adventure is worth pursuing; by the way,
Are you inclined to observe the enterprise
Of the common people?' The ascetic replied,
'Very much lord; otherwise, I would have
Committed suicide by now.' Turning towards
Shri Rama he asked, 'Everyone is awaiting your 30
Deicision, kindly speak.'

'We are eager to meet
Sutheekshna. According to his wish, I would
Like to stay in his hermitage,' said Rama; but
Immediately Dharmabhritya added, 'Forgive me,
My lord, I will tell you one thing; please do not
Mistake my words. You may meet Sage Sutheekshna,
But you cannot stay in his hermitage, because
You cannot destroy the demons from there.
You will understand all this by and by.' 40

A gentle smile adorned
Shri Rama's visage; he nodded his head in assent.
As he stepped forward along with Dharmabhritya's
Companions, men and women came
In droves; they gained courage and were
Excited on the occasion. Looking at the mood
Of joyous celebration, Dharmabhritya said:
'Do you see the unbounded prowess of the
Common people? Their suppressed valour
Has broken the barriers; their heroism 50
Sprouts in abundance; their courage gathers
Like the flood of Ganga in order to end
The exploitation of the oppressed! But if you
See the hermitage now, it is all dull and depressing

As the hermits are forsaking their abodes
And are moving towards towns.'

Saumitri said:
'Dharmabhritya, you have uttered the truth; there are
Reasons too for their helplessness; one is: the fear
Of the demons and they are bothered very much   60
By their long-term anxiety that their exploitation
Would never come to an end. They have inferred
That it is better to take their lives instead of
Leading a humiliating existence. This is the
Second reason. There is one more,
Dharmabhritya, you may forgive me for broaching
Upon this, calling this an act of effrontery;
And that is, the hermits themselves are making
The common man wallow in ignorance
Instilling in them fear and dejection.   70
They have spread pessimism by their lacklustre
Attitude; they have built a wall of slavery
Thereby closing the path of change. If an
Invincible army is not formed, suicide
Will continue without any break.

'If there were to be an organised
Power, the hermitage would have been a centre
Against terrorist attack. Ahalya in the past;
Who can say whose turn it is tomorrow?
These hermits have hugged inaction   80
In the name of peace and they have forgotten
Their obligation; they ought to have galvanised
The common people into a counter-revolutionary
Force. These ascetics steeped in their so called
Spiritual pursuit, they have worked against
Humanity and hence they are guilty of a crime
Unfathomable,' Saumitri uttered these words in pain
And his anger was welling up from within.

Shri Rama was gently amused
Hearing the angry words of Urmila's husband, 90
'Saumitri, you seem to have joined the band of those
Who decry spirituality,' so Rama said to him.
Saumitri replied being overtaken by compassion,
'It is not like that, lord; it is a crime to preach
Spirituality to one who is hungry. What will
Common men make of the cycle of life and death
When they actually are in empty stomach?
When this life is crushed by disease and exploitation
And humiliation; when it is subjected to
The extremes of summer and winter, 100
Can they reach the fruits of spirituality?'

As they were drowned in argument
In this fashion, a villager stopped Saumitri
On the way and said in exhileration, "Dharma-
Bhritya, every now and then, praises a great
Sage and that great soul is Agastya.
Lopamudra is his spouse. It will do good to you
If you meet them.'

Canto Fifty-one

'The Lone Voice of Humanity'

||๏||

In the dead of night, one day,
Two voices were heard penetrating the silence
Of the dark night. They reached the ears of Shri Rama
And Sita in slow pace once and again in a high
pitch; once like a woman's voice and
Again with a male voice; subsequently like
The mingled cry of infants and again like
A man shouting at someone; like a woman
Wailing inconsolably. After some time, it became clear
That it was a scene of domestic discord.   10
'Kill me at once! Choke my neck.
The children are dying of hunger.
You are sailing on the waves of intoxication.
We will die and become one with the soil,
Turning into manure so that crops may
Grow out of our strength,' the wife wept
In deep sorrow.

'What arrogance!
What haughtiness!! you are a quarrelsome
Wench of low status; do you have guts   20

To abuse me? Shut your mouth or else I will
Beat you to death,' thus, when the man blared
The battle drum of the family had been beaten.

The next moment Shri Rama
Rose from his seat and addressed them: 'Come
Dear Saumitri, I will go with Sita and see
What is happening there, the helpless wailing
Of the woman is piercing our ears.' So saying
Rama went there and observed the scene of quarrel
Between the husband and wife.   30

The man had worn round
His waist a piece of rag as a lower garment.
He was a picture of poverty, with sunken
Eyes and sagging jaws; his stomach had stuck
To his back. Being nothing but a skeleton
He was lolling hither and thither, gripped
By the devil of intoxication. 'Hold yourself
Brother, why beat the woman? Tell me
What happened; but stop this beating first.'
So saying Shri Rama intervened and Sita   40
And Saumitri arrived there. They were
Horrified to see that woe-begone sight.

'Who are you to stop me?
This is my wife and I will beat her to death.
I have every right to do so! This is my
House and not your father's. It is our life
And who are you to interfere in our affairs?'
Blurted the man in one breath.

The daughter of the earth
Was so disturbed hearing these words that   50
Her eyes gave out sparks of anger.
Rama felt as if someone had slapped him on his cheeks.
Summoning his usual calm,

He said: 'My brother, I am very well aware
That this is your house; but an abominable
Violence is taking place right now; this is no longer
A home as the dance of death is raging.
Hold on, and be patient!'

'Do we have a home? It is a graveyard.
Home and hearth are for people like you who are well off.   60
Have you come here to pay lip service?
And who is this woman standing beside you?
Is she your wife? Does she also need a bit of thrashing?'
As he rushed forward, saying thus,
Shri Rama held his neck firmly with his fingers,
And said, 'I will forgive your audacity as you are
Inebriated.' But the man did not seem to relent:
'What can you do to me? Do you want to take my life?
When everything is dear, only the life of the poor
Is cheap; the wretched of the earth have barren existence.   70
Let them melt into this earth and become one with the sod.'
While he was shouting thus, his wife came out
And stood leaning against the door.
The clothes she wore were in tatters; her two kids
Watched hiding behind that pathetic raiment,
The wild tantrums of their father in fear and anxiety!

Even as the intoxication subsided,
Attempting to disengage himself from Shri Rama's grip,
The man, at last, said buckling to the ground:
'Who are you, man? Who called you here and   80
What do you want to do?'
Shri Rama replied in a calm and dignified tone:
'I am an ascetic living in the forest,
And I have come here to tell you that women
Must not be treated with violence.
And I am here to protect them. It is against the law
To resort to violence in this fashion.'

'I am her husband and I have
the authority to decide the course of her life.
Are you the owner of the mines that you think   90
You can interfere? Or, are you his kinsman Agnivamshi,
Or, are you a member belonging to the demons
That you persecute us so much?' He said with anger.

'Brother! Should you use such harsh words?
I have the right to protect a helpless woman.
This is merely guided by humane feelings.
Don't be aggressive against a defenceless woman;
You must resist the acts of the wicked people,'
Said Rama with great anguish.

The man floated on the waves of   100
Derisive laughter and said, 'That means, you are
Mandakarni.' 'I do not know who Mandakarni is,
They call me Rama.' But the man reacted quickly,
'You pretend to save the woman
While trying to seduce her. I can mark the frauds
Like you irrespective of your disguise.
You are all demons and Agnivamshis –
You are a Mandakarni; hence be gone.'

Then the daughter of Mithila approached,
Consoled the woman and children, and said: 110
'Sister, we have come to help you; they call me
Sita and Shri Rama is my husband; this is
Saumitri, the blessed one – he is my brother-in-law,'
Sita said this in low tones.
That gentle woman looked at Sita exuding
Gratitude in her eyes. The man slumped
To the ground unable to stand on his legs.

Shri Rama addressed the crowd
That had gathered while the rumbling whisper boomed:
'Why are you all keeping silent while a man is beating   120

His wife to death? It is his domestic affair no doubt,
But you must intervene all the same'.
When they all scattered from the place and the protest
Had also stopped, then the daughter of Janaka touched the woman
Gently again and said, 'Sister, we take our leave of you,
Have no fear.' The woman then saw the fountain of
Human kindness springing from the heart-depths.
Her eyes blossomed in gratitude; the furrows on her
Forehead began to vanish. She nodded her assent.
Then Shri Rama, Saumitri and Vaidehi left for   130
The hermitage of Dharmabhritya.

Canto Fifty-two

'They Have Burnt the Roots of the Creeper of Life'

||๑||

Shri Rama told Dharmabhritya about the domestic quarrel
That he had witnessed, 'That man asked me
Vehemently whether I was "Mandakarni". Who is
This Mandakarni?' Hearing the name from Shri Rama
Dharmabhritya's face registered a mark of sadness.
'Lord, he is a sage and he came as a protector of
The labourers and now he has turned out to be
Their tormentor. These mines have various owners;
They are all sufficiently wealthy. Agnimitra of
Agnivamsha is the richest of them all.' So saying   10
He laid the foundation for the story of Mandakarni.

Saumitri and Sita sat there and Saumitri's
Fondness for such tales was very well-known.
His anger would spring from the stories of exploitation.
'What happened Dharmabhritya, what happened to
Mandakarni?' asked Saumitri.

'Mandakarni came from somewhere.
He is a sage; he is one given to penance, and he really

Pitied the plight of the labourers. The workers
Belonging to the clans of *vanara*, *ruksha*, 20
nishada and *shabara* worked in the mines.
The women, the young and the old and even
The sick worked day and night.
They were all bonded labourers trapped within the confines
Of mines. They worked strenuously but the returns
Were meagre. There was no one to protest on their
Behalf when they suffered greatly due to terrible accidents.

'They were so helpless that they carried on
With total surrender bearing all pain and torture. 30
Mandakarni then alerted them to their plight
By becoming their guide and mentor. He taught
Their children the alphabet. He even encouraged them
To stand united and protest against ill-treatment.
He brought awareness in respect of their rights and freedom.

'The workers rose against Agnivamshi;
And all the attempts of the latter to coax them
To his path failed and the atrocities subsided while
Wages increased marginally. The rays of light
Appeared in the womb of darkness and confinement. 40
They all worshipped Mandakarni; whatever he said
Became law; his utterances were drops of nectar;
His name became a *mantra* and he rose to the
Position of the head of the committee.

'While life went on in this fashion, there was
An earthquake and landslide, and about two
Thousand workers in the mine were buried alive.
The women's wails rose to the sky and the workers
Asked for compensation. Agnimitra's reign was
On a shaky ground. 50

'Not knowing any other way, Agnimitra
Tried to entice Mandakarni to his side.

He approached him with gentleness and humility;
Treated him with utmost respect, lavishing on him
Many gifts. He pleaded with him with folded hands
That he should pacify the workers. He took him to a far off
Land and looked after him with care and respect.
He built a palatial house at a place called
"Panchasara" and told him, "O great one,
This house is for you."   60

'The taste of all that he was provided was
Out of the world; even the women he was provided
Resembled the heavenly nymphs. Comforts
Of every kind along with wealth were offered
On such lavish scale that Mandakarni literally
Wallowed in pleasures that did not seem to end.

'He forgot the interest of the workers,
As he immersed himself in the company of women,
Wine and wealth. The story ahead is all a matter
Of sadness and pity. In the palace of Panchasara   70
The anklets made a tinkling sound, while the fetters
That held the labourers tight in the mines jangled incessantly.

'The women-folk shed tears in the huts;
The children wailed because of hunger; their combined
Cries reached the clouds. The leaders of the workers were
Tied to the posts inside the cottages and were set on fire,
And their bodies were charred in the engulfing flames.

'As the atrocity reached its zenith, they said   80
The workers died in the fire accidentally, thereby they
Buried the truth several fathoms deep. The women's
Modesty was violated, the children were sold to
The outsiders. Thus did Mandakarni sacrifice
The interests of the workers while wallowing in
The excessive pleasures spread before him.'

Saumitri was impatient to learn
What happened further. 'The workers explained
In detail everything that took place to Sharabhanga,
Their head. He understood the deceitful nature 90
Of Mandakarni. Sharabhanga was deeply touched
By this and he took the lead and determined
To respond to their plight. His anger against Mandakarni
Knew no bounds. He organised the workers
Again, promoting their leadership. He made them
Take a pledge that they would fight till they acquired
Ownership of the mines. He formed an association
Of the workers; invited none other than the king of Heaven,
And requested him to guide them. When Devendra
Treated Sharabhanga with scant respect, the latter 100
Put an end to his life unable to bear it. Saumitri,
You are aware of the rest,' so saying Dharmabhritya
Fell silent.

'Would these men have partnership with
The demons?' When Saumitri asked bristling
With anger, Dharmabhritya said again:
'Saumitri, the demons are not staying far away
From us; they are right amidst us, in the form
Of the mine-owners. They are with the *yakshas*
And Aryas, as there is no distinction among 110
The people of wealth. Their eyes are closed
Because of excess of gold they possess and hence
They cannot see the pain of the poor.
'The earth has swallowed the feelings
Of their heart, and they have all turned into stony boors.
Thus, the royal merchant, the trader, the army general
And even the religious head — all have become
Heartless demons. As they are very powerful,
They have the protection of the strong.
What if the gods are ranged against the demons? 120
When the poor are their common enemies, they

Have become allies', so saying Dharmabhritya
Left the place, overcome with emotion.

Early in the morning, one day,
The wife-tormentor, Makhana, approached Shri Rama
And Sita, along with his wife Sudha, after his bath,
Wearing fresh clothes. The splendour of spirit
Shone amidst poverty, and they appeared as if they were
The stars that had passed through thick, dark clouds.

Bowing to the feet of Shri Rama and 130
Sita, Makhana said in all humility: 'Lord,
Forgive my wrongdoing, I behaved in a cruel manner.'

'You have insulted – not me but Sudha,
Beating her black and blue. Who will respect you
In society if you quarrel like this? Ask Sudha's forgiveness,'
Urged Sita. 'He has begged my forgiveness many times.
If he tortures me again and begs my forgiveness,
What is the use of my forgiveness?' said Sudha,
Describing her husband's despicable behaviour.
'What is this Makhana? Why this atrocity against your wife? 140
When will you stop this? Tell me, brother,
Is it right to subject wife and children to cruelty? when
You are in a state of inebriation?

'Liquor destroys the balance of mind,
Polluting the sense of discrimination, it upsets
Your composure; violence takes hold of you
And the house will be in disarray. If you
Refuse the intoxicating drink, wealth grows
And the mind is illuminated resulting in the
Gathering of grace! Why should you undermine 150
Peace, stability and tranquility? Correct yourself,
Makhana, try to lead a respectable life,'
Said Shri Rama to restore balance in the context.

'I want to be a decent man,
I want to be a man of substance; but would these

Heartless men allow me to lead such a life?
Instead of lifting up a man who has fallen into a pit,
Each one will tie a heavy stone or two around his neck.
They will push him to the water and laugh at his plight.
They have burnt the roots of the creeper called life.   160

'When Mandakarni told us
That we too had some ownership over the mines,
And prepared us for the struggle, and thus we got
The grains at a lower rate; the wage was
Increased, they built for us dwelling places,
The hospital came up in the neighbourhood;
They even assured us of a school. When Mandakarni
Caused all this to happen, we worshipped him
As our unfailing kinsman and I appointed
My eldest son for his service. I do not know   170
Where he is, whether in the abode of gods, or
In the domain of the demons as a bonded labourer;
Or he may have been killed and eaten by now.

'What can I say, lord? The owners
Of the mines took away our women and outraged
Their modesty and put them to the life of prostitution.
They all became the pleasure-dolls for the rich.
Our children have suffered endlessly and our
Uprising has proved to be our ruin!

'There was an increase, at the same time,   180
In the number of liquor shops in our village.
The followers of the barons swelled and prospered.
We, on the other hand, were reduced to mere skeletons.
The owners have close contact with the city of Lanka, and
What do we have? Nothing! We know no peace,
No comfort, only labour. We step into our huts
Only to encounter varied apparitions of want.
Our needs are many, but no money to redress;
There is only one way to liberate ourselves from this:

To commit suicide and be done with this life. 190
Hence, lord, we have taken recourse to drinking!' –
Said Makhana in a tone of unimitigated pain.

This tale of exploitation touched
Shri Rama, Sita and Saumitri with its intensity.
They became speechless at Makhana's condition.
They felt sorry for the previous night's incident.
'Forgive me, Makhana, I punished you not
Realising your situation,' said Shri Rama pitying
The man.

'The tale of human beings is a 200
Never-ending one. We are such innocent lot
That we believe easily men's friendship and their
Methods and transactions. Thus, I trusted
Mandakarni and I am suffering as a result.
My wife, Sudha, true to her name "nectar," has protected
Everyone during our time of trouble. But for her support,
I wouldn't be alive now!

'Sage Sharabhanga, our well-wisher,
Tried so many things to rescue us. If he,
Like Mandakarni, had danced to the tune of 210
The exploiters, he too could have lived in a
Palace enjoying all comforts.
He forsook all that and sacrificed everything
For our sake. He achieved life in death; whereas
We are more than dead, though alive! Now
We must take leave of you; we will come again.
We cannot refrain from labour as we have to eke out
A living. Lord, you be the wishing-tree for the
New millennium, we will act as manure for it.'
So saying Makhana and Sudha vanished 220
Out of sight.

Janaki's mind was immersed in thought.
'While the children of the rich are wallowing in plenty

In castle-like buildings, the offsprings of the poor
Play in the dust looking for food in the heap of
leftovers. If Janaka had not saved me while
I was left on the field unattended and crying,
Perhaps, my life would not have been different
From that of Sudha. I would have gazed at the void
In fear and anguish.' That was the chain   230
Of thought in the mind of Maithili.

Angry Saumitri said, 'They are living
Like animals though they are human beings;
The remedy is to raise their spirits; they live in
Slums with empty stomachs and they should be provided
With shelter, food, clothing and education. We
Must motivate them to participate in the movement.
We must weld the common people with the sages,
Savants and the intellectuals, and we have to create
A vigilant society.'   240

The next day Saumitri went to the forest,
Along with Beekhana and brought all the necessary
Wood to build huts over there. Shri Rama, on the other hand,
Started sweeping the streets with Sita; and the workers
Felt ashamed of themselves and joined in the operation
Without wasting any time.

There was some din at that time and
Shri Rama and Sita turned around to see what it was.
Saumitri brought a few men bound who appeared to be
Decent citizens to where Shri Rama was standing.   250

'What is all this, Saumitri?' asked
Shri Rama. 'When we were felling trees for building
Huts, these people stopped us and asked for the reason
And we told them. "We are the protectors of the forest
And you cannot cut trees," they said and a fight
Ensued. These heroes trusted the strength of the swords

And they are the owners of the mines,' said Saumitri
Turning towards the mine barons.

'Did you see our Lord, Shri Ramachandra?
If he so desires, he can award you capital punishment. 260
He subjected Sakalashwa and his son to execution
In Tatakavana, and thus he safeguarded righteousness.'
Hearing this, the owners of the mines were unhinged.

Frightened like deer and trembling,
They all knelt down before Rama and prostrated.
Ugragni implored, 'lord, I am the brother-in-law
Of Agnimitra and they call me Ugragni.
I oversee the mines and that is my job; forgive me
As I have not committed any wrong.'

Shri Rama said in anger, 270
'Why did you stop them? All have equal rights
In the forest. The owners of the mines must build huts
For the workers; but you are wallowing in riches
While pushing them into the mire of poverty and squalor.
The mineral wealth is found in abundance in nature.
If you fail to share equally with the workers,
If you act miserly not providing them any facilities,
You will surely be punished, bear this in mind!'

Ugragni said shaking,
'If all facilities are given along with the increased 280
Wages, they will take to a life of pleasure and waste
Away all they earn and finally slip into indolence.'

Saumitri exploded at this statement
Of Ugragni, 'You are the cruel demons, and you
Are exploiting the workers like animals for your
Comforts. Shri Rama, punish them mercilessly forthwith.'

Rama said to them: 'The workers
Don't need your charity. They work in the mines

Day and night; it is they who should have the ownership.
Right now, I declare that they are the owners of the mines.' 290

Ugragni stuttered: 'Would it be
Possible for the workers to run the mines?
Within four days, they will push it to the brink of loss.
What would be achieved by such a transfer
Of ownership? We don't have any say here,
While Devaraja and Agnideva are all in all;
They will not take this matter lightly. When the gods
And demons join hands, what force can stop their victory?
Gods own some mines, the rest belong to the demons;
And the demons buy all minerals. If the demons lose 300
The ownership of the mines, their coffers will be depleted.
Therefore, they will ally with gods and fight.
Listen, Shri Rama! It will lead all to total ruin.
Permit me to narrate all this to my master.'
So saying, Ugragni went to his place.

Canto Fifty-three

'A Vision of the Community Awareness'

|| ॐ ||

As time passed, one day, Makhana
Came running and said the following in fear:
'Shri Rama, the owners of the mines are planning
To set the mines on fire tonight. This is their
Conspiracy to put an end to those who oppose them.'
Makhana wept inconsolably.

Shri Rama was unperturbed:
'Don't have any fear: I have come here with the definite
Purpose of destroying the unethical union of the gods
And demons.' He said this with such determination   10
In his voice that Makhana shivered further.

Saumitri asked Makhana after understanding
Rama's intentions – 'How many people in this village
Are inclined to fight against the enemy?' 'All
Hold their lives dear, and so I can't see anyone
Ready to fight.' Saumitri enlightened Makhana –
'The reality is something different. Everyone is fed up
With the enemy, and if they are provided with the necessary
Weapons after organising them properly, they will
Take a plunge without any doubt. They have only   20

Two choices now: to die without food confining themselves to
Their cottages or to go over to the battlefield.
Let them decide since it is clear
That death is far better than a life of misery.
Death is knocking at the door; let us get ready.'

When Makhana moved towards his people
Dragging his feet and posed the same question before them,
He was surprised; they all loosened their shoulders and
Showed their readiness to fight. There was no sign
Of fear. The bugle blared at once and all men held 30
The spears in their hands and moved toward the mines.
Women went in the direction of the hermitage along with
Their young ones. The ascetics formed a battle
Formation around the mines tracing a semicircle.
Saumitri was the leader. The swords and daggers,
The shafts and sickles constituted the bulk of weapons.
It was a vision of the awareness of the community.
The mine-owners were terribly scared and hence
They scattered in all directions. Within no time
They vanished into the darkness of the forest. 40

Shri Rama said,
'Can we ever trust the owners of the mines? Can
The enemies turn into friends? They are quite
Organised and as they enjoy the alliance of Ravana's
Army, they are sure to attack us in the night.
Now, we are unencumbered; but it is only temporary,
As it is an uphill task to safeguard liberty.
Weapon-training is compulsory for everyone. We must be
Ever vigilant and retaliate the attackers. Saumitri will
Manage everything with skill and wisdom. There goes 50
The sound of the conch and I wish you all success.
Welcome death and I do not see any alternative.'

'Victory be to lord Shri Rama;
He is the owner of all the mines here,' – that was

The slogan given by the people at the top of their voice.
But Rama shook his head and told them firmly:
'Anyone who becomes a leader will become a demon
As time passes. He will be selfish and an exploiter.
The hunger for money and power will be a terrible obsession;
I don't want leadership! I did not forsake Saketa   60
Only to become a mine owner here. You are the owners
Of the mines. The mines belong to you. You work hard
Without falling a prey to laziness and build a new
Society sans exploitation. The man who tills
The fallow land, he is the owner; I love his coarse
Hands, as he will be a king reigning over the world.
I will remove the weed of exploitation and
The poor will occupy the position of power.
Acquire mastery in science and technology in the temple
Of knowledge.' There was concern in the voice of Rama.   70

Saumitri's plan had already met with success.
He called blacksmiths and built furnaces with new
Designs in order to melt iron. They produced new types
Of weapons moulding them afresh. They cleared all
Slums and built new homes for themselves joining
Hands. Saumitri led the workers in the new direction
Which ensured a new life. The life of comfort was
Theirs in the new arrangement.

Motherly Sita suggested to Rama
That women and children must be taught   80
How to read and write. Learning was extended even to
The elders. When Dharmabhritya's pupils
Became teachers themselves, there was a boy called
Bhulara among the learners! Shubhabuddhi was
Very enthusiastic in teaching and therefore he taught
The boys vigorously and relentlessly. Bhulara resisted,
'I cannot learn at this pace; I am not cut out for this
Rigour; I cannot pick up learning forcefully. I am

Just satisfied with my routine in the mines. I do not
Want this learning. When people learn they also pick up   90
The art of exploiting others. What is the use of learning
If it is geared to exact labour from others?
Leave me alone and you will be doing good to me.
Earlier it was Mandakarni and now it is Saumitri;
No freedom for us anyway. Do we need always
Someone above us as a leader?'

Bhulara questioned with desperation in his voice.
Bhulara's words reached Janaki
And she called him and told him gently, 'Bhulara,
Do not make light of learning; learning is one's father   100
And one's mother; it is an inexhaustible wealth.
The person of learning exudes liveliness.
Look at Shubhabuddhi; he is intelligent
In worldly affairs and also in the enterprise of the mines,
And he offers guidance to the people. A man of learning
Is respected and the one who lacks it is called a beast.
A person of learning rules like a king and you will be
A mere servant always dependent upon his charity,
Always susceptible for fraud and deception,
Waiting for his generosity to offer you food.   110
Without this strength of education, man will be
Just a lump of clay and nothing more.'

Bhulara already felt the vigour
Of the spirit flooding his interior – 'Shubhabuddhi
Did not say anything like this, mother; in the crucible
Of learning blossoms a culture of equality; when
We acquire education, there won't be any difference
Between the labourers and the sages, so said Shri Rama
And his words are still ringing in my ears, mother.
I am enlightened by your guidance; learning is   120
The *mantra* that liberates the workers and I will acquire it.'
So saying, Bhulara surrendered himself to the Goddess
Of Learning!

Many queries cropped up when one day
Shubhabuddhi, Bhulara, Makhana, Sudha and
Many others were in discussion with Rama at the centre.
Shri Rama enlightened them with his answers thus:

'If you really take stock of things,
At every stage of human history there has been a duality
In society: there is selfish motive and there is service 130
Motive. The selfish face is that of a demon; it reveals
In persecuting others; whereas the community-oriented
Mind derives satisfaction serving society,
Safeguarding the well-being of all. You cannot
Divide the society on the basis of caste and creed.
Conflicts are engendered by placing one segment
Above the other; monoculture pushes all to darkness.
There is a need to have a feeling that the entire
Community is one large family. The land belongs
To the people and the tiller of the soil has the sole 140
Right of his crop.

'You need to have weapons;
You need to fight in order to end exploitation.
It is not difficult to overwhelm the demons
Whose moral fibre is weak! They will be surely
Swept aside by the flood of community power!'

The pilgrimage to Dandakaranya
Was still pending and they could not tarry there.
Peace and tranquility prevailed in Dharmabhritya's
Hermitage. The labourers geared themselves to work. 150
There was an end to the persecution of the exploited.
The boys were acquiring learning, and men and women
were also learning assiduously. They were all raising
Themselves to a higher level as the axiom,
'Uddharedatmanatmanam' (One should raise high
Through one's own efforts) suggests. This ensured
The success of Saumitri's plans.

The next day, Bheekana asked:
'Lord, you are moving from one hermitage to another,
And would you not condescend to pay a visit to our   160
Hamlet?' Shri Rama said in compassion after tracing
A sense of desperation in the face of Bheekana: 'I will
Certainly come to your place, Bheekana.'

Bheekana's joy knew no bounds,
And Dharmabhritya was equally elated.
'Bheekana, go and announce the arrival of Rama;
Let everyone gather there, including the demons.
Give invitation to all those who follow the path
Of righteousness,' so said Dharmabhritya.

Canto Fifty-four

'You are Like Fire to The Forest of Desire'

||௬||

Taking their leave of Dharmabhritya
And also the workers, with great difficulty,
Sita, Rama and Lakshmana travelled a long
Distance crossing many rivers, climbing
Several mountains and finally reached
The hermitage of Sage Suthikshna, which
Was situated in the middle of a dense forest.

There were many types of trees,
And many types of flowers and climbers galore;
A variety of trees with luscious fruits and   10
The sage sat there in penance like a statue.
Seeing him all the three pilgrims felt
A thrill of exultation!

'Blessed am I!
Shri Ramachandra, you have come here to give
Your grace though I am an ignoramous
And not adept in observing penance;
And the art of worshipping is beyond my grasp.
It is all your kindness that has condescended
To come in person to this unmerited person.   20

You are a kinsman to the downtrodden;
You are their close associate. Lord, you have
Come to grant me enlightenment, like you
Protected Ajamila. I will offer at your feet
All the merits of my penance. Desire, Anxiety,
Memory, Praise, Emotion, Lament, Excitement,
Disease, Lassitude and Death – these are the ten
Conditions and the last condition is yet to happen.'
So saying, Sage Suthikshana prostrated

At the feet of Shri Rama. 30
As soon as the sage prostrated, he entered
Into a state of trance. Keeping the form of Shri Rama
In his heart, he had attained divine bliss. Shri Rama,
Sita and Saumitri bowed to the sage; and Rama
Uttered these words of reverence: 'We have come here
To see you; open your eyes and give us
Shelter; I will be a bee at your lotus feet,
Hovering there, singing hymns of praise
While you are the divine cow yielding unceasing bliss;
I will distribute to the world what I receive from you. 40
Radiant light that dispels darkness of night
Is emanating from your face; what more can I
Say, O Guru!' said Shri Rama praising the sage.

Suthikshana stood up and
Embraced Shri Rama in utter devotion. He fell
At the feet of Rama all again and floated on the ocean
Of exultation.

'I am a man of little wisdom, lord.
How can I praise you when you are the dazzling sun,
While I am a tiny glow worm. You are veritable 50
Fire to the forest of desire; make the good
People happy; you are like a lion to the elephants
That roam in the night; you are like an eagle
To the serpent called life; you are like a moon
To Vaidehi's eyes which feed, like the *chakora* birds

On moonlight; you are the little swan
That swims in the sea of my mind; you are the ocean
Of compassion granting wealth to one and all.
You are the one without attributes and you are
Also the one with form; you are the one who grants   60
All that the devotees wish for; you erase desire
And anger and enable us to cross this ocean of life.
You are the destroyer of *Kali* and you are the one
Without any blemishes,' thus sang the sage in all humility.

'We have sharp weapons
To destroy wild beasts; but the peace of the
Hermitage would be disturbed if we pick up the bow.
Therefore, it is not right that we stay here for long.
We will spend a night and move on. We are delighted
To have met you and talked to you,' said Saumitri   70
In all reverence and politeness.

Sage Suteekshna treated them
With pleasure and delight, and the night passed
In the elevating divine discourse. Very early in
The morning, next day, they bathed in the pure water
Of the river and ate the fruits offered by the sage.
'We seek your kind permission to take our leave of you,
Revered sir,' implored Rama bowing to the sage's feet.

The sage blessed them with divine
Grace. 'When Sita and Saumitri are with you   80
In this pursuit of Truth, may the success be yours;
Proceed further. You will hear the call of the peacocks
In caves and ravines; similarly, you will hear
The songs of the water-birds on the way;
You will see the grandeur of the rivers,
Lakes and streams; you will see the lotus and lily
Loom; and you will enter into the domain of earthly glory.
You will attain success.' With these words, the sage
Blessed them and sent them on their way.

Canto Fifty-five

'Non-violence is the Shield and the Ultimate God'

||৬||

As the journey was in progress,
Vaidehi told Rama in gentle words thus:
'Did you see, the noble one, how in Sutikshna's
Hermitage the animals live in perfect accord, forgetting
Their traditional enmity? The she-elephant is suckling
The lion's cub; both the young ones of lion and elephant
Are sucking at the cow's udder. This is the essence
Of the non-violent life of a hermitage!

'The enlightened ones think of the good
Of others in word and deed. O noble one! Telling   10
Lies, having illicit relationship with women, persecuting
Others without reason – these are counted as three banes.
As you are the embodiment of Truth, untruth is
Far away from you; you are the ultimate man
With simplicity; you have conquered desire.
Dedicated to one wife. Among the three banes,
Persecution of others is one that bothers you
Though you have committed it inadvertently.
You are caught in the web of violence as you are firm

In your belief that violence is the only way to protect
The labourers and the ascetics at Dandakarnya.

'When you carry bow and arrow,
You cannot resist the temptation of using them.
To corroborate this, I will tell you an episode
Narrated by my father and noble king, Janaka,
When I was a young girl.

'In a sacred forest,
There was a sage, honest and wise. Once a soldier
Approached him with this request: 'O great sage,
I will go on a pilgrimage; kindly keep this sword
Under your custody till I return.' The sage agreed.
Thereafter, he was constantly thinking of its safety;
Being worried about its theft, he kept it on his person
And moved about. Its constant association reduced
The righteous qualities in him and the worldly
Qualities increased which, in turn, provoked
Him to indulge in violence. It eventually
Led him towards hell. Weapons always mean playing
With fire. When you have explosives in the armoury,
You will be tempted to use them; the mind is oriented
Towards destruction; when you have arms close at hand,
The mind cannot guard itself against temptation.

'Forgive me, my lord!
Is it right on your part to kill the demons
In Dandakaranya? What harm have they caused you?
You have come here on exile and you
Indulge in violence; non-violence is the mother
Of the universe and it is the zenith of bliss.'

Shri Rama replied:
'When the demons are tormenting the ascetics,
It is the duty of the martial class to protect
The latter; to protect the penance is expected
Of us kings.'

'As we are in the forest,
How are the weapons valid here? It conflicts
With the environment. You may wield your weapons
Once we go back to Ayodhya. Why worry about
Safeguarding the state in this forest? Picking up arms
Causes depression of the mind; the demons
Crave for violence once they see the weapons; 60
They attack at once and the hermitage will turn
Into a battlefield. It is always good to observe
The righteous ways in the forest. Righteousness leads
To wealth and righteousness causes peace.
Righteousness is the foundation of all action.
Action ceases as a result of contemplation, which
Leads to the realisation of the Ultimate. That is
A state where the body, mind and speech become one.

'Overcoming the pulls of desire,
Those who are in pursuit of Truth, must have mystic 70
Experience as the Ultimate Goal. If you keep
On the track of non-violence, the mind rests
In a mood of penance. Do not think that
I am giving you advice; I have just shared with you
What my father Janaka told me about the nuances
Of righteousness.

'The state that accumulates arms
Indulges in the dance of violence and at the end
Destroys itself. The explosives surely cause
The ruin of everything; and hence throw them 80
To the bottom of the sea nullifying their power.
Put an end to the racial hatred and be
A harbinger of non-violence; let the illumination
Of peace spread to the whole world from the pinnacle
Of light established in the land of Bharata.
What merit is there in the pledge to destroy the demons?
In the process of fulfilling the father's obligations,

Is it right to extend to the south your desire
To conquer through martial advances?

'In the world there are three types of people
And they are – the rigteous, the pleasure-seekers
And downright philistines. The righteous
Always go in pursuit of liberation, the pleasure-
Seekers hanker after pleasure and their indulgence
Causes them to take repeated births. The people
Of the third category go a step further and wallow
In dark passions without any discrimination.
As a result of their excess, they fall into the pit
Of hell and rot there pitifully. That is why, O lord,
Be good and follow the righteous path;
And lead an exemplary life and be a store house
Of values by being an embodiment of purity itself.
Listen to the praise of the Almighty, contemplate on
His form and follow the tenets of equanimity ensured
By the company of the righteous. That will take you
To the pinnacle of bliss. When such is the case,
Why yield yourself blindly to an empty revolution!

'Do not ever forget the sacred ritual of *Putrakameshthi*,
Taught by Sage Jabali to Dasharatha. Do not forget
The grand and divine annals of Raghu dynasty resulting
From the act of entering the wombs of Kausalya,
Sumitra and Kaikeyi! Do not erase the mark of
The philosophy of non-violence of the New Age!

'Violence has many forms and
If you accept violence, then your thought process
Will be violent and that would cause
Unceasing movement from one form of existence
To another. Violence of intention, violence of
Beginning and violence of occupation –
Reject all forms of violence as non-violence
Ensures liberation. Be aware that the transaction

In sword will breed violence. Never forsake
The path of ethics; never be desirous of a cruel path
As it will take you through a cycle of births and deaths.
The nature of fire is to burn, of water to cool, and
Of the wind to blow; similarly, the true nature of the self
Is to possess the ennobling spirit. Following the path
Of non-violence, you be an oarsman helping all
To cross the ocean of life!'

Being an embodiment of peace, 130
Rama listened to Sita's words with great calm, and replied:
'You are knowledge personified, you are super human;
And hence you never lose your balance of mind.
You are a seeker of truth, full of love for life.
I am attached to the land and also to my people;
As I deem my home as an exemplary space,
I must overcome all exploitation. When the master
Of the house is not at home, values vanish and
The home becomes a graveyard.

'Who are these demons ranged against me? 140
They are not innocent creatures like the gazelles;
And these violent men are not really helpless.
They are cowards and known for their dastardly acts.
We can only ignore them at our peril.
Self-confidence must spring in the womb of
Contemplation. King Dasharatha distributed
To all the sweetness of the welfare of all during
His regime. We must continue that and safeguard
The fame of Ikshwaku dynasty.

The warrior must wield his bow and arrow 150
To respond to the cries of the helpless.
When the ascetics have sought my refuge,
It is my bounden duty to protect them;
It is the be all and end all of my life,' said Shri Rama.

Further, he said like a man on a mission:
'Listen, dear wife, listen to my firm resolve.
I will not forsake the path that liberates
The world even if it appears to be erroneous!
I would rather be a beggar wandering
All over with this blemish; I would   160
Willingly carry this muck of sin, and even
If I am to carry the rock of mistake hanging
Around my neck, I will drag it all along
And reach my ultimate destination!

'This is the journey that I have pledged to take;
This is the duty ordained on me by Sage Vishwamitra.
You are the daughter of the sage-king; tell me,
Would chanting the doctrine of peace ever
Put an end to misery? It is appropriate indeed
To quell the demons by wielding arms.   170
Don't stop me, don't make my determination slump;
Don't come in the way of the pledge of the time!
March ahead with me like a great consort,
Without hesitation, in this Great Journey of rare
Pursuit which would at the end reveal a New World,

Where the distinctions of caste, creed and race,
Of inequality and oppression, pain and sorrow,
Are obliterated forever and ever,'
Said Shri Rama, the visionary.

Canto – Fifty-six

'I will Illuminate the Path You Traverse'

||६||

Thus, Shri Rama made Sita understand
The nature of non-violent principle and its
Practical aspect with gentle persuasion;
And then moved in the direction of Agastya's
Hermitage, calmly, followed by Saumitri.

The journey was unbearable,
As they heard the intermittent roar of lions,
And tigers, and their throats were parched
Because of the merciless beating of the sun.
The path was too harsh for Janaki;
She was fatigued beyond words and was breathless,
As her soles cracked and blood started oozing.
Sita, the earth-born, was about to fall on the ground,
Unable to walk any further. At that moment,
Shri Rama ran towards her in a flash, held her, led her
To the shade of a tree, and helped her regain her strength.

'O, Shri Rama! My dear husband!
It is too tiresome and my misery will only increase.
Life appears to take leave of the body, and, I fear,
I cannot walk anymore. This wilderness is impassable;

My limbs are shaking and my will is faltering.
I do not know how my dear father, Janaka, is now.
I saw mother Sunayana in my dream last night!
The memory of having slept on her affectionate lap
Haunts me, relentlessly,' so saying, the gentle lady
Shed inconsolable tears and fainted.

Saumitri's visage was a harbour
Of pain and he lost his speech; looking
At the plight of Janaki, Shri Rama said, 'Did you see,
Brother Lakshmana, the misery of Janaki? 30
She lost her consciousness as she had not eaten enough.
How happily she lived in the palace of Janaka!
Alas! Misery caught up with her since her arrival
In the city of Saketa. She is too tired; fatigued beyond words.
She cannot bear the rigours of life in this wilderness;
Take her to Saketa,' so saying he broke into tears.

Saumitri brought water in a lotus leaf;
Shri Rama sprinkled a little of that on her face;
Caressing her curls he made her drink the water.
Janaki regained consciousness, such was his 40
Treatment, full of concern and kindness!
'You please leave for the palace of Saketa
At once, accompanied by Saumitri,' said Shri Rama.

Sita replied, 'O lord of the Raghu lineage! Listen.
I cannot live even for a moment without you.
What pleasure should I derive going to Ayodhya?
I will overcome all hurdles removing them like weeds.
Neither am I tired nor am I fatigued;
The memory of my parents proved to be taxing.
But my mind now has regained its balance. 50
I will be a ladder to you to ascend to a higher
Order, and I will illumine the path you traverse.
I will buttress and support the bridge you cross;
I will water the roots of the trees on the way.

Even if I am unhinged, will the spirit be destroyed?
I will again enter your body with multiplied
Vigour, inducing inexhaustible sustenance,'
Said Vaidehi.

Shri Rama was thrilled hearing these words
Of Sita; he held her in great love and said: 60
'The path is really uphill and the hideouts of the demons
Lie ahead. At every step they cause untold misery;
We have to forge ahead beyond the mountain ranges
and ocean's vast expanse; there might be wilderness
After comely environs of appealing forest.
The journey is very demanding as the path
Is beset with certain danger. Therefore, I urge you,
Leave for Ayodhya or towards the bank of Sarayu,
Where you will find Urmila, wife of Lakshmana,
Observing penance thinking constantly of our 70
Well-being. You can spend the rest of your life
In the company of this distinguished ascetic.

'The dead bodies of the demons will roll as we have
Ever-changing strategies of war. You cannot
Bear the sight of the dance of violence, neither
You can drink the poison that results in the ocean
Of conflict. There will be rain of fire causing
The destruction of the wealth of nature, turning
Everything into a graveyard. It would be an encounter
Where the epidemic will be chased and hounded.' 80

'Restrain yourself, my lord,
As these words do not suit you! I am not a woman
To return to Saketa even if you try very hard.
I am determined to follow you wherever you go.
If you push me away, you will lose the divine shield
Essential for your journey; and thus the epic
Of *Ramayana* will be curtailed, and transformed
To only *Aranyayana* – the story of the forest.

'I will not allow you to end the great epic
With the saga of exile in the forest; and I will not let you go.   90
Put an end to your attempts to send me either to a palace
Or to a familiar place; either to an abode of pleasure
Or to the environs of separation.
The wife knows no other destination
Than the one followed by her husband! As you are
About to swim in the ocean of victory,
Do not contemplate to confine yourself
In a constricting pot, my lord,' said the daughter
Of Janaka in a determined voice.

Canto Fifty-seven

'Rama's Effulgence Illumines All'

||६||

Everywhere in the hermitage of Agastya,
The trees are full of fruits and berries.
The sacrificial smoke rises in waves
While jackfruit and mangoes fill the atmosphere
With aroma. The birds are singing in ecstasy
While the monkeys hop from branch to branch.
Janaki derived a new spirit looking at all this
As she passed.

The darkness descended and they could not
Continue further and the monk there welcomed
Shri Rama and Saumitri. 'We will see that
You reach the hermitage of Agastya before
Daybreak tomorrow; you spend the night here
Without any worry.' Shri Rama replied, 'We will
Abide by your wishes' and spend time
In great delight receiving the hospitality of
The monks.

The next day the hermits moved
Towards Agastyashrama in a joyous mood.
'Shri Rama has come along with his wife and

His brother and is eager to have the honour of
Seeing you and we have come to inform
You, great teacher.' Hearing this the sage
Said, 'So be it.'

On the way to the hermitage of Agastya
Shri Rama narrated to Sita and Saumitri
The greatness of the sage, 'The Vindhya Mountain
Had posed a problem for the unification of the home of
Bharata. It was so difficult to travel from
The north to the southern region. Sage 30
Agastya came from the Himalayas to the south
Precisely to weld the south and the north in harmony
And Vindhya, his disciple, prostrated before him.
Blessing him the sage said, "It is easy to cross
You over now, you should not rise till I
Return." But Agastya never returned to north
And the Vindhya Mountain never rose again.
Thus the sage accomplished the union of the two
Segments.

His wife Lopamudra was a 40
Great scholar and an expert physician. She knew
The ritual of winning the goddess's blessings.
When the human beings are hit by the weapons
Of fire and wind and serpent, she sucked
All the poison, she mitigated the burning fire.
Agastya's armoury is never penetrated by
The horde of the demons. The sage-couple
Has forsaken enmity and also the sense of hatred.
They both have transcended gender discrimination
And also the distinction of race. 50

When there was a dearth of human values
In the south; while unbridled behaviour reigned,
This great Sage Agastya, the polestar of the land
Of Bharata has emerged as a grand

Agent of unification in the midst of
Secessionist leanings and provincial proclivities.

That is a place where the beasts
Move about in harmony forgetting their
Nature of conflict; fatigue vanishes at once
Bringing the mind to a pleasing balance. 60
This sage protects those who seek refuge in him.
This venerable sage is worshipped by the world.
He has even conquered death in order to
Save this world!

In this hermitage there is no one
Who tells a lie and everyone is restrained.
Let us spend the rest of our lives in this
Land which is the gateway to the beauty of nature.
This is the land that brings blessings to all
Bestowing the harmonious music 70
And the beneficent fruits!'

The hermits brought Shri Rama and Sita
To the hermitage of Agastya and their joy knew no
Bounds. Agastya was equally excited; he stood up
From where he sat and said, 'This is the moment
Of auspiciousness as the effulgence of Shri Rama
Is shining ever brighter. Come dear Shri Rama,
Dear Lakshmana, come; come Sita; I was
Awaiting your arrival with great eagerness.'

Shri Rama, Sita and Saumitri prostrated 80
At the feet of the sage even as the sage lifted
Them up, embracing them he brought tears of joy
About their well-being and soon took them round
The hermitage introducing different spots
Of divinity where Brahma dwelt, where Agni,
Vishnu, Kartikeya, the sun and moon dwelt;
Similarly, the positions of Gayatri, Vasuki,

Kubera, Varunendra, Rudramarutha,
Gananatha and all the immortal gods;
Seeing all this they went into a deep 90
State of meditation as they were overcome by devotion!

The gathering group of monks led them
To the raised platform and made them be seated.
Agastya sat near them while the other monks
Were seated in a circle closeby and they were
A picture of expectation like a *chakora* bird.

'O Rama, we are happy, we are joyful
And we are floating on the ocean of bliss;
May victory be yours! You've traversed
A long distance to have the pleasure of 100
Seeing us. Are you fatigued, is Saumitri
Tired?; Is the daughter of Mithilesha tired?
She was never subjected to any kind of harshness;
She has walked in the burning sun; she has
Climbed up the mountain of difficulties in order to
Dip herself in the river of her husband's love.
The virtuous nature shines ever so splendidly;
It has the velocity of *garuda* and the wind
The sharpness of weapons; it has holiness,
And Sita is like Arundhati; She is a real 110
Effulgent light,' said Agastya praising
Sita from the bottom of his heart.

Raghava bowed before the sage who was
Shining with resplendance and said, 'I am blessed
Indeed, revered teacher; I have come here to stay
For some time making a hut of leaves and so
I seek your permission. I have come here to
Put an end to the army of demons who are tormenting
The world undermining its well-being.

The demons appear in disguise, sometimes 120
As upholders of religion, sometimes as kings;

Thus, they are swallowing the world. To quell
The king of Lanka is our mission. Correct our ways
If we go wrong,' so said Shri Rama and all
The monks welcomed this with great celebration.
'Blessed with a form of divinity,
Your illusion contains all the cosmos and the God of Death
Is waiting to swallow it but he is afraid to approach.
Such is your infinitude and you are asking
Our permission to stay in our hermitage, it sounds   130
Strange! Be kind enough to grant us strength
To meditate on you continuously and bless us
So that we can know your greatness and grandeur,'
Such was their prayer which lodged in their hearts.

At that moment Janaki embraced Lopamudra
With great affection and said, 'Sage-mother, we came
In great haste solely to see you.' Lopamudra
Replied lovingly, 'Where did you learn, daughter,
The wonderful way of addressing me sage-mother?
Prabha was the first one to call me thus; she   140
Is the one who is taking care of this old body.
She calls me "mother, mother" and treats me
In all sincerity; likewise she is treating
Others as well.'

Sita became curious at this and asked
'Is Prabha a physician?' 'She is not merely
A physician, but an expert in treating the wounded
Soldiers, being the wife of a army general
She has saved the lives of so many wounded
Soldiers. Innumerable are those who received   150
Treatment thus.'

Sita was very much impressed and asked
'This Prabha must be your dear daughter?'
Lopamudra agreed at once, 'Yes, she is our
Dear daughter. When there is the dearth of women

Who could share the responsibility of their husbands
Isn't it wonderful that you have come along with him?
You are extraordinary, indeed! I will teach you
How to treat the soldiers who are wounded
In the war. One cannot win wars unless there are 160
Experts in this field.' Lopamudra led Sita to
The quarter where the wounded soldiers were treated.
Like a picture of efficiency Prabha stood there
Among her assistants to treat the patients, and
Sita looked at Prabha and both of them
Were happy beyond words at this event.
Lopamudra enlightened her on this particular treatment
Explaining all the intricacies involved in it.

Canto Fifty-eight

'Bharat Has the Strength to Unify Everything'

||६||

One day Agastya and Shri Rama were in deep
Discussion and neither of them seemed to give
A quarter to the other. Saumitri was elsewhere
And Sita addressed Lopamudra thus: 'Sage-
Mother, what is the nature of discussion between
Agastya and Shri Rama, the discussion appears to be
Grave.' Sita was in real anguish.

'Have no fear, dear child; they are
Both suffering from birth pangs,' when Lopamudra
Said so, Sita responded, 'Sage-mother, I cannot   10
Really make out what you are hinting at. Shri Rama
Is not his normal self ever since we arrived
At this hermitage, and that is my great worry.'
'Don't be ruffled, my dear child, this is how
A sage works,' Lopamudra consoled Sita.

Sage Agastya said thus,
'Unselfishness is on the verge of being erased today,
Ravana's kingdom of selfishness is vast and endless!

He will kill all the intellectuals of all lands!
He is the enemy of magnanimity, hostile he is to 20
Thinking. The good people of Lanka are unable to
Endure him. Relationships depend upon only money
And wealth. When the cruel hands are
Thrashing the world, the celestial Sun-god
Must descend on this earth; no one can face
The ten-headed king so easily.

Shri Rama said bringing a lump in his throat,
'Revered teacher, it is not like before, Dandakaranya
has woken up, even the villagers are ready
With weapons. They will trounce the demons 30
With their strength.'

'The power of the demons is immense.
They have spread themselves all over;
They are gaining strength day by day. Shurpanakhi
Is reigning there. Her army would conquer all
The villages of Dandakaranya. And therefore
Beware, that you may cause the destruction
Of these villages, hamlets and settlements!.'

Shri Rama smiled gently and there was a glint
In his eyes, 'I will not be unhinged at this attack. 40
Will I ever run away in fear? Neither will I
Err on any count! But remember that the demons
Are doomed to die; that is predetermined!'
There was steadfastness in his voice.

The voice of Sage Agastya was equally
Loud: 'This is the battle that is going to either
Save the princes or spell their doom. Shurpanakhi
Is sister to Ravana and she is the reigning queen
To Janasthana; Khara and Dushana are
Stationed there. In the kingdom of Lanka, 50
There are innumerable warriors with invincible armour;

But what is your reckoning before this?
You have neither the horses nor the elephants
Except the half-baked soldiers. When Brahma
And Rudra themselves have bestowed boons on Ravana
How can you face him, the unconquerable king of Lanka!'

Sita said in anger as the sage
Did not take notice of Shri Rama's might:
'It is good that Saumitri is not present at the moment!
I cannot imagine what harm he would have caused you
Listening to your words. Do you think even Brahma
And Vishnu are equal to Shri Rama who is following
The path of righteousness? Can the might of the empire
Stand before the power of the people? Just see
How Shri Rama is going to create armies by his will.
Please stop undermining Shri Rama's strength!.'

Lopamudra then said in a gentle tone,
'Stop subjecting Shri Rama to examination and it is time
For you to bless him.' Then the sage said, 'Raghava,
Move towards Panchavati, there you will have
All the support of armies; be victorious in your
Mission that is the test of the age! Do not forsake
The path of righteousness, it is the affection of people
Which is a great shield.' Lopamudra hugged
Them in affection and blessed, 'Fight on my child, you can
Bring the celestial sun to the world so that
The darkness vanishes at once.'

Janaki then understood the meaning
Of birth-pang referred to by Lopamudra earlier.
Lopamudra's laughter filled Sita's heart.

Then again Janaki's mind went back
To Saketa where the mothers dreamt of having children
And hold them in loving embrace. The toddlers
Would take their first unsure steps even as

The trinkets tied round their ankles made
Pleasing sounds. Their lisping syllables echoed
In homesteads. But Janaki never conceived
Such a child, neither did she give birth to one.
She never took care of a baby attending to all its
Requirements. She is denied of the pleasure of   90
Participating in all the acitivities of a tender child.
Therefore, she was overcome by her maternal instinct!

Thus, in the mind of Sita, Chitrakoota,
Dharmabhritya, Sharabhanga, Sutikshna
All passed like a panorama. 'If Shri Rama
Does not conquer the demons, then every child
Playing in the arms of every mother will be
Eaten away by these demons.' Sita saw Shri Rama's new form
In her mind's eye!

One day, Sage Agastya led Shri Rama   100
To the inner segment of the hermitage and showed
The armoury. Shri Rama became speechless
At this. Then the sage said, 'This bow is created by
None other than Vishwakarma himself; Indra gave this.
Sauthramani gave this to me and Rugmaya
Granted this with all its accessories. With this one could
Conquer the demons and Mahavishnu himself wielded
This in ancient times and quelled his opponents.
Look at this great sword; I am going to hand over
This bow, this arrow and this sword – you may have   110
Them and victory will surely be yours!

'People side themselves with the strong
In an attempt to subjugate the weak; heroism
Is at its low ebb when cowardice reigns supreme;
Duty consciousness has taken a back seat while
Selfish motive is asserting itself. And hence,
Please take all these weapons and wield them
For the good of mankind,' so saying the sage
Handed them over in great affection.

'You are the loving disciple of Vasishtha
And Viswamitra who are always at
Loggerheads with each other; but they have
Bestowed all knowledge on you; Bhargava
Has granted all strength to you. I will narrate my
Experience to you: Though there are many lands
In the world, they call Bharatavarsha the universe
Since Bharat has the strength to unify all segments
Into a unified domain. The principle, that if you
Subtract perfection from perfection, what remains
Is perfection – is realised here!

'It is the self-same divinity that
Divides, himself into *prakriti* and *purusha*, though
In essence formless and without attributes. Creation,
Preservation and destruction are all done by the same
Entity. The wise ones call it *maya* and some understand it
As *lila* or the divine play; that will deceive
The world covering the knowledge of sun.

'The female principle is indispensable
In order to conquer the cruelty that has grown in
The course of time. That is the force of earth's forbearance;
During Sita's wedding it entered the divine bow
You eventually broke and it found its abode in yourself.
Now, the same power has transformed itself into
Your consort, Sita! The gold in the mine becomes
Purified once it is subjected to a process! Otherwise,
It will remain indistinguishable from the mud.
The golden soil of Saketa has turned into Shri Rama
After going through the process of purification.
The wedding ceremony has made it the active power
As you have the goal of lifting the world and upholding
Righteousness; redeeming Ahalya is just a symbolic act!'
So saying the sage conveyed the heart of the mystery.

Canto Fifty-nine

'Go in the Path of the Sun'

||☼||

'Shri Rama, looking at you
One was granted the divine manifestation. Illumination
Filled one's eyes. The ears were filled with the sound
And the touch elevated the body; the fragrance
Filled the nose and the tongue was slaked with the nectar.
The drop merged with the ocean and this was
Made possible by the sight of your divine form.

Emotion, intelligence, stamina and imagination
Are four areas of the mind. Motivation
Yields emotion, intelligence is born of introspection,   10
Stamina accumulates through right conduct
And meditation gives birth to imagination.
It is the individual experience that leads to self-realisation.

If there are countless fissures in the boat
How can the sailors be calm? If there are scorpions
In the bed, would the sleepers repose without being
Disturbed? There is a place called Ashmapuri
Close at hand and it is an abode where the demons
Called Kalakeyas resided. When they killed   20

The innocent people, I smote them. Now everyone
Is living a trouble-free life. Beginning from Chitrakoota
To Atri hermitage and the hermitages of
Sharabhanga, Suthikshna and Dharmabhritya
You have arranged the well-established armies.
Therefore lift the humanity from the rock-bottom
Position it has reached, dear one!

Therefore, I will teach you now
The most essential chanting that is the core of
The ancient path of righteousness. This is 30
The *mantra* that wins the heart of that
Great friend of the world. With the help of that
Mantra, you are going to conquer the enemies
In the battlefield; if you chant it everyday
You will obtain inexhaustible wealth. This
Will grant you everything that is auspicious.
This will erase all sins and put an end to
All sorrows, increasing your life. Your entire
Clan will be protected by Him, who is the life of
This chant, '*Surya aatmaa jagatah*' 40

'The sun is the soul of the world'
Such is the beginning of the *mantra*. He is the
Effulgence who has transported the sages to the world
Of Brahma. The human beings as well as
The demons worship Him as he is the agent
Of all activities. He brings rain to the world
To protect humanity. He causes the harvest
And he is the Lord of the Universe.

'He is Brahma, He is Vishnu, He is Shiva too,
He is Skanda and all the Eight Essences and He is 50
The Lord of the Eight Directions; He is
The Seven Winds and the Ashwini
Deities; He is the Lord of the Cosmos, He is the Lord Infinite,
He is the one who enjoys all material bounties,

He rides the Seven Horses, illuminating all
He has the heart of gold; He is compassionate.
I salute you as you are all this!

'You are the one who has seen the vastness
Of the Vedas; you are the lord who wanders in
The streets of Vindhya; you are the omniscient one, 60
You are the creator of all things; you are
The lord of the stars, planets and all the celestial objects.
I salute you as you destroy all diseases!

'You are the one who destroys the misery of all;
You have the cosmic form containing the fire within;
You are the master of all knowledge. I salute you
As you command the infinite wealth.

'You have the form of Twelve Divinities;
You are the lord of all; you have the form of the eastern-mountain,
So also the western-mountain. 70
You grant victory, bestowing affection
As you are the witness to the world, I salute you.'

Thus the sage chanted the *mantra* of Sun-god
And placed his hand on Shri Rama's head in a gesture
Of benediction; at that moment Shri Rama slipped
Into the realm of contemplation oblivious to the surroundings.
He saw in his mind's eye several galaxies revolving;
The water of the ocean evaporated and turning into
Rain-bearing clouds and eventually descended to the earth
In the form of rain. It filled the rivers, soaked 80
The mountains, then again joining the sea.
Every bit of his body charged with divine touch.
He forgot everything about himself as he was
Nothing but effulgence bringing the entire universe
Into a single focus; he saw only the transcendent energy
And therefore, Shri Rama went deep into a state of meditation.

Then the sage touched Rama and brought him
Back to consciousness and placed him in his original state.
'The great-limbed one, Rama, I have taught you 90
The secret of the righteous path! Chant this *mantra*
Concerning the heart of the Sun-god! It is the most
Auspicious thing! You will conquer all your enemies,
You will achieve all your goals; may the victory be yours.'
When the Sage Agastya blessed him, Shri Rama
Prostrated at his feet.

'The source of Godavari is a land of cruel
Demons. Dandakaranya was under the control of
Dandaka belonging to the Ikshwaku lineage in the past.
He reigned in full splendour possessing 100
All the wealth one could desire, in the city of Madhumanta
Within the ambience of Vindhya mountain-range
Even as Shukracharya guided him at every stage.
But once, owing to unawareness he fell in love with
Araje, the daughter of Sage Shukracharya and incurred
The curse! The city of Madhumanta was erased out of
Existence under an incessant rain of dust that lasted
For seven days. The city became a wilderness and
Dandaka's kingdom was converted into Dandakaranya
And it is the land of the demons now. The advancing 110
Demons took over Ayodhya also as the time passed.
King Anaranya of Raghu dynasty died being
A victim of the demons' aggression. A portion of the
Kingdom belonged to the demons. Subsequently,
They had to beat a retreat as Dasharatha attacked them.

'Therefore, you should always be alert
In controlling the demons, that will enable you to
Establish peace here and everywhere else
In the world. You must walk on the path of 120
Righteousness; unshackle everyone so that peace

Prevails everywhere. The compassionate instrument
Of yours consists not of one string, nor four, nor seven
But thousand; it has several frets and hence
When you pluck it once the resulting divine sound
Pleases everybody.

'For the sacrificial ritual you undertake
Your inner self is the agent; the body itself
Is the offering and your chest is the sacrificial
Pillar. All drinks get converted into divine breweries   130
When you sit, stand and move about – that itself will
Be a part of the ritual.

'Shri Rama, you know, *Yogavashishtha*
Through and through; you have transcended the pulls
Of desire; you have tremendous self-control, always
Mindful of duties. You are a hero among heroes,
Youth among youths, jovial among the pleasure-
Seekers, sharer of sorrow, ancient among the old people,
Unrivalled in courtesy, humble and friendly,
The elevated one, purity personified, the ever-active   140
And hence the liberated one!

'This obligation is the age-old one;
We can only salute Time. No one could alter it,
We have to endure as there is no escape'.
This mindset has gripped mankind so relentlessly that
Inertia has overtaken all; a sense of discrimination
Has deserted men; the spirit of enthusiasm is eclipsed.
Everyday is a new life and everyday is a new beginning.
In the light of new awakening you roll your chariot
Of pursuit by becoming the voice of the New Age!   150
Don't tarry here, restart your journey,
And move towards Panchavati, a place in the wilderness
Blessed by the bounties of Godavari.

'That is where nature dances in earnestness
Best suited to carryout the vow of your father.

Godavari lisps her pleasure there ever so gently
Janaki would certainly be pleased at nature's richness.
The birds fly in large numbers;
All your desires will once again come alive.
When Saumitri is ready at your side, 160
You can easily protect the monks from all encumbrances.

'If you walk southwards, you will
Come across the river Gautami; Panchavati
Is where it takes its birth. That is where the demons
Live too. The atrocities of Ravana have touched
The zenith there. The earth may shudder and there
May be thunder and lightning. The comets may
Presage cataclysm. March forward with great determination,
Let the whirlwinds may become gentle breeze to you!'

Thus, Sage Agastya blessed him. Lopamudra 170
Blessed and so also the rest of the monks. Tying their
Bows and arrows and the sword, the princes bowed to all
In great reverence. Carrying the good wishes
Of the age, they moved in the direction of Panchavati,
A veritable destination of redemption.

When they walked towards Panchavati
On either side of the path, they saw trees
Of innumerable variety. The huge trees have
Spread their branches and the sunlight hardly
Penetrates and reaches the ground. 180
Similar is their wonder at countless animals
That crossed their path. Right from the big bird
To the tiny sparrow, they all hovered over their head
Unmindful of their presence.
Sometimes they would crawl on their stomach,
Sometime, bend and crouch; they would ascend now
Again descend the gradient; step over the fallen trees.
The roar of the wild animals would compete with
Each other. 'Dear Lakshmana, Panchavati is close

At hand, come Sita, come; I can recognise the marks 190
Indicated by Sage Agastya,' so said Rama with
Unbounded enthusiasm.

On the way at some secret bowers
The hidden hermitages caught their attention
As tiny villages surrounded them. The monks said
On seeing Shri Rama and Saumitri, 'Listen,
Shri Rama, the cruel demons have destroyed
The sacrificial platform; they have destroyed
And strewn flesh all over; they have snatched
Away tiger skin; we do not have anyone to turn to; 200
In the absence of a protector we have become listless.'
They shook even as they narrated the devastation.

Consoling them Shri Rama said,
'Don't be afraid, don't be unhinged. I will put an end
To them right now, I will silence them at once.
I have lost my patience; I will not spare anyone;
I will destroy them lock, stock and barrel.
I have Saumitri along with me.'

As they moved ahead Janaki said
In a tone of anxiety, 'It seems it is an 210
Impenetrable wilderness, caves filled with darkness;
The demons have their home there; they have
Carried women and kept them
In those caverns, outraging their modesty at will.
The wives of the monks have narrated this to me.
The demons have become a lawless lot.
Kill them and decimate them with your
Sharp arrows.' Shri Rama smiled at this and said,
'I will not spare them now; I cannot put up
With this anymore; you will see how I am 220
Going to deal with them.' They moved forward
On their path after these words of Shri Rama.

Canto Sixty

'Shine in the Eyes, Sword in Hand'

||๏||

As they moved somehow Shri Rama felt
That somebody is stalking them. He told Lakshmana
That hiding behind the trees, walking along
With them, the person is shadowing them sniffing
Something perking his ears all the time.
Saumitri searched in a hillock for the person
Without wasting words. He saw an old man
In the valley and Shri Rama and Janaki were
Also shown. While his eyes were shining;
He had held a sword in hand; his face betrayed   10
Helplessness; though he appeared a centurion
His arms were firm and strong. 'Who is
This man, who is he?' they murmured to themselves.

But Shri Rama asked him,
'Tell us who you are, why are you
Stalking us in the forest unceasingly?
Come now, we will walk along; you seem to be
All alone; what can I give you in my
Present condition! We are the sons of Dasharatha,
The king of Ayodhya, they call me Rama and   20

This is my brother, Lakshmana, and this is Janaki,
The daughter of Janaka, my wife.'

Joy and wonder at once manifested on his face
And Jatayu said, 'Are you the sons of Dasharatha!
As he is our great friend, you are our well-wishers now.
I am Jatayu belonging to the Gridhra lineage
And Sampati is my elder brother. I am
Blessed after seeing you and my mind
Is free from burden.'

'Permit me to ask why have you 30
Come here forsaking your kingdom and palace
To traverse on this path of stones and thorns?'

After listening to the affectionate words
Of Jatayu Shri Rama replied, 'The revered one,
My father gave two boons to mother Kaikeyi
After Shambara war: one was to coronate Bharata
And another was to send me on exile for fourteen
Years. Therefore we are in exile in the wilderness;
Our father died of grief. Wandering in the forest
We reached the hermitage of Agastya and 40
In accordance with his guidance we have now reached Panchavati.'

'We are greatly blessed, dear one!
Not far from here there is river Godavari
And near to that is Janasthana, where the demons
Have pitched their army camp,' said Jatayu and
Lakshmana in a tone of impatience said,
'We are least bothered, revered one, about what is there
And what is not there.'

'Don't be angry, dear one, that place 50
Contains the reason for my present state; I am eager
To narrate all that to you now. I was ruling
The kingdom as king of Gridhra dynasty. There was

Nothing lacking there. The cities shone in abundance
And the villages were equally endowed.
Everywhere there were noble people and
Culture was seen everywhere, learning
Prevailed in great measure. What can I say;
It is all the game of the fate. The demons
Called the kin of Ravana established themselves 60
There and turned into extremists and destroyed
Everything. Some of the citizens went to the abode
Of death, some vanished leaving their hearth
And home and I lost all my relatives
To the merciless sword of the demons; I remained
At the end all alone; my elder brother is Sampati,
He is wandering all over like a beggar.
Nobody knows whether he is alive or dead!

There is no one to talk to;
I am all alone in this wide forest. 70
This sword is my sole companion, I am
Wandering constantly wielding this weapon!

'Sometime people see me and
Call me a madman and hence keep themselves
Away from me fearing my sword.
The atrocity of the demons has reached the zenith,
Sometime the youth come near me and my
Blood boils. They stand up and show their
Determination to fight, but I see no
Victory to them as the demons are large 80
In number. They are decimated and I remain
Alone again. They have burnt my palace
Into ashes; I have no shelter and I am
Taking refuge in the branches of trees.

'The king of Ikshwaku has risen
To Heaven! Have you seen the fate that has
Overtaken his friend, when is my delivery!

I have nothing to fall upon, except the spirit of
Challenge. I have been waiting for some brave man
Who could throw the demons to the pit of hell 90
After searching for them in relentless intensity.
I am overjoyed seeing you bent on the purpose.
I had determined to put an end to your lives
If I found you were dissemblers, but since
I see you genuinely heroic I will join
Hands with you in this honourable task.

'That is why I followed you Raghuvira
And Saumitri! You are young and tender and
You are accompanied by a delicate young woman,
Would you accept the challenge if the demons 100
Throw one?' asked Jatayu in a breathless manner.

Saumitri smiled and said,
'We have come precisely for the same purpose;
We have come in search of danger as
Fighting is our enterprise.'

Shri Rama addressed Jatayu:
'Apparently we are going to stay here for long;
Our job is cut out for us since we are determined
To erase the demons out of existence. Call all
Your kith and kin who have suffered loss and 110
Damage. We need warriors like you today for
The purpose. Why should they hide themselves
Fearing the enemies? We shall become the tongues
Of flame to consume the demons.'

Jatayu, then, was overcome by emotion
Hearing Shri Rama's assurance, 'Your determination
Is extraordinary; I am going to build huts for you;
We will climb up the hillock yonder and pass,
There is plenty of water over there and the bounty of nature;
The hillock is surrounded on all the four sides 120

By mountain ranges and Godavari flows behind
The forest; Kapila to the left. That is an ideal
Place to fight being ambushed as it is a natural
Barrier. True to the name of 'Panchavati'
There are five huge banyan trees in a grove.
Khara and Dushana have devastated
The hermitages that had come up in that area.'

As Jatayu led the way Shri Rama
Sita and Saumitri followed him and when they
Approached Panchavati, 'Raghuvara, we have   130
Arrived at the place indicated by Sage Agastya.
Everywhere you find fruit-bearing trees;
We will locate the spot where we intend
To build the huts,' said Jatayu in great excitement.

Vaidehi's joy knew no bounds
As she looked at the beauty of nature: 'This is
My favourite space; there is the glory of water,
Flowers galore; there are spots of ceremonial grass.
This appears to be a place closer to the heart of
The damsel called nature.'   140

'That is right Sita,
There are appealing ponds and types of trees,
The lotuses bloom and give out fragrance;
The swans and water birds are swimming
Undisturbed; gazelles drink the water of Godavari;
The peacocks register their joy all over the hillocks
Intertwining creepers design a tapestry around
The trees; this spot rivals with Heaven
Beauty lies here in all its glory and splendour,'
Shri Rama described like a poet indeed.   150

They climbed up the raised ground,
Saw the waves of Godavari lapping against the banks,
Kapila flowed closer to the hillock; that is where

The demons took shelter and the camp of the army
Too was also there and all this caused a sense of wonder.

Shri Rama and Saumitri rested
Their bows and arrows and the swords at
The foot of a tree and relaxed!

They located a particular spot to build
The hut and the monks at once got themselves   160
Busy with the task. Jatayu, Saumitri were
Joined by Shri Rama and Sita. Jatayu was
Wonderstruck at their skill and hardihood
And patient application of their mind to the task.
'Let me have the honour of serving you; you
Just give direction and need not work so hard;
Let me work for Shri Rama,' so saying
Jatayu made Rama and Sita sit and relax
While he along with Lakshmana worked vigorously.

They erected very sturdy pillars and placed   170
Equally sturdy boles across tying with strong creepers
Covering the roof with many types of grass and leaves.
Five leaf cottages came into being, thus,
Rama and Sita will have one, Lakshmana
Will take one; Jatayu will live in another;
One will be dedicated for the arms, while
The other will serve the guests.

Thus the cottages made out of leaves
Came to be erected and beckoned all those who beheld
Them, for they were so beautiful. Shri Rama and   180
Sita took a good look at them, Lakshmana brought
Tears as the thought crossed his mind, 'You
Make everything possible by your will and your
Skill is evident in everything.' Understanding
Lakshmana's mind Shri Rama held him in
Tight embrace. He turned towards Jatayu and

Said, 'It is the result of great merit that we
Are blessed with your friendship; we need your help
In quelling the demons; we are freed from
Worries now, we are greatly relieved,' so saying   190
He hugged Jatayu and shed tears of joy.

The cycle of season moved constantly
And there was beauty in plenty; there was greenery
Everywhere; the cows yielded milk in abundance;
The kings have finished their mission of conquest
Successfully and they have returned to the capital.
The gentle breeze is wafting fragrance on all sides.

As the sun rose in the east the mist
That covered the forest vanished gradually yielding
Place to the golden aura to spread all around.   200
Different birds do sing the songs of ecstasy
While the crops sway their heads in richness
And contentment of their magnanimity.

The look of the evening sun
Has irradiated the vast spread of the grassland
With its golden hew. When the temperature has
Subsided the elephants move towards the waterholes
To slake their thirst; they drop their trunks
Into water and the touch of cold
Water creates a shock and they regain their balance   210
And drink water to their hearts' content.
Water-birds hesitate to get into water
Gathering on the margin like the coward soldiers
Unwilling to take a plunge into the battlefield
Withdrawing from the scene more and more.
The flowers that fall from the trees look like
Those who desire sleep after strenuous labour.
Thick darkness is inching forward to cover
The land and the forest is eager to slip into
A deep slumber.   220

When the sun has completed its southward movement
He is turning to trace the northward path.
The sky wears clear blue. The dead leaves
Are falling from trees and creepers on their own.
Shri Rama, Janaki and Saumitri along with
Jatayu are enjoying the luscious beauty
Of nature in the environs of Parnakuti.

Canto Sixty-one

'The Bond of Brotherhood'

||६||

One day, when Shri Rama, Janaki and Lakshmana
Set out to take bath in Godavari at day-break,
Lakshmana began to sob uncontrollably and Shri Rama
Asked him in great earnest, 'Dear brother, what is
The reason for your sorrow,
Has the image of Urmila crossed your mind?'

'I did not think of Urmila, dear brother,
I thought of Bharata; I thought of the problems and
Miseries he must be facing back home. When Bharata
Goes to the river Sarayu everyday in the morning
For his bath, the people who gather there say, "This is the man   10
Who sent our lord Shri Rama" and treat him harshly.
In order to avoid the crowd Bharata gets up very early
In the morning and goes to the river in the killing chill.
Kaikayi has ruined his life by her ambition; it is a great
Mistake on her part,' said Saumitri in anguish.

Rama felt a lump in his throat!
Again Saumitri added: 'Bharata is grief-stricken,
He takes his bath everyday in the river Sarayu like a
Mendicant forsaking all comforts befitting a king.
He takes scanty food and refuses to sleep on the regal   20

Couch. He thinks constantly of your well-being
And he is in deep penance ever since you left.
One does not know how he is withstanding the rigour;
His sacrifice is unparalleled. He is the lotus-eyed,
Possessing long arms and dark grey body. He is truthful
And he has mastered the senses. He has earned
The merit. He is served by his admirers; he quells
The enemies in battlefields. There is no one to compete
With him in Ikshwaku dynasty. The ocean can be compared
Only with another ocean!   30

'You are doing penance in the forest;
Bharata is doing penance staying in Nandigrama
Of Ayodhyapuri. He does not inherit his mother
Kaikayi's character but possesses father's traits
And hence he upholds the distinction of Ikshwaku lineage,'
So saying Saumitri became pensive and emotional.

'Dear Saumitri, the moment I think of
Bharata, my will power slumps. His words are sweet,
The listener will be overcome at once. His speech
Is dipped in nectar. My heart hankers after Bharata   40
And it longs to join Shatrughna.
The bond of brotherhood stretches back to aeons,'
Said Shri Rama in words of unmatched delicacy.
Saumitri's pain was mitigated a bit.

Shri Rama, Sita and Lakshmana finished
Their bath. They offered prayers to the Sun-god and
Their ancestors and returned to their hut.
Jatayu was guarding everything. Shri Rama meditated
For a while and he opened his eyes afterwards.

Saumitri thought that this is the opportune moment   50
And therefore he inched closer to Shri Rama and said,
'You are omnipotent and you know everything.
Kindly bestow on me the threads of science and knowledge
So that I can smite all the meanness of the world.

The power of the mind is immense and so is
The vastness of truth and the brilliance of beauty.
The world of living beings is immeasurable.
You are a great pursuer who brings all this
Vastness and variety into a indivisible unity;
You know no constraints and hurdles;   60
Enlighten me on all this, I will listen patiently
For that will enrich me in ways I have not fathomed.

'Your words will remove the dross in the divine Ganga;
Your words will make the heart bloom.
They will add strength to the bones
Melting the heart of stone like never before.
They contain the fragrance of jasmine
And the song of a cuckoo,' Saumitri was earnest.

'Listen to me, brother Saumitri,
Real human ethics are to respond to the   70
Universal religion. Whenever the natural
Order is broken that spells doom. If pursued
Relentlessly, the path of truth will reveal itself
And success follows, dear one!

'Knowledge and science will find their ruin
If they are caught in the whirlpool of atheism;
They have built the vast palaces of pleasure
In their endless pursuit of materialism; but they
Have all fallen into the pit of immorality.
They have killed the embryo called   80
Science burning it in the poisonous flames of
Superstition, the black magic of the demons;
The horizons of pure fame has been dimmed.
Covered in the dense darkness of blasphemy
The pursuit of the soul has lost its direction;
Man's heart must orient itself towards
Science and knowledge. That is the only path
For man's welfare; it is the technique of the demons

To rule the world through superstition. The continuous
Remoulding of today, yesterday and tomorrow is called science.   90

'The pursuit of Truth is a long journey.
The knowledge of the world through the senses
Does not reveal what is beyond. Only pure
Wisdom enables us to see the mystery.
The world is an illusion; then what is Truth?
One must ask and seek an answer, otherwise
One wallows in stupidity. The Ultimate Reality
Is the only Truth; it has no second. The experience
Should establish the Absolute Truth as without attributes,   100
Without blemishes and even without form. The limited
Human knowledge cannot be called science. If
Science could leap over the barrier then it will
Acquire the dignity of thought.

'It is the intellectual merchandise
That has hampered the pursuit of Truth.
Everywhere one sees war and there is conflict
Everywhere. Everyone is bothered by the duality
Of life and death. It goes out of sight and again
It reappears. Some call the mind forged images   110
As the absolute and therefore everything has fallen
To the ground as there is a gap between knowledge and action.

'The Illusion has surrounded everything.
Truth is hidden by the veil of unreality.
It cheats the mind by making it believe that
The rope is the snake. The body is temporary.
The world is attached to it. The soul does not
Reckon with the worldly attachments. It knows
Neither life nor death!

'There should be purity in thought, word   120
And deed; be alert in the execution of your duties;
Shun all exaggerated pomp and excessive pleasures.
Knowledge and Science and other regulations

Remoulds the self and enables it to move on the path
Of realisation. That brings redemption at the end.
There is no meanness here;

'Panchavati is an elevating environment where
Treachery and deception have no place. It is the origin
Of mankind. It is where all actions reach their zenith
And hence one must find the path of ascendancy   130
To reach the top-most point. In the absence of adventure
Life resembles a straw caught in the whirlwind.
If hurdles appear one must change direction
And march forward; always in the pursuit of
New path.' When Shri Rama taught him, Saumitri
Was greatly relieved.

Urmila's image passed in the mind
Of Shri Rama. Subjugating the senses, she achieved
The convergence of cosmic power into the ambit of
Terrestrial consciousness; she is the one who welded   140
Force into the field of philosophy. She is the combination
Of beauty and dignity. She is the ocean of peace
Sheltering in the womb the inextinguishable fire
And thus, a veritable image of cosmic response.

And she is his inspiration behind the achievements
Of Saumitri. Her sacrifice has opened the door
For Lakshmana to pursue the path of Truth;
And this voyage is rightly called *Lakshmanayana*.

She is a confluence of all great qualities;
She has conquered all the pulls of worldly distortions;   150
She sees herself wholly and clearly and sees
Her well-being in the well-being of others.
She is a realised person; she is a wise one.
When Saketa is covered by the forest fire called envy
She is standing firmly with undivided attention
Worshipping the image of her husband
With the nectarine light emanating from her eyes.

Canto Sixty-two

'I Will Strive for the Glory of Peace'

||६||

Wandering in the forest near the hermitage of Panchavati
Shurpanakhi's maid saw Shri Rama, Saumitri
And Janaki. She was smitten by their beauty and
Hiding herself behind trees she overheard their words.

As they addressed each other by
Mentioning names, she took note of their identity.
She ran at once to inform her mistress of all that
She saw there. 'If you want to have the company
Of a handsome man, a Cupid called Shri Rama
Has arrived here; you must try right away   10
If you want him. If that materialises, you cannot
Ask for more,' the maid said excitedly.

Hearing those words, Shurpanakhi set out
At once; ordered her guards to stand near the banks
Of Godavari. She crossed the river alone and reached
The hermitage where Rama stayed. She frantically
Searched for Shri Rama peeping through the leaves
And creepers. 'Is Shri Rama here, is he there?
Why is he not seen? Should I ask someone ahead,'

She said this to herself and took a couple of steps 20
Lo and behold, Shri Rama appeared in all his splendour.

Light blue was his complexion; strong
And healthy arms with elegant bulging of sinews;
The back was also erect. 'He is handsome, indeed;
Shall I embrace him and weld him into my breast
And kiss him bringing his chin closer to mine!'
When her mind and heart were bent on this scheme
She swayed her body to lure Shri Rama to her orbit!

She felt as if her breasts were bursting,
And she was hardly able to stand. In this state her mind 30
Dwelt on the person of Shri Rama who had
Wide eyes, elegant tresses, long arms, and effulgence
That he had even overtaken the God of Love, Manmatha.
'How handsome this man is, blessed with luscious
Youth. What my maid said of him is very true.
He is so attractive in the form of a hermit.
What should be his luminosity as a prince!
When I saw Vidyudjihva in the past, I was
Still very young, but even then I was attracted
To him. Again, I am overwhelmed by such longing. 40
I need a shelter in Shri Rama's heart;
Only then my life would be fulfilled and I will
Acquire all worldly pleasure and wealth.'

Shurpanakhi's jealousy was roused beyond words
As she saw Shri Rama engaged in a pleasant conversation.
'Why doesn't he glance towards me, why doesn't he
Talk to me, why, why?' was the refrain on her lips.
She longed for moments of privacy with him.

Before long she was gripped by the fever
Of love; even as the erotic passion welled-up 50
From within she muttered to herself again;
'I want this man to be my husband and I will

Not rest contented until I get him. This man
Has won my heart and he is a veritable thief.
When will I embrace him and when will I possess
Him completely, when, when? I cannot allow
Any other person to own him, no!'
She burned relentlessly in the heat of love.

'I must disburden to him
All that is stored in my heart. I must embrace him,   60
Drinking from his lips the nectar and I must swim
In the pond of pleasure. I cannot live in a world
Without Rama and nothing pleases me where Rama
Is not there; I cannot live even for a single minute
Without him.' So saying, the sister of the king of Lanka
Swam in the ocean of love waiting to meet
Shri Rama in solitude.

Shri Rama is a veritable monk
And Sita is his female counterpart; Saumitri is
Matching them in austerity. He has overcome   70
All sensual pulls. Although he is with Janaki
Shri Rama too has overcome the lure of the senses.
He is observing all discipline residing in the ambience
Of love of an elevated kind.

Janaki moved inside the forest a bit
Picking flowers and Shri Rama tarried behind.
Shurpanakhi thought this is the opportune moment.
'How can I drew his attention now?' she said to
Herself and at that point Shri Rama approached
The coral tree and shook its branches causing   80
A gentle rain of the fragrant blossoms. He looked
To be enjoying this coronation even as Shrupanakhi
Watched with jealousy swelling in her heart.

There was a sudden gathering of dark clouds
In the sky, thunder and lightning followed.

Hailstones rained aplenty and there was the actual
Rain. The Wind-god swept across kindly.
Shurpanakhi chose that moment to appear
Before Rama summoning her skills in walking
Voluptuously with a purpose of attracting him.   90
Even as the perfume she had smeared on her body
Wafted across as if it flowed from the fountain
Of love, she declared openly, 'Look at me,
I am Shurpanakhi.'

There was no distortion of body to suit a demoness.
She had lotus-feet and her walk was swan-like;
The arms were round and smooth; the eyes were
Like that of a gazelle; the face resembling the moon
And her eyebrows bent like a bow; the rich tresses
Adorned her head, while the lips were picture of   100
Redness; the delicate waist was a source of attraction.
The creator must have fashioned a woman
So perfectly for the first time – that was the feeling
One got looking at her.

Shri Rama summoned words
To match his surprise at the moment and said,
'This is an impenetrable jungle, why have you come here,
Respected lady; there are wild animals here; you must
Have been tired and you look like a princess.
Have you been forsaken by your father; your resemble   110
A divine creature; who are you actually?
You look like a deserted deer; this place is not safe,
It is infested with extremists and demons.
When the flood of darkness sweeps, it is difficult to
Safeguard one's dignity! When coarseness prevails
Kindness will be in short supply! This wilderness
Will only protect the law of the jungle and hence
You better go back and join your people or else
Till they come to take you safely stay in the hermitage,

But never put your foot forward; the way is dangerous!' 120
Shurpanakhi found herself in a state of utter
Confusion as she hardly knew the antecedents of Rama.
She only desired him strongly to be her husband; the welding
Of two bodies did not necessitate the harmony of the minds,
According to her. She became a victim of one-sided love;
She hankered after Raghuvara who resembled god Indra.

She addressed Shri Rama thus:
'You are most welcome, king, I am the sister of Lankesha;
They call me Shurpanakhi. This is the southern region
Of Ravana's kingdom. As you are a guest, you are 130
Entitled to all grand treatment; my father is
Sage Vishravasu, mother is Kaikase and I am blessed with
The brothers Ravaneshwara, Kumbhakarna and Vibhishana.
The eldest one, Dashashira is most powerful.
He has conquered all the fourteen worlds by his prowess;
He is learned in all the Vedas; he is an adept at all arts
And a warrier par excellence; there is no one to match him
In logic and argument and philosophical disquisition.
Kumbhakarna is equally powerful; Vibhishana is virtue
Personified; my husband, Vidyudjihva died in the battle, 140
By chance he was severed by the sword of Lankesha;
"He begged my forgiveness" and permitted me to love
A man of my desire and he has granted me sufficient
Land as well. I am a queen possessing the assistance
Of Khara and Dushana. It is my good fortune that you
Have manifested before me; come, you are a sun in my sky!'
Her words were gentle and persuasive.

'I have come to the forest to fulfill
The vow of my father; my brother is Lakshmana and
The daughter of Janaka is my wife. We are observing 150
Penance here.' Shri Rama said and narrated his life history
Very briefly and his intention was to send her away
As quickly as possible.

'O Ramachandra, when my
Pleasure-seeking mind was at its lowest ebb, you came to me
And the ocean inside swelled in response.
You are a wishing-tree to all those who seek your help.
The mind's peacock has spread its wings;
The parrots and cuckoos are singing from the branches
Of mango trees and the heart resembles a stringed   160
Instrument ready to be plucked by an artist.
The river is thirsting to join the sea.
When the Aryans and Dravidians join together
There will be a permanent cessation of conflict
And Saketa and Lanka will come together and
Be a philosopher's stone to the world.
Let all quarrels come to an end heralding peace.
Erase the distinction that some are humans,
Others demon and yet there is a third category
Called apes. Be my lover and we will wander   170
In love all over the valley, hillside and the lakes
And river beds taking deep and long dip into
The domain of love. Honour my request that I am
Love-lorn. We will dance in unison and bring
The earth and Heaven together, come,' so said
Shurpanakhi being forgetful of everything.
She was inviting her own destruction undermining
All rules of decorum and propriety.
Rama was flabbergasted at Lankesha's
Sister's blabberings. He said in utter calmness: 180
'Do not desire something that will be never be yours.
I have a wife, Janaki, from a noble family.
Can anyone put two swords into a single
Sheath, tell me, dear lady!'

Shurpanakhi thought the words of Rama
To be cruel and incivil. She burned more and more
In unrequited love and continued her appeal:
'Do not cut the cords that bind the hearts in love.

When there is Spring in nature, it is the season of
Amorousness; even Himagiri itself melts at its heat.
I have wandered through all the forests in search of
A loving-heart even in nature the birds do join their
Loved ones. Life itself turns into a blossom and
Love creates the nectar and hence the bees sing
Searching for their partners. I am dependent on you,
Grant me shelter in you. Look at all the creations
Of nature, they all are enhancing the mingling
Of hearts and there is a roaring river inside me.
I am the abode of beauty and so are you; therefore
Pluck the string so that the instrument may vibrate!'

Shri Rama understood Shurpanakhi's
State of mind and her love-lorn condition and said:
'This desire is an anathema; you are pulled
More and more inside the well of sin; why should you
Commit a blunder knowing fully well where it leads?
When the sun has already dipped in the ocean.
Why do you think you can bring him back from
The bosom of the blue? This desire is unnatural;
Do not swim in illusion, sister to the king of Lanka.
This does not befit the queen of Janasthana!"

Not willing to lose the argument
Shurpanakhi threw the sharp questions at
Shri Rama thus: 'Even Aryans are not known
To be loyal to their wives. What about Dasharatha?
Didn't he have three wives and who knew how
Many beloveds he had in his palace besides these?
Do not refuse me as you have conquered my
Heart and mind. Once you go away forsaking me
My body will be engulfed by a fire. If you accept me
My life would turn into gold; the whole world
Would be a realm of unending love.'

Shri Rama said again: 'Why should
You cross the limit being overcome by lust? You have
Virtue, character and beauty in abundance and
A young man of equal merit will come and claim you.
Do not entertain any doubt. You will have plenty
Of opportunities to select your suitors, being the sister
Of Ravana. Why should you hanker for the position
Of a maid to a wife, when you can command
The best of men being a queen of an independent kingdom!' 230

Shurpanakhi hardly saw the meaning
Of his advice as the waves of lust engulfed her:
'You are an emperor of the kingdom of beauty;
You are a regal bird flying freely in the sky of my
Heart. You are the rising sun and I would like you
To ascend the throne of my heart. The blooms of the wild
Are giving out fragrance and the bees are sucking
The nectar incessantly; when birds and beasts and
Bees are in full swing realising their dream 240
In this terrestrial Heaven refrain from shutting
The door of love!'

'What are you saying dear lady,
Should you value the physical appearance
So much! When once the oil gets exhausted
The lamp loses its life and there will be darkness again;
Such is the fate of beauty. When the spirit departs
The body withers underlining the impermanence
Of everything. Do not crave for the association
Of this body. Coming closer to love you may lose your
Equanimity. The penalty is too much; is it worth it? 250

'The vow of celibacy is a great discipline.
I will not forsake the path; do not persist;
You will not succeed. You cannot unhinge
A man devoted to his wife.

Coyness is a jewel for a woman; do not throw it away.
Caught in this whirlwind of lust you will surely
Reach the nadir of sin, beware,' so Shri Rama said
In his attempt to lead her to the sunshine of reason
Away from the world of darkness into which she was
Preparing to enter.   260

'The mind is full of your pleasing image
And your words echo in the heart with
Their melody. The nature is full of greenery
And all the senses are ready to pulsate with
The call of love. I have ascended the highest
Level of amorousness and if you separate the hearts
That are welded at this stage I will not live any longer;
Take note of that!' so saying Shurpanakhi made
Her love-lorn condition much more clear before Rama.

'Dear lady, this so called beauty is not   270
Caught within the ambit of the physical eye;
It is lodged deep within; it is invisible, so to say
It is the tiny particle indeed, descending from
Shiva's tresses. If you search for it and succeed
In realising it, then you have reached the goal.
Do not follow the path of impermanent pleasure;
That will only land you in great misery!
Take a vow to see the Bhagirathi or divine Ganga
Who is lodged within your heart!'
This was how Rama instructed her in all sincerity.   280
'When a man of inexhaustible beauty
Is standing right in front of me, should I let go
This opportunity and make a fool of myself?
Every being is craving for union in nature;
The desert land itself is turning into a domain
Of nectar. Are you not witnessing this yourself?
I will merge in you and you will merge in me
To achieve indivisibility, you be my marshall
Shri Rama, my lord!' Shurpanakhi implored again.

'The secret of all beauty lies there, see 290
Formless beauty is without any parallel.
This creation has manifested itself out of bliss.
It lives in bliss and it will end in bliss.
Listen to the divine music of harmony,
The effulgent entity has occupied the earth
And the sky. Think about it withdrawing
Inside yourself. The sun will not shed his light there
And similarly, the moonbeams do not enter;
Neither the stars and galaxies
Extend their luminosity there; but that world 300
Is the world of the self. Therefore, do not fall
Into the pit of the pull being a victim of illusion.
If you rise from this sense of mortality
You can realise what is truth.'

'Rama, the jewel of the world'
Why do you mix the mundane and the other-worldly!
Let my beauty bloom and raise to the highest point.
The heart craves for a union that is predestined.
Do not be blind to my plight and show a deaf ear
To my implorings; do not break the golden mirror 310
Of pleasing dreams; be an emperor of pleasure galore,
I will take you to the rarefied realm of happiness;
I too have tried to swim in the ocean of family life
And a woman is not an obstacle for someone
In pursuit of higher order; never entertain the idea
That a woman will take on a downward path of doom.

'I will beg of you Shri Rama,
Come as a rain to the desert of a woman's life,
Bereft of a husband; save my life like an elixir.
After having enjoyed the dazzling damsel of the north 320
Nothing should deter you from taking a damsel from the south.
I will be a necklace around your neck;
I will follow like a shadow without ever deserting you;

I will make you forget your land and sleep shall
Not approach you any more, granting all pleasures
On the royal bed in the palace; while I am
Rati, the consort of God of Love, you will be
Manmatha himself. I will be lotus and you
Will be the sun; I am the parched earth
While you are the rain from Heaven.   330

'If you forsake me still, you will be
Called a heartless man; instead, be a bridge
Between Saketa and Lanka and be a herald of peace
To the world.

'Being a kinsman of the whole world,
Grant life to countless lives by avoiding wars
And upholding peace; the people of Saketa will
Praise you; while Janaki will take care of the household,
I will absorb all thoughts of envy and hatred
By being a source of redemption!   340

'When peace prevails in the world
I will be an instrument of harmony. My brother,
Ravana, will pay ransom to the flag of Saketa,'
Shurpanakhi was overcome by emotion; she prostrated
At Rama's feet and declared that she would end her life;
Should he shun her with coarseness.

Canto Sixty-three

'You Know How to Blossom My New Poem'

||६||

Not knowing how to persuade Shurpanakhi
Shri Rama decided to send her away forcefully. 'I have
Overcome desire in Saketa itself. As I am an ascetic now
Lust is far away from me. This is the place where carnal
Passions are a taboo. Look at Saumitri, he is young and
Handsome and he will match you in all respects.
His wife Urmila is in Saketapuri and he suffers from
Pangs of separation. He has just come back from swimming
And you may both enjoy like the birds of the wild in full
Freedom,' said Rama.   10

Shurpanakhi's desire became awake
When her heart was brimming with passion, she failed to
Notice that Rama suggested this in jest. She combed her locks
And set her veil to resemble elegance and walked
Towards Saumitri as her steps were meant to attract him!

'This man is Cupid personified;
He is made for me; what bearing, what physique!
I will ransack all pleasures in the world being with him.

Rama lacks the sense of romance and this one seems
To be an adept in amorousness and I will drink   20
The fountain of joy and be a queen of erotic passions!'
That was Shurpanakhi's daydream.

Saumitri asked her a series of questions
In a tone of dignity. 'Who are you young lady?
This is a terrible wilderness and what brought you here?
Which is your place and in which direction is it situated?
Do you belong to *Yakshaloka* or *Nagaloka*? Do not forsake
Decorum; let me know your background.'

Shurpanakhi narrated all her antecedents: 'I cannot
Approach Rama as he is with his wife. But he has told   30
Me that you are alone here and a man with
A romantic bent of mind. You have everything
One looks for – you are young, intelligent and handsome,
You are like a flame of pearl in the ocean of beauty.
I like you and whatever Rama said is true;
You have the heart to understand the mind of a lady;
You can make my new poem bloom.
I have come to you to obtain the treasure of life!

'O god-like Lakshmana, shelter me in your heart
And sing the song of pleasure. I will extend   40
My well-rounded hands; hold me tight and place me
In love in the cushion of romance; light a lamp of
Cool illumination and sing a song of feeling,
Thereby take away all the burden from my heart.

'Do not refuse me. I will adorn you
With perfume of many kind; I will adore you
Placing you in my lap and mend your forelocks;
I will make you feel as if you are floating with the breeze
Bringing all the melodious tunes along so that
You may sway to its lilting rhythm and dance   50
In ecstasy; I will go round in a gyre showing

All my dancing prowess showering the petals
On you competing with the beats of the instruments.'

Saumitri understood at once
That Shurpanakhi is overtaken by a sense of lust;
He also realised that his brother has sent her
To him in jest. He changed his tune to rouse
Expectations and continued the strain of humour;
But put it across in his usual manner.

'When I am caught in the arms of a woman,   60
I will be like a kite without the central thread.
We must catch hold of a woman and then
Catch hold of gold; but woman and gold and
Land and all that will make a man rust;
And if someone wants to dazzle in splendour
He must follow the path of righteousness.'

'Why have you become an ascetic?
"There is no happiness in smaller things; it is only
Assured in grand things" – don't you know this
Observation of the learned? Renunciation is small   70
Really; one must drink the pleasures of life
In full measure as this life is not insignificant.
Living means to nurture all ambitions and to work
Towards its realisation. All our creativity
Is inspired by our desire. Desire promotes the progress
Of life and without it life is a desert indeed.
Do not destroy that which is life-giving.
It is the law of nature that the Ganga of Himalaya
Must flow towards the sea and no one should try to
Hold it back. Likewise when the Ganga of life   80
Aspires to join the vast ocean, no one should
Attempt to stop it!' so said Shurpanakhi.

Saumitri elaborated, changing the line of thought:
'You have studied the Vedas and related tomes;

You have also mastered logic and grammar;
But do you know what culture is? Scholarship
Is not culture. You may collect the axioms
From various sources which will only enhance
Your cleverness; you may also develop
The art of communication; even the learned talk 90
About music and painting does not amount
To obtaining culture!

'What is culture? It is nothing but knowledge that
Promotes the welfare of the world; that which
Enhances virtues; that which harmonises
Both external and internal existence together with
Balancing the beauty and bonds of brotherhood
Alone is entitled to be called culture and anything
That does not measure up to this estimation
Is a mere distortion of culture,' he told 100
The nature of culture in this manner.

'Leave alone the talk of culture,
The noble one; thinking that this life is
Impermanent and the body is doomed to perish.
Should one forget the dictum "That this body is
The instrument to achieve virtue." Should you praise
Renunciation at the cost of life! Culture is
Nothing but taking birth in bliss and growing
In bliss and to moving ahead in bliss!

'The principle of bliss is all pervasive. 110
It is evident in argument; it lends energy
To the limbs and enables them to be active.
It is there in lightning, in rain and in sunshine;
It is in the galaxy and in all things material.
When this principle of bliss is there everywhere
Do not indulge in wasteful argument Saumitri,'
Said Shurpanakhi with force and assurance.

'What is the nature of lust?
It weaves the cocoon of passion around itself
And invites death in the manner of a silkworm 120
And hence passion is a distortion of love. Therefore,
Cut all the roots of the poison-tree called passion;
Rise to the summit of success and do not slide
Into the trough of the valley. Let the Ganga of inner
Beauty fill all your heart; may you see the treasure
Of honour in the light of truth and dignity. Illumine
Your heart and reach the celestial world.
If you win over earthly aberrations
You will have domain of new life. Let the sacred fire
Burn eternally in your heart enabling you 130
To have good thoughts,' such was Saumitri's advice.

'The life of the spirit understands
What is *yajna* or the sacrificial ritual; intertia
Cannot reach it. Hunger has many faces.
The hunger of the mind leads to knowledge;
Hunger of the earth begets greenery; hunger creates will
And hunger spells *yajna*.
In one word, hunger itself is *yajna*.
The seeker after knowledge knows
The worth of life. The desire and anger are twin forms 140
In the world and they propel it forward.

'Why this renunciation, why this indifference?
Why bothered by the thought of sin and merit?
When the soul is covered by the five sheaths:
The sheaths of food, breath, mind, knowledge and bliss,
Why should you live undermining the worldly aspect?
Love binds everything and it is the reigning principle.

'Love engulfs all. Love moves the river
Towards the sea; it is the divine chanting to cause
The evolution of the world. Beginning from the atom 150

To the milky way, love motivates all. The Unmanifest
Divine is in the form of love and it knows
No limitation of the cycle of birth and death!

'This is strange indeed.
The life of the world is like a flowing river,
If it stops it will rot and the miasma spreads;
If it flows it redeems everything, so is life
Flowing is a struggle and it is not less than conflict.
The fundamental principle of life is hunger.
Even the flow of blood is a friction of tiny particles. 160
There is incessant grating in all activities
Which keeps everything fresh. If this is stopped
Life flies away leaving behind the dead body,'
So said Shurpanakhi explaining the mystery
Of the concept of *yajna*!

'What is there for me to add, noble lady,
I am the servant of Shri Rama and Janaki;
And therefore I have no right to fall in love
With you. When I am a servant myself,
You will be a servant's wife and that will not 170
Suit as you are Ravana's sister. This unequal
Wedding will lead to conflict. Since I am bound
To discipline I cannot break it. I am an entity
Bereft of passion. Draw Rama into your orbit
As he is the king of Saketa, you will be the queen
Of the kingdom,' so said Saumitri and sent her to Shri Rama.

Approaching Rama Shurpanakhi narrated
All that Saumitri had told her.
Listening to her words Rama said: 'He is
The lord of everything and why would he be a servant? 180
I have no kingdom when my brothers are
Reigning in Ayodhya? If I want to say
"I am a king" I can only claim that this forest

Is my kingdom! But Saumitri's case is different:
If he becomes your husband he will be the lord
Of Dandaka. He is free and untrammelled
And a warrior of immense power; you better
Go and persuade him again.'

Canto Sixty-four

'There Goes The Call For The War'

|| ६ ||

She went to Saumitri again as she made up
Her mind to try her luck for the second time.
She was at a loss to understand the minds of Shri Rama
And Lakshmana as she was overcome by passion.
She had missed the tone of jest in the dialogue.
'I have won the approval of my brother.
You wear the crown and shun the status of servitude,
Then I won't be a serving maid as you fear.
I will declare the war of liberation. I will conquer
Ayodhya itself. The gentle breeze is blowing   10
Across the sandal trees; the cuckoos are singing
Their songs of mirth; there is beauty everywhere
In the forest.

'Dear Saumitri, why do you think
That it is easy to conquer the God of Love!
Without the help of a woman no one can safeguard *dharma*.
In this world, that is created by god,
Duality is the reigning principle. When a drop
Of water descends from the cloud and enters
The mother-of-pearl, it becomes a shining   20

Precious thing; if it falls into the sea, it merges
In saltish water; if it falls in the well,
It acquires the character of sweetness. Though the water
Is one it attains many tastes.
Grant the nectar of your love, I will fashion
A different pearl out of it, my lord!' said Shurpanakhi.

'What more should I tell you'
Do not get into the pit of passion; do not neglect
The self being bogged down in the lust; more than
The form or appearance you have the self of fragrance. 30
You must know the difference between love and lust.
Life demands detachment; you plant your feet
On the ground but you must look towards the sky;
If you remove the thorn of lust that will be the end
Of pain; attain total vision by overcoming passion.'
Advised Saumitri ever more calmly.

She was deaf to his words: 'Come,
I will bind within my beautiful arms and hold you
In the luminosity of my eyes; I will subject you to
The golden shackles and worship you in my heart; 40
Come, let us sport and gambol in the forest and
Jump into the lake and swim. Be kind enough not to
Disappoint me by saying no to my entreaties.'
Shurpanakhi begged him virtually.

'I tell you with a voice of finality
That my entire self is immersed in the vow of celibacy
And that state is heavenly; as such
Do not pester me; put an end to all your attempts
At once; why do I need the glory of the city when I am
Here in this forest following a path of an ascetic. 50
If you really want to love someone go to Ramachandra;
He answers anyone who prays him with devotion
Not for nothing he is called the "Ocean of Mercy."'
Advised Saumitri again.

Shurpanakhi became angry:
'There is a strong streak of sadism in you both;
You are not to blame as you inherit it from your ancestors.
They have subjected women to misery even in their
Old age. Just to promote one culture, you do not hesitate
To trample upon other cultures. There is double standard   60
In your dealing; you are not plain and straightforward.
I will burst the bubble of your aggressive principle
And save multi-culture. Are you torturing the sister
Of the king of Lanka? What have you gained?
Rama is obsessed with his devotion to his wife
And you worship celibacy. I am a fool to have been
Caught between you two.

'This is nothing but atrocity that you
Are making fun of a woman craving for your love.
You are both mean and irredeemable; I will swallow   70
You lock, stock and barrel. Can you live peacefully
After rejecting me as I am the most beautiful woman
In the world. It is enough that you are
A eunuch who has run away from Saketa.
That cleverness is cheap and worthless;
If there is a co-wife there I will erase her within
No time,' she roared breathlessly and leaving
Aside Lakshmana she went to Rama again.

Shri Rama saw her visage which exuded
Anger. He could not control his laughter and he   80
Looked towards Sita and laughed again. Maithili
Smiled in response while Saumitri stood behind
Laughing at what he saw. Shurpanakhi's anger
Increased several folds and she thought clearly
That they were laughing at her cost!

'During the period of exile, you have
Come in the southern direction without obtaining permission
And I am not going to spare you so easily. You like

The women of dessicated bones without an iota of flesh
On their body; you are dedicated to your wife   90
And you, you say that celibacy is your *mantra*.
It is all play-acting as I can see. You wallow
In the company of many wives and you hide
That fact from others; I will expose your fraud
And trick so that the world may know your worth,'
Said Shurpanakhi.

The harsh words of Shurpanakhi
Brought more laughter to Shri Rama and Lakshmana.
Her childish prattle created humour at that moment.
All the three laughed unable to control it and Shurpanakhi   100
Got wild beyond words:

'I am the sister of Lanka,
Do you think I am a sheep or a beggar? Many
Crowns of kings will fall at my feet, if I so desire.
When I ask for your love, you make fun of me;
You are after all a king of a small area and your ego
Knows no bound, killing all my desires. I will not spare
This weakling called Janaki,' so saying Shurpanakhi
Rushed to the spot where Sita was standing!

Saumitri at once jumped wielding   110
The sword in hand standing between the two. The sword
Touched Shurpanakhi but still she advanced with
Rage. Her ears were cut and the nose impaired.
Shurpanakhi's face was splashed with blood and her anger
Sprang in all its viciousness.

'Nothing could redeem you all. What right
Have you to punish me? I will not spare you who have
Transgressed the land of Lanka. Darkness will
Engulf your lives forthwith and all the richness and
Bounty of Saketa will vanish at once. The Ikshwaku   120
Dynasty will be ruined as if it did not exist;

You will lose the goal of your pursuit and you will
Not be left with anyone to call your own.

'The age will come to an end;
Shri Rama being the last link will fall into hell,
My brother will swallow everything in revenge;
He will go round all the fourteen worlds and
Erase the trace of your lineage whenever he finds it.

'I came in search of love and this is
The reward you gave me – a wounded face! 130
You have exposed my life to the graveyard;
While I craved for the elevating nectar
You made me drink deadliest poison of a black cobra;
You have given a call to the war and invited
The wave of violence. There will be a fountain of
Poison in this churning; when you have exploded
The volcano, lava would flow in full fury,
Everything that is harmonious will be swallowed by fire;
The source of nectar will be lost in the heap
Of sands now! 140

'You are veritable fools
Who tarry without savouring the ambrosia when
It is fresh. This body, this beauty and this youth
Are all given for a purpose; as they are fleeting
And impermanent they must be enjoyed without
Delay. You have invited trouble by insulting
A lady and who will save you now that you have
Caused a great havoc?' So saying Shurpanakhi
Descended on them like a thunderbolt. She was wild
In anger and was disoriented in passion; she writhed 150
In pain and rushed to the spot where Khara and Dushana
Stayed; she was in a hurry to provoke
Them to take revenge against her enemies.

Canto Sixty-five

'Do You Wish to Fight Against a Black Cobra?'

||๑||

Khara and Dushana, the sons of Sage Vishravasu,
And the demoness Raka, are the generals of the army of which
Shurpanakhi is the queen and the Lanka glory was enhanced
During her reign. The good people and the ascetics wailed
In misery and they implored Rama to save them.

When Khara was in the embrace of sleep
One night he was unnerved at the dream he had:
A chariot was drawn by the tigers and it rolled on
Youth innocence and happiness. It was a night of chaos
In which the dark clouds gathered in the sky causing thunder,   10
Lightning and hailstorm raged viciously.
A female jackal is caught in the rain; it had not
Eaten any food and it ran behind the chariot breathlessly.
At that time a huge wave of water struck the beast
So hard that it went down into a valley within no time.

The demon woke up suddenly from his dream
And heaved a sigh of relief that it was not real and only
A dream! He was worried about the condition of Shurpanakhi.

But Shurpanakhi appeared right then with her ears and
Nose profusely bleeding; she had fallen on the ground
Before him. Looking at this cruel sight he said in utter
Disbelief, 'What am I witnessing sister, what is all this,
Tell me, who has caused this?' asked Kharasura.

'I am drenched in blood; see how
I am disfigured. In this world of men do I have freedom
Being a woman? Why should I live in this world at all;
I will put an end to my life. My whole body is burning.
Two brothers called Rama and Lakshmana are staying
At Panchavati hermitage and they say they are the sons
Of Dasharatha; they are arrogant and egoistic beyond words.
They are mere mortals and they have committed this atrocity
On me; they have caused terrible damage to the empress of Lanka,
Pride and self-respect of the demons has received a death blow;
They have extended protection to the sages, thereby provoking
The dignity of Lanka.

'Look at me brother, how they have
Outraged my modesty; I have become the mark
Of the attacks of the Aryans; they have caused anxiety
To the assembly of demons; the whirlwind is blowing
Spelling the doom of all; how can I show my face to
The king of Lanka?' so saying she fell on the ground
Just as a lonely female elephant falls after being
Hit by an arrow.

The demon at once became angry:
'Who could be so insolent as to cause this damage
To the great sister of Lankesha! Is it their wish to
Put her hand into the mouth of a black cobra?
They will be burnt into ashes in the flame of my anger,
I will break their back with my sharp arrows
I will take only their lives in the battlefield;
I will pour their blood on the earth that she may consume it;

I will throw away their bodies for the wild birds and beasts,
Who would protect them then?' he said in a thundering voice.

The brother's words gave her strength and
Tears Rolled down her cheeks even as she said, 'Brother dear, I am
Lost forever; the young brothers resemble the God of Love;
Their charm knows no bound; though they are gentle
In demeanour, they are tough warriors; they wear
The raiment of ascetics and their tufts of hair is attractive too.
They wield bows and arrows and they shine in martial splender.   60

'With the death of my husband, I have become rudderless.
Lankesha has permitted me to marry a man of my choice.
These young men, I thought, would suit me
Though I could not place them among mortals
Or immortals or the dwellers of the angelic world.
It was a great shock to find a damsel beside them
Whom they call by name Sita. I must drink her blood
Only then will I rest contented. How long will I live
Begging for love; as life brings weariness I will
Walk into the sea,' so saying Shurpanakhi cried inconsolably.   70

Hearing about the arrival of Shri Rama and
Lakshmana, the face of Khara perspired profusely.
The bones rattled; anger turned into fire; the thirst for
Blood and battle soared. He called the leaders of
The demons and said: 'Two human beings of no consequence
Have entered into Panchavati and they have cut the ears
And nose of our sister; that is undermining the reign
Of Lankesha; I must hunt them and my sister must
Drink their blood!'   80

The army of the demons marched with
Shurpanakhi leading them. They surged forward
Like the clouds being pushed by the force of whirlwind.
The demons who worship violence as the ultimate
Principle, turn their back to elevating culture;

Nurturing hatred and intolerance they have become blind!
They are incapable of judging pros and cons.
Their army looked like wild elephants caught
In the forest fire and like butterflies fluttering by roaring flame.

Shri Rama and Lakshmana saw 90
At a distance the haste and hurry of the demons!
Shri Rama said even as the picture of Viradha
Flitted across his mind: 'When the demon caught
Hold of Janaki in the past, it caused havoc and
I do not want to see the repetition of such a thing.
I will take on the army of the demons.
You just watch how I fight them and I call you
Only if I need your help. Believe my words;
Have faith in my prowess; I will overcome the demons;
I will decimate them; reducing the burden of the earth 100
I will convert Dandakaranya into a hermitage;
I will make it a demon-free zone.'

He held his great bow in readiness
Taking a good look at the demons. 'Why do you
Torture the monks in this fashion; they live only on
Roots and shoots; they pray for the good of all
And have the thought of others' well-being constantly.
They are the upholders of *dharma*; what harm have
They caused? Violence appears to be your creed.
Stop these atrocities; this is violation of law and it will 110
Only swallow you; there is a deep gorge ahead.'
When Shri Rama thus tried to bring them around,
They only showed their deaf ear.

They held their spears and rushed
Fiercely and thundered loudly, 'Khara is our master,
And we will suck your life at once; you will surely fall
On the ground being subjected to the metallic lashes.
We care less for your bow and tiny arrows as we
Possess immense power and strength.'

Shri Rama shot his arrows at 120
The advancing demons; they found the targets
With unfailing sureness and they all fell to the ground
As a consequence. The arrows burned in the air
Before hitting their chests and the giants dropped
Into pools of blood.

Even as her people met with death
Shurpanakhi's wailing increased. She uttered loud
Sounds mixing sorrow and anger thus: 'I still
Have my brother Khara and he will erase all of you
In one go.' Her voice only produced an unbearable 130
Noise and she ran shouting these words as if
She was a woman possessed.

'No words can console me;
I will not hear anything pertaining to peace.
The weapons like spear, sword and metal lash do not count,
They have all fallen in the ponds of blood
As a result of Rama and Lakshmana's arrows.
I have seen Dasharathi's valour;
The waves of fear lash at me incessantly; 140
Only you can conquer this enemy, surely.

'The decimators of the demon lineage have
Dealt a deadly blow to the reign of Lankesha.
If you are afraid of facing the fire of Rama
Tell me, I myself will go and face him.
I will encounter both of them like a female elephant
Determined to destroy the castle in fury.
The people should not say that there is a dearth
Of heroes in the kingdom of Lankesha and therefore
I am prepared to die, let me go,' so said 150
Shurpanakhi as there was a combination of anger
And fear in her voice.

Thus she provoked Khara with her words of
Taunt and tantrums and Khara thundered thus:

'Would you allow Lankesha's flag of victory to be stamped
In the mud? Don't have any anxiety. Look at my prowess;
Do you think Rama and Lakshmana are my equals?
I will cut them and send them to the abode of death,
I will pour their hot blood into your palms;
You may drink it to your heart's content and dance;
I will prepare victuals out of their flesh and blood;   160
I will be an earthquake causing the vibration
Of the world. I will bury the Aryan's
Way of aggression. We will march forward
Uprooting fear and anxiety from our mind.
Self-confidence and determination are our precious shields.'
Khara's utterance was like the thunderbolt
From the sky and it echoed and re-echoed all around.

Hearing Khara's words, Shurpanakhi brought tears and said,
'You are supreme, and I uttered something without realising
Your prowess, your valour conquers all,' in awe and admiration.   170

Shurpanakhi's words added fuel to the fire and
Kharasura sent for Dushana at once and said when
He appeared before him: 'You must start without wasting
Time for the battlefield; call all those who are skilled in
Warfare to go with you. The miscreants must be punished
Duly. Prepare well for the confrontation. All types of weapons
We must carry and they should be in an excellent condition.
Swords, spears and arrows of sharp points and sure aim.
When I am the tested warrior who can compete with me
I will accomplish the ethnic cleansing?'   180
Before the brother completed his words, Dushana
Kept the chariot ready hitching the horses of great merit.
The chariot was embellished all around and it dazzled
Like the veritable Meru mountain. To invoke auspiciousness
They had kept the golden images of fishes, flowers, trees and
Hills; sun, moon and the stars. Swords were hung and the stem of

The flag was surrounded by trinkets. It heralded
The glory of Dashashira, the ten-headed demon king.

Khara ascended the chariot with a serious face.
Dushana arranged the army of demons into a particular formation. 190
He fastened the sword to his side and wore the armour.
He left in great spirit following Khara in his great chariot.

The demons carried the weapons which suited
Them, and they included the mace, the sword, the bow and many
Lashes of metallic extraction. They rushed in all four directions
Shouting that they would conquer the enemy in no time.

The army had marched from Janasthana
And they encountered many bad omens on the way. The beasts
And birds cried strangely facing the soldiers of Khara and Dushana.
Crows, jackals and kites too made strange noises
Scattering in all directions. 200
There was a thick cloud of dust in the atmosphere;
The horses stumbled and the chariot almost tumbled;
The solar zone was without light or lustre,
Darkness enveloped the region during day-time itself.
It was as if Rahu had caught hold of the sun in the eclipse.
In the darkness impenetrable the stars twinkled
Like glowworms, the shooting stars fell from their positions
To the ground; the fishes and water-birds hid themselves
Being stunned. Fruits and flowers were swept from the
Branches and the trees were uprooted in large numbers. 210
The hills, the forest and the whole wilderness shook caught
In the violent wind. The demon Khara's left arm quaked
Relentlessly and tears welled up in his eyes; his body was baked
In high temperature; he had been gripped by fear
Like never before.

He did not show his anxiety to the world outside
And spoke with a determined voice thus:
'Listen to me, fearless soldiers, let this shooting star

Not bother you. It is the cowards who see such a phenomenon
As a premonition of destruction. They are mere coincidences 220
And they warrant no anxiety. The effulgence of valour
Springs within me; I will sweep the stars with my
Sharp weapons. If I am angered I will stop
The normal process of the world; I will cut
Those handsome duo into pieces and even as they bleed
I will fulfil the wishes of my sister. Let the chief of gods
Descend wielding his *vajra* weapon on his *Airavata*
Elephant, I will not spare him as I know no defeat.
I will show to the whole world the prowess of Dashashira.'

That assurance from Khara's words gave immence power 230
To his followers; they flexed their muscles cheering with joy.
The invisible rope of death had stretched its noose around
The necks of Khara-Dushana and all others who were
At their command.

Khara forged forward in his chariot ahead
Of his men. Shyenagami, Prithugriva, Yajnashatru
Durjaya, Purusha, Karaviraksha, Vihangama,
Kalakarmuka, Meghamali, Sarpasya, Rudhirashana
And innumerable others stood on either side of Khara!
Mahakapala, Sthulaksha, Pramathi and Trishira 240
Were four other soldiers who stood near Dushana.

'It is the cowards who fear the omens
And the valiant ones never take note of them.
We always win in the battle and fighting is our second nature,'
Said Dushana in a thundering voice.

They rushed to the vicinity of the cottage
In Panchavati. The end of the dark night heralded
The arrival of the celestial sun with his glory
Of dawn and the pink of the sky indicated
The cessation of the earthly journey to the horde of demons. 250

Looking at the vehemence and violent words
Of the demons Shri Rama said in calmness: 'The sun
That went down yesterday has appeared again today.
In the background of "yesterday" there is an evolution
Of "today". The sun rising itself is a sign of
Auspiciousness. It is time for you to hide yourselves
In the caves. The arrows vie with each other
To be used first; they are fidgety inside the quiver.'

They flew to the caves without speaking a word
And Saumitri and Sita appeared to be flames of fire 260
Adorned with divine raiments and Rama with his bow
Resembled Rudra himself.

Canto Sixty-six

'Fragrant Breeze is Blowing Gently'

||६||

Shri Ramachandra being a warrior par excellence
Stretched his divine bow to the limit and cut all the arrows
Shot by Khara midway. Rama needs no assistance
And he stood there like an awe-inspiring mountain
Decimating everything.

At the feet of Shri Rama all arrows
Are melting like innumerable rivers merging in the ocean.
Though drenched in blood he quells the enemy camp
Relentlessly with his sharp weapons; he has caused the bodies
Of the demons to roll throwing the noose of death around their neck. 10

The forest of dry wood is raging with fire
And the demons who had ascended the horses and elephants
Are falling to the ground bereft of life-force. The arms
Only with armlets and other decorations are scattered.
But still the demons marched ahead in full fury
Swaying their swords and axes; but Shri Rama took
No notice of their aggression as he attacked them
Separating limbs from their bodies sending them all
To the abode of death.

Like snakes caught in the attack of eagles,
The demons quaked in the face of Rama's arrows
And Khara and Dushana gave them courage
And boosted their sagging morale to fight.

They threw spears and hurled rocks
And trees; shot arrows. The battle reached the zenith;
Shri Rama roared like a lion and meditated a while
He transmitted a sea of arrows covering all the demons.
Even the directions became indiscernible and hence darkness
Descended. The whole of the battlefield contained the dead
Bodies of the demons. Heads with crowns in tact, shoulders
With the corresponding ornament, the broken legs and torn flags
Along with embellished umbrellas all over
And Parnakuti had become a zone of pitched battle.

Dushana's anger was explosive; he rushed
Forward saying that he would kill Rama then and there
Shooting arrows like lightning. Rama was a picture of courage.
He evoked Vasishtha and Viswamitra and other teachers of eminence.
Then he cut the horses of Dushana as they stood
Tracing the design of a half-moon. He cleared the head
Of the charioteer at once! When Dushana was about to
Swing a weapon at Shri Rama, the latter cut the arms
Of the demon in a flash; like an elephant breathing its last
After the removal of the tusks, Dushana's breath went away
Forsaking the body.

The news of Dushana's death brought immense sorrow
To Khara; he delved deep into the slough of sadness;
The enormous pain had caused his bones to crack.
At that point sorrow turned into anger. Just as the disturbed
Lion hardly thinks of the imminent harm, Khara
Advanced hurriedly, Trishira refrained him thus:

'You the mighty one, don't rush forward;
Assign the job to me; I will smite Rama in a trice.

I am veritable death, trust my words.' At his imploring
Khara agreed and sent Trishira to the battlefield.

The thought of Dushana's death covered him again.
'Dear brother, fate has cheated you; you had been my
Support; like an invincible armour you protected me;
You were the redoubtable sword in my sheath!
I am drowned in the sea of sorrow;
Come, dear child, I have placed the lion-throne near me 60
For you to sleep; I have spread a vast bed for your
Comfort, see for yourself,' so saying, he cried.

The chariot of Trishira thundered like the
Trikuta mountain; he rained arrows in the manner
Of a great cloud. When one of the arrows touched
Shri Rama's forehead, his anger sprang at once!

Raghava stood there like a curse to his enemies
And roared. 'What a great wrestler you are!' said he
In mocking admiration. Four arrows were enough to
Quell the horses and eight more to kill the charioteer; 70
One more was needed to destroy the flag and fourteen
Arrows were planted in Trishira's chest and the chariot
Was pulverised at the end!

Trishira's breath struggled to leave the body
And he tried to move towards Rama in his desperate bid
To attack him, but Rama used three more arrows to put
An end to the demon. The three necks appeared to represent
Lust, anger and treachery. Thus he was eliminated
By Rama in the heart of the hermitage of Panchavati!

Just as the deer run helter-skelter after 80
Hearing the roar of a tiger, the demons began
To run and Khara understood the prowess of Shri Rama;
But still he said: 'Don't be afraid brothers; I will
Smite him shortly; I will plant arrows in his chest,
They will penetrate and will be seen at his back; that will

Herald my heroism, you wait'. So saying he stopped
The demons from running away.

In the manner Namuchi faced Devendra,
Khara held his bow and stretched the string
To the maximum shooting the arrows in quick succession.   90
He aimed at Rama's chest and succeeded in planting
Some; the arrows called Naleeka and Vikarni, known
For their sharpness did their job. When he thought
He had cornered Rama, Khara became wild and uncontrollable.

Rama's anger reached its peak.
He shot six arrows in a row from the Vaishnava bow,
As he resembled the Sun-god with dazzling splendour.
He killed the horses; the charioteer lost his head;
The wheels of the chariot were destroyed;
The elephant died; in the absence of a chariot   100
And a bow the demon stood on the ground
Holding a mace in utter confusion.

'You are a terrible menace to the people
Causing untold suffering; the snake
That has sneaked into the house must be killed
At any cost; otherwise the ascetics cannot live.
You must pay for your sins. You cannot eat food
Made out of poison and live. The account must be
Settled in this life itself. It would be a fruitful
Existence if you can travel on the path of progress   110
Hoping for re-creation and new thinking
That will transform this Janasthana into an abode
Of peace bestowing all auspiciousness.'
Said Shri Rama indicating the course future would take.

'Hold on, stop and no more about
Your self-aggrandisement; you lack culture
And enough of your egoistic boastings. I am standing
Here like an immovable mountain; I will torture

All the three worlds,' so saying Khara swung
His mace that was burning like a shooting star   120
At Shri Rama. When the weapon was coming
At a lightning speed Shri Rama cut it midway
With his arrow!

'Worthless demon, don't I know
Your prowess? Look at the battlefield, it is parched
And dry; I will make it drink blood as much
As it needs; don't you see the noose tightening
Around your neck?' Hearing this Khara not
Finding any other weapon uprooted a tree nearby
And threw it at Rama with great speed!   130

As Khara shouted to his people
'Bring the weapon,' they brought the bludgeon and
Javelin; wielding the same the demon spat fire
And his body shook in anger and the spark
Of hidden vengeance gave out a huge flame.
The demon summoned all strength and rushed
Towards Rama like a mammoth mountain
After hurling his weapons one after another.

Shri Rama thought that it is time to put an end
To the demon and hence he set his arrow to the bow and   140
Stretched the string to the limit; took two steps backwards,
standing firmly
Shot the arrow which went like a *Brahmastra* and penetrated
His chest and the demon fell to the ground not able to withstand
The pain; Khara resembled a huge mountain as he collapsed.

The demons' anger had exploded the towns,
Cities and villages until now; killings were a daily affair
And many had become handicapped because of radiation
And many had suffered trauma; the good people
Looked at the sky in utter helplessness. There may be

One Ravana to be counted; but there are uncountable ones 150
Seen everywhere who aspire for position and luxurious life.
They would like to have absolute control over others;
The all-devouring war had erased the natural treasure
All over the world. Who is responsible for this?

The power of the soul is asserting again
The faded dreams have started blooming again
The clouds that had hidden the sun are passing away
The waterfall of happiness is gurgling again
The breeze is carrying the perfume all around
The trees, on their own, scatter the flowers 160
At the feet of Shri Ramachandra.

Peace prevailed again; in the realm of Janasthana
Virtue manifested again; the Goddess of Forests
Bestowed on Rama the golden ears of corn in humility;
It appeared as if the harvest festival had arrived.

The demons have immense power, but
They are great deceivers; they harbour hatred and
Ill-will annulling good thoughts and good deeds;
The assembly of sages rejoiced at the end of
The dance of demons in Dandakaranya. 170

'Lord, you protected the group of monks
By erasing Khara, Dushana and Trishira; you broke
The bow of Shiva and married Sita; you contained
The luminosity of Bhargava and protected the earth
By wielding the bow of Vishnu; we will sing for your
Victory and will sing for auspiciousness. We pour
The oil of devotion to the lamp of Padmanabha's
Divine name so that it may burn eternally.

'Lord, we are redeemed, we are redeemed;
Your valour knows no equal; you have 180
Protected the *dharma*; hail Raghavendra,
Hail Shri Ramachandra; hail the conqueror

Of the demon; hail the nourisher of the good;
Hail him who ended the curse on Ahalya;
He is the jewel of the solar dynasty and he is
The destroyer of Tataka. May victory be yours, the Lord of
Heavens; may victory be yours being a sun for the lotus
Of the devotees' heart; hail the lord of Saketa;
Hail the protector of the cosmos; hail the resplendent moon
To Kausalya; you are the divine icon; you are   190
The one who causes good things to all. Hail Shri Rama,'
So did the monks praise Shri Rama.

Sita and Saumitri came out of the cave and
Saw for themselves what all Shri Rama had accomplished.
They took pride in what Rama had done.
Saumitri embraced his elder brother;
Janaka's daughter was joy personified and she
Forgot herself when Rama took her in his arms!
Sita became the confluence of three fortunes,
Namely the fortune of the state, the fortune of victory   200
And the fortune of mobility! The wounds on Rama's body
Had vanished; Sita, Rama and Lakshmana looked at
The ascetics, the wish of victory echoed and re-echoed
In all directions.

Canto Sixty-seven

'Ravana is Comparable Only to Ravana'

||⦿||

When the leader of the *yakshas* were ruling Lanka
The descendents of Yaksha and Kubera dominated;
They were proud of their position and power and
The lineage of the demons laboured day and night
As servants; they spent their time in anguish and anxiety
While Ravana, their leader, contemplated on conquering
Yaksha and Kubera in a bid to regain his throne.

The demons were not allowed inside the palace;
The inner chamber of Vaishravana, the king of the *yakshas*,
Was well secured with iron bars. 10

He had punished and reduced Kaikase to the position
Of a concubine and they looked down upon her threatening her
No end. Everywhere there was cold indifference
And warmth and civility had vanished once and for all.
The relatives of Kubera enjoyed all the power of the state
Cornering the coffers and commanding respect and comfort.
The children of Kaikase did not have anything
To fall back upon; they wallowed in misery.

The son of Vaivaswata was granted
The coveted position by Vishravasu and that went 20

Eventually to Kubera. The followers of the demons
Were subjected to all kinds of atrocities. They were
Tormented beyond words at the hands of the *yakshas*
And there was no assurance of a good turn of events for them.

The monks in *gurukulas* and hermitages
Were clever enough to praise Kubera and Ravana
Seethed in anger. They were all caught in the
Web of fraud and deception. The seed of poison
Spread like a weed. Everyday
He thought of getting back his kingdom from Kubera   30
And therefore the spark of rebellion was waiting
For an opportune moment to explode.

The demons too contemplated the rebellion;
There was total absence of harmony, there was
Imbalance of every kind. Dashakandhara
Is pushing days in meditating on the moment
That will free them from this menacing
Thrall and exploitation. Their
Pent up desire came to the surface and danced.

When good thoughts are absent inside   40
Love will escape too, making room dreariness
And pain. When the realm of the mind is free
And pure excellent thoughts grow aplenty; feelings
Would be like unshackled birds twittering in the sky.
Good thoughts breed happiness and love, kindness,
Forgiveness result where there is no malice;
Generosity, compassion, bliss and peace take root
In such a place and remain there forever.

It is the bad thoughts that beget hatred,
Ill-will, selfishness, indifference, vengeance and   50
All such negativities multiplying thorns amidst
Growing crops. Vaishravana cared little of
The sentiment of the demons and they, in turn,

Spat venom and waited for an opportune moment
To attack.

The power of Ravana acquired
Vast dimensions of rebellion; the seed of revolt
Grew into a huge tree; Ravana would be a breeze
Enlarging the flames of the uprising. He is the symbol
Of vengeance and his enmity with the *yakshas*   60
Would pit them against each other in a pitched battle.

'We are the workers and
Yaksha and Kubera have been enjoying at our cost.
Our labour must yield happiness to us. We are
Without food in our own land. We will rally together
And win it back. We will concentrate all our strength
And overcome Yaksha and Kubera and make their blood
Flow on the ground and win our freedom. This land
Of our ancestors will be ours once again,' said Ravana.

'This rebellion is decided and   70
Hence no one can stop us; even Yama, Devendra
And Trivikrama cannot restrain us; neither
Is it possible to our father Vishravasu himself.
Surge ahead and we will smite the God of Death!'
So saying he set afire the veins of the demons
With the fire of revolt. He taught them many
Strategies, techniques and ideas by playing
The role of a teacher. He was the motivator
In matters of martial courage. Still, his inordinate
Leaning towards lust proved to be invincible.   80

His mind is like a monkey and it has
Caused so much disturbance that he cannot be quiet
And composed anymore. When there is a dance of
Mediocrity, excellence must take a back seat.
Ravana built castles in his fancy; there was
A museum, art galleries, theatres and a design to lay

The bridge across the ocean. The veritable rainbow
Danced before him and eventually everything
Lay there scattered.

But Ravana persisted in the hope of encountering   90
Good days ahead after wading through the darkness,
He visualised a new path as the days passed by.

The whole of Lanka hated the Kubera dynasty
Because of their corruption, exploitation and excessive
Egoism coupled with their heterodox ways. That
Made Ravana's advance easier.

Ravana had acquired distinguished swords
And charged weapons and the shackles binding the demons
Were broken at once; he put an end to oppression completing
The process of establishing an independent kingdom.   100
Thus he had overcome the nightmare of seeking
Shelter under Kubera.

The golden Lankan empire came into being.
Ravana's triumphant clarion deafened the ears;
The sound of explosions reached the sky; the flag
Of the demons fluttered in the air opening
The gate of power widely.

His determination was to inspire his army
To build a great future, clearing the path
Removing thorns and stones and other hurdles.   110
He told them that there is no rest till they
Achieved the desired goal.

The dazzling prowess of the demons
Had stunned the *yakshas*. 'I will show to the world
That I am the worthy son of Vishravasu.
I will throw the whole of Yaksha dynasty into the valley;
I will bury them filling it with rocks and boulders;
This would be the end of their journey; they will not

Be able to exploit others anymore; I will
Throw him and all his belongings to the fire; 120
I will erase everyone that has caused havoc
And suffering.' Thus he spread the message
Of a new life and lighted the lamp of freedom in Lanka.
This was the proclamation:
'If the women and children are not alert, the enemy
Will harass us no end; before we smite the enemy without
We must quell the enemy within as our
Aim is to move towards a wider horizon!' Thus,
Ravana, transcending the human limit, assumed
Gigantic proportions. 130

He had full faith in war,
He was proud that he had
Conquered the whole world; war is everything;
War is for its own sake and that was Ravana's
Stance and hence dialogue was rendered impossible.
He was a warrior par excellence and he declared
That he would offer his head to Shankara.
He is known for his power of penance and determination.
He cares little of gods and humans and *vanaras;*
Likewise he dares even the demi-gods and *dramilas;* 140
He is not afraid of war, neither is he scared
Of death and he is free from worries.

He has caused happiness
To his mother Kaikase. Even as he prostrated
Before his mother on obtaining the *chandrahasa* weapon.
She hugged him, overcome with joy; she nodded
Her head in great appreciation of their prowess.
'You are my worthy son, you are an achiever.'
She praised him in full measure.

Ravana assumed the charge 150
Of the reign as he was destined to rule.
The distinguished minister Prahastana was his advisor,

Whose guidance had obtained him
Lanka without necessitating the war.
They achieved their aim and the leader of *yakshas*
And *kuberas* had disappeared from the scene.

'We must be on our guard as we
Have deadly enemies; they will be jealous of
Our glory; this is the time to enlarge our
Kingdom; a coward has no right to rule the world.   160
I have observed intense penance obtaining
All merit and I will start my journey of conquest,'
He said and getting the blessings of his mother
Kaikase, the huge army of the demons marched
Forward in great enthusiasm.

As they marched beyond their capital,
Those who opposed them initially, accepted defeat
And paid ranson by surrendering! He met with
Success wherever he went and his valour was
Duly honoured and hence he shone with glory.   170

They got their empire back. Let the warrior
Clan grow from strength to strength; may Ravana
Protect the world with elan; Dashakanta is a real
Protector; let all the pleasures that are available in Heaven
Prevail in Lanka as all the lands have
Surrendered to Ravana. 'King of demons, we salute you.'
So praise the eulogists and that proclamation has filled
All the ten directions and Ravana has illumined
The golden Lanka!

Kumbhakarna is the general of the army,   180
And Vibhishana, the virtuous, is the prince, Prahasta
Is the minister as he is well-versed in diplomacy,
Mandodari, the daughter of Maya who is a great sculptor,
Is the queen of Dashakandhara.

Kumbakharna's wife is Vritrajwale, the daughter
Of Bali; Surame is the daughter of Shailusha and she is

The wife of Vibhishana; whereas Shurpanakhi has married
Vidyudjihva; Lankini has volunteered to guard Lanka
And Lanka knows no threat from any quarter.

The gardens are new and so are the 190
Bowers; new are the royal streets; new is the
Hall of entertainment; everything is new in Lanka
Which is wallowing in richness being the creation
Of Vishwakarma. Lanka is dazzling as the centre of the world.

Ravana is resplendent as the bright lamp.
He harassed the divine guards of eight directions.
He dared the assault by Indra with his *vajra* weapon.
Likewise, he never cowered but withstood bravely the attacks
Of Airavata elephant; when gods cornered him
And hence his courage in the battlefield 200
Is exemplary. He defied gods and encountering
Mount Meru, he smote Vasuki and hence he is
Unparalled in prowess; that is why one may say
Ravana can be compared only to himself
And hence is unconquerable. He is the great fighter
In the world who has bound even the sun and the moon.

Canto Sixty-eight

'Why Go After Somebody's Wife'

||௬||

One day Vaishravana sent a message to Ravana
Through an emissary with ransom. Ravana opened the seal
And read the content, which ran thus:

'This is the message sent by the leader
Of the *yakshas*, Vaishravana, to you, the lord of Lanka.
Being an elder brother, I am prompted to give these words of
Advice to you in the fond hope that you would not mistake me.
We are all foster-children to Sage Vishravasu and
We are ruling different kingdoms at present.
But the bond of brotherhood is intact wherever we are;   10
And I will narrate the sad story that is a part of my life.

'One day in the environs of the White Peak where Shiva resides,
I saw Parvati while roaming aimlessly.
I was completely captivated by her resplendent beauty.
Eyes stayed on her form without moving a bit;
Then suddenly I felt as if somebody poked my eyes
With a live brand and I lost an eye and thus I became
A one-eyed man! I begged Shiva for mercy and forgiveness.
Being kindness personified, Shiva forgave me, but
My status as a one-eyed being is a permanent one!   20

'You are a sovereign king known for your valour,
Courage and conquest; you have been fortunate
To have the discipleship of Shiva Himself; you being
A great adventurer and achiever, should you run
After the wife of another person exhibiting lust?
Why should you keep in your palace another's wife?
Do not follow my way of life, dear one!

'The hungry senses pull you hither and thither,
And you must restrain them carefully; lust is a surest
Way of ruining an individual; cut all the channels   30
That transmit lust and as you are the son of a sage
You must walk with caution to obtain fame, dear one!'

His immediate reaction was to call
The members of the inner circle to tell them how
Angry he was at the impudence of the message.
For, he had read the message from a different angle,
Which ran contrary to the intended meaning. He ordered
At once: 'Let the army march towards Alkapuri
Right now; I cannot wait to take revenge and burn
And destroy it.'   40

Ravana ransacked all the riches of Alkapuri
And carried the great chariot *Pushpaka* to Lanka
With him. Out of brotherly love, Vaishnava had advised
Him, but that caused a terrible disaster to his kingdom
And he endured the consequences in silence.

Kushadhwaja had his hermitage
In the Himachala region and his wonderful daughter
Vedavati lived there; her knowledge of the Vedas
And such lore had made her wisdom personified.
Kushadhwaja had left for rigorous penance   50
After blessing her with the words: 'May Shrihari
Be your consort, worship him!'

In penance, Vedavati appeared to be
As elegant as a celestial bloom; she possessed

A never-fading splendour of youth, and
The luminosity emanating from her body spread
In the vicinity and as she prayed for Narayana
To be her husband. One day, Ravana happened to
Pass that way; being arrested at once by her beauty,
He stood glued in the chariot and took a good look at her. 60
He had not encountered that kind of beauty before;
Her effulgence overflowed the coarse white raiment
She wore; her body acquired a golden hue
Because of the intensity of her penance; her locks
Tied over the head appeared to be divinely ornamental;
Deerskin covered her breasts and the elegant arms
Were surrounded by strings of beads; the holy ash
On her forehead exuded sacredness; she had arrested
All her senses in complete control and thus Vedavati
Dazzled rendering words incapable in describing her state. 70

Eyes glued on her person in the manner
Of a serpent smelling the fragrance of a flower,
Dashashira then looked at her; he was not
Satisfied and in the act of gazing at her he forgot
Himself; he sat at different positions to view her
From different angles; but every angle yielded its
Rich share of glory; he was stung by her beauty
To his depth and the mind lost its control then!

Vedavati, the daughter of the sage,
Was meditating on the form of Hari to have him 80
As her consort. But he made rough overtures
With matching words, 'Dear lady, accept me
As your man, and we would have pleasure to the hilt.'
Shyness forsook him as he was caught in the net of lust.

Vedavati was horrified and as she stayed away
From him not yielding to his advances.
He put his hand to her hair, appearing
Like a huge tiger ready to pounce on

A tiny gazelle at that moment. He tried to drag
Her in his attempt to kiss her; encountering   90
A beastly burden at close quarters she shouted!
To disengage herself from the coil of his arms,
She used all her strength. When Ravana
Seemed oppressively near, thinking that offence
Was the best way to achieve possession, Vedavati
Eluded him and ran and fell into the sacrificial pit.

When she was burning herself
With fire, she cursed him: 'By offending
Me, you have incurred my wrath and you will lose
All your wealth and status.' He invited a terrible curse   100
For yielding himself to lustful overtures. He moved
Towards Lanka in great disappointment of his unrequited advances!

Dhanyamalini, the wife of a sage,
Answered the lustful call of Dashamukha and,
As a result, she gave birth to a son called Atikaya.
She only surrendered her body to Ravana while
All the time meditating on the sage. Ravana made no
Distinction between women as long as they slaked his thirst.   110

At another time Rambha, the damsel
Of paradise, came down to the earth along with
A celestial beauty and played in water as soon as she
Saw a divine lake. Coming face to face with a lotus,
She said, 'This is really dull compared to my face,'
And she laughed loudly!

Another beauty was drawing water
Through the stem of a lotus. They rejoiced to their
Heart's content throwing water on each other.
Drenched fully, their bodies turned into water,   120
And their legs into fish; their hair spread in waves
While their visages resembled lotuses; hands

Became stems and breasts the water-birds;
Every beauty resembled the lake itself!

The water sport had ended and they
All put on their raiments and walked in the garden,
Shining like lightning. They picked flowers
And gathered them in garlands; they tucked
Them in their hair and tucked them in others' hair.
Admired and being admired, they forgot everything,   130
Immersed in the celebration.

Ravana looked at the bevy of beauties
Even as they played in water and saw Rambha
In their midst; he was smitten by the arrow
Of the God of Love and wished strongly to possess her.
Rambha had actually come to entice Nalakubara,
The son of Kubera, and now she was cornered by Ravana.

When Rambha tried to swerve away,
From him, he thought that it was a part of her
Play. As she was a celestial damsel, she was clean   140
And spotless. She had worn *parijata* and *mandara*
Blossoms on her hair. Her blue-silk raiment
Had a white border. Her beauty was striking
With a delicate waist, well-developed breasts, and
Posterior; comely face and manicured eyebrows;
Plaited hair; half-closed eyes, sweet-smelling body,
The luminous personality of a woman on a journey
Of sexual conquest, appeared to subjugate even
Those who have overcome the arrows of Cupid!

Like a man gloating over the gold   150
He has earned, Ravana gazed at Rambha as
Madness engulfed him from all sides. The assault
Of sexual desire proved to be too much;
The power and courage of the conquest of the world
Had receded and the celestial beauty shivered in fear.

But Ravana snatched her into the loop of his
Strong arms; she pleaded trying to disengage herself
From his grip, 'I have come here to join Nalakubara,
The son of your brother, and therefore, release me
As I am like your daughter.' Dashamukha was 160
Deaf to her words and blind to her predicament.
He only wished to possess her then and there!

As Rambha shouted in utter helplessness, the other
Nymphs scattered in all directions like parrots do,
When attacked by a wild hawk. Unmindful of
These happenings, Ravana went ahead
And translated his design into action, Rambha
Appeared like a crushed sugarcane!

Nalakubara learnt about this,
And exploded in anger when he encountered Ravana: 170
'You will invite your ruin while you indulge in
Sexually defiling maids in this fashion.' Showing
Utter indifference to his curse, said Ravana:
'Your words of anger will not reach me,' and entered Lanka
Buffeted by joy and mirth.

Canto Sixty-nine

'The Forest is Withering Away;
No promise of Bloom'

||๑||

Akampana, the minister, was a close associate of Khara.
He was a witness to the destruction of demons
At Janasthana; he was deeply disturbed.
He went running to deliver the news to Ravana
About all this and narrated in a breathless manner:
'Janasthana is on fire, my lord, Khara,
Dushana and Trishira are dead and so also
Other demons; this spells the doom of Lanka
Heralding the reign of Ayodhya; I have
Come running to communicate the news   10
In the guise of a woman. They say Rama
Is a brother to all other women and he didn't
See me; only one man massacred the entire
Army including Khara and Dushana.
They are the sons of Dasharatha
And are called Rama and Lakshmana; this Rama
Is a handsome one, with a lion-like body and
Long arms, he is the resplendent one and his
Fame has spread far and wide.'

Ravaneshwara's anger exploded at once, 20
His eyes became red: 'Enough, enough, stop praising him;
His earthly journey will end soon. Even if he is
God of Death, I will conquer him being stronger
Than him. I have the power of pulverising
Indra, Kubera, Surya and Agni!
How dare he kill Khara, Dushana and Trishira
At Janasthana. This is unbelievable that someone
Walks into Lanka and causes death and destruction!
Has Lanka's fort become weak and porous?
The thirst on the part of the Aryans to extend 30
Their empire is decimating the demons? But
Even if Indra ensures his support to him
Will he survive after killing our kith and kin?'
Akampana then begged for mercy and praised
The destruction of Shri Rama thus: 'Rama is foremost
Among the archers, equal to Indra and in the battlefield
He dazzles with invincibility!
His brother Lakshmana is equally renowned for his valour;
His eyes are marked by red lines. He is graceful
And his voice is unmatched in its clarity; 40
Just as fire is inseparable from wind, he is attached
To Rama. He is supported neither by the soldiers
Nor by the divinities, but he is an embodiment
Of power unshackled and unhampered.
The rain of arrows has engulfed everyone
And wherever you stretch your eyes there
You will see Rama; and our people find no escape
From his relentless attack and the castle of strength
Is ruined and there is total devastation!'
Ravanendra's anger sprang from his brain 50
Which was a home of lightning: 'Whoever came
To Lanka, were crushed mercilessly and whoever
Rose against Lanka was decimated in no time.
But no one who came with an intention to harass us

Ever went back alive! I care little for pedigree
But I will surely cut him to pieces;
Bind his legs with shackles
I will dip that fire in the ocean, it is certain!
Why do you shudder fearing the enemy?
I will smite him and put his entrails around   60
The neck of Dakini and fill the vessel brought
By Shakini with his gore. I will be an endless
Wave of the ocean of war and this is the beginning
Of the fiercest fight, I tell you,' so shouting
He waved a sabre indicating his intent.
'The atom of anger explodes burning
The cities and villages and consuming all living beings
Leaving mounds and mounds of ash behind.
In the heat of radiation many are born with handicaps
And life falls in jeopardy everywhere.   70
One Ravana has bred many Ravanas;
Why this war, why this conflict!
Is it to achieve mastery over the land;
Is it to acquire enormous wealth;
The will to dominate will burn everything eventually.
The harmony of the world is at an end;
The giant shadow of anxiety envelops all;
Love and trust have vanished from the world;
The garden of dreams is charred beyond recognition.'
Akampana thought all this and much more.   80
Ravana roared; 'I will go to Janasthana
And kill Rama and Saumitri without mercy.'
But Akampana stopped him thus, 'Hold on, king
You are unaware of the strength of Rama and Saumitri.
Today it is Janasthana and tomorrow it will be
Lanka which will be a part of the city of Ayodhya.
Has anyone stopped the river in full fury
With only bare hands? Understand your limitation;
Shri Rama is capable of penetrating the galaxies;

If this earth drowns he will lift it up.   90
He can keep under his control both the Wind-god
And Fire-god. Though you know the art of war
You cannot conquer him.
But there is only one strategy to defeat
Rama. His wife, Janaki, is the most beautiful woman
In the world; if you abduct her, Rama is sure to
Suffer and his strength will be reduced. He will languish
And waste away in the wilderness constantly
Thinking of her. He will only be a manure to the trees
Of the forest; thus he sowed the seeds of lust.'   100

'I admire you a great deal;
You know the art of governance. I will go to Panchavati
Province right now and I will not return without Sita;
She will sit on my lap in all her glory.' Ravana
Said imagining his future triumph.
Ravana's journey progressed and he saw
Gokarna in the midst of the forest; appreciated
The mountain of fragrance for its beauty and grace
He saw the snakes playing intoxicated by the heady smell
Of flowers; the sandal trees pressed against each other   110
Emanating wonderful scent; the flowing river carried
The perfumed *lavancha* grass through its course;
Following which Ravana reached the hermitage of Maricha.
Sage Maricha enquired Ravana about
His well-being and treated him with affection and
Asked the reason for his arrival and Lankesha replied:
'I have no one to seek help except you. You are
Beyond comparison in the art of wizardry and other
Strategies; you are second to none is valour, wisdom
War and courage! It seems, he is called Rama,   120
The son of Dasharatha; he has killed Khara and Dushana
Alone and quelled the army at the border alone
And hence it is a hard task to conquer him
Fighting face to face; the option is that he must

Be overcome through indirect methods of cunning.
Abducting Rama's wife Janaki is the only way to bring
About his debility and eventual defeat. We seek
Your advice and guidance to achieve this end.'
'O, king of the *rakshasas*, all those
Who wandered with nowhere to stay, found moorings 130
Through you and you became the supreme king of
The Rakshasa kingdom. You ensured their safety
And well-being at Janasthana. Rule over Lanka
In peace and contentment; keeping your mind free
From sensual allurements, eschew enmity with Rama.
Why desire other man's wife? It is not done
To upset somebody's conjugal life. He is a great warrior
And he will decimate the *rakshasas* completely.
I hope you have not forgotten the way he chased
Me from Kaushika hermitage using *vayavyastra*, 140
The redoubtable weapon. Reject all strategies
Proferred by the enemies in the guise of friends.
I wandered for seven nights and seven days
Not able to withstand the attacks of the arrows.
Rama and Saumitri are unconquerable
And hence the abduction of Sita will spell
The doom of Lanka and it will carry you
To the nether world. Refrain from this fatal game
Of encountering the venomous serpent!
This is the way for the doom of Vishravasu clan. 150
Shri Rama, the great elephant, has descended
From Saketa to the south; his valour is the juice
In rut, his hands are the tusks and his hunger
For expansion is like the trunk and therefore
He will not spare anyone who opposes him.
Why disturb the lion who is asleep?
Should you press the trap that harbours death?
Provoking death is a sign of stupidity;
All your kingdom would be burnt into ashes

Like a structure built of lac. Believe me, 160
Do not listen to those who mislead you.
You must respect the guidance
Given by the elders and well-meaning relatives
That will ensure safe journey through life;
Fighting bereft of reason will take you nowhere.'
Said Maricha in his attempt to enlighten Lankesha.
His words seemed to make temporary impact on Ravana.

Canto Seventy

'The Arrows of Cupid Pierced into the Heart'

||૬||

Fate appeared in the form of Shurpanakhi.
She had seen with her own eyes the death
Of Khara, Dushana, Trishira and the rest of
The *rakshasa* and she was unnerved!
She came to narrate what all she saw to Ravana
And on seeing him glorying on his throne
Her anger sprang at once and she uttered
Words of intensity:
'You are wallowing in indulgence
Floating on the ocean of desire; the end of your 10
Clan is close at hand; it will surely be rudderless.
There is the growth of mono-culture spelling
The end of multi-culture. The ascetics
In Dandakaranya have grown uncontrollable.
They have scant respect for you.
They treat you as the fire in the graveyard.
The ministers have forgotten their work and everything
Has come to a stand still. As you are overtaken by lust
Your enemies have grown; women and wine

Have ruined you. After the death of such warriors
As Khara, Dushana and Trishira, should you
Be so careless and indifferent? In the heart of
Janasthana the flag of Lanka has fallen on the ground.
Do you think the citizens will save you
When you have turned your back on them.
They will turn against you, surely.
Shri Rama has assured the ascetics that
He will smite the demons relentlessly.
Khara, Dashana, Trishira and such other soldiers
Have given their lives by fighting against the enemy.
When the kingdom is shaking out of fear, you are
Indifferent to the anxiety of the people.
Forgetting the responsibility of governance
You have sold your soul at the altar of lust.
Have you forgotten how countless kings have bitten dust
Because they indulged in unethical ways? I am no longer
Proud that I am the sister of Lankesha!

'A kingdom sans ethics; conjugal life
Without love; religion without devotion; learning
Without knowledge; asceticism with association;
Kingship with a bad minister; friendship
Without trust – all lead to destruction.
There is a death-knell pealing at the city-gate.'
So said Shurpanakhi raining the arrows
Of indelicate words in the presence of
The minister Amathya in great anger!
Ravana exploded at once:
'Why did this Rama come to Dandakaranya,
The impenetrable zone, and how did he kill
Our men?' Lankesha, being an expert
In the art of multiple-combat, said these words
Of ignorance not realising Rama's prowess in archery.
'Brother, you do not know
How powerful Rama is when he wields his bow.

The dazzling sharpness of arrows is like
Poisonous serpents, they rush towards you;
How would I describe them? It is hard to realise
With what speed and finesse he holds the arrow
Close to Kodanda, the great bow and finally releases it!
Only I have seen the tumbling of the dead-bodies   60
Of the demons. I have seen this devastation
As something unique and beyond any comparison.
He has killed all except me; he only has
Disfigured me, probably fearing the consequences of my end!

'Saumitri is resplendent
And he is equal to Rama in valour and courage.
His devotion to Rama is legendary. He is quick
To react and he knows no defeat; he is the principal
Support to Rama and one can say that he is
The life-breath of Rama!   70

'Rama's wife is Janaki,
Very devoted and dedicated to him. Her beauty
Is unsurpassed; her tresses are long and
Attractive; her complexion is of golden hue
With a delicate waist and elegant posterior.
I have not seen a damsel as graceful as her!
Brother dear, she is made for you. Her body
Is like a jasmine; a parrot belonging to Cupid;
Her curved brows and her gentle smile
Gives birth to countless suns, in reality.   80
Her neck resembles a conch; redness of her lips
Is proverbial; she walks like a swan and
She is the home of beauty. A mere touch would
Create a cascade; her gestures could send
An individual to the world of romance.
I cannot summon words to describe her grace!

'Flavour rejects description,
Only experience is the witness; everything

Is echoing in the depth of my heart. This beauty has caused
A cosmic reasonance. If Janaki opens her eyes   90
There is daylight and it is night if she closes them.
She is a royal swan floating on the chariot of lotus.

'The countless damsels
In your palace are mere glass beads when
Compared to this Sita who is so dazzling.
If one remembers her, the arrows of Cupid
Hit the centre of the heart; the parrots and cuckoos
Fall silent hearing her voice. The gazelles
Lower their sight before the brightness of her eyes.
The elephants in rut also escape not able   100
To compete with her.
She has a face of a full moon
And hence she is made for you; if she
Decorates your right thigh on the golden throne
The whole world would sing and rejoice.
If you tarry now, there will be doom of everything.
I tried my best to bring her here myself
But, I have not succeeded. You start your
Campaign march. By killing those who have
Caused the death of Khara, Dushana and Trishira   110
You pray for the souls of the latter!
If they fail to conquer Dandakaranya
Rama and Lakshmana would attack Lankapuri
And Bharatavarsha would belong to the Aryans;
Thereby the self-respect of Lanka would be dragged in the dust.
Brother, douse now the flames of imperialism that may
Stretch in future. Arise, arise and be the protector
Of Lankan culture. You alone could achieve that,
Be ready for the great compaign,' thus Shurpanakhi
Provoked her brother to instantaneous action.   120
The descriptions of Janaki's beauty floated
In Ravana's heart; he decided on the abduction
Of Sita as Cupid's arrows penetrated the depth

Of his heart; the fact that they humiliated his sister
Was only an alibi.
Meeting his wife Mandodari, he said:
'It seems, she is the daughter of Janaka
And the jewel among women; I will fetch her,
The wife of Raghava here.'
She was shocked: 130
'Why should you bring the honoured wife of Shri Rama?
It is not done, it is not done, do not get
Carried away by your illusion. Has anyone
Lived after stepping on Adishesha? Rama will
Erase the *rakshasa* clan out of existence.
He has killed Khara, Dushana and others alone
And his prowess is unfathomable. Don't play,
What would happen to an ant if it tries to
Kiss fire? Should you drink poison because
You are attracted to someone's wife? I beg of you, 140
Do not approach her and harass her;
It is not good to sever this great alliance.
Should you fall into the pit during the day
Which you saw during the night? Would fire
Even burn in water; can you expect the tree
To stand once you cut its roots? You have
Ascended the throne of glory after conquering
Desires and accomplishing intense penance!
The Cupid is lying in wait to avenge his defeat;
Would you allow yourself to burn in the flames 150
Of Sita's conjugal loyalty? You are brother to Kubera.
When such is the case, should you stoop so low, lord?'
Thus Mandodari advised him.

'Why fear, dear wife,
Have you ever heard of a deer killing a lion?
When I have been a master of all the three worlds
Should I care for the worthless kingdom of Ayodhya!
For the sin of humiliating the sister of Lankesha

Abduction of Sita is the only answer,' said Ravana.
Mandodari countered, 'Is it ethically right 160
To abduct somebody's wife? Since I, as your wife,
Have to share the honour and dishonour
You kindly listen to my words: I am your
Wedded wife and similarly, Janaki is to Rama.
Is it right, then, to violate the ethical balance?
Do not rush to commit a sin; hold on.
Instead, traverse on the righteous path
And work for the success of the good.
What you are doing is wrong and only
A coward accomplishes it.' Mandodari said this 170
With a lot of pain and anguish.
Not heeding to her plea, Lankesha
Prepared himself to leave ascending the *Pushpaka*
Chariot. Taking the northern direction he advanced
In pride. Countless young women have succumbed
To Ravana's sexual indulgences. Whoever has
Risen must fall and that being the law of nature.
Countdown for Ravana's downfall has begun.
The axles of his chariot are doomed to be shattered;
Rama's great aim was about to be accomplished. 180

Canto Seventy-one

'Let Rama's Arrow Bring the Auspicious Death'

||๖||

In order to meet Maricha, the relative, Ravana
Is moving fast in the direction of the dense forest.
The trees galore laden with flowers and fruits;
Coconut and arecanut trees are swaying their heads;
Birds are singing soulfully;
Many trees are spreading their fragrance.
'The scene is so attractive and
Nature is beckoning! This is really captivating.
The kingdom of Lanka is the home of Goddess of Wealth!'
So Ravana praised the land and entered   10
The hermitage of Maricha situated in the midst of forest
At the end of his journey!
Sage Maricha, the ascetic par excellence,
Renunciation incarnate, welcomed Ravana
And enquired about his well-being thus:
'You were here four days ago; what made you
Undertake a journey here again in such a haste?
Let me know Lankesha, if the matter is serious
I pray for your well-being.

I am bothered by a nightmare
That has gripped me now in which I saw myself
Playing the role of a charioteer while you were
Seated in it and both of us traversed in the Himalayan
Valley; the path became narrower and narrower as we
Went along and the horses stopped not able to advance
Further. I looked back and I could not see the way.
The road ahead was steeped in darkness;
Out of fear I felt like shouting, but my voice failed me;
Then the chariot fell down and slid down the slope
Rushing into the womb of the valley below;
It was smashed into smithereens and we too were
Pulverised. The cold stream ran with force
Pushing us with equal speed. If you have come
Here again thinking of possessing Janaki,
Forget about it; you cannot escape disaster
If you hanker after somebody's wife!'
Ravana listened to Maricha's word
Carefully and replied: 'Rama and Saumitri
Are destroying Dandakaranya like an elephant
In rut. They are moving uncontrollably
Filling rebellious spirit in the minds of sages,
Hunters and the common people.
As a consequence, anarchy and
Disorder have raised their ugly head in the minds
Of the citizens of Lanka making governance
A tough task. We cannot tolerate Rama and
Saumitri who have come with an intention
Of expanding the kingdom of Ayodhya!
The self-respect of Lanka has been trampled upon.
You are aware of the devastation that has occurred
In Tatakavana. They must be quelled, otherwise
The golden Lanka will be burnt into ashes!
Rama's enmity knows no bound.
Why did he cut Shurpanakhi's nose?

It seems, he has acquired all the powers
Earned by a sage through penance. That has gone
To his head and he is wreaking havoc, as a result.
He has mastered black magic and he boasts
That he would win over the world.
The wealth of freedom that I have won 60
From Kubera is about to be lost.
Maricha, you are the one closest to my heart;
I have suffered in pain and anguish,
Guide me what should I do, as you are
A supreme master in valour and strategy,
I have no other master to extend succour.
Show me a way; you are everything to me
In the world. If I abduct Sita, he is sure to
Suffer endlessly because of separation from her
And would die in the course of time! 70

'Shurpanakhi's humiliation
Has caused a great damage to the clan of demons.
Can I safeguard the status of an emperor?
Time has passed and I cannot worry about it;
We must end his insatiable thirst to extend
The territory of Ayodhya!
Make a golden deer saunter
In the vicinity of Rama's cottage; when Sita
Sees it, she will be attracted to it; she will
Crave for the golden deer; when Rama and 80
Saumitri leave the hermitage to catch hold of it
I will wait for my chance, just as Rahu
Engulfs the luminosity of the moon,
And abduct Sita to Lanka!
Maricha, who is not lured to the
Resplendent beauty and glory of golden Lanka!
The Aryan women indulge in drinking *soma*;
They are not cut out for life of hardship.
They are easily drawn to the delicateness of

Romantic living. And hence Janaki would be 90
Drawn into the alluring orbit of my life
And she will forget everything about her past
In my company.
The flame of racial hatred
Would be cooled and the lives of the innocent people
Would be saved. I will be a link to the chain
Of harmony. I will herald peace in the world
Being a master of righteous living.
I will conquer everything, Maricha.'
Maricha became unhinged 100
Listening to the wicked words of Ravana.
His lips and tongue became dry and looked at Ravana
In humbleness. All the earlier happenings
Moved in his mind in a panoramic fashion
That unsettled him and he started perspiring
Profusely; he said in a tone of melancholy thus:
'King of the demons, listen
In the world, many people utter words that please
But the words that bring goodness are not respected.
Shri Rama is a great warrior, he is like Indra 110
And Varuna; he has come to the forest to fulfil
The vow of his father; do not fall into the flame
Of Shri Rama's weapons; if Rama gets angry
He will decimate all the *rakshasas*; take guidance
From Vibhishana and others; an indisciplined king
Would ruin himself and drag his country
Also into the pit of ignominy. This Rama
Who is a compendium of virtues is not rejected
By his father; he is neither a miser;
He is a warrior par excellence, following 120
Always a righteous path; When Kaikayi's net
Of cheating caught the king, Rama showed his readiness
To bail his father out following the path of truth.
He has come to the forest along with his wife and brother.

Just as Devendra is worshipped by the gods,
He is the lord of the Aryan clan and his wife
Vaidehi is an embodiment of conjugal loyalty.
If she is carried away, Lanka would be ruined.
Is it ever possible to steal the illumination of the sun?
Do not become an instrument of destruction   130
To the *rakshasa* clan.
Do not even forget the misfortune
I invited while daring Rama; I had the strength
Of a thousand elephants in the world; my body
Was filled with the power of a mountain;
I had worn the divine crown, swaying the sword
Raised the waves of anxiety in the enemy camp;
I thought no end of my power as I made a road
Where none existed, as my speech became law!
When Sage Viswamitra was preparing   140
To conduct *yajna*, we barged into the hermitage
With great aplomb. But Shri Rama was the protector
Of the *yajna* there and I was harassed by his arrows
And I was thrown far far away.
Rama's arrow will pulverise Lanka;
Rama's arrow will burn Lanka;
Your clan will be decimated by Rama's arrow.
I cannot see the way you will be killed
By Rama's arrow; I cannot tolerate it either
Save your life, save your clan; save the wealth   150
And richness of Lanka. Look at this forest,
Everything has the stamp of Rama here.
There is Rama in the trees
Rama is seen in the flowers and fruits;
The gentle breeze is full of Rama
The flowing rivers sing the name of Rama;
Every bit is filled with Rama.
Free yourself from hatred, come out of wicked thoughts!'
Listening to the words of Maricha

Ravana became angry: 'I have not come here to 160
Listen to your advice. I am the son of Vishravasu
And I know what is right and what is not.
Would I ever surrender to the villain of Saketa?
Death is far better than humiliation;
Dying on the battlefield ensures heroic Heaven.
The royal doctrine suggests that Rama's wife
Should be abducted as a reparation for the humiliation
Of my sister!

My pledge is irrevocable
I have won all the elements; I have conquered 170
The divine guards of the Eight Directions.
You fulfil all the necessary strategies;
Suggest the ways of victory even without the war.
This is the king's order and I will kill you at once
If you refuse the same!' so roared the demon-king.

'Ravaneshwara, listen
This is the surest path to lead the subjects to destruction.
Whose guidance is this, whose machination?
Is it Yaksha who is behind this wicked instruction?
Why knock at the doors of death unnecessarily! 180
Should you rush forward without knowing the strength
Of your enemy? Leave this path, leave this intention.
Sita will not fall for you, you will not survive, for sure.'
Said Maricha in a tone of certainty.
Ravana is the king indulging in
Entrapping women and Maricha is a sage
Ascending from the demon clan to a higher order
And he is now located in Gajakachchapa area
In search of divine peace in the company of seekers
After Truth; but that became a mirage due to 190
Ravana's presence; did the fate save him
From the onslaught he experienced at Tatakavana!
The company of the wicked came in the form

Of Ravana. The advice had gone a waste
And Ravana was brandishing his sword
Threatening to kill. 'I will be killed surely.
Death should not come in the guise of Ravana's sword.
Let me die with the auspicious touch of Rama's arrow.'
So Maricha decided then and there!
Maricha, not knowing any other way, 200
Bowed his head to the march of the Wheel of Time.
'If you achieve harmony, I will not be a hurdle
On the path of your pursuit,' when Maricha
Said thus, Ravana was overjoyed and he embraced him.
Then both of them sat in a great chariot
And arrived at Dandakaranya.

Canto Seventy-two

'My Life-breath is Lodged in that Deer'

||६||

When Sita was spending her time pleasantly
With Rama at Panchavati, one day while picking up flowers
She saw an elephant along with its young one.
It was a hot day.
The baby elephant was unable
To stand at one place; it would go near the mother now,
Now move over and again come back – this happened
Repeatedly for a while. The mother elephant patted
Gently on its back as if to suggest: 'Don't wander;
Be alert; there are enemies here.' Just as a sharp   10
Arrow stays put in a quiver, the baby elephant
Stationed itself now at its mother's side. Then the mother
Made amends by fondling the baby with her trunk
As if to say that 'Should not have beaten you
So hard.' She embraced the baby by placing her trunk
On its head.
The baby stood close to the mother
And started drinking milk and there was a feeling
On its part that the ocean of milk was close at hand.
The fondling of the mother-elephant   20
And the response of the baby raised waves of maternal

Instinct within the heart of Janaki. She could not name
The nature of feelings, but they were connected
With the womb of a mother. When her pain became
Acute she ran into the cottage of leaves and fell on
The ground unable to stand. Tears flowed incessantly
From her eyes!
There was the roll of the seasons
And with the dawn of Spring everywhere
There was the touch of the season and the plants, 30
Trees and climbers – all bore the stamp of the month.
Fruits and flowers were aplenty on the trees
The breeze wafted fragrance all around
The parrots and cuckoos sang songs of pleasant glee
The face of the Forest-goddess resembled
The full moon of the Spring season.
On the ninth day of this pleasant month
Fell Shri Rama's birthday. Janaki was
In a mood of celebration. She rose from her bed
Even before dawn and took a dip in the river 40
Wearing ritual raiment! She decorated the vicinity
Of the cottage with festoons; drew *rangoli* pattern
On the floor; she herself assisted Rama
To take a bath in the river, joyously
She lifted a palmful of water to bathe him ritually;
Prepared the platform inside the cottage
With necessary things for the *yajna*
Caused Rama to conduct the *homa* ritual.
She decorated Shri Rama with sandal paste
Poured over his head with flowers of many kinds, 50
Put a garland around his neck and bowed before
Him with love. Observing all this Saumitri
Did likewise and prostrated before Shri Rama.
Then Shri Rama walked beside Janaki
Enjoying the beauty of the Spring, he attempted
To touch her curly locks near the forehead.

The bees buzzed around her face; Janaki
Swerved quickly to avoid the attack.
She leaned on Rama's chest losing her balance;
Raghava surrounded Janaki with his arms   60
And held her close to him!
It was like supporting a jasmine climber.
The fruit-laden plantain had found its buttress.
One day, when Shri Rama and Sita
Were on a hillock enjoying the beauty of nature
They saw a herd of elephants playing in water
And found the scene very elevating.
If someone disturbed her the queen-elephant
Would raise her trunk exuding anger.
From her eyes and would scatter mud   70
With her legs.

The sun went down
And the moon emanated her gentle rays.
They saw a tiger lying in wait. The robust
Teeth and the alert head; the power of smell,
The listening capacity; the lightning eyes;
The sharp paws! The tiger is nothing but
A moving death. 'You must live like a tiger.'
That truth abides in the forest. The elephant
On this side and the tiger on the other side.   80
Though they are opposite in nature and form and
Everything in nature has a magic of its own!
After their romantic confabulation was over
They came to the cottage. Shri Rama completed
His evening ablutions. After they finished
Their food which consisted of roots and fruits
Their eyes yielded to the embrace of the Goddess of Sleep.
As life went on in this fashion;
Janaki saw an elegant golden deer moving close at hand!
Sita was attracted to the beast irresistibly. It had a shining 90
Coat resembling brilliant sapphire; a belly like jasmine.

The sides were as soft as flower petals. The colour
Of lotus, saffron and ruby have combined there
Or, in one word, there is a confluence of the colours
Of the rainbow. The golden hair and the silver dots,
The elegance and wonder of horns; and Sita
Looked at the beckoning beast without batting her eye lids.
'Shri Rama, look at that deer,
I have seen any number of them in the forest;
This is unique and a like of which I have not seen.   100
Is this a creature from the world of *yakshas*
And *kinnaras!* Its form and its complexion!
The eyes dazzle and the face shines; the ears
And horns are balanced and symmetrical;
The hooves are of golden hue; the shimmer
Of the delicate neck; the calves of legs sans muscles
Are fetching!
Oh, Ramachandra
I want that golden deer right now; could you not
Please get it for me? After our exile when we move over   110
To Saketa again, this creature would be a great
Attraction in our city. Did you see its graceful
Anatomy! It has pushed me into the vortex of desire.
I beg of you, kindly bring the deer at once
Even if you cannot catch it alive, bring it dead;
At least let me have its coat; I will spread it
On the floor and sit with you,' so she implored Shri Rama.
'Do not get caught in the net of desire,
Dear wife, that will spell our doom; do not yield to it.
Filial attachment claimed my revered father   120
Mother Kaikayi's attachment to her son
Caused the death of her husband. Tell me
Whether one could hope for catching hold of the moon
Looking at its reflection in placid water. That which
We cannot possess would lead to the ruin of all.
This is not a real deer, but it is the fraud

Being played by the demons; this is their machination,
Undoubtedly. I will tell you now without an iota of doubt
That it is no use if one becomes wise after disaster. 130
What is the use of the oven burning once the food
Is cooked? Don't be stubborn; don't aspire for it.
Do you wish to wander carrying live-coal in your garment,'
Rama reminded her.
With her eyes brimming with tears
Sita leaned against Shri Rama's chest and said,
'My inner voice tells me that there is no danger
And I am not going to refrain from desiring it.
This is my last hankering in this Dandakaranya.'
'Saumitri, Vaidehi's desire has
Pushed her to the zone of wonder; what can I say? 140
It has even engulfed me; the breathtaking
Beauty of the golden creature; can I not bring
This beast which is unusual in this mortal
World as it possesses signs of divinity?' said Rama.
Lakshmana was astonished
At the fickleness of Shri Rama and Janaki's mind:
'Brother, attachment of this nature is not good.
The *rakshasas* allure the mortals in many ways;
Have you forgotten how Vatapi and Ilvala harassed
The ascetics. After the obsequial dinner when 150
Vatapi tried to come out of the stomach
Sage Agastya anticipated the *rakshasa's* strategy
And said, "Let Vatapi be digested" and thus
Put an end to the excessive torture by the demon.
Haste is not good in anything; we have to
Take a step forward after deliberation; we must
Undertake the task in consonance with ethics.
The demons have spread the net all around;
Remember what Shurpanakhi did; who would
Mount a mad horse? We shall not fall prey 160
To their machinations,' said Lakshmana wisely.
'This is a beast that is most beautiful;

I want this, I want this divine deer; do not give
Any excuse; you are afraid of the consequences,
Your courage is fast vanishing; this deer will enhance
The fame of Saketa; this is a fountain of wonder
And my heart and mind are lodged in the creature.
You are a hero of the world and I don't aspire
For anything; only I want this deer; if you don't
Bring it I may die instantaneously,' said Sita 170
Determined to possess the divine deer.
He could not set aside Janaki's desire,
Lakshmana's advice touched him not; the wish to
Possess the golden deer had occupied the mind,
He couldn't figure that it is all the demon's strategy.
'Do not despair Vaidehi, as you are
My fellow-traveller in this Great Pursuit of mine
It is my duty to fulfil your wish and hence
You please come out from the depth of despair;
I will bring the golden deer which is so dear to you'. 180
Said Rama in consoling his wife.
'Saumitri, do not move anywhere
You must guard Janaki very carefully.
Jatayu, the most loyal kinsman, will be with you.
I will fetch the deer which Janaki wants so desperately.
Do not say "send me for this paltry purpose",
Neither you ask me to refrain from going;
I have no mind to send you there,
I will come back with the beast in a minute.
Do not worry,' so saying the wielder of Kodanda bow 190
Vanished in the forest chasing the deer!
Even when Shri Rama, the most beautiful person
Of the world was beside her, Sita wished to possess
The deer thinking that to be more beautiful.
Rama was also covered by the cloud of attachment.
Lakshmana is the courageous one; he did not
Budge. But Sita's allurement proved to be a trap
That was about to be set by Ravana.

Canto Seventy-three

'He Followed the Arc Drawn by Fate'

||৬||

The movement of the golden deer was a wonder indeed.
It seemed so close now and again went very far;
In this fashion it deceived Raghava and drew him
Far far away; the pursuit of the deer became a mirage.
At that time Maricha imitated Rama's voice
And shouted, 'O Sita, O Lakshmana'.
This voice echoed and re-echoed throughout
The length and breadth of the forest while the caves
Repeated the words umpteen number of times!
Thinking that it is Rama's voice   10
Vaidehi became anxious and inconsolable.
'O god, what happened to my Rama! I am unhinged
Really. He must be in deep trouble, otherwise
He would not shout in utter helplessness. Arise Lakshmana,
You must protect your elder brother; run fast, there is
Something amiss. Do not tarry thinking that it is all
The subterfuge of the *rakshasas*; my right eyelid
Is twitching – this, surely, is an ominous sign.'
She said all this shaking in fear.
Saumitri is a veritable hero   20
And he was sure that it is all the deceit of the demons.

'Have no fear mother; who is there in all the three worlds
Who could confront Rama! I am guarding you
And I cannot transgress my brother's orders.
He is the jewel of the Solar dynasty and his prowess
Knows no bound; that should bring peace to the mind.
This agitation is all because of excessive attachment
Ignoring that you will only fall into the pit of illusion.'
So saying Saumitri tried to dispel the dark clouds
Of anxiety.   30
Shri Rama, on the other side, realised
That it is the work of the *rakshasas*; he got wild
At the sight of the golden deer; he set the dazzling
Arrow to the bow and let it go in the direction from which
The sound 'O Sita, O Lakshmana' came. The arrow
Pierced the heart of Maricha after traversing
With great speed. Maricha fell like a huge tree
On the ground and he soon found himself in a pool of blood.
Then Maricha realised that
His end came because of Rama's arrow; but still   40
He was conscious of his duty and hence again
Shouted 'O Sita, O Lakshmana' in a tone of
Unmitigated anguish.
Shri Rama started worrying:
'Ignoring the good advice of Lakshmana
I am caught in the whirlpool of deceit!
What is in store for me further and what about
Sita and Lakshmana,' so saying he suffered a great deal.
When that heart-rending shout
Reached Sita again, she became utterly unhinged.   50
Thinking that Shri Rama is caught in the death-trap
Posed by the *rakshasas* she begged Lakshmana:
'Why do you tarry Lakshmana, am I not familiar
With the voice of Shri Rama? Why have fallen
Silent, though he is suffering, surely?
Why are you sitting like a statue? Run, run

And see what is bothering Shri Rama!'
'Why worry mother, Shri Rama
Will return unharmed; this surely is the trick
Of the *rakshasas* and you should not fall a victim. 60
You pestered Rama being attracted by the deer,
Now you are pushing me into the pit of sorrow.
As Shri Rama is a great warrior no one could
Confront him. I am duty-bound to protect you;
I cannot leave you alone in the forest; can I really
Overrule the instruction of Rama? If he is angered
By my disobedience will he ever spare me?
Mother, be at peace,' said Saumitri to pacify Sita.
Janaki did not relish Lakshmana's advice;
She used barbed words to hurt him thus: 70
'You only pretend to be a well-wisher of brother
But you are his enemy in reality. You think
You can live happily after the death of Shri Rama.
This is wickedness, this is deception; why do you
Hesitate to protect Rama; why are you passive?
Are you a stone-hearted man?
This stance of yours is like a snake-bite,
It burns within me. Have you no love for
Rama, the one who is admired by the whole world?
As he is surrounded by death why are you so unmoved? 80

'Why this obstinacy; have you no mercy?
You are the enemy of your clan. Your behaviour
Is unnatural as you are related to Rama! You seem to
Rejoice in his difficulty; if you do not rush to rescue Rama
I will cut the net of your deception at once;
I will merge with Rama, who is Raghurama,
And the most elegant one in all the world.' Sita uttered
These words with great intensity.
'Enough mother, please stop
Your barbed words; you are like my own mother, 90
Shri Rama is like my father and this forest is Saketa.

I am the servant ever at your service,
My heart burns with pain listening to your words!
Mother, I can get my head sawn
Into two halves; I can fight with a hungry lion;
I can take a plunge into a cauldron of boiling oil;
I can allow someone to pour into my ears molten lead,
But I cannot bear these unkind words of yours.
Why this punishment, what is my crime?
If I am in the wrong, cut my head here and now! 100
Who is there to stand againt Rama?
Why fall a prey to the subterfuge of the demons?
They are still nursing the grudge against Rama
For killing Khara. I cannot leave you alone
And go, mother.' So saying Lakshmana tried to console her.
She could not tolerate this and Janaki
Said shaking with anger: 'You have turned out
To be a wicked man; you are without an iota of kindness.
Rama's misery is the source of joy for you,
You may have other schemes in your head! 110
I cannot live without Rama even for a minute
I cannot accommodate anyone in my heart except him
I am prepared to die if I am separated from Rama.
If you do not go to rescue him I will jump
Into the fire and burn myself. You are an enemy
To Rama and you must be a spy partial to Bharata.'
Said she becoming a veritable Durga.
Janaki's verbal arrows harassed
Lakshmana endlessly; it was like a thousand
Scorpions biting at one go; it was like the strike 120
Of thunderbolt and the balls of fire
Emanating from a full-blooded volcano. The flow
Of lava was felt in every bit of his body.
Saumitri, the conqueror of the senses said:
'I cannot bear with your cruel
Accusations, I am undone; I am on a righteous path

And you will be the cause of the tragedy of the Age.
What is the provocation to suspect my integrity?
I am only carrying out the order of my brother
And you are misinterpreting my action; 130
You will face misery in future and you will
Vanish in the womb of the earth! Attributing motives
You are pushing the wheel of the Age into the mine
Distorting history, ruining *dharma*, you will
Immerse yourself in the ocean of sorrow!
As you are determined to die
By entering into fire, what is the use of my living?
I will leave now according to your wishes
I will translate into action your intentions
I will enter the forest and join Rama. 140
May the Goddess of Wilderness protect you till I return
May the sun and the moon protect you
May the deities of the direction protect you.
I have lost courage now
And I will rush forward knowing fully well
What is to happen in future; mother, I cannot
Think of anything now as my consciousness is blocked.'
So saying Lakshmana drew seven lines
In front of the cottage, 'Mother, do not cross
These lines till I return. These are Lakshmana Lines; 150
O Five Elements, you are all witness to this.' Said
Lakshmana touching her feet with his head.
Even as he was overcome by feeling, he left in pursuit
Of Rama; he forgot following the arc
Drawn by the fate!

Canto Seventy-four

'Man Cannot Cross the Lines Drawn by the Merited One'

||๏||

Soon after Lakshmana left Parnakuti
Desire sprouted in the mind of Ravana.
He gazed at Janaki hiding behind.
Her beauty was not of this world,
It captivated him at once and he was like a fish
In the ocean of her charm; it distracted his mind
Which was like a drop of water on a lotus leaf.
Ravana was gripped by unquenchable lust;
It was like poison resulting from the churning of that ocean!
To deceive Sita, Ravana appeared   10
In the guise of a monk; baldness of his head,
The saffron raiment, sacred ash on the forehead,
Rudrakshi beads around the neck; a stick for meditation
And a vessel and with his wooden sandals he manifested
Himself before Janaki at a distance!
Janaki, the most beautiful one,
Was like Lakshmi, the Goddess of Wealth in simple raiment.
The lotus eyes, the graceful lips, dazzling teeth
And her full-moon face – he gazed at her undisturbed.

'She will be the presiding deity of Lanka; I will possess her
Quickly,' so he contemplated from where he stood
Just like a worthless star looking at magnificent Rohini.
The evil appeared in the guise of virtue
Mocking at the raiments of a monk,
Everywhere there is dance of wickedness and sham;
It is as though the multiplying demons have descended
Again; politics needs the guise of religion,
Religion has the pretension of service;
Everything is moving in the wrong direction
Caused by this make-believe. One must tear this smoke-screen
Of pretension and obtain the full view of Truth.
Ravana appeared chanting the mantras;
He said: '*Bhavati Bhikshandehi*; hunger is gnawing me,
Noble lady, give alms; I do not ask you to provide me
With ambrosia; I will rest contented with roots and
Fruits,' so he requested in great humility.
'Rama is not at home and Lakshmana
Has gone in search of his brother; he has drawn
Seven lines and has warned me not to cross
Those lines. There are fruits and roots aplenty
And I also wish to give them to you; but these lines
Will thwart the advance of wicked people and protect
The good; kindly cross them over as I can't do.'
Sita pleaded thus.
'Should you give these lines as an excuse
While I have suffered hunger for three days? I cannot
Cross the lines as I am the recipient of the alms;
Neither does it suit a monk to do so; one who gives
The alms should come closer to the ascetic; why should
You suspect me? I am a monk immersed in meditation
And penance and I belong to the lineage of Kashyapa;
I am a scholar par excellence mastering all the texts
On Religion, Yoga, Economics and Law!
But if you cross the lines, you won't suffer

From any adversity as you are beyond all boundaries!
You cross the lines if you are kind to me!
Otherwise I will die of hunger at your door.'
So he exhibited humility.
Janaki was caught in a dilemma
Listening to the words of Ravana. Lakshmana's   60
Lines were meant to protect the women. The manifest
And the unmanifest lines are these which create
The world; they also indicate the evils of the future.
There are lines of sorrow just as there are lines of happiness,
There are lines seen by the inner eye which stand for
Righteous path; the lines there are for distortion
And there are lines for good fortune; the lines thrust
Their presence at the borders of nations; but man
Cannot cross the lines drawn by a merited one;
If that is overruled, it will surely cause misery.   70

Janaki said: 'I do not know
Why Saumitri drew these lines; I cannot summon
Courage to cross them.' 'When your heart has turned
Into stone who can make it mellow; I will tell
The world that Saket is the symbol of stone-heartedness
And move forward,' said Ravana with determination.
Hearing those words compassion
Lodged in Sita's heart awoke; she feared that great
Name of Saketa would be erased, 'If you protect *dharma*,
Dharma will protect you; if you   80
Give alms to an ascetic that will ensure plenty.'
She said this to herself and arranging the alms.
She crossed the lines to give the same!
'You are the meritorious one,
Noble lady, narrate the saga,' said the deceiver
In disguise. 'As the wife of Shri Rama, I spent a period
Of twelve years in the city with pomp and glory,
That seems inaccessible to the mortals. When Rama's
Coronation was close at hand, Kaikayi demanded

That right to Bharata and exile for Rama. Rama 90
Known for keeping the vow of his father, has come
To this forest along with me and his brother, Lakshmana.
Our life of penance is moving peacefully. Please
Accept these roots and fruits, relax for a while.
Rama will come; I do not know what he brings!
As this is the zone of the demons, they will attack the ascetics;
You are alone, be on your guard,' said Janaki warning him.
'I am not afraid of anyone,
Listen now, I will tell you who I am; the gods,
Angels and demi-gods fear to hear my name; 100
I am the king of *rakshasas* and I am Ravaneshwara,
I am the lord of Lanka surrounded by the great ocean.
As you are a divine beauty, no poet can describe
You adequately; this exile is not meant for you!
You are a beauty of a rare mould!
Are you Gauri, or are you Lakshmi, the giver of wealth?
You must be the presiding deity who grants
All success; are you Rati, the consort of Kama,
The God of Love? You have overwhelmed me so much
Like a rushing river that erodes the banks 110
On either side; this is the place where live lions,
Leopards, tigers and the elephants in rut,
They move with speed and ferocity; and hence
Life here is dangerous at every moment.
Be a queen at Lanka possessing all glory,
Wealth and unending riches, being surrounded
By innumerable maids and that will
Make your life a celebration,' said Ravana
Becoming voluble at the sight of Sita.

Sita was unnerved and 120
Anger gushed hearing the words of the deceiver.
'Who do you think is Shri Rama? He is a warrior
Par excellence and a confluence of all virtues.
He is the greatest among mortal men. You desire

To possess a lioness, bringing shame to the raiments
Of a monk. Is it ever possible for you to separate
Me from Rama; you are piercing your eyes
In your desire to have me; you are drowning
In the ocean by tying a rock round your neck.
Why do you attempt to fold a ball of fire with a veil? 130
You are a coward, really.
There cannot be any comparison between a fox and
A lion; likewise an ocean is different from a rivulet
Just as nectar is far away from poison; why compare
The sandalwood with a tree of thorn?
Can there be a relationship between an eagle and an owl?
The hawk cannot aspire for the glory of a swan,
A housefly cannot swallow a diamond,' said Sita
In anger like Kali, the Supreme Mother.
Suppressing violent reaction 140
Lankesha tried to win her over with mild words:
'Dear lady, I will tell you the tale of my prowess;
Vasava himself ran away from me being defeated
Kubera was equally disoriented at my attack
I am an indomitable tiger, always waiting to fight.
Since I am the unquestioned hero
Of the world, gods and demi-gods run away
On seeing me in fear. The Wind-god becomes gentle
Wherever I walk; the Sun-god forgets his nature 150
Of burning pitilessly and acquires gentle coolness
In my vicinity. The rivers seldom roar in my presence,
The trees stand still without quivering their leaves.
The great Lanka is shimmering
In majesty transcending even the grandeur of
Amaravati of Indra, situated amidst the ocean.
The imposing structures and palaces,
The orchards with full of fruit-bearing trees
You can enjoy all bounties with me over there.

Is he the dear son of Dasharatha? 160
When he is in exile what wealth can he boast of!
Is it right on the part of the warrior to renounce
The throne and lead the life of an ascetic?
He lacks discernment, he lacks valour,
He will vanish permanently from the history of the Age
Turning into manure for the trees of the forest.
Without his kingdom and the martial force
He is like a fish thrown out of water.
Will ever a dry stick sprout and a barren cow
Become a milch-cow? 170
I am the king of *rakshasas*
And I have come here to win your heart.
Look at me, I have been hit by the arrows of Cupid,
Do not shun me, do not run away from me.
Dear lady, you may not get a like opportunity again,
Great moments do not occur again and again.
Your Rama is no patch on me. The bud of your fortune
Has blossomed now; come and occupy my heart
And drink the nectar to your heart's content.
Pluck the instrument of my life to produce great music, 180
Do not cut the cord of harmony!'
Sita became wrathful hearing
Ravana's speech; her eyes burned like live coal.
She exploded like thunder and lightning:
'You are steeped in deception in the guise of a monk
Sowing the seeds of disharmony you cannot
Escape the consequences; hatred will grow to be
A big tree and swallow you entirely. The moment
You desire me is also the moment of your ruin.
If you afflict me, you can never hope to live, 190
If you abduct me, your clan will collapse
Certainly; you will surely burn into ash
In the flame of Rama's anger!'
Being an expert in logic, Ravana said:

'Do not condemn me; do not invite death and delusion,
I will lift the globe from beneath; drink the ocean
In one gulp; I will choke the neck of death,
I will order the sun to stop; I am Kama, the God of Love.
Assuming Rama's form I will provide you
The joy of ecstasy! I am the emperor of the world! 200
As I am the most handsome one
Countless damsels have come to me forsaking
Their husbands and children. The whole world
Dances to my tune,' so saying Ravana shed
The raiment of an ascetic, appeared like Shiva
At the time of the Great Flood; he exuded the fire
Of anger and gazed at Janaki to instill fear in her.
'Are you not inclined to love?
You are a beauty beyond comparison and I am 210
The conqueror of three worlds; consign that Rama
Into the valley of the Age seek shelter in me,
Let the stream of love flow in the veins.
The man who has forsaken the kingdom
Will surely forsake you one day; your well-being
Is not ensured in his company; I am the conqueror
Of all the warriors, believe me!'
'I am no longer a woman now
I am a veritable flame; I will burn the entire
Clan of the demons; I will plant a sharp arrow 220
Into the womb of the world. So that Ravana
Will not be born again I will sow the fire
Of revolution in Lanka; I will churn
The ocean of sin of your life, then you will see
The springing of nectar in Rama's life.
I will fill love into the heart of Rama so that
He blesses the world with bounty!' Said the one
Who is not born of a woman.
Listening to her words

Ravana decided that abduction is the only way 230
Since she refused to yield to his gentle plea
And hence he made a ravishing stride and
Caught hold of her locks and dragged her to him
Violently. He lifted her to his chariot and pushed
Her indelicately like a tiger gathering a deer
Within his paws. As he rushed towards Lanka
In a great hurry, he appeared as though
He had fallen in love with death itself!

Canto Seventy-five

'Your Remembrance is My Divine Refuge'

||६||

Sita became a victim of Ravana's deceit,
She suffered a great deal in his custody.
She wailed inconsolably: 'O Lakshmana of great arms,
I condemned you out of ignorance and held my head
To the fetters of Yama; I have been punished
For my desire of the golden deer; I have been punished
For blaming you; come to my rescue, time is running out!
Trees of Janasthana, tell me
Where is Saumitri and whither Shri Rama?
Prasravana, the great mountain, I salute you,   10
Tell my plight to Rama, tell him that I have been
Abducted by Ravana; you must protect *dharma* by doing so.
Mother Godavari, you are my companion,
I salute you; I salute you swan and other avian friends,
I salute you the celestial clouds; I have no one
Except you; I am steeped in sorrow; I am orphaned.
Communicate this news of abduction at once!
I am the daughter of the great King Janaka
And wife of Rama, the cynosure of the Solar dynasty;
Though I have entered the forest, misery is chasing me.   20
I have been ruined being attracted by the evil deer,

Let the world learn a lesson from my mistake.'
So saying Sita shed tears in great sorrow.
Hearing the sound of that cry
Jatayu, the traveller on the righteous path, approached
Her in order to extend succour! 'Stop, Stop' he said
To the demon and continued: 'Do you know who I am?
They call me Jatayu, I belong to *gridhra* clan.
I was a king, but now I am in exile along with my
Younger brother, Sampati; I am determined to destroy   30
You and your clan!
Though belonging to the time-honoured
Family of distinguished individuals, you have abducted
The wife of some other person like a thief! Yours is
Pulastya clan and you have given a go by to reason.
The king must show a way to the citizens,
He must lead them on a proper path; but you have
Forsaken all the obligation and this abduction is the meanest
And most sinful act reflecting the extent of your lust!
Snatching away Janasthana   40
You have ruined tribal culture, spreading all around
The ways of the demons; the opportune moment
Has come for your annihilation. The king is expected
To protect women, but violating their honour
Is unpardonable; belonging to Kubera-clan, you cannot
Indulge in stealing other's riches and other's wives.
If the fence eats the crop then all values and virtues will vanish
From the face of the earth!
What has Shri Rama done to you that you
Have committed such a crime against him?   50
When Khara, Dushana and others had become lawless
Torturing the good and honourable citizens, in the name
Of avenging Shurpanakhi, Shri Rama, the restorer of *dharma*,
Killed them and established peace!
Leave Sita forthwith, otherwise
Shri Rama will burn you to ashes. He will subject you

To sharpest arrows just like Indra condemned
Vritra. You will only vanish in the womb of history
Like an inconsequential creature. I will not spare you
Even if I die; what if I am old, I have the fire of 60
Strength still intact; I will not be over-awed by your
Chariot and the coruscating armour. I swear on
The father and the great sun, on Pulastya and Vishwavasu
You shall not abduct Sita!'
'Make room begone you wretch!
Who gave you the governance of Janasthana?' said Lankesha
In great anger.
'I will not allow you to escape
So easily as you are taking Rama's dear wife away
Without confronting him. I will make you tumble from 70
The chariot just like fruits roll on the ground.
There is a great culture which has sacrificed
Everything for the sake of protecting the women's honour.
Righteousness is protected through the war of *dharma*
As we see in history; this is the land known for the ultimate
Sacrifice; in order to facilitate the growth of good crop
There is a necessity to erase the weed. You are now
An instrument of destruction of righteousness, running away
Stealing the invaluable treasure!'
Ravana lost his mind out of anger. 80
He seemed to breathe fire from all the twenty eyes
And he attacked the king of birds. The fire of the battle
Spread all over the forest; it looked as if the two Meru
Mountains were locked in the fight. Ravana rained
Sharp and gigantic weapons; the king of birds was not relenting
Either; he attacked Ravana's person from all sides.
There was the flood of blood everywhere. The Goddess
Of War wallowed in blood to her heart's content.
Jatayu stood there as if a mountain was installed.
Ravana realised that Jatayu was not an 90
Ordinary enemy; his anger multiplied. 'This foe is

Formidable and I must finish him,' so saying he drew
The sharp arrow till his ear and shot it!
Arrows followed in quick succession
And they were all planted in Jatayu's body who shook
Them violently and said, 'I will hold Ravana
In my firce grip and choke him to death.' He rushed
Forward appearing as if he is an incarnation of death.
Ravana, the great adept in the art of war,
Shot the arrows with the speed of lightning; but Jatayu 100
Replied by plying the weapons in equal measure
Eventually succeeding in breaking his redoubtable
Armour. The white umbrella was ruined and Ravana's
Huge bow dashed against the chariot; the mules fell
On the ground in large numbers.
Ravana was clearly unnerved.
'Though he is aged, he is the king of birds; though
The tamarind tree gets old, the fruits have not lost
Their sourness; if I don't destroy him, I am ruined
Beyond doubt; this one is a real plague to devastate Lanka 110
If he is allowed to live; even if I die I must
Kill him at any cost," so saying, he forsook his chariot
And jumped on the ground tucking Janaki in his arms.
'What if you thwart me? I will break your
Back and throw your dead body to evil spirits; but I will
Carry Sita to Lanka, come what may,' so saying, he swung
His great sword at the king of birds.
He was fatigued indeed, but anger
Lent him energy and he lurched forward: 'You wretch,
Stealing the honourable wife of Shri Rama; you just 120
Wait and see how you and your people are going
To be harassed by Shri Rama's arrows; whoever is
Thirsty must drink water; but since you have
Drunk poison, death is sure to engulf you.
When a fish swallows the bait being attracted,
Its breath bids good-bye, certainly – likewise, as you have

Bitten the bait of lust, the gates of hell await your arrival!'
Said Jatayu condemning Ravana and
At the same time attacking him with sword like
An elephant tamer pierces the animal with his hook. 130
'Leave the Mother at once, or else I will kill you,' he roared and
Broke Ravana's sword into two.
But Dashakanta became ferocious
Like a tiger wounded by the arrow of a hunter and
He lowered Sita on the ground deciding to fight with
Bare hands. When he attacked the king of birds with
All his strength the latter slumped and his bones were crushed!!
He gazed at the visage of Janaki
Who was meditating on Rama and said in all humility:
'I surrender my breath, but I have failed to protect you 140
But do not be afraid, Mother, he cannot win,
Rama would cut his ten-heads in one go; he will
Come to your rescue soon; Shri Rama, victorious Rama,
Grant your grace to all; those who seek refuge in you
Certainly deserve your mercy; quell all these demons
So that the weight of the earth is reduced; I will find
Refuge in your divine vicinity,' so said Jatayu
Even as he slipped gradually into the realm of death.
Looking at Jatayu who was in the pool
Of blood, Janaki said suffering at his misery: 150
'You are dear to me; you have sacrificed your life
For my sake; who will protect me now that you are
Receding fast,' said she rushing towards Jatayu
And she kept his head on her lap crying all the time!
Jatayu was immersed in the devotion of Rama
Whose meditation had elevated him to the zenith of knowledge
When he had the full awareness of divine closeness.
He said: 'Mother, I could not fulfil the task of
Safeguarding you; forgive me; what if my breath
Escapes from my body – I will attain freedom 160
As a result of having the divine vision of Shri Rama.

This body I surrender at your feet with the
Complete awareness that it is meant for the service
Of others. I will attain the highest state if Shri Rama
And Saumitri themselves could conduct the last rites.
May you be blessed, may Rama be victorious,
May Lakshmana win,' so saying he slipped into silence.
The birds wailed forsaking the trees
And nests and the wild animals ran helter-skelter
Everywhere there were signs of premonition.   170
The world seemed to share the sorrow of an individual;
The omens indicated all this at that time!

Canto Seventy-six

'Would the Swan Associate Itself with a Sea-Crow'

||६||

'Shri Rama, where are you, where are you Lakshmana
Don't you hear my voice and my wailing?
Enough of this mirage of a golden deer.'
So cried the earth-born Sita like an orphan.

Dashakanta tugged at her tresses
In anger and moved on carrying her in his chariot.
There was an earthquake and the world was alarmed,
Dark clouds enveloped and the sun was eclipsed;
The Wind-god came to a standstill. The whole world
Appeared to be barren to Janaki.   10

She wiped her tears
With her coarse raiment of golden hue
Even as she shone like lightning on the mountain top
Beside Ravana. She tried to wriggle herself out
Of his grip but she only became tired.
She appeared like a lotus bereft of the foot-stalk,
Her fair looks spread on her smooth visage
And she dazzled like the moon behind sable clouds.

All the flowers she wore on her hair fell off
On the ground and the ornaments made a jingling sound. 20

The bejewelled anklet slipped
From Sita's foot and fell down on the ground like a bunch
Of lightning. When the necklace of pearls fell
It was like the stars dropping from the sky
And the Ganga descending downward in all her radiance.

There was a series of premonitions
Starting from a hurricane to the cry of birds
And the closing of lotuses; all the creatures
Living in water went and hid themselves at the bottom,
Tigers, lions and deer went over a long distance 30
Chasing the winged chariot.

Anger sprang in Janaki;
Dishevelled hair and the red eyes indicated her mind
And fierce words issued from her mouth: 'You are
A coward escaping in stealth and my curse on you:
You have forsaken all paths of virtue and as a result
The good name of your clan is trampled in the mud.
 As this is a the time of your doom your consciousness
Is beclouded; hell awaits you and you can see
Vaitharini over there; you are doomed to dwell 40
In that part of the hell called *Asipatra* where
The forest has swords as leaves on the trees.
This decidedly is the end of your earthly journey!'

She saw Rushyamaka on the way
And a group of *vanaras* was there; she shouted
At the top of her voice 'Rama, Rama'; tying her
Ornaments into a cloth she dropped it on the ground
So that the *vanaras* could see the same!
Dashashira moved with great speed,
He crossed the rivers and mountains and the forests. 50
Entering Lanka created by great architect Maya

Ravana placed Sita in the crowded part of the palace.
He called the maids and ordered everyone:
'Guard her vigilantly; no one should move
Without my permission; console Sita, giving her
Jewels and raiments and no one should speak
Words that are not to her liking.'

Right then he called the heroes among
The demons: 'Janasthana is today the scene of destruction
And Khara, and said Dushana, Trishira and others 60
Have been quelled; Rama, being a mere mortal,
Is questioning my very authority on Lanka
After decimating all my people!
There goes the clarion for war sending vibrations
I cannot tolerate anymore, neither can I suppress
My anger; the fire of enmity has exploded now,
The enemies must be smitten in the battle;
Walk towards Janasthana and show your prowess;
Watch carefully Rama's movements; report to me
All his deeds; you are the heroes and you are 70
The ideal ones and you are the masterminds
Preparing for the eventuality of the war!'

Ravana is gushing in triumph
Already thinking that the whole of Aryavarta
Is under his custody since he is in possession of Sita;
It is nothing but illusion. Having Sita in the vicinity
Is be all and end all to him. Janaki, amidst the maids,
Is like a deer that is separated from its herd;
She is lost and has become rudderless!

Ravana is showing the vastness 80
And grandeur of Lanka, though she is least inclined
To see anything there. The splendour of the palace,
Festoons made of gold; the pillars decorated with
Inlay-works of ivory and gold are so fetching.
Ornaments of many kind; crowns and coronets

The extending terrace. Myriad flowers
In beckoning ponds, and Ravana thought that Maithili
Would be drawn to him seeing his glory. He is spreading
The net of cunning everywhere in his illusory pursuit.

'Listen to my glory and prowess   90
I do possess an army of a hundred million demons and
A population of two hundred million people. This city of Lanka
Is cynosure situated in the middle of an ocean;
It is about a hundred leagues away from the land
Being secure and impenetrable.

If you orient favourably to me
You will be the mistress of all women here
And the whole of the empire, they will be your servants,
Attending to your beck and call;
You are dearer to my heart and hence forsake all worries   100
And be one with me so that you shall enjoy
Pleasure of every kind being the empress of the Golden Lanka
As I am in full possession of the land of Bharata as well!

That Rama is an ordinary mortal
And he is a wanderer without a kingdom and what wealth
Does he have at his command and what felicity?
He is a weak man who could not protect the treasure
Under his custody; I am a master of three realms;
I am beyond compare and no one will have courage
To touch you as long as you are with me!   110

You will be reigning queen
And everything will be under your command,
Coronation will bring great contentment to you
As you have overcome all sins during the years
In exile. This is the moment of your glory
Since I desire you so intensely, absorb
With keenness as pleasures consenting to my advances.
I will inaugurate a new era of a woman's reign

Framing a new constitution to suit the wonder
Of the time. What is there in Aryavarta, after all,   120
The woman is ever dependent and she has no right
To speak of – it is an existence akin to that of beasts,
It is all barren and sterile looking upwards
In an eternal anticipation.
In the Golden Lanka there is fragrance everywhere;
Everywhere there are flowers galore; plenty of jewels
And ornaments to enhance pleasure of every kind.
Why renounce when you are a lotus-faced damsel,
Be mine sailing in the ship of carnal pleasure!'
So said he explaining the routes of excitement in detail.   130
This is the refrain he indulged everyday
To draw Sita to his orbit of love but Janaki covered
Her face in silence not listening to his words crying
All the time. Ravana's wealth is beneath her contempt
And would she ever look at it with desire!
She forgets herself being immersed in the meditation
Of Rama and she utters the name of Rama incessantly
And she has no respite for other thoughts indeed.
In anticipation of her favourable inclination
He sometimes cajoles her and sometimes coerces   140
But he tries again and again without giving up hope
He describes his wealth and expanse of his kingdom.
He employs many strategies, but without any success.
Sita is not the one to yield to the wicked Ravana's lures
As she had transcended being a devoted wife to Rama!
Janaki would tell him condemning in harsh words:
'Rama is a being beyond your comprehension;
He is virtue personified; you have forsaken righteousness
And whatever your trick in showing and speaking
I will not budge from my position.   150

As you want to live
Put an end to enmity with Rama; do not fall a prey
To sensual attraction; just as Kama was brought to ashes

By the third eye of Shiva, you will meet the same fate
When Rama's anger corners you; you are facing danger
And the presiding deity of Lanka will be orphaned.
The sin of separating a virtuous woman from her husband
Would swallow you completely and this is my curse!
Let me not waste words on you
Rama is be all and end all to me; he is the jewel   160
In the crown of Raghu dynasty; his mind
Is as stable as a mountain; he is unconquerable
And his fame has spread far and wide.
Stop your attempts to woo me; Rama is god to me
And he is everything to me.
The arrogance of your people
Met the deserving ate in Dandakaranya;
Is there a comparison between a fox and an eagle?
Rama's arrow will destroy everything
Just as the unnumbered waves of the ocean swallow   170
The land opposite, Rama's fire will burn
Your kingdom engulfing gradually.
Shri Rama will surely melt all your arrogance,
Pride and insolence as you are a depraved demon.
We have achieved inseparable union and hence
A swan would never desire the company of a sea-crow.
Leave this longing and save your life and thus
Try to protect the presiding deity of Lanka!'
Ravana hearing this blustered in anger:
'Mind your words, and be aware of the person   180
With whom you are speaking. Maids, listen to me,
Take her and confine her in Ashokavana,
Just as they tame a wild elephant you bring her around;
If she does not yield herself to your cajoling
Use threatening words but change her you must!'
The servant maids led Sita
To Ashokavana in a rude manner. Sita shook
Like a deer cornered by a herd of female tigers.

She is chanting the name of Rama day and night,
She is unyielding to the threat of the maids.   190
She becomes unconscious and regains alertness once again
Concentrating her mind on Rama. Sita is spending
Her bad days thus surrounded by unmitigated danger.

Canto Seventy-seven

'Alas! The Lamp of My Life is Put Out'

||๑||

Killing the demon who had appeared in the guise of a deer
Rama returned all the while worried that the demon's
Cunning call 'O Sita, O Lakshmana' might have misled
Them into believing that he is facing danger.
Twitching of his left eye along with other ominous signs
Indicated that the demons must have woven a web
To trap the innocent ones.

Lakshmana appeared at that time
In deep sorrow and that enhanced Rama's anxiety;
'What happened to Janaki and why have you   10
Left her side? Is it right to leave her alone?
Sita has been tricked by the love of the golden deer
And I too am a victim of the deceit; we did not
Listen to your words of warning and that has been
Our undoing; the demons must have killed her by now.
Maricha, the wizard, shouted "O Sita, O Lakshmana"
Imitating my voice and that is the source of trouble.
Tell me what all has happened.'
Asked Rama with anxious urgency.

Saumitri, unable to face Rama,
Looked downwards being speechless; the earth and sky
Appeared to revolve incessantly. He sent a silent cry
'Let the ground beneath swallow me here and now,
I cannot bear this', he was unhinged beyond words.

'What can I say, brother
Sister-in-law believed the voice which shouted
"O Sita, O Lakshmana" to be yours and urged me thus:
"Wake up Lakshmana, save your brother who is in deep
Trouble because of the demons," she was inconsolable.
She was not convinced when I insisted that this
Was not Rama's voice as he would overcome the demons
And come back after killing them; this is the trick played
By them to deceive us!
She abused me, instead, using
Words I cannot repeat: "Can I not recognise Rama's voice,
It is Rama wailing; he is in deep trouble; now it is clear
That you followed us to the forest anticipating Rama's
Destruction; you seem to rejoice at Rama's end,
You have forgotten your fraternal duties enshrining
Bestial qualities". As she was stubborn that I know
Very well the machinations of the demons and your
Superior strength in overcoming any kind of trouble.
Dear brother, forgive me as I am blameless;
I came because of sister-in-law's insistence,' said Lakshmana
In a tone of unmitigated sorrow.
'Is that how it happened Saumitri?
What is the fate of Janaki; is she alive or dead?
She must have been caught in the net of the demons;
She came to the forest with me being a dutiful
Companion; she became a part of myself; she was
Unmindful of my crownless condition being ready to face
The hardship of the forest; she is my refuge and tell me
If she is no more so that I can put an end
To this life by entering into fire. Ever-dependable and

A wise man you are and you too forgot your
Obligation to guard Sita at all cost.'
Said Shri Rama in spite of Lakshmana's explanation.

Both Rama and Lakshmana rushed
To the leaves cottage with great speed. The auspicious
Environment wore a bleak look; it was like a lake 60
Bereft of lotuses; the blossoms picked by Janaki
Had been faded; the ritual grass and the deer's skin
Were scattered, everything was thrown helter-skelter
As if somebody had looted the place; the cottage was empty
And there was no sign of Maithili; they ran here,
They ran there and nowhere did they find her.
They even entertained the idea that Maithili must be
Hiding in jest; at last Shri Rama as if his forehead
Hit against the doorframe of the world. 'No, there is no Janaki
Here, everything is gone; The forest fire is raging 70
And my body is burning; brother I trusted you
And you have betrayed that trust,' so saying Shri Rama
Sank to the ground and became unconscious.

Lakshmana too burned in the fire of sorrow
And tended his brother sprinkling on him water
That was cool and he wiped his eyes gently; he waved
The fan and caused pleasant breeze to blow; at this
Rama regained his consciousness and sat down.
'It was a great mistake that she was left alone,
You forgot your duties and now the damage is done. 80
Did you doubt my prowess, brother! Should you
Be exercised by the harsh words of Maithili!
Should you push her into the jaws of the demons
Forgetting my order? You became an uncultivated boor;
Being a wise man with intelligence, you fell a prey
To illusion; you caused the wheel of the great chariot
Of Time to be stuck in the bog; whither did Sita go?
What might have happened to her?' wailed Shri Rama.

He was overcome by weakness:
'Where is my consort; where is my companion 90
Brother, I have lost the light of my eyes.
My throat aches as if it is being squeezed;
I feel the giddiness and my stomach is churned.
Will I ever get my Janaki back – the one
Who came with me to the forest forsaking the palace
And all the attendant comforts; to obtain her was
An extraordinary event that occurred as a result
Of great merit; but what will I do now!' so he said
Lost his consciousness and regained it again!

Saumitri said possessing undimmed equanimity: 100
'We must have the balance of mind and feeling,
No amount of wailing and weeping would bring Janaki
Back. We must take our step forward thinking
About the work on hand. Being a great hero
And a warrior why are you unnerved:
You are worshipped by all the worlds; leave all this worry;
Leave all the anxiety; even if she is in *Brahmaloka*,
Or *Vishnuloka* or in any realm among the fourteen worlds
I am sure to find Sita overcoming all the enemies.
I swear on your feet, I will accomplish this,' so saying 110
Lakshmana took up his bow and arrows and prepared to leave!

Shri Rama stood up and requested him gently:
'Restrain yourself dear brother, I will not allow
You to go; I am suffering already without Janaki;
Do not forsake me, I have none to take care of me,
I am losing control over myself; my breath is deserting me,
I am now like a bird whose wings have been chopped;
With you, I still can hold my life.'
Tears rolled down in quick succession
Like pearls sliding from a necklace after the string 120
Is cut; Lakshmana could not contain his sorrow!
Somebody seemed to walk on the dead leaves

And Rama raised his head to look at the person;
The deer that was tended by Sita was taking steps!
'Would Sita ever return
The unfortunate being who was drawn by illusion
Did she think of the glory of the palace life?
Why did she yield to the attraction of the golden deer!
When I told Shurpanakhi just to prod me a bit.'
Shri Rama said all this while suffering at the separation.   130
'Brother, do not suffer the pangs.
Let us search for the sister-in-law; nothing will come
Of this weakness, have confidence,' so saying
Lakshmana took Rama and they both went
In search of Sita.
Shri Rama enquired all the trees
Of the forest! 'Did you see my Sita who loved you
So much; who loved each and every tree so dearly.
Tell me whether you saw my Sita; if you know
Her whereabouts tell me; I am totally exhausted;   140
I am a weak man now; you only have to tell me
Where my Sita is!
The trees won't answer me;
Let me ask the wild animals; sweet deer tell me
Whether you have seen Maithili; where did she go?
The one who had the eyes of a gazelle. When you
Walked in her vicinity not willing to go closer to her
She herself fondled you in a pleasant camaraderie,
You must have seen Sita, tell me whither did she go.
Tell me tiger if you have seen Sita who came   150
To your cave once and made you drink milk
Caressing your head in great affection,' Raghava
Murmured solicitously.
'Has she slipped into the river?
Has she gone to pick fruits and flowers; has she been bitten
By a poisonous snake; have the barbarians taken her away
Or has she been caught by the cruel animals of the forest?'

Shri Rama thought on these lines and wandered
From hill to hill and from river to the plain
Along with Saumitri; he did not stop; he moved on   160
And on and finally entered into the ocean of sorrow.
He had the hallucination that he saw Janaki:
'Come, come closer; why do you move away from me,
I have seen you now; but we cannot play
In the thick of the forest; do you remember
One day you enticed me in the game of hide-and-seek,
Why do you repeat the torture today without kindness?
Do not go away, my beautiful one, stop, stop;
Do not indulge in this jest: I saw your raiment!
Do not run as I swear on my love.'   170
So saying he cried bitterly.
'Alas, there is no Maithili here
Would she really have stood aloof while I suffered!
She would run to me and hold me in embrace.
Her ornaments and her lips and nose and dazzling
Teeth and her blooming face. What happened to her?
Did the demons take her away and killed her?
Have they eaten her delicate body? Great-limbed Saumitri,
Do you see Sita, I cannot see her and I don't know
Where she has gone, dear brother.' Rama uttered   180
These words of sorrow and wandered in the forest aimlessly.
He searched all over – on the river banks,
In the hills and dales and there was no answer.
He wailed endlessly: 'I do not want to live in the world
Where Vaidehi is not there; She is the light of my eyes
And she is the breath of my life; the dream of my life
Is trampled in the mud and the musical instrument
Of my life is without the string; the lamp of my life
Is gone and the fountain of my love has dried up.   190
My father Dasharatha is gazing at me
Dilating his eyes; he is mocking at me as I was not

Able to guard Janaki, the treasure of the Age.
Kausalya would ask me "Where is Sita"; so will
Urmila ask and Janaka would repeat the question
Along with the people of Saketa. What would I answer
Them, how would I face them; would I say
That I could not protect her in the forest and
Hence I lost her; after having lost the divine consort
He has come to rule Saketa – they would mock at me; 200
They would brand me as a man without substance
And push me to the bottom of the pit,' so saying
Rama wailed and wailed.

Canto Seventy-eight

'The Ocean of Sorrow is Beating its Waves'

||๖||

Lakshmana consoled his brother in many ways
As he went deep into the ocean of sorrow: 'You are
A wise man and let us search for the Mother Sita
All over Dandakaranya, that itself is our Great Pursuit.
You are a supreme being. Bhagiratha,
Who brought Ganga to the earth, is our model; he is our
Ancestor and let us not back out from adventure.
You be a symbol of the power of the Age: you be
Narasimha to pulverise the clan of the demons
You be the Varaha; you be a great mountain   10
To produce the sculpture of the Time; you be the great
Voice for the response of the Age; running away
Is no answer!'
Shri Ramachandra had lost all his strength
Under the burden of sorrow; so he said imploringly:
'Dear brother, I have lost the desire to see Sita; there is fire
In the emptiness of the mind; the waves of the ocean of sorrow
Are hitting relentlessly; the seed of sin sprouted and has
Grown into a huge tree; I have become weak and darkness
Envelops from all sides; tears of the deer merge   20
In the waters of Godavari; the gates of Mithila and

Saketa have closed and my determination to undertake
The Great Pursuit has deserted me. I have lost
That 'Rama-hood' and I will enter deep into the forest.
Janaka had said "This daughter has lost her mother
And you have to protect her like you protect righteousness."
Those words are cleaving my heart; I do not know
How much she wept when she was abducted by demons;
They must have snatched her like Rahu that eclipses the moon.
This atmosphere of pleasant surroundings has indeed   30
Made this separation sharp and keen.
Oh lord, the Sun-god, what is there
In the world that you do not know; when you are a witness
To everything, why are you so silent; tell me where is Sita?
The Wind-god Maruta, you tell me where is Sita as you
Travel over all the three worlds; tell me O mountain Peak
Where is Sita, as you hold the vibrations of the people
Of the world!
Mother Godavari, you are the mother
Of the world and a veritable life-giver; there are   40
Innumerable civilisations and their mystery hidden
In your banks. Many empires have blossomed and folded
In the sands that you have scattered; great poetry
Has spread its richness; your long arms have
Embraced great culture and now dear mother
Enfold me in your arms that all my miseries
May dissolve at once,' so he begged her.
Experiencing the pangs of separation
Shri Rama was deeply immersed in a state of renunciation,
Every bit of the body is occupied by poison of a terrible   50
Snake. Every bit of the body is stung by the pain.
There was a rain of fire. Saumitri tried to douse
The fire of separation of his brother by hugging
Him close to his chest like a mother gives all the succour
To her infant!
'Enough, stop crying brother

Even a small quantity of excessive salt will ruin the food
A tiny scar will disfigure the wholeness of a face
A word spoken in excess will lead to dissension.
The line between elegance and ugliness is very thin, 60
Let us not deviate from the path of righteousness and let us
March forward without staying at once place!
Isn't it strange that the birds
And beasts communicate their mental state in their eyes,
They are crying and leaping and running looking
In the direction of the south; they indicate that somebody
Has carried Janaki away in that direction; they are
The wise beings carrying the message of nature;
It is a message foreboding that Janaki is safe somewhere.'
When Saumitri said this, they both prepared themselves 70
And went southwards in search of Sita.
When they progressed on the path of the Great Pursuit
They encountered many signs: 'The string of flowers
I tucked with my own hands is seen here and there;
Brother see here, the marks of Maithili's steps;
The pearls and rubies are scattered here, see!
Signs of a terrible fight are everywhere,
The bow is broken and the arrows are lying.
This is a torn armour and there lies a white umbrella
Broken into two halves! 80
We shall not spare the demons now,
We must take out the divine weapons; we must
Burn the demons into ashes travelling all over three worlds.
Even if the solar system, the moon and the stars,
The Fire-god and the Wind-god come to a stand-still
And even if the forests, the seven oceans reach their
End-points, we must show to the world the magnificence
Of Rama! Let there be cataclysm and let the celestial
Object roll down from their spheres! Till we see Sita
Let all the three worlds burn and vanish 90
Out of sight!' so saying he set his divine arrow

To the bow.
Saumitri saw this:
'What is this anger, control yourself; you are
Known for your kindness; let not your natural sweetness
Desert you in this overflowing anger. You are a confluence
Of the moon's brightness and the sun's luminosity.
Just because a paltry demon committed a crime
Should you punish the whole nature? That act would
Surely eclipse your name and fame. Do not be a victim 100
Of emotion as that would undermine your wisdom.
You shall not curse or imprecate anyone as you have to
Protect and carry the human beings of the world
To the other shore. The boatman is not supposed
To be angry with the travellers. Separation from your
Wife is a limited damage; but you have larger
Responsibility to shoulder. Why should you punish
The innocent people?
Why this anxiety, why this impatience;
You are not alone – I am with you; Shri Rama, 110
After all, is born as a result of great *yajna*.
Your misery is not unique and unparalleled.
The sun and the moon, being the eyes of the world
Suffer eclipse and are subjected to humiliation.
Very many emperors have won the kingdom of India
And eventually they have lost everything.
You be the treasure of the world
And the conscience of the Age; all these difficulties
That you are facing are a passing phenomenon
And you be the visionary of the world.' so saying 120
Saumitri doused the fire of anger of his elder brother.

Canto Seventy-nine

'I Have Become a Nest of Misery sans Love'

||๖||

When Shri Rama set out with Saumitri in search
Of Sita's whereabouts in Dandakaranya, he saw
Jatayu's body lying on the ground in a pool of blood.
The wounds were still oozing blood and was wailing due to pain.
On seeing Jatayu Shri Rama was overcome
By sorrow and he kept the bow aside and took Jatayu
In his arms shedding tears at Jatayu's condition.
Likewise, Saumitri was equally moved at Jatayu's loyalty!
'Did you see Saumitri, how I have lost all my people,   10
Though I came to the forest ignoring the adverse events of my life
The game of life has turned into a game of chess indeed.
I lost my father and Janaki is yet to be traced
And now this king of birds who is like my father
Has breathed his last!
I am caught in the web of misery
I am being burnt in the chain of unfortunate events
I have not saved my people; I am subjected
To pain and excessive sorrow; look at this
Great soul who has offered his life to safeguard   20

My honour,' so saying he grieved a great deal.
Shri Rama held Jatayu's body close to him
And removed the arrows planted all over; with the help
Of the herbs brought by Saumitri he treated Jatayu
In all urgency. He used all his acumen in order
To heal the wounds of the most loyal of his followers.
But Jatayu slipped further and further away
Without showing any sign of recovery.
Shri Rama spoke to him in affection:
'O, the most powerful one, tell me what happened;   30
Who is responsible for your present condition
Who harassed you undermining your prowess?
Sita is not to be found in her cottage,
Somebody has abducted her; tell me about her
If you happen to know about it,' so he asked
Bringing a lump in his throat.
Jatayu uttered these words
Even as his life breath was about to exit: 'The jewel of Arya clan,
The meritorious wife Janaki has been carried away
By the cruel Ravana. I fought against him in order   40
To save the mother; you see how his weapons have been
Destroyed, but still I could not protect the mother!
It is my great fortune that I am able
To see you. Lord, now I can depart from this world
Enshrining your divine image in my heart!
You are like a lion in valour
You are an eternal guide to the world
You are peace incarnate with a cosmic form
You dispel sorrow at once; you will enable us
To cross this ocean of life; you are an embodiment   50
Of a heroic being; you are an epitome of love
You become one with everyone; you extend refuge to all
You give every pleasure; you are more resplendent
Than a thousand suns; you are a veritable wishing-tree
Granting everything we wish; you are the one

Who cuts the threads of bondage; you have made
The hearts of the *yogis* and *tapasvins* your abode
And you grant liberation being wisdom personified!
I have earned my merit now
As I have overcome the darkness of life in the midst of light. 60
This is a real fortune that I remember you
At the time of my death; I cannot ask for
Anything more! I had the great fortune to serve you
Along with Saumitri! Dear one, Saumitri fill my heart
And wash away my sins; how can I describe
The moments I spent in your friendship, you are
My soul-brother! Kindly give a fraction of love
That you bear in your heart to Rama.
Shri Ramachandra, you start your journey
In the direction of the south; put an end to Ravana 70
And save the mother. When Saumitri is with you
Nothing is insurmountable; Shri Rama will win
Lakshmana will be victorious; virtuous life will win
And let victory be theirs who always meditate on you.'
So saying Jatayu breathed his last in peace
And contentment!
The help of the king of birds made
Shri Rama and Saumitri bring tears; they offered the
Lotuses of their hearts in great affection; they conducted
All the funeral ceremonies with discipline. Rama told 80
Saumitri: 'Now that Jatayu is like our father we
Must perform filial duties,' and likewise they conducted
The ceremony and Jatayu's body was consumed by fire.
Even as the body of the meritorious hero was disappearing
The eyes were filled with tears of fulfilment.
The sting of Janaki's separation was forgotten for the moment!
Jatayu is fortunate indeed as he offered
His very life for the service of Rama and hence
The latter conducted the last rites. Maricha's body
Was base and it was eaten by dogs and foxes! 90

It is the sacrifice that brings success and liberation.
It is Jatayu's sacrifice that won him Rama's attention
Bringing him to the orbit of Goddess of Liberation.
Rama and Saumitri went in search of Sita
In the south-westerly direction. An impenetrable forest it was;
'My adventurous journey would be wasted now
As my determination to find Sita is not sturdy.
Her attachment protected me hitherto; she shared
Joy and sorrow in equal measure and now
She deserted me and I am all alone;   100
Now I am a nest of misery sans love; darkness
Pervades everywhere and I am totally lost, brother
My breath is about to leave and I am in deep despondency.'
Said Rama with confidence reaching the lowest ebb.
Saumitri said sprinkling the nector
Of consolation: 'Brother, this dejection is not becoming
Of a hero like you; you are the one transcending
The limits of mortal frame; your pursuit is beyond
The expectation of any result; you are beyond the reach
Of desire and hate. You have the power of the mind   110
That can understand the heart of the world. You are
The herald of the divine message! What if the flames
Engulf like waves from all sides, forge ahead;

Exploding all hurdles on the path of your Great Pursuit.
Are you not the tempest that scatters the clouds of sorrow!'
'Brother, I am caught in the whirlpool
Of misery. My breath has no strength and my senses
Are weak; the mind slumps; there is a python ahead
And a tiger behind; should anyone venture to move   120
On the raft on the violent waves of a flood!
The pond is deep and there is a venomous serpent,
In the absence of kindness from any side I am in distress
Brother! The cruel fate has pushed me to the life
Of grief cutting my neck. The life force has dried
Up and everything appears to be hopeless and barren!'

Said Shri Rama again in utter pain and agony.
'Why are you worried so much brother;
I am with you, a sure companion in the pursuit.
The path is certainly harsh and rough; we shall 130
Be vigilant day and night against cruel animals,
You be the philosopher of the Age by treading
A new path in the pursuit of a new vision.
What if we spend the rest of our life in the forest!
Many great deeds have already been accomplished.
We shall move in the direction where we will realise
The great experience!' so said Saumitri consoling Rama
And leading him in the intended direction.

Canto Eighty

'Chanting of Supreme Sacrifice on a Daily Basis'

||६||

On the other side great *tapasvin* Urmila addressed Ganga
In her grief caused by separation: 'Mother, you
Are the witness to my love and you are the witness
To the distress caused by it; the agony runs into a flood
And I cannot bear this pang; my feelings are exposed
To the violent blowing of wind; I will offer all my tears
To you like pearls; I have surrendered everything
Into your watery womb and likewise I have entered
Into Saumitri's love.'
Urmila, the one steeped in penance,
Remembered the incidents of her girlhood days
And especially the one she had said while playing
With a toy: why are you keeping quiet doll, speak, speak,
Tear the curtain of silence, come to life, get up,
Come and play with me, dance with me; everywhere
There is music, everywhere there is pleasing sound;
Raining the pleasures into the heart; so she muttered
To herself in her attempt to address her husband
Who was lodged within her like a statue.

On another day, she found a couple   20
Of *chakravaka* birds in the Sarayu river
While they were together in love; suddenly a wave
Hit them and they were separated at once;
They cried aloud to be together again; but their
Voice was never heard any more.
The utterance of love emanating from Urmila
Combined with that coming from Saumitri and
Both were dissolved in the war cry of Saket.
Urmila told him as he set out
That day: 'Do not forget me; I will weep and   30
Remember you always; my cry is equal to pearls
And your laughter is equal to flowers; pearls
And flowers labour together for the success of
The Great Pursuit. I will not be destroyed
And surely I will stand up drawing sustenance
From the power of your union.'
Another day after the passage of time
While she was in meditation in the cottage,
She saw two lamps burning side by side and
The one at the right flickered and it appeared as if   40
It was about to go out; 'Why is this flickering;
Does it augur ill for Shri Rama and Janaki.'
This anguish gripped her.
There is no fear, success is sure to accrue;
I will send the power of my penance to Rama
I will send the power of my penance to Janaki
I will send the power of my penance to my husband.'
Thus Urmila's energy flowed in the forest and protected
Everyone deciding the path of the Age and I can
Hardly describe the magnificence of that power!   50
An incomparable vigil has established itself
In the form of Urmila on the bank of Sarayu in a cottage.
It is experiencing a great agony; there is a lonely light
In the kingdom of darkness; it possesses a divine

Patience, contemplating on the Great Path, it is moving on.
That wealth she had depended
Was elsewhere, far away from her; but still this
Loneliness has kept the doors of the heart wide open.
When memory opens for the new winds to blow
The divine steadfastness in floating on white radiance 60
Time passes as the mind dwells more and more within
There is a daily chant of supreme sacrifice
While the time of Truth is accompanying this chant
The mute attraction of Urmila and Saumitri
Are silent and thus they resemble the ocean of peace.
Some deep rhythm goes on below the surface,
The night wakes up to this celestial song;
There is an eternal light emanating from the spirit
There is no meeting point and the poles are apart.
She has forgotten herself being immersed in deep penance. 70
In this theatre of Great Pursuit, Urmila
Is like an actress without a role.
She wishes to take birth in the realm
Of Saumitri, attuning herself to his orientation
She is yielding completely. She is lighting the lamp everyday
Thinking about him. She bears all the pain of separation
Incorporating the peace that prevails in Saumitri's heart;
She understands that it is her life's mission to walk
On the path trodden by him. She has risen to infinity
In the dream of immortality. As Saumitri is 80
Floating on the ocean of eternity, she hopes
For the day when he would swim into her ken.
The wind in the ocean is pushing
The boat relentlessly; it is moving at all times;
All the waters of the world are hitting against it.
This gives rise to the question, when would
This mysterious journey end.
Urmila is an island amidst an
Unrecognisable island; the waves of separation

Are attacking her incessantly; the unknown hands 90
Surround her and that embrace pleases her.
She commands ineffable peace like a queen.
She has reached the Solar and to Lunar realms
In ascending the stairs of the Great Pursuit
She has already reached the blissful state
Crossing the preceding four conditions!
She wanders in her mind in silence.
Footsteps do not leave a mark. The heart is
Anxious. The song of separation has turned into
A song of experience, thereby enriching the bliss 100
Of the world and Urmila has dissolved herself in all this.
Urmila shows the way even as Saumitri
Is leading Rama on the pathless tracks. She is the guard
And protector to the castle of Rama; she is the charioteer
Of the conscience: 'May this light of my inner self
Be your torch; let my determination and my unswerving
Mind lead you with steadfastness,' she is sending this
Prayer every day.
When in deep meditation, Urmila sees
Lakshmana in her heart every now and then 110
It appears as if the peacocks dance in ecstasy
And the stars of the sky walked along holding
Their hands in perfect accord.
'O, dearest lady, you have
Illumined our path day and night; you are
A golden maid in the temple of solitude;
Your celestial song lures me beyond words;
That sweet laughter and that elegant tumult,
It falls like a cascade in intoxicating tunes.
You have filled nectar into this life of wilderness 120
You are a *kaustubha* pearl around my neck
Your memory is enough to cause the stability of the mind
Lead like this on the path of Divine Pursuit.'
She would feel as if Saumitri uttered these words.

'Continue, and never stop your pleasant conversation
Dear husband, speak feeding me with nectar;
Speak till this mortal mind sees the immortal world,
Walk in the golden realm of my life; be a flute
To answer the call of my heart,' so Urmila
Will pray in response. 130
O, the blissful one, you have descended
From above in a chariot of light; you have illumined
The province of desire spreading the lingering sound of
Unalloyed sweetness; you are pervading all over
Like undiluted fragrance.' so would Saumitri celebrate.
The great *tapasvini* is in deep meditation
In the cottage of leaves; her body is a container of bliss;
The golden hue surrounds her person; she sheds tears
Not for herself, but for the sake of Shri Rama, Saumitri
And Janaki as they are treading the path of gravel and thorns. 140
'Let everything turn into flowers taking away the roughness'
She prays incessantly!
Life is turning like a top without stopping
Since aeons; she has forsaken all association
In her madness of sacrifice; she has borne in solitude.
All the ambitions of those who are walking in wilderness.
She is praying for their well being; though she is soft
Like a blossom she is as strong as a diamond.
She is showing the way for the turning time.
She is pouring the result of her penance on them 150
Forgetting her own pain; she desires the good of the world
Believing that sacrifice paves the way for immortality.
She is offering everything at the feet of Saumitri!

The glory of the palace in Saketa
Is a forgotten chapter. Mural paintings,
Music halls, dancing halls – all have receded
Into background. Even the gentle smile for her
Husband, the beckoning lower lip, the musical
Droning of the bees, the exhilarating touch of

All have vanished from memory like an illusion.   160
The cottage on the Sarayu
Itself has become Urmila's world; sun-rising
Is Brahma, the afternoon is Vishnu and the evening
Is Shiva – they manifest in their glory and these hours!
In that silent zone of the forest; the cottage
Is immersed in unswerving concentration.
Sometimes she becomes unnerved
As the wave of pain of all the world approaches her;
Complex sounds in the dead of the night
Becomes wide awake and delving deeper into love   170
Emerges victorious!
That day when Saumitri was about to
Take leave of her, she placed her wet cheeks
On his feet. 'We have two bodies
But the soul is one. Give me love and give again
A stamp on every bit of my body as the sign
Of the Great Pursuit. When the great wheel
Is turning I do not know when we are destined
To meet again, my lord,' so saying she swam   180
In a lake of unfathomable desire; what next,
What again!
The inexhaustible pain of countless aeons
Was lodged within the heart in the fear of explosion.
Looking at the sky in mute movement of the feet
She is awaiting the expense of ten and four years
Beyond which period her husband would join her!
Sometimes Urmila's mind becomes
An arena of conflicting thoughts: 'You are like
A beast tied to the ceremonial pillar; what   190
Strength do you possess to carry on the struggle?
The spirit is dead and it is all covered in darkness;
All valves are closed and no ray of hope penetrates.
Where is the refuge and what is the way out
When the flood is raging how would I cross.'

All these questions come to the surface and dance.
The inner self again would say as if it found
An answer: 'Come, you spirit, breaking the bastion
Of constricting framework and out of a chocking cage
Outgrow the castle's restrictions and run   200
To the freedom of eternity in order to hold
The earthen lamp lit by Saumitri; come you light
Of an infinite world of unfathomable energy!'
In that deep meditation she felt
The embrace of her dear husband. It welded
The earth and Heaven fusing all the constituents
In universal love and Urmila bore the divine
Burden in her womb to give birth to myriad
Wonders. It opened the valves of happiness
Of the world. The spirit saw all the beings   210
With eyes wide open. The immense power of women
Had plucked the strings of a divine instrument.
There was cascade of love which engulfed
The world like unending mystery!

Canto Eighty-one

'Bharatavarsha is Greater than Heaven for Us'

||६||

The western sky dazzled with unusual radiance
And appeared like a raiment of silk dipped in blood
Amidst the dense trees. The edge of the clouds
Had an aura of blood-red. The brilliance of evening
In the forest deserved the description of 'blood-red evening'.
Shri Rama and Saumitri walked over
A long distance amidst the mountain range and
Finally reached Krauncharanya. There were tall trees
Competing with the height of the peaks and they appeared
To overcome evil and wickedness; the mountain ranges   10
Appeared to be giants reclining. The uninhabited
Forest was scary. The wind that blew across trees
Seemed like long sighs emanating from a giant.
The affliction caused by the separation of Sita
Ate into the very vitals of Shri Rama in the forest
Environment; the wilderness is licking the brothers
With its tongue. The world is burning with the fire of the sun.
They traversed very far in the dense
Darkness of the forest. A frog was leaping swallowing

All along the insects it encountered and the frog was 20
Caught by a snake which was attacked by a hawk;
At that time the frog in the mouth of the snake stretched
Its tongue to snap up an insect. The snake was unaware
Of the hawk that was attacking it while the frog was its target.
Shri Rama saw the nature of hunger in the world,
Hunger in the face of death, hate in the vicinity of death
Is an enduring culture and this cannot be rectified,
He thought. Creatures live by swallowing the weak ones
And they die by fighting engendered by hate. This activity
Of the world is strange. The animals with intelligence 30
And the creatures sans intelligence – if they all fight
And perpetuate hatred what is the value of life!
There is not an iota of selfishness
In Jatayu's service; he is the protector of *dharma*,
He fought against Ravana protesting his cruelty;
He sacrified his life fighting a person of meanness.
There is a perpetual fight between virtue and vice
Between justice and injustice – that is most necessary
For peace to prevail.
In the Krauncharanya Shri Rama 40
Encountered disappointment everywhere! The mango-grove
Is almost singed and it appears to have acted as a ritual
Lamp to the mother nature; pomegranate which always
Shone with a brightness of undimmed red, today has lost
All the colour and freshness and it only resembles
Cactus of a barren land!
The nature is indulging in malicious
Laughter, as if mocking 'I know you but you cannot
Understand me'. Is the value of deep vision is undermined?
When Janaki was there everything looked wholesome, 50
Everything was filled with light in that ineffable
Comeliness. That radiance was beyond the province of darkness;
Beauty was in the mould of form always agreeable!
But the story is different today – the door is kept closed.

Who has fed the sour water to all the plants irrespective of
Their nature? Destroying the taste? The mind was in a turmoil.
'Brother, what is left now? Everything
Is destroyed. I was gearing myself to cleanse the domain
Of man, but a thunderbolt struck me at once;
Everything was washed away in the terrible flood.
Whatever I sowed 60
After preparing the field is gone forever and only
The pain of my labour I experience; peace is hidden
In the urn of hate!

What is the use of my prattle?
Rama without Sita is just a wandering singer.
Where is life? Stars fall, the clouds move violently;
Tempest is roaring; the demonic dance of darkness is on;
It seems the undying apparition has come out of the cage
And wreaking havoc.
Lightning forks in the sky; the sea swells 70
To the borders of the clouds; pain and anguish
Send its hideous laughter; death strides uncontrollably
All over and I have no inclination to live!'
Shri Rama uttered these words in sorrow.
Saumitri said in ever-attending calmness:
'In the process of the Great Pursuit, the seed of creation
Will be in a hidden state; there is a need to nurture it
With concentration of the mind; then only the lotus
Of the heart will bloom! Look at the myriad petals
Of that lotus. When you are the guide, why worry 80
You have filled immortality in this evanescent body;
I have dissolved myself in the boundless bliss
That you have granted; all illusion of the mind
Is gone and I am experiencing a rare serenity!
Lord you have burned all things fearful
And terrible into ashes and the sway of selfishness is too gone.
Cause the light of the heart to radiate in the midst of sorrow
You are everything to me; I cannot exist without you,

This life bereft of kindness must be won at any cost.
This world is an ancient *peepul* tree; though it appears　　　90
To shrivel at the top, it sprouts again with shoots afresh;
Plenitude is an indication of the zest for life!
Life should go on like a river rising and falling,
Turning and swirling in an unstoppable flow. Anxiety,
Haste, ambition and wrath are not good! The splendour of
Sunrise and the magic of a tree acquiring leaves anew,
Are all natural in the world; life should be like that.
Hedonism is not the ideal, pleasure-seeking is unacceptable.
Virtue gets established if there is skill and efficiency
In the work we do; in its absence the self suffers.　　　100
The world is a veritable god; valour is god; the expansion
Of the soul is a greatest triumph and hence we must face
The indomitable evils with courage.
Friendliness with the world is an antidote
To all ills. Brother, why dance to the tune of fate;
It is untrue that man lives according to the way
Determined by fate. Righteous living and the will
To follow the path are the sole supporters of life. Why depend
On outside power as you are holding the reins yourself?
Brother, let us combine in equal measure, happiness　　　110
And sorrow; we will win at the end as we follow
The path of perfection! We will march forward
Breaking all shackles; Bharatavarsha is greater
Than Heaven for us; this cradle for the beginning
Of life is a pleasant garden in our adult life,
Let us forsake fear as you are a leader of men!
Zest for life, splendour of manliness,
And amity with the world and the rewards accruing thereof
Are the three delivering ways and this is the sum and
Substance of recondite philosophy,' so said Saumitri　　　120
Elaborating on his ideas. There is nothing Shri Rama
Does not know. As he had a great deal of pain and sorrow
The consoling words of Saumitri rejuvenated him!

Canto Eighty-two

'That is the Blessed Place – the Destination'

॥६॥

Shri Rama and Lakshmana crossed Kraunchadhama
Then entered into an impenetrable forest where
They found a variety of birds and animals! There was a huge
Gorge that went right into the womb of the valley
Disappearing in darkness.
When they moved along the gorge
They heard violent sounds as if the hills exploded all around.
There was a tempest in the sky. At that moment
The brother set the arrows to their bows; soon they saw
Gigantic demons resembling dark clouds! Their bodies   10
Had grown like huge tress. Their eyes were tawny and sharp
Was their vision; their mouths were so big that they would swallow
The wild animals at once; they were savagery personified!
One of the demons stretched his hand
Across the path on which Rama and Saumitri were moving
Snatched them and pressed them against his body even as
Their ribs made a breaking sound. The brothers became
Unconscious in his deadly grip.
When the squeeze became unbearable
Saumitri shivered and told Rama, 'O Rama,   20
Save yourself somehow, don't worry about me.

This demon is a veritable savage and you do not tarry,
Go in search of Vaidehi; you shall not forget
The call of the Age being pulled by the bond of a brother.'
The demon roared and said: 'Who are you
Walking in this fearful forest? You look like heroes
And you are carrying the bows and arrows on your
Strong shoulders; what brings you here? I have been
Starved without food. They call me Kabandha and
I have found today's food and you are my banquet. 30
No one has escaped my hold,' he uttered these words
And he was about to swallow them.
'Did you see Saumitri, how strong
Is his grip! Too difficult to wriggle out. This is the end
Of our attempt to find Sita. When bad times arrive
Fate mocks at our heroism,' said Shri Rama in anguish.

Saumitri flexed himself;
All fear that had gripped his mind vanished at once.
He understood quickly the source of the demon's strength:
'Hurry up Raghava, the demon depends only on his arms; 40
He won't spare us if we fail to cut them now,' so said
Saumitri explaining the secret.
Being alert Shri Rama drew
His sword and it appeared as if a fish leapt
Out of a constricting net; at that moment
Saumitri also drew his sword and they swayed their
Swords simultaneously; the demon's right hand was cut
By Rama's sword while the left one was chopped off
By Lakshmana's weapon; and then they both subjected
The body to vivisection. That was the end of the hell 50
Called Kabandha's grip!
All the ten directions shivered
As the demon roared at the top of his voice, falling
On the ground losing his limbs. That groan
Sent out by the demon made their hearts melt
And Rama and Saumitri went in a hurry to see

His visage.
They took pity on the demon after
Seeing ugliness. As they stood in silence he himself
Began to speak: 'O, the great-armed one, 60
Forgive my sin; I was a prince born into the
Clan of demi-gods but I harassed people being
Proud of my handsomeness and youth; I stretched
My arms for wine, women and wealth; that excessive
Leanings to a lustful life gave me the title of Kabandha
And thus I have been relegated to this forest.
I hunted women relentlessly as my
Thirst for them grew day by day; in the process of
My enjoyment I made a weird dance which
Caused the earthquake. 70
I resembled Manmatha during
The time of my youth. I even transcended the handsomeness
Of Indra and Chandra; but I soon fell into my doom
Chasing a life of lust being a complete rake.
I burned in the fire of physical pleasure
And went down the slippery slope;
The diseases followed one after another; all my dreams
Were shattered and my life became a tale of sorrow.
The ocean of milk had turned into a flood of blood;
The head was broken when I dived into a deep pond 80
Swimming in the overwhelming flood of lust;
I contracted myriad deadly diseases and lost all my
Charm; being caught in the stranglehold of Cupid
I myself became Kabandha!
All my handsomeness is gone and now
I am totally shrivelled. Fate has erased me
In the game Cupid yelling triumphantly
I have become an ugly creature, my lord!
The eye on the forehead was sunken and dead;
The ears too had shrunken and the nose was flat, 90
The chest was a concave while the back jetted out.

The buttocks were thin and the belly was loose
And I became a dark of lump flesh.
My mental disfigurement gave birth to bodily deformity.'
Shri Rama and Saumitri shed tears in silence.
Shri Rama narrated his tale of woe in brief. Then
Kabandha said, 'I will tell you the strategy
To bring back Sita from Ravana,' and he explained in detail.
To surmount pain and sorrow you need a trustworthy
Friend; there is a supreme *vanara* called Sugriva;   100
His elder brother Vali has exiled him from the kingdom.
He is experiencing the pang of separation from his wife
And biding his time at Rushyamuka. He follows Truth,
And very efficient in everything he does; he is wise
And humble; he is radiant. He has some four followers
And you two are facing the same predicament.
If you cultivate friendship with Sugriva
He will be the beneficiary. That will pave the way for
Finding Sita. Sugriva is the younger son of the Sun-god,
He is wise and knows all skills meticulously; Sugriva   110
Will reveal Sita wherever she is hidden – whether
Atop Mount Meru or in the womb of the earth or in the
Depth of the sea. He is capable of bringing Sita searching
Every nook and corner of the city of Dashakanta.'
Kabandha explained the way that leads to
Rushyamuka: 'You see Shri Rama and Saumitri!
In the western direction there are trees with thick foliage
And the path is quite conducive; you keep moving
Till you see a land that resembles Kubera's
Chaitrarathavana where all seasons meet; that is   120
Karnataka, a land of sandalwood where the honey
Flows like a river.
Wherever you see there are trees
Bearing fruits and trees are lined like a wall.
If you continue to walk you will see a pond and that will be a
Fountain of your Great Pursuit.

That is Pampasarovar, the most divine spot.
There is no crumbling bank or the gravel-stones
Nor swamp; wherever you stretch your eyes you will
Only see crystal-clear water. There are many types of birds 130
Singing their sweet melodies; the place derives its name
Because of the pleasant sounds produced by the avian world;
The birds and beasts move about freely as there is no anxiety
Of being chased by hunters; the land of Karnataka
Is an abode of truth and peace and happiness
And the language they speak there is Kannada.
Near Pampasarovar congregate
Monkeys, elephants, tigers and bears along with myriad
Birds to drink water – that particular sight
Is delightful indeed; it is a crystal mirror to Bharatavarsha; 140
It is Manasasarovar of the south. The trees of the bank
Imbibe cool water and grant to the world fruits in abundance,
There is a virtual rain of flowers from the fragrant trees
And there is no one to tuck them in their hair.
The people of Kannadaland are bearing
Other's pain and praying for their well-being;
They will win the world following the path of non-violence.
There is Matangashrama which redeems the world;
There are devotees to serve the ascetics; a great
Devotee called Shabari lives there; she is awaiting 150
Your arrival to have a glimpse and to leave her mortal coil!
Matangavana is like a heavenly garden.
The wild elephants worship gods there; it is an
Abode of peace, indeed. You will see in the east
Rushyamuka where there are trees with flowers!
As you relax on the peak you will be seeing
In the dream that you acquired wealth and
That will be transformed into a reality. That is
A divine land where all wishes come true. 160
That is the land of great culture

In the context of Bharatavarsha. One who is not
Righteous cannot climb the peak of Rushyamuka.
Looking at the sapphire-coloured antelopes all sorrows
Would come to an end,' so saying Kabandha closed his eyes.

Canto Eighty-three

'Protect the Compassionate One'

||६||

Shri Rama and Lakshmana went in search of
Pampasarovara with peace in their heart. The nature
Was a veritable paradise as there were trees full of fruits,
The climbers entwining the trees; the rivulets and streams
Descending from the hills would swell into full-fledged
Rivers; the gentle breeze wafting all around.
When they moved in the burning sunshine they saw
A ramshackle cottage. Trees not very tall surrounded
The hut even as they bear fruits and berries of many kind.
A little distance away, there was a ceremonial fire-place;   10
Closely was a pond with crystal-clear water; all this
Indicated that it was a place made auspicious by
The presence of a great person.
Shri Rama bowed and moved
Forward near the cottage in great reverence.
The cool shade and the gentle breeze elevated
One's spirit. An old woman with unfathomable radiance
Was seated in front of the cottage. She had stretched
Her legs and supported herself with her hands;   20
She had a staff to lean on as if it was her companion.
Her body shone beneath numberless tatters of her coarse raiment

Her hair descended as if they were strings of crystals;
The eyes were burning brighter as if to spill
The feelings of her mind.
The woman who was sitting like a statue
Without batting the eye-lids is none other than Shabari!
She is in a state of meditation and she is ancient
Her age has matured with her penance; she belongs
To the assembly of hunters, but she is of a superior culture: 30
'Rama is my god, Rama is everything to me,
When will I see him, when will I talk to him,
When will I place the dust of his feet on my head,'
She is spending her days in this thought alone.
Innocent devotion is great, great is knowledge
And meditation and equally distinguished is prayer and worship.
Rama likes the purity of heart and Shabari knows this very well.
Rama is attracted to Shabari's devotion. Just like a thousand suns
Descending on the earth and the divine cow coming in search of
Its young one Shri Rama came to Shabari at that time!   40
All directions were illuminated; peace engulfed
Like the ocean of milk in flood. Shabari who was lost in
Meditation awoke at once and she uttered the name of Rama
Several times and gazing at the idols in front of her
Said to herself, 'Is what I see is real, am I dreaming or awake?'
Days, months and years have rolled by
But the belief in Rama's arrival is as strong as ever;
She has grown gray and the skin is wrinkled and
She has become really old. She has installed in her heart
The image of Shri Rama. Will he come today, won't he come
Tomorrow; but he is sure to come one day.   50
She has drawn the sacred pattern and lit the lamp of devotion
And she is waiting for the Blissful One eternally.
Her breath awaits his arrival;
She is picking fruits everyday to give to Rama, the riped ones.
She tests them by tasting and she keeps them aside,
If they are ripe adequately guarding them carefully.

If Rama did not turn up she would offer them
To birds and animals rejoicing that Rama
Himself ate the fruits.
She would look at the horizon and gaze 60
Intently again bringing her palm near the eye; she would
Climb up the hillock sometimes tumbling down; she would
Crawl down slowly. 'He didn't come today and tomorrow
He is sure to come' listening to her inner voice
She is keeping her calm.
She was waiting for this day for a long time;
Her wish was fulfilled; her aged eyes saw the duo
'Who came now, open the door' she pressed her eyes of
Dim vision. She moved a little closer and shading her
Palms near the eyes still gazed at them. 70
The raiments had been soiled and their bodies were
Covered with dust and perspiration; they were utterly tired
Walking continuosly in the forest; they wore matted hair;
They had their coarse raiments: 'Who are these two?
They are so radiant, who are these! Curiosity increased
In her mind; is this, by any chance, my Rama
Who has lodged himself in my heart so firmly.'
She put a question to herself and asked at the end:
'Who are you boys, from where
Have you come? May victory be unto Rama; are you Rama? 80
My heart assures me and who is this handsome one
Who resembles you.' As an answer Shri Rama
The ever-polite person said: 'Grandma Shabari,
I am Rama; this is Lakshmana my younger brother.
We have come from far to see you mother!
We have understood the meaning of the word
Steadfastness after seeing you.'
Hearing Rama's words the wrinkled visage
Of Shabari acquired a rare shine; she danced
Like a young girl in enthusiasm: 'Shri Rama, 90
My lord, come; I have spent years in meditating

About your arrival; your kindness has redeemed me!
The chief of the Raghu-clan; the divine
Consort of Lakshmi, the Goddess of Wealth, the Great
Ghanashyam; the unrivalled warrior, the bestower
Of fearlessness; you are omnipotent, the redeemer
From all sins; I am immersed in the world;
Lift me up; as you are the liberator of the world
Grant my wish, O lord!
What is happiness, after all, happiness 100
Is remembering you; to see you is happiness.
Everything is evanescent, only you are enduring,
You are Parabrahma, Paramatma and Parameshwara,
The supreme god; you are the one who installs us
In the realm of liberation; you are a support
To the fallen people, you are a protector of the downtrodden,
O my lord redeem me, forgive me!
You are a mother-bird to me while I am your offspring,
When mother-bird is bringing corns as your offspring
I am waiting for the food from your mouth. Lord, you 110
Have come to save the child from the burning fire
To which it has fallen!
I have overcome my ignorance today
That I thought god was an illusion. You are the limit
For everything, nothing is there beyond you;
You are the storehouse of knowledge, giver of power and
Happiness; come and cut all chains of bondage
And make my mind focus on you beyond all distractions!
You are known by the scriptures alone
I have suffered being burnt in three types of sorrow; 120
The flame of grief and enticement is ablaze,
God of kindness rains on me the grace and protect me;
I am caught in the cage of sins, protect me,
Sheltering me in your heart; protect me
Before I am swallowed by pride and arrogance,
Bind me in the cord of love and protect me

Being a chief among the *yogis*, protect the poor.
The end is nearing fast every moment, protect me,
You have the cosmic form, you have the cosmic face.
You are bliss personified and you are the home of happiness,   130
The world is filled with you. Everything is full of Rama.
You are with quality and you are also beyond quality.
Did you manifest yourself in the concrete form
To make yourself available for seeing, for touch and conversation?
You walk without legs, you hold without hands
You see without eyes, you hear without ears
Did you take birth in the land without the earth?
Were you born in the tree without leaves?
Your grace is grand. The whole cosmos is your body,
But did you come to bless me in the form of a boy!   140
I am immersed in the water of love;
I see Rama if I close my eyes and see Rama on opening them.
My entire body is filled with Rama and my mind
Is full of Rama. Lord you are the essence of light
And I am redeemed after seeing you,' so she praised
Him being immersed in the ocean of devotion.
She prostrated at the feet of Shri Rama
And Lakshmana. Rama embraced Shabari
In great reverence. 'Mother, tell me how your
Penance has progressed, we are blessed that we saw you.'   150
When Shri Rama said, grandma Shabari enquired
About his well-being. Shri Rama narrated the tale
Of his life at an appropriate length to suit the occasion.
Shabari said being excited about
The proximity of Shri Rama: 'O, the kindest one,
The end and aim of my penance is to see you,
That is achieved and this body shrivelled awaiting
Your arrival. I was in great agony all these days
Like a caged bird; my wish is fulfilled now.
What more do I want? The vessel of fulfilment   160
Is filled to the brim. I have the greatest of bliss.'

So saying she washed the feet of Shri Rama
And Saumitri in great devotion and worshipped.
'Look there Saumitri, look at Shabari;
What radiance in that emaciated body;
There is a citadel of devotion in her heart,
Devotion is overflowing in her body,' so said
Shri Rama in praise of Shabari.

Canto Eighty-four

'Listen, Mother I am Beyond Caste, Class and Clan'

||६||

'I have brought the best fruits for you
Selecting the ones just ripe and juicy
Lord, do not ignore me because I belong to a lower caste;
Kindly accept this as if it is ambrosia,' Shabari prayed to
Him with devotion. 'I am completely overwhelmed by
Your devotion, mother; you are a pure soul and
A blessed being; you deserve to be worshipped
Like my mother Kausalya; you have illumined
The world by the radiance of the soul.
I will not count on caste, class and clan, mother   10
Does water have a caste, does the land have a caste,
Likewise does the fruit have caste; does devotion
Have caste; difference and dissension are ephemeral
In the absence of *bhakti*; wealth, knowledge
And family – all are meaningless like a barren cloud.
Be courageous mother, leaving servile disposition.'
So that Shri Rama appreciating the fruits
A great deal.
'They are very tasty,' praised

Saumitri and continued: 'Devotion dissolves all 20
Deformities or differences; sugarcane is crooked
But the juice is not crooked; the river is serpentine
But water is not; the bow is curved and
The arrow is not; the external accoutrements
Are the screens of illusion; listen mother,
You have planted the tree of devotion,
We have eaten the fruits borne by it.
Mother, all caste consideration is washed out
Before your devotion and steadfastness;
You have opened the era of devotion afresh, 30
You are the empress to the world of devotion.
We would like to hear your life history, mother
Kindly narrate it to us,' so asked Saumitri
In great earnestness.
The sun went down in the west
And Shabari prepared rice out of bamboo seeds
And a sweet dish from mango fruit; she made plates
Out of leaves and approached the brothers: 'You must
Be very hungry, you must be very tired, please
Come and have your food,' so saying she asked 40
Them very affectionately.
The brothers partook of the food
Relishing every morsel of it. Shabari looked
At the way they ate their food: 'It must have
Been quite a long time ago that you ate
Food served by your mother; you haven't had
Sufficient sleep, you are very tired, I am sure.'
When grandma Shabari uttered those words
Tears rolled down the cheeks of Rama and Lakshmana
As they remembered their mothers Kausalya and Sumitra! 50
Grandma Shabari gave them
The mat woven out of coarse grass; after
The food that was veritable ambrosia, the brothers
Stretched their limbs even as their minds were

Filled with peace; they shed tears of joy and Shabari
Too did likewise; love that was beyond words
Had filled the heart; there was steadfastness
In the mind and they were all tongue-tied!
Grandma Shabari said breaking the silence:
'Where is Janaki, the Goddess of Wealth of Saketa? 60
My mind is greatly pained not seeing her,
Tell me where is that invaluable jewel.'
Then Shri Rama narrated the entire saga.
While he narrated how Ravana had abducted
The one who was earth-born Rama brought a lump in his throat
And he became unconscious. At that moment Shabari placed his
Head on her lap and nursed him till he regained his consciousness.
Saumitri said again, 'Why don't you
Share your story.' Shabari remembered her
Life story and said, 'I have almost forgotten 70
My tale, everything has receded into the realm
Of forgetfulness, but wait, I will manage
To remember as much as possible. Shri Rama
And Saumitri, this is the holy place where the great
Matanga Sage is living; look at the resplendent
Nature of this zone; the fragrant flowers borne
On the creepers and climbers and innumerable trees;
You have seen with your eyes the grandeur
Of fruits and rivers and ponds!
Sage Matanga has observed 80
Penance continuously for a period of one hundred years.
The lake that you see here is the sacred water
Of seven seas; one day the sage wanted to take
A dip in all the seven seas; but since he was
Desperate, looking at their teacher's earnestness
All the disciples collected water from all the seven seas
And created a pond here. When Sage Matanga
Blessed them being contented this place became
Known as "Holy Water of the Seven Seas"!

I belong to the hunters' caste and I was
Born in the forest. I lost my mother quite early
And my father was killed by a wild elephant!
I became an orphan. The ascetics and sages
And the learned ones have relegated us to a lower
Order branding us as beneath their attention.
We suffered a great deal even without names
Like beasts, we were subjected to unfold misery.
When everyone rejected me I was steeped in sorrow.
I had fallen on the ground without any food
And at that time Sage Matanga lifted me up
Like a father and protected me and nursed me
With great affection. As I belonged to the hunters'
Caste he called me Shabari. I have obtained
A new life being bathed in his kindness.
He is father and mother to me; he is
All the relatives I have in the world; he is
The *sadguru* for me. This hermitage is built by him;
In the service of my great teacher;
Therefore, you have been my great teacher I acquired
Inner refinement and I attained knowledge.
I became determined to cross the ocean of the world
Therefore, you have been my pole-star;
You have kept me in the boat of kindness
You have illumined the heart of love
Filling it with devotion.
The great Guru said one day, "Instal a divine idol
In your mind and he is everything to you"
And from that moment onwards I enshrined
In my heart an elegant image of the one with
Bow and arrow as I had seen them from my
Childhood days. I told my Guru dancing with frenzy.
The great teacher, understanding my heart at that
Moment, placed his palm on my head and said,
"Dear daughter, wait for the divine form that will

Manifest before you in flesh and blood one day.
Do your penance keeping the form in your heart
As you have obtained now." At this blessing I danced
Thinking about my good fortune.
Years rolled by as I contemplated on the image
Of the divinity within me day and night; and Sage Matanga's   130
Physical condition got deteriorated as well. He had decided
To leave his mortal coil. When I was in his service
One day at the hour of dawn he called me 'Shabari'
And when I went closer to him he moved his fingers
Through my hair in great affection, "You are fortunate
And soon your wish will be fulfilled; the divine image
You are worshipping enshrining in your heart
Is born in Saket and he is called by the name of Shri Rama.
I am not destined to have that luck. After having
Obtained his *darshan* attain divine merit and come   140
To the world of liberation.
So saying he took a dip in the holy waters
Of *saptasagara* and sat on the platform
In meditation! A radiant light went out of his body
And vanished in the sky!
We shed tears and conducted
The last rites. The God of Fire consumed his body.
Then the disciples went in different directions.
I have spent the time in uttering "Shri Rama, Shri Rama",
Your divine name. The desire to see you had filled   150
Every bit of my body; all my breath was full of
Rama; all my wishes are fulfilled by your *darshan*.
Lord, you are the self, same form which Sage
Matanga had blessed me to carry in my heart
All these years!
O lord, who is reigning in my heart,
My ambition of aeons has been fulfilled.
My eyes are satisfied; all the fourteen worlds will
Attain permanent peace after obtaining your *darshan*.

You are a resplendent light to the waiting world.   160
Meditating on your name constantly,
There was a divine music emanating, listening
To that music I gained freedom from all kinds of
Diseases! I was totally ignorant about the metre and

Beats of the songs, but I sang all the same and
Finally emerged as singer par excellence, my lord!
Even as the fountain of music sprang
I saw the divine form with my own eyes; when the radiance
Of your heart had filled my heart there was happiness
Brimming. It is a brightness not depending on the sun   170
Neither on the moon and it is beyond the light emanating
From the galaxies and the milky way; now I am standing
In that light beyond description.

Canto Eighty-five

'The Vessel of Devotion is Brimful'

||৬||

'Lord, the giver of auspiciousness, I have grown very old,
My eyes are unable to see your perfect form
My ears cannot hear the tender words of your divinity
The nose is unable to smell the divine fragrance
I cannot worship your feet either; Shri Raghurama
Protect me!
The whole world is caught in the sorrow;
It cannot understand; it has fallen into the valley.
There is anarchy everywhere and despondency reigns supreme,
The world is suffering chasing the mirage of desire; 10
Shri Raghurama, protect the world!
Though you are inaccessible to meditation even
You have granted *darshan* to me out of kindness,
I know neither chanting nor other techniques
Of strict discipline; but still I have attained
Liberation winning your grace; Lord of lords,
Protect me Shri Raghurama!
I have surrendered my all at your feet
As your are all pervading – you are in every bit
Of the soil; in my breath and being. What more 20
Do I need to achieve? Protect me Shri Raghurama!

When you shine, the whole world shines,
Your light is the source of everything and you are
The sculptor of the world. Devotion alone welds hearts;
Devotion alone leads one to the highest condition
Of spirituality. You have made this truth clear
Lord of lords; Protect me Shri Raghurama!
I have attained the divine world after your *darshan*;
This body is the temple and the heart is your seat
The eyes are lamps and the palms are fans; 30
All are dedicated to your worship, my lord;
Protect me Shri Raghurama!
You are the Supreme Lord among the gods,
I prostrate at your feet and I will merge in you;
I am emaciated and all my senses are not
Under my control; the mind is at rest at your
Holy feet now after wandering incessantly
For quite a long time. Protect me Shri Raghurama!
Your *veena* will vibrate at the touch of the fingers,
Your flute will sing when the lips touch it; 40
You are the source of all music, kindly make
Me sing your name, my lord; Protect me Shri Raghurama!
There cannot be a greater penance than patience,
They say and that has yielded good results.
I remained indifferent to the harsh and uncouth
Words of the people. I believed in the rewards
Of patience, I believed in the adage that the young plant
Requires to grow to yield fruits in future.
Lord of the universe protect me, Shri Raghurama!
Ahalya was saved by trusting your grace, 50
This body will not end its journey without your *darshan*;
The vessel of devotion is overflowing now;
There is nothing equal to the treasure called your feet,
You are the raft and you are the boatman,
Protect me, Shri Raghurama!
When Ravana abducted the jewel among women

He spelled the doom of demons. The demons will be
Destroyed by the great weapons shot from your bow.
Good will result with your association of Sugriva.
The unwise Vali will be slain by you and that also 60
Awaits your arrival. The good people will live in peace,
They will attain their desire through you. Protect me
Lord Shri Raghurama!
The land of Karnata is the abode of great heroes,
The lamp of morality is lit in every house;
Culture is in every bit of the soil; when Vali
Has committed a heinous crime of deceiving his own brother
Rushyamuka Karnata is awaiting your arrival;
Protect me, Shri Raghurama!'
When Shabari praised Shri Rama with her 70
Unbounded devotion, he said overwhelmed
By her appreciation: 'What need is there of intense
Penance; counting of rosary, bodily suffering
Resulting from fasting? It is necessary to overcome the feeling
That "the body is me"; one must remember constantly
The divine image of the lord; the fear of birth and death should not
Bother; always think of the service of the poor and the needy,
If we take this life forward in devotion that is an ideal
Existence, you listen, mother Shabari!
All possess the power of will, knowledge 80
And action; but still one will be called a *jnani*
Only when he transcends distorted actions;
Otherwise, he will be called a demon of darkness.
What is *dharma*, after all, it is the capacity to bear.
You have already attained perfection by bearing
Dharma, listen mother Shabari!
Great is the world of devotion – it is nine-fold
Really. Devotion brings happiness, plenitude and
It is the source of creation. The path of devotion
Reveals what is sin and what is merit; what is action 90
And what is inaction; what is bondage and what is

Redemption. The path of *bhakti* assures a sense of equality
Just as the descending rains are essential for the crops
Beneath, the water of devotion is essential for *dharma*;
Listen mother, Shabari!
You are devotion personified. By controlling
The senses and pleasures one must stay rooted in *dharma*
At the same time being detached from indulgence
Nurture orientation to righteousness and one must immerse
Constantly in the nine-fold devotion, listen mother, Shabari! 100
If one understands oneself what else
Is there to be understood. Everything manifest will
Melt away; the world will recede and there will be
Divine revelation; there will not be any difference
Between the self and the Supreme Self; listen mother, Shabari!
Shabari was not alone who stood and waited
For the *darshan* of the lord; people have been
Waiting since ages making their bodies shrines;
They are keeping in their hearts' container all offerings
To surrender at Rama's feet; listen mother, Shabari!' 101

Canto Eighty-six

'The Great Land of Kannada'

|| ६ ||

'Mother, tell us more about the hermitage
Of the sage,' when Saumitri requested her, Sabari
Explained in detail: 'Rama and Saumitri, how shall I
Describe the place which is covered by a dense cluster
Of clouds. That Matangavana is full of birds and beasts,
Shri Guru forsook his body in that hermitage. He undertook
The great worship on the platform which faces the west
Even as he offered flowers his hands shook. These are
The flowers that the great sage offered, the lilies are still fresh,
As you can see!'   10
The Guru had asked me to "wait till
You see Shri Rama here" and that penance is over now.
I have seen the divine image that I had enshrined
In my heart. Your brother Lakshmana has followed you
Like a shadow and seeing him is an additional grace,
I should say.
Matanga Sage is my protector and saviour,
He is my Sadguru; he brought me to the path of devotion.
I will end my life's journey now; this body is emaciated,
I will renounce it now,' so she said decidedly.   20
She bowed at the feet of Rama after she bathed

In the sacred water of *saptasagara*. She fell at the feet of Saumitri:
'Who can be compared to you in brotherly love
And affection; Saumitri do I have your permission to end my
Earthly journey,' so saying she closed her eyes sitting near the
Platform. 'Do I have your permission for my journey,
Shri Rama, Jaya Rama, Jaya Jaya Rama, Om,' she
Uttered the chant of Rama raising to the highest level.
Even as her breath hovered in the province of faintness
The name of Rama sheltered in her heart; she ascended
The elevated seat of perfect peace; she joined the 30
Horizon of the path of devotion. The great mother
Shabari's soul attained the feet of Shri Rama at that moment.
Remembering Rama, seeing Rama, and becoming
Rama in every bit of her body she attained
Divinity. In the Great Pursuit of Shri Rama
The flood of victory had merged in the confluence
Of meritorious light!
It was the sunset time and just
As he descended into the ocean the spirit left the body.
Joining hands with Saumitri, Shri Rama placed 40
Shabari's body on the pyre and conducted the last rites.
How fortunate was Shabari!
'She showered on us motherly affection
Yesterday; but that Shabari is not there today,' said the brothers
During the night remembering the departed grandmother.
They finished their morning ablutions before dawn
And offered the ash of Shabari's body in the sacred
Waters of *saptasagara* and bowed reverentially.
The tears of Shri Rama joined with the waters of
Saptasagara turning it into *ashtasagara*! 50
Shri Rama went near the ritual platform
And shed tears copiously remembering Shabari
All the time. 'Where am I and where is Saketa,
Where is the hermitage of Matanga, where is Shabari
How to understand this bond that binds all this!'

So saying Shri Rama was sitting unmoved like a statue.
At that time Saumitri expressed his joy and remembered
Shabari with a great sense of satisfaction. He spoke
To his brother in gentle words: 'Brother, it is getting late,
Let us get going; we shall salute Matangashram and
Take leave of it; a lot of work to do; a long distance
To traverse. We have acquired merit and had the
Divine *darshan* and now we have gathered strength
To forge ahead on the path of Great Pursuit and Rama's
Strength has increased several folds now.'
Shri Rama opened his eyes like a blooming
White lotus and talked to the gentle brother: 'Did you see
Saumitri, our fortune is great that we could see Shabari!
Look there the tigers and deer have forgotten their traditional
Enmity and are playing together in peace and harmony;
This land of Karnataka is an abode of culture!
Hurry up Saumitri, since the Wind-god
Is really propitious in the heart there springs
An unalloyed enthusiasm of goodness. Now our fortune
Will be enhanced in the company of Sugriva!'
Shri Rama and Lakshmana walked ahead and reached
The banks of the lake Pampa! It was a spot most beautiful
And peace prevailed all over! There were white lotuses,
Red lotuses and the blue ones; and it was surrounded by a grove
In which myriad trees of various kinds beckoned
The onlookers with ineffable elegance and the lake Pampa
Appeared to be a zone of ethereal beauty!
'Thunga and Bhadra, the most
Auspicious rivers, though born together, flow in two as they
Move on and come together again in joyous abandon.
Look there Saumitri, we have been
Blessed to have the *darshan* of Virupaksha. The fragrant
Flowers and the twitter of the birds presage the possibility
Of seeing Sita. This land of Kannada is really enticing,
This is exactly like what Shabari described;

There is no fraud and deceit here; neither is there the sting
Of hatred and anger; there is no ambition, blind
Imitation and disappointments, neither there is rivalry,
One-upmanship and backbiting.
The people of Kannada land are living
In perfect accord without yielding to flattery,
Fraud, sleight-of-hand and unhealthy competition.
They do not look at others' wives with evil intentions,
They do not utter lies; they do not ill treat their parents.
This is how they have safeguarded the culture of Kannada land!   100
Shabari dropped like a leaf and a ripe fruit
In the manner of the sky-enveloping clouds descending
On the earth; she attained the end of her life when she
Joined the great ocean of Shri Rama's love; she planted
The divine tree of Karnataka culture and when the light
Emerging from her opened the eyes of the world
She passed into a new world beyond all coverings!'

Canto Eighty-seven

'In Anticipation of Seeing the Blessed Lady'

||๑||

Remembering Shabari and praising Sage Matanga
Shri Rama and Lakshmana continued their journey. On the way
The ascetics showed the direction extending all hospitality.
'Our aim is to see the lake Pampa and to obtain
The friendship of Sugriva and our sole aim is to search Sita.'
When they walked with this determination they saw
The divine lake at that time!
'Saumitri, you see the crystal-clear water
Of the lake Pampa; the lotuses and lilies have bloomed,
The fishes swim and flash as they move in water joyously; 10
The forest of huge trees with their strong boughs look grand;
Many types of flowers have blossomed and have fallen on
The ground and they have created a multi-coloured mat.
Everything is beautiful here as the climbers have clutched
The stems in inseparable love!
The snakes in groups are crawling here and there,
The deer are grazing in the grassland; with the advent
Of the Spring the breeze blows making a gentle sound.
The fragrance of flowers is engulfing the atmosphere

Giving pleasure to the senses. When the flowers fall from
The trees, it appears as if they are raining blooms.
The wind and the blossoms are playing with each other.
What is this ethereal sight brother, how wonderful it is!
As the breeze sails forward the bees fly behind
Singing in groups. The cuckoo in intoxication calls
And there is music everywhere in this wilderness!
Brother, looking at this great plenitude of nature
My mind thinks of Sita and sorrow wells from within.
I am now a poor supplicant. The determination slumps,
My eyes moisten with tears. Everything is mocking
At me augmenting my agony.
The singing cuckoos are making fun of me in their
Pride and happiness. The waterfowl murmurs causing
Sadness in me again. Even as the birds of the hermitage sing
They remind me of Janaki's dance of mirth and it pains
Me as if a knife entered my heart. Look at the ineffable
Joy of the birds in romance. When all the creatures

Of the forest have reached the zenith of ecstasy
I am doomed to despair!
The arrival of Spring has only spelled sorrow
To me. The *ashoka*-flower has only increased my pain,
The droning of bees has pierced my ears;
The russet colour of the leaves appears like flames
Brother, how shall I live now!
When I look at the eyes of the antelopes
I am reminded of Janaki's unstopping eyes.
Understanding the heart of the mates peacocks
Are readying themselves for amatory advances;
That torments me. When the whole nature is
Susceptible to love, my mind contemplates
On the universal love; this fetching wind
Is a source of great pain, indeed.
Look at that mango tree, how it has
Grown tall and huge as if to mock at my

Condition with its indifference; in the light
Of the young sun the elves are dancing and
Lotuses and lilies are smiling with their bloom.
The bees drink nectar hopping from flower to flower,
Chakravaka's call of romance is raucous indeed
To my ears; the herd of deer flocking to slake
Their thirst at the waterhole brings pain again.
Everything is beautiful, but it reminds me of
My consort and as such I am unhinged!'
Thus Raghava disburdened himself forgetting
The world, forgetting himself but only the thought of Janaki
Is churning him. 'Did you see the lotus-eyed lady
Who hankers after lotuses? Did you see, fragrant
Mint and jasmine the one who was as delicate as the flowers.
Why are you silent, tell me if you have seen her;
Those eyes are fortunate which see the auspicious lady
And the eyes have become blind not seeing such a woman!
The lotus have bloomed like Janaki's eyelashes
The Wind-god who carries the saffron pollens is bringing
The fragrant breath of Janaki's when the real blossoms
Adorn the trees it appears as if the very hill is on fire.
The happy garden of mine is also burning and shrivelling,'
So saying he drowned in the ocean of sorrow.
'Why should I grieve and why should I suffer
Thinking of Janaki again and again; when my mind
Is despondent these beautiful scenes themselves
Are a source of pain to me. These creatures of the wild
Are teaching us to be joyous with their mirthful
Existence. The bees drone in the sky and the deer
Gambols incessantly and that is a great lesson for us!
Undimmed enthusiasm is needed for the successful
Accomplishment of the task on hand and hence banish
The sorrowful thoughts,' said Lakshma in order to
Bring him back to the mood of salubriousness.
As the sun had already set they

Completed their daily routine and Lakshmana said, 90
'Let us eat these fruits which have fallen from
The trees attaining ripeness.' They ate the fruits
And Lakshmana spread the mat and they spent their night.
The whole world is gearing up to welcome
The sun. The breeze is blowing thereby telling the world
That an interrelation is necessary among creatures.
The bamboo trees bend and sway and support one another
Producing the pleasing sound touching the neighbours.
They teach us to grow tall.
The stars in the firmament are 100
Receding into background one by one as the sky is filled
With the crimson light before the dawn. Millions of golden
Rays in the east radiate all around. That has made
The green of the leaves shine ever so brighter.
The sun is lending new rays to the new day
Spreading newness to this world charged with divinity.
The eyes of Rama and Saumitri who
Had been tired blossomed, the sun went up in the sky
As if the gates of Heaven were opened wide,
The brothers rejoiced within themselves anticipating 110
The good forgot themselves for a while, but soon
Became alert again and they walked towards Rushyamuka!

Canto Eighty-eight

'I Offer Myself At Your Feet'

|| ६ ||

Sugriva, the chief of *vanaras* stood on the mountain top
And looked at Shri Rama and Lakshmana
At a distance; he was astonished and became
Melancholic again; his mind was anxious. Who are these
Individuals? They look like heroes; they are carrying
The weapons and coming in this direction; they are wearing
The raiments of coarse fibres but what made them
Come to this wild forest.' He addressed Hanuma who was
With him at that time:
'Are they our well-wishers or what   10
I am caught in a vortex of confusion. They must
Have been sent by Vali and there is something
Amiss and I surmise that all is not well.'
Hanumanta being an eloquent scholar
Said consoling Sugriva: 'Why do you worry,
This is not Vali's machination. The hermitage of
Matanga and Rushyamuka are not accessible
To Vali! It is propitious for us, always conducive
For our meditation. Have no fear. Get ready
To work in wisdom as you are full of self-confidence.'   20
'They look like the children of god;

But Vali has friends everywhere. He is a great
Strategist and I feel he has sent the extraordinary
Individuals here. The spies are known to work
In invidious ways roaming all over in secrecy.
We must unlock this mystery without being indifferent.
Hanuma, go ahead and find out their nature
Observing them at close quarters; you are an adept
In understanding their heart engaging in intimate
Conversation,' so said Sugriva with great enthusiasm. 30
Within a minute the son of Maruta flew over
And reached them like a cloud messenger.
He is a great hero who was a manifestation of all
Creativity combining in himself the colours of a rainbow.
Accepting the order of Saugreeva he approached Shri Rama
And Lakshmana in great speed attaining the guise
Of a mendicant leaving aside his *vanara* appearance.
On approaching Rama, Hanuma experienced a shock
Of lightning and a profound attraction of soul's intimacy,
The wonder of creation. It is like the eyes encountering 40
The effulgence of light after eternal blindness;
Like the lotus of heart blooming; he felt as if
He was alerted at once from utter loneliness; the tender
Shoot was enabled to grow; he had stumbled upon
A treasure that had been hidden from view
Since aeons; the celestial moon of infinite beauty
Radiated in the sky; truth was revealed to him
Then and there. The concealed channels of energy
Opened up and there was a great flood. He bowed
And began to speak 50
'Individuals of great merit, may I have your permission to ask,
Where are you from and whither are you going?
You are supreme human beings; you are philosopher-kings,
You have come to the forest in the guise of ascetics
Determined to undergo severe discipline; it is indeed
A great fortune to see you! You are examining everything

With great curiosity. It seems you have come to quell
The enemy with your bows and arrows. Your dignified
Steps and your stance is a source of wonder to us!
You are the greatest among the heroes,　　　　　　　　　60
You possess long arms like the trunks of elephants;
You have the aura of royalty; the eyes are
Like lotus petals; you look like the sun and the moon
Descended to the earth; you are the demi-gods
In the form of human beings. Your elegant quivers
Contain the deadly arrows which will smite the enemies
In a trice; the swords resemble the *vajrayudha*.
Why are you struggling in this daunting path of wilderness?
You look as if you are tired walking on this way.
May I ask the purpose of your journey?　　　　　　　　　70
You are so tender and I wonder
How you would withstand the onslaught of violent wind
And severe sunshine; isn't this path of thorns and stones
Difficult for you to walk; are you the Nara and Narayana
Coming to lessen the burden of the earth;
You are the lords of the world and you have come
To redeem the world; somehow I feel this is your task
And hence I bow before you!'
Saumitri said being overjoyed at
The words he spoke: 'Brother, listen, we feel as if　　　　80
We are meeting a long-lost kin. We belong to
Ikshwaku clan and we are the sons of Dasharatha
Who was a king of Saket with regal effulgence.
He treated all creatures with equal affection,
He had undertaken many *yajnas* of great magnitude.
Kausalya, Sumitra and Kaikayi are our mothers;
Kaikayi demanded coronation rights to Bharata
And Rama was exiled for fourteen years; this is
Our elder brother and I am Lakshmana younger to him.
Sita is our sister-in-law and she followed　　　　　　　　90
Us like a shadow! Her merit is boundless as she is virtue

Personified. As we traversed in the south, the demon
Ravana abducted her and probably he must have
Kept her in Lanka! This atrocity is too much
And we have come this far searching for the mother.
The good people have said that we can find her
With the help of Sugriva. It seems he has suffered
A great deal at the hands of Vali; he is the chief
Of *vanaras*; let us know more about him if you can tell us!'
Listening to Lakshmana'a words Hanuma 100
Felt as if he got back all the lost treasure. He went
Round Rama being overwhelmed by devotion; washed his feet
And worshipped in great reverence. He stood up and
Looked at him intently: 'May victory be Rama's,
May victory be Janaki's husband's; victory to
Kodandarama and to the lord of Saket; I had been
Waiting for you for so long; the merit earned is ripe now
My lord; your name has filled my ears; your form
Has filled my eyes! You are the wishing-tree; you are
Kamadhenu; you are the wishing-gem; you have granted me 110
Darshan answering my prayers; is there anyone in
The world as fortunate as I am? After listening to your words
What needs to be listened to? After touching you what
Remains to be touched? When I say Rama Rama what need
Is there to utter anything else?
You are my treasure-trove, you are the source
Of my happiness; you are my mind's inclination and
You are my source of strength; I have no one to call
My own; you are everything to me; you are my father,
You are my mother,' so praising he danced with joy! 120
Shri Rama embraced Hanuma at that
Moment in great ecstasy. He fondled his forehead and cheeks
And rained on him love and affection. Hanuma brought
His hands together being overwhelmed by the experience
And said: 'I have been waiting for your *darshan*
All these years; the *vanara*-hero Kesari is my father

And Anjana is my mother and I am called Anjaneya
As I have been born with the spirit of Maruta, the
Wind-god; I am also called Maruti; therefore, I am
Pavanaja and also Mukhyaprana. I leapt to the sphere 130
Of sun during my childhood!
I have mastered the Vedas and other
Scriptures from the learned teachers. I have
Attained mastery over my senses worshipping Sun-god
With purity of mind. Looking at the setting sun
Without batting the eyelids I have enshrined in my
Heart the divine spirit; I have the bliss unalloyed
Within me!
I have acquired *yoga* and control
Of breath. I have understood the movement of the solar 140
System. Realising the relationship between the earth
And the sun I have acquired power to achieve everything
In this mortal world.
I joined the hermitage. I gathered
All knowledge sitting at the feet of great mystics.
I heard the maxim that the face of truth is hidden
With a golden lid and it is revealed at once if opened.
In order to understand the complete truth, I am
Moving on the path of pursuit.
When I felt that all penance was a waste 150
I encountered a great teacher who reassured me:
"Enough this penance, you take the path of action
And you will achieve that with Sugriva; when the
Auspicious moment arrives you will be blessed by
A great being and then you will reap the benefits
Of your penance and then you will shine with a radiance
Incomparable; he will be your master and will receive
Your services with great enthusiasm and you will
Attain name and fame in the worlds.
That lord will make you realise 160
The cosmic experience within you; that will be your

Life's fulfilment and you will attain perfection.
He said: "A great being will come, he will be your
Lord and you will realise the Ultimate within you."
Echoed my mother Anjana too; being associated
With Sugriva, O lord, I have seen your feet.
This is the moment of great auspiciousness,
I will offer myself at your wonderful feet;
This is the fulfilment of many lives, indeed
Being a ocean of kindness grant me the honour   170
Of serving your feet,' so saying he prostrated
At Shri Rama's feet.
Shri Rama embraced Hanuma in unmitigated love.
'May all your wishes come true, may your mother's
Wishes also meet with success! You have acquired
The complete grace; your association itself elevates.
Your wishes are noble, indeed. You have attained
The highest state of devotion. You are my guide
In my Great Pursuit; you are equal to Lakshmana
And equal to my breath and I will not forsake you.'   180
So saying he blessed Hanuma.
Anandamurty, Mukhyaprana
Shed tears of joy copiously: 'The brothers Vali and Sugriva
Are so strong that the whole world trembles hearing
Their names; but now hatred has separated them
From each other. Vali has sent away Sugriva
From his kingdom in arrogance and has seduced
His wife; the culture of Karnata has descended
To the nadir; the golden cupolas of Karunadu's virtue
Are tumbling to the ground.   190
Listen prince, Vali is overtaken by the lust
Of other's wife and he has become blind to everything else.
We must decimate those who commit atrocities.
There will be a song of the new dawn in the hearts
Of the virtuous and they will run to you in the groups
And praise your greatness; you will dispel gloom

Engulfing their hearts and you will be the light
Of the land of Karnataka and you will have to shine
Like the sun. I have now seen the mystery
Of the world in the deep blue eyes!   200
You have ascended the Himalayan mountain!
By the swing of the bow you have built a kingdom
Obtaining nectar in the churning of *dharma*.
The new vision will be yours as you have set out
On your Great Pursuit blending the light of the North
With the devotion of the South. You have won the hearts
Of the Goddesses of Power, Knowledge and Wealth
And thus you have become the herald of a new dawn.
Protect Sugriva who is suffering a great deal
From the fear of his vicious brother! Punish Vali!   210
Before your splendour we are like atoms, indeed!

I am your servant, kindly
Lead me on the path of love; there is no time
To waste and this is the moment to wage a war
Of liberation,' so Hanuma implored Rama.

Canto Eighty-nine

'You are the Sun and I am the Ray'

||⑥||

Listening to the words of Anjaneya
Shri Rama forgot himself! 'Did you hear Saumitri,
What humility, what nobility; everything is so dignified.'
He praised at length thus: 'This person has mastered
The art of speech, he has mastered all the Vedas too;
He has served the Goddess of Learning devotedly,
Otherwise he could not have summoned such a finish
To his articulation? He uses words appropriately
And not a syllable out of place. He has understood
The mystery of creation! He is a sun burning   10
With the effulgence of the divine words; he needs
No external law to guide him!
He possesses the voice that captivates the hearts
Of those who listen to him; no room for ambiguity
In his sentences. While he delivers no distracting gestures of the face,
Forehead, eyes or eye brows. The style of his dialogue
Is astonishing indeed. He has the disarming
Art of winning the heart of the enemy so much so
That the enemy will lower the sword even if
He is about to raise to kill him. That is the grand   20
Nature of this person's eloquence. There is politeness

In his voice and his mastery of the Vedas is reflected
In every syllable he utters. If a king has a minister
Like him he will not encounter defeat. He being
The minister of Sugriva the latter is extremely
Fortunate, so to say!
Crossing over Aryavarta he has seen
The horizon of the culture of Bharatavarsha; he is
A visionary par excellence and a jewel in the crown
Of Karnata. That's why the land is called Hanumanadu   30
And Kannada language has shone with undimmed lustre.
Hanuma is such a *karmayogin* that his devotion
For Rama is flowing in his veins!
Hanuma is truth personified,
He is empowering Sugriva in his dire needs
As he believes in the dictum that "no man should be
Ignored when he is down". He is away from the
Politics of strategy and hence he is serving his master
With devotion waiting for the moment of triumph
With patience and steadfastness; he is not exulting in his   40
Power, neither is he slipping into despondency
And he is exemplary in his total detachment.
He is an achiever of Ultimate Goal,
He has never abused the power of virtue; devotion is not
The agitation of the mind; devotion is nothing but
The power of intuition that flows to the hands
Through intelligence. One leg is rooted in the heart
While the other is rooted in the brain. What if you
Decorate the doorway with festoons? There should be
Victuals to eat in the kitchen! When we say Hanuma   50
He is the presiding deity of devotion; when we say
Hanuma, he is the embodiment of wisdom; when we
Say Hanuma, he is the power of the mind, achievement
And the energy of the world!
He is the teacher to the clan of the poets,
He is the master of music and an intuitive reflector;

He knows the art of speech and in matters of morals he is supreme
In purity of heart and concentration; Hanuma is
Comparable only to Hanuma. The bodies are two
But the souls are one and the souls of Rama and
Anjaneya have been fused in *yogic* meditation!
He is a great ascetic who understood
That though people follow many paths ultimately
They all meet at the feet of the same lord.
Being a mystic of great magnitude, he has ascended
To the great height. He is a visionary par excellence
Who sprinkled spirituality on the fires of the world
And averted the explosion!
He is the greatest among the greats. When in the world
We see the poison of enmity and the malicious laughter
This Hanumanta lit the lamp and stretched the hand
Of help in an attempt at nullify the pain of people.
He forged ahead to find a solution like a veritable hero!'
When Shri Rama was praising him thus
Hanumanta shed tears of gratitude and it was
An occasion of great celebration for him too. He praised
The lord, in turn, being overwhelmed by devotion:
'Great teacher, you are being worshipped by the world
I have been blessed with the merit of myriad lives.
Kindly pluck the string of new life; as you are
The visionary of a new creation I have overcome
All doubts and diffidence. You have installed
A new cupola in my heart's shrine and I
Surrender at your feet, lord!
You are the embodiment of truth,
You are the idol of love descended to awaken the soul
Motivating it to imbibe the nectar of spirituality.
I am the dullard always enamoured of things worldly,
Now I am awashed with your kindness
And I have surrendered to you, the great light!
You are of the cosmic form,

As you have occupied the whole world I will revolve
Around you; when you have filled yourself
With me, I will be one with you; you are great
To the world, but I am greater than you
In the rhythmic beating of the heart; I will dance
In the equal music of the mind; as you have
Come in the form of light I have surrendered to you!
The ocean of grace, cut all bondages
And grant freedom; make me think of you constantly.   100
Let your name fill my ears; make my heart
Your permanent abode; as you are making me
Melt in the ocean of love I surrender to you, lord!
Giver of all treasures and happiness,
Saviour of the voiceless you are, but I am a fool
When I see you I become speechless; there are
So many sects and so many paths; but lord, your
Splendour is everywhere though it is called by
Different names. You are accessible to the Vedas
And can be grasped by experience, I surrender to you!   110
You are the primordial spirit.
In the womb of the sea the oyster will wait for a drop
Of rain and the moment it receives it the oyster
Will close the lid and go down. As time passes
The drop of rain will turn into pearl and attain
Fulfilment; now I have become that pearl
And stand as a significant being and what more
Need I ask, I prostrate before you, lord!
You are the ocean of bliss and
Possessor of all good qualities and you are an independent   120
Dignified being; you are the buttress to the citadel
Of devotion; love alone is the sturdy raft that
Takes closer to you; Janaki's husband, you are
My breath; you will be drawn to those who

Surrender unconditionally to you and hence
I salute you, my lord!

The giver of the good, O sun
What sweetness is there in your name, O lord
The more I taste it the more I crave for it.
You are positioned strongly among myriad names, 130
I have filled the nectar of your name within me;
You have come without my prayer, what is this fortune!
I am completely astonished and I surrender to you!
The most beautiful lord,
I am in possession of a distinguished pearl
And I have kept it in the casket of devotion
With great care; I have a feeling that I am
On the verge of attaining perfection;
Just as the hills and rivers lose their names and forms
Myself in the ocean of Rama, I surrender to you! 140
You are always pure and blameless,
In the heart there is the echo of this truth;
It has filled inside and outside and there is
Bliss whichever way I look; devotion swells
In every bit of my body; I have raised
My breath from my navel to the zenith,
I will attain permanent redemption, I salute you!
You are a complete teacher;
Just as the elephant shines inside a mirror
Be shining in my heart, O lord; do not stir 150
From the shrine of my body even for a moment;
I will install you in the *mandap* of nine precious stones.
When you are the sun, I being a ray, could I
Dream of a separate existence? You are
The strongest among the strong, I surrender O lord!
The beautiful one for the eyes
You are a great embellishment for the three worlds,
You are the protector of the needy and cynosure for all;
You are the most celebrated by the devotees; you are
The sun among the clouds, you are the crest-jewel; 160
For the wicked you are nightmare, for the good a sure

Source of succour; you are a jewel of quality,
A jewel of happiness and I surrender before you!
The beautiful one of all the world;
You punished the wicked and protected the good
And to achieve this end you made many incarnations
As Fish, as Tortoise, as Boar and also you came down
In the form of Man-Lion and also a Dwarf and again
As Parashurama, I bow down to you lord!
You are the unparalleled one 170
I am like a poor cow fallen into the swamp
Looking in all directions helplessly always expecting you;
You lifted me from the quagmire becoming the lord
Of beasts; I do not have even an iota of devotion;
I will be a vehicle of devotion hereafter and my body
Will carry nothing but devotion, I surrender to you lord!
Sure kinsman of the devotees, I saw
Your effulgence in all the fourteen worlds,
I saw in my heart a Brindavan and I saw you
Enjoying yourself being seated there; I saw the 180
Unfurling of the sail of my boat; lord, make it reach
The other shore in everlasting bliss; make
The river of virtuous mind to flow, I salute you lord!
The primordial spirit of the world,
I have not approached you thinking that I am
Without food and shelter; the absence of wife and children
Is also not the reason for my coming; I have not come
As the cascade of devotion is in full flow within me.
Hence I have kept you in the lotus-heart, O lord,
I am immensely fortunate, I surrender to you! 190
You are accessible to all the chants
When all my feelings are disturbed and chaotic,
When life is beyond tolerance, the body is emaciated;
I am like a solitary elephant, you came and arranged
Everything in an order and showed a new path;
I salute you, O lord!

You are the abode of all strategems,
I have not come to you praying for jewels and ornaments
Neither I crave for pleasures of any kind;
Lord, I have come solely in search of devotion,   200
I have come to you with a desire of liberation
Take me to a world free from illusion and enticement.
I surrender to you O lord!'

Canto Ninety

'You Be the Charioteer to the Great Pursuit'

||৬||

Shri Rama asked Hanuma with affection: 'Hanumanta,
Are you willing to come to a new world where light reigns supreme;
Where there is no sorrow, pain and attachment, neither there is
Illusion and desire; there flows the Ganga of Love unceasingly!
All are equal there; the distinction of master and servant,
Rich and poor does not exist; everywhere there is goodness
And success attends everything, everywhere virtue prevails.
That is the place of *Ramarajya*; would you come there
Hanuma!
The way is very steep   10
And you should have overcome hunger and thirst;
You should have achieved victory over your mind after
Observing intense penance; you should have transcended
The pull of the senses; you should have the stamina
To tread the path of thorns and stones; there will be
Lightning and thunderbolts; dark nights and whirlwinds;
The frightening path of blood and gore; would you come
Along with me without hesitation? We will ascend together
To a new gathering, a new era and a new horizon, Hanuma!
Wherever you see, the law of the jungle prevails,   20
Everywhere the dictates of law and prisons galore, everywhere

One encounters shackles and cruelty; we have to engender
Love in the shrivelled hearts, filling the nectar of
Reassurance; we must give food to the one who
Gives a drink of water; and silver coin to the one
Who gives just a nickel; that is why you become
Mukhyaprana to have the cosmic vision!
The serpent of the ego is raising its arrogant hood
And you be the antidote to it; you be the charioteer
To the Great Pursuit and become a source of inspiration   30
For the pursuit of Truth as well.'
Listening to Shri Rama's words intently Hanumanta said:
'Sugriva is waiting for you extending the hand
Of friendship. I will cement the friendship further
Between you two. Permit me lord to proceed;
We will climb up Rushyamuka and I will raise
The bridge of friendship now; since it is a daunting path
I request you to sit on my shoulder,' when he said

So Shri Rama and Saumitri agreed gladly and they
Sat on each shoulder!   40
Hanuma climbed up the mountain slowly and
Steadily just as a *yogi* ascends the mystic zones one by one
During the course of his spiritual journey. He is a great
Accomplisher, the radiant one. Appreciating his son the Wind-god
Blew gently; like the king of eagles carrying Shri Hari
Hanuma bore the flowers of the garden of Saket and
Moved forward. When a man achieves merit in life
And reaches a point of maturity, he traces the path
Of upward movement and that was demonstrated
By Hanuma now. He moved ahead to show that   50
The service of the lord was a great fortune indeed.
As he ascended further and further and when he
Looked below the valley and the raised ground appeared
Plain; everything was smooth and appealing;
Hanuma was overwhelmed by joy and he went round
A big rock and hopped over a boulder; he went forward

Dancing and leaping and singing and gyrating without stopping.
To break the wave of the Age, Maruti resembled
The wind that blew in the world and went
Towards Rushyamuka.   60
As he moved in this fashion the feet of Shri Rama
And the feet of Saumitri touched the back and the chest
Of Hanuma and that brought great ecstasy to him.
He appeared like the one who has realised Brahman
After reaching the Ultimate Goal being a pure soul.
Rama is father to all and Janaki is mother to all.
All men are brothers; give up quarrels and squabbles
And harsh words, bow down your head to justice;
Struggle hard, never forsaking virtue; install the name
Of Shri Rama on the tongue and if you can live winning   70
The love of the world that life would be a life of fulfilment!
Hanuma's life is of great value.

He took pride of being the servant of Shri Rama. He contained
Securely within himself the ten qualities like effulgence,
Success, courage, delicateness, capacity, humility,
Efficiency, heroism, victory and good sense!
The remembrance of Hanuma's name
Is like a philosopher's stone to India which has
Suffered from slavery, humiliation, despair and disunity.
Karnata, the land where Hanuma was born, is shining,   80
The land is fulfilled and people are also fulfilled
And everyone who is passing through the experience of
Shri Ramayana Mahanveshanam is fortunate, indeed!

BOOK THREE

Canto Ninety-one

'He Carries All to the Height He Reaches'

||௬||

He is of divine origin, Hanuma the son of Anjana.
Can anyone rival him in his service to Shri Rama,
In his character unblemished, and in his dedication?
Competent he is in his job, expert in his endeavours,
A fountain of spirit – and a terror to his enemies.
He carries every one to the heights he reaches,
Dispersing all clouds of despair and disappointment.
Of valour and wisdom, he is the embodiment.
Power of body, wisdom and spirituality –
Being a confluence of all these three, he glories; 10
He is, indeed, a symbol of human perfection.
He is the polestar in the darkness of the world,
He is the tower of the edifice of all ideals,
He is the ruby that shines in the *Ramayana*-necklace.

Listen to his exploits as a boy.
Once, the small boy, Hanuma, beheld the sun's orb,
And, deeming it a ripe fruit, to pluck it and eat,
He leapt to the sky. The *vanaras* were taken aback
With this exploit. The king of all gods, so it is said,
Hit him hard with his weapon *vajra* and knocked him down. 20
Due to the fall, his left jaw broke and swelled,

And everyone began to shout '*hanu – hanu –*'.
Since '*hanu*' means jaw, this brave man, therefore,
Was called Hanuma, the man with the broken jaw.

Be this story of the jaw truth or fiction,
'Hanuma' is, truly speaking, a symbol of genius;
'Hanuma' is a metaphor for fulfilment;
'Hanuma' is a name for commitment to action;
And a symbol for awakened consciousness.
He is the pinnacle of expanse and magnanimity; 30
He is the divine flash of intelligence that has dropped
From Heaven to the earth.

Thus, good people talked about his childhood,
And they savoured, with pleasure, his heroic stories.
The child Hanuma grew up in course of time;
But, alas! As if enveloped in forgetfulness,
Dumbfounded, he used to sit, alone and lost.
Struck with anxiety, his mother Anjana, hurried
To the great Sage Matanga, bowed to him humbly,
And prayed to him to bless her and her son. 40
Assuaging her fears, he said,
'Why do you worry, my daughter?
Not being wasted here and there, the energy in
Hanuma is getting stored and preserved in him,
To be harvested later in his service to Shri Rama.
Like a flash, the sight of Rama will revitalise him,
And enlighten him. Of the great things to come
When Rama's spiritual strength fuses with Hanuma's
Physical strength, this is only a prophecy.

'With the age-old wisdom, 50
And the newly awakened energy, Hanuma, truly,
Will be the harbinger of the new millennium.
Listen! The Dravidian society will be the source
Of the great flow of *bhakti*; and Karnataka will nourish it.
And, there will converge in Rama and Hanuma,

The triple principle of devotion, wisdom and
Asceticism; and there, on the Dravida horizon,
Will arise the energised and the glorious sun of *dharma*.'

True to the words of the sage,
Hanuma grew – the one to ameliorate the world,   60
The one who knew no fear, a man of truth,
Competent in his duty, and an expert in all arts;
He is an ocean of virtues, and a master of words,
The one who has moulded the core of our culture.
An expert in many tongues, and a model of behaviour,
He is the polestar of all – to the harbour of knowledge.

Canto Ninety-two

'His Heart Blossomed with Pure Joy'

||๖||

'Listen, O the noblest of Raghu dynasty! My mind
Is quickened in your presence. Without you,
I am nothing and you are the force sustaining the universe.
Your creation is dynamic, inspiring to move ahead,
And from you, all people draw their living breath.
All the flowers, plants and trees now stand still,
Given to the ecstasy of silence and stillness.
This silence of their's is not a sign of death;
It is pregnant with a meaning transcending words.
You are the light, ever-shining in pitch darkness.　　　　　　10

'When the demon, mad with rage,
Smashed the pillar, you manifested yourself anew,
Breathing fire, from the pillar, O God!
Protector of devotees, when the little boy Prahlada cried for your help,
You came out, at once, to protect him, O Lord!
You manifested yourself breaking the pillar
Of passive mind; you came out from the dark mines
Of human heart, smiling blissfully, O Master!

'In that lovely morning, sparkling milky white,
And the night knitting pearls on the edges of clouds,　　　　　　20

You, the monarch of all, sovereign of the world,
When you set your feet on the soil of Karnataka,
Everyone's heart blossomed with great joy,
And I, like one such flower, am now at your feet.
You are Truth incarnate, you are the treasure of wisdom;
Such a great companionship is my fortune.'

With these words charged with emotion,
Hanuma surrendered himself to the great man, Rama.
No weapon could hurt his soul and no fire burn;
No water could wet it and no wind dry it.   30
Indestructible was his soul. When he surrendered
His mind and body to Shri Rama and became one
With his radiance, it was a union of two great souls;
It was then that Hanuma achieved self-realisation.

Like the moon emerging from the dark clouds,
Like the sweet cuckoo-song pouring into one's ears,
Like the peacock dancing in full moonlight,
Like the flight of doves in the vast ocean of sky,
Divinity sprang up from the depths of the earth,
And all matter, lifeless and living, became one.   40
That was the moment, aiding as well as nourishing,
Of divine illumination.

Then said Hanuma, again:
'Out of the caverns of anguish hidden in my heart,
Out of the depths of pain, O Lord, you have freed me.
Self-knowledge, expanding like the endless sky,
Has yielded joy, rippling in all directions.
Fear, hidden in the unconscious regions,
You have expelled, and brought forth a new world.

'The terrifying war drums not beaten and the trumpets   50
Not blown, the swords are sheathed. The future age
Of non-violence, cleansed of partisan minds
And self-indulgence, you have proclaimed,
And caused everyone to work towards universal

Happiness. Your story is so edifying, your acts
So unparalleled. O Master! I surrender to you.

'What doubts can I have, you being perfect!
Sin and piety, right and wrong – having transcended
All such dualities, having surrendered myself to you,
I have no life of my own apart from yours, O God!   60
When you have given me a new mind, a new life,
The ever-turning wheel of *karma* cannot bother me.
I am your devotee and you are my god;
Rama and Hanuma are but mirrors of each other;
I am freed forever from all turmoils of the heart.

'Endless reflections spreading joy everywhere,
When you make yourself visible to your devotees,
You appear all around, wherever one casts one's glance.
You are there, here, everywhere; you are omnipresent;
You have myriad forms and limitless manifestations.   70
With just your touch, I have become one with you;
And I only hope not to be swayed by any temptations.

'Your name and nobility are found everywhere;
All I desire is to pray to you and serve you.
That is my aim, the governing principle of my life.

'Your speech, true and convincing,
Resounding like thunder amidst clouds,
Clears illusions and presents new visions.
Your love and compassion, like a lamp,
Light my mind and heart, and guide my word and deed.   80
The vesicas of *anna* or food, *prana* or breath,
Mana or mind, and *vigyana* or true knowledge,
And finally, the vesica of *ananda* or supreme joy,
it has permeated.

'New worlds are opened, new visions created,
And new directions to explore the meaning of life;
And, you are there to guide me, with affection.

'You are my noble Guru;
You are the Kamadhenu, the all-yielding heavenly cow.
I receive the divine nectar of joy from you, 90
And I will happily apportion it among all good people.
You are all harmony and you are all radiance –
It is beyond me to describe your endless virtues.

'You are beyond attributes!
You are the living truth, you are formless.
I, like a honey bee hovering around your lotus feet,
Seek, while singing your praises, the honey of highest Truth.
Sometimes in silence and sometimes in words,
I drown, blissfully, in the ocean of wisdom.
Like the legendary eagle, Garuda, covering its eaglets 100
Under its huge wings, you are protecting me now.
I am freed now, from begging all sorts of kings
And living in obligation for their largesse.'

Thus said Hanuma, the son of Wind,
Unrivalled in strength and magnificent in physique,
Unequalled in valour, and free from all sensual drives.
Noblest in resolve, untouched by bonds of carnal
Affection, blessed with all virtuous qualities,
Humblest, and always striving for the good of all,
Fearless in mind and the champion of truth, 110
An expert in his tasks, and a great scholar,
He is the vast ocean of all noble virtues,
Eloquent in speech, and moving in his words.
He is the one who gave the essence of culture
To this country, the land of Bharata. A man of
Many languages, he is the lodestar, the ever-burning
Lamp of wisdom.

Having praised Rama, thus,
And having prepared the ground for friendship
Between Sugriva and Rama, Hanuma departed. 120

Canto Ninety-three

'Racial Amity Blossomed'

||ॐ||

Hanuma, the messenger, stood before Sugriva,
Straight and courteous, and addressed him thus:
'Listen! O King Sugriva! Having had a sight
Of Shri Rama, dear to the whole world and perfect,
I feel blessed and supremely fulfiled.

'Shri Rama is the saviour of the weak and the needy;
He destroys the wicked and protects good people;
He is the follower of truth, one to keep his words.
What does one gain drowned in selfish pleasures?
Only the lineage of Kabandha, Viradha, and Vali   10
Will increase. If you forsake truth and hope for
A counter revolution, you will invite disaster.

'Who is Shri Rama?
He is a revolutionary on the path of munificence.
Tell me, can even thousands of Valis and Ravanas
Be equal to him? He is a personification of
Valour and fame. He protects those who trust him.
He is neither overjoyed nor depressed by his power;
And he is never given to despair. He is always
Courteous and humble.   20

'Listen! He is the perfect man.
He has studied the Vedas, is well-versed in treatises;
And he is here to spread the culture of Ayodhya.
To teach everyone that civilisation is only the husk,
And that the inner core of every society is culture,
He has undertaken an endless journey of the quest
Throughout the length and breadth of this country.'

In his boundless enthusiasm, Hanuma continued:
'I have brought Rama and Lakshmana, and made them
Stay on the summit of Malayagiri. They belong   30
To the Ikshvaku clan and they are Dasharatha's sons.
Truthful, obedient to their parents, and virtuous
They are; and they are brave and courageous.
To uphold truth, they are ready to go through
The ordeal of fire. Having left their capital,
They have come here, accompanied by Sita.
Alas! The lustful Ravana has kidnapped Sita,
Rama's spouse, and has, thereby, provoked death.

'To slay Ravana and free Sita, Rama needs your help;
He has come here seeking your friendship.   40
He will be the seer to help us discover this new age,
And it will be for the good of all. Let's welcome him.'
Then, Hanuma bowed to Sugriva respectfully.

These words gladdened Sugriva's heart, and the dark
Clouds of fear being dispelled, his face brightened.
Thinking that great fortune had come his way,
He said: 'Where? Where is Shri Rama? Show him,
And I will immediately stretch my hand of friendship
To him.' He was beaming with joy.

Then went Hanuma and brought Shri Rama   50
And Lakshmana to Sugriva; he introduced them
To him and stood by. Sugriva's heart overflowed
With joy. 'O Rama, the noblest of the Aryans,

I am fortunate that you have come seeking me.
You are compassionate and I depend on you;
Guide me to what is good and meritorious.'

With these loving words, he approached Rama
His hands outstretched; and Rama, gladly
And firmly, embraced him close to his heart.
Then Sugriva, with the same affection,   60
Embraced Lakshmana.

Maruti, in the meanwhile, got a fire ready, and,
With the fire as witness, both sealed their friendship.
Then, both Sugriva and Rama, with folded hands,
Went around the fire and vowed mutual friendship.
The blossom of amity between the two races
Sparkled in the sky.

Shri Rama and Sugriva looked at each other for long;
The more they saw each other, the more they wanted to.
'Your pleasure is my pleasure; your pain my pain;   70
You have been my kith since many previous births;
Having met you, this life has acquired a new meaning,
And you have opened the doors, closed for ages,'
So said Sugriva, gratefully.

Then Sugriva broke a branch of a *sala* tree,
Studded with flowers, and spreading it on the ground,
Seated Rama there, and then he sat near him.
Hanuma brought a branch of a sandalwood tree,
And spread it on the ground as a seat for Lakshmana.
All sat down together, and the world became quiet.   80
Surrounding then, there were huge rocks and crags,
And smooth stone slabs that served as seats.

Clean and unsullied, calm and peaceful,
That charming place seemed to invite one and all.
Merry were the flowering plants and creepers there;
Merry were the glorious lakes, full of pure water;
There were the tall trees weighed down with fruits;

Verily, it was the home of the Goddess of Nature.
The name of that kingdom was Rushyamuka,
Sugriva its king, and his followers his subjects, 90
His palace was a hill-cave and his throne a huge rock.
There were no war cries, no place for tyranny,
No slaves shedding tears; it was a haven of peace.
The divine peace that reigned near the Pampa lake

Was reflected in the heart of Sugriva.
Full of joy, Sugriva
Brought a water-pot and washed Shri Rama's feet.
He offered them water and jaggery, juicy fruits,
And served the brothers with love and respect.
He took out a fan, made of *lamancha* roots, 100
Dipped it in cool water, and fanned them with that.
After exchanging a few words of courtesy humbly,
Sugriva folded his hands respectfully, and said:

'O, Shri Rama! You were kind to bless Hanuma;
And, because of him, I have now got the fortune
Of your presence, O glory of the sun's lineage!

'Vali my elder brother, a man of supreme power,
Has forcibly taken Ruma, my wife, and has banished
Me from my kingdom. Separated from my wife,
I am forlorn; wandering here and there, I am lost. 110
Full of hatred towards me, if he just sights me,
He will kill me with his arrows, sharp and swift.
With my spirit destroyed by the fear of Vali,
I am in hiding, in this impregnable forest.
I have lost everything, as you can see for yourself;
Grant me shelter – You are the protector of *dharma*.'

Listening to the words of Sugriva,
Rama took pity on him, and got enraged
By Vali's wicked deeds. Assuringly, he said:
'I will not forgive Vali, who has taken your wife. 120
My arrows, sharp and sparkling as the sun,

That resemble the *vajra* weapon in Indra's hands,
And hiss like an angry python, will pierce his body,
And knock him down; have no fear.'
Assured with those words of Rama,
Sugriva said, happily: 'I am blessed today.
No more anxiety I have and no further fears.
When you are prepared to help me thus,
It is my duty to offer you some help too.
I am aware of the whole story, why 130
You had to come to the forest and how Sita,
The earth-born was abducted – the whole
Sad story of the misdeeds of the king of Lanka
Hanuma has recounted to me.

'The story of noble Jatayu, who fought
Ravana bravely and eventually died,
Saddens me. But, O Rama, you don't feel sad.
I am with you; and I won't rest till I rescue Sita,
The princess of Mithila, and bring her to you.
Nobody can get away with such a crime, 140
Be they gods like Indra, *rakshasas*, or *yakshas*.
Be she in the depths of the nether world or high
In the abode of gods; I will search her out.
Such is my vow, firm and truthful. Trust me.
Sir, have faith; I have a huge army of mine,
And all of us are resolved. Why this sorrow then?
When the *rakshasas* Madhu and Kaitabha hid
The holy Vedas, the great god Narayana freed them.
My task will be similar to that.

'Some time in the past, 150
We, from a distance, heard pitiful cries
Like "O Rama! O Lakshmana," and sobbing.
Now we know they were the cries of "Mother" Sita.
A helpless captive on Ravana's lap in his chariot,
She appeared like a snake wriggling for freedom
In the snake charmer's hands, O Raghava.

Are criminal acts new to the king of Lanka?
Every day, his carnal acts are on the rise;
The lives of all beauteous women are being
Ruined; and we are helpless and sad. 160
'Once, when we were standing in a valley,
Overcome with despair, Hanuma roared
In rage: "I will destroy this wicked man's chariot,
And reduce it to pieces." When he was about to leap
Intent on his task, I stopped him and said:
"What is Ravana's strength and what is ours?
Unless you consider this difference, it is foolish
To engage him in a fight." Ravana is a friend
Of Vali, and Kishkindha is very close to him.
Hence, I lacked the will power to oppose him. 170

'Like a vulture holding a fish in its beak,
When Ravana was carrying Sita, speedily,
She took out the ornaments on her body and
Threw them to us. The pearl necklace she threw
Appeared, while falling, like a string of tear-drops,
Like drops of snow. The sun rays, taking them for
Heavenly ornaments, brought them to the earth.'

The words of Sugriva
Brightened Rama's face immeasurably.
'O Sugriva! Your words give me great solace. 180
My curiosity grows; get the ornaments at once.'
Then Sugriva went to his cave and brought
A cloth bundle; Shri Rama's heart lay inside it.
The son of Sumitra quickly opened the bundle.
Pairs of toe-rings, armlets, pearl necklaces,
Golden bracelets studded with precious rubies –
The son of Sumitra took them one by one
And showed them to his brother, lovingly.

Shri Rama took the ornaments in his hand,
Touched them tenderly, looked at them, quietly. 190

Surprise and sorrow shook him, and, like a pearl
Necklace, tears streamed down from his eyes.
His saddened face wrenched Lakshmana's heart.
Sugriva, shaken, looked at Rama, at Lakshmana,
At Hanuma, and then, casting his eyes heavenward,
Was lost in his own thoughts.
Silence enveloped everyone,
And all of them, confused and worried,
Were drowned in sorrow.

Pained and in anguish, 200
Rama gave vent to his grief thus:
'How is my wife? Has her smiling face paled?
Is her long and beautiful *champaka*-nose the same?
Have her honeyed words lost their sweetness?
What has become of her cuckoo-sweet voice?
How are her hands now, once as tender as new leaves?
How is her body now, once as delicate as a creeper,
Radiant and fragrant?

'Alas, my wife, as dear as my life!
You are the one who left behind all of 210
Your ornaments and flowers at Saketa –
Those that your mother, Sunayana, gave you!
Without any kind of attachment to them,
You have thrown out all of them here.
Bereft of all such jewellery, like an orphan,
You must be leading a wretched life, now,
Under cruel controls.

'O virtuous woman!
When we lived in the forest, every moment,
You revelled in the beauty of nature, and 220
Declared that the real Heaven was on earth.
Where is that charming and happy face?
Full of despair that he who wasn't there
To protect you in distress, was of no use to you,
Did you just discard me, O Devi?'

Repeating such words,
Looking at the ornaments often, sadly
Clasping them to his heart, as if the queen
Of his heart lay there; tears streaming down,
He, the master of the earth, collapsed on the earth. 230
The son of Sumitra, then, with a heavy heart,
Lifted his brother Rama, and consoled him thus:

'Arise, O first-born!
Why do you put the Raghu-clan to such shame?
Let the flame of valour in you blaze up bright;
Let the light within you illumine all that's dark.
You are the very radiance to enlighten this world.
'The lightning of Varuna, the God of Rain,
And the thunderous uproar were all quieted
Disdainfully by your inner strength and peace 240
Prevailed. How did you lose that strength?'

These soothing words of the son of Sumitra
Had their effect; Rama regained his spirit
And said: 'Look, my brother; look at these
Ornaments that Vaidehi, the daughter of Videha has thrown out:
This is the necklace that danced round her neck;
This is the bracelet, studded with precious gems,
That sparkled round her wrists; but, where
Is the precious earring that lit up her face
Like the rising sun? Where, O where 250
Is her crest-jewel studded with sparkling sapphires?
When the demonic Ravana was carrying her away,
She has discarded these, in her wisdom, as signs.
She is beyond any praise.'

Examining all those ornaments,
Rama felt very sad and remorseful. But,
Immediately, as if he awoke after a nightmare,
He recovered, forgetting all his sorrow.

Canto Ninety-four

'Fellowship of Many Lives was Renewed'

||௬||

That Shri Rama might come out of his anguish,
Lakshmana and Hanuma took him to a nearby hill,
And strolling here and there, they rejoiced
In the evening splendour.
Clouds, pure white and thick, were ranged
Against the vast blue expanse of the sky, as if
They formed a lid to the sky. The west-bound sun
Strew crimson colour on the clustered clouds
As if he wished to build a lustrous fort there.
The river Pampa, full of pure, clear water,   10
Gliding over the uneven ground and levelling it,
Shone like a crystal garland worn by Mother Earth.
The virtuous people bathed in it and were sanctified,
While sinners, bathing in it, washed their sins off.

When the sky looked like an umbrella,
Held high over the earth, burning in the sun's heat,
The cool breeze from the Malaya hill was soothing;
The refreshing fragrance of flowers on trees
And plants spread everywhere, and announced
The arrival of a new season.   20

The evening sun, tired of his long journey,
Slipped into the womb of the dense forest,
Resolved that he would rise again and defeat
The thick forces of darkness – a symbol of
Indefatigable spirit against heavy odds.

The sun and the moon, stars and fire, of course,
Give outer Light; but they have no place near
Inner light. Shri Ramachandra, moving ahead on
The path of the great search for self-knowledge,
Can guide the world on the path of right action.   30
Like all great men, who practise *dharma*, and
Who, while treading the difficult path of *dharma*,
Sacrifice their lives and thus show the path
For others, the sun set behind the hill, happily.
Standing on the peak of Rushyamuka hill till
Sunset, Rama watched everything, sighing
Now and then; and before it got dark, lest he
Be consumed by it, shook himself awake,
And got down from the hill.

Sugriva, the soft-spoken,   40
Led Shri Rama to his cave; so that the lamp
Of hope in Rama may not die, he poured into it
The oil of his fellowship. He so contrived that
The Rama-ocean, being bountiful with tides, was full
Of life. Thus Sugriva, born into the sun-clan,
Devoted to his duty and blessed with divine
Radiance, led Rama in the right path.
With him is Lakshmana,
Like the amber hue glowing on the eastern sky;
There is Hanuma, like the gentle breeze that   50
Caresses one to happiness. With them, like the sun
Of amity rising in the east, is Shri Rama.
After Hanuma lighted the lamp of friendship
Between Rama and Sugriva, both of them,

With fire as witness to their fellowship,
Their hearts beating together in harmony,
Continued on the path of auspicious love.

To them,
Friendship was light and friendship was water;
Their very breath was friendship; with mutual   60
Affection, they led each other on the path of success;
Affection of many births bound them together.
With one view, one aim, and one mind,
They moved together, full of divine happiness.
The flag of Saketa, rising above the watery
Clouds, spread itself spanning the vast sky,
Like saffron, in which, rind, seed, and petal
Become one fruit; like all great rivers flowing
With the same holy water; like the hidden Ganga
Meeting the ocean of one's heart.   70

The camaraderie between Rama and Sugriva,
Cleansing the age-old filth of distrust, nurtured
The tree of friendship, which will bear flowers
And fruits, in the years to come; which, nourished
By devotion of many years, will yield a rich
Harvest, anticipating the New Age to come.
Like the confluence of the rivers Tunga and Bhadra,
Like wealth following success, like emotions
Fusing with intellect, the blind and uneventful
Life of Sugriva shone in the light of friendship   80
Of Shri Rama, the divine light.

Anxiously, once, Shri Rama said to Sugriva:
'Let us not wait any longer, my friend. Let us find out
Who it is that has abducted Sita, and where he
Has hidden her captive. I am burning in the fire
Of anger that swells day by day. Ravana,
In fact, has opened the doors of death wide.
I will attack him from all directions, and I will

Dispatch everyone to the city of death.
I will reduce to dust the cruel peaks of crime. 90
The molten lava of my rage and resentment
Will flow and swallow the whole of Lanka.'
His words were like a thunderbolt;
The face of Saketa-king was flushed with anger,
And also sorrow. Sugriva's eyes were moist.
Sobbing, he said: 'Sorrow is worse than an enemy;
It lessens one's will power and weakens one physically.
A ship full of water can only sink to the bottom.
Come out of your sorrow. I won't rest till I restore
"Mother" Sita to you. I will destroy the entire clan 100
Of the Lankan king, and I will plant the victory flag
In Lanka. Trust the words of a bosom friend.
'My affection and regard for you
Are, indeed, firm. In your company, confidence
In myself has been augmented. When you are near me,
Tell me, is there anything impossible? I can even
Seize the kingdom of gods. With your blessings,
Would I be scared of anyone's aggression?

'Here, in Rushyamuka,
You are grieving, Shri Rama, alone and silent. 110
Whereas, I am destroyed by Vali's misdeeds.
He has stolen my wedded wife, Ruma;
My name and honour are completely ruined;
Impotent that I am, I could not protect even my wife;
And, hence, drowned in despair, I am lost.
Like a refugee, I have wandered from land to land;
A victim of my brother's anger, I am drained.
O Sire! Assist me, a poor and lonely man.'

Listening to these helpless words of the *vanara* king,
Rama consoled him: 'Meeting friends 120
Means help is near; it presages danger only
When you come across enemies. Listen to me!

I will not allow Vali, villainous and the abductor
Of your wife, to go unpunished. All of my arrows,
Kept in a golden quiver, are both shining and swift.
They are as awesome as the *vajra* wielded by Indra;
They are as sharp and furious as the enraged snake.
Just as even a huge mountain is crushed by the *vajra*,
Vali, struck down by my arrows, will fall, dead.

Shedding tears of joy, Sugriva, reassured, said: 130
'Great. You are the refuge to those in sorrow.
The thought that I wasn't the husband my wife
Could be proud of gnawed at my heart, sharply.
But today, my king, all my agony has ended;
Your words are the life-giving springs to me.
I shall now forget those wretched days
As a bad dream. Is it a common thing
That I am associated with you in your
Noble Quest of truth?

'Hanuma built the bridge of fellowship between us, 140
And making him your trusted servant was how you rewarded him.
Now, none but you can help me, O Lord!
I am as good as dead bereft of my kingdom.

'Once, the ten-headed Ravana,
Vainglorious, challenged Vali for combat;
My elder brother bound him hand and foot,
And tied him to his son's cradle as a toy.
When he understood the power of Vali,
Ravana, humbly, begged for friendship with him.
His bonds were gone and their friendship grew; 150
Both, since then, became unquestioned tyrants
And harassed the world, endlessly.

'Anxiety was widespread;
Panic grew; shrieks and cries were always heard.
When I couldn't bear it, I fought with Vali;

But I got defeated, condemned for a living death;
My life, without my wife, lost its meaning.
Only you can understand my agony and suffering.

'They were autumnal nights. The moon was full;
And the gentle breeze of April, carrying the fragrance   160
Of flowers, brought with it my wife's memories,
And my spirit sank. Thus passed in succession
Days and nights, months and years;
My suffering seemed endless. I survived, only
With the hope of better days. My tears have dried up.
Now, with your arrival, the creeper of my desire
Has put on new leaves.

'Bitter words he spoke;
Chased me out of my kingdom, Ruma is a captive,
And threw all of my friends into dark dungeons.   170
These four alone including Hanuma are with me,
They have cared for me with love, and a part of me
They are. They have an equal share in my misery.
They stand if I stand, they sit when I sit;
And if I weep, they also shed profuse tears.
You are my refuge, now; there is none but you.

'The path to vanquish Vali is hard and painful,
To free Ruma is, by no means, easy and simple.
But I am unconcerned, as I have surrendered to you;
And you have to protect me, I seek shelter in you.   180
I am alive now, breathing through your body.'

Canto Ninety-five

'The Vanara Army is Very Impressive'

||☉||

Touched deep with the misery of Sugriva,
'Tell me, Sugriva, the reason for your enmity,
And thus help me to decide what is *dharma*.
The tale of your misfortune and suffering
Has inflamed me. My heart is shaken and
My patience ended. Recount the story quickly,
And I will kill him,' – thus spoke Shri Rama,
In a stern but soothing voice.

'Listen, then, Shri Rama,' recounted Sugriva;
'My elder brother was valiant, and hence, our father 10
Loved him dearly; I admired and respected him.
After the death of father, Vali succeeded him
As the ruler of Kishkindha.

'Once, due to the enmity with Mayavi,
The son of Dundhubi, a *rakshasa*, a terrible war
Was waged. Mayavi, stood in the portals
Of Kishkindha and, insolently, challenged Vali.
It was a dark night; and, taken by surprise,
Vali got up, and, hissing like an enraged python,
Got ready to rush at his enemy. 20

'But then, Tara, my sister-in-law,
Stopped him and counselled: "Sir, what is the hurry?
It is not advisable to fight at night; better
Wait for the dawn to break and then enter
The battlefield. The fight is going to be hard,
And my heart forebodes untoward ills."
But unheeding her advice, my brother Vali,
Courageous like the Sahyadri Mountain, dashed
Seeking his enemy.

'I was with him for his support. 30
When we faced the *rakshasa*, he panicked and ran;
And we pursued him, in darkness, relentlessly.
With spirit in our hearts, and strength in our legs,
We followed him on a path, dim and confusing.
When the moon came out again, we pressed hard.
The *rakshasa*, an expert conjurer, dashed speedily,
And escaped into a cave.

'Vali, looking terrible in anger, ordered me:
"My brother, Sugriva, guard the cave-mouth;
I will go in, beat the enemy to pulp and return. 40
If I don't return, presume that I am dead; and,
Closing the cave-mouth, go and reign supreme."

'I desisted him in his pursuit and pleaded:
"Elder brother, why have you to enter this cave?
The passage is arduous and the *rakshasa* cruel;
If he gets the better of you, Kishkindha
Will be orphaned. Permit me; I shall go in
And fight this *rakshasa*."

'But, stroking my back lovingly, Vali said:
"No, I will not sacrifice my brother. You cannot 50
Understand the demonic tricks he may play in
The cave. The demon may not be alone there;
And you are yet to learn the ways of fighting

Inside a cave. But I am fully conversant
With the tricks and stratagems of *rakshasas*.

'"I shall confront him inside the cave;
If his followers come, you stop them here,
Engage them in fight, and destroy them.
Guard this cave-mouth for six months, and,
If I don't return, go back and accept the kingship. 60
Supposing both of us enter the cave, and
Fighting the demon both of us lose our lives,
The *vanara* kingdom will cease to exist.
Now, Kishkindha, totally independent,
Flourishes, an island among many kingdoms;
The *vanara* force is famed as all-conquering.
The onus is on you, now, to preserve this fame.
Forget your love for me; it is childish;
Cultivate love for the country, and engage
Yourself in the defence of our motherland. 70

'"Protect with love
My wife Tara and my dear son Angada.
This is my order; swear on our father and me
Not to violate it. There are many tasks ahead,
And many victories; don't be hasty and await me,"
So said he, determined.

'What could I do? Whom could I consult?
I carried out my brother's orders and sat there,
Guarding the entrance. It wasn't easy. Waiting
For him was more painful than death. Days passed 80
Into weeks and weeks to months, and thus
Six months passed, and Vali had not returned.
I suffered in anxiety and fear. Though I could
Espy no sign of his coming back from the cave,
With the fond hope that he would surely return,
I still waited and continued to wait for him.
My anxiety, growing like a huge tree, cracked

The earth with its roots; and I had limited force
With me.

'In the meanwhile, there in Kishkindha,   90
Lack of knowledge about the whereabouts
Of the king and his brother, bred dark clouds
Of lawlessness. Scholars and ministers,
Relatives, queens, and citizens – all, terror-struck,
Spent their days staring at the sky, vacantly.
When the spies brought the news that the army
Was considering a quick coup, and the fear of
Neighbouring states invading the kingdom was rife,
I began to ponder over the situation, gravely.

'Thus six months and two more were spent,   100
When, one day, the demon's terrible roar inside
The cave was heard; huge drums and trumpets
Were sounded, and in the wake of that noise,
Blood, hot and bubbling, streamed from the cave.
There was no sign of brother and his war-cries
Were also absent. The demon's bellowing
Broke my heart.

'There, in the capital,
The ministers, subjects, and women panicked.
Fearing that further waiting was in vain,   110
And that if we did, our enemies would capture
Our land, despite my pleadings to the contrary,
They closed the cave's mouth with a huge rock,
As if they were closing my heart.

'I sent my men in all directions to trace Vali,
In forests and caves, in towns and hamlets.
I got the crumbling fort repaired, and I
Vanquished the enemies covetous of our land.

'Then, I approached my sister-in-law, Tara,
And assured her: "Have no fear; having killed   120

All those *rakshasas*, Vali will certainly return.
His valour is incomparable. If he does not,
I shall go out myself and snatch him even from
The jaws of death. This is nothing new. You know,
He used to be away for days on a hunting trip.
It is impossible for anyone to defeat him."

'But there was no sign of him;
Dull days were followed by duller nights;
Even after many more months, he wasn't seen.
I was ruling as his deputy, and every one was passive.

'Again, I went to my sister-in-law:
"Listen, if we continue waiting for elder brother,
The whole administration will go awry.
Let us declare the child Angada as the king;
And you can rule as the regent, king's mother,"
I suggested to her in earnest.

'But my sister-in-law, Tara, disagreed:
"I have lost hopes of Vali's returning here;
I don't know if that's what fate has willed.
In Vali's absence, power doesn't interest me.
Tell me, is it that simple to rule a kingdom?
Angada is still a boy and he doesn't know much.
When you are the crown prince, is it proper
To bring Angada to the throne?

'"He is like a son to you, and he is your pupil.
He is going to learn how to rule from you.
O my brother-in-law, do you think Vali's soul
Will be happy if Angada is made the king?
Your brother deemed you his son and declared
You the crown prince; would you disobey him?"

'Worried, I said to her again:
"This is not right, mother. People with mean minds
Will gossip that I deceived an innocent queen.

In future, if Angada too does not see eye to eye
With me, our subjects will rise in rebellion."

'Then Tara said: "Sugriva, what you say is true.
Let the council of ministers approve your kingship;
My brother Tara will propose it and my father
Sushena will second it. Do you have any objections?"
Thus, they forced this position on me and said: 160
"You, the crown-prince have a right to kingship,
As approved by all codes." Then, they put the crown
On my unwilling head, and held coronation.

'Still, I ruled
In the name of my elder brother. But the throne
Became a bed of thorns, and many pushed me into
Some of the worst moments of my life. The fear
That the infamy of having cheated my brother
Might be hurled at me any time, singed me
Till I withered.' Thus Sugriva recounted to Rama 170
His sad past.

Canto Ninety-six

'Open the Doors of Knowledge for All'

||௬||

After Sugriva ascended the throne of Kishkindha,
The new policies he introduced, the new laws
He enforced, and the new projects he launched,
All that as he conveyed them to Shri Rama,
I will narrate here to the lovers of poetry.

Once, with his council of ministers, he voiced forth
His thoughts, thus: 'For Kishkindha to achieve
Progress, all men and women should get education.
When we have the great Guru Agastya and
His disciples, why should anyone lead a
Life of ignorance? If co-education is available
In Lanka, why should the women, denied of it
In Kishkindha, live in the cesspool of darkness
As parasites? None should be condemned
To dwell in an island of illiteracy. Everyone
Should be given education and military training.

'This is the new education policy, which offers to all
General education, training in sciences and
Military art. If all the ministers, officials, and their
Children get this new education, our country will

Progress; and the culture of Karnataka will be enriched.
This new education policy that I have charted,
Will make our country an ideal welfare state.

'Hanuma, Angada, Nila, Nala, Tara, and
Mainda will be responsible for implementation.
This Kishkindha kingdom will equal Ayodhya
In culture, and, with expertise in science and
Technical education, it will put Lanka to shame.
It will be a land of work-culture and it will
Transform itself into a modern nation, 30
Full of self-confidence; it will indeed open
A new chapter in history,' thus confided Sugriva.

But the minister called Kataksha intervened:
'My king, where are scholars, teachers, and experts,
Who have the competence to put all this into practice?'

'Don't be so pessimistic,' replied Sugriva:
'There are famous scholars and experts here.
Karnataka is blessed by both saints and scholars;
And, it is also a land of brave warriors.

'We have Sushena, a scholar in Ayurveda; 40
Nala and Nila are renowned in architecture.
In sculpture, our land is the testing ground,
And there are great epic poets and writers.
Can Hanuma, Angada and Jambavanta
Be equalled in valour? Also, this is the land
Where Hanuma and Shabari taught the path
Of *bhakti* to the whole world.

'The sages Agastya and Sutikshna are
Great scholars who have explicated *bhakti*
And knowledge, and continue to explore 50
That field. Given to prayers and meditation,
And imparting education to all, they have striven
To establish an egalitarian society.

'Build special cottages to the institution-heads.
This land of ours is the origin of formal education,
And curriculam of worldwide knowledge. In future,
Kishkindha will become the knowledge-capital of
Karnataka; it will be the tall Meru Mountain
In culture and the sacred ocean of arts. Have faith;
Our *vanaras* will all be experts in varied fields.' 60

In a mocking tone, Dhumra said: 'Pardon me,
King. If all *vanara* children go to school,
Who will toil in our gardens and fields?
If there are no ignorant masses, how will our
Households function? Alas! This culture
Of comfort, then, will crumble. If the *dasyus*
Rise and equal us, *dharma* will be violated.

'O King! You are building castles in the air.
Why do you attempt to break the fort built
By countless workers? Don't you know the adage 70
That "when a monkey moves in the garden of
A crazy mind, dogs and jackals eat away everything"?
Lawlessness will reign in Kishkindha.
Free your mind from the illusion that everyone
Can be a master. Unless there are subjects to sweat
And do menial jobs, ours will become an idle land.
Attempting to follow Lanka, people will go hungry.'

Sugriva smiled knowingly, and said:
'You have to understand that the world is
As we view it. Can anybody be a minister? 80
Of course, not. But all are human beings,
Not animals or birds living in caves and tree-tops.
They can understand the way the government
Functions, and they can judge. In fact, they are
The explorers of new paths the country has to tread.

'Vigilance is the shield of administration.
Education is not required only to run the state;

We need it to run a family as well.
Can the *vanara* community, isolated,
Live like an island, cut off from the rest? 90
If we desire to wipe out ignorance from our minds,
And to free ourselves from the chains of bondage,
We have to, first, examine our own hearts.

'What is salvation? It is to plunge into the ocean
Of our consciousness and expand it. Scholars
Are those that have toiled hard for it, devoted.
An institution-head earns his position by hard work.
The sage Sharabhanga, like Matanga, though
Of the hunter's tribe, has devoted his life
To austere studies, and has earned his position 100
Only by his scholarship. Listen! Incessant
Labour is the highway of Great Quest.'

'If wisdom is got only through meditation, what
Other means are there to reinforce it?,' queried Hanuma.

'Good that you asked me this question.
There are many ways to supplement this path.
These are my orders to be enforced strictly:
Immediately, close down all bars, houses
Of prostitution, and gambling centres. 120
All these should come under the police control;
Remove all the roots of crime and throw them out,'
Sugriva spoke firmly.

Darimukha, another minister, burst out,
Boiling with rage: 'Don't be hasty, my king.
Better to discuss these in a cabinet meeting.
If you try to cut down the tree of corruption in a hurry,
While falling, it may crush you to the ground.'

'Give up I will not,' retorted Sugriva,
'I will root it out, I am not afraid of death. 130
My final goal is the happiness of people.

Even a king cannot afford to forget
The common people and their welfare.

'When Vali was the king, what was his wont
If his orders were disobeyed? They would be
Caught and thrown into dungeons. I warn you,
These are royal orders, not to be violated.'

Subdued, Darimukha said again:
'O King! Weigh the pros and cons of this policy.
If there is no prostitution, adultery will flourish   140
In every house; if bars are closed, each house
Will be a bar; and poisonous liquor will flow
On all streets and roads.

'If you prohibit gambling, every home
Will turn into a gambling den. Also, the state
Exchequer will lose huge revenue, coming from
Liquor and gambling now. And, without any
Amusement and relief, people's lives will be dull.'

'I am amused by your words,' said Sugriva,
'Liquor, prostitution, and gambling houses   150
Destroy people; they spread crime and diseases,
Exploitation and violence, and, finally, unrest.
Do we need the money got through such means?
In our attempts to build a new society,
A new order, we must focus on work-culture.
Like the Sun-god, I, of the Sun-dynasty,
Will dispel darkness and all social evils.
I shall dispense justice with an even hand.
Life is to live together, full of understanding;
It is death if one lives destroying others.'   160
With these words, he ended his meeting.

When Ruma came to know of the decisions
Of the council, she told Sugriva, in a tone of
Mixed joy and anxiety: 'You are attempting

To cleanse Kishkindha of all evils and vices.
But, in the process, putting an end to the selfish
Luxury and comforts of the powerful rich,
You will antagonise them. They will hate you
And oppose you in every manner. Those lustful
Animals, who exploit the innocent women,   170
Will revolt and destroy your mental peace.'

Angada intervened:
'What step-mother fears is true. Vested interests
Will certainly plot against you. Before they do so,
Unless we empower common people, disaster
Will fall on the kingdom; the royal umbrella,
Alas, will break and fall down.'

Hanuma, the minister, viewed all the others
And spoke grimly: 'O King! Listen to my proposal.
Let us formulate a new economic policy. Unless   180
We do so, the wheel of transformation won't roll;
And people's power can't be geared toward the new order.'

'I shall at once come up with a new economic
Policy; and it will eventually nourish culture
During transition,' declared Sugriva agitated.
All were relieved and happy.

Later, while Sugriva lay on his couch, thoughtful,
Ruma, his wife, approached him; stroked him gently,
And said: 'My dear! When you know your path is right,
Why do you worry? The burden on your head is bound   190
To be heavy. Authority is a huge tree, on which
Parasitical creepers have grown and flourished.
Uprooted, while falling, it will surely destroy
All those surrounding it. You can't achieve much
Through minor changes. Why this fear? This worry?
Move on with courage on your chosen path,
Full of challenge and determination.'

Canto Ninety-seven

'I Will Build a New Society, Free from Exploitation'

||६||

As days of Sugriva's reign rolled on, once,
In the council meeting, Hanuma begged for
Permission to report: 'Sir, our academies
Are empty. They lack students though there are
Teachers and all other facilities needed for study.
Rich students are unwilling to study together
With those from poor families; and the poor ones,
Out of ignorance or carelessness, do not study.

'Lanka, the land of pleasure-culture, is very near;
And the rich young men go there, drawn by its gold.   10
They study there and then return to rule here.
Thus, the *dasyu* class is on the increase, sir,
Causing a huge divide. How will you solve this?'

'Why should our institutions be ignored?
Why this division on the lines of workers and
Masters in our *vanara* community? I will not
Rest till I end such exploitation of our children.
Listen! I will immediately issue an order

Prohibiting study in foreign countries. When we
Provide good education in our own country,   20
Why do we need Lankan education, inimical
To our national culture. Stop this whispering
And murmuring, and state your views boldly.
Be frank and honest,' said Sugriva.

Then Durmukha stood up boldly, and said:
'O King! This education policy is oppressive.
Why should we make it a rule that every one
Should study only in Kishkindha? This way, Sir,
You will push everyone into the well of darkness.
Those who can afford will send their wards   30
To study the courses they choose in Lanka.
If you ban such choices, we will stagnate
And our subjects will become dumb sheep.
If freedom is curtailed, there will be unrest.'

'I will never accept it,' replied Sugriva sternly,
'The kind of education acquired in other countries
Destroys national morality. That education,
Which teaches one hierarchical inequality,
Which breeds contempt for labour and vanity,
Which gives birth to an acquisitive society –   40
I refuse to approve such education.

'Those who study abroad and return home,
Lead a life of vainglorious luxury and comfort,
And supersede meritorious people, ruthlessly.
I consider them, though of *vanara* clan, aliens;
And, it is for their own good that I speak thus,'
Said Sugriva, full of love for his land.

When he inquired why poor children
Did not attend schools, Hanuma said gravely:
'Some of the boys work in fields and gardens,   50
And some labour hard in back-breaking mines.

Girls, on their part, do menial household chores
In wealthy homes, and thus spend painful lives.
Being strangers to the ways of acquiring money,
And struggling hard only to eke out a living,
They discard slates and pencils as not for them.
With no hopes for future, helpless, they just exist.

'But, you needn't despair, sir;
I have thought of ways to remedy their misery.
Let's open residential schools, everywhere. 60
The pupils, assured of food and shelter there,
Will assuredly get the education they need,
And, hence, Kishkindha-culture will be nurtured.
Once, boys and girls are trained in vocations like
Basket-making, cloth-weaving, tending cattle-ranches
And horse-studs, farming and agriculture, they will become
Self-sufficient, ready to lead a prosperous and happy life.
A part of their earning in these tasks, we can send
To their parents, and thus they will also be happy.'

Sugriva, pleased with Hanuma's plans, said 70
In approval: 'Yes, we shall certainly do as you suggest,
In the field of education; and thus open a new era.'

Just then, before they could disperse, Tara said:
'Please permit me to speak about a grave matter.
In Kishkindha, the *rakshasas* are dumping ornaments
And clothes, manufactured in the *yaksha* land.
Hence, there is a shortage of rice and food grains,
And the prices of all these are on increase.

'The middlemen are thriving on huge profits,
While the poor, unable to buy these food grains, 80
Are suffering in hunger; and quite a few, eating
Poisonous seeds for want of food, have died.
It is the Trade Pact between Lanka and our land,
It is the policy of unequal export and import,
That has shattered our system and bred suffering.

'The crops grown in wet and dry fields
Go to the rich owners; and the landless
Farmers are denied the fruit of their labour.
Our vassals, army generals, and those
That have inherited huge wealth, entering 90
Into a secret pact with the *rakshasas* and *yakshas,*
Have developed vast businesses and trade.
Unwilling to contribute to the state coffers,
They just hoard wealth, and get richer and richer.
The poor labour and the rich reap the fruits;
It is like the very fence destroying the field it is
Supposed to protect. Power of money, men,
And muscle – lies concentrated only in them.'

Sugriva was enraged:
'I will now destroy all their power and arrogance. 100
Let everyone know that these are Sugriva's orders:
I will build a new state freed from exploitation;
The tiller of the land is its owner; all will share equally;
Those who export luxury goods to other states
Will need a special license from the government;
And the exchange will have to guard state interests.
This is the law, and whoever transgresses it
Will be sentenced to death.' When these laws
Were framed, all the common people rejoiced.

As days passed thus, once, an intelligence 110
Report reached Sugriva and disturbed him.
'A *rakshasa* possessing magical powers,' the report said,
'Had killed Vali and discarded his body on the war-field;
Heeding this moment as opportune, the enemy forces
Were getting ready to invade and occupy Kishkindha.
The army being resentful of Sugriva's harsh orders,
Leaders are ready to bring down the Sugriva-tower.
The entire *vanara* force is about to crumble,
And Vali's kingdom has developed cracks.'

The news of Vali's death spread, 120
And all the citizens and servants began to gossip:
'Is it true that Vali is dead or is it a wicked trick
Played by Sugriva, in order to hide truth from us?
Who can believe that Vali's body has disappeared?
He, who had defeated Ravana and humbled him,
How can such a brave man die like a nameless person,
Unrecognised, alone and helpless?'

Reminiscing his childhood days, Sugriva grieved:
'We grew up together and played together. Whenever,
Getting defeated, I pouted and shrieked that I had won, 130
Declaring that I had truly won, he consoled me,
And guided me with love. How can I forget him?
How could his valour decline, leaving him
To die like an orphan in a dark cave?

'Could it be really true that he is dead?
Or, is he, firm and resolute, wandering
In valleys and caverns, fighting the demon?'

The new measures introduced by Sugriva,
Had yielded only mixed results. The rich businessmen,
Feudatories, ministers, and army commanders, 140
All had become selfish, oblivious to people's welfare.
The poor, as in the past, were given to mute suffering,
Their passive emotions finding no legitimate outlet.
Alas! Patriotism had almost become extinct.

It takes, indeed, ages and ages
For the people to awaken to new realities.
People dream of future for a world non-existent today;
And they yearn for an impossible future world –
Thus we find flights of fancy in an illusory sky.
Sugriva, now, is only a figurehead as a king; 150
And none else shares his concerns and ideals.

The hungry, forsaking their ancestral homes
In villages and towns, come to this city-hell, seeking
Food and shelter. They live in old forts and fords,
And eke out a life of animals; they feed on garbage
And leftovers, and lead a miserable life. The splendour
Of Kishkindha now is akin to a city of illusions.
Joining hands with the *rakshasas* and *yakshas*,
The rich buy and sell land at exorbitant prices, and
Collect huge profits. Powerless to buy land, the poor,   160
Continue to exist and suffer, in silence.

If a few poor ones, occasionally, raise their voice
And protest, their poor dwellings are reduced to ashes;
And they are beaten up, ruthlessly. In this devil-dance,
All the royal edicts and laws are ignored and forgotten.

Sugriva mused ruefully:
'The awakening that I caused among all, how did it
Die out so quickly? The golden dawn, why did it
Lose its light so soon? Why did the laws to ameliorate
The marginalised fall dead in the vale of time?   170
How could the flag of justice be brought down to dust?'

Sugriva summoned an urgent meeting and said:
'Fellow citizens of the *vanara* clan, listen to me.
If we live at the cost of another's life, it is not "living";
It is only "nature" if we live, preyed by lust and avarice;
It becomes "culture" when we co-exist, full of understanding.
It is nature to be plagued by anger and enemity;
It is culture to be guided by reason and justice.
It is nature if a tiger lives, feeding upon a cow;
It is culture if the tiger admires the cow's truthfulness.   180
Nature makes the cow wallow in its domestic troubles,
Culture makes the tiger sympathise with the cow.
It is such culture that enlightens a civilised society.

'I am aware of the condition of our forts and fords;
And I know that our land's peace is disturbed.
Now it is for us all to analyse and discover
What has gone wrong with our defence measures;
And those that break our laws will surely be punished.

'Agitated people's grievance has exploded.
How long will the weak meekly suffer injustice!   190
Be it in the peace-meet or the warfield,
I will destroy the arrogance of those vain groups.
I will stamp out the wicked that kill our spirits,
And I will build shelters for the homeless refugees.
When the innocent are meted out pain and death,
They will surely arise and surge ahead, determined.
Why should we put out the sparks of revolution?
And, why should we allow the wealthy to build
Palaces, violating the spirit of justice?

'The poor are exploited everywhere: 200
They are there, to labour in fields and farms;
They are there, to lose their lives on the war-front.
Now, they have arisen out of their age-old silence;
Should we become, deaf and blind to the cry of the age?
Now it is a spark, but very soon it will be a huge fire;
And when that agony of so many ages turns into a volcano,
To remain unconcerned is only foolishness.
We have to give an equal share to all those
Who toil in war and peace, in life and death.
If they also want to build good houses for themselves,   210
It is fine. Enough of cheating them with lies.'

Listening to the words of Sugriva,
Impatient and angry, Durmukha burst out:
'Who stops them, O King, and who opposes them?
Why houses? Let them build heavenly palaces;
Let them pay and buy whatever land they fancy;
And let them sit on high thrones and preen themselves.

But, if they encroach on our ancestral lands,
We will oppose them, like hard rocks, with
All our might.'   220
Sugriva noticed the cruel sarcasm carved
On the face of Durmukha, and said testily:
'They have no money, and you say, "let them earn";
This is the *vanara* kingdom. Do you know
Where the wealth has come from? The whole land
Belongs to the kingdom and there is nothing
Like "yours" and "mine". We have to create
Opportunities for all to work and earn money.
The process of tax-collection has to be simplified
And attack on human rights has to be ended.   230
The kind of dictatorship prevailing in Lanka,
Which curtails individual freedom, I will not tolerate here.
There is no place for vested interests and their games.
This land of Karnataka is a holy land; and
No one should wish for unequal power and rights?

'Should the ministers and other privileged people
Hoard all the wealth of this country? Distribution
Of that wealth among the poor is what *dharma* dictates.
Thereby, we will return what justly belongs to them.
Exploitation and arrogance won't be tolerated   240
For long; and when the revolution explodes,
None of you will survive its force and horror,
And the common people will usher in a new age.'

Hiding his anger and feigning tolerance,
Kataksha asked: 'What is your plan, O king?
In the place of rich edifices, do you desire
To construct dirty huts and cottages?'

'Dirty huts? On the contrary, I will issue orders
Not to bring down existing structures and
Not to do anything to spoil beautiful parks,   250
And to build suitable two-storeyed houses

Only on vacant land, wherever it is available.
I will extend the "Healthy Home" scheme
For the common people of Kishkindha,
And establish the principle of "live and let live".'

'Those *vanaras*, who are used to living
In tree hollows and shoots, in nooks and niches,
How can they understand what a house is?
All of your projects are merely day-dreams.
Again, to build houses for all, do we have enough   260
Resources? This is not Golden Lanka,' responded
Kataksha, contemptuously.

Then Hanuma intervened, breaking his silence:
'Why rake up the question of resources now?
It is not a question having no answer. Do all the generals,
Ministers, and their attendants own the land, water,
And wealth of this country? They belong to the people.'
'Now you have the answer,' said Sugriva, relieved.
But, the faces of the nobles there were etched
With worry and despair.   270

Canto Ninety-eight

'Once Rage Subsides, Joy will be There'

||௬||

'A few months passed by, and then, O Shri Rama,
One night, Vali appeared before us, suddenly.
I was, at that time, engaged in consultations
With Tara, my sister-in-law, regarding state-matters.

'Vali rushed in,
Banging the doors, in uncontrollable rage,
Nursing all kinds of untoward thoughts,
And his red eyes emitting sparks of fire.
"Are you plotting against me, together with my wife?"—
He roared, casting a killing glance at me, and, 10
Harbouring suspicions about Tara's fidelity,
He fell upon me, with an intent to kill me.
Disturbed and hurt, I fell on his feet, and
Stretched my arms to embrace him.

'"Get out, I know your affection.
Getting me killed treacherously, you planned
To ascend the throne, didn't you, rogue?
I will chop off your tail and break your jaws,"
So saying, he leapt on me like a tiger.

'Trembling with fear, I tried to explain: 20
"I bless my stars that I see you again, my brother,
Listen to me. No need to lose your patience.
I am your liegeman and I will humbly serve you.
Why do you suspect me and sister-in-law?
I stood, near the cave-door, waiting for you,
For a whole year, without food and sleep.
But when you didn't come out, the demon's
Roar was heard, and blood streamed out,
All the ministers, presuming that you were dead,
Forced me to shut the cave door against the *rakshasa*. 30
Despite my pleadings to the contrary, they put me
On the throne. I have no desire or ambition
To rule. I am ruling now only as your agent.
Now that you have destroyed the enemy,
The throne is yours; I beg you to accept it.
You have brought me up like a father, and now
Show me the same love and trust. You are,
Indeed, a mine of generosity."

'But he was adamant. "You are not to be trusted,"
He said and continued angrily, "You feign love 40
Outwardly; but at heart you nurse hatred.
I wandered, aimlessly, in that spacious cave.
It was a colourful world and lacked nothing.
I forgot everything and thus years rolled on.
Then, one day, my kingdom flashed in my mind,
And, remembering everything, I returned,
Dragging Dundubhi's body to the cave-entrance.
It was only a skeleton, without any flesh anywhere.
When I saw the rock, barring exit, my heart also
Turned into a stone. I kicked the rock to pieces, 50
I came out; thrilling it was to set foot on my homeland.

'"But you turned out to be a knave.
I will cut you to pieces and throw them to jackals;
I will hang you from a tall post, and then, your body,

Tied to the chariot, will be drawn by asses
Through all the streets, violently. If he can,
Let Yama, the God of Death, come down to save you.
Catching hold of his black robes, I will punch his face."

'Hearing these angry and hateful words, frightened,
I left the palace, immediately, and ran out. 60
I took to my heels like a coward, and since then,
I am leading a life of death.

'Had I fought with my elder brother, either
I would have defeated him or met a courageous
Death. But brotherly love held me back; and hence,
I have to lead throughout a life of infamy.
Hoping that once he comes to know the truth, his anger
Will subside and that he will accept me
As his brother, I am here in hiding.

'I am tired of endless wandering 70
Through forests, hills and rivers, I have wandered
Everywhere. There is no hill I haven't climbed,
No river I haven't crossed, and no people
I haven't met. My feet have measured the length
And breadth of our country. I am a tramp now.
How can I forget, O Lord, those ecstatic moments
I spent with Ruma and my yearning for her?

'All alone in forests,
I used to be scared of my own shadow.
As months passed by, I was a living corpse, 80
And I couldn't recognise myself in the mirror.
My dreams have dried up now, leaving no traces,
And I have sought refuge in this Rushyamuka.
I am counting days and months, wondering
Who will come to my succour and save me.'

'Why did you choose to seek refuge
In Rushyamuka? I am just curious,'
Saumitri, the son of Sumitra, asked him.

'It is good that you asked me,' said Sugriva,
'Listen. Vali is a strong man – he is so strong that
During the period between sunrise and sunset,
He can touch both the eastern and the western oceans.
He can break the tall forest trees with his bare hands,
And, from mountain-tops, he can jump down.

'Once, the *rakshasa* Dundhubi, bestowed with
The strength of an elephant, used to enter hermitages,
And harass the hermits there; he would attack
Hunters and other forest-dwellers. Vainglorious,
He believed that none could equal him in strength.

'Once, a hermit told him: "Why do you fight
With unequal people? It doesn't behove you.
There lives in Kishkindha, one Vali, the king
Of *vanaras*; and, radiant as the king of gods,
He is an expert in wrestling. You should fight
With him and prove your strength."

'Hearing those words, Dundubhi set out at once,
And, rushing like a wild bison, he reached Kishkindha.
Standing on the outskirts of the city, he roared
A deafening challenge to Vali. Provoked,
Vali rushed out and faced the *rakshasa* with fury.
And a royal battle ensued between the two.

'Dundubhi, accounting for the soldiers easily,
Stood before Vali and roared; Vali, drawing himself
To the full, and measuring the *rakshasa's* strength
Like a trained hunter, said to himself: "He equals
Me in both age and physique. Let me show him
What I am," and fell on him like a thunderbolt.

'Dundubhi, with equal rage and force,
Hissing like a huge cobra, dashed against Vali
With the intent of throwing him down. But Vali
Dodged his thrust and raised his fist to punch

And break open his head; but Dundubhi ducked
The punch. Thus they fought a terrible battle,
Like two intoxicated bulls butting each other,
As if both were figures of fire, or sharp arrows
Sparkling, exchanging blow for blow.
Dundubhi, unable to bear the crushing blows,
Staggering, jumping to evade the blows, ran
For his life to a distant jungle.

'Once Dundubhi entered the forest, there isn't much   130
To recount. After a prolonged fight, finally,
The matchless Vali killed the *rakshasa*, Dundubhi.
Then, he lifted his lifeless body, whirled it round,
And flung it far; the body fell in the hermitage
Of the great sage, Matanga, in Rushyamuka.

'All the bones in the demon's body, broken,
Were scattered there, turning the holy place unholy.

'There, Vali beheld a huge herd of elephants,
Stamping the ground and trumpeting loudly,
Coming down the slope of the Rushyamuka hill,   140
As if to wipe him out of the earth. Scared,
Vali left the place and returned to Kishkindha.

'The venerable sage, Matanga saw the dead body,
And flew into a rage. Coming to know that it was
Vali's deed, he cursed Vali thus: "How could anyone
Foul this holy place by his barbaric doings?
If such a wicked person steps into this place
Again, may he die at once, vomiting blood.
This is my curse and it will never fail."

'Listen, Saumitri; this is the reason   150
Why, fearing the sage's curse, he won't come here;
And I am safe. This cave is hidden there, and
In front of it, lies the tank full of sweet water,
Hence a safe haven for me. But a strange place

This is – a pious man, sleeping, sees good dreams;
But an impious man gets only nightmares.
I am yet to see one who can defeat Vali;
But, owing to the sage's penance, this is
A strong fortress for me.'

Canto Ninety-nine

'The World's Illnesses Cured, Peace Reigned Supreme'

||௬||

Sugriva had a nagging doubt still;
He wasn't sure if Rama possessed all the necessary
Strength and skill to defeat Vali. Hence, he said:

'Pardon me, Rama, for these words.
Vali is the one who bound Ravana head and foot;
He is a world-conqueror, unmatched in warfare;
And Lanka shivers due to his valorous accounts.
Rama, you are my friend and I have no intent
Of testing your valour. On the contrary,
I am curious to witness your matchless strength. 10
If you can cut all those seven *sala* trees
With just a single arrow, I will be doubly assured.
Take out your sharp arrow; let it fly high.
After being repeatedly beaten, I am here in hiding,
Scared of Vali's cruelty. Your soothing words
Have kindled in me the desire to see your strength.'

Listening to those words,
Saumitri flared up: 'O, Sugriva! Stop this blabber.

I am patient only because you are Rama's friend,
Sworn so in the presence of fire; otherwise,
I would have slit your tongue and killed you
Horribly. How can you entertain doubts about
Rama? Don't demean yourself with such words.'
With these words, when Lakshmana took out an arrow
And moved forward, Rama stopped him and said:
'It doesn't become you to blame Sugriva, our friend.
He is overcome with fear and his spirits are low.
But once I display my skill and strength, he will
Surely banish his doubts and regain confidence.'

Then, Rama, took out a shaft,
Fixed it on his bow, and aiming it on the tree cluster,
Shot it. At once, the shaft flew, swift and whistling,
And cut all the trees. Bewildered with such an act,
The *vanaras*, along with Sugriva, hailed Rama's
Achievement, and bowed to him respectfully.

After having hit its mark, the shaft,
With the same speed, returned to Rama's scabbard.
Rama's bowmanship had pleased one and all.
As though it had traversed the whole universe,
As though it had destroyed the whole demon-clan,
It lay in the scabbard, quietly, like a swan.
It looked as if the inert matter had come to life,
And, then, resolved to reach its holy objective,
It had explored in all the directions, and then,
Gaining wisdom, it had returned to its master.

Can anybody rival Rama?
As the sunrays dispel the world's darkness,
And provide every being health and happiness,
Rama, who struck seven trees down with a single arrow,
He who had earlier broken the bow of Shiva and
Enlivened everyone's heart, he will kill Vali,
And Vali will fall like the seven *sala* trees –

With such thoughts drifting through his mind,
Free from all fears and doubts, and sure of victory,
Sugriva told Rama:

'Pardon me, Rama.
You are the delight of all eyes; you are full
Of love for your devotees; you fulfil the needs
Of all those who come seeking you. You are
The heartthrob of Lakshmi and you have made   60
The souls of sages and hermits your holy home.
It isn't that I had any doubts about your valour,
I greatly yearned to witness your brave deeds.
Now, there is neither fear nor any doubt in my mind;
All sorrow and despair have vanished into thin air.
I will swim, henceforth, in the lake of devotion to Rama,
And I will carry out all my master's tasks, faithfully.
You are the greatest warrior, and who can stand
Face to face with you on the battlefield?'

Shri Rama answered majestically, like thunder: 70
'Be not frightened, be not hesitant;
I will destroy Vali and protect the code of *dharma*;
It is the duty of a king.'

Shri Rama shone, at that moment,
Like the arc of the sun, rising in the east;
He shone, then, as the ocean of good fortune.
Being rid of all ills, the enchanting earth,
Gleamed then, suffused with new radiance.

Then, Sugriva got up and proclaimed:
'I will go now to the city of Kishkindha,   80
And I will provoke Vali immediately.
I will challenge him, who equals Indra's son,
For a battle; he who defeated Ravana, I will
Challenge him.' With these words, he left
Without any delay, for Kishkindha.

Like an enraged elephant in rut,
Stamping the ground heavily, Sugriva roared,
Hearing which Kishkindha trembled and the sky echoed:
'Come, come out Vali; I will not leave you alone;
Get ready to battle or surrender to me.'   90
At once, adding force to his challenge, the trumpets
Blared, and all the four corners echoed them.
The city cowered as if there was an earthquake;
The mountain-tops quivered; and, shrieking in panic,
Animals fled and birds flew helter-skelter.

Vali heard it.
That ear-splitting and heart-breaking roar he heard,
And, immediately, with the valour of a lion,
The vengeful anger of a serpent, and
The majesty of an elephant, he reached   100
The battle-ground. Burning with anger,
Like the death at the end of the world,
Like the wild forest fire with its bloody tongue
Outstretched, ready to consume everything,
Vali rushed forth to assault.

Then ensued a wrestling bout between the two.
Like two huge black clouds clashing with each other,
Trembling with anger, roaring with resentment,
They clashed, pounded, parried, and struck each other.

When both of them, equal in strength,   110
Extended their arms, and battered each other's head,
It appeared as if the planets were in fierce fray,
As if gods and *rakshasas* clashed with each other.

While they fought intent to kill each other,
Neither could get the better of the other; so equal
Were they in strength and skill. While Rama
And Hanuma watched them silently, Hanuma's
Eyes were tearful. Casting his glance once at the sky,

And once at his king, heaving a deep sigh, Hanuma
Approached Rama and bathed his feet with his tears. 120
Rama was in a dilemma: should he hide himself
And kill Vali like a thief? Would it be proper?
It was a grave matter of what is right and wrong.

He thought of Janaki, the daughter of Janaka,
And said to himself: 'I am caught in a web of
Confusion; without your counsel, I am powerless.

'Behold them, Saumitri; both of them,
Like black clouds, whirlwinds, and raging fires,
Are engaged in a war of death; and, caught
In a dilemma of right and wrong, I am sitting helpless. 130
My eyes are dim and I cannot take up arms.'
With these words, Shri Rama plunged into silence.

Canto One Hundred

'Egalitarian Culture of the New Millennium'

||6||

Shri Rama, with downcast eyes and depressed,
Looked at Lakshmana and confided in him: 'O brother!
I am confused; how can I shoot the arrow in this state?
Those two look alike, they are fighting an equal war;
I am unable to distinguish Vali from Sugriva.

'My mind is full of conflicting ideas. Killing Vali
Will be a beastly act, an act of cowardice and one fit
Only for a butcher. It doesn't become a king; and
If he does such a sinful act, he will perish losing
His kingdom.'   10

The son of Sumitra understood
The conflict-ridden mind of Rama and said:
'O lord! Do not falter on the road of righteous action.
Your closed eye-lids also cover a vision dimmed;
In your un-opened ears, there is a drum-beat unheard.
Remember, spiritual strength is greater than physical.
When you have lost peace of mind and will-power,

When the smiling mask outside hides an anguished heart,
You have to harmonise your inner and outer self, and
Put an end to all of your conflicts.

'You being the Creator, who else but you
Can save men and matter from vices and crimes?
Who else but you can lead them towards light?
You have to come out of this state like the winter sun.

'When one gets power and authority from people,
If one fails in his duty, one loses that support of people;
And the fountain of people's love will dry up.

'When invaders attack a land,
To gather together soldiers and ready a strong army,
To strengthen all forts and fortresses, and to store
Necessary food-grains and drinking water, and such
And to make them easily available for both the soldier
And citizen: when these duties are carried out properly,
The invading enemy will lose his heart and run away.

'Shri Rama,
Why do you suffer this conflict of right and wrong?
Why this fear? You are the one to cleanse the sins of all.
Hear the call of the duty of a Kshatriya and awake.
Don't fall into a whirlpool of eternal infamy;
And, don't choose the path worse than death.
Take up your bow and arrows; get ready for the fight.
Let the outcome be happiness or pain, or even death;
Let the valley of profit and loss stare at you;
Let the pit of fire, of victory and defeat, leap up;
Ignore them and get ready for the battle.

'Some rulers, in their religious fanaticism,
Destroy the peace of all; and some, thirsty to extend
Their empire, lead to death and destruction.
Vali is one such; he has utilised all his strength
To spread violence. Does one become a great king

Vanquishing weaker kings? Having lost his balance,
And submerged in evil designs, he is vainglorious.
Could such a one, an enemy to the world, be a king?

'When barbaric rulers get ready for war,
The evolution of a new world gets jeopardised;
And the progressive king becomes all alone,
Standing on the summit of change, imperilled.

'O Shri Rama! You are all-knowing!
You are not the one to be taught these lessons.
Give up the easy path and tread the difficult one;   60
Forsake the world of rest and choose one of action.
Remember the initiation given by the noble sages,
Vishwamitra and Agastya, and march ahead.'

Having listened to Saumitri's words,
Breaking his stony silence, Shri Rama answered:
'Being well-versed in economics, when one treads
The moral and altruistic path, if one faces problems,
Should one, intent on safeguarding one's power
And position, take recourse to intrigues to survive?
If one, in the pretext of political strategy, accepts   70
The principles of animal-world, gives up human
Values under the excuse of fate and destiny,
Chooses the path of war, and goes astray,
One ceases to be human; he will be no different
From a wild beast, and will be destroyed in the end.
How do we protect *dharma* in an immoral world?
Is it proper for us to sow the seeds of *adharma*?'

Saumitri pleaded:
'O Rama! Don't forget the spirit of the age to come.
The king, knowing full-well the complexities   80
Of right and wrong, should control the vainglorious
With the fear of rod, and, to such needy people caught
Helpless in troubles, he should extend support and aid.
Such is the ethical code of conduct of a king.'

Canto One Hundred and One

'Only Through Strife does Life Become Meaningful'

||6||

'Use of force is but natural to cruel beasts;
The lion cannot break through the hunter's nets by itself;
And the wolf won't give up preying upon jackals.
Sympathy, proper expression, faith, honesty,
And loyalty – these five are the qualities that enrich all,
And the state marked by these will flourish in peace.
No king can rule under the shadows of intrigue.
A ruler should be diamond-hard towards enemies;
Passivity leads to the loss of authority.
One should identify and respect talent;   10
He should commend the assembly of scholars;
And he should applaud and help the virtuous –
Only such a one would be worthy of a minister's seat.
If, to the contrary, tempted by luxury, he ignores
The state-interests, he is doomed to be corrupt.

'A king, listen to me, brother,
Should keep flatterers and hangers-on at a distance;
Should reject hypocrites who concoct gossip,
And should listen to the advice of the good people.

Lest, caught up in the alluring pulls, he goes astray,
He should stand firm amidst temptations.
Averse to hypocritical games, he should strive,
To uplift the common people in the new system.

'O incarnation of Vishnu! Truthful Soul!
The naked dance of the *rakshasa*-power,
Is now shaking the world and ringing in the sky;
It is burying deep below the earth the poor,
Who, with no hope in their hearts, writhe in pain.
O Lord! Bring sunlight to the numberless
Young and green plants sporting new leaves.
O Lord! You should strive that new hopes sprout
And new desires send their roots deep in people's
Hearts.

'You are the one, O Lord, who could usher in
The new age full of new sights and new thoughts.
Today, idolatry is on the rise in order to grab power;
And all intellectual achievements are swept away
Through intrigue and plotting. It is your bounden
Duty to subdue beastly acts and thoughts.'

'In the past,' replied Shri Rama,
'Defeated in his endeavour to emancipate
The labourers from oppression, the Sage Sharabhanga
Had to end his life, voluntarily, in despair.
Now, when my mind is ridden with conflicts,
How can I follow truth if I kill Vali?

'When, following Sage Vishwamitra,
I left Saketa and reached the forest of Tataka,
I saw new horizons and beheld new visions.
But now, wherever I cast my eyes, I see only
White clouds, stone-heaps, and parched earth;
I see only piles and piles of old and white bones;
And the new horizon I once beheld has vanished.
How can I confront Vali and kill him deceitfully?'

Saumitri, aware of the conflict-ridden mind
Of Shri Rama, continued: 'You are the king of kings;
You are above reason and logic; what are you afraid of?
You are an abstraction; how can we measure you?
Be the founder of a New World and lead others to it;
Be the explorer of new paths and guide others on it.
Vali is doomed to die; why do you torment yourself?
Birth is an accident, but death is a certainty. 60
He is wicked, drowned deep in the well of sin;
He is but a burden to the earth, better that he dies.
When your goal is fixed, how can you betray doubts?
Now, is Vali a man of virtue and righteousness?
He exploits and torments those who are innocent.
If you leave him unharmed, won't he
Rush to Lanka and join hands with Ravana?
Then, within no time, there will be a blood-tide
That will sweep through Kishkindha; and
This country, Karnataka, will be wiped out 70
In the ensuing tragic massacre of men and women.
Be the charioteer of your own soul and proceed
On the narrow path of Quest.'

Still, Shri Rama was hesitant:
'Spying on others in forts and bastions, weaving
Intricate webs and waiting like a spider
For the poor flies that are tempted and trapped,
Appropriating all the achievements of good people
And enjoying the wealth hard-earned by others,
Defiling the youth of maidens, lustfully, 80
And flourishing in violence – if a ruler indulges
In all these, is there anything to be sought for?
It is like a fence itself eating up the whole field.

'Vali is such a ruler.
If he is killed, will the people applaud it?
Supposing all of them rebel and declare war,
And the cruel war touches all the *vanaras*,

How will I safeguard the values and morals?
To stop the growing menace of Lanka-culture,
If I accept the principle of invading the language, 90
Territory, and people of others, I will also be
Treading the path of suppression and hatred.
My heart sinks, my mind flinches from such a task.'

Lakshmana replied: 'It is true,
Freedom and peace are the twin principles
Bharata, our country, has preached and practiced.
But now, the whole edifice is crumbling due
To the folly of a few; and the whole society is afflicted
With cancer and bodily organs are rotting.
The king of Lanka and Vali, like huge spectres, 100
Are haunting our country. Arise, O Shri Rama,
And, destroying the roots of violence, establish
A healthy nation like the physician of gods.
The whole age awaits you.'

Tortured with doubts of right and wrong,
Shri Rama was still uneasy: 'If I have to kill Vali,
I have to declare war. In order to establish *dharma*,
Do we have to take the path of destruction?
If Vali shows deep devotion toward me, and if,
During war, he bows to me very humbly, 110
How can I, a guardian of my devotees, kill him?
Again, I have taken a vow before fire as my witness
That I will destroy him; hence, how can I save him?
Should I keep my vow or falsify my reputation?'

'You belong to the lineage of the sun.
Why do you limit yourself only to Ayodhya?
You have to fly high and wide, spreading your rays
All over the world, infusing new blood and energy.
Let the intellect, truthfulness and humane
Values blossom under your protecting hand. 120
How can you forget your vow for the new age?

'The time for the world's decline has been set,
And the black horse of total destruction is on the run;
Vali's death is the last act in this course of conflicts.
Strife and conflict are nature's laws, inviolable.
Why are you still wavering?

'Once, a farmer
In utter despair, complained to god:
"When the crops are full and ripe, why this endless rain?
If it is now burning sun, it is floods some other time;   130
And some times, it is fog that buries everything,
Besides worms and insects that eat up the crops.
You, god, have become an enemy of all."

'Having heard the farmer's words, god said:
"Don't get so angry; I will hand over nature to you,
And you can control it throughout the year.
You are the master and nature will obey your wishes;
Do whatever you want."

'The farmer was very happy.
He planned his work carefully, and with enthusiasm,   140
He ploughed the fields and planted seeds, and,
In course of time, rich crops danced in the sun.
But, alas, the crops did not contain any seeds.
"O God! What have you done? Why are the crops seedless?"
He inquired with god, in anguish.

'God smiled and said:
"The way you have farmed, how can you get good crops?
You have to have rain and storm and floods;
Cold fog has to set in and hot sun has to burn.
Otherwise, your plants will not develop seeds."   150

'That is why, Shri Rama, think it over.
If the fear of future death makes us weak today,
We cannot achieve anything significant and holy.
Only through strife does life become meaningful,

And it is strife that begets new energy.
Vali has to die and Sugriva has to win,
And, under the aegis of Ayodhya, Kishkindha
Has to prosper with Sugriva as the ruler.
This is the prologue for the future war against Lanka.

'Before Ravana brings together all of his   160
Neighbouring kings and erects an invincible army,
Before the *vanaras* build the great Lanka-bridge,
Put an end to Vali's reign and restore peace and order.
Demonstrate to the world your righteous acts,
And become a model of truth and culture.'

Weighed down by the moral dilemmas, Shri Rama sighed:
'The special army units to guard the king
And the allied armies are distrustful of the king.
If they lack patriotism, all our efforts will be in vain,
And they will cause untold harm during war,   170
As if the subjects have to pay for their king's faults.
I will not sow the seeds of destruction in Kishkindha.
Occupying one state after another, extending Ayodhya,
Instigating revolt in states, now here now there,
Should I erase the principle of "live and let live,"
Disturbing peace and destroying happiness?'

Canto One Hundred and Two

'Augment the Fruitfulness of this Ever Fertile Earth'

||৬||

Saumitri continued thus to persuade Rama:
'There lived Sakalashwa and his son Devapriya,
In Tataka forest. As the chieftains of wicked forces,
They, grown arrogant, harassed the sages and molested
Their wives and daughters. Have you forgotten them?
The Lankan culture, vain in its cerebral achievements,
Is destroying the democratic values of our country.
It was Vishwamitra, the great sage, who entrusted
The responsibility of establishing world-peace.
We have already freed Janasthana and   10
Standing on the Rushyamuka hill, we are ready
To march out, and save the rest of the world.

'This war, I know, "mother" Sita, Janaka's daughter,
Does not approve of. But, in our path of amelioration,
War has become inevitable, without an alternative.
This is but the first step in rebuilding the world;
This is the need and desire of the New Age.
Listen, you cannot help destroying Vali.

Otherwise, the innocent blood of the *vanaras*
Will mix with the river Tungabhadra, join the ocean 20
Of mankind, and pollute it horribly.

'The death of Vali is but the beginning
Of peace and comfort to come in future.
Don't throw away the clarion of world peace.
It will be a great service to the nation to crush
Wicked forces and hoist the flag of people's force.
Listen, this is the lighthouse leading to peace.
Don't tell me that the *vanara* king Vali
Cannot be an enemy of Saketa, and that you,
A man of high morals, won't kill one hiding. 30
If, in a country of blind people, he with one eye
Becomes the king, he cultivates cruelty,
Harasses people and pushes them to misery.
When Vali is an ally of the king of Lanka,
He deserves to be punished, have no doubts.
Good people like Hanuma, Nala, Nila,
And Jambava are with us. If ill-tempered and
Cruel people were to be with us, we would have been
Caught in whirls of anger and sunk to the bottom.
A life of failure will drive all to be thrown 40
To the ocean-bottom.'

Aware that his hard-hitting words
Touched Shri Rama's heart, Lakshmana continued:
'Listen, elder brother! Being always introspective,
And soul-searching, you have nothing to fear.
If you boldly face the crisis and engage yourself
In a one-to-one confrontation, all misgivings
Will disappear and the sky of your mind will be pure.
Like a satellite, man's mind will rise very high,
And then will settle down on a fixed spot. 50

'Don't you ever pause here and there;
Tired or pained, even when you are all alone,

Trusting the battle-ground and discarding rest,
Move, move forward, boldly move ahead.
What though the path is beset with danger,
What though the troubles are mountain high,
Move, move forward, boldly move ahead.
Maybe the land lying ahead is totally barren,
Maybe the whole world is in the womb of darkness,
Move, move forward, boldly move ahead. 60
Let the wind be blowing, carrying burnt ashes,
Let the desert be growing, swallowing all life,
Move, move forward, boldly move ahead.
Even if the boundless ocean, intoxicated,
Hurls gigantic waves of bubbling water,
Move, move forward, boldly move ahead.

'Why do you delay?
Himachala lies to the north and on its other side
Lies China; to the north-east Burma, and to the east
Bay of Bengal; the Indian Ocean to the south, and, 70
The Arabian Sea to the west – that land is called
Jambu Dwipa or Bharata. Traverse this land far
And wide, and rule in the mind of the whole nation.
You are not to waste yourself in the Rushyamuka.
Arise, O son of Dasharatha; and put an end to Vali.
You will succeed in your search for mother Sita.
Arise, O Hari, like fire hidden in water.
Setting the saddle on the chosen horses,
Enriching the fruitfulness of this fertile earth,
Cutting through the curtain of darkness, 80
Shedding light on the earth below and the sky above,
Become the sun, become the Narasimha,
O Shri Rama the radiant, continue your Great Quest.'

Canto One Hundred and Three

'Let Hanuma Put the Garland Around Your Neck'

॥૬॥

While the duel between Sugriva and Vali continued,
Sugriva, unable to fight further and hurt,
Blood gushing out and pain getting unbearable,
In despair, feeling that his trust in Shri Rama
Led him to this condition, approached Rama and said:
'I am taken in by your valour, O Raghava;
Do not continue to test my might and strength.
O Lord of Saketa! I have trusted only you;
My life depends on you, and my honour too.

'O ocean of compassion! Protect me.   10
I am drowned in the sea of my past deeds.
My hope that had sprouted trusting you has dried;
And the huge tree of asylum has fallen to the ground.
While I was hoping to get back my wife, Ruma,
I was only a toy for you to play with, O Lord;
I was only a means of entertainment for you, Lord.
I have now become a blind hawk that cannot
Enjoy the moonlight of the autumnal full moon.
What do I get blaming others?

'The bird,
That flies high near the sky and sings in joy,
Is all alone. Why do you mock at me?
Foolishly I trusted you. Why do you tease me now?
I commenced the duel trusting your support,
And now, I am in pain, fatally wounded.'

Comforting Sugriva, Lakshmana said:
'Don't use empty words without understanding
The awful dilemma Rama is in. In his wisdom,
He has established the reign of *dharma* throughout
The south of this country. Now, when he is caught
In the vicious circle of right and wrong, how can he
Stab Vali at his back?'

Then Rama explained to Sugriva:
'When friendship and culture are forged together,
How can I cut the creeper of brotherly love?
Having enjoyed the honey of brotherly love,
Killing Vali is a hard fact to accept. I know,
Without Vali's death, you won't get Ruma back.
But the use of force has to be undertaken
Only when it becomes inevitable. I have given you
My promise; but should I follow it blindly?
I don't know how I am going to ready my arrow.

'Do you know what I felt when, during the battle,
I beheld Hanuma? His eyes were wet with acute pain.
Could I ignore a good man's tears and go ahead?
His mind is my mind, his opinion is my opinion.
Painful it was for me to witness the end of heroic
Age in the duel between brothers; and that anguish
Held back my arms; and, in the meanwhile, you
Were hurt. You are fighting for your wife,
And, my fight is to establish *dharma* in the world.
When I was thus sunk deep in despair, Lakshmana

Came there to clear the doubts and dilemmas.
Hence, now Hanuma's tears have dried up.

'Since both of you look alike,
I need some mark to recognise you when you fight.
Vali has worn a golden chain round his neck;
Let Hanuma put a garland of flowers on you.
Then, invite Vali for a duel and fight
Without fear. I give you my word that 60
I will slay Vali. Now I am free from doubts.'
Hearing those words of Shri Rama, and putting
A garland of flowers round his neck, Sugriva,
With renewed spirit, rushed to the fray.

Bearing the bow Kodanda, which sparkled
In the bright sunrays, quickly went Shri Rama
And stood in the middle of the forest; by his side,
Stood Lakshmana, Hanuma, Nala and Nila.
'I have told him to bring Vali here,' mused Rama,
'But how is he faring? Can he succeed in his task?' 70
When he stood there, musing, the vernal beauty
Around him caught his sight and heart.

On the trees and plants, thickly ranged together,
Flowers blossomed, spreading their aroma.
A stream with crystal-clear water flowed
Murmuring, at the foot of a hill. Above the stream,
On the plateau, there were lovely lakes and tanks.
Swans, geese, and cuckoos crooned happily;
Deer chewed young grass free from any fear;
Here and there were seen thick banana groves; 80
Herds of huge elephants trumpeted loudly, and,
Breaking down the bamboo, feasted on them;
And dark clouds shone with the sun on their rims.

'What a beautiful sight! O Hanuma, this place
Must be one blessed by gods,' Rama exclaimed;

And Hanuma answered him thus: 'Sir, it is said
That the holy seven sages live here. They eat
Only once a week and indulge in hard penance.
Here is where they achieved the eight-fold Yoga,
And here they achieved bodily salvation.   90
All consider this a place sanctified by gods;
And, gods are supposed to come here, often,
And enjoy themselves with heavenly women.
It is said that, many times, echoes of the anklet-bells
Of those women and their singing are heard;
And that, all through the year, the very air is fragrant.
Now, my Lord, your feet have sanctified this place
More than before,' said Hanuma.

Canto One Hundred and Four

'Is it Proper to be Carried Away by Unbridled Rage?'

||૭||

With the assurance of Shri Rama, Sugriva
Forgot his pain, and again challenged Vali for a duel.
In great fervour, he roared like a lion,
Hearing which Vali, fond of wars, got up at once.

Stamping the ground hard,
As if the whole earth was about to split into two,
As if a huge serpent, provoked, came hissing,
His face fierce, his eyes flaming with anger,
Impatient and roaring, Vali also sprang for the duel.

Tara was frightened, and she implored Vali:
'O my love! Control yourself; don't be hasty;
Tell me, is it right to be swept off by rage?
Sugriva has already been hurt and beaten;
If he still comes there and challenges you,
There has to be some hidden strategy in his move.

'He must have received someone's support;
Otherwise, would he challenge you, roaring?
Would he come back unless he is sure of his strength?

Would he accept defeat and dishonour again?
Listen to this news brought by Angada. 20
Spies reveal that Sugriva is not alone now,
And that he has got ready for a long battle.

'Listen to me, my master.
Why should you have enmity with your brother?
He is intelligent, competent, and brave.
He never saw me with lustful eyes; on the contrary,
He always respected me as his sister-in-law.
Appoint him as the crown prince, master,
And save this country from total ruin.
It will be in the interests of all and good for all. 30

'It seems, they are the sons of Dasharatha,
By name Rama and Lakshmana; and they are famous
As great warriors, invincible in any war.
Shri Rama, though as strong as Rudra, the destroyer,
Protects all good people and blesses them,
And assists all people – poor and suffering.
Obedient to his father and full of worldly wisdom,
He is a rich mine of virtues.

'Shri Rama, glorious and great, equals the king
Of gods; why foster enmity with such a man? 40
He punishes the wicked; why rivalry with him?
While Sugriva is under the protection of Shri Rama,
You cannot defeat him. Extend brotherly love
To him, and lead all in the path of friendship.'

'My dear wife, do not fear,' Vali assured Tara,
'You are my brave wife and I have won over fear;
Why, then, do you give me the counsel of escape?
Rama and Lakshmana are here as Sugriva's friends,
Are they? All right; I will find out their motive.
If they have come here to end sinful life on earth, 50
I will give up my enmity, and bow to them respectfully;

And, I will welcome them, hear me, with devotion.
Let both of us settle those idols of love
In the temples of our hearts – do you hear me?

'If they, Rama and Lakshmana, have come here
With Sugriva, full of hatred and enmity,
And fall upon me with an intent to kill me,
I will fight with them and cut them to pieces,
I will pluck out their intestines, and drink their blood.
Give up your fears unworthy of Vali's wife.' 60

'Please, do not go, my husband.
Listen to this news brought by Angada.
Ravana, it's said, has abducted Sita, Rama's wife,
And has kept her captive at Lanka. To rescue her,
Sugriva has promised his help to Rama; and,
In return, Rama has agreed to kill you
And free Ruma from your hands. Listen!
If Rama has cut off seven *sala* trees
With just a single arrow, isn't his prowess great?
It's his faith in Shri Rama's power and strength 70
That has encouraged Sugriva to challenge you, again.
Do not leave for battle now,' Tara pleaded,
Falling on his feet, piteously.

But Vali was unmoved:
'Strange are your words, my wife. Afraid
Of my brother, should I run away from battle?
I, born of the sun, will die if I have to die.
This Kishkindha is the place of fearless warriors.
Be it Rama or Bhima the terrible, I will
Neither bow to anyone nor seek shelter of anybody. 80
Free your mind from fears and doubts, unfounded.
One step forward, it is Heaven; one backward, it is hell;
Death is great and glorious.

'Is my valour any less?
The Lankan king is my friend, out of fear;

And proffering Kishkindha an equal status
With the kingdom of Lanka, he lies quiet.
Who is Rama, the king of some tiny region?
All these Ramas are just hollow humans;
How can they equal me in strength and stature? 90
Brave wife, don't come in the way of my strength;
Have you become deaf to Sugriva's vain roars?
With no excuse, if he challenges me for war,
I cannot sit quiet like a coward. I have to accept
His challenge; this is my vow.

'I will not step back into the inner chambers.
Dear wife, hear my words; nothing untoward
Will befall me. I have not wronged Rama.
I am angry with Sugriva because of his fraud;
And though I have kept Ruma a captive, 100
I have looked upon her as my daughter,
With no trace of lust or desire.

'In fact, I have already served the cause of Rama;
I have stopped Ravana from crossing the Vindhyas,
And I have limited his victories only to the south.
He dare not go against any of my will and wish.
If Shri Rama so desires, I am ready to help him further;
It isn't a great task to bring back Sita from Lanka, is it?
When things stand thus, why should Rama oppose me?

'This is foolishness. 110
Should he listen to mean people and come here?
Dasharatha became a victim of mean people.
Does Rama, in the same manner, want to take my life?
Does it befit one reputed as a righteous person?
Without any knowledge of what is true or false,
Drowned in the sorrow of having lost his wife,
If he takes my life, listen, the whole of Treta *yuga*
Will be besmirched in infamy.

'Rahu and Ketu afflict the sun and the moon
Unfailingly; Brahma's skull torments Shiva always; 120
Similarly, this evil deed will haunt Rama, who glories
As the "Man of the Millennium," for ever.

'Rama, the lord of the Raghu clan,
Is supposed to be balanced and equal-minded.
How can he be "Rama" without the essence of Rama?
Rama he is not; he is now Ravana; and,
Pining for his wife Sita, he has lot his sense of right and wrong.
Be it god, if he forsakes the righteous path,
I will curb his pride and humble him. I will remove
The veil of wrong-thinking that has made him forget 130
His noble task – the task of ushering in a New Age.

'If he proves to be a virtuous man,
I have no quarrels with him; during discussions,
I will wash his feet like a devotee, and bow to him.
But he is not Shri Rama, it is somebody else.'

Like a mango tree, full of fruits,
Falling down suddenly, Tara collapsed onto
The feet of Vali, and bathed them with her tears.
He, who was deaf to her advice, lifted her up,
And, tenderly, caressed her. 140

Then, Tara said:
'Shri Rama is a friend to all. Send Angada
Immediately to Rama; let him praise
And worship Rama, and then bring him here,
To Kishkindha, with all pomp befitting a king.
If, following Rama's orders, Sugriva agrees
For any kind of mediation, the *vanara* clan
Will indeed be blessed.'

'My dear wife, listen,' said Vali, determined,
'Should I turn my back to the warfield like a eunuch? 150
Shall I sneak in, like a thief, and beg for my life?
When the whole world praises Shri Rama as a man

Of mercy, why would he do me any treachery?
Even if he kills me, does it matter? I shall discard
My corporeal frame, intent on eternal salvation.'

'Bad omens are seen everywhere, my lord:
My right eye quivers; crows are crowing in despair;
Jackals shriek, and different shapes that resemble
Comets, now appear and now disappear in the sky,
And, thus mock me like ghosts of dead women. 160
They open their huge mouths, hungrily, like whales,
Intent on devouring the earth, and yawn, and thus
Raise waves of anxiety and concern in my heart.
How can I send you for war?' – Tara asked,
Making vain efforts to stop her tears.

But Vali persisted: 'Why do you stop me?
You being a brave wife, would it suit you? Be bold;
Draw on my forehead the mark of a brave man,
And pour on my head the seeds of victory,
And, smiling, send me to the warfield. 170
I have defeated Ravana, and now would I fear
This common man?'

Unable to respond to his words, the loyal wife,
Tara, ran to Vali and held him tight in her arms.
Then, she circled him respectfully as one would
In a temple, bowed to him. 'Be victorious,
On the field, my lord; may god protect you,'
With those words, seeking god's blessings on him,
She sent him to the fray.

With his ego swollen like a dome, 180
Suppressed rage seething in his mind,
Like a volcano, like Bhairava on doomsday,
Like an enraged lion, like Rahu to blot out the moon,
His heart beating loudly and his head aching,
Vali, steeling his mind to kill Sugriva,
Stepped out, taut and ready to explode.

Canto One Hundred and Five

'Lord of All Hearts, Why this Enmity with Me?'

||૬||

Hissing with anger, in a loud and stern voice,
Vali shouted: 'Where are you, Sugriva?
One hard hit from my clenched fist, and you die.
Give up your hollow bravado. Even before
The earlier wounds on your body are healed,
You have returned; have you learnt any new trick?
Earlier, I left you alive because you are my brother;
But now, without any such thought, I will send you
To a world from where you will not return.'

Strong fighters both, 10
They battered each other, trading hard punches;
And many a deadly hit each gave the other.

Wheeling slyly, stretching his arms, dragging,
Shrieking, roaring, clenching his fist hard,
When Vali smote him angrily, Sugriva
Was grievously wounded; and from his chest
Sprang a fountain of hot, red blood.

Seething in fury,
Sugriva pulled up a tall tree and struck Vali
With it Vali tottered like a ship caught in a whirl,   20
And then, after a while, steadied himself.
Being equally powerful and nimble-footed,
They continued to fight with no respite.
But, as the fight advanced, and they smote each other,
Sugriva began to sink before Vali's ferocity.
'Shri Rama, save me; I am quite humbled;
I am tired, and I cannot fight any longer,'
So prayed Sugriva, mentally.

At once, Shri Rama,
Fixed the shaft to his bow, with total intent,   30
And, aiming to pierce Vali's chest and kill him,
He stretched his bow and, with speed, shot the arrow.
It was the garland of flowers that saved Sugriva.
Like the arrow shot by Rudra on the doomsday,
Sparkling and flashing, spitting out fire,
It pierced the chest of the *vanara* king.

Like the majestic flagstaff,
That falls on the ground at the festival's end,
Like the tall tree uprooted on the ground by storm,
Like a meteor that falls from the sky, flashing,   40
Howling, Vali collapsed on the ground.
Like a fountain, blood sprang high, continuous.
As if he could not see his son's plight any more,
The sun, in distress, sank in the western ocean.

The bird of life was still surviving in its nest;
Vali cast his eyes here and there, searching for some one.
'What deceptive game is this? Who shot the arrow?
Has the Lankan king come here or is it Rama's work?
Ignoring the ethical codes of kings and gods,
Alas, Shri Rama has killed me,' said Vali,   50
Writhing in pain.

Shri Rama, accompanied by Lakshmana,
Approached Vali and stood by him, gravely.
Vali realised that it was Rama's work, and,
Enduring great pain, he questioned Rama:
'Where is your valour and what deed have you done?
Learning two languages, coming down from north,
And cheating the innocent people here – is it proper?
Tell me, where did you learn this kind of warfare?
Indeed your fame has spread – none to equal you – 60
Was born earlier, and will be born in future.
It is certainly a model of practicing impotent
Art, in a manner befitting thieves and rogues.

'Being known as "the man of model conduct,"
Would anyone break the cultural constitution?
Not only today, even in the coming New Age,
You will be the director of "the drama of delusion."
You have given ample evidence of such conduct.
Shooting the fatal arrow, hiding yourself,
What have you gained? What fame or fortune? 70
Having defaulted in your duty to this world,
How will you defeat and subdue the king of Lanka?
Now has set the dull sun of fortune, in this age;
Now has collapsed the great bridge of Quest,
And has sunk deep into the womb of pitch dark time.

'The qualities befitting a king are:
Sympathy, restraint, courage and forgiveness.
You reign in the hearts of all; why enmity with me?
When I was full of devotion towards you, and,
When I came running, yearning to meet you, 80
What have you done to me, O lord!

'Why are you hostile to me?
I have not lied to you, neither have I slandered you;
Have I defamed you? Have I declared war on you
With the intent of occupying your capital, Ayodhya?

Quarrels are common for women, gold, and land;
But, without any of these at stake, you have come here,
And, moved by prejudice, you have fouled *dharma*.
Politics bereft of *dharma* can only lead to evil.

'Alas! This lusty elephant of Saketa, intoxicated
By its passion for a woman, has broken the chains
Of proper conduct, and, unheeding the mahout's hook,
Has rushed ahead and trampled on righteousness.
Had you so desired, I would have put a noose on
Ravana's neck and dragged him to your presence.
That I bound him hand and foot and hung him
Above Angada's cradle is not unknown to you.
As Vishnu, incarnate as a fish, restored Vedas,
When Hayagriva ran away stealing them,
Had you ordered me, be she at the ocean bottom
Or in the nether world, I would have found her,
The Lakshmi of Saketa, and given her to you.

'Who can justify your action?
Born in the sun-lineage, renowned as a great man,
How could you, tell me, attack a weaponless person?

'What crime have I committed?
Have I harassed the sages, disturbing their rites?
Have I appropriated money or gold of others?
Have I looted and destroyed the wealth of nature?
If you were impartial, you could have invited me,
Given me loving advice on amity and brotherhood,
And could have brought both the brothers together.
"Friendship among equals, loans from the richer,
And protection from the powerful" – so goes a saying.
Tell me, what do you get from Sugriva's friendship?
How do you hope to cross the bridge of this world?
How could you become so mean? The good fortune
Of meeting death while fighting I am denied.
I have lost the chance of a "warrior's death."

'Affection, glory, 120
Sympathy and mercy, righteousness and truth,
These are the ideals a great king should hold.
But, hiding, you have killed an innocent person.
The Saketa flagpost of honour has fallen down;
And, possessed by demonic imperial lust,
You are caught now in a poisonous whirl.'

Canto One Hundred and Six

'Haste is the Cause of Fall, Restraint is Rejuvenating'

||६||

Having listened to the words of the *vanara* king,
Shri Rama replied patiently, free from any rancour:
'If you blame me, O Vali, I will not feel sad.
Is it right to banish a brother to suffer in forests?
Why have you kept Sugriva's wife, Rumaa,
A captive in your harem? Answer me.

'I have no intention of expanding my empire;
I have no desire to accumulate wealth;
What is good for humanity is my good;
What benefits the whole world is my benefit.   10
Saumitri is my sceptre, I am the royal flag;
The world is my royal garden, this forest palace;
Roots and fruits constitute to me a royal feast.
My path of victory leads to the Truth and *dharma*,
And I am going on that path.

'Where there are no caste-creed differences,
Where there are no differences of borders, and
Wicked domes of politics, free from violence

Born of fear, and where good people are happy –
Establishing such a nation is my goal.   20

'Colluding with Ravana, you have built,
Between him and yourself, a bridge of friendship.
Hence, in my attempts to get back Janaki,
How could you build up friendship with me?
In my quest for the new order, whatever thorns
And snags appear, I will uproot them and move.
This is what the Sage Vishwamitra taught me,
And this is the *"aditya hridaya"* Agastya
Expounded to me.

'*Dharma* is what I have to follow.   30
Just as they use nets and ropes and other tricks,
To catch wild beasts and put an end to them,
I had to catch you, who were no different from them.
Slaying you was in accordance with *dharma*.

'If I need help to free Janaki, I have
Sugriva, Hanuma, Jambava, and Neela.
I will destroy Ravana without your help;
Need I your help who snatched a brother's wife?
You are like Ravana; how can you be a friend?
Still, before shooting the arrow, to forewarn,   40
I did sound my bow-string; birds and beasts, scared,
Ran hither and thither. Tell me, truly:
Did you not hear it? Did you not see it?
Had you come to me then, I would have saved you.

"I am innocent," you say;
But, being an ally of Lanka-king, you also share
Whatever crimes he has committed against women.
Months have passed since I came here; and, still,
You did not bother to enquire why I was here and
What I needed. Courtesy is not a part of your behaviour.   50

It is a king's duty to discover if some one is a friend
Or an enemy or neutral; you failed in that duty.

'When Sita was being abducted,
By that thief Lanka-king, you did not stop him.
But Sugriva, collecting all the ornaments,
Thrown down by Sita, stood by me, humbly.
Jatayu sacrificed his life fighting atrocity.
You and your friend Ravana who prides himself
On abducting another's wife are of the same mettle
Your own indifference to evil has destroyed you.   60
True, I am perturbed by the absence of my wife;
For, it is a husband's duty to care for his wife.

'Yours was unruly behaviour;
Owing to your strength, you developed arrogance.
Kabandha and Shabari have recounted your misdeeds,
And Hanuma has briefed me about your wicked rule.
When I left Saketa, I vowed I would devote my life
To punish the wicked and protect the virtuous.
I had decided then to kill you and free Ruma.
But, being drowned in sensual, sadistic pleasures,   70
How could you lend your ears to sane advice?

'Ravana and such other evil forces
Are with you; sensuality has destroyed your soul.
When the *rakshasas*, furious and angry, churned the ocean,
What did they get? – only poison, fuming and bubbling.
But, since the gods churned the ocean with love,
They were fortunate enough to taste ambrosia.
Haste is the cause of fall; restraint is rejuvenating
Restraint is *dharma*, it is culture.

'Even when the news reached you   80
Of my coming here, you did not wait for me.
Biding one's time is fruitful; it is penance.

Biding one's time is auspicious; it purifies one.
There is Urmila, ascetic of the era, calmly waiting;
Shabari, the hoary woman, waited, yearning for me;
There waited Jatayu for long, intent on salvation.
We have to wait, and yet wait, restraining
Our doubts and fears and dreams.

'You have violated the bond of brotherhood;
You have destroyed the holy bond of marriage. 90
Blinded by delusion, how could you see truth?
It is easy to talk about truth, practice so demanding.
Truth, austerity, renunciation, and learning –
These are the steps leading to noble achievements.
With a heart cleansed of blemishes, and with a
Clear mind, if you so desire, I shall withdraw my shaft;
And you can lead a life, happy and contented.'

His tongue was getting dry, his breath was feeble;
Still, reluctant to give up his argument, Vali said: 100
'That it makes one happy, is it proper to kill?
Is the Rama-Ravana conflict unavoidable?
And, is my death a forerunner of many such deaths?
I wonder when the Aryans' thirst for conquest
Is going to be quenched.'

Shri Rama answered:
'When a strong man like you was in the South,
How did Ravana and his ilk plunder Janasthana?
Why was Janaka's daughter forcefully abducted?
The *danava* culture is preying upon *vanara* culture.
This is what your glorious reign has led to. 110
Fallen into the well of sin, why do you blame others?

'The prelude to my friendship with Sugriva
Is not of recent origin. Kabandha himself had told me:
"Sugriva, living in Rushyamuka, is an earth-scientist;

Being sensitive, he knows much about the chain of life.
He also is aware about Ravana's life.
Friendship with him will be highly profitable to you."
That is the reason why our friendship sprouted.

'Only those who are in pain
Can appreciate the pain of others. How could you,   120
Lost in the carnival of carnal pleasures, respond
To the helpless cries of women like Sita and Rumaa?
You were drunk with power and position.

'Extending your hand of friendship to Ravana,
You tightened the noose yourself around your neck.
With a man like you, who, breeding fear and anxiety,
Forces women to accept him, who would fight straight?
Whether you blame others or mock at others,
Your own crimes, I tell you, have destroyed you.

'Enough of this argument.   130
You are an acknowledged expert in boxing;
You are unrivalled in jungle warfare;
But I am adept with bows and arrows, you are not.
Then, tell me, how can we fight face to face?
As with an animal, the only way left was
To kill you with cunning. You are unworthy of trust.

'You could have been a lighthouse on a dark sea;
You could have hoisted high the flag of work culture;
You could have empowered the weak and helpless;
You could have been the dome of Karnataka;   140
But – but you negated all these possibilities.

'Still, despite these limitations,
I regret that I was the cause of your death;
Drowned in sorrow, I am depressed.

Canto One Hundred and Seven

'Ravana's Company Cost Vali his Life'

||☉||

The news that Vali was dead spread in the city;
And all the *vanaras* got together and went to Tara.
'Shri Rama has killed our king,' they said to Tara,
'Now, act quickly and save Angada.
Anoint him as the king immediately.
We will not tolerate the Aryan intrigues.

'We are ready to sacrifice our lives;
But, we will not allow the *vanara* kingdom to fall.
What does it matter if our Kannada blood
Gets mixed with the waters of Kaveri, Kali,   10
Netravati, and Tungabhadra? This we vow:
We will not let the unity of Karnataka to be undone.
Tighten up all the strings of power and authority;
Once they are lost, they cannot be regained.
The Dravida king, Ravana, will halt the Aryans
Near the Vindhyas, and will save our racial unity.
You, on your part, safeguard Vali's kingdom
Like a cobra safeguarding a treasure.'

Tara heard their brave words,
And at once came running to see her husband.   20

Vali was on his death bed; Rama stood there
Silently, and so did, by his side, Lakshmana,
Hanuma, and her brother-in-law, Sugriva.
Like a plucked bird, Tara collapsed there,
And rolled on the ground writhing, like a star
That, slipping from its group, had fallen down.

'O valiant man! You have collapsed here
Like a mountain hit by Indra's weapon *Vajra*.
You, who crushed enemy clusters and roared,
And shone like the king of gods, how could you fall? 30

'O bravest of the brave!
I am humbled; why are you angry with me?
I am your wedded wife; forgive me and arise.
You are a great king; how can you lie like this?
The very husband of the earth-born has killed you,
And, hence, earth will devour you impassively.
O the first among the brave! O lone fighter!
Tell me, have you taken to the path of Heaven
In order to build there another new empire?
Has the rich garden of nectar dried up for ever? 40
Have I lost my wedded status and left alone?'
Thus Tara wailed, sad and helpless.

Staring at Rama's face, she questioned:
'Confronting each other on the battle-field,
Killing or getting killed is the motto of brave kings.
But, hiding yourself, why did you kill in subterfuge?
If your wife is abducted, should you punish me?
You will not escape infamy. This sinful act, for ages,
Will haunt you, like *Brahma kapala*.
Having done a heinous act, how can you be calm? 50
Just because you wanted your wife back, you killed
My husband, and reduced me to a life of widowhood.

'In the pretext of spreading *dharma*,
You have spread sorrow, and, deem it victory;

Do you feel satisfied having killed Vali?
Have you, who redeemed Ahalya, forgotten mercy?
Has your heart hardened because you do not have sisters?
Kill me also, as you have killed my husband, Vali?
Let Sugriva's ambition be fulfilled, and,
Together with Rumaa, let him enjoy his rule, 60
Sitting on the royal throne of my widowhood.'

Hearing the words of Tara, Shri Rama said sadly:
'Following the path of *dharma*, I have been cruel;
My sympathy for you is greater than your sorrow.
Be they *vanaras, danavas,* or humans,
They deserve death if they violate *dharma*.
Vali has fallen into the pit dug by himself.
Your words have becalmed my disturbed heart;
You have taught me what is right and wrong.
I do not have sisters, and now you are my sister. 70
Forget your pain and grief, and protect Angada.'
Thus, he tried to pacify Tara; and consoling her,
He said: 'Your husband did not desire a rebirth;
Do not break his intention. You are a mother;
You have a son, Angada, and take care of him;
Anoint him as the crown prince immediately.
As you are a brave mother, fulfil your duty;
And assist the *vanara* race to prosper.'

Having slightly recuperated,
Vali opened his eyes and beheld Tara and Angada: 80
'Come, Sugriva, erase my faults from your mind.
Accept this kingdom and safeguard the *vanaras*.
I would have invited you, sooner or later,
Made you the crown prince, which is your position,
And lived happily. But fate ruled otherwise.
I have not lusted for Rumaa; I have looked after her
As my own daughter. Companionship of Ravana
Has led to my death.

'Had Shri Rama fought with me directly,
Not only I but the whole *vanara* race   90
Would have become extinct. Shri Rama, wisely,
Forestalled such a tragedy; and the whole state
Is indebted to Shri Rama for it. Even though one Vali
Is dead, thousands of Valis are saved.

'In order to put down Ravana's rule,
If Kishkindha could be of any help, there cannot be
Greater prospects. Look after and console Angada.
He has grown up happily; he is wise, virtuous,
And equal to you in power. He can discuss issues
With you on an equal footing.   100

'Tara is an expert in taking wise decisions.
Her hard decisions will be of great help to you.
Devote yourself to the service of Shri Rama;
Otherwise, *adharma* will ruin everthing.'

Sugriva blamed himself for having suspected
His elder brother. 'I thought wrongly that, lustful
Of Rumaa, you took her captive; and spread infamy.
I am a great sinner; forgive me. I do not want
To live any longer. Lift your sword and cut my head.'
With such words, Sugriva took out his sword,   110
But Vali stopped him.

Vali held his brother's head on his chest,
Kissed his forehead, brushed his curls affectionately,
And said: 'This is the fruit of my irrational rage.
Had I finished off the Lanka-king, I would have
Nurtured the tree of *dharma*. In fact, the rise of *adharma*
Is the cause for the birth of Shri Rama. You should not die,
As your death will jeopardise future actions.
What is unpleasant today will be pleasant tomorrow,
And the *vanaras* will be famous for their achievements.   120
O brother, be patient and hopeful.'

Sugriva held Vali's feet and bathed them with tears.
In great anguish, he said: 'Listen, my brother.
In the name of our father, Shri Rama, and your dear son
Angada, I swear that I do not want the throne.
I will give it to Angada, and till he comes of age,
Tara, as caretaker, will look after the state affairs.
She will be the queen-mother and I her servant.
I shall stake even my life and protect the throne.
If you disagree, I shall ascend to the Heaven with you. 130

'O brother! I cannot bear to be slandered
That, covetous of the throne and lusting for Tara,
I got my elder brother killed. I want to die in your hands.
Life without you is death to me. Grant me death.
Let the world learn a lesson from my life. Dying,
I shall light up the lamp of Karnataka-culture.
I shall demonstrate that Dravida culture is in no way
Inferior to Aryan culture.'

Then, Vali replied to Sugriva:
'Sugriva, do not be childish; and do not fritter away 140
The *vanara* lineage. Will you not put out, by your act,
The light of friendship with Shri Rama? The New Age
Will not forgive you for that. Listen to my words;
You are the main figure in the Great Quest of Shri Rama.
You have to steer ahead the Ramayana-chariot.

'Drowned in your sentiments,
Do not be deaf to the call of the new age.
You were the crown-prince; it is only proper that now
You ascend the throne as the king. Be free from fears.
This is inevitable for you to assist Shri Rama. 150
In the name of our father, do not dispute;
It is my order and you are the king.'

Canto One Hundred and Eight

'The Blessed Name of Rama Rings in my Heart'

||೬||

Death approaching him fast, his breath weak,
Vali tenderly caressed Angada, and advised him thus:
'My dearest son, Angada! Pay heed to my words.
Let not wealth elate you or poverty depress you;
Being free from jealousy, never abandoning truth,
Never deeming the corporeal frame as your true self,
You have to live. Be alert towards all kinds of enemies.
If some one blames you, why should you retaliate?
Why should you, for that reason, lose your equanimity?
It is always better to love all establish relationships.   10
Listen! Regarding gold, cattle, horses, gems,
And slaves, do not trust them unless you test them.
Blind trust in them leads, always, to suffering.

'The greatest disaster is anger;
And tolerance is real wealth. Do not you ever lie.
In success or failure, in all kinds of misfortune,
Maintain equanimity.

'Mean people may twist and turn your words;
Do not fear them. When afflictions attack you,

When you are defeated and when you succeed,
Accept all of them with an equal frame of mind,
And show the world your mental calibre.

'Be transparent like a pure crystal.
Rebuild and enrich the broken worlds of others;
And sharpen those minds that have gone rusted and blind.
Be careful, very careful in both your words and acts;
And move, move forward, lighting up the dark world.
Be aware that there is life beyond the pomp and the power,
Authority and luxury granted by kingship.
Otherwise, when you lose position and power,
You will, in distress, ruin your life.

'Do not preen yourself
That you know everything and you can do anything.
Discuss with elders and debate with ministers,
And, then, formulate all of your action-plans;
And, do not ignore, lost in your power and glory,
The administrators and officials.

'Anger is red,
Love is blue, renunciation is saffron, and
White symbolises purity and peace.
The string is broken and the tune is cut;
The thousand-headed Adishesha calls me now.'

Then, he folded his hands to Rama and said:
'O Shri Rama! With enchanting musical notes,
Beyond the quest for the sparkling rubies,
I shall travel far, far away into the divine land.
I never desired either land or life on this earth.
Free my soul and bid me farewell with love.
The blessed name of Rama rings in my heart,
And calls me waving its hand.'

Then Shri Rama approached Vali quickly,
Laid Vali's head on his lap, and told him lovingly:
'You had strength that equalled the strength of Ravana;

Had you chosen the path of righteousness, you could have
Evolved into Rama. Having lost her brave son,
Earth condoles your death. Do not regret or be sad;
I admire you, and assure you that I will protect
Your son, Angada, like my younger brother.'

'You have achieved freedom from the bondage
Of this corporeal frame. Bless me, my elder brother,
I shall unite North and South through true conquest;
We will become the staff of support for Rama's quest,
And prove that the soul of the *Ramayana* is the strength
Of the *vanaras*. We will recount everywhere
Your noble sacrifice,' Sugriva said in ringing words.

The sky turned pale and dim.
Then, there was seen a round and crimson ball,
Which burnt itself out and, being immersed
In the waters of the sea, gave out a last ray,
Which shone again for a moment. Like the hopes
Of a dead person rekindled in those that survive him,
The sun shone for a second, and then disappeared
Into the womb of the ocean.

Unable to control her grief, Tara burst out:
'Alas, brave man! Should you lie down, thus, helpless?
Has the fountain of loving words dried up now?
Deaf to the cries and blind to the streaming tears
Of your loving son Angada and other chieftains,
Should you, who was brave and cherished war,
Disintegrate to the five primal elements?'

Then she called Angada and told him:
'Come, my son; bow to the feet of your father.
He was the bravest and the brightest of all;
He who is sinking now, was the seer of the New Age.'
Angada, hearing the words of his mother,
Like a calf that approaches its mother defeated by

The king of animals, went near his father, sobbing,
And, touching his feet, shed profuse tears.
That touching sight wrenched Sugriva's heart,
And made him weep along with other *vanaras*.   80
There was moaning everywhere, and Lakshmana's
Eyes also were full of tears.

Neela, stepping forward,
Took out the arrow stuck deep in Vali's body.
That arrow, shedding bright rays like the sun,
Was now painted red with the blood of Vali.
Immediately, blood streamed out from the body,
And Vali looked like a red flower falling from its stalk.

Overcome with grief, Sugriva confessed to Rama:
'Caught in the wild dance of ghosts of ambition,   90
I killed Vali; sister-in-law's sorrow stabs me now.
When the city of Kishkindha is burning in sorrow,
I do not know whether Angada can survive it.
Now, you have to show me the way to cleanse
Myself of these sins. I wish to renounce everything,
Go to Rushyamuka, and undertake penance.

'Memories come crowding.
My elder brother did not kill me; instead, he said:
"My heart does not allow me to kill you; go and save
Your skin." But I did not grasp the intent of his words.   100
Once, when he hit me with a tree-branch and I staggered
From pain, he commanded me not to fight with him,
In future, and saved me. How could I forget that love?
On that day, Vali displayed what an elder brother is.

'But, fickle-minded as I am,
I tarnished the image of the *vanara* community.
Having fallen deep into the well of sins and crimes,
Do I have the moral authority to rule this kingdom?
Waves of sorrow lash against me and consume me;

Like a rogue elephant smashing against the river-bank,   110
Elephantine sin smothers me.

'I, sinful and responsible
For all these unfortunate events, will leap into fire.
Do not fear; Angada, Hanuma, and such others
Will search for mother Sita and will find her,
And you will triumph. I cannot live any longer.'

Rama, valour incarnate, stood there,
Silent and pensive; and the assembled crowd
Stared at him in wonder. Tara, sad and sorrowful,
Approached Rama, idol of all people, and said: 120
'O you of the Raghu lineage, can I grasp your greatness?
You are a man of virtues; you have triumphed over senses;
You are the divine soul beyond human form and traits.
Kill me also with the arrow with which you killed Vali;
And I will be re-united with my husband at Heaven.
He does not lust for other women, does not even see them;
Even if the bevy of nymphs, decked with red flowers,
Invites him and tempts him, he will be unmoved.
Such a strong-willed man and so chaste a husband,
He is full of love and altruism. You do not know him;   130
But I know Vali through and through.

'The bond between him and me is cut.
Having lost Sita, you know the pangs of separation;
How can I live, tell me, bereft of Vali's company.
If you can understand that pain, kill me at once.
It will be an act of mercy, not murder, and legal also;
And you will not be tainted with a woman's blood.
You are the statesman who formulates new laws;
Listen, uniting a sorrowful wife with her husband
Is a virtuous act; and separating them a sin.'   140

Shri Rama consoled her with loving words:
'Why do you, a brave wife, lose your courage thus?
The bold words that Vali uttered at the time of his death –

Do not forget them; and do not undo your vow, in the heat
Of passions. You have to walk on the path of fire,
Lead unto a New Age, and protect *vanara* honour.'

Having understood Shri Rama's feelings,
The son of Sumitra said: 'Enough of such tears.
Get rid your sorrow, and, as befitting a king,
Conduct the proper rites now, without any delay.   150

'Time is running out. Together with Tara
And Angada, you Sugriva, conduct the funeral rites
And protect Angada. You have to get quickly sandal
Paste, flowers, oil and *ghee*, along with camphor.
You have to make a wooden bier, fast.'

No sooner did Lakshmana pronounce thus than
A bier, that resembled the aero-plane of holy saints,
Was got ready like a majestic chariot.

Canto One Hundred and Nine

'The Dark Clouds over Kishkindha have Passed'

||۶||

Sugriva, Angada, and all the other *vanara* elders
Laid Vali's body, bedecked with garlands, on the bier.
'Listen, all of you,' Sugriva told them with a heavy heart;
'My brother's funeral rites have to be conducted
In a royal manner; pearls and rubies have to be given
Away in charity.' As the funeral procession continued,
All the men, women, and children of the city followed
The procession, in utter silence.

As the procession reached its end,
Suddenly, breaking the heavy silence, there erupted 10
A loud cry, reaching the surrounding hills and trees.
When Vali's body was laid on the pyre, and Angada
Set fire to it, as if the age of darkness was over,
Surpassing numberless suns and moons in brilliance,
The flame went up, and a huge fire burned.

The whole world condoled the death of a brave man;
The Bharata nation shook, as if in an earthquake.
As if none in future would be born to equal Vali,

Heavy black clouds gathered; and it rained
Continuously, to cleanse the whole earth. 20

Then, Shri Rama consoled all with his loving words:
'You brave people, listen to me. I understand your grief.
Vali, a man who did not cry even at the time of death,
Intent on salvation, has conquered death itself.
We are the four sons of Dasharatha; but, at the time
Of his death, none of us was near him. Pining,
Sad and disconcerted, he left this world,
And vanished in the womb of time, as if to mock
This world. What did it matter that I was the first born?
I did not have the fortune to conduct his last rites. 30

'I am the one ill-fated.
Shabari, the sage, lived for hundred years due to
Her desire to see me; she saw me and then she died.
Sage Sharabhanga, entered fire and ended
His life, of his own will. Jatayu, the brightest
Of the Gridhra community, fought to save Janaki
And died. Now, the king of *vanaras*, Vali,
Unable to distinguish good people from the bad,
Allied himself with the wicked Ravana, and died.
Alas! With doubtful behaviour and open to public 40
Judgment, he suffered; and now he is a part of history.

'Unfortunate that I am,
I do not know how many more innocent lives
I am going to take, and how many hangman's nooses
I am going to tighten. This fear haunts me always.
"Give up violence and cultivate non-violence,"
So said my wife; and, unheeding her advice,
I am now caught in the whirl of doubts and dilemmas.

'What shall I do now?
The Ikshwaku lineage is now tarnished; 50
And I am haunted by sin like the skull of Brahma.

Moving from place to place, I have become a nomad,
With blind courage and the pretext of *dharma*.
I cannot distinguish now *dharma* from *adharma*;
I do not know what is truth and what is not, and.
What is violence and what is non violence.
I am blindly moving ahead.

'What is over is over.
Let Sugriva be the king and Angada crown-prince,
And let both of them work for the welfare of people.
Let them work together, and grow together;
Let the work-culture be honoured and spread.
May the egalitarian winds of world-peace,
Of equal share for all and equal life for all,
Begin to blow from Kishkindha, and satisfy
The needs and expectations of the world.'
Listening to these words of Shri Rama,
All of them came out of grief, and busied themselves
In the varied activities of the state.

All the ministers and elders of the state
Went to Shri Rama, bowed to him, and said:
'O Raghava! With your permission, we will
Install Sugriva as the king and Angada
As the crown-prince. You have to be present
On that occasion.' Shri Rama told them:
'You know my father's command, not to be broken:
I cannot enter cities for fourteen years. Hence,
I will send Hanuma my soul-mate, and Saumitri,
My life-breath; you can conduct the coronation
Ceremony in their presence.'

The spectacular coronation ceremony
Took place in the beginning of the rainy season,
In the month of Shravana. White royal umbrellas
Were held; a pair of white cloud-like royal fans
Were flaunted; fruits, flowers, and precious stones

From ten different directions were collected there;
Sandal paste, coloured paddy seeds, honey, and
Grains were brought there; tiger-skins and curds
Were also got. Joyous notes of music arose from
Musical instruments. Beaming with pleasure, 90
They brought holy water, in ruby-studded vessels,
From all the rivers and oceans. Many virgin girls,
Radiant and happy, carried holy *kalasha* on their heads.

The coronation ceremony of Sugriva was held
Amidst holy chants, in great pomp and jubilation,
As if all the *vasus* thronged and conducted
The coronation of Indra, the king of Heaven, with great joy.
Angada was anointed as the crown-prince. The entire
Community of the *vanaras* rejoiced.
The black clouds over Kishkindha had passed 100
And the sun's rays spakled everywhere.

Canto One Hundred and Ten

'The Question of Angst was in the Forefront'

||๑||

Since the rainy season approached, Sugriva
And Angada sent their army away for four months.
Saumitri stayed there to look after the future tasks;
He was indeed the Adishesha carrying,
The three worlds on his head.

Shri Rama, who had been burdened
With doubts and regrets about having killed Vali,
Finally reconciled himself to it and was calm of mind.
He thought over it at length, and realised the demands
Of the New Age; the wheels of quest rolled on.   10

The task of bringing together and infusing
New spirit in the lives of the forest-dwellers
Like *vanara, dasyu, nishada,* and *bhilla*
Tribes occupied the minds of Saumitri and Hanuma.

As the summer ended, came the cool rainy season.
Black clouds gathered thickly and fierce storms

Began to blow, uprooting huge trees everywhere.
Clouds clashed thunderously, lightnings flashed,
And thunder-bolts struck, and heavy rains poured,
Discouraging all human activities. 20

Shri Rama and Lakshmana,
Like turtles, withdrew into themselves, calmly.
Cogitating on the future steps of their quest,
And the rain flooding everything, inside and out,
They quietly went into an emotive trance.

No pressing work to be done.
The woodland was charming with colourful flowers;
Hungry for honey, the bees hovered over the flowers,
Sipped nectar happily, and rejoiced gleefully;
And Shri Rama, along with the son of Sumitra, 30
Lived peacefully on the hill of Prasravana.

Lions and tigers, cooped in their caves,
Roared loudly to frighten other animals nearby;
Bears, apes, and wild cats wandered here and there;
Natural springs poured clear water and nourished
The pretty plants, creepers and bushes.

Gazing at the pleasing sights of nature,
Shri Rama said to his brother: 'Behold, Saumitri!
What a variety of trees, of different sizes, heights,
And colours, grows in this land of Karnataka! 40
With hundreds of boughs and numberless branches,
The trees have stretched to the clouds and the moon;
Searching for the stars and kissing the clouds, they are
Tasting the nectar of Heaven.

'Everything is beauteous, here.
Beautiful are the hills and caves, and beautiful
Are the valleys. By the side of hills and rivers,
Bloom the jasmine and the *champak*, the scent of which

Reaches the lake, in which lotuses, in full bloom,
And water-lilies of blue and white hues rejoice. 50

'Creepers, laden with flowers,
Remind me of Sita, earth's tender daughter.
Here the pairs of ruddy geese, there the pairs of swans,
And there partridges, the inseparable couples,
The curlew-pairs, as white as the moonshine,
The water-birds – all are aflutter, cooing with joy.
Their youthful vigour gives them unbridled spirit.
The cool sandy places on the river banks serve
As the playground for all those bird-couples.
Their chirping and twittering and humming 60
Are so sweet and lulling, like a mother's lullaby.

'The kingdom of Kishkindha,
Encircled by the graceful seas, looks like a girdle,
On the waist of the Goddess Earth. The carpet of fresh
And green grass rolled out here is so refreshing.
How many varied sights and sounds are here!
Look! The snake, having swallowed a mouse,
Slowly slithers into its pit, its long, curved body
Sparkling in the early morning sun.

'Wherever our eyes turn, 70
They behold hill-tops and beautiful crags,
White, black, brown, of all colours ands shades.
Be it the black colour of collyrium, or,
The blazing red of the *palaasha* trees,
A whole world of colours and hues lies before us.
As if to increase this splendour hundredfold,
A stream of cool water flows in the east, the vale
Encircling.

'At nights, what an enchanting sight it is!
The clusters of stars, sparkling on the milky path, 80
Appear like a golden mat spread on a black curtain.

The stars shine on the casks of heavenly nectar,
Like the fanciful flights in the wombs of dream.

'Brother, I find it hard to speak.
It is as if the entire glory here mocks at me.
The waves of music and instruments, coupled
With pleasure and joy, have overflown Kishkindha.
I alone am unfortunate; how shall I live?
As if in a dark dungeon, I am here in hiding;
And the mattress of pleasure has become a mirage. 90
Memories of Sita, whom I love more than my life,
Pierce my heart, like sharp and pointed arrows.
When I see the rising moon above the eastern hill,
Painful sorrow swells in my heart, like a river in flood.
How shall I endure this pain, these burning wounds?'
Thus groaned Shri Rama, in pain and suffering.

Canto One Hundred and Eleven

'As Radiant as the Sun, as Fearless as the Mountain'

||6||

'Why do you grieve and suffer, O my lord?
If Shri Rama suffers, the whole world will grieve.
Does the darkness of a black night stay on for ever?
The world's desire will burst out from its womb.
When you are happy, the whole earth will be happy.
You have to come out of this grief, rain happiness,
And bring to the lives of all hope and happiness,'
Thus the son of Sumitra pleaded.

'What shall I say, my brother?
When will I set my eyes on Janaki, whose eyes 10
Are as quick and sparkling as those of the deer?
Once, after Guha took us across the river in his boat,
And the princess of Mithila walked for some time,
She got tired and said: "How far have we to walk
On this path? Where is the place called Chitrakoota?"
She was hurt and weary; and her legs, as delicate
As the *mimosa* flower, had cracked and blood
Oozing out, had reddened the entire path; and my
Sad tears had wetted the path.

'If I sleep, it is Janaki;
When I wake up, it is Janaki; even in my dreams,
I see Janaki; and, in any state I can think only of her.

'I am drowned in anguish.
The wheel of violence, that I set rolling,
Approaches me, now, to wreak vengeance.
Poisonous from head to foot, it has ruined the present,
And is getting ready to crush my future under it.
It's burning me with its red-hot embers.

'See the wound deep enough
Caused by the sharp arrow I shot at Vali's heart.
Now, where can I see light? The lamp of my life?
The words of warning, uttered by Janaka's daughter,
Are stabbing me in the depths of my heart:
"Put an end to this kind of quest,
Which drives thousands of women into widhowhood,
Which reduces thousands of children into orphans,
Which puts on you the medallion of victory,
Mark of blood on your forehead, and makes me
Shed unending and helpless tears – put an end
To this bloody quest". But, ignoring her words,
I stood on the top of the volcano called Kishkindha,'
So grieved Shri Rama, full of remorse.

Then, the son of Sumitra, consoled him:
'Arise, O Shri Rama! Do not lead a life of fear.
Do not be caught in the swirling whirls of the past;
Think of the future, and move forward, with a free mind.
Cut through the curtain of darkness, raise your head,
And set the wheels of change rolling.

'Burning out this black night,
Safeguarding the dove carefully in your dream-cage,
Vanquishing wicked swordsmen and evil hunters,
Move ahead, with steady intent. Be the messenger
Of new tidings and of new designs of tomorrow.

'You should go ahead.
You are the *veena*-player of the earth and sky;
You should arise and move so that water flows
On the parched, cracked earth, and the wounds
Of time strike the heart.'

Shri Rama replied pensively:
'Ravana has abducted the daughter of Janaka; 60
And, nobody knows for sure if she is alive or not
Why should I live when I could not protect my wife?
When I get back Sita, I will accept her and rejoice,
As I would when divine nectar comes out of ocean.
I will not rest till I destroy Ravana and his
Followers. If I have to walk twenty miles,
I will walk ten miles with enthusiasm, and rest.
But if the distance runs to thousands of miles,
How do I continue my journey?

'Having no fellow-travellers, 70
Wondering how many Lanka-kings there are
On this steep slope, I get confused, depressed.
I see only thorns all through the path of journey;
A giant spider-web confronts me ominously;
Tree-branches, thick with thorns, stab my eyes;
And blood from the blue ocean springs high.

'Lightning mocks at my conflicts; is this living?
Gazing far at the road, deviating from the path,
Reaching a fork in a yellow forest, I am there,
Under the delusion that I am on a noble quest, 80
When harsh reality wakes me up to the truth.
The lake is frozen; hills are covered with snow;
Cities have turned into rocks; the river of desire
Has dried up; and all my dreams have vanished.

'Now, my heart fears the loud noises of thunder;
What do we do if the clouds pour down bubbling oil?

You have deserted Urmila; and, the fears that Sita
May or may not be found torture my heart.
My mind has become unsteady, and it desires
The support of love.   90

'I have tolerated everything.
Just as the saints and virtuous people tolerate
The abuses of the wicked, just as the mountain
Tolerates storms and heavy rains, with the hope
That some day the clouds may pour down sweet water,
I tolerate everything.

'I think of Hanuma.
Full of enthusiasm and incomparable strength,
Of courteous behaviour, serious and skilful, in him
Are blended all the qualities of mind and heart.   100
Resplendent like the sun, fearless as the mountain,
Hanuma is firm like the rain-water becoming a river
That joins the ocean. He firmly believes in *nishkama
karma,* action free from any expectations of reward.
He is all set for the Quest of Truth; and, like you,
Though separate bodily, he is one with me in soul.
Noblest among *yogis,* he stands majestic.

'To my mind, the rainy season has this to teach us:
Just as the trees, clad with new leaves, stand glorious,
The place where virtuous people stay, is the abode of peace. 110
The wicked, and hypocrites will never succeed.
To show that an altruist's money belongs to others,
The crops stand erect and proud, full of grains.
The swarm of glow-worms, twinkling weakly,
Tells us that half-knowledge can never root out
Ignorance. The very heavy rain shows us that
Unlicensed behaviour surely destroys one's life.

'That the weeds have to be removed to get good crops,
Teaches us that we have to weed out such passions

As lust, arrogance, and ignorance to make life 120
Meanigful. Rich crops show us that women with
Good character always enrich home and society.
One has to be awake and watchful always.

'These are the lessons the rainy season teaches us.'

Canto One Hundred and Twelve

'I am Crushed by the Burden of the Pangs of Separation'

॥६॥

'Can you not hear, my brother, the call of the earth?
Full of maternal affection, silently, stretching
Her long arms to embrace me and caress me,
She, the earth-mother glories. Cool is her refuge,
And so loving her bosom; she sings lullabies to me,
Sweet and affectionate. Clothed in pretty flowers,
She smiles blissfully.

'The woman, in whose womb seeds grow, is the force
Of creation. That is why, proud of her pregnancy,
Displaying the charm of motherhood, she moves about. 10
Where has my beloved, earth's daughter, disappeared?
Like the ruddy swan disappearing from the lake,
Sita has disappeared from the lake of my mind.

'Saketa, the noble kingdom, comes to my mind
Often. In a noble kingdom, the essence of *dharma*
And culture, shines by itself, without any hindrance;
And, evil forces decay and die by themselves.
Such is *Ramarajya*, the ideal kingdom, as the wise say.

In such a kingdom, the king is the servant of people.
If a son, a blot on his lineage, is born, owing to him, 20
Listen, *dharma*, piety, and all such are ruined.
Even the lineage loses its name,' said Shri Rama.

Saumitri tried to cheer him up:
'In your shelter, all the elements like water
And earth are happy. Then, why do you grieve?
You are a pious man and a man of action.
Come autumn, show the world your valour.
The entire family of Ravana is going to be
Destroyed by you. Be firm in your mind.'

Rama replied to Lakshmana with affection: 30
'O Saumitri! You have told me, like a good friend,
What is good for me. You are now the catalyst of
My thoughts; and thus you have served the world.
I will not be inactive in the coming autumn.'

There, in Ayodhya,
Urmila thought only of Rama and Saumitri.
With her loved one away, she found everything
Dry and lifeless. When her maid brought her milk,
She laid it aside, saying, 'Being drowned in
The ocean of sorrow, why do I need milk? 40
I do not, I do not want it.' Occasionally, when
Her mother told her that being free from forest-life,
She had no reason to give up the palace too, she replied:

'I am not fortunate to live with my husband.
I had nursed a great desire to follow my dear
Husband to the forest. Now, it is only my body
That is here; my spirit is with my loved one, there.
There is none to listen to the story of my anguish;
And none to hear the sad story of my husband.
Pains of separation have dried up now, mother. 50
My life-creeper, having grown up in Mithila,

And, having flourished freely in Saketa,
Is now, like the river Sarayu, flowing fast,
In search of my loved one, with the hope of
Meeting him.'

And, Urmila talked to herself:
'O Chitrakoota! O Panchavati!
O trees and plants! O flowers and bowers!
You gave shelter to my loving husband;
The peacocks danced, the cuckoos sang, 60
And rain, storm and sunlight nursed his body.
I recall the story of Shri Rama's sacrifice,
And console myself.

'In this world of selfishness, there is Bharata,
An idol of renunciation, who, at present, is doing
Penance. His love for his brother, like fire-ordeal,
Has enabled him to burn all lust and temptations.
He has left the capital and is living in Nandigram.
The banner of brotherly love is raised very high,
And the stream of sacrifice is flowing far. 70

'Saumitri is in the forest, and Bharata in a hamlet.
They are there not due to their weakness, but due to
Their spirit of sacrifice. They have bowed to Shri Rama
With love. All through these seven years, people
Themselves have ruled the kingdom of Saketa,
And have been living contented. This is what
Makes me proud and happy.

'The history of Shri Rama
Is grand, divine, and the pinnacle of culture.
His story subsumes the principles of courtesy, 80
Co-existence, and aesthetic pleasure, in great
Measure. He causes the wheels of *dharma* move,
And, like a gentle stream, makes the earth happy.'

Here, on Malyavat hill, Shri Rama
Said to Lakshmana: 'Look at the glory of the clouds.
Absorbing the essence of oceans, the sky-woman
Has become pregnant. The Earth-goddess carries
The *kedage* scent. The rain is conducting the ritual
Of *abhisheka* with great joy. Water-drops stream down
From the sky, like the broken pearl-necklaces of nymphs 90
Of Heaven, come down to the earth seeking pleasure.
All these augment my pain of separation;
And I am done.

'Amidst the clash and noise of thunders,
Who is it that lashes the sky with a gold-whip?
Lightning, flashing amidst black clouds, stabs me,
As if to question me if Sita is, really, a captive
Of the king of Lanka. Hills and valleys, trees
Laden with flowers welcome the new rainy season.
All these augment my pain of separation; 100
And I am undone.

'Dear brother, behold there!
The stream, full of new water, flows down the hill;
And the flowers, fallen down into it, are floating.
With majestic steps, peacocks strut forward;
The black *nerile* fruits are strewn on the ground;
There, the procession of huge elephants, trumpeting;
Here, files of playful cranes, coming toward us;
See, see them, they look like long garlands of lilies.
All these augment my pain of separation; 110
And I am undone.

'All these rivers – look, Saumitri –
Are rushing to meet Narayana, who lies
In a yogic trance in the ocean of milk.
Carrying gifts of flowers, eroding their banks
These rivers run to meet their lover, the ocean.

All these augment my pain of separation;
And I am undone.

'See the honey-bees there!
On branches and trunks, and drunk with nectar, 120
The bees, intoxicated, are flitting around vainly.
To quench their thirst, partridges lap up water;
The long mountain-line, rejoicing in glory,
Has gone through coronation, meant for kings.
O look! The God of Wind, obediently, carries
The cloud-water-pots, given him by Indra.
All these augment my pain of separation;
And I am undone.

'And I remember, there in Ayodhya,
The way the river Sarayu flows in floods, 130
Like the power of penance of Urmila, the *yogin*.
Like the river-banks, eroded by the floods,
I am getting shattered in the floods of sorrow.
All these augment my pain of separation;
And I am undone.'

Thus, in the rainy season,
Shri Rama moaned and suffered in Sita's absence.
Lakshmana continued to console him softly:
'Be patient, elder brother.
The new water of this season will sweep away 140
All dirt and waste. Likewise, all impediments
Shall disappear. In the path of the Great Quest,
Let us move ahead, kill Ravana, free mother Sita,
And, flourishing high the flag of victory,
Let us live happily.'

Canto One Hundred and Thirteen

'Cupid Himself, the God of Love, Dances in Rapture'

||๑||

The autumn was there, in all its glory.
Water was clear in all the rivers and oceans,
As if they were cleansed of lust and arrogance.
Birds of varied colours and plume sang in ecstasy,
As if virtuous deeds had their fruits in the right time.
Not a speck of dust was there; and the lotuses
In lakes were beautiful. Buzzing of the bees
And the coy cooing of birds enthralled every one.
Thick bamboo groves, then, developed pith.

Black clouds having disappeared, 10
And everything being tinged with pleasing blue,
The Earth-goddess wore a crown, gem-studded.
The dusky veil was taken out from the earth,
And the sun shone in glory and splendour.

New dreams and new values,
Manifested themselves with renewed faith,
Waking up consciousness from a state of passivity.
The world, dark at night, witnesses in the morning
A glorious procession of torch lights from the east.

The autumn was dressed up like a new bride.
Pairs of peacocks revel, dancing and strutting;
And royal swans flew freely, their wings spread.
Flowers of many kinds spread their varied scents:
Sugandharaja glowed with regal pomp; and,
The fragrance of jasmine filled the whole forest.
The moon, at night, cast his cool rays everywhere,
And spread blithe bliss all around.

Intoxicated, bees in pairs, whispering,
Are busy sucking nectar from the flower-cups;
The black antelope, craving for its mate's touch,
With half-closed eyes, scratches its beloved,
With its long horns.

Love is in the air.
The female elephant sprouts water from its trunk
To its lover; the male partridge gives its beloved
The lotus stalk, lovingly; Time climbs up and sits
On the autumn-chariot; and, in order to cleanse
The world, sends wind as his first messenger.

The small bells round the neck
Of calves, ringing, give out pleasing notes.
The sounds of huge bells in temples are echoed,
Farmers and cowherds practice in mild tones
Folk songs and folk rhythms.

Autumn is in a riotous glory.
Wherever one turns, one sees dazzling flowers;
Wherever one turns, one sees golden forest;
At every turn, one hears cuckoos singing
At every turn, one finds a bride's adornment

The wind, loitering in the scented forest,
Full of *kodasu* and *matti* blossoms, has lain down
Still, exhausted. All the water here is pure, and
All the hills are unsullied; the dancing creepers,

Picturesque flowers and new foliage, statuesque
Tree stems and branches – all are so exquisite.
Most trees stand together like a married couple,
But a few are, for some reason, standing alone.
Here is an exhibition of the enormous wealth,
Hidden in the womb of the Kannata region.

If you cast your eyes on the wet fields,
You will find paddy fields with luxurious growth, 60
From which, birds pick up grains and eat, merrily.
When they fly in the sky, they draw charming
Lines of garlands.

There is new life, throbbing everywhere.
Hot sun here, there the dried up soft clay;
Lusty bulls in the herds of cows, kicking
Dust from the earth, ready to enter into fray.
While the she-elephant, amorous, moves slowly,
The he-elephant follows her, with regal airs.
There are no rivers in floods, no roaring falls, 70
And no scope for tempests.

The gentle breeze, that carried the scent
Of *saugandhika* flowers to Sita and tempted her,
Is cool and refreshing. The sky, clean and clear,
Shines like a sword burnished.

The lilies smile;
The tall grass and the crimson amaranth
Are inviting; Cupid, whose bow is sugarcane,
Himself dances in rapture. The streams that
Flow round sandy dunes that resemble the derriere of 80
Women who walk shyly. The rich paddy fields,
Ready for harvest, wave their heads, happily.

'Look there, Lakshmana,' said Shri Rama,
'Herds of deer graze their contented;

And so are mountain ebony and hibiscus plant.
Feel the sun's heat now, it is so torrid;
But come the night, and the moon then,
Who bears the deer on his chest, cools everything.
Sita, whose eyes are like those of a deer, and
Who is moon-faced – where is she now?   90

'The daughter of Janaka is beautiful.
Arms soft as flowers, gait of a royal swan,
Face as radiant as the full moon, deer-like
Eyes, bow-shaped eye-brows, hair long and soft
Like the hair of a yak – who can rival her?
The rival of Janaki in beauty is only Janaki.'

Canto One Hundred and Fourteen

'We are not the Ones Who Wove the Web of Life'

||๖||

With the blessings of Shri Rama,
Sugriva is happily the king of Kishkindha.
His long suffering has now got him rich rewards.
The sad clouds of Vali's death being blown away,
The *vanara* community is, now, bathing in joy.
Considering the holy state Vali is going to get
In course of time, Hanuma, contented, is in peace.
Like gold purified by fire, all the people,
Now, are full of joy and spirits.

Being sad and sorrowful, 10
Rama feels he has walked for a long time
On a craggy path, and only for a moment
On a happy path. Owing to the pangs of
Separation, he suffers every moment and
Pines for Sita. Despairing of ever meeting her,
He gazes at the sky, full of anguish and pain.
When the white cranes, stretching their long necks,
Utter sweet notes, old memories haunt Shri Rama:
The way, listening to the same crane-notes, and

Carried away, Janaki had joined her voice to theirs;
The way she had danced in rapture, when she saw
Flowers strewn thickly all over, beneath the trees.

Shree Rama began to think –
'Once, when she had gone to the river Godavari
To bathe, and, in the company of swans, she lost
Herself, singing and jumping, while I was angry,
Unable to see where she was, she tiptoed
Towards me and, suddenly, sprinkled water
On me and smiled. Enraged, when I stared
At her with blood-shot eyes, she, gripped with fear,
Sank down like a creeper and begged me,
With folded hands, to forgive her. My lips
Trembled and my heart went to her. I enfolded her
With my arms stretched, and her soft, wet cheeks
Transported me to the world of love.

'Janasthana had a surprise for me.
In all those places, where I had strolled with Sita,
There is no water, and there are no rivers, any more.
There is sand, and nothing but sand everywhere.
Emptiness. There are no trees, nothing of the kind.
The hills are bare, the forest is empty,
And, my heart also is bare and empty.

'What has happened to me? Where am I?
A hot wind blows through the joyful forest.
Janaki's hot sighs fan the fire of separation;
And, it seems, the treasure of beauty has vanished.
My heart is emptied of all emotions,
As if the springs of feelings have dried up.

I am away from one who was not born of a woman.
The whole world appears to me an empty bubble;
And I feel I have spent ages, lonely and all alone.
Like the male elephant separated from its herd,
I am emaciated and broken.

'One day, her eyes wide open
And her brows dancing, clapping her hands
With innocent joy, coaching peacocks to dance
Rhythmically, the sweet words of love she spoke –
How can I forget those words and that moment?

'The day we left for the forest,
After we left Saketa and covered some distance
On foot, looking at me innocently, she asked:
"How far is the place, still, where we are headed?"
Her words were weak and helpless.

I asked her: "Our destination
Is far, far off; it is a long way and the path
Is rocky and thorny. Your feet are so soft;
How will you cross that distance?" She said:
"I have no fears, and I don't regret.
This is what I desired, what I dreamed of.
I am not tired." But her tears belied her.

The son of Sumitra came running.
"What are you thinking of so deeply? What is it
That worries you?" he inquired.

"Life is the home of sorrow," Shri Rama mused:
'We are caught in illusions, love and hatred.
If, once, we appear bold, next we are frightened.
Life is a hard knot, a riddle impossible to solve,

'It is the mind.
Mind is the cause for both birth and death;
We have to enrich it and control it.
We have to protect it so that it nurtures
Dharma, knowledge, science, and culture.
We are not the ones who wove this web of life;
And we have no right to destroy it any time.
Indian culture proclaims that it is right
And proper to safeguard the *dharma* of nature. –

These are the thoughts that were passing through
My mind. I have no worries since you are with me;
You, my brother, can solve all of my problems,'
Thus Shri Rama confided in Lakshmana.

Canto One Hundred and Fifteen

'Free the Birds to Fly; Captivity is Painful'

||६||

There, in Saketa, all alone, Urmila
Lives in her world of memories: 'O Lakshmana!
You are the summit of honour and a rich treasure
Of greatness. In this season of autumn, the stream
Of great love flows in your heart. Your body is hard;
But your heart is soft. Happiness and misery
Are equal to you; and you are the refuge of
Peace, joy, and contentment. But, I am alone
Here, and none is there to console me.'

She called her friend near and told her: 10
'I wish to paint a picture now, my friend;
Suggest to me what scene I should paint.
Shall I depict the scene of Rama and Sita
Walking on a path while Saumitri climbs
Down to a river? Or, the sight of Rama and
Sita, leaning against a tree, peacefully?

'I had this experience in my childhood:
When the chariot of happiness moves on
A smooth road, and the feathery tribe sings,

Suddenly, I open my eyes and see – what?
The garden of beauty and joy has disappeared.

'All joy just evaporated.
There are no cuckoos singing melodiously,
There is no love in the eastern or western horizon,
The golden necklace pours down hot embers.
The creeper, studded with flowers, is dusty, and,
The whole earth, cracked up, stares at the sky.
Time is the cause of every thing.

'Some say, the sun sinks into the ocean;
Some say, he brightens another world with his light
At the end of the day, the powerful rays of the sun
Enter Agni, the God of Fire, they say.
Whatever be it; the truth is, the setting sun enters
The hearts of lovers separated from each other.

'Tell me; will this darkness of my heart be over?
Here I am like the ruddy swan; will the sun rise?
Free these birds; captivity is very painful.
"Why are you angry, my queen?" this parrot asks me,
Imitating the lessons Saumitri taught it, playfully.
'O, parrot! Fly, fly far away, and reach Panchavati;
And see my loved one.

'O, rabbit! Where are you?
Tell me, where is your master who caresses you?
O you dove! Go to wherever he is, and get me
The golden chalice of love that lies in his heart.
You are always full of praise for my loving
Husband; how are you now away from him?
Reading my husband's letter of love, I used to
Come out of my grief; What do I do now?

'O, you partridge, who feeds upon moonlight
And rest contented! Now, you are also suffering

Pains of separation. Share now my sorrow,
When sharp shafts pierce my heart deep.

'Listen, my friend!
Do not light the lamps; why should we kill moths?
Do I need any light when those I love are not there?
I, you, this perfume – none and nothing has any meaning.
O dreams! Come and unite me with my loved one.
O deep sleep! Come; you are my treasure now;
And taste my salty tears, streaming from my eyes. 60
Without you, often, I have counted endless stars.'

Urmila fancies her husband Saumitri
Consoling her: 'I see in the betel creeper
Your tender form, in the deer-eyes your own,
Your radiant face in the orb of the moon,
Your shining hair in the peacock's long tail,
And your lovely eyebrows in the flowing stream.
But, will I ever see you in your real form?
Afraid that I may not see you again, my body
Is full of sweat, my mind hot and burning. 70
But, my wife, don't you worry and suffer;
Shri Rama is merciful and so is Sita; with their
Blessings, our yearning to see each other is
Going to be fulfilled. Till then, you are there,
High on the dais of my heart.'

Canto One Hundred and Sixteen

'He has Forgotten Himself – and Me Too'

||६||

When both the earth and the sky throbbed with new life,
Hanuma gauged the situation in Kishkindha.
Satisfied that he had retrieved his wife and power,
Sugriva, closeted in his harem, had forgotten
His kingly duties and his promise to Shri Rama.
Drowned in sensual pleasures with Rumaa,
He was oblivious of the whole world.

Sugriva was well-built: tall and broad-chested,
He possessed muscular shoulders, and arms
As straight and long as *sala* trees. He was a picture   10
Of bubbling spirit and valour.

The son of Wind, Hanuma,
Came to the palace, bowed to Sugriva, and said:
'Why this delay in the work of Shri Rama?
Why are you careless in searching for the "mother"?
Remember; you have secured your kingdom
And your harem with Rama's help.

'What can I tell you?
It is better to act in time and not postpone it;
You have to protect your name and fame intact.   20

Be a man of character; take the virtuous path;
Is it proper to forget oneself in sensual pleasures?
Do not, ever, forget what happened to Vali.

'Shri Rama is not an ordinary person;
He is a godly person, one who can accomplish
Any hard task, and he is an ocean of all virtues.
Neglect of your duties is improper; get ready
To fulfil Shri Rama's exigency.

'Take upon yourself to fulfil the vow
To search for and locate Sita, a "mother" for all of us. 30
Rama will appreciate it, and so will Saumitri,
And all of your friends and relatives.'

Sugriva, scared by the words of Hanuma,
Sent for his general immediately, and ordered:
'The big task of searching for Sita is before me;
Get the army ready under Angada's leadership.'
However, having given such commands, Sugriva
Forgot everything and plunged himself in pleasures,
Like a fish caught in the net of sensuality.

When he could not see any active steps, 40
On Sugriva's part, toward search for Sita,
In the presence of Saumitri and Hanuma,
Rama confided:

'I have spent months worrying about Sita;
I have spent months in pangs of separation;
How can he sit idle, forgetting Rama's friendship?
Has he become heartless or does he ignore me?
That ungrateful wretch! When he wept before me,
Having lost his kingdom and his wife, I seated him
On the throne again. My dreams are shattered 50
And the cruelty of the king of Lanka is sky-high.
Due to this forest-life, I am sick and emaciated;
Does he now regard me as nothing?

'Deluded by physical pleasures,
And lost in carnal delight, has he forgotten me?
Is he so mean as to thwart my wishes and desires?
Is his promise to help me in my task out of his mind?
Doesn't he even weigh what is good or bad for him?
He whose words and deeds match is the noblest man.

'The highest virtue is to be free from all obligations.   60
You challenge him now with all your force;
And let the values of this age be scrutinised, quickly.

'Does Sugriva yearn
To witness, again, the might of my majestic bow?
Does the king of *vanaras* desire to face me,
In my fierce form, on the battleground? Would he like
To hear the terrible sound when I strike my bow-string?

'O son of Sumitra, listen to me.
Though I bear the burden of this entire world
Like Adishesha, I will again jump to the fray;   70
And I will break the bones of him who is lost
In sensual pleasures. Go now and wake him up.
Otherwise, he may tread the same path of Vali.
If he continues to be drowned in carnal pleasures,
Giving up the path of truth, his end is certain,
And Kishkindha will be reduced to dust.

'He, who said he had no desire for kingship,
Who declared that his be all and all was to search
For Sita, the cheat, where is he now hiding?
When my boat is being rocked by harsh winds,   80
Is he indulging in his pleasure-boat, forgetting
The courtesy of helping his friend in dire times?
Surrounded by wine and women, for sure, he is
Oblivious of both me and himself; and I am forced
To beg him for his helpful hand. Announce it now
Aloud that he is tracing the path Vali trod,'
Thus burst out Shri Rama, in great anger.

Canto One Hundred and Seventeen

'Soft Words, Like the Divine Crystal, will Conquer the World'

||ॐ||

Hearing the words of Shri Rama,
Lakshmana exploded like an angry volcano.
'I will put an end to the whole lineage of Sugriva;
I will drag him out of his throne and install Angada,
The son of Vali, on it. I will teach every human being
What happens to ungrateful wretches,' thus roared
The son of Sumitra, the incarnation of Adishesha.

When Shri Rama heard those angry words,
He realised at once that things were going wrong.
He feared that Lakshmana might kill Sugriva,   10
And repented for his words spoken in anger.
He knew he had to somehow calm down Lakshmana.

'Do not misread my anger,' he said,
'My anger is only for a fleeting moment; and,
Because of it, we cannot ignore Sugriva's friendship.
Can Sugriva face your rage and remain unhurt?
Control the volcano of your anger now; otherwise,
The whole world will be reduced to ashes.

'Be large-hearted.
Live in peace and allow others to live in peace.
When you conquer your mind, you will have
Conquered the whole world, with love and affection.
Killing the son of the sun will equal patricide;
And we are forbidden to kill innocent people.

'Remember that Sita, the daughter of Janaka,
Threw her ornaments to Sugriva – a sign of trust.
Could we break that bridge of trust and friendship?
He has sealed his friendship with fire as witness;
Should we destroy it now in the fire of suspicion?
It is my anxiety that made my words harsh;
They should not lead to any enmity with Sugriva.
Words of love, like nectar, are life-giving;
And sweet words do conquer the whole world.'

Still Saumitri was not to be pacified:
'The wintry sun has risen now in the sky, and
The same evil force that had gripped Vali earlier
Has now seized Sugriva – the evil of kingship.
Being now a wicked politician, he has forgotten
His promise to us, that hypocritical knave.
You killed Vali and, now, I will kill Sugriva.
Just give me your permission, and I will let loose
A bloodbath, and a new dawn will follow it.'

'Do not be hasty, brother,' Shri Rama pacified,
'Separated from his wife for many, many years,
Sugriva has got back his wife now; let us understand
His feelings and behaviour. As a matter of fact,
The *vanara* race is very different from us.
They live in islands, hills and valleys, woods
And forests, and their land is wide-spread.

'It is not easy to bring all of them all together,
Speedily; do not be impatient, my brother.

Having suffered during Vali's wicked reign,
They are angry and desperate; it takes time
And patience to pacify and unite them.

'Again, Sugriva, having drunk the bitter cup
For a long time, now has sweet sugarcane juice
To taste; let us bear with him. After some time,
I am sure he will come out of it and do his duties.

'He who is patient lives a good life.
Killing friends will throw us into the well of sin.   60
Be guided by reason and rein in your anger.
Let us have a heart-to-heart dialogue with him.
Why this excessive haste and why this anger?
Endeavour to make Sugriva see reason;
Talk to him with affection, and set him on
The quest for Sita.'

His anger unabated with Rama's words,
His eyes red with rage, Saumitri, taking long steps,
Stamping on the earth, moving here and there,
Breaking a few branches here and crushing rocks   70
To powder, there his forehead striking a rock and bleeding,
Shouted in passion:

'What is this, my elder brother?
Having incited me, why do you now pacify me?
I cannot understand this behaviour, my brother!
Why do you stop me and dissuade me?
Has your mind gone soft in the absence of "mother"?
I shall surely punish him who has betrayed his friends.

'I shall raise the flames,
And shall teach the world a hard lesson or two.   80
O Shri Rama! At the time of war, accident, and fire,
One should not be slow and patient; one has to be
Quick in one's thinking and action. Being slow
And wasting time will be criminal. I will advise him

Certainly. If he heeds it, good for him; if he does not,
I will take up cudgels.' With such angry words,
Agitated, he strode with rapid steps to Kishkindha,
Like the Mandara Mountain moving, speedily.

Canto One Hundred and Eighteen

'The People of Karnataka are Known for their Pride'

||௬||

Fiery in his terrible rage, moving like a storm,
Chopping off the shrubs and rolling away the rocks
That blocked his way, keen to confront Sugriva,
He, the son of Sumitra, reached the portals of
Kishkindha, and stood there like the God of Death.

Looking at his threatening figure,
The guards of the fort got panicky and ran away.
They went running to Sugriva and begged him:
'Sir, death stands here, fierce and angry;
Pacify Lakshmana and ask him what his orders are. 10
Fearing that if we stood there he would butcher us,
We have come to you running and trembling.'

Angada approached the son of Sumitra,
Who stood there spitting fire, and bowed to him.
'Listen Angada,' Lakshmana commanded,
'Go and inform Sugriva that Saumitri is here,
And unless he, Sugriva, wakes up, Saumitri
Will write his death sentence. Pound his ears
With this message.'

Angada slipped away and reached the palace. 20
'Father, alas! Horrible danger faces us now.
Enraged, Lakshmana is there hissing like a cobra.
Before he destroys this city and everything else,
Before the ocean of anger crosses its limits,
Come quickly and pacify Lakshmana,'
So begged Angada.

'Yes, my son; I will come immediately,'
So saying, Sugriva tried to get up. But, unsteady
Owing to his state of intoxication, he fell down.
He could not grasp the seriousness of the situation. 30
Here, in the meanwhile, Lakshmana approached,
Like a volcano about to explode.
Angada cast a look at him and ran away.

The ministers came running and advised Sugriva:
'Rama and Saumitri are men of truth; they have
Given you back your kingdom. Renouncing
All kingly ambitions, they have anointed you;
And thus have saved this kingdom in dire times.
They are the models of righteousness and culture.
When Lakshmana is here, with a message from Rama, 40
Listen to him and ready yourself for your duties.
He stands there near the door, with bloodshot eyes;
Welcome him humbly, and plead for his forgiveness.'

'O hear me, you ministers!' pleaded Sugriva;
'I do not wish any harm to Dasharatha's sons.
I do not see any reason why they should get angry.
I have passed orders for the whole army to assemble;
I have not done anything amiss. It is easy to form
Friendship, but difficult to put it into practice.'

Then, Maruti said: 'Listen to me, O king! 50
We cannot forget that he has got us Rumaa back.
Drowned in sensuality, let us not lose our directions.

The rainy season is over and autumn is here;
The banana tree with seven leaves has turned green;
Free of black clouds, the sky is clear and pure;
Stars shine with royal splendour, and rivers, rivulets,
And streams flow freely – without noticing any of these,
Is it proper to drown yourself in carnal pleasures?
Saumitri is here, and he is burning with rage;
It is proper to forget anger, and, with loving words   60
And tolerance, to beg his forgiveness humbly.
It is proper to pacify him with affection, and
Assure him that we will set about mother Sita's quest.
Once Rama gets angry, neither gods nor *danavas*,
Neither *gandharvas* nor others can oppose him.
Only Rama we can depend upon, and trust
The son of Sumitra.' Hearing these words of Maruti,
Sugriva became aware of the situation, and got ready
For future action.

Then, Angada approached Lakshmana and said: 70
'Come, O my lord! Listen to the friendly words
Of my uncle Sugriva, and come to us. Our city
Is fortunate to have in it; drums and pipes welcome
You with joy. Notes of music have spread this joy
Everywhere, and waves of amity are rising very high.'
Lakshmana, pleased with Angada's courtesy, slowly
Moved ahead; and *vanaras* saluted him with their
Arms and weapons. When he of the Raghu dynasty
Stepped majestically into the city, all were relieved.

Lakshmana moved in the city, surveying all.   80
Kishkindha rivalled Amaravati, the city of gods.
It was the treasure-house of Karnataka, and wealth
In plenty was displayed everywhere. Victorious
Trumpets were sounded throughout the city.
The city had risen on the banks of the river
Tungabhadra; lakes and gardens, hills and

Tall buildings, all displayed signs of wealth
And expensive objects.

It was the ocean of virtuous deeds.
All the citizens played and sang happily; 90
Women indulged in amorous games on terraces,
As if the moon was the ball they played with.
All the people were well-built and free from malice.
Pearls, rubies, and other precious stones were heaped
On roadsides, to be bought and sold like goods.
There was no fear from thieves and robbers.
There were to be seen perfumes of varied aroma;
There were seen varied clothes and ornaments;
There were swimming pools and fresh fountains; 100
There were huge canals, carrying water to the fields;
And there were tall temples and palaces of generals.

As Lakshmana walked through the city,
He saw Angada's house there, Mainda's here;
And the houses of the *vanara* elite, like Nala,
Hanuma, Kumuda, Tara, and Neela.

As if the entire wealth of Kubera was given over
To it, Kishkindha shone more resplendent
Than Amaravati, the city of gods. A high wall
Encircled the palace, the storeys of which rose 110
As high as the peak of the Mount Kailasa. The domes
Of pure white, the ornamental tassels hanging
From them, the numerous creepers laden with flowers,
The glorious trees studded with colourful fruits –
Words fail to describe their beauty and grace.

As Saumitri moved ahead, there rose before him
The tall and grand palace of Sugriva, the king.
The splendour of the harem inside it was beyond
Words. It was a huge place, guarded by soldiers;
And inside it were carved cots of gold and silver, 120

Attractive chairs and stools, and splendid curtains.
Gentle notes of *veena* filled the ears with joy.
Walls were painted with new and varied colours;
And colourful festoons were hung here and there.
There were festoons of jasmine of Venupura,
Of ears of corn, *mallika* flowers, and betel sheafs.
With anklet-bells tinkling, glass bangles ringing,
And toe-rings chiming rhythmically, the lustful
Women there indulged in games of love and pleasure.

When Sugriva beheld the fiery form of Lakshmana, 130
He confided in Rumaa: 'Saumitri has come here,
Angry and vengeful. I do not understand the cause
Of his anger or resentment. I have not done or said
Anything unpleasant. If he sees me, he will explode.
But I have heard that he respects all women, and that,
Since he does not have sisters, he deems every woman
His sister. Hence, my dear wife, you go to him, talk
To him softly, and find out why he is here.'

Rumaa, accordingly, approached Saumitri,
Knelt before him, and begged: 'My lord, calm down. 140
Being laymen, we lack understanding, sir.
Forgive our faults and protect us kindly.
Sir, you order us what we should do, and we will
Obey you and do it without a second thought.'

Pretending to be still angry,
Lakshmana spoke harshly: 'Where is Sugriva?
I shall carry him, bound hand and foot, with me.
Why is he dilly dallying in the work of Shri Rama?
Be they brothers or sisters or parents, if they
Destroy one's peace of mind, they are enemies; 150
I shall punish them and, if anybody tries to stop me,
He or she also will meet the same fate.'

But Rumaa did not lose her courage; bathing
His feet with her streaming tears, she said to Saumitri:

'It is well-known that the kings of Raghu lineage
Consider all women as their sisters. Why are you,
Then, so resentful? Be merciful towards me.

'Has the culture of the Raghu lineage cracked up?
Tell me, why has their flag of fame fallen down?
I will not let go your feet until you promise me, lord,   160
That you will save my husband's life and my marriage.
If you so desire, give up my husband and take my life;
If you take away my life, I will deem it my fortune;
And, I will reach Heaven as a married woman.
If I die in your hands, I will achieve salvation;
And I will bedeck the hair of Lakshmi as a flower.
You being the incarnation of Adishesha, the bed
On which lies Vishnu, bestow on me the fortune
Of reaching Vishnu's feet in your presence.

'Sugriva is faultless.   170
He has sent *vanaras* to all the four corners
To search for Sita. Can't you hear the noise
Of the army's movement, the twang of the bows,
The clang of swords, and the thunderous sounds
Of the maces? Give up your anger, my lord.'

Still Saumitri shouted:
'Time is running out and preparation is not enough.
He, forgetting friendship, indulges in pleasures.
I will root out the entire *vanara* race,
Reduce the city of Kishkindha to an arid land,   180
And will send Sugriva to the God of Death.'

Rumaa lost her patience.
'What did you say, Sumitra's son?' she shot back.
'Is Sugriva a lad? Are we all slaves of Saketa?
We have humbled the proud Ravana, and have built
An independent country of *vanaras*; the proud flag
Of this country is held high throughout the world.

We are bold people; if you provoke us, it will be
The ruin of the kingdom called Saketa.

'The people of Karnataka are honourable people;   190
They will rather die than break their promises.
We will not compromise with our honour; and,
We will not be tempted by the momentary lures
Of political strategies and personal gains.
Tell me, are these your words or of Rama?
Among friends, does anybody flash anger?

'The rainy season is just over;
Is it easy to mobilise an army, when the rivers
Are full, and the landslides block the roads?
Now, the message-bearers have gone, far and wide.   200
Just because one is suffering from separation,
Does it become that one begins to act like a child?
Words like "you will kill all, destroy everything"
Sound only childish to me. What more shall I say?
These words do not suit the sons of the clan of the sun.
Whether it is the effect of the age or of this soil
That the kings of the Raghu dynasty utter such words,
I cannot decide.

'My lord! Control your anger.
Does anyone act like fire in a dried-up forest?   210
Tell us, immediately, what your orders are.
We are Rama's servants; look at us with love.
I bow to the Destroyer; I bow to his arrows.
Destroy the king of Lanka, and the six-fold
Passions; and lead us in the propitious path.'

Canto One Hundred and Nineteen

'Life Originates In Pain'

||๖||

Rumaa's words becalmed Lakshmana
And he said: 'Listen; you are a woman of equanimity.
Only because Sugriva was lost in his sensual pleasures,
I have come here to wake him up. You are a woman
Who commands respect; you know the urgency of
The task ahead. What more can I say?'

'Yes, we were at fault,' Rumaa responded:
'But, Saumitri, does one get angry with people
Who are near to him? If we are at fault, forgive us.
You are aware of the demands of flesh; but,   10
You do not know what it is to be away from one's wife;
I realise it, the intensity of libidinal thirst, when
I think of your wife, Urmila.

'Lustful people are blind to
What is proper and improper, pride and shame.
The God of Love, Manmatha, traps even sages.
Orders have been passed and the *vanara* leaders
Have been arriving from all the four corners

To begin their quest for Sita. At least now, be calm.
Like Ganga coming down from the Himalayas 20
To bless the sons of Sagara, you have come here.
Punishing the wicked and protecting the good,
Upholding the culture of world-citizenship, and
The principles of "Sympathy as the core of *dharma*,"
And *datta – dayadhwam – damyata*
"Give, Sympathy, and Control" everywhere,
You are going ahead.

'This world is the home for sorrow;
We have suffered in sorrow and that is the truth of life.
Is happiness everlasting? It vanishes in no time. 30
The wise ones consider both as one, indivisible.
We have suffered in pain, we are thirsty for relief;
And, out of pain arises new life.

'O my lord, Saumitri!
Your life has been moulded by suffering; and
Your life, like the grave ocean, resonates
The yeaning of the age. Have mercy on us.
Sugriva has been waiting for you.'

Rumaa's words pacified Lakshmana.
However, he decided not to let Sugriva go 40
Unpunished for his lapses. He strode into the hall
Where Sugriva sat on the royal throne, in great pomp.
With total disdain for the royal pomp, with his eyes
Burning like the eye of the Destroyer, when he stood
There, unmoved like Adishesha, Sugriva got up
From his golden throne immediately, his hands
Folded in supplication. Saumitri spoke to him
Thus, harshly:

'Sugriva, if the world acknowledges
That you are a man of truth, why are you treading 50
The path of falsehood? Being false is as sinful
As killing a hundred horses or a hundred cows.

'Listen, Sugriva!
Ingratitude is the worst sin one can commit.
There is expiation for the murder of a Brahmin
Or a cow; there is expiation for drinking liquor
Or not doing a ritual. But, there is no expiation
For ingratitude. Does one, drowned in animal
Pleasures, forget one's promise, and face
The anger of the lord of the Ikshwaku lineage?　　　　60
Before you follow the path of Vali, wake up;
Before the whale of pleasures swallows you, wake up;
Before the python of lust crushes you, wake up
And attend to your duties ordained by Rama.'

In the meanwhile, there came running Tara,
Together with Angada, worried; and they implored:
'O Saumitri, enough of these harsh words and anger.
He is neither ungrateful, not is he wicked;
And, he is not the one to indulge in lies.

'Since he has got back his wife,　　　　70
Owing to the blessings of Shri Rama, he is indulgent,
As Vishwamitra was indulgent towards Menaka.
None is free from the pulls of the body, of libido.
You are the noblest of all; forgive Sugriva;
And give up your anger.

'The *vanara* leaders, all, will assemble here,
Within a day or two. Vali had captured Ravana;
And who was there to equal him among Aryas
And Dravidas? Sugriva has grown on Vali's model.
Arms are in plenty and Ravana's army is huge:　　　　80
And his fort lies in the middle of the ocean.
Conquering him is not easy.

'Before we understand the secrets of Lanka,
Before we assemble the army and discuss plans,
Should we leap into the fire-pit, Saumitri?
Sugriva is an expert, like Chanakya, in planning;

Even when he is in harem, he does not forget his duty.
Is it a child's game to face Ravana on the warfield?
I am disturbed by your uncontrolled anger;
O lord! Be patient.' 90

When the son of Sumitra found all of them
Pleading humbly, he pacified himself and smiled.
Sugriva, free from fear, explained to him softly:
'O son of Sumitra! I bow to you; you are merciful.
I know this is your kingdom and you are unequalled.
I have no doubt, Rama, a brave man and virtuous,
Will certainly destroy Lanka. He is so strong
That he cut seven *sala* trees with just one arrow.
You have lifted me up, like Adishesha from the ocean
Of sensuality into which I had fallen. Be merciful 100
Towards me and take me to Shri Rama's presence.'

Lakshmana responded to him calmly: 'Be a man
Of character. You deserve to enjoy this world,
And you are fit to destroy your enemies. Why do you
Delay? Come to the aid of Shri Rama and console him
Who is now plunged in sorrow. His grief hurt me,
And hence harsh words came out of my mouth.
Do not take it to heart and forgive me.' So saying,
He embraced Sugriva, thrilled and satisfied.

Life is indeed strange. 110
Whereas anger rises high once, calm surfaces next;
And one's mind wavers between high and low.
Prosperity and decline, the good and bad,
Both are like the ebbs and tides of the life's ocean.
Once the sky is clear and then it's cloudy and dark;
Once the clouds clash and thunder, and then silence.
If one does not get sound advice or does not heed it,
One's life is surely doomed to fall.

Canto One Hundred and Twenty

'Let All Brave Men Assemble'

||๑||

Reassured and cheerful, Sugriva called Hanuma
And said to him: 'O son of Anjana! Pay attention.
Summon all the brave men of the *vanara* race,
That live on the five hills, named Mahendra, Vindhya,
Himavanta, Sahyadri, and Bilishikhara, to assemble
Here, immediately. Let them come from all the regions.
Let them know that time is ripe to wipe out Lanka
And sing the glory of Saketa.

'Call them wherever they are:
Be they on the Mount Meru or the Anjana hill, 10
On the Maharuna hill or Dhumra hill,
Be they on any hill or inside any cave,
Or in any eye-catching forests and gardens;
They have to assemble here within ten days,
Or, they will be dealt with harshly.
These are the orders of Sugriva, and whoever
Violates the orders will be sentenced to death.
Let them all understand it.'

Then Sugriva ordered that a palanquin be brought
In order to go and receive Rama. Then, he sat in it, 20

Accompanied by Saumitri. Holding white umbrellas,
And fanning them with white fans, two liegemen
Ran on both sides of the palanquin. Conches, bugles,
And trumpets were blown, huge drums were beaten,
And pipes were sounded. Thus, he approached Rama,
And stood facing him, with his hands folded humbly.
The entourage looked like a sea full of lotuses and lilies.

With courtesy personified,
Sugriva said: 'May the lord be victorious.
O the noblest of Raghu dynasty! Be merciful. 30
When I told you that I do not need the throne,
And that quest for Sita was my first priority,
You forced me to occupy the throne and rule.
Have I subdued my senses? It is an illusion.
The fact is, senses have triumphed over me.
Brahma himself has confessed, "*imdriyaani mayaa jetum
Purushottuma*" (O the noblest, senses have indeed
Conquered me).

'Listen to Indra, the king of Heaven;
Look at Kaushika; consider all the great sages— 40
Is anyone of them free from the sensual pulls?
Do you not know that Shiva, the enemy of the God
Of Lust, ran after the charming Mohini? You also know
The story of the Moon-god who lusted after his
Teacher's wife. Monkey-mind is fickle;
And I am an ordinary being; you know my fate.

'You are one who has subdued all the senses.
Can I ever be equal to you? Cords of passion
Are strangling my throat. Tell me, does such a cord
Loosen its hold even when one's hair gets white, 50
Teeth fall, the waist is bent, and eyes get weak?

'The base of lust is woman, of anger is desire,
And the base of avidity is jealousy.

He who wins against all these becomes one like you;
And, with your blessings, will achieve salvation.
But I will achieve salvation while I am alive.
I bow to you, the crown of the Raghu dynasty;
I bow to you, the delight of Sita;
I bow to you whose very name is propitious;
I bow to you who is the home of all virtues. 60
Forgive my faults; I seek refuge in you.

'I have summoned all the brave men,
And they have all assembled here, in great number.
They will go in different directions in search of Sita,
And will surely seek her out.

'There are unequalled brave men,
Like Kumuda, Maindapa, and many others.
How can Ravana stand before them?
Like blades of grass, he will be blown afar.'

Shri Rama, overcome by Sugriva's affection 70
And devotion, replied to him: 'I admire
Your way of thinking; you have woken up in time.
Like Hanuma and Lakshmana, you are my brother;
We were brothers four; and now you are the fifth.
There is work ahead, and go about it determined.

'When there are friends like you,
·The king of gods will send good rains and crops;
The sun with his bright rays will dispel darkness;
And the moon will bestow cool light at night.
With your help, I have no doubt, I will vanquish 80
Enemy-hosts. O Sugriva, you are soft-spoken
And a man of character.' By this time, the *vanara*
Army, as vast as the ocean, assembled before Shri Rama.

Canto One Hundred and Twenty-one

'Staking Your Lives, Explore the Whole World'

||६||

In Kishkindha, the entire *vanara* army
Assembled, and, guided by Shri Rama, Sugriva,
And Saumitri, shaped clear strategies to search
For mother-like Sita.

All the brave leaders were there:
The brave Shatabali, Sushena, the father
Of Tara, Kesari, the father of Hanuma,
Tara Angada's uncle, Gavaksha of
The Golangula lineage, Dhumra, the destroyer
Of enemies, Panasa, the valiant, Gavaya 10
Who resembled the golden hill, Darimukha,
Mainda, Jambava, Gandhamadana, Baladitya,
Durmukha, and many more generals were there.

Leaping and jumping, this huge army
Stood before Sugriva, heads bent in courtesy;
And they all bowed to Shri Rama in devotion.
Nodding his head in admiration for Sugriva's
Power and friendship, Shri Rama felt that he
Had erred in judging Sugriva, and felt sad.

'Behold them, O Ramachandra! 20
They are brave leaders and love adventures;
They are such veterans of war that they can move
On land, in water, or anywhere and wage war.
Now, they are your servants, bent on serving you;
And their motto is to defend their country even
At the cost of their lives.

'They are not the ones who will break temples,
Neither will they sow hatred between religions.
They are the beacons of Karnataka culture.
They will build bridges between north and south, 30
And sculpt a new nation,' said Sugriva proudly.

Bathed in the ocean of friendship of Sugriva,
Shri Rama responded happily: 'You are not a novice;
You are knowledgeable, experienced, and an expert
Politician. Who can vie with you in breaking the
mystery of Lanka?'

While Shri Rama taught Sugriva
The hidden mysteries of the political path,
Other leaders assembled there nodded their heads,
And praised both: 'Shri Rama is well-versed in political 40
Philosophy and Sugriva is worldly-wise.
When both are united, Ravana will bite the dust.'

'Listen to me, O *vanara* king,'
Rama explained: 'The location of Lanka
Has to be discovered quickly; and, after we know
How the daughter of Janaka is, ill or well,
We should formulate our future strategies.
You as a king know how to get things done;
And you are intelligent. Show these brave men
Their course of action that lies ahead.' 50

Listening to the words of Rama and pleased,
Sugriva sent for the commander, Vinuta,

And told him: 'Take the army of hundred thousand
Soldiers and go to the east. You have to discover
Quickly, where Ravana stays and where Sita is.

'On the eastern coast of the ocean, there lies
A region of vast mines; explore that region.
On the hilltops there, live people, rough and black-faced.
Their ears are so long that they touch their lips. They are
The people who walk fast on bare feet; and they do not 60
Have homes and hearths; they are nomadic people.
They are fierce cannibals. Then, on the islands there
Live rough-haired hunters; and there are yellow-
Coloured people, as ferocious as striped tigers.
Be bold, be free, and look for our "mother."

'From there, you have to go
To the Yava island; it is a picturesque place.
It is a region where gold is mined, and it is
As spectacular as the floor of Heaven. Search there
The hills and fortresses, also woods and forests. 70

'In your wanderings there, if you turn right,
You will find the red water of Ghataprabha
Of Karnataka. You will come across many other
Rivers: Krishna, Bheema, Godavari, Netravati,
Malaprabha, Kapila, Harangi and Kali,
Kaveri, Vedavati, Sharavati and Hemavati.
Explore all those river banks.

Explore, explore
In forests and flower-gardens, on the hills
And in the valleys, mountain passes, caves, 80
And tunnels, in the ocean roaring with red water.
You have only one month's time. If you exceed
This term, Kishkindha will be put to shame,
And I will not continue to live. I will accept
Voluntary death, and my body will float on
The waters of the Pampa river.

'To the southern regions,
Let Angada, known for his speed, go for his quest.
Andhra, Chola, Tuluva and Kerala – he should pass
Through all these regions and look for Sita.
Where sandalwood trees give out sweet fragrance,
Where the river Kaveri meanders gently,
Where the Malaya mountain rises high and proud,
And where Sage Agastya stands in meditation—
He has to search for Sita in all those places.

'There is a river called Tamraparni, in which
Pearls are found. But, be very careful there as it is
Infested with terrible crocodiles. If you go further,
There, you will find the capital of the Pandya king.
It is famed for wealth and culture; its people are brave.
At the foot of the Mahendra hill, you will find trees
Of couple colours. The land, there, juts far into the sea.
On auspicious days, saints and monks, even gods
From Heaven arrive there for a holy dip in the ocean.

'There, beyond the ocean,
Lies a golden island; it is called the island of Lanka.
Strong and impregnable, and *rakshasas* live there.
There is a demoness called Angarake, who
Devours humans alive.

'Beyond the island of Lanka, southward,
In the middle of the ocean, lies Pushpagiri.
It is the home of enlightened hermits, and its
Peaks rise so high as to penetrate the sky.
It is invisible – or so it is said – to those
Who are ungrateful or violent or atheists.
All of you, brave men, bow with whole-hearted
Devotion to the sacred mountain, and go
In search of Sita, like searching for a ruby.

'If you proceed further, after some distance,
You will behold the Suryavan mountain.

It is a charming mountain, surrounded by varied
Fruit-trees, and plants and roots. You can eat them,
And drink honey, and enjoy yourselves to the full.
Then, after some rest there, move towards Kunjanagiri.

'There is a mansion on that hill, huge and spacious,
That Vishwakarma, the architect of Heaven,
Planned and built for the great Sage Agastya.
It is resplendent with gold and the nine precious gems.
Just adjacent to it, there lies the city of Bhogavati.
It is home for the serpent race and it is spread out;   130
Vasuki, the king of serpents, lives there.
Vicious and poisonous serpents guard the city,
Day and night, alert. There are a few hidden places
In its neighborhood.

'If you continue your journey,
You will see a bull-shaped hill full of rubies.
All types of rubies – *goshirshaka, padmaka,*
And *harishyama* – are found there. Divine
Sandalwood trees grow in plenty there. Five types
Of *gandharvas*, by name Shailusha, Gramani,   140
Shigru, Babhru, and Surya, live there.
Do not touch anything there, do not be tempted;
If you touch them, you will be burnt.

'To the east, there are many rivers:
Yamuna, Ganga, Sarayu, Kaushaki, Narmada,
Saraswati and Gomati. On the banks of those rivers
Lie many cities like Kashi, Kosala, and Paundra.
Look for our "mother" in the buildings of all
Those cities.

'All of you have to finish your quest   150
Within a month and return to Kishkindha.
It is the order of Sugriva, inviolable.
He who discovers Sita will be deemed by me

As my best friend, my intimate kin, my king.
Stake your lives and explore the whole world.'
With these words, Sugriva, administered to them
The oath of duty.

Sugriva's orders are formidable.
What should one do, where should one go to,
What is the punishment for default and what   160
Reward for success – all such details together
Have made "Sugriva's order" synonymous
With Draconian laws.

Jambavanta was wise, good, and strong.
He gave a piece of advice to the *vanara* host:
'Move always in groups; never go alone, anywhere.
Unity should be your watchword. Let your thoughts,
Speech, and action be one; and let there be total
Dedication in your work.

'The witness to all of our actions is the sun.   170
He is the conscience of the whole universe;
And he is the patron-god of eyes. He is Narayana.
Pray to him and move forward without any fear.
Agni is the patron-god of word and the moon
Is the patron of heart. Let your mind be firm;
Ignore comforts. May Rama be in your hearts,
And may success crown you.'

Canto One Hundred and Twenty-two

'Explore all the Hills and Deep Ravines'

||६||

The brave, blue-coloured leaders,
Sushena and others, approached the radiant
Sugriva and stood before him, their hands folded.
Sugriva addressed them thus: 'Hear me, O leaders!
Get ready to search for Sita and these are the details
Of your expedition. In the land of Bharata,
There are many rivers such as Ganga, Sindhu,
Brahmaputra, Yamuna, Narmada, Krishna,
And Kaveri; before they join the ocean, they bathe
Vast stretches of dry land and transform them   10
Into rich fertile fields. They fill the hearts of people
With delight and pleasure.

'There is also a desert, called Thar,
Where dusty storms blow noisily, and where
People live in fear, their hearts burning.

'In contrast, here, the ocean water,
Evaporates, joins the clouds as vapour, and
Pours down as rain; and the Himalayan snow
Melts, flows down, and, in the form of rivers,

Quenches the nation's thirst. People rejoice, 20
And rich nature, shooting forth new leaves and buds,
Makes people happy.
'You *vanara* leaders! You will see many kingdoms
In your journey: Vanga, Kalinga, Kashi,
Kamboja, and such; you will see the different
Parts of a city called Mahishapura and its wealth;
You will see there the gifted artisans who make
Sarees with gold borders, ceremonial dresses of silk,
Soft rugs, and the skilled goldsmiths who make 30
Gold ornaments of varied patterns.

'Let the army, two-lakh-strong, go to the west
Under the command of Sushena. You will go through
Regions like Saurashtra, and Bahlika. You will find
There a kingdom known as Kukshi, where, trees like
Punnaga, bakula, and *uddalaka* grow in plenty.
There you will find glorious rivers, hermitages
Of sages, very tall fortresses and mountain-ranges.
You have to go through the whole kingdom, looking
For Sita. Further, of course, lies the desert.

'There lies the western ocean, home for numberless 40
Water-creatures including whales and crocodiles.
There are, along its coast, *ketaki* groves, coconut
And betel-nut gardens, and rows of *tamala* trees.
If you go further, you will find the charming city of
Avanti, and, by its side, a huge mountain, Hemagiri.
Lions and tigers live there freely, and there are birds
Which are named after lions. There may live people
Who can change their forms at will. Look at them
Closely.

'There is one mountain range by name Pariyatra, 50
The peaks of which are sky-high; and on that lives
Fierce *gandharva* race. The *gandharvas* are experts
In changing their appearance, and they move in groups.

The orchards there yield fruits in all seasons; but,
Do not eat those fruits or pluck any flowers there.
They are guarded by the invincible *gandharvas*.

'If you go further, you will come across
The Vajra mountain, which is huge; and on it
Are found innumerable caves and grottos.
Search each one of them carefully. 60

'If you go beyond the western ocean,
You will find a hill called Chakravanta. On it,
There is a curious wheel which was fashioned
By Vishwakarma himself. It was there that Vishnu,
The god of all gods, killed five *rakshasas* known as
Hayagrivas. Go through each one of the caves and
Caverns there, and look for "mother" Sita.

'When you go ahead, you will find
A divine mountain called Varaha, which rises
In the middle of the ocean. Its peak sparkles 70
Like gold; and there lies the city by name Pragjotisha.
It is home for the wicked ruler Naraka. When you cross
The city, you will come across spectacular hills,
Forests, and huge caves, home for tigers and cheetas,
Which move about freely and proudly, roaring.

'Interesting accounts are narrated,
That, once, all the gods came together and conducted
The coronation ceremony of Indra on that hill.
Hence, that hill came to be known as "Maghavan".

'When you look at the distant horizon, 80
You will notice a long mountain-range, Swarnashaila.
Its endless peaks are so bright that they daze the eyes
Like the sunrays. To its north lies the Mount Meru,
Of which it is said that it has the boon to shine
Forever, with the lustre of gold.

'The eight *vasus* and the seven *marutas*, it is said,
Pray to the evening sun on the Mount Meru. On its summit,
There are glorious mansions built by Vishwakarma.
Around the mansion, there are colourful birds
And clusters of thick trees. These are the places,   90
Where you have to look for Mother Sita.'

Then, the noble *vanara* king, Sugriva,
Called Shatabali near him and said: "Come near,
Shatabali! You have with you a contingent of
One lakh soldiers; and your task is to go northwards.
In the countries like Shurasena, Madra, and Matsya,
In the mountain-ranges of the Himalayas, Kalagiri,
Tamrataka and Gandhamadana, Krauncha
and Mainaka – in all those mountains and forests,
Caverns and valleys, you have to search for Sita,   100
Shri Rama's wife. We have to fulfill our obligations
As soon as possible, and be contented.

'In the Krauncha mountain,
You will find a huge hollow carved by Skanda.
You have to go inside it with caution, and explore.
When you cross Krauncha, you will see before you
The Mainaka mountain, on which lies the abode
Of Maya. Explore the abode and nearby caves
Thoroughly. You will also see there the holy
Hermitage of Vaikhanasa and Valakhilya,   110
And such others who have achieved strange powers
Through their continued meditation. Bow to them
Humbly, and convey to them my regards.

'In the Vaikhanas lake, you will see
Golden lotuses and royal swans that glow like
The early morning sun. Male elephants play there
In the company of many female elephants.

'Beyond that lake, you will find
A vast field, enveloped in silence, where no sun
Or moon shines and no stars sparkle. Near it,   120
There lies the Shailoda river, on both the banks
Of which an empire of bamboo groves flourishes.

'There is a country on the other bank of the river,
By name Uttarakuru, through which flow scores of
Rivers; and they flaunt precious gems on golden
Lotuses. Lakes full of lilies are seen everywhere.

'The glory of the sand-dunes there
Is beyond words. They seem to be the golden
Dust sprayed by unknown hands. Birds flock,
The fruits on trees and flowers send forth alluring   130
Aroma. Happiness reigns there supreme.

'Nearby lies Somagiri,
From the top of which, it is said, one can see
The world of Indra and the world of Brahma.
It is also said, the sun, having set, rests there.

'You are bestowed with the speed of wind;
Go to all the three worlds and search for Sita.
Who knows where Ravana has kept her hidden,
In Janasthana, or in the north or south, or in
The underworld? The king of Lanka possesses   140

Magical powers, and the fear that he may take
Away the life of Janaki haunts me. Why delay?
Go round the world and look for her.'

Canto One Hundred and Twenty-three

'We Will Pull up the Hills, We Will Break the World'

||६||

Sugriva deemed Hanuma, the son of the God of Wind,
A man of action and efficient in his work.
Hence, he called him near and addressed him thus:
'O noble one! You know how to travel through
Both this world and the sky, without any problem.
Who else but you has the ability to go through
The demon-world as well as the world of gods,
The world of *nagas* and that of *gandharvas?*
You are also a man of strategies and unrivalled
Strength. Go and see Rama before leaving for   10
The quest.'

Hanuma, thrilled by the sight of Rama, said:
'My lord! As commanded by my king, I am
Leaving now for the adventure. Bless me.'
Then Shri Rama said: 'All living beings are born
Of the soul, and wind is a part of the soul. Hence,
It is wind that keeps all beings breathing. You are
The son of wind, and hence you are called "Primeval
Breath," Mukhyaprana. My son, I know you have

The ability to find out the daughter of Janaka.
I give you my royal ring; and when you show this
To Sita, she will immediately trust you.

'You are very close to my heart, and hence,
I will confide in you a few things concealed in my heart.
If you tell them, Sita will trust you. These are certain
Signs of Sita's body which none but I am aware of.'
With these words, Shri Rama shared those secrets with
Hanuma, and continued:

'Give this message to Janaki:
"I am like a fish discarded on the sands; who else
But you can care for me? The thought hurts me
Every moment: of what use is my power
when you are a captive of others? Come, come quickly to me,
And revive me before my body dries up. Show me
Your divine smile, you woman of good fortune.

"Your name itself is auspicious.
The parched earth has cracked up and the world
Gazes at the sky expectantly. With a tired mind,
With a future dim and dark, groping in darkness,
Shrieking as if holding a serpent, I stand aflame
As if touched by a comet. The rain of fire joins
The rivers and they together erode the ground
On which I stand. Come to me like the river Saraswati.
If the raft of your love gives me shelter, I can
Float on these horrid waters and reach you safely.

"I will not be daunted if there are millions
Of *rakshasas*, and Ravana does not frighten me.
I shall send all of them to the underworld, easily.
Whoever comes between us is doomed to die.
I shall wait for you till the end of this world."
Give this message to Janaka's daughter, and
Try to console her.

'You are the first among brave men,
And I know you won't leave any task unfulfilled.
Janaka's daughter will receive you with affection,
And, with complete trust, will give you her message.
May you be successful in your endeavour.' Thus
Shri Rama blessed him. Hanuma bowed to him
Respectfully, and carrying the signet ring
On his head, he took his leave of Rama.   60

Sugriva, then, said to them:
'Listen to me carefully; this is my final message.
This country of ours, Bharatavarsha, has people
And wealth. But, it is burning with the fire of hatred
And envy; the Tree of Love and sympathy is charred.
We have to weed out the deadly elements, and
Develop our country in egalitarian spirit.
Let us trust one another, let us work together,
Let us learn together, and let us live together.
Let us follow the noble path of quest, set for us   70
By Shri Rama, in his great mercy.'

The *vanaras* set forth with great enthusiasm.
Their cry, 'we will discover "mother" and destroy
Ravana,' rent the sky. Leaping and jumping,
Screaming and shrieking, they ran in different
Directions.

'We will break the trees;
We will uproot the hills and crush this globe;
We will disturb the ocean and jump long and high;
We will enter the underworld and roar there,' thus   80
The huge army of *vanaras* shrieked on its way.
Then, Shri Rama asked Sugriva:
'Your knowledge of geography is surprising.
How did you get these minute details?'

Sugriva replied to him humbly:
'You know my story. Afraid that my elder brother
Might catch me and kill me, I wandered everywhere,
Along with my ministers; and saw all the rivers
And oceans.

'All lakes I have seen; 90
The Udaya mountain, rich with ore, I have seen;
I have wandered from one island to another;
Hence, this world is as familiar to me as the mirror
Held on my palm.'

Canto One Hundred and Twenty-four

'No Sign of the Earth-born, No Trace of her Hideout'

||⊚||

The *vanaras* that had gone to the north
Searching for Sita, became aware of the ideal system
Of democracy in practice there. All the people's
Representatives in that system got elected, once in
Five years, by people both urban and rural. *Vox populi*
Or people's voice mattered in that system; and women
Too became people's representatives.

During the spring season, sages, students,
Ministers, and all representatives got together
And indulged in weeklong deliberations, regarding 10
The progress of the nation.

As they went further in north,
They beheld the Himalayan range, a glorious
Umbrella held above the country. Its crimson-
Lined peaks and metals of varied colours make it
A glorious sight. The wind sings there melodiously,
And the *kinnara* maidens, attuned to that rhythm,
Sing joyously.

The *surabhi* creeper rises high there, embracing
The tall trees; the river Jahnavi flows with royal
Majesty; and the moist, gentle breeze becalms
Every one's heart.

In the deep ravine, the mountain-walls
Rising on both the sides, beneath the rope-bridge
Built for crossing, flows the murmuring stream,
That never goes dry.

Through the rock-hollows, at the uneven bottom,
Flow the rivulets, once calm and once roaring,
Once in a slow pace, and once rushing fast,
Dashing against the rocks on both the sides. 20
The music of these streams and rivulets –
Of which scale is it and set to which beat?
Whose riotous imagination has created
This glorious poetry? And, to please whom?
In all such places, the *vanaras* search
For Sita, day and night.

When they reached Gandhara,
They saw the Sindhu and Konera rivers flowing
Playfully. To the south of Gandhara, there lay
Purushapura, narrow in the south and broad in 30
The north. It was a beautiful and cultured kingdom.

Then, they reached the Solimani mountain,
In Gandhara; it was like a holy vase in the middle
Of the Sindhu river. The *vanaras* rested there,
Slept in the open space, and, mixing with the people
There, they laughed and leapt with them.

To the east of Gandhara, stretched the Thar
Desert, as far as one could see. No rain or dew
Fell there, no greenery or crops. The sun pierced
Everyone like a sharp arrow. Further, to the east, 40

They went through Kosala, Shravasti, and
Kapilavastu; but they did not find any trace of Sita.

Further, they reached the land of five rivers.
To the east lay Magadha and rich Pataliputra,
Cradled on the banks of Ganga. The city of Nala
And Magadhapur were also there; and, coming
Downwards, the holy Gaya was there.
Further to the east, as they proceeded,
They saw the kingdom of Kashi, the very sight
Of which thrilled them. They rejoiced in the company 50
Of the people of Kashi. They looked for Sita in
Kausambi and Kosala. There were women of great
Charm and graceful form; their lips were red, their
Palms as soft as tender leaves, face like a lily, and
Their talk as sweet as nectar. Their physique,
Like lightning, could entice any youth; and their
Sidelong glances were enough to tempt any person.

Men, in those regions, were ambitious.
They carried as merchandise pearls and rubies
To distant lands, earned a lot money selling them, 60
And returned home very rich. But, due to their
Business, they ignored their wives, unashamed.

Through Tamralipti and the Anga kingdom,
The *vanaras* wandered everywhere till they were
Tired and dejected.

Thus, they spent a month,
Exploring cities and hills, rivers and lakes,
Various regions and also the coastline of the sea
And the ocean; but they did not find Sita;
And they were plunged in despair. 70

One by one, Vinuta, Shatabali, and Sushena,
Returned to Kishkindha from different directions,
And confessed to Sugriva, full of regret:

'There is not a city we haven't gone to; there is not
Any hill we haven't explored. Disdaining any
Danger, we have wandered through thick forests,
And searched caves and coasts. Pardon us, lord,
There is no sign of the earth-born anywhere, and
No trace of her.'

Looking at the sad and shrunk faces   80
Of the *vanaras*, Rama and Saumitri were plunged
Into sorrow, pained and anguished.

Canto One Hundred and Twenty-five

'If We Shut Our Eyes, the Whole World Disappears'

||६||

Along with Angada and Tara,
Hanuma went southwards and searched for Sita.
Wherever there were hills and mountain peaks,
Wherever there were rivers and lakes,
Wherever there were forests and deep valleys,
In all those places, Hanuma carried out
An intense search for the princess of Mithila.

However, the journey became harder,
More agonising, and the path arduous
As days went by. In some places, they were lucky   90
To get good fruits and sweet water, after partaking
Of which, they would rest and then continue
Their quest.

But, in many places, they did not find
Either fruits or flowers or roots or water.
Dry were the rivers and the surrounding land
Drier and burnt out. No signs of animals and
No nests of birds were there; no sounds of bees

And no trace of flowers or nectar. Confronted
With such a wasteland, they suffered out of 100
Hunger and thirst.

'Why is the land here so dead?' they asked
The villagers and this is what they replied:
'This was the place of sages and monks in the past.
Once, for some reason, a sage's son disappeared;
And the sage, burning with rage, cursed thus:
"May this forest be destroyed forever;
May no animal or bird inhabit this land;
And, let this region turn into a wasteland."
Owing to that curse, the land here is dead.' 110

Once, during their search, they found
A cruel demon in a cave; and the *vanaras*,
Deluded that he was Ravana himself, chased
And caught hold of him, dashed him against
A huge rock, and killed him.

Angada, intending to enthuse the *vanaras*
Dejected and dispirited, said to them: 'Listen!
We cannot afford to despair; we have to continue
Our task even if we have to give up food and sleep.
Enthusiasm, competence, and an iron will 120
Not to accept defeat – these are the three principles
Of success in any task. If we close our eyes,
The world also will be blind towards us.
Time is passing fast, and my uncle, Sugriva's
Orders are very stringent. If there are any
Alternative ways, tell me.'

Hearing the words of the crown-prince,
Gandhamadana said: 'There is no other way
But to continue our search despite hurdles.'
The *vanaras,* got up instantly as if a storm 130
Arose there, as if lightning struck them, and
Continued their search more intensely.

Anjaneya and others continued their journey,
And left behind the kingdoms of Andhra, Pandya,
Kerala and Tuluva. Of all of them, the land of
The Kodavas was the most picturesque. A brave
Land, it gave birth to many valiant men who,
For the sake of their nation, sacrificed their lives.
They are famed that they have drunk tiger's milk;
That they have used a python as catapult's string;   140
That they have played with ruttish-elephant's trunk;
That they have ruled the region from Bommagiri
To Pushpagiri, in a righteous and generous way.

The land of the Kodavas is the holy land
Where Sage Agastya conducted his penance;
Where the people, dressed in bodice and sash,
Sing the songs of harvest; and where, men and women
Indulge in varied dances with spirit.

The majesty of the river Kaveri
Is beyond words; it appears as if the heavenly   150
Ganga, leaping from above, flows triumphantly.
Flowing through hard rocks boulders with a roar,
Like a huge bow bent, full of whirls and pools,
Now invisible here, and now visible there,
Looping and dancing, it appears like a maiden
Anxious and excited to meet her lover.

But the daughter of Janaka is not there.
The palace-doors of the sky are shut; and the cuckoo's
Songs are muted. Desirous of playing in water,
Elephants are moving slowly; and the wild bisons   160
Are running fast. Nights have lost their charm,
And the breeze is no longer gentle. When lightning
Flashes slicing the sky, the cuckoo-chicks, scared,
Fold their wings closely.

Is there any end for a quest?
In the Sahyadri-forests and in deep caverns,

Hanuma and others searched for "mother" in vain.
Gaja, Gavaya, Gavaksha, Gandhamadana,
Sharabha, Sushena, Dwivida, Mainda, and
The crown-prince Angada climbed the boulders, 170
And entered into the dark caves looking for Sita.

Then, they reached the heart of Tulunadu;
And witnessed, spellbound, the glory of the rainy
Season in coastal Karnataka. Oh, what a scene!
The whole sky was a pageantry of hectic movements.
The defiant noise of thunder and lightning; the devious
Flashes of streaks of lightning; the rain that pours down
Day and night with a vengeance; it is beyond any words.
Filling up tanks and causing floods in rivers,
Drilling holes in hills and eroding valleys, 180
Noisy, hectic, wet, and life-giving,
Was the rainy season there.

Who can describe it in full?
Like the streams of tears, shed profusely by the sad
Beloved, frightened by the blood-red eyes and words
Of her enraged lover, rivulets of rain water flew
Everywhere, in mixed colours. But, after some time,
Rivers and rivulets calmed down; the soft mud
Settled down at the bottom; and water, clear
And transparent, displayed webs of foam, on which 190
The sunrays broke into seven colours. The earth,
Putting on a thick saffron saree, fixed, merrily,
The nose-ring on her nose.

Having worn a new saree, bedecked to visit
A crowded fair, the Taulava-queen, the daughter
Of Parashurama, rejoiced fearlessly.

The *vanaras* gazed awe-struck:
The sea-birds, like brilliant garlands, were flying
Silently toward the coast, proudly displaying

Their sparkling wings tinged with crimson, and 200
The sun, in a hurry to set, was plunging into
The sea, his face reddened, as if he was anxious
To meet his beloved speedily.

The huge sea waves, on the coast,
Rushed toward land roaring, stood still for
A moment, and withdrew, again to rush forward.
Here and there in whirls, the foam churned,
In fury, as if there was a decisive battle going on.
The *vanara* company pressed ahead, climbing
Up the hills and entering the caves, hoping 210
To see some sign of the "mother."

Then they saw a huge hollow on the ground,
From where birds like *krauncha* and *sarasa*
Came out flying, spraying cool water-drops.
A cool breeze blew, carrying a sweet scent with it.
They suggested that there, somewhere inside,
Might be a lake full of water.

'Let us go in and see,' said Hanuma;
And, slowly and cautiously, all went inside.
The cave was pitch dark and frightening. Afraid 220
That they might lose their way, they held each other's
Hand, and moved slowly. For hours and hours,
They walked and felt tired and thirsty.

Being hungry and exhausted,
And some even swooned. Caught between
Scylla and Charybdis, they couldn't either go
Ahead or go back. Thus they walked on and on,
When, finally, they saw some light at a distance;
Their hopes were revived, their breath returned.

A divine world, unseen and unheard of till then, 230
Manifested itself before them. They saw a grove,
Full of varied trees, different kinds of creepers,
And flowers of innumerable colours.

There lay a lotus pond,
In which red coloured lotuses had bloomed
In plenty, on which bees hovered buzzing and
Drinking nectar. Swans and cranes swam there
Lazily; and fish dipped into water and came up,
Flashing their white bellies.

There lay a city, 240
That had neat roads and multi-storeyed buildings,
Resplendent open halls, and big public offices.
Inside them were kept many idols of gold and silver;
And varied pictures had been painted on their walls.
There were rich clothes and exquisite drinks;
Floors were studded with precious stones, and
Festoons of pearls were hung everywhere.
Wonder-struck, the *vanaras* saw them, and
With unknown fear, trembled.

Canto One Hundred and Twenty-six

'You Have Shown Us the Path of Search for Salvation'

||๖||

'We have lost our way and we do not know where
We are. There are, of course, plenty of fruits and roots;
But we are not sure if we can eat them safely. What
Do we do now?' – thus the *vanaras* were worried.

'Answer – Are there any human beings here?
Answer us,' thus shouting, when they moved ahead,
They suddenly faced a holy woman in meditation.

Hanuma approached her and asked her politely:
'Mother, who are you? We are the messengers of
Rama, the Lord of Saketa, who, to fulfil his father's   10
Promise, gave up his throne and, accompanied by
Saumitri and Janaki, began to live in forest.
Ravana, the king of Lanka, kidnapped Janaki.
Sugriva, the ruler of Kishkindha, is our master;
And he, due to his friendship with Rama, ordered
Us to locate where Sita is kept captive. Having
Searched for her almost everywhere, unsuccessfully,
We have landed ourselves here unknowingly.

We are happy that we have met you here. Hunger
And thirst are distressing us. Having lost our way,
We have entered this hollow; and we pray to you
To show us the right path.

'Tell us who you are;
And why you are here, all alone. Trees are glowing
Here like rays of the rising sun, and the golden
Mansions strike one with wonder. Golden fish here,
Golden tortoise there; being a sage, how did you
Achieve all this? Who built this city and why is it
Totally deserted? Could you, kindly, tell us?

'I am the son of Anjana, and this man, here,
Is Jambavanta, senior to all of us. This youth
Is Angada, the son of Vali and Tara,
Presently, the crown-prince of Kishkindha.
Sugriva has given us only a month to finish
Our task; and time is running out in the quest.
We haven't found either a sign or a trace of Sita;
And we have lost our way. Kindly guide us.
Sage that you are, if you know where Sita is,
Tell us and help us,' said Hanuma humbly.

Listening to the words of the Son of Wind,
The sage felt very happy and said: 'Blessed am I,
And blessed is my life. Stop worrying and I
Will guide you. I am devotee of Rama, and
My name is Swayamprabha; I have been waiting
Anxiously to see Rama. As you are the messengers
And devotees of Rama, meeting you is as good as
Meeting Rama. You are hungry, thirsty, and tired;
Please accept these fruits, sweet water, and drinks.'
Swayamprabha, thus, treated them hospitably.

When all of them, revived with food and water,
Rested there satisfied, she narrated to them her story:

'An architect of the *danavas*, by name Maya,
Built this city; it is glorious and full of gold.
Having lost his heart to a heavenly being, called
Hema, he lived here with her. But once, due to
That woman, Hema, he got into a fierce war with
Indra, the king of Heaven; and Maya died fighting.
Now, this city is in the possession of Hema; and
I am her handmaid. She has gone to Heaven, and
Has forgotten everything in the presence of Indra. 60
I, given the responsibility of guarding
This city, am here doing penance.

'My inner voice told me: "Fix the form of
Shri Rama in your heart, and immerse yourself in
His meditation; your life's goal will be reached."
I have been waiting for Rama here, and now
I see you. My prayers have been rewarded,'
Said Swayamprabha, with joy and excitement.

She, who had been yearning for a glimpse
Of Shri Rama, rejoiced when she saw Hanuma as if 70
She had seen Rama himself, and danced with joy.
'O Rama! I had been waiting for you,' she sang;
'I had been meditating on you, when you granted
Me your divine vision in the form of Hanuma,
And, dispelling my heart's darkness, have filled it
With light. O ocean of virtues! I bow to you.

'When great sages and monks
Long for your vision, how did you lean towards me
With love? You have shown me the great path
Of salvation. O ocean of virtues! I bow to you. 80

'You have given me boundless wealth;
You have transported me to the divine world,
Which can neither be described not observed.
O ocean of virtues! I bow to you.

'I have bathed in the lake of your blessings;
My life is meaningful now and I am satisfied.
You are truth incarnate, you are omnipresent;
O ocean of virtues! I bow to you.

'Who knows but you
What the ends and means of human life are!
There is none higher than you; you are the king.
O ocean of virtues! I bow to you.

'You are
The moon in beauty, the earth in forgiveness;
In anger, you are the God of Fire on the doomsday.
Once one is blessed with your vision, one finds
All equal. O ocean of virtues! I bow to you.

'The sky is your seat, the sun and the moon the lamps;
The galaxies of stars are your necklace of rubies;
The southern breeze fans you like a royal fan.
O ocean of virtues! I bow to you.

'You are
Unequalled in strength, lustrous like the golden hill;
You are the master of the wise, home for all virtues.
I sing forgetting myself, you are a lover of melody;
O ocean of virtues! I bow to you.

'The whole world knows the story of your life;
None suffers who believes you; only a non-believer suffers;
If one trusts you heart and soul, one is blessed by you;
O ocean of virtues! I bow to you.

'Ahalya awaited you for long, in the form of soil;
Shabari awaited you for long, in the form of fruit;
Waiting itself is penance, a whetstone of devotion;
O ocean of virtues! I bow to you.

'To the lake of Rama, morality is the bank;
Restraint is its water, truth is its deep bottom.

I shall bathe in the waves of your mercy, and
Achieve salvation. O ocean of virtues! I bow to you.

'A serpent's food is air;
Leaves and grass are the food of the elephants;
To me, devotion is food, which satisfies
My hunger. O ocean of virtues! I bow to you.

'I experience now a state of total contentment;
I now shine as gold tested in fire; the devotion for
Rama has cleansed me of all acts, past and present;
And has prepared me to take the path of salvation.
Your sight has sanctified my life; you are the ocean
Of mercy; you are the father of the whole world.'
Thus Swayamprabha praised Rama in the form of
Hanuma, with great joy.

Then, she showed them the way and said:
'Those who enter this hollow cannot return; listen,
I will give you the fruit of my penance and lead
You out of this place.' Then she conducted them
All out of the hole, bowed to Hanuma, and said:
'See the ocean there. In the middle of it lies Lanka.
It is famous by the name of "Golden Lanka,"
Since the wealth of the entire world is heaped there;
Ravana is its king, and it is impossible to enter it.
But, Hanuma will overcome all hurdles,
And will discover "mother"; no doubts about it,'
Thus spoke Swayamprabha, wished them well,
And went back to the hole.
'Victory to Shri Rama, victory to Swayamprabha,
Victory to Sugriva, victory to Saumitri,
Victory to Jambavanta, victory to Angada,
And victory to Hanuma who succeeds in all,'
Thus the *vanaras* hailed Rama and others.

Canto One Hundred and Twenty-seven

'May the Rule of the People Be Celebrated'

||௬||

'When will the *vanaras*, who have gone away
Seeking Sita, return? Will they bring any good news?'
Wondering thus, Shri Rama, Sugriva and Saumitri
Waited for them at Kishkindha, anxioiusly.

Besides the quest, Saumitri is intent
On a grand vision of building a new society.
He contemplates a synthesis of the cultures
Of Kishkindha and Ayodhya, for which
Rushyamuka seems to him the ideal place.

Man's progress has to reach the sky;   10
All the human potential hidden in him has to be
Manifested; and, rising higher than the material
World, a man should aspire for a spiritual world
In the New Age – this was Saumitri's vision.

Once, when he was in the company of Sugriva,
Saumitri unburdened himself on the preparations
For the coming war, thus:

'Scores of rivers join the ocean of war.
One individual cannot do much; revolutions

Are the result of the uprising of the masses.
A war means the construction of a new path;
A war means the arousal of new ideas and emotions;
A war means the establishment of egalitarianism;
A war means forging together the culture of ancient
Sages and that of modern scientists.

'Even if we have to wage a war,
We should fight to save the honour of women;
We should fight to save the lives of helpless children;
We should fight to keep the flame of freedom burning;
We should fight to oppose tyranny and oppression,
And to usher in peace and welfare.

'O Sugriva, listen!
Wars shouldn't result in total destruction;
Blood-thirst is totally foreign to a war.
Unaware of this truth, nations today are caught
In mutual hatred, and are racing toward ruin.
Such aggressive nations will soon disappear
Like dust in the womb of Time.

'The rule in Lanka is barbaric;
Such autocratic rule has to be terminated.
It is not enough if we free "mother" from
The captivity of Ravana; we have to establish
People's rule in Lanka and make it a seat of *dharma*.
Once we achieve this task, automatically,
Heartless and lustful men like Ravana will be
No more; ideals and principles will take root
And root out corruption.

'Consider this: war should be an instrument
To end the horrible tradition of forceful
Occupation, bloodshed and rampage. May the values
Of righteousness be established and may the people

Get the kind of rule they desire in this southern
Island, leading to joy and prosperity.'

Sugriva responded to the ideas of Saumitri
Enthusiastically: 'Let us stop, Saumitri,
The propagation of Lanka-culture, speedily.
Cowardice and weakness have no place here.
Let us try to find out the kind of warfare Ravana
Practices, and then let us root out the evil imposed
On that country.' 60

'Good people say,' Saumitri rejoined;
'When equal powers clash, it leads to great ruin.
Ravana has perpetuated this myth of "racial
Difference between Arya and Dravida," and
The myth that "Aryans are aliens to this country."
This myth has the potential to give birth to explosive
Hatred between communities; it is a conspiracy
To destroy the nation. He is a fool, who does not
Know the difference between a revolution and
Mutiny. He has done enough evil to deserve death. 70
Let us pull aside the false curtain of "Arya-Dravida"
Difference; let us celebrate the vision of the "oneness"
Of the world and the divine fusion of mind and heart.'

Sugriva agreed with him and said:
'The stream of freedom is flowing now intensely
In the hearts of all the *vanaras*. The Tungabhadra
River is rushing toward its goal, roaring confidently.
Drops of water thrown up by it display on all sides
Rainbow colours; the fount of revolutionary
Spirit is springing up, and limitless joy has filled 80
All hearts. Drums proclaim that *vanaras* are awake,
And that their poetry contains sparks of revolution.
Whereas Lanka is noted for its war-culture,
Ayodhya is proud of its culture of peace.

'We stand now between life and death;
But the ambition to live in peace and fuse heart
And mind is very strong.'

Canto One Hundred and Twenty-eight

'We Have To Light the Lamp of Joy and Contentment'

||6||

Saumitri said to Sugriva:
'The human being has been endowed with
The rational faculty to improve the world;
He has the consciousness of truth and values.
While the animals have to depend on their instincts
To make choices and denial, man has reason
To make right choices. If men follow the path of
Animals, murder and violence will unsettle
The whole world, killing humane feelings.

'During peace, one has to prepare for war. 10
Present war-strategies have to be evaluated,
And, through short-term, mid-term, and long-
Term plans, infrastructure has to be perfected.
Common people have to be empowered, and
Their collective strength has to be harnessed.
Such planning guarantees victory.'

Sugriva replied dejected:
'Terrible weapons are being forged. Chemical
Weapons that spit poison, deadly weapons that
Can burn a whole region, doomsday weapons   20
That strew disease-viruses – all potent weapons
To destroy the whole of mankind are in use.
How do we fight such a bloody war?'

But Saumitri consoled him: 'In this country
Of Bharata, while the kings of the Ikshwaku
Lineage preach peace, the demoniac groups
Are hastening to break this country and subjugate
Ayodhya. Aware that Vali is no more; Ravana
Intends to occupy Kishkindha and raise
The flag of victory on the Rushyamuka peak.   30
The famed towers of Karnataka he hopes
To topple and reduce the kingdom to dust.

'But, being knowledgeable about such
Intentions, sages like Vishwamitra, Agastya,
And Parashurama have bestowed on Rama
And me powerful, divine arms and weapons;
And have taught us many war strategies.

'Disarmament, if it is one-sided, is fruitless.
Ravana has planted explosives in different
Parts of this country; and he hopes to explode   40
Them from Lanka itself. This is his strategy.
Fear and anxiety are increasing every day.
Hence, how can we disarm ourselves and fight
The king of Lanka? Is there any alternative
To war? Poisonous seeds sown by Ravana
Have now become plants and huge trees;
Can we now create a world free from fears?

'The king of Lanka is vainglorious.
Water in this world is ten times more than the earth;

Fire ten times more than water; air ten times 50
More than fire, and space ten times more than air.
The wicked king of Lanka has vanity ten times
More than others; and that is driving the world
To the brink of disaster.

'There are also signs of external forces
Interfering with the affairs of our country.
Their goal is to encourage internal frictions,
And, thereby, usurp our land. As the wise put it,
Eternal vigilance is the price we pay in order
To protect our freedom. 60

'We should be proud of ourselves,
And also possess self-respect; but these have to be
United with strong willpower. Only then, they will
Become the bastion of a nation's freedom.

'Victory is assured in a war,
If there is an army motivated, commanders
With stony willpower, and common people,
Who are alert and ready to aid the army.

'If the common people are corrupt,
And their lives are disturbed, the ruler has to 70
Use his power to punish the guilty. If law-breakers
Commit crimes, the ruler's rod has to be used
To put an end to their crimes.

'What the ancient dictum "*raja pratyaksha
Devata*" means is that the king is equal to god
On earth. This dictum becomes true only when
The king protects good people, punishes the wicked,
And grants economic help to the poor.

'On the contrary,
If the king becomes a victim of lust and anger, 80
Hatred and passions, rules the people using

Deceit and falsehood, uncaring of the people,
Doesn't heed anybody's advice, and lives in
Luxury, people will rise against him and kingship
Will collapse. The king, who remains a wicked ruler,
Is worse than a murderer, and deserves punishment.

'The king alone has to look after the weak
And widowed women, orphans, and old people.
He has to wipe out the tears of helplessness,
And light the lamp of joy and contentment.   90
On the path of progress, pain and sorrow follow
One like bees and sting. What the age demands
Is to renounce the comforts of this world, and
Dedicate oneself to the amelioration
Of others' suffering. A life of revolution stands
On the base of sacrifice and renunciation.
That is the greatest reward for a dedicated soul.'

Canto One Hundred and Twenty-nine

'New Precepts are Needed to Save this World'

||6||

Sugriva, having listened to the words of Saumitri,
Asked him: 'Where can we find humanitarian concerns?
Where are fellow-feeling, love and peace? Who can
Save us from the jaws of war, that has taken a toll of
Innumerable people who are buried in time's womb?
How do we quench the thirst for war? There are now
Arms and weapons that can totally destroy everything?

'Any number of saints and god's incarnations
Took birth in different countries and in different ages;
They preached the principles of peace and friendship,   10
And then they went back behind the curtains of
Life's play. But, have we learnt anything from them?
They are only memories now, and incarnations
Have disappeared into thin air like mist.

'How do we deal with man's egotism,
Which urges him only to think of himself
And his possessions? My strength is limited:
I want freedom but not any exploitation;

I want co-operation and not hatred;
I need a new precept, the one that can save
The world; the precept of noble love, that can
Bring cheer to everyone's heart and root out
Violence. But, when there are the enemies
To peace, contentment is only a mirage.'

Saumitri replied calmly:
'The vow to ban wars is indeed noble; but,
The war against Lanka is before us, unavoidable.
Ravana, who believes that the policy of aggression
Is his political philosophy, has destroyed peace,
And has spread, everywhere, his deceitful net.

'It is not practicable to ban by law all wars.
The desire for peace should grow within oneself,
And one must be determined to that end.
Otherwise, the "no-war-policy" will be one-sided and of
No use. There are many ways to control violence
Even in war; we have to defeat enemy's plans and
Strategies so that there will be no bloodshed.

'Once you enter into a war,
You should have total faith in your commander;
Soldiers' training should be complete and our
Stores of arms must be full and ready. All should have
Sense of time and discipline. If all these are satisfactory,
You can defeat any enemy. Faultless preparation
For war is a sign of victory.

'We should be competent to pinpoint our enemy;
Otherwise, success will always elude us. War cannot be
Synonymous with the commander; and if we trust
Only the commander, we will find victory elusive.

'A leader who can inspire his followers,
Should possess a vision, courage to take novel
Decisions, and he should be outstanding in his

Determination and readiness to sacrifice everything.
In the absence of such an able commander, we will be
Like cactus growing on desert land.

'In the new reign, all should have equal share
And protection. If one selfish class oppresses
All other classes, there will be revolution,
Burning and destroying all; and it will be
A prologue for the birth of a new system.
Once the subjects are happy, everything else
Will be under control.

'What should be in the forefront is the people's will
That there is no place for discussions, and that
War is inevitable since freedom is in jeopardy.
The skill and sincerity of the taskforce that carries
Out our plans must be strong and well-founded;
And intelligent spies should reveal to us all
The enemy movements and strategies.

'During a war, all of your plans and operations
Should be new. They should be based on your
Secrets, and they should be practicable. Based
On past experience, our soldiers' training should be
Revised from time to time; future visions should be
Based on past experiences.

'If we prepare for war very hard during peace,
War, when it becomes inevitable, will be easy
To manage.

'The *Golden Lanka* possesses
A huge arsenal and experienced soldiers.
The commanders, of course, are highly intelligent.
You cannot pit against Ravana your proficiency
In boxing or wrestling. The art of war has progressed;
New weapons and newer strategies are striking.
Only when spiritual power is coupled with mechanical
Power, one can be sure of victory.

'Both the Aryans and the *vanaras*
Are loath to learn the new ways of war. They are
Entrenched in their own old plans and ways of war;
They are like fossils submerged in desert sands.
How can they fight a war against Ravana? 90

'That *vanara* army is huge and Ravana's
Small is nothing to be complacent about. An army,
Well-equipped and trained, can inflict defeat on
Bigger armies, as history documents. O Sugriva!
We have to make perfect preparations if we wish
To be victorious against Ravana.

'Get ready for a great war.
Get together all the *vanara* army units.
They should know all the hiding places of the enemy;
And they should know how to change their fields 100
And formations during war. War does breed fear
Of death; but they have to fight ignoring this fear.
War implies pain, exhaustion, and suffering.
Only when the body and the mind are blended,
Enemy's heart is broken.

'The two great sages,
Vishwamitra and Agastya have taught me
The secrets of great weapons; they are known as
Mukta, amukta, yantramukta, and *muktamukta*.
Call immediately your skilful smiths to make 110
These weapons.

'Let them make strong bow-strings,
Iron bows, bamboo bows, and sharp shafts of
Ivory. I will invite the teachers from the hermitage
Of Agastya; they will teach your army everything
About archery.'

Canto One Hundred and Thirty

'A Festival for the Brave, a Carnival of Patriots'

||❂||

Saumitri continued to impart the intricate
Art of warfare to Sugriva: 'Among the arrows shot,
Depending on their speed and direction, there are
Nine types: *unmukhi, abhimukhi, tiryak, manda,*
Gomutrika, dhruva, skhalita, yamakakanta,
And *krushta*. One has to study them deeply.

'The shape of the sharp arrows shot by soldiers
Can be of many different types: *karnika, nalika,*
Vasti, suchi, kapisha, lipta, shlishta, kshurapra,
Puti, jihmaga, vaitasti, naaraacha, ardha-
Naraacha, bhallavipata, anjali, ardhachandra,
And so on. With an arrow called *shataghni*,
One can kill a hundred people at a time.

10

'Inside the fort of Lanka,
There are weapons like *shatagni*, tridents, and
Those that are moved in machines on wheels.
To defend the fort and at the time of attack, there are
Implements to noisily rain stones on the enemy and
Force him to retreat.

'There are, in Lanka, many modern weapons,
By name *kampana, kanapa, rushti, nakhara,
Danda, salake, goshirsha, ulukhila,
Sarvatobhadra,* and there are huge metal balls.

'There are such sophisticated weapons like rockets
In his arsenal, such as *Indrastra, vayavya, salila,
Indrajaala, nagasampada, shaila, pashupata,
Bhargava, sthulakarna,* and *Mahendrastra.*
Ravana has trained his army in the use of these weapons.

'Consequently, we should also be ready
To use the great weapons given by Brahma,
Like *Rudrastra, Narayanastra,* and
Brahmashirostra.

'In addition to our arsenal of weapons,
We should get ready various types of equipment
To protect the chest, arms and head of soldiers,
Such as helmets and breastplates, and shields
Made of the thick skin and horns of elephants,
Rhinos, and bulls. We should also get prepared
Armours and coats of mail, and those known as
*Kurpasa, kanchuka, varavana, patta,
Nagodarika, hastikarna, talamoori,
Dhamanika, kavata, apratihata, kitika,
Balahakanta,* and such other items
Of protection.

Besides such weapons as spears and lances,
There are canons called *sarvayasam* and *danda.*
To smash through the enemy forces, we have to
Have *tomara* or iron maces. To force the elephants
Also to retreat, maces are necessary; without maces,
No fighting can be complete. Scimitars are necessary
In single combat. *Pasha* or the long chain with

A noose, that flashes suddenly like glow worms,
Is of great use for cavalry. Then there are stakes
And tridents, mallets, swords, bludgeons, and pikes.

'When there is the fear of assault,
One should devise suitable different formations:
If the enemy is in front, we need alligator-formation;
If the enemy frightens from behind, cart-formation;
If it harasses from the flanks, diamond-formation;
If the attack is from all sides, the only formation
One can go for is *sarvatobhadra*.

'Call all the blacksmiths, Sugriva,
And order them to prepare different types of carts.
We need carts to carry weapons and ammunition,
Carts to carry food-items and treasury, carts to
Carry chariots, and carts to carry medical supplies.

'We need huge pots full of oil,
And pots full of snakes; protectors for elephants;
Resin and allied chemicals to produce fire,
Honey-wax, liquid jaggery, and bamboo fans
To cleanse foodgrains.

'On level grounds, position horse-drawn chariots;
On water, boats; and the foot-soldiers in forests.
They should carry with them bows and arrows,
Swords and spears.'

Then Sugriva said in admiration:
'O Saumitri, the war-preparations you have
Explained at length is great. See there, in the outer
Parts of Kishkindha, both defence and offence,
Deployment of the army and use of arms, all these
Are being rigorously taught by the expert instructors
Who have come from Janasthana.

'The entire workforce of weapons and other arms,
That belongs to Sage Agastya has come here.
So has Prabha, the instructor of Shalya.

'Whether it is elephant-training or horse-training,
Be it single combat – the experts are here
To teach. There are masters in the use of bows,
Swords, and maces; there are those adept in taming
Elephants and horses; there are veterans to teach
The use of *mukta* and *amukta* weapons. In fact,
There is a huge gathering itself engaged in
Preparations prior to war.

'Look at those horses!
There is the white horse called Karka, the one
Blood-red in colour is called Shona, and that
Of brown colour is known as Hema. The horse
With white eyes is known as Mallikaksha; and
The horse that is all white is called Bolla.
You will see there horses of all types and colours.

'Look at those brave soldiers!
Highly excited, leaping and jumping, they have
Turned into real apes. They cannot wait for the war
To begin.

'There, you can see
The various kinds of formations you explained:
Naga, Mandala, Bhoga, Durjaya, and
Sarvatobhadra. Devising strategies to attack
And counterattack, they have forgotten themselves.
This is a festival for the brave, a carnival for patriots;
They await, impatiently the war against Lanka.'

Saumitri was happy to hear these words;
And he added: 'First, the infantry should attack
Fiercely; and they should go ahead notwithstanding
The enemy force; and they should be followed by

Another unit of infantry. Thus, in waves, like
The roaring waves of the ocean, they should
Press forward.

'In a righteous war,   120
Fighting at night is not right, but it is unavoidable.
Get your army trained to both during day and night.
All the *vanaras* have to imbibe the strategies
Of army movements and army deployment.
See those that have to fight in valleys and
River-banks are highly motivated. Let all these
War preparations continue with full force.

'Pay special attention to train soldiers
In wars on open fields and an assault on fortified
Strongholds. All the seven organs of the force,   130
Namely, king, minister, advisor, treasury,
Army, nation and castle must be involved in
All such wars.

'Castles are of four types:
Those on hill, in water, in a forest, and on land.
A capital without a fortified castle will easily fall
Like clouds driven by storm, hither and thither.

'Experts are needed to build bastions on forts,
With wood, tiles, and bricks. Holes through which
Archers can shoot should cleverly be carved on   140
The fort walls. Importantly, the fort's main portal
Has to be very strong.

'The passages to enter and come out of forts
Should have a "tiger-face" at entrance, and huge
Bolts. Compared to a battle on open field,
Battle around the fort is very hard. Before assault,
One should have a complete idea of the enemy's castle.
One should also find out and mark the weak points
Of the fort, and where water-holes, horse-holes, and

Escape holes are situated. Only when one is sure 150
Of all these, one should mount an assault.

'One should fuse together both offence and
Defence; otherwise, combat will be fruitless.
While launching an assault on a fort, one should have
Different types of ladders, ropes, cords, and flagstaffs
Of the bastion.

'The bastion-doors have always to be closed;
Here and there on the battlements, one should fix
Pikes and pointed stakes, and in between bags of
Sand. Huge catapults to throw stone balls should be 160
Kept ready.

'One should also keep ready boiling gruel
And oil, wooden logs, hot sand, and such to pour
On the enemy attempting to scale the fort and
Force him to retreat.

'*Howdahs* for elephants,
And saddles for horses should always be ready.
Also, drums big and small, double drums, horns,
Trumpets, metallic gongs, and such should be ready.
They should be so played that their ear-splitting 170
Noise scares the enemy and motivates our army.

'While undertaking a war-expedition,
One should have only one goal in mind: enemy's
Defeat. Hence, one should take into account
The enemy-strength, right season and time, and then
Proceed. The best to launch a war is autumn; next
Comes spring, and summer is the least preferred.
The rainy season is the worst.

'While the army is on the march, the following
Support-staff should accompany it: artisans, smiths, 180
Carpenters, weapon-sharpeners, stone-cutters,

And those that work with axes, spades, crow-bars,
Cleavers, and sickles. Also, water-carriers and cooks
Shouldn't be forgotten. Most importantly, an army
On the march should have a host of experienced
Physicians; and merchants selling a variety of
Eatables and grocery should accompany the army.

Canto One Hundredn and Thirty-one

'Prabha the Physician Shone Like the Pole Star'

||૬||

There was a young woman from Agastya's hermitage,
An expert surgeon and highly knowledgeable in
The field of poisons. Her name was Prabha; she was, now,
In Kishkindha, to conduct a workshop for men and women
About the ways of nursing, and thus to prepare them
For the coming war.

One day, she called the veteran general
Of the *vanara* army, and propounded to him:
'O general, listen to me attentively. I will
Teach you how to protect food from poisoning.
When Rama, Lakshmana, and Sugriva march ahead,
Followed by their army, ready for war, there should be
Physicians, always. Do not use any clothes or food
Gifted by others; there is a chance of food-poisoning,
Which may threaten life.

'Any kind of food, liquid or solid,
If it is found that it contains poison, immediately,
Should be buried under the earth to keep it away
From men and animals.

'Those who are poisoned behave thus:
They stammer and their words are incoherent;
They shake with pain and scratch the ground;
And their whole behaviour gets suspicious.
Such behaviour ought to be examined keenly.

'As soon as poisonous food is sighted,
Flies die, crows' cawing gets weak, and birds
Like parrots, sparrows and cranes fly skyward
Shrieking; swans' legs falter; partridges' eyes
Redden; cats scared run helter skelter; monkeys
Urinate and get uneasy; and peacocks dance
In fear. One has to observe all these phenomena;
Otherwise, one's life will be endangered.

'If you throw poisoned objects into fire,
There will be a result in crackling sound, followed by
A flame as blue as a peacock's neck; and the stench
Will be as strong as that of a burning corpse.

'If one touches any poisoned object,
One's skin begins to itch, followed by swelling
And fever. The remedy for this is to apply the paste
Of ground sandalwood and *lavancha* grass.
Also, one should rinse one's mouth with the potion
Of moon creeper and palmyra leaves. No sooner does
The potion reach stomach, than one vomits, giving him
Relief. There are many other potions that pacify
The poisoned person. Our ancient sages
Have given us fifty types of roots that contain
Cure against poisoning; and you better know
All of them.'

Then, Jambagi the *vanara* healer asked her:
'Respected Prabha, tell us what we should do
If one, poisoned, loses his consciousness.'

Prabha thought about it for a while, and then said:
'The method to be followed in such a case is called

Sanyasthapana. If you make the patient sniff
The powder prepared from asafoetida, curry leaves,
Nettles, *kachora* roots, black hellebore, bdellium,
And many such other roots, the patient will gain
Consciousness at once.

'Again, after you burn the roots smoke will arise;
And if you blow that smoke through a small pipe 60
Into the nose of the patient, he becomes conscious
At once, and returns to the battle ground to fight.'

Another in the gathering, by name Pasanara,
Interested in nursing the wounded, requested
Prabha to tell them how to treat wounds. Prabha
Enumerated: 'Wounds are of two types: expected
And unexpected, and different forms of wounds
Are caused by different sources: man-bites, bites
Of animals and birds, and bites of creatures like
Snakes, centipedes, and scorpions. Even the bites 70
Are different: *prahara, agni, kshara, visha,*
Tikshnaushadha, kapala and *aghata.*
Among the battle-wounds, there are different
Kinds of wounds caused by different weapons
Like the wheel and the axe. If one immediately
Applies honey to the wound, it relieves pain,
And also acts as antiseptic. If medicinal leaves
Are tied in a piece of cloth and the wound is tied
With that cloth, the wound dries up slowly.
If the substance called *vayuvidanga* is heated 80
On hot embers, along with neem leaves and
Turmeric, the resulting smoke can dry up
The wounds quickly.

'Grinding gall nut in goat's milk,
And applying it on the wound for seven days
Is one method. Another is to powder egg-shell
Of hens, *jyeshtha* root, *chillada* nuts and tiny

Cowries, mix it with cow urine, and applying it,'
Prabha explained.

Then Durbhara got up and said: 'Please explain 90
To us the different kinds of instruments used
In surgery.' Prabha complimented him on his
Interest and explained in detail: 'Listen, Durbhara!
That which is sharp on one side is *ardhadharaa*
Shastr; if the blade is curved it is *suchi shastr;*
That which is pointed at the end like sacrificial
Grass is called *kushapatra shastr.* If you have to
Prick, that instrument is known as *achimukha*
Shastr; one that is used to slice off rotten flesh
Is *kartarikamukha shastr;* the one used for 100
Cleaning teeth is *dantashanku shastr;* to suck out
Puss, *eshani shastr* or *trikurcha shastr.*

'There are instruments of many shapes:
That which is shaped like a snake is *kankamukha;*
The one that resembles a bee is *bhrungamukha;*
Sandarshana yantra is used to peel off skin;
Jalodara yantra sucks out water from the womb;
The one used to take out a dead foetus from womb
Is called *garbhashansu yantra.* To remove kidney
Stones *ashwariharana yantra* is used. Tweezer- 110
Shaped is *munchundi yantra;* what is used to
Operate on piles is *arsho yantra.* Oh, there are
So many types and kinds of surgical instruments.
Send at once for all skilfull blacksmiths and
Organise a workshop; and collect steel and
Gold to prepare the necessary instruments.
And, they must be in plenty. For what we have
Ahead is a great war,' said Prabha, the physician.

The senior-most healer among the *vanaras,*
Muchchandi, got up and said: 'Although I am 120
A physician, I am an amateur and, by joining

Broken bones forcefully and causing pain to
My patients, I am eking out a living for me.
O respectable one! Tell us what we should do
On the warfield.' Prabha the physician told him
Lovingly: 'Listen to me. If the bones are broken
In thighs, or collar, or hands, or arms, or neck,
Or jaw, you have to bandage medicinal roots
Very carefully. No other medicine is required,
And, in course of time the bones will set,' she said,   130
And she demonstrated different kinds of bandages
And how to wrap them.

Thus, that brilliant woman
Opened a new era in medical treatment,
And continued to discover new ways and means
In that field through research. Because of her,
Medical education of Bharata achieved new
Laurels, and opened a new chapter in that field.

The physicians in the *vanara* community
Turned out to be modern *dhanvantaris*,   140
The heavenly physicians; and they shone
Like radiant lamps on the horizon of medical
Sciences. Thus, during the period of war-
Preparations, Prabha the physician sparkled
Like the pole star in the sky.

Canto One Hundred and Thirty-two

'Like the Hawks, Let them Attack the Enemy'

||६||

While Saumitri discussed with Sugriva
Serious plans regarding the forthcoming war,
One brave warrior approached them, and told them
With spirit: 'Victory to Saumitri! I am the one
Fed upon the corn of Karnataka. Like lightning
Flashes, we flourish our swords and win battles.
We will prove our prowess in Shri Rama's army,
And we will triumph against any mighty enemy.
Even when our heads are cut off, we will crawl
On our headless trunks and slaughter the enemy.' 10

Before he could complete his words,
There came a courageous woman with her husband,
And said: 'Listen, Saumitri! My husband is
Very brave and valiant.
The pearls on the forehead of the enemy elephants
In rut, and bring them to me. He has pawned my
Status of a married woman to free "mother" Sita
From Ravana's captivity. In order to save the honour

Of "the woman of this epoch," alas, he has staked
My fortune and happiness.   20

'Fate's decree decides everything.
But I will be united with my husband, here or there;
If he returns victorious, here in Kishkindha,
Or, if he dies on the warfield, there in Heaven.
I will practice "*Sati*," and, ceremonioiusly,
Like a nymph of Heaven, I will welcome him there.
This is how Kannada people exhibit their courage.'
Listening to her brave words, Saumitri rejoiced.

Then, Saumitri continued his discussion
Of the art of war with Sugriva: 'If you are aware   30
Of the enemy formation on the battleground, you can
Fight him in many different ways. Unless you engage
The enemy units on your left, you cannot escape
From his units on your right; in such a situation,
Your front units will be hit and defeated by the enemy.
Just as one gauges the dimensions of the ground
While projecting water-carriers, you have to weigh
The size of enemy forces with those of yours and
Then adopt the right strategy of war. This is
The basic principle of war.   40

'When you march with your army
Through mountains and hills, through low and
Marshy places, through forests and slushy land,
Unless the locals there enlist themselves in your
Service and guide you properly, you cannot win
Any war. Even if you win, it will be a defeat
In victory.

'O Sugriva, listen!
First, subdue the mind of the enemy generals;
And destroy their will-power completely.   50

Otherwise, even your victory will be futile,
Like carrying a hot ember in your pocket.

'Most importantly, you should know yourself;
You should weigh your military strength with that
Of your enemy, and only when you are confident
That you can win the war, you should go ahead.
In such a situation, there will be none to stop you.
On the contrary, if you hasten for a war you will
Meet defeat and you will disappear in Time's womb.

'A war is very demanding   60
You should consider the terrain of the battlefield,
And then choose the right weapon for battles;
The war-terrain you choose should suit weather.
You should proceed only after you have discerned
The enemy mind and plans and, before you proceed,
You should mark clear places of safety and dangers.
Whether it is to invade or to withdraw, appropriate
Decisions should be taken from time to time.

'Attack on the battlefield should be quick
And sudden, like a hawk swooping down in a flash,   70
Like water gushing out roaring when the crest-doors
Of a dam are all opened. Bewildered, the enemy-force
Will run hither and thither, and will come to naught.
Your movements should be such that the enemy cannot,
Ever, surmise what your plans are. This is called genius,
And, with commanders, genius gets the pride of place.
On the contrary, if you think tall forts and deep moats
Guarantee you victory, give it up; it is an illusion.

'If you disregard those loyal to you,
Internal strength goes down, leading to defeat.   80
Army operations are like playing with fire;
Unless you are ever watchful and plan, they
Reduce the planners themselves into ashes.

'Art of warfare does not care
For either age or senior positions. If you want
To master it, give up short temper and focus
Only on victory. A merchant thinks of only
Profits in his work; a sculptor dedicates himself
Totally to his work until his imagination takes form.
"Preparation, and more preparation" should be   90
Undertaken like a revolution; only then, O Sugriva,
You can be sure of victory.

'We should identify who our enemy is;
We should have a total knowledge of his strength;
Our plans should be complete and faultless;
The time of when we enter into war should be
Well-known to everyone concerned in our forces;
And, when our enemy is busy with his preparations,
We should invade the enemy camp and destroy it.
These are the "Five Principles" of success in war'.   100

Canto One Hundred and Thirty-three

'Show All the Paths to Reach the Peak of Peace'

||๑||

The war-preparations being done with great fervour,
Once, Shri Rama unburdened his heart to Sugriva
And Saumitri: 'Who knows who wins this cruel war?
Time does not distinguish between friends and foes,
Right and wrong, and justice and injustice.
The harsh truth is – on the battlefield, all are victims.
Once you pull the trigger of weapons of mass destruction,
It has no end; everyone gets reduced to mere dust.

'I saw a dream yesterday night; it was a nightmare.
A huge army of countless soldiers, equipped with 10
All kinds of destructive weapons, marched on
The battle-ground, like the furious Jog Falls.
Immediately, like cancer patients, soldiers in tents
And shelters, nooks and corners, collapsed on the ground.
So did all the army commanders.

'There I saw a devastated scene;
There were men and beasts, half-dead and writhing.
With eyes burnt and bodies charred and blackened,

Burnt-down hair piled up on the ground, struggling
To hold on to life, soldiers moaned and groaned.   20
None was there to nurse them, to give them water;
And no kith and kin to lift up and carry the dead;
No one was there to cremate or bury the dead.
The air was rent with cries, shrieks, and piteous sobs.
In the course of mindless invasion, millions
Had been reduced to dust.

'Driven with the mad ambition
Of conquering all, and oblivious of the world,
Countless people have fallen on the warfield,
And, their threatening voices muted and wings slashed,   30
Have been buried in the womb of man's history.

'Such a nightmare has painted before my eyes
The coming war with Lanka. Do we really need
Such a war that may obliterate this glorious age?
The Goddess of Death stands there, her mouth wide open,
Hungry to devour the whole world. Life on this earth
May come to an end, total, with Rama and Ravana.
We stand on the edge of doomsday.'

Saumitri, the son of Sumitra, consoled him:
'My elder brother, we have to go ahead on the war path;   40
We are left with no choice, and no alternatives.
No peaceful ways left to subdue Ravana, and no chance
Of treaty; and, following Sugriva's orders, all are ready.
How can we withdraw from war, in this juncture?'

Hearing these words, the son of Dasharatha
Raised his arms to the skies, and said in agony:
'O wise men and sages! O you men of science!
Tell me, exploring new paths, would you lead all
To the deep ravine of ruin? You have to show all
The path that takes them all to the summit of peace.   50
The river of fire will carry all, eating away the banks,

Homes and hearths, fields, crops, beasts and men,
All to the ocean of total destruction.

'Why should the search for knowledge
And science lead us to this path of annihilation?
Where is that Narasimha, who wore the demon's
Intestines like a garland to protect the virtuous?
Do we really need this science that laughs at
The total ruin caused by it and mocks us?

'Time is ripe now for serious reflection.
Mind is the primary base for wars and conflicts;
And, from the mind, it spreads to kingdoms
And countries; and, in known and unknown forms,
It appears in different physical and political
Dimensions in this world. When do we learn
The art of living without any hostilities?

'There is no point or meaning in war.
What is there in a war to make us happy and proud?
Victory is but an illusion and an army is a symbol
Of what is not good. Only that art of warfare,
Which enables us to live long and in prosperity,
Is meaningful.'

'Since there is no alternative for war,
We are ready for it. But, even on the field,
If there is any way we can limit bloodshed,
Kindly, tell us and we will follow your words,'
Said Sugriva, humbly.

Shri Rama responded to him in these words:
'If you can gauge the extent of war and grasp
The enemy movements, and proceed accordingly,
We will be victorious with minimum efforts.
Let alone physical prowess if you go ahead
With a strong will and break, intelligently,
Enemy plans and strength, you can minimise

Bloodshed. If you limit the war zone, violence
Will be limited and, if you wage an equal fight,
You can keep off defeat. However, even defeated,
Strong men will survive it and continue to live.

'If the principles of war and virtuous behaviour
Are blended, all arms and weapons get nullified, 90
And peace and prosperity will reign in the world.
One should have compassion along with courage;
One should be simple enough not to expect honour.
If you can cultivate these three qualities, carefully,
Even on the warfield, you will find a resting place.
Experts in the art of war raise the flag of victory,
Without much bloodshed; but the ignorant, lacking
Will power, fight, get defeated, will be reduced
To nothing, and will soon be forgotten.'

Canto One Hundred and Thirty-four

'May Victory Be Yours, May You Be Propitious'

||৬||

Angada and all the others came out of their shelters,
And marched by the side of Kaveri. Kaveri, like a bride
Going to her in-laws from her parental house, bedecked,
Gleamed in her charm.

Kaveri is the patron of Karnataka;
She is known by various names like Marutvrudha
And Kaveri. She is imbued with divine spirit
Like the *yogis*' mind, philosophical and peaceful.
She excels Ganga, the queen of the ocean-king.
Many small rivers like the black-shaded Asiknia
Kapila join her and, enriched by them, proudly,
She flows in the sacred land of Karnataka.

10

On both the sides of Kaveri,
There lie tall trees covered with flowers, and they
Look like travellers who wear their own *dhotra*
Wrapped round their head like a turban.

What words can describe the majesty
Of the varied trees, that thrust into the sky!

The tall coconut trees appear to reach the sun,
And honour him with their gifts of devotion and faith.
The betel-nut trees, tall and slender, heads bowed,
Look like monks immersed in doctrinal discussions.

The river-banks are lined with fig, mango, and
Nelli trees; amidst them are plants and creepers
Such as jasmine, *mandara, nagasampige, tumbe,*
And *alambi*. Here and there, flourish *palasha* trees,
Packed with blood-red flowers.

Bees swarm around the flowers, singing happily,
Sucking nectar and getting refreshed. Swans sport
In princely lakes proudly, like princesses bathing.
Lustfully, they chase their loved ones, impatient
To catch them and caress them.

With the nectar in the flowers fallen on her lap,
Kaveri prepares sweet water with a delicious aroma.
She is a siren for aesthetes, and to monks and sages,
She is the holy river Ganga; she is the one
Who cleanses the sins of all seeking refuge in her.
She, the daughter of Kavera, holy and pure,
Soothes and becalms all those, weary with travel.

She puts on new forms and newer shades of charm,
As she moves from one lovely city to another
Carrying Lord Shiva's compassion as water,
She flows southward, looking like a girdle,
Round the waist of Hastigiri hill.

She passes through the city of Kanchi,
Famed for its bewitching belles. Glowing like the moon,
Connoisseurs opine, they mock the stars and mirrors.
How beautiful this land is, by name Karnataka!
How beautiful this country is, by name Bharata!
Holy and blessed are the cities here – Tirupati,
Shriranga, Kumbhakona, Madhurai, Udupi,

Melukote, Kuduma, Kollur and Shringeri,
Shringeri the seat of Sharada, Goddess of Arts –
This country, Bharata, is the most beautiful,
And the holiest country in the world.

Searching for mother Sita,
And the period fixed by Sugriva almost over,
Hanuma, Angada, and all the others, desperate,
Lay on the ground in anguish. Then, Angada said:

'The time given us to locate "mother"   60
Is coming to an end. All of you are devoted,
And in completing any assignment given to you,
You are unrivalled. Your fame has spread far
And wide. But, violation of Sugriva's orders
Leads only to death.

'Even if we are not put to death,
The king will punish us and torture us, surely.
Alas! What shall we do now? You, Jambava,
Senior to all of us, advise us about possible
Course of action, open to us.'   70

Then, Jambava said:
'Sugriva is not the one to indulge in torture;
And, Shri Rama will not have anything like that;
Blessed is he, our lord, and he will protect us.
Again, we are helpless; let them kill us if they wish.
In the past, Jatayu breathed his last as soon as
He had a glimpse of Rama; it is our turn, now.
Let us reach the city of gods, and rejoice that
Our lives have been sanctified. Evil times,
Surely, lie in wait for Ravana.'   80

At that time, they saw
A very old and emaciated man, lying under a tree,
Crawling towards them, following their voices.
'Who are you people? Huddled together in this

Dense forest, what are you doing? My hearing is weak;
But I fancied I heard the name of Rama. Dasharatha,
Rama's father and the crown of Ikshwaku clan,
Is a dear friend of mine.

'Also, I thought you took the name of Ravana.
He is a wicked creature; having robbed us of our
Kingdom, he has harassed us to no end. He stays
In an island, in the midst of this ocean, and, however
Vengeful I am, my chances of destroying him
Are getting weaker as the days go by. I do not know,
Alas, when he and his progeny will meet their doom.
But, the name of Jatayu falling on my ears,
My hopes are rising, like an old tree sporting
New leaves in the autumnal season.'

No sooner did Hanuma hear those words,
Than he approached the old man speedily and said:
'Sir, you seem to be all alone in this wild jungle;
Could we inquire of you the reason for this state?
In majesty, you are a lion; and we are blessed
Meeting you. What are you thinking of? In despair,
We were all awaiting death; but your words have
Rekindled new hopes and new promises in us.
Because of you, our spirits are soaring to the sky.
Tell us your story and cleanse us off our sins.'

Fixing his eyes at the distant horizon,
The old man said: 'Unless I know who you are,
How can I tell you my story? This world is full of
Traitors; and I have suffered for trusting others.
Who are trustworthy and whom I can depend on,
I do not at all know. You may be tricksters, for all
I know. How can I confide in you?'

Then, Hanuma replied to him very politely:
'Why do you suspect us? We are weak creatues.

In order to keep his fathers's promise, when Shri Rama,
Together with Saumitri and Janaki, exiled himself
From the city and entered forest, while living in 120
Panchavati, Ravana the imposter, kidnapped
Sita. At that time, Jatayu the head of the eagle clan,
Challenged Ravana; and in the ensuing fierce fight,
Jatayu met his death.' Even before Hanuma could
Complete his sentence, the old man swooned
And collapsed on the ground.

After the *vanaras*, surprised and concerned,
Ministered to him tenderly, he woke up, and moaned:
'Alas! I am undone. Is my brother Jatayu dead?
Have my dreams of subduing the wicked *rakshasas* 130
And anointing my brother as the king of the Gruddhra
Kingdom come to nothing? Now, there is no meaning
For my life.' With these words, when he went up
A hill and was ready to jump down to death, Hanuma
And others ran after him and caught up with him.

Old though he was, he was not an ordinary man;
By name Sampati, he was Jatayu's elder brother.
Even when the *vanaras* tried to drag him back,
Freeing himself, he got to the hill-peak and leapt.
But Hanuma extended his arm and held his waist. 140
Others, in a line, tried to pull back Hanuma.
It appeared as if they were churning the ocean
With the Mount Mandara. Even though a tamarind
Tree gets old, does its fruit lose its fresh taste?

Finally, when Jambavanta,
Unrivalled in strength, took the name of Shri Rama,
And pulled back with all his strength, every one,
Including Sampati fell back on Jambava,
And he lay beneath that heap, unable to breathe.
After a moment or two, all of them got up and 150
Jambava, finally, stood up and breathed free.

The utter confusion caused by Sampati being over,
All got up, dusted their clothes, and felt both
Angry and happy. They were also intrigued. Finally,
All burst out with laughter loudly.

Angada tried to pacify the old man:
'O noble man! Why this anguish? Why this haste
To end your precious life? We are all with you, and
So are Rama, Saumitri and the forces of Sugriva.
What is the matter? Why are you so desperate? 160
Life is always full of new turns and twists. Let us all
Sit together and make something meaningful
Out of our lives.'

Sampati, still sad and grief-stricken, said:
'Jatayu is my brother and I am Sampati, elder
To him. Tell me everything about Jatayu and
Your plans to put an end to Ravana.'

Then, Hanuma replied to him:
'The last rites of Jatayu were conducted by Rama
And Saumitri. Searching for Sita being his sole goal, 170
Rama and Saumitri arrived at Kishkindha,
And became friends of Sugriva; consequently,
Rama killed Vali.

'Then, Sugriva became the king and Angada
The crown prince. The king has given us one month
To locate Sita; if we fail, death sentence awaits us.
And, we do not have a single clue as to where or
How Sita is; hence, we are all sunk in despair.
But now, having met you, our hopes have revived.'

Sampati listened to these painful words, 180
And said, his eyes tearful: 'Then, listen to my story.
When Ravana abducted Sita and was taking her
With him, she cried: "O Rama! O Saumitri!"

I heard those words, and saw the flashing ornaments
Thrown down by Sita.

'She could be the daughter of king Janaka.
But, whoever she was, Indian culture told me that
To help a woman in distress was everyone's duty.
What could I do, being alone? Ravana flew past
In great speed; my legs were tottering and my arms   190
Weak. The history of the Gruddhra-clan is one of
Self-sacrifice. I was utterly defeated and Jatayu's
Luck evaded me. He became a martyr and I lay
There, a helpless and silent spectator.

'Ravana has kept Sita a captive in Lanka;
And many *rakshasis* guard her day and night.
But, you can find her; and, with Rama's blessings,
You will be successful in your heroic endeavour.
But that bloodthirsty thief has to be killed.
My life-breath reaches its end today.   200
May you be successful, may you be propitious.'

With these words, Sampati, sitting in a posture
Called *padmasana*, ended his life in the yogic way.

Canto One Hundred and Thirty-five

'He Grew so High as to Reach the Skies'

||௬||

Hanuma and the other *vanaras* gave a tearful
Farewell to brave Sampati, and conducted his
Last rites with devotion. The news of Sita's whereabouts
Had brought back joy and spirits.

They all assembled by the sea-shore
In the evening. The crimson sky appeared as if
A box full of *kumkum*, being carried by a boy,
Had its lid taken out, spraying its contents everywhere.

With the wild and mammoth beings
Rising out of the ocean with their jaws open,
With mighty waves, enraged, lashing at the shore,
The roaring ocean seemed to mirror the turmoil
Of the world.

How do we cross this vast ocean
And reach Lanka? When do we get any news
About Sita? Has anyone amongst us the strength
To leap over this ocean? Who will succeed in this
Challenging task? – Such thoughts kept the *vanaras*
Awake throughout the night.

When the sun arose in the morning, 20
Like the army of gods standing in a circle
Around the king of gods, the *vanaras* surrounded
Angada, and stood silently. They were troubled
With thoughts about their daunting task.

Then Angada said:
'Don't allow worries and fears to kill you. Let us show
What we are capable of and cross the ocean.
It is hundred *yojanas* in width; who can leap over it?
If you do, you will raise high the banner of Kishkindha
Through your courage and valour; and you will be 30
Honoured. Who is there amongst you, unrivalled in
Strength, to take up this challenge? Speak up.'

Staring at the huge waves,
Jambava said in anguish: 'Have you seen
The ocean that is roaring loudly? See the foam
Gathering up, the waves chasing each other, and
The majesty with which the ocean welcomes all
Sacred rivers to come unto it. Look at its pride,
That it has sheltered mammoth sharks and whales.
Have all of you observed fully the rising waves, 40
Huge enough to frighten any brave person?

'Now, the master of the "milk-ocean,"
Vishnu who sleeps on a serpent, he alone knows
How to cross this ocean. If we cannot cross it,
Sugriva is going to demand our heads; if we try
To cross it, we will be food for sharks and whales.
O Mother! Primeval Energy! Be merciful to us.
You have hung the sun and the moon on the sky;
You are the protector of the world, omnipresent
And omniscient. Listen to our prayers; give us 50
The strength to overcome our fears. Light the torch
Of courage in our hearts, and fasten on us the armour
Of your assurance and protect us.

'You *vanaras*, why are you so hesitant?
Having a noble Quest ahead, does anyone
Sleep over it? We have a long, very long journey ahead;
Don't you take to the path of self-destruction!

'Let no impediments scare you.
Remember Sugriva's commands, always.
Even if all the cruel sea-beasts kill and feed on us, 60
Even if the ocean, crossing its limits, reaches us
And drags all of us into its depths, let us preserve
The protective mail of our will power, undying.
Let us devote our lives to the task of Shri Rama,
And, let us sacrifice our lives for that cause.
Such a path of action will bring us glory, and
Contentment. It is a bliss to search for "mother".'

'O venerable Jambava!
We know neither fear nor anxiety,' said Hanuma.
'We will uproot the earth, pluck out the sun and the moon, 70
And, throw out Shiva from his abode in Kailasa.
We will unseat Indra, the king of Heaven, and banish him;
We will bind and throw out Java, the God of Death;
And, we will defeat the terrible Bhairava, and dance.
Within a wink of time, we will leap over the ocean,
Cut the *rakshasa* to pieces, and arrange a grand
Feast to the spirits of death.

'We will sport in blood, reach "our mother,"
And stand before her with folded hands. Humbly,
We will give her the message of Shri Rama, and 80
Fulfil the expectations of the new era.'

'True; all of you are truly brave and courageous,'
Said Jambava and cautioned them: 'However,
Never forget that your fight is against Ravana,
The most powerful king of Lanka.
You have to face him with both power and tact.

Do not forget that we are the messengers of
The king of Ayodhya.

'Hanuma is the bravest among the brave,
And the boldest among the bold. He is well-versed 90
In scriptures and also in political philosophy.
There is none in this world who can rival Hanuma
In intuitive intelligence and valour.

'To cross the ocean and reach Lanka,
To meet "mother" and give her Rama's message,
To subdue the *rakshasas* and destroy Lanka,
To accomplish our task without bloodshed,
To bring fame and name to the *vanara* lineage,
And to raise high the repute of Karnataka –
To achieve all this, there is none but Hanuma. 100
Victory to Hanuma, the son of the Wind-god;
Victory to the messenger of Shri Ramachandra.'

Hearing these words of Jambava,
All of them, full of endless joy and confidence,
Lifted up Hanuma high, and, hailing the name
Of Rama, Lakshmana, and Janaki, they danced
Merrily, singing of their glory.

Amidst all this noise and festivity,
Hanumanta sat there, calmly like a stoic figure,
Neither elated nor sad. Looking at him, Jambava said: 110
'You, an ocean of valour, why are you so quiet?
Would you be a mute spectator when Aryans and we
Are going through the fire-ordeal? Are you unaware
Of your latent powers? Don't you realise that you are
A hot ember covered with ashes?

'Why this lack of self-confidence?
You, the charmer, can sport with the whole world;
An ardent devotee of Rama, you are an achiever.
You are equal in strength to Rama, Saumitri, and

Sugriva. None can rival your speed or strength.
Is there anyone to equal your courage or wisdom?
In competence, you are one with the son of Vinuta.
Now, save our lives and achieve immortality.

'Arise! Arise, O mighty!
Arise! Arise, O the noblest of the *vanaras*!
Arise! Arise, O Trivikrama, who measured
The entire universe with just two steps!
O Rama's messenger, arise; O Rama's servant, arise;
O the dearest friend of Saumitri, Great Soul, arise.
To see your great accomplishments, the whole
World stands, eager and expectant.'

The words of Jambava had the power
To provoke and augment Hanuma's vigour;
They were like light to bring to light latent strength.
They were invigorating enough to cleanse
The great man's mind of lethargy and fear.

Hanuma, then, rousing himself
From his feeling of inferiority, rejoiced.
He realised his real strength and the task
That lay before him. His self-confidence,
That none but he could accomplish the task,
That none but he could cross the vast ocean,
That none but he could reach the city of Lanka,
And, that none but he could see the "mother",
Such a self-confidence vitalised his mind.

He shrugged himself out of his passivity,
And grew so high as to reach the skies,
Becoming omnipresent, and as colossal
As Trivikrama. His corporeal frame was
As radiant as the Mount Meru; and valour streamed
Out from his body and affected all.

Astounded by this glorious vision, in silence,
All gazed at him, speechless and wide-eyed.
Then, with folded hands, Hanuma bowed and said:

'End all of your worries now.
No more fear and no more suffering from delusions.
Give up your piteous looks and gaze boldly.
With your blessings on my head, I will surely
Cross the ocean and meet the "mother." Cities
Like Lanka may be there countless, but I shall   160
Reduce them all to dust and ashes.

'The sacred name of Rama is the bridge;
I move fast and, kissing the skies, I shall uproot
All the hills. I shall circle even the Meru many times;
And with my strong arms, I will throw the earth
To the ocean.

'My speed, beyond any words,
Will shake the ocean and cause the water-beasts
Like the sharks, crocodiles, and huge whales
Tremble with fear. Thousand times more speedily   170
Than the eagle-king swooping down on snakes,
I shall swoop down on the ocean.

'Beginning my race with the rising sun,
I shall reach the western mountain before him,
And retracing my path, shall greet the sun at noon.
I have the strength to go beyond the galaxies; and
I can pound the earth and throw it to the ocean.
To churn the ocean, why does one need gods and
Demons? Why the Mandara mountain and Vasuki?
Why do we need Vishnu and Shiva and Mohini?   180
Like Shiva, I myself shall drink the deadly poison,
And present the nectar "mother" to Shri Rama.'

When Hanuma ascended the Mount Mahendra,
And stamped it with his feet, the mountain itself

Was crushed, unable to bear his weight. As when
A mighty lion assaults an elephant, and it collapses,
A loud noise erupted. Keeping his feet one on
Each peak, when Hanuma pressed hard, rocks came
Rolling down, resulting in a catastrophe.
Gods gathered in the sky to witness the glorious 190
Act, hailed him and showered flowers on him.

With total concentration,
When he was moving his legs and getting ready
For that mammoth leap, all sang his paeans:
'Victory! Victory to you, O Hanuma!
You are merciful, and you have rained nectar;
You are beyond the binding wheel of birth and death;
You are dear to all, and you are virtue personified.
Smaller than the atom, you are bigger than the biggest;
And you are born only to give succour to the world. 200

'O Great Soul!
Destroying vice, you have protected *dharma*;
You are the founder of the path of devotion
You have fused all doctrines with that of Rama.
In your land of birth, all trees and plants are divine;
In your land of birth, all stones are alchemic;
In your land of birth, all water is heavenly nectar;
In your land of birth, all towns are holy places.
In you, all virtues and noble qualities have come
Together, with love. 210

'You are the usherer of the new epoch.
New knowledge is dawning because of you;
New horizons are opening because of you;
New light is flowing because of you; and,
New truths are flashing because of you.'
Thus, all of them hailed Hanuma, with great joy.